GREEK PHILOSOPHY

A COLLECTION OF TEXTS

WITH NOTES AND EXPLANATIONS

BY

C. J. DE VOGEL

PH.D., PROFESSOR OF ANCIENT AND MEDIAEVAL
PHILOSOPHY IN THE UNIVERSITY OF UTRECHT

VOLUME III

THE HELLENISTIC-ROMAN PERIOD

SECOND EDITION

LEIDEN
E. J. BRILL
1964

The publication of this volume is facilitated by a subvention granted by "The Netherlands Organization for Pure Research" (Z.W.O.)

Printed in the Netherlands

GUILELMO VOLLGRAFF

MAGISTRO – COLLEGAE – AMICO

CONTENTS

BOOK VI—THE THEOLOGICAL OR THEOSOPHICAL SCHOOLS

PREFACE

With the present volume this history of Greek philosophy, as much as possible composed by the texts, is completed. I might simply repeat the sober words written in the preface of the second volume: "the purpose of the book will be easily understood by those who take the trouble of reading it." Meanwhile, since it happens that even reviewers do not, or hardly, take this trouble, or, if they do, may fail to understand essential things, it might be better to add a few words.

The leading principles of this work have been: first, that the study of Greek philosophy can be practised only on the texts; second, though the study of special parts and, say, of details is always, and should be, the basis, the philosopher's interest is to have a view of the whole. Ὁ γὰρ συνοπτικὸς διαλεκτικός. And lastly, the right understanding of the part is promoted and deepened by as wide as possible a knowledge of the whole. The present work has been undertaken to serve this purpose. As some of the reviewers rightly observed, it is by no means sufficiently characterized by saying that it is "ein Buch für den Unterricht",— a formula which, as it seems, may be easily understood in such a sense that the work denoted by it would be of a more or less elementary character, and as such of no interest to the scholar. With regard to the present work this might prove to be, indeed, rather a strange and regrettable misunderstanding, and it would be better, therefore, not to apply the said formula to it. The work is evidently not what is called in the Anglo-American world a "text-book". It is a source-book in the largest sense, giving ample documentation on the whole of Greek philosophy. After all, the comparison with Ritter and Preller could better be dropped, since the present work was conceived in an entirely independent way.

A word must be said on the character of personal interpretation which is—and should be—found in a work like this. It has been there from the beginning, though always with a certain discretion and often compressed into a very short form. So it is in the present volume. Evidently such paragraphs as those on Posidonius, Antiochus of Ascalon, questions such as the Logos theory of Philo, Albinus' Platonism, the three Gods of Numenius and many points of detail required a considerable amount of personal interpretation. But *where* in Greek philosophy—or in whatever piece of human thought in past or present days—is this not the case if anybody is to write its history, be it a history composed of the texts, with marginal notes, introductions and explanations? I am well aware that the present volume, too, contains a good deal of personal interpretation. I can only say: I did it as carefully and well as possible, though always limiting my remarks to a very moderate space; i.e. keeping them as short as possible. The essential thing is always to have the texts, and to have them well ordered, so that the whole forms a readable history, with due information as to literature, with some explanation as far as necessary, and—last not least—with copious indexes for the use of everybody who might consult the work with profit: the historian and the philosopher, the medievalist, the ethicist, the theologian, and the historian of various sciences, including law, logic and philology.

A volume like this, which contains a history of eight centuries of very varied thought—from the atomism of Epicurus, the great system of the Stoa with its many aspects, and the subtle criticism of the sceptic thinkers to the wide-spread complex of what we call prae-neo-platonism, the mature and profound philosophy of Plotinus, and to that of his followers—such a volume must be equipped with good indexes, where the history of all kinds of concepts, theories and terms can be easily found. Now and then such an index has to do more than just sum up the passages where a certain word occurs,—though this too may evidently be quite revealing. There may be more in it. For it happens not unfrequently that the equivalent of a modern concept—or what is approximately so—is expressed in Greek by different terms or circum-scriptions. Sometimes historians have been inclined to conclude from this that "the Greeks did not know this or that concept" because, as it seemed to them, "they did not have a word for it". Such was, e.g., the case of the concept of *person* and *personality*. It has been said by some illustrious historians of philosophy that the Greeks did not know this concept, and that it was formally discovered by Christian thinkers, since it was first defined by Boëthius.

Now this is—it must be said—rather strange, and even alarming, information to those who know something of Greek literature and of the life in the Greek philosophers' Schools, where obviously a true cult of the personality was practised. Briefly speaking, the above-quoted statement was erroneous; moreover, it was an error springing from lack of knowledge both of Greek philosophy and of the terms used by its representatives. The notion of "person" and "personality" existed. The "concept" was, formally speaking, "discovered" by Panaetius,—only, under a name so common, that it appears to have escaped the notice even of such scholars as E. Gilson and R. Klibanski.—But, once we are paying attention to such a notion, we shall find that it occurs again very clearly in the writings of certain other authors, be it once more under names so common, that they *might* pass unobserved. For not only is Panaetius' expression *propria natura* (indicating the natural aptitude or disposition of the individual man, as opposed to the "nature of man"-as-a-species) found literally in Plotinus' οἰκεία φύσις, but we shall find this author seeking for an exact definition of "what are *we*": not *we* in the vegetative or animal sense, but "we" as morally responsible and spiritual beings; "we" as—*persons* or, say, *personalities*.

But once we have arrived at this point we shall have to observe that the "concept of personality" found in such late Greek authors as Plotinus and Porphyry, was already explicitly present in Aristotle, who obviously took it from Plato (whether we think the *Alcibiades maior* authentic or not),—and that Gilson was very wrong indeed when writing that the metaphysical basis of personality was not discovered by the Greeks.

I hope to expound this question more explicitly. It is one point out of many. May the sample indicate somehow both the need for and the use of a work like this, which in its three volumes taken together offers to the scholar the opportunity of a σύνοψις of Greek philosophical thought; the opportunity of finding quickly and safely where, and how, many a concept and many a philosophical term was used first, how it spread and how it developed. For this purpose the author made the indexes of "concepts" and of "Greek words". If anything is lacking in them, the benevolent reader will realize that an enormous work has been done, and that it was done by one person.

To me it has been and always is a thing of great delight to live in the world of Greek philosophical thought and its vehicle, the Greek language, and to penetrate more and more deeply into it. Especially the reading and re-reading of Plotinus has been and always is to me a great delight. The fact that I shared it since several years with a circle of young friends interested in these matters, certainly increased the joy of this spiritual intercourse.

As has been said above, many questions of detail had to be considered and now and then compressed into a very short formula. To expound certain points more explicitly will be a task for coming years, which I hope to carry out myself.

In achieving this laborious task of many years, I think it both an honour and a joy to dedicate this third volume of my *Greek Philosophy* to the man who, in past years, was my venerated master in Greek philology, and always stayed a good and faithful friend, full of interest in my work, not the least in this part of it which is now reaching its term.

In preparing this volume for the press I have been kindly assisted by Dr. W. Wiersma who, though finding himself at the beginning of a new task of university teaching, took the trouble of reading a complete series of proofs with me. I thank him sincerely for his kind help.

It was Mr. B. L. Hijmans, at present lecturer in the university of Capetown who, before leaving Europe, did the preparatory work for composing the index of names. I wish to express my gratitude to him in this place. I also thank Mr. M. T. P. van Buijtenen, Mr. T. H. Janssen and Mr. Th. G. Sinnige, who each took their share in the laborious task of reading the proofs.

C. J. d. V.

PREFACE TO THE SECOND EDITION

In the second edition a few small corrections have been made. The Bibliography was completed.

Utrecht, nov. 1963.   C. J. d. V.

EDITIONS AND ABBREVIATIONS

As in my previous volumes, I have used the best modern editions. Since the authors cited are numerous and the texts are all mentioned in the bibliography, it is hardly necessary to give a complete list of them. The following indications may be sufficient.

For Epicurus I used Bailey [1]), for the ancient Stoa Von Arnim SVF, for Sextus Emp. Mutschmann and Mau; for Cicero, Seneca, Musonius, Epictetus, M. Aurelius, Plutarchus, Maximus Tyrius, Apuleius, Porphyrius and Iamblichus the Teubner editions mentioned in the bibliography; for Philo Cohn-Wendland, for Albinus P. Louis, for the *Hermetica* Nock-Festugière, for Irenaeus (Valentinus) Stieren, for Numenius Leemans, for Plotinus *Enn.* I-III Henri-Schwyzer, for *Enn.* IV-VI Bréhier; for Proclus' *Elementa* Dodds, for the Timaeus commentary Diehl, and for the other commentaries the editions mentioned in the bibliography. For Damascius Ruelle.

Where I chose a reading different from those editions, I usually said so in a note.

I did not abuse of abbreviations. Those which are used require hardly any explanation. In the indexes of concepts and Greek words such formulas as "according to" and "small print" are written: *acc. to* and *sm. pr.*

---

[1]) A copy of *The extant remains*, which was out of print for several years, was procured for me by the great kindness of Dr. Bailey himself, when I had the pleasure of meeting him in Oxford, May 1951.

GENERAL INTRODUCTION

805—The profound political change in the Greek world after Alexander had its reflexion in philosophical thought. The disappearance of the polis, the loss of freedom, the utter uncertainty of all outward circumstances of life, lead on the one hand to a narrowing of the interests (individualism and culture of the personality as an aim in itself), on the other hand to an extension of the ken (universalism). On the whole, they lead to a striving for inner peace, which consists of being freed from passions and desires (ἀπάθεια and ἀταραξία).

(1)   a. The note of individualism appears strongly in Epicureanism, **Individualism** which might even be defined as "living to oneself". See our XXth chapter, especially nrs. **860a, 861a, 878, 879**.

b. It appears also in the Stoa, which is, after all, a philosophy aiming at a certain moral or spiritual training of the individual man, hardening him against the vicissitudes of life. Ch. XXI, nrs. **942, 1006-1011, 1044**.

c. It may be seen, also in Pyrrho's utter indifferentism to anything happening round about him. Ch. XXII, nr. **1082b**.

(2)   The note of universalism appears most strikingly in the greatest **Universalism** dogmatical system of the period: the Stoa, which may be rightly called *a cosmic religion.*

Festugière, *Le dieu cosmique*, especially chapters IX-XIV.
Our ch. XXI, nrs. **919-934**.

I do not think Festugière is right in denying any oriental influence on the Stoic cosmic religion. It is quite true that Plato taught a cosmic religion in his later dialogues (*Tim.* and *Nom.*), and that, with an important modification, Aristotle taught it in his II. φιλ. Yet, why should not persons like Zeno of Citium, Chrysippus of Soli, Diogenes called the Babylonian, Antipater of Tarsus and Posidonius of Apamea in their general attitude of mind have been more or less influenced by that spiritual climate from which they came by birth? The room dedicated to Cyprian art in the Louvre-Museum, adjacent to the compartment of Syria and Anatolia, speaks an eloquent language as to the character of this civilization.

(3)   Our third note, which means that during this period happiness is **A negative** defined in a negative way, may be first observed in Epicureanism: **definition of happiness** ch. XX, nrs. **860a, 864a**; next in the Stoic striving after ἀπάθεια (ch. XXI, nrs. **1059-1062**; XXIII, nrs. **(1166), 1211**, and finally in the

ἀταραξία of Pyrrho and Arcesilaus and of the later Sceptics (XXII, nr. **1087a**).

School-philosophy

806—During the Hellenistic-Roman period philosophy remains a school-discipline, and as such preserves a technical character. E.g. the letters of Epicurus, especially those to Herodotus and to Pythocles, and the discussions between Stoics and Sceptics. Even a man like Epictetus shows himself to be interested in purely theoretical questions (*Diss.* III 9, 21). Therefore, one would be mistaken in thinking that after Aristotle Greek philosophy was made popular and preached for everyman. It was, but during the last three centuries B.C. only occasionally, by some few individuals, (Bion of Borysthenes etc., ch. XXIII, nrs. **1249** ff.); more generally during the Roman Empire, but even then not so as to take the place of the school-philosophy, in its more technical sense.

and world-philosophy

Thus, next to the school-philosophy, the Hellenistic-Roman age knew a more popular form of philosophy addressed to every man of good intention. The Cynical device ὅτι πᾶσι φιλοσοφητέον, later found in Musonius Rufus (nr. **1227bc**) and Epictetus, expresses another kind of *universalism*.

Number of students

807—We know something about the number of students of philosophy during the generation directly after Aristotle [1].

Diog. Laert. V 37 (about Theophrastus): ᾿Απήντων δ᾿ εἰς τὴν διατριβὴν αὐτοῦ μαθηταὶ πρὸς δισχιλίους.

Now Theophr. directed the school for 34 years, so there was an average of 60 students a year. Consequently we have to imagine that in the Lyceum lectures were held for hundreds of people. To this one must take into account that at the same time three other flourishing schools of philosophy existed at Athens (the Academy, that of Epicurus and of the Stoa), and besides that outside of Athens Stilpo of Megara attracted many people, while others went to Eretria and heared Menedemus.

Synopsis of Epicurus and the Stoa

808—Both Epicurus and Zeno try to give an answer to the same question, namely: *How to live? How to be happy in a so uncertain world?* Their replies are opposed the one to the other on the following points:

(1) In defining the *telos* or *summum bonum*: according to Epicurus it is pleasure, according to Zeno virtue.

---

[1] The remark was made by G. Verbeke, *Kleanthes* p. 12, who gives a good introduction into the Hellenistic period in his first chapter.

(2)   In physics: both systems are a kind of materialism, but Epicurus teaches a mere mechanicism (nothing exists but the atoms moved by a merely mechanical force), Zeno vitalism (matter is animated); Epicurus holds that organisms are fortuitous combinations, Zeno is a finalist; Epicurus teaches the contingency of all things, Zeno defends fatalism (the rule of a fixed and inexorable law of the universe which is the Divine Logos); Epicurus admits innumerable worlds, once to be dissolved into their elements, the Stoa one kosmos, either eternal (Panaetius) or periodically perishing and rebuilt (the general Stoic doctrine).

(3)   In theology: Epicurus teaches that the gods live in the intermundia and are not concerned with the world; the Stoa holds that the Divine penetrates the world and leads it by *pronoia*.

(4)   In theory of knowledge: Epicurus teaches consequent sensualism (every sense-impression is true); according to Zeno the intellect has to judge about the value of sense-impressions.

(5)   The soul: for Epicurus it is merely material and therefore perishing with the body; the Stoa, in spite of its materialistic starting point, tends to spiritualism. Later Stoics believe in the soul's immortality.

(6)   Political life: According to Epicurus it is normally to be avoided; according to Stoics only exceptionally (in perfectly desperate cases).

809—Pyrrho and the later Sceptics give a third reply to the questions **A third reply** of "how to live" and "how to be happy": by suspending one's judgment (ἐποχή). In practical life they either showed a complete indifferentism (Pyrrho), or were lead by practical evidence (Arcesilaus and Carneades). Later Sceptics elaborated a systematical empiricism.

Chronologically Pyrrho precedes Epicurus, but I hardly think he influenced him. Epicurus, on the other hand, preceded Zeno, and I do think the founder of the Stoa was influenced by Epicurus' doctrine.

Preferring to follow the lines of the different schools to a disposition of the stuff according to succession in time, I treat first Epicurus and his school, next the Stoa and thirdly scepticism.

BOOK V

POST-ARISTOTELIAN DOGMATISM AND THE SCEPTICAL REACTION

TWENTIETH CHAPTER

EPICURUS AND HIS SCHOOL

I—THE MAN AND HIS WORKS

Life

810—a. Diog. Laert. X, 1-2:

Ἐπίκουρος Νεοκλέους καὶ Χαιρεστράτης Ἀθηναῖος, τῶν δήμων Γαργήττιος, γένους τοῦ τῶν Φιλαϊδῶν, ὥς φησι Μητρόδωρος ἐν τῷ περὶ εὐγενείας. τοῦτόν φασιν ἄλλοι τε καὶ Ἡρακλείδης ἐν τῇ Σωτίωνος ἐπιτομῇ, κληρουχησάντων Ἀθηναίων τὴν Σάμον, ἐκεῖ τραφῆναι, ὀκτωκαιδεκέτη δ' ἐλθεῖν εἰς Ἀθήνας, Ξενοκράτους μὲν ἐν Ἀκαδημείᾳ, Ἀριστοτέλους δ' ἐν Χαλκίδι διατρίβοντος [1]. τελευτήσαντος δὲ Ἀλεξάνδρου τοῦ Μακεδόνος καὶ τῶν Ἀθηναίων ἐκπεσόντων [2] ὑπὸ Περδίκκου, μετελθεῖν εἰς Κολοφῶνα πρὸς τὸν πατέρα. (2) χρόνον δέ τινα διατρίψαντα αὐτόθι καὶ μαθητὰς ἀθροίσαντα [3] πάλιν ἐπανελθεῖν εἰς Ἀθήνας ἐπὶ Ἀναξικράτους [4], καὶ μέχρι μέν τινος κατ' ἐπιμιξίαν τοῖς ἄλλοις φιλοσοφεῖν, ἔπειτα ἰδίᾳ ἀπο‹φαίνεσθαι› τὴν ἀπ' αὐτοῦ κληθεῖσαν αἵρεσιν συστήσαντα. ἐφάψασθαί τε φιλοσοφίας αὐτός φησιν ἔτη γεγονὼς τέτταρα καὶ δέκα· Ἀπολλόδωρος δ' ὁ Ἐπικούρειος ἐν τῷ πρώτῳ περὶ τοῦ Ἐπικούρου βίου φησὶν ἐλθεῖν αὐτὸν ἐπὶ φιλοσοφίαν καταγνόντα τῶν γραμματιστῶν, ἐπειδὴ μὴ ἐδυνήθησαν ἑρμηνεῦσαι αὐτῷ τὰ περὶ τοῦ παρ' Ἡσιόδῳ χάους.

How he came to philosophy

b. Sextus, *Math.* X (*Against the Physicists* II) 18-19:

Ὁ μὲν γὰρ εἰπών

ἤτοι μὲν πρώτιστα χάος γένετ', αὐτὰρ ἔπειτα
γαῖ' εὐρύστερνος, πάντων ἔδος,

ἐξ αὐτοῦ περιτρέπεται [5]. ἐρομένου γάρ τινος αὐτὸν ἐκ τίνος γέγονε τὸ χάος,

---

[1] In the year 322.

[2] Sc. ἐκ τῆς Σάμου.

[3] Vid. sub *c*.

[4] In the year 307/6.

[5] „is refuted by himself".

οὐχ ἕξει λέγειν. καὶ τοῦτό φασιν ἔνιοι αἴτιον γεγονέναι Ἐπικούρῳ τῆς ἐπὶ τὸ φιλοσοφεῖν ὁρμῆς. κομιδῇ γὰρ μειρακίσκος ὢν ἤρετο τὸν ἐπαναγινώσκοντα αὐτῷ γραμματιστὴν "ἤτοι μὲν πρώτιστα χάος γένετ'", ἐκ τίνος χάος ἐγένετο, εἴπερ πρῶτον ἐγένετο. τούτου δὲ εἰπόντος μὴ αὑτοῦ ἔργον εἶναι τὰ τοιαῦτα διδάσκειν ἀλλὰ τῶν καλουμένων φιλοσόφων, τοίνυν, ἔφησεν ὁ Ἐπίκουρος, ἐπ' ἐκείνους μοι βαδιστέον ἐστίν, εἴπερ αὐτοὶ τὴν τῶν ὄντων ἀλήθειαν ἴσασιν.

c. Diog. Laert. X 15: First school

Ὑπάρχοντα δ' αὐτὸν ἐτῶν δύο καὶ τριάκοντα πρῶτον ἐν Μυτιλήνῃ καὶ Λαμψάκῳ συστήσασθαι σχολὴν ἐπὶ ἔτη πέντε· ἔπειθ' οὕτως εἰς Ἀθήνας μετελθεῖν..

811—He shows a marked hostility towards learning and disparages all other philosophers in a rather disagreeable way. He is said to have heard the lectures of the Democritean *Nausiphanes* at Teos, but has no good word for him either.

a. Sextus, *Math.* I 1-4, says that both Epicurus and the School of Pyrrho were hostile towards the μαθηματικοί ("professors of Arts and Sciences"), and this for different reasons: Hostility towards learning

Οἱ μὲν περὶ τὸν Ἐπίκουρον ὡς τῶν μαθημάτων μηδὲν συνεργούντων πρὸς σοφίας τελείωσιν, ἢ ὥς τινες εἰκάζουσι, τοῦτο προκάλυμμα τῆς ἑαυτῶν ἀπαιδευσίας εἶναι νομίζοντες (ἐν πολλοῖς γὰρ ἀμαθὴς Ἐπίκουρος ἐλέγχεται, οὐδὲ ἐν ταῖς κοιναῖς ὁμιλίαις καθαρεύων), τάχα δὲ καὶ διὰ τὴν πρὸς τοὺς περὶ Πλάτωνα καὶ Ἀριστοτέλη καὶ τοὺς ὁμοίους δυσμένειαν πολυμαθεῖς γεγονότας. οὐκ ἀπέοικε δὲ καὶ διὰ τὴν πρὸς Ναυσιφάνην τὸν Πύρρωνος ἀκουστὴν ἔχθραν· πολλοὺς γὰρ τῶν νέων συνεῖχε καὶ τῶν μαθημάτων σπουδαίως ἐπεμελεῖτο, μάλιστα δὲ ῥητορικῆς. γενόμενος οὖν τούτου μαθητὴς ὁ Ἐπίκουρος ὑπὲρ τοῦ δοκεῖν αὐτοδίδακτος εἶναι καὶ αὐτοφυὴς φιλόσοφος ἠρνεῖτο ἐκ παντὸς τρόπου, τήν τε περὶ αὐτοῦ φήμην ἐξαλείφειν ἔσπευδε, πολύς τε ἐγίνετο τῶν μαθημάτων κατήγορος, ἐν οἷς ἐκεῖνος ἐσεμνύνετο. φησὶ γοῦν ἐν τῇ πρὸς τοὺς ἐν Μυτιλήνῃ φιλοσόφους ἐπιστολῇ "οἶμαι δὲ ἔγωγε τοὺς βαρυστόνους καὶ μαθητήν με δόξειν τοῦ πλεύμονος εἶναι, μετὰ μειρακίων τινῶν κραιπαλώντων ἀκούσαντα," νῦν πλεύμονα καλῶν τὸν Ναυσιφάνην ὡς ἀναίσθητον. καὶ πάλιν προβὰς πολλά τε κατειπὼν τἀνδρὸς ὑπεμφαίνει τὴν ἐν τοῖς μαθήμασιν αὐτοῦ προκοπὴν λέγων "καὶ γὰρ πονηρὸς ἄνθρωπος ἦν καὶ ἐπιτετηδευκὼς τοιαῦτα ἐξ ὧν οὐ δυνατὸν εἰς σοφίαν ἐλθεῖν," αἰνισσόμενος τὰ μαθήματα.

b. Cicero, who is not a friend of Epicurus, says in *N.D.* I, 26, 73: pupil of Nausiphanes
In Nausiphane Democriteo tenetur: quem cum a se non neget auditum, vexat tamen omnibus contumeliis.

We have to admit either that Epic. studied philosophy between the age of 20 and 30, till he started to teach himself at the age of 32 (Bailey), and that he heard Nausiphanes after his 20th year[1], roaming, either alone or with his parents, through the towns of Mikrasia,—or to imagine, as Festugière[2] does, that the young Epicurus at the age of 14 was sent to Teos by his father and stayed there till 17, following the lectures of Nausiphanes among the "jeunesse dorée" that surrounded this teacher. In favour of this view F. adduces the following text:

The school of Nausiphanes   c. *Vol. Herc.* 2 I, 132 ff. (probably from Epicurus' Letter *To the friends at Mytilene*):

"<Αὐτοῦ> ταῖς ἡμερ<οκ>ωμίαις ἐν Τέῳ συσχόμενος π<ρὸ> τοῦ σοφιστεῦσαι, τοῦ τ' 'Αναξαγόρου ἀναγινώσκοντος καὶ 'Εμπεδοκλέους καὶ περὶ ταῦτα τερθρευομένου κατατεταμένωσ" ἢ πάλιν "ὁ τοὺς 'Ερμοκοπίδας ἐν Τέῳ συ<σ>τήσα<ς> κατὰ Δ>ημόκριτον καὶ <Λεύκιπ>πον πραγματευ<ομένου ἀκουσομένους>".

The word ἡμεροκωμίαι suggests revels at an unusually early hour. Nausiphanes seems to have arranged such parties "before lecturing", and is said to have gathered "the lawless young people" (τοὺς 'Ερμοκοπίδας) in Teos, who were going to hear his lectures in which he followed Democritus and Leucippus.

I think Bailey's opinion as to the youth of Epicurus is much more probable. He may, of course, have got some books of Democritus at an early age. This is less romantical than Festugière's picture, but probably more true.

Epicurus' personality   812—Diogenes, after having mentioned a whole series of unelegant predicates, lavished by Epicurus on his colleagues-philosophers—e.g. he called Nausiphanes "the jelly-fish", an illiterate, a fraud and a trollop; Plato he called ironically "the golden", Aristotle a profligate, who after devouring his patrimony took to soldiering and selling drugs, Heraclitus a muddler (κυκητής), Democritus Lerocritus etc.—mentions some interesting features of the character of Epicurus and of the life in his school.

his philanthropia   a.   Diog. X, 9-10:

Τῷ γὰρ ἀνδρὶ μάρτυρες ἱκανοὶ τῆς ἀνυπερβλήτου πρὸς πάντας εὐγνωμοσύνης ἥ τε πατρὶς χαλκαῖς εἰκόσι τιμήσασα οἵ τε φίλοι τοσοῦτοι τὸ πλῆθος ὡς μηδ' ἂν πόλεσιν ὅλαις μετρεῖσθαι δύνασθαι· οἵ τε γνώριμοι πάντες ταῖς δογματικαῖς αὐτοῦ σειρῆσι προσκατασχεθέντες, πλὴν Μητροδώρου τοῦ Στρατονικέως πρὸς Καρνεάδην ἀποχωρήσαντος, τάχα βαρυνθέντος ταῖς ἀνυπερβλήτοις αὐτοῦ χρηστότησιν· ἥ τε διαδοχὴ πασῶν σχεδὸν ἐκλιπουσῶν τῶν ἄλλων[3] ἐς ἀεὶ

---

[1] He is called a Democritean in several other places: Cic., *N.D.* I 26, 73; Suidas, *Life of Epic.*; *Vol. Herc.* 2 IV f. 206 (cited by Usener, p. 414).

[2] *Epicure et ses dieux*, p. 25.

[3] This statement is exaggerated: probably in the Sceptic School there has been an interruption, in other schools certainly not.

διαμένουσα καὶ νηρίθμους ἀρχὰς ἀπολύουσα ἄλλην ἐξ ἄλλης τῶν γνωρίμων·
ἥ τε πρὸς τοὺς γονέας εὐχαριστία καὶ ἡ πρὸς τοὺς ἀδελφοὺς εὐποιία πρός τε
τοὺς οἰκέτας ἡμερότης, ὡς δῆλον κἀκ τῶν διαθηκῶν αὐτοῦ καὶ ὅτι αὐτοὶ
συνεφιλοσόφουν αὐτῷ, ὧν ἦν ἐνδοξότατος ὁ προειρημένος Μῦς· καθόλου τε ἡ
πρὸς πάντας αὐτοῦ φιλανθρωπία. Τῆς μὲν γὰρ πρὸς θεοὺς ὁσιότητος καὶ πρὸς
πατρίδα φιλίας ἄλεκτος ἡ διάθεσις· ὑπερβολῇ γὰρ ἐπιεικείας οὐδὲ πολιτείας
ἥψατο.

b. He spent nearly his whole life at Athens. Only once or twice he
went to Ionia to see his friends there. *The community of the friends*

Diog. ib., 10-11:

Οἳ καὶ πανταχόθεν πρὸς αὐτὸν ἀφικνοῦντο καὶ συνεβίουν αὐτῷ ἐν τῷ κήπῳ,
καθά φησι καὶ Ἀπολλόδωρος, [ὃν καὶ ὀγδοήκοντα μνῶν πρίασθαι. Διοκλῆς
δὲ ἐν τῇ τρίτῃ τῆς ἐπιδρομῆς φησιν] εὐτελέστατα καὶ λιτότατα διαιτώμενοι.
"Κοτύλῃ γοῦν, φησίν, οἰνιδίου ἠρκοῦντο, τὸ δὲ πᾶν ὕδωρ ἦν αὐτοῖς ποτόν."
τόν τε Ἐπίκουρον μὴ ἀξιοῦν εἰς τὸ κοινὸν κατατίθεσθαι τὰς οὐσίας, καθάπερ
τὸν Πυθαγόραν κοινὰ τὰ φίλων λέγοντα· ἀπιστούντων γὰρ εἶναι τὸ τοιοῦτον,
εἰ δ᾽ ἀπίστων, οὐδὲ φίλων. αὐτός τέ φησιν ἐν ταῖς ἐπιστολαῖς ὕδατι μόνον
ἀρκεῖσθαι καὶ ἄρτῳ λιτῷ. καί, "Πέμψον μοι τυροῦ, φησί, κυθριδίου, ἵν᾽ ὅταν
βούλωμαι πολυτελεύσασθαι δύνωμαι." τοιοῦτος ἦν ὁ τὴν ἡδονὴν εἶναι τέλος
δογματίζων.

813—a. *To Leontion*, ap. Diog. X 5 (fr. 143 Us.): *his cordiality*

Παιὰν ἄναξ, φίλον Λεοντάριον, οἵου κροτοθορύβου ἡμᾶς ἐνέπλησας ἀνα-
γνόντας σου τὸ ἐπιστόλιον.

Plut., *De recta ratione audiendi* 15, p. 45 f., is displeased with this κροτοθόρυβος
of Epic. and calls him ἀηδής.

b. *To Themista*. Ap. Diog., ib. (fr. 125 Us.):

Οἷός τέ εἰμι, ἐὰν μὴ ὑμεῖς πρός με ἀφίκησθε, αὐτὸς τρικύλιστος, ὅπου ἂν
ὑμεῖς καὶ Θεμίστα παρακαλῆτε, ὠθεῖσθαι.

c. *To a child*: Vol. Herc. 176, col. 18 (fr. 176 Us.):

Ἀ>φείγμεθα εἰς Λάμψακον ὑγιαίνοντες ἐγὼ καὶ Πυθοκλῆς κα<ὶ Ἕρμ>αρχος
καὶ Κ<τή>σιππος, καὶ ἐκεῖ κατειλήφαμεν ὑγ<ι>αίνοντας Θεμίσταν καὶ τοὺς
λοιποὺς <φί>λο<υ>ς. εὖ δὲ ποιε<ῖ>ς καὶ σὺ εἰ<ἱ ὑ>γιαίνεις καὶ ἡ μ<ά>μμη <σ>ου,
καὶ πάπαι καὶ Μάτρω<ν>ι πάντα πε<ί>θη<ι>, <ὥσπ>ερ καὶ ἔ<μ>προσθεν. εὖ γὰρ
ἴσθι, ἡ αἰτία, ὅτι καὶ ἐγὼ καὶ ο<ἱ> λοιποὶ πάντες σε μέγα φιλοῦμεν, ὅτι τούτοις
πείθη πάντα * *.

814—As we saw in **812b**, soberness was one of the essential features *Soberness* of the Epicurean style of life. The principle is put forth in the following lines.

a. *Letter to Idomeneus*. Stob. *Flor*. XVII 24 (fr. 135 Us.):

Εἰ βούλει πλούσιον Πυθοκλέα ποιῆσαι, μὴ χρημάτων προστίθει, τῆς δὲ ἐπιθυμίας ἀφαίρει.

b. Aelianus, *Var. Hist*. IV 13 (fr. 602 Us.):

Ὁ αὐτὸς ἔλεγεν ἑτοίμως ἔχειν καὶ τῷ Διὶ ὑπὲρ εὐδαιμονίας διαγωνίζεσθαι μᾶζαν ἔχων καὶ ὕδωρ.

c. The reason why Epic. thought it good to strive after αὐτάρκεια, is expressed in the following lines.

To Idomeneus. Stob., *Flor*. XVII 14 (Bailey V 28):

Ἐζηλώσαμεν τὴν αὐτάρκειαν οὐχ ὅπως τοῖς εὐτελέσι καὶ λιτοῖς πάντως χρώμεθα, ἀλλ᾽ ὅπως θαρρῶμεν πρὸς αὐτά.

Cheerfulness **815—a.** Epicurus prescribed that at regular times there should be feasts. To this purpose he made some arrangements in his testament. Diog. X 18:

Ἐκ δὲ τῶν γινομένων προσόδων τῶν δεδομένων ἀφ᾽ ἡμῶν Ἀμυνομάχῳ καὶ Τιμοκράτει κατὰ τὸ δυνατὸν μεριζέσθωσαν μεθ᾽ Ἑρμάρχου σκοπούμενοι εἴς τε τὰ ἐναγίσματα τῷ τε πατρὶ καὶ τῇ μητρὶ καὶ τοῖς ἀδελφοῖς καὶ ἡμῖν εἰς τὴν εἰθισμένην ἄγεσθαι γενέθλιον ἡμέραν ἑκάστου ἔτους τῇ προτέρᾳ δεκάτῃ τοῦ Γαμηλιῶνος, ὥσπερ καὶ εἰς τὴν γινομένην σύνοδον ἑκάστου μηνὸς ταῖς εἰκάσι τῶν συμφιλοσοφούντων ἡμῖν εἰς τὴν ἡμῶν τε καὶ Μητροδώρου μνήμην κατατεταγμένην.

b. We learn something about the spirit and the organization of these feasts in a text of Philodemus.

Vogliano, *Epicuri et Epicureorum scripta*, p. 70, fr. 8, col. I:

.... μή[τε τοῖς δι]ὰ ταράχους μ[ο]χθοῦσι, τάς τ᾽ ἰ[δέας τ]ῶν ἀρίστων καὶ μακ[α]ρισ[τοτάτ]ων φύσεων ἐν μ[νήμῃ ἔχοντας κ]αλεῖν εὐωχ[εῖσ]θαι [1] αὐτοὺς καὶ γελᾶν ὡς καὶ τ[οὺς] ἄλλους, τούς γε [κ]ατὰ τὴν οἰκ[ίαν] ἅπαντας καὶ [τ]ῶ[ν] ἔξωθεν [μηδέν᾽ ὅλ]ω[ς] παραλείποντας, ὅσοι τ[ὰ]ς [εὐ]νοίας [καὶ] τὰς ἑαυτοῦ κ[α]ὶ τὰ[ς τ]ῶν ἑαυτοῦ φίλων ἔχουσιν· οὐ γὰρ δημαγωγήσειν, τοῦτο πράττοντας, τὴν κενὴν καὶ ἀφυσιο[λ]όγητον δ[η]μαγ[ωγ]ίαν, ἀλλ᾽ ἐν τοῖς τῆς φύσεω[ς οἰκ]είοις ἐνεργοῦντας μνη[σθ]ήσεσθαι πάντων τῶν τὰς εὐν[οίας] ἡμῖν ἐχόντων

---

[1] Non-members of the School to be invited: 1. ...... (text unreadable). 2. no grumblers. 3. "such persons as have a remembrance of the best and most blessed beings", i.e. the gods.

ὅπως συ[γκαθ]αγίζωσιν τὰ τοῖς ἐπὶ τῆι ἑαυτ[ῶν μα]καρίαι συ[μφι]λοσ[ο]φο[ῦσι
καθ]ήκοντα.

The sense of these ritual meals is not, as Cic. thinks (De fin. II 31, 101), that
Epic., in spite of his theory, attributed some form of survival to the dead, but
that he wished the sphere of cheerfulness and friendship in his school to be continued after his death.

   c. Epic., Sent. Vat. XLI (Bailey VA, XLI):

Γελᾶν ἅμα δεῖν καὶ φιλοσοφεῖν *.

816—Epicurus intends to give a philosophy of life for the simple ones.   **Dislike**
His first principle is that for being happy very few things are required.   **of learning**
Hence he shows a certain dislike of learning and scholarly pretentions.

   a. *To Pythocles*. Ap. Diog. X 6 (Bailey V B, 33):

Παιδείαν δὲ πᾶσαν, μακάριε, φεῦγε τἀκάτιον ἀράμενος.

   b. It is from this attitude of mind that we can understand the less
agreeable predicates attributed by Epic. to former and contemporary
philosophers (**811a**, **812**). On the other hand we find him writing and
reproaching Timocrates, who left his school and wrote against it, for
despising the philosophers who certainly do not deserve such contempt.
   Philodemus, π. κακιῶν I, col. IV, l. 25-29 [1]:

Καὶ [τ]ῶν φι[λ]οσόφων δὴ καθυπε[ρ]ηφανεῖ, περὶ ὧν ἀποπληξία λέ[γε]ιν ὡς
εἰσὶν ἐπιτήδειοι καταφρονεῖσθαι.

817—The same letter gives, in opposition to Timocrates' ὑπερηφανία,   **Simplicity**
a short summary of Epicurus' attitude in life.
   Philodemus, ib., col. IX, 1. 1-28 (Jensen, o.c., p. 31):

..... [μηδὲ τῶν ἀλλ]ων ἀνθρ[ώπω]ν ἐξ[ευτε]λιστὴν μηδ' ἑαυτοῦ θαυμαστήν,
καὶ μάλιστα ἐ[πὶ] τοῖς ἐκ τύχη[ς · μ]ηδ' ἐξηλ[λα]γμένον ἐν μηδενὶ φαίνεσθαι· μηδὲ
δ[υσ]πρόσδεκτον εἰς ο[ἰκί]αν καὶ ὁμιλίαν καὶ τῶν λοι[π]ῶν μετάδοσιν· μ[ηδ]ὲ
ἀναξίους ἀποφαίν[ειν ἑ]αυτοῦ πάντας· καὶ τατ[τόν]τ[ω]ν [ὑπα]κού[ει]ν δ[υνά]μεων
[καὶ] θε[ῶν]· ὠφ[ελία]ς [τε λέγ]ε[ιν ὑπ'] ἐνίων εὐ[εργετῶν γεγο]νένα[ι] καὶ
εὐ[χαριστ]εῖν [ἐπ'] αὐταῖς, ἀλ[λὰ] μὴ κατα[ξ]ιοῦν ἐκ[εί]νους μέγα νομίζειν, ὅτι
προσδέδεκταί τι παρ' αὐτῶν· κἂν χρείαν τινὸς [π]οιῆται μείζονος, αὐτὸν
θεραπεύειν, ὁπότ[αν] ἁνδάνηι, μὴ θεραπεύεσθαι ζητεῖν· πρόνοιαν δ' ἔχειν καὶ
πε[ρὶ] τῶν οἰκετῶν [καὶ] τῶν ὑπηρετούντων ἐ[λε]υθέρων ἢ συνόντων ἄλλων·

---

* γελᾶν om. Usener.
[1] Jensen, *Ein neuer Brief Epikurs*, p. 21.

Veneration of friends

818—*To Colotes*. Plut., *Adv. Coloten* 17, p. 1117 b (fr. 141 Us.):

Colotes, on hearing Epicurus' teaching, suddenly knelt before him and venerated him as a god. Epicurus answers him with a glimpse of irony.

ὡς σεβομένῳ γάρ σοι τὰ τότε ὑφ' ἡμῶν λεγόμενα προσέπεσεν ἐπιθύμημα ἀφυσιολόγητον τοῦ περιπλακῆναι ἡμῖν γονάτων ἐφαπτόμενον καὶ πάσης τῆς εἰθισμένης ἐπιλήψεως γίνεσθαι κατὰ τὰς σεβάσεις τινῶν καὶ λιτάς· ἐποίεις οὖν καὶ ἡμᾶς ἀνθιεροῦν σὲ αὐτὸν καὶ ἀντισέβεσθαι. ἄφθαρτός μοι περιπάτει καὶ ἡμᾶς ἀφθάρτους διανοοῦ.

Last letter to Idomeneus

819—On the day of his death Epicurus writes to Idomeneus the following letter. Diog. X 22 (fr. 138 Us.):

Τὴν μακαρίαν ἄγοντες καὶ ἅμα τελευτῶντες ἡμέραν τοῦ βίου ἐγράφομεν ὑμῖν ταυτί· στραγγουρικά τε παρηκολούθει καὶ δυσεντερικὰ πάθη ὑπερβολὴν οὐκ ἀπολείποντα τοῦ ἐν ἑαυτοῖς μεγέθους· ἀντιπαρετάττετο δὲ πᾶσι τούτοις τὸ κατὰ ψυχὴν χαῖρον ἐπὶ τῇ τῶν γεγονότων ἡμῖν διαλογισμῶν μνήμῃ. σὺ δὲ ἀξίως τῆς ἐκ μειρακίου παραστάσεως πρὸς ἐμὲ καὶ φιλοσοφίαν ἐπιμελοῦ τῶν παίδων Μητροδώρου.

Works

820—Of the works of Epic. we possess in the tenth book of Diog. Laert. the three great epistles (that *to Herodotus*, which is a treatise on physics, that *to Pythocles*, on the celestial phenomena, and the letter *to Menoeceus* on ethics), the *Kyriai doxai* and a considerate number of fragments. Of the great work π. φύσεως important fragments have been found on papyri, published by Vogliano. The *Letter to Idomeneus*, cited sub **816**, **817**, on Timocrates' ὑπερηφανία was admirably reconstructed and explained by Chr. Jensen.

2—BASIC PRINCIPLES: THE CANONICE

The Canon

821—Diog. X 30:

Διαιρεῖται τοίνυν (sc. philosophy, according to Epic.) εἰς τρία, τό τε κανονικὸν καὶ φυσικὸν καὶ ἠθικόν. τὸ μὲν οὖν κανονικὸν ἐφόδους ἐπὶ τὴν πραγματείαν ἔχει καὶ ἔστιν ἐν ἑνὶ τῷ ἐπιγραφομένῳ Κανών.

Ἡ κανονική: the doctrine of the leading principles. It was concerned with the criterium (or criteria) of truth. The title seems to have been inspired by a work of Democr.: Π. λογικῶν κανών.

All sensibles are true and existent

822—The summary of Epicurus' theory of knowledge, which forms the basis of his doctrine, is expressed by Sextus, *Adv. Math.* VIII (*Against the Logicians* II) 9:

Ὁ δὲ Ἐπίκουρος τὰ μὲν αἰσθητὰ πάντα ἔλεγεν ἀληθῆ καὶ ὄντα. οὐ διήνεγκε γὰρ ἀληθὲς εἶναί τι λέγειν ἢ ὑπάρχον· ἔνθεν καὶ ὑπογράφων τἀληθὲς καὶ ψεῦδος "ἔστι" φησὶν "ἀληθὲς τὸ οὕτως ἔχον ὡς λέγεται ἔχειν," καὶ "ψεῦδός ἐστι" φησὶ "τὸ οὐχ οὕτως ἔχον ὡς λέγεται ἔχειν."

Which means: there is one means of knowledge, and one only, namely sense-perception, which is in itself our last and only guarantee of truth.—This solution of the problem of knowledge is, after Plato's *Theaet.* and Aristotle's *Post. Anal.*, incredibly simplistic. We can agree with Bailey that Epicurus' atomic theory shows a certain genius; yet, it must be granted that his philosophical basis was extremely weak.

823—a.   In Diog. X 31 three or even four criteria are mentioned: αἰσθήσεις, προλήψεις, πάθη

Ἐν τοίνυν τῷ Κανόνι λέγων ἐστὶν ὁ Ἐπίκουρος κριτήρια τῆς ἀληθείας εἶναι τὰς αἰσθήσεις καὶ προλήψεις καὶ τὰ πάθη, οἱ δ' Ἐπικούρειοι καὶ τὰς φανταστικὰς ἐπιβολὰς τῆς διανοίας.

It is hardly possible that Epic. should have intended to introduce other standards of truth besides the senses.

b.   Cf. *Kyriai doxai* XXIII (Diog. X 146):

Εἰ μάχῃ πάσαις ταῖς αἰσθήσεσιν, οὐχ ἕξεις οὐδ' ἃς ἂν φῇς αὐτῶν διεψεῦσθαι πρὸς τί ποιούμενος τὴν ἀναγωγὴν κρίνῃς.

c.   Also *K.D.* XXIV (Diog. ib. 147):

Εἴ τιν' ἐκβαλεῖς ἁπλῶς αἴσθησιν, . . . συνταράξεις καὶ τὰς λοιπὰς αἰσθήσεις, . . . ὥστε τὸ κριτήριον ἅπαν ἐκβαλεῖς.

d.   Lucr. IV, 469-70, 472-79:

> Denique nil sciri siquis putat, id quoque nescit
470   an sciri possit, quoniam nil scire fatetur.
> Et tamen hoc quoque uti concedam scire, at id ipsum
> quaeram, cum in rebus veri nil viderit ante,
475   unde sciat quid sit scire et nescire vicissim,
> notitiam veri quae res falsique crearit
> et dubium certo quae res differre probarit.
> Invenies primis ab sensibus esse creatam
> notitiem veri neque sensus posse refelli.

e.   *To Herod.*, ap. Diog. X 38:

Ἔτι τε κατὰ τὰς αἰσθήσεις δεῖ πάντα τηρεῖν.

We can hardly admit that the following words of this passage should retract anything of the first principle. The text runs:

Καὶ ἁπλῶς ‹κατὰ› τὰς παρούσας ἐπιβολὰς εἴτε διανοίας εἴθ' ὅτου δήποτε τῶν κριτηρίων. ὁμοίως δὲ κατὰ τὰ ὑπάρχοντα πάθη, ὅπως ἂν καὶ τὸ προσμένον καὶ τὸ ἄδηλον ἔχωμεν οἷς σημειωσόμεθα.

What is meant by ἐπιβολὰς τῆς διανοίας and by other criteria will be explained in the following numbers.

What are
προλήψεις? **824**—What then are προλήψεις and in what sense can they be called criteria?

a. Diog. X 33:

Τὴν δὲ πρόληψιν λέγουσιν οἱονεὶ κατάληψιν ἢ δόξαν ὀρθὴν ἢ ἔννοιαν ἢ καθολικὴν νόησιν ἐναποκειμένην, τουτέστι μνήμην τοῦ πολλάκις ἔξωθεν φανέντος, οἷον τὸ Τοιοῦτόν ἐστιν ἄνθρωπος· ἅμα γὰρ τῷ ῥηθῆναι ἄνθρωπος εὐθὺς κατὰ πρόληψιν καὶ ὁ τύπος αὐτοῦ νοεῖται προηγουμένων τῶν αἰσθήσεων.

Thus, the general notion called πρόληψις is a sediment of various sensations. Having such a notion in our mind, we are able to identify new individual perceptions.

b. Same passage, continued:

Παντὶ οὖν ὀνόματι τὸ πρώτως ὑποτεταγμένον ἐναργές ἐστι· καὶ οὐκ ἂν ἐζητήσαμεν τὸ ζητούμενον, εἰ μὴ πρότερον ἐγνώκειμεν αὐτό, οἷον Τὸ πόρρω ἑστὼς ἵππος ἐστὶν ἢ βοῦς· δεῖ γὰρ κατὰ πρόληψιν ἐγνωκέναι ποτὲ ἵππου καὶ βοὸς μορφήν· οὐδ' ἂν ὠνομάσαμέν τι μὴ πρότερον αὐτοῦ κατὰ πρόληψιν τὸν τύπον μαθόντες. ἐναργεῖς οὖν εἰσιν αἱ προλήψεις καὶ τὸ δοξαστὸν ἀπὸ προτέρου τινὸς ἐναργοῦς ἤρτηται, ἐφ' ὃ ἀναφέροντες λέγομεν, οἷον Πόθεν ἴσμεν εἰ τοῦτό ἐστιν ἄνθρωπος;

The explanation is, of course, a circulus: perception is explained by perception.

c. Cf. Clem. Alex., *Strom*. II 4, 16, 3 (Stählin II, p. 121, 10-13):

Πρόληψιν δὲ ἀποδίδωσιν ἐπιβολὴν ἐπί τι ἐναργὲς καὶ ἐπὶ τὴν ἐναργῆ τοῦ πράγματος ἐπίνοιαν.

Epic. in the passage cited sub **823e** speaks of ἐπιβολὰς εἴτε διανοίας εἴθ' ὅτου δήποτε τῶν κριτηρίων: directing one's attention (either of the mind or of whatever other means of knowledge) to a thing.

Notitia
or *notities*
in Lucr. **825**—In Lucr. the πρόληψις appears as a *notitia veri falsique*, by which alone we are able to distinguish between what is doubtful and what is certain.

a. Lucr. IV 474 ff., cited sub **823d**.

b. How would the gods have brought forth a world, if they had not had a *notities* of it?
Lucr. V 181 f.:

Exemplum porro gignundis rebus et ipsa
notities divis hominum unde est insita primum?

The passage will be quoted at length sub 85 4 b.

c. And how could man have invented language, if he had not a notion of it by a language already existing round about him?

Lucr. V 1046-49:

> Praeterea si non alii quoque vocibus usi
> inter se fuerant, unde insita notities est
> utilitatis et unde data est huic prima potestas,
> quid vellet facere ut sciret animoque videret?

826—The πάθη, finally, are a criterium in ethics, and they too can be reduced to the senses, for "good" is what is agreeable to them, and "bad" what is not. The
πάθη as
a criterium

a. Diog. X 34:

Πάθη δὲ λέγουσιν εἶναι δύο, ἡδονὴν καὶ ἀλγηδόνα, ἱστάμενα περὶ πᾶν ζῷον· καὶ τὴν μὲν οἰκεῖον, τὴν δὲ ἀλλότριον· δι' ὧν κρίνεσθαι τὰς αἱρέσεις καὶ φυγάς.

b. *To Menoeceus*, ap. Diog. X 129:

Ταύτην γὰρ (sc. τὴν ἡδονὴν) ἀγαθὸν πρῶτον καὶ συγγενικὸν ἔγνωμεν, καὶ ἀπὸ ταύτης καταρχόμεθα πάσης αἱρέσεως καὶ φυγῆς, καὶ ἐπὶ ταύτην καταντῶμεν ὡς κανόνι τῷ πάθει πᾶν ἀγαθὸν κρίνοντες.

827—In Diog. X 31 there is spoken of ἐπιβολὰς τῆς διανοίας as a fourth criterium, introduced not by Epic. himself but in his School (nr. **823a**; cf. **824c**, with note 1). We find the term used by Epic: ἐπιβολὴ
τῆς διανοίας

a. in the letter to Herod., Diog. X 38, cited above, sub **823e**; cp. **824c**.

b. in K.D. XXIV (Diog. X 147):

Εἴ τιν' ἐκβαλεῖς ἁπλῶς αἴσθησιν καὶ μὴ διαιρήσεις τὸ δοξαζόμενον κατὰ τὸ προσμένον καὶ τὸ παρὸν ἤδη κατὰ τὴν αἴσθησιν καὶ τὰ πάθη καὶ πᾶσαν φανταστικὴν ἐπιβολὴν τῆς διανοίας, συνταράξεις καὶ τὰς λοιπὰς αἰσθήσεις τῇ ματαίᾳ δόξῃ.

τὸ προσμένον: that which awaits to be confirmed by experience.

τὸ παρὸν: "that which is already present, whether in sensation or in feelings or in any presentative perception of the mind" (Hicks).

Epic. means that certain beings, e.g. the gods, send out *eidola* so fine, that they can only be perceived by the finer atoms of the mind, provided it directs its attention to them. Thus, here again we have a kind of aisthesis, be it of a subtler form.

828—Epic. supports his criteriology by two arguments: Epicurus'
arguments

**for his
sensualism**

(1) sensation is irrational and therefore immediate,

(2) we do not possess any other criterium by which we could refute it.

Diog. X 31-32:

Πᾶσα γάρ, φησίν, αἴσθησις ἄλογός ἐστι καὶ μνήμης οὐδεμιᾶς δεκτική·
οὔτε γὰρ ὑφ’ αὑτῆς οὔτε ὑφ’ ἑτέρου κινηθεῖσα δύναταί τι προσθεῖναι ἢ ἀφελεῖν
οὐδὲ ἐστὶ τὸ δυνάμενον αὐτὰς διελέγξαι. οὔτε γὰρ ἡ ὁμοιογενὴς αἴσθησις τὴν
ὁμογενῆ διὰ τὴν ἰσοσθένειαν, οὔθ’ ἡ ἀνομογένεια τὴν ἀνομογένειαν· οὐ γὰρ
τῶν αὐτῶν εἰσι κριτικαί· οὔτε μὴν λόγος, πᾶς γὰρ λόγος ἀπὸ τῶν αἰσθήσεων
ἤρτηται· οὔθ’ ἡ ἑτέρα τὴν ἑτέραν· πάσαις γὰρ προσέχομεν.

A criticism of this theory may be found in Plato's *Theaet*. "Αἴσθησις ἀεὶ τοῦ ὄντος
ἐστίν" is said in that dialogue. So far Epic. is right. The senses do not lie. But
how then to explain ψευδὴς δόξα?

3—THE ATOMIC THEORY

829—In principle Epic. adopted the atomic theory of Democr., though
it might seem not to be compatible with his standard of knowledge.
In fact Epic. holds that the senses first give us positive σημεῖα for the
atomic theory, and secondly procure us a method of negative control:
κατὰ τὰς αἰσθήσεις δεῖ πάντα τηρεῖν (*To Herod.* 38), which means, our

**The
ἄδηλα
Nothing is
created out
of nothing,
nothing
destroyed
into nothing**

theories are never allowed to be against sense data.

    a.   *To Herod.*, ap. Diog. X 38-41:

Ταῦτα δεῖ διαλαβόντας συνορᾶν ἤδη περὶ τῶν ἀδήλων, πρῶτον μὲν ὅτι
οὐδὲν γίνεται ἐκ τοῦ μὴ ὄντος· πᾶν γὰρ ἐκ παντὸς ἐγίνετ’ ἄν, σπερμάτων γε
οὐθὲν προσδεόμενον. καὶ εἰ ἐφθείρετο δὲ τὸ ἀφανιζόμενον εἰς τὸ μὴ ὄν, πάντα
ἂν ἀπωλώλει τὰ πράγματα, οὐκ ὄντων τῶν εἰς ἃ διελύετο. καὶ μὴν καὶ τὸ πᾶν
ἀεὶ τοιοῦτον ἦν οἷον νῦν ἐστι καὶ ἀεὶ τοιοῦτον ἔσται. οὐθὲν γάρ ἐστιν εἰς ὃ
μεταβάλλει. παρὰ γὰρ τὸ πᾶν οὐθέν ἐστιν ὃ ἂν εἰσελθὸν εἰς αὐτὸ τὴν μεταβολὴν
ποιήσαιτο. Ἀλλὰ μὴν καὶ τὸ πᾶν ἐστι <σώματα καὶ τόπος>*· τὰ μὲν γὰρ
σώματα ὡς ἔστιν αὐτὴ ἡ αἴσθησις ἐπὶ πάντων μαρτυρεῖ καθ’ ἣν ἀναγκαῖον τὸ
ἄδηλον τῷ λογισμῷ τεκμαίρεσθαι (ὥσπερ προεῖπον τὸ πρόσθεν). εἰ γὰρ μὴ ἦν ὃ κενὸν καὶ χώραν καὶ ἀναφῆ φύσιν ὀνομάζομεν, οὐκ ἂν εἶχε τὰ σώματα ὅπου ἦν οὐδε
δι’ οὗ ἐκινεῖτο, καθάπερ φαίνεται κινούμενα. παρὰ δὲ ταῦτα οὐθὲν ἐπινοηθῆναι
δύναται οὔτε περιληπτῶς** οὔτε ἀναλόγως τοῖς περιληπτοῖς, ὡς τὰ καθ’ ὅλας
φύσεις λαμβανόμενα καὶ μὴ ὡς τὰ τούτων συμπτώματα ἢ συμβεβηκότα [1]

---

[1] By συμπτώματα Epic. means *accidents*, by συμβεβηκότα however he designs
permanent properties, not separable from the thing.

  *   <σώματα καὶ τόπος> Usener, followed by Bailey.

 **   περιληπτικῶς corr. Bailey.

λεγόμενα. — καὶ τῶν σωμάτων τὰ μέν ἐστι συγκρίσεις, τὰ δ' ἐξ ὧν αἱ συγ- **Bodies and** κρίσεις πεποίηνται. ταῦτα δέ ἐστιν ἄτομα καὶ ἀμετάβλητα, εἴπερ μὴ μέλλει πάντα **space** εἰς τὸ μὴ ὂν φθαρήσεσθαι, ἀλλ' ἰσχύοντα* ὑπομένειν ἐν ταῖς διαλύσεσι τῶν συγ- κρίσεων, πλήρη τὴν φύσιν ὄντα καὶ οὐκ ἔχοντα ὅπη ἢ ὅπως διαλυθήσεται. ὥστε τὰς ἀρχὰς ἀτόμους ἀναγκαῖον εἶναι σωμάτων φύσεις.

b. Ib., 41: **Infinity of the universe**

Ἀλλὰ μὴν καὶ τὸ πᾶν ἄπειρόν ἐστι· τὸ γὰρ πεπερασμένον ἄκρον ἔχει· τὸ δὲ ἄκρον παρ' ἕτερόν τι θεωρεῖται. ὥστε οὐκ ἔχον ἄκρον πέρας οὐκ ἔχει, πέρας δὲ οὐκ ἔχον ἄπειρον ἂν εἴη καὶ οὐ πεπερασμένον. καὶ μὴν καὶ τῷ πλήθει τῶν σωμάτων ἄπειρόν ἐστι τὸ πᾶν καὶ τῷ μεγέθει τοῦ κενοῦ.

830—a. Ib., 42: **Differences of shape in the atoms**

Πρός τε τούτοις τὰ ἄτομα τῶν σωμάτων καὶ μεστά, ἐξ ὧν καὶ αἱ συγκρίσεις γίνονται καὶ εἰς ἃ διαλύονται, ἀπερίληπτά ἐστι ταῖς διαφοραῖς τῶν σχημάτων· οὐ γὰρ δυνατὸν γενέσθαι τὰς τοσαύτας διαφορὰς ἐκ τῶν αὐτῶν σχημάτων περιειλημμένων. καὶ καθ' ἑκάστην δὲ σχημάτισιν ἁπλῶς ἄπειροί εἰσιν αἱ ὅμοιαι, ταῖς δὲ διαφοραῖς οὐχ ἁπλῶς ἄπειροι, ἀλλὰ μόνον ἀπερίληπτοι.

The question will be explained sub 832 b.

b. Ib., 43: **Motion of the atoms**

Κινοῦνταί τε συνεχῶς αἱ ἄτομοι τὸν αἰῶνα.

831—a. Besides shape and size the atoms must possess weight. **Shape,** Diog. X 54: **wheight and size**

Καὶ μὴν καὶ τὰς ἀτόμους νομιστέον μηδεμίαν ποιότητα τῶν φαινομένων προσφέρεσθαι πλὴν σχήματος καὶ βάρους καὶ μεγέθους καὶ ὅσα ἐξ ἀνάγκης σχήματι συμφυῆ ἐστι· ποιότης γὰρ πᾶσα μεταβάλλει, αἱ δὲ ἄτομοι οὐδὲν μεταβάλλουσιν, ἐπειδήπερ δεῖ τι ὑπομένειν ἐν ταῖς διαλύσεσι τῶν συγκρίσεων στερεὸν καὶ ἀδιάλυτον, ὃ τὰς μεταβολὰς οὐκ εἰς τὸ μὴ ὂν ποιήσεται οὐδ' ἐκ τοῦ μὴ ὄντος, ἀλλὰ κατὰ μεταθέσεις <τινῶν>, τινῶν δὲ καὶ προσόδους καὶ ἀφόδους. ὅθεν ἀναγκαῖον τὰ μὴ μετατιθέμενα ἄφθαρτα εἶναι καὶ τὴν τοῦ μεταβάλλοντος φύσιν οὐκ ἔχοντα.

Cf. our nr. **141**: Democr. admitted only shape and size in his atoms.

b. [Plut.], *Plac.* I 3, 26 (285, 15 Dox.): **Difference from Democr.**

Ὁ δὲ Ἐπίκουρος τούτοις καὶ τρίτον βάρος προσέθηκεν· ἀνάγκη γάρ, φησί, κινεῖσθαι τὰ σώματα τῇ τοῦ βάρους πληγῇ.

Bailey, *The Gr. atomists* p. 289, thinks that this third property of the atoms was introduced not by Epic., but before him, perhaps by Nausiphanes, because

* ἰσχῦόν τι corr. Bailey.

Lucr. ii 225-242 explains the atomic movement not by weight but by the lack of resistance in the void. In fact, the passage of Lucr. does not tend to deny that the downward motion of the atoms is caused by their weight. What he says is that the *meeting* of the atoms in their downward fall cannot be accounted for by their weight, because in the void, which offers no resistance, all bodies, whatever be their weight, move with equal speed.

Other points of difference 832—Epicurus' theory is original on two other points. The second is his doctrine of the *minimae partes*, by which he can explain the difference in shape of the atoms. Epic. rejects the theory of infinite divisibility of the atoms, because it is against experience.

a. *To Herod.*, ap. Diog. 56-59:

Theory of minimae partes

Πρὸς δὲ τούτοις οὐ δεῖ νομίζειν ἐν τῷ ὡρισμένῳ σώματι ἀπείρους ὄγκους εἶναι οὐδ' ὁπηλικουσοῦν· ὥστε οὐ μόνον τὴν εἰς ἄπειρον τομὴν ἐπὶ τοὔλαττον ἀναιρετέον, ἵνα μὴ πάντα ἀσθενῆ ποιῶμεν καὶ ὡς ἐν ταῖς περιλήψεσι τῶν ἀθρόων εἰς τὸ μὴ ὂν ἀναγκαζώμεθα τὰ ὄντα θλίβοντες καταναλίσκειν· ἀλλὰ καὶ τὴν μετάβασιν μὴ νομιστέον γίνεσθαι ἐν τοῖς ὡρισμένοις εἰς ἄπειρον μηδ' <ἐπὶ> τοὔλαττον. οὔτε γὰρ ὅπως, ἐπειδὰν ἅπαξ τις εἴπῃ ὅτι ἄπειροι ὄγκοι ἔν τινι ὑπάρχουσιν ἢ ὁπηλικοιοῦν, ἔστι νοῆσαι πῶς τ' ἂν ἔτι τοῦτο πεπερασμένον εἴη τὸ μέγεθος·—

Τό τε ἐλάχιστον τὸ ἐν τῇ αἰσθήσει δεῖ κατανοεῖν ὅτι οὔτε τοιοῦτόν ἐστιν οἷον τὸ τὰς μεταβάσεις ἔχον οὔτε πάντως ἀνόμοιον, ἀλλ' ἔχον μέν τινα κοινότητα τῶν μεταβατῶν*, διάληψιν δὲ μερῶν οὐκ ἔχον·—

Ταύτῃ τῇ ἀναλογίᾳ νομιστέον καὶ τὸ ἐν τῇ ἀτόμῳ ἐλάχιστον κεχρῆσθαι· μικρότητι γὰρ ἐκεῖνο δῆλον ὡς διαφέρει τοῦ κατὰ τὴν αἴσθησιν θεωρουμένου, ἀναλογίᾳ δὲ τῇ αὐτῇ κέχρηται.

cf. Lucr. I 599-634. Bailey, *The Gr. Atomists*, p. 285-287.

b. As we saw sub **830a**, Epic. admitted a large number of shapes of the atoms. The theory of *minimae partes* enables us to explain this point further. I cite Bailey, *The Gr. Atomists*, p. 287 f.:

"An ingenious critic [1] has worked out some of these differences. If, for instance, we suppose the *minimae partes* to be cubes of exactly the same size, then, if an atom contains two only, it can have but one shape ; if it contains three, two shapes and ; if four, five shapes on one plane, and two more in two planes, according as one of the parts in the last figure be placed on top either of one of its neighbours, or of that at the opposite corner: with five or six parts the possibilities are very largely increased".

---

* Corr. Schneider; μεταβάντων codd. [1] Brieger, *Jahrb. Fleck.*, 1875, p. 630.

833—The third point on which Epic. differs from Democr. is his *the clinamen*
theory of the παρέγκλισις: a "tiny swerve" of the atoms, which is to
account for their meeting and collisions, i.e. for the forming and for
the dissipation of bodies. Bailey, *Gr. At.* p. 316 says: "It is curious that
there is no mention of the "swerve" of the atoms in the Letter to Herodotus: it must have been there either at the beginning of par. 43, where
some words have been lost, or in another section which has perished.
But we have evidence enough for it elsewhere."

    a.   *Diogenes of Oenoanda*, fr. 33, col. II l. 14-col. III, 19:

[Οὔκουν] οἶδας, ὅστις ποτὲ εἶ, καὶ ἐλευθέραν τινὰ ἐν ταῖς ἀτόμοις κείνησιν
εἶναι, ἣν Δημόκριτος μὲν οὐχ εὗρεν, Ἐπίκουρος δὲ εἰς φῶς ἤγαγεν, παρεγκλιτι-
κὴν ὑπάρχουσαν, ὡς ἐκ τῶν φαινομένων δείκνυσιν;

    b.   Aetius I 12, 5 (p. 311a 10 Dox.):

Κινεῖσθαι δὲ τὰ ἄτομα τότε μὲν κατὰ στάθμην τότε δὲ κατὰ παρέγκλισιν.

    c.   Ib. I 23, 4 (p. 319 Dox.):

Ἐπίκουρος δύο εἴδη τῆς κινήσεως, τὸ κατὰ στάθμην καὶ τὸ κατὰ παρέγκλισιν.

834—The connexion with ethics is clearly brought out by Diog. **Connexion**
Oenoand. fr. 33, col. III, l. 9-14 (directly after the above cited lines): **with ethics**

Τὸ δὲ μέγιστον πιστευθείσης γὰρ εἱμαρμένης αἴρεται πᾶσα νουθεσία καὶ
ἐπιτείμησις καὶ οὐδὲ τοὺς πονηροὺς [ἐξέσται κολάζειν] [1].

    b.   Lucr. II, 289-293:

> Sed ne mens ipsa necessum
> intestinum habeat cunctis in rebus agendis
> et devicta quasi cogatur ferre patique,
> id facit exiguum clinamen principiorum
> nec regione loci certa nec tempore certo.

    c.   Plut., *De sollertia an.* 7, 964c:

Ἄτομον παρεγκλῖναι μίαν ἐπὶ τοὐλάχιστον, ὅπως ἄστρα καὶ ζῷα καὶ τύχη
παρεισέλθη καὶ τὸ ἐφ᾽ ἡμῖν μὴ ἀπόληται.

835—This theory has been criticized very severely, both in ancient **Objections**
and in modern times.

---

[1] The last words have been supplied by Usener.

a. Cic., *De fato* X 22 (281 Us.):

Epicurus declinatione atomi vitari necessitatem fati putat. Itaque tertius quidam motus oritur extra pondus et plagam, cum declinat atomus intervallo minimo—id appellat ἐλάχιστον—; quam declinationem sine causa fieri si minus verbis, re cogitur confiteri. Non enim atomus ab atomo pulsa declinat. Nam qui potest pelli alia ab alia, si gravitate feruntur ad perpendiculum corpora individua rectis lineis, ut Epicuro placet? Sequitur enim ut, si alia ab alia numquam depellatur, ne contingat quidem alia aliam. Ex quo efficitur, etiamsi sit atomus eaque declinet, declinare sine causa. Hanc Epicurus rationem induxit ob eam rem, quod veritus est ne, si semper atomus gravitate ferretur naturali ac necessaria, nihil liberum nobis esset, cum ita moveretur animus, ut atomorum motu cogeretur. Id Democritus, auctor atomorum, accipere maluit, necessitate omnia fieri, quam a corporibus individuis naturalis motus avellere.

b. Ib. XX, 46 (Us., ib.):

Declinat, inquit, atomus. Primum cur? Aliam enim quandam vim motus habebant a Democrito impulsionis, quam plagam ille appellat, a te, Epicure, gravitatis et ponderis. Quae ergo nova causa in natura est, qua declinet atomus? Aut num sortiuntur inter se, quae declinet, quae non? Aut cur minimo declinent intervallo, maiore non? Aut cur declinent uno minimo, non declinent duobus aut tribus? Optare hoc quidem est, non disputare.

c. In *De finibus* I 6, 19 he calls it a *res ficta pueriliter* and in *De N.D.* I 25, 70 he even says:

hoc dicere turpius est quam illud quod volt non posse defendere.

On the value of the theory and modern analogies see Bailey, *Gr. At.* p. 320-327.

Atomic speed   **836—a.** All atoms move at equal rate, because the void offers no resistance.

To Herod. ap. Diog. X 61:

Καὶ μὴν καὶ ἰσοταχεῖς ἀναγκαῖον τὰς ἀτόμους εἶναι, ὅταν διὰ τοῦ κενοῦ εἰσφέρωνται μηδενὸς ἀντικόπτοντος· οὔτε γὰρ τὰ βαρέα θᾶττον οἰσθήσεται τῶν μικρῶν καὶ κούφων, ὅταν γε δὴ μηδὲν ἀπαντᾷ αὐτοῖς· οὔτε τὰ μικρὰ τῶν μεγάλων, πάντα πόρον σύμμετρον ἔχοντα, ὅταν μηθὲν μηδὲ ἐκείνοις ἀντικόπτῃ· οὔθ' ἡ ἄνω οὔθ' ἡ εἰς τὸ πλάγιον διὰ τῶν κρούσεων φορὰ οὔθ' ἡ κάτω διὰ τῶν ἰδίων βαρῶν· ἐφ' ὁπόσον γὰρ ἂν κατίσχῃ ἑκάτερα αὐτ>ῶν, ἐπὶ τοσοῦτον

ἅμα νοήματι τὴν φορὰν σχήσει, ἕως <ἄν τι> ἀντικόψῃ ἢ ἔξωθεν ἢ ἐκ τοῦ
ἰδίου βάρους πρὸς τὴν τοῦ πλήξαντος δύναμιν.

This theory of Epic. has been confirmed by modern physics.

b. Lucr., II 238-239:

> Omnia quapropter debent per inane quietum
> aeque ponderibus non aequis concita ferri.

c. *To Herod.*, ap. Diog. X 46b (placed by Bailey after c. 61):

Καὶ μὴν καὶ ἡ διὰ τοῦ κενοῦ φορὰ κατὰ μηδεμίαν ἀπάντησιν τῶν ἀντικοψόντων * γινομένη πᾶν μῆκος περιληπτὸν ἐν ἀπερινοήτῳ χρόνῳ συντελεῖ·
βράδους γὰρ καὶ τάχους ἀντικοπὴ καὶ οὐκ ἀντικοπὴ ὁμοίωμα λαμβάνει.

837—What becomes of the motions of atoms imprisoned in compounds?
—"It is one of the most striking of Epicurus' acts of "mental apprehension"," Bailey says (*Gr. At.* p. 331), "that he saw that the motion of the
atom through the void at 'atomic' speed is not in any way diminished
or altered by its entry into a compound body". *(margin: Motion in compound bodies)*

To Herod., ap. Diog. X 43:

Κινοῦνταί τε συνεχῶς αἱ ἄτομοι τὸν αἰῶνα, καὶ αἱ μὲν...** εἰς μακρὰν ἀπ'
ἀλλήλων διιστάμεναι, αἱ δ' αὐτὸν τὸν παλμὸν ἴσχουσιν, ὅταν τύχωσιν τῇ
περιπλοκῇ κεκλιμέναι ἢ στεγαζόμεναι παρὰ τῶν πλεκτικῶν.

Bailey, l.l., explains: "The only result of the density of formation (sc. of a
compound body) is that the atom, as it moves at absolute speed, more immediately
comes into conflict with other atoms and is again changed in direction: its "trajects"
—if this term may be applied to its infinitely minute journeyings to and fro—are
made shorter and its collisions more frequent." This perpetual interior vibration
of a compound body is called by Epic. παλμός. Lucr. described it in II 308-332.

838—The compound body (ἄθροισμα, *concilium*) is not a mere aggre-
gate, but a new unity endowed with properties which do not belong to
the atoms themselves, e.g. colour. Lucr. II 766-775 argues that, if the
atoms had colour, changes of colour could not possibly be accounted for.
We cite II. 772-775: *(margin: Properties of compound bodies)*

> Quod si caeruleis constarent aequora ponti
> seminibus, nullo possent albescere pacto.
> Nam quocumque modo perturbes caerula quae sint,
> numquam in marmoreum possunt migrare colorem.

---

* ἀντικοψόντων Usener, Bailey; ἀντικοψάντων codd.

** Bailey, following Bignone, indicates a lacuna here. It might be supplied by
the words <κατὰ στάθμην, αἱ δὲ κατὰ παρέγκλισιν, αἱ δὲ κατὰ παλμόν. τούτων δὲ αἱ μὲν
φέρονται>, as has been suggested by Bignone.

Bailey, *Gr. At.* p. 354 ff., rightly points to the difference between Democr. and Epic. in the appreciation of the so-called secondary qualities: for Democr. only primary qualities were essential and the object of true knowledge; for Epic. however sense-perception is true, and therefore, also secondary qualities are real.

Definition of time

839—We saw (sub **829a**) that Epic. uses the term σύμπτωμα in the sense of *accident*. He defines *time* as "an accident of accidents".

Sextus, *Adv. Math.* X (Against the Physicists II) 219 (294 Us.):

Ἐπίκουρος δὲ . . . τὸν χρόνον σύμπτωμα συμπτωμάτων εἶναι λέγει, παρεπόμενον ἡμέραις τε καὶ νυξὶ καὶ ὥραις καὶ πάθεσι καὶ ἀπαθείαις καὶ κινήσεσι καὶ μοναῖς.

Which means: time is not *essentially* connected with things, as is, for instance, weight; and as, for instance, colour is a συμβεβηκός of *visible* things.

Infinite number of worlds

840—Since there is a countless number of atoms, there is an infinite number of worlds.

a. *To Herod.* ap. Diog. X 45:

Ἀλλὰ μὴν καὶ κόσμοι ἄπειροί εἰσιν, οἵ θ' ὅμοιοι τούτῳ καὶ οἱ ἀνόμοιοι· αἵ τε γὰρ ἄτομοι ἄπειροι οὖσαι, ὡς ἄρτι ἀπεδείχθη, φέρονται καὶ πορρωτάτω· οὐ γὰρ κατανήλωνται αἱ τοιαῦται ἄτομοι, ἐξ ὧν ἂν γένοιτο κόσμος ἢ ὑφ' ὧν ἂν ποιηθείη, οὔτ' εἰς ἕνα οὔτ' εἰς πεπερασμένους, οὔθ' ὅσοι τοιοῦτοι, οὔθ' ὅσοι διάφοροι τούτοις· ὥστ' οὐδὲν τὸ ἐμποδοστατῆσόν ἐστι πρὸς τὴν ἀπειρίαν τῶν κόσμων.

formed by agglomerations of matter and dissolved again

b. Ib. 73:

Ἐπί τε τοῖς προειρημένοις τοὺς κόσμους δεῖ καὶ πᾶσαν σύγκρισιν πεπερασμένην, τὸ ὁμοειδὲς τοῖς θεωρουμένοις πυκνῶς ἔχουσαν νομίζειν γεγονέναι ἀπὸ τοῦ ἀπείρου, πάντων τούτων ἐκ συστροφῶν ἰδίων ἀποκεκριμένων καὶ μειζόνων καὶ ἐλαττόνων· καὶ πάλιν διαλύεσθαι πάντα, τὰ μὲν θᾶττον, τὰ δὲ βραδυτέρον· καὶ τὰ μὲν ὑπὸ τοιῶνδε, τὰ δ' ὑπὸ τοιῶνδε τοῦτο πάσχοντα.

metakosmia

c. The space between the different worlds is called by Epicurus μετακόσμια, by Lucr. *intermundia*. It is firstly the place where new worlds may come into being, secondly the dwelling place of the gods.

To Pythocles, ap. Diog. X 89:

Ὅτι δὲ καὶ τοιοῦτοι κόσμοι εἰσὶν ἄπειροι τὸ πλῆθος, ἔστι καταλαβεῖν, καὶ ὅτι ὁ τοιοῦτος δύναται κόσμος γίνεσθαι καὶ ἐν κόσμῳ καὶ μετακοσμίῳ, ὃ λέγομεν μεταξὺ κόσμων διάστημα, ἐν πολυκένῳ τόπῳ καὶ οὐκ ἐν μεγάλῳ εἰλικρινεῖ καὶ κενῷ, καθάπερ τινές φασιν.

The coming into being of a world is picturesquely described by Lucr. V 416-508. Cp. also Vergil's Ecl. VI. Bailey explains the theory in his *Gr. At.*, p. 364 ff.

841—Lucr. speaks at great length on the ultimate destruction of worlds: V 64-109, 235-415. He thinks that our world is already on the path of decay.

Lucr. V 104-109:

> Dictis dabit ipsa fidem res
> fortisan et graviter terrarum motibus ortis
> omnia conquassari in parvo tempore cernes.
> Quod procul a nobis flectat fortuna gubernans,
> et ratio potius quam res persuadeat ipsa
> succidere horrisono posse omnia victa fragore.

Our aging world

842—Lucr. describes the early development of the animal kingdom in the same way as Empedocles did (our nr. **111**): arbitrary combinations arise, of which the fittest survive.

Formation of organisms

a. Lucr. V 837-850:

> Multaque tum tellus etiam portenta creare
> conatast mira facie membrisque coorta,
> androgynum, interutrasque nec utrum, utrimque remotum,
> 840 orba pedum partim, manuum viduata vicissim,
> muta sine ore etiam, sine vultu caeca reperta,
> vinctaque membrorum per totum corpus adhaesu,
> nec facere ut possent quicquam nec cedere quoquam
> nec vitare malum nec sumere quod foret usus.
> 845 Cetera de genere hoc monstra ac portenta creabat,
> nequiquam, quoniam natura absterruit auctum
> nec potuere cupitum aetatis tangere florem
> nec reperire cibum nec iungi per Veneris res.
> Multa videmus enim rebus concurrere debere,
> 850 ut propagando possint procudere saecla.

b. Lucr. denies the possibility of the existence of such mythical beings as centaurs, scyllas and chimaeras, and does this by applying the criterium of experience. The passage shows a remarkably keen observation.

Lucr. V 878-894:

> Sed neque Centauri fuerunt, nec tempore in ullo
> esse queunt duplici natura et corpore bino
> 880 ex alienigenis membris compacta, potestas

no centaurs and chimaeras

hinc illinc par, vis ut sat par * esse potissit.
Id licet hinc quamvis hebeti cognoscere corde.
Principio circum tribus actis impiger annis
floret equus, puer haudquaquam; nam saepe etiam nunc
885   ubera mammarum in somnis lactantia quaeret.
Post ubi equum validae vires aetate senecta
membraque deficiunt fugienti languida vita,
tum demum puerili aevo florente iuventas
occipit et molli vestit lanugine malas.
890   Ne forte ex homine et veterino semine equorum
confieri credas Centauros posse neque esse,
aut rabidis canibus succinctas semimarinis
corporibus Scyllas et cetera de genere horum,
inter se quorum discordia membra videmus.

843—Since there is no other kind of being than the atoms and the
void, the soul must be a body consisting of fine atoms.

The soul a body consisting of fine atoms

a. *To Herod.*, ap. Diog. X 63:

Μετὰ δὲ ταῦτα δεῖ συνορᾶν ἀναφέροντα ἐπὶ τὰς αἰσθήσεις καὶ τὰ πάθη·
οὕτω γὰρ ἡ βεβαιοτάτη πίστις ἔσται, ὅτι ἡ ψυχὴ σῶμά ἐστι λεπτομερές,
παρ᾽ ὅλον τὸ ἄθροισμα παρεσπαρμένον, προσεμφερέστατον δὲ πνεύματι
θερμοῦ τινα κρᾶσιν ἔχοντι καὶ πῆ μὲν τούτῳ προσεμφερές, πῆ δὲ τούτῳ.
ἔστι δὲ τὸ μέρος πολλὴν παραλλαγὴν εἰληφὸς τῇ λεπτομερείᾳ καὶ αὐτῶν
τούτων, συμπαθὲς δὲ τούτῳ μᾶλλον καὶ τῷ λοιπῷ ἀθροίσματι. τοῦτο δὲ
πᾶν αἱ δυνάμεις τῆς ψυχῆς δηλοῦσι καὶ τὰ πάθη καὶ αἱ εὐκινησίαι καὶ αἱ
διανοήσεις καὶ ὧν στερόμενοι θνήσκομεν.

b. The soul has sensation, yet not in itself but by its being en-
closed in a body.

Interdependence of soul and body

To Herod., ib. 63-65:

Καὶ μὴν καὶ ὅτι ἔχει ἡ ψυχὴ τῆς αἰσθήσεως τὴν πλείστην αἰτίαν δεῖ κατέχειν.
οὐ μὴν εἰλήφει ἂν ταύτην, εἰ μὴ ὑπὸ τοῦ λοιποῦ ἀθροίσματος ἐστεγάζετό πως·
τὸ δὲ λοιπὸν ἄθροισμα παρασκευάσαν τὴν αἰτίαν ταύτην μετείληφε καὶ αὐτὸ
τοιούτου συμπτώματος παρ᾽ ἐκείνης, οὐ μέντοι πάντων ὧν ἐκείνη κέκτηται.
διὸ ἀπαλλαγείσης τῆς ψυχῆς οὐκ ἔχει τὴν αἴσθησιν· οὐ γὰρ αὐτὸ ἐν ἑαυτῷ
ταύτην ἐκέκτητο τὴν δύναμιν, ἀλλ᾽ ἑτέρῳ ἅμα συγγεγενημένῳ αὐτῷ παρε-
σκεύαζεν·—65. διὸ δὴ καὶ ἐνυπάρχουσα ἡ ψυχὴ οὐδέποτε, ἄλλου τινὸς μέρους
ἀπηλλαγμένου, ἀναισθητεῖ, ἀλλ᾽ ἃ ἂν καὶ ταύτης ** ξυναπόληται, τοῦ στε-

---

* par, vis ut sat par *Giussani;* partis *Lachmann, Bailey.*
** ταύτης Usener; ταύτῃ codd.

γάζοντος λυθέντος εἴθ' ὅλου εἴτε καὶ μέρους τινός, ἐάν περ διαμένῃ, ἕξει τὴν
αἴσθησιν· τὸ δὲ λοιπὸν ἄθροισμα διαμένον καὶ ὅλον καὶ κατὰ μέρος οὐκ ἔχει
τὴν αἴσθησιν, ἐκείνου ἀπηλλαγμένου ὅσον ποτέ ἐστι τὸ συντεῖνον τῶν ἀτόμων πλῆθος εἰς τὴν τῆς ψυχῆς φύσιν. καὶ μὴν καὶ διαλυομένου τοῦ ὅλου
ἀθροίσματος ἡ ψυχὴ διασπείρεται καὶ οὐκέτι ἔχει τὰς αὐτὰς δυνάμεις οὐδὲ
κινεῖται, ὥστε οὐδ' αἴσθησιν κέκτηται.

    c. Why the soul cannot be incorporeal:

the soul
cannot be
incorporeal

Ib. 67:

'Αλλὰ μὴν καὶ τόδε γε δεῖ προσκατανοεῖν, ὅτι τὸ ἀσώματον λέγεται * κατὰ
τὴν πλείστην ὁμιλίαν τοῦ ὀνόματος ἐπὶ τοῦ καθ' ἑαυτὸ νοηθέντος ἄν· καθ' ἑαυτὸ
δὲ οὐκ ἔστι νοῆσαι τὸ ἀσώματον πλὴν τοῦ κενοῦ. τὸ δὲ κενὸν οὔτε ποιῆσαι
οὔτε παθεῖν δύναται, ἀλλὰ κίνησιν μόνον δι' ἑαυτοῦ τοῖς σώμασι παρέχεται.
ὥσθ' οἱ λέγοντες ἀσώματον εἶναι τὴν ψυχὴν ματαΐζουσιν.

844—The above point is of great importance for man, since its direct
consequence is that death is nothing to us.

Death is
nothing to us

    a. *Kyr. dox.* II, ap. Diog. X 139:

'Ο θάνατος οὐδὲν πρὸς ἡμᾶς· τὸ γὰρ διαλυθὲν ἀναισθητεῖ, τὸ δ' ἀναισθητοῦν
οὐδὲν πρὸς ἡμᾶς.

    b. *To Menoeceus,* ap. Diog. X 125:

Τὸ φρικωδέστατον οὖν τῶν κακῶν ὁ θάνατος οὐθὲν πρὸς ἡμᾶς, ἐπειδήπερ
ὅταν μὲν ἡμεῖς ὦμεν, ὁ θάνατος οὐ πάρεστιν· ὅταν δὲ ὁ θάνατος παρῇ, τόθ'
ἡμεῖς οὐκ ἐσμέν.

Together with the message that the gods are not concerned with human
affairs this is the gospel of Epicurus to humanity. Lucr. explains the
physical theory at length in his third book (416-829) and then concludes
with a great paean on the mortality of the soul, opening with the following verses:

    c. Lucr. III 830 f.:

    Nil igitur mors est ad nos neque pertinet hilum,
    quandoquidem natura animi mortalis habetur.

4—THE GODS

845—Epicurus was an atheist not in the sense of denying the existence
of God(s), but in the sense of denying providence.

Francis Bacon, in his Essay XVI (Of Atheism) [1], speaks very precisely of
Epicurus, saying:

---

[1] The Philosophical Works of Francis Bacon edited by J. M. Robertson,
p. 754 f.

* λέγεται Bignone; λέγει γὰρ codd.

"Epicurus is charged that he did but dissemble for his credit's sake, when he affirmed there were blessed natures, but such as enjoyed themselves without having respect to the government of the world. Wherein they say he did temporize; though in secret he thought there was no God. But certainly he is traduced; for his words are noble and divine: Non Deos vulgi negare profanum; sed vulgi opiniones Diis applicare profanum. Plato could have said no more. And although he had the confidence to deny the administration, he had not the power to deny the nature."

The gods exist, but are not such as is mostly supposed

To Menoeceus, ap. Diog. X 123-124:

῍Α δέ σοι συνεχῶς παρήγγελον, ταῦτα καὶ πρᾶττε καὶ μελέτα, στοιχεῖα τοῦ καλῶς ζῆν ταῦτ' εἶναι διαλαμβάνων. Πρῶτον μὲν τὸν θεὸν ζῷον ἄφθαρτον καὶ μακάριον νομίζων, ὡς ἡ κοινὴ τοῦ θεοῦ νόησις ὑπεγράφη, μηθὲν μήτε τῆς ἀφθαρσίας ἀλλότριον μήτε τῆς μακαριότητος ἀνοίκειον αὐτῷ πρόσαπτε [1]· πᾶν δὲ τὸ φυλάττειν αὐτοῦ δυνάμενον τὴν μετὰ ἀφθαρσίας μακαριότητα περὶ αὐτοῦ δόξαζε. θεοὶ μὲν γάρ εἰσιν. ἐναργὴς δέ ἐστιν αὐτῶν ἡ γνῶσις· οἵους δ' αὐτοὺς οἱ πολλοὶ νομίζουσιν οὐκ εἰσίν· οὐ γὰρ φυλάττουσιν αὐτοὺς οἵους νομίζουσιν. ἀσεβὴς δὲ οὐχ ὁ τοὺς τῶν πολλῶν θεοὺς ἀναιρῶν, ἀλλ' ὁ τὰς τῶν πολλῶν δόξας θεοῖς προσάπτων. (124) οὐ γὰρ προλήψεις εἰσίν, ἀλλ' ὑπολήψεις ψευδεῖς [2] αἱ τῶν πολλῶν ὑπὲρ θεῶν ἀποφάσεις, ἔνθεν αἱ μέγισται βλάβαι [αἴτιαι] τοῖς κακοῖς ἐκ θεῶν ἐπάγονται καὶ ὠφέλειαι <τοῖς ἀγαθοῖς>. ταῖς γὰρ ἰδίαις οἰκειούμενοι διὰ παντὸς ἀρεταῖς τοὺς ὁμοίους ἀποδέχονται, πᾶν τὸ μὴ τοιοῦτον ὡς ἀλλότριον νομίζοντες.

846—Cic., De N.D. I 43-44, gives an Epicurean "proof of the existence of God(s)".

Having spoken of the "error of the poets", to which he adds Chaldaean and Egyptian superstition, and also "popular opinions" which are "more inconsistent and ignorant", Velleius continues:

"Ea qui consideret quam inconsulte ac temere dicantur, venerari Epicurum et in eorum ipsorum numero, de quibus haec quaestio est, habere debeat. Solus enim vidit [3] primum esse deos, quod in omnium animis eorum notionem impressisset ipsa natura. Quae est enim gens aut quod genus hominum quod non habeat sine doctrina anticipationem quandam deorum? quam appellat πρόληψιν Epicurus, id est, anteceptam animo rei quandam informationem, sine qua nec intelligi quidquam

---

[1] Cf. *Kyr. dox*. I, sub nr. **865a**.
[2] "Not conceptions derived from sensation" (προλήψεις), "but false suppositions" (Bailey). See sub **848a**, **b**.
[3] On this point we have to correct Velleius: Epicurus was certainly not *the only* one to have seen this, for the Stoics too used this proof and counted the notion of God among their κοιναὶ ἔννοιαι. But he may have been the first.

nec quaeri nec disputari potest.—Cum enim non instituto aliquo aut more aut lege sit opinio constituta maneatque ad unum omnium firma consensio, intelligi necesse est esse deos, quoniam insitas eorum vel potius innatas cognitiones habemus. De quo autem omnium natura consentit, id verum esse necesse est. Esse igitur deos confitendum est."

Now a πρόληψις according to Epicurus is founded in sense experience. How then is it possible for man to have a πρόληψις of the gods?

847—The following texts explain how Epic. thinks that man comes to have a πρόληψις of the gods.

Human
experience
of the gods

a. Sextus, *Adv. Math.* IX (*Against the Phys.* I) 25:

Ἐπίκουρος δὲ ἐκ τῶν κατὰ τοὺς ὕπνους φαντασιῶν οἴεται τοὺς ἀνθρώπους ἔννοιαν ἐσπακέναι θεοῦ· μεγάλων γὰρ εἰδώλων, φησί, καὶ ἀνθρωπομόρφων κατὰ τοὺς ὕπνους προσπιπτόντων ὑπέλαβον καὶ ταῖς ἀληθείαις ὑπάρχειν τινὰς τοιούτους θεοὺς ἀνθρωπομόρφους.

b. Cf. *Aetius* I 7, 34 (Dox. 306):

Ἐπίκουρος ἀνθρωποειδεῖς μὲν τοὺς θεούς, λόγῳ δὲ πάντας θεωρητοὺς διὰ τὴν λεπτομέρειαν τῆς τῶν εἰδώλων φύσεως.

c. Cf. Cic., *N.D.* I 19, 49:

Epicurus...... docet eam esse vim et naturam deorum ut..... non sensu sed mente cernatur.

The passage will be treated at length sub nr. **849**. Cp. also Lucr. V 148 f.:

> Tenuis enim natura deum longeque remota
> sensibus et nostris animi vix mente videtur.

848—a. How to explain these images? May we assume that they come from real beings?—To this Epic. replies: the fact that these appearances occur very frequently and generally is a guarantee that they come indeed from real beings. Hence Epic. says that the belief in gods is founded on an ἐναργὴς γνῶσις (see the passage quoted sub **845**): the repeatedly occurring images cause in the mind of man a durable general notion (πρόληψις) of divine beings.

Ἐναργὴς
γνῶσις

b. In contemplating the order of celestial phaenomena men are inclined to think that sun, moon and stars are divine beings. [1] These

---

[1] A widely spread belief in Hellenistic times. It can be traced back directly to Plato's later dialogues (*Tim.* and *Nom.*) and to Aristotle's Π. φιλ.; further back to Alcmaeon of Croton and probably to Socrates. Festugière treats the subject amply in *Le dieu cosmique*.

προλήψεις however, are not notions founded on sense experience (προλήψεις),
and
ὑπολήψεις Epic. says, but false suppositions (ὑπολήψεις ψευδεῖς); and philosophy
has the task of rooting them out.

Lucr. V 114-116:
> Religione refrenatus ne forte rearis
> terras et solem et caelum, mare sidera lunam
> corpore divino debere aeterna manere.

c. Also Lucr. V 1183-1197:
> Praeterea caeli rationes ordine certo
> et varia annorum cernebant tempora verti
> 1185 nec poterant quibus id fieret cognoscere causis.
> Ergo perfugium sibi habebant omnia divis
> tradere et illorum nutu facere omnia flecti.
> In caeloque deum sedis et templa locarunt,
> per caelum volvi quia nox et luna videtur,
> 1190 luna dies et nox et noctis signa severa
> noctivagaeque faces caeli flammaeque volantes,
> nubila sol imbres nix venti fulmina grando
> et rapidi fremitus et murmura magna minarum.
> O genus infelix humanum, talia divis
> 1195 cum tribuit facta atque iras adiunxit acerbas!
> Quantos tum gemitus ipsi sibi, quantaque nobis
> vulnera, quas lacrimas peperere minoribu' nostris!

The nature of 849—How does Epic. imagine those material beings from which
the gods spring the eidola grasped by the human mind during sleep?

Cic., N.D. I 19, 49:
Epicurus autem, qui res occultas et penitus abditas non modo viderat
animo, sed etiam sic tractat, ut manu [1], docet eam esse vim et naturam
deorum, ut primum non sensu, sed mente cernatur *, nec soliditate quadam
nec ad numerum [2], ut ea, quae ille propter firmitatem στερέμνια appellat,

---

[1] Cic. speaks with a slight irony, though this does not suit the person of Velleius.
[2] The gods are "neither solid nor a unity by numerical identity". "Non solid"
means: mere outlines (liniamenta, Cic. N.D. I 44, 123, i.e. void forms. *Soliditate
quadam* is an abl. qual. with *vim et naturam deorum*.

The expression κατ' ἀριθμὸν ἕν (*ad numerum*), is opposed by Ar. (Metaph. Δ 6,
1016 b 32) to κατ' εἶδος ἕν. The first is a material unity, the latter a notional one.—
Epic. applies the distinction in this way: there are things in which matter is permanent (solid bodies, called στερέμνια, e.g. a stone), and others in which form only

sed imaginibus similitudine et transitione perceptis[1]: quum infinita
simillimarum imaginum species ** ex innumerabilibus individuis exsistat[2]
et ad deos *** adfluat[3], tum maximis voluptatibus in eas imagines
mentem intentam infixamque nostram intelligentiam capere, quae sit
et beata natura et aeterna.

The passage is treated at length by Bailey, *Gr. At.*, pp. 443-467.

850—Next to the proof *ex consensu gentium* Epic. introduced another   **Second**
proof of the existence of gods, namely, there must be an equilibrium in   **proof of the**
                                                                            existence
the universe: therefore, the existence of destructive forces in our world   **of gods**
implies the existence of conserving forces elsewhere.

   a. Cic., *N.D.* I 19, 50:

Summa vero vis infinitatis et magna ac diligenti contemplatione

---

is permanent (e.g. a flame, a river, a waterfall). Of the last kind are the gods.

This is Epicurus' solution of the problem how material beings can be imperishable: in the *intermundia* there is an unlimited quantity of atoms, everlastingly
streaming through the "forms" of the gods, like water through a waterfall (Bailey,
p. 452).

[1] *Sed imaginibus perceptis* belongs to the preceding *cernatur*. I propose to
translate: "It is rather perceived by images apprehended by their being equal
and by a direct passing over from the intermundia to our mind".

The images are perceived or apprehended by their similarity (*similitudine*),
i.e. single "idols" are too thin to be perceived, but by a succession of similar idols
the image can be apprehended by the mind.

My translation of *transitione* is based on a text in Philodemus' treatise π. θεῶν,
the fragments of which have been edited by Diels in *Abhandl. d. Kön. Preuss. Akad.*
1916, vol. 4 and 6. In col. IX l. 20 (Diels vol. 6, p. 28) the term ὑπέρβασις is used
to indicate a direct passing over from the *intermundia* to the human mind, without
passing through the atomic world where they might be crushed and distorted.
Bailey, *Gr. At.* p. 449, hesitates to adopt this interpretation and prefers to explain
similitudine et transitione as a hendiadys: "by a succession of similar idols", taking
transitione as a translation of the Greek μετάβασις which should mean succession.
Cp. Cic. *N.D.* I 39, 109: fluentium frequenter transitio fit visionum, ut e multis
una videatur. To this my first objection is that μετάβασις does not mean *succession*,
nor does *transitio*.

[2] Cum . . . . . . existat: "For an infinite number of very similar images spring
from innumerable atoms" (individua). Series, as Brieger proposed, is easier to
understand than *species*.

[3] "And stream to the gods". This is perfectly unintelligible. Bailey, o.c., p. 459,
says: "Cicero may fairly be convicted of an inaccuracy due to brevity of expression. He ought rather to have said: "an infinite succession of similar images is
formed out of innumerable atoms, which flow together to make in successive
instants the forms of the gods"."

*   Perhaps *cernantur*.
* *   Brieger: *series*.
* * *   Some mss have *eos*. Lambinus reads: *nos*.

dignissima est, in qua intelligi necesse est eam esse naturam, ut omnia omnibus paribus paria respondeant. Hanc ἰσονομίαν appellat Epicurus, id est, aequabilem tributionem. Ex hac igitur illud efficitur, si mortalium tanta multitudo sit, esse immortalium non minorem et, si quae interimant innumerabilia sint, etiam ea quae conservent infinita esse debere.

the principle of isonomy **b.** Lucr. speaks frequently on this principle of isonomy. He even thinks that every species must be represented by an equal number of copies.

Lucr. II 532-540:

> Nam quod rara vides magis esse animalia quaedam
> fecundamque minus naturam cernis in illis,
> at regione locoque alio terrisque remotis
> 535   multa licet genere esse in eo numerumque repleri;
> sicut quadrupedum cum primis esse videmus
> in genere anguimanus elephantos, India quorum
> milibus e multis vallo munitur eburno,
> ut penitus nequeat penetrari: tanta ferarum
> 540   vis est, quarum nos perpauca exempla videmus.

the equilibrium of destructive and conserving forces **c.** Lucr. II 569-576:

> Nec superare queunt motus itaque exitiales
> 570   perpetuo neque in aeternum sepelire salutem,
> nec porro rerum genitales auctificique
> motus perpetuo possunt servare creata.
> Sic aequo geritur certamine principiorum
> ex infinito contractum tempore bellum.
> 575   Nunc hic nunc illic superant vitalia rerum
> et superantur item.

Objections against this theory **851**—Cotta is not convinced, either by Epicurus' arguments for the eternity of the gods or by his second argument for their existence.

Cic., N.D. I 39, 109:

Fluentium frequenter transitio fit visionum, ut e multis una videatur. Puderet me dicere non intelligere, si vos ipsi intelligeretis, qui ista defenditis. Quo modo enim probas continenter imagines ferri? aut, si continenter, quo modo aeternae? Innumerabilitas, inquis, suppeditat atomorum. Num eadem ergo ista faciet ut sint omnia sempiterna? Confugis ad aequilibritatem—sic enim ἰσονομίαν, si placet, appellemus—

et ais, quoniam sit natura mortalis, immortalem etiam esse oportere.
Isto modo, quoniam homines mortales sunt, sint aliqui immortales, et
quoniam nascuntur in terra, nascantur in aqua. "Et quia sunt quae
interimant, sint quae conservent". Sint sane, sed ea conservent, quae
sunt. Deos istos esse non sentio.

852—With Epic. the standing predicates of the gods are: μακάριον **Properties of the gods**
καὶ ἄφθαρτον (K. Δ. I; Ep. III 123). Hence follows directly that the gods
are not concerned with governing the universe and with human affairs;
for happiness, according to Epic., is ἀπονία and ἀταραξία.

Kyr. Dox. I, ap. Diog. X 139:

Τὸ μακάριον καὶ ἄφθαρτον οὔτε αὐτὸ πράγματα ἔχει οὔτε ἄλλῳ παρέχει,
ὥστε οὔτε ὀργαῖς οὔτε χάρισι συνέχεται· ἐν ἀσθενεῖ γὰρ πᾶν τὸ τοιοῦτον.

By this Epic. denied firstly that the kosmos is created (i.e. arranged) by a
Demiurge, such as Plato introduced in his *Tim.*; secondly, the existence of a *pronoia*,
as was taught by the Stoics.

853—There are too many bad things in the world that it could be **Pessimistic view of the world**
the work of almighty gods.

    a. Lucr. V 196-199:

        Hoc tamen ex ipsis caeli rationibus ausim
        confirmare aliisque ex rebus reddere multis,
        nequaquam nobis divinitus esse paratum
        naturam rerum: tanta stat praedita culpa.

    b. Lactantius, *Div. inst.* III 17, 16 cites Epic. in this way: "Nulla",
inquit, "dispositio est. Multa enim facta sunt aliter quam fieri debuerunt".

854—**a.** Firstly the gods had no reason to create a world and human **No reason for creation**
beings.

Lucr. V 165-174:

        Quid enim immortalibus atque beatis
      gratia nostra queat largirier emolumenti,
      ut nostra quicquam causa gerere aggrediantur?
      Quidve novi potuit tanto post ante quietos
      inlicere ut cuperent vitam mutare priorem?
170   Nam gaudere novis rebus debere videtur
      cui veteres obsunt; sed cui nil accidit aegri

tempore in anteacto, cum pulchre degeret aevum,
quid potuit novitatis amorem accendere tali?
Quidve mali fuerat nobis non esse creatis?

b. Finally, they *could* not create a world unless they had a *notities* of what they were going to make, and this they could not have unless a world existed already.

Impossibili-
ty of
creation

Ib., 181-186:

Exemplum porro gignundis rebus et ipsa
notities divis hominum unde est insita primum,
quid vellent facere ut scirent animoque viderent,
quove modost umquam vis cognita principiorum
185   quidque inter sese permutato ordine possent,
si non ipsa dedit specimen natura creandi?

The idea of
teleology
criticized

855—The teleological view of nature is very sharply criticized by Lucr., IV 822-842:

Illud in his rebus vitium vementer avessis
effugere, errorem vitareque praemetuenter,
825   lumina ne facias oculorum clara creata,
prospicere ut possimus, et ut proferre queamus
proceros passus, ideo fastigia posse
surarum ac feminum pedibus fundata plicari,
bracchia tum porro validis ex apta lacertis
830   esse manusque datas utraque (ex) parte ministras,
ut facere ad vitam possemus quae foret usus.
Cetera de genere hoc inter quaecumque pretantur
omnia perversa praepostera sunt ratione,
nil ideo quoniam natumst in corpore ut uti
835   possemus, sed quod natumst id procreat usum.
Nec fuit ante videre oculorum lumina nata
nec dictis orare prius quam lingua creatast,
sed potius longe linguae praecessit origo
sermonem multoque creatae sunt prius aures
840   quam sonus est auditus, et omnia denique membra
ante fuere, ut opinor, eorum quam foret usus.
Haud igitur potuere utendi crescere causa.

The gods an
example of
happiness

856—For Epic. the religious sense of the existence of the gods is, that for man they are an example of happiness.

a. Philodemus, Π. εὐσεβείας 28 (Gomperz, *Herc. Stud.* p. 148):

Οἱ δὲ πεισθέντες οἷς ἐχρησμωιδήσαμεν περὶ θεῶν πρῶτον μὲν ὡς θνητοὶ μειμεῖσθαι τὴν ἐκείνων εὐδαιμονίαν θελήσουσιν,—

b. In this sense Epicureans can say that a blessing comes from the gods to man.

Atticus ap. Euseb., *Praep. Ev.* XV 5:

Ἤδη δὲ ταύτῃ γε καὶ κατ' Ἐπίκουρον ὄνησις τοῖς ἀνθρώποις ἀπὸ θεῶν γίνεται.

Atticus, quite consistently, explains the coming of this blessing in a merely physical way (ib.):

Τὰς γοῦν βελτίονας ἀπορροίας αὐτῶν φασι τοῖς μετασχοῦσι μεγάλων ἀγαθῶν παραιτίας γίνεσθαι.

857—Epicurus knew in his way a kind of ὁμοίωσις τῷ θεῷ κατὰ τὸ δύνατον (cp. our nr. **318**). **Epicurean mysticism**

Philodemus, *De deorum victu*, Vol. Herc. VI, col. I:

... Καὶ θαυμάζει τὴ[ν] φύσιν [αὐτῶν κ(αὶ)] τὴν διάθεσιν καὶ πειρᾶται συνεγγί[ζειν] αὐτῇ καὶ καθαπερεὶ γλίχεται θιγε[ῖν καὶ συ]νεῖναι, καλεῖ τ[ε] καὶ τοὺς σοφοὺς τῶν [θεῶ]ν φίλους καὶ τοὺς θεοὺς τῶν σοφῶν.

Cp. also our nr. **815b**: among those who are to be invited for dinner belongs the group of "such persons as have a remembrance of the best and most blessed beings".

858—In the first column of Philodemus' Περὶ κακιῶν we find Epicurus talking with the god Asklepios. **Epicurus favoured by the gods**

Philodemus, Π. κακιῶν I, col. I, l. 11-26 (Jensen, *Ein neuer Brief Epikurs*, p. 15):

... Τὸ]ν θε[ὸν δ'] εἰπὼ[ν ἐθ]έ[λειν] ἄν[ευ λ]ύπη[ς] μένε[ιν οὐ πρ]οσ[δεχόμενον τοὺ[ς π]ό[νους] ε[ὐδαίμων] ἔφην εἶν[αι. "Τί γ]άρ", [ἀντ]εῖπε[ν] "περ[ίεσ]ταί μοι; [δεδίδ]αχα[ς] τοὺς θεοὺς [τὴ]ν [ἀταρ]αξίαν [ἐθ]έλο[ντάς] τ[ι πάσχ]ε[ιν] διὰ τὴ[ν κ]αταφ[ρόνησιν·] κα[ὶ] τῆς τ[ινω]ν ἐνίο[τ' εὐμ]ενεία[ς μετ]ασχὼν ἀνέχ[ου] ζῶντα[ς αὐ]το[ὺς με]τ' ἀ[ταραξί]ας ὅλως [παρ' ἤ[ν τηρο]ῦσι δίκην, ἐ[πειδ]ὴ δι' ἀ[δικία]ν [Τυ]φώνι[ον πο]νεῖν τ[ι] τὸν Π[ρο]μη[θέα φής·] ἢ οὐ [φή]σε[ι]ς προ[ο]ρᾷ[ν] ἐ[μὲ] τοῦ τοιούτο[υ] πό[νου δι]ὰ [σ]ωτηρίας·—

Jensen asks: How can it be that Asklepios speaks of the benevolence of certain gods towards Epicurus, and that he even assures him of his salutary cares?— As a parallel he cites the wellknown words of the *Letter to Menoeceus*, Diog. X 124: ταῖς γὰρ ἰδίαις οἰκειούμενοι διὰ παντὸς ἀρεταῖς τοὺς ὁμοίους ἀποδέχονται, πᾶν τὸ μὴ τοιοῦτον ὡς ἀλλότριον νομίζοντες (cited above, sub **845**), which he translates: "For the gods are always only familiar with their own virtues and therefore accept only those men who are similar to them, while they consider all that is different as alien."

Thus he makes *the gods* subject of ἀποδέχονται, while usually the text is understood as saying that *men* are always accustomed to their own virtues and therefore welcome only those like themselves (see Bailey in *Epicurus, The extant Remains*). The latter translation must be the right one, since in the preceding lines it is rejected as a false supposition that great misfortunes befall the wicked and great blessings the good by the gift of the gods. The meaning of the following lines is: "for men make to themselves their gods according to their own image."

So I do not think the Letter to Menoeceus offers a good parallel to the passage restituted by Jensen. But we can grant him that, supposing the restitution is right, Epic. admitted that certain persons are more or less favoured by the gods.

5—ETHICS

859—Epicurus, together with the other post-aristotelian Schools, uses Aristotle's terminology in speaking of "the end" to which all conduct should be subordinated. Generally speaking, the end is: the happy life, and of this the first principle is, according to Epic., pleasure.

The telos

To Menoec., Diog. X 128:

Τὴν ἡδονὴν ἀρχὴν καὶ τέλος λέγομεν εἶναι τοῦ μακαρίως ζῆν.

860—The above statement in the *Letter to Menoeceus* is not the beginning but the end of an argument. The passage begins by a division of desires (our nr. **866**): of desires some are natural, others vain; of the natural some are necessary, others just natural. Now of the necessary some are so for happiness, others for the repose of the body, still others for very life. The author continues:

Diog. X 128:

Τούτων γὰρ ἀπλανὴς θεωρία πᾶσαν αἴρεσιν καὶ φυγὴν ἐπανάγειν οἶδεν ἐπὶ τὴν τοῦ σώματος ὑγίειαν καὶ τὴν τῆς ψυχῆς ἀταραξίαν, ἐπεὶ τοῦτο τοῦ μακαρίως ζῆν ἐστὶ τέλος. τούτου γὰρ χάριν ἅπαντα πράττομεν, ὅπως μήτε ἀλγῶμεν μήτε ταρβῶμεν· ὅταν δὲ ἅπαξ τοῦτο περὶ ἡμᾶς γένηται, λύεται πᾶς ὁ τῆς ψυχῆς χειμών, οὐκ ἔχοντος τοῦ ζῴου βαδίζειν ὡς πρὸς ἐνδέον τι καὶ ζητεῖν ἕτερον ᾧ τὸ τῆς ψυχῆς καὶ τὸ τοῦ σώματος ἀγαθὸν συμπληρωθήσεται. τότε γὰρ ἡδονῆς χρείαν ἔχομεν, ὅταν ἐκ τοῦ μὴ παρεῖναι τὴν ἡδονὴν ἀλγῶμεν· ὅταν δὲ μὴ ἀλγῶμεν, οὐκέτι τῆς ἡδονῆς δεόμεθα. καὶ διὰ τοῦτο τὴν ἡδονὴν ἀρχὴν καὶ τέλος λέγομεν εἶναι τοῦ μακαρίως ζῆν.

861—According to Diog. Epicurus based this principle on the same argument as was used by Eudoxus (see our nr. **786**).

Diog. X 137:

'Αποδείξει δὲ χρῆται τοῦ τέλος εἶναι τὴν ἡδονὴν τῷ τὰ ζῷα ἅμα τῷ γεννηθῆναι τῇ μὲν εὐαρεστεῖσθαι, τῷ δέ πόνῳ προσκρούειν φυσικῶς καὶ χωρὶς λόγου.

862—a. The *Letter to Menoec.* continues (Diog. X 129):

Ταύτην γὰρ ἀγαθὸν πρῶτον καὶ συγγενικὸν ἔγνωμεν, καὶ ἀπὸ ταύτης καταρχόμεθα πάσης αἱρέσεως καὶ φυγῆς, καὶ ἐπὶ ταύτην καταντῶμεν ὡς κανόνι τῷ πάθει πᾶν ἀγαθὸν κρίνοντες.

Pleasure the standard of good

b. Ib. (same passage, continued):

Καὶ ἐπεὶ πρῶτον ἀγαθὸν τοῦτο καὶ σύμφυτον, διὰ τοῦτο καὶ οὐ πᾶσαν ἡδονὴν αἱρούμεθα, ἀλλ' ἔστιν ὅτε πολλὰς ἡδονὰς ὑπερβαίνομεν, ὅταν πλεῖον ἡμῖν τὸ δυσχερὲς ἐκ τούτων ἔπηται· καὶ πολλὰς ἀλγηδόνας ἡδονῶν κρείττους νομίζομεν, ἐπειδὰν μείζων ἡμῖν ἡδονὴ παρακολουθῇ, πολὺν χρόνον ὑπομείνασι τὰς ἀλγηδόνας. πᾶσα οὖν ἡδονή, διὰ τὸ φύσιν ἔχειν οἰκείαν, ἀγαθόν, οὐ πᾶσα μέντοι αἱρετή· καθάπερ καὶ ἀλγηδὼν πᾶσα κακόν, οὐ πᾶσα δὲ ἀεὶ φευκτὴ πεφυκυῖα. τῇ μέντοι συμμετρήσει καὶ συμφερόντων καὶ ἀσυμφόρων βλέψει ταῦτα πάντα κρίνειν καθήκει.

But not every pleasure is to be chosen

c. Since all pleasure as such is good, the standard of selection is one of quantity.

Aristocles ap. Euseb., *Praep. Ev.* XIV 21, 3:

Μετρεῖσθαι γὰρ αὐτὰ τῷ ποσῷ καὶ οὐ τῷ ποιῷ.

Standard of selection

863—According to this standard the pleasure of the body is the greatest.

a. Epic. ap. Athenaeum VII, p. 280a:

Κἂν τῷ Περὶ τέλους δέ φησιν οὕτω πως· οὐ γὰρ ἔγωγε ἔχω τί νοήσω ἀγαθόν, ἀφαιρῶν μὲν τὰς διὰ χυλῶν ἡδονάς, ἀφαιρῶν δὲ τὰς δι' ἀφροδισίων, ἀφαιρῶν δὲ τὰς δι' ἀκροαμάτων, ἀφαιρῶν δὲ καὶ τὰς διὰ μορφῆς κατ' ὄψιν ἡδείας κινήσεις.

The pleasure of the body is the greatest

The passage is translated by Cicero, *Tusc.* III 18, 41.

b. The pleasure of the stomach according to Epicurus' standard takes the first place.

Athenaeus XII, p. 546 f.:

'Αρχὴ καὶ ῥίζα παντὸς ἀγαθοῦ ἡ τῆς γαστρὸς ἡδονή· καὶ τὰ σοφὰ καὶ τὰ περιττὰ ἐπὶ ταύτην ἔχει τὴν ἀναφοράν. [1]

---

[1] "Even wisdom and culture must be referred to this" (Bailey).

c. Cf. Plut., *Contra Epicuri beatitudinem* 17, p. 1098d:

Οἱ ἄνθρωποι ("those people" sc. Epicureans) τῆς ἡδονῆς τὸ μέγεθος καθάπερ κέντρῳ καὶ διαστήματι τῇ γαστρὶ περιγράφουσι. [1]

864—It is Epicurus' originality to have taught that bodily pleasure is limited, and even very restrained: it is satisfying the most elementary, strictly bodily needs. The aponia and analgia resulting from this satisfaction are already pleasure, and therefore perfect happiness.

Pleasure defined by absence of pain

a. *Kyr. dox.* III, ap. Diog. 139:

"Ορος τοῦ μεγέθους τῶν ἡδονῶν ἡ παντὸς τοῦ ἀλγοῦντος ὑπεξαίρεσις. ὅπου δ᾽ ἂν τὸ ἡδόμενον ἐνῇ, καθ᾽ ὃν ἂν χρόνον ᾖ, οὐκ ἔστι τὸ ἀλγοῦν ἢ τὸ λυπούμενον ἢ τὸ συναμφότερον.

Cp. also our nr. **860a**, supra.

Therefore limited

b. Plut., *Contra Epic. beat.* 3, p. 1088c:

Καὶ πέρας (ταῖς ἡδοναῖς) κοινὸν Ἐπίκουρος τὴν παντὸς τοῦ ἀλγοῦντος ὑπεξαίρεσιν ἐπιτέθεικεν, ὡς τῆς φύσεως ἄχρι τοῦ λῦσαι τὸ ἀλγεινὸν αὐξούσης τὸ ἡδύ, περαιτέρω δὲ προελθεῖν οὐκ ἐώσης κατὰ μέγεθος.

Reason sets bounds to the pleasure of the body

c. The judgment of reason about pleasure.

Kyr. dox. XX (Diog. X 145):

Ἡ μὲν σὰρξ ἀπέλαβε τὰ πέρατα τῆς ἡδονῆς ἄπειρα, καὶ ἄπειρος αὐτὴν χρόνος παρεσκεύασεν. Ἡ δὲ διάνοια τοῦ τῆς σαρκὸς τέλους καὶ πέρατος λαβοῦσα τὸν ἐπιλογισμὸν καὶ τοὺς ὑπὲρ τοῦ αἰῶνος φόβους ἐκλύσασα τὸν παντελῆ βίον παρεσκεύασεν καὶ οὐθὲν ἔτι τοῦ ἀπείρου χρόνου προσεδεήθημεν· ἀλλ᾽ οὔτε ἔφυγε τὴν ἡδονήν, οὔθ᾽ ἡνίκα τὴν ἐξαγωγὴν ἐκ τοῦ ζῆν τὰ πράγματα παρεσκεύαζεν ὡς ἐλλείπουσά τι τοῦ ἀρίστου βίου κατέστρεφεν.

See our nr. **869**.

865—Epicurus is well aware that man, in any case civilized man, has very different aspirations from satisfying his most elementary bodily needs, and other concerns than merely for physical pain. Therefore, his doctrine of pleasure is preceded by two preliminary points.

Two preliminary points

1. The gods are not concerned with human affairs

a. The gods are not concerned with the world and with human affairs. *To Menoec.*, ap. Diog. X 123, see above, nr. **845**. The meaning of the words "μηθὲν μήτε τῆς ἀφθαρσίας ἀλλότριον μήτε τῆς μακαριό-

---

[1] "measure the amount of pleasure as with compasses from the stomach as centre" (Bailey).

τητος ἀνοίκειον αὐτῷ πρόσαπτε" is clearly explained in *Kyr. dox.* I (Diog. X 139):

Τὸ μακάριον καὶ ἄφθαρτον οὔτε αὐτὸ πράγματα ἔχει οὔτε ἄλλῳ παρέχει, ὥστε οὔτε ὀργαῖς οὔτε χάρισι συνέχεται· ἐν ἀσθενεῖ γὰρ πᾶν τὸ τοιοῦτον.

b. There is nothing terrible in death.

To Menoec., Diog. X 124:

Συνέθιζε δὲ ἐν τῷ νομίζειν μηθὲν πρὸς ἡμᾶς εἶναι τὸν θάνατον, ἐπεὶ πᾶν ἀγαθὸν καὶ κακὸν ἐν αἰσθήσει, στέρησις δέ ἐστιν αἰσθήσεως ὁ θάνατος. ὅθεν γνῶσις ὀρθὴ τοῦ μηθὲν εἶναι πρὸς ἡμᾶς τὸν θάνατον ἀπολαυστὸν ποιεῖ τὸ τῆς ζωῆς θνητόν, οὐκ ἄπειρον προστιθεῖσα χρόνον, ἀλλὰ τὸν τῆς ἀθανασίας ἀφελομένη πόθον. οὐθὲν γάρ ἐστιν ἐν τῷ ζῆν δεινὸν τῷ κατειληφότι γνησίως τὸ μηθὲν ὑπάρχειν ἐν τῷ μὴ ζῆν δεινόν. ὥστε μάταιος ὁ λέγων δεδιέναι τὸν θάνατον, οὐχ ὅτι λυπήσει παρών, ἀλλ' ὅτι λυπεῖ μέλλων. ὃ γὰρ παρὸν οὐκ ἐνοχλεῖ, προσδοκώμενον κενῶς λυπεῖ.

Follows the text cited above, sub **844b**.
Cp. also *Kyr. dox.* II, sub **844a**.

2. Death is nothing to us

866—a. Having established these two points, Epic. begins the exposition of his theory of pleasure by an analysis of desires.

To Menoec., ap. Diog. X 127:

'Αναλογιστέον δὲ ὡς τῶν ἐπιθυμιῶν αἱ μέν εἰσι φυσικαί, αἱ δὲ κεναί. καὶ τῶν φυσικῶν αἱ μὲν ἀναγκαῖαι, αἱ δὲ φυσικαὶ μόνον· τῶν δὲ ἀναγκαίων αἱ μὲν πρὸς εὐδαιμονίαν εἰσὶν ἀναγκαῖαι, αἱ δὲ πρὸς τὴν τοῦ σώματος ἀοχλησίαν, αἱ δὲ πρὸς αὐτὸ τὸ ζῆν.

Analysis of desires

b. The division is explained in a scholion in Arist., *E.N.* III 13, 1118b[8] (456 Us.):

'Επίκουρος καὶ οἱ ἀπ' αὐτοῦ οὕτω διαιροῦσι· τῶν ἐπιθυμιῶν αἱ μέν τινες ἀναγκαῖαι, αἱ δὲ φυσικαὶ μὲν οὐκ ἀναγκαῖαι δέ, αἱ δὲ οὔτε ἀναγκαῖαι οὔτε φυσικαὶ ἀλλὰ κατὰ κενὴν γινόμεναι δόξαν. ἡ μὲν οὖν τῆς τροφῆς ἐπιθυμία καὶ τῆς ἐσθῆτος ἀναγκαία· ἡ δὲ τῶν ἀφροδισίων φυσικὴ μὲν οὐκ ἀναγκαία δέ· ἡ δὲ τῶν τοιῶνδε σιτίων ἢ τοιᾶσδε ἐσθῆτος ἢ τοιῶνδε ἀφροδισίων οὔτε φυσικὴ οὔτε ἀναγκαία.

Cp. *Kyr. dox.* XXIX (Diog. X 149).

c. Cic., *Tusc.* V 33, 93:

Vides, credo, ut Epicurus cupiditatum genera diviserit, non nimis fortasse subtiliter, utiliter tamen: partim esse naturalis et necessarias, partim naturalis et non necessarias, partim neutrum. Necessarias satiari posse paene nihilo, divitias enim naturae esse parabilis; secundum autem genus cupiditatum nec ad potiendum difficile esse censet nec vero ad carendum; tertias, quod essent plane inanes neque necessitatem modo, sed ne naturam quidem attingerent, funditus eiciendas putavit.

The pleasures of love

d. As to the pleasures of love, though they belong to the middle category, it should be noticed that Epic. rather declined them.

Epic., *Sent. Vat.* LI:

Πυνθάνομαί σου τὴν κατὰ σάρκα κίνησιν ἀφθονώτερον διακεῖσθαι πρὸς τὴν τῶν ἀφροδισίων ἔντευξιν. σὺ δὲ ὅταν μήτε τοὺς νόμους καταλύῃς μήτε τὰ καλῶς ἔθη κείμενα κινῇς μήτε τῶν πλησίον τινὰ λυπῇς μήτε τὴν σάρκα καταξαίνῃς μήτε τὰ ἀναγκαῖα καταναλίσκῃς, χρῶ ὡς βούλει τῇ σεαυτοῦ προαιρέσει. ἀμήχανον μέντοι γε τὸ μὴ οὐχ ἑνί γέ τινι τούτων συνέχεσθαι· ἀφροδίσια γὰρ οὐδέποτε ὤνησεν· ἀγαπητὸν δὲ εἰ μὴ ἔβλαψεν.

Epicurean ascetism

867—Thus, Epicurus' attitude of life is, in fact, ascetical: a voluntary limitation of desires to that which is strictly necessary.

a. *Kyr. dox.* XV (Diog. X 144):

Ὁ τῆς φύσεως πλοῦτος καὶ ὥρισται καὶ εὐπόριστός ἐστιν· ὁ δὲ τῶν κενῶν δοξῶν εἰς ἄπειρον ἐκπίπτει.

b. *Sent. Vat.* XXXIII:

Σαρκὸς φωνὴ τὸ μὴ πεινῆν, τὸ μὴ διψῆν, τὸ μὴ ῥιγοῦν. Ταῦτα γὰρ ἔχων τις καὶ ἐλπίζων ἕξειν κἂν <Διὶ> ὑπὲρ εὐδαιμονίας μαχέσαιτο.

Judgment of Clemens Alex.

868—**a.** The Epicurean asceticism was violently opposed by Clem. Alex., *Strom.* II 21 (602 Us.):

Ἐπίκουρος δὲ ἐν τῷ μὴ πεινῆν μηδὲ διψῆν μηδὲ ῥιγοῦν τὴν εὐδαιμονίαν τιθέμενος τὴν ἰσόθεον ἐπεφώνησε φωνήν, ἀσεβῶς εἰπὼν ἐν τούτοις κἂν Διὶ πατρὶ μάχεσθαι, ὥσπερ ὑῶν σκατοφάγων καὶ οὐχὶ τῶν λογικῶν καὶ φιλοσόφων τὴν μακαρίαν νικᾶν δογματίζων.

b. Seneca, *Ep.* 25, 4, speaks with more comprehension about it:

Ad legem naturae revertamur: divitiae paratae sunt. Aut gratuitum est quo egemus aut vile: panem et aquam natura desiderat. Nemo ad haec pauper est. Intra quae quisquis desiderium suum clusit, cum ipso Iove de felicitate contendat, ut ait Epicurus.

869—In fact, Epicurus' reduction of desires to that which is most elementary is the triumph of reason over the flesh.

Kyr. dox. XVIII (Diog. X 144):

Οὐκ ἐπαύξεται ἐν τῇ σαρκὶ ἡ ἡδονή, ἐπειδὰν ἅπαξ τὸ κατ' ἔνδειαν ἀλγοῦν ἐξαιρεθῇ, ἀλλὰ μόνον ποικίλλεται· τῆς δὲ διανοίας τὸ πέρας τὸ κατὰ τὴν ἡδονὴν ἀπεγέννησεν ἥ τε τούτων αὐτῶν ἐκλόγησις καὶ τῶν ὁμογενῶν τούτοις [1], ὅσα τοὺς μεγίστους φόβουσ παρεσκεύαζε τῇ διανοίᾳ.

The triumph of reason over the flesh

870—A direct consequence of the principle enunciated in the first line of the above text is, that infinite time does not increase pleasure.

Infinite time does not increase pleasure

Kyr. dox. XIX (Diog. X 145):

Ὁ ἄπειρος χρόνος ἴσην ἔχει τὴν ἡδονὴν καὶ ὁ πεπερασμένος, ἐάν τις αὐτῆς τὰ πέρατα καταμετρήσῃ τῷ λογισμῷ.

871—The elementary needs being satisfied, the "fullness of life" is reached.

Epicurean wisdom

Kyr. dox. XXI (Diog. X 146):

Ὁ τὰ πέρατα τοῦ βίου κατειδὼς οἶδεν ὡς εὐπόριστόν ἐστι τὸ <τὸ> ἀλγοῦν κατ' ἔνδειαν ἐξαιροῦν καὶ τὸ τὸν ὅλον βίον παντελῆ καθιστάν· ὥστ' οὐδὲν προσδεῖται πραγμάτων ἀγῶνας κεκτημένων.

872—**a.** Epic. speaks on autarkeia (independence of desire) in much the same way as the Stoics.

To Menoec., ap. Diog. X 130 f.:

αὐτάρκεια

Καὶ τὴν αὐτάρκειαν δὲ ἀγαθὸν μέγα νομίζομεν, οὐχ ἵνα πάντως τοῖς ὀλίγοις χρώμεθα, ἀλλ' ὅπως, ἐὰν μὴ ἔχωμεν τὰ πολλά, τοῖς ὀλίγοις χρώμεθα, πεπεισμένοι γνησίως ὅτι ἥδιστα πολυτελείας ἀπολαύουσιν οἱ ἥκιστα ταύτης δεόμενοι, καὶ ὅτι τὸ μὲν φυσικὸν πᾶν εὐπόριστόν ἐστι, τὸ δὲ κενὸν δυσπόριστον. οἵ τε λιτοὶ χυλοὶ ἴσην πολυτελεῖ διαίτῃ τὴν ἡδονὴν ἐπιφέρουσιν, ὅταν ἅπαν τὸ ἀλγοῦν κατ' ἔνδειαν ἐξαιρεθῇ· καὶ μᾶζα καὶ ὕδωρ τὴν ἀκροτάτην ἀποδίδωσιν ἡδονήν, ἐπειδὰν ἐνδέως τις αὐτὰ προσενέγκηται.

b. He proclaims φρόνησις to be the greatest good and the root of all other virtues. I cite the whole passage. Epic. here clearly opposes the popular misinterpretation of his doctrine.

φρόνησις

Diog. X 131 f.:

῞Οταν οὖν λέγωμεν ἡδονὴν τέλος ὑπάρχειν, οὐ τὰς τῶν ἀσώτων ἡδονὰς καὶ τὰς ἐν ἀπολαύσει κειμένας λέγομεν, ὥς τινες ἀγνοοῦντες καὶ οὐχ ὁμολογοῦντες ἢ κακῶς ἐκδεχόμενοι νομίζουσιν, ἀλλὰ τὸ μήτε ἀλγεῖν κατὰ σῶμα μήτε ταράτ-

---

[1] "And of the emotions akin to them" (Bailey).

τεσθαι κατὰ ψυχήν. οὐ γὰρ πότοι καὶ κῶμοι συνείροντες οὐδ' ἀπολαύσεις
παίδων καὶ γυναικῶν οὐδ' ἰχθύων καὶ τῶν ἄλλων ὅσα φέρει πολυτελὴς τράπεζα,
τὸν ἡδὺν γεννᾷ βίον, ἀλλὰ νήφων λογισμὸς καὶ τὰς αἰτίας ἐξερευνῶν πάσης
αἱρέσεως καὶ φυγῆς καὶ τὰς δόξας ἐξελαύνων ἀφ' ὧν πλεῖστος τὰς ψυχὰς καταλαμβάνει θόρυβος. τούτων δὲ πάντων ἀρχὴ καὶ τὸ μέγιστον ἀγαθὸν φρόνησις·
διὸ καὶ φιλοσοφίας τιμιώτερον ὑπάρχει φρόνησις, ἐξ ἧς αἱ λοιπαὶ πᾶσαι πεφύκασιν ἀρεταί, διδάσκουσαι ὡς οὐκ ἔστιν ἡδέως ζῆν ἄνευ τοῦ φρονίμως καὶ
καλῶς καὶ δικαίως, <οὐδὲ φρονίμως καὶ καλῶς καὶ δικαίως> ἄνευ τοῦ ἡδέως·
συμπεφύκασι γὰρ αἱ ἀρεταὶ τῷ ζῆν ἡδέως, καὶ τὸ ζῆν ἡδέως τούτων ἐστὶν
ἀχώριστον.

873—It may be seen from the above passage, as it might be concluded
from *Ad Menoec.* 129 (our nr. **861a**) that, for Epicurus, the passing over
from the doctrine of pleasure to that of moral good is hardly a *metabasis*,
in any case no passing over to another genos.

Virtue sub-ordinated to pleasure

a. Alex. Aphr., *De anima* II 22, p. 156, 9 (515 Us.):
('Η ἀρετὴ) περὶ τὴν ἐκλογήν ἐστι τῶν ἡδέων κατ' 'Επίκουρον.

b. Virtue, consequently, is nothing in itself.

Cic., *Tusc.* V 26, 73 (511 Us.):
Epicuro qui ... haec nostra honesta turpia irrideat dicatque nos in
vocibus occupatos inanis sonos fundere.

Cf. Laelius 23, 86: A multis virtus ipsa contemnitur et venditatio quaedam atque
ostentatio esse dicitur.

c. Athenaeus XII, p. 547a cites Epicurus in this way:
Προσπτύω τῷ καλῷ καὶ τοῖς κενῶς αὐτὸ θαυμάζουσιν, ὅταν μηδεμίαν
ἡδονὴν ποιῇ.

τὸ καλόν means here *honestum*, i.e. virtue.

Correlation between pleasure and virtue

874—Epic. teaches that, in fact, there is a correlation between pleasure
and virtue.

Kyr. dox. V (Diog. X 140):
Οὐκ ἔστιν ἡδέως ζῆν ἄνευ τοῦ φρονίμως καὶ καλῶς καὶ δικαίως <οὐδὲ
φρονίμως καὶ καλῶς καὶ δικαίως> ἄνευ τοῦ ἡδέως. ὅτῳ δὲ τοῦτο μὴ ὑπάρχει,
οὐ ζῇ φρονίμως καὶ καλῶς καὶ δικαίως, <καὶ ὅτῳ ἐκεῖνο μὴ> ὑπάρχει, οὐκ ἔστι
τοῦτον ἡδέως ζῆν.

The four virtues

875—That, of the four classical virtues, wisdom, selfrestraint, and
bravery contribute something to the right selection of pleasure, might
be fairly clear; but concerning justice the theory reveals its weakness.

a. *Kyr. dox.* XXXI (Diog. X 150):   Justice

Τὸ τῆς φύσεως δίκαιόν ἐστι σύμβολον τοῦ συμφέροντος εἰς τὸ μὴ βλάπτειν
ἀλλήλους μηδὲ βλάπτεσθαι.

b. Ib. XXXIII:

Οὐκ ἦν τι καθ' ἑαυτὸ δικαιοσύνη, ἀλλ' ἐν ταῖς μετ' ἀλλήλων συστροφαῖς καθ'
ὁπηλίκους δή ποτε ἀεὶ τόπους συνθήκη τις ὑπὲρ τοῦ μὴ βλάπτειν ἢ βλάπτεσθαι.

c. Ib. XXXIV:

Ἡ ἀδικία οὐ καθ' ἑαυτὴν κακόν, ἀλλ' ἐν τῷ κατὰ τὴν ὑποψίαν φόβῳ, εἰ μὴ   Injustice
λήσει τοὺς ὑπὲρ τῶν τοιούτων ἐφεστηκότας κολαστάς.

Lucr. III 1011-23 describes this fear of punishment, of which Epic. says in
Kyr. dox. XXXV that it never leaves anyone who has committed injustice.

The theory recalls that of Callicles and Thrasymachus, who taught that nothing
is better for man than doing as much injustice as possible, provided that he remains
unpunished.

d. Epic. only hesitates with his reply when asking himself "whether   Epic.
the wise man will do things forbidden by law, if he is sure that he will   shrinks
escape punishment".   from the
                                                                               conse-
Plut., *Adv. Col.* 34, p. 1127d: quences

Ἀποκρίνεται, "οὐκ εὔοδον τὸ ἁπλοῦν ἐστι κατηγόρημα·" τοῦτ' ἔστι, πράξω
μέν, οὐ βούλομαι δὲ ὁμολογεῖν.

In fact, Epic. shrinks from drawing the consequences of his own theory.

876—Cicero criticized Epicurus' theory of virtues judiciously.   The theory
                                                                               criticized
De off. III 33, 117:   by Cic.

Si illum (Epicurum) audiam de continentia et temperantia, dicit ille quidem multa multis locis, sed aqua haeret, ut aiunt. Nam qui potest temperantiam laudare is, qui ponat summum bonum in voluptate? . . . . .
Atque in his tamen tribus generibus, quoquo modo possunt, non incallide
tergiversantur. Prudentiam introducunt scientiam suppeditantem volup-
tates, depellentem dolores. Fortitudinem quoque aliquo modo expediunt,
cum tradunt rationem neglegendae mortis, perpetiendi doloris. Etiam
temperantiam inducunt, non facillime illi quidem, sed tamen quoquo
modo possunt: dicunt enim voluptatis magnitudinem doloris detractione
finiri. Iustitia vacillat vel iacet potius omnesque eae virtutes quae in
communitate cernuntur et in societate generis humani. Neque enim
bonitas nec liberalitas nec comitas esse potest, non plus quam amicitia,
si haec non per se expetantur, sed ad voluptatem utilitatemve referantur.

Friendship 877—Friendship however, though it can be reduced, indeed, to reasons of material interest and, thus, to primitive ἡδονή, takes a very important place in Epicurean life and is taxed high in the ranks of value.

a. *Kyr. dox.* XXVII (Diog. X 148):

Ὧν ἡ σοφία παρασκευάζεται εἰς τὴν τοῦ ὅλου βίου μακαριότητα, πολὺ μέγιστόν ἐστιν ἡ τῆς φιλίας κτῆσις.

Cp. our first paragraph, nrs. **812-819**.

b. *Sent. Vat.* XXIII:

Πᾶσα φιλία δι' ἑαυτὴν αἱρετή· ἀρχὴν δ' εἴληφεν ἀπὸ τῆς ὠφελείας.

878—Clem. Alex., *Strom.* II 23, 138 (St. II, p. 189, 15-18):

Marriage Δημόκριτος δὲ γάμον καὶ παιδοποιΐαν παραιτεῖται διὰ τὰς πολλὰς ἐξ αὐτῶν ἀηδίας τε καὶ ἀφολκὰς ἀπὸ τῶν ἀναγκαιοτέρων. συγκατατάττεται δὲ αὐτῷ καὶ Ἐπίκουρος καὶ ὅσοι ἐν ἡδονῇ καὶ ἀοχλησίᾳ, ἔτι δὲ καὶ ἀλυπίᾳ τἀγαθὸν τίθενται.

The principle 879—Since the wise man will try to avoid βλάβας ἐξ ἀνθρώπων (Diog.
of avoiding X 117), he will keep aloof from public life. The Λάθε βιώσας is a well
public life known Epicurean principle. It is mentioned or referred to by many later writers.

a. Plutarch wrote a few pages (1128-1130) on the subject:
Εἰ καλῶς εἴρηται τὸ Λάθε βιώσας.

Cp. Julianus ad Themistium, p. 471 Pet.; Themistius, *Or.* 26, p. 390, 21 Dind.; Philostr., *Vit. Apoll.* VIII 28, p. 368; Hor., Ep. I 17, 10; I 18, 102-103.

b. Lucretius expresses it in these lines (V 1127 f.):

ut satius multo iam sit parere quietum
quam regere imperio res velle et regna tenere.

c. The principle is connected with Epicurus' view that man is naturally not a social being.

Themistius, *Or.* XXVI, p. 390 Dind.:

Ἐπίκουρος λάθρα βιώσας ἐπῃνεῖτο καὶ ἔθετο δόγμα μὴ φύσει εἶναι τὸν ἄνθρωπον κοινωνικόν τε καὶ ἥμερον.

By this principle Epic. continues the line of certain Sophists, such as Critias (our nr. **195b**) and stands against the view of Plato (Rep. II, 369b, our nr. **277**) and of Aristotle.

d. The principle itself of avoiding public life is found in Epicurus' Sent. Vat., tr. LVIII Bailey:

Ἐκλυτέον ἑαυτοὺς ἐκ τοῦ περὶ τὰ ἐγκύκλια καὶ πολιτικὰ δεσμωτηρίου.

880—From Aristippus and his School Epicurus differs on three main points:

Differences from the Cyrenaics

1) Against Aristippus, who considered the pleasure of the moment as being the end (our nr. **255**), Epic. holds that the end is happiness, which is a permanent condition of equilibrium (ἀταραξία), as well of the mind as of the body.

1. Happiness a permanent condition

Olympiodorus in Plat. *Philebum*, p. 274 Stallb.:

Καὶ ὁ Ἐπίκουρος λέγει τὴν κατὰ φύσιν ἡδονήν, καταστηματικὴν αὐτὴν λέγων.

2) In defining pleasure as absence of pain, Epicurus views it essentially as implying a state of rest, and in this he is opposed to Aristippus, who defined pleasure as a λεία κίνησις (our nr. **256c-e**). Diog., however says that Epic. admitted both.

2. As such opposed to Aristippus' λεία κίνησις

Diog. X 136:

Διαφέρεται δὲ πρὸς τοὺς Κυρηναϊκοὺς περὶ τῆς ἡδονῆς· οἱ μὲν γὰρ τὴν καταστηματικὴν οὐκ ἐγκρίνουσι, μόνην δὲ τὴν ἐν κινήσει· ὁ δ' ἀμφοτέραν, ψυχῆς καὶ σώματος, ὥς φησιν ἐν τῷ Περὶ αἱρέσεως καὶ φυγῆς καὶ ἐν τῷ Περὶ τέλους καὶ ἐν τῷ πρώτῳ Περὶ βίων καὶ ἐν τῇ πρὸς τοὺς ἐν Μυτιλήνῃ φιλοσόφους ἐπιστολῇ. ὁμοίως δὲ καὶ Διογένης ἐν τῇ ἑπτακαιδεκάτῃ τῶν Ἐπιλέκτων καὶ Μητρόδωρος ἐν τῷ Τιμοκράτει λέγουσιν οὕτω· "Νοουμένης δὲ ἡδονῆς τῆς τε κατὰ κίνησιν καὶ τῆς καταστηματικῆς." ὁ δὲ Ἐπίκουρος ἐν τῷ Περὶ αἱρέσεως οὕτω λέγει· " Ἡ μὲν γὰρ ἀταραξία καὶ ἀπονία καταστηματικαί εἰσιν ἡδοναί, ἡ δὲ χαρὰ καὶ εὐφροσύνη κατὰ κίνησιν ἐνεργείᾳ βλέπονται."

3) Next, the mind is not limited to the sensation of the present moment, as Aristippus argued it is (our nr. **256b**): it can look "before and after". Therefore,

3. The mind not limited to the present

a. the memory of past pleasures may overwhelm, at least diminish, present distress.

Plut., *Contra Epic. beat.* 18, p. 1099d:

Ὥσπερ λέγουσι τὸ μεμνῆσθαι τῶν προτέρων ἀγαθῶν μέγιστόν ἐστι πρὸς τὸ ἡδέως ζῆν.

Value of pleasures

Cf. Hieronymus, *in Esaiam* b. XI c. 38 (t. IV, p. 473e Vall.): Unde stulta Epicuri sententia est, qui asserit recordatione praeteritorum bonorum mala praesentia mitigari.

Epic.' last letter to Idomeneus (our nr. **819**) illustrates the doctrine referred to in these texts.

b. The hope of pleasure to come is a source of happiness next to "the stable condition of rest in the flesh".

of future pleasures

Epic. fr. 11 Bailey, ap. Plut., *Contra Epic. beat.* 4, 1089d:

Τὸ γὰρ εὐσταθὲς σαρκὸς κατάστημα καὶ τὸ περὶ ταύτης πιστὸν ἔλπισμα τὴν ἀκροτάτην χαρὰν καὶ βεβαιοτάτην ἔχει τοῖς ἐπιλογίζεσθαι δυναμένοις.

Pains of the mind worse than bodily pains

c. Accordingly pains of the mind, embracing past, present and future, are worse than those of the body.

Diog. X 137:

῎Ετι πρὸς τοὺς Κυρηναϊκούς· οἱ μὲν γὰρ χείρους τὰς σωματικὰς ἀλγηδόνας τῶν ψυχικῶν· κολάζεσθαι γοῦν τοὺς ἁμαρτάνοντας σώματι [1]· ὁ δὲ τὰς ψυχικάς. τὴν γοῦν σάρκα τὸ παρὸν μόνον χειμάζειν, τὴν δὲ ψυχὴν καὶ τὸ παρελθὸν καὶ τὸ παρὸν καὶ τὸ μέλλον.

Pleasures of the mind greater

d. Thus, the pleasures of the mind are greater than those of the body.

Ib. (same passage continued):

Οὕτως οὖν καὶ μείζονας ἡδονὰς εἶναι τὰς τῆς ψυχῆς.

881—We conclude from the preceding points that, in spite of his starting point (vid. **863**), happiness for Epicurus essentially transcends the body.

For Epic. happiness transcends the body

Plut., *Contra Epic. beat.* 5, p. 1089d:

῞Ορα δὴ πρῶτον μὲν οἷα ποιοῦσιν τὴν εἴτε ἡδονὴν ταύτην εἴτε ἀπονίαν ἢ εὐστάθειαν ἄνω καὶ κάτω μεταίροντες ἐκ τοῦ σώματος εἰς τὴν ψυχήν, εἶτα πάλιν ἐκ ταύτης εἰς ἐκεῖνο, τῷ μὴ στέγειν ἀπορρέουσαν καὶ περιολισθάνουσαν ἀναγκαζόμενοι τῇ ἀρχῇ συνάπτειν καὶ τὸ μὲν ἡδόμενον, ὥς φησι, τῆς σαρκὸς τῷ χαίροντι τῆς ψυχῆς ὑπερείδοντες, αὖθις δ᾽ ἐκ τοῦ χαίροντος εἰς τὸ ἡδόμενον τῇ ἐλπίδι τελευτῶντες.

General characteristic of Epic. ethics

882—Bailey, *Gr. At.* p. 525 f., rightly qualifies Epicurus' ethics as a system of uncompromising egoistic hedonism. Most modern hedonistic systems, he remarks, have preferred to abandon egoism in favour of a social utilitarianism aiming at the "greatest happiness of the greatest number". Epicurus however is prepared to stand by his principles and take their consequences.

Epicureanism as a gospel

883—a. How his doctrine was accepted by his followers as a real gospel may appear first in the exordium of Lucretius' third book (1-30) [2]:

> E tenebris tantis tam clarum extollere lumen
> qui primus potuisti inlustrans commoda vitae,
> te sequor, o Graiae gentis decus, inque tuis nunc
> ficta pedum pono pressis vestigia signis,
> 5   non ita certandi cupidus quam propter amorem
> quod te imitari aveo; quid enim contendat hirundo

---

[1] Our nr. **256g**.
[2] A highly poetical translation of this wonderful passage was given by the Dutch poet J. H. Leopold.

cycnis, aut quidnam tremulis facere artubus haedi
consimile in cursu possint et fortis equi vis?
tu, pater, es rerum inventor, tu patria nobis,
10   suppeditas praecepta, tuisque ex, inclute, chartis,
floriferis ut apes in saltibus omnia libant,
omnia nos itidem depascimur aurea dicta,
aurea, perpetua semper dignissima vita.
nam simul ac ratio tua coepit vociferari
15   naturam rerum, divina mente coorta,
diffugiunt animi terrores, moenia mundi
discedunt, totum video per inane geri res.
apparet divum numen sedesque quietae
quas neque concutiunt venti nec nubila nimbis
20   aspergunt neque nix acri concreta pruina
cana cadens violat semperque innubilus aether
integit, et large diffuso lumine ridet.
omnia suppeditat porro natura neque ulla
res animi pacem delibat tempore in ullo.
25   at contra nusquam apparent Acherusia templa
nec tellus obstat quin omnia dispiciantur,
sub pedibus quaecumque infra per inane geruntur.
his ibi me rebus quaedam divina voluptas
percipit atque horror, quod sic natura tua vi
30   tam manifesta patens ex omni parte retecta est.

b. Five centuries after Epicurus the great inscription, which Diogenes of Oenoanda in Lycia ordered to be placed in the wall of a stoa "to help the strangers passing by", shows the same appreciation: men are considered as suffering from a general and widely spread disease, and Epicurus' doctrine is "the medicine of salvation".

Diog. Oenoand., fr. II, col. IV, 1. 3-col. VI l. 2:

Ἐπεὶ δέ, ὡς προεῖπα, οἱ πλεῖστοι καθάπερ ἐν λοιμῷ τῇ περὶ τῶν πραγμάτων ψευδοδοξίᾳ νοσοῦσι κοινῶς, γείνονται δὲ καὶ πλείονες — διὰ γὰρ τὸν ἀλλήλων ζῆλον ἄλλος ἐξ ἄλλου λαμβάνει τὴν νόσον, ὡς τὰ πρόβατα —, δίκαιο[ν δ' ἐστὶ καὶ] τοῖς μεθ' ἡμᾶς ἐσομένοις βοηθῆσαι — κἀκεῖνοι γάρ εἰσιν ἡμέτεροι καὶ εἰ [μὴ] γεγόνασί πω —, πρὸς δὲ δὴ φιλάνθρωπον καὶ τοῖς παραγεινομένοις ἐπικουρεῖν ξένοις, — ἐπείδη οὖν εἰς πλείονας διαβέβηκε τὰ βοηθήματα τοῦ συνγράμματος, ἠθέλησα τῇ στοᾷ ταύτῃ καταχρησάμενος ἐν κοινῷ τὰ τῆς σωτηρίας προθε[ῖναι φάρμα]κα.

TWENTY-FIRST CHAPTER
THE STOA

I—GENERAL ASPECT, CHIEF PERSONALITIES

884—a. Diog. VII, 1:

Ζήνων Μνασέου ἢ Δημέου Κιτιεὺς ἀπὸ Κύπρου, πολίσματος Ἑλληνικοῦ, Φοίνικας ἐποίκους ἐσχηκότος. — Ἀπολλώνιος δέ φησιν ὁ Τύριος ὅτι ἰσχνὸς ἦν, ὑπομήκης, μελάγχρους — ὅθεν τις αὐτὸν εἶπεν Αἰγυπτίαν κληματίδα.

Probably Pohlenz is right in thinking that Zeno was a Phoenician. In fact all our testimonies agree on the point (see Diog. VII, 3, 15, 25 and 30; also Cic., *De Fin.* IV, 56). Festugière, *Le Dieu cosm.* 266 n. 1 argues that the point is uncertain and that nothing can be concluded from Crates' words "Τί φεύγεις, Φοινικίδιον;" (Diog. VII, 3).

Date

b. Zeno came to Athens in the year 311/0 at the age of 22, as appears from the testimony of his disciple Persaeus, the year of his death being known from the honorary decree to be cited sub **887b**.

Diog. VII 28:

Περσαῖος δέ φησιν ἐν ταῖς ἠθικαῖς σχολαῖς δύο καὶ ἑβδομήκοντα ἐτῶν τελευτῆσαι αὐτόν, ἐλθεῖν δ' Ἀθήναζε δύο καὶ εἴκοσιν ἐτῶν·

885—Since he studied philosophy under the direction of Crates and others during a period of some ten years, he started to teach not earlier than in the year 301/0.

Disciple of Crates and of Polemo

a. Diog. VII 2:

Διήκουσε δέ, καθὰ προείρηται, Κράτητος· εἶτα καὶ Στίλπωνος ἀκοῦσαί φασιν αὐτὸν καὶ Ξενοκράτους ἔτη δέκα, ὡς Τιμοκράτης ἐν τῷ Δίωνι· ἀλλὰ καὶ Πολέμωνος.

The Crates here mentioned was the well known disciple of Diogenes the Cynic (Diog. Laert. VI 85-93). His *floruit* was, according to Diog. VI 87, about 328-324. Probably he was the man who was Zeno's teacher during ten years [1]. That Zeno heard Xenocrates, is impossible, for the latter died 314. Polemo was head of the Academy 314-270.

---

[1] Three philosophers of the name Crates are known to us. The first, Crates the Cynic, was a Theban (Diog. VI 85). He cannot be identified with Crates the inti-

b. Ib. 2-3:

Τῷ οὖν Κράτητι παρέβαλε τοῦτον τὸν τρόπον. πορφύραν ἐμπεπορευμένος ἀπὸ τῆς Φοινίκης πρὸς τῷ Πειραιεῖ ἐναυάγησεν. ἀνελθὼν δ' εἰς τὰς Ἀθήνας ἤδη τριακοντούτης ἐκάθισε παρά τινα βιβλιοπώλην· ἀναγινώσκοντος δ' ἐκείνου τὸ δεύτερον τῶν Ξενοφῶντος Ἀπομνημονευμάτων, ἡσθεὶς ἐπύθετο ποῦ διατρίβοιεν οἱ τοιοῦτοι ἄνδρες. εὐκαίρως δὲ παριόντος Κράτητος, ὁ βιβλιοπώλης δείξας αὐτόν φησι, "τούτῳ παρακολούθησον." ἐντεῦθεν ἤκουσε τοῦ Κράτητος, ἄλλως μὲν εὔτονος πρὸς φιλοσοφίαν, αἰδήμων δὲ ὡς πρὸς τὴν Κυνικὴν ἀναισχυντίαν.

c. The rest of the story is a clear indication that the Crates who was Zeno's teacher was no other than the Cynic Crates.

Ib. 3:

Ὅθεν ὁ Κράτης βουλόμενος αὐτὸν καὶ τοῦτο θεραπεῦσαι δίδωσι χύτραν φακῆς διὰ τοῦ Κεραμεικοῦ φέρειν. ἐπεὶ δ' εἶδεν αὐτὸν αἰδούμενον καὶ παρακαλύπτοντα, παίσας τῇ βακτηρίᾳ κατάγνυσι τὴν χύτραν· φεύγοντος δ' αὐτοῦ καὶ τῆς φακῆς κατὰ τῶν σκελῶν ῥεούσης, φησὶν ὁ Κράτης, "τί φεύγεις, Φοινικίδιον; οὐδὲν δεινὸν πέπονθας".

d. He seems to have still frequented Polemo's lectures when already teaching himself.

Diog. VII 25:

Ἤδη δὲ προκόπτων εἰσήει καὶ πρὸς Πολέμωνα ὑπ' ἀτυφίας, ὥστε φασι λέγειν ἐκεῖνον, "οὐ λανθάνεις, ὦ Ζήνων, ταῖς κηπαίαις παρεισρέων θύραις καὶ τὰ δόγματα κλέπτων Φοινικικῶς μεταμφιεννύς."

886—He starts teaching in the Stoa Poikile.

Diog. VII 5:

Ἀνακάμπτων δὴ ἐν τῇ ποικίλῃ στοᾷ τῇ καὶ Πεισιανακτείῳ καλουμένῃ, ἀπὸ δὲ τῆς γραφῆς τῆς Πολυγνώτου ποικίλῃ, διετίθετο τοὺς λόγους. —

Προσήεσαν δὴ λοιπὸν ἀκούοντες αὐτοῦ καὶ διὰ τοῦτο Στωϊκοὶ ἐκλήθησαν καὶ οἱ ἀπ' αὐτοῦ ὁμοίως, πρότερον Ζηνώνειοι καλούμενοι, καθά φησι καὶ Ἐπίκουρος ἐν ἐπιστολαῖς.

Since Zeno started to teach in the Stoa some six years after Epicurus opened his School at Athens, we may be sure that he was influenced by Epicurus' teaching:

mate friend of Polemo and his successor in the Academy (Diog. IV 21 f.; *Index Acad.* ed. Mekler, p. 56, 58 f., 62. See our nr. **797**). This second Crates was an Athenian and apparently much younger than Polemo. Zeno must have known him as a συσχολαστής. The *Index Acad.* (p. 87 M.) mentions a third Crates, of Tarsus, who lived more than a century later and was the head of the School between Carneades and Clitomachus.

doubtless in Zeno's doctrine we have to see a reaction against Epicurus' teaching
that pleasure is the end and that the universe is a product of chance. Both theses
must have offended Zeno's belief in a rational Power (logos) ruling the universe
and dwelling also in man.

Honoured   **887—a.**   Diog. VII 6:
by the
Athenians   Ἐτίμων δὴ οὖν Ἀθηναῖοι σφόδρα τὸν Ζήνωνα, οὕτως ὡς καὶ τῶν τειχῶν
αὐτῷ τὰς κλεῖς παρακαταθέσθαι καὶ χρυσῷ στεφάνῳ τιμῆσαι καὶ χαλκῇ εἰκόνι.

     b.   Decree of the Athenians after Zeno's death.

Diog. VII 10-11:

Ἐπειδὴ Ζήνων Μνασέου Κιτιεὺς ἔτη πολλὰ κατὰ φιλοσοφίαν ἐν τῇ πόλει
γενόμενος ἔν τε τοῖς λοιποῖς ἀνὴρ ἀγαθὸς ὢν διετέλεσε καὶ τοὺς εἰς σύστασιν
αὐτῷ τῶν νέων πορευομένους παρακαλῶν ἐπ' ἀρετὴν καὶ σωφροσύνην παρώρμα
πρὸς τὰ βέλτιστα παράδειγμα τὸν ἴδιον βίον ἐκθεὶς ἅπασιν, ἀκόλουθον ὄντα
τοῖς λόγοις οἷς διελέγετο, τύχῃ ἀγαθῇ δεδόχθαι τῷ δήμῳ, ἐπαινέσαι μὲν Ζήνωνα
Μνασέου Κιτιέα καὶ στεφανῶσαι χρυσῷ στεφάνῳ κατὰ τὸν νόμον ἀρετῆς
ἕνεκεν καὶ σωφροσύνης, οἰκοδομῆσαι δὲ αὐτῷ καὶ τάφον ἐπὶ τοῦ Κεραμεικοῦ
δημοσίᾳ. τῆς δὲ ποιήσεως τοῦ στεφάνου καὶ τῆς οἰκοδομῆς τοῦ τάφου χειρο-
τονῆσαι τὸν δῆμον ἤδη τοὺς ἐπιμελησομένους πέντε ἄνδρας ἐξ Ἀθηναίων·
ἀναγράψαι δὲ <τόδε> τὸ ψήφισμα τὸν γραμματέα τοῦ δήμου ἐν στήλαις <λιθίναις>
δύο καὶ ἐξεῖναι αὐτῷ θεῖναι τὴν μὲν ἐν Ἀκαδημείᾳ, τὴν δὲ ἐν Λυκείῳ. τὸ δὲ
ἀνάλωμα τὸ εἰς τὰς στήλας γινόμενον μερίσαι τὸν ἐπὶ τῇ διοικήσει, ὅπως
ἅπαντες εἰδῶσιν ὅτι ὁ δῆμος ὁ τῶν Ἀθηναίων τοὺς ἀγαθοὺς καὶ ζῶντας τιμᾷ
καὶ τελευτήσαντας.

Favoured   **888—a.**   Antigonus Gonatas also favoured him. Diog. VII 6:
by king
Antigonus   Ἀπεδέχετο δ' αὐτὸν καὶ Ἀντίγονος καὶ εἴ ποτ' Ἀθήναζε ἥκοι, ἤκουεν
αὐτοῦ πολλά τε παρεκάλει ἀφικέσθαι ὡς αὐτόν. ὁ δὲ τοῦτο μὲν παρῃτήσατο,
Περσαῖον δὲ ἕνα τῶν γνωρίμων ἀπέστειλεν. [1]

A. praizes   **b.**   Antigonus' words after Zeno's death. Diog. VII 15:
Zeno's
character   Λέγεται δὲ καὶ μετὰ τὴν τελευτὴν τοῦ Ζήνωνος εἰπεῖν τὸν Ἀντίγονον οἷον
εἴη θέατρον ἀπολωλεκώς. —
Ἐρωτηθεὶς δὲ διὰ τί θαυμάζει αὐτόν, "ὅτι, ἔφη, πολλῶν καὶ μεγάλων αὐτῷ
διδομένων ὑπ' ἐμοῦ οὐδέποτ' ἐχαυνώθη οὐδὲ ταπεινὸς ὤφθη.

Comic poets   **c.**   His soberness. Diog. VII 27:
on Zeno
   Οἵ γε μὴν κωμικοὶ ἐλάνθανον ἐπαινοῦντες αὐτὸν διὰ τῶν σκωμμάτων.
ἵνα καὶ Φιλήμων φησὶν οὕτως ἐν δράματι Φιλοσόφοις:

---

[1] On this Persaeus see below, nrs. **890, 924.**

εἷς ἄρτος, ὄψον ἰσχάς, ἐπιπιεῖν ὕδωρ.
φιλοσοφίαν καινὴν γὰρ οὗτος φιλοσοφεῖ,
πεινῆν διδάσκει καὶ μαθητὰς λαμβάνει·
— ἤδη δὲ καὶ εἰς παροιμίαν σχεδὸν ἐχώρησεν. ἐλέγετο γοῦν ἐπ' αὐτοῦ·
Τοῦ φιλοσόφου Ζήνωνος ἐγκρατέστερος.

889—Zeno was succeeded by his faithful disciple Cleanthes of Assos. **Cleanthes**
Diog. VII 168, 170:

Κλεάνθης Φανίου "Ασσιος. οὗτος πρῶτον ἦν πύκτης, ὥς φησιν 'Αντισθένης
ἐν Διαδοχαῖς· ἀφικόμενος δ' εἰς 'Αθήνας τέσσαρας ἔχων δραχμάς, καθά
φασί τινες, καὶ Ζήνωνι παραβαλὼν ἐφιλοσόφησε γενναιότατα καὶ ἐπὶ τῶν
αὐτῶν ἔμεινε δογμάτων. διεβοήθη δ' ἐπὶ φιλοπονίᾳ, ὅς γε πένης ὢν ἄγαν
ὥρμησε μισθοφορεῖν· καὶ νύκτωρ μὲν ἐν τοῖς κήποις ἤντλει, μεθ' ἡμέραν δ'
ἐν τοῖς λόγοις ἐγυμνάζετο· ὅθεν καὶ Φρεάντλης ἐκλήθη. —
Ἦν δὲ πονικὸς μέν, ἀφύσικος δὲ καὶ βραδὺς ὑπερβαλλόντως. —
Καὶ σκωπτόμενος δ' ὑπὸ τῶν συμμαθητῶν ἠνείχετο· καὶ ὄνος ἀκούων
προσεδέχετο, λέγων αὐτὸς μόνος δύνασθαι βαστάζειν τὸ Ζήνωνος φορτίον.

Of Cleanthes' works, as of Zeno's, only fragments have survived. His *Hymn
to Zeus*, preserved by Stobaeus (our nr. **943**) is the longest authentic text we
possess of the Ancient Stoa.

890—Herillus and Aristo of Chios were more or less heretical Stoics. **Herillus,**
We shall speak of them in dealing with the doctrine of adiaphora (nr. **Aristo of**
1021) and with the definition of virtue (nrs. **1028c**, **1030a**, **b**). **Chios,**
Persaeus

Persaeus, too, is frequently considered as a heretic (e.g. by Goedeckemeyer [1]) or as a practically unworthy Stoic (Verbeke [2]). It may be
questioned, however, whether this view is justified (below, under **924c**).

891—Cleanthes was succeeded by Chrysippus, a famous dialectician
who truly rebuilt the Stoic philosophy as a solid and well ordered system.

a. Diog. VII 179, 180: **Chrysippus**

Χρύσιππος 'Απολλωνίου Σολεὺς ἢ Ταρσεύς, ὡς 'Αλέξανδρος ἐν Διαδοχαῖς,
μαθητὴς Κλεάνθους. οὗτος πρότερον μὲν δόλιχον ἤσκει, ἔπειτ' ἀκούσας
Ζήνωνος ἢ Κλεάνθους, ὡς Διοκλῆς καὶ οἱ πλείους, ἔτι τε ζῶντος ἀπέστη
αὐτοῦ καὶ οὐχ ὁ τυχὼν ἐγένετο κατὰ φιλοσοφίαν· ἀνὴρ εὐφυὴς καὶ ὀξύτατος
ἐν παντὶ μέρει οὕτως ὥστε καὶ ἐν τοῖς πλείστοις διηνέχθη πρὸς Ζήνωνα,

---

[1] Barth-Goedeckemeyer, *Die Stoa*[5] 1941, p. 37, 41.
[2] *Kleanthes*, p. 32 f. On p. 16 the author even cites Persaeus' writing Π. θεῶν
under the title *On impiety* ("Over de goddeloosheid").

ἀλλὰ καὶ πρὸς Κλεάνθην, ᾧ καὶ πολλάκις ἔλεγε μόνης τῆς τῶν δογμάτων διδασκαλίας χρήζειν, τὰς δὲ ἀποδείξεις αὐτὸς εὑρήσειν. — οὕτω δ' ἐπίδοξος ἐν τοῖς διαλεκτικοῖς ἐγένετο, ὥστε δοκεῖν τοὺς πλείους ὅτι εἰ παρὰ θεοῖς ἦν διαλεκτική, οὐκ ἂν ἄλλη ἦν ἢ ἡ Χρυσίππειος.

His writings   **b.** Ib. 180:

Πλεονάσας δὲ τοῖς πράγμασι τὴν λέξιν οὐ κατώρθωσε. πονικώτατός τε παρ' ὁντινοῦν γέγονεν, ὡς δῆλον ἐκ τῶν συγγραμμάτων αὐτοῦ· τὸν ἀριθμὸν γὰρ ὑπὲρ πέντε καὶ ἑπτακόσιά ἐστιν. ἐπλήθυνε δ' αὐτὰ πολλάκις ὑπὲρ τοῦ αὐτοῦ δόγματος ἐπιχειρῶν καὶ πᾶν τὸ ὑποπεσὸν γράφων καὶ διορθούμενος πλεονάκις πλείστῃ τε τῶν μαρτυριῶν παραθέσει χρώμενος· ὥστε καὶ ἐπειδή ποτ' ἔν τινι τῶν συγγραμμάτων παρ' ὀλίγον τὴν Εὐριπίδου Μήδειαν ὅλην παρετίθετο καὶ τις μετὰ χεῖρας εἶχε τὸ βιβλίον, πρὸς τὸν πυθόμενον τί ἄρα ἔχοι, ἔφη, "Χρυσίππου Μήδειαν".

Style   **c.** Dionys. Halic., *De comp. verb.* p. 30 Re. (SVF II, 28):

Καὶ τί δεῖ τούτους θαυμάζειν, ὅπουγε καὶ οἱ τὴν φιλοσοφίαν ἐπαγγελλόμενοι καὶ τὰς διαλεκτικὰς ἐκφέροντες τέχνας οὕτως εἰσὶν ἄθλιοι περὶ τὴν σύνθεσιν τῶν ὀνομάτων, ὥστ' αἰδεῖσθαι καὶ λέγειν; ἀπόχρη δὲ τεκμηρίῳ χρήσασθαι τῷ λόγῳ Χρυσίππου τοῦ Στωϊκοῦ· περαιτέρω γὰρ οὐκ ἂν προβαίην. τούτου γὰρ οὔτ' ἄμεινον οὐδεὶς τὰς διαλεκτικὰς τέχνας ἠκρίβωσεν, οὔτε χείρονι ἁρμονίᾳ συνταχθέντας ἐξήνεγκε λόγους τῶν ὀνόματος καὶ δόξης ἀξιωθέντων.

Merits for Stoic philosophy   **892—a.** His merits for Stoic philosophy are expressed in the popular verse (Diog. VII 183):

Εἰ μὴ γὰρ ἦν Χρύσιππος, οὐκ ἂν ἦν Στοά.

In fact, Stoic doctrine is known to us almost entirely in the form Chrysippus gave it, and it is often difficult to decide what exactly was the founder's opinion. On some important points however (e.g. in the theory of knowledge) we can see that Chrys. altered Zeno's doctrine considerably.

b. Cf. Origenes, *Contra Cels.* II 12 (SVF II 21):

Ἀλλὰ καὶ ὁ Χρύσιππος πολλαχοῦ τῶν συγγραμμάτων αὐτοῦ φαίνεται καθαπτόμενος Κλεάνθους, καινοτομῶν παρὰ τὰ ἐκείνῳ δεδογμένα, γενομένῳ αὐτοῦ διδασκάλῳ ἔτι νέου καὶ ἀρχὰς ἔχοντος φιλοσοφίας.

Vid. sub **896**.

Diogenes of Seleucia and Antipater of Tarsus   **893**—Of Chrysippus' disciples the best known were *Diogenes the Babylonian*, together with Carneades ambassador to Rome in the year 156/5, and *Antipater of Tarsus*, who succeeded Diogenes as the head of the school ± 150.

Both are considered by von Arnim as belonging to the Ancient Stoa and accordingly treated in *Stoicorum Veterum Fragmenta III*.

894—A new period starts with *Panaetius*, who lived a part of his life in Rome, where he belonged to the circle of Scipio and Laelius. His disciple *Posidonius* had his school on Rhodes, where he was heard by Cicero in the year 78 and visited by Pompeius coming from his victory over Mithradates. *(margin: Middle period of the Stoa)*

Both Panaetius and Posidonius were important thinkers and scholars. We shall come back to them after having expounded the Stoic doctrine as a whole.

895—A third period in the history of the Stoa is that of the Roman Empire. Its chief representatives are: *(margin: The Roman Stoa)*

- **a.** Seneca
- **b.** Musonius Rufus
- **c.** Epictetus
- **d.** the emperor Marcus Aurelius.

We shall deal with them and with later Cynicism in a special chapter (XXIII).

896—As opposed to Epicurus' School the Stoa contained, from the very beginning, a variety of opinions. *(margin: Unity and diversity in Stoic doctrine)*

Numenius ap. Eusebium, *Praep. ev.* XIV, p. 728a:

Τὰ δὲ τῶν Στωϊκῶν ἐστασίασται, ἀρξάμενα ἀπὸ τῶν ἀρχόντων καὶ μηδέπω τελευτῶντα καὶ νῦν. ἐλέγχουσι δ' ἀγαπώντως ὑπὸ δυσμενοῦς ἐλεγχοῦ, οἱ μέν τινες αὐτῶν ἐμμεμενηκότες ἔτι, οἱ δ' ἤδη μεταθέμενοι. εἴξασιν οὖν οἱ πρῶτοι ὀλιγαρχικωτέροις, οἳ δὴ διαστάντες ὑπῆρξαν εἰς τοὺς μετέπειτα πολλῆς μὲν τοῖς προτέροις, πολλῆς δὲ τῆς ἀλλήλοις ἐπιτιμήσεως αἴτιοι, εἰσέτι ἑτέρων ἕτεροι Στωϊκώτεροι·

In fact, the term ἐστασίασται is too strong: there is one Stoic doctrine we find from Zeno and the Ancient Stoics down to the Roman period. Aristo of Chios and Herillus differed too much from Zeno to be considered as Stoics at all. However, there have been alterations of Zeno's doctrine, first by Chrysippus (under the influence of Arcesilaus' criticism), next by Panaetius, who was influenced by Carneades. Posidonius restored the ancient doctrine on several points but had his own strong individuality. Ancient Stoic doctrine is found again in Seneca, Musonius and Epictetus; it is found essentially also in Marcus Aurelius, though with an individual accent. Therefore, we shall treat Stoic doctrine as such, illustrating it by texts of ancient and later Stoics, and marking the chief points of its development.

Division of philosophy

897—The well known tripartition of philosophy is generally ascribed to the Stoa.

a. Diog. VII 39:

Τριμερῆ φασιν εἶναι τὸν κατὰ φιλοσοφίαν λόγον· εἶναι γὰρ αὐτοῦ τὸ μέν τι φυσικόν, τὸ δὲ ἠθικόν, τὸ δὲ λογικόν. οὕτω δὲ πρῶτος διεῖλε Ζήνων ὁ Κιτιεὺς ... καὶ Χρύσιππος ... καὶ Διογένης ὁ Βαβυλώνιος καὶ Ποσειδώνιος.

b. The same sequence of the three parts appears in Aëtius, *Plac.* I, Prooem. 2 (273, 11 Dox.):

Οἱ μὲν οὖν Στωϊκοὶ ἔφασαν τὴν μὲν σοφίαν εἶναι θείων τε καὶ ἀνθρωπίνων ἐπιστήμην, τὴν δὲ φιλοσοφίαν ἄσκησιν ἐπιτηδείου τέχνης· ἐπιτήδειον δὲ εἶναι μίαν καὶ ἀνωτάτω τὴν ἀρετήν, ἀρετὰς δὲ τὰς γενικωτάτας τρεῖς, φυσικὴν ἠθικὴν λογικήν. δι' ἣν αἰτίαν καὶ τριμερής ἐστιν ἡ φιλοσοφία, ἧς τὸ μὲν φυσικὸν τὸ δὲ ἠθικὸν τὸ δὲ λογικόν· καὶ φυσικὸν μὲν ὅταν περὶ κόσμου ζητῶμεν καὶ τῶν ἐν κόσμῳ, ἠθικὸν δὲ τὸ κατησχολημένον περὶ τὸν ἀνθρώπινον βίον, λογικὸν δὲ τὸ περὶ τὸν λόγον, ὃ καὶ διαλεκτικὸν καλοῦσιν.

c. Varro, ap. Cic., *Acad. post.* 5, 19, about to expound what he calls the *veterum philosophia* (i.e. that of the early Academy and the first Peripatetics), introduces the same tripartition, saying:

"Fuit ergo iam accepta a Platone philosophandi ratio triplex: una de vita et moribus, altera de natura et rebus occultis, tertia de disserendo et quid verum sit, quid falsum, quid rectum in oratione pravumve, quid consentiens, quid repugnans iudicando".

Sextus, *Adv. math.* VII (= *Ag. the logicians I*) 16 says more accurately that Plato is "virtually" the pioneer (δυνάμει μὲν Πλάτων ἐστὶν ἀρχηγός), but it was Xenocrates who introduced it explicitly (ῥητότατα). Cp. Xenocr., fr. 1 H. (our nr. **753a**) [1].

Likenesses

898—The following likenesses were used.

Diog. VII 40:

Εἰκάζουσι δὲ ζῴῳ τὴν φιλοσοφίαν, ὀστοῖς μὲν καὶ νεύροις τὸ λογικὸν προσομοιοῦντες, τοῖς δὲ σαρκοδεστέροις τὸ ἠθικόν, τῇ δὲ ψυχῇ τὸ φυσικόν. ἢ πάλιν ᾠῷ· τὰ μὲν γὰρ ἐκτὸς εἶναι τὸ λογικόν, τὰ δὲ μετὰ ταῦτα τὸ ἠθικόν, τὰ δ' ἐσωτάτω τὸ φυσικόν. ἢ ἀγρῷ παμφόρῳ· οὗ τὸν μὲν περιβεβλημένον φραγμὸν τὸν λογικόν, τὸν δὲ καρπὸν τὸ ἠθικόν, τὴν δὲ γῆν ἢ τὰ δένδρα τὸ φυσικόν. ἢ πόλει καλῶς τετειχισμένῃ καὶ κατὰ λόγον διοικουμένῃ.

---

[1] The same definition of wisdom appears in Seneca, *Ep.* 89. Also ap. Sext., *Adv. math.* IX (= *Ag. the phys.* I) 13.

If we might perhaps wonder why in a living being *the body* is compared with ethics, while *physics* is said to be like the soul, and again, why in the egg the yolk is compared with physics, while ethics is said to resemble the white, we shall find that in the above cited passage of Sextus *physics* is compared with the white of the egg and with the body of a living being, while *ethics* is said to resemble the yolk of the egg and the soul of a living being, the latter comparison being attributed to Posidonius.

b. Sextus, *Adv. Math.* VII (= *Against the Logicians* I) 19:

Ὁ δὲ Ποσειδώνιος, ἐπεὶ τὰ μὲν μέρη τῆς φιλοσοφίας ἀχώριστά ἐστιν ἀλλήλων, τὰ δὲ φυτὰ τῶν καρπῶν ἕτερα θεωρεῖται καὶ τὰ τείχη τῶν φυτῶν κεχώρισται, ζώῳ μᾶλλον εἰκάζειν ἠξίου τὴν φιλοσοφίαν, αἵματι μὲν καὶ σαρξὶ τὸ φυσικόν, ὀστέοις δὲ καὶ νεύροις τὸ λογικόν, ψυχῇ δὲ τὸ ἠθικόν.

c. It seems that the sequence and appreciation of the three parts is subject to variation. Cp. Diog. VII 40 (the passage cited sub a. continued):

Variation in sequence

Καὶ οὐθὲν μέρος τοῦ ἑτέρου ἀποκεκρίσθαι, καθά τινες αὐτῶν φασιν, ἀλλὰ μεμίχθαι αὐτά. καὶ τὴν παράδοσιν μικτὴν ἐποίουν. ἄλλοι δὲ πρῶτον μὲν τὸ λογικὸν τάττουσι, δεύτερον δὲ τὸ φυσικόν, καὶ τρίτον τὸ ἠθικόν· ὧν ἐστι Ζήνων ἐν τῷ Περὶ λόγου καὶ Χρύσιππος καὶ Ἀρχέδημος καὶ Εὔδρομος.

The sequence *logic, ethics, physics* is found in Sext., *Math.* VII 22. Also in the fr. of Chrys. ap. Plut., *Stoic. repugn.* 9, p. 1035a (SVF II 42)

Since Chrysippus himself seems to have varied the order of the three parts of philosophy, I think it better not to follow the direction of the last cited passage, but to choose the order which seems most rational to me, namely 1. physics, 2. logic, 3. ethics. After all the orchard is there before the enclosure, and usually the enclosure is made before the fruits are there.

Order to be followed

2—PHYSICS: (1) GENERAL PRINCIPLES

899—a. Diog. VII 134:

First principles

Δοκεῖ δ' αὐτοῖς ἀρχὰς εἶναι τῶν ὅλων δύο, τὸ ποιοῦν καὶ τὸ πάσχον. τὸ μὲν οὖν πάσχον εἶναι τὴν ἄποιον οὐσίαν, τὴν ὕλην· τὸ δὲ ποιοῦν τὸν ἐν αὐτῇ λόγον, τὸν θεόν. τοῦτον γὰρ ἀΐδιον ὄντα διὰ πάσης αὐτῆς δημιουργεῖν ἕκαστα. τίθησι δὲ τὸ δόγμα τοῦτο Ζήνων μὲν ὁ Κιτιεὺς ἐν τῷ Περὶ οὐσίας, Κλεάνθης δὲ ἐν τῷ Περὶ τῶν ἀτόμων, Χρύσιππος δὲ ἐν τῇ πρώτῃ τῶν Φυσικῶν.

b. Aëtius, I 3, 25 (Dox. 289):

Ζήνων Μνασέου Κιτιεὺς ἀρχὰς μὲν τὸν θεὸν καὶ τὴν ὕλην, ὧν ὁ μέν ἐστι τοῦ ποιεῖν αἴτιος, ἡ δὲ τοῦ πάσχειν, στοιχεῖα δὲ τέσσαρα.

Diog., l.c., adds a note on the difference between ἀρχαί and στοιχεῖα:

Τὰς μὲν γὰρ εἶναι ἀγενήτους καὶ ἀφθάρτους, τὰ δὲ στοιχεῖα κατὰ τὴν ἐκπύρωσιν φθείρεσθαι. ἀλλὰ καὶ ἀσωμάτους εἶναι τὰς ἀρχὰς καὶ ἀμόρφους, τὰ δὲ μεμορφῶσθαι.

c. Seneca, *Ep.* 65, 2:

Dicunt, ut scis, Stoici nostri duo esse in rerum natura, ex quibus omnia fiant, causam et materiam. Materia iacet iners, res ad omnia parata, cessatura si nemo moveat. Causa autem, id est ratio, materiam format et quocumque vult versat, ex illa varia opera producit. Esse ergo debet, unde aliquid fiat, deinde a quo fiat. Hoc causa est, illud materia.

The difference from Aristotle's doctrine of εἶδος and ὕλη may be easily seen from the Stoic principle mentioned sub **901**.

Πρώτη ὕλη and λόγος

900—a. Zeno speaks on πρώτη ὕλη as follows.

Stob., *Ecl.* I 11, 5a, p. 132, 26W. (SVF I 87):

Ζήνωνος· οὐσίαν δὲ εἶναι τὴν τῶν ὄντων πάντων πρώτην ὕλην, ταύτην δὲ πᾶσαν ἀΐδιον καὶ οὔτε πλείω γιγνομένην οὔτε ἐλάττω· τὰ δὲ μέρη ταύτης οὐκ ἀεὶ ταὐτὰ διαμένειν ἀλλὰ διαιρεῖσθαι καὶ συγχεῖσθαι. διὰ ταύτης δὲ διαθεῖν τὸν τοῦ παντὸς λόγον, ὃν ἔνιοι εἱμαρμένην καλοῦσιν, οἷόνπερ καὶ ἐν τῇ γονῇ τὸ σπέρμα.

God inseparable from matter

b. Cp. Chalcid. *in Tim.* c. 294 (SVF ib.):

Stoici deum scilicet hoc esse quod silva sit vel etiam qualitatem inseparabilem deum silvae, eundemque per silvam meare, velut semen per membra genitalia.

c. Epiphan., *Adv. Haer.* I 5 (Dox. 588), SVF, ib.:

Φάσκει οὖν καὶ οὗτος (Ζήνων) τὴν ὕλην σύγχρονον καλῶν τῷ θεῷ ἴσα ταῖς ἄλλαις αἱρέσεσιν. εἱμαρμένην τε εἶναι καὶ γένεσιν ἐξ ἧς τὰ πάντα διοικεῖται καὶ πάσχει.

Stoics never speak of God and matter as being two substances. They always consider them as two aspects of the same nature which is one. Thus, for the Stoa in a sense God "is" matter, or at least inseparably connected with matter.

Everything which operates is a body

901—God and soul must be matter according to the Stoic principle that everything which operates is a body.

a. Diog. VII 56:

Πᾶν γὰρ τὸ ποιοῦν σῶμά ἐστι.

b. Cic., *Acad. Post.* I 11, 39:

Discrepabat etiam ab his (sc. Zeno ab Academicis et Peripateticis) quod nullo modo arbitrabatur quicquam effici posse ab ea quae expers esset corporis, cuius generis Xenocrates et superiores etiam animum esse dixerant, nec vero aut quod efficeret aliquid aut quod efficeretur posse esse non corpus.

c. Clem. Alex., *Strom.* V 14, p. 384 St. (SVF II 1035):

Φασὶ γὰρ σῶμα εἶναι τὸν θεὸν οἱ Στωϊκοὶ καὶ πνεῦμα κατ' οὐσίαν, ὥσπερ ἀμέλει καὶ τὴν ψυχήν.

Cp. Theodoretus, *Graec. aff. cur.* p. 37, 33, who speaks of τῶν Στωϊκῶν τὴν ἀπρεπῆ περὶ τοῦ θείου δόξαν: σωματοειδῆ γὰρ οὗτοι τὸν θεὸν ἔφασαν εἶναι. (SVF II 1028).

902—In fact, the Stoic monism tends to wipe out the opposition of "matter" to "spirit" or "mind": God is defined as πῦρ τεχνικόν, but this creative fire a is kind of metaphysical fire,—corporeal, yet spiritual.

a. Aëtius, *Plac.* I, 7, 33 (SVF II 1027):

God defined
as
πῦρ τεχνικόν

Οἱ Στωϊκοὶ νοερὸν θεὸν ἀποφαίνονται, πῦρ τεχνικόν, ὁδῷ βαδίζον ἐπὶ γένεσιν κόσμου, ἐμπεριειληφὸς πάντας τοὺς σπερματικοὺς λόγους, καθ' οὓς ἕκαστα καθ' εἱμαρμένην γίνεται· καὶ πνεῦμα μὲν διῆκον δι' ὅλου τοῦ κόσμου, τὰς δὲ προσηγορίας μεταλαμβάνον κατὰ τὰς τῆς ὕλης, δι' ἧς κεχώρηκε, παραλλάξεις. θεοὺς δὲ καὶ τὸν κόσμον καὶ τοὺς ἀστέρας καὶ τὴν γῆν, τὸν δ' ἀνωτάτω πάντων νοῦν ἐν αἰθέρι.

The definition Πῦρ τεχνικόν, etc. is also found in Diog. VII 156. On the notion of σπερματικοὶ λόγοι vid. infra, sub nrs. **904a, 919**. That the Spirit alters its names according to the different forms of the matter which it pervades, is a typically pantheistic view. We shall find it again in Seneca, *De benef.* IV 7-8 (our nr. **924a**).

b. Cicero, *N.D.* II 22, 57 (SVF I 171):

Zeno igitur naturam ita definit, ut eam dicat ignem esse artificiosum ad gignendum progredientem via. Censet enim artis maxime proprium esse creare et gignere, quodque in operibus nostrarum artium manus efficiat, id multo artificiosius naturam efficere, id est, ut dixi, ignem artificiosum, magistrum artium reliquarum.

c. Stob., *Ecl.* I p. 213, l. 17 ff. W.:

Two kinds
of fire

Ζήνωνος. — Δύο γὰρ γένη πυρός, τὸ μὲν ἄτεχνον καὶ μεταβάλλον εἰς ἑαυτὸ τὴν τροφήν, τὸ δὲ τεχνικόν, αὐξητικόν τε καὶ τηρητικόν, οἷον ἐν τοῖς φυτοῖς ἐστι καὶ ζῴοις, ὃ δὴ φύσις ἐστὶ καὶ ψυχή.

Cf. Cic., *N.D.* II 15, 41.

903—Contrary to Aristotle's doctrine in Π. φιλ. that noûs consists of the same element as the celestial bodies, namely aether (our nr. **431d**), Zeno held that the soul is fire or pneuma.

Soul is not aether but fire

a. Cic., *Ac. Post.* I 11, 39:

De naturis autem sic sentiebat, primum, ut in quattuor initiis rerum illis quintam hanc naturam, ex qua superiores sensus et mentem effici rebantur, non adhiberet. Statuebat enim ignem esse ipsam naturam, quae quidque gigneret, etiam mentem atque sensus.

Idem, *de Fin.* IV 12:

Cum autem quaereretur res admodum difficilis, num quinta quaedam natura videretur esse, ex qua ratio et intellegentia oriretur, in quo etiam de animis cuius generis essent quaereretur, Zeno id dixit esse ignem.

or
πνεῦμα
ἔνθερμον

b. Diog. VII 157:

Ζήνων δ' ὁ Κιτιεὺς καὶ 'Αντίπατρος ἐν τοῖς Περὶ ψυχῆς καὶ Ποσειδώνιος πνεῦμα ἔνθερμον εἶναι τὴν ψυχήν· τούτῳ γὰρ ἡμᾶς εἶναι ἐμπνόους καὶ ὑπὸ τούτου κινεῖσθαι.

Consitus Spiritus

c. We find the doctrine of Zeno again in Tertull., *De anima* 5 (SVF I 137):

Denique Zeno "consitum spiritum" definiens animam hoc modo instruit, "quo" inquit "digresso animal emoritur, corpus est: consito autem spiritu digresso animal emoritur: ergo consitus spiritus corpus est: consitus autem spiritus anima est: ergo corpus est anima".

On the consequences of the Stoic doctrine of materiality of the soul, see our nrs. **914-915**.

904—In what sense God or the Logos is called Demiurge or Builder of the world.

How the world comes into being

a. Diog. VII 135 f.:

"Εν τ' εἶναι θεὸν καὶ νοῦν καὶ εἱμαρμένην καὶ Δία· πολλάς τ' ἑτέρας ὀνομασίας προσονομάζεσθαι. κατ' ἀρχὰς μὲν οὖν καθ' αὑτὸν ὄντα τρέπειν τὴν πᾶσαν οὐσίαν δι' ἀέρος εἰς ὕδωρ· καὶ ὥσπερ ἐν τῇ γονῇ τὸ σπέρμα περιέχεται, οὕτω καὶ τοῦτον σπερματικὸν λόγον ὄντα τοῦ κόσμου τοιόνδ' ὑπολείπεσθαι ἐν τῷ ὑγρῷ, εὐεργὸν αὑτῷ ποιοῦντα τὴν ὕλην πρὸς τὴν τῶν ἑξῆς γένεσιν, εἶτ' ἀπογεννᾶν πρῶτον τὰ τέσσαρα στοιχεῖα, πῦρ, ὕδωρ, ἀέρα, γῆν. λέγει δὲ περὶ αὐτῶν Ζήνων τ' ἐν τῷ Περὶ τοῦ ὅλου καὶ Χρύσιππος ἐν τῇ πρώτῃ τῶν Φυσικῶν.

How it is meant that the world comes into being when "God" transforms "the whole of substance" through air into water, may become somewhat clearer from the passage cited sub *b* We have to remember Heraclitus' downward and upward way (our nr. **55**). Zeno who adopts the theory of the four elements, introduces air into Heraclitus' scheme. That God who is called by Zeno "the seminal Reason of the Universe", remains behind in cosmic moisture as an agent "adapting matter to himself with a view to the next stage of creation", reminds us of a passage in Seneca, *Nat. queast.*, to be cited sub **905c**.

b.   Diog., ib. 142: *ὁδὸς κάτω, ὁδὸς ἄνω*

Γίνεσθαι δὲ τὸν κόσμον, ὅταν ἐκ πυρὸς ἡ οὐσία τραπῇ δι' ἀέρος εἰς ὑγρότητα, εἶτα τὸ παχυμερὲς αὐτοῦ συστὰν ἀποτελεσθῇ γῆ, τὸ δὲ λεπτομερὲς ἐξαερωθῇ, καὶ τοῦτ' ἐπὶ πλέον λεπτυνθὲν πῦρ ἀπογεννήσῃ· εἶτα κατὰ μίξιν ἐκ τούτων φυτά τε καὶ ζῷα καὶ τὰ ἄλλα γένη.

That this generation of the universe, and its destruction, is meant as *a periodical process*, appears both from the praesens γίνεσθαι and from the ὅταν. It is expressed explicitly in Stob., *Ecl.* I 17, 3, p. 152, 19 (see Pearson, *The fragments of Zeno*, nr. 52). See also the next nr.

905—a.   Aristocles ap. Euseb., *Praep. Evang.* XV, p. 816d, (SVF I 98), having summarized Zeno's doctrine of the active and the passive principle, continues:

῎Επειτα δὲ καὶ κατά τινας εἱμαρμένους χρόνους ἐκπυροῦσθαι τὸν σύμπαντα   *Periodical conflagration*
κόσμον, εἶτ' αὖθις πάλιν διακοσμεῖσθαι. τὸ μέντοι πρῶτον πῦρ εἶναι καθαπερεί τι σπέρμα, τῶν ἁπάντων ἔχον τοὺς λόγους καὶ τὰς αἰτίας τῶν γεγονότων καὶ τῶν γιγνομένων καὶ τῶν ἐσομένων·

b.   Heracles who, tired by his works, gave himself death by fire appears as a symbol of the "creative fire" from which everything springs and to which everything returns periodically.

Seneca, *De benef.* IV 8:
Herculem quia vis eius invicta sit, quandoque lassata fuerit operibus editis in ignem recessura.

c.   Seneca describes the process of conflagration and regeneration of the world in such a way that, when fire is extinguished humour remains, in which a germ for a new world is present.

Sen., *Nat. quaest.* III 13:   *and regeneration*
Nihil relinqui aliud in rerum natura igne restincto quam umorem, in hoc futuri mundi spem latere. Ita ignis exitus mundi est, umor primordium.

Cp. Cleanthes' description of the regeneration of the kosmos, to be cited sub **908**.

906—Hence the curious doctrine of the periodical repetition of history   *Reiteration of history*
(cp. our nr. **23c**), called by later writers ἀποκατάστασις.

Nemesius, *De nat. hom.* 38, p. 277 (SVF II 625):

Οἱ δὲ Στωϊκοί φασιν ἀποκαθισταμένους τοὺς πλάνητας εἰς τὸ αὐτὸ σημεῖον κατά τε μῆκος καὶ πλάτος, ἔνθα τὴν ἀρχὴν ἕκαστος ἦν, ὅτε τὸ πρῶτον ὁ κόσμος συνέστη, ἐν ῥηταῖς χρόνων περιόδοις ἐκπύρωσιν καὶ φθορὰν τῶν ὄντων ἀπεργάζεσθαι· καὶ πάλιν ἐξ ὑπαρχῆς εἰς τὸ αὐτὸ τὸν κόσμον ἀποκαθίστασθαι· τῶν ἀστέρων ὁμοίως πάλιν φερομένων ἕκαστον ἐν τῇ προτέρᾳ περιόδῳ γινόμενον ἀπαραλλάκτως ἀποτελεῖσθαι. ἔσεσθαι γὰρ πάλιν Σωκράτη καὶ Πλάτωνα καὶ ἕκαστον τῶν ἀνθρώπων σὺν τοῖς αὐτοῖς καὶ φίλοις καὶ πολίταις· καὶ τὰ αὐτὰ πείσεσθαι καὶ τὰ αὐτὰ μεταχειριεῖσθαι, καὶ πᾶσαν πόλιν καὶ κώμην καὶ ἀγρὸν ὁμοίως ἀποκαθίστασθαι· γίνεσθαι δὲ τὴν ἀποκατάστασιν τοῦ παντὸς οὐχ ἅπαξ, ἀλλὰ πολλάκις· μᾶλλον δ᾽ εἰς ἄπειρον καὶ ἀτελεύτητον τὰ αὐτὰ ἀποκαθίστασθαι. τοὺς δὲ θεοὺς τοὺς μὴ ὑποκειμένους τῇ φθορᾷ, ταύτῃ παρακολουθήσαντας μιᾷ περιόδῳ, γινώσκειν ἐκ ταύτης πάντα τὰ μέλλοντα ἔσεσθαι ἐν ταῖς ἑξῆς περιόδοις. οὐδὲν γὰρ ξένον ἔσεσθαι παρὰ τὰ γενόμενα πρότερον, ἀλλὰ πάντα ὡσαύτως ἀπαραλλάκτως ἄχρι καὶ τῶν ἐλαχίστων.

Later development of the doctrine

907—Panaetius, influenced by Carneades' criticism, abandoned the theory of πῦρ τεχνικόν and periodical conflagration. He adopts the Aristotelian doctrine of the eternity of the world and the aether hypothesis. Posidonius restores the Ancient Stoic theory. It is found again with later Stoics, though in a more ethical version: both Seneca and Marcus Aurelius view the conflagration as a renewal of the world ordered by Providence [1].

a. Seneca, *Nat. quaest.* III 28, 7 and 30, 8.

Speaking on great floods inundating the world without rules or measure (*solutus legibus sine modo fertur*) Seneca says:

Qua ratione? inquis. Eadem qua conflagratio futura est. Utrumque fit, cum deo visum ordiri meliora, vetera finiri.

And again, in 30, 8:

Omne ex integro animal generabitur dabiturque terris homo inscius scelerum et melioribus auspiciis natus. Sed illis quoque innocentia non durabit, nisi dum novi sunt; cito nequitia subrepit.

b. Cf. Marcus Aurelius XII 23, 3:

Τὸν δὲ καιρὸν καὶ τὸν ὅρον δίδωσιν ἡ φύσις, ποτὲ μὲν καὶ ἡ ἰδία, ὅταν ἐν

---

[1] The same view was, however, already taken by Chrysippus, as appears from a passage in Origenes, *Contra Celsum*. See sub. **938**.

γήρᾳ, πάντως δὲ ἡ τῶν ὅλων, ἧς τῶν μερῶν μεταβαλλόντων νεαρὸς ἀεὶ καὶ ἀκμαῖος ὁ σύμπας κόσμος διαμένει.

Cp. also VII 25, and Seneca, *Ep.* 90, 44.

908—a. Cleanthes describes the periodical renewal of the kosmos in the following passage.

Stob. *Ecl.* I 17, 3, p. 153, 7W. (SVF I 497):

The periodical renewal of the kosmos

Κλεάνθης δὲ οὕτω πώς φησιν· ἐκφλογισθέντος τοῦ παντὸς συνίζειν τὸ μέσον αὐτοῦ πρῶτον, εἶτα τὰ ἐχόμενα ἀποσβέννυσθαι δι' ὅλου. τοῦ δὲ παντὸς ἐξυγρανθέντος, τὸ ἔσχατον τοῦ πυρός, ἀντιτυπήσαντος αὐτῷ τοῦ μέσου, τρέπεσθαι πάλιν εἰς τοὐναντίον, εἶθ' οὕτω τρεπόμενον ἄνωθέν φησιν αὔξεσθαι καὶ ἄρχεσθαι διακοσμεῖν τὸ ὅλον· καὶ τοιαύτην περίοδον ἀεὶ καὶ διακόσμησιν ποιούμενον[1] τὸν ἐν τῇ τῶν ὅλων οὐσίᾳ τόνον μὴ παύεσθαι. ὥσπερ γὰρ ἑνός τινος τὰ μέρη πάντα φύεται ἐκ σπερμάτων ἐν τοῖς καθήκουσι χρόνοις, οὕτω καὶ τοῦ ὅλου τὰ μέρη, ὧν καὶ τὰ ζῷα καὶ τὰ φυτὰ ὄντα τυγχάνει, ἐν τοῖς καθήκουσι χρόνοις φύεται. καὶ ὥσπερ τινὲς λόγοι τῶν μερῶν εἰς σπέρμα συνιόντες μίγνυνται καὶ αὖθις διακρίνονται γινομένων τῶν μερῶν, οὕτως ἐξ ἑνός τε πάντα γίνεσθαι καὶ ἐκ πάντων ἓν συγκρίνεσθαι, ὁδῷ καὶ συμφώνως διεξιούσης τῆς περιόδου.

After the conflagration, the whole mass of fire is gradually extinguished, the process spreading from the centre to the periphery. A last sparklet of fire remains at the outskirts of the kosmos.[2] Thus, all things are reduced to the sperma whence they came, and it is from this cosmic sperma that a new process of generation comes forth: the resistance of the moist mass is overcome and again matter is transformed into the diversity of a kosmos.

Τὸ ἔσχατον τοῦ πυρός — τρέπεσθαι πάλιν εἰς τοὐναντίον: if the text is sound, τρέπεσθαι is a medial form, as Verbeke, *Kleanthes* p. 126, rightly explains it. Therefore in the next line τρεπόμενον gives a better sense than τρεπομένου.

b. The notion of a τόνος in the universe which entertains the cosmic process is found again in Cornutus, c. 31 (SVF I 514):

---

[1] A necessary correction, made by Meerwaldt (*Mnem.* 1951, p. 53). The codd. have ποιουμένου.

[2] This is, at least what our text, as it has come to us, says. J. D. Meerwaldt (in *Mnem.* 1951, p. 46 ff.) thinks the text must be emended by cancelling the words τοῦ πυρός, because all texts agree on the point that *the whole mass of fire* is extinguished, turning through air into water, and no part of it remains. Cp. however Diog. VII, 136 (sub **904a**), where it is said that "he", i.e. God or the creative fire, "who is the σπερματικὸς λόγος of the universe", *remains behind as such in the moisture* (τοιόνδ' ὑπολείπεσθαι ἐν τῷ ὑγρῷ), which seems to mean: as creative fire, which is cosmic sperma. Cp. also SVF II 717 (τοὺς σπερματικοὺς λόγους ... ἀφθάρτους ἐποίησαν), and Epict. III 13, 4-7 (Zeus is alone at the conflagration), to be cited sub **924b**.

Ἡρακλῆς δ' ἐστὶν ὁ ἐν τοῖς ὅλοις τόνος, καθ' ὃν ἡ φύσις ἰσχυρὰ καὶ κραταιά ἐστιν, ἀνίκητος καὶ ἀπεριγένητος οὖσα, μεταδοτικὸς ἰσχύος καὶ τοῖς κατὰ μέρος καὶ ἀλκῆς ὑπάρχων.

Seneca, *Nat. quaest.* II 8, speaks of *intentio spiritus*.

909—The doctrine of periodical destruction and renewal of the world is connected with the view of the kosmos as a living being, springing up, growing, perishing, and arising again from the original sperma whence it came.

The kosmos endowed with soul and reason

Diog. L. VII 138-139:

Τὸν δὴ κόσμον διοικεῖσθαι κατὰ νοῦν καὶ πρόνοιαν, καθά φησι Χρύσιππός τ' ἐν τῷ πέμπτῳ Περὶ προνοίας καὶ Ποσειδώνιος ἐν τῷ τρίτῳ Περὶ θεῶν, εἰς ἅπαν αὐτοῦ μέρος διήκοντος τοῦ νοῦ, καθάπερ ἐφ' ἡμῶν τῆς ψυχῆς· ἀλλ' ἤδη δι' ὧν μὲν μᾶλλον, δι' ὧν δὲ ἧττον. δι' ὧν μὲν γὰρ ὡς ἕξις κεχώρηκεν, ὡς διὰ τῶν ὀστῶν καὶ τῶν νεύρων· δι' ὧν δὲ ὡς νοῦς, ὡς διὰ τοῦ ἡγεμονικοῦ. οὕτω δὴ καὶ τὸν ὅλον κόσμον ζῷον ὄντα καὶ ἔμψυχον καὶ λογικόν, ἔχειν ἡγεμονικὸν μὲν τὸν αἰθέρα, καθά φησιν Ἀντίπατρος ὁ Τύριος ἐν τῷ ὀγδόῳ Περὶ κόσμου. Χρύσιππος δ' ἐν τῷ πρώτῳ Περὶ προνοίας καὶ Ποσειδώνιος ἐν τῷ Περὶ θεῶν τὸν οὐρανόν φασι τὸ ἡγεμονικὸν τοῦ κόσμου, Κλεάνθης δὲ τὸν ἥλιον.

On Cleanthes' doctrine see Verbeke, *Kleanthes*, p. 135 f. V. is quite right in rejecting the necessity of oriental influence on this point. Cp. Plato, *Symp.* 220d: Socrates, after that famous night in the camp near Potidaea, adores the sun (our nr. **208c**, the end).

910—Zeno seems to have "proved" the intelligent character of the kosmos by three arguments.

First argument

a. Sext., *Adv. math.* IX (= *Against the Physicists* I) 104:

Καὶ πάλιν ὁ Ζήνων φησίν, "τὸ λογικὸν τοῦ μὴ λογικοῦ κρεῖττόν ἐστιν· οὐδὲν δέ γε κόσμου κρεῖττόν ἐστιν· λογικὸν ἄρα ὁ κόσμος. καὶ ὡσαύτως ἐπὶ τοῦ νοεροῦ καὶ ἐμψυχίας μετέχοντος. τὸ γὰρ νοερὸν τοῦ μὴ νοεροῦ καὶ τὸ ἔμψυχον τοῦ μὴ ἐμψύχου κρεῖττόν ἐστιν· οὐδὲν δέ γε κόσμου κρεῖττον· νοερὸς ἄρα καὶ ἔμψυχός ἐστιν ὁ κόσμος."

Cf. Cic., *N.D.* II, 8. 21: Quod ratione utitur, id melius est quam id quod ratione non utitur. Nihil autem mundo melius: ratione igitur mundus utitur.

The argument is severely criticized by Carneades (our nr. **1117a**).

Second argument

b. Sextus, ib. 101:

Ζήνων δὲ ὁ Κιτιεὺς ἀπὸ Ξενοφῶντος τὴν ἀφορμὴν λαβὼν οὑτωσὶ συνερωτᾷ. τὸ προϊέμενον σπέρμα λογικοῦ καὶ αὐτὸ λογικόν ἐστιν· ὁ δὲ κόσμος προΐεται σπέρμα λογικοῦ· λογικὸν ἄρα ἐστὶν ὁ κόσμος.

Cf. Cic., *N.D.* II 22: nihil quod animi, quodque rationis est expers, id generare ex se potest animantem compotemque rationis. Mundus autem generat animantes compotesque rationis. Animans est igitur mundus composque rationis.

c. Sextus, ib. 85:

Third
argument

Ἀλλὰ καὶ ἡ τὰς λογικὰς περιέχουσα φύσεις πάντως ἐστὶ λογική· οὐ γὰρ οἷόν τε τὸ ὅλον τοῦ μέρους χεῖρον εἶναι.

Cf. Cic., *N.D.* II 22: Idemque (Zeno) hoc modo: nullius sensu carentis pars aliqua potest esse sentiens. Mundi autem partes sentientes sunt. Non igitur caret sensu mundus.

911—In this sense then Zeno could call the logos δημιουργὸς τοῦ ὅλου or τοῦ παντός, as was implied in the passage of Diog. Laërt. cited sub **899a**.

In what
sense the
Logos is
δημιουργός

a. Lactantius, *De vera sap.* c. 9:

Zeno rerum naturae dispositorem atque artificem universitatis λόγον praedicat, quem et fatum et necessitatem rerum et deum et animum Iovis nuncupat.

b. Cf. Philodemus, Π. εὐσ. c. 11 (Dox. 545 b 12):

Ἀλλὰ μὴν καὶ Χρύσιππος ... ἐν μὲ)ν τῷ πρώτ(ῳ Περὶ θεῶ)ν Δία φη(σὶν εἶναι τὸ)ν ἄπαντ(α διοικοῦ)ντα λόγον κ(αὶ τὴν) τοῦ ὅλου ψυχὴ(ν κα)ὶ τῇ τούτου μ(ετοχ)ῇ πάντα (ζῆν)·

912—To the question of "How it is possible that God being a body penetrates the universe which is a body too" the Stoa replies by its theory of the interpenetration of bodies.

a. Simplicius, *Phys.* p. 530, 9 Diels (SVF II 467):

Theory of
the inter-
penetration
of bodies

Τὸ δὲ σῶμα διὰ σώματος χωρεῖν οἱ μὲν ἀρχαῖοι ὡς ἐναργὲς ἄτοπον ἐλάμβανον, οἱ δὲ ἀπὸ τῆς Στοᾶς ὕστερον προσήκαντο ὡς ἀκολουθοῦν ταῖς σφῶν αὐτῶν ὑποθέσεσιν, ἃς ἐνόμιζον παντὶ τρόπῳ δεῖν κυροῦν· σώματα γὰρ πάντα λέγειν δοκοῦντες, καὶ τὰς ποιότητας καὶ τὴν ψυχήν, καὶ διὰ παντὸς ὁρῶντες τοῦ σώματος καὶ τὴν ψυχὴν χωροῦσαν καὶ τὰς ποιότητας, ἐν ταῖς κράσεσι συνεχώρουν σῶμα διὰ σώματος χωρεῖν.

b. The theory of mixture according to Chrysippus is expounded in Stob., *Ecl.* I 17, 4 (p. 153-155 W.), SVF II 471. Four kinds of "mixture" are distinguished, namely παράθεσις, μῖξις, κρᾶσις and σύγχυσις. Only in the last kind the two substances and their qualities disappear, being transformed into a new substance [1]. The connexion of soul and

---

[1] It is to be noticed that the Stoic texts do not use the term "substance" but only speak of "qualities" which are or are not transformed into a new "quality".

body proves to be a form of μῖξις, which is an interpenetration of bodies preserving their own qualities, like iron in fire.

Παράθεσιν μὲν γὰρ εἶναι σωμάτων συναφὴν κατὰ τὰς ἐπιφανείας, ὡς ἐπὶ τῶν σωρῶν ὁρῶμεν . . .

Μῖξιν δ' εἶναι δύο ἢ καὶ πλειόνων σωμάτων ἀντιπαρέκτασιν δι' ὅλων, ὑπομενουσῶν τῶν συμφυῶν περὶ αὐτὰ ποιοτήτων, ὡς ἐπὶ τοῦ πυρὸς ἔχει καὶ τοῦ πεπυρακτωμένου σιδήρου, ἐπὶ τούτων γὰρ <δι'> ὅλων γίγνεσθαι τῶν σωμάτων τὴν ἀντιπαρέκτασιν. Ὁμοίως δὲ κἀπὶ τῶν ἐν ἡμῖν ψυχῶν ἔχειν· δι' ὅλων γὰρ τῶν σωμάτων ἡμῶν ἀντιπαρεκτείνουσιν, ἀρέσκει γὰρ αὐτοῖς σῶμα διὰ σώματος ἀντιπαρήκειν. Κρᾶσιν δὲ εἶναι λέγουσι δύο ἢ καὶ πλειόνων σωμάτων ὑγρῶν δι' ὅλων ἀντιπαρέκτασιν τῶν περὶ αὐτὰ ποιοτήτων ὑπομε- νουσῶν· [Τὴν μὲν μῖξιν καὶ ἐπὶ ξηρῶν γίγνεσθαι σωμάτων, οἷον πυρὸς καὶ σιδήρου, ψυχῆς τε καὶ τοῦ περιέχοντος αὐτὴν σώματος· τὴν δὲ κρᾶσιν ἐπὶ μόνων φασὶ γίνεσθαι τῶν ὑγρῶν] συνεκφαίνεσθαι γὰρ ἐκ τῆς κράσεως τὴν ἑκάστου τῶν συγκραθέντων ὑγρῶν ποιότητα, οἷον οἴνου, μέλιτος, ὕδατος, ὄξους, τῶν παραπλησίων. Ὅτι δ' ἐπὶ τοιούτων κράσεων διαμένουσιν αἱ ποιό- τητες τῶν συγκραθέντων, πρόδηλον ἐκ τοῦ πολλάκις ἐξ ἐπιμηχανήσεως ἀπο- χωρίζεσθαι ταῦτα ἀπ' ἀλλήλων. Ἐὰν γοῦν σπόγγον ἡλαιωμένον καθῇ τις εἰς οἶνον ὕδατι κεκραμένον, ἀποχωρίσει τὸ ὕδωρ τοῦ οἴνου, ἀναδραμόντος τοῦ ὕδατος εἰς τὸν σπόγγον. Τὴν δὲ σύγχυσιν δύο ἢ καὶ πλειόνων ποιοτήτων περὶ τὰ σώματα μεταβολὴν εἰς ἑτέρας διαφερούσης τούτων ποιότητος γένεσιν, ὡς ἐπὶ τῆς συνθέσεως ἔχει τῶν μύρων καὶ τῶν ἰατρικῶν φαρμάκων.

Again, the theory is expounded in Alex. Aphrod., *De mixtione* p. 216, 14 Bruns (SVF II 473). It is combated by Plutarchus, *De comm. not.* 37, p. 1077e (SVF II, 465) and discussed by Plotinus, *Enn.* II, 7, 1.

c. Alex. Aphr., *De mixt.* p. 226 (SVF II 475) rightly points to the importance of the doctrine with regard to the theory of εἱμαρμένη and of cosmic sympathy.

He speaks of the "absurdity of the doctrine".

(Τῆς ἀτοπίας τῶν ὑφ' αὑτῶν λεγομένων), οἷς καὶ τὰ κυριώτατα καὶ μέ- γιστα τῶν κατὰ φιλοσοφίαν δογμάτων ἤρτηται καὶ τὴν κατασκευὴν ἀπὸ τοῦ θαυμαστοῦ δόγματος ἔχει τοῦ σῶμα χωρεῖν διὰ σώματος. Ὅ τε γὰρ περὶ κράσεως αὐτοῖς λόγος οὐκ ἐν ἄλλῳ τινί. ἀλλὰ καὶ τὰ περὶ ψυχῆς ὑπ' αὐτῶν λεγόμενα ἐντεῦθεν ἤρτηται. ἥ τε πολυθρύλητος αὐτοῖς εἱμαρμένη καὶ ἡ τῶν πάντων πρόνοια δὲ <ἐντεῦθεν> τὴν πίστιν λαμβάνουσιν. ἔτι τε ὁ περὶ ἀρχῶν τε καὶ θεοῦ <λόγος> καὶ ἡ τοῦ παντὸς ἕνωσίς τε καὶ συμπάθεια πρὸς αὐτό. πάντα γὰρ αὐτοῖς ταῦτ' ἐστὶν ὁ διὰ τῆς ὕλης διήκων θεός.

913—The notion of a κρᾶσις δι' ὅλου or δι' ὅλων, famous by Chrysippus' instance of the drop of wine, appears already with Zeno.

a. Galenus, *in Hippocr. de humoribus* I (XVI 32 K.), SVF I 92:

Ζήνων τε ὁ Κιτιεὺς ὡς τὰς ποιότητας οὕτω καὶ τὰς οὐσίας δι' ὅλου κεράννυσθαι ἐνόμιζεν.

Cf. Themistius, *De anima* f. 68 II, p. 30, 17 Spengel (SVF I 145).

b. Diog. VII 151 (SVF II 479):

Καὶ τὰς κράσεις δὲ διόλου γίνεσθαι, καθά φησιν ὁ Χρύσιππος ἐν τῇ τρίτῃ τῶν Φυσικῶν, καὶ μὴ κατὰ περιγραφὴν καὶ παράθεσιν· καὶ γὰρ εἰς πέλαγος ὀλίγος οἶνος βληθεὶς ἐπὶ ποσὸν ἀντιπαρεκταθήσεται, εἶτα συμφθαρήσεται.

c. Plut., *Comm. not.* 37, p. 1078e (SVF II 480):

Καὶ ταῦτα προσδέχεται Χρύσιππος εὐθὺς ἐν τῷ πρώτῳ τῶν Φυσικῶν ζητημάτων "οὐδὲν ἀπέχειν φάμενος, οἴνου σταλαγμὸν ἕνα κεράσαι τὴν θάλατταν," καὶ ἵνα δὴ μὴ τοῦτο θαυμάζωμεν, "εἰς ὅλον, φησί, τὸν κόσμον διατενεῖν τῇ κράσει τὸν σταλαγμόν."

The image, and the text itself, became famous in Dutch litterature by the poem of J. H. Leopold, *Verzen*, (2) 1920, p. 137-141, a late expression of the Stoic doctrine of cosmic sympathy.

914—Consequences of Stoic materialism.

To the principle mentioned sub **901** and the definition of soul sub **903** must be referred the Stoic doctrine that virtues and all mental activities are bodies.

Virtues and mental activities are bodies

a. Alex. Aphr., *De anima libri mant.* p. 115 Bruns (SVF II 797):

Καὶ γὰρ καί, ἐπεὶ αἱ τῆς ψυχῆς ποιότητες σώματα κατ' αὐτοὺς (sc. τοὺς Στωϊκοὺς) καὶ αἱ τοῦ σώματος, πολλὰ σώματά ἐστιν ἐν τῷ αὐτῷ καὶ διάφορα δι' ἀλλήλων διήκοντα καὶ ἐν τῷ αὐτῷ τόπῳ.

116, 13: ἔτι εἰ καὶ αἱ ἀρεταὶ σώματα καὶ αἱ τέχναι, πῶς οὐ προσγενόμενα ταῦτά τινι στενοχωρήσει τὸ σῶμα ἢ αὐξήσει;

b. Plut., *De comm. not.* c. 45, p. 1084a (SVF II 848):

and even animals

Ἄτοπον γὰρ εὖ μάλα τὰς ἀρετὰς καὶ τὰς κακίας, πρὸς δὲ ταύταις τὰς τέχνας καὶ τὰς μνήμας πάσας, ἔτι δὲ φαντασίας καὶ πάθη καὶ ὁρμὰς καὶ συγκαταθέσεις σώματα ποιουμένους, ἐν μηδενὶ φάναι κεῖσθαι μηδ' ὑπάρχειν τόπον τούτοις, ἕνα <δὲ> τὸν ἐν τῇ καρδίᾳ πόρον στιγμιαῖον ἀπολιπεῖν, ὅπου τὸ ἡγεμονικὸν συστέλλουσι τῆς ψυχῆς, ὑπὸ τοσούτων σωμάτων κατεχόμενον, ὅσων τοὺς πάνυ δοκοῦντας ἀφορίζειν καὶ ἀποκρίνειν ἕτερον ἑτέρου πολὺ πλῆθος

διαπέφευγε. τὸ δὲ μὴ μόνον σώματα ταῦτα ποιεῖν, ἀλλὰ καὶ ζῷα λογικὰ —
ὑπερβολή τίς ἐστιν — παρανομίας εἰς τὴν — συνήθειαν. 1084c. ἀλλὰ πρὸς
τούτοις ἔτι καὶ τὰς ἐνεργείας σώματα καὶ ζῷα ποιοῦσι.

c. Seneca, *Ep.* 113, 1 discusses the question

quid sentiam de hac questione iactata apud nostros: an iustitia
fortitudo prudentia ceteraeque virtutes animalia sint.

SVF III 307. Seneca rejects Chrysippus' consequence that mental qualities and
activities are ζῷα, but he does not doubt of their corporeality. Cp. *Ep.* 106, 5:
*Non puto te dubitaturum an adfectus corpora sint ..., an vultum nobis mutent, an
frontem adstringant* etc.

Pohlenz, *Stoa* I p. 66, explains the doctrine as a Semitic view of things. Cp.
certain expressions in the A.T., such as "bad face" for sadness, and "sniffing" for
wrath. In any case it is connected with Chrysippus' doctrine of the ἡγεμονικόν
πως ἔχον, the πως ἔχον being one of his four categories of being.

four kinds   **915**—Chrysippus admits four categories of being.
of being
    a. Simpl., *in Ar. Categ.* f. 16 Δ ed. Bas. (SVF II 369):

Οἱ δέ γε Στωϊκοὶ εἰς ἐλάττονα συστέλλειν ἀξιοῦσι τὸν τῶν πρώτων γενῶν
ἀριθμόν. — ποιοῦνται γὰρ τὴν τομὴν εἰς τέσσαρα· εἰς ὑποκείμενα καὶ ποιὰ
καὶ πως ἔχοντα καὶ πρὸς τί πως ἔχοντα.

The four γένη are discussed by Plotinus in *Enn.* VI, 1, 25.

τὸ   **b.** The πως ἔχον means: a certain state or condition. Therefore
ἡγεμονικόν   Chrysippus, tracing all πάθη and ὁρμαί and mental activities back to
πως ἔχον   the hegemonikon, could call ἐπιστήμη or ὀργή or ἐπιθυμία: τὸ ἡγεμονικόν
πως ἔχον. Alex. Aphrod., *De anima libri mant.* p. 118, 6 Bruns (SVF
II 823):

Ὅτι μὴ "μία ἡ τῆς ψυχῆς δύναμις, ὡς τὴν αὐτήν πως ἔχουσαν ποτὲ μὲν
διανοεῖσθαι, ποτὲ δὲ ὀργίζεσθαι, ποτὲ δ' ἐπιθυμεῖν παρὰ μέρος" δεικτέον.

    c. Cf. Sextus, *Pyrrh.* II 81:

Ἡ δὲ ἐπιστήμη πως ἔχον ἡγεμονικόν, ὥσπερ καὶ ἡ πως ἔχουσα χεὶρ πυγμή,
τὸ δὲ ἡγεμονικὸν σῶμα· ἔστι γὰρ κατ' αὐτοὺς πνεῦμα.

Chrysippus' doctrine of the ἡγεμονικόν πως ἔχον is expounded by Pohlenz in
Zenon und Chrysipp, p. 181 ff.

Stoic   **916**—Plotinus in combating the Stoic materialism, argues that before
materialism the bodies there must exist some other kind of being: according to the
criticized   Stoics themselves soul is not merely pneuma (for there are many πνεύματα
by Plotinus ἄψυχα), but pneuma πως ἔχον, which either is nothing or introduces some
other kind of being.

a. *Enn.* IV 7, 4:

Soul as
πνεῦμά
πως ἔχον

Μαρτυροῦσι δὲ καὶ αὐτοὶ ὑπὸ τῆς ἀληθείας ἀγόμενοι, ὡς δεῖ τι πρὸ τῶν σωμάτων εἶναι κρεῖττον αὐτῶν ψυχῆς εἶδος, ἔννουν τὸ πνεῦμα καὶ πῦρ νοερὸν τιθέμενοι, ὥσπερ ἄνευ πυρὸς καὶ πνεύματος οὐ δυναμένης τῆς κρείττονος μοίρας ἐν τοῖς οὖσιν εἶναι, τόπον δὲ ζητούσης εἰς τὸ ἱδρυθῆναι, δέον ζητεῖν, ὅπου τὰ σώματα ἱδρύσουσιν, ὡς ἄρα δεῖ ταῦτα ἐν ψυχῆς δυνάμεσιν ἱδρῦσθαι. Εἰ δὲ μηδὲν παρὰ τὸ πνεῦμα τὴν ζωὴν καὶ τὴν ψυχὴν τίθενται, τί τὸ πολυθρύλητον αὐτοῖς πως ἔχον, εἰς ὃ καταφεύγουσιν ἀναγκαζόμενοι τίθεσθαι ἄλλην παρὰ τὰ σώματα φύσιν δραστήριον; Εἰ οὖν οὐ πᾶν μὲν πνεῦμα ψυχή, ὅτι μυρία πνεύματα ἄψυχα, τὸ δέ πως ἔχον πνεῦμα φήσουσι, τό πως ἔχον τοῦτο καὶ ταύτην τὴν σχέσιν ἢ τῶν ὄντων τι φήσουσιν, ἢ μηδέν. Ἀλλ' εἰ μὲν μηδέν, πνεῦμα ἂν εἴη μόνον, τὸ δέ πως ἔχον ὄνομα. Καὶ οὕτως συμβήσεται αὐτοῖς οὐδὲ ἄλλο οὐδὲν εἶναι λέγειν ἢ τὴν ὕλην, καὶ ψυχὴν καὶ θεὸν ὀνόματα πάντα, ἐκεῖνο δὲ μόνον <ὄν>. Εἰ δὲ τῶν ὄντων ἡ σχέσις καὶ ἄλλο παρὰ τὸ ὑποκείμενον καὶ τὴν ὕλην, ἐν ὕλῃ μέν, ἄϋλον δὲ αὐτὸ τῷ μὴ πάλιν αὖ συγκεῖσθαι ἐξ ὕλης, λόγος ἂν εἴη τις καὶ οὐ σῶμα καὶ φύσις ἑτέρα.

We need not infer from this passage that soul was explicitly defined by the Stoics as πνεῦμά πως ἔχον: Plotinus, adopting their terminology, rather seems to urge on them the necessity of this consequence.

The same definition of soul is attributed to the Stoics by Porphyrius ap. Euseb., *Praep. ev.* XV, p. 813c:

Πῶς δὲ οὐκ αἰσχύνης γέμων ὁ πνεῦμά πως ἔχον αὐτὴν (sc. τὴν ψυχὴν) ἀποδιδούς, ἢ πῦρ νοερόν, τῇ περιψύξει καὶ οἷον βαφῇ τοῦ ἀέρος ἀναφθὲν ἢ στομωθέν;

Indeed, the Stoics imagined that the πῦρ νοερόν or πνεῦμα ἔνθερμον at the birth of a child was cooled by the air and "stimulated" and thus became a living being: hence the name of ψυχή, παρὰ τὴν ψῦξιν [1].—This is the account of the soul's origin we find in Plut., *Stoic. repugn.* 41 (SVF II 806):

Τὸ βρέφος ἐν τῇ γαστρὶ φύσει τρέφεσθαι νομίζει καθάπερ φυτόν· ὅταν δὲ τεχθῇ, ψυχόμενον ὑπὸ τοῦ ἀέρος καὶ στομούμενον τὸ πνεῦμα μεταβάλλειν καὶ γίνεσθαι ζῷον· ὅθεν οὐκ ἀπὸ τρόπου τὴν ψυχὴν ὠνομάσθαι παρὰ τὴν ψῦξιν.

It is clear, then, that soul was not the πῦρ νοερόν or cosmic pneuma, which Zeno called also νοῦς, as such; it was πνεῦμά πως ἔχον, to say it in Chrysippus' terminology.

b. Again, in another passage of the *Enneads* Plotinus says that the Stoics went so far as to define God as "prime matter πως ἔχουσαν".

Enn. II, 4, 1:

God as
(πρώτη)
ὕλη πως
ἔχουσα

Καὶ οἱ μὲν σώματα μόνον τὰ ὄντα εἶναι θέμενοι καὶ τὴν οὐσίαν ἐν τούτοις, μίαν τε τὴν ὕλην λέγουσι καὶ τοῖς στοιχείοις ὑποβεβλῆσθαι, καὶ αὐτὴν εἶναι

---

[1] We find this Stoic doctrine later in Origenes, who frequently declares that "soul" is "cooled νοῦς".

τὴν οὐσίαν· τὰ δ' ἄλλα πάντα οἷον πάθη ταύτης, καί πως ἔχουσαν αὐτὴν καὶ τὰ στοιχεῖα εἶναι. καὶ δὴ καὶ τολμῶσι καὶ μέχρι θεῶν αὐτὴν ἄγειν· καὶ τέλος δὴ καὶ αὐτὸν τὸν θεὸν ὕλην ταύτην πως ἔχουσαν εἶναι.

That Chrysippus or other Stoics really defined God as (πρώτη) ὕλη πως ἔχουσα seems hardly credible. Pohlenz, *Stoa* II p. 41 qualifies it as a "natürlich unzulässige Folgerung" and remarks that in fact, Stoics must consider *qualified things* as ὕλη πως ἔχουσα. However, it should be noticed that *in a sense* (as we remarked sub **900c**) for Stoics God *is* matter. And this is what Plotinus, using Stoic terminology, expresses in the terms: God is to them ὕλη πως ἔχουσα, just as he could say that soul is to them πνεῦμά πως ἔχον.

The definition of God as prime matter occurs again in the beginning of the 13th century with David of Dinant (but without the addition of a πως ἔχουσα!): *Deus et materia prima sunt omnino simplicia. Ergo nullo modo differunt.* The argument is mentioned by Thomas Aquinas, *Summa theol.* I qu. 3, art. 8, ad 3, who rejects it mainly because God does not mix with anything ("Non est possibile Deum aliquo modo in compositionem alicuius venire,—nec sicut principium formale nec sicut principium materiale".)

3—PHYSICS: (2) GOD, PROVIDENCE, MANTIC

God
1. τὸ ποιοῦν,
Λόγος,
πῦρ τεχνικόν

917—Various aspects of the Deity.

1. The active principle in Nature, called Logos and defined as πῦρ τεχνικόν:

Nrs. **899-902**.

2. Εἱμαρμένη

918—Since the Logos rules all that is and happens, it is identified with the Εἱμαρμένη of popular faith: the inexorable Law of the Universe.

a. Schol. in Hom. *Il.* VIII 69 (SVF II 931):

Οἱ Στωϊκοὶ δέ φασιν ὡς ταὐτὸν εἱμαρμένη καὶ Ζεύς.

b. Stob., *Ecl.* I 79, 1 W. (SVF II 913):

Χρύσιππος δύναμιν πνευματικὴν τὴν οὐσίαν τῆς εἱμαρμένης, τάξει τοῦ παντὸς διοικητικήν. Τοῦτο μὲν οὖν ἐν τῷ δευτέρῳ Περὶ κόσμου. Ἐν δὲ τῷ δευτέρῳ Περὶ ὅρων καὶ ἐν τοῖς Περὶ τῆς εἱμαρμένης καὶ ἐν ἄλλοις σποράδην πολυτρόπως ἀποφαίνεται λέγων· "Εἱμαρμένη ἐστὶν ὁ τοῦ κόσμου λόγος" ἢ "λόγος τῶν ἐν τῷ κόσμῳ προνοίᾳ διοικουμένων" ἢ "λόγος καθ' ὃν τὰ μὲν γεγονότα γέγονε, τὰ δὲ γινόμενα γίνεται, τὰ δὲ γενησόμενα γενήσεται."

c. Plut., *Stoic. repugn.* c. 34 p. 1049f (SVF II 937):

"Ὅτι δ' ἡ κοινὴ φύσις καὶ ὁ κοινὸς τῆς φύσεως λόγος εἱμαρμένη καὶ πρόνοια καὶ Ζεύς ἐστιν, οὐδὲ τοὺς ἀντίποδας λέληθε· πανταχοῦ γὰρ ταῦτα θρυλεῖται ὑπ' αὐτῶν· καὶ τὸ

(A5) Διὸς δ' ἐτελείετο βουλή,

τὸν Ὅμηρον εἰρηκέναι φησὶν ὀρθῶς, ἐπὶ τὴν εἱμαρμένην ἀναφέροντα καὶ τὴν τῶν ὅλων φύσιν, καθ' ἣν πάντα διοικεῖται.

d. The same view of the universe is expressed in Cleanthes' *Hymn to Zeus* (our nr. **943**), but in such a way that Zeus is addressed as the *Ruler* of the κοινὸς λόγος which pervades the Universe (vs. 12). This λόγος then, or νόμος, is identic with the *Will* of Zeus, and thus may be said to be identic with Zeus. Seneca's *semper paret, semel iussit* is a less philosophical expression of the same view. For the rest the passage has a somewhat different accent.

Seneca, *De Prov.* 5, 8:
Grande solacium est cum universo rapi; quicquid est quod nos sic vivere, sic mori iussit, eadem necessitate et deos alligat. Irrevocabilis humana pariter ac divina cursus vehit: ille ipse omnium conditor et rector scripsit quidem fata, sed sequitur, semper paret, semel iussit.

On the problem of *Fate and Liberty* (of man) see below nr. **944**.

919—The Logos is also called Λόγος σπερματικός and is said to contain all λόγοι σπερματικοί: our nr. **902a** (the creative fire contains all the "seminal reasons") and **904a** (God or the fire as the "seminal reason" which, when "the whole of substance" is transformed through air into water, remains behind "as such"—i.e. as fire, which is cosmic sperma— in the moisture).

3. λόγος σπερματικός and λόγοι σπερματικοί

a. In the text cited sub **902a** the λόγοι σπερματικοί are described as a kind of *exemplary forms* of things coming into being:

exemplary forms

Τοὺς σπερματικοὺς λόγους καθ' οὓς ἕκαστα καθ' εἱμαρμένην γίνεται.

The expression is also used by *Athenagoras, Presb.* c. 6 (to be cited sub **924b**). It reminds us of the Platonic Idea, the difference being evidently that Plato's ideal world is transcendent, while the stoic seminal reasons are immanent.

b. They are imperishable. Proclus in Plat. *Parm.* V, p. 135 Cousin (SVF II 717):

imperishable

In order to warrant the permanent character of participation, a cause is required which should be beyond motion and instability.

Ταύτης γὰρ ἐφιέμενοι πάντες τῆς αἰτίας, οἱ μὲν τοὺς σπερματικοὺς λόγους εἶναι τούτους οἰηθέντες, ἀφθάρτους αὐτοὺς ἐποίησαν, ὡς οἱ ἀπὸ τῆς Στοᾶς.

c. They are immanent in matter.

immanent

Origenes, *Contra Celsum* IV 48 (SVF II 1074):
Λέγει γὰρ ἐν τοῖς ἑαυτοῦ συγγράμμασιν ὁ σεμνὸς φιλόσοφος (sc. Chrysip-

pus), ὅτι τοὺς σπερματικοὺς λόγους τοῦ θεοῦ ἡ ὕλη παραδεξαμένη ἔχει ἐν ἑαυτῇ εἰς κατακόσμησιν τῶν ὅλων.

One and many

d. Like Plato's Ideas formed one kosmos noètós, which is (according to *Soph.* 249a [1]) an intelligent and living being, thus the Stoic seminal reasons, which are many, form the seminal Reason which is one. E.g. Marcus Aurelius, who declares that soul originates from "the seminal Reason" as a part of it and will return to it after death (IV, 14), elsewhere says that soul goes back to the σπερματικοὶ λόγοι.

Soul originates from the logos sperm.

Marc. Aur. IV, 14:

'Ενυπέστης ὡς μέρος. 'Εναφανισθήσῃ τῷ γεννήσαντι· μᾶλλον δὲ ἀναληφθήσῃ εἰς τὸν λόγον αὐτοῦ τὸν σπερματικὸν κατὰ μεταβολήν.

or logoi sperm.

Cf. VI 24, where the plural is used in exactly the same sense: ἀνελήφθησαν εἰς τοὺς αὐτοὺς τοῦ κόσμου σπερματικοὺς λόγους.

920—The Logos is also, but less frequently, called Νοῦς. Thus in:

a. Diog. VII 135, cited sub **904a**:

Έν τ' εἶναι θεὸν καὶ νοῦν καὶ εἱμαρμένην etc.

b. Epiphanius, *Adv. haer.* III 2, 9 (SVF I 146):

Ζήνων ὁ Κιτιεὺς ὁ Στωϊκὸς ἔφη μὴ δεῖν θεοῖς οἰκοδομεῖν ἱερά, ἀλλ' ἔχειν τὸ θεῖον ἐν μόνῳ τῷ νῷ, μᾶλλον δὲ θεὸν ἡγεῖσθαι τὸν νοῦν. ἔστι γὰρ ἀθάνατος.

In spite of these words, Zeno, as we shall see, did not oppose popular belief, but tried to assimilate it. Pohlenz supposes that the above text, belonging to his Ideal State, was still near to Antisthenes' influence.

c. Cp. Diog. VII 138:

Τὸν δὴ κόσμον διοικεῖσθαι κατὰ νοῦν καὶ πρόνοιαν, καθά φησι Χρύσιππός τ' ἐν τῷ πέμπτῳ Περὶ προνοίας καὶ Ποσειδώνιος ἐν τῷ τρίτῳ Περὶ θεῶν, εἰς ἅπαν αὐτοῦ μέρος διήκοντος τοῦ νοῦ, καθάπερ ἐφ' ἡμῶν τῆς ψυχῆς· ἀλλ' ἤδη δι' ὧν μὲν μᾶλλον, δι' ὧν δὲ ἧττον.

Thus, Alex. Aphrod. could say that τὸν νοῦν καὶ ἐν τοῖς φαυλοτάτοις εἶναι, θεῖον ὄντα, was Stoic doctrine (SVF II 1038).

In using the terms νοῦς and πρόνοια the Stoics follow Plato's terminology in *Tim.* and *Nom.*, while usually they follow Heraclitus in speaking of the Logos.

921—Since God the Logos pervades the kosmos, he may be called φύσις, giving vital force and various abilities to various beings.

5. φύσις

---

[1]   Nr. **315c**.

Seneca, *De benef.* IV 7:

Having mentioned various arts and talents, such as music, song and poetry, the natural development of the body and its various functions, the author continues:

"Natura", inquit, "haec mihi praestat". Non intellegis te, cum hoc dicis, mutare nomen Deo? Quid enim aliud est natura quam Deus et divina ratio, toti mundo partibusque eius inserta?

922—a. From the unity of the Logos follows firstly the unity of the kosmos. **Unity of the kosmos**

Diog. VII 140:

Ἕνα τὸν κόσμον εἶναι καὶ τοῦτον πεπερασμένον, σχῆμ' ἔχοντα σφαιροειδές. — Ἐν δὲ τῷ κόσμῳ μηδὲν εἶναι κενόν, ἀλλ' ἡνῶσθαι αὐτόν.

Also in Cornutus, *Compendium* c. 27; Plut. *Stoic. repugn.* c. 9.

b. Next, the unity of God might be concluded from it. And in fact, we find the doctrine ascribed to Zeno and to Stoics in general. **Unity of God**

Philodemus, Π εὐσεβ. p. 84 G.:

Πάντες οὖν οἱ ἀπὸ Ζήνωνος, εἰ καὶ ἀπέλειπον τὸ δαιμόνιον . . . , ἕνα θεὸν λέγουσιν εἶναι.

Cp. also Lactantius, *De ira Dei* c. 11: Antisthenes . . . unum esse naturalem Deum dixit, quamvis gentes et urbes suos habeant populares. Eadem fere Zeno cum Stoicis suis.

923—On the other hand, the existence of *gods* is defended, both by Zeno and Cleanthes. **Combined with polytheism**

a. Sextus, *Adv. Math.* IX (Ag. the Phys. I) 133:

Ζήνων δὲ καὶ τοιοῦτον ἠρώτα λόγον· "τοὺς θεοὺς εὐλόγως ἄν τις τιμῴη. τοὺς δὲ μὴ ὄντας οὐκ ἄν τις εὐλόγως τιμῴη· εἰσὶν ἄρα θεοί."

b. Cleanthes wrote a book Π. θεῶν (Diog. VII 174).

Ap. Cicero, *N.D.* I 14, 37, Velleius says that he, in his books against pleasure, "tum fingit formam quandam et speciem deorum, tum divinitatem omnem tribuit astris, tum nihil ratione censet divinius."

924—Popular polytheism is not as such rejected by the Stoa, but explained in a syncretistic spirit. This is what we find in the above cited passage of Seneca, *De Benef.* IV (sub **921**), where God is identified with nature. **Syncretistic explanation of popular religion**

a. Seneca, *De benef.* IV, 7-8. Deus — natura — divina ratio.

The passage cited sub **921** continues as follows:

Quotiens voles, tibi licet aliter hunc auctorem rerum nostrarum compellare. Et Iovem illum optimum ac maximum rite dices, et Tonantem et Statorem: qui non, ut historici tradiderunt, ex eo quod post votum susceptum acies Romanorum fugientium stetit, sed quod stant beneficio eius omnia, stator stabilitorque est: hunc eundem et Fatum si dixeris, non mentieris. Nam cum fatum nihil aliud sit quam series implexa causarum, ille est prima omnium causa, ex qua ceterae pendent. Quaecunque voles illi nomina proprie aptabis, vim aliquam effectumque coelestium rerum continentia. Tot appellationes eius possunt esse quot munera.

Hunc et Liberum patrem et Herculem ac Mercurium nostri putant. Liberum patrem quia omnium parens sit, quod *ab eo* primum inventa seminum vis est, consultura per voluptatem. Herculem, quia vis eius invicta sit, quandoquė lassata fuerit operibus editis, in ignem recessura. Mercurium, quia ratio penes illum est, numerusque et ordo et scientia. Quocumque te flexeris, ibi illum videbis occurrentem tibi. Nihil ab illo vacat: opus suum ipse implet. Ergo nihil agis, ingratissime mortalium, qui te negas Deo debere, sed naturae: quia nec natura sine Deo est, nec Deus sine natura; sed idem est utrumque, nec distat officio. Si quid a Seneca accepisses, Annaeo te diceres debere, vel Lucio: non creditorem mutares, sed nomen. Quoniam sive praenomen eius, sive nomen dixisses, sive cognomen, idem tamen ille esset. Sic hunc naturam voca, fatum, fortunam: omnia eiusdem dei nomina sunt, varie utentis sua potestate.

The doctrine is summarized by Servius ad Verg. *Aen.* IV 638: Et sciendum Stoicos dicere unum esse deum, cui nomina variantur pro actibus et officiis.

b. The Christian writer Athenagoras speaks on Stoic "monotheism" in the following passage.

Presbeia c. 6, p. 7 B:

Οἱ δὲ ἀπὸ τῆς Στοᾶς κἂν ταῖς προσηγορίαις κατὰ τὰς παραλλάξεις τῆς ὕλης, δι᾽ ἧς φασι τὸ πνεῦμα χωρεῖν τοῦ θεοῦ, πληθύνωσι τὸ θεῖον τοῖς ὀνόμασι, τῷ γοῦν ἔργῳ ἕνα νομίζουσι τὸν θεόν· εἰ γὰρ ὁ μὲν θεὸς πῦρ τεχνικὸν ὁδῷ βαδίζον ἐπὶ γενέσεις κόσμου ἐμπεριειληφὸς ἅπαντας τοὺς σπερματικοὺς λόγους καθ᾽ οὓς ἕκαστα καθ᾽ εἱμαρμένην γίνεται, τὸ δὲ πνεῦμα αὐτοῦ διήκει δι᾽ ὅλου τοῦ κόσμου, ὁ θεὸς εἷς κατ᾽ αὐτοὺς Ζεὺς μὲν κατὰ τὸ ζέον τῆς ὕλης ὀνομαζόμενος, Ἥρα δὲ κατὰ τὸν ἀέρα καὶ τὰ λοιπὰ καθ᾽ ἕκαστον τῆς ὕλης μέρος δι᾽ ἧς κεχώρηκεν καλούμενος.

c. Minucius Felix, *Octav.* 19, 10:

Idem (sc. Zeno) interpretando Iunonem aera, Iovem caelum, Neptunum mare, ignem esse Vulcanum et ceteros similiter vulgi deos elementa esse monstrando publicum arguit graviter et revincit errorem.

The method of allegorizing

The method of allegorizing, inaugurated by Antisthenes and generally practiced by the Stoics, may be called a kind of rationalisation of popular religion. Yet, it is done in a spirit different from Prodicus' rationalism mentioned sub **192**. The latter's argument tends to "humanize" the gods by proving that they are not φύσει but by human institution, useful things being *considered* by man as gods. The Stoics, however, intend to say that Nature and her various forces *are indeed* divine and thus rightly venerated [1].

925—God the Logos or Physis is called Zeus by Zeno (**904a**) and Cleanthes (*Hymn to Zeus*, to be cited as a compendium of Stoic theology at the end of this paragraph).

6. Zeus

a. *Epictetus* usually speaks of ὁ θεός, e.g. in *Diatr.* I 16, the end. Having spoken of the gifts of God to man he concludes:

or
ὁ θεός

Τί οὖν; ἐπεὶ οἱ πολλοὶ ἀποτετύφλωσθε, οὐκ ἔδει τινὰ εἶναι τὸν ταύτην ἐκπληροῦντα τὴν χώραν καὶ ὑπὲρ πάντων ᾄδοντα τὸν ὕμνον τὸν εἰς τὸν θεόν; τί γὰρ ἄλλο δύναμαι γέρων χωλὸς εἰ μὴ ὑμνεῖν τὸν θεόν; εἰ γοῦν ἀηδὼν ἤμην, ἐποίουν τὰ τῆς ἀηδόνος, εἰ κύκνος, τὰ τοῦ κύκνου. νῦν δὲ λογικός εἰμι· ὑμνεῖν με δεῖ τὸν θεόν. τοῦτό μου τὸ ἔργον ἐστίν, ποιῶ αὐτὸ οὐδ' ἐγκαταλείψω τὴν τάξιν ταύτην, ἐφ' ὅσον ἂν διδῶται, καὶ ὑμᾶς ἐπὶ τὴν αὐτὴν ταύτην ᾠδὴν παρακαλῶ.

b. But e.g. in the following passage he speaks of Zeus and his government of the universe.

Epict., *Diatr.* III 13, 4-7.

Loneliness (ἐρημία) is, the author says, a feeling of helplessness: not just being alone, but feeling bereft and threatened.

Ἐπεὶ εἰ τὸ μόνον εἶναι ἀρκεῖ πρὸς τὸ ἔρημον εἶναι, λέγε ὅτι καὶ ὁ Ζεὺς ἐν τῇ ἐκπυρώσει ἔρημός ἐστι καὶ κατακλαίει αὐτὸς ἑαυτοῦ· "τάλας ἐγώ, οὔτε τὴν Ἥραν ἔχω οὔτε τὴν Ἀθηνᾶν οὔτε τὸν Ἀπόλλωνα οὔτε ὅλως ἢ ἀδελφὸν ἢ υἱὸν ἢ ἔγγονον ἢ συγγενῆ". ταῦτα καὶ λέγουσί τινες ὅτι ποιεῖ μόνος ἐν τῇ ἐκπυρώσει. οὐ γὰρ ἐπινοοῦσι διεξαγωγὴν μόνου καὶ ἀπό τινος φυσικοῦ ὁρμώμενοι, ἀπὸ τοῦ φύσει κοινωνικοῦ εἶναι καὶ φιλαλλήλου καὶ ἡδέως συναναστρέ-

---

[1] For this reason I do not think it quite convincing to put Persaeus, Zeno's disciple, on a level with Prodicus, as is done by Philodemus, II. εὐσεβ. 9 (our nr. **192a**).

φεσθαι ἀνθρώποις. ἀλλ' οὐδὲν ἧττον δεῖ τινα καὶ πρὸς τοῦτο παρασκευὴν ἔχειν τὸ δύνασθαι αὐτὸν ἑαυτῷ ἀρκεῖν, δύνασθαι αὐτὸν ἑαυτῷ συνεῖναι· ὡς ὁ Ζεὺς αὐτὸς ἑαυτῷ σύνεστι καὶ ἡσυχάζει ἐφ' ἑαυτοῦ καὶ ἐννοεῖ τὴν διοίκησιν τὴν ἑαυτοῦ οἵα ἐστὶ καὶ ἐν ἐπινοίαις γίνεται πρεπούσαις ἑαυτῷ, οὕτως καὶ ἡμᾶς δύνασθαι αὐτοὺς ἑαυτοῖς λαλεῖν, μὴ προσδεῖσθαι ἄλλων [1].

The passage is instructive. Zeus is alone at the conflagration; as soon as there is a world, there are many gods. Epict. does not reject them, he believes in all good gods and all good daemons: Πάντα θεῶν μεστὰ καὶ δαιμόνων, he says (III, 13, 15). He rejects only the bad ones (I, 22, 16). The same may be seen in Marc. Aurel.: he speaks of Asklepios (VI 43) and Demeter, of "Helios and the other Gods" (VIII 19) as really existing beings. But he does not believe in bad spirits and in exorcisms (I 6).

Good spirits or daemons

926—Do Seneca, Epictetus and Marcus Aurelius imagine good spirits as existing exterior to man? The point is not quite clear.

a. Epict. I 14, 12-14. In a paragraph entitled ὅτι πάντας ἐφορᾷ τὸ θεῖον Epict. says (to a man who complains that, by the limitation of his abilities, he is not able to understand Providence):

Τοῦτο δέ σοι καὶ λέγει τις, ὅτι ἴσην ἔχεις δύναμιν τῷ Διί; ἀλλ' οὖν οὐδὲν ἧττον καὶ ἐπίτροπον ἑκάστῳ παρέστησεν τὸν ἑκάστου δαίμονα καὶ παρέδωκεν φυλάσσειν αὐτὸν αὐτῷ καὶ τοῦτον ἀκοίμητον καὶ ἀπαραλόγιστον. τίνι γὰρ ἄλλῳ κρείττονι καὶ ἐπιμελεστέρῳ φύλακι παρέδωκεν ἡμῶν ἕκαστον; ὥσθ', ὅταν κλείσητε τὰς θύρας καὶ σκότος ἔνδον ποιήσητε, μέμνησθε μηδέποτε λέγειν ὅτι μόνοι ἐστέ· οὐ γὰρ ἐστέ, ἀλλ' ὁ θεὸς ἔνδον ἐστὶ καὶ ὁ ὑμέτερος δαίμων ἐστίν.

b. *Marc. Aur.* identifies the daemon with the hegemonikon. V 27:
"Συζῆν θεοῖς". συζῇ δὲ θεοῖς ὁ συνεχῶς δεικνὺς αὐτοῖς τὴν ἑαυτοῦ ψυχὴν ἀρεσκομένην μὲν τοῖς ἀπονεμομένοις, ποιοῦσαν δὲ ὅσα βούλεται ὁ δαίμων, ὃν ἑκάστῳ προστάτην καὶ ἡγεμόνα ὁ Ζεὺς ἔδωκεν, ἀπόσπασμα ἑαυτοῦ. οὗτος δέ ἐστιν ὁ ἑκάστου νοῦς καὶ λόγος.

c. Cp. also Seneca, *ad Lucil.* 41, 1:

Non sunt ad caelum elevandae manus nec exorandus aedituus, ut nos ad aurem simulacri, quasi magis exaudiri possimus, admittat: prope est a te deus, tecum est, intus est. ita dico, Lucili: sacer intra nos spiritus sedet, malorum bonorumque nostrorum observator et custos.

---

[1] The passage may be quoted, I think, in order to illustrate such passages as Diog. VII 136 (sub **904a**) and Cleanthes' description of the renewal of the kosmos ap. Stob., *Ecl.* I 17, 3 (sub **908a**): at the conflagration of the kosmos, *Zeus alone* remains, i.e. "God" who is the creative fire.

927—Zeus, the creative fire, Logos, Heimarmene, Nature, is also *Providence*.

7. πρόνοια

Later Stoics speak very frequently on it, but the doctrine is certainly ancient Stoic.

a. *Theodoretus, Graec. aff. cur.* VI 14, p. 153 Raeder (SVF I 176):

Ζήνων δὲ ὁ Κιτιεὺς δύναμιν κέκληκε τὴν εἱμαρμένην κινητικὴν τῆς ὕλης· τὴν δὲ αὐτὴν καὶ πρόνοιαν καὶ φύσιν ὠνόμασεν.

The same is said by Aëtius I 27, 5 (SVF I ib.).

b. Cleanthes confines the field of Providence: everything happens by Fate, not everything by Providence.

Chalcidius *in Tim.* c. 144 (SVF I 551):

Ex quo fieri ut, quae secundum fatum sunt, etiam ex providentia sint, eodemque modo quae secundum providentiam, ex fato, ut Chrysippus putat. alii vero quae quidem ex providentiae auctoritate, fataliter quoque provenire, nec tamen quae fataliter, ex providentia, ut Cleanthes.

According to this passage, Chrysippus returned to Zeno's doctrine of the identity of Fate and Providence. But cp. Plut., *Stoic. repugn.* (SVF II 1178), to be cited sub **939a**.

928—In the later Stoa Providence takes a very important place. Besides in *De Prov.*, Seneca speaks amply of it in the introduction to his *Nat. quaest.*

Seneca, *Nat. quaest.*, praef. 13-15:

Quid est deus? Mens universi. Quid est deus? Quod vides totum et quod non vides totum. Sic demum magnitudo illi sua redditur, qua nihil maius cogitari potest, si solus est omnia, si opus suum et intra et extra tenet. Quid ergo interest inter naturam dei et nostram? Nostri melior pars animus est; in illo nulla pars extra animum est. Totus est ratio, cum interim tantus error mortalia tenet, ut hoc, quo neque formosius est quicquam nec dispositius nec in proposito constantius, existiment homines fortuitum et casu volubile ideoque tumultuosum inter fulmina nubes tempestates et cetera quibus terrae ac terris vicina pulsantur. Nec haec intra vulgum dementia est, sed sapientiam quoque professos contigit. Sunt qui putent ipsis animum esse, et quidem providum, dispensantem singula et sua et aliena, hoc autem universum, in quo nos quoque sumus, expers consilii ferri *aut* temeritate quadam aut natura nesciente quid faciat.

929—Epictetus' *Diatribae* are full of it. He writes at least four special treatises on Providence.

a. Epict., *Diatr.* I 16, 15-18:

Τίς ἐξαρκεῖ λόγος ὁμοίως αὐτὰ (sc. τὰ ἐφ' ἡμῶν ἔργα τῆς προνοίας) ἐπαινέσαι ἢ παραστῆσαι; εἰ γὰρ νοῦν εἴχομεν, ἄλλο τι ἔδει ἡμᾶς ποιεῖν καὶ κοινῇ καὶ ἰδίᾳ ἢ ὑμνεῖν τὸ θεῖον καὶ εὐφημεῖν καὶ ἐπεξέρχεσθαι τὰς χάριτας; οὐκ ἔδει καὶ σκάπτοντας καὶ ἀροῦντας καὶ ἐσθίοντας ᾄδειν τὸν ὕμνον τὸν εἰς τὸν θεόν; "μέγας ὁ θεός, ὅτι ἡμῖν παρέσχεν ὄργανα ταῦτα δι' ὧν τὴν γῆν ἐργασόμεθα· μέγας ὁ θεός, ὅτι χεῖρας δέδωκεν, ὅτι κατάποσιν, ὅτι κοιλίαν, ὅτι αὔξεσθαι λεληθότως, ὅτι καθεύδοντας ἀναπνεῖν." ταῦτα ἐφ' ἑκάστου ἐφυμνεῖν ἔδει καὶ τὸν μέγιστον καὶ θειότατον ὕμνον ἐφυμνεῖν, ὅτι τὴν δύναμιν ἔδωκεν τὴν παρακολουθητικὴν τούτοις καὶ ὁδῷ χρηστικήν.

Divine providence extended to all human conduct

b. I 14, 1-10:

Πυθομένου δέ τινος, πῶς ἄν τις πεισθείη, ὅτι ἕκαστον τῶν ὑπ' αὐτοῦ πραττομένων ἐφορᾶται ὑπὸ τοῦ θεοῦ, Οὐ δοκεῖ σοι, ἔφη, ἡνῶσθαι τὰ πάντα; — Δοκεῖ, ἔφη. — Τί δέ; συμπαθεῖν τὰ ἐπίγεια τοῖς οὐρανίοις οὐ δοκεῖ σοι; — Δοκεῖ, ἔφη. — Πόθεν γὰρ οὕτω τεταγμένως καθάπερ ἐκ προστάγματος τοῦ θεοῦ, ὅταν ἐκεῖνος εἴπῃ τοῖς φυτοῖς ἀνθεῖν, ἀνθεῖ, ὅταν εἴπῃ βλαστάνειν, βλαστάνει, ὅταν ἐκφέρειν τὸν καρπόν, ἐκφέρει, ὅταν πεπαίνειν, πεπαίνει, ὅταν πάλιν ἀποβάλλειν καὶ φυλλο‹ρ›ροεῖν καὶ αὐτὰ εἰς αὑτὰ συνειλούμενα ἐφ' ἡσυχίας μένειν καὶ ἀναπαύεσθαι, μένει καὶ ἀναπαύεται; πόθεν δὲ πρὸς τὴν αὔξησιν καὶ μείωσιν τῆς σελήνης καὶ τὴν τοῦ ἡλίου πρόσοδον καὶ ἄφοδον τοσαύτη παραλλαγὴ καὶ ἐπὶ τὰ ἐναντία μεταβολὴ τῶν ἐπιγείων θεωρεῖται; ἀλλὰ τὰ φυτὰ μὲν καὶ τὰ ἡμέτερα σώματα οὕτως ἐνδέδεται τοῖς ὅλοις καὶ συμπέπονθεν, αἱ ψυχαὶ δ' αἱ ἡμέτεραι οὐ πολὺ πλέον; ἀλλ' αἱ ψυχαὶ μὲν οὕτως εἰσὶν ἐνδεδεμέναι καὶ συναφεῖς τῷ θεῷ ἅτε αὐτοῦ μόρια οὖσαι καὶ ἀποσπάσματα, οὐ παντὸς δ' αὐτῶν κινήματος ἅτε οἰκείου καὶ συμφυοῦς ὁ θεὸς αἰσθάνεται; ἀλλὰ σὺ μὲν περὶ τῆς θείας διοικήσεως καὶ περὶ ἑκάστου τῶν θείων, ὁμοῦ δὲ καὶ περὶ τῶν ἀνθρωπίνων πραγμάτων ἐνθυμεῖσθαι δύνασαι καὶ ἅμα μὲν αἰσθητικῶς ἀπὸ μυρίων πραγμάτων κινεῖσθαι, ἅμα δὲ διανοητικῶς, ἅμα δὲ συγκαταθετικῶς, τοῖς δ' ἀνανευστικῶς ἢ ἐφεκτικῶς, τύπους δὲ τοσούτους ἀφ' οὕτω πολλῶν καὶ ποικίλων πραγμάτων ἐν τῇ σαυτοῦ ψυχῇ φυλάττεις καὶ ἀπ' αὐτῶν κινούμενος εἰς ἐπινοίας ὁμοειδεῖς ἐμπίπτεις τοῖς πρώτως τετυπωκόσι τέχνας τ' ἄλλην ἐπ' ἄλλῃ καὶ μνήμας ἀπὸ μυρίων πραγμάτων διασῴζεις· ὁ δὲ θεὸς οὐχ οἷός τ' ἐστὶ πάντα ἐφορᾶν καὶ πᾶσιν συμπαρεῖναι καὶ ἀπὸ πάντων τινὰ ἴσχειν διάδοσιν; ἀλλὰ φωτίζειν οἷός τ' ἐστὶν ὁ ἥλιος τηλικοῦτον μέρος τοῦ παντός, ὀλίγον δὲ τὸ ἀφώτιστον ἀπολιπεῖν ὅσον οἷόν τ' ἐπέχεσθαι ὑπὸ

σκιᾶς, ἣν ἡ γῆ ποιεῖ· ὁ δὲ καὶ τὸν ἥλιον αὐτὸν πεποιηκὼς καὶ περιάγων μέρος
ὄντ' αὐτοῦ μικρὸν ὡς πρὸς τὸ ὅλον, οὗτος δ' οὐ δύναται πάντων αἰσθάνεσθαι;

930—a. Marcus Aurelius II 11 (speaking on the possibility of passing
away):

Τὸ δὲ ἐξ ἀνθρώπων ἀπελθεῖν, εἰ μὲν θεοὶ εἰσίν, οὐδὲν δεινόν· κακῷ γάρ
σε οὐκ ἂν περιβάλοιεν· εἰ δὲ ἤτοι οὐκ εἰσὶν ἢ οὐ μέλει αὐτοῖς τῶν ἀνθρωπείων,
τί μοι ζῆν ἐν κόσμῳ κενῷ θεῶν ἢ προνοίας κενῷ; ἀλλὰ καὶ εἰσὶ καὶ μέλει αὐτοῖς
τῶν ἀνθρωπείων.

b. Ib. IV 10:

Ὅτι πᾶν τὸ συμβαῖνον δικαίως συμβαίνει· ὃ ἐὰν ἀκριβῶς παραφυλάσσῃς,
εὑρήσεις· οὐ λέγω μόνον κατὰ τὸ ἑξῆς, ἀλλ' ἔτι κατὰ τὸ δίκαιον καὶ ὡς ἂν
ὑπό τινος ἀπονέμοντος τὸ κατ' ἀξίαν.

931—Marc. Aur. speaks repeatedly of the hierarchic order in nature. **The principle**
V 16: **of teleology**

Ἢ οὐκ ἦν ἐναργὲς ὅτι τὰ χείρω τῶν κρειττόνων ἔνεκεν, τὰ δὲ κρείττω
ἀλλήλων; κρείττω δὲ τῶν μὲν ἀψύχων τὰ ἔμψυχα, τῶν δὲ ἐμψύχων τὰ λογικά.

Cp. also VII 55.

932—a. How the principle of teleology was applied by Chrysippus, **Its**
may appear from a few instances cited by Plutarch, *Stoic. repugn.* 21, **application**
p. 1044d:

Οἱ κόρεις εὐχρήστως ἐξυπνίζουσιν ἡμᾶς, καὶ οἱ μύες ἐπιστρέφουσιν ἡμᾶς
μὴ ἀμελῶς ἕκαστα τιθέναι.

This anthropocentric interpretation reminds us of the rather narrow views of
Chr. Wolff and his school. With regard to such interpretations Heine wrote, refer-
ring to the suitable organization of the body of man:

> Hätte er der Mäuler zwei,
> lüge er sogar beim Fressen.

In Greek philosophy the teleological explanation of nature was introduced by
Diogenes of Apollonia (our nr. **163a**). Cf. Xen. *Mem.* I 4. Chrysippus' teleological
explanations were criticized by Carneades. We find his arguments in the following
passage of Porphyrius.

b. Porphyrius, *De abstinentia* III 20:

Ἀλλ' ἐκεῖνο, νὴ Δία, τοῦ Χρυσίππου πιθανὸν ἦν, ὡς ἡμᾶς αὐτῶν καὶ ἀλλήλων
οἱ θεοὶ χάριν ἐποιήσαντο, ἡμῶν δὲ τὰ ζῷα, συμπολεμεῖν μὲν ἵππους καὶ συν-
θηρεύειν κύνας, ἀνδρείας δὲ γυμνάσια παρδάλεις καὶ ἄρκτους καὶ λέοντας.

ἡ δὲ ὗς, ἐνταῦθα γάρ ἐστι τῶν χαρίτων τὸ ἥδιστον, οὐ δι' ἄλλο τι πλὴν θύεσθαι ἐγεγόνει, καὶ τῇ σαρκὶ τὴν ψυχὴν ὁ θεὸς οἷον ἅλας ἐνέμιξεν, εὐοψίαν ἡμῖν μηχανώμενος. ὅπως δὲ ζωμοῦ καὶ παραδειπνίων ἀφθονίαν ἔχωμεν, ὄστρεά τε παντοδαπὰ καὶ πορφύρας καὶ ἀκαλήφας καὶ γένη πτηνῶν ποικίλα παρεσκεύασεν.

In spite of the reminiscence of Diog. of Apoll., Pohlenz (*Stoa* I p. 100) thinks that Chrysippus' anthropocentrism is a new element in Greek thought and hence must be of Semitic origin.

c. According to Chrysippus, however, not everything is made for the sake of its utility: nature makes many things for beauty's sake and rejoicing in variation.

Plut., *Stoic. repugn.* 21, 1044c:

Γράψας τοίνυν ἐν τοῖς περὶ Φύσεως, ὅτι "πολλὰ τῶν ζῴων ἕνεκα κάλλους ἡ φύσις ἐνήνοχε, φιλοκαλοῦσα καὶ χαίρουσα τῇ ποικιλίᾳ", καὶ λόγον ἐπειπὼν παραλογώτατον, ὡς "ὁ ταὼς ἕνεκα τῆς οὐρᾶς γέγονε, διὰ τὸ κάλλος αὐτῆς."

And in a literal quotation, directly after the words cited sub **a**:

Γένοιτο δ' ἂν μάλιστα τούτου ἔμφασις ἐπὶ τῆς κέρκου τοῦ ταώ.

d. Marc. Aurel. considers everything firstly as a part of a whole. II 3:

Παντὶ δὲ φύσεως μέρει ἀγαθόν, ὃ φέρει ἡ τοῦ ὅλου φύσις καὶ ὃ ἐκείνης ἐστὶ σωστικόν.

This is also the point of view of Leibniz' teleology.

Mantic and providence   **933**—The belief in Providence is connected with the belief in *omina*. Cp. Socrates' belief in signs and mantic (nr. **217**).

a. Cic., *de Div.* II 63, 130:

Definition of mantic   Chrysippus quidem divinationem definit his verbis: vim cognoscentem et videntem et explicantem signa quae a dis hominibus portendantur.

b. We find the Greek text of this definition in Sextus, *Adv. Math.* IX (*Ag. the Phys.* I) 132:

Ἐπιστήμη θεωρητικὴ καὶ ἐξηγητικὴ τῶν ὑπὸ θεῶν ἀνθρώποις διδομένων σημείων.

A similar definition is given in Stob., *Ecl.* II 67, 13 W.

its possibility   **c.** Cicero founds the possibility of mantic firstly on the existence of gods and providence. *Div.* I 38, 82:

Quam quidem esse re vera hac Stoicorum ratione concluditur: "si sunt di neque ante declarant hominibus quae futura sint, aut non diligunt homines, aut quid eventurum sit ignorant, aut existumant nihil interesse hominum scire quid sit futurum, aut non censent esse suae maiestatis praesignificare hominibus quae sint futura, aut ea ne ipsi quidem di significare possunt. at neque non diligunt nos: sunt enim benifici generique hominum amici; neque ignorant ea quae ab ipsis constituta et designata sunt; neque nostra nihil interest scire ea quae eventura sint: erimus enim cautiores si sciemus; neque hoc alienum ducunt maiestate sua: nihil est enim beneficentia praestantius; neque non possunt futura praenoscere.

934—Stoics distinguished between *natural and artificial mantic*. The first, being by dreams and by words spoken in *trance* or by chance (φῆμαι), is dealt with by Cic. in *Div*. I. He follows Posidonius in his work on dreams. **Natural and artificial mantic**

a. Cic., *Div*. I 33, 72; 49, 109-110:

Quae vero aut coniectura explicantur aut eventis animadversa ac notata sunt, ea genera divinandi, ut supra dixi, non naturalia sed artificiosa dicuntur; in quo haruspices augures coniectoresque numerantur. haec improbantur a Peripateticis, a Stoicis defenduntur.

49, 109-110: Quid, si etiam ratio exstat artificiosae praesensionis facilis, divinae autem paulo obscurior? quae enim extis, quae fulgoribus, quae portentis, quae astris praesentiuntur, haec notata sunt observatione diuturna. adfert autem vetustas omnibus in rebus longinqua observatione incredibilem scientiam; quae potest esse etiam sine motu atque impulsu deorum, cum quid ex quoque eveniat et quid quamque rem significet crebra animadversione perspectum est.

Altera divinatio est naturalis, ut ante dixi, quae physica disputandi subtilitate referenda est ad naturam deorum, a qua, ut doctissimis sapientissimisque placuit, haustos animos et libatos habemus; cumque omnia completa et referta sint aeterno sensu et mente divina, necesse est contagione divinorum animorum animos humanos commoveri.

b. How to understand artificial mantic. Cic., *Div*. I 118:

Nam non placet Stoicis singulis iecorum fissis aut avium cantibus interesse deum: neque enim decorum est nec dis dignum nec fieri ullo pacto potest; sed ita a principio inchoatum esse mundum, ut certis rebus certa signa praecurrerent, alia in extis, alia in avibus, alia in fulgoribus, alia in ostentis, alia in stellis, alia in somniantium visis, alia in furentium vocibus. ea quibus bene percepta sunt, ii non saepe falluntur; male coniecta maleque interpretata falsa sunt non rerum vitio sed interpretum inscientia.

Artificial mantic based on cosmic συμπάθεια 935—As appears from the "sed ita a principio inchoatum esse mundum" in the above quotation, artificial mantic is founded on the theory of cosmic συμπάθεια. The sceptic criticism (doubtless of Carneades) attacks this point.

Cic., *Div.* II 14, 33:

Cum rerum autem natura quam cognationem habent (sc. exta e quibus haruspices futura praedicunt)? quae ut uno consensu iuncta sit et continens, quod video placuisse physicis eisque maxume qui omne quod esset unum esse dixerunt, quid habere mundus potest cum thesauri inventione coniunctum? si enim extis pecuniae mihi amplificatio ostenditur idque fit natura, primum exta sunt coniuncta mundo, deinde meum lucrum natura rerum continetur. Nonne pudet physicos haec dicere?

34. Sescenta licet eiusdem modi proferri, ut distantium rerum cognatio naturalis appareat—demus hoc; nihil enim huic disputationi adversatur; num etiam, si fissum cuiusdam modi fuerit in iecore, lucrum ostenditur? qua ex coniunctione naturae et quasi concentu et consensu, quam συμπάθειαν Graeci appellant, convenire potest aut fissum iecoris cum lucello meo aut meus quaesticulus cum caelo terra rerumque natura? [1]

936—Panaetius, under the impression of Carneades' arguments, rejects mantic. His influence may be seen in the behaviour of C. Blossius of Cumae ap. Plut., *Tiberius Gracchus* 17.

Though several bad signs have happened on the morning of that day, Tiberius sets out, on learning that the people were assembled on the Capitol.

---

[1] A curious instance of modern belief in "signs" by fortuitous events based on cosmic "sympathy" may be found in R. H. Benson's novel *Initiation*, [5]1914, p. 229 f.: ,,I suppose you notice how things happen," he said, ,,like birds flying, or a shadow over the sun, and think they're signs?" — ,,How do you know?" she asked, amazed. — ,,Because I used to do it myself," he said, ,,until I learned how useless it was." — ,,You think it all nonsense, then? Just as I do? — at least, just as I know it is, really?" ,,Not all nonsense," he said imperturbably. ,,I am entirely convinced, from simple observation, that there is some connection between — well, between different things that seem to have no connection. That there are laws that are true and active in all realms at once; and that sensitive or intuitive people can sometimes perceive them."

Μικρὸν δ' αὐτοῦ προελθόντος ὤφθησαν ὑπὲρ κεράμου μαχόμενοι κόρακες ἐν ἀριστερᾷ· καὶ πολλῶν ὡς εἰκὸς ἀνθρώπων παρερχομένων, κατ' αὐτὸν τὸν Τιβέριον λίθος ἀπωσθεὶς ὑπὸ θατέρου τῶν κοράκων ἔπεσε παρὰ τὸν πόδα. τοῦτο καὶ τοὺς θρασυτάτους τῶν περὶ αὐτὸν ἐπέστησεν· ἀλλὰ Βλόσσιος ὁ Κυμαῖος παρὼν αἰσχύνην ἔφη καὶ κατήφειαν ἂν εἶναι πολλήν, εἰ Τιβέριος, Γράχχου μὲν υἱὸς Ἀφρικανοῦ δὲ Σκηπίωνος θυγατριδοῦς, προστάτης δὲ τοῦ Ῥωμαίων δήμου, κόρακα δείσας οὐχ ὑπακούσειε τοῖς πολίταις καλοῦσι.

937—Posidonius restores the belief in mantic. We find it again in the later Stoa. Seneca believes in "signs".

a. Seneca, *Nat. quaest.* II 32, 2:

Hoc inter nos et Tuscos, quibus summa est fulgurum persequendorum scientia, interest: nos putamus, quia nubes collisae sunt, fulmina emitti; ipsi existimant nubes collidi ut fulmina emittantur; nam, cum omnia ad deum referant, in ea opinione sunt tamquam non, quia facta sunt, significent, sed quia significatura sunt, fiant. Eadem tamen ratione fiunt, sive illis significare propositum, sive consequens est.

b. Ib. 6-7:

Astrology accepted on the same grounds

Quinque stellarum potestates Chaldaeorum observatio excepit; quid? tu tot illa milia siderum iudicas otiosa lucere? Quid est porro aliud quod errorem maximum incutiat peritis natalium quam quod paucis nos sideribus assignant, cum omnia quae supra nos sunt partem nostri sibi vindicent? Summissiora forsitan propius in nos vim suam dirigunt et ea quae frequentius mota aliter nos aliterque prospiciunt; ceterum et illa quae aut immota sunt aut propter velocitatem universo parem immotis similia non extra ius dominiumque nostri sunt.

The belief in the connexion between human life and the heavenly bodies, which might seem to be an arbitrary assumption to the modern mind, was for the Stoic rationally founded on cosmic "sympathy."

938—If the identity of God and Providence with Nature be admitted, the problem of the origin of evil presents certain obvious difficulties. The Stoic philosophers do not confine themselves to the teaching that all outward events are adiaphora, but propose three arguments in order to meet the said difficulties.

The problem of evil

1. "Evil" is an instrument in the hands of God for the education of man.
Thus, Chrysippus says, ap. Plut., *Stoic. repugn.* 15, p. 1040c, citing the verses of Hesiod, *Erga* 242:

First solution

Τοῖσιν δ' οὐρανόθεν μέγ' ἐπήλασε πῆμα Κρονίων,
λιμὸν ὁμοῦ καὶ λοιμόν· ἀποφθινύθουσι δὲ λαοί·

ταῦτά φησι τοὺς θεοὺς ποιεῖν, ὅπως κολαζομένων τῶν πονηρῶν οἱ λοιποὶ
παραδείγμασι τούτοις χρώμενοι ἧττον ἐπιχειρῶσι τοιοῦτόν τι ποιεῖν.

Cp. the view that God "purifies" the world by floods and conflagration, ὅταν
πολλὴ ἡ κακία γένηται ἐν αὐτῷ (Origenes, *Contra Celsum* IV 64, SVF II 1174).

Difficulties   **939**—Here, of course, the question arises as to why so many innocent
people are struck by evil.

a.   Both Cleanthes (Vid. **926b**) and Chrysippus admit a certain
limitation of Providence. Plut., *Stoic. repugn.* 37, p. 1051b:

Ἔτι περὶ τοῦ μηδὲν ἐγκλητὸν εἶναι μηδὲ μεμπτὸν κόσμῳ κατὰ τὴν ἀρίστην
φύσιν ἁπάντων παραγομένων πολλάκις γεγραφώς (sc. Chrys.), ἔστιν ὅπου πάλιν
ἐγκλητάς τινας ἀμελείας οὐ περὶ μικρὰ καὶ φαῦλα ἀπολείπει. Ἐν γοῦν τῷ τρίτῳ
Περὶ οὐσίας, μνησθεὶς ὅτι συμβαίνει τινὰ τοῖς καλοῖς καὶ ἀγαθοῖς τοιαῦτα
"Πότερον, φησίν, ἀμελουμένων τινῶν, καθάπερ ἐν οἰκίαις μείζοσι παραπίπτει
τινὰ πίτυρα καὶ ποσοὶ πυροί τινες, τῶν ὅλων εὖ οἰκονομουμένων· ἢ διὰ
τὸ καθίστασθαι ἐπὶ τῶν τοιούτων δαιμόνια φαῦλα, ἐν οἷς τῷ ὄντι γίνονται
καὶ ἐγκλητέαι ἀμέλειαι;" φησὶ δὲ πολὺ καὶ τὸ τῆς ἀνάγκης μεμῖχθαι.

Hence the Epicurean Philodemus reproaches the Stoics that they, first, hold
the almightiness of God, and afterwards confine it by saying that God is not the
cause of accidental things.

b.   The doctrine that matter has its own causality, was accepted
in the School. We find it in Seneca, *Nat. Quaest.* VI 3, who, speaking of
men perishing in catastrophes of nature, says:

Illud quoque proderit praesumere animo nihil horum deos facere nec
ira numinum aut caelum converti aut terram; suas ista causas habent.

Cf. *De Prov.* 5, 9: Quare tamen deus tam iniquus in distributione fati fuit, ut
bonis viris paupertatem et vulnera et acerba funera ascriberet? non potest artifex
mutare materiam: hoc passa est.

c.   Marcus Aurelius VI 36:

Πάντα ἐκεῖθεν ἔρχεται, ἀπ' ἐκείνου τοῦ κοινοῦ ἡγεμονικοῦ ὁρμήσαντα ἢ
κατ' ἐπακολούθησιν¹. καὶ τὸ χάσμα οὖν τοῦ λέοντος καὶ τὸ δηλητήριον καὶ
πᾶσα κακουργία ὡς ἄκανθα, ὡς βόρβορος, ἐκείνων ἐπιγεννήματα τῶν σεμνῶν
καὶ καλῶν. μὴ οὖν αὐτὰ ἀλλότρια τούτου οὗ σέβεις φαντάζου, ἀλλὰ τὴν πάντων
πηγὴν ἐπιλογίζου.

---

¹ ὁρμήσαντα ἢ κατ' ἐπακολούθησιν—be it directly or by accident.

d. Thus, according to Chrysippus diseases are κατὰ παρακολούθησιν. Gellius, *N.A.* VII 1, 7:

Chrysippus in eodem libro (i.e. quarto Περὶ προνοίας) tractat consideratque dignumque esse id quaeri putat, εἰ αἱ τῶν ἀνθρώπων νόσοι κατὰ φύσιν γίνονται, id est, si natura ipsa rerum vel providentia, quae compagem hanc mundi et genus hominum fecit, morbos quoque et debilitates et aegritudines corporum, quas patiuntur homines, fecerit. Existimat autem non fuisse hoc principale naturae consilium, ut faceret homines morbis obnoxios, nunquam enim hoc convenisse naturae auctori parentique omnium rerum bonarum. "Sed cum multa", inquit, "atque magna gigneret pareretque aptissima et utilissima, alia quoque simul adgnata sunt incommoda his ipsis quae faciebat cohaerentia", eaque neque per naturam, sed per sequellas quasdam necessarias facta dicit, quod ipse appellat "κατὰ παρακολούθησιν". "Sicut", inquit, "cum corpora hominum natura fingeret, ratio subtilior et utilitas ipsa operis postulavit, ut tenuissimis minutisque ossiculis caput compingeret. Sed hanc utilitatem rei maiorem alia quaedam incommoditas extrinsecus consecuta est, ut fieret caput tenuiter munitum et ictibus offensionibusque parvis fragile. Proinde morbi quoque et aegritudines partae sunt, dum salus paritur.

By the above cited passage of Marcus Aurelius P. Barth, *Die Stoa* p. 66, feels reminded of J. Stuart Mill who, in his *Three Essays on Religion*, wrote that "on the ground of natural theology" almightiness cannot be attributed to God.—Which, after all, does not mean anything else than that divine Providence is incomprehensible for man. Cp., for the rest, the "gnostical" solution of the problem, followed e.g. by the Dutch poet Frederic van Eeden (before he became a Catholic): that the world cannot be the work of "the highest God" but must have been made by some minor Spirits.

940—2. The cosmological point of view: the universe is an organical whole; therefore, what happens to the individual man should not be considered as an isolated phenomenon. It may serve for preserving the whole.

Second solution

a. Chrysippus ap. Plut., *Stoic. repugn.* 35, p. 1050 e:

Ποτὲ μὲν τὰ δύσχρηστα συμβαίνειν φησὶ τοῖς ἀγαθοῖς οὐχ ὥσπερ τοῖς φαύλοις κολάσεως χάριν, ἀλλὰ κατ' ἄλλην οἰκονομίαν, ὥσπερ ἐν ταῖς πόλεσι.

What he means by this, appears from c. 32, p. 1049a:

Ὡς δὲ αἱ πόλεις πλεονάσασαι εἰς ἀποικίας ἀπαίρουσι τὰ πλήθη καὶ πολέμους ἐνίστανται πρός τινας, οὕτως ὁ θεὸς φθορᾶς ἀρχὰς δίδωσι. καὶ τὸν Εὐριπίδην μάρτυρα καὶ τοὺς ἄλλους προσάγεται τοὺς λέγοντας ὡς ὁ Τρωϊκὸς πόλεμος ὑπὸ τῶν θεῶν ἀπαντλήσεως χάριν τοῦ πλήθους τῶν ἀνθρώπων γένοιτο.

b. Seneca, *Ep.* 74, 20:

Nihil indignetur sibi accidere sciatque illa ipsa, quibus laedi videtur, ad conservationem universi pertinere et ex iis esse quae cursum mundi officiumque consummant.

c. Marc. Aur. IX 39:

῎Ητοι ἀπὸ μιᾶς πηγῆς νοερᾶς πάντα ὡς ἑνὶ σώματι ἐπισυμβαίνει καὶ οὐ δεῖ τὸ μέρος τοῖς ὑπὲρ τοῦ ὅλου γινομένοις μέμφεσθαι· ἢ ἄτομοι καὶ οὐδὲν ἄλλο ἢ κυκεὼν καὶ σκεδασμός.

He means that, evidently, in this alternative only the first is possible.

Third solution

941—3. The bad is correlate of the good, just as left is the correlate of right.

This view of the problem is certainly connected with Heraclitus' doctrine of the harmony of opposites (our nrs. **53** and **54**).

a. Gellius, *N.A.* VII 1 (SVF II 1169):

Quibus non videtur mundus dei et hominum causa institutus neque res humanas providentia gubernari, gravi se argumento uti putant, cum ita dicunt: "si esset providentia, nulla essent mala". Nihil enim minus aiunt providentiae congruere, quam in eo mundo, quem propter homines fecisse dicatur, tantam vim esse aerumnarum et malorum. Adversus ea Chrysippus cum in libro Περὶ προνοίας quarto dissereret "nihil est prorsus istis", inquit, "insubidius, qui opinantur bona esse potuisse, si non essent ibidem mala. Nam cum bona malis contraria sint, utraque necessum est opposita inter sese et quasi mutuo adversoque fulta nisu consistere; nullum adeo contrarium est sine contrario altero. Quo enim pacto iustitiae sensus esse posset, nisi essent iniuriae? aut quid aliud iustitia est quam iniustitiae privatio? quid item fortitudo intellegi posset, nisi ex ignaviae adpositione? quid continentia, nisi ex intemperantiae? quo item modo prudentia esset, nisi foret contra imprudentia? Proinde", inquit, "homines stulti cur non hoc etiam desiderant, ut veritas sit et non sit mendacium? Namque itidem sunt bona et mala, felicitas et importunitas, dolor et voluptas. Alterum enim ex altero, sicuti Plato ait [1], verticibus inter se contrariis deligatum est; si tuleris unum, abstuleris utrumque."

In this passage we have primarily to do with a logical thesis: *nullum contrarium est sine contrario altero.* Now this thesis is wrong, as may be seen from Aristotle, *Categ.* 10. Various kinds of opposites are distinguished in this chapter. The first,

---

[1] *Phaedo* 60 c.

called ἀντικείμενα πρός τι, are correlates: they depend on each other and do not have a μέσον. The second group however, consisting of things which do not depend on each other (ὧν μὴ ἀναγκαῖον θάτερον ὑπάρχειν), do possess a middle term: οὐ γὰρ πᾶν ἤτοι λευκὸν ἢ μέλαν ἐστίν. Of this kind are φαῦλον καὶ σπουδαῖον (good and bad): where the one is, the other must not necessarily be too. There is a μέσον.

b. It appears as a metaphysical principle in Plut., *St. repugn.* 35, p. 1050f, where Chrys. is cited in this way:

'Η δὲ κακία πρὸς τὰ δεινὰ συμπτώματα ἴδιόν τινα ἔχει λόγον· γίνεται μὲν γὰρ καὶ αὐτή πως κατὰ τὸν τῆς φύσεως λόγον, καί, ἵν' οὕτως εἴπω, οὐκ ἀχρήστως γίνεται πρὸς τὰ ὅλα· οὐδὲ γὰρ τἀγαθὰ ἦν.

This explanation tends to legitimate evil, by making it metaphysically necessary, and thus creates a contradiction in the notion of God. A systematical exposition of the objections against Providence and their refutation by the Stoics is given by Philo, *Provid.* II.

942—In Seneca's *De prov.* Providence is defended according to the first view, which might be called the paedagogical principle. *(Seneca's defense of Providence)*

Hence he says (II 2) that the good man *omnia adversa exercitationes putat.* From this point of view it may be understood that on the very best the hardest training is imposed, so that it is an honour and an election to be on hard trial. *De Prov.* IV 8:

Quare deus optimum quemque aut mala valitudine aut luctu aut aliis incommodis afficit? quia in castris quoque periculosa fortissimis imperantur: dux lectissimos mittit, qui nocturnis hostes aggrediantur insidiis aut explorent iter aut praesidium loco deiciant. Nemo eorum qui exeunt dicit: "male de me imperator meruit", sed "bene iudicavit". item dicant quicumque iubentur pati timidis ignavisque flebilia: "digni visi sumus deo in quibus experiretur quantum humana natura posset pati".

Two remarks must be made here.

1—The difference between the Stoic and the Christian attitude towards suffering appears clearly from such a passage as *De prov.* II, 1: *Quare multa bonis viris adversa eveniunt? nihil accidere bono viro mali potest: non miscentur contraria. quemadmodum tot amnes, tantum superne deiectorum imbrium, tanta medicatorum vis fontium non mutant saporem maris, ne remittunt quidem, ita adversarum impetus rerum viri fortis non vertit animum: manet in statu et quicquid evenit in suum colorem trahit; est enim omnibus externis potentior. nec hoc dico: non sentit illa.*

The Christian accepts suffering as such and wishes to pass through it, the Stoic denies its existence and thus tries to make himself immune to it. Cp. our nrs. **1013, 1017a, 1018.**

2—Seneca's God looks at human suffering with the delight of the spectator in an arena. *De prov.* II 9: *Ecce spectaculum dignum ad quod respiciat intentus operi suo deus, ecce par deo dignum, vir fortis cum fortuna mala compositus, utique si et provocavit. non video, inquam, quid habeat in terris Iuppiter pulchrius, si eo conver-*

tere animum velit, quam ut spectet Catonem iam partibus non semel fractis stantem nihilominus inter ruinas publicas rectum.

Very different is the attitude of "God and the holy Angels" at the sight of the Christian's trial, as for instance Newman represents it (*Parochial and Plain Sermons*, vol. VII, p. 54 ed. Longmans): "They rejoice over one sinner that repenteth; how must they mourn over those who fall away! What interest, surely, is excited among them by the sight of the Christian's trial, when faith and the desire of the world's esteem are struggling in his heart for victory! what rejoicing if, through the grace of God, he overcomes! what sorrow and pity if he is overcome by the world!"

A compendium of Stoic theology

943—Cleanthes, *Hymn to Zeus*, ap. Stob., *Ecl.* I 1, 12, p. 25 W. (SVF I 537).

Κύδιστ' ἀθανάτων, πολυώνυμε, παγκρατὲς αἰεί,
Ζεῦ, φύσεως ἀρχηγέ, νόμου μέτα πάντα κυβερνῶν,
χαῖρε· σὲ γὰρ πάντεσσι θέμις θνητοῖσι προσαυδᾶν.
ἐκ σοῦ γὰρ γένος εἶσ' ἤχου μίμημα λαχόντες [1]
5 μοῦνοι, ὅσα ζώει τε καὶ ἕρπει θνήτ' ἐπὶ γαῖαν·
τῷ σε καθυμνήσω καὶ σὸν κράτος αἰὲν ἀείσω.
σοὶ δὴ πᾶς ὅδε κόσμος, ἑλισσόμενος περὶ γαῖαν [2],
πείθεται, ᾗ κεν ἄγῃς, καὶ ἑκὼν ὑπὸ σεῖο κρατεῖται·
τοῖον ἔχεις ὑποεργὸν ἀνικήτοις ὑπὸ χερσὶν
10 ἀμφήκη, πυρόεντα, ἀειζώοντα κεραυνόν·
τοῦ γὰρ ὑπὸ πληγῆς φύσεως πάντ' ἔργα ‹τελεῖται›·
ᾧ σὺ κατευθύνεις κοινὸν λόγον, ὃς διὰ πάντων
φοιτᾷ, μιγνύμενος μεγάλοις μικροῖς τε φάεσσι·
ᾧ σὺ τόσος γεγαὼς ὕπατος βασιλεὺς διὰ παντός.
15 οὐδέ τι γίγνεται ἔργον ἐπὶ χθονὶ σοῦ δίχα, δαῖμον,
οὔτε κατ' αἰθέριον θεῖον πόλον οὔτ' ἐνὶ πόντῳ,
πλὴν ὁπόσα ῥέζουσι κακοὶ σφετέραισιν ἀνοίαις·
ἀλλὰ σὺ καὶ τὰ περισσὰ ἐπίστασαι ἄρτια θεῖναι,
καὶ κοσμεῖν τἄκοσμα καὶ οὐ φίλα σοὶ φίλα ἐστίν.
20 ὧδε γὰρ εἰς ἓν πάντα συνήρμοκας ἐσθλὰ κακοῖσιν,
ὥσθ' ἕνα γίγνεσθαι πάντων λόγον αἰὲν ἐόντα,
ὃν φεύγοντες ἐῶσιν ὅσοι θνητῶν κακοί εἰσι,

---

[1] ἤχου μίμημα λαχόντες "for they have got an image of Thee within themselves, namely language". Human logos is an image of Divine Logos. Because he has an image of divine Logos in himself, man is "of God's race" (Verbeke). Others explain ἤχου μίμημα as "language which imitates things".

[2] Cleanthes was a declared enemy of Aristarchus, and this on religious grounds: the heliocentric hypothesis seemed to him in contradiction with the divine order of things.

δύσμοροι, οἵ τ' ἀγαθῶν μὲν ἀεὶ κτῆσιν ποθέοντες
οὔτ' ἐσορῶσι θεοῦ κοινὸν νόμον, οὔτε κλύουσιν,
25 ᾧ κεν πειθόμενοι σὺν νῷ βίον ἐσθλὸν ἔχοιεν.
αὐτοὶ δ' αὖθ' ὁρμῶσιν ἄνοι κακὸν ἄλλος ἐπ' ἄλλο,
οἱ μὲν ὑπὲρ δόξης σπουδὴν δυσέριστον ἔχοντες,
οἱ δ' ἐπὶ κερδοσύνας τετραμμένοι οὐδενὶ κόσμῳ,
ἄλλοι δ' εἰς ἄνεσιν καὶ σώματος ἡδέα ἔργα.
30 <ἀλλὰ κακοῖς ἐπέκυρσαν>*, ἐπ' ἄλλοτε δ' ἄλλα φέρονται
σπεύδοντες μάλα πάμπαν ἐναντία τῶνδε γενέσθαι.
ἀλλὰ Ζεῦ πάνδωρε, κελαινεφές, ἀργικέραυνε,
ἀνθρώπους <μὲν> ** ῥύου ἀπειροσύνης ἀπὸ λυγρῆς,
ἣν σύ, πάτερ, σκέδασον ψυχῆς ἄπο, δὸς δὲ κυρῆσαι
35 γνώμης, ᾗ πίσυνος σὺ δίκης μέτα πάντα κυβερνᾷς,
ὄφρ' ἂν τιμηθέντες ἀμειβώμεσθά σε τιμῇ,
ὑμνοῦντες τὰ σὰ ἔργα διηνεκές, ὡς ἐπέοικε
θνητὸν ἐόντ', ἐπεὶ οὔτε βροτοῖς γέρας ἄλλο τι μεῖζον,
οὔτε θεοῖς, ἢ κοινὸν ἀεὶ νόμον ἐν δίκῃ ὑμνεῖν.

The prayer in vs. 28 ff. aims at realizing the Stoic ideal of virtue: to live in inner harmony with the divine Law. For this purpose the poet asks the help of God, and he feels that, without this help, we, on our side, are not able to honour God truly (ὄφρ' ἂν τ ι μ η θ έ ν τ ε ς ἀμειβώμεσθά σε τιμῇ) [1].

The hymn has been recently explained by G. Verbeke, *Kleanthes*, p. 235-251, by A. J. Festugière in *Le Dieu Cosmique*, p. 310-332, and finally by J. D. Meerwaldt in *Mnemosyne* 1951, p. 58-69, 1952 p. 1-12.

Festugière rightly qualifies Cleanthes' religious attitude as a *mystique du consentement*. It is the same philosophy of life which is expressed more than four centuries later by Marcus Aurelius in these words: ὅτι μόνῳ τῷ λογικῷ ζῴῳ δέδοται τὸ ἑκουσίως ἕπεσθαι τοῖς γινομένοις, τὸ δὲ ἕπεσθαι ψιλὸν πᾶσιν ἀναγκαῖον (Χ 28).

944—a. The discussion on the problem "Fate and Liberty" to which the Stoic doctrine gave rise, is summarized in the following passage of Gellius, *N.A.* VII 2:

Fatum quod εἱμαρμένην Graeci vocant, ad hanc ferme sententiam Chrysippus, Stoicae princeps philosophiae, definit (fr. 33 G.): "Fatum

Fate and Liberty

---

[1] Festugière, *Le Dieu cosmique* p. 324 f., commented excellently on these lines. Note the expression τιμᾶσθαι: *recevoir une faveur divine*.

* I give the text according to Von Arnim's reconstruction *exempli causa* (SVF I 537). Meerwaldt (in *Mnem.* 1952 p. 7) proposed: πᾶσιν δ' ἄλγε' ἑτοῖμα or πάντες δ' ἄλγε' ἐφεῦρον.

** μὲν was added by Scaliger, followed by Pearson and Von Arnim. Meerwaldt (o.c., p. 8) proposed: σούς.

est", inquit "sempiterna quaedam et indeclinabilis series rerum et catena volvens semetipsa sese et implicans per aeternos consequentiae ordines, ex quibus apta nexaque est." Ipsa autem verba Chrysippi, quantum valui memoria, ascripsi, ut, si cui meum istud interpretamentum videbitur esse obscurius, ad ipsius verba animadvertat. In libro enim Περὶ προνοίας quarto (fr. 33 G.) εἱμαρμένην esse dicit φυσικήν τινα σύνταξιν τῶν ὅλων ἐξ ἀϊδίου τῶν ἑτέρων τοῖς ἑτέροις ἐπακολουθούντων καὶ μεταπολουμένων ἀπαραβάτου οὔσης τῆς τοιαύτης ἐπιπλοκῆς.

Aliarum autem opinionum disciplinarumque auctores huic definitioni ita obstrepunt: "Si Chrysippus" inquiunt "fato putat omnia moveri et regi nec declinari transcendique posse agmina fati et volumina, peccata quoque hominum et delicta non suscensenda neque inducenda sunt ipsis voluntatibusque eorum, sed necessitati cuidam et instantiae, quae oritur ex fato, omnium quae sit rerum domina et arbitra, per quam necesse sit fieri, quicquid futurum est; et propterea nocentium poenas legibus inique constitutas, si homines ad maleficia non sponte veniunt, sed fato trahuntur".

Contra ea Chrysippus tenuiter multa et argute disserit; sed omnium fere, quae super ea re scripsit, huiuscemodi sententia est (fr. 30 G.): "Quamquam ita sit", inquit "ut ratione quadam necessaria et principali coacta atque conexa sint fato omnia, ingenia tamen ipsa mentium nostrarum proinde sunt fato obnoxia, ut proprietas eorum est ipsa et qualitas. Nam si sunt per naturam primitus salubriter utiliterque ficta, omnem illam vim, quae de fato extrinsecus ingruit, inoffensius tractabiliusque transmittunt. Sin vero sunt aspera et inscita et rudia nullisque artium bonarum adminiculis fulta, etiam si parvo sive nullo fatalis incommodi conflictu urgeantur, sua tamen scaevitate et voluntario impetu in assidua delicta et in errores se ruunt. Idque ipsum ut ea ratione fiat, naturalis illa et necessaria rerum consequentia efficit, quae fatum vocatur. Est enim genere ipso quasi fatale et consequens, ut mala ingenia peccatis et erroribus non vacent."

Huius deinde rei exemplo non hercle nimis alieno neque inlepido utitur (fr. 31 G.). "Sicut" inquit "lapidem cylindrum si per spatia terrae prona atque derupta iacias, causam quidem ei et initium praecipitantiae feceris, mox tamen ille praeceps volvitur, non quia tu id iam facis, sed quoniam ita sese modus eius et formae volubilitas habet: sic ordo et ratio et necessitas fati genera ipsa et principia causarum movet, impetus vero consiliorum mentiumque nostrarum actionesque ipsas voluntas cuiusque propria et animorum ingenia moderantur". Infert deinde verba haec his, quae dixi, congruentia (fr. 32 G.): Διὸ καὶ ὑπὸ τῶν Πυθαγορείων (χρύσ. ἔπ. 54) εἴρηται·

γνώσει δ' ἀνθρώπους αὐθαίρετα πήματ' ἔχοντας,

ὡς τῶν βλαβῶν ἑκάστοις παρ' αὐτοῖς γινομένων καὶ καθ' ὁρμὴν αὐτῶν ἁμαρτανόντων τε καὶ βλαπτομένων καὶ κατὰ τὴν αὐτῶν διάνοιαν καὶ θέσιν.

Propterea negat oportere ferri audirique homines aut nequam aut ignavos et nocentes et audaces, qui, cum in culpa et in maleficio revicti sunt, perfugiunt ad fati necessitatem tamquam in aliquod fani asylum et, quae pessime fecerunt, ea non suae temeritati, sed fato esse attribuenda dicunt.

Primus autem hoc sapientissimus ille et antiquissimus poetarum dixit hisce versibus (Hom. Od. I 32):

ὢ πόποι, οἷον δή νυ θεοὺς βροτοὶ αἰτιόωνται.
ἐξ ἡμέων γάρ φασι κάκ' ἔμμεναι· οἱ δὲ καὶ αὐτοὶ
σφῇσιν ἀτασθαλίῃσιν ὑπὲρ μόρον ἄλγε' ἔχουσιν.

b. Chrysippus holds that Fate does not exclude liberty. His view is illustrated by the following example.

Hippolyt., *Philos.* 21 (SVF II 975):   **the draughtdog**

Καὶ αὐτοὶ δὲ (sc. Zeno and Chrys.) τὸ καθ' εἱμαρμένην εἶναι πάντα διεβεβαιώσαντο παραδείγματι χρησάμενοι τοιούτῳ, ὅτι ὥσπερ ὀχήματος ἐὰν ᾖ ἐξηρτημένος κύων, ἐὰν μὲν βούληται ἕπεσθαι, καὶ ἕλκεται καὶ ἕπεται, ποιῶν καὶ τὸ αὐτεξούσιον μετὰ τῆς ἀνάγκης [οἷον τῆς εἱμαρμένης]· ἐὰν δὲ μὴ βούληται ἕπεσθαι, πάντως ἀναγκασθήσεται· τὸ αὐτὸ δήπου καὶ ἐπὶ τῶν ἀνθρώπων· καὶ μὴ βουλόμενοι γὰρ ἀκολουθεῖν ἀναγκασθήσονται πάντως εἰς τὸ πεπρωμένον εἰσελθεῖν.

c. Cp. Cleanthes' prayer, cited by Epict., *Ench.* 53:

Ἄγου δέ μ', ὦ Ζεῦ, καὶ σύ γ' ἡ Πεπρωμένη,
ὅποι ποθ' ὑμῖν εἰμι διατεταγμένος·
ὡς ἕψομαί γ' ἄοκνος· ἢν δέ γε μὴ θέλω,
κακὸς γενόμενος, οὐδὲν ἧττον ἕψομαι.

Pohlenz argues for the oriental character of this "feeling" of fate, as displayed in the Stoic doctrine of heimarmene: *Stoa* I p. 107 f.; *Stoa und Semitismus*, 263 ff.

4—PHYSICS: (3) SOUL AND ITS VARIOUS FUNCTIONS; IMMORTALITY

945—Contrary to Epicurus the Stoa teaches that the animal's first impulse is not towards pleasure but towards selfpreservation.

οἰκείωσις   **a.**   Diog. VII 85:

Τὴν δὲ πρώτην ὁρμήν φασι τὸ ζῷον ἴσχειν ἐπὶ τὸ τηρεῖν ἑαυτό, οἰκειούσης αὐτῷ τῆς φύσεως ἀπ' ἀρχῆς, καθά φησιν ὁ Χρύσιππος ἐν τῷ πρώτῳ Περὶ τελῶν, πρῶτον οἰκεῖον εἶναι λέγων παντὶ ζῴῳ τὴν αὐτοῦ σύστασιν καὶ τὴν ταύτης συνείδησιν· οὔτε γὰρ ἀλλοτριῶσαι εἰκὸς ἦν αὐτὸ τὸ ζῷον, οὔτε ποιήσασαν αὐτό μήτ' ἀλλοτριῶσαι μήτ' οἰκειῶσαι. ἀπολείπεται τοίνυν λέγειν συστησαμένην αὐτὸ οἰκειῶσαι πρὸς ἑαυτό· οὕτω γὰρ τά τε βλάπτοντα διωθεῖται καὶ τὰ οἰκεῖα προσίεται. ὃ δὲ λέγουσί τινες, πρὸς ἡδονὴν γίγνεσθαι τὴν πρώτην ὁρμὴν τοῖς ζῴοις, ψεῦδος ἀποφαίνουσιν.

The oikeiosis is common to man and irrational animals.

b.   Cic., *De Fin.* III 16:

Placet his quorum ratio mihi probatur, simulatque natum sit animal, ipsum sibi conciliari et commendari [1] ad se conservandum et ad suum statum [2] eaque quae conservantia sint eius status diligenda, alienari [3] autem ab interitu iisque rebus quae interitum videantur afferre.

c.   Hierocles I 38:

Διὸ φαίνεται τὸ ζῷον ἅμα τῇ γενέσει αἰσθάνεσθαί τε αὐτοῦ καὶ οἰκειοῦσθαι ἑαυτῷ καὶ τῇ ἑαυτοῦ συστάσει.

That the doctrine reaches back to Zeno, is argued by Pohlenz (*Zeno u. Chrysipp*, p. 199 ff.) against Dirlmeier. The doctrine is found in Arius Didymus' account of peripatetic ethics, which according to H. von Arnim [4] goes back directly to Theophrastus. Against this Dirlmeier [5] argued that, because (on p. 126, 12 ff. of the treatise) Critolaus is referred to, it must go back to a later peripatetic. He agrees however with von Arnim in ascribing the oikeiosis-doctrine to Theophrastus: from him it was borrowed by the peripatetic who was Arius Didymus' source. Pohlenz, *Grundfragen*, p. 8 ff., argues on good grounds that Didymus' source was "contaminated" with Stoic doctrine and terminology, Didymus being also influenced by the Stoa on other points. For these reasons Pohlenz maintains the Stoic origin of the doctrine of oikeiosis. See further below, under **999c**.

Instinct
and reason   **946**—The Stoa makes a sharp distinction between non rational animals and man.

---

[1]   *sibi conciliari et commendari* is Cicero's translation of οἰκειοῦσθαι.
[2]   σύστασιν.
[3]   ἀλλοτριοῦσθαι.
[4]   H. von Arnim, *Arius Didymus' Abriss der peripatetischen Ethik*, Sitzungsberichte Wien, Philol.-hist. Kl. 204 (1926), 3.
[5]   O. Dirlmeier, *Die Oikeiosislehre Theophrasts*, in *Philologus*, Suppl. XXX (1937), nr. 1.

a. Origenes, *Contra Celsum* IV 87 (SVF II 725):

Ἔστω δὲ καὶ ἄλλα ὑπὸ τῶν ζῴων γιγνώσκεσθαι ἀλεξιφάρμακα, τί οὖν τοῦτο πρὸς τὸ μὴ φύσιν ἀλλὰ λόγον εἶναι τὸν εὑρίσκοντα ταῦτα ἐν τοῖς ζῴοις; εἰ μὲν γὰρ λόγος ἦν ὁ εὑρίσκων, οὐκ ἂν ἀποτεταγμένως τόδε τι μόνον εὑρίσκετο ἐν ὄφεσιν, ἔστω καὶ δεύτερον καὶ τρίτον, καὶ ἄλλο τι ἐν ἀετῷ καὶ οὕτως ἐν τοῖς λοιποῖς ζῴοις· ἀλλὰ τοσαῦτα ἂν ὅσα καὶ ἐν ἀνθρώποις· νυνὶ δὲ φανερὸν ἐκ τοῦ ἀποτεταγμένως πρός τινα ἑκάστου φύσιν ζῴου νενευκέναι βοηθήματα, ὅτι οὐ σοφία οὐδὲ λόγος ἐστὶν ἐν αὐτοῖς, ἀλλά τις φυσικὴ πρὸς τὰ τοιάδε σωτηρίας ἕνεκεν τῶν ζῴων κατασκευή, ὑπὸ τοῦ λόγου γεγενημένη.

b. Philo, *De animalibus adv. Alex.*, p. 147 Aucher (SVF II 726):

Canis cum persequebatur feram, perveniens ad fossam profundam, iuxta quam duae erant semitae, una ad dextram, altera in sinistram, paululum se sistens, quo ire oporteat, meditabatur. Currens autem ad dexteram et nullum inveniens vestigium, reversus per alteram ibat. Quando vero neque in ista aperte appareret aliquod signum, transiliens fossam curiose indagat, praeter odoratum cursum accelerans; satis declarans non obiter haec facere, sed potius vera inquisitione consilii. Consilium autem talis cogitationis dialectici appellant demonstrativum evidens quinti modi: "Quoniam vel ad dextram fera fugit vel ad sinistram aut demum transsiliit, <atqui neque ad dextram fugit neque ad sinistram; ergo transsiliit>."

Idem p. 166 Aucher. Proscribenda et opinio eorum, qui canem venaticum bestias persequentem autumarunt quinto argumenti modo uti. Idem dicendum de collectoribus conchyliorum deque quaerentibus quidquam; indicia enim rerum sequentur, apparenter sub specie dialectica, verum tamen nec per somnium quidem philosophentur; alioquin dicendum esset de omnibus aliquid quaerentibus, quod quintum illum modum usurpent. —

Nos enim dicimus, quod ex decentibus bonisque sibi convenientibus multisque rebus iuvantibus ad sanitatem perseverationemque valetudinis habent appetitionem et universali comprehensione universorum carentes eam possident certitudinem, quae in propria specie cernitur. Verum tamen rationalis habitus necesse est illa nullam habere participationem. Rationalis autem habitus est syllogismus ex apprehensione entium, quae minime adsunt; ut intellectus de deo, de mundo, de lege, de patrio more, de civitate, de politica — quorum nihil percipiunt bestiae.

c. Cp. Plut., *De E apud Delphos*, p. 386 f.:

Τῆς μὲν ὑπάρξεως τῶν πραγμάτων ἔχει καὶ τὰ θηρία γνῶσιν, ἀκολούθου δὲ...
κρίσιν ἀνθρώπῳ μόνῳ παραδέδωκεν ἡ φύσις.

**The soul
of man**

947—a. Zeno distinguishes eight "parts" or faculties of the soul
of man.

Nemesius, *De natura hominis* p. 96 (SVF I 143):

Ζήνων δὲ ὁ Στωϊκὸς ὀκταμερῆ φησιν εἶναι τὴν ψυχήν, διαιρῶν αὐτὴν εἰς
τε τὸ ἡγεμονικὸν καὶ εἰς τὰς πέντε αἰσθήσεις καὶ εἰς τὸ φωνητικὸν καὶ τὸ
σπερματικόν.

**Its eight
parts or
faculties**

b. Aëtius explains the division as it was made by Chrysippus.
Aëtius, *Plac.* IV 21 (SVF II 836):

Πόθεν αἰσθητικὴ γίνεται ἡ ψυχὴ καὶ τί αὐτῆς τὸ ἡγεμονικόν. Οἱ
Στωϊκοί φασιν εἶναι τῆς ψυχῆς ἀνώτατον μέρος τὸ ἡγεμονικόν, τὸ ποιοῦν
τὰς φαντασίας καὶ συγκαταθέσεις καὶ αἰσθήσεις καὶ ὁρμάς· καὶ τοῦτο λογισμὸν
καλοῦσιν. — Ἀπὸ δὲ τοῦ ἡγεμονικοῦ ἑπτὰ μέρη ἐστὶ τῆς ψυχῆς ἐκπεφυκότα
καὶ ἐκτεινόμενα εἰς τὸ σῶμα καθάπερ αἱ ἀπὸ τοῦ πολύποδος πλεκτάναι· τῶν
δὲ ἑπτὰ μερῶν τῆς ψυχῆς πέντε μέν εἰσι τὰ αἰσθητήρια, ὅρασις ὄσφρησις ἀκοὴ
γεῦσις καὶ ἀφή. — Ὧν ἡ μὲν ὅρασίς ἐστι πνεῦμα διατεῖνον ἀπὸ τοῦ ἡγεμονικοῦ
μέχρις ὀφθαλμῶν, ἀκοὴ δὲ πνεῦμα διατεῖνον ἀπὸ τοῦ ἡγεμονικοῦ μέχρις ὤτων,
ὄσφρησις δὲ πνεῦμα διατεῖνον ἀπὸ τοῦ ἡγεμονικοῦ μέχρι μυκτήρων [λεπτῦνον],
γεῦσις δὲ πνεῦμα διατεῖνον ἀπὸ τοῦ ἡγεμονικοῦ μέχρι γλώττης, ἀφὴ δὲ πνεῦμα
διατεῖνον ἀπὸ τοῦ ἡγεμονικοῦ μέχρις ἐπιφανείας εἰς θίξιν εὐαίσθητον τῶν
προσπιπτόντων. — Τῶν δὲ λοιπῶν τὸ μὲν λέγεται σπέρμα, ὅπερ καὶ αὐτὸ
πνεῦμά ἐστι διατεῖνον ἀπὸ τοῦ ἡγεμονικοῦ μέχρι τῶν παραστατῶν· τὸ δὲ
"φωνᾶεν" ὑπὸ τοῦ Ζήνωνος εἰρημένον, ὃ καὶ φωνὴν καλοῦσιν, ἔστι πνεῦμα
διατεῖνον ἀπὸ τοῦ ἡγεμονικοῦ μέχρι φάρυγγος καὶ γλώττης καὶ τῶν οἰκείων
ὀργάνων. αὐτὸ δὲ τὸ ἡγεμονικὸν ὥσπερ ἐν κόσμῳ <ἥλιος> κατοικεῖ ἐν τῇ
ἡμετέρᾳ σφαιροειδεῖ κεφαλῇ.

c. Cp. the quotation of Chrysippus in *Chalcidius*, in *Tim.* c. 220
(SVF II 879):

Porro animae partes velut ex capite fontis cordis sede manantes per
universum corpus porriguntur omniaque membra usque quaque vitali
spiritu complent reguntque et moderantur innumerabilibus diversisque
virtutibus nutriendo, adolendo, movendo, motibus localibus instruendo,
sensibus compellendo ad operandum, totaque anima sensus, qui sunt
eius officia, velut ramos ex principali parte illa tamquam trabe pandit,

futuros eorum quae sentiunt nuntios, ipsa de iis quae nuntiaverint
iudicat ut rex.

The same image is used by St. Augustine.

948—Zeno, and after him Chrysippus, placed the hegemonikon in **The seat of the hegemonikon**
the heart.

    a. *Chalc.*, in *Tim.* c. 220 (SVF II 879 the beginning):

Stoici vero cor quidem sedem esse principalis animae partis consen-
tiunt, nec tamen sanguinem, qui cum corpore nascitur.

    b. Chalcidius (in the same chapter) cites Chrysippus in this way:

Sicut aranea in medietate cassis omnia filorum tenet pedibus exordia,
ut, cum quid ex bestiolis plagas incurrerit ex quacunque parte, de
proximo sentiat, sic animae principale, positum in media sede cordis,
sensuum exordia retinere, ut cum quid nuntiabunt de proximo recog-
noscat.

    c. Not long before Chrysippus Herophilus of Alexandria discovered
the nervous system and the function of the brain. The following passage
of Chrysippus refers to the discussions about the seat of the hegemonikon
going on in those days.

    Galenus, *De Hippocr. et Platonis Plac.* III 1 (112), p. 251 Müller (SVF
II 885):

Ἡ ψυχὴ πνεῦμά ἐστι σύμφυτον ἡμῖν συνεχὲς παντὶ τῷ σώματι διῆκον,
ἔστ' ἂν ἡ τῆς ζωῆς εὔπνοια παρῇ ἐν τῷ σώματι. ταύτης οὖν τῶν μερῶν ἑκάστῳ
διατεταγμένων μορίῳ, τὸ διῆκον αὐτῆς εἰς τὴν τραχεῖαν ἀρτηρίαν φωνήν
<φαμεν> εἶναι, τὸ δὲ εἰς ὀφθαλμοὺς ὄψιν, τὸ δὲ εἰς ὦτα ἀκοήν, τὸ δὲ εἰς ῥῖνας
ὄσφρησιν, τὸ δ' εἰς γλῶτταν γεῦσιν, τὸ δ' εἰς ὅλην τὴν σάρκα ἁφήν, καὶ τὸ
εἰς ὄρχεις ἕτερόν τιν' ἔχον τοιοῦτον λόγον σπερματικόν, εἰς ὃ δὲ συμβαίνει
πάντα ταῦτα, ἐν τῇ καρδίᾳ εἶναι, μέρος ὂν αὐτῆς τὸ ἡγεμονικόν. οὕτω δὲ
ἐχόντων αὐτῶν, τὰ μὲν λοιπὰ συμφωνεῖται, περὶ δὲ τοῦ ἡγεμονικοῦ μέρους
τῆς ψυχῆς διαφωνοῦσιν, ἄλλοι ἐν ἄλλοις λέγοντες αὐτὸ εἶναι τόποις. οἱ μὲν
γὰρ περὶ τὸν θώρακά φασιν εἶναι αὐτό, οἱ δὲ περὶ τὴν κεφαλήν.

949—Chrysippus supports Zeno's thesis by the following arguments. **Chrysippus' arguments**
    a. Thinking must be situated in the place whence the word comes.
Galenus, o.c. II 5 (98), p. 203 M. (SVF II 894):

Εὔλογον δέ, εἰς ὃ γίγνονται αἱ ἐν τούτῳ [1] σημασίαι, καὶ ἐξ οὗ <ὁ> λόγος,

---

[1] Müller seems to have found difficulties in the ἐν τούτῳ and brackets it. In

ἐκεῖνο εἶναι τὸ κυριεῦον τῆς ψυχῆς μέρος. οὐ γὰρ ἄλλη μὲν [ἡ] πηγὴ λόγου
ἐστίν, ἄλλη δὲ διανοίας, οὐδὲ ἄλλη μὲν φωνῆς πηγή, ἄλλη δὲ λόγου, οὐδὲ τὸ
ὅλον ἁπλῶς ἄλλη φωνῆς πηγή ἐστιν, ἄλλο δὲ τὸ κυριεῦον τῆς ψυχῆς μέρος. —
τοιούτοις δὲ καὶ τὴν διάνοιαν συμφώνως ἀφοριζόμενοι λέγουσιν αὐτὴν πηγὴν
εἶναι λόγου. — Τὸ γὰρ ὅλον ὅθεν ὁ λόγος ἐκπέμπεται, ἐκεῖσε δεῖ καὶ τὸν δια-
λογισμὸν γίγνεσθαι καὶ τὰς διανοήσεις καὶ τὰς μελέτας τῶν ῥήσεων, καθάπερ
ἔφην. ταῦτα δὲ ἐκφανῶς περὶ τὴν καρδίαν γίγνεται, ἐκ τῆς καρδίας διὰ φάρυγγος
καὶ τῆς φωνῆς καὶ τοῦ λόγου ἐκπεμπομένων. πιθανὸν δὲ καὶ ἄλλως, εἰς ὃ
ἐνσημαίνεται τὰ λεγόμενα, καὶ σημαίνεσθαι ἐκεῖθεν, καὶ τὰς φωνὰς ἀπ' ἐκείνου
γίγνεσθαι κατὰ τὸν προειρημένον τρόπον.

b. In saying "I am it", we usually point to the breast.

Galenus, o.c. II 2, p. 172 M. (SVF II 895):

Οὕτως δὲ καὶ τὸ ἐγὼ λέγομεν κατὰ τοῦτο, δεικνύντες αὐτοὺς ἐν τῷ <λέγειν·
"ἐμοὶ τοῦτο προσήκει, τοῦτο ἐγώ σοι λέγω" εἰς τὸ> ἀποφαίνεσθαι <ἐκεῖ>
τὴν διάνοιαν εἶναι [1], τῆς δείξεως φυσικῶς καὶ οἰκείως ἐνταῦθα φερομένης.

c. Chrysippus adduced even a selfmade etymology in support of
his thesis.

Galenus, o.c. III 5 (124), p. 295 M. (SVF II 896):

Τούτοις πᾶσι συμφώνως καὶ τοὔνομα τοῦτ' ἔσχηκεν ἡ καρδία κατά τινα
κράτησιν καὶ κυρείαν, ἀπὸ τοῦ ἐν αὐτῇ εἶναι τὸ κυριεῦον καὶ κρατοῦν τῆς
ψυχῆς μέρος, ὡς ἂν κρατία λεγομένη.

d. Besides these arguments Chrys. could cite a good number of
verses of Homer and of other poets in support of his thesis, and Galenus
shows us that he did (SVF II 890, 904-906). We mention only *Od.*
XX 17 f.:

Στῆθος δὲ πλήξας κραδίην ἠνίπαπε μύθῳ·
Τέτλαθι δὴ κραδίη, καὶ κύντερον ἄλλο ποτ' ἔτλης.

Chrysippus tries to refute Herophilus

950—Chrysippus tries to refute Herophilus, who holds that the
brain is the seat of the hegemonikon.

a. Galenus, o.c. II 5 (102), p. 215 M. (SVF II 898):

Παραγράψω δὲ καὶ τὴν ῥῆσιν αὐτήν, ἐν ᾗ δείκνυσιν ὁ Χρύσιππος,

---

my opinion it is an instance of the well known paratactical construction, the
meaning of the sentence being: εἰς ὃ καὶ ἐν ᾧ γίγνονται αἱ σημασίαι (to put it in bad
Greek).

[1] Müller restituted the text by adding λέγειν — εἰς τὸ between ἐν τῷ and ἀποφαίνεσθαι. It seems necessary to me to add ἐκεῖ after ἀποφαίνεσθαι.

ὡς οὐκ ἔστιν ὁ προγεγραμμένος λόγος ἀποδεικτικός. ἔστι δὲ τοιάδε·
'"Ἔχει δ' ὡς ἔφην πλείονα αὐτοῖς ἐπὶ πᾶσι, μήποτ' εἰ καὶ τοῦτο δοθείη,
καθάπερ ἐπιπορεύονται, ἀπὸ τῆς κεφαλῆς εἶναι τὴν ἀρχὴν ἐπὶ τὰ εἰρημένα
μέρη, ἐπιζητήσομεν. σχεδὸν γάρ, οἷα ἄν τινα λέγοιεν περὶ τοῦ τὴν φωνὴν ἐκ
τοῦ στήθους φέρεσθαι διὰ τῆς φάρυγγος, ἀπὸ τῆς κεφαλῆς ποιᾶς τινος καταρ-
χῆς γιγνομένης, τοιαῦτ' ἔξεστι λέγειν, ἐν τῇ καρδίᾳ μὲν τοῦ ἡγεμονικοῦ ὄντος,
τῆς δὲ τῶν κινήσεων ἀρχῆς ἀπὸ τῆς κεφαλῆς οὔσης."

b. Galenus in introducing this passage remarks that, being in
fact forced to grant his opponent's argument, Chrysippus prefers to
destroy his own with it. Ib., the beginning:

Κατὰ μὲν γὰρ ἄλλην τινὰ (sc. ῥῆσιν) μετ' οὐ πάνυ πολὺ ταύτης γεγραμμένην
ἠναγκάσθη τὸ ἀληθὲς ὁμολογῆσαι. ἀναγκασθῆναι δὲ εἶπον αὐτόν, ὅτι λόγον
ἕτερον ἀνατρέψαι βουλόμενος ὡς οὐκ ἀληθῆ, κἄπειτα τὸ τῆς ἀντιλογίας εἶδος
αἰσθόμενος οὐδὲν ἧττον ἐπιστρέψον καὶ καθ' ἑαυτοῦ, συνανατρέψαι καὶ τὸν
ἴδιον οὐκ ὤκνησε τῷ τῶν ἑτεροδόξων.

c. Galenus concludes, after having cited the passage and explained
it (ib., p. 224 M.):

Ταῦτα μὲν οὖν ὀρθῶς εἴρηται τῷ Χρυσίππῳ καὶ διὰ τοῦτο ἄν τις αὐτῷ καὶ
μᾶλλον μέμψαιτο, διότι κατιδὼν τὸ ἀληθὲς ὅμως οὐ χρῆται· τὰ δὲ ἀπὸ τῆς
θέσεως ἐπικεχειρημένα, καὶ τούτων μᾶλλον ὅσα ποιηταὶ μαρτυροῦσιν ἢ οἱ
πολλοὶ τῶν ἀνθρώπων ἢ ἐτυμολογία τις ἤ τι τοιοῦτον ἕτερον, οὐκ ὀρθῶς.

951—Everything which happens in the soul—φαντασίαι, ὁρμαί, πάθη—
is explained by Chrysippus as a ἑτεροίωσις τῆς ψυχῆς. Zeno speaks of
a τύπωσις. Ὁρμή is explained in this way.

a. Philo, *Quod deus sit immut.* 41 (SVF II 458):

Τὸ δὲ φανὲν καὶ τυπῶσαν τότε μὲν οἰκείως, τότε δὲ ὡς ἑτέρως διέθηκε τὴν
ψυχήν. Τοῦτο δ' αὐτῆς τὸ πάθος ὁρμὴ καλεῖται, ἣν ὁριζόμενοι πρώτην ἔφασαν
εἶναι ψυχῆς κίνησιν.

b. Stob., *Ecl.* II 86, 17 W. (SVF III 169):

Τὴν δὲ ὁρμὴν εἶναι φ ο ρ ὰ ν ψ υ χ ῆ ς ἐ π ί τι κατὰ τὸ γένος. ταύτης
δ' ἐν εἴδει θεωρεῖσθαι τήν τε ἐν τοῖς λογικοῖς γιγνομένην ὁρμὴν καὶ τὴν ἐν
τοῖς ἀλόγοις ζῴοις· οὐ κατωνομασμέναι δ' εἰσίν· ἡ γὰρ ὄρεξις οὐκ ἔστι λογικὴ
ὁρμή, ἀλλὰ λογικῆς ὁρμῆς εἶδος.

Τὴν δὲ λογικὴν ὁρμὴν δεόντως ἄν τις ἀφορίζοιτο, λέγων εἶναι φορὰν διανοίας ἐπί τι τῶν ἐν τῷ πράττειν· ταύτῃ δ' ἀντιτίθεσθαι ἀφορμήν, φοράν τινα
<διανοίας ἀπό τινος τῶν ἐν τῷ πράττειν>.

c. Cf. Clem. Alex., *Strom.* II 13, p. 145 St. (SVF III 377):

Ὁρμὴ μὲν οὖν φορὰ διανοίας ἐπί τι ἢ ἀπό του.

πάθος **952—a.** In the same passage πάθος is defined:

Clem. Alex., ib.:

Πάθος δὲ πλεονάζουσα ὁρμὴ ἢ ὑπερτείνουσα τὰ κατὰ τὸν λόγον μέτρα· ἢ
ὁρμὴ ὁρμὴ ἐκφερομένη καὶ ἀπειθὴς λόγῳ. Παρὰ φύσιν οὖν κινήσεις ψυχῆς κατὰ
πλεονάζουσα τὴν πρὸς τὸν λόγον ἀπείθειαν τὰ πάθη.

b. Cf. Diog. VII 110 (SVF I 205):

Ἔστι δὲ αὐτὸ τὸ πάθος κατὰ Ζήνωνα ἡ ἄλογος καὶ παρὰ φύσιν ψυχῆς
κίνησις, ἢ ὁρμὴ πλεονάζουσα.

c. Again, in Stob., *Ecl.* II 7, 10, p. 88, 8 W.:

Πάθος δ' εἶναί φασιν ὁρμὴν πλεονάζουσαν καὶ ἀπειθῆ τῷ αἱροῦντι λόγῳ
ἢ κίνησιν ψυχῆς <ἄλογον> παρὰ φύσιν.

On the ground of this text Zeller defended the irrationality of the πάθη according
to Zeno. After him R. Philippson supported the same thesis (in *Rhein. Mus.* 86,
1937, p. 140-179), but his argument is not conclusive. See under **953d.**

d. Stob., Ib. 7, 1, p. 39, 5 W.:

πτοία Ὡρίσατο δὲ κἀκείνως· "πάθος ἐστὶ πτοία ψυχῆς", ἀπὸ τῆς τῶν πτηνῶν
φορᾶς τὸ εὐκίνητον τοῦ παθητικοῦ παρεικάσας.

Chrysippus' **953**—Chrysippus' doctrine that all psychical functions, actions and
theory qualities—not only φαντασία, ὁρμή and πάθος, but also knowledge, virtue
and vice, and even walking—are a certain state or condition of the
hegemonikon, appears in the following passages.

a. Plut., *De virtute morali* c. 3, p. 441c (SVF III 459):

Κοινῶς δὲ ἄπαντες οὗτοι (sc. Zeno, Aristo, Menedemus and Chrysippus [1])
τὴν ἀρετὴν τοῦ ἡγεμονικοῦ τῆς ψυχῆς διάθεσίν τινα καὶ δύναμιν, γεγενημένην
ὑπὸ λόγου, μᾶλλον δὲ λόγον οὖσαν αὐτὴν ὁμολογούμενον καὶ βέβαιον καὶ
ἀμετάπτωτον, ὑποτίθενται· καὶ νομίζουσιν οὐκ εἶναι τὸ παθητικὸν καὶ ἄλογον
διαφορᾷ τινι καὶ φύσει ψυχῆς τοῦ λογικοῦ διακεκριμένον, ἀλλὰ τὸ αὐτὸ τῆς
ψυχῆς μέρος, ὃ δὴ καλοῦσι διάνοιαν καὶ ἡγεμονικόν, διόλου τρεπόμενον καὶ

---

[1] Plutarchus gives it certainly as an ancient Stoic theory. This means: he
explains Zeno's ἄλογος κίνησις in such a way, that soul would not contain any irrational part. Doubtless, this was Chrysippus' view. Whether it was Zeno's too, is
a more complicated question.

μεταβάλλον ἔν τε τοῖς πάθεσι καὶ ταῖς κατὰ ἕξιν ἢ διάθεσιν μεταβολαῖς, κακίαν
τε γίγνεσθαι καὶ ἀρετήν, καὶ μηδὲν ἔχειν ἄλογον ἐν ἑαυτῷ· λέγεσθαι δὲ ἄλογον,
ὅταν τῷ πλεονάζοντι τῆς ὁρμῆς, ἰσχυρῷ γενομένῳ καὶ κρατήσαντι, πρός τι
τῶν ἀτόπων παρὰ τὸν αἱροῦντα λόγον ἐκφέρηται· καὶ γὰρ τὸ πάθος εἶναι λόγον
πονηρὸν καὶ ἀκόλαστον, ἐκ φαύλης καὶ διημαρτημένης κρίσεως σφοδρότητα
καὶ ῥώμην προσλαβούσης.

b. Thus Clem. Alex., *Strom.* II 16, p. 151 St., calls such feelings
as χαρά and ἔλεος, τροπὰς ψυχῆς (SVF III 433):

Τὴν μὲν γὰρ χαρὰν εὔλογον ἔπαρσιν ἀποδιδόασι· καὶ τὸ ἀγάλλεσθαι χαίρειν
ἐπὶ καλοῖς· τὸ δὲ ἔλεος λύπην ἐπὶ ἀναξίως κακοπαθοῦντι· τροπὰς δὲ εἶναι
ψυχῆς καὶ πάθη τὰ τοιαῦτα.

c. Alex. Aphrod., *De anima libri mant.*, p. 118, 6 Bruns (SVF II 823): ψυχή πως
ἔχουσα
"Ὅτι μὴ "μία ἡ τῆς ψυχῆς δύναμις, ὡς τὴν αὐτήν πως ἔχουσαν ποτὲ μὲν
διανοεῖσθαι, ποτὲ δὲ ὀργίζεσθαι, ποτὲ δ' ἐπιθυμεῖν παρὰ μέρος", δεικτέον.

d. Cp. Stob., *Ecl.* I 49, 33, p. 368, 17 W.:

Ὥσπερ γὰρ τὸ μῆλον ἐν τῷ αὐτῷ σώματι τὴν γλυκύτητα ἔχει καὶ τὴν
εὐωδίαν, οὕτω καὶ τὸ ἡγεμονικὸν ἐν ταὐτῷ φαντασίαν, συγκατάθεσιν, ὁρμήν,
λόγον συνείληφε.

According to this theory all ὁρμαί are essentially rational, and there is no irrational part in the soul.—If this was also Zeno's view, his definition of πάθος as
κίνησις ψυχῆς ἄλογος must be explained in this sense that the πάθη are essentially
rational but accidentally revolting against reason [1].

954—a. The "rational" interpretation of Zeno's definition of πάθος Did Zeno
might seem to be supported by the following text. hold that
πάθη
Themistius, *De anima* 90b, Spengel II 197, 24 (SVF I 208): are
κρίσεις?
Καὶ οὐ κακῶς οἱ ἀπὸ Ζήνωνος τὰ πάθη τῆς ἀνθρωπίνης ψυχῆς τοῦ λόγου
διαστροφὰς εἶναι τιθέμενοι καὶ λόγου κρίσεις ἡμαρτημένας.

b. But in fact, Posidonius' controversy against Chrysippus' intellectualism, preserved in Galenus' *De placitis Hippocratis et Platonis*,
gives us reason to doubt of the correctness of this interpretation.

Galenus, o.c. V 1, p. 405 Müller:

Χρύσιππος μὲν οὖν ἐν τῷ πρώτῳ Περὶ παθῶν ἀποδεικνύναι πειρᾶται κρίσεις

---

[1] Thus, M. van Straaten, *Panaetius*, p. 108 ff. The author refers to Pohlenz'
earlier study *Antikes Führertum* (1934) and to R. Philippson's article in the *Rhein.
Mus.* 1937, but apparently he does not know Pohlenz' later study *Zenon u. Chrysipp.*
See our following numbers.

τινὰς εἶναι τὰ πάθη, Ζήνων δὲ οὐ τὰς κρίσεις αὐτάς, ἀλλὰ τὰς ἐπιγινομένας αὐταῖς συστολὰς καὶ διαχύσεις ἐπάρσεις τε καὶ πτώσεις τῆς ψυχῆς ἐνόμιζεν εἶναι τὰ πάθη.

From this and similar texts Pohlenz infers that, while for Zeno the πάθη were irrational, Chrysippus rationalized them, in behalf of his theory of the unity of the hegemonikon (Pohlenz, *Zeno u. Chrys.* p. 188 f..).

λύπη
defined as
δόξα
πρόσφατος

955—Again, Zeno's definition of λύπη might be cited in favour of his intellectualism.

    a. Galenus, *De Plac. Hipp. et Plat.* IV 7, p. 391 M. (SVF I 212):
Δόξαν γὰρ εἶναι πρόσφατον τοῦ κακὸν αὐτῷ παρεῖναί φησι τὴν λύπην.

Pohlenz explains this formula as a brachylogy: Zeno had so often and so clearly defined πάθος in a non rationalistic way, that he needed not always add "the feelings accompanying" δόξα.

Opinion the
cause of
πάθη

    b. The "opinion" which produces the affect is not truth, but error: it is a perversion of reason (τοῦ λόγου διαστροφαί and κρίσεις ἡμαρτημέναι). Thus Cicero could say in *Tusc.* IV 37, 80:

Ut constantia scientiae, sic perturbatio erroris est.

    c. Cf. *Tusc.* III 11, 24, where he says that *the cause* of *aegritudo* and of all perturbations is in "opinion":

Nam cum omnis perturbatio sit animi motus vel rationis expers vel rationem aspernans vel rationi non oboediens, isque motus aut boni aut mali opinione citetur, bifariam quattuor perturbationes aequaliter distributae sunt.

And having described these four as *praeter modum elata laetitia* and *libido* on the one hand, *metus and aegritudo* on the other [1], he goes on:

(Ib. 25) His autem perturbationibus, quas in vitam hominum stultitia quasi quasdam furias immittit atque incitat, omnibus viribus atque opibus repugnandum est, si volumus hoc quod datum est vitae tranquille placideque traducere.

Treatment
This statement, then, gives an indication for the treatment of the perturbations: it is *persuasion*. E.g. in the case of libido. *Tusc.* IV 35, 74:

Sic igitur affecto haec adhibenda curatio est, ut et illud quod cupiat ostendatur quam leve, quam contemnendum, quam nihil sit omnino, quam facile vel aliunde vel alio modo perfici, vel omnino neglegi possit. Abducendus est etiam nonnumquam ad alia studia, sollicitudines, curas,

---

[1] The four πάθη were, according to Zeno's doctrine: λύπη, φόβος, ἐπιθυμία, ἡδονή (Diog. VII 110; Stob., *Ecl.* II 7, 10).

negotia. Loci denique mutatione, tamquam aegroti non convalescentes, saepe curandus est.

956—a. That Chrysippus really changed the meaning of Zeno's formulas, as is argued by Posidonius, appears also in Sextus' treatment of the Stoic doctrine of φαντασία, ὁρμή etc. He remarks that, while Zeno explains presentation as an *impression* in the soul (τύπωσις), Chrysippus speaks of an *alteration* of the ruling part (ἑτεροίωσις ἐν ἡγεμονικῷ): *Ag. the Logicians* I 233 (see below our nr. **986b**). **Chrysippus altered the sense of Zeno's formulas**

Sextus, *Adv. Math.* VII (*Ag. the Log.* I) 237:
Καὶ γὰρ ἡ ὁρμὴ καὶ ἡ συγκατάθεσις καὶ ἡ κατάληψις ἑτεροιώσεις μέν εἰσι τοῦ ἡγεμονικοῦ.

b. Cp. also the discussion between Cleanthes and Chrysippus on the nature of "walking".
Seneca, *Ep.* 113, 18 (SVF I 525):
Inter Cleanthem et discipulum eius Chrysippum non convenit quid sit ambulatio: Cleanthes ait spiritum esse a principali usque in pedes permissum; Chrysippus ipsum principale.
Which means that Chrysippus—not yet Cleanthes—explained "walking" too as "the ἡγεμονικόν πως ἔχον".

c. That Cleanthes did not conceive the πάθη as a part of reason, was deduced by Posidonius from the following verses of Cleanthes (SVF I 570), where a dialogue is held between λογισμός and θυμός:
ΛΟΓ. Τί ποτ' ἔσθ' ὃ βούλει, θυμέ; τοῦτό μοι φράσον.
ΘΥΜ. <Σ>έ γ', ὦ λογισμέ, πᾶν ὃ βούλομαι ποιεῖν.
ΛΟΓ. Βασιλικὸν <εἶ>πε<ς>· πλὴν ὅμως εἰπὸν πάλιν.
ΘΥΜ. Ὦν ἂν ἐπιθυμῶ, ταῦθ' ὅπως γενήσεται.

Zeller thinks the argument not conclusive, but Pohlenz (*Stoa* I p. 91) rightly remarks that the obvious sense of Cleanthes' words is as Posidonius understands them.

957—When reading in Epiphanius, as cited under **920b**, that Zeno said noûs is immortal, we certainly do not have to imagine that he meant, *a part of soul*, say the hegemonikon, is immortal. When speaking of noûs in the above cited passage Zeno means the *cosmic pneuma* or πῦρ νοερόν which he calls God. Now surely this pneuma is in man (and even in every being), but as we saw above (**916a**), "cooled". What Zeno thought about the durability of this cooled pneuma which is soul, is this: **The soul not immortal**

a. Epiphanius, *Adv. Haer.* III 2, 26 (SVF I 146):

Ἔλεγε δὲ καὶ μετὰ χωρισμὸν τοῦ σώματος ‹χρόνον τινὰ διαμένειν› [1] καὶ ἐκάλει τὴν ψυχὴν πολυχρόνιον πνεῦμα, οὐ μὴν δὲ ἄφθαρτον δι' ὅλου ἔλεγεν αὐτὴν εἶναι. ἐκδαπανᾶται γὰρ ὑπὸ τοῦ πολλοῦ χρόνου εἰς τὸ ἀφανές, ὥς φησι.

b. Cf. Arius Didymus, *Epit. phys.* fr. 39 Diels (SVF II 809):

Τὴν δὲ ψυχὴν γενητήν τε καὶ φθαρτὴν λέγουσιν. οὐκ εὐθὺς δὲ τοῦ σώματος ἀπαλλαγεῖσαν φθείρεσθαι, ἀλλ' ἐπιμένειν τινὰς χρόνους καθ' ἑαυτήν· τὴν μὲν τῶν σπουδαίων μέχρι τῆς εἰς πῦρ ἀναλύσεως τῶν πάντων, τὴν δὲ τῶν ἀφρόνων πρὸς ποσούς τινας χρόνους. — Τὰς δὲ τῶν ἀφρόνων καὶ ἀλόγων ζῴων ψυχὰς συναπόλλυσθαι τοῖς σώμασι.

c. Diog. VII 157:

Κλεάνθης μὲν οὖν πάσας ἐπιδιαμένειν μέχρι τῆς ἐκπυρώσεως, Χρύσιππος δὲ τὰς τῶν σοφῶν μόνον.

958—Panaetius, influenced by the sceptic criticism of Carneades, draws a stricter consequence from the Stoic materialism.

a. Cic., *Tusc. Disp.* I 32, 79:

Vult enim, quod nemo negat, quidquid natum sit, interire: nasci autem animos, quod declaret eorum similitudo, qui procreentur: quae etiam in ingeniis, non solum in corporibus, appareat.

b. Ib.:

Alteram autem affert rationem: nihil esse, quod doleat, quin id aegrum esse quoque possit: quod autem in morbum cadat, id etiam interiturum; dolere autem animos; ergo etiam interire.

In this Cic. follows Posidonius, who accepted Plato's tripartition of soul and considered the hegemonikon as immortal.

959—Contrary to Panaetius, Posidonius held that soul does not come into being with the body, but enters into it θύραθεν (like Aristotle said in *De gen. anim.* II 3), while after death it ascends into aether and feeds on the same substance as the stars [2].

a. Cic., *Tusc.* I 18, 42-19, 43:

The soul, by its fiery nature, must seek higher regions.

Calidior est enim vel potius ardentior animus quam est hic aër, quem modo dixi crassum atque concretum, quod ex eo sciri potest, quia cor-

---

[1] Something like this must have been dropped (restitution of Diels).
[2] Cp. our nr. *431 d*.

pora nostra terreno principiorum genere confecta ardore animi concalescunt. Accedit ut eo facilius animus evadat ex hoc aëre, quem saepe iam appello, eumque perrumpat, quod nihil est animo velocius, nulla est celeritas quae possit cum animi celeritate contendere. Qui si permanet incorruptus suique similis, necesse est ita feratur, ut penetret et dividat omne caelum hoc, in quo nubes imbres ventique coguntur, quod et umidum et caliginosum est propter exhalationes terrae.

Quam regionem cum superavit animus naturamque sui similem contigit et adgnovit, iunctis ex anima tenui et ex ardore solis temperato ignibus insistit et finem altius se ecferendi facit. Cum enim sui similem et levitatem et calorem adeptus est, tamquam paribus examinatus ponderibus nullam in partem movetur, eaque ei demum naturalis est sedes, cum ad sui simile penetravit; in quo nulla re egens aletur et sustentabitur isdem rebus, quibus astra sustentantur et aluntur.

Most probably this is Posidonius' doctrine, which is founded on Plato's in the *Tim.* [1] and Aristotle's in Π. φιλ. [2].

b. The same doctrine is found in the *Somnium Scipionis* (Cic., *De re publ.* VI 26-28), where the spirit of Scipio Africanus, *de excelso et pleno stellarum, illustri et claro quodam loco*, speaks to the younger Scipio as follows:

"Tu vero enitere et sic habeto, non esse te mortalem sed corpus hoc; nec enim tu is es quem forma ista declarat, sed mens cuiusque is est quisque [3], non ea figura quae digito demonstrari potest. deum te igitur scito esse, siquidem est deus qui viget qui sentit qui meminit qui providet, qui tam regit et moderatur et movet id corpus cui praepositus est, quam hunc mundum ille princeps deus; et ut mundum ex quadam parte mortalem ipse deus aeternus, sic fragile corpus animus sempiternus movet. nam quod semper movetur, aeternum est; quod autem motum adfert alicui quodque ipsum agitatur aliunde, quando finem habet motus, vivendi finem habeat necesse est. solum igitur quod se ipsum movet, quia numquam deseritur a se, numquam ne moveri quidem desinit; quin etiam ceteris quae moventur hic fons, hoc principium est movendi. principii autem nulla est origo; nam ex principio oriuntur omnia, ipsum autem nulla ex re alia nasci potest; nec enim esset id principium quod gigneretur aliunde; quodsi numquam oritur, nec occidit quidem umquam. nam principium exstinctum nec ipsum ab alio renascetur,

---

[1] 42b (our nr. **354b**). [2] Cp. our nr. **431d**.
[3] Cp. Ar., EN X 7, 1178a 2: Δόξειε δ' ἂν καὶ εἶναι ἕκαστος τοῦτο, εἴπερ τὸ κύριον καὶ ἄμεινον (above, under **418d**).

nec ex se aliud creabit, siquidem necesse est a principio oriri omnia.
Ita fit ut motus principium ex eo sit quod ipsum a se movetur; id autem
nec nasci potest nec mori; vel concidat omne caelum omnisque natura
et consistat necesse est nec vim ullam nanciscatur qua a primo inpulsa
moveatur. cum pateat igitur aeternum id esse quod se ipsum moveat,
quis est qui hanc naturam animis esse tributam neget? inanimum est
enim omne quod pulsu agitatur externo; quod autem est animal, id
motu cietur interiore et suo; nam haec est propria natura animi atque
vis; quae si est una ex omnibus quae se ipsa moveat, neque nata certe
est et aeterna est.

Discussion
To this passage the following remarks must be made.

I—The immortality advocated in the *Somn. Sc.* has been rightly called "celestial
immortality": the soul of Africanus is situated on the Milky Way cp. Heraclides
Ponticus, our nr. **775a**) and shows to the younger Scipio the order of the universe
(c. 16 ff.).

II—This kind of immortality is first promised to those who have served their
country well: *omnibus qui patriam conservaverint, adiuverint, auxerint, certum esse
in caelo ac definitum locum, ubi beati aevo sempiterno fruantur* (c. 13). But in the
above cited passage the soul as such is said to be immortal, because it is a self-
moving principle.

III—The author knows a supreme God who rules the world, and he regards the
soul as god, but of a lower degree. Hence it does not follow that the supreme God
should be considered as transcendent. The background of the *Somn. Sc.* is doubtless
the Stoic doctrine of God-the fiery pneuma pervading the universe and being
present in the hegemonikon of man in a higher degree than in non-rational beings,
even in anorganic nature (cf. Diog. VII 138-139, our nr. **909**; cf. **920c**).

IV—The *Somn. Sc.* (c. 15) contains a condemnation of suicide borrowed from
Plato's *Phaedo*.

V—The doctrine of the *Somn. Sc.* was generally attributed by modern scholars
to Posidonius, until Edelstein [1] denied it him, because the fragments bearing the
name of Posidonius explicitly, should not give any indication in this direction.

That this argument is not conclusive, will appear below (nrs. **1192-1195**).
Moreover, the following points make it probable that, for a part at least, Posidonius
is behind the doctrine of immortality set forth in the *Somn. Sc.*

(1) Similar thoughts are found with the Stoic Cato of Utica (Plut., *Cato minor*
68 f.); (2) in Diog. VII 138-139, where Posidonius is mentioned, the view that the
hegemonikon, being noûs, is immortal, is in any case *very near*; (3) We know
from Galenus that Posid. in his anthropology was to a great extent inspired by
Plato; (4) the *neque nata et certe aeterna* of our text contains clearly a polemic
against Panaetius.

VI—Litterature on the *Somn. Sc.*:

F. Cumont, *After life in Roman paganism*, New Haven 1922, pp. 91 ff. (Celestial
immortality).

R. M. Jones, *Posidonius and the flight of the mind*, in *Class. Philol.* XXI (1926),
p. 97-113.

P. Boyancé, *Etudes sur le Songe de Scipion*, Paris 1936.

---

[1]   In the *Amer. Journal of Philol.*, 1936.

Tends to eliminate the influence of Posid. by maintaining that Cicero himself is a disciple of Plato and quite able to be the author of the theory.

A. J. Festugière, *Le dieu cosmique*, Paris 1949, pp. 441-459.

A. A. C. Sier, Cicero's *Somnium Scipionis*, Diss. Utrecht 1945, gives a survey of the problem and a bibliography.

See also the important "Rapport" of P. Boyancé at the Budé-congress of 1953: *Le Platonisme à Rome. Platon et Cicéron*, in: *Congrès de Tours et Poitiers*, 3-9 Sept. 1953, Actes du Congrès, Paris 1954, p. 195-222.

960—With Seneca, immortality takes an important place. He speaks frequently about it, and in terms which remind us of Plato (especially of the *Phaedo*).

The same belief in Seneca

a. Sen., *Ep.* 65, 16:

Nam corpus hoc animi pondus ac poena est: premente illo urgetur, in vinculis est, nisi accessit philosophia, et illum respirare rerum naturae spectaculo iussit, et a terrenis dimisit ad divina. Haec libertas eius est, haec evagatio: subducit interim se custodiae in qua tenetur, et caelo reficitur.

b. Sen., *Ep.* 102, 22:

Cum venerit dies ille, qui mixtum hoc divini humanique secernat, corpus hic, ubi inveni, relinquam: ipse me dis reddam. nec nunc sine illis sum, sed gravi terrenoque detineor.

c. Id., *Nat. quaest.*, Praef. 11-12:

Sursum ingentia spatia sunt, in quorum possessionem animus admittitur, et ita si secum minimum ex corpore tulit, si sordidum omne detersit et expeditus levisque ac contentus modico emicuit. Cum illa tetigit, alitur, crescit ac velut vinculis liberatus in originem redit et hoc habet argumentum divinitatis suae, quod illum divina delectant, nec ut alienis, sed ut suis interest. Secure spectat occasus siderum atque ortus et tam diversas concordantium vias; observat ubi quaeque stella primum terris lumen ostendat, ubi columen eius summum cursus sit, quousque descendat; curiosus spectator excutit singula et quaerit. Quidni quaerat? Scit illa ad se pertinere.

d. Id., *Ad Marciam de consolatione* 25:

Proinde non est quod ad sepulcrum fili tui curras: pessima eius et ipsi molestissima istic iacent, ossa cineresque, non magis illius partes quam vestes aliaque tegimenta corporum. integer ille nihilque in terris relinquens sui fugit et totus excessit; paulumque supra nos commoratus, dum expurgatur et inhaerentia vitia situmque omnem mortalis aevi excutit, deinde ad excelsa sublatus inter felices currit animas. excepit illum coetus sacer, Scipiones Catonesque, interque contemptores vitae et beneficio . . liberos parens tuus, Marcia. ille nepotem suum — quamquam illic omnibus omne cognatum est — adplicat sibi nova luce gaudentem et vicinorum siderum meatus docet, nec ex coniectura sed omnium ex vero peritus in arcana naturae libens ducit; utque ignotarum urbium monstrator hospiti gratus est, ita sciscitanti caelestium causas domesticus interpres.

Also the Christian Origenes imagines that in "paradise" the souls will be initiated into the secrets of the kosmos [1]; and, as we remarked already in treating Aristotle's Π. φιλ. [2], the conviction that the heavenly bodies are a kind of reality superior to our world, remained until the days of Kepler and Galilei: they still regarded the celestial bodies with the eye of Plato in the *Tim.* and of the ancient Stoics, such as Seneca.

The difference between Stoics and Christians longing for "heaven" lies chiefly in these two points: 1) For the Christian, God is *above* creation, and even a perfect knowledge of the heavenly bodies can never be more than an initiation preparing for a higher vision, as it was for Plato, too. For the Stoics, however, the clear vision of the heavenly bodies was in the fullest sense the vision of God. 2) Stoics, such as Seneca, expect this vision as *a right* which will be given to them in consequence of their virtue. Seneca (*Ep.* 95, 10) writes: "*Merui quidem admitti* et iam inter illos (sc. deos) fui animumque illo meum misi et ad me illi suum miserant."— This view is strange to the Christian who prays:

"*Nobis quoque peccatoribus*, famulis tuis, de multitudine miserationum tuarum sperantibus, partem aliquam et societatem donare digneris, cum tuis sanctis apostolis et martyribus, et omnibus sanctis tuis, intra quorum nos consortium, *non aestimator meriti, sed veniae quaesumus largitor admitte*, per Christum dominum nostrum" (h. mass).

Moreover, it should be noticed that the above mentioned belief is not the only aspect of the problem of immortality with Seneca. See below, our nr. **1223b-c**.

5—LOGIC: (1) GRAMMATICAL SCIENCE

The foundation of grammatical science   **961**—From Zeno onwards, Stoics have been always well aware that, since λόγος means both *word* and *thought*, philosophy and language can be hardly separated. By their reflexions on the elementary facts of language, by their definitions and divisions, they laid the foundation of grammatical science. The Grammar of Dionysius Thrax is founded for the greater part on Diogenes the Babylonian's Τέχνη περὶ φωνῆς, and Roman grammarians borrowed still more from him.

---

[1] *Contra Celsum* II 62. It should be noticed that this initiation, which is equal to that of the Stoic "celestial immortality", according to Origenes takes place *not in heaven* but ἐν μεθορίῳ τινί.

[2] Our nr. **431d**.

See: K. Barwick, *Remmius Palaemon u. die römische ars grammatica*, Leipzig 1922
(*Philologus*, Suppl. Bd. XV). pp. 90-101.
Also: M. Pohlenz, *Die Begründung der abendländischen Sprachlehre durch die Stoa.*
Nachr. d. Göttinger Gesellschaft d. Wissensch., phil.-hist. Kl., Fachgruppe I,
N.F. III 6 (1939).
——, *Die Stoa* I, p. 37-47.
Diog. Laert. VII 55-59 gives a survey of Diogenes' Τέχνη. That Zeno himself
was already occupied with these problems, may appear from our next nrs., and
from the fact that he considered dialectic as being only a more concentrated form
of rhetoric (**964a**), while Cleanthes made rhetoric a part of philosophy next to
dialectic (**964c**).

962—a. Eustath. *in Iliad.* Σ 506, p. 1158, 37 (SVF I 74):

Zeno's definition of φωνή

Ἡεροφώνους κήρυκας "Ομηρος κἀνταῦθα εἰπὼν τὸν κατὰ Ζήνωνα τῆς
φωνῆς ὅρον προϋπέβαλεν εἰπόντα· "φωνή ἐστιν ἀὴρ πεπληγμένος."

b. Diog. Laërt. VII 55 (SVF III, Diog. Bab. 17):

repeated by Diog.

Ἔστι δὲ φωνὴ ἀὴρ πεπληγμένος ἢ τὸ ἴδιον αἰσθητὸν [1] ἀκοῆς, ὥς φησι Διογένης ὁ Βαβυλώνιος ἐν τῇ περὶ τῆς φωνῆς τέχνῃ. <καὶ> ζῴου μέν ἐστι φωνὴ
ἀὴρ ὑπὸ ὁρμῆς πεπληγμένος, ἀνθρώπου δέ ἐστιν ἔναρθρος καὶ ἀπὸ διανοίας
ἐκπεμπομένη, ὡς ὁ Διογένης φησίν, ἥτις ἀπὸ δεκατεσσάρων ἐτῶν τελειοῦται.

c. From this definition follows directly that voice is something
corporeal.

voice is corporeal

Diog. Laërt., ib. (SVF III, Diog. Bab. 18):

Καὶ σῶμα δ' ἐστὶν ἡ φωνὴ κατὰ τοὺς Στωϊκούς, ὥς φησιν Ἀρχέδημός τ' ἐν
τῇ Περὶ φωνῆς καὶ Διογένης καὶ Ἀντίπατρος καὶ Χρύσιππος ἐν τῇ δευτέρᾳ
τῶν Φυσικῶν. πᾶν γὰρ τὸ ποιοῦν σῶμά ἐστι, ποιεῖ δὲ ἡ φωνὴ προσιοῦσα τοῖς
ἀκούουσιν ἀπὸ τῶν φωνούντων.

963—From the fact that voice proceeds from the throat Zeno, followed by Diogenes the Babylonian, concluded that thought does not
originate from the brain, but from the heart.

Both thought and voice spring from the heart

Galenus, *De plac. Hippocr. et Plat.* II 5, p. 201 Müller (SVF III,
Diog. Bab. 29):

Καὶ μὴν ὁ θαυμαζόμενος ὑπὸ τῶν Στωϊκῶν λόγος ὁ Ζήνωνος, ὃν καὶ πρῶτον
ἁπάντων ἔγραψεν ἐν τῷ Περὶ τοῦ τῆς ψυχῆς ἡγεμονικοῦ Διογένης ὁ Βαβυλώνιος, — εἴσῃ δ' ἐναργέστερον, εἰ παραγράψαιμεν αὐτόν, ἔχει γὰρ ὧδε. "Φωνὴ
διὰ φάρυγγος χωρεῖ. εἰ δὲ ἦν ἀπὸ τοῦ ἐγκεφάλου χωροῦσα, οὐκ ἂν διὰ φάρυγγος
ἐχώρει. ὅθεν δὲ λόγος, καὶ φωνὴ ἐκεῖθεν χωρεῖ. λόγος δὲ ἀπὸ διανοίας χωρεῖ,

---

[1] τὸ ἴδιον αἰσθητὸν—"the proper object of the sense of hearing". Cp. nr. **641**.

ὥστ' οὐκ ἐν τῷ ἐγκεφάλῳ ἐστὶν ἡ διάνοια." τὸν αὐτὸν δὴ τοῦτον λόγον Διογένης οὐ κατὰ τὴν αὐτὴν ἐρωτᾷ λέξιν, ἀλλ' ὧδε· ,,Ὅθεν ἐκπέμπεται ἡ φωνή,
καὶ ἡ ἔναρθρος, οὐκοῦν καὶ ἡ σημαίνουσα ἔναρθρος φωνὴ ἐκεῖθεν. τοῦτο δὲ ὁ
λόγος. καὶ λόγος ἄρα ἐκεῖθεν ἐκπέμπεται, ὅθεν καὶ ἡ φωνή. ἡ δὲ φωνὴ οὐκ ἐκ
τῶν κατὰ τὴν κεφαλὴν τόπων ἐκπέμπεται, ἀλλὰ φανερῶς ἐκ τῶν κάτωθεν
μᾶλλον. — καὶ ὁ λόγος ἄρα οὐκ ἐκ τῆς κεφαλῆς ἐκπέμπεται, ἀλλὰ κάτωθεν
μᾶλλον. ἀλλὰ μὴν κἀκεῖνο ἀληθὲς τὸ τὸν λόγον ἐκ τῆς διανοίας ἐκπέμπεσθαι. —
καὶ ἡ διανοία ἄρα οὐκ ἔστιν ἐν τῇ κεφαλῇ, ἀλλ' ἐν τοῖς κατωτέρω τόποις,
μάλιστά πως περὶ τὴν καρδίαν."

Dialectic is
linked with   **964**—Since, then, language and thought are so closely related, dialec-
rhetoric   tic is, according to Zeno, essentially linked with rhetoric.

    a.   Sextus Emp., *Adv. math.* II 7 (SVF I 75):

    Ἔνθεν γοῦν καὶ Ζήνων ὁ Κιτιεὺς ἐρωτηθεὶς ὅτῳ διαφέρει διαλεκτικὴ ῥητο-
ρικῆς, συστρέψας τὴν χεῖρα καὶ πάλιν ἐξαπλώσας ἔφη "τούτῳ", κατὰ μὲν
τὴν συστροφὴν τὸ στρογγύλον καὶ βραχὺ τῆς διαλεκτικῆς τάττων ἰδίωμα,
διὰ δὲ τῆς ἐξαπλώσεως καὶ ἐκτάσεως τῶν δακτύλων τὸ πλατὺ τῆς ῥητορικῆς
δυνάμεως αἰνιττόμενος.

    b.   Cp. Cicero, *De fin.* II 17 (SVF I ib.):

    Zenonis est, inquam, hoc Stoici. Omnem vim loquendi, ut iam ante
Aristoteles, in duas tributam esse partes, rhetoricam palmae, dialecticam pugni similem esse dicebat, quod latius loquerentur rhetores, dialectici autem compressius.

    c.   Diog. Laërt., after having mentioned the well-known tripar-
tition of philosophy with Zeno and his followers (see above, nr. **897a**),
adds that "some Stoics" used to divide logic into rhetoric and dialectic,
as we know Cleanthes did, who introduced rhetoric as a part of philosophy
next to dialectic.

    Diog. Laërt. VII 41:

    Ὁ δὲ Κλεάνθης ἓξ μέρη φησί, διαλεκτικόν, ῥητορικόν, ἠθικόν, πολιτικόν,
φυσικόν, θεολογικόν. —

    Τὸ δὲ λογικὸν μέρος φασὶν ἔνιοι εἰς δύο διαιρεῖσθαι ἐπιστήμας, εἰς ῥητορικὴν
καὶ διαλεκτικήν·

λόγος
ἐνδιάθετος   **965**—Later, the terms ἐνδιάθετος and προφορικός are generally used to
and   indicate the different functions of the logos as thought and the logos
προφορικός   as voice.

a. Galenus in *Hippocr. de med. officina*, vol. XVIII B, p. 649 K. (SVF II 135):

Τῶν αἰσθήσεων ἀπάσαις τὴν γνώμην ἐφεξῆς ἔταξεν, ὅπερ ἐστὶ τὴν διάνοιαν, ἥν τε καὶ νοῦν καὶ φρένα καὶ λόγον κοινῶς οἱ ἄνθρωποι καλοῦσιν. ἐπεὶ δὲ καὶ τῶν κατὰ φωνήν ἐστί τις λόγος, ἀφορίζοντες οὖν τοῦτον τὸν προειρημένον λόγον οἱ φιλόσοφοι καλοῦσιν ἐνδιάθετον, ᾧ λόγῳ τά τε ἀκόλουθα καὶ τὰ μαχόμενα γιγνώσκομεν.

b. Sextus Emp., *Adv. math.* VIII (*Against the logicians* II) 275:

... φασὶν ὅτι ἄνθρωπος οὐχὶ τῷ προφορικῷ λόγῳ διαφέρει τῶν ἀλόγων ζῴων (καὶ γὰρ κόρακες καὶ ψιττακοὶ καὶ κίτται ἐνάρθρους προφέρονται φωνάς) ἀλλὰ τῷ ἐνδιαθέτῳ, οὐδὲ τῇ ἁπλῇ μόνον φαντασίᾳ — ἀλλὰ τῇ μεταβατικῇ καὶ συνθετικῇ.

It should be noted that in these passages no indication occurs that these terms have been used already in the Ancient Stoa. Probably they date from the days of Carneades and his discussions with Stoics on the question as to whether animals possess speech and thought, too. See Pohlenz, *Begründung* p. 191 ff.

966—Having defined voice, Diogenes the Babylonian went on by defining the elements of language.

The elements of language

Diog. Laërt. VII 56-57 (SVF III, Diog. Bab. 20):

Λ έ ξ ι ς δέ ἐστι κατὰ τοὺς Στωϊκούς, ὥς φησιν ὁ Διογένης, φωνὴ ἐγγράμματος, οἷον "ἡμέρα".

Λ ό γ ο ς δέ ἐστι φωνὴ σημαντικὴ ἀπὸ διανοίας ἐκπεμπομένη, ‹οἷον "ἡμέρα ἐστί"›.

Δ ι ά λ ε κ τ ο ς δέ ἐστι λέξις κεχαραγμένη ἐθνικῶς τε καὶ Ἑλληνικῶς· ἢ λέξις ποταπή, τουτέστι ποιά κατὰ διάλεκτον, οἷον κατὰ μὲν τὴν Ἀτθίδα "θάλαττα", κατὰ δὲ τὴν Ἰάδα "ἡμέρη".

Τ ῆ ς δὲ λ έ ξ ε ω ς σ τ ο ι χ ε ῖ ά ἐστι τὰ εἰκοσιτέσσαρα γράμματα. —

Φ ω ν ή ε ν τ α δέ ἐστι τῶν στοιχείων ἑπτά· α, ε, η, ι, ο, υ, ω.

Ἄ φ ω ν α δὲ ἕξ· β, γ, δ, π, κ, τ.

Διαφέρει δὲ φ ω ν ὴ καὶ λ έ ξ ι ς , ὅτι φωνὴ μὲν καὶ ὁ ἦχός ἐστι, λέξις δὲ τὸ ἔναρθρον μόνον.

Λ έ ξ ι ς δὲ λ ό γ ο υ διαφέρει, ὅτι λόγος ἀεὶ σημαντικός ἐστι, λέξις δὲ καὶ ἀσήμαντος, ὡς ἡ "βλίτυρι", λόγος δὲ οὐδαμῶς.

967—Diog. now proceeds to define the five parts of speech.

The five parts of speech

Diog. Laërt. VII 57-58 (SVF III, Diog. Bab. 21, 22):

Τοῦ δὲ λόγου ἐστὶ μέρη πέντε, ὥς φησι Διογένης τε ἐν τῷ Περὶ φωνῆς καὶ Χρύσιππος· ὄνομα, προσηγορία, ῥῆμα, σύνδεσμος, ἄρθρον. —

῎Εστι δὲ προσηγορία μέν, κατὰ τὸν Διογένην, μέρος λόγου σημαῖνον κοινὴν ποιότητα, οἷον "ἄνθρωπος" "ἵππος".

῎Ονομα δέ ἐστι μέρος λόγου δηλοῦν ἰδίαν ποιότητα, οἷον Διογένης, Σωκράτης.

῾Ρῆμα δέ ἐστι μέρος λόγου σημαῖνον ἀσύνθετον κατηγόρημα, ὡς ὁ Διογένης, ἢ ὥς τινες, στοιχεῖον λόγου ἄπτωτον [1] σημαῖνόν τι συντακτὸν περί τινος ἢ τινῶν, οἷον "γράφω" "λέγω".

Σύνδεσμος δέ ἐστι μέρος λόγου ἄπτωτον, συνδοῦν τὰ μέρη τοῦ λόγου.

῎Αρθρον δέ ἐστι στοιχεῖον λόγου πτωτικόν, διορίζον τὰ γένη τῶν ὀνομάτων καὶ τοὺς ἀριθμούς· οἷον "ὁ, ἡ, τό, οἱ, αἱ, τά".

According to Dion. Halic., *De verb. comp.* 2, the Stoics started by admitting four parts of speech: ὄνομα, ῥῆμα, σύνδεσμος, ἄρθρον, the same that were also mentioned by Aristotle in *Poet.* 20. Aristotle, however, did not separate them from other elements of language, saying:

Τῆς δὲ λέξεως ἁπάσης τάδ᾽ ἐστι μέρη· στοιχεῖον, συλλαβή, σύνδεσμος, ἄρθρον, ὄνομα, ῥῆμα, πτῶσις, λόγος.

Therefore, Pohlenz (*Stoa* I, p. 44) seems to be right in stating that it was Zeno who first distinguished "the four parts of speech" as such, and separated them from other elements. Later, Chrysippus divided ὄνομα into ὄνομα and προσηγορία.

The excellences and vices of speech

968—Next, Diog. deals with the excellences and vices of speech. Diog. Laërt. VII 59 (SVF III, Diog. Bab. 24):

᾽Αρεταὶ δὲ λόγου εἰσὶ πέντε· ἑλληνισμός, σαφήνεια, συντομία, πρέπον, κατασκευή.

῾Ελληνισμὸς μὲν οὖν ἐστι φράσις ἀδιάπτωτος ἐν τῇ τεχνικῇ καὶ μὴ εἰκαίᾳ συνηθείᾳ.

Σαφήνεια δέ ἐστι λέξις γνωρίμως παριστᾶσα τὸ νοούμενον.

Συντομία δέ ἐστι λέξις αὐτὰ τὰ ἀναγκαῖα περιέχουσα πρὸς δήλωσιν τοῦ πράγματος.

Πρέπον δέ ἐστι λέξις οἰκεία τῷ πράγματι.

Κατασκευὴ δέ ἐστι λέξις ἐκπεφευγυῖα τὸν ἰδιωτισμόν.

῾Ο δὲ βαρβαρισμός, ἐκ τῶν κακιῶν, λέξις ἐστὶ παρὰ τὸ ἔθος τῶν εὐδοκιμούντων ῾Ελλήνων.

Σολοικισμὸς δέ ἐστι λόγος ἀκαταλλήλως συντεταγμένος.

The ἀρεταὶ and κακίαι of speech were not adopted by Dion. Thr., but they were by Latin grammarians.

The doctrine of declension

969—Zeno seems to have been the author of the doctrine of declension, the term πτῶσις having been used by Aristotle in a more general sense (for every form deduced by alteration from another, for verbal

---

[1] ἄπτωτον-*indeclinable.*

forms, comparatives and adverbs as well as for the cases of a noun). Pohlenz, *Stoa* I 44, admits that Zeno limited the term to the sense it has until the present day [1]. Chrysippus wrote a book Π. τῶν πέντε πτώσεων.

a. The *casus obliqui* are mentioned in Diog. Laërt. VII 65:

Πλάγιαι δὲ πτώσεις εἰσὶ γενικὴ καὶ δοτικὴ καὶ αἰτιατική.

It must be noticed that in the preceding chapter the term πτῶσις is used for verbal forms.

b. There seems to have been a controversy between Stoics and Peripatetics on the question as to whether the nominative can be called a "case" at all.

Ammonius in Ar. *De interpret.* p. 42, 30 Busse (SVF II, 164):

Περὶ τῆς κατ' εὐθεῖαν γινομένης τῶν ὀνομάτων προφορᾶς εἴωθε παρὰ τοῖς παλαιοῖς ζητεῖσθαι, πότερον πτῶσιν αὐτὴν προσήκει καλεῖν ἢ οὐδαμῶς, ἀλλὰ ταύτην μὲν ὄνομα, ὡς κατ' αὐτὴν ἑκάστου τῶν πραγμάτων ὀνομαζομένου, τὰς δὲ ἄλλας πτώσεις ὀνόματος ἀπὸ τοῦ μετασχηματισμοῦ τῆς εὐθείας γινο- μένας. τῆς μὲν οὖν δευτέρας προΐσταται δόξης ὁ Ἀριστοτέλης —τῆς δὲ προτέρας οἱ ἀπὸ τῆς Στοᾶς καὶ ὡς τούτοις ἀκολουθοῦντες οἱ τὴν γραμματικὴν μετιόντες τέχνην. λεγόντων δὲ πρὸς αὐτοὺς τῶν Περιπατητικῶν — "τὴν εὐθεῖαν κατὰ τίνα λόγον πτῶσιν ὀνομάζειν δίκαιον, ὡς ἀπὸ τίνος πεσοῦσαν;" — ἀποκρίνονται οἱ ἀπὸ τῆς Στοᾶς ὡς ἀπὸ τοῦ νοήματος τοῦ ἐν τῇ ψυχῇ καὶ αὕτη πέπτωκεν· ὃ γὰρ ἐν ἑαυτοῖς ἔχομεν τοῦ Σωκράτους νόημα δηλῶσαι βουλόμενοι τὸ "Σω- κράτης" ὄνομα προφερόμεθα· καθάπερ οὖν τὸ ἄνωθεν ἀφεθὲν γραφεῖον καὶ ὀρθὸν παγὲν πεπτωκέναι τε λέγεται καὶ τὴν πτῶσιν ὀρθὴν ἐσχηκέναι, τὸν αὐτὸν τρόπον καὶ τὴν εὐθεῖαν πεπτωκέναι μὲν ἀξιοῦμεν ἀπὸ τῆς ἐννοίας, ὀρθὴν δὲ εἶναι διὰ τὸ ἀρχέτυπον τῆς κατὰ τὴν ἐκφώνησιν προφορᾶς.

Doubtless Pohlenz (*Stoa* II p. 26) is right in noticing that the *casus rectus* prob- ably has got its name from being the *normal* form of the word, in which the noun "remains erect".

970—As to the conjugation of verbs, Stoics had their chief merits in composing a new system of the *tempora*.   *System of the tempora*

a. As we are informed by later grammarians (*Stephanus* in the scholia on Dionys. Thr., p. 250, 26 and *Priscianus* VIII 51 ff.), they made their main distinction between *definite* and *indefinite tenses*, and thus came to the following scheme:

---

[1]　See also Pohlenz, *Begründung*, p. 167 ff.

A.

B.

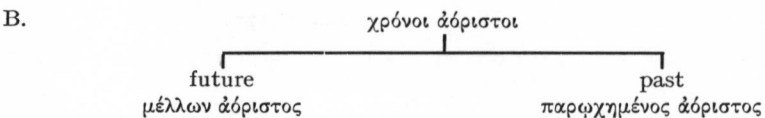

To this, Pohlenz (*Stoa* II, p. 27) remarks that probably the system reaches back to Zeno, since it presupposes the sharp distinction between *perfectum* and *aoristus*, a distinction which began to disappear as early as the middle of the third century.

Meaning of the durativum   **b.** The meaning of the *durativum* (or *imperfectum*) is explained by Priscianus, VIII, p. 414, 24:

... praesens tempus hoc solemus dicere, quod contineat et coniungat quasi puncto aliquo iuncturam praeteriti temporis et futuri nulla intercisione interveniente, unde Stoici iure hoc tempus *praesens imperfectum* vocabant.

c. Cp. Scholia in Dionys. Thr., Bekker, *Anecd. Gr.* II, p. 891 (SVF II, 165):

Τὸν ἐνεστῶτα οἱ Στωϊκοὶ ἐνεστῶτα παρατατικὸν ὁρίζονται, ὅτι παρατείνεται καὶ εἰς μέλλοντα· ὁ γὰρ λέγων "ποιῶ" καὶ ὅτι ἐποίησέ τι ἐμφαίνει καὶ ὅτι ποιήσει.

Words are φύσει   **971**—As to their general idea of language, Stoics held that words are φύσει, while Aristotle taught they are θέσει.

a. Origenes, *Contra Celsum* I 24 (SVF II 146):

Ἐμπίπτει εἰς τὸ προκείμενον λόγος βαθὺς καὶ ἀπόρρητος, ὁ περὶ φύσεως ὀνομάτων, πότερον, ὡς οἴεται Ἀριστοτέλης, θέσει ἐστὶ τὰ ὀνόματα ἤ, ὡς νομίζουσιν οἱ ἀπὸ τῆς Στοᾶς, φύσει, μιμουμένων τῶν πρώτων φωνῶν τὰ πράγματα, καθ' ὧν τὰ ὀνόματα, καθὸ καὶ στοιχεῖά τινα τῆς ἐτυμολογίας εἰσάγουσιν.

Cp. the expression ἤχου μίμημα in Cleanthes' *Hymn to Zeus*, which might be explained in this way (above, nr. **943**, n. 1).

Etymology   **b.** Hence their interest in etymology. Some instances may be found in SVF II 156-163.

972—From the thesis that words are φύσει one might deduce that there is an exact congruity between words and thought. Now this is what is called *analogy* and was defended by Aristarchus of Alexandria. Chrysippus however opposed him, holding that there is *anomaly*.

Analogy and anomaly

a. Varro, *De lingua Latina* IX 1 (SVF II 151):

<Insignis eorum est error qui malunt quae> nesciunt docere quam discere quae ignorant: in quo fuit Crates, nobilis grammaticus, qui fretus Chrysippo, homine acutissimo qui reliquit Περὶ ἀνωμαλίας III libros, contra analogian atque Aristarchum est nixus, sed ita, ut scripta indicant eius, ut neutrius videatur pervidisse voluntatem, quod et Chrysippus de inaequabilitate cum scribit sermonis, propositum habet ostendere similes res dissimilibus verbis et dissimiles similibus esse vocabulis notatas, id quod est verum, et quod Aristarchus, de aequabilitate cum scribit ei<us>de<m> verborum similitudinem quandam <in> inclinatione sequi iubet, quoad patiatur consuetudo.

Varro argues that both anomaly and regularity must be admitted, both having sprung from a certain usage in speech [1].

b. By what kind of reasons Chrysippus was brought to this thesis, may be seen from the following passage of Simplicius, which deals with negation.

Simpl. in Ar. *Categ.* f. 100 Z ed. Bas. (SVF II 177, towards the end):

Καὶ τοῦτο δὲ ἰστέον ὅτι ἐνίοτε μὲν οὐ στερητικὰ ὀνόματα στέρησιν δηλοῖ, ὡς ἡ πενία τὴν στέρησιν τῶν χρημάτων καὶ ὁ τυφλὸς στέρησιν ὄψεως. ἐνίοτε δὲ στερητικὰ ὀνόματα οὐ στέρησιν δηλοῖ· τὸ γὰρ ἀθάνατον, στερητικὸν ἔχον τὸ σχῆμα τῆς λέξεως, οὐ σημαίνει στέρησιν.

Doubtless, the fact that there is often not a complete congruity between the form of a word and its meaning, as is suggested by the above cited passage of Varro, was explained by the Stoics by historical development (*consuetudo*): originally there was analogy, but the later usage of speech changed many things. Thus fem. words having a masc. ending, such as *mater, soror*; plural forms indicating singular notions, such as *nuptiae*, etc.

6—LOGIC (2): FORMAL LOGIC

973—Stoics took great care of accurate expression. They distinguished between the modalities of single sentences, between the various kinds of composed sentences and between the different forms of negation.

---

[1] See further on the conflict between Analogy and Anomaly: H. Steinthal, *Geschichte der Sprachwissenschaft b. d. Griechen und Römern*, Vol. I (2), Berlin 1890, p. 357.

Judgement or proposition

a. Definition of judgement. Diog. Laërt. VII 65:

Ἀξίωμα δέ ἐστιν ὅ ἐστιν ἀληθὲς ἢ ψεῦδος ἢ πρᾶγμα αὐτοτελὲς ἀποφαντὸν ὅσον ἐφ᾽ ἑαυτῷ, ὡς ὁ Χρύσιππός φησιν ἐν τοῖς Διαλεκτικοῖς ὅροις· ,,ἀξίωμά ἐστι τὸ ἀποφαντὸν ἢ καταφαντὸν ὅσον ἐφ᾽ ἑαυτῷ, οἷον Ἡμέρα ἐστί, Δίων περιπατεῖ.'' ὠνόμασται δὲ τὸ ἀξίωμα ἀπὸ τοῦ ἀξιοῦσθαι ἢ ἀθετεῖσθαι· ὁ γὰρ λέγων Ἡμέρα ἐστίν, ἀξιοῦν δοκεῖ τὸ ἡμέραν εἶναι. οὔσης μὲν οὖν ἡμέρας, ἀληθὲς γίνεται τὸ προκείμενον ἀξίωμα· μὴ οὔσης δέ, ψεῦδος.

Modalities of the sentence

b. Diog. Laërt. VII 66-68 (SVF II 186):

Διαφέρει δὲ ἀξίωμα καὶ ἐρώτημα καὶ πύσμα <καὶ> προστακτικὸν καὶ ὁρκικὸν καὶ ἀρατικὸν καὶ ὑποθετικὸν καὶ προσαγορευτικὸν καὶ πρᾶγμα ὅμοιον ἀξιώματι. ἀξίωμα μὲν γάρ ἐστιν ὃ λέγοντες ἀποφαινόμεθα, ὅπερ ἢ ἀληθές ἐστιν ἢ ψεῦδος. ἐρώτημα δέ ἐστι πρᾶγμα αὐτοτελὲς μέν, ὡς καὶ τὸ ἀξίωμα, αἰτητικὸν δὲ ἀποκρίσεως, οἷον "ἆρά γ᾽ ἡμέρα ἐστί;" τοῦτο δὲ οὔτε ἀληθές ἐστιν οὔτε ψεῦδος· ὥστε τὸ μὲν "ἡμέρα ἐστίν" ἀξίωμά ἐστι, τὸ δὲ "ἆρά γ᾽ ἡμέρα ἐστίν;" ἐρώτημα. πύσμα δέ ἐστι πρᾶγμα πρὸς ὃ συμβολικῶς οὐκ ἔστιν ἀποκρίνεσθαι, ὡς ἐπὶ τοῦ ἐρωτήματος, "ναί", ἀλλὰ <δεῖ> εἰπεῖν "οἰκεῖ ἐν τῷδε τῷ τόπῳ". προστακτικὸν δέ ἐστι πρᾶγμα, ὃ λέγοντες προστάσσομεν, οἷον·

"σὺ μὲν βάδιζε τὰς ἐπ᾽ Ἰνάχου ῥοάς"[1].

ὁρκικὸν****[2] <προσαγορευτικὸν> δέ ἐστι πρᾶγμα, ὃ εἰ λέγοι τις, προσαγορεύοι ἄν, οἷον

"Ἀτρείδη κύδιστε, ἄναξ ἀνδρῶν Ἀγαμέμνων"[3].

ὅμοιον δέ ἐστιν ἀξιώματι, ὃ τὴν ἐκφορὰν ἔχον ἀξιωματικὴν παρά τινος μορίου πλεονασμὸν ἢ πάθος ἔξω πίπτει τοῦ γένους τῶν ἀξιωμάτων, οἷον·

"καλός γ᾽ ὁ παρθενών".

"ὡς Πριαμίδησιν ἐμφερὴς ὁ βουκόλος"[4] ἔστι δὲ καὶ ἐπαπορητικόν τι πρᾶγμα διενηνοχὸς ἀξιώματος, ὃ εἰ λέγοι τις, ἀποροίη ἄν·

"ἆρ᾽ ἔστι συγγενές τι λύπη καὶ βίος;"[5]

οὔτε δὲ ἀληθῆ ἐστιν οὔτε ψευδῆ τὰ ἐρωτήματα καὶ τὰ πύσματα καὶ τὰ τούτοις παραπλήσια, τῶν ἀξιωμάτων ἢ ἀληθῶν ἢ ψευδῶν ὄντων.

c. More precisely, Ammonius says that, to the five traditional modalities, Stoics added five others.

Ammonius in Ar. *De interpr.*, p. 2, 26 Busse (SVF II 188):

Καλοῦσι δὲ οἱ Στωϊκοὶ τὸν μὲν ἀποφαντικὸν λόγον ἀξίωμα, τὸν δὲ εὐκτικὸν

---

[1] Nauck, *Trag. Graec. Fragm.*, Adesp. 177.
[2] The lacuna must have covered the definitions of the ὁρκικόν, ἀρατικόν and ὑποθετικόν.
[3] *Iliad* IX 96.   [4] Nauck, T.G.F., Adesp. 286.
[5] Menander, fr. 281, 9 Kock.

ἀρατικόν, τὸν δὲ κλητικὸν προσαγορευτικόν, προστιθέντες τούτοις [1] ἕτερα πέντε λόγων εἴδη σαφῶς ὑπό τινα τῶν ἀπηριθμημένων ἀναφερόμενα· λέγουσι γὰρ τὸ μέν τι εἶναι ὁμοτικόν, οἷον·

"Ἴστω νῦν τόδε γαῖα,"
τὸ δὲ ἐκθετικόν, οἷον "ἔστω εὐθεῖα γραμμὴ ἥδε", τὸ δὲ ὑποθετικόν, οἷον "ὑποκείσθω τὴν γῆν κέντρον εἶναι τῆς τοῦ ἡλίου σφαίρας" τὸ δὲ ὅ μ ο ι ο ν ἀ ξ ι ώ - μ α τ ι, οἷον

"ὡς ὡραΐζεται ἡ τύχη εἰς τοὺς βίους" [2].
ἅπερ ἅπαντα δεκτικὰ ὄντα ψεύδους τε καὶ ἀληθείας ὑπάγοιντο ἂν τῷ ἀποφαντικῷ. — πέμπτον δέ τι τούτοις εἶναί φασι τὸ ἐ π α π ο ρ η τ ι κ ό ν. —

974—To the fundamental thesis that every proposition must be either true or false, the Sceptics opposed the famous "Liar" [3].
The Stoic basis of dialectic opposed by Sceptics

Thus, Cic. in *Acad. pr.* (*Lucullus*) 29, 95:

Nempe fundamentum dialecticae est, quidquid enuntietur (id autem appellunt ἀξίωμα; quod est quasi effatum) aut verum esse aut falsum. Quid igitur? Haec vera an falsa sunt? "Si te mentiri dicis idque verum dicis, mentiris" *et* "*si te mentiri dicis idque mentiris*, verum dicis"? Haec scilicet inexplicabilia esse dicitis. Quod est odiosius quam illa, quae nos incomprehensa et non percepta dicimus. Sed haec omitto. Illud quaero, si ista explicari non possunt nec eorum ullum iudicium invenitur, ut respondere possitis verane an falsa sint: ubi est illa definitio "effatum esse id, quod aut verum aut falsum sit"?

975—a. Diog. Laërt. VII 75-76 (SVF II 201):
Various kinds of propositions

Πιθανὸν δέ ἐστιν ἀξίωμα τὸ ἄγον εἰς συγκατάθεσιν, οἷον "εἴ τίς τι ἔτεκεν, ἐκείνη ἐκείνου μήτηρ ἐστί." ψεῦδος δὲ τοῦτο· οὐ γὰρ ἡ ὄρνις ᾠοῦ ἐστι μήτηρ. ἔτι τὰ μέν ἐστι δυνατά, τὰ δὲ ἀδύνατα, καὶ τὰ μὲν ἀναγκαῖα, τὰ δ' οὐκ ἀναγκαῖα. δυνατὸν μὲν τὸ ἐπιδεκτικὸν τοῦ ἀληθὲς εἶναι, τῶν ἐκτὸς μὴ ἐναντιουμένων πρὸς τὸ ἀληθὲς εἶναι, οἷον "ζῇ Διοκλῆς". ἀδύνατον δὲ ὃ μή ἐστιν ἐπιδεκτικὸν τοῦ ἀληθὲς εἶναι, οἷον "ἡ γῆ ἵπταται". ἀναγκαῖον δέ ἐστιν, ὅπερ ἀληθές ὂν οὐκ ἔστιν ἐπιδεκτικὸν τοῦ ψεῦδος εἶναι, ἢ ἐπιδεκτικὸν μέν ἐστι, τὰ δ' ἐκτὸς αὐτῷ ἐναντιοῦται πρὸς τὸ ψεῦδος εἶναι, οἷον "ἡ ἀρετὴ ὠφελεῖ". οὐκ ἀναγκαῖον δέ ἐστιν ὃ καὶ ἀληθές ἐστι καὶ ψεῦδος οἷόν τε εἶναι, τῶν ἐκτὸς μηδὲν ἐναντιουμέ-

---

[1] Of the five modalities admitted by Peripatetics he mentions here only three, omitting the ἐρώτημα or αἰτητικόν, and the προστακτικόν. Cp. Ammonius in *Anal. pr.*, p. 2, 3 Wallies: ἤτοι τῶν πέντε κατὰ τοὺς Περιπατητικοὺς ἢ τῶν δέκα κατὰ τοὺς Στωϊκοὺς πλὴν τοῦ ἀποφατικοῦ—which is correct, since they introduced the πύσμα as a special kind next to the ἐρώτημα.

[2] Menander, fr. 855.   [3] Our nr. **231b**.

νων, οἷον τὸ "περιπατεῖ Δίων". εὔλογον δέ ἐστιν ἀξίωμα τὸ πλείονας ἀφορμὰς
ἔχον εἰς τὸ ἀληθὲς εἶναι, οἷον "βιώσομαι αὔριον". καὶ ἄλλαι δέ εἰσι διαφοραὶ
ἀξιωμάτων καὶ μεταπτώσεις αὐτῶν ἐξ ἀληθῶν εἰς ψεύδη καὶ ἀντιστροφαί,
περὶ ὧν ἐν τῷ πλάτει λέγομεν.

Stoic doctrine
of modalities
criticized by
Boëthius

b. The Stoic doctrine about "possible" and "necessary" is opposed
by Boëthius, ad Ar. *De interpr.*, p. 429 (SVF II ib.):

Illud autem ignorandum non est, quod Stoicis universalius videatur
esse possibile a necessario; dividunt enim enuntiationes hoc modo:
"enuntiationum, inquiunt, aliae sunt possibiles, aliae impossibiles; pos-
sibilium aliae sunt necessariae, aliae non necessariae; rursus non neces-
sariarum aliae possibiles, etc." stulte atque improvide idem possibile et
genus non necessarii et speciem constituentes.

Different
kinds of
negation

976—Diog. Laërt. VII 69-70 (SVF II 204):

. . . ἀποφατικὸν μὲν οἷον "οὐχὶ ἡμέρα ἐστίν". εἶδος δὲ τούτου τὸ ὑπεραποφατικόν. ὑπεραποφατικὸν δέ ἐστιν ἀποφατικὸν ἀποφατικοῦ, οἷον "οὐχὶ
ἡμέρα <οὐκ> ἔστιν. τίθησι δὲ τὸ "ἡμέρα ἐστίν". ἀρνητικὸν δέ ἐστι τὸ συνεστὸς
ἐξ ἀρνητικοῦ μορίου καὶ κατηγορήματος, οἷον "οὐδεὶς περιπατεῖ", στερητικὸν
δέ ἐστι τὸ συνεστὸς ἐκ στερητικοῦ μορίου καὶ ἀξιώματος κατὰ δύναμιν, οἷον
"ἀφιλάνθρωπός ἐστιν οὗτος".

Division
of compound
sentences

977—Simple propositions may be linked to one another by different
conjunctions. Thus, six kinds are distinguished:

1. συνημμένον - hypothetical
2. παρασυνημμένον - inferential
3. συμπεπλεγμένον - coupled (also called *conjunctive* [1])
4. διεζευγμένον - disjunctive
5. αἰτιῶδες - causal
6. διασαφοῦν τὸ μᾶλλον ⎫ comparative (also called ⎰a. preferential [2].
   — τὸ ἧττον ⎭   ⎱b. quantitative [2]).

Diog. Laërt. VII 71-73 (SVF II 207):

Τῶν δ' οὐχ ἁπλῶν ἀξιωμάτων συνημμένον μέν ἐστιν, ὡς ὁ Χρύσιππος ἐν
ταῖς Διαλεκτικαῖς φησι καὶ Διογένης ἐν τῇ Διαλεκτικῇ τέχνῃ, τὸ συνεστὸς διὰ
τοῦ "εἰ" συναπτικοῦ συνδέσμου. ἐπαγγέλλεται δ' ὁ σύνδεσμος οὗτος ἀκολουθεῖν

---

[1] Mme A. Virieux-Reymond, *La logique et l'épistémologie des Stoïciens*, p. 138,
speaks of "le type conjonctif".

[2] Mme Virieux-Reymond calls them "le type préférentiel" and "le type quantitatif".

τὸ δεύτερον τῷ πρώτῳ, οἷον "εἰ ἡμέρα ἐστί, φῶς ἐστι." παρασυνημμένον δέ ἐστιν, ὡς ὁ Κρῖνίς φησιν ἐν τῇ Διαλεκτικῇ τέχνῃ, ἀξίωμα ὃ ὑπὸ τοῦ "ἐπεί" συνδέσμου παρασυνῆπται ἀρχόμενον ἀπ' ἀξιώματος καὶ λῆγον εἰς ἀξίωμα, οἷον "ἐπεὶ ἡμέρα ἐστί, φῶς ἐστιν". ἐπαγγέλλεται δ' ὁ σύνδεσμος ἀκολουθεῖν τε τὸ δεύτερον τῷ πρώτῳ καὶ τὸ πρῶτον ὑφεστάναι. συμπεπλεγμένον δέ ἐστιν ἀξίωμα ὃ ὑπό τινων συμπλεκτικῶν συνδέσμων συμπέπλεκται, οἷον "καὶ ἡμέρα ἐστί, καὶ φῶς ἐστιν." διεζευγμένον δέ ἐστιν ὃ ὑπὸ τοῦ "ἤτοι" διαζευκτικοῦ συνδέσμου διέζευκται, οἷον "ἤτοι ἡμέρα ἐστὶν ἢ νύξ ἐστιν. ἐπαγγέλλεται δ' ὁ σύνδεσμος οὗτος τὸ ἕτερον τῶν ἀξιωμάτων ψεῦδος εἶναι. αἰτιῶδες δέ ἐστιν ἀξίωμα τὸ συντασσόμενον διὰ τοῦ "διότι", οἷον "διότι ἡμέρα ἐστί, φῶς ἐστιν"· οἱονεὶ γὰρ αἴτιόν ἐστι τὸ πρῶτον τοῦ δευτέρου. διασαφοῦν δὲ τὸ μᾶλλον ἀξίωμά ἐστι τὸ συνταττόμενον ὑπὸ τοῦ διασαφοῦντος τὸ μᾶλλον συνδέσμου καὶ τοῦ <,,ἤ"> μέσου τῶν ἀξιωμάτων τασσομένου, οἷον "μᾶλλον ἡμέρα ἐστὶν ἢ νύξ ἐστι. διασαφοῦν δὲ τὸ ἧττον ἀξίωμά ἐστι τὸ ἐναντίον τῷ προκειμένῳ, οἷον "ἧττον νύξ ἐστιν ἢ ἡμέρα ἐστίν."

978—Disjunctive and hypothetical propositions became the basis of Stoic syllogistic and of their doctrine of proof. The function of hypothetical propositions with a view to acquiring knowledge may be understood from the following passage of Sextus.

The importance of hypothetical propositions

Sextus Emp., *Adv. math.* VIII (*Against the logicians* II) 108-111 (SVF II 216):

Καὶ δὴ οὐχ ἁπλᾶ μέν ἐστιν ἀξιώματα τὰ ἀνώτερον προειρημένα, ἅπερ ἐξ ἀξιώματος διαφορουμένου [1] ἢ ἀξιωμάτων διαφερόντων συνέστηκε καὶ ἐν οἷς σύνδεσμος ἢ σύνδεσμοι ἐπικρατοῦσιν. λαμβανέσθω δὲ ἐκ τούτων ἐπὶ τοῦ παρόντος τὸ καλούμενον συνημμένον. τοῦτο τοίνυν συνέστηκεν ἐξ ἀξιώματος διαφορουμένου ἢ ἐξ ἀξιωμάτων διαφερόντων διὰ τοῦ "εἰ" ἢ "εἴπερ" συνδέσμου, οἷον ἐκ διαφορουμένου μὲν ἀξιώματος καὶ τοῦ "εἰ" συνδέσμου συνέστηκε τὸ τοιοῦτον συνημμένον "εἰ ἡμέρα ἔστιν, ἡμέρα ἔστιν", ἐκ διαφερόντων δὲ ἀξιωμάτων καὶ διὰ τοῦ "εἴπερ" συνδέσμου τὸ οὕτως ἔχον "εἴπερ ἡμέρα ἔστι, φῶς ἔστιν". τῶν δὲ ἐν τῷ συνημμένῳ ἀξιωμάτων τὸ μετὰ τὸν ,,εἰ" ἢ τὸν ,,εἴπερ" σύνδεσμον τεταγμένον ἡγούμενόν τε καὶ πρῶτον καλεῖται, τὸ δὲ λοιπὸν λῆγόν τε καὶ δεύτερον, καὶ ἐὰν ἀναστρόφως ἐκφέρηται τὸ ὅλον συνημμένον, οἷον οὕτως "φῶς ἔστιν, εἴπερ ἡμέρα ἔστιν"· καὶ γὰρ ἐν τούτῳ λῆγον μὲν καλεῖται τὸ "φῶς ἔστιν" καίπερ πρῶτον ἐξενεχθέν, ἡγούμενον δὲ τὸ "ἡμέρα ἔστιν" καίπερ δεύτερον λεγόμενον, διὰ τὸ μετὰ τὸν ,,εἴπερ" σύνδεσμον

---

[1] ἀξιώματος διαφορουμένου - a duplicated proposition, as in the example given *infra*. The true name of tautological syllogisms, such as are meant here, is διφορούμενοι. Later they were called erroneously διαφορούμενοι.

τετάχθαι. ἡ μὲν οὖν σύστασις τοῦ συνημμένου, ὡς ἐν συντόμῳ εἰπεῖν, ἐστὶ τοιαύτη, ἐπαγγέλλεσθαι δὲ δοκεῖ τὸ τοιοῦτον ἀξίωμα ἀκολουθεῖν τῷ ἐν αὐτῷ πρώτῳ τὸ ἐν αὐτῷ δεύτερον καὶ ὄντος τοῦ ἡγουμένου ἔσεσθαι τὸ λῆγον. ὅθεν σῳζομένης μὲν τῆς τοιαύτης ἐπαγγελίας καὶ ἀκολουθοῦντος τῷ ἡγουμένῳ τοῦ λήγοντος ἀληθὲς γίνεται καὶ τὸ συνημμένον, μὴ σῳζομένης δὲ ψεῦδος.

Proof **979**—Proof, then, is defined as follows.

Sextus Emp., *Adv. math.* VIII (*Against the logicians* II) 310-314:

Τούτων δὴ οὕτως ἐχόντων ἡ ἀπόδειξις πρὸ πάντος ὀφείλει λόγος εἶναι, δεύτερον συνακτικός [1], τρίτον καὶ ἀληθής, τέταρτον καὶ ἄδηλον ἔχων συμπέρασμα, πέμπτον καὶ ἐκκαλυπτόμενον τοῦτο ἐκ τῆς δυνάμεως τῶν λημμάτων [2]. ὁ γοῦν τοιοῦτος λόγος ἡμέρας οὔσης "εἰ νὺξ ἔστι, σκότος ἔστιν· ἀλλὰ μὴν νὺξ ἔστι· σκότος ἄρα ἔστιν" συνακτικὸς μὲν καθειστήκει (δοθέντων γὰρ αὐτοῦ τῶν λημμάτων ὑπάρχειν συνάγεται καὶ ἡ ἐπιφορά [3]), οὐκ ἀληθής δέ γε ἦν (εἶχε γὰρ ἐν αὐτῷ λῆμμα ψεῦδος τὸ "νὺξ ἔστι")· διόπερ οὐδὲ ἀποδεικτικός ἐστιν. πάλιν ὁ τοιοῦτος "εἰ ἡμέρα ἔστι, φῶς ἔστιν· ἡμέρα δ' ἔστιν· φῶς ἄρα ἔστιν" πρὸς τῷ συνακτικὸς ἔτι καὶ ἀληθής ἐστιν, ἐπείπερ δοθέντων αὐτοῦ τῶν λημμάτων δίδοται καὶ ἡ ἐπιφορά, καὶ δι' ἀληθῶν ἀληθές τι δείκνυσιν. τοιοῦτος δὲ ὢν πάλιν οὐκ ἔστιν ἀπόδειξις τῷ πρόδηλον ἔχειν τὸ συμπέρασμα τὸ "φῶς ἔστιν", ἀλλὰ μὴ ἄδηλον. κατὰ ταὐτὰ δὲ καὶ ὁ οὕτως ἔχων "εἴ τίς σοι θεῶν εἶπεν ὅτι πλουτήσει οὗτος, πλουτήσει οὗτος· οὑτοσὶ δὲ ὁ θεὸς εἶπέ σοι ὅτι πλουτήσει οὗτος· πλουτήσει ἄρα οὗτος" ἄδηλον μὲν ἔχει συμπέρασμα τὸ πλουτήσειν τοῦτον, οὐκ ἔστι δ' ἀποδεικτικὸς διὰ τὸ μὴ ἐκ τῆς τῶν λημμάτων δυνάμεως ἐκκαλύπτεσθαι, ἀλλ' ἐκ τῆς τοῦ θεοῦ πίστεως παραδοχῆς τυγχάνειν. συνδραμόντων οὖν πάντων τούτων, τοῦ τε συνακτικὸν εἶναι τὸν λόγον καὶ ἀληθῆ καὶ ἀδήλου παραστατικόν, ὑφίσταται ἡ ἀπόδειξις. ἔνθεν καὶ οὕτως αὐτὴν ὑπογράφουσιν "ἀπόδειξίς ἐστι λόγος δι' ὁμολογουμένων λημμάτων κατὰ συναγωγὴν [1] ἐπιφορὰν ἐκκαλύπτων ἄδηλον", οἷον ὁ τοιοῦτος "εἰ ἔστι κίνησις, ἔστι κενόν· ἀλλὰ μὴν ἔστι κίνησις· ἔστιν ἄρα κενόν". τὸ γὰρ εἶναι κενὸν ἄδηλόν τ' ἐστί, καὶ δι' ἀληθῶν δοκεῖ, τοῦ τε "εἰ ἔστι κίνησις, ἔστι κενόν" καὶ τοῦ "ἔστι δὲ κίνησις", κατὰ συναγωγὴν ἐκκαλύπτεσθαι.

λόγοι **980**—When it happens that an argument is not conclusive (ἀπέραντος).
ἀπέραντοι Sextus Emp., *Adv. math.* VIII (*Ag. the log.* II) 429-434 (SVF II 240):

---

[1] The term συνακτικός is used by Stoic logicians for "conclusive", συναγωγή for deduction or inference.

[2] λήμματα is used by Stoics for the premises. Aristotle mostly called them προτάσεις, but sometimes he also spoke of λήμματα.

[3] ἐπιφορά is the Stoic term for "what follows from premisses", ergo the conclusion.

Τοίνυν φασὶ τετραχῶς γίγνεσθαι τὸν ἀπέραντον λόγον, ἤτοι κατὰ διάρτησιν [1]
ἢ κατὰ παρολκὴν [2] ἢ κατὰ τὸ ἐν μοχθηρῷ ἠρωτῆσθαι σχήματι ἢ κατὰ ἔλλειψιν.
ἀλλὰ κατὰ διάρτησιν μέν, ὅταν μηδεμίαν ἔχῃ κοινωνίαν καὶ συνάρτησιν τὰ
λήμματα πρὸς ἀλληλά τε καὶ πρὸς τὴν ἐπιφοράν, οἷον ἐπὶ τοῦ τοιούτου λόγου
"εἰ ἡμέρα ἔστι, φῶς ἔστιν· ἀλλὰ μὴν πυροὶ ἐν ἀγορᾷ πωλοῦνται· φῶς ἄρα
ἔστιν." ὁρῶμεν γὰρ ὡς ἐπὶ τούτου οὔτε τὸ "εἰ ἡμέρα ἔστι" ἔχει τινὰ σύμπνοιαν
καὶ συμπλοκὴν πρὸς τὸ "πυροὶ ἐν ἀγορᾷ πωλοῦνται", οὔτε ἑκάτερον αὐτῶν πρὸς
τὸ "φῶς ἄρα ἔστιν", ἀλλ' ἕκαστον ἀπὸ τῶν ἄλλων διήρτηται. κατὰ δὲ παρολκὴν
ἀπέραντος γίνεται ὁ λόγος, ὅταν ἔξωθέν τι καὶ περισσῶς παραλαμβάνηται τοῖς
λήμμασι, καθάπερ ἐπὶ τοῦ οὕτως ἔχοντος "εἰ ἡμέρα ἔστι, φῶς ἔστιν· ἀλλὰ μὴν
ἡμέρα ἔστι, ἀλλὰ καὶ ἡ ἀρετὴ ὠφελεῖ· φῶς ἄρα ἔστιν". τὸ γὰρ τὴν ἀρετὴν
ὠφελεῖν περισσῶς συμπαρείληπται τοῖς ἄλλοις λήμμασιν, εἴ γε δυνατόν ἐστιν
ἐξαιρεθέντος αὐτοῦ διὰ τῶν περιλειπομένων, τοῦ τε "εἰ ἡμέρα ἔστι, φῶς ἔστιν"
καὶ τοῦ "ἀλλὰ μὴν ἡμέρα ἔστι", συνάγεσθαι τὴν ἐπιφορὰν τὸ "φῶς ἄρα
ἔστιν". διὰ δὲ τὸ ἐν μοχθηρῷ ἠρωτῆσθαι σχήματι ἀπέραντος γίνεται <ὁ> λόγος,
ὅταν ἔν τινι τῶν παρὰ τὰ ὑγιῆ σχήματα θεωρουμένων ἐρωτηθῇ σχήματι·
οἷον ὄντος ὑγιοῦς σχήματος τοῦ τοιούτου "εἰ τὸ πρῶτον, τὸ δεύτερον, τὸ δέ γε
πρῶτον, τὸ ἄρα δεύτερον", ὄντος δὲ καὶ τοῦ "εἰ τὸ πρῶτον, τὸ δεύτερον, οὐχὶ
δέ γε τὸ δεύτερον, οὐκ ἄρα τὸ πρῶτον", φαμὲν τὸν ἐν τοιούτῳ σχήματι ἐρωτη-
θέντα "εἰ τὸ πρῶτον, τὸ δεύτερον, οὐχὶ δέ γε τὸ πρῶτον, οὐκ ἄρα τὸ δεύτερον"
ἀπέραντον εἶναι, οὐχ ὅτι ἀδύνατόν ἐστιν ἐν τῷ τοιούτῳ σχήματι λόγον συν-
ερωτᾶσθαι δι' ἀληθῶν ἀληθὲς συνάγοντα (δύναται γάρ, οἷον ὁ τοιοῦτος "εἰ τὰ
τρία τέσσαρά ἐστι, τὰ ἓξ ὀκτώ ἐστι· οὐχὶ δέ γε τὰ τρία τέσσαρά ἐστι, οὐκ
ἄρα τὰ ἓξ ὀκτώ ἐστι"), τῷ δὲ δύνασθαί τινας λόγους ἐν αὐτῷ τάττεσθαι
μοχθηρούς, καθάπερ καὶ τὸν τοιοῦτον "εἰ ἡμέρα ἔστι, φῶς ἔστιν· ἀλλὰ μὴν
οὐκ ἔστιν ἡμέρα· οὐκ ἄρα ἔστι φῶς". κατ' ἔλλειψιν δὲ ἀπέραντος γίνεται ὁ
λόγος, ὅταν ἐλλείπῃ τι τῶν συνακτικῶν λημμάτων. οἷον "ἤτοι κακόν ἐστιν ὁ
πλοῦτος ἢ ἀγαθόν ἐστιν ὁ πλοῦτος· οὐχὶ δέ γε κακόν ἐστιν ὁ πλοῦτος· ἀγαθὸν
ἄρα ἐστὶν ὁ πλοῦτος." ἐλλείπει γὰρ ἐν τῷ διεζευγμένῳ τὸ ἀδιάφορον εἶναι τὸν
πλοῦτον, ὥστε τὴν ὑγιῆ συνερώτησιν τοιαύτην μᾶλλον ὑπάρχειν "ἤτοι ἀγαθόν
ἐστιν ὁ πλοῦτος ἢ κακόν ἐστιν ἢ ἀδιάφορον· οὔτε δὲ ἀγαθόν ἐστιν ὁ πλοῦτος
οὔτε κακόν· ἀδιάφορον ἄρα ἐστίν."

981—For Chrysippus, the chief task of dialectic is: determining the **The five**
τρόποι in which a correct conclusion is possible. He finds five forms which **anapodeiktoi**
are evident without any proof.

---

[1] By διάρτησις he means *incoherence*, as will appear in the following explanation.
[2] παρολκή means that "strange" elements are introduced into the argument, as
will be explained below.

Diog. Laërt. VII 79-81 (SVF II 241):

Εἰσὶ δὲ καὶ ἀναπόδεικτοί τινες, τῷ μὴ χρῄζειν ἀποδείξεως, ἄλλοι μὲν παρ' ἄλλοις, παρὰ δὲ τῷ Χρυσίππῳ πέντε, δι' ὧν πᾶς λόγος πλέκεται. — πρῶτος δέ ἐστιν ἀναπόδεικτος, ἐν ᾧ πᾶς λόγος συντάσσεται ἐκ συνημμένου καὶ τοῦ ἡγουμένου, ἀφ' οὗ ἄρχεται τὸ συνημμένον, καὶ τὸ λῆγον ἐπιφέρει, οἷον "εἰ τὸ πρῶτον, τὸ δεύτερον· ἀλλὰ μὴν τὸ πρῶτον, τὸ ἄρα δεύτερον". δεύτερος δ' ἐστὶν ἀναπόδεικτος ὁ διὰ συνημμένου καὶ τοῦ ἀντικειμένου τοῦ λήγοντος τὸ ἀντικείμενον τοῦ ἡγουμένου ἔχων συμπέρασμα, οἷον "εἰ ἡμέρα ἐστί, φῶς ἐστιν· ἀλλὰ μὴν νύξ ἐστιν· οὐκ ἄρα ἡμέρα ἐστίν". ἡ γὰρ πρόσληψις γίνεται ἐκ τοῦ ἀντικειμένου τῷ λήγοντι καὶ ἡ ἐπιφορὰ ἐκ τοῦ ἀντικειμένου τῷ ἡγουμένῳ. τρίτος δέ ἐστιν ἀναπόδεικτος ὁ δι' ἀποφατικῆς συμπλοκῆς καὶ ἑνὸς τῶν ἐν τῇ συμπλοκῇ ἐπιφέρων τὸ ἀντικείμενον τοῦ λοιποῦ, οἷον "οὐχὶ τέθνηκε Πλάτων καὶ ζῇ Πλάτων· ἀλλὰ μὴν τέθνηκε Πλάτων· οὐκ ἄρα ζῇ Πλάτων". τέταρτος δέ ἐστιν ἀναπόδεικτος ὁ διὰ διεζευγμένου καὶ ἑνὸς τῶν ἐν τῷ διεζευγμένῳ τὸ ἀντικείμενον τοῦ λοιποῦ ἔχων συμπέρασμα, οἷον "ἤτοι τὸ πρῶτον ἢ τὸ δεύτερον· ἀλλὰ μὴν τὸ πρῶτον· οὐκ ἄρα τὸ δεύτερον". πέμπτος δέ ἐστιν ἀναπόδεικτος, ἐν ᾧ πᾶς λόγος συντάσσεται ἐκ διεζευγμένου καὶ ἑνὸς τῶν ἐν τῷ διεζευγμένῳ ἀντικειμένου καὶ ἐπιφέρει τὸ λοιπόν, οἷον "ἤτοι ἡμέρα ἐστὶν ἢ νύξ ἐστιν· οὐχὶ δὲ νύξ ἐστιν· ἡμέρα ἄρα ἐστίν."

Mme Virieux-Reymond gives the list in the above cited work, p. 141 f. Cp. also Sextus, *Ag. the Log.* II 223-230 (SVF II 242).

Originality of Chrysippus' logic
982—That, after Aristotle, and even for the greater part after Theophrastus and Eudemus, Chrysippus went a new way, is confirmed by the following passage of Boëthius.

Boëthius, *De syllogismo hypoth.* I, Prooem. (Patrol. Lat. LXIV 831):

De hypotheticis syllogismis ... ab Aristotele nihil est conscriptum, Theophrastus vero ... rerum tantum summas exsequitur; Eudemus latiorem docendi graditur viam, sed ita ut veluti quaedam seminaria sparsisse, nullum tamen frugis videatur extulisse proventum. Nos igitur ... quae ab illis vel dicta breviter vel funditus omissa sunt, elucidanda diligenter suscepimus.

About Theophr. and Eudemus, cp. our nr. **675**.

Modern estimation of it
983—In the nineteenth century, Stoic logic has been seriously underestimated by German scholars, first of all by Prantl in his *Geschichte der Logik im Abendlande*, Vol. I, Leipzig 1885. Prantl was followed only too much by Zeller and by Überweg.

V. Brochard was the first to appreciate Stoic logic in a more intelligent way, in his article *La logique des Stoïciens*, first published in the *Archiv für Geschichte der Phil.*, 1892; reprinted in *Etudes de phil. ancienne et de phil. moderne*, Paris 1912, pp. 220 ff.

He was followed by E. Bréhier, *Chrysippe*, Paris 1910;

A. Reymond, *La logique stoïcienne* in the Swiss *Revue de théol. et de phil.* 1929, pp. 161-171;

J. Lukasiewicz, *Zur Geschichte der Aussagenlogik*, in *Annalen der Phil.*, Bd. XIII, Heft 1 (Congress of Prague, 1935);

M. Pohlenz, *Die Stoa* I, Göttingen 1948, pp. 47-51;

Mme A. Virieux-Reymond, *La logique et l'épistémologie des Stoïciens*, Lausanne, sans date (1949).

Finally, there is a recent American publication on Stoic logic: B. Mates, *Stoic Logic* (Univ. of California publications in phil.), Berkeley 1953.

Mme Virieux summarizes her judgement on Stoic logic in the following lines **The value of** (o.c., p. 153): **Stoic Logic**
"Elle (i.e. la logique stoïcienne) s'apparente à celle de Stuart Mill: données **according to** concrètes et individuelles du jugement; définitions purement nominales (énumé- **A. Virieux-** ration des propriétés d'un sujet); inférences et propositions conditionnelles, etc. **Reymond** La logique du Portique tendait ainsi à être inductive. —
Il y a un certain flottement dans la logique stoïcienne entre une tendance à l'empirisme et une autre vers la formalisation logique: c'est à propos de cette dernière — sur le terrain de la logique pure — que MM. Lukasiewicz et Reymond ont découvert simultanément la similitude indéniable qui existe entre la logistique et la dialectique stoïcienne."

7—LOGIC (3): THEORY OF KNOWLEDGE

984—Stoic theory of knowledge is usually qualified as "sensualism", a qualification which, as we shall see, is not correct, i.e. if by "sensualism" a doctrine is meant which makes the senses the criterium of knowledge. What is true is, first, that in their theory of knowledge the Stoics *started from* the senses; secondly that Zeno defined his φαντασία quite materially as an impression in "the soul"; thirdly, that the decisive act, called κατάληψις, was itself named αἴσθησις; fourthly that Chrysippus, altering Zeno's account of the process of knowledge, did not call κατάληψις but φαντασία καταληπτική the standard of knowledge, conceiving it in a different way which, in any case, came nearer to sensualism.

    a. Sextus Emp., *Adv. math.* VII (*Ag. the logicians* I) 236 (SVF   φαντασία I 58): **defined by** **Zeno**
"Ὅταν λέγῃ ὁ Ζήνων φαντασίαν εἶναι τύπωσιν ἐν ψυχῇ, —

φαντασία   **b.** Sextus Emp., *Adv. math.* VII (*Ag. the log.* I) 248 (SVF I 59):
καταληπτική

Φαντασία καταληπτική ἐστιν ἡ ἀπὸ τοῦ ὑπάρχοντος καὶ κατ' αὐτὸ τὸ ὑπάρχον ἐναπομεμαγμένη καὶ ἐναπεσφραγισμένη, ὁποία οὐκ ἂν γένοιτο ἀπὸ μὴ ὑπάρχοντος.

That, according to Zeno's conception, φαντασία καταληπτική should not be translated by "fetching" or "arresting presentation", but "liable to κατάληψις", i.e. comprehension, may be understood from the following nr.

The meaning   **985—a.** Cic., *Acad. post.* (I) 11, 40-42:
of
κατάληψις   ... primum de sensibus ipsis quaedam dixit nova; quos iunctos [1] esse censuit e quadam quasi impulsione oblata extrinsecus: quam ille φαντασίαν, nos visum appellemus licet;—sed ad haec, quae visa sunt et quasi accepta sensibus, adsensionem adiungit animorum [2]: quam esse vult in nobis positam et voluntariam. Visis [3] non omnibus adiungebat fidem, sed iis solum, quae propriam quandam haberent declarationem earum rerum, quae viderentur: id autem visum, cum ipsum per se cerneretur, comprehensibile. Feretis haec? Nos vero, inquit. Quonam enim modo καταλημπτόν diceres?—Sed, cum acceptum iam et approbatum esset, comprehensionem [4] appellabat, similem iis rebus, quae manu prenderentur: ex quo etiam nomen hoc duxerat, cum eo verbo ante nemo tali in re usus esset: plurimisque idem novis verbis (nova enim dicebat) usus est. Quod autem erat sensu comprehensum, id ipsum sensum [5] appellabat, et si ita erat comprehensum, ut convelli ratione non posset, scientiam: sin aliter, inscientiam nominabat [6]: ex qua exsisteret etiam opinio, quae esset imbecilla et cum falso incognitoque communis. Sed inter scientiam et inscientiam comprehensionem illam, quam dixi, collocabat.

b. How the relation between φαντασία, συγκατάθεσις, κατάληψις and ἐπιστήμη was illustrated by Zeno by a gesture.

---

[1] iunctos esse - The senses are "affected by" some impulsion from outside, which makes them "joint" and, in a sense, united: *perception* (αἴσθησις), which is one, comes from the, thus affected, αἰσθήσεις.

[2] adsensio animorum - the συγκατάθεσις, which is free and in our power.

[3] φαντασίαις.

[4] κατάληψις. Zeno speaks of "comprehension"—we should rather say *apprehension*— only when the "presentation" of the senses has been accepted by Reason.

[5] In this sense, αἴσθησις contains the rational element of the συγκατάθεσις.

[6] The Stoic conception of knowledge as τὴν ἀσφαλῆ καὶ βεβαίαν καὶ ἀμετάθετον ὑπὸ λόγου κατάληψιν and of "opinion" as τὴν ἀσθενῆ καὶ ψευδῆ συγκατάθεσιν, while the κατάληψις stands between them, may be clearly seen in Sextus, *Ag. the Log.* I 151, who (at the end of 152) confirms explicitly that κατάληψις was made the standard of truth (καὶ ταύτην κριτήριον ἀληθείας καθεστάναι).

Cic., *Acad. pr.* (*Lucullus*) 47, 145:

Et hoc quidem Zeno gestu conficiebat. Nam cum extensis digitis adversam manum ostenderat, "*visum*, inquiebat, huiusmodi est". Deinde, cum paulum digitos constrinxerat, "*assensus* huiusmodi". Tum, cum plane compresserat pugnumque fecerat, *comprehensionem* illam esse dicebat: quae ex similitudine etiam nomen ei rei, quod ante non fuerat, κατάλημψιν imposuit. Cum autem laevam manum admoverat et illum pugnum arte vehementerque compresserat, *scientiam* talem esse dicebat; cuius compotem, nisi sapientem, esse neminem.

On the division of mankind into σοφοί and φαῦλοι, see *Ethics*.

c. That φαντασία καταληπτική, as it is usually called, is the same as what Cicero, in the passage cited sub **a**, called καταληπτός and consequently had a passive sense, at least originally, may be clearly seen from the following passage of Sextus. The double aspect of apprehension, according to Zeno's conception, is keenly noticed in this passage.

Sextus Emp., *Adv. math.* VIII (*Ag. the log.* II) 397 (SVF II 91): **Double aspect of apprehension**

Ἔστι μὲν οὖν ἡ κατάληψις, ὡς ἔστι παρ' αὐτῶν ἀκούειν, καταληπτικῆς φαντασίας συγκατάθεσις, ἥτις διπλοῦν ἔοικεν εἶναι πρᾶγμα, καὶ τὸ μέν τι ἔχειν ἀκούσιον, τὸ δὲ ἑκούσιον καὶ ἐπὶ τῇ ἡμετέρᾳ κρίσει κείμενον. τὸ μὲν γὰρ φαντασιωθῆναι ἀβούλητον ἦν· καὶ οὐκ ἐπὶ τῷ πάσχοντι ἔκειτο ἀλλ' ἐπὶ τῷ φαντασιοῦντι τὸ οὑτωσὶ διατεθῆναι, οἷον λευκαντικῶς λευκοῦ ὑποπεσόντος χρώματος ἢ γλυκαντικῶς γλυκέος τῇ γεύσει προσαχθέντος· τὸ δὲ συγκατατίθεσθαι τούτῳ τῷ κινήματι ἔκειτο ἐπὶ τῷ παραδεχομένῳ τὴν φαντασίαν.

986—Since, according to the Stoics, κατάληψις was the standard of truth, and κατάληψις presupposing the φαντασία καταληπτική, it was against this notion that Arcesilaus, head of the Academy after Polemo and Crates, directed his criticism. He simply states that such a presentation, the definition of which has been given sub **984b**, does not exist, since there is not true presentation which could not be confounded with an untrue one [1]. In general, the Sceptics attacked the Stoic definition of φαντασία as an impression, because, if it were so, the idea of μνήμη as a θησαυρισμὸς φαντασιῶν, as Zeno called it [2], would become impossible [3]. Chrysippus,

The φαντασία καταληπτική criticized by Arcesilaus

---

[1] The argument of Arcesilaus, found in Sextus, *Math.* VII (*Ag. the Log.* I) 247-252, will be given in our next chapter, nr. **1104**.

[2] The expression has become famous by the well known passage of St. Augustine, *Conf.* X 8, 12: "et venio in campos et lata praetoria memoriae, ubi sunt thesauri innumerabilium imaginum de cuiuscemodi rebus sensis invectarum."

[3] The Sceptic argument ap. Sextus, *Math.* VII (*Ag. the Log.* I) 372. Below, nr. **1134**.

therefore, first altered Zeno's idea of "presentation", next his conception of the presentation called kataleptic.

a. Sextus Emp., *Adv. math.* VII (*Ag. the log.* I) 228-231 (SVF II 56):

The φαντασία explained as ἑτεροίωσις ψυχῆς

Φαντασία οὖν ἐστι κατ' αὐτοὺς (sc. τοὺς Στωϊκούς) τύπωσις ἐν ψυχῇ. περὶ ἧς εὐθὺς καὶ διέστησαν· Κλεάνθης μὲν γὰρ ἤκουσε τὴν τύπωσιν κατὰ εἰσοχήν τε καὶ ἐξοχήν [1], ὥσπερ καὶ <τὴν> διὰ τῶν δακτυλίων γινομένην τοῦ κηροῦ τύπωσιν. Χρύσιππος δὲ ἄτοπον ἡγεῖτο τὸ τοιοῦτον. πρῶτον μὲν γάρ, φησί, τῆς διανοίας δεήσει ὑφ' ἕν ποτε τρίγωνόν τι καὶ τετράγωνον φαντασιουμένης τὸ αὐτὸ σῶμα κατὰ τὸν αὐτὸν χρόνον διαφέροντα ἔχειν περὶ αὐτῷ σχήματα ἅμα τε τρίγωνον καὶ τετράγωνον γίνεσθαι ἢ καὶ περιφερές, ὅπερ ἐστὶν ἄτοπον· εἶτα, πολλῶν ἅμα φαντασιῶν ὑφισταμένων ἐν ἡμῖν παμπληθεῖς καὶ τοὺς σχηματισμοὺς ἕξειν τὴν ψυχήν, ὃ τοῦ προτέρου χεῖρόν ἐστιν. αὐτὸς οὖν τὴν τύπωσιν εἰρῆσθαι ὑπὸ τοῦ Ζήνωνος ὑπενόει ἀντὶ τῆς ἑτεροιώσεως, ὥστ' εἶναι τοιοῦτον τὸν λόγον "φαντασία ἐστὶν ἑτεροίωσις ψυχῆς", μηκέτι ἀτόπου ὄντος <τοῦ> τὸ αὐτὸ σῶμα, ὑφ' ἕν [κατὰ τὸν αὐτὸν χρόνον] * πολλῶν περὶ ἡμᾶς συνισταμένων φαντασιῶν, παμπληθεῖς ἀναδέχεσθαι ἑτεροιώσεις· ὥσπερ γὰρ ὁ ἀήρ, ὅταν ἅμα πολλοὶ φωνῶσιν, ἀμυθήτους ὑπὸ ἓν καὶ διαφερούσας ἀναδεχόμενος πληγὰς εὐθὺς πολλὰς ἴσχει καὶ τὰς ἑτεροιώσεις, οὕτω καὶ τὸ ἡγεμονικὸν ποικίλως φαντασιούμενον ἀνάλογόν τι τούτῳ πείσεται.

or ἑτεροίωσις ἐν ἡγεμονικῷ

b. The definition is formulated more explicitly in Sextus, *Adv. math.* VII (*Ag. the Log.* I) 233:

... ὅταν λέγωμεν τὴν φαντασίαν τύπωσιν ἐν ψυχῇ, συνεμφαίνομεν καὶ τὸ περὶ ποιὸν μέρος γίνεσθαι τῆς ψυχῆς τὴν τύπωσιν, τουτέστι τὸ ἡγεμονικόν, ὥστε ἐξαπλούμενον γίνεσθαι τὸν ὅρον τοιοῦτον "φαντασία ἐστὶν ἑτεροίωσις ἐν ἡγεμονικῷ".

Cp. our nr. **956a, b**, where it was argued that Chrysippus explained all mental activities, such as ὁρμή, συγκατάθεσις, κατάληψις, and even movements of the body, such as walking, as ἑτεροιώσεις τοῦ ἡγεμονικοῦ, technically called also: the ἡγεμονικόν πως ἔχον.

c. We find the formula later in Seneca's definition of virtue. Seneca, *Ep.* 113, 2:

Virtus autem nihil aliud est quam animus quodammodo se habens.

d. Cp. Plut., *De virt. mor.* 3:

Κοινῶς δὲ ἅπαντες οὗτοι (sc. οἱ Στωϊκοί) τὴν ἀρετὴν τοῦ ἡγεμονικοῦ τῆς ψυχῆς διάθεσίν τινα καὶ δύναμιν γεγενημένην ὑπὸ λόγου, μᾶλλον δὲ λόγον

---

[1] "by way of intaglios and of embossed figures". Cp. *Pyrrh. Hyp.* II 70.
* del. Mutschmann.

οὖσαν αὐτὴν ὁμολογούμενον καὶ βέβαιον καὶ ἀμετάπτωτον, ὑποτίθενται· καὶ νομίζουσιν οὐκ εἶναι τὸ παθητικὸν καὶ ἄλογον διαφορᾷ τινι καὶ φύσει ψυχῆς τοῦ λογικοῦ διακεκριμένον, ἀλλὰ τὸ αὐτὸ τῆς ψυχῆς μέρος, ὃ δὴ καλοῦσι διάνοιαν καὶ ἡγεμονικόν, διόλου τρεπόμενον καὶ μεταβάλλον ἔν τε τοῖς πάθεσι καὶ ταῖς κατὰ ἕξιν ἢ διάθεσιν μεταβολαῖς, κακίαν τε γίνεσθαι καὶ ἀρετήν, καὶ μηδὲν ἔχειν ἄλογον ἐν ἑαυτῷ· —

And again in c. 7:

Ἔνιοι δέ φασιν οὐχ ἕτερον εἶναι τοῦ λόγου τὸ πάθος, οὐδὲ δυοῖν διαφορὰν καὶ στάσιν, ἀλλὰ ἑνὸς λόγου τροπὴν ἐπ᾽ ἀμφότερα.

From these passages may be inferred that, indeed, Chrysippus held a kind of psychological monism, in which the different psychical functions—φαντασία, συγκατάθεσις, ὁρμή and πάθος—and also moral dispositions such as virtue and vice, are considered each as a ἡγεμονικόν πως ἔχον.

As we shall see later, Posidonius opposed this doctrine of the πάθη and, according to Pohlenz, came back to Zeno's conception.

987—a.   The following description of φαντασία καταληπτική, ascribed by Sextus to νεώτεροι, is by some scholars attributed to Chrysippus [1].

The character of the φαντασία καταληπτική is changed

Sextus Emp., *Adv. math.* VII (*Ag. the log.* I) 257:

Αὕτη γὰρ ἐναργὴς οὖσα καὶ πληκτικὴ μόνον οὐχὶ τῶν τριχῶν, φασί, λαμβάνεται, κατασπῶσα ἡμᾶς εἰς συγκατάθεσιν, καὶ ἄλλου μηδενὸς δεομένη εἰς τὸ τοιαύτη προσπίπτειν ἢ εἰς τὸ τὴν πρὸς τὰς ἄλλας διαφορὰν ὑποβάλλειν.

Pohlenz, *Zeno und Chrysipp*, p. 181, notices that, while in Zeno's conception the συγκατάθεσις is a free and active decision of the intellect, to be clearly distinguished from the φαντασία, in which the soul is entirely passive, Chrysippus explains the process of knowledge in such a way that the presentation, if it is "kataleptic", is in itself decisive and *compels* the intellect to assent. This, then, is indeed what we call *sensualism*.

It should be noticed, however, that these very νεώτεροι, to whom the above description is attributed, added the condition "μηδὲν ἔχουσαν ἔνστημα" to Zeno's definition [2]. Which means that a man may receive a kataleptic presentation—but reject it because he thinks it improbable διὰ τὴν ἔξωθεν περίστασιν [3]. Thus, the assent, which is normally given, in special cases may be held back. And in this our decision is free.

Whether, then, Chrys. was or was not the author of the above expressed view, this much is sure, that he differed from Zeno as to the theory of knowledge not so much in that he should have abolished the freedom of the intellect with regard to presentation, while Zeno upheld it, but rather in that Chrys. was more strictly

---

[1]   Thus by Pohlenz in *Zeno und Chrysipp*. Later, in *Die Stoa* I p. 62, he says that "later, in the days after Chrysippus", the kataleptic presentation was explained as being a "fetching" or "arresting" presentation, which "lays hold of us, almost by the very hair, and drags us off to assent" (Bury).

[2]   Sextus, o.c., 253.

[3]   E.g. Admetus when Alcestis is brought back to him from the grave, or Menelaus when he sees Helen at Proteus' house in Pharos.

a psychological monist, and therefore regarded presentation and assent both as
rational, both being functions of the hegemonikon. We can understand, that, by
this doctrine, Chrys. was led to making the kataleptic presentation itself the
criterium of truth, as is mentioned repeatedly by Sextus and by Diog. Laërt.

φαντασία   **b.** While according to Zeno the κατάληψις is the criterium of truth,
καταληπτική
the criterium and only indirectly the kataleptic presentation which underlies it, in
of knowledge Chrysippus' conception it is the kataleptic presentation itself that
becomes the criterium.

Diog. Laërt. VII 54:

Κριτήριον δὲ τῆς ἀληθείας φασὶ τυγχάνειν τὴν καταληπτικὴν φαντασίαν,
τουτέστι τὴν ἀπὸ ὑπάρχοντος, καθά φησι Χρύσιππος ἐν τῇ δυοδεκάτῃ τῶν
Φυσικῶν καὶ 'Αντίπατρος καὶ 'Απολλόδωρος.

988—Later Stoics, such as Epictetus and Marcus Aurelius, lay great
stress on the freedom of personality, also with regard to presentations.

Active rôle   **a.** Epict., *Diss.* III 12, 15:
of the
intellect   'Ως γὰρ ὁ Σωκράτης ἔλεγεν ἀνεξέταστον βίον μὴ ζῆν, οὕτως ἀνεξέταστον
stressed by φαντασίαν μὴ παραδέχεσθαι, ἀλλὰ λέγειν "ἔκδεξαι, ἄφες ἴδω, τίς εἶ καὶ
later Stoics πόθεν ἔρχῃ", ὡς οἱ νυκτοφύλακες "δεῖξόν μοι τὰ συνθήματα". "ἔχεις τὸ παρὰ
τῆς φύσεως σύμβολον, ὃ δεῖ τὴν παραδεχθησομένην ἔχειν φαντασίαν;"

b. Again he stresses the rôle of the active intellect in the process
of knowledge in a passage like the following, where he is speaking on
the organization of the human mind as a proof of Providence.

Epict., *Diss.* I 6, 10:

'Η δὲ τοιαύτη τῆς διανοίας κατασκευή, καθ' ἣν οὐχ ἁπλῶς ὑποπίπτοντες
τοῖς αἰσθητοῖς τυπούμεθα ὑπ' αὐτῶν, ἀλλὰ καὶ ἐκλαμβάνομέν τι καὶ ἀφαιροῦμεν καὶ προστίθεμεν καὶ συντίθεμεν τάδε τινὰ δι' αὐτῶν καὶ νὴ Δία μετα-
βαίνομεν ἀπ' ἄλλων ἐπ' ἄλλα τ<ιν>ὰ οὕτω πως παρακείμενα, οὐδὲ ταῦτα ἱκανὰ
κινῆσαί τινας καὶ διατρέψαι πρὸς τὸ ἀπολιπεῖν [1] τὸν τεχνίτην;

c. Marc. Aur., VII 54, mentions three things which are the task
of a piously living man. The third is: "carefully working at your presentations, lest anything not liable to reasonable confirmation should
intrude."

Πανταχοῦ καὶ διηνεκῶς ἐπί σοί ἐστι καὶ τῇ παρούσῃ συμβάσει θεοσεβῶς
εὐαρεστεῖν καὶ τοῖς παροῦσιν ἀνθρώποις κατὰ δικαιοσύνην προσφέρεσθαι
καὶ τῇ παρούσῃ φαντασίᾳ ἐμφιλοτεχνεῖν, ἵνα μή τι ἀκατάληπτον παρεισρυῇ.

---

[1] ἀπολιπεῖν is used a.o. by Chrysippus for "leaving undisputed", hence for
"admitting".

989—Since Schmekel, the spiritualistic tendency of the later Stoa is usually explained by saying that, after Carneades' criticism, the materialism and sensualism of the older Stoa was overcome by Posidonius, who, returning to Plato and Aristotle, introduced the notion of ὀρθὸς λόγος into Stoic theology and theory of knowledge.

Posidonius the author of later spiritualism?

Schmekel [1] argues that, by ὀρθὸς λόγος, Posid. meant: Reason not dependent on the body; consequently God, or the κοινὸς λόγος pervading the Universe. This Logos being evidently faultless, our presentations must be checked by comparing them with it. This is what Posid. says in criticizing Chrysippus' doctrine of the πάθη.

a. Galenus, *De plac. Hippocr. et Plat.* ed. Müller p. 448, 15:

Τὸ δὴ τῶν παθῶν αἴτιον, τουτέστι τῆς τε ἀνομολογίας καὶ τοῦ κακοδαίμονος βίου, τὸ μὴ κατὰ πᾶν ἕπεσθαι τῷ ἐν αὐτοῖς δαίμονι συγγενεῖ τε ὄντι καὶ τὴν ὁμοίαν φύσιν ἔχοντι τῷ τὸν ὅλον κόσμον διοικοῦντι, τῷ δὲ χείρονι καὶ ζῳώδει ποτὲ συνεκκλίνοντας φέρεσθαι.

To this text three points should be noticed.

1. The view that human intellect is connected with, and even part of, the κοινὸς λόγος in the Universe, is ancient Stoic doctrine. Cp. Cleanthes' *Hymn to Zeus* (above, nr. **943**).

2. The identification of the hegemonikon with an inward "daemon", connected with the Spirit of the Universe, is a more personal and religious interpretation of the ancient Stoic doctrine of the fiery pneuma. Marcus Aurelius speaks in the same way. It must be asked, however, whether it is not exactly the same view, and even the same terminology, which in the next cited passage of Diog. Laërtius seems to belong to Chrysippus himself.

3. In his doctrine that the intellect judging must be ranked essentially higher than the senses furnishing presentations Posid. agrees with Zeno's doctrine of συγκατάθεσις.

To these three notes, tending to show that Posid. in his opposition to Chrysippus, and what may be surely called a spiritualizing tendency, was not utterly strange to ancient Stoic doctrine, a fourth note must be added, namely, that Posid. was probably not the first to introduce the Platonic-Aristotelian notion of ὀρθὸς λόγος into Stoic doctrine.

b. The following passage on the *telos* may show that, most probably, Chrys. himself spoke of ὀρθὸς λόγος and expressed himself in almost the same terms as Posid. did in the above cited lines.

The term ὀρθὸς λόγος probably used by Chrysippus

Diog. Laërt. VII 87-88:

Πάλιν δ' ἴσον ἐστὶ τὸ κατ' ἀρετὴν ζῆν τῷ κατ' ἐμπειρίαν τῶν φύσει συμβαινόντων ζῆν, ὥς φησι Χρύσιππος ἐν τῷ πρώτῳ Περὶ τελῶν· μέρη γάρ εἰσιν αἱ ἡμέτεραι φύσεις τῆς τοῦ ὅλου. διόπερ τέλος γίνεται τὸ ἀκολούθως τῇ φύσει

---

[1] *Die mittlere Stoa*, p. 266 ff.

ζῆν, ὅπερ ἐστὶ κατά τε τὴν αὑτοῦ καὶ κατὰ τὴν τῶν ὅλων, οὐδὲν ἐνεργοῦντας
ὧν ἀπαγορεύειν εἴωθεν ὁ νόμος ὁ κοινός, ὅσπερ ἐστὶν ὁ ὀρθὸς λόγος διὰ πάντων
ἐρχόμενος, ὁ αὐτὸς ὢν τῷ Διί, καθηγεμόνι τούτῳ τῆς τῶν ὄντων διοικήσεως
ὄντι· εἶναι δ᾽ αὐτὸ τοῦτο τὴν τοῦ εὐδαίμονος ἀρετὴν καὶ εὔροιαν βίου, ὅταν
πάντα πράττηται κατὰ τὴν συμφωνίαν τοῦ παρ᾽ ἑκάστῳ δαίμονος πρὸς τὴν
τοῦ τῶν ὅλων διοικητοῦ βούλησιν.

Cp. also the papyrusfragment of Chrys. cited in SVF II 131, p. 41, l. 27 f., where
philosophy is called ἐπιτήδευσις λόγου ὀρθότητος.

Again, we shall find the term ὀρθὸς λόγος attributed to "some of the older Stoics"
in Diog. Laërt. VII 54 (to be cited sub **990**).

c. It must be stressed that Zeno's doctrine of the criterium was
not a sensualistic theory of knowledge. By his doctrine of assent Zeno
wanted to oppose Epicurus' sensualism, and he did so consciously and
explicitly.

Chrysippus indeed, by his doctrine of kataleptic presentation came
very near to sensualism. Hence, after Carneades' criticism, a certain
spiritualistic reaction appears among later Stoics. Posidonius, who,
as we shall see in dealing with Ethics, opposed Chrysippus' monism as
to the doctrine of the πάθη, may as well have opposed him concerning
the relation of the senses and the intellect in the theory of knowledge,
and by doing so, may have determined the character of later Stoic
doctrine.

Other "criteria" are mentioned **990**—Diog. Laërt. VII 54, having declared that, according to Chrysippus and his disciples, the kataleptic presentation was the criterium of
truth, continues as follows:

Ὁ μὲν γὰρ Βόηθος [1] κριτήρια πλείονα ἀπολείπει, νοῦν καὶ αἴσθησιν καὶ
ὄρεξιν καὶ ἐπιστήμην· ὁ δὲ Χρύσιππος διαφερόμενος πρὸς αὐτὸν ἐν τῷ πρώτῳ
Περὶ λόγου κριτήριά φησιν εἶναι αἴσθησιν καὶ πρόληψιν· ἔστι δ᾽ ἡ πρόληψις
ἔννοια φυσικὴ τῶν καθόλου. ἄλλοι δέ τινες τῶν ἀρχαιοτέρων Στωϊκῶν τὸν
ὀρθὸν λόγον κριτήριον ἀπολείπουσιν, ὡς ὁ Ποσειδώνιος ἐν τῷ Περὶ κριτηρίου
φησί.

To this passage it should be noticed that κριτήριον does not only mean "standard" or "test" of truth, but also the *means* of acquiring knowledge. Cp. Sextus,
Adv. Math. VII 35 ff. on the different meanings of the term. Cp. also Epict.,
Diss. I 11, 9 ff., where first is asked for a "criterium" for distinguishing black and
white, etc. For these things and for other αἰσθητά the criteria prove to be the senses.
For the distinction of moral principles, however, another criterium is required.

---

[1] Boëthus of Sidon, a disciple of Diogenes the Babylonian.

It is determined in I 18, 6, where the γνώμη διακριτικὴ τῶν ἀγαθῶν καὶ κακῶν is opposed to the ὄψις διακριτικὴ τῶν λευκῶν καὶ μελάνων.

Instead of γνώμη he also speaks of διάνοια or λόγος. Here then we have fundamentally the same criteria as those attributed to Chrysippus in the above cited passage of Diog. Laërt. [1]

Our next task is to see what is exactly the meaning of ἔννοια and πρόληψις.

991—The katalepsis is only the beginning of the work of the mind at the presentations of the senses. Do they stay, they become ἔννοιαι or ἐννοήματα, *notions or concepts of the mind*. Our clearest account of this process is in Aëtius, *Plac.* IV 11 (SVF II 83):

ἔννοιαι
or
ἐννοήματα

Πῶς γίνεται ἡ αἴσθησις καὶ ἡ ἔννοια καὶ ὁ κατὰ ἐνδιάθεσιν λόγος. Οἱ Στωϊκοί φασιν· ὅταν γεννηθῇ ὁ ἄνθρωπος, ἔχει τὸ ἡγεμονικὸν μέρος τῆς ψυχῆς ὥσπερ χάρτην εὔεργον εἰς ἀπογραφήν· εἰς τοῦτο μίαν ἑκάστην τῶν ἐννοιῶν ἐναπογράφεται. — Πρῶτος δὲ [ὁ] τῆς ἀναγραφῆς τρόπος ὁ διὰ τῶν αἰσθήσεων. αἰσθανόμενοι γάρ τινος οἷον λευκοῦ, ἀπελθόντος αὐτοῦ μνήμην ἔχουσιν· ὅταν δὲ ὁμοειδεῖς πολλαὶ μνῆμαι γένωνται, τότε φαμὲν ἔχειν ἐμπειρίαν· ἐμπειρία γάρ ἐστι τὸ τῶν ὁμοειδῶν φαντασιῶν πλῆθος. — Τῶν δὲ ἐννοιῶν αἱ μὲν φυσικῶς γίνονται κατὰ τοὺς εἰρημένους τρόπους καὶ ἀνεπιτεχνήτως, αἱ δὲ ἤδη δι᾽ ἡμετέρας διδασκαλίας καὶ ἐπιμελείας· αὗται μὲν οὖν ἔννοιαι καλοῦνται μόνον, ἐκεῖναι δὲ καὶ προλήψεις. — Ὁ δὲ λόγος, καθ᾽ ὃν προσαγορευόμεθα λογικοί, ἐκ τῶν προλήψεων συμπληροῦσθαι λέγεται κατὰ τὴν πρώτην ἑβδομάδα. ἔστι δ᾽ ἐννόημα φάντασμα διανοίας λογικοῦ ζῴου· τὸ γὰρ φάντασμα ἐπειδὰν λογικῇ προσπίπτῃ ψυχῇ, τότε ἐννόημα καλεῖται, εἰληφὸς τοὔνομα παρὰ τοῦ νοῦ. — Διόπερ τοῖς ἀλόγοις ζῴοις ὅσα προσπίπτει, φαντάσματα μόνον ἐστίν· ὅσα δὲ ἡμῖν καὶ τοῖς θεοῖς, ταῦτα καὶ φαντάσματα κατὰ γένος καὶ ἐννοήματα κατ᾽ εἶδος· ὥσπερ τὰ δηνάρια καὶ οἱ στατῆρες αὐτὰ μὲν καθ᾽ αὑτὰ ὑπάρχει δηνάρια <καὶ> στατῆρες· ἐὰν δὲ εἰς πλοίων δοθῇ μίσθωσιν, τηνικαῦτα πρὸς τῷ δηνάρια εἶναι καὶ ναῦλα λέγεται.

In this account we have first the *tabula rasa* image, later adopted by Locke.

The account of ἐμπειρία as preceding concepts reminds us of Aristotle, *Anal. Post.* II 19 and *Metaph.* A 1 (our nr. **465** and **519**).

The relation between ἔννοια and προλήψεις can be hardly other than this: that ἔννοιαι are the more general notion, while only a part of them—namely, those occurring "naturally" and without instruction, in early youth—are called προλήψεις.

As to ἐννοήματα, one might hesitate as to whether they are simply synonymous with ἔννοιαι, or these become ἐννοήματα only at a later state of reflexion, say after the age of 14, when a man is in the full possession of his reason. Pohlenz, *Stoa* I p. 56, seems to be of the latter opinion [2]. Yet, the way in which we find both terms

---

[1] The question of the criteria is discussed at length by Bonhöffer, *Epiktet u. die Stoa*, p. 223 ff.

[2] „Der Begriff, die Ennoia, und die Allgemeinvorstellung wird zum Ennoëma, dem geistig geschauten Bilde" ...

used rather gives the impression that they are synonyms, both indicating "general idea" or "concept".

The ennoema a mere abstraction

992—The Stoic *ennoëma* is merely a *concept of the mind*. It is not supposed to have any "physical" or metaphysical existence.

a. Stobaeus, *Ecl.* I, p. 136, 21 W. (SVF I 65):

Ζήνωνος ‹καὶ τῶν ἀπ᾽ αὐτοῦ›. τὰ ἐννοήματά φασι μήτε τινὰ εἶναι μήτε ποιά, ὡσανεὶ δέ τινα καὶ ὡσανεὶ ποιὰ φαντάσματα ψυχῆς· ταῦτα δὲ ὑπὸ τῶν ἀρχαίων ἰδέας προσαγορεύεσθαι. τῶν γὰρ κατὰ τὰ ἐννοήματα ὑποπιπτόντων εἶναι τὰς ἰδέας, οἷον ἀνθρώπων, ἵππων, κοινότερον εἰπεῖν πάντων τῶν ζῴων καὶ τῶν ἄλλων ὁπόσων λέγουσιν ἰδέας εἶναι. ταύτας δὲ οἱ Στωϊκοὶ φιλόσοφοί φασιν ἀνυπάρκτους εἶναι.

b. Cp. Diog. Laërt. VII 61:

Ἐννόημα δέ ἐστι φάντασμα διανοίας, οὔτε τι ὂν οὔτε ποιόν, ὡσανεὶ δέ τι ὂν καὶ ὡσανεὶ ποιόν, οἷον γίνεται ἀνατύπωμα ἵππου καὶ μὴ παρόντος.

In the same sense Descartes speaks of *perceptio generalis*, and many after him of *idea generalis*. Berkeley rejects it, saying that such schematical general notions (e.g. a triangle being neither rectangular nor equilateral) are not really representable. A real representation is always concrete (Stoics would have said τὶ ἢ ποιόν).

The doctrine of κοιναὶ ἔννοιαι

993—A special class of these general notions are the κοιναὶ ἔννοιαι. Since they are said to be "natural" or "given to us by nature", and criteria of truth, it is likely that they are identic with the προλήψεις, of which was said that they φυσικῶς γίνονται καὶ ἀνεπιτεχνήτως (**991**) and that Chrys. admitted them as a criterium next to sense perception (**990**).

They are „natural" and criteria of truth

a. Alex. Aphrod., *De mixtione*, p. 217, l. 2-4 Bruns (SVF II 473). Having expounded Chrysippus' theory on the different kinds of mixture, he continues:

Τὸ δὲ ταύτας τὰς διαφορὰς εἶναι τῆς μίξεως, πειρᾶται πιστοῦσθαι διὰ τῶν κοινῶν ἐννοιῶν, μάλιστα δὲ κριτήρια τῆς ἀληθείας φησὶν ἡμᾶς παρὰ τῆς φύσεως λαβεῖν ταύτας.

b. Cp. Plut., apud Olympiodorum in Plat. *Phaed.* p. 156, 8 ed. Norvin (SVF II 104) who is speaking on the aporia broached in Plato's *Meno* (80e) εἰ οἷόν τε ζητεῖν καὶ εὑρίσκειν, solved by Plato by his anamnesis theory.

Οἱ δὲ ἀπὸ τῆς Στοᾶς τὰς φυσικὰς ἐννοίας αἰτιῶνται.

994—They comprise first a certain knowledge of moral principles in general, next of the existence and the nature of God(s).

a.　Origenes, *Contra Celsum* VIII 52 (SVF III 218):

Οὐδὲ γὰρ τὰς κοινὰς ἐννοίας περὶ καλῶν καὶ αἰσχρῶν καὶ δικαίων <καὶ ἀδίκων> εὕροι τις ἂν πάντως ἀπολωλεκότας.

b.　Plut., *De Stoic. repugn.* c. 17, p. 1041e (SVF III 69):

Τὸν περὶ ἀγαθῶν καὶ κακῶν λόγον ὃν αὐτὸς (sc. Chrysippus) εἰσάγει καὶ δοκιμάζει "συμφωνότατον εἶναί φησι τῷ βίῳ καὶ μάλιστα τῶν ἐμφύτων ἅπτεσθαι προλήψεων."

When the προλήψεις are called here ἔμφυτοι, this should not be understood in the sense of *ideae innatae* of Descartes and Leibniz or of Spinoza's *notiones communes*, which were meant as being inborn as to their contents. Now this would have been impossible to Stoics, who held that man's soul at birth is like a *tabula rasa*. What they meant is apparently that the human mind is naturally *predisposed* to having these notions. In my opinion, therefore, P. Barth was right in speaking here of a *formal a priori* (as opposed to a "material" one).

995—**a.**　Doubtless, the ἔννοια θεῶν, elsewhere called a πρόληψις, belonged to the κοιναὶ ἔννοιαι, too.

Aëtius I 6 (SVF II 1009):

Ἔσχον δὲ ἔννοιαν τούτου (sc. of God as πνεῦμα νοερόν) πρῶτον μὲν ἀπὸ τοῦ κάλλους τῶν ἐμφαινομένων προσλαμβάνοντες. οὐδὲν γὰρ τῶν καλῶν εἰκῇ καὶ ὡς ἔτυχε γίνεται, ἀλλὰ μετά τινος τέχνης δημιουργούσης.

b.　Cp. Plut., *De comm. not.* 32, p. 1075:

Καὶ μὴν αὐτοί γε πρὸς τὸν Ἐπίκουρον οὐδὲν ἀπολείπουσι τῶν πραγμάτων, ἰού, ἰού, φεῦ, φεῦ βοῶντες, ὡς συγχέοντα τὴν τῶν θεῶν πρόληψιν, ἀναιρουμένης τῆς προνοίας· "οὐ γὰρ ἀθάνατον καὶ μακάριον μόνον, ἀλλὰ καὶ φιλάνθρωπον καὶ κηδεμονικὸν καὶ ὠφέλιμον προλαμβάνεσθαι καὶ νοεῖσθαι τὸν θεόν."

Which means: "This prolepsis, namely, does not only include the immortality and beatitude of the gods, but also that they love man and care for him and look after their interests".

996—**a.**　According to Cicero, also the opinion that death is an evil and that there is some form of a life hereafter—though not its mode—belong to them.

Cic., *Tusc. disp.* I 13, 30 - 14, 31:

Ut porro firmissimum hoc adferri videtur, cur deos esse credamus, quod nulla gens tam fera, nemo omnium tam sit inmanis, cuius mentem non imbuerit deorum opinio:—multi de dis prava sentiunt (id enim

vitioso more effici solet), omnes tamen esse vim et naturam divinam
arbitrantur, nec vero id conlocutio hominum aut consessus efficit, non
institutis opinio est confirmata, non legibus; omni autem in re consensio
omnium gentium lex naturae putanda est:—quis est igitur qui suorum
mortem primum non eo lugeat, quod eos orbatos vitae commodis arbi-
tretur? Tolle hanc opinionem, luctum sustuleris. Nemo enim maeret
suo incommodo: dolent fortasse et anguntur; sed illa lugubris lamentatio
fletusque maerens ex eo est, quod eum, quem dileximus, vitae commodis privatum arbitramur idque sentire. Atque haec ita sentimus
natura duce, nulla ratione nullaque doctrina.

Maxumum vero argumentum est naturam ipsam de immortalitate
animorum tacitum iudicare, quod omnibus curae sunt et maxumae
quidem, quae post mortem futura sint.

And in 16, 36:

Sed ut deos esse natura opinamur, qualesque sint ratione cognoscimus,
sic permanere animos arbitramur consensu nationum omnium, qua in
sede maneant qualesque sint ratione discendum est.

From the consensus gentium concerning the matter of the *notiones communes*,
their truth is concluded. Cp. *ND* I 44: *de quo omnium natura consentit, id verum
esse necesse est.*

b. Cp. Seneca, *Ep*. 117, 6:

Multum dare solemus praesumptioni omnium hominum, et apud nos
veritatis argumentum est aliquid omnibus videri. tamquam deos esse
inter alia hoc colligimus, quod omnibus insita de dis opinio est nec ulla
gens usquam est adeo extra leges moresque proiecta, ut non aliquos deos
credat. cum de animarum aeternitate disserimus, non leve momentum
apud nos habet consensus hominum aut timentium inferos aut colentium.

We shall find the Sceptics opposing this argument. In the 16th and 17th century it became very popular: the so called *natural religion* was built on it.

The categories   **997**—Evidently, the *notiones communes* differ from the categories.
As to the latter, Stoics reduced the number of Aristotle's categories [1] to four.

Simpl. in Ar. *Categ.* p. 66, 32K (SVF II 369):

Οἱ δέ γε Στωϊκοὶ εἰς ἐλάττονα συστέλλειν ἀξιοῦσι τὸν τῶν πρώτων γενῶν
ἀριθμόν. καί τινα ἐν τοῖς ἐλάττοσιν ὑπηλλαγμένα παραλαμβάνουσι. ποιοῦνται
γὰρ τὴν τομὴν εἰς τέσσαρα· εἰς ὑποκείμενα καὶ ποιὰ καί πως ἔχοντα καὶ
πρός τί πως ἔχοντα.

---

[1] Cp. nr. **437b**.

Aristotle's first category, the οὐσία, is understood here as ὑποκείμενον. The πὼς ἔχον (Aristotle's ἔχειν) includes all possible attributes: κεῖσθαι, ἔχειν, ποιεῖν, πάσχειν, and even quantity (ποσόν). Place and time belong to the category of relation: the πρός τί πως ἔχοντα.

Since Chrysippus, this was generally accepted Stoic doctrine. It is criticized by Plotinus in *Enn.* VI 1, 25-34 (after his criticism of Aristotle's doctrine of the categories, ib. 1-24).—Modern logicians feel nearer to the Stoic theory than to Aristotle's.

998—Francis Bacon, *Novum organum* I, art. 95, apparently inspired by a passage in Seneca's *Epist.* 84, 3, writes the following lines on the method of philosophy.

Qui tractaverunt scientias, aut empirici aut dogmatici fuerunt. *Empirici* formicae more congerunt tantum et utuntur; *rationales* (we should say "idealists") aranearum more telas ex se conficiunt. Apis vero ratio media est, quae materiam ex floribus horti et agri elicit, sed tamen eam propria facultate vertit et digerit. Neque absimile philosophiae verum opificium est, quod nec mentis viribus tantum aut praecipue nititur, neque ex historia naturali et mechanicis experimentis praeditam materiam, in memoria integram, sed in intellectu mutatam et subactam reponit.

P. Barth, *Die Stoa,* [4] 1922, p. 85, declares that, in Ancient philosophy, it was Stoic theory of knowledge that came nearest to the demands pitched by Bacon.— In fact, this judgement is founded on a highly insufficient knowledge and understanding of Plato and Aristotle. The author assumes that, in Aristotle's theory, knowledge does not really start from the senses—which, in fact, it does, and even to a certain extent in Plato's theory, where seeing certain objects "reminds" one of the Idea. Finally, we should ask ourselves whether the active part of the intellect in the process of knowledge is sufficiently understood and analyzed by Stoics.

A modern judgement on Stoic theory of knowledge

8—ETHICS (1): THE STARTING-POINT AND THE END

999—Like Epicurus, Zeno starts from the question of "what is the primary impulse of man". Believing, however, that man's *proprium* lies in Reason and its full development, he opposes Epicurus by holding that man's primary impulse is not for pleasure (which, being an animal instinct, cannot be of primary value for man), but for selfpreservation. Cp. above, our nr. **945**.

a. Diog. Laërt., VII 85 (SVF III 178):

The oikeiosis doctrine

Τὴν δὲ πρώτην ὁρμήν φασι τὸ ζῷον ἴσχειν ἐπὶ τὸ τηρεῖν ἑαυτό, οἰκειούσης αὐτῷ τῆς φύσεως ἀπ' ἀρχῆς· καθά φησιν ὁ Χρύσιππος ἐν τῷ πρώτῳ Περὶ τελῶν, πρῶτον οἰκεῖον λέγων εἶναι παντὶ ζώῳ τὴν αὐτοῦ σύστασιν καὶ τὴν ταύτης συνείδησιν. οὔτε γὰρ ἀλλοτριῶσαι εἰκὸς ἦν αὐτῷ τὸ ζῷον, οὔτε ποιήσασαν αὐτὸ μήτε ἀλλοτριῶσαι μήτε [οὐκ] οἰκειῶσαι. ἀπολείπεται τοίνυν λέγειν συστησαμένην αὐτὸ οἰκειῶσαι πρὸς ἑαυτό. οὕτω γὰρ τά τε βλάπτοντα διωθεῖται καὶ τὰ οἰκεῖα προσίεται. ὃ δὲ λέγουσί τινες, πρὸς ἡδονὴν γίγνεσθαι τὴν πρώτην ὁρμὴν τοῖς ζῴοις, ψεῦδος ἀποφαίνουσιν. ἐπιγέννημα γάρ φασιν, εἰ ἄρα ἐστίν, ἡδονὴν εἶναι ὅταν αὐτὴν καθ' αὑτὴν ἡ φύσις ἐπιζητήσασα τὰ ἐναρμόζοντα τῇ συστάσει ἀπολάβῃ· ὃν τρόπον ἀφιλαρύνεται τὰ ζῷα καὶ θάλλει τὰ φυτά.

This passage, which will be continued under nr. **1003**, is not a direct quotation of Zeno, but, as has been recognized by W. Wiersma, Π. τέλους p. 27 ff., from Chrysippus' work Π. τέλους.

b. Cp. Plut., *Stoic. repugn.* 12, p. 1038b (SVF III 179):

Πῶς οὖν ἀποκναίει πάλιν (sc. Chrysippus) ἐν παντὶ βιβλίῳ φυσικῷ, νὴ Δία, καὶ ἠθικῷ γράφων ὡς "οἰκειούμεθα πρὸς αὐτοὺς εὐθὺς γενόμενοι καὶ τὰ μέρη καὶ τὰ ἔκγονα τὰ ἑαυτῶν";

c. In Cicero's *De finibus* III, 5, 16, Cato begins his survey of Stoic doctrine by speaking of *oikeiosis* (sibi conciliari). (SVF III 182).

Placet his, quorum ratio mihi probatur, simulatque natum sit animal (hinc enim est ordiendum) ipsum sibi conciliari et commendari ad se conservandum et ad suum statum eaque quae conservantia sunt eius status diligenda: alienari autem ab interitu iisque rebus, quae interitum videantur afferre. Id ita esse sic probant, quod, ante quam voluptas aut dolor attigerit, salutaria appetant parvi aspernenturque contraria: quod non fieret nisi statum suum diligerent, interitum timerent. Fieri autem non posset, ut appeterent aliquid, nisi sensum haberent sui eoque se diligerent. Ex quo intellegi debet, principium ductum esse a se diligendo.

The words *ipsum sibi conciliari - ad suum statum* correspond exactly to the Greek οἰκειοῦσθαι ἑαυτῷ καὶ τῇ ἑαυτοῦ συστάσει, as is found e.g. with Hierocles I 38.

The term οἰκειοῦσθαι, *to be familiarized to*, is used in the perfect (ᾠκειῶσθαι) simply in the sense of *feeling an affection for*, while the substantive, οἰκείωσις, means *attachment* or *affection*. The opposite is ἀλλοτρίωσις. Thus, Posidonius opposes Chrysippus' doctrine that, by nature, man has no *oikeiosis* for pleasure, but only for the moral good (Galenus, *De Hippocr. et Plat. plac.*, 437 M.): μηδεμίαν οἰκείωσιν εἶναι πρὸς ἡδονὴν ἢ ἀλλοτρίωσιν πρὸς πόνον—

And in 439 M.: ἡμᾶς ᾠκειῶσθαι πρὸς μόνον τὸ κάλον.

Does this doctrine originate from Zeno or from Theophr.? In the last decads, there has been some discussion about the origin of the oikeiosis doctrine, as was mentioned above (sub **945c**). Against H. von Arnim (*Arius Didymus' Abriss der peripatetischen Ethik*, SB. Wien, Ph.-Hist. Kl. 204, 1926, 3) and F. Dirlmeier (*Die Oikeiosislehre Theophrasts*, in *Philol.*, Suppl. XXX, 1937, 1) Pohlenz holds (*Grundfragen*, p. 1-47; *Die Stoa* II p. 66) that the doctrine originates from Zeno, not from Theophrastus. It is true that Arius Didymus' account of peripatetic ethics (preserved by Stobaeus, *Ecl.* II, 116 sqq.) shows some traces of Stoic doctrine and terminology, not only on the topic of oikeiosis. But, first, Arius' account of oikeiosis is not exact and clear, and, secondly, his speaking of ἐκλογὴ τῶν κατὰ φύσιν and ἀπεκλογὴ τῶν παρὰ φύσιν betrays some later Stoic influence, the doctrine of ἐκλογή having been developed not before Diogenes the Babylonian and Antipater in their controversy with Carneades. Pohlenz thinks, Antiochus of Ascalon is the source of the kind of doctrine of oikeiosis we find with Arius (cp. Cic., *De fin.* V 65 ff.).

In the seventeenth century, the doctrine of oikeiosis was adopted by Herbert of Cherbury (s. Pohlenz, *Stoa* II p. 469 f.). We even find traces of it in modern psychology [1]).

1000—In man, oikeiosis is not limited to our own offspring, but applies to all human beings.

Oikeiosis extends to all human beings

a. Cic., *De fin.* III 19, 62-63:

Pertinere autem ad rem arbitrantur intellegi natura fieri, ut liberi a parentibus amentur; a quo initio profectam communem humani generis societatem persequimur. Quod primum intellegi debet figura membrisque corporum, quae ipsa declarant procreandi a natura habitam esse rationem. Neque vero haec inter se congruere possent ut natura et procreari vellet et diligi procreatos non curaret. Atque etiam in bestiis vis naturae perspici potest; quarum in fetu et in educatione laborem cum cernimus, naturae ipsius vocem videmur audire. Quare ut perspicuum est natura nos a dolore abhorrere, sic apparet a natura ipsa, ut eos quos genuerimus amemus, impelli. Ex hoc nascitur, ut etiam communis hominum inter homines naturalis sit commendatio, ut oporteat hominem ab homine ob id ipsum quod homo sit, non alienum videri.

It must be remarked that this aspect of oikeiosis is already present in Aristotle, *Eth. Nic.* VIII 10, 1161 b 1-8.

b. The practical consequences of this principle are drawn in *De officiis* III, ch. V-VI, espec. V 25 and VI 27-28:

Ex quo efficitur hominem naturae oboedientem homini nocere non posse. —

(27) Atque etiam, si hoc natura praescribit, ut homo homini, quicumque sit, ob eam ipsam causam, quod is homo sit, consultum velit, necesse est secundum eandem naturam omnium utilitatem esse communem. Quod si ita est, una continemur omnes et eadem lege naturae, idque ipsum si ita est, certe violare alterum naturae lege prohibemur. Verum autem primum; verum igitur extremum. —

(28) Qui autem civium rationem dicunt habendam, externorum negant, ii dirimunt communem humani generis societatem, qua sublata beneficentia, liberalitas, bonitas, iustitia funditus tollitur. Quae qui tollunt, etiam adversus deos inmortales impii iudicandi sunt; ab iis enim

---

[1] Pohlenz cites Aug. Bier, *Die Seele*, 1939, p. 78: "Der Grundtrieb des Menschen ist der Begehrungstrieb, d.h. der Wille etwas zu besitzen und zu erreichen, was angenehm oder nützlich ist. Am stärksten äussert sich dieser Wille im Trieb zur Erhaltung der eigenen Person und der eigenen Art."

constitutam inter homines societatem evertunt. Cuius societatis artissimum vinculum est magis arbitrari esse contra naturam hominem homini detrahere sui commodi causa quam omnia incommoda subire vel externa vel corporis.

See further the idea of *humanity* with *Panaetius*, infra, nr. **1159b**, and of natural law, nrs. **1066, 1069f.**

but not to animals

1001—Though man shares with the lower animals the instinct of selfpreservation, there cannot exist any moral community between man and animals, the latter being devoid of reason. In other words, by lack of natural affinity the oikeiosis in man does not extend to animals. Hence follow three consequences:

a. Man has no duties towards animals. Cic., *De fin.* III 20, 67:

Et quomodo hominum inter homines iuris esse vincula putant, sic homini nihil iuris esse cum bestiis. Praeclare enim Chrysippus, cetera nata esse hominum causa et deorum; eos autem communitatis et societatis suae: ut bestiis homines uti ad utilitatem suam possent sine iniuria.

In the same way Plutarch, *De esu carnium* 2, 6 (p. 999) makes the Stoics reply to the reproach of "the barbarity of extravagance and of cruelty" in their habits of eating meat:

"Ναί, οὐδὲν γὰρ ἡμῖν πρὸς τὰ ἄλογα δίκαιόν ἐστι."

Iamblichus, *Vita Pyth.* 168, says he extended oikeiosis to animals. Also Porphyry, *De abst.* III 19.

b. Animals do not possess any moral principles.
Philo, *De opif. mundi* 73 (SVF III 372):

Τῶν ὄντων τὰ μὲν οὔτε ἀρετῆς οὔτε κακίας μετέχει, ὥσπερ φυτὰ καὶ ζῷα ἄλογα, τὰ μὲν ὅτι ἄψυχά τέ ἐστι καὶ ἀφαντάστῳ φύσει διοικεῖται, τὰ δὲ ὅτι νοῦν καὶ λόγον ἐκτέτμηται. Κακίας δὲ καὶ ἀρετῆς ὡς ἂν οἶκος νοῦς καὶ λόγος, ᾧ πεφύκασιν ἐνδιαιτᾶσθαι. Τὰ δὲ αὖ μόνης κεκοινώνηκεν ἀρετῆς, ἀμέτοχα πάσης ὄντα κακίας, ὥσπερ οἱ ἀστέρες. Οὗτοι γὰρ ζῷά τε εἶναι λέγονται καὶ ζῷα νοερά . . . . . Τὰ δὲ τῆς μικτῆς ἐστι φύσεως, ὥσπερ ἄνθρωπος, ὃς ἐπιδέχεται . . . ἀρετὴν καὶ κακίαν.

A certain analogy with the communal sense of rational beings may be noticed in such cases as the symbiosis of the *pinoteres*, and in the behaviour of bees and ants (mentioned by Cic., *De fin.* III 19, 63); yet, these things are no more than a μίμησις πρὸς τὰ λογικά, as it is called by Origenes (*C. Celsum* IV 81).

c. There is a *civitas communis deorum atque hominum*. Lower animals do not belong to it.
Cic., *De leg.* I 7, 22:

Animal hoc providum, sagax, multiplex, acutum, memor, plenum rationis et consilii, quem vocamus hominem, praeclara quadam con-dicione generatum esse a supremo deo. Solum est enim ex tot animantium generibus atque naturis particeps rationis et cogitationis, cum cetera sint omnia expertia. Quid est autem, non dicam in homine, sed in omni caelo atque terra ratione divinius? quae cum adulevit atque perfecta est, nominatur rite sapientia. Est igitur, quoniam nihil est ratione melius, eaque <est> et in homine et in deo, prima homini cum deo rationis societas. Inter quos autem ratio, inter eosdem etiam recta ratio communis est. Quae cum sit lex, lege quoque consociati homines cum diis putandi sumus. Inter quos porro est communio legis, inter eos communio iuris est. Quibus autem haec sunt [inter eos] communia, ei civitatis eiusdem habendi sunt. Si vero iisdem imperiis et potestatibus parent, multo iam magis. Parent autem huic caelesti descriptioni mentique divinae et praepotenti deo: ut iam universus hic mundus una civitas communis deorum atque hominum existimanda <sit>.

I do not think—as Wiersma did in his above cited work (II. τέλους)—that Stoicism became a social philosophy only off Chrysippus, and especially *after* him. The principle of oikeiosis, which certainly comes from Zeno, makes it very probable that the founder of the Stoa himself, opposing Epicurus' asocial doctrine, very consciously laid the foundation of a philosophy of humanity on the basis of Reason. Wiersma considers Zeno too exclusively as starting from Cynicism, and almost suggests that the controversy with Epicureanism began only with Cleanthes.
    On the main difference between man and non rational animals, see also Cic., *De off.* I 4, 11. On law and state, below, nrs. **1066-1074**.

1002—Reason, then, being the proprium of man, man feels attach-   **Reason the proprium of man**
ment for himself as a rational being.
    Seneca, *Ep.* 121, 14:
    Dicitis, inquit, omne animal primum constitutioni suae conciliari, hominis autem constitutionem rationalem esse et ideo conciliari hominem sibi non tamquam animali, sed tamquam rationali. ea enim parte sibi carus est homo qua homo est.

1003—Since, on the basis of lower nature, reason has been given to man as his proper characteristic, *living according to nature*, for man, means *living according to Reason*. Hence, virtue being regarded, since Plato and Aristotle [1], as a perfection of nature, "living according to

---

[1] Plato, *Laches* 190b, describes virtue as a thing by the presence of which a man becomes better as to his soul. *Republ.* 353b he states that everything, which has

nature" means: *virtuous life*,—though in itself the first impulse of man is not for virtue, and the so called "primary objects of nature" (τὰ πρῶτα κατὰ φύσιν) are not yet of the level of morality.

a. How Stoics pass on from the first impulse to virtuous life. Diog. Laert. VII 86-87 (the passage cited sub **999a** continued):

Οὐδέν τε, φασί, διήλλαξεν ἡ φύσις ἐπὶ τῶν φυτῶν καὶ ἐπὶ τῶν ζῴων, ὅτι χωρὶς ὁρμῆς καὶ αἰσθήσεως κἀκεῖνα οἰκονομεῖ καὶ ἐφ' ἡμῶν τινα φυτοειδῶς γίνεται. ἐκ περιττοῦ δὲ τῆς ὁρμῆς τοῖς ζῴοις ἐπιγενομένης, ᾗ συγχρώμενα πορεύεται πρὸς τὰ οἰκεῖα, τούτοις μὲν τὸ κατὰ φύσιν τῷ[1] κατὰ τὴν ὁρμὴν διοικεῖσθαι. τοῦ δὲ λόγου τοῖς λογικοῖς κατὰ τελειοτέραν προστασίαν δεδομένου, τὸ κατὰ λόγον ζῆν ὀρθῶς γίνεσθαι <τού>τοις κατὰ φύσιν· τεχνίτης γὰρ οὗτος ἐπιγίνεται τῆς ὁρμῆς. διόπερ πρῶτος ὁ Ζήνων ἐν τῷ Περὶ ἀνθρώπου φύσεως τέλος εἶπε τὸ ὁμολογουμένως τῇ φύσει ζῆν, ὅπερ ἐστὶ κατ' ἀρετὴν ζῆν· ἄγει γὰρ πρὸς ταύτην ἡμᾶς ἡ φύσις.

„Living according to nature" a moral principle

Probably Zeno did not use the formula ὁμολογουμένως τῇ φύσει ζῆν, but simply ὁμολογουμένως. See the text of Stobaeus, below (**1004a**). Diog., in the above cited text, follows Chrysippus, who only said that Zeno's formula had to be explained in this sense.

b. Cicero, who, in his IIIrd book *De finibus*, doubtless follows ancient Stoic sources, clearly marks the difference of level between the "primary objects of nature" and the *honestum*, which arises only on a later stage of development.

Man's first impulse not yet on the level of morality

Cic., *De finibus* III 6, 20-21:

a special function has its proper virtue, namely that property by which they fulfill that function well, e.g. the eyes the function of seeing, the ears that of hearing. Now, according to Plato, what he calls "justice" is the special virtue of the soul, which enables it to fulfill its function (i.e. *living*) well.—Thus, for Plato virtue is undoubtedly a perfection of nature. By Aristotle, *Phys.* VII 3, 246a, 13-17, virtue and vice are explicitly defined in this way:

Ἡ μὲν ἀρετὴ τελείωσίς τις—ὅταν γὰρ λάβῃ τὴν ἑαυτοῦ ἀρετήν, τότε λέγεται τέλειον ἕκαστον· τότε γὰρ μάλιστά ἐστι τὸ κατὰ φύσιν, ὥσπερ κύκλος τέλειος ὅταν μάλιστα γένηται κύκλος καὶ ὅταν βέλτιστος—, ἡ δὲ κακία φθορὰ τούτου καὶ ἔκστασις.

Thus, man possesses his proper virtue, when he fully realizes his essence.

Cp. Thomas Aquinas who, in his *S. Th.* II[1], qu. 71, refers to the above cited passage of Aristotle, and concludes, quoting Dionysius Areop. (*De div. nom.* 22, 4): *Bonum autem hominis est secundum rationem esse, et malum hominis est praeter rationem esse.*

See also St. Augustine, *De lib. arb.* III 13, 38: "Omne vitium, eo ipso quo vitium est, contra naturam est. Si enim naturae non nocet, nec vitium est; si autem quia nocet ideo vitium est, ideo vitium est quia contra naturam est."—Hence, in 14, 41: "Quod ergo perfectioni naturae deesse perspexeris, id vocas vitium".—*Virtus*, then, in a general sense, must be defined as *perfectio naturae.*

---

[1] τῷ corr. Von Arnim; codd. τό.

Initiis igitur ita constitutis, ut ea quae secundum naturam sunt ipsa propter se sumenda sint contrariaque item reicienda, primum est officium (id enim appello καθῆκον), ut se conservet in naturae statu, deinceps ut ea teneat quae secundum naturam sint, pellatque contraria; qua inventa selectione et item rejectione sequitur deinceps cum officio selectio, deinde ea perpetua, tum ad extremum constans consentaneaque naturae, in qua primum inesse incipit et intellegi quid sit quod vere bonum possit dici. Prima est enim conciliatio hominis ad ea quae sunt secundum naturam; simul autem cepit intellegentiam vel notionem potius, quam appellant ἔννοιαν illi, viditque rerum agendarum ordinem et, ut ita dicam, concordiam, multo eam pluris aestimavit quam omnia illa quae prima dilexerat, atque ita cognitione et ratione collegit, ut statueret in eo collocatum summum illud hominis per se laudandum et expetendum bonum. Quod cum positum sit in eo quod ὁμολογίαν Stoici, nos appellemus convenientiam, si placet, cum igitur eo sit id bonum quo omnia referenda sint, honeste facta ipsumque honestum, quod solum in bonis ducitur, quamquam post ortitur, tamen id solum vi sua et dignitate expetendum est; eorum autem quae sunt prima naturae propter se nihil est expetendum.

By the ὁμολογία mentioned in this text is meant: the ὁμολογουμένως ζῆν, i.e. "living in inner harmony", or "living consistently". See under our next nr.

1004—The following text of Stobaeus gives us some more precise information about the telos formula.

Stobaeus, *Ecl.* II 75, 11 W.:

The telos formula

Τὸ δὲ τέλος ὁ μὲν Ζήνων οὕτως ἀπέδωκε· "τὸ ὁμολογουμένως ζῆν". τοῦτο δ' ἐστὶ καθ' ἕνα λόγον καὶ σύμφωνον ζῆν, ὡς τῶν μαχομένως ζώντων κακοδαιμονούντων. Οἱ δὲ μετὰ τοῦτον προσδιαρθροῦντες οὕτως ἐξέφερον "ὁμολογουμένως τῇ φύσει ζῆν" ὑπολαβόντες ἔλαττον εἶναι κατηγόρημα τὸ ὑπὸ τοῦ Ζήνωνος ῥηθέν[1]. Κλεάνθης γὰρ πρῶτος διαδεξάμενος αὐτοῦ τὴν αἵρεσιν προσέθηκε "τῇ φύσει" καὶ οὕτως ἀπέδωκε· "τέλος ἐστὶ τὸ ὁμολογουμένως τῇ φύσει ζῆν". Ὅπερ ὁ Χρύσιππος σαφέστερον βουλόμενος ποιῆσαι, ἐξήνεγκε τὸν τρόπον τοῦτον· "ζῆν κατ' ἐμπειρίαν τῶν φύσει συμβαινόντων".

The passage continues by reporting the definitions of telos by Diogenes of Seleucia, Archedemus and Antipater, who are all occupied with "choosing what is according to nature" (the so-called πρῶτα κατὰ φύσιν) and rejecting what is against it (ἐκλογή and ἀπεκλογή). Wiersma, Π. τέλους, remarked rightly that in these formula's a more active attitude of life is expressed than in the classical formula of ὁμολογου-

---

[1] "since they thought the formula, as it was said by Zeno, incomplete".

μένως τῇ φύσει (at least as Cleanthes took it). But at the same time, there is a certain inconsistency about a so great interest in adiaphora! We shall come back to these questions in dealing with καθήκοντα and with Carneades' criticism.

Zeno's formula explained

1005—a. The explanation given in the above cited text of Zeno's telos formula is supported by the Stoic definition of virtue as it is found, for instance, in Diog. Laërt. VII 89:

Τήν τε ἀρετὴν διάθεσιν εἶναι ὁμολογουμένην·

b. Or in Clem. Alex., *Paed.* I 13 (p. 150 St.):

Ἡ ἀρετὴ ... διάθεσίς ἐστι ψυχῆς σύμφωνος ὑπὸ τοῦ λόγου περὶ ὅλον τὸν βίον.

c. If anything must be supplied to the ὁμολογουμένη or σύμφωνος— and, in fact, we do supply something mentally—, it can be nothing but a ἑαυτῇ, as we read in Stob. II p. 60, 7-8 W.:

Τὴν ἀρετὴν διάθεσιν εἶναί φασι ψυχῆς σύμφωνον αὐτῇ περὶ ὅλον τὸν βίον.

d. Cleanthes, in adding τῇ φύσει to Zeno's formula, does not seem to have thought primarily of the individual "nature" of the subject, but of universal Nature, the κοινὸς νόμος (Hymn to Zeus, l. 20 f.) with which the individual must agree, if it will live a good and happy life. Now, evidently, since the individual is rooted essentially in universal Nature and is congenial with this, there is no essential difference between the one and the other. Therefore, Cleanthes could without any difficulty interpret Zeno's formula as he did. As is told us explicitly in the following passage of Diogenes, Chrysippus thought equally of the individual and of universal nature.

Diog. Laert. VII 89:

Φύσιν δὲ Χρύσιππος μὲν ἐξακούει, ᾗ ἀκολούθως δεῖ ζῆν, τήν τε κοινὴν καὶ ἰδίως τὴν ἀνθρωπίνην· ὁ δὲ Κλεάνθης τὴν κοινὴν μόνην ἐκδέχεται φύσιν, ᾗ ἀκολουθεῖν δεῖ, οὐκέτι δὲ καὶ τὴν ἐπὶ μέρους.

The distinction between the individual and the "common" nature was made, in any case, explicitly by Panaetius. We find it in Cic., *De off.* I 30, 107, where great stress is laid on the principle of following one's individual character and endowments. See below, nr. **1163**.

Constantia with Cic.

1006—The formal principle of selfconsistency plays a great rôle with Cic. and later Stoics. The first, in his *De legibus* I 17, 45, defines *virtus* as *constans et perpetua ratio vitae*, while *vitium* is equalized to *inconstantia*.

and Seneca

With Seneca, *constantia* is the first thing required for a philosophical state of mind.

a. Sen., *Ep.* 35, 4:

Profice et ante omnia hoc cura, ut constes tibi. quotiens experiri voles an aliquid actum sit, observa an eadem hodie velis quae heri: mutatio voluntatis indicat animum natare, aliubi atque aliubi apparere, prout tulit ventus. non vagatur quod fixum atque fundatum est. istud sapienti perfecto contingit, aliquatenus et proficienti provectoque. quid ergo interest? hic commovetur quidem, non tamen transit, sed suo loco nutat; ille ne commovetur quidem.

b. Sen., *Ep.* 120, 22:

Sic maxime coarguitur animus inprudens: alius prodit atque alius et, quo turpius nihil iudico, impar sibi est. magnam rem puta unum hominem agere. praeter sapientem autem nemo unum agit, ceteri multiformes sumus. modo frugi tibi videbimur et graves, modo prodigi et vani. mutamus subinde personam et contrariam ei sumimus, quam exuimus. hoc ergo a te exige, ut, qualem institueris praestare te, talem usque ad exitum serves. effice ut possis laudari, si minus, ut adgnosci.

c. Sen., *De vita beata* 8, 3 (of the man of a philosophical state of mind):

Maneant illi semel placita nec ulla in decretis eius litura sit.

1007—The ideal of selfconsistency with Epictetus. **Selfconsistency with Epictetus**

a. For Epict., the first principle of philosophy is: to distinguish between the things that are in our power (τὰ ἐφ' ἡμῖν) and those which are not (τὰ οὐκ ἐφ' ἡμῖν). Now this is a fundamental dilemma: you choose either τὰ ἐκτός, or you choose τὰ σά. In the first case you have to do it always and radically. It is a choice for slavery.

Epict., *Diss.* II 2, 12-13:

"Όταν γὰρ ὑποθῇς τὰ σὰ τοῖς ἐκτός, δούλευε τὸ λοιπὸν καὶ μὴ ἀντισπῶ καὶ ποτὲ μὲν θέλε δουλεύειν, ποτὲ δὲ μὴ θέλε, ἀλλ' ἁπλῶς καὶ ἐξ ὅλης τῆς διανοίας ἢ ταῦτα ἢ ἐκεῖνα.

b. To what results this principle might lead, and, in fact, did lead sometimes, may be seen from the 15th ch. of the same book of Epict., where he says: there are some people who fancy they must, in any case, stick to their decisions. But first the decision must be sound!

Epict., *Diss.* II 15, 4-7, 8:

Οἷος καὶ ἐμός τις ἑταῖρος ἐξ οὐδεμιᾶς αἰτίας ἔκρινεν ἀποκαρτερεῖν. ἔγνων ἐγὼ ἤδη τρίτην ἡμέραν ἔχοντος αὐτοῦ τῆς ἀποχῆς καὶ ἐλθὼν ἐπυνθανόμην

τί ἐγένετο. — Κέκρικα, φησίν. — Ἀλλ' ὅμως, τί σε ἦν τὸ ἀναπεῖσαν; εἰ γὰρ
ὀρθῶς ἔκρινας, ἰδοὺ παρακαθήμεθά σοι καὶ συνεργοῦμεν, ἵν' ἐξέλθῃς· εἰ δ'
ἀλόγως ἔκρινας, μετάθου. — Τοῖς κριθεῖσιν ἐμμένειν δεῖ. — Τί ποιεῖς, ἄνθρωπε;
οὐ πᾶσιν, ἀλλὰ τοῖς ὀρθῶς. —

Οὐ θέλεις τὴν ἀρχὴν στῆσαι καὶ τὸν θεμέλιον, τὸ κρῖμα σκέψασθαι πότερον
ὑγιὲς ἢ οὐχ ὑγιές, καὶ οὕτως λοιπὸν ἐποικοδομεῖν αὐτῷ τὴν εὐτονίαν, τὴν
ἀσφάλειαν;

"Now this man let himself be persuaded. But of the present generation there are
some people whose mind you cannot change" . . . .

with
Marc Aurel **1008—a.** Marc. Aur. X 11 says of the wise man:

. . . καὶ οὐδὲν ἄλλο βούλεται ἢ εὐθεῖαν περαίνειν διὰ τοῦ νόμου καὶ εὐθεῖαν
περαίνοντι ἔπεσθαι τῷ θεῷ.

b. Cp. Marc. Aur. XI 21:

"Ὧ μὴ εἷς καὶ ὁ αὐτός ἐστιν ἀεὶ τοῦ βίου σκοπός, οὗτος εἷς καὶ ὁ αὐτὸς
δι' ὅλου τοῦ βίου εἶναι οὐ δύναται." οὐκ ἀρκεῖ τὸ εἰρημένον, ἐὰν μὴ κἀκεῖνο
προσθῇς, ὁποῖον εἶναι δεῖ τοῦτον τὸν σκοπόν. ὥσπερ γὰρ οὐχ ἡ πάντων τῶν
ὁπωσοῦν τοῖς πλείοσι δοκούντων ἀγαθῶν ὑπόληψις ὁμοία ἐστίν, ἀλλ' ἡ τῶν
τοιῶνδέ τινων, τουτέστι τῶν κοινῶν, οὕτω καὶ τὸν σκοπὸν δεῖ τὸν κοινωνικὸν
καὶ πολιτικὸν ὑποστήσασθαι. ὁ γὰρ εἰς τοῦτον πάσας τὰς ἰδίας ὁρμὰς ἀπευθύ-
νων πάσας τὰς πράξεις ὁμοίας ἀποδώσει καὶ κατὰ τοῦτο ἀεὶ ὁ αὐτὸς ἔσται.

The in-
consistency
of sin **1009**—As we found with Cicero that vitium was equalized to *inconstantia*, thus, Epictetus writes in his diatribe ,,What is the true nature of
sin" (*Diss.* II 26, 1-3, 7):

Πᾶν ἁμάρτημα μάχην περιέχει [1]. ἐπεὶ γὰρ ὁ ἁμαρτάνων οὐ θέλει ἁμαρτάνειν, ἀλλὰ κατορθῶσαι, δῆλον ὅτι ὃ μὲν θέλει οὐ ποιεῖ. τί γὰρ ὁ κλέπτης θέλει
πρᾶξαι; τὸ αὐτῷ συμφέρον. οὐκ οὖν, εἰ ἀσύμφορόν ἐστιν αὐτῷ τὸ κλέπτειν,
ὃ μὲν θέλει ποιεῖ. πᾶσα δὲ ψυχὴ λογικὴ φύσει διαβέβληται πρὸς μάχην· καὶ
μέχρι μὲν ἂν μὴ παρακολουθῇ τούτῳ, ὅτι ἐν μάχῃ ἐστί, οὐδὲν κωλύεται τὰ
μαχόμενα ποιεῖν· παρακολουθήσαντα δὲ πολλὴ ἀνάγκη ἀποστῆναι τῆς μάχης
καὶ φυγεῖν οὕτως ὡς καὶ ἀπὸ τοῦ ψεύδους ἀνανεῦσαι πικρὰ ἀνάγκη τῷ αἰσθα-
νομένῳ, ὅτι ψεῦδός ἐστιν· μέχρι δὲ τοῦτο μὴ φαντάζηται, ὡς ἀληθεῖ ἐπινεύει
αὐτῷ. —

(7) Λογικῷ ἡγεμονικῷ δεῖξον μάχην καὶ ἀποστήσεται· ἂν δὲ μὴ δεικνύῃς,
αὐτὸς σαυτῷ μᾶλλον ἐγκάλει ἢ τῷ μὴ πειθομένῳ.

---

[1] "Contains an inconsistency".

1010—Selfconsistency, then, being the true nature of virtue, we can understand that, according to Stoics, the wise man never repents.

a. Cic., *Tusc.* V 81:

The wise man never repents

Sapientis enim est proprium nihil quod paenitere possit facere, nihil invitum, splendide, constanter, graviter, honeste omnia.

b. Seneca, *Ep.* 115, 18:

Hoc tibi philosophia praestabit, quo equidem nihil maius existimo: numquam te paenitebit tui.

c. Sen., *De benef.* IV 34, 4:

Non mutat sapiens consilium omnibus his manentibus, quae erant cum sumeret. ideo numquam illum poenitentia subit, quia nihil melius illo tempore fieri potuit quam quod factum est, nihil melius constitui quam quod constitutum est. ceterum ad omnia cum exceptione venit: si nihil inciderit quod impediat.

d. Marc. Aur. VIII 53:

Repentance not a virtue

Ἐπαινεῖσθαι θέλεις ὑπὸ ἀνθρώπου τρὶς τῆς ὥρας ἑαυτῷ καταρωμένου; ἀρέσκειν θέλεις ἀνθρώπῳ ὃς οὐκ ἀρέσκει ἑαυτῷ; ἀρέσκει ἑαυτῷ ὁ μετανοῶν ἐφ' ἅπασι σχεδὸν οἷς πράσσει;

Cp. also the portrait of the wise man in Cicero's *Pro Murena* 60 ff., our nr. **1050b**.—Similar thoughts may be found later with Spinoza.

1011—As we found in the passage of Stobaeus quoted sub **1004**, those who live inconsistently live unhappily (ὡς τῶν μαχομένως ζώντων κακοδαιμονούντων). To put it in positive terms: the harmonious life is the happy life.

The harmonious life is happy

a. Thus, Diog. Laërt. says, in his description of the telos according to Chrysippus (VII 88):

Διόπερ τέλος γίνεται τὸ ἀκολούθως τῇ φύσει ζῆν, ὅπερ ἐστὶ κατά τε τὴν αὑτοῦ καὶ κατὰ τὴν τῶν ὅλων, οὐδὲν ἐνεργοῦντας ὧν ἀπαγορεύειν εἴωθεν ὁ νόμος ὁ κοινός, ὅσπερ ἐστὶν ὁ ὀρθὸς λόγος διὰ πάντων ἐρχόμενος, ὁ αὐτὸς ὢν τῷ Διὶ καθηγεμόνι τούτῳ τῆς τῶν ὅλων διοικήσεως ὄντι· εἶναι δ' αὐτὸ τοῦτο τὴν τοῦ εὐδαίμονος ἀρετὴν καὶ εὔροιαν βίου, ὅταν πάντα πράττηται κατὰ τὴν συμφωνίαν τοῦ παρ' ἑκάστῳ δαίμονος πρὸς τὴν τοῦ τῶν ὅλων διοικητοῦ βούλησιν.

In this fr. of Chrysippus we find many things which play an important rôle with later Stoics.

(1) "Nature" is taken as well in the sense of individual nature as in that of universal.

(2) The νόμος κοινός is called ὀρθὸς λόγος, a term much used e.g. by Epict.

(3) Every man is said to have a daimon who, in the wise man, is in harmony with the will of the Governor of the universe. —

The idea of a good or evil spirit following every individual man throughout his life is ancient [1]. The formula ὁ παρ᾽ ἑκάστῳ δαίμων can, doubtless, mean: the spirit *dwelling in* the individual man. This is what we find with Posidonius (infra nr. **1055**). Marc. Aur. identifies the daimon within us with the hegemonikon (our nr. **1266a**).

Wiersma, Π. τέλους p. 30 f., thinks that Chrysippus' conception of the daimon differs from Posidonius', in that Chrys. thought the daimon could be against the will of the Governor of the universe, while according to Posidonius such a dis-agreement is essentially excluded. It seems, however, that W. reads here more in Chrysippus' text, than is in it.

Happiness a concomitant state **b.** It must be noticed that, unlike Aristotle, Stoics emphatically did not regard *eudaimonia* as the telos, but simply as a concomitant state.

Seneca, *De vita beata* 8, opposes Stoic doctrine to Epicurus in this way:

Quid, quod tam bonis quam malis voluptas inest nec minus turpes dedecus suum quam honestos egregia delectant? ideoque praeceperunt veteres optimam sequi vitam, non iucundissimam, ut rectae ac bonae voluntatis non dux sed comes sit voluptas. natura enim duce utendum est; hanc ratio observat, hanc consulit. idem est ergo beate vivere et secundum naturam.

And again, at the end of ch. 13:

Agedum, virtus antecedat, tutum erit omne vestigium. et voluptas nocet nimia: in virtute non est verendum, ne quid nimium sit, quia in ipsa est modus; non est bonum, quod magnitudine laborat sua. rationalem porro sortitis naturam quae melius res quam ratio proponitur? et si placet ista iunctura, si hoc placet ad beatam vitam ire comitatu, virtus antecedat, comitetur voluptas et circa corpus ut umbra versetur: virtutem quidem, excelsissimam dominam, voluptati tradere ancillam nihil magnum animo capientis est.

The last sentence refers to the picture Cleanthes used to draw, representing

---

[1] It occurs frequently in Plato, e.g.

Phaed. 107d: ὁ ἑκάστου δαίμων ὅνπερ ζῶντα εἴληχεν.

Phaed. 108b: ὑπὸ τοῦ προστεταγμένου δαίμονος οἴχεται ἀγομένη (ἡ ψυχή).

Phaed. 113d: οἷ ὁ δαίμων ἕκαστον κομίζει.

Resp. X 617e: Οὐχ ὑμᾶς δαίμων λήξεται, ἀλλ᾽ ὑμεῖς δαίμονα αἱρήσεσθε.

Polit. 274b: τοῦ κεκτημένου καὶ νέμοντος ἡμᾶς δαίμονος.

In *Tim.* 90a he says that God gave "the most sovereign form of soul in us" (τὸ κυριώτατον ἐν ἡμῖν ψυχῆς εἶδος) as a daimon to each of us.

Pleasure, dressed as a queen and seated on a throne, surrounded by the Virtues, ministering to her as humble servants.

c. Cp. Cic., *De fin.* II 21, 69:

Pudebit te, inquam, illius tabulae, quam Cleanthes sane commode verbis depingere solebat. Iubebat eos, qui audiebant, secum ipsos cogitare pictam in tabula Voluptatem pulcherrimo vestitu et ornatu regali in solio sedentem, praesto esse Virtutes ut ancillulas, quae nihil aliud agerent, nullum suum officium ducerent, nisi ut Voluptati ministrarent et eam tantum ad aurem admonerent, si modo id pictura intellegi posset, ut caveret, ne quid faceret imprudens, quod offenderet animos hominum, aut quicquam, e quo oriretur aliquis dolor. "Nos quidem Virtutes sic natae sumus, ut tibi serviremus, aliud negoti nihil habemus."

Wiersma, Π. τέλους, p. 19 ff., considers Zeno as a pure eudaemonist: eudaimonia, according to him, should have been the true "end" of life. I think this view is not justified by the texts.

9—ETHICS (2): BONUM, BONA, AND RELATIVELY VALUABLE THINGS

1012—a. Diog. Laërt. VI 1, 14 cites the following lines of the epigrammatist Athenaeus:

> Ὦ Στωϊκῶν μύθων εἰδήμονες, ὦ πανάριστα,
>   δόγματα ταῖς ἱεραῖς ἐνθέμενοι σελίσιν,
> τὰν ἀρετὰν ψυχᾶς ἀγαθὸν μόνον· ἅδε γὰρ ἀνδρῶν
>   μούνα καὶ βιοτὰν ῥύσατο καὶ πόλιας.

In fact, the doctrine that "the virtue of the soul is the only good" has been from the beginning a main dogma of the Stoa, or even, next to the formal principle of ὁμολογουμένως ζῆν, *the* fundamental principle. Zeno expressed it as follows.

b. Stob., *Ecl.* II p. 57, 18 W. (SVF I 190):

Τῶν δ᾽ ὄντων τὰ μὲν ἀγαθά, τὰ δὲ κακά, τὰ δὲ ἀδιάφορα. ἀγαθὰ μὲν τὰ τοιαῦτα· φρόνησιν, σωφροσύνην, δικαιοσύνην, ἀνδρείαν καὶ πᾶν ὅ ἐστιν ἀρετὴ ἢ μετέχον ἀρετῆς· κακὰ δὲ τὰ τοιαῦτα· ἀφροσύνην, ἀκολασίαν, ἀδικίαν, δειλίαν, καὶ πᾶν ὅ ἐστι κακία ἢ μετέχον κακίας· ἀδιάφορα δὲ τὰ τοιαῦτα· ζωὴν θάνατον, δόξαν ἀδοξίαν, πόνον ἡδονήν, πλοῦτον πενίαν, νόσον ὑγίειαν, καὶ τὰ τούτοις ὅμοια.

A similar division was made by Xenocr., who said, according to Sextus, *Adv. math.* XI (= *Ag. the Ethicists*) 4:

Πᾶν τὸ ὂν ἢ ἀγαθόν ἐστιν ἢ κακόν ἐστιν ἢ οὔτε ἀγαθόν ἐστιν οὔτε κακόν ἐστιν.

In the preceding chapter Sextus says that the Stoic division was common to the Ancient Academy, Peripatetics and Stoics. However, the term ἀδιάφορα for the third group is specifically Stoic, and it is most characteristic.

c. Thus, Tacitus, when speaking about Helvidius Priscus and Paetus Thrasea, qualifies Stoics by these terms (*Hist.* IV 5):

Doctores sapientiae secutus est (Priscus), qui bona quae honesta, mala tantum quae turpia, potentiam nobilitatem ceteraque extra animum neque bonis neque malis adnumerant.

d. Seneca, *Ep.* 71, 4:

Summum bonum est quod honestum est. Et quod magis admireris: *unum* bonum est quod honestum est. Ceteri falsa et adulterina bona sunt.

1013—To this only good belongs that which is essentially linked up with it.

Reason its ground

a. *Reason* is its ground. Therefore, Seneca could say in *Ep.* 76, 9:

In homine optimum quid est? — Ratio. Hoc antecedit animalia, deos sequitur.

Freedom its outward aspect

b. *Freedom* may be called its visible or outward aspect: for wisdom, which implies all virtues, liberates man from outward things. Epictetus, therefore, calls the non-philosophical man δοῦλος, and says that Antisthenes "liberated" him, viz. by teaching him not to desire outward things, which are not in our power.

Epict., *Diatr.* III 24, 67 ff.:

Διὰ τοῦτο ἔλεγεν ὅτι "ἐξ οὗ μ' Ἀντισθένης ἠλευθέρωσεν, οὐκέτι ἐδούλευσα". πῶς ἠλευθέρωσεν; ἄκουε, τί λέγει· "ἐδίδαξέν με τὰ ἐμὰ καὶ τὰ οὐκ ἐμά."

Cp. supra, **1007a**.

Happiness its inner aspect

c. *Happiness* might be called its inner aspect or psychological reverse. It depends wholly and exclusively on virtue.

Cic., *Acad. post.* I 35:

Zeno ... qui omnia quae ad beatam vitam pertinerent, in una virtute poneret.

See also *Tusc. disp.* V 48.

The autarkeia of virtue

1014—Virtue, therefore, is considered as self-sufficient by Stoics.

a. Diog. Laert. VII 127:

Αὐτάρκη τε εἶναι αὐτὴν (sc. τὴν ἀρετὴν) πρὸς εὐδαιμονίαν, καθά φησι Ζήνων.

b. Cp. Cic., *De fin.* V 79:

A Zenone hoc magnifice tamquam ex oraculo editur: "Virtus ad beate vivendum se ipsa contenta est".

1015—The absolute character of virtue implies that there are no degrees of it, just as there are no degrees of sin.

No degrees of bonum

a. Seneca, *Ep.* 66, 12:

Mortalia minuuntur, cadunt, deteruntur, crescunt, exhauriuntur, inplentur. itaque illis in tam incerta sorte inaequalitas est: divinorum una natura est. ratio autem nihil aliud est quam in corpus humanum pars divini spiritus mersa. si ratio divina est, nullum autem bonum sine ratione est, bonum omne divinum est. nullum porro inter divina discrimen est: ergo nec inter bona. paria itaque sunt et gaudium et fortis atque obstinata tormentorum perpessio. in utroque enim eadem est animi magnitudo, in altero remissa et laeta, in altera pugnax et intenta.

Thus, Diog. Laert. summarizes Stoic doctrine in these words (VII 101):

Δοκεῖ δὲ πάντα τὰ ἀγαθὰ ἴσα εἶναι καὶ πᾶν ἀγαθὸν ἐπ' ἄκρον εἶναι αἱρετὸν καὶ μήτ' ἄνεσιν μήτ' ἐπίτασιν ἐπιδέχεσθαι.

b. The reverse of this thesis is that sins are equal, as we find it in Cicero's *Pro Munera* 61: *omnia peccata esse paria*.

Peccata paria

Diog. Laërt. VII 120:

Ἀρέσκει τ' αὐτοῖς ἴσα ἡγεῖσθαι τὰ ἁμαρτήματα, καθά φησι Χρύσιππος . . . καὶ Ζήνων. —

Καὶ γὰρ ὁ ἑκατὸν σταδίους ἀπέχων Κανώβου καὶ ὁ ἕνα ἐπίσης οὐκ εἰσὶν ἐν Κανώβῳ· οὕτω καὶ ὁ πλέον καὶ ὁ ἔλαττον ἁμαρτάνων ἐπίσης οὐκ εἰσὶν ἐν τῷ κατορθοῦν.

The doctrine is also mentioned in Sextus, *Adv. math.* VII 422. It is explained by Cicero, *De fin.* III 14, 45-48, as we shall see in dealing with the κατόρθωμα (below, nr. **1036**).

1016—For the Stoics, virtue has a strictly interior character: it is a question of intention, not of any practical result.

A good action has its value in itself

a. Cic., *De fin.* III, 6, 22:

Ut enim si cui propositum sit conliniare hastam aliquo aut sagittam, sic nos ultimum in bonis dicimus, [sic illi facere omnia, quae possit, ut conliniet]. Huic in eius modi similitudine omnia sint facienda, ut conliniet, et tamen, ut omnia faciat, quo propositum assequatur, sit hoc quasi ultimum quale nos summum in vita bonum dicimus: illud autem ut feriat quasi seligendum, non expetendum.

Plut., *De comm. not.* 26, mentions this point among the "strange and puzzling things" in Stoic doctrine. In fact, it is inherent in the view that a good action has its value in itself, as is also explained in the following passage.

b. Cic., *De fin.* III 7, 24:

Ut enim histrioni actio, saltatori motus non quivis, sed certus quidam est datus, sic vita agenda est certo genere quodam, non quolibet; quod genus conveniens consentaneumque dicimus. Nec enim gubernationi aut medicinae similem sapientiam esse arbitramur, sed actioni illi potius quam modo dixi et saltationi, ut in ipsa insit, non foris petatur extremum, id est artis effectio. — Sola enim sapientia in se tota conversa est, quod idem in ceteris artibus non fit.

We shall come back to this passage again in dealing with *katorthomata* (nrs. **1033-1036**).

Bonum defined as ὠφέλεια

1017—a. Ἀγαθόν, in general, is defined by Stoics as ὄφελος or ὠφέλεια, e.g. in Diog. Laert. VII 94 (SVF III 76); cp. Sextus, *adv. Math.* XI 22 (SVF III 75); by which they mean, of course, not outward things— for there is no help in these—, but virtue and what belongs to it. See our nr. **1013**; also **1018a**.

or as a natural perfection

b. Or again, the good is defined by them as *the natural perfection of a rational being*:

Τὸ τέλειον κατὰ φύσιν λογικοῦ ὡς λογικοῦ (Diog. Laërt. VII 94).

in which they follow the line of Plato (*Laches* 190b, *Resp.* 353b sqq.) and of Aristotle (*Phys.* VII 3), as indicated *supra* (n. 1 to nr. **1003**).

„that which is absolute by nature"

c. The clearest expression of the Stoic view is given in Diogenes' definition mentioned by Cicero, *De fin.* III 10, 33:

Ego assentior Diogeni qui bonum definierit *id quod esset natura absolutum*.

By this definition is clearly indicated that the good is of a level different from relatively valuable things, as is explained in the following passage.

As such, it is superior to relatively valuable things

d. Cic., *De fin.* III 10, 34:

Hoc autem ipsum bonum non accessione neque crescendo aut cum ceteris comparando, sed propria vi sua et sentimus et appellamus bonum.

ut enim mel, etsi dulcissimum est, suo tamen proprio genere saporis, non comparatione cum aliis dulce esse sentitur, sic bonum hoc, de quo agimus, est illud quidem plurimi aestimandum, sed ea aestimatio genere valet, non magnitudine. Nam cum aestimatio, quae ἀξία dicitur, neque in bonis numerata sit nec rursus in malis, quantumcumque eo addideris, in suo genere manebit. Alia est igitur propria aestimatio virtutis, quae genere, non crescendo valet.

To this absolute character of the good we shall come back, again, in dealing with *katorthomata.*

1018—Zeno's division of all things into three classes—good, bad and morally indifferent—, as mentioned under **1012b**, is maintained by Chrysippus and other Stoics. The third class is not deprived of any value (ἀξία); only, this value is not of the moral level. Two arguments are given to support this view: (1) these things are not profitable to man; (2) both good and bad use can be made of them. *The doctrine of adiaphora*

Diog. Laërt. VII 101 (the end)-103:

Τῶν δ' ὄντων φασὶ τὰ μὲν ἀγαθὰ εἶναι, τὰ δὲ κακά, τὰ δ' οὐδέτερα. Ἀγαθὰ μὲν οὖν τάς τ' ἀρετάς, ... κακὰ δὲ τὰ ἐναντία ... Οὐδέτερα δὲ ὅσα μήτε ὠφελεῖ μήτε βλάπτει· οἶον ζωή, ὑγίεια, ἡδονή, κάλλος, ἰσχύς, πλοῦτος, εὐδοξία, εὐγένεια· καὶ τὰ τούτοις ἐναντία, θάνατος, νόσος, πόνος, αἶσχος, ἀσθένεια, πενία, ἀδοξία, δυσγένεια καὶ τὰ τούτοις παραπλήσια· καθά φησιν Ἑκάτων ἐν ἑβδόμῳ Περὶ τέλους καὶ Ἀπολλόδωρος ἐν τῇ Ἠθικῇ καὶ Χρύσιππος. μὴ γὰρ εἶναι ταῦτα ἀγαθά, ἀλλ' ἀδιάφορα, κατ' εἶδος προηγμένα· ὡς γὰρ ἴδιον θερμοῦ τὸ θερμαίνειν, οὐ τὸ ψύχειν, οὕτω καὶ ἀγαθοῦ τὸ ὠφελεῖν, οὐ τὸ βλάπτειν. οὐ μᾶλλον δὲ ὠφελεῖ ἢ βλάπτει ὁ πλοῦτος καὶ ἡ ὑγίεια· οὐκ ἄρα ἀγαθὸν οὔτε πλοῦτος οὔτε ὑγίεια. ἔτι τέ φασιν· ᾧ ἔστιν εὖ καὶ κακῶς χρῆσθαι, τοῦτο οὐκ ἔστιν ἀγαθόν· πλούτῳ δὲ καὶ ὑγιείᾳ ἔστιν εὖ καὶ κακῶς χρῆσθαι· οὐκ ἄρα ἀγαθὸν πλοῦτος καὶ ὑγίεια.

1019—This, then, being presupposed, ἀδιάφορα are again divided. *προηγμένα and ἀποπροηγ-μένα*

a. Diog. Laërt. VII 105:

Τῶν ἀδιαφόρων τὰ μὲν λέγουσι προηγμένα, τὰ δὲ ἀποπροηγμένα· προηγμένα μὲν τὰ ἔχοντα ἀξίαν, ἀποπροηγμένα δὲ τὰ ἀπαξίαν ἔχοντα.

b. What is meant by ἀξία. Diog. L., ib.: *What is ἀξία*

Ἀξίαν δὲ τὴν μέν τινα λέγουσι σύμβλησιν πρὸς τὸν ὁμολογούμενον βίον, ἥτις ἐστὶ περὶ πᾶν ἀγαθόν, τὴν δὲ εἶναι μέσην τινὰ δύναμιν ἢ χρείαν συμβαλλο-μένην πρὸς τὸν κατὰ φύσιν βίον, ὅμοιον εἰπεῖν ἥν τινα προσφέρεται πρὸς τὸν κατὰ φύσιν βίον πλοῦτος ἢ ὑγίεια· τὴν δ' εἶναι ἀξίαν ἀμοιβὴν δοκιμαστοῦ, ἣν ἂν ὁ ἔμπειρος τῶν πραγμάτων τάξῃ, ὅμοιον εἰπεῖν ἀμείβεσθαι πυροὺς πρὸς τὰς σὺν ἡμιόνῳ κριθάς.

The text will be further explained sub **1020b**.

Instances   **c.** Instances of προηγμένα and of ἀποπροηγμένα.

Diog. Laërt. VII 106:

Προηγμένα μὲν οὖν εἶναι ἃ καὶ ἀξίαν ἔχει, οἷον ἐπὶ μὲν τῶν ψυχικῶν εὐφυΐαν, τέχνην, προκοπὴν καὶ τὰ ὅμοια· ἐπὶ δὲ τῶν σωματικῶν ζωήν, ὑγίειαν, ῥώμην, εὐεξίαν, ἀρτιότητα, κάλλος· ἐπὶ δὲ τῶν ἐκτὸς πλοῦτον, δόξαν, εὐγένειαν καὶ τὰ ὅμοια. ἀποπροηγμένα δὲ ἐπὶ μὲν τῶν ψυχικῶν ἀφυΐαν, ἀτεχνίαν καὶ τὰ ὅμοια· ἐπὶ δὲ τῶν σωματικῶν θάνατον, νόσον, ἀσθένειαν, καχεξίαν, πήρωσιν, αἶσχος καὶ τὰ ὅμοια· ἐπὶ δὲ τῶν ἐκτὸς πενίαν, ἀδοξίαν, δυσγένειαν καὶ τὰ παραπλήσια. οὔτε δὲ προήχθη οὔτε ἀποπροήχθη τὰ οὐδετέρως ἔχοντα.

The last group is specified as μήτε ὁρμῆς μήτε ἀφορμῆς κινητικά (Diog. VII 104) and instanced as follows:

Τὸ ἀρτίας ἔχειν ἐπὶ τῆς κεφαλῆς τρίχας ἢ περιττάς, ἢ ἐκτεῖναι τὸν δάκτυλον συστεῖλαι.

The first two groups (proegmena and apoproegmena) are ὁρμῆς καὶ ἀφορμῆς κινητικά.

The proegmenon not of the level of morality **1020—a.** That the *proegmenon* is not of the level of the agathon, is illustrated by the simile of the king and his courtiers.

Stob., *Ecl.* II p. 84, 21 (SVF I 192):

Προηγμένον δ' εἶναι λέγουσιν, ὃ ἀδιάφορον ⟨ὂν⟩ ἐκλεγόμεθα κατὰ προηγού-μενον λόγον. τὸν δὲ ὅμοιον λόγον ἐπὶ τῷ ἀποπροηγμένῳ εἶναι. .... οὐδὲν δὲ τῶν ἀγαθῶν εἶναι προηγμένον διὰ τὸ τὴν μεγίστην ἀξίαν αὐτὰ ἔχειν. τὸ δὲ προηγμένον, τὴν δευτέραν χώραν καὶ ἀξίαν ἔχον, συνεγγίζειν πως τῇ τῶν ἀγαθῶν φύσει· οὐδὲ γὰρ ἐν αὐλῇ τῶν προηγμένων εἶναι τὸν βασιλέα, ἀλλὰ τοὺς μετ' αὐτὸν τεταγμένους.

Cic. mentions the simile in *De fin.* III 16, 52.

b. The same text continued:

Προηγμένα δὲ λέγεσθαι οὐ τῷ πρὸς εὐδαιμονίαν τινὰ συμβάλλεσθαι συνεργεῖν τε πρὸς αὐτήν, ἀλλὰ τῷ ἀναγκαῖον εἶναι τούτων τὴν ἐκλογὴν ποιεῖσθαι παρὰ τὰ ἀποπροηγμένα.

The proegmena, then, come under the second kind of ἀξία mentioned sub **1018b**. The first class, evidently, is of the agatha, which by definition contribute some-thing to the ὁμολογουμένως ζῆν. That the second kind is said to contribute to "the life according to nature", be it in an indirect way (μέσην τινὰ δύναμιν ἢ χρείαν), does not imply that, in fact, they should be good, too. It should be remembered that those things which by Stoics were called τὰ πρῶτα κατὰ φύσιν, (see **1003b**) are not yet of the moral level. Now, it is exactly to these *prima naturae* that the proegmena must be referred.

c. Thus, we can understand the following passage, on the reasons why things are preferred. Diog. Laërt. VII 107:

Why certain things are preferred

Ἔτι τῶν προηγμένων τὰ μὲν δι᾽ αὑτὰ προῆκται, τὰ δὲ δι᾽ ἕτερα, τὰ δὲ καὶ δι᾽ αὑτὰ καὶ δι᾽ ἕτερα. καὶ δι᾽ αὑτὰ μὲν εὐφυΐα, προκοπὴ καὶ τὰ ὅμοια· δι᾽ ἕτερα δὲ πλοῦτος, εὐγένεια καὶ τὰ ὅμοια· δι᾽ αὑτὰ δὲ καὶ δι᾽ ἕτερα ἰσχύς, εὐαισθησία, ἀρτιότης. δι᾽ αὑτὰ μέν, ὅτι κατὰ φύσιν ἐστί· δι᾽ ἕτερα δέ, ὅτι περιποιεῖ χρείας οὐκ ὀλίγας. ὁμοίως δ᾽ ἔχει καὶ τὸ ἀποπροηγμένον κατὰ τὸν ἐναντίον λόγον.

1021—Aristo of Chios differed from Zeno in rejecting any distinction between the adiaphora. Cicero mentions him repeatedly together with Pyrrho (cp. infra, nr. **1088b, c**) and Herillus.

The heresy of Aristo of Chios

a. Cic., *De fin.* II 13, 43 (SVF I 364):

Quae (sc. prima naturae) quod Aristoni et Pyrrhoni omnino visa sunt pro nihilo, ut inter optime valere et gravissime aegrotare nihil prorsus dicerent interesse, recte iam pridem contra eos desitum est disputari. Dum enim in una virtute sic omnia esse voluerunt, ut eam rerum selectione exspoliarent nec ei quicquam aut unde oriretur darent, aut ubi niteretur, virtutem ipsam, quam amplexabantur, sustulerunt.

b. Cic., *De off.* I 2, 6:

Quoniam Aristonis, Pyrrhonis, Erilli iam pridem explosa sententia est; qui tamen haberent ius suum disputandi de officio, si rerum aliquem dilectum reliquissent, ut ad officii inventionem aditus esset.

c. Chrysippus opposed this doctrine energetically. Cic., *De fin.* IV 25, 68:

Cum enim, quod honestum sit, id solum bonum esse confirmatur, tollitur cura valetudinis, diligentia rei familiaris, administratio rei publicae, ordo gerendorum negotiorum, officia vitae, ipsum denique illud honestum, in quo uno vultis esse omnia, deserendum est. Quae diligentissime contra Aristonem dicuntur a Chrysippo.

1022—The Stoic thesis that outward things do not contribute anything to happiness, was opposed by Peripatetics; later by Carneades. Cicero speaks of it in *De fin.* III 12, 41:

The great controversy between Stoics and Peripatetics

Tum ille (sc. Cato); "His igitur ita positis", inquit, "sequitur magna contentio, quam tractatam a Peripateticis mollius (est enim eorum consuetudo dicendi non satis acuta propter ignorationem dialecticae) Carneades tuus egregia quadam exercitatione in dialecticis summaque eloquentia rem in summum discrimen adduxit, propterea quod pugnare non destitit in omni hac quaestione, quae de bonis et malis appelletur, non esse rerum Stoicis cum Peripateticis controversiam, sed nominum. Mihi autem nihil tam perspicuum videtur, quam has sententias eorum philosophorum re inter se magis quam verbis dissidere; maiorem multo inter Stoicos et Peripateticos rerum esse aio discrepantiam quam verborum, quippe cum Peripatetici omnia quae ipsi bona appellant pertinere dicant ad beate vivendum, nostri non ex omni quod aestimatione aliqua dignum sit compleri vitam beatam putent."

Carneades' essential argument was that Zeno, in distinguishing proegmena and apoproegmena, in fact reintroduced the notion of relatively good things, rejected by him in principle. It is clear that Stoics never could grant this.

10—ETHICS (3): VIRTUE, VIRTUES, ABSOLUTE AND RELATIVE MORALITY

Virtue a perfection of nature

1023—Virtue, then, is defined by the Stoics, as by Aristotle, as a perfection of each individual's nature. Cp. our nr. **1003** n. 1.

a. In general: Diog. Laërt. VII 90 (SVF III 197):

Ἀρετὴ δέ τοι ἡ μέν τις κοινῶς παντὶ τελείωσις, ὥσπερ ἀνδριάντος· καὶ ἡ ἀθεώρητος, ὥσπερ ὑγίεια· καὶ ἡ θεωρηματική, ὡς φρόνησις.

Cp. the definition of ἀγαθόν given sub **1017b** (Diog. VII 94).

b. In man: Galenus defends against Chrysippus the unity of virtue, because it is a perfection, "as he (Chrys.) himself grants".
De plac. Hippocr. et Plat. V 5, p. 446 M. (SVF III 257):

Μία γὰρ ἑκάστου τῶν ὄντων ἡ τελειότης, ἡ δ' ἀρετὴ τελειότης ἐστὶ τῆς ἑκάστου φύσεως, ὡς αὐτὸς ὁμολογεῖ.

Not a ἕξις but a διάθεσις

1024—Stoics do not follow Aristotle in considering virtue as a ἕξις. They call it a διάθεσις.

a. Plut., *De virt. mor.* 3 (SVF I 202):

Κοινῶς δὲ ἅπαντες οὗτοι (sc. Menedemus, Aristo, Zeno, Chrys.) τὴν ἀρετὴν τοῦ ἡγεμονικοῦ τῆς ψυχῆς διάθεσίν τινα καὶ δύναμιν γεγενημένην ὑπὸ λόγου.

Cp. also Diog. Laërt. VII 89: τήν τε ἀρετὴν διάθεσιν εἶναι ὁμολογουμένην.

b. The reason of this preference for the term διάθεσις may be seen from the following text.

Simpl., *in Ar. Categ.* f. 61b ed. Bas. (SVF II 393):

Τὰς μὲν ἕξεις ἐπιτείνεσθαί φασι δύνασθαι καὶ ἀνίεσθαι· τὰς δὲ διαθέσεις ἀνεπιτάτους εἶναι καὶ ἀνανέτους.

1025—According to Stoics, man has by nature an aptitude for virtue.

Natural aptitude for virtue

a. Cleanthes, SVF I fr. 566 (Stob., *Ecl.* II, p. 65, 8 W.):

Πάντας γὰρ ἀνθρώπους ἀφορμὰς ἔχειν ἐκ φύσεως πρὸς ἀρετήν.

b. Cp. *Anced. graeca Paris.* ed. Cramer, Vol. I p. 171, l. 28 (SVF III 214):

Φύσει δὲ πάντες πρὸς ἀρετὴν γεννώμεθα, καθ' ὅσον ἀφορμὰς ἔχομεν.

1026—This view of the origin of virtue is rather well in agreement with Aristotle's, expounded in EN II 1, where virtue is said not to come to us φύσει, but may be said to be κατὰ φύσιν, because human nature is made so, that virtue may arise in it by practice. As might be expected, we find it in Stoic as well as in Peripatetic, may be more or less mixed, sources.

a. Cic., *Tusc. disp.* III 1, 2:

Sunt enim ingeniis nostris semina innata virtutum, quae si adolescere liceret, ipsa nos ad beatam vitam natura perduceret. Nunc autem, simul atque editi in lucem et suscepti sumus, in omni continuo pravitate et in summa opinionum perversitate versamur, ut paene cum lacte nutricis errorem suxisse videamur. Cum vero parentibus redditi, dein magistris traditi sumus, tum ita variis imbuimur erroribus, ut vanitati veritas et opinioni confirmatae natura ipsa cedat.

Semina innata virtutum

Cp. Diog. Laërt. VII 89 (SVF III 228):
Διαστρέφεσθαι δὲ τὸ λογικὸν ζῷον ποτὲ μὲν διὰ τὰς τῶν ἔξωθεν πραγμάτων πιθανότητας, ποτὲ δὲ διὰ τὴν κατήχησιν τῶν συνόντων· ἐπεὶ ἡ φύσις ἀφορμὰς δίδωσιν ἀδιαστρόφους.

See our next nr.

b. Cic., *De fin.* V 18, 43:

Est enim natura sic generata vis hominis, ut ad omnem virtutem percipiendam facta videatur, ob eamque causam parvi virtutum simulacris, quarum in se habent semina, sine doctrina moventur; sunt enim prima

elementa naturae, quibus auctis virtutis quasi germen efficitur. nam
cum ita nati factique simus, ut et agendi aliquid et diligendi aliquos et
liberalitatis et referendae gratiae principia in nobis contineremus atque
ad scientiam, prudentiam, fortitudinem aptos animos haberemus a
contrariisque rebus alienos, non sine causa eas, quas dixi, in pueris
virtutum quasi scintillas videmus, e quibus accendi philosophi ratio
debet, ut eam quasi deum ducem subsequens ad naturae perveniat
extremum. nam, ut saepe iam dixi, in infirma aetate inbecillaque mente
vis naturae quasi per caliginem cernitur; cum autem progrediens confirmatur animus, agnoscit ille quidem naturae vim, sed ita, ut progredi
possit longius, per se sit tantum inchoata.

In this book the ethics of Antiochus of Ascalon is expounded. A certain contamination of Stoic and Aristotelian doctrine in this passage must be noticed.

c. Cp. Arius Didymus in Stob., *Ecl.* II, p. 116, 21 W.:

Τὸ μὲν οὖν ἦθος τοὔνομα λαβεῖν φησιν ἀπὸ τοῦ ἔθους· ὧν γὰρ ἐκ φύσεως
ἀρχὰς ἔχομεν καὶ σπέρματα, τούτων τὰς τελειότητας περιποιεῖσθαι τοῖς ἔθεσι
καὶ ταῖς ὀρθαῖς ἀγωγαῖς· δι' ὃ καὶ τὴν ἠθικὴν ἐθικὴν εἶναι καὶ περὶ μόνα τὰ
ζῷα γίνεσθαι καὶ μάλιστα περὶ ἄνθρωπον.

On the sources of Arius Didymus' survey of peripatetic ethics, see under nr. **999**
(on the origin of the oikeiosis theory).

d. Seneca, *Ep.* 108, 8:

Facile est auditorem concitare ad cupidinem recti: omnibus enim
natura fundamenta dedit semenque virtutum.

Sin a
perversio
naturae
(διαστροφή) **1027**—The reverse of this thesis is, evidently, that sin comes from
without and is a perversion of nature.

a. Galenus, Π. τῶν τῆς ψυχῆς ἠθῶν ed. Bas. I 351 (SVF III 235):
Οὐ γάρ, ὡς οἱ Στωϊκοί φασιν, ἔξωθεν ἐπέρχεται ταῖς ψυχαῖς ἡμῶν τὸ
σύμπαν τῆς κακίας.

b. As we saw in Diog. Laërt. VII 89, cited under **1026a**, Stoics
spoke of a διαστροφή of the reasonable being, caused by two reasons.
The same is found in Galenus, *De plac. Hipp. et Plat.* V 5, p. 437 M.:

Διττὴν γὰρ εἶναι τῆς διαστροφῆς τὴν αἰτίαν, ἑτέραν μὲν ἐκ κατηχήσεως
τῶν πολλῶν ἀνθρώπων ἐγγιγνομένην, ἑτέραν δ' ἐξ αὐτῆς τῶν πραγμάτων
τῆς φύσεως.

c. Chalcidius *in Timaeum* c. 165 ff. (SVF III 229) gives a long
description of this double perversion.

Dicunt porro non spontanea esse delicta, ideo quod omnis anima particeps divinitatis naturali adpetitu bonum quidem semper expetit, errat tamen aliquando in iudicio bonorum et malorum. namque alii nostrum summum bonum voluptatem putant, divitias alii, plerique gloriam et omnia magis quam ipsum verum bonum. Est erroris causa multiplex. Prima quam Stoici duplicem perversionem vocant. haec autem nascitur tam ex rebus ipsis quam ex divulgatione famae. Quippe mox natis exque materno viscere decidentibus provenit ortus cum aliquo dolore, propterea quod ex calida atque umida sede ad frigus et siccitatem aëris circumfusi migrent. Adversum quem dolorem frigusque puerorum opposita est, medicinae loco, artificiosa obstetricum provisio, ut aqua calida confoveantur recens nati adhibeanturque vices et similitudo materni gremii ex calefactione atque fotu, quo laxatum corpus tenerum delectatur et quiescit. Ergo ex utroque sensu, tam doloris quam delectationis, opinio quaedam naturalis exoritur, omne suave ac delectabile bonum, contraque quod dolorem adferat malum esse atque vitandum. Par atque eadem habetur sententia de indigentia quoque et exsaturatione, blanditiis obiurgationibusque, cum aetatis fuerint auctioris. proptereaque confirmata eadem aetate in anticipata sententia permanent: omne blandum bonum, etiamsi sit inutile, omne etiam laboriosum, etiamsi conmoditatem adferat, malum existimantes. Consequenter divitias, quod praestantissimum sit in his instrumentum voluptatis, eximie diligunt, gloriamque pro honore amplexantur. Natura quippe omnis homo laudis atque honoris est adpetens. est enim honor virtutis testimonium. Sed prudentes quidem versatique in sciscitatione sapientiae viri sciunt, quam et cuiusmodi debeant excolere virtutem. Vulgus vero imperitum propter ignorationem rerum pro honore gloriam popularemque existimationem colunt. pro virtute vero vitam consectantur voluptatibus delibutam, potestatem faciendi quae velint regiam quandam esse eminentiam existimantes; —

simul quia beatum necesse est libenter vivere, putant etiam eos, qui cum voluptate vivant, beatos fore. Talis error est, opinor, qui ex rebus ortus hominum animos possidet. ex divulgatione autem succedit errori supra dicto ex matrum et nutricum votis de divitiis gloriaque et ceteris falso putatis bonis insusurratio, in terriculis etiam, quibus tenera aetas vehementius commovetur, nec non in solaciis et omnibus huiusmodi perturbatio. Quin etiam corroboratarum mentium delinitrix poëtica et cetera scriptorum et auctorum opera magnifica quantam animis rudibus invehunt, iuxta voluptatem laboremque, inclinationem favoris?

Quid? pictores quoque et fictores, nonne rapiunt animos ad suavitatem ab industria?

Similar things are said by Cicero in *De legibus* I 11, 31 and 17, 47. Cp. also Seneca, *Ep.* 94, 53 and *Ep.* 115, 11-12.

The unity
of virtue
maintained
by Zeno

1028—a. How Zeno maintained the unity of virtue, may be seen from the following passage of Cicero, *Ac. post.* I 10, 38:

Cumque superiores non omnem virtutem in ratione esse dicerent, sed quasdam virtutes natura aut more perfectas, hic (scil. Zeno) omnes in ratione ponebat; cumque illi ea genera virtutum, quae supra dixi, seiungi posse arbitrarentur, hic nec id ullo modo fieri posse disserebat, nec virtutis usum modo, ut superiores, sed ipsum habitum per se esse praeclarum, nec tamen virtutem cuiquam adesse, quin ea semper uteretur.

By *superiores* Aristotle and his school are meant, and the distinction between διανοητικαί and ἠθικαὶ ἀρεταί (EN I 13, 1103 a 5).
Also the last sentence refers to Aristotle who, having defined the ἀνθρώπινον ἀγαθόν as "an activity of the soul according to virtue" (EN I 7, 1098 a 17), posits that displaying virtue is much more than possessing it (EN I 8, 1098 a 32-b 7).

The four
main virtues

b. Zeno admitted the four main virtues as distinct one from the other, but inseparable. Plut., *Stoic. repugn.* 7, p. 1034c:

Ἀρετὰς ὁ Ζήνων ἀπολείπει πλείονας κατὰ διαφοράς, ὥσπερ ὁ Πλάτων, οἷον φρόνησιν ἀνδρείαν σωφροσύνην δικαιοσύνην, ὡς ἀχωρίστους μὲν οὔσας, ἑτέρας δὲ καὶ διαφερούσας ἀλλήλων.

φρόνησις
used in the
general sense

c. He seems to have used the term φρόνησις also in the general sense of "practical reason", which is the basis of all virtue, as Socrates does in Xen.'s *Mem.* III 9.

Plut., *De virt. mor.* 2, p. 441a:

Ἔοικε δὲ καὶ Ζήνων εἰς τοῦτό πως ὑποφέρεσθαι ὁ Κιτιεύς, ὁριζόμενος τὴν φρόνησιν ἐν μὲν ἀπονεμητέοις δικαιοσύνην, ἐν δ' αἱρετέοις σωφροσύνην, ἐν δ' ὑπομενετέοις ἀνδρείαν. ἀπολογούμενοι δ' ἀξιοῦσιν ἐν τούτοις τὴν ἐπιστήμην φρόνησιν ὑπὸ τοῦ Ζήνωνος ὠνομάσθαι.

Aristo of Chios found an inconsistency in accepting a plurality of virtues. He rejected any distinction between them and, defining them as ἐπιστήμη, maintained their strict unity (see **1030a**).

Cleanthes'
view of
virtue

1029—Cleanthes described virtue as a force and a tension of the soul.

a. Plut., *Stoic. repugn.* 7, p. 1034d (SVF I 563):

Ὁ δὲ Κλεάνθης ἐν ὑπομνήμασι φυσικοῖς εἰπὼν ὅτι "πληγὴ πυρὸς ὁ τόνος ἐστί, κἂν ἱκανὸς ἐν τῇ ψυχῇ γένηται πρὸς τὸ ἐπιτελεῖν τὰ ἐπιβάλλοντα, ἰσχὺς καλεῖται καὶ κράτος", ἐπιφέρει κατὰ λέξιν "ἡ δ' ἰσχὺς αὕτη καὶ τὸ κράτος, ὅταν μὲν ἐν τοῖς φανεῖσιν ἐμμενετέοις ἐγγένηται, ἐγκράτειά ἐστιν· ὅταν δ' ἐν τοῖς ὑπομενετέοις, ἀνδρεία· περὶ τὰς ἀξίας δὲ δικαιοσύνη· περὶ τὰς αἱρέσεις καὶ ἐκκλίσεις σωφροσύνη."

b. Stob., *Ecl.* II 7, 5, p. 62, 24 W. (SVF I ib.):

Καὶ ὁμοίως ὥσπερ ἰσχὺς τοῦ σώματος τόνος ἐστὶν ἱκανὸς ἐν νεύροις, οὕτω καὶ ἡ τῆς ψυχῆς ἰσχὺς τόνος ἐστὶν ἱκανὸς ἐν τῷ κρίνειν καὶ πράττειν ἢ μή.

1030—Of Chrysippus, we have some more intellectual definitions of virtue and virtues.

a. In spite of his fundamentally monistic view of the soul, whence follows that every virtue is nothing but the hegemonikon in a certain state or condition—the ἡγεμονικόν πως ἔχον—(supra, nrs. **953** and **986c**) Chrys. opposed Aristo's view of virtue as an undifferentiated unity, though holding essentially the same definition.

Galenus, *De plac. Hippocr. et Plat.* VII 2, 591 M. (SVF III 256): **Virtue is knowledge**

Νομίσας γοῦν ὁ Ἀρίστων μίαν εἶναι τῆς ψυχῆς δύναμιν, ᾗ λογιζόμεθα, καὶ τὴν ἀρετὴν τῆς ψυχῆς ἔθετο μίαν, ἐπιστήμην ἀγαθῶν καὶ κακῶν. ὅταν μὲν οὖν αἱρεῖσθαί τε δέῃ τἀγαθὰ καὶ φεύγειν τὰ κακά, τὴν ἐπιστήμην τήνδε καλεῖ σωφροσύνην· ὅταν δὲ πράττειν μὲν τἀγαθά, μὴ πράττειν δὲ τὰ κακά, φρόνησιν· ἀνδρείαν δ' ὅταν τὰ μὲν θαρρῇ, τὰ δὲ φεύγῃ· ὅταν δὲ τὸ κατ' ἀξίαν ἑκάστῳ νέμῃ, δικαιοσύνην· ἑνὶ δὲ λόγῳ γινώσκουσα μὲν ἡ ψυχὴ χωρὶς τοῦ πράττειν τἀγαθά τε καὶ κακὰ σοφία τέ ἐστι καὶ ἐπιστήμη, πρὸς δὲ τὰς πράξεις ἀφικνουμένη τὰς κατὰ τὸν βίον, ὀνόματα πλείω λαμβάνει τὰ προειρημένα, φρόνησίς τε καὶ σωφροσύνη καὶ δικαιοσύνη καὶ ἀνδρεία καλουμένη. τοιαύτη μέν τις ἡ Ἀρίστωνος δόξα περὶ τῶν τῆς ψυχῆς ἀρετῶν.

Ὅ γε μὴν Χρύσιππος οὐκ οἶδα ὅπως ἀντιλέγειν ἐπιχειρεῖ τἀνδρὶ τὴν κοινὴν πρὸς αὐτὸν ὑπόθεσιν ἀκριβῶς διαφυλάττοντι. καλῶς γὰρ ἅπαντα γινωσκόντων τε καὶ πραττόντων ἡμῶν ἂν ὁ βίος διοικοῖτο κατὰ ἐπιστήμην, κακῶς δὲ καὶ ψευδῶς γινωσκόντων τε καὶ πραττόντων κατὰ ἄγνοιαν. ὡς αὐτὸς ὁ Χρύσιππος βούλεται, καὶ διὰ ταῦτα μία μὲν ἀρετὴ γίνοιτο ἄν, ἡ ἐπιστήμη, μία δὲ ὡσαύτως ἡ κακία, προσαγορευομένη καὶ ἥδε ποτὲ μὲν ἄγνοια, ποτὲ δὲ ἀνεπιστημοσύνη.

b. How this general definition was meant, is explained by Galenus in the next passage (ib., 592 M.):

Ἐὰν οὖν τις τὸν θάνατον ἢ τὴν πενίαν ἢ τὴν νόσον ὡς κακὰ δεδιὼς ᾖ, δέον θαρρεῖν, ὡς ἐπὶ ἀδιαφόροις, ἐνδείᾳ μὲν ἐπιστήμης αὐτὸν τίθενται ἀγνοεῖν

τάληθές, ὡς ἂν Ἀρίστων τε καὶ Χρύσιππος εἴποι, κακίαν δὲ ἔχειν ψυχῆς,
ἣν ὀνομάζουσι δειλίαν, ἢ ἐναντίαν ἀρετὴν αὐτοί φασιν εἶναι τὴν ἀνδρείαν,
ἐπιστήμην οὖσαν ὧν χρὴ θαρρεῖν ἢ μὴ θαρρεῖν, τουτέστιν ἀγαθῶν τε καὶ
κακῶν τῶν ὄντως δηλονότι τοιούτων, οὐ κατὰ ψευδῆ δόξαν ὑπειλημμένων,
οἷάπερ ἐστὶν ὑγίεια καὶ πλοῦτος καὶ νόσος καὶ πενία. τούτων γὰρ οὐδὲν οὔτε
ἀγαθὸν οὔτε κακὸν εἶναί φασιν, ἀλλὰ ἀδιάφορα πάντα. καὶ τοίνυν, εἰ τὸ μὲν
ἡδὺ νομίσας τις ἀγαθόν, τὸ δὲ ἀνιαρὸν κακὸν ἀκολουθῶν τῇ δόξῃ τῇδε τοῦ μὲν
τὴν αἵρεσιν ποιοῖτο, τοῦ δὲ τὴν φυγήν, ἀμαθής ἐστιν οὐσίας ἀγαθοῦ καὶ διὰ
ταῦτα ἀκόλαστος. ἐν ἁπάσαις γὰρ πράξεσιν αἱρουμένων ἡμῶν τὸ φαινόμενον
ἀγαθόν, φευγόντων δὲ τὸ φαινόμενον κακόν, ἐχόντων δὲ φύσει τὰς ὁρμὰς
ταύτας ἐφ᾽ ἑκάτερον ἡ φιλοσοφία διδάσκουσα τὸ κατὰ ἀλήθειαν ἀγαθόν τε καὶ
κακὸν ἀναμαρτήτους ἐργάζεται.

Definitions of the four cardinal virtues   **c.**   The following definitions of the four cardinal virtues are due to Chrysippus [1].

Stob., *Ecl.* II, p. 59, 4 W. (SVF III 262):

Φρόνησιν δ᾽ εἶναι ἐπιστήμην ὧν ποιητέον καὶ οὐ ποιητέον καὶ οὐδετέρων, ἢ
ἐπιστήμην ἀγαθῶν καὶ κακῶν καὶ οὐδετέρων φύσει πολιτικοῦ ζῴου (καὶ ἐπὶ
τῶν λοιπῶν δὲ ἀρετῶν οὕτως ἀκούειν παραγγέλλουσι). σωφροσύνην δ᾽ εἶναι
ἐπιστήμην αἱρετῶν καὶ φευκτῶν καὶ οὐδετέρων· δικαιοσύνην δ᾽ ἐπιστήμην
ἀπονεμητικὴν τῆς ἀξίας ἑκάστῳ· ἀνδρείαν δὲ ἐπιστήμην δεινῶν καὶ οὐ δεινῶν
καὶ οὐδετέρων.

Inseparability of virtue   **1031—a.**   From the fundamental unity of virtue follows that he who possesses one virtue possesses all of them.

Stob., ib., p. 63, 6 W.:

Πάσας δὲ τὰς ἀρετὰς ὅσαι ἐπιστῆμαί εἰσι καὶ τέχναι κοινά τε θεωρήματα
ἔχειν καὶ τέλος, ὡς εἴρηται, τὸ αὐτό· διὸ καὶ ἀχωρίστους εἶναι· τὸν γὰρ μίαν
ἔχοντα πάσας ἔχειν, καὶ τὸν κατὰ μίαν πράττοντα κατὰ πάσας πράττειν.

b.   The same doctrine is found in Seneca, *Ep.* 67, 10:

Cum aliquis tormenta fortiter patitur, omnibus virtutibus utitur.
Fortasse una in promptu sit et maxime appareat, patientia: ceterum
illic est fortitudo, cuius patientia et perpessio et tolerantia rami sunt;
illic est prudentia, sine qua nullum initur consilium, quae suadet quod
effugere non possis quam fortissime ferre; illic est constantia, quae
deici loco non potest et propositum nulla vi extorquente dimittit;

---

[1]   See Dyroff, *Die Ethik der alten Stoa*, p. 82 ff., also Wachsmuth in his apparatus.

illic est individuus ille comitatus virtutum. Quicquid honeste fit, una virtus facit.

c.   The reverse of this thesis is, evidently, that he who lacks one virtue lacks all; whence the division of mankind into wise men and fools (our next paragraph).

1032—The absolute character of virtue implies also that he who possesses it cannot lose it. This was, in general, the Stoic thesis. A point of discussion among Stoics was the question whether or not virtue can be lost by intoxication or melancholy. Cleanthes held it could not, Chrysippus thought it could [1].

Virtue cannot be lost

a.   Simplicius in Ar. *Categ.* f. 102 A ed. Bas. (SVF III 238):

('Εκ μὲν φαύλου σπουδαῖος γίνεται) τὸ δ' ἀνάπαλιν οἱ Στωϊκοὶ οὐ διδόασιν. οὐκ εἶναι γάρ φασιν ἀποβλητὴν τὴν ἀρετήν.

b.   Ib. B:

(Aristotle and Theophr. thought it above the human condition that virtue could not be lost.)

Ἔτι δὲ καὶ οἱ Στωϊκοὶ ἐν μελαγχολίαις καὶ κάροις καὶ ληθάργοις καὶ ἐν φαρμάκων λήψεσι συγχωροῦσιν ἀποβολὴν γίνεσθαι μεθ' ὅλης τῆς λογικῆς ἕξεως καὶ αὐτῆς τῆς ἀρετῆς, κακίας μὲν οὐκ ἀντεισαγομένης, τῆς δὲ βεβαιότητος χαλωμένης καὶ εἰς ἣν λέγουσιν ἕξιν μέσην οἱ παλαιοὶ μεταπιπτούσης.

c.   Cp. Diog. Laërt. VII 127 (SVF III 237):

Καὶ μὴν τὴν ἀρετὴν Χρύσιππος μὲν ἀποβλητήν, Κλεάνθης δὲ ἀναπόβλητον· ὁ μὲν ἀποβλητὴν διὰ μέθην καὶ μελαγχολίαν, ὁ δὲ ἀναπόβλητον διὰ βεβαίους καταλήψεις.

1033—Virtuous acts are called by Stoics κατορθώματα. Now, since virtue is a certain state of mind (διάθεσις), the first thing to be stressed is that katorthomata are not defined by what is done, but by the state of mind which is behind the action. As such, they are distinct from καθήκοντα, which are, in general, "befitting acts", for which a reasonable defence can be adduced. The katorthoma, however, can be (and in fact, was) regarded as the perfect kathekon.

Virtuous acts: katorthomata

---

[1]   Later, we shall find the problem in Plotinus, *Enn.* I 4, 9-10 and IV 4, 43-44; infra, our nrs. **1422c** and **1432c**.

καθήκοντα:
τέλεια
and μέσα κ.

a. Stob., *Ecl.* II 85, 13 W. (SVF III 494):

Ἀκόλουθος δ᾽ ἐστὶ τῷ λόγῳ τῷ περὶ τῶν προηγμένων ὁ περὶ τοῦ καθήκοντος τόπος. Ὁρίζεται δὲ τὸ καθῆκον· "τὸ ἀκόλουθον ἐν ζωῇ, ὃ πραχθὲν εὔλογον ἀπολογίαν ἔχει·" παρὰ τὸ καθῆκον δὲ τὸ ἐναντίως. Τοῦτο διατείνει καὶ εἰς τὰ ἄλογα τῶν ζῴων, ἐνεργεῖ γάρ τι κἀκεῖνα ἀκολούθως τῇ ἑαυτῶν φύσει· ἐπὶ ⟨δὲ⟩ τῶν λογικῶν ζῴων οὕτως ἀποδίδοται· "τὸ ἀκόλουθον ἐν βίῳ". Τῶν δὲ καθηκόντων τὰ μὲν εἶναί φασι τέλεια, ἃ δὴ καὶ κατορθώματα λέγεσθαι. Κατορθώματα δ᾽ εἶναι τὰ κατ᾽ ἀρετὴν ἐνεργήματα, οἷον τὸ φρονεῖν, τὸ δικαιοπραγεῖν. οὐκ εἶναι δὲ κατορθώματα τὰ μὴ οὕτως ἔχοντα, ἃ δὴ οὐδὲ τέλεια καθήκοντα προσαγορεύουσιν, ἀλλὰ μέσα, οἷον τὸ γαμεῖν, τὸ πρεσβεύειν, τὸ διαλέγεσθαι, τὰ τούτοις ὅμοια.

b. Stob., ib., p. 93, 14 W. (SVF III 500):

Κατόρθωμα δ᾽ εἶναι λέγουσι καθῆκον πάντας ἐπέχον τοὺς ἀριθμούς, ἢ ... τέλειον καθῆκον.

Cp. Cic., *De fin.* III 7, 24, where wisdom is compared with other arts: it differs from the arts of acting and of dancing, the author says, in this, that a movement perfectly executed does not include all the parts which together constitute the subject matter of the art, whereas the *katorthoma*, indeed, contains the whole of virtue.

..."est etiam alia cum his ipsis artibus sapientiae dissimilitudo, propterea quod in illis, quae recte facta sunt, non continent tamen omnis partis, e quibus constant: quae autem nos aut recta facta dicamus, si placet, illi autem appellant κατορθώματα, *omnis numeros virtutis continent*".

The
kathekon
and the
κατὰ φύσιν

1034—The καθῆκον is connected with the πρῶτα κατὰ φύσιν, and as such, not yet of the moral level (cp. supra, nrs. **1017-1020**).

a. Diog. Laërt. VII 108-109:

Ἐνέργημα δ᾽ αὐτὸ εἶναι ταῖς κατὰ φύσιν κατασκευαῖς οἰκεῖον. τῶν γὰρ καθ᾽ ὁρμὴν ἐνεργουμένων τὰ μὲν καθήκοντα εἶναι, τὰ δὲ παρὰ τὸ καθῆκον, τὰ δ᾽ οὔτε καθήκοντα οὔτε παρὰ τὸ καθῆκον. καθήκοντα μὲν οὖν εἶναι ὅσα λόγος αἱρεῖ ποιεῖν, ὡς ἔχει τὸ γονεῖς τιμᾶν, ἀδελφούς, πατρίδα, συμπεριφέρεσθαι φίλοις· παρὰ τὸ καθῆκον δέ, ὅσα μὴ αἱρεῖ λόγος, ὡς ἔχει τὰ τοιαῦτα, γονέων ἀμελεῖν, ἀδελφῶν ἀφροντιστεῖν, φίλοις μὴ συνδιατίθεσθαι, πατρίδα ὑπερορᾶν καὶ τὰ παραπλήσια· οὔτε δὲ καθήκοντα οὔτε παρὰ τὸ καθῆκον, ὅσα οὔθ᾽ αἱρεῖ λόγος πράττειν οὔτ᾽ ἀπαγορεύει, οἷον κάρφος ἀνελέσθαι, γραφεῖον κρατεῖν ἢ στλεγγίδα καὶ τὰ ὅμοια τούτοις.

not yet of the
moral level

b. Cic., *De fin.* III 6, 22:

Cum vero illa, quae officia esse dixi, proficiscantur ab initiis naturae, necesse est ea ad haec referri, ut recte dici possit omnia officia eo referri, ut adipiscamur principia naturae, nec tamen ut hoc sit bonorum ultimum, propterea quod non inest in primis naturae conciliationibus honesta actio; consequens enim est et post oritur, ut dixi. Est tamen ea secundum naturam multoque nos ad se expetendam magis hortatur quam superiora omnia.

In fact, the doctrine of the καθῆκον, which is, in principle, the question of choosing **Importance** what is to be "preferred" among the ἀδιάφορα, took a great place in Stoic philosophy **of the** since Chrysippus. Wiersma, Π. τέλους, p. 65 ff., expounds how Diogenes of Seleucia, **καθήκοντα** by wording the telos as εὐλογιστεῖν ἐν τῇ τῶν κατὰ φύσιν ἐκλογῇ—a formula in which **stressed by** the προηγμένα are shortly called τὰ κατὰ φύσιν—, gave a remarkable development **Chrysippus'** to Chrysippus' doctrine of the καθήκοντα. Chrysippus' immediate successors— **successors** Diogenes, Archedemus and Antipater—appear to have considered the choice of the right kind of adiaphora as the essential thing in life, and therefore could define the telos by the ἐκλογὴ τῶν κατὰ φύσιν and ἀπεκλογή of what was opposed to these. Thus Stoicism became a philosophy of the προκόπτοντες, though never forgetting that the προκόπτων is essentially not of the level of the wise man, as the προηγμένον is not of the level of the ἀγαθόν.

c. Cic., ib. 17, 58:

Sed cum quod honestum sit, id solum bonum esse dicamus, consenta-neum tamen est fungi officio, cum id officium nec in bonis ponamus nec in malis. Est enim aliquid in rebus probabile, et quidem ita, ut eius ratio reddi possit, ergo ut etiam probabiliter acti ratio reddi possit. Est autem officium, quod ita factum est, ut eius facti probabilis ratio reddi possit. Ex quo intelligitur officium medium quiddam esse, quod neque in bonis ponatur neque in contrariis.

In this text the term *probabile* is used as a translation of the Greek εὔλογον which, with Stoic writers, has not a sceptical sense, but means simply "reasonable" or "justifiable by reason".

d. We possess a text of Chrysippus himself on the (relative) value of καθήκοντα.

Stob., *Florileg.* 103, 22 (SVF III 510):

Χρυσίππου. Ὁ δ' ἐπ' ἄκρον, φησί, προκόπτων ἅπαντα πάντως ἀποδί-δωσι τὰ καθήκοντα καὶ οὐδὲν παραλείπει.

Τὸν δὲ τούτου βίον οὐκ εἶναί πώ φησιν εὐδαίμονα, ἀλλ' ἐπιγίγνεσθαι αὐτῷ τὴν εὐδαιμονίαν ὅταν αἱ μέσαι πράξεις αὗται προσλάβωσι τὸ βέβαιον καὶ ἑκτικὸν καὶ ἰδίαν πῆξιν τινὰ λάβωσι.

The text reminds us of Aristotle's teaching in the *Eth. Nic.* II, that virtue arises from habit (our nr. **567a**), but only then, ἐὰν ὁ πράττων πως ἔχων πράττῃ, and ἐὰν καὶ βεβαίως καὶ ἀμετακινήτως ἔχων πράττῃ (EN II 4; our nr. **570a**).
Chrysippus was not so far from Aristotle as he might seem to have been!
Wiersma cites the above text of Chrysippus and comments on it, Π. τέλους p. 61 f.

See also, on the relation between καθῆκον and κατόρθωμα, the article of G. Nebel, *Hermes* 70, 1935, p. 439-460.

Morality depends on the inner man

1035—The katorthoma proceeds from the inner man.

a. Seneca, *Ep.* 95, 57:

Actio recta non erit, nisi recta fuerit voluntas: ab hac enim est actio. Rursus voluntas non erit recta, nisi habitus animi rectus fuerit: ab hoc enim est voluntas. Habitus porro animi non erit in optimo, nisi totius vitae leges perceperit et quid de quoque iudicandum sit exegerit.

Cp. Stob., *Ecl.* II 7, 1, p. 38, 15 W. (SVF I 203):
Οἱ δὲ κατὰ Ζήνωνα τὸν Στωϊκὸν τροπικῶς· ἦθός ἐστι πηγὴ βίου, ἀφ' ἧς αἱ κατὰ μέρος πράξεις ῥέουσι.

No outward conditions

b. No outward conditions are required for it.

Seneca, *De benef.* III 18:

Refert enim cuius animi sit qui praestat, non cuius status: nulli praeclusa virtus est, omnibus patet, omnes admittit, omnes invitat, ingenuos, libertinos, servos, reges, exules. non eligit domum nec censum, nudo homine contenta est.

In this Stoic ethics stands opposite to Aristotle, who, in his EN I 8 (1099 a 31-b 2; cp. 1098 b 32 - 1099 a 7) taught that outward means are necessary for the exercise of virtue, the χρῆσις of which seemed to him far superior to its κτῆσις.

Hence, for Aristotle, it is a question whether or not slaves, women and children can have virtue. He replied that, indeed, none of them can in full sense, and that the virtue of a woman is different from that of a man, and the virtue of slaves different from that of freeborn people (our nr. **611**).

To this view, Stoics opposed energetically ὅτι ἡ αὐτὴ ἀρετὴ ἀνδρὸς καὶ γυναικός, etc., or, as it was said by Musonius Rufus [1] and later, e.g., by Clement of Alexandria: ὅτι πᾶσι φιλοσοφητέον [2]. In this, the Stoics were preceded by Antisthenes and his school.

Not increased by duration

1036—The value of morality being something absolute, right conduct, which depends on a certain inner disposition, is not capable of increase, and therefore independent of duration.

Cic., *De fin.* III 14, 45-47:

Ut enim obscuratur et offunditur luce solis lumen lucernae et ut interit in magnitudine maris Aegaei stilla mellis et ut in divitiis Croesi teruncii accessio et gradus unus in ea via, quae est hinc in Indiam, sic,

---

[1] Musonius c. 3, "Οτι καὶ γυναιξὶ φιλοσοφητέον.
[2] Clem. Alex., *Strom.* IV 8, p. 590 and 592 (SVF III 254). Cp. Lactantius, *Inst.*, III 25.

cum sit is bonorum finis, quem Stoici dicunt, omnis ista rerum corporearum aestimatio splendore virtutis et magnitudine obscuretur et obruatur atque intereat necesse est; et quem ad modum opportunitas—sic enim appellemus εὐκαιρίαν—non fit maior productione temporis—habent enim suum modum quae opportuna dicuntur—, sic recta effectio—κατόρθωσιν enim ita appello, quoniam rectum factum κατόρθωμα—, recta igitur effectio, item convenientia, denique ipsum bonum, quod in eo positum est ut naturae consentiat, crescendi accessionem nullam habet. ut enim opportunitas illa, sic haec, de quibus dixi, non fiunt temporis productione maiora, ob eamque causam Stoicis non videtur optabilior nec magis expetenda beata vita, si sit longa, quam si brevis, utunturque simili: ut, si cothurni laus illa esset, ad pedem apte convenire, neque multi cothurni paucis anteponerentur nec maiores minoribus, sic, quorum omne bonum convenientia atque opportunitate finitur, nec plura paucioribus nec longinquiora brevioribus anteponent. nec vero satis acute dicunt: "si bona valetudo pluris aestimanda sit longa quam brevis, sapientiae quoque usus longissimus quisque sit plurimi." non intellegunt valetudinis aestimationem spatio iudicari, virtutis opportunitate, ut videantur qui illud dicunt idem hoc esse dicturi, bonam mortem et bonum partum meliorem longum esse quam brevem. Non vident alia brevitate pluris aestimari, alia diurnitate.

1037—As to the outward appearance, the man who does not possess virtue may do the same things as he who possesses it. The difference is in the inner man.

A non-moral action may be seemingly the same as a katorthoma

a. Clem. Alex., *Strom.* VII 10, p. 43 St. (SVF III 511):

Καίτοι πράσσεταί τινα καὶ πρὸς τῶν μὴ γνωστικῶν ὀρθῶς, ἀλλ' οὐ κατὰ λόγον· οἷον ἐπὶ ἀνδρείας· ἔνιοι γὰρ ἐκ φύσεως θυμοειδεῖς γενόμενοι, εἶτα ἄνευ τοῦ λόγου τοῦτο θρέψαντες, ἀλόγως ἐπὶ τὰ πολλὰ ὁρμῶσι καὶ ὅμοια τοῖς ἀνδρείοις δρῶσιν, ὥστε ἐνίοτε τὰ αὐτὰ κατορθοῦν οἷον βασάνους ὑπομένειν εὐκόλως· ἀλλ' οὔτε ἀπὸ τῆς αὐτῆς αἰτίας τῷ γνωστικῷ οὔτε καὶ τὸ αὐτὸ προθέμενοι, οὐδ' ἂν τὸ σῶμα ἅπαν ἐπιδιδῶσιν. — Πᾶσα οὖν ἡ διὰ τοῦ ἐπιστήμονος πρᾶξις εὐπραγία, ἡ δὲ διὰ τοῦ ἀνεπιστήμονος κακοπραγία, κἂν ἔνστασιν σῴζῃ. ἐπεὶ μὴ ἐκ λογισμοῦ ἀνδρίζεται μηδὲ ἐπί τι χρήσιμον τῶν ἐπὶ ἀρετὴν καὶ ἀπὸ ἀρετῆς καταστρεφόντων τὴν πρᾶξιν κατευθύνει. Ὁ δὲ αὐτὸς λόγος καὶ ἐπὶ τῶν ἄλλων ἀρετῶν.

What Clement calls the γνωστικός is the spiritually fullgrown, or deeply initiated, Christian, as opposed to the "simple believer" (ἁπλῶς πιστός) who is at a lower stage of spiritual development. The actions of the first, whom he calls also the ἐπιστήμων, are always right—Clement calls them εὐπραγία, or also κατορθώματα (see sub *b*)—, those of the latter, who does not possess "knowledge", never.

In this and the following passage we find Stoic views and terminology adopted by a Christian.

b.   Clem. Alex., *Strom.* VI 14, p. 487 St. (SVF III 515):

Οὕτως καὶ πᾶσα πρᾶξις γνωστικοῦ μὲν κατόρθωμα, τοῦ δὲ ἁπλῶς πιστοῦ μέση πρᾶξις λέγοιτ' ἄν, μηδέπω κατὰ λόγον ἐπιτελουμένη μηδὲ μὴν κατ' ἐπίστασιν κατορθουμένη.

c.   That there is a true analogy between the Stoic and the Christian view of moral perfection, may be seen from the following well-known text.

Paulus, *ad Rom.* 14, 23:

Πᾶν δὲ ὃ οὐκ ἐκ πίστεως ἁμαρτία ἐστίν.

Which means: those actions which do not spring from the right state of the inner man, cannot be called good actions.

11—ETHICS (4): WISE MEN AND FOOLS

No medium between virtue and vice

1038—Stoics did not admit of any medium between virtue and vice.

a.   Diog. Laërt. VII 127 (SVF III 536):

Ἀρέσκει δὲ αὐτοῖς μηδὲν μέσον εἶναι ἀρετῆς καὶ κακίας, τῶν Περιπατητικῶν μεταξὺ ἀρετῆς καὶ κακίας εἶναι λεγόντων τὴν προκοπήν· ὡς γὰρ δεῖν φασιν ἢ ὀρθὸν εἶναι ξύλον ἢ στρεβλόν, οὕτως ἢ δίκαιον ἢ ἄδικον, οὔτε δὲ δικαιότερον οὔτε ἀδικώτερον, καὶ ἐπὶ τῶν ἄλλων ὁμοίως.

b.   Cp. Cleanthes, fr. 566 SVF I (ap. Stob., *Ecl.* II 65, 7 W.):

Ἀρετῆς δὲ καὶ κακίας οὐδὲν εἶναι μεταξύ. πάντας γὰρ ἀνθρώπους ἀφορμὰς ἔχειν ἐκ φύσεως πρὸς ἀρετήν, καὶ οἰονεὶ τὸν τῶν ἡμιαμβείων λόγον ἔχειν, κατὰ Κλεάνθην· ὅθεν ἀτελεῖς μὲν ὄντας εἶναι φαύλους, τελειωθέντας δὲ σπουδαίους.

The προκόπτοντες classed as ἀνόητοι

1039—The προκόπτοντες are classed as ἀνόητοι.

a.   Plut., *De comm. not.* 10, p. 1063a (SVF III 539):

Ναί, φασίν, ἀλλὰ ὥσπερ ὁ πῆχυν ἀπέχων ἐν θαλάττῃ τῆς ἐπιφανείας, οὐδὲν ἧττον πνίγεται τοῦ καταδεδυκότος ὀργυιὰς πεντακοσίας, οὕτως οὐδὲ οἱ πελάζοντες ἀρετῇ τῶν μακρὰν ὄντων ἧττόν εἰσιν ἐν κακίᾳ· καὶ καθάπερ οἱ τυφλοὶ τυφλοί εἰσι, κἂν ὀλίγον ὕστερον ἀναβλέπειν μέλλωσιν, οὕτως οἱ προκόπτοντες, ἄχρις οὗ τὴν ἀρετὴν ἀναλάβωσιν, ἀνόητοι καὶ μοχθηροὶ διαμένουσιν.

b. Likewise, Cicero in *De finibus* III 14, 48, when expounding that wisdom does not admit of degrees, says:

Ut enim qui demersi sunt in aqua nihilo magis respirare possunt, si non longe absunt a summo, ut iam iamque possint emergere, quam si etiam tum essent in profundo, nec catulus ille, qui iam adpropinquat ut videat, plus cernit quam is, qui modo est natus, item qui processit aliquantum ad virtutis habitum nihilo minus in miseria est quam ille, qui nihil processit.

c. Plut. finds some difficulties in the abrupt transition from φαυλότης to wisdom. *Quomodo quis in virtute sentiat profectum*, c. 1, p. 75c (SVF III ib.):

Οὕτως ἐν τῷ φιλοσοφεῖν οὔτε προκοπὴν οὔτε τινὰ προκοπῆς αἴσθησιν ὑποληπτέον, εἰ μηδὲν ἡ ψυχὴ μεθίησι μηδ᾽ ἀποκαθαίρεται τῆς ἀβελτερίας, ἄχρι δὲ τοῦ λαβεῖν ἄκρατον τὸ ἀγαθὸν καὶ τέλειον ἀκράτῳ τῷ κακῷ χρῆται. Καὶ γὰρ ἀκαρεῖ χρόνου καὶ ὥρας ἐκ τῆς ὡς ἕνι μάλιστα φαυλότητος εἰς οὐκ ἔχουσαν ὑπερβολὴν ἀρετῆς διάθεσιν μεταβαλὼν ὁ σοφός, ἧς οὐδ᾽ ἐν χρόνῳ πόλλῳ μέρος ἀφεῖλε κακίας ἅμα πᾶσαν ἐξαίφνης ἐκπέφευγε. καίτοι ἤδη τοὺς ταῦτά γε λέγοντας οἶσθα δήπου πάλιν πολλὰ παρέχοντας αὐτοῖς πράγματα καὶ μεγάλας ἀπορίας περὶ τοῦ διαλεληθότος, ὃς αὐτὸς ἑαυτὸν οὐδέπω κατείληφε γεγονὼς σοφός. — Εἰ δέ γε ἦν τάχος τοσοῦτον τῆς μεταβολῆς καὶ μέγεθος, ὥστε τὸν πρωὶ κάκιστον ἑσπέρας γεγονέναι κράτιστον, ἢ ἂν οὕτω τινὶ συντύχη τὰ τῆς μεταβολῆς, καταδαρθόντα φαῦλον ἀνεγρέσθαι σοφὸν καὶ προσειπεῖν ἐκ τῆς ψυχῆς μεθεικότα τὰς χθιζὰς ἀβελτερίας καὶ ἀπάτας

"ψευδεῖς ὄνειροι, χαίρετ᾽· οὐδὲν ἦτ᾽ ἄρα",

τίς ἂν ἀγνοήσειεν αὐτοῦ διαφορὰν ἐν αὐτῷ τοσαύτην γενομένην καὶ φρόνησιν ἀθρόον ἐκλάμψασαν;

1040—Stoics themselves made a certain difference between the ἁμαρτήματα though they are fundamentally equal.

Fundamental equality of ἁμαρτήματα

a. Stob., *Ecl.* II 7, p. 106, 21 W. (SVF III 528):

Ἴσά τε πάντα λέγουσιν εἶναι τὰ ἁμαρτήματα, οὐκέτι δ᾽ ὅμοια. Καθάπερ γὰρ ἀπὸ μιᾶς τινος πηγῆς τῆς κακίας φέρεσθαι πέφυκε, τῆς κρίσεως οὔσης ἐν πᾶσι τοῖς ἁμαρτήμασι τῆς αὐτῆς· παρὰ δὲ τὴν ἔξωθεν αἰτίαν τῶν ἐφ᾽ οἷς αἱ κρίσεις ἀποτελοῦνται μέσων διαλλαττόντων, διάφορα κατὰ ποιότητα γίνεσθαι τὰ ἁμαρτήματα. Λάβοις δ᾽ ἂν εἰκόνα σαφῆ τοῦ δηλουμένου τῷδ᾽ ἐπιστήσας· πᾶν γὰρ τὸ ψεῦδος ἐπ᾽ ἴσης ψεῦδος συμβέβηκεν, οὐ γὰρ εἶναι ἕτερον ἑτέρου μᾶλλον διεψευσμένον· τὸ [τε] γὰρ νύκτ᾽ ⟨ἀεὶ⟩ εἶναι ψεῦδός ἐστι, καθάπερ

τὸ ἱπποκένταυρον ζῆν· καὶ οὐ μᾶλλον εἰπεῖν ἔστι ψεῦδος εἶναι θάτερον θατέρου·
ἀλλ᾽ οὐχὶ τὸ ψεῦδος ἐπίσης ψεῦδός ἐστιν, οὐχὶ δὲ καὶ οἱ διεψευσμένοι ἐπίσης
εἰσὶ διεψευσμένοι. Καὶ ἁμαρτάνειν δὲ μᾶλλον καὶ ἧττον οὐκ ἔστιν, πᾶσαν γὰρ
ἁμαρτίαν κατὰ διάψευσιν πράττεσθαι. Ἔτι, οὐχὶ κατόρθωμα μὲν μεῖζον καὶ
ἔλαττον οὐ γίγνεσθαι, ἁμάρτημα δὲ μεῖζον καὶ ἔλαττον γίγνεσθαι· πάντα γάρ
ἐστι τέλεια, διόπερ οὔτ᾽ ἐλλείπειν οὔτ᾽ ὑπερέχειν δύναιτ᾽ ἂν ἀλλήλων.

Fools are equally fools

b. Stob., ib., 113, 18 W. (SVF III 529):

Πάντων τε τῶν ἁμαρτημάτων ἴσων ὄντων καὶ τῶν κατορθωμάτων, καὶ τοὺς
ἄφρονας ἐπίσης πάντας ἄφρονας εἶναι, τὴν αὐτὴν καὶ ἴσην ἔχοντας διάθεσιν.
ἴσων δὲ ὄντων τῶν ἁμαρτημάτων εἶναί τινας ἐν αὐτοῖς διαφοράς, καθ᾽ ὅσον
τὰ μὲν αὐτῶν ἀπὸ σκληρᾶς καὶ δυσιάτου διαθέσεως γίνεται, τὰ δ᾽ οὔ.

Moral progress admitted by Zeno

1041—a. That Zeno admitted a προκοπή, may be seen from the
following passage.

Plut., *De prof. in virt.* 12, p. 82 f. (SVF I 234):

Ὅρα δὴ καὶ τὸ τοῦ Ζήνωνος ὁποῖόν ἐστιν. ἠξίου γὰρ ἀπὸ τῶν ὀνείρων
ἕκαστον αὐτοῦ συναισθάνεσθαι προκόπτοντος, εἰ μήθ᾽ ἡδόμενον αἰσχρῷ τινι
ἑαυτὸν μήτε τι προσιέμενον ἢ πράττοντα τῶν δεινῶν καὶ ἀτόπων ὁρᾷ κατὰ
τοὺς ὕπνους, ἀλλ᾽ οἷον ἐν βυθῷ γαλήνης ἀκλύστου καταφανεῖ διαλάμπει τῆς
ψυχῆς τὸ φανταστικὸν καὶ παθητικὸν διακεχυμένον ὑπὸ τοῦ λόγου.

The same doctrine in Seneca

b. Seneca treats at some length of moral progress. *Ep.* 75, 8:

Quid ergo? infra illum nulli gradus sunt? statim a sapientia praeceps
est? Non, ut existimo: nam qui proficit, in numero quidem stultorum
est, magno tamen intervallo ab illis diducitur. Inter ipsos quoque proficientes sunt magna discrimina.

He then proceeds to divide the *proficientes* into three classes, of which we shall
speak again in dealing with the πάθη and their treatment.

Wise men and fools

1042—Mankind, then, is divided by Stoics into two classes: wise men
and fools.

a. Stob., *Ecl.* II 7, 11g; p. 99, 3 W. (SVF I 216):

Ἀρέσκει γὰρ τῷ τε Ζήνωνι καὶ τοῖς ἀπ᾽ αὐτοῦ Στωϊκοῖς φιλοσόφοις δύο
γένη τῶν ἀνθρώπων εἶναι, τὸ μὲν τῶν σπουδαίων, τὸ δὲ τῶν φαύλων· καὶ τὸ
μὲν τῶν σπουδαίων διὰ παντὸς τοῦ βίου χρῆσθαι ταῖς ἀρεταῖς, τὸ δὲ τῶν
φαύλων ταῖς κακίαις· ὅθεν τὸ μὲν ἀεὶ κατορθοῦν ἐν ἅπασιν οἷς προστίθεται,
τὸ δὲ ἁμαρτάνειν. καὶ τὸν μὲν σπουδαῖον ταῖς περὶ τὸν βίον ἐμπειρίαις χρώμενον
ἐν τοῖς πραττομένοις ὑπ᾽ αὐτοῦ πάντ᾽ εὖ ποιεῖν, καθάπερ φρονίμως καὶ σωφρόνως

καὶ κατὰ τὰς ἄλλας ἀρετάς· τὸν δὲ φαῦλον κατὰ τοὐναντίον κακῶς. καὶ τὸν
μὲν σπουδαῖον μέγαν καὶ ἁδρὸν καὶ ὑψηλὸν καὶ ἰσχυρόν. μέγαν μὲν ὅτι δύναται
ἐφικνεῖσθαι τῶν κατὰ προαίρεσιν ὄντων αὐτῷ καὶ προκειμένων· ἁδρὸν δέ, ὅτι
ἐστὶν ηὐξημένος πάντοθεν· ὑψηλὸν δ᾽, ὅτι μετείληφε τοῦ ἐπιβάλλοντος ὕψους
ἀνδρὶ γενναίῳ καὶ σοφῷ. καὶ ἰσχυρὸν δ᾽, ὅτι τὴν ἐπιβάλλουσαν ἰσχὺν περιπε-
ποίηται, ἀήττητος ὢν καὶ ἀκαταγώνιστος. παρ᾽ ὃ καὶ οὔτε ἀναγκάζεται ὑπό
τινος οὔτε ἀναγκάζει τινα, οὔτε κωλύεται οὔτε κωλύει, οὔτε βιάζεται ὑπό
τινος οὔτ᾽ αὐτὸς βιάζει τινα, οὔτε δεσπόζει οὔτε δεσπόζεται, οὔτε κακοποιεῖ
τινα οὔτ᾽ αὐτὸς κακοποιεῖται, οὔτε κακοῖς περιπίπτει ‹οὔτ᾽ ἄλλον ποιεῖ κακοῖς
περιπίπτειν›, οὔτε ἐξαπατᾶται οὔτε ἐξαπατᾷ ἄλλον, οὔτε διαψεύδεται οὔτε
ἀγνοεῖ οὔτε λανθάνει ἑαυτόν, οὔτε καθόλου ψεῦδος ὑπολαμβάνει· εὐδαίμων δέ
ἐστιν μάλιστα καὶ εὐτυχὴς καὶ μακάριος καὶ ὄλβιος καὶ εὐσεβὴς καὶ θεοφιλὴς
καὶ ἀξιωματικός, βασιλικός τε καὶ στρατηγικὸς καὶ πολιτικὸς καὶ οἰκονομικὸς
καὶ χρηματιστικός. τοὺς δὲ φαύλους ἅπαντα τούτοις ἐναντία ἔχειν.

b. Athenaeus IV 158b (SVF I 217):

Στωϊκὸν δὲ δόγμα ἐστίν· ὅτι πάντα τε εὖ ποιήσει ὁ σοφὸς καὶ φακῆν φρονίμως
ἀρτύσει· διὸ καὶ Τίμων ὁ Φλιάσιος ἔφη (fr. 72 Wachsm.) [καὶ]

   "Ζηνώνειόν γε φακῆν ἕψειν ὃς μὴ φρονίμως μεμάθηκεν"

ὡς οὐκ ἄλλως δυναμένης ἑψηθῆναι φακῆς εἰ μὴ κατὰ τὴν Ζηνώνειον ὑφήγησιν,
ὃς ἔφη

   "εἰς δὲ φακῆν ἔμβαλλε δυωδέκατον κοριάννου".

The wise
man does
every thing
well

1043—The wise man never fails, neither in judgment nor in action;
consequently, he never repents and never changes his opinion.

a. Stob., *Ecl.* II, p. 111, 18 W. (SVF III 548):

He is never
in error

Ψεῦδος δ᾽ ὑπολαμβάνειν οὐδέποτέ φασι τὸν σοφόν, οὐδὲ τὸ παράπαν ἀκαταλήπτῳ τινὶ συγκατατίθεσθαι, διὰ τὸ μηδὲ δοξάζειν αὐτὸν μηδ᾽ ἀγνοεῖν μηδέν.
τὴν γὰρ ἄγνοιαν μεταπτωτικὴν εἶναι συγκατάθεσιν καὶ ἀσθενῆ. Μηδὲν δ᾽
ὑπολαμβάνειν ἀσθενῶς, ἀλλὰ μᾶλλον ἀσφαλῶς καὶ βεβαίως, διὸ καὶ μηδὲ
δοξάζειν τὸν σοφόν. Διττὰς γὰρ εἶναι δόξας, τὴν μὲν ἀκαταλήπτῳ συγκατάθεσιν, τὴν δὲ ὑπόληψιν ἀσθενῆ· ταύτας ‹δ᾽› ἀλλοτρίους εἶναι τῆς τοῦ σοφοῦ
διαθέσεως· δι᾽ ὃ καὶ τὸ προπίπτειν πρὸ καταλήψεως ‹καὶ› συγκατατίθεσθαι
κατὰ τὸν προπετῆ φαῦλον εἶναι καὶ μὴ πίπτειν εἰς τὸν εὐφυῆ καὶ τέλειον
ἄνδρα καὶ σπουδαῖον. Οὐδὲ λανθάνειν δὲ αὐτόν τι, τὴν γὰρ λῆσιν εἶναι ψεύδους
ὑπόληψιν ἀποφαντικὴν πράγματος. Τούτοις δ᾽ ἀκολούθως οὐκ ἀπιστεῖν, τὴν
γὰρ ἀπιστίαν εἶναι ψεύδους ὑπόληψιν· τὴν δὲ πίστιν ἀστεῖον ὑπάρχειν, εἶναι
γὰρ κατάληψιν ἰσχυράν, βεβαιοῦσαν τὸ ὑπολαμβανόμενον. Ὁμοίως δὲ καὶ τὴν
ἐπιστήμην ἀμετάπτωτον ὑπὸ λόγου· διὰ ταῦτά φασι μήτε ἐπίστασθαί τι τὸν

φαῦλον μήτε πιστεύειν. Ἐχομένως δὲ τούτων οὔτε πλεονεκτεῖσθαι τὸν σοφὸν οὔτε βουκολεῖσθαι οὔτε διαιτᾶσθαι οὔτε παραριθμεῖν οὔτε ὑφ' ἑτέρου παραριθμεῖσθαι. ταῦτα γὰρ πάντα τὴν ἀπάτην περιέχειν καὶ τοῖς κατὰ τὸν τόπον ψεύδεσι πρόσθεσιν. Οὐδένα δὲ τῶν ἀστείων οὔθ' ὁδοῦ διαμαρτάνειν οὔτ' οἰκίας οὔτε σκοποῦ· ἀλλ' οὐδὲ παρορᾶν [ἀλλ'] οὐδὲ παρακούειν νομίζουσι τὸν σοφόν, οὐδὲ τὸ σύνολον παραπαίειν κατά τι τῶν αἰσθητηρίων· καὶ γὰρ τούτων ἕκαστον ἔχεσθαι νομίζουσι τῶν[δε] ψευδῶν συγκαταθέσεων. οὐδ' ὑπονοεῖν δέ φασι τὸν σοφόν· καὶ γὰρ τὴν ὑπόνοιαν ἀκαταλήπτῳ εἶναι τῷ γένει συγκατάθεσιν· οὐδὲ μετανοεῖν δ' ὑπολαμβάνουσι τὸν νοῦν ἔχοντα· καὶ γὰρ τὴν μετάνοιαν ἔχεσθαι ψευδοῦς συγκαταθέσεως, <ὡς> ἂν προδιαπεπτωκότος. οὐδὲ μεταβάλλεσθαι δὲ κατ' οὐδένα τρόπον οὐδὲ μετατίθεσθαι οὐδὲ σφάλλεσθαι· ταῦτα γὰρ εἶναι πάντα τῶν τοῖς δόγμασι μεταπιπτόντων, ὅπερ ἀλλότριον εἶναι τοῦ νοῦν ἔχοντος· οὐδὲ δοκεῖν αὐτῷ τί φασι παραπλησίως τοῖς εἰρημένοις.

and
possesses
all virtues

b. Stob., ib. 65, 12 W. (SVF III 557):

Φασὶ δὲ καὶ πάντα ποιεῖν τὸν σοφὸν <κατὰ> πάσας τὰς ἀρετάς. πᾶσαν γὰρ πρᾶξιν τελείαν αὐτοῦ εἶναι, διὸ καὶ μηδεμιᾶς ἀπολελεῖφθαι ἀρετῆς.

Relation
with
Cynicism

1044—In his ideal of the wise man, Zeno was doubtless inspired by Cynicism, as appears clearly from the following passage.

a. Diog. Laërt. VII 121-122:

Πολιτεύσεσθαί φασι τὸν σοφὸν ἂν μή τι κωλύῃ, ὥς φησι Χρύσιππος ἐν πρώτῳ Περὶ βίων· καὶ γὰρ κακίαν ἐφέξειν καὶ ἐπ' ἀρετὴν παρορμήσειν. καὶ γαμήσειν, ὡς ὁ Ζήνων φησὶν ἐν Πολιτείᾳ, καὶ παιδοποιήσεσθαι. ἔτι τε μὴ δοξάσειν τὸν σοφόν, τουτέστι ψεύδει μὴ συγκαταθήσεσθαι μηδενί. κυνιεῖν τ' αὐτόν· εἶναι γὰρ τὸν κυνισμὸν σύντομον ἐπ' ἀρετὴν ὁδόν, ὡς Ἀπολλόδωρος ἐν τῇ Ἠθικῇ. γεύσεσθαί τε καὶ ἀνθρωπίνων σαρκῶν κατὰ περίστασιν. μόνον τ' ἐλεύθερον, τοὺς δὲ φαύλους δούλους. εἶναι γὰρ τὴν ἐλευθερίαν ἐξουσίαν αὐτοπραγίας, τὴν δὲ δουλείαν στέρησιν αὐτοπραγίας. —

(122) Οὐ μόνον δ' ἐλευθέρους εἶναι τοὺς σοφούς, ἀλλὰ καὶ βασιλέας, τῆς βασιλείας οὔσης ἀρχῆς ἀνυπευθύνου, ἥτις περὶ μόνους ἂν τοὺς σοφοὺς συσταίη, καθά φησι Χρύσιππος, ἐν τῷ Περὶ τοῦ κυρίως κεχρῆσθαι Ζήνωνα τοῖς ὀνόμασιν· ἐγνωκέναι γάρ φησι δεῖν τὸν ἄρχοντα περὶ ἀγαθῶν καὶ κακῶν, μηδένα δὲ τῶν φαύλων ἐπίστασθαι ταῦτα.

Ὁμοίως δὲ καὶ ἀρχικοὺς δικαστικούς τε καὶ ῥητορικοὺς μόνους εἶναι, τῶν δὲ φαύλων οὐδένα. ἔτι καὶ ἀναμαρτήτους, τῷ ἀπεριπτώτους εἶναι ἁμαρτήματι.

In this portrait of the sage, the notes of *freedom* and of *kingship* are of Cynic origin [1], as is copiously shown by R. Höistad, *Cynic hero and Cynic King*, Uppsala

---

[1] See *Gr. Ph.* I, nrs. **244b** (the example of Heracles), and **248a**.

1948. We shall find them again in Dio Chrysostomus. See also our nr. **1013b**, where Epictetus says that he is no more a slave since Antisthenes liberated him by teaching him what is, and what is not, in our power.

The Cynic tradition knows also the ideal of the philosopher as a ruler and an educator. Cp. the story of Diogenes as the educator of the sons of Xeniades (Diog. Laërt. VI 30). On this theme: Höistad, o.c., p. 118-126; on *paideia* in Dio Chrys., ib. p. 156-179. The ancient Cynic ideal of education, however, has an ethical-individual character; with the Stoics, it becomes more social and political. See our next nr.

b. The following chapter of Diog. Laërt. (VII 123) shows us the hardness of the Stoic sage.

The wise man does not feel compassion

Ἐλεήμονάς τε μὴ εἶναι συγγνώμην τ' ἔχειν μηδενί· μὴ γὰρ παριέναι τὰς ἐκ τοῦ νόμου ἐπιβαλλούσας κολάσεις, ἐπεὶ τό γ' εἴκειν καὶ ὁ ἔλεος αὐτή θ' ἡ ἐπιείκεια οὐδένειά ἐστι ψυχῆς πρὸς κολάσεις προσποιουμένης χρηστότητα· μηδ' οἴεσθαι σκληροτέρας αὐτὰς εἶναι.

We shall find this feature again in Cicero's description of the sapiens in *Pro Murena* 61 ff. (infra, **1050b**).
On ἐπιείκεια, nrs. **589** and **658a**.

1045—a. With the Stoics, παιδεία shows more a political character than it had in ancient Cynicism.

Political character of paideia with the Stoics

Stob., *Ecl.* II, p. 94, 7 W. (SVF III 611):

Τό τε δίκαιόν φασι φύσει εἶναι καὶ μὴ θέσει. Ἐπόμενον δὲ τούτοις ὑπάρχειν καὶ τὸ πολιτεύεσθαι τὸν σοφὸν καὶ μάλιστ' ἐν ταῖς τοιαύταις πολιτείαις ταῖς ἐμφαινούσαις τινὰ προκοπὴν πρὸς τὰς τελείας πολιτείας· καὶ τὸ νομοθετεῖν δὲ καὶ τὸ παιδεύειν ἀνθρώπους.

b. In Stoicism, again, the ideal of the *basileus* acquires a cosmic and religious character, which was alien to the ancient Cynic conception. This specifically Stoic character of the *basileus* may be seen in Dio Chrys.' *Or.* 3, 51-85, where the earthly being is a copy of Zeus-basileus, ὁ πρῶτος καὶ ἄριστος θεός (50).

We cite the beginning of Dio's exposition, c. 51 ff.:

Cosmic and religious character of the Stoic basileus

Πρῶτον μέν ἐστι θεοφιλής, ἅτε τῆς μεγίστης τυγχάνων παρὰ θεῶν τιμῆς καὶ πίστεως. καὶ πρῶτόν γε καὶ μάλιστα θεραπεύσει τὸ θεῖον, οὐκ ὁμολογῶν μόνον, ἀλλὰ καὶ πεπεισμένος εἶναι θεούς, ἵνα δὴ καὶ αὐτὸς ἔχῃ τοὺς κατ' ἀξίαν ἄρχοντας. ἡγεῖται δὲ τοῖς ἄλλοις ἀνθρώποις συμφέρειν τὴν αὐτοῦ πρόνοιαν οὕτως ὡς αὐτῷ τὴν ἐκείνων ἀρχήν. —

(53) Ἡγεῖται δὲ τὴν μὲν ἀρετὴν ὁσιότητα, τὴν δὲ κακίαν πᾶσαν ἀσέβειαν. εἶναι γὰρ ἐναγεῖς καὶ ἀλιτηρίους οὐ μόνον τοὺς τὰ ἱερὰ συλῶντας ἢ λέγοντάς

τι βλάσφημον περὶ τῶν θεῶν, ἀλλὰ πολὺ μᾶλλον τούς τε δειλοὺς καὶ ἀδίκους καὶ ἀκρατεῖς καὶ ἀνοήτους καὶ καθόλου τοὺς ἐναντίον τι πράττοντας τῇ τε δυνάμει καὶ βουλήσει τῶν θεῶν.

See on this passage: Höistad o.c., p. 190 f.

The wise man is rich

1046—a. Stob., *Ecl.* II, p. 101, 14 W. (SVF III 593):

Τὸν δὲ κατ' ἀλήθειαν πλοῦτον ἀγαθὸν εἶναι λέγουσι καὶ τὴν κατ' ἀλήθειαν πενίαν κακόν. καὶ τὴν μὲν κατ' ἀλήθειαν ἐλευθερίαν ἀγαθόν, τὴν δὲ κατ' ἀλήθειαν δουλείαν κακόν· δι' ὃ δὴ καὶ τὸν σπουδαῖον εἶναι μόνον πλούσιον καὶ ἐλεύθερον, τὸν δὲ φαῦλον τοὐναντίον πένητα, τῶν εἰς τὸ πλουτεῖν ἀφορμῶν ἐστερημένον, καὶ δοῦλον διὰ τὴν ὑποπτωτικὴν ἐν αὐτῷ διάθεσιν.

He alone is beautiful

b. Sextus Emp., *Adv. math.* XI (= *Ag. the ethicists*) 170:

Cp. Cic., *De fin.* III, 22, 75: recte etiam pulcher appellabitur; animi enim lineamenta sunt pulchriora quam corporis.

Καὶ ὁ ἀξιέραστός ἐστι καλός, μόνος δὲ ὁ σοφὸς ἀξιέραστος· μόνος ἄρα ὁ σοφός ἐστι καλός.

and happy

c. Gregorius Nazianzenus, *Ep.* 32 (SVF III 586):

Ἐπαινῶ δὲ τῶν ἀπὸ τῆς Στοᾶς τὸ νεανικόν τε καὶ μεγαλόνουν, οἳ μηδὲν κωλύειν φασὶ πρὸς εὐδαιμονίαν τὰ ἔξωθεν, ἀλλ' εἶναι τὸν σπουδαῖον μακάριον, κἂν ὁ Φαλάριδος ταῦρος ἔχῃ καιόμενον.

εὔλογος ἐξαγωγή

1047—He has the right to dispose of his own life.

a. Diog. Laërt. VII 130 (SVF III 757):

Εὐλόγως τέ φασι ἐξάξειν ἑαυτὸν τοῦ βίου τὸν σοφόν, καὶ ὑπὲρ πατρίδος καὶ ὑπὲρ φίλων, κἂν ἐν σκληροτέρᾳ γένηται ἀλγηδόνι ἢ πηρώσεσιν ἢ νόσοις ἀνιάτοις.

b. Stob., *Ecl.* II, p. 110, 9 W. (SVF III 758):

Φασὶ δέ ποτε καὶ τὴν ἐξαγωγὴν τὴν ἐκ τοῦ βίου τοῖς σπουδαίοις καθηκόντως ‹γίγνεσθαι› κατὰ πολλοὺς τρόπους, τοῖς ‹δὲ› φαύλοις μονὴν ‹τὴν› ἐν τῷ ζῆν καὶ εἰ μὴ μέλλοιεν ἔσεσθαι σοφοί· οὔτε γὰρ τὴν ἀρετὴν κατέχειν ἐν τῷ ζῆν οὔτε τὴν κακίαν ἐκβάλλειν· τοῖς δὲ καθήκουσι καὶ τοῖς παρὰ τὸ καθῆκον ‹παρα›μετρεῖσθαι τήν τε ζωὴν καὶ τὸν θάνατον.

c. Cf. Plut., *De Stoic. repugn.* 18, p. 1042d:

Ἀλλ' οὐδ' ὅλως, φασίν, οἴεται δεῖν Χρύσιππος οὔτε μονὴν ἐν τῷ βίῳ τοῖς ἀγαθοῖς, οὔτ' ἐξαγωγὴν τοῖς κακοῖς παραμετρεῖν, ἀλλὰ τοῖς μέσοις κατὰ φύσιν·

διὸ καὶ τοῖς εὐδαιμονοῦσι γίνεταί ποτε καθῆκον ἐξάγειν ἑαυτούς, καὶ μένειν αὖθις ἐν τῷ ζῆν τοῖς κακοδαιμονοῦσιν.

d. The doctrine is explained at some length by Cato in Cicero's *De fin*. III 18, 60:

Sed cum ab his (i.e. a principiis naturalibus sive *primis naturae*) omnia proficiscantur officia, non sine causa dicitur ad ea referri omnis nostras cogitationes, in his et excessum e vita et in vita mansionem: in quo enim plura sunt quae secundum naturam sunt, huius officium est in vita manere; in quo autem aut sunt plura contraria aut fore videntur, huius officium est e vita excedere; e quo adparet et sapientis esse aliquando officium excedere e vita, cum beatus sit, et stulti manere in vita, cum sit miser. nam bonum illud et malum, quod saepe iam dictum est, postea consequitur; prima autem illa naturae, sive secunda, sive contraria, sub iudicium sapientis et dilectum cadunt, estque illa subiecta quasi materia sapientiae. itaque et manendi in vita et migrandi ratio omnis iis rebus, quas supra dixi, metienda. nam neque virtutem qui habet virtute retinetur in vita, nec iis, qui sine virtute sunt, mors est oppetenda; et saepe officium est sapientis desciscere a vita, cum sit beatissimus, si id opportune facere possit. sic enim censent, opportunitatis esse beate vivere, quod est convenienter naturae vivere; itaque a sapientia praecipitur, se ipsam, si usus sit, sapiens ut relinquat. quam ob rem cum vitiorum ista vis non sit, ut causam adferant mortis voluntariae, perspicuum est etiam stultorum, qui idem miseri sint, officium esse manere in vita, si sint in maiore parte rerum earum, quas secundum naturam esse dicimus; et quoniam excedens e vita et manens aeque miser est, nec diuturnitas magis ei vitam fugiendam facit, non sine causa dicitur iis, qui pluribus naturalibus frui possint, esse in vita manendum.

1048—The wise man is the absolute example. Practically speaking, he is as rare as the phoenix.

The wise man a very rare phaenomenon

a. Plut., *De Stoic. repugn*. 31 (SVF III 662):

Καὶ μὴν οὔθ᾽ αὐτὸν ὁ Χρύσιππος ἀποφαίνει σπουδαῖον οὔτε τινὰ τῶν αὐτοῦ γνωρίμων ἢ καθηγεμόνων.

b. Cp. Seneca, *De tranqu*. 7, 4, who says, speaking of the importance of selecting friends carefully:

Nec hoc praeceperim tibi, ut neminem nisi sapientem sequaris aut adtrahas; ubi enim istum invenies, quem tot saeculis quaerimus?

c. Seneca, *Ep.* 42, 1:

Iam tibi iste persuasit virum se bonum esse? atqui vir bonus tam cito nec fieri potest nec intellegi. Scis quem nunc virum bonum dicam? huius secundae notae. Nam ille alter fortasse tamquam phoenix semel anno quingentesimo nascitur. Nec est mirum ex intervallo magna generari: mediocria et in turbam nascentia saepe fortuna producit, eximia vero ipsa raritate commendat.

Value of the absolute example

1049—In general, a very great value was attributed by ancient philosophers to the moral example. This attitude, which appears in the Stoic ideal of the wise man, may be seen e.g. in the following texts.

a. Clem. Alex., *Strom.* II 20, 125; p. 178 St. (SVF I 241):

Καλῶς ὁ Ζήνων ἐπὶ τῶν Ἰνδῶν ἔλεγεν ἕνα Ἰνδὸν παροπτώμενον ἐθέλειν ⟨ἂν⟩ ἰδεῖν ἢ πάσας τὰς περὶ πόνου ἀποδείξεις μαθεῖν.

b. Seneca, *Ep.* VI 5-6:

Plus tamen tibi et viva vox et convictus quam oratio proderit: in rem praesentem venias oportet, primum quia homines amplius oculis quam auribus credunt, deinde quia longum iter est per praecepta, breve et efficax per exempla. Zenonem Cleanthes non expressisset, si tantummodo audisset; vitae eius interfuit, secreta perspexit et observavit illum, an ex formula sua viveret. Platon et Aristoteles et omnis in diversum itura sapientium turba plus ex moribus quam ex verbis Socratis traxit: Metrodorum et Hermarchum et Polyaenum magnos viros non schola Epicuri sed contubernium fecit. Nec in hoc te accerso tantum, ut proficias, sed ut prosis: plurimum enim alter alteri conferemus.

Philosophy has always been for the Ancients first of all a certain style of life. Only by this attitude we can explain the rôle of a man like Pyrrho in ancient philosophy. See our nr. **1082** ff.

Ancient criticism of the wise man

1050—**a.** Evidently, the Stoic sage was a grateful object of mockery and satire. This is what we find in Lucianus, *Bion prasis* 20:

ΖΕΥΣ. Ἄλλον κάλει, τὸν ἐν χρῷ κουρίαν ἐκεῖνον, τὸν σκυθρωπόν, τὸν ἀπὸ τῆς Στοᾶς.

ΕΡΜ. Εὖ λέγεις· ἐοίκασι γοῦν πολύ τι πλῆθος αὐτὸν περιμένειν τῶν ἐπὶ τὴν ἀγορὰν ἀπηντηκότων. αὐτὴν τὴν ἀρετὴν πωλῶ, τῶν βίων τὸν τελειότατον. τίς πάντα μόνος εἰδέναι ἐθέλει;

ΩΝΗΤΗΣ. Πῶς τοῦτο φής;

ΕΡΜ. Ὅτι μόνος οὗτος σοφός, μόνος καλός, μόνος δίκαιος ἀνδρεῖος βασιλεὺς ῥήτωρ πλούσιος νομοθέτης καὶ τἄλλα ὁπόσα ἐστίν.

ΩΝ. Οὐκοῦν, ὠγαθέ, καὶ μάγειρος μόνος, καὶ νὴ Δία γε σκυτοδέψης καὶ τέκτων καὶ τὰ τοιαῦτα;

ΕΡΜ. Ἔοικεν.

ΩΝ. Ἐλθέ, ὠγαθέ, καὶ λέγε πρὸς τὸν ὠνητὴν ἐμὲ ποῖός τις εἶ, καὶ πρῶτον εἰ οὐκ ἄχθη πιπρασκόμενος καὶ δοῦλος ὤν.

ΧΡΥΣΙΠΠΟΣ. Οὐδαμῶς· οὐ γὰρ ἐφ' ἡμῖν ταῦτά ἐστιν. ὅσα δὲ οὐκ ἐφ' ἡμῖν, ἀδιάφορα εἶναι συμβέβηκεν.

ΩΝ. Οὐ μανθάνω ᾗ καὶ λέγεις.

ΧΡΥΣ. Τί φής; οὐ μανθάνεις ὅτι τῶν τοιούτων τὰ μέν ἐστι προηγμένα, τὰ δ' ἔμπαλιν ἀποπροηγμένα;

ΩΝ. Οὐδὲ νῦν μανθάνω.

ΧΡΥΣ. Εἰκότως· οὐ γὰρ εἶ συνήθης τοῖς ἡμετέροις ὀνόμασιν οὐδὲ τὴν καταληπτικὴν φαντασίαν ἔχεις, ὁ δὲ σπουδαῖος ὁ τὴν λογικὴν θεωρίαν ἐκμαθὼν οὐ μόνον ταῦτ' οἶδεν, ἀλλὰ καὶ σύμβαμα καὶ παρασύμβαμα ὁποῖα καὶ ὁπόσον ἀλλήλων διαφέρει.

ΩΝ. Πρὸς τῆς σοφίας, μὴ φθονήσῃς κἂν τοῦτο εἰπεῖν τί τὸ σύμβαμα καὶ τί τὸ παρασύμβαμα· καὶ γὰρ οὐκ οἶδ' ὅπως ἐπλήγην ὑπὸ τοῦ ῥυθμοῦ τῶν ὀνομάτων.

ΧΡΥΣ. Ἀλλ' οὐδεὶς φθόνος· ἦν γάρ τις χωλὸς ὢν αὐτῷ ἐκείνῳ τῷ χωλῷ ποδὶ προσπταίσας λίθῳ τραῦμα ἐξ ἀφανοῦς λάβῃ, ὁ τοιοῦτος εἶχε μὲν δήπου σύμβαμα τὴν χωλείαν, τὸ τραῦμα δὲ παρασύμβαμα προσέλαβεν.

ΩΝ. Ὦ τῆς ἀγχινοίας. —

b. A serious criticism of the Stoic conception of the wise man is found in Cicero, *Pro Murena* 29, 60 - 31, 64, where he addresses Cato in this way:

Ego tuum consilium, Cato, propter singulare animi mei de tua virtute iudicium vituperare non possum: nonnulla forsitan conformare et leviter emendare possim. "non multa peccas", inquit ille fortissimo viro senior magister, "sed peccas: te regere possum". at ego non te: verissime dixerim peccare te nihil neque ulla in re te esse huius modi, ut corrigendus potius quam leviter inflectendus esse videare; finxit enim te ipsa natura ad honestatem, gravitatem, temperantiam, magnitudinem animi, iustitiam, ad omnis denique virtutes magnum hominem et excelsum. accessit doctrina non moderata nec mitis, sed, ut mihi videtur, paulo asperior et durior quam aut veritas aut natura patitur. et quoniam non est nobis haec oratio habenda aut in imperita multitudine aut in aliquo conventu agrestium, audacius paulo de studiis humanitatis, quae et mihi et vobis nota et iucunda sunt, disputabo. In M. Catone, iudices, haec bona quae videmus divina et egregia, ipsius scitote esse propria: quae nonnumquam requirimus, ea sunt omnia non a natura, verum a magistro. fuit enim quidam summo ingenio vir, Zeno, cuius inventorum aemuli Stoici nominantur. huius sententiae sunt et praecepta huius modi: sapientem gratia numquam moveri, numquam cuiusquam delicto ignoscere; neminem misericordem esse nisi stultum et levem ; viri non esse neque exorari neque placari; solos sapientes esse, si distortissimi sint, formosos; si mendicissimi, divites; si servitutem serviant, reges; nos autem, qui sapientes non sumus, fugitivos, exules, hostis, insanos denique esse dicunt; omnia peccata esse paria; omne delictum scelus esse nefarium, nec minus delinquere eum, qui gallum gallinaceum, cum opus non fuerit, quam eum qui patrem suffocaverit; sapientem nihil opinari, nullius rei paenitere, nulla in re falli, sententiam mutare numquam. —

(30, 63) Nostri autem illi, — fatebor enim, Cato, me quoque in adulescentia diffisum ingenio meo quaesisse adiumenta doctrinae — nostri, inquam, illi a Platone et Aristotele, moderati homines et temperati, aiunt apud sapientem valere aliquando gratiam; viri boni esse misereri; distincta genera esse delictorum et disparis poenas; esse apud hominem constantem ignoscendi locum; ipsum sapientem saepe aliquid opinari quod nesciat; irasci nonnumquam; exorari eundem et placari; quod dixerit, interdum, si ita rectius sit, mutare; de sententia decedere aliquando; omnis virtutes mediocritate quadam esse moderatas. hos ad magistros si qua te fortuna, Cato, cum ista natura detulisset, non tu quidem vir melior esses nec fortior nec temperantior nec iustior — neque enim esse potes, — sed paulo ad lenitatem propensior.

12—ETHICS (5): THE ΠΑΘΗ AND HOW TO TREAT THEM

1051—Before Zeno, the notion of πάθος ἐν ψυχῇ was used, but not precisely defined, by Aristotle. The πάθη had a certain function in his ethics (see our nrs. **571a** and **572**) and their nature was inquired into in his psychology (**633c**, **d**; **634**). But Zeno was the first to develop a full doctrine of the πάθη, to define the notion precisely and give it a very important place as well in theoretical as in applied ethics.

πάθος
defined

a. Zeno's definition of πάθος. Diog. Laërt. VII 110 (SVF I 205):
Ἔστι δὲ αὐτὸ τὸ πάθος κατὰ Ζήνωνα ἡ ἄλογος καὶ παρὰ φύσιν ψυχῆς κίνησις, ἢ ὁρμὴ πλεονάζουσα.

b. Cp. Stob., *Ecl.* II 7, 10, p. 88, 8 W. (SVF I ib.):

Πάθος δ' εἶναί φασιν ὁρμὴν πλεονάζουσαν καὶ ἀπειθῆ τῷ αἱροῦντι λόγῳ, ἢ κίνησιν ψυχῆς <ἄλογον> παρὰ φύσιν.

Cicero mentions these definitions of *perturbatio* in *Tusc. disp.* IV 11 and IV 47: (perturbatio est) *aversa a recta ratione contra naturam animi commotio*, vel brevius *appetitus vehementior*.
And again in *De off.* I 136: perturbationes, id est *motus animi nimios rationi non obtemperantes*.

1052—Zeno gave also the following definition of πάθος, found in Stob., *Ecl.* II 7, 1, p. 39, 7 W. (SVF I 206):

Other definition

Ὡρίσατο δὲ κἀκείνως· "πάθος ἐστὶ πτοία ψυχῆς", ἀπὸ τῆς τῶν πτηνῶν φορᾶς τὸ εὐκίνητον τοῦ παθητικοῦ παρεικάσας.

1053—Chrysippus, in defining the πάθη as judgments, seems to have differed from Zeno, on this point as well as in his theory of knowledge.

a. Galenus, *De plac. Hippocr. et Plat.* V 1, p. 405 M. (SVF III 461):

Chrysippus defined the πάθη as κρίσεις

Χρύσιππος μὲν οὖν ἐν τῷ πρώτῳ Περὶ παθῶν ἀποδεικνύναι πειρᾶται, κρίσεις τινὰς εἶναι τοῦ λογιστικοῦ τὰ πάθη, Ζήνων δ' οὐ τὰς κρίσεις αὐτάς, ἀλλὰ τὰς ἐπιγιγνομένας αὐταῖς συστολὰς χύσεις, ἐπάρσεις τε καὶ πτώσεις τῆς ψυχῆς ἐνόμιζεν εἶναι τὰ πάθη.

b. Plutarchus, though speaking (in his already cited chapter 3 of the *De virtute morali* [1]) of Stoics in general, expounds in fact Chrysippus' doctrine of the ἡγεμονικόν πως ἔχον, when he says, after having qualified virtue as a διάθεσις τοῦ ἡγεμονικοῦ or rather "Reason itself, harmonious and steady and inalterable" (SVF III 459):

Καὶ νομίζουσιν οὐκ εἶναι τὸ παθητικὸν καὶ ἄλογον διαφορᾷ τινι καὶ φύσει ψυχῆς τοῦ λογικοῦ διακεκριμένον, ἀλλὰ τὸ αὐτὸ τῆς ψυχῆς μέρος, ὃ δὴ καλοῦσι διάνοιαν καὶ ἡγεμονικόν, διόλου τρεπόμενον καὶ μεταβάλλον ἔν τε τοῖς πάθεσι καὶ ταῖς κατὰ ἕξιν ἢ διάθεσιν μεταβολαῖς, κακίαν τε γίγνεσθαι καὶ ἀρετήν, καὶ μηδὲν ἔχειν ἄλογον ἐν ἑαυτῷ· λέγεσθαι δὲ ἄλογον, ὅταν τῷ πλεονάζοντι τῆς ὁρμῆς, ἰσχυρῷ γενομένῳ καὶ κρατήσαντι, πρός τι τῶν ἀτόπων παρὰ τὸν αἱροῦντα λόγον ἐκφέρηται· καὶ γὰρ τὸ πάθος εἶναι λόγον πονηρὸν καὶ ἀκόλαστον, ἐκ φαύλης καὶ διημαρτημένης κρίσεως σφοδρότητα καὶ ῥώμην προσλαβούσης.

The difference between Zeno and Chrysippus as to the conception of the πάθη, which is chiefly known to us by Posidonius' polemic against Chrysippus, recorded

---

[1] See above, nr. **953a**, **1024a**.

by Galenus in his above cited work, is very clearly expounded by Pohlenz, *Zenon u. Chrysipp*, p. 182 ff., 187 ff., summarized in *Die Stoa* I, p. 143. Cp. our nrs. **953-955**.

1054—Posidonius, opposing Chrysippus' doctrine of the πάθη as κρίσεις, cites the following dialogue of λογισμός and θυμός, to show that its author, Cleanthes, was on his side.

Cleanthes, unlike Chrys., admitted a dualism in man

Galenus, *De plac. Hippocr. et Plat.*, p. 456 M. (SVF I 570):

Τὴν μὲν οὖν τοῦ Κλεάνθους γνώμην ὑπὲρ τοῦ παθητικοῦ τῆς ψυχῆς ἐκ τῶνδε φαίνεσθαί φησι τῶν ἐπῶν.

ΛΟΓΙΣΜΟΣ. τί ποτ' ἔσθ' ὃ βούλει, θυμέ; τοῦτό μοι φράσον.

ΘΥΜΟΣ. <σ>έ γ', ὦ λογισμέ, πᾶν ὃ βούλομαι ποιεῖν.

Λ. βασιλικὸν <εἶ>πε<ς>· πλὴν ὅμως εἰπὸν πάλιν.

Θ. ὧν ἂν ἐπιθυμῶ, ταῦθ' ὅπως γενήσεται.

ταυτὶ τὰ ἀμοιβαῖα Κλεάνθους φησὶν εἶναι Ποσειδώνιος ἐναργῶς ἐνδεικνύμενα τὴν περὶ τοῦ παθητικοῦ τῆς ψυχῆς γνώμην αὐτοῦ, εἴ γε δὴ πεποίηκε τὸν Λογισμὸν τῷ Θυμῷ διαλεγόμενον ὡς ἕτερον ἑτέρῳ.

1055—The reason why Posidonius opposes Chrysippus' monism so vigorously, going back essentially to Zeno's view, may be seen from the following passage.

Posidonius opposes Chrys.' doctrine of the πάθη

Galenus, o.c., p. 448 M.:

Τὸ δὴ τῶν παθῶν αἴτιον, τουτέστι τῆς τε ἀνομολογίας καὶ τοῦ κακοδαίμονος βίου, τὸ μὴ κατὰ πᾶν ἕπεσθαι τῷ ἐν αὑτοῖς δαίμονι συγγενεῖ τε ὄντι καὶ τὴν ὁμοίαν φύσιν ἔχοντι τῷ τὸν ὅλον κόσμον διοικοῦντι, τῷ δὲ χείρονι καὶ ζῳώδει ποτὲ συνεκκλίνοντας φέρεσθαι. οἱ δὲ τοῦτο παριδόντες οὔτε ἐν τούτοις βελτιοῦσι τὴν αἰτίαν τῶν παθῶν, οὔτ' ἐν τοῖς περὶ τῆς εὐδαιμονίας καὶ ὁμολογίας ὀρθοδοξοῦσι. οὐ γὰρ βλέπουσιν, ὅτι πρῶτόν ἐστιν ἐν αὐτῇ τὸ κατὰ μηδὲν ἄγεσθαι ὑπὸ τοῦ ἀλόγου τε καὶ κακοδαίμονος καὶ ἀθέου τῆς ψυχῆς.

Posid., then, holds that there is, indeed, an irrational part in the soul. He blames Chrys. for having overlooked, or at least undervalued this, and hence for not having understood the real character of the moral struggle in man. Infra, nrs. **1181-1188**.

Seneca holds it

1056—a. In Seneca we find again Chrysippus' doctrine of the ἡγεμονικόν πως ἔχον. *De ira* I 8, 2-3:

In primis, inquam, finibus hostis arcendus est; nam cum intravit et portis se intulit, modum a captivis non accipit. neque enim sepositus est animus et extrinsecus speculatur adfectus, ut illos non patiatur ultra quam oportet procedere, sed in adfectum ipse mutatur ideoque non potest utilem illam vim et salutarem proditam iam infirmatamque revocare.

non enim, ut dixi, separatas ista sedes suas diductasque habent, sed affectus et ratio in melius peiusque mutatio animi est.

From this passage it may be easily understood that Chrysippus, in his way, gave a very strong expression to the Stoic view that, indeed, πάθη cannot be moderated, but can be only extirpated: as soon as πάθος is introduced, Reason has lost its power. Indeed, Zeno taught that πάθη are παρὰ φύσιν, and are ἄλογα in the sense of ἀπειθῆ τῷ λόγῳ.

b. Cp. Stob., *Ecl.* II 89, 4 W. (SVF III 389), where the violent character of the πάθη is brought out.

Violent character of the πάθη

Τὸ δὲ "ἄλογον" καὶ τὸ "παρὰ φύσιν" (sc. in πάθους definitione) οὐ κοινῶς, ἀλλὰ τὸ μὲν "ἄλογον" ἴσον τῷ "ἀπειθὲς τῷ λόγῳ". πᾶν γὰρ πάθος βιαστικόν ἐστι, ὡς πολλάκις ὁρῶντας τοὺς ἐν τοῖς πάθεσιν ὄντας ὅτι οὐ συμφέρει τόδε ποιεῖν, ὑπὸ τῆς σφοδρότητος ἐκφερομένους, καθάπερ ὑπό τινος ἀπειθοῦς ἵππου, ἀνάγεσθαι πρὸς τὸ ποιεῖν αὐτό, παρ' ὃ καὶ πολλάκις τινὰς ἐξομολογεῖσθαι λέγοντας τὸ θρυλούμενον τοῦτο·

γνώμην δ' ἔχοντα μ' ἡ φύσις βιάζεται· [1]

γνώμην γὰρ λέγει νῦν τὴν εἴδησιν καὶ γνῶσιν τῶν ὀρθῶν πραγμάτων. καὶ τὸ "παρὰ φύσιν" δ' εἴληπται ἐν τῇ τοῦ πάθους ὑπογραφῇ, ὡς συμβαίνοντος παρὰ τὸν ὀρθὸν καὶ κατὰ φύσιν λόγον. πάντες δ' οἱ ἐν τοῖς πάθεσιν ὄντες ἀποστρέφονται τὸν λόγον, οὐ παραπλησίως δὲ τοῖς ἐξηπατημένοις ἐν ὁτῳοῦν, ἀλλ' ἰδιαζόντως. οἱ μὲν γὰρ ἠπατημένοι λόγου χάριν περὶ <τοῦ> τὰς ἀτόμους ἀρχὰς εἶναι, διδαχθέντες ὅτι οὐκ εἰσίν, ἀφίστανται τῆς κρίσεως· οἱ δ' ἐν τοῖς πάθεσιν ὄντες, κἂν μάθωσι, κἂν μεταδιδαχθῶσιν ὅτι οὐ δεῖ λυπεῖσθαι ἢ φοβεῖσθαι, ἢ ὅλως ἐν τοῖς πάθεσιν εἶναι τῆς ψυχῆς, ὅμως οὐκ ἀφίστανται τούτων, ἀλλ' ἄγονται ὑπὸ τῶν παθῶν εἰς τὸ ὑπὸ τῆς τούτων κρατεῖσθαι τυραννίδος.

1057—Plotinus, *Enn.* III 6, 3, opposes Chrysippus' doctrine more fundamentally than Posidonius did, saying that it is not the soul itself that changes, but that the πάθη proceed from it, while the soul, being a substance, stays what it is.

Plotinus' criticism of the doctrine

Τὰς δ' οἰκειώσεις καὶ ἀλλοτριώσεις [2] πῶς; Καὶ λῦπαι καὶ ὀργαὶ καὶ ἡδοναὶ ἐπιθυμίαι τε καὶ φόβοι πῶς οὐ τροπαὶ καὶ πάθη ἐνόντα καὶ κινούμενα; Δεῖ δὴ καὶ περὶ τούτων ὧδε διαλαβεῖν. Ὅτι γὰρ ἐγγίγνονται ἀλλοιώσεις καὶ σφοδραὶ τούτων αἰσθήσεις μὴ οὐ λέγειν ἐναντία λέγοντός ἐστι τοῖς ἐναργέσιν. Ἀλλὰ χρὴ συγχωροῦντας ζητεῖν ὅ τι ἐστὶ τὸ τρεπόμενον. Κινδυνεύομεν γὰρ περὶ ψυχὴν ταῦτα λέγοντες ὅμοιόν τι ὑπολαμβάνειν, ὡς εἰ τὴν ψυχὴν λέγομεν ἐρυθριᾶν

---

[1] Eur. fr. 837 Nauck. [2] Affections and aversions.

ἢ αὖ ἐν ὠχριάσει γίγνεσθαι, μὴ λογιζόμενοι, ὡς διὰ ψυχὴν μὲν ταῦτα τὰ πάθη, περὶ δὲ τὴν ἄλλην σύστασίν ἐστι γιγνόμενα.

The four main πάθη

1058—The four main πάθη.

    a.   Diog. Laërt. VII 110 (SVF I 211):

Τῶν παθῶν τὰ ἀνωτάτω (καθά φησιν ... Ζήνων ἐν τῷ Περὶ παθῶν) εἶναι γένη τέτταρα, λύπην, φόβον, ἐπιθυμίαν, ἡδονήν.

Their causes

    b.   Aspasius in Aristot. *Eth. Nic.* p. 45, 16 Heylb. (SVF III 386):

Γενικὰ δὲ πάθη οἱ μὲν ἐκ τῆς Στοᾶς ἔφασαν εἶναι ἡδονὴν καὶ λύπην, φόβον <καὶ> ἐπιθυμίαν· γίνεσθαι μὲν γὰρ τὰ πάθη ἔφασαν δι' ὑπόληψιν ἀγαθοῦ καὶ κακοῦ, ἀλλ' ὅταν μὲν ὡς ἐπὶ παροῦσι τοῖς ἀγαθοῖς κινῆται ἡ ψυχή, ἡδονὴν εἶναι, ὅταν δὲ ὡς ἐπὶ παροῦσι τοῖς κακοῖς, λύπην· πάλιν δὲ ἐπὶ τοῖς προσδο-κωμένοις ἀγαθοῖς ἐπιθυμία συμβαίνει, ὄρεξις οὖσα ὡς φαινομένου ἀγαθοῦ, κακῶν δὲ προσδοκωμένων τὸ συμβαῖνον πάθος φόβον ἔλεγον εἶναι.

    c.   Andronicus, Π. παθῶν 1 (SVF III 391) defines them as follows:

Definitions   Λύπη μὲν οὖν ἐστιν ἄλογος συστολή· ἢ δόξα πρόσφατος κακοῦ παρουσίας, ἐφ' ᾧ οἴονται δεῖν συστέλλεσθαι.

Φόβος δὲ ἄλογος ἔκκλισις· ἢ φυγὴ ἀπὸ προσδοκωμένου δεινοῦ.

Ἐπιθυμία δὲ ἄλογος ὄρεξις· ἢ δίωξις προσδοκωμένου ἀγαθοῦ.

Ἡδονὴ δὲ ἄλογος ἔπαρσις· ἢ δόξα πρόσφατος ἀγαθοῦ παρουσίας, ἐφ' ᾧ οἴονται δεῖν ἐπαίρεσθαι.

1059—Since the πάθη destroy the harmony of the soul and obstruct the right function of Reason, they are essentially unnatural and must be extirpated. On this point, too, Stoic doctrine is opposite to Aristotelian.

The πάθη must be extirpated

    a.   Seneca, *Ep.* 116, 1:

Utrum satius sit modicos habere adfectus an nullos, saepe quaesitum est: nostri illos expellunt, Peripatetici temperant.

    b.   Lactantius, *Div. inst.* VI 14:

Nam Stoici affectus omnes, quorum impulsu animus commovetur, ex homine tollunt, cupiditatem, laetitiam, metum, moestitiam: quorum duo priora ex bonis sunt aut futuris aut praesentibus; posteriora ex malis. Eodem modo haec quattuor morbos (ut dixi) vocant, non tam natura insitos, quam prava opinione susceptos: et idcirco eos censent extirpari posse radicitus, si bonorum malorumque opinio falsa tollatur.

c. Cp. Lactantius, *De ira* c. 17:

Sed Stoici non viderunt esse discrimen recti et pravi; esse iram iustam, esse et iniustam; et quia medelam rei non inveniebant, voluerunt eam penitus excidere.

1060—Since there is an exact parallel between body and soul, philosophy is the healing art of the soul like medicine is of the body. As such, it has essentially to treat the πάθη.

a. Galenus, *De plac. Hippocr. et Plat.* V 2, p. 413 M. (SVF III 471) cites Chrysippus in his ethical treatise Π. παθῶν:

Philosophy the healing art of the soul

Οὔτε γὰρ περὶ τὸ νοσοῦν σῶμά ἐστί τις τέχνη, ἣν προσαγορεύομεν ἰατρικήν, οὐχὶ δὲ καὶ περὶ τὴν νοσοῦσαν ψυχήν ἐστί τις τέχνη, οὔτ' ἐν τῇ κατὰ μέρος θεωρίᾳ τε καὶ θεραπείᾳ δεῖ λείπεσθαι ταύτην ἐκείνης. διὸ καί, καθάπερ τῷ περὶ τὰ σώματα ἰατρῷ καθήκει τῶν τε συμβαινόντων αὐτοῖς παθῶν ἐντὸς εἶναι, ὡς εἰώθασι τοῦτο λέγειν, καὶ τῆς ἑκάστῳ οἰκείας θεραπείας, οὕτω καὶ τῷ τῆς ψυχῆς ἰατρῷ ἐπιβάλλει, ἀμφοτέρων τούτων ἐντὸς εἶναι, ὡς ἔνι ἄριστα. καὶ ὅτι οὕτως ἔχει, μάθοι ἄν τις τῆς πρὸς ταῦτα ἀναλογίας παρατεθείσης ἀπ' ἀρχῆς. ἡ γὰρ πρὸς ταῦτα ἀντιπαρατείνουσα οἰκειότης παραστήσει, ὡς οἴομαι, καὶ τὴν τῶν θεραπειῶν ὁμοιότητα, καὶ ἔτι τὴν ἀμφοτέρων τῶν ἰατρειῶν πρὸς ἀλλήλας ἀναλογίαν.

b. Cp. Cic., *Tusc. disp.* II 4, 11:

Nam efficit hoc philosophia: medetur animis, inanes sollicitudines detrahit, cupiditatibus liberat, pellit timores.

As may be clear from the preceding chapters, this conception of philosophy, though Cicero had it doubtless from his Stoic preceptors, is not exclusively Stoic. It was also Epicurean, Platonic and Aristotelian and, as will appear from our next chapter, even Sceptic.

1061—The general treatment of the πάθη is: to set before the patient's mind the irrational character of the πάθος.

a. Galenus, *De plac. Hippocr. et Plat.* IV 7, p. 397 M. (SVF III 467), where Chrysippus, Π. τῶν παθῶν, is cited as follows:

General treatment of the πάθη

"Περὶ δὲ τῆς λύπης [καὶ] ὡς ἂν ἐμπλησθέντες τινὲς ὁμοίως φαίνονται ἀφίστασθαι, καθάπερ καὶ ἐπὶ 'Αχιλλέως ταῦτα λέγει ὁ ποιητὴς πενθοῦντος τὸν Πάτροκλον· (δ 541. Ω 514)

> 'Αλλ' ὅτε δὴ κλαίων τε κυλινδόμενός τ' ἐκορέσθη,
> Καί οἱ ἀπὸ πραπίδων ἦλθ' ἵμερος ἠδ' ἀπὸ γυίων,

ἐπὶ τὸ παρακαλεῖν ὥρμησε τὸν Πρίαμον, τὴν τῆς λύπης ἀλογίαν αὐτῷ παριστάς.''

εἶτ' ἐφεξῆς ἐπιφέρει καὶ ταῦτα·

''Καθ' ὃν λόγον οὐκ ἂν ἀπελπίσαι τις οὕτως τῶν πραγμάτων ἐγχρονιζομένων, καὶ τῆς παθητικῆς φλεγμονῆς ἀνιεμένης, τὸν λόγον παρεισδυόμενον καὶ οἱονεὶ χώραν λαμβάνοντα παριστάναι τὴν τοῦ πάθους ἀλογίαν.''

Galenus rightly observed that Chrys.—and doubtless Zeno before him, as may be seen in his definition of λύπη as δόξα πρόσφατος κακοῦ παρουσίας [1]—paid due attention to the fact that affects lose their force by time and then, growing weaker, may be overcome by reason.

Prevention of violent impressions   **b.**   Therefore, to prevent violent impressions, it is useful to familiarize oneself with things beforehand (προενδημεῖν τοῖς πράγμασι).

Galenus, o.c., IV 7, p. 392 M. (SVF III 482):

Καί φησι διότι πᾶν τὸ ἀμελέτητον καὶ ξένον ἀθρόως προσπῖπτον ἐκπίπτει τε καὶ τῶν παλαιῶν ἐξίστησι κρίσεων, ἀσκηθὲν δὲ καὶ συνεθισθὲν καὶ χρονίσαν ἢ οὐδ' ὅλως ἐξίστησιν, ὡς κατὰ πάθος κινεῖν, ἢ ἐπὶ μικρὸν κομιδῇ· διὸ καὶ προενδημεῖν δεῖν φησι τοῖς πράγμασι μήπω τε παροῦσιν οἷον παροῦσι χρῆσθαι. βούλεται δὲ τὸ προενδημεῖν ῥῆμα τῷ Ποσειδωνίῳ τὸ οἷον προαναπλάττειν τε καὶ προτυποῦν τὸ πρᾶγμα παρ' ἑαυτῷ τὸ μέλλον γενήσεσθαι καὶ ὡς πρὸς ἤδη γενόμενον ἐθισμόν τινα ποιεῖσθαι κατὰ βραχύ. διὸ καὶ τὸ τοῦ Ἀναξαγόρου παρείληφεν ἐνταῦθα, ὡς ἄρα τινὸς ἀναγγείλαντος αὐτῷ τεθνάναι τὸν υἱὸν εὖ μάλα καθεστηκότως εἶπεν ''ᾔδειν θνητὸν γεννήσας''.

c.   Evidently, the true medicine against sorrow according to the Stoic view is always: convincing people that there is no evil except what is morally bad. Thus, Cicero says in *Tusc. disp.* III 76:

Nihil esse malum quod turpe non sit   Sunt qui unum officium consolantis putant ''malum illud omnino non esse'', ut Cleanthi placet.

Cp. also our nr. **955b, c**.

The wise man is ἀπαθής   **1062**—The wise man is passionless, but not insensible to impressions.

a.   Diog. Laert. VII 117:

Φασὶ δὲ καὶ ἀπαθῆ εἶναι τὸν σοφόν, διὰ τὸ ἀνέμπτωτον εἶναι. εἶναι δὲ καὶ ἄλλον ἀπαθῆ, τὸν φαῦλον, ἐν ἴσῳ λεγόμενον τῷ σκληρῷ καὶ ἀτέγκτῳ.

b.   Cp. Stob., *Flor.* 7, 21 (SVF III 574):

Χρυσίππου. ἔλεγεν δὲ ὁ Χρύσιππος ἀλγεῖν μὲν τὸν σοφόν, μὴ βασανίζεσθαι δέ· μὴ γὰρ ἐνδιδόναι τῇ ψυχῇ. Καὶ δεῖσθαι μέν, μὴ προσδέχεσθαι δέ.

---

[1]   In its fuller form the definition is cited in our nr. **955a**.

c.   In a passage cited in our first volume (nr. **239**) Seneca opposes the Stoic wise man to that of Stilpo and certain others "quibus summum bonum visum est animus impatiens", saying (*Ep.* I 9, 3):

Hoc inter nos et illos interest: noster sapiens vincit quidem incommodum omne, sed sentit, illorum ne sentit quidem.

The representatives of ἀταραξία, meant by *illi*, were doubtless, besides Stilpo, Cynics who professed a complete indifference to outward things (cp. our nr. **248**), and, perhaps even stronger, a man like Pyrrho who, without making a "doctrine" of it, displayed a radical indifferentism in daily life. Below, nr. **1082b**.

The Stoic attitude towards *externa* may be also illustrated by Seneca, *De prov.* 2, 1, where he says: *nec hoc dico: "non sentit illa"*, sed vincit, e.q.s.—See also, on Stoic ἀπάθεια, Wiersma, Π. τέλους p. 15.

1063—The Stoics do acknowledge right feelings.

a.   Diog. Laërt. VII 116 (SVF III 431):

The three
εὐπάθειαι

Εἶναι δὲ καὶ εὐπαθείας φασὶ τρεῖς, χαράν, εὐλάβειαν, βούλησιν. καὶ τὴν μὲν χαρὰν ἐναντίαν φασὶν εἶναι τῇ ἡδονῇ, οὖσαν εὔλογον ἔπαρσιν, τὴν δὲ εὐλάβειαν τῷ φόβῳ, οὖσαν εὔλογον ἔκκλισιν· φοβηθήσεσθαι μὲν γὰρ τὸν σοφὸν οὐδαμῶς, εὐλαβηθήσεσθαι δέ. τῇ δὲ ἐπιθυμίᾳ ἐναντίαν φασὶν εἶναι τὴν βούλησιν, οὖσαν εὔλογον ὄρεξιν. καθάπερ οὖν ὑπὸ τὰ πρῶτα πάθη πίπτει τινά, τὸν αὐτὸν τρόπον καὶ ὑπὸ τὰς πρώτας εὐπαθείας· καὶ ὑπὸ μὲν τὴν βούλησιν εὔνοιαν, εὐμένειαν, ἀσπασμόν, ἀγάπησιν, ὑπὸ δὲ τὴν εὐλάβειαν αἰδῶ, ἀγνείαν, ὑπὸ δὲ τὴν χαρὰν τέρψιν, εὐφροσύνην, εὐθυμίαν.

b.   Cp. the definitions in Andronicus, Π. παθῶν, c. 6 (SVF III 432):

Definitions

Εὐπαθείας εἴδη γ΄·

Βούλησις μὲν οὖν ἐστιν εὔλογος ὄρεξις.

Χαρὰ δὲ εὔλογος ἔπαρσις.

Εὐλάβεια δὲ εὔλογος ἔκκλισις.

Βουλήσεως εἴδη δ΄.

Εὔνοια μὲν οὖν ἐστι βούλησις ἀγαθῶν ⟨ἑτέρῳ⟩ αὐτοῦ ἕνεκεν ἐκείνου.

Εὐμένεια δὲ εὔνοια ἐπίμονος.

Ἀσπασμὸς δὲ ἀδιάστατος ⟨εὔνοια⟩.

Ἀγάπησις — — —

Χαρᾶς εἴδη γ΄.

Τέρψις μὲν οὖν ἐστι χαρὰ πρέπουσα ταῖς περὶ αὐτὸν ὠφελείαις.

Εὐφροσύνη δὲ χαρὰ ἐπὶ τοῖς τοῦ σώφρονος ἔργοις.

Εὐθυμία δὲ χαρὰ ἐπὶ διαγωγῇ ἢ ἀνεπιζητησίᾳ παντός.

Εὐλαβείας εἴδη β΄.

Αἰδὼς μὲν οὖν ἐστιν εὐλάβεια ὀρθοῦ ψόγου.

Ἁγνεία δὲ εὐλάβεια τῶν περὶ θ⟨εοὺς⟩ ἁμαρτημάτων.

1064—As we noticed before, the Stoics neither classed compassion nor repentance as right feelings.

Rejection of
compassion

a. On compassion, cp. Cicero, *Tusc. disp.* IV 26, 56:

An sine misericordia liberales esse non possumus? Non enim suscipere ipsi aegritudines propter alios debemus, sed alios, si possumus, levare aegritudine.

See also our nr. **1044b**: The wise man does not feel compassion.

and of
repentance

b. On repentance, see Stob., *Ecl.*, II 102, 25 W. (SVF III 563):

Εἶναι δὲ τὴν μεταμέλειαν λύπην ἐπὶ πεπραγμένοις ὡς παρ' αὐτοῦ ἡμαρτη-μένοις, κακοδαιμονικόν τι πάθος ψυχῆς καὶ στασιῶδες· ἐφ' ὅσον γὰρ ἄχθεται τοῖς συμβεβηκόσιν ὁ ἐν ταῖς μεταμελείαις ὤν, ἐπὶ τοσοῦτον ἀγανακτεῖ πρὸς ἑαυτὸν ὡς αἴτιον γεγονότα τούτων.

Cp. also our nr. **1010a-d**: The wise man never repents, etc.

13—ETHICS (6): LAW, STATE AND HUMANITY

Nature the
basis of
morality
and law

1065—Morality is founded on "nature", as it is conceived by Stoic philosophers.

a. Diog. Laërt. VII 128:

Φύσει τε τὸ δίκαιον εἶναι καὶ μὴ θέσει, ὡς καὶ τὸν νόμον καὶ τὸν ὀρθὸν λόγον, καθά φησι Χρύσιππος ἐν τῷ Περὶ τοῦ καλοῦ.

b. In Cicero's *De fin.* III 21, 71, Cato expounds Stoic doctrine on law and justice as follows:

Ius autem, quod ita dici appellarique possit, id esse natura, alienumque esse a sapiente non modo iniuriam cui facere, verum etiam nocere. Nec vero rectum est cum amicis aut bene meritis consociare aut coniungere iniuriam. Gravissimeque ... defenditur numquam aequitatem ab utilitate posse seiungi, et, quicquid aequum iustumque esset, id etiam honestum, vicissimque quicquid esset honestum, iustum etiam atque aequum fore.

c. In general, what is morally good is natural.

Cic., *De leg.* I 16, 44:

Nec solum ius et iniuria natura diiudicantur, sed omnino omnia honesta ac turpia. Nam et communis intelligentia notas nobis res efficit easque in animis nostris inchoavit, ut honesta in virtute ponantur, in vitiis turpia. Haec autem in opinione existimare, non in natura posita, dementis est. Nam nec arboris nec equi virtus, quae dicitur (in quo abutimur nomine) in opinione sita est, sed in natura. Quodsi ita est, honesta quoque et turpia natura diiudicanda sunt. Nam si opinione universa virtus, eadem etiam eius partes probarentur. Quis igitur prudentem, et, ut ita dicam, catum non ex ipsius habitu, sed ex aliqua re externa iudicet? Est enim virtus perfecta ratio; quod certe in natura est. Igitur omnis honestas eodem modo.

1066—a.   Cic., *De leg.* I 6, 18, gives the following definition of law: Lex defined
as ratio
summa

Lex est ratio summa, insita in natura, quae iubet ea quae facienda sunt prohibetque contraria.

b.   Human law is derived from divine Reason.

Cic., *De leg.* II 4, 8:

Hanc igitur video sapientissimorum fuisse sententiam, legem neque hominum ingeniis excogitatam nec scitum aliquod esse populorum, sed aeternum quiddam, quod universum mundum regeret imperandi prohibendique sapientia. Ita principem legem illam et ultimam mentem esse dicebant omnia ratione aut cogentis aut vetantis dei; ex quo illa lex, quam di humano generi dederunt, recte est laudata; est enim ratio mensque sapientis ad iubendum et ad deterrendum idonea. —

Sed vero intellegi sic oportet, ... iussa ac vetita populorum vim habere ad recte facta vocandi et a peccatis avocandi, quae vis non modo senior est quam aetas populorum et civitatium, sed aequalis illius caelum atque terras tuentis et regentis dei. — Neque enim esse mens divina sine ratione potest, nec ratio divina non hanc vim in rectis pravisque sanciendis habet. — Quam ob rem lex vera atque princeps apta ad iubendum et ad vetandum ratio est recta summi Iovis.

c.   Cic., *De re publ.* III 33:   True law is
eternal

Est quidem vera lex recta ratio, naturae congruens, diffusa in omnes, constans, sempiterna; quae vocet ad officium iubendo, vetando a fraude deterreat, quae tamen neque probos frustra iubet aut vetat, nec improbos iubendo aut vetando movet. Huic legi nec obrogari fas est, neque derogari ex hac aliquid licet, neque tota abrogari potest: nec vero aut per senatum aut per populum solvi hac lege possumus: neque est quaerendus explanator aut interpres eius alius: nec erit alia lex Romae, alia Athenis, alia nunc, alia posthac; sed et omnes gentes et omni tempore una lex et sempiterna et immutabilis continebit; unusque erit communis quasi magister et imperator omnium deus, ille legis huius inventor, disceptator, lator; cui qui non paiebit, ipse se fugiet ac naturam hominis aspernatus, hoc ipso luet maximas poenas, etiam si cetera supplicia, quae putantur, effugerit.

The passage is cited by Lactantius, *Div. inst.* VI 8. For the notion of eternal law in the Stoa, cp. Cleanthes' κοινὸς νόμος in the Hymn to Zeus (our nr. **943**). The notion goes back to Heraclitus' conception of Law (fr. 114 Diels; our nr. **62d**). Cp. also Plato, *Laws* IV 713e-714a, where he says that God and Reason which follows Him must rule our public and our private life:

Καὶ ὅσον ἐν ἡμῖν ἀθανασίας ἔνεστι, τούτῳ πειθομένους δημοσίᾳ καὶ ἰδίᾳ τάς τ᾽ οἰκήσεις καὶ τὰς πόλεις διοικεῖν, τ η ν τ ο ῦ Ν ο ῦ δ ι α ν ο μ ὴ ν ἐ π ο ν ο μ ά ζ ο ν τ α ς ν ό μ ο ν.

Only, when Plato says that God, and not man, must be the measure of all things (*Laws* IV 716c), he certainly thought of a *transcendent* Reason, which can be only "imitated" by man, i.e. which is not directly and as such in man, but only by participation. Thus, between Plato and the Stoics, though the words are similar, there is a considerable distance.

Pindarus' wellknown words Νόμος πάντων βασιλεύς were cited by Chrysippus in the beginning of his book Π. νόμου (quoted by Marcianus, l. I *Instit.*, SVF III 314).

As to the notion of eternal law in Aristotle, see our nrs. **589** and **658a**.

d.   Plut., *St. repugn.* 9 (SVF III 326), cites the following lines of Chrysippus, where we find the basis of Cicero's doctrine.

Ἄκουε δὲ ἃ λέγει περὶ τούτων ἐν τῷ τρίτῳ Περὶ θεῶν· "οὐ γάρ ἐστιν εὑρεῖν τῆς δικαιοσύνης ἄλλην ἀρχήν, οὐδ᾽ ἄλλην γένεσιν, ἢ τὴν ἐκ τοῦ Διὸς καὶ τὴν ἐκ τῆς κοινῆς φύσεως· ἐντεῦθεν γὰρ δεῖ πᾶν τὸ τοιοῦτον τὴν ἀρχὴν ἔχειν, εἰ μέλλομέν τι ἐρεῖν περὶ ἀγαθῶν καὶ κακῶν".

Empirical law

1067.   Empirical law as such has no authority. It derives its force exclusively from eternal law, and must be judged after the latter.

a.   Cic., *De leg.* I 15, 42:

Iam vero illud stultissimum, existimare omnia iusta esse, quae sancita sint in populorum institutis aut legibus. Etiamne si quae leges sint tyrannorum? — Est enim unum ius, quo devincta est hominum societas et quod lex constituit una; quae lex est recta ratio imperandi atque prohibendi: quam qui ignorat, is est iniustus, sive est illa scripta uspiam, sive nusquam.

b.   Ib., I 16, 43:

Quodsi populorum iussis, si principum decretis, si sententiis iudicum iura constituerentur: ius esset latrocinari, ius adulterare, ius testamenta falsa supponere, si haec suffragiis aut scitis multitudinis probarentur.

Quod si tanta potestas est stultorum sententiis atque iussis, ut eorum suffragiis rerum natura vertatur: cur non sanciunt, ut quae mala perniciosaque sunt habeantur pro bonis ac salutaribus? aut cur ius ex iniuria lex facere possit, bonum eadem facere non possit ex malo? Atqui nos legem bonam a mala nulla alia nisi naturae norma dividere possumus.

Cp. *Tusc. Disp.* I 45, 108, where Cicero says that Chrysippus collected a great number of instances of immoral laws, in order to show that empirical law as such has no authority.

Permulta alia colligit Chrysippus, ut est in omni historia curiosus: sed ita tetra sunt quaedam, ut ea fugiat et reformidet oratio.

1068—The *katorthoma*, however, is a commandment of Nomos. Hence, by Nomos nothing is commanded to the φαῦλοι, though many things are prohibited to them. Cp. our nrs. **1033** ff.

a. Plut., *Stoic. repugn.* 11, p. 1037c (SVF III 520):

Τὸ κατόρθωμά φασι νόμου πρόσταγμα εἶναι· τὸ δ' ἁμάρτημα νόμου ἀπαγόρευμα, διὸ τὸν νόμον πολλὰ τοῖς φαύλοις ἀπαγορεύειν, προστάττειν δὲ μηδέν· οὐ γὰρ δύνανται κατορθοῦν.

The katorthoma a command-ment of Law

b. The following text of Origenes shows how much this Christian author was penetrated by Stoic views and terminology.

Orig., *Comment. in Matth.*, vol. III p. 494 Delarue (SVF III 523):

Καὶ πρέπον γέ ἐστι θεοῦ νόμῳ ἀπαγορεύειν τὰ ἀπὸ κακίας καὶ προστάσσειν τὰ κατ' ἀρετήν, τὰ δὲ τῷ ἰδίῳ λόγῳ ἀδιάφορα ταῦτα ἐᾶν ἐπὶ χώρας, δυνάμενα διὰ τὴν προαίρεσιν καὶ τὸν ἐν ἡμῖν λόγον ἁμαρτανόμενα μὲν κακῶς πράττεσθαι, κατορθούμενα δὲ γίνεσθαι καλῶς.

The same terminology is used by Origenes

1069—**a.** Stoics taught with a certain emphasis the natural equality of men, as well as their social character. The doctrine is found in Cicero, *De leg.* I 10, 28-30:

Men are equal by nature

Nihil est profecto praestabilius, quam plane intellegi, nos ad iustitiam esse natos, neque opinione, sed natura constitutum esse ius. Id iam patebit, si hominum inter ipsos societatem coniunctionemque perspexeris. Nihil est enim unum uni tam simile, tam par, quam omnes inter nosmet ipsos sumus: quod si depravatio consuetudinum, si opinionum vanitas non imbecillitatem animorum torqueret et flecteret, quocunque coepisset, sui nemo ipse tam similis esset quam omnes sunt omnium. Itaque quaecunque est hominis definitio, una in omnes valet. Quod argumenti satis est, nullam dissimilitudinem esse in genere: quae si esset, non una omnes definitio contineret. Etenim ratio, qua una praestamus beluis, per quam coniectura valemus, argumentamur, refellimus, disserimus, conficimus aliquid, concludimus, certe est communis, doctrina differens, discendi quidem facultate par. Nam et sensibus eadem omnia comprehenduntur: et ea quae movent sensus, itidem movent omnium: quaeque in animis imprimuntur, de quibus ante dixi, inchoatae intelligentiae, similiter in omnibus imprimuntur: interpresque mentis oratio verbis discrepat, sententiis congruens. Nec est quisquam gentis ullius, qui ducem ‹naturam› nactus ad virtutem pervenire non possit.

Natural community of mankind   **b.** That humanity is the first and most fundamental community founded on nature, is a principle more than once repeated by Cicero. Violating it is considered by him as a transgression of the divine Order.

Cic., *De fin.* III 19, 62-63; *De off.* III 5, 25-6, 27 and 28, all cited under nr. **1000**.

1070—Cicero founds a certain international law on the principle of the natural community of men.

International law based on this principle   **a.** Justice prevails, not only among citizens of the same state, but also in intercourse with foreigners.

Cic., in the last cited passage, *De off.* III 6, 28:

Qui autem civium rationem dicunt habendam, externorum negant, ii dirimunt communem humani generis societatem; e.q.s.

Vid. sub nr. **1000b**.

b. It counts, too, in the case of a state in its external relations.

Cic., *De off.* I 11, 34-35:

Atque in re publica maxime conservanda sunt iura belli: nam cum sint duo genera decertandi, unum per disceptationem, alterum per vim, cumque illud proprium sit hominis, hoc beluarum, confugiendum est ad posterius, si uti non licet superiore. qua re suscipienda quidem bella sunt ob eam causam, ut sine iniuria in pace vivatur, parta autem victoria conservandi ii, qui non crudeles in bello, non inmanes fuerunt, ut maiores nostri Tusculanos, Aequos, Volscos, Sabinos, Hernicos in civitatem etiam acceperunt, at Karthaginem et Numantiam funditus sustulerunt.

c. We are bound by certain moral obligations, also towards enemies.

Cicero fills five chapters of his third book *De officiis* (27-31) with the famous case of Regulus, who kept his oath towards a bitter and treacherous enemy, at the sacrifice of what seemed to be expedient for himself.

1071—Since men are equal by nature, Chrysippus, and Stoics in general, do not make any distinction between what is called a noble or ignoble birth, between free men and slaves.

Class distinction rejected

a. Seneca, *De benef.* III 28:

Eadem omnibus principia eademque origo, nemo altero nobilior, nisi cui rectius ingenium et artibus bonis aptius.

Cp. Plut., *Pers. de nobil.*, c. 12, where Chrysippus is cited (SVF III 350).

b. Seneca, *De benef.* III 22:

Nobody is a slave by nature

Servus, ut placet Chrysippo, perpetuus mercennarius est.

c. Cp. Philo, *De septen. et fest. dieb.*, p. 283 vol. II Mang.:

Ἄνθρωπος γὰρ ἐκ φύσεως δοῦλος οὐδείς.

This Stoic doctrine is also found with Eratosthenes, ap. Strabo I, 66.

1072—As we noticed earlier, Stoics admitted a *civitas* of all reasonable beings, including men as well as gods, animals being excluded. Our nr. **1001**.

Civitas communis deorum atque hominum

1073—In their principle of the natural equality of men and their notion of humanity founded on this principle, Stoics were anticipated by the older Cynics. In fact, Zeno's *Politeia*, and even that of Chrysippus, showed (not only on this point) some rather marked Cynic features. A certain congeniality with Cynicism may be found in the following texts, the first of which displays Zeno's ideal of a practical community of mankind, the other his spiritualized conception of God and worship.

Congeniality with Cynics on this and other points

a. Plut., *De Alex. virt.* I 6, p. 329a (SVF I 262):

Καὶ μὴν ἡ πολὺ θαυμαζομένη πολιτεία τοῦ τὴν Στωϊκῶν αἵρεσιν καταβαλομένου Ζήνωνος εἰς ἓν τοῦτο συντείνει κεφάλαιον, ἵνα μὴ κατὰ πόλεις μηδὲ κατὰ δήμους οἰκῶμεν, ἰδίοις ἕκαστοι διωρισμένοι δικαίοις, ἀλλὰ πάντας ἀνθρώπους ἡγώμεθα δημότας καὶ πολίτας, εἷς δὲ βίος ᾖ καὶ κόσμος, ὥσπερ ἀγέλης συννόμου νόμῳ κοινῷ συντρεφομένης. τοῦτο Ζήνων μὲν ἔγραψεν ὥσπερ ὄναρ ἢ εἴδωλον εὐνομίας φιλοσόφου καὶ πολιτείας ἀνατυπωσάμενος· —

b. Clem. Alex., *Strom.* V 12, 76, p. 377 St. (SVF I 264):

Λέγει δὲ καὶ Ζήνων, ὁ τῆς Στωϊκῆς κτίστης αἱρέσεως, ἐν τῷ τῆς Πολιτείας βιβλίῳ μήτε ναοὺς δεῖν ποιεῖν μήτε ἀγάλματα· μηδὲν γὰρ εἶναι τῶν θεῶν ἄξιον κατασκεύασμα, καὶ γράφειν οὐ δέδιεν αὐταῖς λέξεσι τάδε· ἱερά τε οἰκοδομεῖν οὐδὲν δεήσει· ἱερὸν γὰρ μὴ πολλοῦ ἄξιον καὶ ἅγιον οὐδὲν χρὴ νομίζειν· οὐδὲν δὲ πολλοῦ ἄξιον καὶ ἅγιον οἰκοδόμων ἔργον καὶ βαναύσων.

1074—In spite of their tendency towards cosmopolitism, Stoics had a high appreciation of existing laws and states.

Appreciation of existing laws and states

a. Stob., *Ecl.* II 7, p. 103, 9 W. (SVF III 328):

Λέγουσι δὲ καὶ φυγάδα πάντα φαῦλον εἶναι καθ' ὅσον στέρεται νόμου καὶ πολιτείας κατὰ φύσιν ἐπιβαλλούσης. Τὸν γὰρ νόμον εἶναι, καθάπερ εἴπομεν, σπουδαῖον, ὁμοίως δὲ καὶ τὴν πόλιν.

Definition of „state"

b. "State" is defined by Stoics as πλῆθος ἀνθρώπων ὑπὸ νόμου διοικούμενον. The definition is found in Clem. Alex., *Strom.* IV 26, p. 324 St., and in Dio Chrysost., *Or.* 36, 20 (SVF III, 327, 329).

Aristotle too, in *Pol.* I 1, set a high value on the polis (1253 a 2-5). He described it as γινομένη μὲν τοῦ ζῆν ἕνεκεν, οὖσα δὲ τοῦ εὖ ζῆν, but did not define it by law.

1075—In principle, neither Zeno nor Chrysippus was against taking part in political life, though neither of them did.

Zeno and Chrys. not against taking part in politics

a. Seneca, *De otio* 3, 2 Gertz:

Zenon ait: accedet ad rem publicam (sapiens), nisi si quid impedierit.

b. Diog. Laërt. VII 121:

Πολιτεύσεσθαί φασι τὸν σοφὸν ἂν μή τι κωλύῃ, ὥς φησι Χρύσιππος ἐν πρώτῳ Περὶ βίων· καὶ γὰρ κακίαν ἐφέξειν καὶ ἐπ' ἀρετὴν παρορμήσειν.

Panaetius' attitude

c. Panaetius laid great stress on the duty of public service for a special class of people, but did not set more value on these duties than on those of pure theory.

Cic., *De off.* I 21, 71-72:

The author thinks some persons excused by special reasons for having retired from the service of the state. He continues (72):

Sed iis qui habent a natura adiumenta rerum gerendarum, abiecta omni cunctatione adipiscendi magistratus et gerenda res publica est; nec enim aliter aut regi civitas aut declarari animi magnitudo potest.

Probably the whole passage has been more or less worked over by Cicero, who may well be the author of the last cited words.

In any case, as we know from ch. 6 of the same work, Panaetius placed the first of the four cardinal virtues, "qui in veri cognitione consistit", at the top, as "touching human nature most closely" (*maxime naturam attingit humanam*).

d. Cicero went a step further, in grading social duties as such higher than theoretical.

De off. I 6, 19:

After having praised certain persons for their knowledge of astronomy, geometry, dialectics and law, he says:

Cuius studio a rebus gerendis abduci contra officium est.

In practice, from Panaetius onwards Stoicism has been for a large part the philosophy of the leading statesmen of Rome. By its very attitude towards political life, and by its moral severity in general, it was much more adapted to the Roman mind than Epicureanism was.

1076—The notion of natural law, as established by the Stoics, who continued on this point the line of Plato's and Aristotle's thought, was adopted by the classical jurists of the Roman Empire.
Later influence

a. Though *Ulpianus* (Dig. I 1, 1, 3; Inst. I 2) extends natural law to all living beings, with the clear purpose of distinguishing *ius naturale* from *ius gentium*, on the whole, he stands on Stoic ground, e.g. in his definitions of *iustitia* and *iuris prudentia*.
In the Digestae

Dig. I 1, 10:

Iustitia est constans et perpetua voluntas ius suum cuique tribuendi. Iuris praecepta sunt haec: honeste vivere, alterum non laedere, suum cuique tribuere. Iuris prudentia est divinarum atque humanarum rerum notitia, iusti atque iniusti scientia.

b. *Florentinus* (*Dig.* I 1, 3) deduces natural law from the πρώτη ὁρμή of self-preservation and from mutual relationship of men.

In *Inst.* I 2, 2 we find the Stoic principle that, according to natural law, every man is born free; and *Marcianus* began his *Institutions* by quoting Chrysippus as the highest authority of Stoic wisdom (*Dig.* I 3, 2).

c. In the 13th Century, the principle of natural law is adopted by Thomas Aquinas. It is kept up till our days in scholastical philosophy.
In Thomas Aquinas

See, for instance, Thomas Aq., *Summa theol.* II, 1, qu. 93, art. 3, Resp.:

Cum ergo lex aeterna sit ratio gubernationis in supremo gubernante, necesse est quod omnes rationes gubernationis, quae sunt in inferioribus gubernantibus, a lege aeterna deriventur. Hujusmodi autem rationes inferiorum gubernantium sunt quaecumque aliae leges praeter aeternam; unde omnes leges, inquantum participant de ratione recta, intantum derivantur a lege aeterna. Et propter hoc Augustinus dicit in l. *De Lib. Arb.* (cap. 6), quod in temporali lege nihil est iustum ac legitimum, quod non ex lege aeterna homines sibi derivaverunt.

Cp. also *S. Th.* II, 1, qu. 91, art. 2, Resp.:
Natural law a participation of eternal law

... Cum omnia, quae divinae providentiae subduntur, a lege aeterna regulentur et mensurentur, ut ex dictis patet (art. praec.), manifestum est, quod omnia participant aliqualiter legem aeternam, inquantum scilicet ex impressione eius habent inclinationes in proprios actus et fines. Inter cetera autem rationalis creatura excellentiori quodam modo divinae providentiae subjacet, inquantum et ipsa fit providentiae particeps, sibi ipsi et aliis providens. Unde et in ipsa participatur ratio aeterna, per quam habet naturalem inclinationem ad debitum actum et finem: et talis participatio legis aeternae in rationali creatura *lex naturalis* dicitur.

That S. Thomas speaks here of *participation*, shows us the difference between his and the Stoic view of eternal law: for Stoics, eternal Law is directly immanent in nature; for S. Thomas, it is essentially transcendent, and only indirectly immanent, as a regulative principle.

TWENTY-SECOND CHAPTER
SCEPTICISM

i—INTRODUCTORY REMARKS

What is
meant by
Sceptics **1077**—By Sceptics we mean those philosophers who deny the possibility of any knowledge and think that wisdom consists in withholding assent (ἐποχή). Since Pyrrho of Elis was the first to take this attitude, he is considered as the founder of the Sceptical School, and Sceptics were also called Πυρρώνειοι.

In the following passage of Sextus "Sceptics" are distinguished from those philosophers who, being members of the Academy, took the sceptical attitude. Certain points of difference between the two Schools are noticed by Sextus in the same book, 229-231. Arcesilaus, however, is said to have been on the side of the Sceptical School (232). Later both groups are practically identified in being σκεπτικοί or ἐφεκτικοί. St. Augustine, in combating scepticism, wrote *Contra Academicos*.

**Academics
and Sceptics
opposed to
dogmatists** **a.** Sextus, *P.* I 1, 1-4:

Τοῖς ζητοῦσί τι πρᾶγμα ἢ εὕρεσιν ἐπακολουθεῖν εἰκὸς ἢ ἄρνησιν εὑρέσεως καὶ ἀκαταληψίας [1] ὁμολογίαν ἢ ἐπιμονὴν ζητήσεως. διόπερ ἴσως καὶ ἐπὶ τῶν κατὰ φιλοσοφίαν ζητουμένων οἱ μὲν εὑρηκέναι τὸ ἀληθὲς ἔφασαν, οἱ δ' ἀπεφήναντο μὴ δυνατὸν εἶναι τοῦτο καταληφθῆναι, οἱ δὲ ἔτι ζητοῦσιν. καὶ εὑρηκέναι μὲν δοκοῦσιν οἱ ἰδίως καλούμενοι δογματικοί, οἷον οἱ περὶ Ἀριστοτέλην καὶ Ἐπίκουρον καὶ τοὺς Στωϊκοὺς καὶ ἄλλοι τινές, ὡς δὲ περὶ ἀκαταλήπτων ἀπεφήναντο οἱ περὶ Κλειτόμαχον καὶ Καρνεάδην καὶ ἄλλοι Ἀκαδημαϊκοί, ζητοῦσι δὲ οἱ σκεπτικοί. ὅθεν εὐλόγως δοκοῦσιν αἱ ἀνωτάτω φιλοσοφίαι τρεῖς εἶναι, δογματικὴ Ἀκαδημαϊκὴ σκεπτική.

**Various
names of
scepticism** **b.** Besides the above-mentioned names, scepticism is also qualified as ζητητική or ἀπορητική.

Sextus, *P.* I 3, 7:

Ἡ σκεπτικὴ τοίνυν ἀγωγὴ καλεῖται μὲν καὶ ζητητικὴ ἀπὸ ἐνεργείας τῆς κατὰ τὸ ζητεῖν καὶ σκέπτεσθαι, καὶ ἐφεκτικὴ ἀπὸ τοῦ μετὰ τὴν ζήτησιν περὶ τὸν σκεπτόμενον γινομένου πάθους, καὶ ἀπορητικὴ ἤτοι ἀπὸ τοῦ περὶ παντὸς ἀπορεῖν καὶ ζητεῖν, ὡς ἔνιοί φασιν, ἢ ἀπὸ τοῦ ἀμηχανεῖν πρὸς συγκατάθεσιν ἢ

---

[1] The impossibility of κατάληψις, as it is taught by Stoics (above, nrs. **984-985**).

ἄρνησιν, καὶ Πυρρώνειος ἀπὸ τοῦ φαίνεσθαι ἡμῖν τὸν Πύρρωνα σωματικώτερον καὶ ἐπιφανέστερον τῶν πρὸ αὐτοῦ προσεληλυθέναι τῇ σκέψει.

1078—There seems to have been an interruption in the Sceptical School: Menodotus, a later Sceptic of the empirical school, says that Pyrrho's successor Timon had no successor himself.

Probable interruption of the School after Timon

a. Diog. Laërt. IX 115:

Τούτου (sc. Τίμωνος) διάδοχος, ὡς μὲν Μηνόδοτός φησι, γέγονεν οὐδείς, ἀλλὰ διέλιπεν ἡ ἀγωγὴ ἕως αὐτὴν Πτολεμαῖος ὁ Κυρηναῖος ἀνεκτήσατο.

Ptolemaeus of Cyrene lived towards the end of the second century or in the beginning of the first.

b. Others filled the gap between Timon and Ptolemaeus.

Diog. Laërt., ib.:

'Ὡς δ' Ἱππόβοτός φησι καὶ Σωτίων, διήκουσαν αὐτοῦ Διοσκουρίδης Κύπριος καὶ Νικόλοχος Ῥόδιος καὶ Εὐφράνωρ Σελευκεὺς Πραῦλος τ' ἀπὸ Τρωάδος, ὃς οὕτω καρτερικὸς ἐγένετο, καθά φησι Φύλαρχος ἱστορῶν, ὥστ' ἀδίκως ὑπομεῖναι ὡς ἐπὶ προδοσίᾳ κολασθῆναι, μηδὲ λόγου τοὺς πολίτας καταξιώσας. Εὐφράνορος δὲ διήκουσεν Εὔβουλος Ἀλεξανδρεύς, οὗ Πτολεμαῖος, οὗ Σαρπηδὼν καὶ Ἡρακλείδης, Ἡρακλείδου δ' Αἰνεσίδημος Κνώσιος, ὃς καὶ Πυρρωνείων λόγων ὀκτὼ συνέγραψε βιβλία· οὗ Ζεύξιππος ὁ πολίτης, οὗ Ζεῦξις ὁ Γωνιόπους, οὗ Ἀντίοχος Λαοδικεὺς ἀπὸ Λύκου· τούτου δὲ Μηνόδοτος ὁ Νικομηδεύς, ἰατρὸς ἐμπειρικός, καὶ Θειωδᾶς Λαοδικεύς· Μηνοδότου δὲ Ἡρόδοτος Ἀριέως Ταρσεύς· Ἡροδότου δὲ διήκουσε Σέξτος ὁ Ἐμπειρικός, οὗ καὶ τὰ δέκα τῶν Σκεπτικῶν καὶ ἄλλα κάλλιστα· Σέξτου δὲ διήκουσε Σατορνῖνος ὁ Κυθηνᾶς, ἐμπειρικὸς καὶ αὐτός.

Probably this list was fabricated later, as is admitted by Brochard, *Les sceptiques grecs*, Paris 1887, ²1932, p. 229. See also L. Robin, *Pyrrhon*, Paris 1944, p. 137-139; Zeller III 2, p. 2. C. W. Vollgraff, in his interesting study on the life of Sextus Empiricus (*Revue de Philologie* 1902, p. 195-210) defends the authenticity of this list. In fact, the space of time between Timon and Ptolemaeus is exactly filled if a period of 30 years is attributed to every schoolhead. Now, this is certainly not impossible, yet rather suspect.

c. That an interruption has happened in at least one philosophers school, is confirmed by the following passage from the life of Epicurus. Diog. Laërt. X 9:

As a witness in favour of Epicurus' character he mentions i.a.:

Ἥ τε διαδοχὴ πασῶν σχεδὸν ἐκλιπουσῶν τῶν ἄλλων ἐσαεὶ διαμένουσα καὶ νηρίθμους ἀρχὰς ἀπολύουσα ἄλλην ἐξ ἄλλης τῶν γνωρίμων.

Moreover, we know that neither in the Stoa, nor in the Academy or Peripatos
was the succession ever interrupted.

When did
Sextus
Empiricus
live?
1079—Usually the life of Sextus Empiricus is dated c. 180-210.
Vollgraff, in his above cited article, identified this Sextus with Sextus of
Chaeronea, nephew of Plutarchus and teacher of Marcus Aurelius. If
this identification is right—and, indeed, it does not depend on the list
of Hippobotus and Sotion—, we possess a description of Sextus' character
by the emperor's hand.

a. Marcus Aurelius, *Meditations* I 9:

Παρὰ Σέξτου τὸ εὐμενές· καὶ τὸ παράδειγμα τοῦ οἴκου τοῦ πατρονομουμένου·
καὶ τὴν ἔννοιαν τοῦ κατὰ φύσιν ζῆν· καὶ τὸ σεμνὸν ἀπλάστως· καὶ τὸ στοχα-
στικὸν τῶν φίλων κηδεμονικῶς· καὶ τὸ ἀνεκτικὸν τῶν ἰδιωτῶν καὶ <διὰ> τὸ
ἀθεώρητον οἰομένων· καὶ τὸ πρὸς πάντας εὐάρμοστον, ὥστε κολακείας μὲν
πάσης προσηνεστέραν εἶναι τὴν ὁμιλίαν αὐτοῦ, αἰδεσιμώτατον δὲ αὐτοῖς
ἐκείνοις παρ' αὐτὸν ἐκεῖνον τὸν καιρὸν εἶναι· καὶ τὸ καταληπτικῶς καὶ ὁδῷ
ἐξευρετικόν τε καὶ τακτικὸν τῶν εἰς βίον ἀναγκαίων δογμάτων· καὶ τὸ μηδὲ
ἔμφασίν ποτε ὀργῆς ἢ ἄλλου τινὸς πάθους παρασχεῖν, ἀλλὰ ἅμα μὲν ἀπαθέ-
στατον εἶναι, ἅμα δὲ φιλοστοργότατον· καὶ τὸ εὔφημον καὶ τοῦτο ἀψοφητί·
καὶ τὸ πολυμαθὲς ἀνεπιφάντως.

Doubtless, the feature of ἀπάθεια in this portrait does not prove at all that the
philosopher was a Stoic. As to the words καὶ τὴν ἔννοιαν τοῦ κατὰ φύσιν ζῆν, as a
general rule of life this formula was evidently Stoic. In a sense, however, the
sceptic Sextus did speak of the "guidance of Nature", too (*Pyrrh. Hyp.* I 23-24,
see under nr. **1140b**), and it is quite possible that Marcus Aurelius, on hearing
the well-known formula used by Sextus in a more limited sense, took it, as Stoics
did, δογματικῶς.
Thus, I do not think there is anything against the identification in this passage.

b. The identification is confirmed by Suidas:

Σέξτος Χαιρωνεὺς ἀδελφιδοῦς Πλουτάρχου γεγονὼς κατὰ Μάρκον Ἀντω-
νῖνον τὸν Καίσαρα φιλόσοφος μαθητὴς Ἡροδότου τοῦ Φιλαδελφαίου. Ἦν δὲ
τῆς Πυρρωνείου ἀγωγῆς. Καὶ τοσοῦτον πρὸς τιμῆς τῷ βασιλεῖ ἦν ὥστε καὶ
συνδικάζειν αὐτῷ. Ἔγραψεν Ἠθικὰ καὶ [1] Σκεπτικὰ βιβλία δέκα.

Division of
the Sceptical
School
1080—The Sceptical School may be divided into three periods:

  I. *The older Sceptics*, Pyrrho and Timon: *an anti-dialectical philosophy
    of life*;

  II. The *dialectical scepticism* of Aenesidemus and Agrippa;

---

[1] The traditional reading is: ἐπί.

III. The *empirical phenomenism* of the later Sceptical School, to which belongs Sextus Empiricus.

This later Scepticism is prepared and certainly influenced by the philosophers of the so-called *Middle and Third Academy*, Arcesilaus and Carneades. We shall deal with them between (I) and (II).

1081—The question may be asked whether or not Pyrrho's scepticism was a new philosophy. I think, it was, for

Is scepticism a new philosophy?

(1) Presocratic philosophers, on the whole, did not so much confide in the senses, but they had great confidence in reason (Heraclitus, our nr. **66**; Parmenides, nrs. **80**, l. 33-37, **81-83**; Anaxagoras, nr. **133a, b**; Democritus, **142a d**).

(2) The Sophists displayed a beginning of scepticism: Protagoras' principle of ἀντιλογική (nr. **172**), and Gorgias' three nihilistic theses (**182-184**). All sophists, however, differ from Pyrrho in that their scepticism had no bearing on their conduct, and from the scepticism of the Academy and later members of the Sceptical School by its not being intellectually full-grown.

(3) The socratic dialogues, certainly, were ἀπορητικοί. Yet, neither Socrates nor Plato were sceptics. They both believed firmly in many things, such as the superiority of soul to body, the not only objective but even absolute value of moral principles, the existence of good and righteous Gods and their providence; and all this, they believed on rational grounds (**215, 217, 223**; cp. **198-199, 388** and **394**).

Therefore, the Sceptics and those philosophers of the Academy who are on their side can appeal to Socrates and Plato only *per accidens*. The mental attitude both of Socrates and of Plato differs very much from Pyrrho's and his followers' attitude in life. The latter were interested in dialectic, much more and deeper than the Sophists were. Yet, it may be said that the Sceptics developed certain principles laid down somewhat provisionally by the older Sophists, especially Protagoras.

2—THE OLDER SCEPTICS: PYRRHO AND TIMON

1082—Antigonos of Karystos, a contemporary of Timon, a physician who wrote biographies of philosophers, was inter alia the author of a life of Pyrrho and of Timon. These biographies were used by Diogenes Laërtius.

a. Diog. Laërt. IX 61:

Life of Pyrrho

Πύρρων Ἡλεῖος Πλειστάρχου μὲν ἦν υἱός, καθὰ καὶ Διοκλῆς ἱστορεῖ· ὡς φησι δ᾽ Ἀπολλόδωρος ἐν Χρονικοῖς, πρότερον ἦν ζωγράφος, καὶ ἤκουσε Βρύσωνος τοῦ Στίλπωνος, ὡς Ἀλέξανδρος ἐν Διαδοχαῖς, εἶτ᾽ Ἀναξάρχου [1] ξυνακολουθῶν πανταχοῦ, ὡς καὶ τοῖς Γυμνοσοφισταῖς ἐν Ἰνδίᾳ συμμίξαι [2]

---

[1] Anaxarchus of Abdera, who accompanied Alexander on his expedition to the Orient, is described as a man of a very strong and independent character, who impressed Alexander. Diog. L. IX 58-60.

[2] On the Gymnosophists, see Plutarch, *Life of Alexander*, cc. 64-65 and 69, 3-4,

καὶ τοῖς Μάγοις. ὅθεν γενναιότατα δοκεῖ φιλοσοφῆσαι, τὸ τῆς ἀκαταληψίας [1]
καὶ ἐποχῆς εἶδος [2] εἰσαγαγών, ὡς Ἀσκάνιος ὁ Ἀβδηρίτης φησίν· οὐδὲν γὰρ
ἔφασκεν οὔτε καλὸν οὔτ' αἰσχρὸν οὔτε δίκαιον οὔτ' ἄδικον· καὶ ὁμοίως ἐπὶ
πάντων μηδὲν εἶναι τῇ ἀληθείᾳ, νόμῳ δὲ καὶ ἔθει πάντα τοὺς ἀνθρώπους
πράττειν· οὐ γὰρ μᾶλλον τόδε ἢ τόδε εἶναι ἕκαστον.

His indif-
ferentism

b. Diog. L., ib., c. 62:

Ἀκόλουθος δ' ἦν καὶ τῷ βίῳ, μηδὲν ἐκτρεπόμενος μηδὲ φυλαττόμενος, ἅπαντα
ὑφιστάμενος, ἁμάξας, εἰ τύχοι, καὶ κρημνοὺς καὶ κύνας καὶ ὅλως μηδὲν ταῖς αἰσθήσεσιν ἐπιτρέπων. σῴζεσθαι μέντοι, καθά φασιν οἱ περὶ τὸν Καρύστιον Ἀντίγονον, ὑπὸ τῶν γνωρίμων παρακολουθούντων. Αἰνεσίδημος δέ φησι φιλοσοφεῖν
μὲν αὐτὸν κατὰ τὸν τῆς ἐποχῆς λόγον, μὴ μέντοι γ' ἀπροοράτως ἕκαστα πράττειν. Ὁ δὲ πρὸς τὰ ἐνενήκοντα ἔτη κατεβίω.

1083—Antigonos gave some more explicit information about Pyrrho's
life and conduct.

a. Diog. L., ib., ·c. 62 (continued):

Ἀντίγονος δέ φησιν ὁ Καρύστιος ἐν τῷ Περὶ Πύρρωνος τάδε περὶ αὐτοῦ,
ὅτι τὴν ἀρχὴν ἄδοξός τ' ἦν καὶ πένης καὶ ζωγράφος. σῴζεσθαί τ' αὐτοῦ ἐν
Ἤλιδι ἐν τῷ γυμνασίῳ λαμπαδιστὰς μετρίως ἔχοντας. ἐκπατεῖν τ' αὐτὸν καὶ
ἐρημάζειν, σπανίως ποτ' ἐπιφαινόμενον τοῖς οἴκοι. τοῦτο δὲ ποιεῖν ἀκούσαντα
Ἰνδοῦ τινος ὀνειδίζοντος Ἀναξάρχῳ ὡς οὐκ ἂν ἕτερόν τινα διδάξαι οὗτος
ἀγαθόν, αὐτὸς αὐλὰς βασιλικὰς θεραπεύων. ἀεί τ' εἶναι ἐν τῷ αὐτῷ καταστήματι,
ὥστ' εἰ καί τις αὐτὸν καταλίποι μεταξὺ λέγοντα, αὐτῷ διαπεραίνειν τὸν λόγον,
καίτοι κεκινημένον τε <τῷ τοῦ ὄχλου κρότῳ καὶ φιλόδοξον> [3] ὄντα ἐν νεότητι.
πολλάκις, φησί, καὶ ἀπεδήμει, μηδενὶ προειπών, καὶ συνερρέμβετο οἷστισιν
ἤθελεν, καί ποτ' Ἀναξάρχου εἰς τέλμα ἐμπεσόντος, παρῆλθεν οὐ βοηθήσας·
τινῶν δ' αἰτιωμένων, αὐτὸς Ἀνάξαρχος ἐπῄνει τὸ ἀδιάφορον καὶ ἄστοργον
αὐτοῦ.

b. Ib., c. 64:

Καταληφθεὶς δέ ποθ' ἑαυτῷ λαλῶν καὶ ἐρωτηθεὶς τὴν αἰτίαν ἔφη μελετᾶν

---

where it is told how the gymnosophist Calanos burned himself on a pyre. Pyrrho
seems to have been greatly impressed by these Indian sages.

[1] See **1077a** n. 1.
[2] The term ἐποχή, which is much used by later Sceptics, seems not to have been
used by Pyrrho. It does not occur, at least, in the fragment of Aristocles, which
goes back to Timon (our nr. **1087a**).
[3] The lacuna was filled in this way by Diels.

χρηστὸς εἶναι. ἔν τε ταῖς ζητήσεσιν ὑπ' οὐδενὸς κατεφρονεῖτο διὰ τὸ διεξοδικῶς λέγειν καὶ πρὸς ἐρώτησιν· ὅθεν καὶ Ναυσιφάνην ἤδη νεανίσκον ὄντα θηραθῆναι [1]. ἔφασκε γοῦν γίνεσθαι δεῖν τῆς μὲν διαθέσεως τῆς Πυρρωνείου, τῶν δὲ λόγων τῶν ἑαυτοῦ. ἔλεγέ τε πολλάκις καὶ Ἐπίκουρον θαυμάζοντα τὴν Πύρρωνος ἀναστροφὴν συνεχὲς αὐτοῦ πυνθάνεσθαι περὶ αὐτοῦ. οὕτω δ' αὐτὸν ὑπὸ τῆς πατρίδος τιμηθῆναι ὥστε καὶ ἀρχιερέα καταστῆσαι αὐτὸν καὶ δι' ἐκεῖνον πᾶσι τοῖς φιλοσόφοις ἀτέλειαν ψηφίσασθαι.

1084—Other witnesses.

a. Diog. L. IX 66:

Εὐσεβῶς δὲ καὶ τῇ ἀδελφῇ συνεβίω μαίᾳ οὔσῃ, καθά φησιν Ἐρατοσθένης ἐν τῷ Περὶ πλούτου καὶ πενίας, ὅτε καὶ αὐτὸς φέρων εἰς τὴν ἀγορὰν ἐπίπρασκεν ὀρνίθια, εἰ τύχοι, καὶ χοιρίδια, καὶ τὰ ἐπὶ τῆς οἰκίας ἐκάθαιρεν ἀδιαφόρως. λέγεται δὲ καὶ δέλφακα λούειν αὐτὸς ὑπ' ἀδιαφορίας. καὶ χολήσας τι ὑπὲρ τῆς ἀδελφῆς, Φιλίστα δ' ἐκαλεῖτο, πρὸς τὸν ἐπιλαβόμενον εἰπεῖν ὡς οὐκ ἐν γυναίῳ ἡ ἐπίδειξις τῆς ἀδιαφορίας. καὶ κυνός ποτ' ἐπενεχθέντος διασοβηθέντα εἰπεῖν πρὸς τὸν αἰτιασάμενον, ὡς χαλεπὸν εἴη ὁλοσχερῶς ἐκδῦναι τὸν ἄνθρωπον.

b. Ib., c. 68:

Ποσειδώνιος δὲ καὶ τοιοῦτόν τι διέξεισι περὶ αὐτοῦ. τῶν γὰρ συμπλεόντων αὐτῷ ἐσκυθρωπακότων ὑπὸ χειμῶνος, αὐτὸς γαληνὸς ὢν ἀνέρρωσε τὴν ψυχήν, δείξας ἐν τῷ πλοίῳ χοιρίδιον ἐσθίον καὶ εἰπὼν ὡς χρὴ τὸν σοφὸν ἐν τοιαύτῃ καθεστάναι ἀταραξίᾳ.

1085—Timon expressed his admiration for Pyrrho in the following lines.

a. In the *Silloi*, fr. 48 Diels (ap. Diog. L. IX 65):
Ὦ γέρον, ὦ Πύρρων, πῶς ἢ πόθεν ἔκδυσιν εὗρες
λατρείης δοξῶν τε κενοφροσύνης τε σοφιστῶν,
καὶ πάσης ἀπάτης πειθοῦς τ' ἀπελύσαο δεσμά;
οὐδ' ἐμέλέν σοι ταῦτα μετ' ἄλλοισιν, τίνες αὖραι
Ἑλλάδ' ἔχουσι, πόθεν τε καὶ εἰς ὅ, τι κυρεῖ ἕκαστα.

b. In the *Indalmoi*, fr. 67 Diels (partly ap. Diog. L., ib., more completely ap. Sext. Emp., *Adv. math.* I 305):

---

[1] Nausiphanes, Epicurus' teacher, is mentioned among Pyrrho's pupils ap. Diog. L. IX 69 (our nr. **1099**).

Τοῦτό μοι, ὦ Πύρρων, ἱμείρεται ἦτορ ἀκοῦσαι,
   πῶς ποτ' ἀνὴρ ὅτ' ἄγεις [1] ῥᾶστα μετ' ἡσυχίης
μοῦνος ἐν ἀνθρώποισι Θεοῦ τρόπον ἡγεμονεύων,
   ὃς περὶ πᾶσαν ἐλῶν γαῖαν ἀναστρέφεται,
δεικνὺς εὐτόρνου σφαίρας πυρικαύτορα κύκλον.

1086—Brochard thinks (as Diels seems to do) that the next fragment may have been written by Timon as Pyrrho's reply to the question asked in the last lines.

Pyrrho's reply?

Timon, fr. 68 Diels (ap. Sext., *Adv. math.* XI 20):
   Ἦ γὰρ ἐγὼν ἐρέω ὥς μοι καταφαίνεται εἶναι,
   μῦθον ἀληθείης ὀρθὸν ἔχων κανόνα,
   ὡς ἡ τοῦ θείου τε φύσις καὶ τἀγαθοῦ αἰεί,
   ἐξ ὧν ἰσότατος γίνεται ἀνδρὶ βίος.

Now, this might seem to us a curious sceptic who, when about to reveal "how the nature of God and of goodness is", pretends to have an exact standard of truth in his speech!—Most of this form of expression must be put down, doubtless, to Timon's account. Later Sceptics make use of the fragment without any reserve, e.g. Sextus Empiricus l.l., who precedently remarks that, the word "is" having two meanings, namely first "really exists", and secondly "appears", sentences like ours are, of course, used in the sense of appearance.

Cp. Timon's fr. 69D (ap. Diog. L. IX 105):
   ἀλλὰ τὸ φαινόμενον πάντη σθένει, οὕπερ ἂν ἔλθη.

Pyrrho's doctrine

1087—a. Of fundamental importance is the following fragment, which, according to the text, goes back to Timon.

Aristocles ap. Euseb., *Praep. ev.* XIV 18, 2:
Ὁ δέ γε μαθητὴς αὐτοῦ (sc. Πύρρωνος) Τίμων φησὶ δεῖν τὸν μέλλοντα εὐδαιμονήσειν εἰς τρία ταῦτα βλέπειν· πρῶτον μέν, ὁποῖα πέφυκε τὰ πράγματα· δεύτερον δέ, τίνα χρὴ τρόπον ἡμᾶς πρὸς αὐτὰ διακεῖσθαι· τελευταῖον δέ, τί περιέσται τοῖς οὕτως ἔχουσι. Τὰ μὲν οὖν πράγματά φησιν αὐτὸν ἀποφαίνειν ἐπίσης ἀδιάφορα καὶ ἀστάθμητα καὶ ἀνεπίκριτα, διὰ δὲ τοῦτο μήτε τὰς δόξας ἀληθεύειν ἢ ψεύδεσθαι. Διὰ τοῦτο οὖν μηδὲ πιστεύειν αὐταῖς δεῖν, ἀλλ' ἀδοξάστους καὶ ἀκλινεῖς καὶ ἀκραδάντους εἶναι, περὶ ἑνὸς ἑκάστου λέγοντας ὅτι οὐ μᾶλλον ἔστιν ἢ οὐκ ἔστιν, ἢ καὶ ἔστι καὶ οὐκ ἔστι, ἢ οὔτ' ἔστι οὔτ' οὐκ ἔστιν. Τοῖς μέντοι διακειμένοις οὕτω περιέσεσθαι Τίμων φησὶ πρῶτον μὲν ἀφασίαν, ἔπειτα δ' ἀταραξίαν.

---

[1] Most mss. read ἀνὴρ ἔτ' ἄγεις. Now, this would mean, as Diels remarks: *etiam virili aetate incuriosus tamquam infans*. This is, however, against the view the Ancients took of infancy; and further, in this case ἀνήρ is rather opposed to θεός. Hence there is no parallel with the lines "δολίη δ' ὁδῷ ἐξαπατήθη / πρεσβυγενὴς ἔτ' ἐών", (fr. 59 D., ap. Sext., P. I 224), as there might *seem* to be!

From this passage we may conclude:

(1) Pyrrho replied in his way to the question of "how to live happily". In this sense, he may be considered as a moralist,—and a very severe one—, as he was e.g. by Cicero.

(2) He replies: We must be aware that we do not know things as they are. Neither by the senses nor by thinking do we touch reality. Therefore, we must live without any opinions or preference for anything. The result will be: first, *aphasia*; next, *ataraxia*.

(3) Thus, ἐποχή, which is a theoretical attitude, was not aimed at by Pyrrho, but *ataraxia*, which is a practical attitude in life and means *indifferentism*, as complete as possible. Hence Cicero's view of Pyrrho (next nr.).

The theoretical consequences of what may be called Pyrrho's doctrine will be developed later by Carneades (probabilism) and Menodotus (empirical phenomenism). Cp. the so-called sensualism (better: *phenomenism*) of Aristippus of Cyrene, who taught that our knowledge is strictly confined to our own πάθη (Vol. I, nr. **260**).

b. Cp. Aenesidemus ap. Diog. Laërt. IX 106:

Καὶ Αἰνεσίδημος ἐν τῷ πρώτῳ τῶν Πυρρωνείων λόγων οὐδέν φησι ὁρίζειν τὸν Πύρρωνα δογματικῶς διὰ τὴν ἀντιλογίαν, τοῖς δὲ φαινομένοις ἀκολουθεῖν.

c. Cp. also the following description of the sceptical attitude.

Diog. L. IX 74:

Διετέλουν δὴ οἱ Σκεπτικοὶ τὰ τῶν αἱρέσεων δόγματα πάντ' ἀνατρέποντες, αὐτοὶ δ' οὐδὲν ἀπεφαίνοντο δογματικῶς, ἕως δὲ τοῦ προφέρεσθαι τὰ τῶν ἄλλων καὶ διηγεῖσθαι μηδὲν ὁρίζοντες, μηδ' αὐτὸ τοῦτο. ὥστε καὶ τὸ μὴ ὁρίζειν ἀνῄρουν, λέγοντες οἷον ,,Οὐδὲν ὁρίζομεν'', ἐπεὶ ὥριζον ἄν· προφερόμεθα δέ, φασί, τὰς ἀποφάσεις εἰς μήνυσιν τῆς ἀπροπτωσίας, ὡς εἰ καὶ νεύσαντας τοῦτο ἐνεδέχετο δηλῶσαι· διὰ τῆς οὖν ,,Οὐδὲν ὁρίζομεν'' φωνῆς τὸ τῆς ἀρρεψίας πάθος δηλοῦται· ὁμοίως δὲ καὶ διὰ τῆς ,,Οὐδὲν μᾶλλον'' καὶ τῆς ,,Παντὶ λόγῳ λόγος ἀντίκειται'' καὶ τῶν ὁμοίων.

1088—a. In morals, certainly, Pyrrho did not teach any theoretically more positive doctrine, as may appear clearly from the above cited passage of Diog. (**1082a**), IX 61:

Οὐδὲν γὰρ ἔφασκεν οὔτε καλὸν οὔτ' αἰσχρὸν οὔτε δίκαιαν οὔτ' ἄδικον· e.q.s.

b. Cicero repeatedly mentions him on a level with a most rigorous moralist such as Aristo of Chios, who refused to admit of any distinction between *adiaphora*. Thus, he says in *De finibus* II 13, 43:

Quae (sc. external goods) quod Aristoni et Pyrrhoni omnino visa sunt pro nihilo, ut inter optime valere et gravissime aegrotare nihil prorsus dicerent interesse, recte iam pridem contra eos desitum est disputari. Dum enim in una virtute sic omnia esse voluerunt, ut eam rerum selectione exspoliarent nec ei quicquam aut unde oriretur darent, aut ubi niteretur, virtutem ipsam, quam amplexabantur, sustulerunt.

Cp. also *De fin.* III 3, 11 and III 4, the beginning.

c. Again, *De finibus* IV 16, the beginning:

Itaque mihi videntur omnes quidem illi errasse qui finem bonorum esse dixerunt honeste vivere, sed alius alio magis, Pyrrho scilicet maxime, qui virtute constituta nihil omnino quod appetendum sit relinquat, deinde Aristo, e.q.s.

Now it is clear how Pyrrho, being a practical indifferentist of great rigorism, could be placed on a level with Aristo. If the question is asked how then, after all, "virtue was constituted" by the sceptical philosopher who denied that anything was honourable or dishonourable, just or unjust, one answer only can be given, namely: that, for Pyrrho, "virtue" was this very attitude of utter indifference towards everything.

Cicero, evidently, "translated" Pyrrhonism into the terminology of dogmatists.

A modern judgment on Pyrrho

1089—V. Brochard, at the end of his excellent chapter on Pyrrho, gives the following characteristic of his personality [1].

"On a vu bien des hommes, dans l'histoire de la philosophie et des religions, pratiquer le détachement des biens du monde et le renoncement absolu; mais les uns étaient soutenus par l'espoir d'une récompense future; ils attendaient le prix de leur vertu, et les joies qu'ils entrevoyaient réconfortaient leur courage et les assuraient contre eux-mêmes. Les autres, à défaut d'une telle espérance, avaient au moins un dogme, un idéal, auquel ils faisaient le sacrifice de leurs désirs et de leur personne; le sentiment de leur perfection était au moins une compensation à tant de sacrifices. Tous avaient pour point d'appui une foi solide. Seul, Pyrrhon n'attend rien, n'espère rien, ne croit à rien; pourtant il vit comme ceux qui croient et espèrent [2]. Il n'est soutenu par rien et il se tient debout.—

Quelques réserves qu'on puisse faire, il y a peu d'hommes qui donnent une plus haute idée de l'humanité. En un sens, Pyrrhon dépasse Marc-Aurèle et Spinoza. Et il n'y a plus qu'un pas à faire pour dire, comme quelques-uns de ses disciples l'ont dit, que la douceur est le dernier mot du scepticisme."

The reference at the end is to Diog. L. IX 108:

Gentleness the end of scepticism

Τινὲς καὶ τὴν ἀπάθειαν, ἄλλοι δὲ τὴν πραότητα τέλος εἰπεῖν φασι τοὺς σκεπτικούς.

1090—Diog. L. IX 69:

Pyrrho's pupils

Πρὸς τούτοις διήκουε τοῦ Πύρρωνος Ἑκαταῖός θ' ὁ Ἀβδηρίτης [3] καὶ

---

[1]   *Les sceptiques grecs*[1], p. 73.

[2]   This, certainly, is not quite true: compared with those who believe and hope, Pyrrho's greatness is a tragic one. It lacks all joy.

[3]   Hecataeus of Abdera wrote a history of Egypt under Ptolemaus I (= 300), later followed by Manetho. Jacoby, *Fr. Gr. Hist.* III A, p. 12.

Τίμων ὁ Φλιάσιος ὁ τοὺς Σίλλους πεποιηκώς, περὶ οὗ λέξομεν, ἔτι τε Ναυσι-
φάνης <ὁ> Τήιος, οὗ φασί τινες ἀκοῦσαι Ἐπίκουρον.

1091—Diog. L. IX 109-111; 112:

Timon

Ἀπολλωνίδης ὁ Νικαεὺς ὁ παρ' ἡμῶν [1] ἐν τῷ πρώτῳ τῶν Εἰς τοὺς Σίλλους
ὑπομνημάτων, ἃ προσφωνεῖ Τιβερίῳ Καίσαρι, φησὶ τὸν Τίμωνα εἶναι πατρὸς
μὲν Τιμάρχου, Φλιάσιον δὲ τὸ γένος· νέον δὲ καταλειφθέντα χορεύειν, ἔπειτα
καταγ·όντα ἀποδημῆσαι εἰς Μέγαρα πρὸς Στίλπωνα· κἀκείνῳ συνδιατρίψαντα
αὖθις ἐπανελθεῖν οἴκαδε καὶ γῆμαι. εἶτα πρὸς Πύρρωνα εἰς Ἦλιν ἀποδημῆσαι
μετὰ τῆς γυναικὸς κἀκεῖ διατρίβειν ἕως αὐτῷ παῖδες ἐγένοντο, ὧν τὸν μὲν
πρεσβύτερον Ξάνθον ἐκάλεσε καὶ ἰατρικὴν ἐδίδαξε καὶ διάδοχον τοῦ βίου
κατέλιπε. ὁ δ' ἐλλόγιμος ἦν, ὡς καὶ Σωτίων ἐν τῷ ἑνδεκάτῳ φησίν. ἀπορῶν
μέντοι τροφῶν ἀπῆρεν εἰς τὸν Ἑλλήσποντον καὶ τὴν Προποντίδα· ἐν Χαλκηδόνι
τε σοφιστεύων ἐπὶ πλέον ἀποδοχῆς ἠξιώθη· ἐντεῦθέν τε πορισάμονος ἀπῆρεν
εἰς Ἀθήνας, κἀκεῖ διέτριβε μέχρι καὶ τελευτῆς, ὀλίγον χρόνον εἰς Θήβας
διαδραμών. ἐγνώσθη δὲ καὶ Ἀντιγόνῳ τῷ βασιλεῖ καὶ Πτολεμαίῳ τῷ Φιλα-
δέλφῳ, ὡς αὐτὸς ἐν τοῖς ἰάμβοις αὐτῷ μαρτυρεῖ. Ἦν δέ, φησιν ὁ Ἀντίγονος,
καὶ φιλοπότης καὶ ἀπὸ τῶν φιλοσόφων εἰ σχολάζοι ποιήματα συνέγραφε καὶ
ἔπη καὶ τραγῳδίας καὶ σατύρους καὶ δράματα κωμικὰ τριάκοντα, τραγικὰ
δὲ ἑξήκοντα, σίλλους τε καὶ κιναίδους. — Τῶν δὲ σίλλων τρία ἐστίν, ἐν οἷς His works
ὡς ἂν σκεπτικὸς ὢν πάντας λοιδορεῖ καὶ σιλλαίνει τοὺς δογματικοὺς ἐν παρῳδίας
εἴδει. — 112. Ἐτελεύτησε δ' ἐγγὺς ἐτῶν ἐνενήκοντα.

Timon died in the year 235 (later than Arcesilaus, see under **1093**). Of his prin-
cipal work, the *Silloi*, Wachsmuth published the remains and tried to reconstruct
the whole (*De Timone Phliasio*, Leipzig 1859). Later, these fragments were inserted
in Diels' *Poetarum philosophorum fragmenta*, Berlin 1901.

1092—The first book of the *Silloi* seems to have been a *Nekyia*: the the Silloi
philosophers were distinguished in the crowd of souls and characterized
by Timon in a hardly flattering way.

Zeno, the founder of the Stoa, is introduced as a sneeky and greedy Phoenician
old woman, sitting in a dark place full of (dogmatical) smoke and bearing a very
small fishbasket (an allusion to the dialectical subtleties of the Stoa), too tiny
to contain all the fishes and hence swept away by the river. She was not quite as
intelligent as a guitar . . .

---

[1] This Apollonides is unknown to us. The words ὁ παρ' ἡμῶν either mean that
Diogenes himself was a sceptic, or that he used a sceptic's work without indicating
that it was a citation.

a. Fr. 38 D. (ap. Diog. L. VII 15):

Καὶ Φοίνισσαν ἴδον λιχνόγραυν σκιερῷ ἐνὶ τύφῳ
πάντων ἱμείρουσαν· ὁ δ' ἔρρει γυργαθὸς αὐτῆς
σμικρὸς ἐών, νοῦν δ' εἶχεν ἐλάσσονα κινδαψοῖο.

b. Xenophanes, writer of Silloi, finds most favour in Timon's eyes.
He is introduced in this way.

Fr. 60 D. (ap. Sext., P. I 224):

Ξεινοφάνης ὑπάτυφος, ὁμηραπάτης ἐπισκώπτης,
ἐκτὸς * ἀπ' ἀνθρώπων θεὸν ἐπλάσατ' ἴσον ἀπάντῃ,
<ἀτρεμῆ> ἀσκηθῆ, νοερώτερον ἠὲ νόημα.

Relation to Arcesilaus   **1093**—Arcesilaus, though not far from him in philosophy, was handled not much better in the *Silloi*, but gloriefied after his death.

Diog. L. IX 115:

Ἐρωτηθεὶς δέ ποθ' ὑπὸ τοῦ Ἀρκεσιλάου διὰ τί παρείη ἐκ Θηβῶν, ἔφη,
"ἵν' ὑμᾶς ἀναπεπταμένους ὁρῶν γελῶ". ὅμως δὲ καθαπτόμενος Ἀρκεσιλάου
ἐν τοῖς σίλλοις ἐπήνεκεν αὐτὸν ἐν τῷ ἐπιγραφομένῳ Ἀρκεσιλάου περιδείπνῳ.

The Indalmoi   **1094**—By Ἰνδαλμοί the writer probably meant the deceptive images or appearances of wisdom, brought forward by philosophers.

Sextus, *Adv. math.* XI (= *Ag. the eth.*) 1, fr. 67 D., cited under **1085b**, l. 4:

Μὴ προσέχων δίνοις ** ἡδυλόγου σοφίης.

He sneers at Stoic κατάληψις   **1095**—The following passage of Diogenes shows us his way of attacking the Stoic theory of κατάληψις.

Diog. L. IX 114:

Συνεχές τ' ἐπιλέγειν εἰώθει πρὸς τοὺς τὰς αἰσθήσεις μετ' ἐπιμαρτυροῦντος
τοῦ νοῦ ἐγκρίνοντας,

Συνῆλθεν Ἀτταγᾶς τε καὶ Νουμήνιος.

εἰώθει δὲ καὶ παίζειν τοιαῦτα.

According to Diogenianus Attagas and Numenius were two notorious thieves.
R. D. Hicks translates elegantly:

Conclusion   "Birds of a feather flock together".

Timon appears to have been more a fighting spirit and a scoffer than Pyrrho was, but not yet a dialectician.

---

* ἐκτὸς Bekker; εἰ τὸν Diels; ἔα τὸν codd.
** δίνοις corr. Nauck, followed by Diels; δειλοῖς codd. R. G. Bury proposes αἴνοις: "sweet-voiced Science's tales".

3—THE SECOND OR MIDDLE ACADEMY: ARCESILAUS

1096—Arcesilaus is said to have first taught to suspend judgment by developing opposite arguments, and to have first restored in the Academy the Socratic-Platonic method of question and reply.

Arcesilaus introduced scepticism in the Academy

a. Diog. L. IV 28:

Ἀρκεσίλαος Σεύθου, ὡς Ἀπολλόδωρος ἐν τρίτῳ Χρονικῶν, Πιτάνης τῆς Αἰολίδος. Οὗτός ἐστιν ὁ τῆς μέσης Ἀκαδημίας κατάρξας, πρῶτος ἐπισχὼν τὰς ἀποφάσεις διὰ τὰς ἐναντιότητας τῶν λόγων. πρῶτος δὲ καὶ εἰς ἑκάτερον ἐπεχείρησε, καὶ πρῶτος τὸν λόγον ἐκίνησε τὸν ὑπὸ Πλάτωνος παραδεδομένον καὶ ἐποίησε δι' ἐρωτήσεως καὶ ἀποκρίσεως ἐριστικώτερον.

b. At Athens, he heard first Theophrastus, later Crantor in the Academy (see our nrs. **798** ff.) and succeeded to Crates. We may admit that by Crantor he was introduced into Plato's works, and, as to his sceptical attitude, that he was greatly influenced by Pyrrho.

Crates' successor

Diog. L. IV 32-33:

Κράτητος δὲ ἐκλιπόντος κατέσχε τὴν σχολήν, ἐκχωρήσαντος αὐτῷ Σωκρα-τίδου τινός. Διὰ δὲ τὸ περὶ πάντων ἐπέχειν οὐδὲ βιβλίον, φασί τινες, συνέ-γραψεν. — Ἐῴκει δὴ θαυμάζειν καὶ τὸν Πλάτωνα καὶ τὰ βιβλία ἐκέκτητο αὐτοῦ. ἀλλὰ καὶ τὸν Πύρρωνα κατά τινας ἐζηλώκει. Καὶ τῆς διαλεκτικῆς εἴχετο καὶ τῶν Ἐρετρικῶν ἥπτετο λόγων· ὅθεν καὶ ἐλέγετο ἐπ' αὐτοῦ ὑπ' Ἀρίστωνος·

Πρόσθε Πλάτων, ὄπιθεν Πύρρων, μέσσος Διόδωρος. [1]

1097—In the Academy, Arcesilaus' method meant a radical change, as may appear from the following passages of Cicero.

A revolution in the Academy

a. Cicero, *Ac. post.* I 17:

Utrique (sc. both Academics and Peripatetics), Platonis ubertate completi, certam quandam disciplinae formulam[2] composuerunt, et eam quidem plenam ac refertam: illam autem Socraticam dubitationem de omnibus rebus et nulla affirmatione adhibita consuetudinem disserendi reliquerunt. Ita facta est [disserendi] (quod minime Socrates probabat) ars quaedam philosophiae, et rerum ordo, et descriptio disciplinae[3].

---

[1] The famous dialectician Diodorus Cronus of the Megarian School. See vol. I, **232** ff.
[2] A definite dogmatical form.
[3] A technical philosophy, systematically divided and with a positive doctrinary contents.

b. Cic., *De Oratore* III 67:

(Arcesilaum) quem ferunt eximio quodam usum lepore dicendi ... primum instituisse (quamquam id fuit Socraticum maxime) non quid ipse sentiret ostendere, sed contra id quod quisque se sentire dixisset disputare.

I.e.: he expounded different views, the one opposite to the other, without coming to any positive result;—exactly what was done by Carneades at Rome in the year 155 (below, nr. **1111**).

and in the history of scepticism **1098**—In the history of scepticism, too, Arcesilaus marks an epoch. From the early sceptics he differs by being a dialectician, and this for the sake of pure theory: for him, suspense of judgment was the end, *ataraxia* a concomitant symptom.

Sext. Emp., P. I 232:

Ὁ μέντοι Ἀρκεσίλαος, ὃν τῆς μέσης Ἀκαδημίας ἐλέγομεν εἶναι προστάτην καὶ ἀρχηγόν, πάνυ μοι δοκεῖ τοῖς Πυρρωνείοις κοινωνεῖν λόγοις, ὡς μίαν εἶναι σχεδὸν τὴν κατ' αὐτὸν ἀγωγὴν καὶ τὴν ἡμετέραν. οὔτε γὰρ περὶ ὑπάρξεως ἢ ἀνυπαρξίας τινὸς ἀποφαινόμενος εὑρίσκεται, οὔτε κατὰ πίστιν ἢ ἀπιστίαν προκρίνει τι ἕτερον ἑτέρου, ἀλλὰ περὶ πάντων ἐπέχει. καὶ τέλος μὲν εἶναι τὴν ἐποχήν, ᾗ συνεισέρχεσθαι τὴν ἀταραξίαν ἡμεῖς ἐφάσκομεν.

For Pyrrho, as we saw, *ataraxia* was the end, non-judging the means to reach it.

Arcesilaus' character **1099**—Arcesilaus was a wealthy man and certainly not an ascetic. Diog. L. IV 40 says, he was πολυτελὴς ἄγαν, fond of dining well and of certain other pleasures. For the rest, he and others tell many good things about A.: he was very generous, an excellent friend and discrete in his liberality. Cleanthes defends him when he is censured.

a. Diog. L. VII 171:

Εἰπόντος δέ τινος Ἀρκεσίλαον μὴ ποιεῖν τὰ δέοντα, "Παῦσαι," ἔφη, "καὶ μὴ ψέγε· εἰ γὰρ καὶ λόγῳ τὸ καθῆκον ἀναιρεῖ, τοῖς γοῦν ἔργοις αὐτὸ τιθεῖ.

b. A., on his side, showed great regards for Cleanthes.

Plut., *De discernendo adulatore ab amico* c. 11, p. 55c:

Καὶ Βάττῳ τὴν σχολὴν ἀπεῖπεν Ἀρκεσίλαος, ὅτε πρὸς Κλεάνθην στίχον ἐποίησεν ἐν κωμῳδίᾳ, πείσαντος δὲ τὸν Κλεάνθην καὶ μεταμελομένου διηλλάγη.

---

¹ In this passage, Sextus opposes Arcesilaus, as being a pure sceptic, to Carneades and Critolaus who, in his opinion, were no pure ἐφεκτικοί (cp. our nr. **1077**; infra, **1116**).

1100—a. Plut., in the same work, c. 22, p. 63 D, tells the following story.

Τοιοῦτος Ἀρκεσίλαος περί τε τἆλλα καὶ νοσοῦντος Ἀπελλοῦ τοῦ Χίου τὴν πενίαν καταμαθὼν ἐπανῆλθεν αὖθις ἔχων εἴκοσι δραχμάς, καὶ καθίσας πλησίον "ἐνταῦθα μέν," εἶπεν, "οὐδὲν ἢ τὰ Ἐμπεδοκλέους στοιχεῖα ταυτί·

πῦρ καὶ ὕδωρ καὶ γαῖα καὶ αἰθέρος ἤπιον ὕψος.

ἀλλ᾽ οὐδὲ κατάκεισαι σὺ δεξιῶς," ἅμα δὲ διακινῶν τὸ προσκεφάλαιον αὐτοῦ, λαθὼν ὑπέβαλε τὸ κερμάτιον. ὡς οὖν ἡ διακονοῦσα πρεσβῦτις εὗρε καὶ θαυμάσασα τῷ Ἀπελλῇ προσήγγειλε, γελάσας ἐκεῖνος "Ἀρκεσιλάου", εἶπε, "τοῦτο τὸ κλέμμα".

b. It seems that he was well-known for such-like benefits. Diog. L. IV 37 says:

Ἔν τε τῷ βίῳ κοινωνικώτατος ἐγένετο καὶ εὐεργετῆσαι πρόχειρος ἦν καὶ λαθεῖν τὴν χάριν ἀτυφότατος. —

Follows a similar story as sub **a**. And again, in c. 38:

Καί ποτέ τινος ἀργυρώματα λαβόντος εἰς ὑποδοχὴν φίλων καὶ ἀποστεροῦντος οὐκ ἀπῄτησεν οὐδὲ προσεποιήθη [1].

c. Cp. also Diog. L. IV 32:

Διήκουσε δὲ καὶ Ἱππονίκου τοῦ γεωμέτρου· ὃν καὶ ἔσκωψε τὰ μὲν ἄλλα νωθρὸν ὄντα καὶ χασμώδη, ἐν δὲ τῇ τέχνῃ τεθεωρημένον, εἰπὼν τὴν γεωμετρίαν τοῦ χάσκοντος εἰς τὸ στόμα ἐμπτῆναι. τοῦτον καὶ παρακόψαντα ἀναλαβὼν οἴκοι ἐς τοσοῦτον ἐθεράπευσεν, ἐς ὅσον ἀποκαταστῆσαι.

1101—He was very able in discussion, and very good for his pupils. Diog. L. IV 37:

Ἦν δὲ καὶ εὑρεσιλογώτατος ἀπαντῆσαι εὐστόχως καὶ ἐπὶ τὸ προκείμενον ἀνενεγκεῖν τὴν περίοδον τῶν λόγων καὶ ἅπαντι συναρμόσασθαι καιρῷ. πειστικός τε ὑπὲρ πάνθ᾽ ὁντινοῦν· παρὸ καὶ πλείους πρὸς αὐτὸν ἀπήντων εἰς τὴν σχολήν, καίπερ ὑπ᾽ ὀξύτητος αὐτοῦ ἐπιπληττόμενοι. ἀλλ᾽ ἔφερον ἡδέως· καὶ γὰρ ἦν ἀγαθὸς σφόδρα καὶ ἐλπίδων ὑποπιμπλὰς τοὺς ἀκούοντας.

1102—Two arguments against the Stoic doctrine of assent (see above, nr. 985a, b).

(1) Since it is by assent only that we come to κατάληψις, this assent itself is a judgment which precedes knowledge.

---

[1] "and pretended it had not been borrowed".

a. The argument is given very shortly by Cicero, *Acad. pr.* (*Lucullus*) 18, 59:

Si enim percipi nihil potest—as is held by sceptics, such as Arcesilaus—tollendus assensus est; quid enim est tam futtile quam quicquam appiobare non cognitum?

b. More explicitly in *Acad. post.* (I) 12, 45:

— Arcesilas negabat esse quicquam, quod sciri posset, ne illud quidem ipsum, quod Socrates sibi reliquisset: sic omnia latere censebat in occulto. Neque esse quicquam quod cerni aut intellegi posset: quibus de causis nihil oportere neque profiteri, necque affirmare quemquam, neque assensione approbare. cohibereque semper, et ab omni lapsu continere temeritatem, quae tum esset insignis, cum aut falsa, aut incognita res approbaretur, neque hoc quicquam esse turpius quam cognitioni et perceptioni assensionem approbationemque praecurrere.

Second argument   **1103**—(2) The doctrine of assent is in conflict with the Stoic doctrine of the wise man.

a. Cic., *Acad. pr.* (*Lucullus*) 66-67:

Quid igitur loquar de firmitate sapientis? quem quidem nihil opinari tu quoque, Luculle, concedis. Quod quoniam a te probatur,— haec primum conclusio, quam habeat vim, considera. 67. Si ulli rei sapiens assentietur unquam, aliquando etiam opinabitur. Nunquam autem opinabitur, nulli igitur rei assentietur. Hanc conclusionem Arcesilas probabat.

b. Sextus Emp., *Adv. math.* VII (*Ag. the log.* I) 156:

Πάντων ὄντων ἀκαταλήπτων διὰ τὴν ἀνυπαρξίαν τοῦ Στωϊκοῦ κριτηρίου, εἰ συγκαταθήσεται ὁ σοφός, δοξάσει ὁ σοφός· μηδενὸς γὰρ ὄντος καταληπτοῦ εἰ συγκατατίθεταί τινι, τῷ ἀκαταλήπτῳ συγκαταθήσεται, ἡ δὲ τῷ ἀκαταλήπτῳ συγκατάθεσις δόξα ἐστίν.

Against kataleptic presentation   **1104**—The concept of kataleptic presentation as it was defined by Zeno (see above, **984b**) is criticized by saying shortly that such a presentation does not exist; for there is no true presentation which could not be confounded with an untrue one.

Sextus, *Adv. math.* VII, 249; 252:

— Πρῶτον μὲν τὸ ἀπὸ ὑπάρχοντος γίνεσθαι· πολλαὶ γὰρ τῶν φαντασιῶν προσπίπτουσιν ἀπὸ μὴ ὑπάρχοντος ὥσπερ ἐπὶ τῶν μεμηνότων, αἵτινες οὐκ ἂν εἶεν καταληπτικαί. δεύτερον δὲ τὸ καὶ ἀπὸ ὑπάρχοντος εἶναι καὶ κατ' αὐτὸ τὸ ὑπάρχον· ἔνιαι γὰρ πάλιν ἀπὸ ὑπάρχοντος μέν εἰσιν, οὐκ αὐτὸ δὲ τὸ ὑπάρχον ἰνδάλλονται, ὡς ἐπὶ τοῦ μεμηνότος Ὀρέστου μικρῷ πρότερον ἐδείκνυμεν. εἷλκε μὲν γὰρ φαντασίαν ἀπὸ ὑπάρχοντος τῆς Ἠλέκτρας, οὐ κατ' αὐτὸ δὲ τὸ ὑπάρχον· μίαν γὰρ τῶν Ἐρινύων ὑπελάμβανεν αὐτὴν εἶναι, καθὸ καὶ προσιοῦσαν καὶ τημελεῖν αὐτὸν σπουδάζουσαν ἀπωθεῖται λέγων

μέθες μί' οὖσα τῶν ἐμῶν Ἐρινύων. [1]

καὶ ὁ Ἡρακλῆς [2] ἀπὸ ὑπάρχοντος μὲν ἐκινεῖτο τῶν Θηβῶν, οὐ κατ' αὐτὸ δὲ τὸ ὑπάρχον· καὶ γὰρ κατ' αὐτὸ τὸ ὑπάρχον δεῖ γίνεσθαι τὴν καταληπτικὴν φαντασίαν.

— 252. Τὸ δὲ "οἷα οὐκ ἂν γένοιτο ἀπὸ μὴ ὑπάρχοντος" προσέθεσαν, ἐπεὶ οὐχ ὥσπερ οἱ ἀπὸ τῆς Στοᾶς ἀδύνατον ὑπειλήφασι κατὰ πάντα ἀπαράλλακτόν τινα εὑρεθήσεσθαι, οὕτω καὶ οἱ ἀπὸ τῆς Ἀκαδημίας. ἐκεῖνοι μὲν γάρ φασιν ὅτι ὁ ἔχων τὴν καταληπτικὴν φαντασίαν τεχνικῶς προσβάλλει τῇ ὑπούσῃ τῶν πραγμάτων διαφορᾷ, ἐπείπερ καὶ εἶχέ τι τοιοῦτον ἰδίωμα ἡ τοιαύτη φαντασία παρὰ τὰς ἄλλας φαντασίας καθάπερ οἱ κεράσται παρὰ τοὺς ἄλλους ὄφεις· οἱ δὲ ἀπὸ τῆς Ἀκαδημίας τοὐναντίον φασὶ δύνασθαι τῇ καταληπτικῇ φαντασίᾳ ἀπαράλλακτον εὑρεθήσεσθαι ψεῦδος.

1105—To the question of "How to regulate practical life" A. replies that conduct will be directed rightly by the rule of the εὔλογον.

The εὔλογον a rule for practical life

Sextus, *Adv. math.* VII 158:

Ἀλλ' ἐπεὶ μετὰ τοῦτο ἔδει καὶ περὶ τῆς τοῦ βίου διεξαγωγῆς ζητεῖν, ἥτις οὐ χωρὶς κριτηρίου πέφυκεν ἀποδίδοσθαι, ἀφ' οὗ καὶ ἡ εὐδαιμονία, τουτέστι τὸ τοῦ βίου τέλος, ἠρτημένην ἔχει τὴν πίστιν, φησὶν ὁ Ἀρκεσίλαος ὅτι ὁ περὶ πάντων ἐπέχων κανονιεῖ τὰς αἱρέσεις καὶ φυγὰς καὶ κοινῶς τὰς πράξεις τῷ εὐλόγῳ, κατὰ τοῦτό τε προερχόμενος τὸ κριτήριον κατορθώσει· τὴν μὲν γὰρ εὐδαιμονίαν περιγίνεσθαι διὰ τῆς φρονήσεως, τὴν δὲ φρόνησιν κεῖσθαι ἐν τοῖς κατορθώμασιν, τὸ δὲ κατόρθωμα εἶναι ὅπερ πραχθὲν εὔλογον ἔχει τὴν ἀπολογίαν. ὁ προσέχων οὖν τῷ εὐλόγῳ κατορθώσει καὶ εὐδαιμονήσει.

The wording of this passage is Stoic, e.g. "eudaimonia, i.e. the end of life". Surely, this is not what was taught by Arcesilaus; but we may infer from the passage that A. replied to Stoic opponents saying that sceptics do have a rule for practical life in the εὔλογον, and that happiness, *which according to Stoics is the end of life*, depends on it, since it is attained by φρόνησις.—It should be noticed, further, that A., replying to Stoics, called "right action" (the κατόρθωμα) ὅπερ πραχθὲν εὔλογον ἔχει τὴν ἀπολογίαν. Now this is the formula used by Stoics not to qualify the κατόρθωμα but the καθῆκον. Arcesilaus, then, appears to have opposed Stoic doctrine by saying that, indeed, actions which can be reasonably justified are *moral* actions in the full sense (κατορθώματα), not only *befitting* (καθήκοντα).

---

[1] Eur. *Orest.* 264.
[2] The author seems to confound the mad Heracles with the mad Pentheus who, according to Eur., *Bacch.* 918, saw the image of a "doubled Thebes and a doubled sun".

1106—a. Later, Carneades will speak of πιθανόν to indicate probability. This principle differs from Arcesilaus' εὔλογον by being an *experimental* principle, while the εὔλογον depends entirely on reason. Below, nr. **1116.** Cp. Brochard, *Les sceptiques grecs*, p. 110 f.

b. Numenius ap. Euseb., *Praep. ev.* XIV 6, p. 731 b4, says about A.:
— ἀναιροῦντα καὶ αὐτὸν τὸ ἀληθές, καὶ τὸ ψεῦδος, καὶ τὸ πιθανόν.

Evidently, Arc. rejected the πιθανόν in the sense the Stoics gave to it, viz. of ἀξίωμα τὸ ἄγον εἰς συγκατάθεσιν.

1107—a. Cic., *Acad. pr.* (*Lucullus*) 18, 60, alludes to a kind of esoterical dogmatism of Arc. The method of arguing pro and contra would have been used by him and Carneades as a heuristic method and for the larger circle of their students.

— dicunt veri inveniendi causa contra omnia dici oportere, et pro omnibus. Volo igitur videre quid invenerint. Non solemus, inquit, ostendere. Quae sunt tandem ista mysteria? aut cur celatis, quasi turpe aliquid, sententiam vestram?

b. Cp. Sextus Emp., *P.* I 234:

Εἰ δὲ δεῖ καὶ τοῖς περὶ αὐτοῦ λεγομένοις πιστεύειν, φασὶν ὅτι κατὰ μὲν τὸ πρόχειρον Πυρρώνειος ἐφαίνετο εἶναι, κατὰ δὲ τὴν ἀλήθειαν δογματικὸς ἦν· καὶ ἐπεὶ τῶν ἑταίρων ἀπόπειραν ἐλάμβανε διὰ τῆς ἀπορητικῆς, εἰ εὐφυῶς ἔχουσι πρὸς τὴν ἀνάληψιν τῶν Πλατωνικῶν δογμάτων, δόξαι αὐτὸν ἀπορητικὸν εἶναι, τοῖς μέντοι γε εὐφυέσι τῶν ἑταίρων τὰ Πλάτωνος παρεγχειρεῖν.

c. A far echo of this pretended dogmatism of Arc. is heard in Augustinus, *Contra Acad.* I 17, 38, and in one of his letters, viz. *Ad Diosc.* 118, 16. This is, however, not an independent witness: it depends on Cicero.

d. As to the truth of the story, certainly there has not been anything like a *disciplina arcani* with Arcesilaus. The Academy did not know any secrete doctrine, and Arc. least of all. What is true, is that Arc. intended to restore *Platonism* in the School;—surely not dogmatic Platonism, but there may have been some misunderstanding about the point. This is the explanation offered by Robin, *Pyrrhon*, p. 69, which is in fact most satisfactory. Brochard, p. 117 f., thinks of probabilism, but here we are with Carneades, not with Arc.

4—THE THIRD OR NEW ACADEMY: CARNEADES

1108—Diog. L. IV 62, 63, 65:

Καρνεάδης Ἐπικώμου ἢ Φιλοκώμου ὡς Ἀλέξανδρος ἐν Διαδοχαῖς, Κυρηναῖος. οὗτος τὰ τῶν Στωϊκῶν βιβλία ἀναγνοὺς ἐπιμελῶς καὶ μάλιστα τὰ τοῦ

Χρυσίππου, ἐπιεικῶς αὐτοῖς ἀντέλεγε καὶ εὐημέρει τοσοῦτον, ὥστε ἐκεῖνο ἐπιλέγειν·

Εἰ μὴ γὰρ ἦν Χρύσιππος, οὐκ ἂν ἦν ἐγώ.

Φιλόπονος δ' ἄνθρωπος γέγονεν εἰ καί τις ἄλλος, ἐν μὲν τοῖς φυσικοῖς ἧττον φερόμενος, ἐν δὲ τοῖς ἠθικοῖς μᾶλλον. ὅθεν καὶ ἐκόμα καὶ ἔτρεφεν ὄνυχας ἀσχολίᾳ τῇ περὶ τοὺς λόγους. τοσοῦτον δ' ἴσχυσεν ἐν φιλοσοφίᾳ, ὥστε καὶ τοὺς ῥήτορας ἀπολύσαντας ἐκ τῶν σχολῶν παρ' αὐτὸν ἰέναι καὶ αὐτοῦ ἀκούειν. — Δεινῶς τ' ἦν ἐπιπληκτικὸς καὶ ἐν ταῖς ζητήσεσι δύσμαχος· τά τε δεῖπνα λοιπὸν παρῃτεῖτο διὰ τὰς προειρημένας αἰτίας. —

Φησὶ δὲ Ἀπολλόδωρος ἐν Χρονικοῖς ἀπελθεῖν αὐτὸν ἐξ ἀνθρώπων ἔτει τετάρτῳ τῆς δευτέρας καὶ ἑξηκοστῆς καὶ ἑκατοστῆς Ὀλυμπιάδος (a. 129-128), βιώσαντα ἔτη πέντε πρὸς τοῖς ὀγδοήκοντα. Φέρονται δ' αὐτοῦ ἐπιστολαὶ πρὸς Ἀριαράθην τὸν Καππαδοκίας βασιλέα. τὰ δὲ λοιπὰ αὐτοῦ οἱ μαθηταὶ συνέγραψαν· αὐτὸς δὲ κατέλιπεν οὐδέν.

We know his arguments mainly from Cicero and from Sextus Empiricus, who both go back to Clitomachus, a direct pupil of Carneades, acute and precise. Clitomachus succeeded to Carneades as head of the School and wrote many books. Cp. Diog. L. IV 67.

1109—In the year 155 Carneades and two other philosophers came to Rome as ambassadors from Athens.

Carneades at Rome

Plut., *Cato maior* c. 22, p. 349:

Ἤδη δὲ αὐτοῦ (sc. Cato maior) γέροντος γεγονότος πρέσβεις Ἀθήνηθεν ἦλθον εἰς Ῥώμην οἱ περὶ Καρνεάδην τὸν Ἀκαδημαϊκὸν καὶ Διογένη τὸν Στωϊκὸν φιλόσοφον, καταδίκην τινὰ παραιτησόμενοι τοῦ δήμου τῶν Ἀθηναίων. — εὐθὺς οὖν οἱ φιλολογώτατοι τῶν νεανίσκων ἐπὶ τοὺς ἄνδρας ἵεντο, καὶ συνῆσαν ἀκροώμενοι καὶ θαυμάζοντες αὐτούς, μάλιστα δ' ἡ Καρνεάδου χάρις, ἧς δύναμίς τε πλείστη καὶ δόξα τῆς δυνάμεως οὐκ ἀποδέουσα, μεγάλων ἐπιλαβομένη καὶ φιλανθρώπων ἀκροατηρίων ὡς πνεῦμα τὴν πόλιν ἠχῆς ἐνέπλησε. καὶ λόγος κατεῖχεν, ὡς ἀνὴρ Ἕλλην εἰς ἔκπληξιν ὑπερφυὴς πάντα κηλῶν καὶ χειρούμενος ἔρωτα δεινὸν ἐμβέβληκε τοῖς νέοις, ὑφ' οὗ τῶν ἄλλων ἡδονῶν καὶ διατριβῶν ἐκπεσόντες ἐνθουσιῶσι περὶ φιλοσοφίαν. ταῦτα τοῖς μὲν ἄλλοις ἤρεσκε Ῥωμαίοις γινόμενα, καὶ τὰ μειράκια παιδείας Ἑλληνικῆς μεταλαμβάνοντα καὶ συνόντα θαυμαζομένοις ἀνδράσιν ἡδέως ἑώρων. ὁ δὲ Κάτων ἐξ ἀρχῆς τε τοῦ ζήλου τῶν λόγων παραρρέοντος εἰς τὴν πόλιν ἤχθετο φοβούμενος, μὴ τὸ φιλότιμον ἐνταῦθα τρέψαντες οἱ νέοι τὴν ἐπὶ τῷ λέγειν δόξαν ἀγαπήσωσι μᾶλλον τῆς ἀπὸ τῶν ἔργων καὶ τῶν στρατειῶν, ἐπεὶ δὲ προὔβαινεν ἡ δόξα τῶν φιλοσόφων ἐν τῇ πόλει καὶ τοὺς πρώτους λόγους αὐτῶν πρὸς τὴν σύγκλητον ἀνὴρ ἐπιφανὴς

σπουδάσας αὐτὸς καὶ δεηθεὶς ἡρμήνευσε, Γάϊος Ἀκίλιος, ἔγνω μετ’ εὐπρεπείας
ἀποδιαπομπήσασθαι τοὺς φιλοσόφους ἅπαντας ἐκ τῆς πόλεως. καὶ παρελθὼν
εἰς τὴν σύγκλητον ἐμέμψατο τοῖς ἄρχουσιν, ὅτι πρεσβεία κάθηται πολὺν χρόνον
ἄπρακτος ἀνδρῶν, οἳ περὶ παντὸς οὗ βούλοιντο ῥαδίως πείθειν δύνανται· δεῖν
οὖν τὴν ταχίστην γνῶναί τι καὶ ψηφίσασθαι περὶ τῆς πρεσβείας. ὅπως οὗτοι
μὲν ἐπὶ τὰς σχολὰς τραπόμενοι διαλέγωνται παισὶν Ἑλλήνων, οἱ δὲ Ῥωμαίων
νέοι τῶν νόμων καὶ τῶν ἀρχόντων ὡς πρότερον ἀκούωσι.

His fame as a dialectician **1110—a.** Lactantius, *Inst.* V 14:

Carneades Academicae sectae philosophus, cuius in disserendo quae
vis fuerit, quae eloquentia, quod acumen, qui nescit ipsum, ex praedica-
tione Ciceronis intelleget aut Lucilli, aput quem disserens Neptunus de
re difficillima ostendit non posse id explicari,

non Carneaden si ipsum Orcus remittat, —

b. Cp. Cic., *De oratore* II 38, 161:

Carneadis vero vis incredibilis illa dicendi, et varietas, perquam esset
optanda nobis: qui nullam unquam in illis suis disputationibus rem
defendit quam non probarit; nullam oppugnavit quam non everterit.

c. Numenius ap. Euseb., *Praep. Ev.* XIV 8, p. 738 b4:

Καὶ μέντοι λέγων ὁ Καρνεάδης ἐψυχαγώγει καὶ ἠνδραποδίζετο.

His method **1111**—What was his method, can be inferred fairly well from what
Lactantius says about Carneades’ expositions on justice, held at Rome,—
the report of Furius Philus in Cicero’s *Republic* III is lost—, if it is
combined with a passage in Cicero’s *De finibus*.

a. Lactantius, *Inst.* V 14:

(The beginning of the sentence was cited under **1110a**).

— Is cum legatus ab Atheniensibus Romam missus esset, disputavit
de iustitia copiose audiente Galba et Catone Censorio maximis tunc
oratoribus. sed idem disputationem suam postridie contraria disputatione
subvertit et iustitiam quam pridie laudaverat sustulit, non quidem
philosophi gravitate, cuius firma et stabilis debet esse sententia, sed
quasi oratorio exercitii genere in utramque partem disserendi. quod ille
facere solebat, ut alios quidlibet adserentes posset refutare. eam disputationem, qua iustitia evertitur, aput Ciceronem Lucius Furius recor-
datur, credo quoniam de re publica disserebat, ut defensionem laudatio-

nemque eius induceret, sine qua putabat regi non posse rem publicam. Carneades autem ut Aristotelem refelleret ac Platonem iustitiae patronos, prima illa disputatione collegit ea omnia quae pro iustitia dicebantur, ut posset illam, sicut fecit, evertere.

Carn., then, appears to have expounded on the first day of his disputation all the arguments in favour of justice, following the line of the three great dogmatic Schools, viz. those of Plato, Aristotle and the Stoa. On the second day he developed all the arguments against it. That such was his usual way of proceeding, may be inferred from what Cicero says on the *Carneadea divisio*.

b. Cic., *De fin.* V 6, 16, says, speaking of the means of finding a rule of happiness:

Quod quoniam in quo sit magna dissensio est, Carneadea nobis adhibenda divisio est, qua noster Antiochus libenter uti solet. Ille igitur vidit, non modo quot fuissent adhuc philosophorum de summo bono, sed quot omnino esse possent sententiae.

1112—Against the kataleptic presentation Carneades repeats Arcesilaus' argument that an untrue presentation can present itself to us with as much evidence as a true one [1]. It is expounded by Cicero in *Acad. pr.* (*Lucullus*) 26, 84 - 28, 90, and by Sextus Emp., *Adv. math.* VII (= *Ag. the log.* I) 401-411. Here are the main points of the argument.

Arguments against the Stoic criterium of truth

a. Sextus Emp., *Adv. math.* VII 403-405, 410-411:

Καὶ τεκμήριον τῆς ἀπαραλλαξίας τὸ ἐπ' ἴσης ταύτας ἐναργεῖς καὶ πληκτικὰς εὑρίσκεσθαι, τοῦ δὲ ἐπ' ἴσης πληκτικὰς καὶ ἐναργεῖς εἶναι τὸ τὰς ἀκολούθους πράξεις ἐπιζεύγνυσθαι. ὥσπερ γὰρ ἐν τοῖς ὕπαρ ὁ μὲν διψῶν ἀρυόμενος ποτὸν ἥδεται, ὁ δὲ θηρίον ἢ ἄλλο τι τῶν δειμαλέων φεύγων βοᾷ καὶ κέκραγεν, οὕτω καὶ κατὰ τοὺς ὕπνους ἡ μὲν διάχυσίς ἐστι τοῖς διψῶσι καὶ ἀπὸ κρήνης πίνειν δοκοῦσιν, ἀνάλογον δὲ φόβος τοῖς δειματουμένοις·

ταφὼν γὰρ ἀνόρουσεν Ἀχιλλεύς
χερσί τε συμπλατάγησεν, ἔπος τ' ὀλοφυδνὸν ἔειπεν· [2]

καὶ ὃν τρόπον ἐν καταστάσει τοῖς τρανότατα φαινομένοις πιστεύομεν καὶ συγκατατιθέμεθα, οἷον Δίωνι μὲν ὡς Δίωνι, Θέωνι δὲ ὡς Θέωνι προσφερόμενοι, οὕτω καὶ ἐν μανίᾳ τὸ παραπλήσιον πάσχουσί τινες. ὁ γοῦν Ἡρακλῆς μανείς, καὶ λαβὼν φαντασίαν ἀπὸ τῶν ἰδίων παίδων ὡς Εὐρυσθέως, τὴν ἀκόλουθον πρᾶξιν ταύτῃ τῇ φαντασίᾳ συνῆψεν. ἀκόλουθον δ' ἦν τὸ τοὺς τοῦ ἐχθροῦ παῖδας ἀνελεῖν, ὅπερ καὶ ἐποίησεν. εἰ οὖν καταληπτικαί τινές εἰσι φαντασίαι παρόσον ἐπάγονται ἡμᾶς εἰς συγκατάθεσιν καὶ εἰς τὸ τὴν ἀκόλουθον αὐταῖς πρᾶξιν

---

[1] Above, nr. **1104**.   [2] *Iliad* 23, 101.

συνάπτειν, ἐπεὶ καὶ ψευδεῖς τοιαῦται πεφήνασι, λεκτέον ἀπαραλλάκτους εἶναι ταῖς καταληπτικαῖς φαντασίαις τὰς ἀκαταλήπτους. —

Ὁ δ᾽ αὐτὸς λόγος ἐστὶ καὶ ἐπὶ διδύμων· λήψεται γὰρ ψευδῆ φαντασίαν ὁ σπουδαῖος καὶ ἀπὸ ὑπάρχοντος καὶ κατ᾽ αὐτὸ τὸ ὑπάρχον ἐναπομεμαγμένην καὶ ἐναπεσφραγισμένην ἔχων τὴν φαντασίαν, ἐὰν ἀπὸ Κάστορος ὡς ἀπὸ Πολυδεύκους φαντασιωθῇ. ἐντεῦθεν γοῦν καὶ ὁ ἐγκεκαλυμμένος συνέστη λόγος· ἐὰν γὰρ προκύψαντος δράκοντος θέλωμεν τῷ ὑποκειμένῳ ἐπιστῆναι, εἰς πολλὴν ἀπορίαν ἐμπεσούμεθα, καὶ οὐχ ἕξομεν λέγειν πότερον ὁ αὐτός ἐστι δράκων τῷ πρότερον προκύψαντι ἢ ἕτερος, πολλῶν ἐνεσπειραμένων τῷ αὐτῷ φωλεῷ δρακόντων. οὐ τοίνυν ἔχει τι ἰδίωμα ἡ καταληπτικὴ φαντασία ᾧ διαφέρει τῶν ψευδῶν τε καὶ ἀκαταλήπτων φαντασιῶν.

b. To these arguments, the first of which were, in any case, already brought forward by Arcesilaus, Carneades added two others: first that of colour there is no kataleptic presentation, since colour changes with time and circumstances; but not of other sensible qualities either.

Sextus, ib. 411-414:

Πρὸς τούτοις, εἴ τι ἄλλο καταληπτικόν τινός ἐστι, καὶ ἡ ὅρασις. οὐχὶ δέ γ᾽ αὕτη καταληπτική τινός ἐστιν, ὡς παραστήσομεν· οὐκ ἄρα ἔστι τι καταληπτικόν τινος. ἡ γὰρ ὅρασις λαμβάνειν μὲν δοκεῖ χρώματα καὶ μεγέθη καὶ σχήματα καὶ κινήσεις, τούτων δὲ οὐδὲν λαμβάνει, καθάπερ εὐθὺς ἀπὸ τῶν χρωμάτων ἀρξαμένοις ἡμῖν φανεῖται. εἴπερ οὖν ἡ ὅρασις καταλαμβάνεταί τι χρῶμα, φασὶν οἱ ἐξ Ἀκαδημίας, καὶ τὸ τοῦ ἀνθρώπου καταλήψεται· οὐ καταλαμβάνεται δὲ τοῦτο· οὐδ᾽ ἄλλο τοίνυν καταλήψεται χρῶμα. καὶ ὅτι οὐ καταλαμβάνεται, πρόδηλον· μεταβάλλει γὰρ κατὰ ὥρας ἐνεργείας φύσεις ἡλικίας περιστάσεις νόσους ὑγείαν ὕπνον ἐγρήγορσιν, ὥστε τὸ μὲν οὕτως αὐτὸ ποικίλλεσθαι γινώσκειν ἡμᾶς, τὸ δὲ τί ἐστι τὸ κατ᾽ ἀλήθειαν ἀγνοεῖν. ταύτῃ τε εἰ τοῦτο μή ἐστι καταληπτόν, οὐδ᾽ ἄλλο τι γενήσεται γνώριμον. καὶ μὴν καὶ ἐπὶ σχήματος τὸ αὐτὸ γένος τῆς ἀπορίας εὑρήσομεν· τὸ γὰρ αὐτὸ λεῖον καὶ τραχὺ ὑποπίπτει ὡς ἐπὶ τῶν γραφῶν, στρογγύλον τε καὶ τετράγωνον ὡς ἐπὶ πύργων, εὐθύ τε καὶ κεκλασμένον ὡς ἐπὶ τῆς ἐξάλου τε καὶ ἐνάλου κώπης, καὶ ἐπὶ κινήσεως κινούμενον καὶ ἠρεμοῦν, ὡς ἐπὶ τῶν ἐν νηὶ καθεζομένων ἢ ἐπὶ τῶν ἐν αἰγιαλοῖς ἑστώτων.

Cp. Berkeley's doctrine of the subjectivity of the sensible qualities.

c. Chrysippus said, one should not lightly give one's assent to a presentation: in doubtful cases one must let the hegemonikon take some rest (ἡσυχάζειν). Now, Carn. asks: How is it possible to find a transition from the last kataleptic presentation to the first non-kataleptic one?

Cic., *Acad. pr.* (Luc.) 29, 93-94:

Placet enim Chrysippo, cum gradatim interrogetur verbi causa tria pauca sint anne multa, aliquanto prius quam ad multa perveniat quiescere. (Id est quod ab his dicitur ἡσυχάζειν). Per me vel stertas licet, inquit Carneades, non modo quiescas. Sed quid proficit? sequitur enim qui te ex somno excitet et eodem modo interroget: quo in numero conticuisti, si ad eum numerum unum addidero, multane erunt? progrediere rursus, quoad videbitur. quid plura? hoc enim fateris, neque ultimum te paucorum neque primum multorum respondere posse. cuius generis error ita manat, ut non videam quo non possit accedere. Nihil me laedit, inquit; ego enim ut agitator callidus priusquam ad finem veniam equos sustinebo, eoque magis si locus is quo ferentur equi praeceps erit. sic me, inquit, ante sustineo nec diutius captiose interroganti respondeo. Si habes quod liqueat neque respondes, superbe; si non habes, ne tu quidem percipis [1].

1113—Next, Carn. attacks the fundamental thesis of Stoic logic: that a proposition must be necessarily true or untrue.

Against the basis of logic, the law of contradiction

a. Cic., *Acad. pr.* (*Luc.*) 29, 95:

Nempe fundamentum dialecticae est, quidquid enuntietur (id autem appellant ἀξίωμα, quod est quasi effatum) aut verum esse aut falsum. Quid igitur? haec vera an falsa sunt: "si te mentiri dicis idque verum dicis, mentiris" et „*si te mentiri dicis idque mentiris*, verum dicis?" haec scilicet inexplicabilia esse dicitis; quod est odiosius quam illa quae nos non comprehensa et non percepta dicimus.—Sed hoc omitto, illud quaero: si ista explicari non possunt nec eorum ullum iudicium invenitur, ut respondere possitis verane an falsa sint, ubi est illa definitio, effatum esse id quod aut verum aut falsum sit?

b. Now this argument overthrows the whole logic.

Cic., ib. 30, 97-98:

"Aut vivet cras Hermarchus aut non vivet." — Si talis disiunctio falsa potest esse, nulla vera est. mecum vero quid habent litium, qui ipsorum disciplinam sequor? cum aliquid huius modi inciderat, sic ludere Carneades solebat: "si recte conclusi, teneo; sin vitiose, minam Diogenes mihi reddet". ab eo enim Stoico dialecticam didicerat; haec autem merces erat dialecticorum.

---

[1] I.e.; you have no more a kataleptic presentation than I have.

Against
proof

1114—In Sextus Emp., *Adv. math.* VIII (= *Ag. the log.* II) 337 ff. we find some arguments against proof which, probably, go back to Carneades.

It has been argued in the preceding passage (322-325) that proof is a non-evident thing, if concerned with non-evident objects. Therefore, the author goes on in the following chapters, proof is not acceptable without a proof,—either a generic or a particular one. But both are impossible, for the generic proof depends on the particular, and the particular proof presupposes the generic.

Sextus, *Adv. math.* VIII 340-343:

'Επεὶ τοίνυν ἄδηλόν ἐστιν ἡ ἀπόδειξις, ὡς ἐπελογισάμεθα, ὀφείλει ἀποδεδεῖχ-θαι· πᾶν γὰρ ἄδηλον ἀναποδείκτως λαμβανόμενόν ἐστιν ἄπιστον. ἤτοι οὖν ὑπὸ γενικῆς ἀποδείξεως καταστήσεται τὸ εἶναί τι ἀπόδειξιν ἢ ὑπὸ εἰδικῆς. ἀλλ' ὑπὸ μὲν εἰδικῆς οὐδαμῶς· οὔπω γὰρ οὐδεμία καθίσταται εἰδικὴ ἀπόδειξις διὰ τὸ μήπω ὡμολογῆσθαι τὴν γενικήν. ὡς γὰρ μηδέπω σαφοῦς ὄντος τοῦ ὅτι ἔστι ζῷον, οὐδὲ ὅτι ἵππος ἔστι γνώριμον καθέστηκεν, οὕτω μηδέπω συν-ομολογηθέντος τοῦ ὅτι ἔστι γενικὴ ἀπόδειξις, οὐκ ἂν εἴη τις τῶν ἐπὶ μέρους ἀποδείξεων πιστή, μετὰ τοῦ καὶ εἰς τὸν δι' ἀλλήλων τρόπον ἡμᾶς ἐμπίπτειν· ἵνα μὲν γὰρ ἡ γενικὴ ἀπόδειξις βεβαιωθῇ, τὴν εἰδικὴν ἡμᾶς ἔχειν δεῖ πιστήν, ἵνα δὲ ἡ εἰδικὴ ὁμολογηθῇ, τὴν γενικὴν ἔχειν βέβαιον, ὥστε μήτε ἐκείνην πρὸ ταύτης ἔχειν δύνασθαι μήτε ταύτην πρὸ ἐκείνης. οὐκοῦν ὑπὸ μὲν εἰδικῆς ἀπο-δείξεως ἀμήχανον τὴν γενικὴν ἀποδειχθῆναι. καὶ μὴν οὐδ' ὑπὸ γενικῆς· αὕτη γάρ ἐστιν ἡ ζητουμένη, ἄδηλος δὲ οὖσα καὶ ζητουμένη οὐκ ἂν εἴη κατασκευασ-τικὴ ἑαυτῆς, ἥ γε καὶ τῶν ἐκκαλυπτόντων αὐτὴν ἔχρῃζεν.

The argument is directed not against Aristotle's conception of proof—for Aristotle taught that proof must depend on ἄμεσα [1]—, but against Chrysippus, who held that proof must be founded on proof.

Akatalepsia

1115—Conclusion: strictly speaking, it is impossible to know anything. Since there is no kataleptic presentation, there are only ἀκατάληπτα.

This means: we are strictly confined to our individual πάθη and can never be sure whether or not there is any exterior object behind them.

a. Cic., *Acad. pr.* (*Luc.*) 15, 48:

— Cum mens moveatur ipsa per sese, ut et ea declarant quae cogitatione depingimus et ea quae vel dormientibus vel furiosis videntur, non, inquiunt, veri simile sit sic etiam mentem moveri, ut non modo non inter-noscat vera illa visa sint anne falsa, sed ut in is nihil intersit omnino, ut si qui tremerent et exalbescerent vel ipsi per se motu mentis aliquo vel objecta terribili re extrinsecus, nihil ut esset qui distingueretur

---

[1] Vol. II, nr. **458a, b.**

tremor ille et pallor, neque ut quicquam interesset <inter> intestinum
et oblatum.

b. Another curious argument of sceptics, may be of Carneades,
is m entioned in the previous lines (15, 47):

Nam cum dicatis, inquiunt, visa quaedam mitti a deo, velut ea quae
in somnis videantur quaeque oraculis auspiciis extis declarentur (haec
enim aiunt probari a Stoicis, quos contra disputant) — quaerunt quonam
modo falsa visa quae sint, ea deus efficere possit probabilia, quae autem
plane proxume ad verum accedant efficere non possit, aut si ea quoque
possit, cur illa non possit quae perdifficiliter internoscantur tamen, et
si haec, cur non inter quae nihil sit omnino?

The argument reminds us of Descartes, who based human knowledge on the
confidence that it is impossible that God should be willing to deceive man. See
on this principle: B. J. H. Ovink, *Philosophie und Sophistik*, Den Haag 1940,
p. 234 f.

1116—a. According to Sextus Emp., *P.* I 227, Carneades differed
from the Sceptics by admitting that some impressions are probable, others **Probability**
improbable.

Τάς τε φαντασίας ἡμεῖς μὲν ἴσας λέγομεν εἶναι κατὰ πίστιν ἢ ἀπιστίαν ὅσον
ἐπὶ τῷ λόγῳ, ἐκεῖνοι δὲ τὰς μὲν πιθανὰς εἶναί φασι, τὰς δὲ ἀπιθάνους.

We may infer from this text that probability, as it was conceived by Carn.,
was not only an ethical-practical principle, but had a theoretical value, too.

b. Carn. distinguished three degrees of probability; the third **Three**
and highest may be called practical certitude. **degrees of**
probability

Sextus, *P.* I 227-229:

Καὶ τῶν πιθανῶν δὲ λέγουσι διαφοράς· τὰς μὲν γὰρ αὐτὸ μόνον πιθανὰς
ὑπάρχειν ἡγοῦνται, τὰς δὲ πιθανὰς καὶ διεξωδευμένας, τὰς δὲ πιθανὰς καὶ
περιωδευμένας καὶ ἀπερισπάστους. οἷον ἐν οἴκῳ σκοτεινῷ ποσῶς κειμένου
σχοινίου ἐσπειραμένου πιθανὴ ἁπλῶς φαντασία γίνεται ἀπὸ τούτου ὡς ἀπὸ
ὄφεως τῷ ἀθρόως ἐπεισελθόντι· τῷ μέντοι περισκοπήσαντι ἀκριβῶς καὶ
διεξοδεύσαντι τὰ περὶ αὐτό, οἷον ὅτι οὐ κινεῖται, ὅτι τὸ χρῶμα τοῖόν ἐστι,
καὶ τῶν ἄλλων ἕκαστον, φαίνεται σχοινίον κατὰ τὴν φαντασίαν τὴν πιθανὴν
καὶ περιωδευμένην. ἡ δὲ καὶ ἀπερίσπαστος φαντασία τοιάδε ἐστίν. λέγεται ὁ
Ἡρακλῆς ἀποθανοῦσαν τὴν Ἄλκηστιν αὖθις ἐξ Ἅιδου ἀναγαγεῖν καὶ δεῖξαι τῷ
Ἀδμήτῳ, ὃς πιθανὴν ἐλάμβανεν φαντασίαν τῆς Ἀλκήστιδος καὶ περιωδευμένην·
ἐπεὶ μέντοι ᾔδει ὅτι τέθνηκεν, περιεσπᾶτο αὐτοῦ ἡ διάνοια ἀπὸ τῆς συγκαταθέσεως καὶ πρὸς ἀπιστίαν ἔκλινεν. προκρίνουσιν οὖν οἱ ἐκ τῆς νέας Ἀκαδημίας

τῆς μὲν πιθανῆς ἁπλῶς τὴν πιθανὴν καὶ περιωδευμένην φαντασίαν, ἀμφοτέρων
δὲ τούτων τὴν πιθανὴν καὶ περιωδευμένην καὶ ἀπερίσπαστον.

It has been rightly observed, both by Brochard and Robin, that what is described
in this passage is a kind of experimental method, the value of which is not confined
to the field of ethics.

**The
existence
of Gods**
1117—The Stoic arguments for the existence of God(s) are criticized
by Carneades as follows.

a. First, he opposes Zeno's argument that the cosmos must be an
intelligent being. Cic., *De n.d.* III 9, 22-23:

**The cosmos
an intelligent
being?**
Zeno enim ita concludit: quod ratione utitur, id melius est quam id
quod ratione non utitur; nihil autem mundo melius; ratione igitur
mundus utitur. Hoc si placet, iam efficies ut mundus optime librum
legere videatur; Zenonis enim vestigiis hoc modo rationem poteris
concludere: quod litteratum est, id est melius quam quod non est litteratum; nihil autem mundo melius; litteratus igitur est mundus. Isto
modo etiam disertus et quidem mathematicus musicus, omni denique
doctrina eruditus, postremo philosophus.

b. In fact, neither the cosmos nor the celestial bodies are divine.
Ib., 23-24:

**Neither the
universe nor
the stars
are gods**
Non est igitur mundus deus; et tamen nihil est eo melius: nihil est
enim eo pulchrius, nihil salutarius nobis, nihil ornatius aspectu motuque
constantius. Quod si mundus universus non est deus, ne stellae quidem,
quas tu innumerabiles in deorum numero reponebas. quarum te cursus
aequabiles aeternique delectabant, nec mehercule iniuria, sunt enim
admirabili incredibilique constantia. sed non omnia, Balbe, quae cursus
certos et constantis habent, ea deo potius tribuenda sunt quam naturae. —
Vide, quaeso, si omnis motus omniaquae quae certis temporibus ordinem
suum conservant divina dicimus, ne tertianas quoque febres et quar-
tanas divinas esse dicendum sit, quarum reversione et motu quid potest
esse constantius?

1118—Next, Chrysippus' argument that the world and what is in it
must be made by God.

**Why should
not the
universe
have been
made by
nature?**
a. Cic., *De n.d.* III 10, 25-26:

Et Chrysippus tibi acute dicere videbatur, homo sine dubio versutus
et callidus —; is igitur: ,,Si aliquid est'', inquit, ,,quod homo efficere non
possit, qui id efficit melior est homine; homo autem haec quae in mundo

sunt efficere non potest; qui potuit igitur, is praestat homini; homini autem praestare quis possit nisi deus? est igitur deus." Haec omnia in eodem quo illa Zenonis errore versantur. quid enim sit melius, quid praestabilius, quid inter naturam et rationem intersit, non distinguitur. Idemque, si dei non sint, negat esse in omni natura quicquam homine melius; id autem putare quemquam hominem, nihil homine esse melius, summae adrogantiae censet esse.

b. Ib., 26:

Et "Si domus pulchra sit, intellegamus eam dominis" inquit "aedificatam esse, non muribus; sic igitur mundum deorum domum existimare debemus". Ita prorsus existimarem, si illum aedificatum, non quem ad modum docebo a natura conformatum putarem.

c. Cp. Cic., *Acad. pr.* (*Lucullus*) 38, 121:

Negas sine deo posse quicquam: ecce tibi e transverso Lampsacenus Strato, qui det isti deo inmunitatem—magni quidem muneris; sed cum sacerdotes deorum vacationem habeant, quanto est aequius habere ipsos deos! negat opera deorum se uti ad fabricandum mundum, quaecumque sint docet omnia effecta esse natura, nec ut ille qui asperis et levibus et hamatis uncinatisque corporibus concreta haec esse dicat interiecto inani: somnia censet haec esse Democriti non docentis, sed optantis. ipse autem singulas mundi partes persequens, quidquid aut sit aut fiat naturalibus fieri aut factum esse docet ponderibus et motibus. ne ille et deum opere magno liberat et me timore. quis enim potest, cum existimet curari se a deo, non et dies et noctes divinum numen horrere et si quid adversi acciderit, quod cui non accidit, extimescere ne id iure evenerit? nec Stratoni tamen adsentior nec vero tibi; modo hoc modo illud probabilius videtur.

1119—The fact that man is a rational being does not prove divine Providence and its benevolence towards man.

Are the Gods benevolent towards man?

a. Cic., *De n.d.* III 31, 78:

Si homines rationem bono consilio a dis immortalibus datam in fraudem malitiamque convertunt, non dari illam quam dari humano generi melius fuit. Ut si medicus sciat eum aegrotum, qui iussus sit vinum sumere, meracius sumpturum statimque periturum, magna sit in culpa, sic vestra ista Providentia reprehendenda, quae rationem dederit iis quos scierit ea perverse et improbe usuros. Nisi forte dicitis eam nescisse. Utinam quidem! sed non audebitis. non enim ignoro quanti eius nomen putetis.

b. If the gods are benevolent towards man, why then so many harmful beings on earth and in the sea?

Cic., *Acad. pr.* (*Luc.*) 38, 120:

Quaero enim cur deus, omnia nostra causa cum faceret (sic enim vultis), tantam vim natricum viperarumque fecerit, cur mortifera tam multa ac perniciosa terra marique disperserit.

Inconsistencies in the Stoic notion of God

1120—a. If the gods are material, they cannot be eternal.

Cic., *De n.d.* III 12, 29:

Illa autem quae Carneades adferebat, quem ad modum dissolvitis? si nullum corpus immortale sit, nullum esse corpus sempiternum: corpus autem immortale nullum esse, ne individuum quidem nec quod dirimi distrahive non possit; cumque omne animal patibilem naturam habeat, nullum est eorum quod effugiat accipiendi aliquid extrinsecus, id est, quasi ferendi et patiendi necessitatem, et si omne animal tale est, inmortale nullum est. Ergo itidem, si omne animal secari ac dividi potest, nullum est eorum individuum, nullum aeternum; atqui omne animal ad accipiendam vim externam et ferundam paratum est; mortale igitur omne animal et dissolubile et dividuum sit necesse est.

b. If the gods are living beings, they must have perception and, consequently, be liable to pain. But then, they must be corruptible.
Ib. 13, 32:

Et, ut haec omittamus, tamen animal nullum inveniri potest quod neque natum umquam sit et semper sit futurum. omne enim animal sensus habet; sentit igitur et calida et frigida et dulcia et amara, nec potest ullo sensu iucunda accipere, non accipere contraria; si igitur voluptatis sensum capit, doloris etiam capit; quod autem dolorem accipit, id accipiat etiam interitum necesse est; omne igitur animal confitendum est esse mortale.

c. If the gods are happy, they must possess virtue. But how could they be self-controlled or brave?

Sextus Emp., *Adv. math.* IX (= *Ag. the phys.* I) 152, 157-160:

Εἴγε μὴν ἔστι τὸ θεῖον, πάντως καὶ ζῷόν ἐστιν. εἰ δὲ ζῷόν ἐστιν, πάντως καὶ πανάρετόν ἐστι καὶ εὐδαῖμον· εὐδαιμονία δὲ χωρὶς ἀρετῆς οὐ δύναται ὑποστῆναι· εἰ δὲ πανάρετός ἐστι, καὶ πάσας ἔχει τὰς ἀρετάς. ἀλλ' οὐ πάσας μὲν ἔχει τὰς ἀρετάς, οὐχὶ δέ γε καὶ ἐγκράτειαν ἔχει καὶ καρτερίαν. οὐχὶ δέ γε ταύτας μὲν ἔχει τὰς ἀρετάς, οὐχὶ δέ γε ἔστι τινὰ δυσαπόσχετα καὶ δυσεγκαρτέρητα τῷ θεῷ. —

Εἰ δὲ ἔστι τινὰ δυσαπόσχετα καὶ δυσυπομένητα τῷ θεῷ, ἔστι τινὰ καὶ τὰ ἐπὶ τὸ χεῖρον αὐτοῦ μεταβλητικὰ καὶ ὀχλήσεως ποιητικά. ἀλλ' εἰ τοῦτο, δεκτικός ἐστιν ὀχλήσεως ὁ θεὸς καὶ τῆς ἐπὶ τὸ χεῖρον μεταβολῆς, διὸ καὶ φθορᾶς. ὥστε εἴπερ ἔστιν ὁ θεός, φθαρτός ἐστιν· οὐχὶ δὲ τὸ δεύτερον, οὐκ ἄρα τὸ πρῶτον. Ἔτι δὲ σὺν τοῖς προκειμένοις, εἰ πανάρετόν ἐστι τὸ θεῖον, καὶ ἀνδρείαν ἔχει· εἰ δὲ ἀνδρείαν ἔχει, ἐπιστήμην ἔχει δεινῶν καὶ οὐ δεινῶν καὶ τῶν μεταξύ, καὶ εἰ τοῦτο, ἔστι τι θεῷ δεινόν. οὐ γὰρ δή γε ὁ ἀνδρεῖος διὰ ταῦτά ἐστιν ἀνδρεῖος ὅτι ἐπιστήμην ἔχει τοῦ ποῖά ἐστι τὰ δεινὰ τῷ γείτονι, ἀλλὰ τὰ αὐτῷ. ἅπερ οὐκ ἀπαράλλακτά ἐστι τοῖς τοῦ πλησίον δεινοῖς. ὥστε ἐπεὶ ἀνδρεῖός ἐστιν ὁ θεός, ἔστι τι αὐτῷ δεινόν. εἰ ἔστι τι θεῷ δεινόν, ἔστι τι τῷ θεῷ ὀχλήσεως ποιητικόν. εἰ δὲ τοῦτο, ἐπιδεκτικός ἐστιν ὀχλήσεως, διὰ δὲ τοῦτο καὶ φθορᾶς. ὅθεν εἰ ἔστι τὸ θεῖον, φθαρτόν ἐστιν. οὐκ ἄρα ἔστιν.

1121—As to the gods of popular religion, adopted by the Stoics, Carneades proceeds by *soritai* [1].

The gods of popular religion ridiculized by soritai

a. Cic., *De n.d.* III 17, 43-44:

Si enim vos sequar, dic quid ei respondeam qui me sic roget: "Si di sunt, suntne etiam Nymphae deae? si Nymphae, Panisci etiam et Satyri; hi autem non sunt; ne Nymphae quidem igitur. at earum templa sunt publice vota et dedicata. ne ceteri quidem ergo di, quorum templa sunt dedicata. Age porro: Iovem et Neptunum deum numeras; ergo etiam Orcus frater eorum deus, et illi qui fluere apud inferos dicuntur, Acheron Cocytus Pyriphlegethon, tum Charon tum Cerberus di putandi. At id quidem repudiandum; ne Orcus quidem igitur; quid dicitis ergo de fratribus?" Haec Carneades aiebat, non ut deos tolleret (quid enim philosopho minus conveniens?), sed ut Stoicos nihil de dis explicare convinceret. itaque insequebatur: "Quid enim?", aiebat, "si hi fratres sunt in numero deorum, num de patre eorum Saturno negari potest, quem volgo maxime colunt ad occidentem? qui si est deus, patrem quoque eius Caelum esse deum confitendum est. quod si ita est, Caeli quoque parentes dii habendi sunt Aether et Dies eorumque fratres et sorores, qui a genealogis antiquis sic nominantur, Amor Dolus

---

[1] See for this kind of arguments Zeno of Elea, nr. **88** f., and Eubulides of the Megarian School (nr. **231e**).

Metus Labor Invidentia Fatum Senectus Mors Tenebrae Miseria Querella Gratia Fraus Pertinacia Parcae Hesperides Somnia; quos omnis Erebo et Nocte natos ferunt. aut igitur haec monstra probanda sunt aut prima illa tollenda.

b. Sextus Emp., *Adv. math.* IX (= *Ag. the phys.* I) 186-188:

Εἴγε μὴν Ἀφροδίτην θεὰν λέγομεν εἶναι, ἔσται καὶ ὁ Ἔρως υἱὸς ὢν Ἀφροδίτης θεός. ἀλλ᾽ εἰ ὁ Ἔρως θεός ἐστι, καὶ ὁ Ἔλεος ἔσται θεός· ἀμφότερα γάρ ἐστι ψυχικὰ πάθη, καὶ ὁμοίως ἀφωσίωται τῷ Ἔρωτι καὶ ὁ Ἔλεος· παρὰ Ἀθηναίοις γοῦν Ἐλέου βωμοί τινές εἰσιν. εἰ δὲ ὁ Ἔλεος θεός ἐστι, καὶ ὁ Φόβος· —

Εἰ δὲ ὁ φόβος, καὶ τὰ λοιπὰ τῆς ψυχῆς πάθη. οὐχὶ δέ γε ταῦτα· οὐδὲ ἡ Ἀφροδίτη ἄρα θεός ἐστι.

c. Cic., *De n.d.* III 20, 51:

Illa autem, Balbe, quae tu a caelo astrisque ducebas, quam longe serpant non vides: solem deum esse lunamque, quorum alterum Apollinem, Graeci alteram Dianam putant. quod si Luna dea est, ergo etiam Lucifer ceteraeque errantes numerum deorum obtinebunt; igitur etiam inerrantes. cur autem arqui species non in deorum numero reponatur? est enim pulcher, et ob eam speciem, quia causam habeat admirabilem, Thaumante dicitur esse nata. cuius si divina natura est, quid facies nubibus? arcus enim ipse e nubibus efficitur quodam modo coloratis; quarum una etiam Centauros peperisse dicitur. quod si nubes rettuleris in deos, referendae certe erunt tempestates, quae populi Romani ritibus consecratae sunt. ergo imbres nimbi procellae turbines dei putandi. —

Ergo hoc aut inmensum serpet, aut nihil horum recipiemus; nec illa infinita ratio superstitionis probabitur; nihil ergo horum probandum est.

Mantic criticized   **1122**—Carneades' arguments against the Stoic doctrine of mantic, expounded by Cic. in *De div.* II (the first book *De div.* contains Chrysippus' doctrine), may be summarized as follows.

1. There is no special object of mantic, though it is said not to be universal.

2. If it is said to be concerned with *fortuita*, either these are incalculable and therefore unpredicable, or they do not exist, since (according to the Stoics) everything is determined by fate.

3. If the possibility of mantic be founded on cosmic sympathy, Carn. replied that a certain coherence of natural phenomena does exist,

but not such a coherence as is admitted by the Stoics (e.g. between the form of a liver of a victim and a certain advantage of mine).

a.   When, now, the Stoics conclude that mantic must be possible **It is based on insuffi- cient grounds** because there are gods, Carn. turns the argument.

Cic., *De div.* II 17, 41:

Ita enim, cum magis properant, concludere solent "si di sunt, est divinatio; sunt autem di; est ergo divinatio." Multo est probabilius "non est autem divinatio; non sunt ergo di".

b.   Neither can mantic be founded on the *consensus omnium*.
Ib. 39, 81:

At omnes reges populi nationes utuntur auspiciis. quasi vero quicquam sit tam valde quam nihil sapere vulgare, aut quasi tibi ipsi in iudicando placeat multitudo. quotus quisque est qui voluptatem neget esse bonum? plerique etiam summum bonum dicunt. num igitur eorum frequentia Stoici de sententia deterrentur? aut num plerisque in rebus sequitur eorum auctoritatem multitudo? quid mirum igitur, si in auspiciis et in omni divinatione inbecilli animi superstitiosa ista concipiant, verum dispicere non possint?

c.   Finally, why should the gods give us signs, and why so obscurely?

Ib. 25, 54-55:

Quae est enim ista a deis profecta significatio et quasi denuntiatio calamitatum? quid autem volunt ea di immortales primum significantes quae sine interpretibus non possimus intellegere, deinde ea quae cavere nequeamus? at hoc ne homines quidem probi faciunt, ut amicis inpenden- tis calamitates praedicant quas illi effugere nullo modo possint, ut medici quamquam intellegunt saepe tamen numquam aegris dicunt illo morbo eos esse morituros; omnis enim praedictio mali tum probatur, cum ad praedictionem cautio adiungitur. quid igitur aut ostenta aut eorum interpretes vel Lacedaemonios olim vel nuper nostros adiuverunt? quae si signa deorum putanda sunt, cur tam obscura fuerunt? si enim, ut intellegeremus quid esset eventurum, aperte declarari oportebat, aut ne occulte quidem, si ea sciri nolebant.

1123—Prodigia, oracles and dreams can be explained by natural   **How to explain prodigia** causes.

a.   Cic., *De div.* II 27, 58; 28, 60:

Sanguine[m] pluisse senatui nuntiatum est, Atratum etiam fluvium

fluxisse sanguine[m] deorum sudasse simulacra. num censes his nuntiis
Thalen aut Anaxagoran aut quemquam physicum crediturum fuisse?
nec enim sanguis nec sudor nisi e corpore. —

An vero illa nos terrent, si quando aliqua portentosa aut ex pecude
aut ex homine nata dicuntur? quorum omnium, ne sim longior, una ratio
est. Quicquid enim oritur qualecumque est, causam habeat a natura
necesse est, ut etiamsi praeter consuetudinem extiterit, praeter naturam
tamen non possit existere. causam igitur investigato in re nova atque
admirabili si poteris; si nullam reperies, illud tamen exploratum habeto,
nihil fieri potuisse sine causa, eumque terrorem quem tibi rei novitas
attulerit naturae ratione depellito.

b.　Cic., ib. 56, 115-116; 57, 117.

Oracles　　Some oracles happen to be true (by chance); others are so ambiguous that they
are never false.

Nam cum sors illa edita est opulentissimo regi Asiae

"Croesus Halyn penetrans magnam pervertet opum vim",

hostium vim se perversurum putavit; pervertit autem suam: utrum
igitur eorum accidisset, verum oraclum fuisset. cur autem hoc credam
umquam editum Croeso, aut Herodotum cur veraciorem ducam Ennio?
num minus ille potuit de Croeso quam de Pyrrho fingere Ennius? quis
enim est qui credat Apollinis ex oraclo Pyrrho esse responsum

"aio te, Aeacida, Romanos vincere posse."

primum latine Apollo numquam locutus est; deinde ista sors inaudita
Graecis est; praeterea Pyrrhi temporibus iam Apollo versus facere
desierat. —

117. Sed quod caput est, cur isto modo iam oracla Delphis non eduntur,
non modo nostra aetate, sed iam diu *tantum modo iam* ut nihil possit
esse contemptius? hoc loco cum urgentur, evanuisse aiunt vetustate
vim loci eius unde anhelitus ille terrae fieret quo Pythia mente incitata
oracula ederet. —

Quando ista vis autem evanuit? an postquam homines minus creduli
esse coeperunt?

Dreams　　**c.**　Cic., ib. 62, 127-128:

Iam vero quis dicere audeat vera omnia esse somnia? Aliquot somnia vera, inquit Ennius, sed omnia non necesse est. Quae est tandem
ista distinctio? quae vera, quae falsa habet? et si vera a deo mittuntur,

falsa unde nascuntur? nam si ea quoque divina, quid inconstantius
deo? quid inscitius autem est quam mentes mortalium falsis et menda-
cibus visis concitare? sin vera visa divina sunt, falsa autem et inania
humana, quae est ista designandi licentia, ut hoc deus hoc natura fecerit
potius quam aut omnia deus, quod negatis, aut omnia natura? quod
quoniam illud negatis, hoc necessario confitendum est. naturam autem
eam dico, qua numquam animus insistens agitatione et motu esse vacuus
potest. Is cum languore corporis nec membris uti nec sensibus potest,
incidit in visa varia et incerta ex reliquis ut ait Aristoteles inhaerentibus
earum rerum quas vigilans gesserit aut cogitaverit; quarum turbatione
mirabiles interdum existunt species somniorum.

Cicero concludes (72, 148) that, by these arguments, not religion but superstition
is extirpated, and this is certainly a gain.

1124—According to Chrysippus, everything is determined by pre- **Fate and**
ceding causes. The problem is: how to find room for free will under this **free will**
system of natural fatality. Carneades solved the problem by introducing
free will as an independent cause [1].

Cic., *De fato* 14, 31 - 15, 35:

Carneades genus hoc totum non probabat et nimis inconsiderate con-
cludi hanc rationem putabat; itaque premebat alio modo nec ullam
adhibebat calumniam. cuius erat haec conclusio "si omnia antecedentibus
causis fiunt, omnia naturali conligatione conserte contexteque fiunt; quod
si ita est, omnia necessitas efficit; id si verum est, nihil est in nostra potestate; est autem aliquid in nostra potestate; at, si omnia fato fiunt, omnia
causis antecedentibus fiunt; non igitur fato fiunt, quaecumque fiunt. —
itaque dicebat Carneades ne Apollinem quidem futura posse dicere
nisi ea quorum causas natura ita contineret, ut ea fieri necesse esset. —
Causis enim efficientibus quamque rem cognitis posse denique sciri,
quid futurum esset. ergo nec de Oedipode potuisse Apollinem praedicere
nullis in rerum natura causis praepositis, cur ab eo patrem interfici
necesse esset, nec quicquam eius modi. —

15, 34. Causa autem ea est, quae id efficit cuius est causa, ut vulnus
mortis, cruditas morbi, ignis ardoris. itaque non sic causa intellegi debet,
ut quod cuique antecedat, id ei causa sit, sed quod cuique efficienter
antecedat, nec quod in campum descenderim, id fuisse causae cur pila

---

[1] Cp. Aristotle, EN III, 3, 1112a 31-34 (above, nr. **577e**, the end); later
Plotinus, *Enn.* III 1, cc. 8-9, below, nr. **1418**; also **1425c, d** and **1430c, d**.

luderem, nec Hecubam causam interitus fuisse Troianis quod Alexandrum genuerit, nec Tyndareum Agamemnoni quod Clytemestram. hoc enim modo viator quoque bene vestitus causa grassatori fuisse dicetur, cur ab eo spoliaretur. ex hoc genere illud est Enni

"utinam ne in nemore Pelio securibus
caesae accidissent abiegnae ad terram trabes"

— licuit vel altius "utinam ne in Pelio nata ulla umquam esset arbor", etiam supra "utinam ne esset mons ullus Pelius" similiterque superiora repetentem regredi infinite licet.

1125—In ethics, Carn. denies that moral principles could be founded on nature, as is done by Stoics and, in a sense, by Plato and Aristotle, who used to consider ἀρετή in general as a perfection of being (cp. above, nr. **1003**, n. 1). Hence, Carn. rejects the notion of *natural law* as rooted in the objective order of things. To this he opposes the following arguments.

Law not rooted in nature

a. If law were rooted in the natural order of things, everybody could find it there and conceptions of law would never be in disagreement. But laws are different in different countries, and man is not just by nature.

Cic., *De republ.* III 8, 13; 11, 18:

Ius enim de quo quaerimus, civile est aliquod, naturale nullum; nam si esset, ut calida et frigida, et amara et dulcia, sic essent iusta et iniusta eadem omnibus. —

(Deus si) sanxisset iura nobis, et omnes isdem et idem non alias aliis uterentur. Quaero autem, si iusti hominis et si boni est viri parere legibus, quibus? an quaecumque erunt? At nec inconstantiam virtus recipit, nec varietatem natura patitur, legesque poena, non iustitia nostra comprobantur; nihil habet igitur naturale ius; ex quo illud efficitur, ne iustos quidem esse natura.

Man is not just by nature

b. That men are not just by nature, can be inferred from their attitude towards animals.

Cic., ib. 11, 18-19:

An vero in legibus varietatem esse dicunt, natura autem viros bonos eam iustitiam sequi, quae sit, non eam, quae putetur? esse enim hoc boni viri et iusti, tribuere id cuique, quod sit quoque dignum. Ecquid ergo primum mutis tribuemus beluis?

1126—Doubtless, Carn. opposed to this the *social contract* theory, held previously by some of the older sophists (cp. our nr. **195b**) and by Epicurus.

a. Lactantius, *Inst.* V 16, 3 summarizes Carn.'s doctrine as follows:

> The social contract theory

Iura sibi homines pro utilitate sanxisse, scilicet varia pro moribus, et aput eosdem pro temporibus saepe mutata, ius autem naturale esse nullum; omnes et homines et alias animantes ad utilitates suas natura ducente ferri; proinde aut nullam esse iustitiam aut, si sit aliqua, summam esse stultitiam, quoniam sibi noceret alienis commodis consulens.

b. Lact., ib. 16, 4:

> Arguments from history

Et inferebat haec argumenta: omnibus populis qui florerent imperio et Romanis quoque ipsis, qui totius orbis potirentur, si iusti velint esse, hoc est si aliena restituant, ad casas esse redeundum et in egestate ac miseriis iacendum.

1127—Thus there is no link either between justice and wisdom, or between wisdom and happiness, as the dogmatists admitted there is.

> Conflict between wisdom and justice

Cic., *De republ.* III 15, 24:

Sapientia iubet augere opes, amplificare divitias, proferre fines — unde enim esset illa laus in summorum imperatorum incisa monumentis "finis imperii propagavit", nisi aliquid de alieno accessisset? — imperare quam plurimis, frui voluptatibus, pollere regnare dominari; iustitia autem praecipit parcere omnibus, consulere generi hominum, suum cuique reddere, sacra publica aliena non tangere. quid igitur efficitur si sapientiae pareas?

1128—Carn. illustrated the conflict of justice and "wisdom" by some famous examples, cited by Lactantius.

a. Lact., *Inst.* V 16, 5-6:

> Carneades' casus con-scientiae

Bonus vir, inquit, si habeat servum fugitivum, vel domum insalubrem ac pestilentem, quae vitia solus sciat, et ideo proscribat ut vendat, utrumne profitebitur fugitivum se servum vel pestilentem domum vendere an celabit emptorem? si profitebitur, bonus quidem, quia non fallet, sed tamen stultus iudicabitur, quia vel parvo vendet vel omnino non vendet; si celabit, erit quidem sapiens, quia rei consulet, sed idem malus, quia fallet.

b. Ib. 16, 10:

Quid ergo iustus faciet, si forte naufragium fecerit et aliquis imbecillior viribus tabulam ceperit? nonne illum tabula deturbabit, ut ipse conscendat eaque nixus evadat, maxime cum sit nullus medio mari testis? si sapiens est, faciet: ipsi enim pereundum est, nisi fecerit; si autem mori maluerit quam manus inferre alteri, iam iustus ille, sed <idem> stultus est, qui vitae suae non parcat, dum parcit alienae.

c. Ib., 16, 11:

Item si acie suorum fusa hostes insequi coeperint, et iustus ille nanctus fuerit aliquem saucium equum insidentem, eine parcet, ut ipse occidatur, an deiciet ex equo, ut ipse hostem possit effugere? quod si fecerit, sapiens, sed idem malus, si non fecerit, iustus, sed idem stultus sit necesse est.

The *casus* of Carneades are treated in a very interesting article by J. Croissant, *La morale de Carnéade*, in *Revue internat. de phil.*, 1939, p. 545-570.

Casuistic in the Stoa As appears from Cicero's *De officiis* III, cc. 12 ff., these and many similar "cases" were discussed by Diogenes the Babylonian and Antipater [1]. Panaetius' pupil Hecaton of Rhodos in his 6th book *De officiis* mentioned a great number of suchlike questions (Cic., *De off.* III 23).

Cicero's attitude Cicero, who *in theoreticis* was an admirer of Carneades, took the part of the Stoics as to ethics and the foundation of law: he defended natural law by the principle of *oikeiosis* (above, nrs. **1065b-c, 1066-1067, 1070**), denied any conflict between the *honestum* and the *utile* (*De off.* III 3), and in cases of a *seeming* conflict, such as the instances introduced by Carn., Cicero even preferred the severe solution of Antipater to the laxer one of Diogenes (ib., cc. 12-23).

Carneades a dogmatist in ethics? As to Carneades' position in ethics, if it is true that he admitted the social contract theory instead of that of "nature" being the basis of moral principles and law, it is clear that he was not a sceptic, but a dogmatist, too.

Remark on „classical naturalism" With regard to those modern philosophers who are inclined to adopt Carneades' arguments against "classical naturalism", saying that "nature" is something neutral and therefore can never furnish us with any moral principles, it should be remarked that, for the ancient philosophers opposed by Carn. (as for those among modern philosophers who follow them), "nature" meant more than "just what happens". Cp. the passages of St. Thomas Aquinas cited under **1076**.

5—DIALECTICAL SCEPTICISM: AENESIDEMUS AND AGRIPPA

Aenedise-mus of Cnossus **1129—a.** In the list of Hippobotus and Sotion (ap. Diog. L. IX 115 f., cited under nr. **1078b**) Aenesidemus of Cnossus is mentioned third after Ptolemaeus of Cyrene and is said to be the author of 8 books of *Pyrrhoneioi logoi*.

b. Aristocles ap. Euseb., *Praep. ev.* XIV 18, 763d, mentions him as the first important man of the Sceptical School after Pyrrho and Timon:

---

[1]   Cp. below, nr. **1143**, sub (5).

Μηδενὸς δ' ἐπιστραφέντος αὐτῶν, ὡς εἰ μηδὲ ἐγένοντο τὸ παράπαν, ἐχθὲς **He lived at**
καὶ πρώην ἐν Ἀλεξανδρείᾳ τῇ κατ' Αἴγυπτον Αἰνεσίδημός τις ἀναζωπυρεῖν **Alexandria**
ἤρξατο τὸν ὕθλον τοῦτον.

c. The patriarch Photius, *Myriobiblon* p. 212, 169 b 17 sqq.,   **Date**
171 a 4 Bekker, in his short analysis of the *Pyrrh. log.* says that Aenesidemus dedicated this work to the Roman L. Aelius Tubero. The identity
of this personage with the friend of Cicero is rejected by Zeller, but
defended by Robin. It is mostly admitted that Aen. lived c. 80-60 B.C.
His arguments are fairly well known to us by Sextus Emp. and by
Diog. Laert., who seems to have possessed the text.

1130—Sextus Emp., *Adv. math.* VIII (= *Ag. the log.* II) 40-47:   **1. Against**
     truth

Εἰ γὰρ ἔστι τι ἀληθές, ἤτοι αἰσθητόν ἐστιν ἢ νοητόν ἐστιν, ἢ καὶ νοητόν
ἐστι καὶ αἰσθητόν ἐστιν. [ἢ] οὔτε δὲ αἰσθητόν ἐστιν οὔτε νοητόν ἐστι, οὔτε
τὸ συναμφότερον, ὡς παρασταθήσεται· οὐκ ἄρα ἔστι τι ἀληθές. ὅτι μὲν οὖν
οὐκ ἔστιν αἰσθητόν, οὕτως ἐπιλογιούμεθα. τῶν αἰσθητῶν τὰ μέν ἐστι γένη
τὰ δὲ εἴδη, καὶ γένη μὲν αἱ ἐνδιήκουσαι ἐν τοῖς κατὰ μέρος κοινότητες, ὡς
ἄνθρωπος ὁ διὰ τῶν κατὰ μέρος ἀνθρώπων πεφοιτηκὼς καὶ ἵππος ὁ διὰ τῶν
κατὰ μέρος ἵππων, εἴδη δὲ καὶ καθ' ἕκαστον ἰδιότητες, ὡς Δίωνος, Θέωνος,
τῶν ἄλλων. εἴπερ οὖν αἰσθητόν ἐστι τὸ ἀληθές, καὶ τοῦτο πάντως κοινὸν
πλειόνων <ἢ ἐν> ἰδιότητι κείμενον ἔσται αἰσθητὸν [τὸ ἀληθές]· οὔτε δὲ
κοινόν ἐστιν οὔτε ἐν ἰδιότητι κείμενον· οὐκ ἄρα αἰσθητόν ἐστι τὸ ἀληθές.
ἔτι ὃν τρόπον τὸ μὲν ὁρατὸν ὁράσει ληπτόν ἐστι, τὸ δὲ ἀκουστὸν ἀκοῇ γνώριμόν
ἐστι, τὸ δὲ ὀσφρητὸν ὀσφρήσει, οὕτω καὶ τὸ αἰσθητὸν κοινῶς αἰσθήσει γνωρίζεται.
οὐ γνωρίζεται δὲ κοινῶς αἰσθήσει <τὸ ἀληθές>· ἡ γὰρ αἴσθησις ἄλογός ἐστιν,
καὶ τὸ ἀληθὲς οὐκ ἀλόγως γνωρίζεται. οὐκ ἄρα αἰσθητὸν τὸ ἀληθές. καὶ μὴν
οὐδὲ νοητόν ἐστιν, ἐπεὶ οὐδὲν ἔσται τῶν αἰσθητῶν ἀληθές· ὃ πάλιν ἄτοπον. —
Ἀλλὰ μὴν οὐδὲ αἰσθητὸν ἅμα καὶ νοητόν. ἤτοι γὰρ πᾶν αἰσθητὸν καὶ πᾶν
νοητὸν ἀληθές ἐστιν ἢ τὶ αἰσθητὸν καὶ τὶ νοητόν. ἀλλὰ τὸ μὲν φάσκειν πᾶν
αἰσθητὸν καὶ πᾶν νοητὸν ἀληθὲς εἶναι τῶν ἀμηχάνων. μάχεται γὰρ τὰ αἰσθητὰ
τοῖς αἰσθητοῖς καὶ τὰ νοητὰ τοῖς νοητοῖς καὶ ἐναλλὰξ τὰ αἰσθητὰ τοῖς νοητοῖς
καὶ δεήσει πάντων ἀληθῶν ὄντων τὸ αὐτὸ εἶναι καὶ μὴ εἶναι, ἀληθές τε ὑπάρχειν
καὶ ψεῦδος. τὶ δὲ αἰσθητὸν ἀληθὲς καὶ τὶ νοητὸν ἀληθὲς ἀξιοῦν πάλιν τῶν
ἀπόρων· ζητεῖται γὰρ τοῦτο. καὶ ἄλλως ἀκόλουθόν ἐστιν ἢ πάντα λέγειν
ἀληθῆ ἢ πάντα λέγειν ψευδῆ τὰ αἰσθητά· ἐπ' ἴσης γάρ ἐστιν αἰσθητά, καὶ
οὐ τὸ μὲν μᾶλλον τὸ δὲ ἧττον, καὶ τὰ νοητὰ πάλιν ἐπ' ἴσης ἐστὶ νοητά, καὶ
οὐ τὸ μὲν μᾶλλον τὸ δὲ ἔλαττον. οὐ πάντα δὲ τὰ αἰσθητὰ λέγεται ἀληθῆ, οὐδὲ
πάντα ψευδῆ· οὐκ ἄρα ἔστι τι ἀληθές.

As to the value of Aenesidemus' arguments against truth and the notion of cause, see under **1134**. Also **1135** (the ten "tropes").

2. Against causality

1131—Sextus Emp., *Adv. math.* IX (= *Ag. the phys.* I) 219-226:

Τὸ γὰρ σῶμα τοῦ σώματος οὐκ ἂν εἴη αἴτιον, ἐπείπερ ἢ ἀγένητόν ἐστι τὸ τοιοῦτον σῶμα καθάπερ ἡ κατ' Ἐπίκουρον ἄτομος, ἢ γενητὸν ὡς ἔθος, καὶ ἢ φανερὸν ὡς σίδηρος καὶ πῦρ, ἢ ἀφανὲς ὡς ἄτομος. ὅ τι δ' ἂν ᾖ τούτων, οὐδὲν δύναται ποιεῖν. ἤτοι γὰρ καθ' ἑαυτὸ μένον ἕτερόν τι ποιεῖ ἢ ἑτέρῳ συνελθόν. ἀλλὰ μένον μὲν καθ' ἑαυτὸ πλεῖον αὑτοῦ καὶ τῆς οἰκείας φύσεως οὐκ ἂν δύναιτό τι ποιεῖν. συνελθὸν δὲ ἑτέρῳ τρίτον οὐκ ἂν δύναιτο ἀποτελεῖν, ὃ μὴ πρότερον ἐν τῷ εἶναι ὑπῆρχεν. οὔτε γὰρ τὸ ἓν γενέσθαι δύο δυνατόν ἐστιν, οὔτε τὰ δύο τρίτον ἀποτελεῖ. εἰ γὰρ τὸ ἓν δύο γενέσθαι δυνατὸν ἦν, καὶ ἑκάτερον τῶν γενομένων ἓν ὂν δύο ἀποτελέσει, καὶ τῶν τεσσάρων ἕκαστον ἓν ὂν δύο ποιήσει, καὶ ὁμοίως τῶν ὀκτὼ ἕκαστον, καὶ οὕτως εἰς ἄπειρον. παντελῶς δέ γε ἄτοπόν ἐστι τὸ ἐξ ἑνὸς ἄπειρα λέγειν γίνεσθαι· ἄτοπον ἄρα καὶ ἐκ τοῦ ἑνὸς λέγειν τι πλεῖον γεννᾶσθαι. τὰ δ' αὐτὰ κἂν ἀξιῶ τις ἐκ τῶν ἡσσόνων κατὰ σύνοδον πλείονα ἀποτελεῖσθαι· εἰ γὰρ τὸ ἓν τῷ ἑνὶ συνελθὸν τρίτον ποιεῖ, καὶ τὸ τρίτον προσγενόμενον τοῖς δυσὶ τέταρτον ἀποτελέσει, καὶ τὸ τέταρτον προσγενόμενον τοῖς τρισὶ πέμπτον ἀποτελέσει, καὶ οὕτω πάλιν εἰς ἄπειρον. οὐκοῦν σῶμα μὲν σώματος οὐκ ἔστιν αἴτιον. καὶ μὴν οὐδὲ ἀσώματον ἀσωμάτου διὰ τὰς αὐτὰς αἰτίας· οὔτε γὰρ ἐξ ἑνὸς οὔτε ἐκ πλειόνων ἢ ἑνὸς γένοιτ' ἄν τι πλεῖον. καὶ ἄλλως· ἀναφὴς φύσις καθεστὼς τὸ ἀσώματον οὔτε ποιεῖν οὔτε πάσχειν δύναται. ὥστε οὐδὲ ἀσώματον ἀσωμάτου ποιητικόν ἐστιν· οὕτως δὲ οὐδὲ τὸ ἐναλλάξ, τουτέστι σῶμα ἀσωμάτου ἢ ἀσώματον σώματος. τό τε γὰρ σῶμα οὐκ ἔχει ἐν αὑτῷ τὴν τοῦ ἀσωμάτου φύσιν, τό τε ἀσώματον οὐκ ἐμπεριεῖχε τὴν τοῦ σώματος φύσιν. διόπερ οὐδέτερον ἐξ οὐδετέρου συστῆναι δυνατόν ἐστιν, ἀλλ' ὡς ἐκ πλατάνου οὐ γίνεται ἵππος διὰ τὸ μὴ εἶναι ἐν τῇ πλατάνῳ τὴν τοῦ ἵππου φύσιν, οὐδὲ ἐξ ἵππου συνίσταται ἄνθρωπος διὰ τὸ μὴ εἶναι ἐν ἵππῳ τὴν τοῦ ἀνθρώπου φύσιν, οὕτως οὐδὲ ἐκ σώματος ἔσται ποτ' ἂν τὸ ἀσώματον διὰ τὸ μὴ εἶναι ἐν τῷ σώματι τὴν τοῦ ἀσωμάτου φύσιν, οὐδὲ ἀνάπαλιν ἐκ τοῦ ἀσωμάτου τὸ σῶμα. — οὐδὲ σῶμα οὖν ἀσωμάτου ἢ ἀσώματον σώματός ἐστιν αἴτιον· ᾧ ἀκολουθεῖ τὸ μηδὲν εἶναι αἴτιον.

σημεῖα
do not lead
to any
certitude
either

1132—Epicurus and the Stoics thought it possibile to find the causes indirectly by the effects. Hence their doctrine of σημεῖα. To this, Aen. opposes the following argument.

a. Sextus Emp., *Adv. math.* VIII (= *Ag. the log.* II) 215:

Εἰ τὰ φαινόμενα πᾶσι τοῖς ὁμοίως διακειμένοις παραπλησίως φαίνεται καὶ τὰ σημεῖά ἐστι φαινόμενα, τὰ σημεῖα πᾶσι τοῖς ὁμοίως διακειμένοις παραπλησίως φαίνεται. οὐχὶ δέ γε τὰ σημεῖα πᾶσι τοῖς ὁμοίως διακειμένοις παραπλησίως φαίνεται· τὰ δὲ φαινόμενα πᾶσι τοῖς ὁμοίως διακειμένοις παραπλησίως φαίνεται· οὐκ ἄρα φαινόμενά ἐστι τὰ σημεῖα.

b. The proposition that "signs do not appear alike to all those in a similar condition" is illustrated by a medical instance: the symptoms of fever are explained differently by different physicians according to their different theories.

Sextus, ib. 219-220:

Τὸ γοῦν ἐπὶ τῶν πυρεσσόντων ἔρευθος καὶ ἡ τῶν ἀγγείων προπάλεια καὶ ὁ ἔνικμος χρὼς καὶ ἡ πλείων θερμασία καὶ ἡ σφοδρότης τῶν σφυγμῶν καὶ τὰ λοιπὰ σημεῖα τοῖς ὁμοίως κατά τε τὰς αἰσθήσεις καὶ τὴν ἄλλην σύγκρισιν διακειμένοις τοῦ αὐτοῦ προσπίπτει σημεῖα, οὐδ᾽ ὡσαύτως πᾶσι φαίνεται, ἀλλ᾽ Ἡροφίλῳ μὲν λόγου χάριν ὡς ἄντικρυς χρηστοῦ αἵματος σημεῖα, Ἐρασιστράτῳ δὲ ὡς μεταπτώσεως τῆς ἐκ φλεβῶν εἰς ἀρτηρίας, Ἀσκληπιάδῃ δὲ ὡς ἐνστάσεως νοητῶν ὄγκων ἐν νοητοῖς ἀραιώμασιν.

Photius says, Aen. taught that signs are no visible things revealing the invisible (φανερὰ τῶν ἀφανῶν).

1133—The books of Sextus contain quite a number of passages containing arguments against proof. In these passages the name of Aenesidemus is not mentioned; but it is highly probable that he had his part in developing the arguments.

3. Against proof

a. Proof, too, is a "sign", and as such to be rejected.

Sextus Emp., *P.* II 134:

Φανερὸν μὲν οὖν ἐκ τούτων ὅτι οὐδὲ ἡ ἀπόδειξις ὁμολογούμενόν τι πρᾶγμά ἐστιν· εἰ γὰρ περὶ τοῦ σημείου ἐπέχομεν, καὶ ἡ ἀπόδειξις δὲ σημεῖόν τί ἐστι, καὶ περὶ τῆς ἀποδείξεως ἐπέχειν ἀνάγκη. καὶ γὰρ εὑρήσομεν τοὺς περὶ τοῦ σημείου λόγους ἠρωτημένους ἐφαρμόζεσθαι δυναμένους καὶ κατὰ τῆς ἀποδείξεως, ἐπεὶ καὶ πρός τι εἶναι δοκεῖ καὶ ἐκκαλυπτικὴ τοῦ συμπεράσματος, οἷς ἠκολούθει τὰ πρὸς τὸ σημεῖον ἡμῖν εἰρημένα σχεδὸν ἅπαντα.

Other passages containing the same argument are: *P.* II 122; *M.* VIII 277, 279 sq.

b. Proof as a conclusion from premisses depends on conditions which must be also proved.

Sextus Emp., *P.* II 113-116:

Καὶ γὰρ ἡ ἀπόδειξις ὑγιὴς εἶναι δοκεῖ, ὅταν ἀκολουθῇ τῇ διὰ τῶν λημμάτων αὐτῆς συμπλοκῇ τὸ συμπέρασμα αὐτῆς ὡς λῆγον ἡγουμένῳ, οἷον οὕτως

"εἰ ἡμέρα ἔστιν, φῶς ἔστιν· ἀλλὰ μὴν ἡμέρα ἔστιν· φῶς ἄρα ἔστιν. εἴπερ
ἡμέρα ἔστι, φῶς ἔστιν· καὶ ἡμέρα ἔστι καὶ φῶς ἔστιν." ζητουμένου δὲ περὶ
τοῦ πῶς κρινοῦμεν τὴν ἀκολουθίαν τοῦ λήγοντος πρὸς τὸ ἡγούμενον [1], ὁ διάλληλος εὑρίσκεται τρόπος [2]. ἵνα μὲν γὰρ ἡ κρίσις τοῦ συνημμένου [3] ἀποδειχ-
θῇ, τὸ συμπέρασμα τοῖς λήμμασι [4] τῆς ἀποδείξεως ἀκολουθεῖ, ὡς προειρή-
καμεν· ἵνα δὲ πάλιν τοῦτο πιστευθῇ, δεῖ τὸ συνημμένον καὶ τὴν ἀκολουθίαν
ἐπικεκρίσθαι. ὅπερ ἄτοπον. ἀκατάληπτον ἄρα τὸ ὑγιὲς συνημμένον.

Ἀλλὰ καὶ τὸ προκαθηγούμενον [5] ἄπορόν ἐστι. τὸ μὲν γὰρ προκαθηγούμενον,
ὥς φασιν, ἐστὶ τὸ ἡγούμενον ἐν τοιούτῳ συνημμένῳ, ὃ ἄρχεται ἀπὸ ἀληθοῦς
καὶ λήγει ἐπὶ ἀληθές. εἰ δὲ ἐκκαλυπτικόν ἐστι τοῦ λήγοντος τὸ σημεῖον, ἤτοι
πρόδηλόν ἐστι τὸ λῆγον ἢ ἄδηλον. εἰ μὲν οὖν πρόδηλον, οὐδὲ τοῦ ἐκκαλύψοντος
δεήσεται, ἀλλὰ συγκαταληφθήσεται αὐτῷ, καὶ οὐκ ἔστιν αὐτοῦ σημειωτόν,
διόπερ οὐδὲ ἐκεῖνο τούτου σημεῖον. εἰ δὲ ἄδηλον, ἐπεὶ περὶ τῶν ἀδήλων δια-
πεφώνηται ἀνεπικρίτως, ποῖα μέν ἐστιν αὐτῶν ἀληθῆ ποῖα δὲ ψευδῆ, καὶ ὅλως
εἰ ἔστι τι αὐτῶν ἀληθές, ἄδηλον ἔσται εἰ εἰς ἀληθὲς λήγει τὸ συνημμένον.
ᾧ συνεισέρχεται καὶ τὸ ἄδηλον εἶναι εἰ προκαθηγεῖται τὸ ἐν αὐτῷ ἡγούμενον.

The argument is directed not against Aristotle's categorical syllogism, but against
hypothetical syllogism, much used in the Stoa. Cp. above nr. **979**.

c. Another argument is given in the following passage.

Sextus Emp., *P.* II 177-179:

Ἔτι ἐκ τούτων τὸ ἀνυπόστατον τῆς ἀποδείξεως ἔνεστιν ὑπομιμνήσκειν. εἰ γὰρ
ἔστιν ἀπόδειξις, ἤτοι φαινομένη φαινομένου ἐστὶν ἐκκαλυπτικὴ ἢ ἄδηλος ἀδήλου
ἢ ἄδηλος φαινομένου ἢ φαινομένη ἀδήλου· οὐδενὸς δὲ τούτων ἐκκαλυπτικὴ
δύναται ἐπινοεῖσθαι· ἀνεπινόητος ἄρα ἐστίν. εἰ μὲν γὰρ φαινομένη φαινομένου
ἐκκαλυπτική ἐστιν, ἔσται τὸ ἐκκαλυπτόμενον ἅμα φαινόμενόν τε καὶ ἄδηλον,
φαινόμενον μέν, ἐπεὶ τοιοῦτον εἶναι ὑπετέθη, ἄδηλον δέ, ἐπεὶ δεῖται τοῦ ἐκκαλύψοντος καὶ οὐκ ἐξ ἑαυτοῦ ὑποπίπτει ἡμῖν σαφῶς. εἰ δὲ ἄδηλος ἀδήλου, αὐτὴ δεήσεται
τοῦ ἐκκαλύψοντος αὐτὴν καὶ οὐκ ἔσται ἐκκαλυπτικὴ ἑτέρων, ὅπερ ἀφέστηκε
τῆς ἐννοίας τῆς ἀποδείξεως. διὰ δὲ ταῦτα οὐδὲ ἄδηλος προδήλου δύναται
εἶναι ἀπόδειξις. ἀλλ' οὐδὲ πρόδηλος ἀδήλου· ἐπεὶ γὰρ πρός τί ἐστιν, τὰ δὲ
πρός τι ἀλλήλοις συγκαταλαμβάνεται, συγκαταλαμβανόμενον τῇ προδήλῳ
ἀποδείξει τὸ ἀποδείκνυσθαι λεγόμενον πρόδηλον ἔσται, ὡς περιτρέπεσθαι τὸν
λόγον καὶ μὴ εὑρίσκεσθαι πρόδηλον αὐτὴν ἀδήλου ἀποδεικτικήν. εἰ οὖν μήτε

---

[1] "the logical sequence of the consequent in its relation to the antecedent."
[2] The argument of the circle.
[3] By συνημμένος (συλλογισμός) the hypothetical syllogism is meant.
[4] λήμματα, as was explained under **979**, is the term for premisses.
[5] "antecedent".

φαινομένη φαινομένου ἐστὶν ἡ ἀπόδειξις μήτε ἄδηλος ἀδήλου μήτε ἄδηλος προδήλου μήτε πρόδηλος ἀδήλου, παρὰ δὲ ταῦτα οὐδὲν εἶναι λέγουσιν, λεκτέον μηδὲν εἶναι τὴν ἀπόδειξιν.

Cp. also *M.* VIII 381-395.

1134—Now, Aristotle was well aware that proof must start from certain ἀρχαὶ ἀναπόδεικτοι (see vol. II, nr. **458**), and Chrysippus admits of certain indemonstrable statements (λόγοι ἀναπόδεικτοι), employed in the construction of every argument (above, **981**). This position of the dogmatists is attacked in the following passage.

Sextus Emp., *Adv. math.* VIII (= *Ag. the log.* II) 367 f.:

The classical argument of the Sceptics

’Αλλ’ οὐ δεῖ, φασί, πάντων ἀπόδειξιν αἰτεῖν, τινὰ δὲ καὶ ἐξ ὑποθέσεως λαμβάνειν, ἐπεὶ οὐ δυνήσεται προβαίνειν ἡμῖν ὁ λόγος, ἐὰν μὴ δοθῇ τι πιστὸν ἐξ αὐτοῦ τυγχάνειν. ἀλλὰ πρῶτον μὲν καὶ ἡμεῖς ἐροῦμεν ὅτι οὐκ ἔστιν ἀναγκαῖον τὰς ἐκείνων δογματολογίας προβαίνειν, πλασματώδεις ὑπαρχούσας. εἶτα καὶ ποῖ προβήσονται; τῶν γὰρ φαινομένων αὐτὸ μόνον παριστάντων ὅτι φαίνεται, τὸ δ’ ὅτι καὶ ὑπόκειται μηκέτι προσισχυόντων διδάσκειν, τιθέσθω καὶ τὰ λήμματα τῆς ἀποδείξεως ὅτι φαίνεται, καὶ ἡ ἐπιφορὰ ὁμοίως. ὧδε δὲ οὐ συναχθήσεται τὸ ζητούμενον καὶ οὐ παραχθήσεται ἡ ἀλήθεια, μενόντων ἡμῶν ἐπὶ ψιλῆς φάσεως καὶ τοῦ οἰκείου πάθους. τὸ δ’ ὅτι οὐ μόνον φαίνεται ἀλλὰ καὶ ὑπόκειται θέλειν παριστᾶν ἀνδρῶν ἐστι μὴ τῷ ἀναγκαίῳ πρὸς τὴν χρείαν ἀρκουμένων, ἀλλὰ καὶ τὸ δυνατὸν συναρπάζειν ἐσπουδακότων.

This is the classical argument of sceptics and "phenomenists", from Pyrrho to Kant and logical positivism of our days: human experience never transcends phenomena; hence we can never say what "is behind" them or reach a truth *in se*. Surely this is what Aenes. intended to say by his arguments against truth and against the notion of a cause. In form they may be rathei sophistical,—as to their tendency they were renewed by Berkeley, Hume and Kant.

1135—The so-called ten "tropes" of Aenedisemus, i.e. ten modes by which suspension of judgment was supposed to be brought about, were all concerned with the difficulties of perception. Diog. L. IX 79-88 describes them shortly (**a**); Sextus, *Pyrrh. hyp.* I 36-163, after a short survey (**b**) deals with them at great length.

a. Diog. L. IX 79-88:

The ten tropoi

[Εἷς] πρῶτος ὁ παρὰ τὰς διαφορὰς τῶν ζώων πρὸς ἡδονὴν καὶ ἀλγηδόνα καὶ βλάβην καὶ ὠφέλειαν. συνάγεται δὲ δι’ αὐτοῦ τὸ μὴ τὰς αὐτὰς ἀπὸ τῶν αὐτῶν προσπίπτειν φαντασίας καὶ τὸ διότι τῇ τοιαύτῃ μάχῃ ἀκολουθεῖ τὸ ἐπέχειν· —

(80) Δεύτερος ὁ παρὰ τὰς τῶν ἀνθρώπων φύσεις καὶ τὰς ἰδιοσυγκρισίας·
Δημοφῶν γοῦν ὁ Ἀλεξάνδρου τραπεζοκόμος ἐν σκιᾷ ἐθάλπετο, ἐν ἡλίῳ δ'
ἐρρίγου. Ἄνδρων δ' ὁ Ἀργεῖος, ὥς φησιν Ἀριστοτέλης, διὰ τῆς ἀνύδρου
Λιβύης ὥδευεν ἄποτος. — Καὶ ταῦτα οὓς μὲν βλάπτει, οὓς δὲ ὠφελεῖ· ὅθεν
ἐφεκτέον.

(81) Τρίτος ὁ παρὰ τὰς τῶν αἰσθητικῶν πόρων διαφοράς. τὸ γοῦν μῆλον
ὁράσει μὲν ὠχρόν, γεύσει δὲ γλυκύ, ὀσφρήσει δ' εὐῶδες ὑποπίπτει. καὶ ἡ αὐτὴ
δὲ μορφὴ παρὰ τὰς διαφορὰς τῶν κατόπτρων ἀλλοία θεωρεῖται. ἀκολουθεῖ
οὖν μὴ μᾶλλον εἶναι τοῖον τὸ φαινόμενον ἢ ἀλλοῖον.

(82) Τέταρτος ὁ παρὰ τὰς διαθέσεις καὶ κοινῶς παραλλαγάς, οἷον ὑγίειαν,
νόσον, ὕπνον, ἐγρήγορσιν, χαράν, λύπην, νεότητα, γῆρας, θάρσος, φόβον, . . .
Ἀλλοῖα οὖν φαίνεται τὰ προσπίπτοντα παρὰ τὰς ποιὰς διαθέσεις. —

(83) Πέμπτος ὁ παρὰ τὰς ἀγωγὰς καὶ τοὺς νόμους καὶ τὰς μυθικὰς πίστεις
καὶ τὰς ἐθνικὰς συνθήκας καὶ δογματικὰς ὑπολήψεις. ἐν τούτῳ περιέχεται τὰ
περὶ καλῶν καὶ αἰσχρῶν, περὶ ἀληθῶν καὶ ψευδῶν, περὶ ἀγαθῶν καὶ κακῶν, περὶ
θεῶν καὶ γενέσεως καὶ φθορᾶς τῶν φαινομένων πάντων. τὸ γοῦν αὐτὸ παρ' οἷς
μὲν δίκαιον, παρ' οἷς δὲ ἄδικον· καὶ ἄλλοις μὲν ἀγαθόν, ἄλλοις δὲ κακόν. —

(84) Ἕκτος ὁ παρὰ τὰς μίξεις καὶ κοινωνίας, καθ' ὃν εἰλικρινῶς οὐδὲν καθ'
αὑτὸ φαίνεται, ἀλλὰ σὺν ἀέρι, σὺν φωτί, σὺν ὑγρῷ, σὺν στερεῷ θερμότητι,
ψυχρότητι, κινήσει, ἀναθυμιάσεσιν, ἄλλαις δυνάμεσιν. — (85) Ἀγνοοῦμεν οὖν
τὸ κατ' ἰδίαν, ὡς ἔλαιον ἐν μύρῳ.

Ἕβδομος ὁ παρὰ τὰς ἀποστάσεις καὶ ποιὰς θέσεις καὶ τοὺς τόπους καὶ τὰ ἐν
τοῖς τόποις. κατὰ τοῦτον τὸν τρόπον τὰ δοκοῦντ' εἶναι μεγάλα μικρὰ φαίνεται,
τὰ τετράγωνα στρογγύλα, τὰ ὁμαλὰ ἐξοχὰς ἔχοντα, τὰ ὀρθὰ κεκλασμένα, τὰ
ὠχρὰ ἑτερόχροα. — (86) Ἐπεὶ οὖν οὐκ ἔνι ἔξω τόπων καὶ θέσεων ταῦτα κατα-
νοῆσαι, ἀγνοεῖται ἡ φύσις αὐτῶν.

Ὄγδοος ὁ παρὰ τὰς ποσότητας καὶ ποιότητας αὐτῶν ἢ θερμότητας ἢ ψυ-
χρότητας ἢ ταχύτητας ἢ βραδύτητας ἢ ὠχρότητας ἢ ἑτεροχροιότητας. ὁ γοῦν
οἶνος μέτριος μὲν ληφθεὶς ῥώννυσιν, πλείων δὲ παρίησιν· ὁμοίως καὶ ἡ τροφὴ καὶ
τὰ ὅμοια. — (87) Ἔνατος ὁ παρὰ τὸ ἐνδελεχὲς ἢ ξένον ἢ σπάνιον. οἱ γοῦν σεισμοὶ
παρ' οἷς συνεχῶς ἀποτελοῦνται οὐ θαυμάζονται, οὐδ' ὁ ἥλιος, ὅτι καθ' ἡμέραν
ὁρᾶται. — (88) Δέκατος ὁ κατὰ τὴν πρὸς ἄλλα σύμβλησιν, καθάπερ τὸ κοῦφον
παρὰ τὸ βαρύ, τὸ ἰσχυρὸν παρὰ τὸ ἀσθενές, τὸ μεῖζον παρὰ τὸ ἔλαττον, τὸ ἄνω
παρὰ τὸ κάτω. τὸ γοῦν δεξιὸν φύσει μὲν οὐκ ἔστι δεξιόν, κατὰ δὲ τὴν ὡς πρὸς
τὸ ἕτερον σχέσιν νοεῖται· μετατεθέντος γοῦν ἐκείνου, οὐκέτ' ἐστὶ δεξιόν.
ὁμοίως καὶ πατὴρ καὶ ἀδελφὸς ὡς πρός τι καὶ ἡμέρα ὡς πρὸς τὸν ἥλιον καὶ
πάντα ὡς πρὸς τὴν διάνοιαν. ἄγνωστα οὖν τὰ πρός τι [ὡς] καθ' ἑαυτά. καὶ
οὗτοι μὲν οἱ δέκα τρόποι.

b. Sextus Emp., *P.* I 36-38, summarizes them very shortly.

Παραδίδονται τοίνυν συνήθως παρὰ τοῖς ἀρχαιοτέροις Σκεπτικοῖς τρόποι, δι᾽ ὧν ἡ ἐποχὴ συνάγεσθαι δοκεῖ, δέκα τὸν ἀριθμόν, οὓς καὶ λόγους καὶ τόπους συνωνύμως καλοῦσιν. εἰσὶ δὲ οὗτοι, πρῶτος ὁ παρὰ τὴν τῶν ζῴων ἐξαλλαγήν, δεύτερος ὁ παρὰ τὴν τῶν ἀνθρώπων διαφοράν, τρίτος ὁ παρὰ τὰς διαφόρους τῶν αἰσθητηρίων κατασκευάς, τέταρτος ὁ παρὰ τὰς περιστάσεις, πέμπτος ὁ παρὰ τὰς θέσεις καὶ τὰ διαστήματα καὶ τοὺς τόπους, ἕκτος ὁ παρὰ τὰς ἐπιμιξίας, ἕβδομος ὁ παρὰ τὰς ποσότητας καὶ σκευασίας τῶν ὑποκειμένων, ὄγδοος ὁ ἀπὸ τοῦ πρός τι, ἔννατος ὁ παρὰ τὰς συνεχεῖς ἢ σπανίους ἐγκυρήσεις, δέκατος ὁ παρὰ τὰς ἀγωγὰς καὶ τὰ ἔθη καὶ τοὺς νόμους καὶ τὰς μυθικὰς πίστεις καὶ τὰς δογματικὰς ὑπολήψεις. χρώμεθα δὲ τῇ τάξει ταύτῃ θετικῶς.

c. Next, Sextus reduces them to three main groups:

(1) those based on the differences in the subject that judges (the first four);

(2) those based on variances in the object (nr. 7 and 10);

(3) those based on both subject and object (nrs. 5, 6, 8 and 9).

Finally, all could be reduced, he says, to one category, viz. that of relation (the πρός τι). Ib., 38-39.

Τούτων δὲ ἐπαναβεβηκότες εἰσὶ τρόποι τρεῖς, ὁ ἀπὸ τοῦ κρίνοντος, ὁ ἀπὸ τοῦ κρινομένου, ὁ ἐξ ἀμφοῖν· τῷ μὲν γὰρ ἀπὸ τοῦ κρίνοντος ὑποτάσσονται οἱ πρῶτοι τέσσαρες (τὸ γὰρ κρῖνον ἢ ζῷόν ἐστιν ἢ ἄνθρωπος ἢ αἴσθησις καὶ ἔν τινι περιστάσει), εἰς δὲ τὸν ἀπὸ τοῦ κρινομένου ⟨ἀνάγονται⟩ ὁ ἕβδομος καὶ ὁ δέκατος, εἰς δὲ τὸν ἐξ ἀμφοῖν σύνθετον ὁ πέμπτος καὶ ὁ ἕκτος καὶ ὁ ὄγδοος καὶ ὁ ἔννατος. πάλιν δὲ οἱ τρεῖς οὗτοι ἀνάγονται εἰς τὸν πρός τι, ὡς εἶναι γενικώτατον μὲν τὸν πρός τι, εἰδικοὺς δὲ τοὺς τρεῖς, ὑποβεβηκότας δὲ τοὺς δέκα.

1136—About Agrippa we do not know anything but the fact that, after Aenesidemus, he introduced 5 modes, which by certain modern critics have been judged to be the sharpest and most radical expression of scepticism [1]. Agrippa's name is mentioned by Diog. Laërt., who adds a short description of the arguments. Sextus, who says that "later Sceptics" (νεώτεροι Σκεπτικοί) handed down these arguments, explains them more clearly.

a. Diog. Laërt. IX 88:　　　　　　　　　　　　　　　　　　The five
　　　　　　　　　　　　　　　　　　　　　　　　　　　　　tropes of
Οἱ δὲ περὶ ᾽Αγρίππαν τούτοις ἄλλους πέντε προσεισάγουσι, τόν τ᾽ ἀπὸ　**Agrippa**

---

[1] Brochard, *Les sceptiques grecs*, p. 306

τῆς διαφωνίας καὶ τὸν εἰς ἄπειρον ἐκβάλλοντα καὶ τὸν πρός τι καὶ τὸν ἐξ ὑποθέσεως καὶ τὸν δι᾽ ἀλλήλων.

Description   **b.** Sextus Emp., *P.* I 165-169:

Καὶ ὁ μὲν ἀπὸ τῆς διαφωνίας ἐστὶ καθ᾽ ὃν περὶ τοῦ προτεθέντος πράγματος ἀνεπίκριτον στάσιν παρά τε τῷ βίῳ καὶ παρὰ τοῖς φιλοσόφοις εὑρίσκομεν γεγενημένην, δι᾽ ἣν οὐ δυνάμενοι αἱρεῖσθαί τι ἢ ἀποδοκιμάζειν καταλήγομεν εἰς ἐποχήν. ὁ δὲ ἀπὸ τῆς εἰς ἄπειρον ἐκπτώσεώς ἐστιν ἐν ᾧ τὸ φερόμενον εἰς πίστιν τοῦ προτεθέντος πράγματος πίστεως ἑτέρας χρῄζειν λέγομεν, κἀκεῖνο ἄλλης, καὶ μέχρις ἀπείρου, ὡς μὴ ἐχόντων ἡμῶν πόθεν ἀρξόμεθα τῆς κατασκευῆς τὴν ἐποχὴν ἀκολουθεῖν. ὁ δὲ ἀπὸ τοῦ πρός τι, καθὼς προειρήκαμεν, ἐν ᾧ πρὸς μὲν τὸ κρῖνον καὶ τὰ συνθεωρούμενα τοῖον ἢ τοῖον φαίνεται τὸ ὑποκείμενον, ὁποῖον δὲ ἔστι πρὸς τὴν φύσιν ἐπέχομεν. ὁ δὲ ἐξ ὑποθέσεως ἔστιν ὅταν εἰς ἄπειρον ἐκβαλλόμενοι οἱ δογματικοὶ ἀπό τινος ἄρξωνται ὃ οὐ κατασκευάζουσιν ἀλλ᾽ ἁπλῶς καὶ ἀναποδείκτως κατὰ συγχώρησιν λαμβάνειν ἀξιοῦσιν. ὁ δὲ διάλληλος τρόπος συνίσταται ὅταν τὸ ὀφεῖλον τοῦ ζητουμένου πράγματος εἶναι βεβαιωτικὸν χρείαν ἔχῃ τῆς ἐκ τοῦ ζητουμένου πίστεως· ἔνθα μηδέτερον δυνάμενοι λαβεῖν πρὸς κατασκευὴν θατέρου, περὶ ἀμφοτέρων ἐπέχομεν.

6—LATER SCEPTICS: MENODOTUS AND SEXTUS

1137—Later Sceptics, such as Menodotus and Sextus Empiricus, were empirical physicians, and this with an elaborate method and a theory on it. They opposed dogmatism, as in our days neopositivists oppose metaphysics: to dogmatical philosophy they opposed experience and observation (τήρησις) as nowadays positive science is often opposed to metaphysics.

Menodotus was not the first to invent empirical method: it went back to Philinos of Cos (middle of the third century), and was represented after him by Serapion of Alexandria (c. 200) and Heraclides of Tarentum (first half of the first century).

The emperi-   **a.** [Galenus], Εἰσαγωγὴ ἢ ἰατρός XIV 683, 11 (Deichgr. 6):
cal school

Τῆς δὲ ἐμπειρικῆς (sc. αἱρέσεως) προέστηκε Φιλῖνος Κῷος ὁ πρῶτος αὐτὴν ἀποτεμόμενος ἀπὸ τῆς λογικῆς αἱρέσεως τὰς ἀφορμὰς λαβὼν παρὰ Ἡροφίλου οὗ καὶ ἀκουστὴς ἐγένετο. — μετὰ δὲ Φιλῖνον ἐγένετο Σεραπίων Ἀλεξανδρεύς, εἶτα Ἀπολλώνιοι δύο πατήρ τε καὶ υἱὸς Ἀντιοχεῖς, μεθ᾽ οὓς Μηνόδοτος καὶ Σέξτος, οἳ καὶ ἀκριβῶς ἐκράτυναν αὐτήν.

b. [Galenus] Ὅροι ἰατρικοί XIX 353, 9 (Deichgr. 11):

Πόσαι (sc. εἰσὶν) κατὰ ἰατρικὴν αἱρέσεις; ἰατρικῆς αἱρέσεις αἱ πρῶται δύο, ἐμπειρική τε καὶ λογική . . . τί ἐστιν ἐμπειρική; ἔστιν ἡ μὲν ἐμπειρικὴ αἵρεσις τήρησις τῶν πλειστάκις κατὰ τὸ αὐτὸ ὡσαύτως ἑωραμένων.

1138—Sextus gives a general description of the empirical method in medicine in the following passages.

a. *Adv. math.* VIII 288:

Κἂν δῶμεν δὲ διαφέρειν τῶν ἄλλων ζῴων τὸν ἄνθρωπον λόγῳ τε καὶ μεταβατικῇ φαντασίᾳ καὶ ἐννοίᾳ ἀκολουθίας, ἀλλ᾽ οὔ τοί γε καὶ ἐν τοῖς ἀδήλοις καὶ ἀνεπικρίτως διαπεφωνημένοις συγχωρήσομεν αὐτὸν εἶναι τοιοῦτον, ἐν δὲ τοῖς φαινομένοις τηρητικήν τινα ἔχειν ἀκολουθίαν, καθ᾽ ἣν μνημονεύων τίνα μετὰ τίνων τεθεώρηται καὶ τίνα πρὸ τίνων καὶ τίνα μετὰ τίνα, ἐκ τῆς τῶν προτέρων ὑποπτώσεως ἀνανεοῦται τὰ λοιπά.

b. Ib., 291:

Τῆς μὲν τῶν ἄλλων θεωρητικῆς τέχνης οὐδέν ἐστι θεώρημα, καθάπερ ὕστερον διδάξομεν, τῆς δὲ ἐν τοῖς φαινομένοις στρεφομένης ἔστιν ἴδιόν τι θεώρημα. διὰ γὰρ τῶν πολλάκις τετηρημένων ἢ ἱστορημένων ποιεῖται τὰς τῶν θεωρημάτων συστάσεις· τὰ δὲ πολλάκις τηρηθέντα καὶ ἱστορηθέντα ἴδια καθεστήκει τῶν πλειστάκις τηρησάντων, ἀλλ᾽ οὐ κοινὰ πάντων.

1139—In *Adv. math.* V the empirical method is applied to astrology. The author concludes as follows.

Adv. math. V 104 f.:

Καὶ ὃν τρόπον ἐν τῇ ἰατρικῇ ἐτηρήσαμεν ὅτι ἡ τῆς καρδίας τρῶσις αἴτιόν ἐστι θανάτου, οὐ τὴν Δίωνος μόνον τελευτὴν αὐτῇ συμπαρατηρήσαντες ἀλλὰ καὶ Θέωνος καὶ Σωκράτους καὶ ἄλλων πολλῶν, οὕτω καὶ ἐν μαθηματικῇ εἰ πιστόν ἐστιν ὅτι ὅδε ὁ συσχηματισμὸς τῶν ἀστέρων τοιούτου βίου μηνυτικὸς καθέστηκεν, πάντως οὐχ ἅπαξ ἐφ᾽ ἑνὸς ἀλλὰ πολλάκις ἐπὶ πολλῶν παρετηρήθη. ἐπεὶ οὖν ὁ αὐτὸς τῶν ἀστέρων συσχηματισμὸς διὰ μακρῶν, ὥς φασι, χρόνων θεωρεῖται, ἀποκαταστάσεως γινομένης τοῦ μεγάλου ἐνιαυτοῦ δι᾽ ἐννεακισχιλίων ἐνακοσίων καὶ ἑβδομήκοντα καὶ ἑπτὰ ἐτῶν, οὐ φθάσει ἀνθρωπίνη τήρησις τοῖς τοσούτοις αἰῶσι συνδραμεῖν ἐπὶ μιᾶς γενέσεως, καὶ ταῦτα οὐχ ἅπαξ ἀλλὰ πολλάκις ἤτοι <τῆς> τοῦ κόσμου φθορᾶς, εἰρήκασιν ὥς τινες, μεσολαβούσης αὐτήν, ἢ πάντως γε τῆς κατὰ μέρος μεταβολῆς ἐξαφανιζούσης τὸ συνεχὲς τῆς ἱστορικῆς παραδόσεως.

1140—Scepticism as a philosophical method.

The
criterium

a. Sextus, *P.* I 22:

Κριτήριον τοίνυν φαμὲν εἶναι τῆς σκεπτικῆς ἀγωγῆς τὸ φαινόμενον, δυνάμει τὴν φαντασίαν αὐτοῦ οὕτω καλοῦντες· ἐν πείσει γὰρ καὶ ἀβουλήτῳ πάθει κειμένη ἀζήτητός ἐστιν. διὸ περὶ μὲν τοῦ φαίνεσθαι τοῖον ἢ τοῖον τὸ ὑποκείμενον οὐδεὶς ἴσως ἀμφισβητεῖ, περὶ δὲ τοῦ εἰ τοιοῦτόν ἐστιν ὁποῖον φαίνεται ζητεῖται.

applied to
practical
life

b. Ib., 23-24:

Τοῖς φαινομένοις οὖν προσέχοντες κατὰ τὴν βιωτικὴν τήρησιν ἀδοξάστως βιοῦμεν, ἐπεὶ μὴ δυνάμεθα ἀνενέργητοι παντάπασιν εἶναι. ἔοικε δὲ αὕτη ἡ βιωτικὴ τήρησις τετραμερὴς εἶναι καὶ τὸ μέν τι ἔχειν ἐν ὑφηγήσει φύσεως [1], τὸ δὲ ἐν ἀνάγκῃ παθῶν, τὸ δὲ ἐν παραδόσει νόμων τε καὶ ἐθῶν, τὸ δὲ ἐν διδασκαλίᾳ τεχνῶν, ὑφηγήσει μὲν φυσικῇ καθ' ἣν φυσικῶς αἰσθητικοὶ καὶ νοητικοὶ ἐσμεν, παθῶν δὲ ἀνάγκῃ καθ' ἣν λιμὸς μὲν ἐπὶ τροφὴν ἡμᾶς ὁδηγεῖ δίψος δ' ἐπὶ πόμα, ἐθῶν δὲ καὶ νόμων παραδόσει καθ' ἣν τὸ μὲν εὐσεβεῖν παραλαμβάνομεν βιωτικῶς ὡς ἀγαθὸν τὸ δὲ ἀσεβεῖν ὡς φαῦλον, τεχνῶν δὲ διδασκαλίᾳ καθ' ἣν οὐκ ἀνενέργητοί ἐσμεν ἐν αἷς παραλαμβάνομεν τέχναις. ταῦτα δὲ πάντα φαμὲν ἀδοξάστως.

1141—Later Sceptics have a dislike of dialectic, whether true or false (i.e., producing fallacies or opposing them): they thought it useless to argue against such arguments as "that you have horns" [2], or "that motion is impossible" [3], "becoming is impossible" [4], or "that snow is black" [5], because experience is against it.

Against
dialectic

a. Sextus, *P.* II 244-245:

Καὶ τοιούτους τινὰς ἀθροίσας ὕθλους συνάγει τὰς ὀφρῦς, καὶ προχειρίζεται τὴν διαλεκτικήν, καὶ πάνυ σεμνῶς ἐπιχειρεῖ κατασκευάζειν ἡμῖν δι' ἀποδείξεων συλλογιστικῶν ὅτι γίνεταί τι καὶ ὅτι κινεῖταί τι καὶ ὅτι ἡ χιών ἐστι λευκὴ

---

[1] The passage shows that Sextus, too, spoke of a "guidance of Nature", be it in a far more limited sense than the Stoics did. Cp. above, our note to **1079a**.

[2] Argument of Eubulides: our nr. **231d**.

[3] Sextus, *P.* II 242, refers to the argument of Diodorus Cronus, our nr. **232**.

[4] The argument referred to by Sextus l.l. goes back to Parmenides, fr. 8 D., l. 7-8, where a lacuna should be marked after the words πῇ πόθεν αὐξηθέν; Diels filled it up as follows:

<οὔτ' ἐκ τευ ἐόντος ἔγεντ' ἄν·
ἄλλο γὰρ ἂν πρὶν ἔην·> οὔτ' ἐκ μὴ ἐόντος κτλ.

[5] This assertion, according to Sextus, *P.* I 33, based by Anagaxoras on the fact that snow is frozen water, and water is black, was with its author not so much a result of dialectic as of a general theory of Nature. Cp. our nrs. **124b, c** and **133a**.

καὶ ὅτι κέρατα οὐκ ἔχομεν, καίτοι γε ἀρκοῦντος ἴσως τοῦ τὴν ἐνάργειαν αὐτοῖς ἀντιτιθέναι πρὸς τὸ θραύεσθαι τὴν διαβεβαιωτικὴν θέσιν αὐτῶν διὰ τῆς ἐκ τῶν φαινομένων ἰσοσθενοῦς αὐτῶν ἀντιμαρτυρήσεως. ταῦτά τοι καὶ ἐρωτηθεὶς φιλόσοφος <τις> [1] τὸν κατὰ τῆς κινήσεως λόγον σιωπῶν περιεπάτησεν, καὶ οἱ κατὰ τὸν βίον ἄνθρωποι πεζάς τε καὶ διαποντίους στέλλονται πορείας κατασκευά-ζουσί τε ναῦς καὶ οἰκίας καὶ παιδοποιοῦνται τῶν κατὰ τῆς κινήσεως καὶ γενέ-σεως ἀμελοῦντες λόγων. φέρεται δὲ καὶ Ἡροφίλου τοῦ ἰατροῦ χαρίεν <τι> ἀπο-μνημόνευμα· συνεχρόνισε γὰρ οὗτος Διοδώρῳ, ὃς ἐναπειροκαλῶν τῇ διαλεκτικῇ λόγους διεξῄει σοφιστικοὺς κατά τε ἄλλων πολλῶν καὶ τῆς κινήσεως. ὡς οὖν ἐκβαλών ποτε ὦμον ὁ Διόδωρος ἧκε θεραπευθησόμενος ὡς τὸν Ἡρόφιλον, ἐχαριεντίσατο ἐκεῖνος πρὸς αὐτὸν λέγων "ἤτοι ἐν ᾧ ἦν τόπῳ ὁ ὦμος ὢν ἐκπέπτωκεν, ἢ ἐν ᾧ οὐκ ἦν· οὔτε δὲ ἐν ᾧ ἦν οὔτε ἐν ᾧ οὐκ ἦν [2]· οὐκ ἄρα ἐκπέ-πτωκεν," ὡς τὸν σοφιστὴν λιπαρεῖν ἐᾶν μὲν τοὺς τοιούτους λόγους, τὴν δὲ ἐξ ἰατρικῆς ἁρμόζουσαν αὐτῷ προσάγειν θεραπείαν.

b. Sextus concludes the above passage by saying that it is possible to live in accordance with "what is generally observed and believed", without affirming anything dogmatically.

Scepticism in accordance with common sense

Ib. 246:

Ἀρκεῖ γάρ, οἶμαι, τὸ ἐμπείρως τε καὶ ἀδοξάστως κατὰ τὰς κοινὰς τηρήσεις τε καὶ προλήψεις βιοῦν, περὶ τῶν ἐκ δογματικῆς περιεργίας καὶ μάλιστα ἔξω τῆς βιωτικῆς χρείας λεγομένων ἐπέχοντας.

1142—The sceptical rejection of the σημεῖον is not against common sense either.

Sextus, *Adv. math.* VIII 156-157:

Ἀλλὰ γὰρ δυοῖν ὄντων σημείων, τοῦ τε ὑπομνηστικοῦ καὶ ἐπὶ τῶν πρὸς καιρὸν ἀδήλων τὰ πολλὰ χρησιμεύειν δοκοῦντος, καὶ τοῦ ἐνδεικτικοῦ, ὅπερ ἐπὶ τῶν φύσει ἀδήλων ἐγκρίνεται, μελλήσομεν πᾶσαν ποιεῖσθαι ζήτησιν καὶ ἀπορίαν οὐ περὶ τοῦ ὑπομνηστικοῦ (τοῦτο γὰρ παρὰ πᾶσι κοινῶς τοῖς ἐκ τοῦ βίου πε-πίστευται χρησιμεύειν), ἀλλὰ περὶ τοῦ ἐνδεικτικοῦ· τοῦτο γὰρ ὑπὸ τῶν δογματι-κῶν φιλοσόφων καὶ τῶν λογικῶν ἰατρῶν, ὡς δυνάμενον τὴν ἀναγκαιοτάτην αὐτοῖς παρέχειν χρείαν, πέπλασται. ὅθεν οὐδὲ μαχόμεθα ταῖς κοιναῖς τῶν ἀνθρώπων προλήψεσιν, οὐδὲ συγχέομεν τὸν βίον, λέγοντες μηθὲν εἶναι ση-μεῖον, καθάπερ τινὲς ἡμᾶς συκοφαντοῦσιν. εἰ μὲν γὰρ πᾶν ἀνηροῦμεν σημεῖον, τάχ' ἴσως ἂν καὶ τῷ βίῳ καὶ πᾶσιν ἀνθρώποις ἐμαχόμεθα· νυνὶ δὲ οὕτω καὶ

---

[1] According to Diog. L. VI 39 this philosopher was Diogenes the Cynic.
[2] See the argument of Diodorus under nr. **232**.

αὐτοὶ ἔγνωμεν, ἐκ μὲν καπνοῦ πῦρ, ἐκ δὲ οὐλῆς προηγησάμενον ἕλκος, ἐκ δὲ προηγουμένης καρδίας τρώσεως θάνατον, ἐκ δὲ προκειμένης ταινίας ἄλειμμα λαμβάνοντας.

Thus with regard to practical life, Sextus comes near to Pyrrho—namely in just doing what everybody does, without any dogmatical assumptions. Though he dislikes the method of dialectics, he stands with Aenesidemus in rejecting truth, causality and indicative signs. With Carneades, finally, he shares the idea of practical certitude on a merely empirical basis.

TWENTY-THIRD CHAPTER

THE STOA AND THE ACADEMY AFTER CARNEADES' CRITICISM; LATER STOICS AND LATER CYNICISM.

1—THE STOA IN DISCUSSION WITH CARNEADES

1143—Stoic philosophy was defended against Carneades by Diogenes the Babylonian and Antipater of Tarsus. Certain points were altered under the influence of Carneades' criticism.

a. The doctrine of *ekpyrosis* was abandoned by Diogenes in his later years. **Ekpyrosis abandoned**

Philo, *De incorrupt. mundi* 15; SVF III, fr. 27 Diog.:

Λέγεται δὲ καὶ Διογένης ἡνίκα νέος ἦν συνεπιγραψάμενος τῷ δόγματι τῆς ἐκπυρώσεως ὀψὲ τῆς ἡλικίας ἐνδοιάσας ἐπισχεῖν.

b. Boëthus of Sidon denied that the cosmos is a living being, but held that the sphere of the fixed stars (aether) is God. **The cosmos divine?**

Diog. L. VII 143, 148:

Βόηθος δέ φησιν οὐκ εἶναι ζῷον τὸν κόσμον. —
Βόηθος δὲ ἐν τῇ Περὶ φύσεως οὐσίαν θεοῦ τὴν τῶν ἀπλανῶν σφαῖραν.

c. Mantic, however, was defended both by Diogenes and by Antipater, as appears in Cic., *Div.* I 39, 84; 54, 123. **Mantic defended**

1144—The wording of the telos formula by Diogenes, Archedemus and Antipater is influenced by Carneades. **The telos formula**

Stob., *Ecl.* II, p. 76, 8 W:

Διογένης δέ· εὐλογιστεῖν ἐν τῇ τῶν κατὰ φύσιν ἐκλογῇ καὶ ἀπεκλογῇ.
Ἀρχέδημος δέ· πάντα τὰ καθήκοντα ἐπιτελοῦντας ζῆν.
Ἀντίπατρος δέ· ζῆν ἐκλεγομένους μὲν τὰ κατὰ φύσιν, ἀπεκλεγομένους δὲ τὰ παρὰ φύσιν διηνεκῶς. Πολλάκις δὲ καὶ οὕτως ἀπεδίδου· πᾶν τὸ καθ᾽ αὑτὸν ποιεῖν διηνεκῶς καὶ ἀπαραβάτως πρὸς τὸ τυγχάνειν τῶν προηγουμένων κατὰ φύσιν.

Doubtless, the increased interest in practical life displayed in these formulae was a result of Carneades' criticism. They tried to find an answer to the question of "How to submit practical life to reason, if the object of our striving does not contribute anything to the end".

Antipater's last cited formula leads to the difficulty that, in this conception, either the striving itself must be said to be the end, or a duplicity of ends is introduced, namely first the right choice of the object, secondly attaining it [1]. The difficulty is touched upon by Cicero, De fin. III 6, 22-7, 24, cited above (nr. **1016a, b**; cp. nrs. **1033-1036**).

The formula of Archedemus means a transition to Panaetius' doctrine of καθή-κοντα, which was, for this philosopher, the essential part of moral philosophy.

Casuistic in the Stoa

1145—As was remarked under nr. **1128c**, Diogenes and Antipater discussed a number of *casus conscientiae* such as those introduced by Carneades. Diogenes, laying stress on the instinct of selfpreservation implied in the principle of *oikeiosis*, held that, in case of a conflict of interests, one is allowed to follow one's own advantage. Antipater, emphasizing the obligations towards our fellow-men, implied in the same principle, defended the opposite rule, coming near in this to what Cicero, following the lead of Panaetius, called *humanitas*.

a. Cicero, *De off.* III 12, 51:

In huius modi causis [2] aliud Diogeni Babylonio videri solet, magno et gravi Stoico, aliud Antipatro, discipulo eius, homini acutissimo. Antipatro omnia patefacienda, ut ne quid omnino, quod venditor norit, emptor ignoret, Diogeni venditorem, quatenus iure civili constitutum sit, dicere vitia oportere, cetera sine insidiis agere et, quoniam vendat velle quam optime vendere.

b. In chapter 23 of the same book Cicero mentions quite a number of "cases", found in Hecaton's 6th book "On moral duties".

De off. III 23, 91:

Quaerit etiam, si sapiens adulterinos nummos acceperit imprudens pro bonis, cum id rescierit, soluturusne sit eos, si cui debeat, pro bonis. Diogenes ait, Antipater negat, cui potius adsentior. Qui vinum fugiens vendat sciens, debeatne dicere. Non necesse putat Diogenes, Antipater viri boni existimat.

---

[1] A distinction is made here between τέλος and σκοπός. See the instance of the archer, mentioned by Plut., *Comm. not.* 26, cited under **1016a**.

[2] Such as Carneades' first instance: how to act in selling a bad house.

1146—Also on other points Antipater laid more emphasis on the social aspect of Stoicism, e.g. in appreciating good fame (εὐδοξία), as is told by Cicero, *De fin.* III 17, 57:

De bona autem fama (quam enim appellant εὐδοξίαν, aptius est bonam famam hoc loco appellare quam gloriam) Chrysippus quidem et Diogenes detracta utilitate ne digitum quidem eius causa porrigendum esse dicebant; quibus ego vehementer assentior. Qui autem post eos fuerunt, cum Carneadem sustinere non possent, hanc, quam dixi, bonam famam ipsam propter se praepositam et sumendam esse dixerunt, esseque hominis ingenui et liberaliter educati velle bene audire a parentibus, a propinquis, a bonis etiam viris, idque propter rem ipsam, non propter usum.

In this, too, Antipater came near to Panaetius and his *humanitas*, as may be seen in Cic., *De off.* I 28, 99:
Adhibenda est igitur quaedam reverentia adversus homines et optimi cuiusque et reliquorum. Nam neglegere, quid de se quisque sentiat, non solum arrogantis est, sed etiam omnino dissoluti.

1147—In his work Π. γάμου, Antipater praised married life as the only *complete* life, which is superior to the so-called ἤθεος βίος, and a duty both towards one's native country and towards the Gods (fr. 63).

a. This is what he says about the way of seeking a companion. *Stob. Flor.* LXX 13; SVF III, fr. 62 Antip.:

Πρῶτον μὲν χρὴ τὴν μνηστείαν μὴ εἰκῆ ποιήσασθαι ἀλλὰ πάνυ πεφροντισμένως, μηδ' εἰς πλοῦτον μηδ' εἰς ὀγκοῦσαν εὐγένειαν μηδὲ εἰς ἄλλην χάσμην μηδεμίαν ἀποβλέπειν, μηδὲ μὰ Δία εἰς κάλλος· καὶ γὰρ τοῦτο ὡς ἐπὶ πᾶν ὄγκον καὶ δεσποτικὸν ἦθος περιποιεῖ· ἀλλὰ πρῶτα μὲν τὸ τοῦ γονέως ἐξετάζειν ἦθος καὶ τρόπον, εἰ πολιτικὸς καὶ ἄφορτος <καὶ> εὐγνώμων, ἔτι δὲ σώφρων καὶ δίκαιος, ἐπὶ δὲ τούτοις ἀκενόσπουδος καὶ <κατ'> ἴχνος καὶ τὰ ἄλλα <ἃ> περὶ τοῦ ποίους τινὰς φίλους κτᾶσθαι δεῖ παραγγέλλεται. ἔπειτα καὶ τὴν μητέρα, ἦ <ἡ> γαμεῖσθαι μέλλουσα συντρέφεται καὶ τὸν ταύτης τρόπον κατὰ τὸ πλεῖστον ἀποπλάττεται. μετὰ ταῦτα εἰ ἀκολούθως τῷ ἑαυτῶν τρόπῳ ἤχασι τὴν θυγατέρα καὶ μὴ ἡττημένοι εἰσὶν καὶ ἀποκεκλικότες ἀπὸ τοῦ συμφέροντος διὰ τὴν ἄγαν φιλοστοργίαν· καὶ τοῦτο ποικίλως ἐξητακέναι καὶ διὰ δούλων καὶ <δι'> ἐλευθέρων τῶν τε ἔνδοθεν καὶ τῶν ἔξωθεν καὶ διὰ γειτόνων καὶ τῶν ἄλλων εἰσιόντων εἴσω διὰ φίλων ἐπιπλοκὰς ἑστιατικὰς ἢ ἄλλως, μαγείρων ἢ δημιουργῶν ἢ ἀκεστριῶν ἢ τῶν ἄλλων τεχνιτῶν καὶ τεχνιτίδων. καὶ λίαν γὰρ προχειρότερον τοὺς τοιούτους εἰσάγουσιν καὶ ὑπὲρ τὴν ἀξίαν μεγάλα πράγματα καὶ πίστιν ἐγχειρίζουσιν.

b. To the traditional view that having a wife is a handicap he opposes the following argument. Fr. 63, SVF III p. 256, 17:

Ὁμοιότατον γάρ ἐστιν ὡς εἴ τις μίαν ἔχων χεῖρα ἑτέραν ποθὲν προσλάβοι ἢ ἕνα πόδα ἔχων ἕτερον ἀλλαχόθεν κτήσαιτο. ὡς γὰρ οὗτος πολὺ ἂν ῥᾷον καὶ βαδίσαι οὗ θέλοι κἀπελάσαι καὶ προσαγάγοιτο, οὕτως ὁ γυναῖκα εἰσαγαγόμενος ῥᾷον ἀπολήψεται τὰς κατὰ τὸν βίον σωτηρίους καὶ συμφερούσας χρείας. ἀντὶ γοῦν δύο ὀφθαλμῶν χρῶνται τέσσαρσι καὶ ἀντὶ δύο χειρῶν ἑτέραις τοσαύταις, αἷς καὶ ἀθρόως πράττοι ἂν <καὶ> ῥᾷον τὸ τῶν χειρῶν ἔργον. διὸ κἂν εἰ αἱ ἕτεραι κάμνοιεν, ταῖς ἑτέραις αὖ θεραπεύοιτο καὶ τὸ σύνολον δύο γεγονὼς ἀνθ᾽ ἑνὸς μᾶλλον ἂν ἐν τῷ βίῳ κατορθοίη. διόπερ τὸν νομίζοντα τὴν εἴσοδον τῆς γυναικὸς καταβαρύνειν τὸν βίον καὶ δυσκίνητον ποιεῖν ὅμοιον <οἶμαι> πάσχειν, ὡς εἴ τις πλείονας πόδας κωλύοι προσλαβεῖν, ἵν᾽ ἐὰν πολὺ δέῃ βαδίζειν μὴ ἐφελκώμεθα πολλούς, ἢ τῷ πλείονας χεῖρας κτωμένῳ μέμφοιτο. ὅταν γάρ τι δέῃ πράττειν ἐμποδίσεσθαι ὑπὸ τοῦ πλήθους αὐτῶν.

2—THE SO-CALLED MIDDLE STOA: (1) PANAETIUS

Panaetius   **1148—a.** Suidas (Fr. 2 V. Str.):

Παναίτιος· ὁ νεώτερος, Νικαγόρου, Ῥόδιος, φιλόσοφος Στωϊκός, Διογένους γνώριμος, ὃς καθηγήσατο καὶ Σκηπίωνος τοῦ ἐπικληθέντος Ἀφρικανοῦ μετὰ Πολύβιον Μεγαλοπολίτην. ἐτελεύτησε δ᾽ ἐν Ἀθήναις.

His ancestors   **b.** Strabo XIV 2, 13 (Fr. 3 V. Str.):

Ἄνδρες δ᾽ ἐγένοντο (sc. ἐν Ῥόδῳ) μνήμης ἄξιοι πολλοὶ στρατηλάται τε καὶ ἀθληταί, ὧν εἰσι καὶ οἱ Παναιτίου τοῦ φιλοσόφου πρόγονοι.

His intimacy with Scipio and Laelius   **c.** Cic., De fin. IV 9, 23 (Fr. 10 V. Str.):

Homo in primis ingenuus et gravis, dignus illa familiaritate Scipionis et Laelii, Panaetius. —

His works   **1149**—P. was a learned man, interested in history, mathematics and natural science, but he chiefly concentrated on metaphysical questions (he wrote a famous work Π. προνοίας, cited by Cic., Ep. ad Att. XIII 8) and was especially concerned with a "philosophy of life" for those who, by birth and talents, were called to take a leading position in the state.

a. We are informed of the contents of Panaetius' work Π. τοῦ καθήκοντος by Cicero, De off. III 2, 7:

Panaetius igitur, qui sine controversia de officiis accuratissime disputavit, quemque nos correctione quadam adhibita potissimum secuti

sumus, tribus generibus propositis, in quibus deliberare homines et con-
sultare de officio solerent, uno, cum dubitarent, honestumne id esset,
de quo ageretur, an turpe, altero, utilene esset an inutile, tertio, si id,
quod speciem haberet honesti, pugnaret cum eo, quod utile videretur,
quo modo ea discerni oporteret, de duobus generibus primis tribus
libris explicavit, de tertio autem genere deinceps se scripsit dicturum
nec exsolvit id, quod promiserat.

b.   That it was a very famous work in Antiquity may be inferred
from the following passage, ib. § 10:

Accedit eodem testis locuples Posidonius, qui etiam scribit in quadam
epistula P. Rutilium Rufum dicere solere, qui Panaetium audierat, ut
nemo pictor esset inventus, qui in Coa Venere eam partem, quam Apelles
inchoatam reliquisset, absolveret (oris enim pulchritudo reliqui corporis
imitandi spem auferebat), sic ea, quae Panaetius praetermisisset et non
perfecisset, propter eorum, quae perfecisset, praestantiam neminem per-
secutum.

c.   His work Π. αἱρέσεων, cited by Diog. Laërt. II 87, was a history Π. αἱρέσεων
of philosophy. In this work he seems to have emphasized the Socratical
character of Stoicism by tracing it back to Socrates as the father of
ethical philosophy.

Hence, the philosopher Iccius, when about to join a military expedition to
Arabia Felix, is addressed by Horatius, *Carm.* I 29, in these words:

—Quis neget arduis
pronos relabi posse rivos
montibus et Tiberim reverti,

cum tu coemptos undique nobilis
libros Panaeti Socraticam et domum
mutare loricis Hiberis,
pollicitus meliora, tendis?

Cp. Diog. Laërt. I 18, where "the ten ethical Schools" are, as such, traced back
to Socrates. Pohlenz, Stoa II p. 98, assumes that the passage is borrowed from
Panaetius, Π. αἱρέσεων.

1150—On the whole, it can be said that P. *humanized* Stoicism by
omitting many of its former characteristics: he was not interested in
logical subtleties, nor in casuistic, rejected mantic and astrology, ἀπάθεια
and the rationalistic view of man; he even abandoned the autarky of
virtue, and was as much interested in Plato and Aristotle and their
Schools as in Stoic philosophers.

General
character
of his
philosophy

a.   Cic., *De fin.* IV 28, 79:

Quam illorum (sc. Stoicorum) tristitiam atque asperitatem fugiens

Panaetius nec acerbitatem sententiarum nec disserendi spinas probavit fuitque in altero genere mitior, in altero illustrior semperque habuit in ore Platonem, Aristotelem, Xenocratem, Theophrastum, Dicaearchum, ut ipsius scripta declarant.

b. Cp. *Stoic. Index Herc.* col. 61 (Fr. 57 V. Str.):

ᵀΗν γὰρ ἰσχυρῶς φιλοπλάτων καὶ φιλοαριστοτέλης, ἀ[λλὰ] (κ)αὶ παρε[ν-έδ]ω[κ]ε τ(ῶ)ν Ζηνων[είω]ν [τι διὰ τὴ]ν 'Ακαδημίαν [καὶ τὸν Περί](π)ατον.

Phil. of nature

1151—Like Posidonius after him, P. started from the philosophy of nature.

a. Diog. Laërt. VII 41:

Παναίτιος δὲ καὶ Ποσειδώνιος ἀπὸ τῶν φυσικῶν ἄρχονται.

Eternity of the cosmos

b. He rejected *ekpyrosis* and held the eternity of the cosmos. Philo, *De aetern. mundi* 76 (Fr. 65 V. Str.):

Βοηθὸς γοῦν ὁ Σιδώνιος καὶ Παναίτιος, ἄνδρες ἐν τοῖς Στωϊκοῖς δόγμασιν ἰσχυκότες, ἄτε θεόληπτοι, τὰς ἐκπυρώσεις καὶ παλιγγενεσίας καταλιπόντες πρὸς ὁσιώτερον δόγμα τὸ τῆς ἀφθαρσίας τοῦ κόσμου παντὸς ηὐτομόλησαν.

c. In Cic., *De n.d.* II 38, 98,-40,103 we find a passage where the beauty and harmony of nature (not only of the heavens) are adduced as an argument for Providence. Pohlenz, *St.* I 195, II 99, attributes the passage to P., as was done by Heinemann, *Posid.* II 183 ff. This is, however, purely conjectural. Cp. Festugière, *Le dieu cosmique*, p. 416 ff. K. Reinhardt attributed the same passage with the following chapters to Posidonius.

Rejection of mantic

1152—P. rejected mantic and popular religion.

a. Epiphanius, *De fide* 9, 45 (Fr. 68 V. Str.):

Παναίτιος ὁ 'Ρόδιος τὸν κόσμον ἔλεγεν ἀθάνατον καὶ ἀγήρω, καὶ τῆς μαντείας κατ' οὐδὲν ἐπεστρέφετο, καὶ τὰ περὶ θεῶν λεγόμενα ἀνῄρει. ἔλεγε γὰρ φλήναφον εἶναι τὸν περὶ θεοῦ λόγον.

b. Diog. Laërt. VII 149 (Fr. 73 V. Str.):

'Ο μὲν γὰρ Παναίτιος ἀνυπόστατον αὐτήν (sc. τὴν μαντικήν) φησιν.

Arguments against astrology

1153—According to Cicero, *De div.* II ch. 42 ff., P. rejected the predictions of astrology. Even Diogenes, he says, made certain restrictions here.

a. *De div.* II 43, 90:

Etenim geminorum formas esse similis, vitam atque fortunam plerumque disparem. Procles et Eurysthenes Lacedaemoniorum reges gemini fratres fuerunt. at ii nec totidem annos vixerunt, anno enim Procli vita brevior fuit, multumque is fratri rerum gestarum gloria praestitit.

b. P.'s strongest argument is that climatic influences must be more important than sidereal ones.

Ib., 44, 93 - 45, 94; 46, 96 f.:

(—necesse est ortus occasusque siderum non fieri eodem tempore apud omnes.)
Quodsi eorum vi caelum modo hoc modo illo modo temperatur, qui potest eadem vis esse nascentium, cum caeli tanta sit dissimilitudo? in his locis quae nos incolimus post solstitium Canicula exoritur et quidem aliquot diebus, at apud Troglodytas, ut scribitur, ante solstitium, ut, si iam concedamus aliquid vim caelestem ad eos qui in terra gignuntur pertinere, confitendum sit illis eos, qui nascuntur eodem tempore, posse in dissimilis incidere naturas propter caeli dissimilitudinem; quod minime illis placet; volunt enim illi omnis eodem tempore ortos qui ubique sint nati eadem condicione nasci. Sed quae tanta dementia est, ut in maxumis motibus mutationibusque caeli nihil intersit qui ventus, qui imber, quae tempestas ubique sit? quarum rerum in proxumis locis tantae dissimilitudines saepe sint, ut alia Tusculi alia Romae eveniat saepe tempestas; quod qui navigant maxume animadvertunt, cum in flectendis promunturiis ventorum mutationes maxumas saepe sentiant — haec igitur cum sit tum serenitas tum perturbatio caeli, estne sanorum hominum hoc ad nascentium ortus pertinere non dicere, quod non certe pertinet, illud nescio quid tenue, quod sentiri nullo modo, intellegi autem vix potest, quae a luna ceterisque sideribus caeli temperatio fiat, dicere ad puerorum ortus pertinere? —
Quid? Dissimilitudo locorum nonne dissimilis hominum procreationes habet? quas quidem percurrere oratione facile est, quid inter Indos et Persas, Aethiopas ‹et› Syros differat corporibus animis, ut incredibilis varietas dissimilitudoque sit. ex quo intellegitur plus terrarum situs quam lunae tactus ad nascendum valere.

1154—P. also denied the immortality of the soul, and this for two reasons.

Arguments against immortality

Cic., *Tusc. disp.* I 32, 79, cited above, nr. **958**.

1155—P. opposes Chrysippus' psychological monism.

He admits an irrational part in the soul

a. Cic., *De off.* I 28, 101:

Duplex est enim vis animorum atque naturae; una pars in adpetitu posita est, quae est ὁρμή Graece, quae hominem huc et illuc rapit, altera in ratione, quae docet et explanat, quid faciendum fugiendumve sit.

b. Ib., I 36, 132:

Motus autem animorum duplices sunt, alteri cogitationis, alteri adpetitus; cogitatio in vero exquirendo maxime versatur, appetitus impellit ad agendum. Curandum est igitur, ut cogitatione ad res quam optimas utamur, adpetitum rationi oboedientem praebeamus.

New interpretation of the telos formula

1156—He took Zeno's telos formula in such a sense, that *natural aspirations* (ἀφορμαί) acquire a very positive sense.

Clem. Alex., *Strom.* II 21 (Fr. 96 V. Str.):

Πρὸς τούτοις ἔτι Παναίτιος τὸ ζῆν κατὰ τὰς δεδομένας ἡμῖν ἐκ φύσεως ἀφορμὰς τέλος ἀπεφήνατο.

Thus the classical Stoic rule of life was interpreted in a decidedly individual sense. Cp. what was noticed under **1005d**. See further **1163**.

Virtues founded on natural strivings

1157—P. finds four natural aspirations or "strivings" in man, on which he founds the four cardinal virtues.

Cic., *De off.* I 4, 12-14:

Having spoken of the instinct of selfpreservation which, in its lower form, is common to all living beings, the author continues as follows.

Eademque natura vi rationis hominem conciliat homini et ad orationis et ad vitae societatem ingeneratque in primis praecipuum quendam amorem in eos, qui procreati sunt, impellitque, ut hominum coetus et celebrationes et esse et a se obiri velit ob easque causas studeat parare ea, quae suppeditent ad cultum et ad victum, nec sibi soli, sed coniugi, liberis ceterisque, quos caros habeat tuerique debeat; quae cura exsuscitat etiam animos et maiores ad rem gerendam facit. In primisque hominis est propria veri inquisitio atque investigatio. Itaque cum sumus necessariis negotiis curisque vacui, tum avemus aliquid videre, audire, addiscere cognitionemque rerum aut occultarum aut admirabilium ad beate vivendum necessariam ducimus. Ex quo intellegitur, quod verum, simplex sincerumque sit, id esse naturae hominis aptissimum. Huic veri videndi cupiditati adiuncta est adpetitio quaedam principatus, ut nemini parere animus bene informatus a natura velit nisi praecipienti aut docenti aut utilitatis causa iuste et legitime imperanti; ex quo magnitudo animi existit humanarumque rerum contemptio. Nec vero illa parva vis naturae est rationisque, quod unum hoc animal sentit, quid sit ordo, quid sit quod deceat, in factis dictisque qui modus. Itaque eorum ipsorum, quae aspectu sentiuntur, nullum aliud animal pulchritudinem, venustatem, convenientiam partium sentit; quam similitudinem natura ratioque ab oculis ad animum transferens multo etiam magis pulchritudinem, constantiam, ordinem in consiliis factisque conservandam putat cavetque, ne quid indecore effeminateve faciat, tum in omnibus et opinionibus et factis ne quid libidinose aut faciat aut cogitet. Quibus ex rebus conflatur et efficitur id, quod quaerimus, honestum, quod, etiamsi nobilitatum non sit, tamen honestum est, quodque vere dicimus, etiamsi a nullo laudetur, natura esse laudabile.

1158—Thus, the *honestum* is displayed in four different fields, the first of which consists in the knowledge of truth.

The intellectual virtue

Cic., *De off.* I 6, 18-19:

Ex quattuor autem locis, in quos honesti naturam vimque divisimus, primus ille, qui in veri cognitione consistit, maxime naturam attingit humanam. Omnes enim trahimur et ducimur ad cognitionis et scientiae cupiditatem, in qua excellere pulchrum putamus, labi autem, errare, nescire, decipi et malum et turpe ducimus. In hoc genere et naturali et honesto duo vitia vitanda sunt, unum, ne incognita pro cognitis habeamus iisque temere adsentiamur; quod vitium effugere qui volet (omnes autem velle debent), adhibebit ad considerandas res et tempus et diligentiam. Alterum est vitium, quod quidam nimis magnum studium multamque operam in res obscuras atque difficiles conferunt easdemque non necessarias.

1159—Next comes social virtue.

Social virtue: justice and generosity

a. Ib., I 7, 20:

De tribus autem reliquis latissime patet ea ratio, qua societas hominum inter ipsos et vitae quasi communitas continetur. Cuius partes sunt duae, iustitia, in qua virtutis splendor est maximus, ex qua viri boni nominantur, et huic coniuncta beneficentia, quam eandem vel benignitatem vel liberalitatem appellari licet. Sed iustitiae primum munus est, ut ne cui quis noceat nisi lacessitus iniuria, deinde ut communibus pro communibus utatur, privatis ut suis.

As may be seen in this definition and in several other passages of the same work, P. accepted the legitimacy of private property as a basic principle of human society (*De off.* I 7, 21). Violating it is a sin against humanity (III 5, 21; III 6, 30). Cp. **1162b** and **1168**.

b. In fact, P.'s social virtue did not stop at the "ne cui quis noceat, nisi lacessitus iniuria". First, he exhorts to moderation towards those who have wronged us (*De off.* I 11, 33) and extends moral obligations to our enemies (cp. our nrs. **1069b** and **1070**, on the natural community of mankind, and on international law founded on this principle; also **1000b**, on the practical consequences of *oikeiosis*). Secondly his social virtue is not only negative in character, but means an active kindness towards man in general and towards special groups of persons in particular. This is the doctrine of *beneficentia* and *liberalitas*, expounded in *De off.* I, ch. 14-18.

Cicero, following P., uses also the term *humanitas*, which includes both the Greek παιδεία and φιλανθρωπία (kindness towards man). A word will be said on it under **1162**.

Fortitudo **1160**—The virtue corresponding to the classical ἀνδρεία is developed by P. in the direction of Aristotle's μεγαλοψυχία. It is not called first, but *splendidissimum*, and is worked by, or even consists in, an *animus magnus elatusque humanasque res despiciens*.

a. Cic., *De off.* I 20, 66-67:

Omnino fortis animus et magnus duabus rebus maxime cernitur, quarum una in rerum externarum despicientia ponitur, cum persuasum sit nihil hominem, nisi quod honestum decorumque sit, aut admirari aut optare aut expetere oportere nullique neque homini neque perturbationi animi nec fortunae succumbere. Altera est res, ut, cum ita sis adfectus animo, ut supra dixi, res geras magnas illas quidem et maxime utiles, sed et vehementer arduas plenasque laborum et periculorum cum vitae, tum multarum rerum, quae ad vitam pertinent. Harum rerum duarum splendor omnis, amplitudo, addo etiam utilitatem, in posteriore est, causa autem et ratio efficiens magnos viros in priore.

b. Under this heading P. probably gave some directions for state-government. He warned against partisanship (citing Plato) and against ambition, and exhorted to gentleness towards political enemies and to humility in favourable conditions of life.

Cic., *De off.* I 26, 90:   Warning against arrogance

Atque etiam in rebus prosperis et ad voluntatem nostram fluentibus superbiam magnopere, fastidium arrogantiamque fugiamus. Nam ut adversas res, sic secundas immoderate ferre levitatis est, praeclaraque est aequabilitas in omni vita et idem semper vultus eademque frons, ut de Socrate idemque de C. Laelio accepimus. —

Panaetius quidem Africanum, auditorem et familiarem suum, solitum ait dicere: "ut equos propter crebras contentiones proeliorum ferocitate exultantes domitoribus tradere soleant, ut iis facilioribus possint uti, sic homines secundis rebus effrenatos sibique praefidentes tamquam in gyrum rationis et doctrinae duci oportere, ut perspicerent rerum humanarum inbecillitatem varietatemque fortunae.

1161—In the fourth kind, which is concerned with moderation and self-   *Temperantia et modestia*
control, is included what is called by Cicero the *decorum* (Gr. τὸ πρέπον).

   a.   Cic., *De off.* I 27, 93-94; 96:
Sequitur, ut de una reliqua parte honestatis dicendum sit, in qua verecundia et quasi quidam ornatus vitae, temperantia et modestia omnisque sedatio perturbationum animi et rerum modus cernitur. Hoc loco continetur id, quod dici Latine decorum potest; Graece enim πρέπον dicitur. Huius vis ea est, ut ab honesto non queat separari; nam et quod decet, honestum est, et quod honestum est, decet. Qualis autem differentia sit honesti et decori, facilius intellegi quam explanari potest. Quidquid est enim quod deceat, id tum apparet, cum antegressa est honestas. Itaque non solum in hac parte honestatis, de qua hoc loco disserendum est, sed etiam in tribus superioribus quid deceat apparet.—

Est autem eius descriptio duplex; nam et generale quoddam decorum intellegimus, quod in omni honestate versatur, et aliud huic subiectum, quod pertinet ad singulas partes honestatis. Atque illud superius sic fere definiri solet: decorum id esse, quod consentaneum sit hominis excellentiae in eo, in quo natura eius a reliquis animantibus differat. Quae autem pars subiecta generi est, eam sic definiunt, ut id decorum velint esse, quod ita naturae consentaneum sit, ut in eo moderatio et temperantia appareat cum specie quadam liberali.

   b.   It completes justice as a social virtue. Ib. 28, 99:
Adhibenda est igitur quaedam reverentia adversus homines et optimi   Reverence towards men
cuiusque et reliquorum. [1] —

------
[1]   Here follows the sentence on the value of good fame, cited above, nr. **1146**.

Est autem quod differat in hominum ratione habenda inter iustitiam et verecundiam. Iustitiae partes sunt non violare homines, verecundiae non offendere; in quo maxime vis perspicitur decori.

Humanity and humanitas 1162—Of P. is certainly the doctrine of degrees of social relationship, and of the natural bond that binds together man and man.

    a. Cic., *De off.* I 16, 50-51; 17, 53:

Est enim primum (principium communitatis), quod cernitur in universi generis humani societate. Eius autem vinculum est ratio et oratio, quae docendo, discendo, communicando, disceptando, iudicando conciliat inter se homines coniungitque naturali quadam societate. Neque ulla re longius absumus a natura ferarum, in quibus inesse fortitudinem saepe dicimus, ut in equis, in leonibus, iustitiam, aequitatem, bonitatem non dicimus; sunt enim rationis et orationis expertes. Ac latissime quidem patens hominibus inter ipsos, omnibus inter omnes, societas haec est. In qua omnium rerum, quas ad communem hominum usum natura genuit, est servanda communitas. —

Gradus autem plures sunt societatis hominum. Ut enim ab illa infinita discedatur, propior est eiusdem gentis, nationis, linguae, qua maxime homines coniunguntur. Interius etiam est eiusdem esse civitatis; multa enim sunt civibus inter se communia, forum, fana, porticus, viae, leges, iura, iudicia, suffragia, consuetudines praeterea et familiaritates multisque cum multis res rationesque contractae. Artior vero colligatio est societatis propinquorum; ab illa enim immensa societate humani generis in exiguum angustumque concluditur.

The idea of *humanity* as a whole is found repeatedly in *De off.* Some passages have been cited under **1000b** and **1096b**. Since certain moral obligations are deduced from it, we find ourselves here in the sphere of that *humanitas* which, through the medium of Cicero, became so famous in later history.

    b. What is "human" and what is "inhuman".

What is „human" Cic., *De off.* III 6, 30; 10, 41; 11, 47; 23, 89:

Si quid ab homine ad nullam partem utili utilitatis tuae causa detraxeris, inhumane feceris contraque naturae legem. —

    (41) Omisit hic (sc. Romulus patricida) et pietatem et humanitatem. —

    (47) Usu vero urbis prohibere peregrinos sane inhumanum est.

    (89) (Hecaton in sexto libro de officiis) ad extremum utilitate, ut putat, officium dirigit magis quam humanitate.

1163—P. distinguished the generic nature of man from the individual nature. By the latter notion he formally discovered the concept of personality. It took an important place in his philosophy. The concept of personality

Cic., *De off.* I 30, 107; 31, 110-112, 114:

Intellegendum etiam est duabus quasi nos a natura indutos esse personis; quarum una communis est ex eo, quod omnes participes sumus rationis praestantiaeque eius, qua antecellimus bestiis, a qua omne honestum decorumque trahitur, et ex qua ratio inveniendi officii exquiritur, altera autem, quae proprie singulis est tributa. Ut enim in corporibus magnae dissimilitudines sunt (alios videmus velocitate ad cursum, alios viribus ad luctandum valere, itemque in formis aliis dignitatem inesse, aliis venustatem), sic in animis existunt maiores etiam varietates. — (110) Admodum autem tenenda sunt sua cuique non vitiosa, sed tamen propria, quo facilius decorum illud, quod quaerimus, retineatur. Sic enim est faciendum, ut contra universam naturam nihil contendamus, ea tamen conservata propriam nostram sequamur, ut, etiamsi sint alia graviora atque meliora, tamen nos studia nostra nostrae naturae regula metiamur; neque enim attinet naturae repugnare nec quicquam sequi, quod adsequi non queas. Ex quo magis emergit, quale sit decorum illud, ideo quia nihil decet invita Minerva, ut aiunt, id est adversante et repugnante natura. Omnino si quicquam est decorum, nihil est profecto magis quam aequabilitas universae vitae, tum singularium actionum, quam conservare non possis, si aliorum naturam imitans omittas tuam. — (112) Atque haec differentia naturarum tantam habet vim, ut non numquam mortem sibi ipse consciscere alius debeat, alius in eadem causa non debeat. Num enim alia in causa M. Cato fuit, alia ceteri, qui se in Africa Caesari tradiderunt? Atqui ceteris forsitan vitio datum esset, si se interemissent, propterea quod lenior eorum vita et mores fuerant faciliores, Catoni cum incredibilem tribuisset natura gravitatem eamque ipse perpetua constantia roboravisset semperque in proposito susceptoque consilio permansisset, moriendum potius quam tyranni vultus aspiciendus fuit. — (114) Suum quisque igitur noscat ingenium acremque se et bonorum et vitiorum suorum iudicem praebeat, ne scaenici plus quam nos videantur habere prudentiae.

1164—In his *De off.* III, Cicero followed P. in holding, first, that the *utile* should not be compared with the *honestum*. Honestum and utile

a. *De off.* III 4, 18:

Qui autem omnia metiuntur emolumentis et commodis neque ea volunt praeponderari honestate, ii solent in deliberando honestum cum eo, quod utile putant, comparare, boni viri non solent. Itaque existimo Panaetium, cum dixerit homines solere in hac comparatione dubitare, hoc ipsum sensisse quod dixerit, "solere" modo, non etiam "oportere". Etenim non modo pluris putare quod utile videatur quam quod honestum sit, sed etiam haec inter se comparare et in his addubitare turpissimum est.

b. Secondly, that there is not any real conflict between the two. *De off.* III 7, 34- 8, 35:

Ac primum in hoc Panaetius defendendus est, quod non utilia cum honestis pugnare aliquando posse dixerit (neque enim ei fas erat), sed ea, quae viderentur utilia. Nihil vero utile, quod non idem honestum, nihil honestum, quod non idem utile sit, saepe testatur negatque ullam pestem maiorem in vitam hominum invasisse quam eorum opinionem, qui ista distraxerint. Itaque, non ut aliquando anteponeremus utilia honestis, sed ut ea sine errore diiudicaremus, si quando incidissent, induxit eam, quae videretur esse, non quae esset, repugnantiam.

The autarchy of virtue abandoned

1165—The πρῶτα κατὰ φύσιν taxed as real values.

a. Diog. Laërt. VII 128 (Fr. 110 V. Str.):

Ὁ μέντοι Παναίτιος καὶ Ποσειδώνιος οὐκ αὐτάρκη λέγουσι τὴν ἀρετήν, ἀλλὰ χρείαν εἶναί φασι καὶ ὑγιείας καὶ χορηγίας καὶ ἰσχύος.

Not an ascetic style of life

b. In fact, P. was not an ascetic, nor did he teach his aristocratic pupils an ascetic style of life. E.g., in *De off.* I 39, 138 f., it is said that a man of rank and station should have a spacious and imposing house, according to his dignity.

Rejection of ἀπάθεια

1166—Rejection of ἀπάθεια and ἀναλγησία.

a. Gellius, *N.A.* XII 5 (Fr. 111 V. Str.):

,,᾿Αναλγησία enim atque ἀπάθεια non meo tantum," inquit, ,,sed quorundam etiam ex eadem porticu prudentiorum hominum, sicuti iudicio Panaetii, gravis atque docti viri, improbata abiectaque est."

Cp. Cic., *De off.* I 29, 103: Ex quibus intellegitur, ... appetitus *omnes contrahendos sedandosque esse.*

Now this was exactly what the Academics and Peripatetics held, as opposed to the Stoic tenets. Our nr. **1059a, b**. Cp. Posidonius, infra, nr. **1187**.

b. Sextus, *Adv. math.* XI (= *Ag. the Eth.*) 73 (Fr. 112 V. Str.): **Pleasure**

Παναίτιος δὲ (φησὶν ἡδονὴν) τινὰ μὲν κατὰ φύσιν ὑπάρχειν, τινὰ δὲ παρὰ φύσιν.

Cp. Cic., *De off.* I 30, 105-106, where it is said—and certainly P. is the author—that sensual pleasure is unworthy of the dignity of man, and that a sober life is in accordance with the superiority and dignity of our nature.

c. He never said that pain is not an evil, but, for the rest, took a **Pain** "Stoic" attitude towards it as much as possible.

Cic., *De fin.* IV 9, 23:

Homo in primis ingenuus et gravis, dignus illa familiaritate Scipionis et Laelii, Panaetius, cum ad Q. Tuberonem de dolore patiendo scriberet, quod esse caput debebat, si probari posset, nusquam posuit non esse malum dolorem, sed quid esset et quale, quantumque in eo inesset alieni, deinde quae ratio esset perferendi.

1167—Seneca, *Ep.* XIX 7, 5 (Fr. 114 V. Str.): **Love**

Eleganter mihi videtur Panaetius respondisse adulescentulo cuidam quaerenti, an sapiens amaturus esset. de sapiente, inquit, videbimus: mihi et tibi, qui adhuc a sapiente longe absumus, non est committendum, ut incidamus in rem commotam, inpotentem, alteri emancupatam, vilem sibi. sive enim non respuit, humanitate eius inritamur, sive contempsit, superbia accendimur. aeque facilitas amoris quam difficultas nocet: facilitate capimur, cum difficultate certamus. itaque conscii nobis imbecillitatis nostrae quiescamus. nec vino infirmum animum committamus nec formae nec adulationi nec ullis rebus blande trahentibus.

1168—On the whole, P.'s moral philosophy displays an essentially **Aristocratic character of** aristocratic character. This appears first in his attitude towards private **P.'s moral** property and what he declares to be the first duty of the statesman and **philosophy** the essential function of the state.

a. Cic., *De off.* III 5, 21: **Private property**

Detrahere igitur alteri aliquid et hominem hominis incommodo suum commodum augere magis est contra naturam quam mors, quam paupertas, quam dolor, quam cetera, quae possunt aut corpori accidere aut rebus externis. Nam principio tollit convictum humanum et societatem.

Since Cicero wrote the third book *De off.* "suo marte", these words cannot be regarded as a literal quotation of P.; they were, however, certainly an expression of his conviction.

b. Cic., *De off.* II 21, 73:

In primis autem videndum erit ei, qui rem publicam administrabit, ut suum quisque teneat neque de bonis privatorum publice deminutio fiat. — Hanc enim ob causam maxime, ut sua tenerentur, res publicae civitatesque constitutae sunt.

1169—P. did not think that his principles of humanity came into conflict with Roman imperialism. On the contrary, he thinks imperialism can and must be justified by the humanity of the rulers. Hence his directions about "humanity" in war, and mildness towards the vanquished.

a. Cic., *De off.* I 11, 34-35:

Atque in re publica maxime conservanda sunt iura belli. Nam cum sint duo genera decertandi, unum per disceptationem, alterum per vim, cumque illud proprium sit hominis, hoc beluarum, confugiendum est ad posterius, si uti non licet superiore. Quare suscipienda quidem bella sunt ob eam causam, ut sine iniuria in pace vivatur, parta autem victoria conservandi ii, qui non crudeles in bello, non inmanes fuerunt. — Et cum iis, quos vi deviceris, consulendum est, tum ii, qui armis positis ad imperatorum fidem confugient, quamvis murum aries percusserit, recipiendi.

Cp. also III, 11, 46 f.
Thus P. defended Roman justice against Carneades' famous attack. And this was, certainly, one of the reasons of his great influence in Rome.

b. An ironical application of P.'s principles— ironical, not to the Roman author, evidently, but to modern appreciation—may be seen in Cicero's praise of Aemilius Paullus who, by bringing all the wealth of Macedonia into the treasury of Rome, provided an ideal solution of all tax problems.

De off. II 22, 76:

Laudat Africanum Panaetius, quod fuerit abstinens. Quidni laudet? Sed in illo alia maiora; laus abstinentiae non hominis est solum, sed etiam temporum illorum. Omni Macedonum gaza, quae fuit maxima, potitus Paulus tantum in aerarium pecuniae invexit, ut unius imperatoris praeda finem attulerit tributorum. At hic nihil domum suam intulit praeter memoriam nominis sempiternam.

3—THE SO-CALLED MIDDLE STOA: (2) POSIDONIUS

1170—a. Suidas: Life

Ποσειδώνιος· Ἀπαμεὺς ἐκ Συρίας ἢ Ῥόδιος· [1] φιλόσοφος Στωϊκός, ὃς ἐπεκλήθη Ἀθλητής. σχόλην δ' ἔσχεν ἐν Ῥόδῳ, διάδοχος γεγονὼς καὶ μαθητὴς Παναιτίου. ἦλθε δὲ καὶ εἰς Ῥώμην ἐπὶ Μάρκου Μαρκέλλου [2]. ἔγραψε πόλλα.

b. Strabo, XIV 2, 13:

Ποσειδώνιος δ' ἐπολιτεύσατο μὲν ἐν Ῥόδῳ καὶ ἐσοφίστευσεν, ἦν δ' Ἀπαμεὺς ἐκ τῆς Συρίας.

c. Strabo XVI 2, 10:   The fame of
                                                                                                         his learning
Ἐντεῦθεν (sc. ἐξ Ἀπαμείας) δ' ἐστὶ Ποσειδώνιος ὁ Στωϊκός, ἀνὴρ τῶν καθ' ἡμᾶς φιλοσόφων πολυμαθέστατος.

Cicero mentions him with pride as his master and friend: *De n.d.* I 3, 6.

1171—a. In 86 he was an ambassador to Rome and met with Marius,   Ambassador
then an old and sick man.   to Rome

Plut., *Marius* 45:

Having described Marius's state of mind as that of an overtired man, full of
fears and anguish, he concludes:

Τέλος δὲ ... εἰς νόσον κατηνέχθη πλευρῖτιν, ὡς ἱστορεῖ Ποσειδώνιος ὁ
φιλόσοφος, αὐτὸς ἐσελθεῖν καὶ διαλεχθῆναι περὶ ὧν ἐπρέσβευεν ἤδη νοσοῦντι
φάσκων αὐτῷ.

b. Pompeius visited him on Rhodes in going to and coming from   Visit of
the war with Mithradates.   Pompeius

Cic., *Tusc. disp.* II 25, 61:

Solebat narrare Pompeius, se, cum Rhodum venisset decedens ex
Syria, audire voluisse Posidonium; sed cum audisset eum graviter esse
aegrum, quod vehementer eius artus laborarent, voluisse tamen nobilissi-
mum philosophum visere: quem ut vidisset et salutavisset honorificisque
verbis prosecutus esset molesteque se dixisset ferre, quod eum non posset
audire, at ille: "tu vero", inquit, "potes, nec committam, ut dolor
corporis efficiat, ut frustra tantus vir ad me venerit." Itaque narrabat
eum graviter et copiose de hoc ipso, nihil esse bonum nisi quod esset

---

[1] More accurately: he was born at Apameia in Syria and had his school on
Rhodes. Cp. **1170b** and **1171b**.
[2] Probably in 51 B.C., when the pact between Rome and Rhodes was renewed.

honestum, cubantem disputavisse, cumque quasi faces ei doloris admo-
verentur, saepe dixisse: "nihil agis, dolor! quamvis sis molestus, numquam te esse confitebor malum."

Cp. Strabo XI 1, 6 and Plut., *Pomp.* 42 (F.Gr.Hist. II, T 8).

The histori-
an and the   1172—He wrote historical and geographical-ethnological works, fre-
geographer quently cited by Strabo, Diodorus and Athenaeus.

a. [Lucian.], *Macrob.* 20 (F. Gr. Hist. II, T 4):

Ποσειδώνιος ὁ 'Απαμεὺς τῆς Συρίας, νόμῳ δὲ 'Ρόδιος, φιλόσοφός τε ἅμα
καὶ ἱστορίας συγγραφεὺς —

b. Athen. IV 36, p. 151 E (F. Gr. Hist. II, T 12a):

Ποσειδώνιος δ' ὁ ἀπὸ τῆς Στοᾶς ἐν ταῖς ἱστορίαις, αἷς συνέθηκεν οὐκ.
ἀλλοτρίως ἧς προῄρητο φιλοσοφίας, πολλὰ παρὰ πολλοῖς ἔθιμα καὶ νόμιμα
ἀναγράφων —

c. Physical geography took an important place in his works.
Strabo VIII 1, 1 (F. Gr. Hist. II, T 14):

Οἱ δ' ἐν τῇ κοινῇ τῆς ἱστορίας.γραφῇ χωρὶς ἀποδείξαντες τὴν τῶν ἠπείρων
τοπογραφίαν, καθάπερ "Εφορός τε ἐποίησε καὶ Πολύβιος, ἄλλοι δ' εἰς τὸν
φυσικὸν τόπον καὶ τὸν μαθηματικὸν προσέλαβόν τινα καὶ τῶν τοιούτων,
καθάπερ Ποσειδώνιός τε καὶ "Ιππαρχος.

d. Cp. Strabo II 3, 8 (F. Gr. Hist. II, T 15b):

Πολὺ γάρ ἐστι τὸ αἰτιολογικὸν παρὰ αὐτῷ καὶ τὸ ἀριστοτελίζον.

Fragments in *F.Gr.Hist.* II A, pp. 225-317. Pohlenz calls him the greatest scientific
explorer of the Ancient world.

1173—In his work Π. 'Ωκεανοῦ, frequently cited by Strabo, he develops
his theory of the form of the earth, the five zones and the climates.

The form of
the earth   a. Strabo II 2, 1-3 (F. Gr. Hist. II, F 28):

Ἔστιν οὖν τι τῶν πρὸς γεωγραφίαν οἰκείων τὸ τὴν γῆν ὅλην ὑποθέσθαι
σφαιροειδῆ, καθάπερ καὶ τὸν κόσμον, καὶ τὰ ἄλλα παραδέξασθαι τὰ ἀκόλουθα
τῇ ὑποθέσει ταύτῃ. τούτων δ' ἐστὶ καὶ τὸ πεντάζωνον αὐτὴν εἶναι. — (3) αὐτὸς
δὲ διαιρῶν εἰς τὰς ζώνας πέντε μέν φησιν εἶναι χρησίμους πρὸς τὰ οὐράνια.
The five
zones   τούτων δὲ περισκίους δύο τὰς ὑπὸ τοῖς πόλοις μέχρι τῶν ἐχόντων τοὺς τροπικοὺς
ἀρκτικούς· ἑτεροσκίους δὲ τὰς ἐφεξῆς ταύταις δύο μέχρι τῶν ὑπὸ τροπικοῖς
οἰκούντων, ἀμφίσκιον δὲ τὴν μεταξὺ τῶν τροπικῶν.

b.   The terms are explained in II 5, 43 (F. Gr. Hist. II, F 76):

'Αμφίσκιοι μέν, ὅσοι κατὰ μέσον ἡμέρας τοτὲ μὲν ἐπὶ τάδε πιπτούσας ἔχουσι τὰς σκιάς, ὅταν ὁ ἥλιος ἀπὸ μεσημβρίας τῷ γνώμονι προσπίπτῃ τῷ ὀρθῷ πρὸς τὸ ὑποκείμενον ἐπίπεδον, τοτὲ δ' εἰς τοὐναντίον, ὅταν ὁ ἥλιος εἰς τοὐναντίον περιστῇ. τοῦτο δὲ συμβέβηκε μόνοις τοῖς μεταξὺ τῶν τροπικῶν οἰκοῦσιν. ἑτερόσκιοι δ' ὅσοις ἢ ἐπὶ τὴν ἄρκτον ἀεὶ πίπτουσιν, ὥσπερ ἡμῖν, ἢ ἐπὶ τὰ νότια, ὥσπερ τοῖς ἐν τῇ ἑτέρᾳ εὐκράτῳ ζώνῃ οἰκοῦσι· τοῦτο δὲ συμβαίνει πᾶσι τοῖς ἐλάττονα ἔχουσι τοῦ τροπικοῦ τὸν ἀρκτικόν. ὅταν δὲ τὸν αὐτὸν ἢ μείζονα, ἀρχὴ τῶν περισκίων ἐστὶ μέχρι τῶν οἰκούντων ὑπὸ τῷ πόλῳ.

c.   He holds that the zone, called "torrid" by his predecessors, is not only inhabited, but even "well-mixed".

The "torrid" zone inhabited

Cleomedes, *De motu circ. corp. cael.* I 6, 31 f., p. 56 Ziegler (F. Gr. Hist. II, F 78):

Καὶ πέντε ζώνας εἶναι τῆς γῆς τῶν εὐδοκίμων φυσικῶν ἀποφηναμένων, αὐτὸς τὴν ὑπ' ἐκείνων διακεκαῦσθαι λεγομένην οἰκουμένην καὶ εὔκρατον εἶναι ἀπεφήνατο. "ὅπου γάρ", φησιν, "ἐπὶ πλέον τοῦ ἡλίου περὶ τοὺς τροπικοὺς διατρίβοντος, οὐκ ἔστιν ἀοίκητα τὰ ὑπ' αὐτοῖς, οὐδὲ τὰ ἔτι τούτων ἐνδοτέρω, πῶς οὐκ ἂν πολὺ πλέον τὰ ὑπὸ τῷ ἰσημερινῷ εὔκρατα εἴη, ταχέως τῷ κύκλῳ τούτῳ καὶ προσιόντος τοῦ ἡλίου καὶ πάλιν ἴσῳ τάχει ἀφισταμένου αὐτοῦ καὶ μὴ ἐγχρονίζοντος περὶ τὸ κλίμα, καὶ μὴν διὰ παντός", φησιν, "ἴσης τῆς νυκτὸς τῇ ἡμέρᾳ οὔσης ἐνταῦθα καὶ διὰ τοῦτο σύμμετρον ἐχούσης πρὸς ἀνάψυξιν τὸ διάστημα; καὶ τοῦ ἀέρος τούτου ἐν τῷ μεσαιτάτῳ καὶ βαθυτάτῳ τῆς σκιᾶς ὄντος, καὶ ὄμβροι γενήσονται καὶ πνεύματα δυνάμενα ἀναψύχειν τὸν ἀέρα· ἐπεὶ καὶ περὶ τὴν Αἰθιοπίαν ὄμβροι συνεχεῖς καταφέρεσθαι ἱστοροῦνται περὶ τὸ θέρος καὶ μάλιστα τὴν ἀκμὴν αὐτοῦ, ἀφ' οὗ καὶ ὁ Νεῖλος πληθύειν τοῦ θέρους ὑπονοεῖται.

1174—a.   The inhabited world is surrounded by the ocean.

The inhabited world

Strabo II 3, 5 (F. Gr. Hist. II, 28):

'Εκ πάντων δὴ τούτων φησὶ (sc. ὁ Ποσειδώνιος) δείκνυσθαι, διότι ἡ οἰκουμένη κύκλῳ περιρρεῖται τῷ ὠκεανῷ·

"οὐ γάρ μιν δεσμὸς περιβάλλεται ἠπείροιο,
ἀλλ' ἐς ἀπειρεσίην κέχυται· τό μιν οὔτι μιαίνει." [1]

b.   The length of the inhabited world is judged by him to be about 70.000 stadia.

Its length

Strabo ib., 6 (F. Gr. Hist., ib.):

'Υπονοεῖ δὲ τὸ τῆς οἰκουμένης μῆκος ἑπτά που μυριάδων σταδίων ὑπάρχον

---

[1]   The author of these verses is unknown.

ἥμισυ εἶναι τοῦ ὅλου κύκλου, καθ᾽ ὃν εἴληπται, "ὥστε", φησίν, "ἀπὸ τῆς
δύσεως εὔρῳ πλέων ἐν τοσαύταις μυριάσιν ἔλθοι ἂν εἰς Ἰνδούς."

The circum-
ference of
the earth **1175**—His method of measuring the circumference of the earth.
Cleomedes, *De motu circ.* I 10, 49-52; Ziegler p. 90 ff. (F. Gr. Hist.
II, F 97):

Περὶ δὲ τοῦ μεγέθους τῆς γῆς πλείους μὲν γεγόνασι δόξαι παρὰ τοῖς φυσικοῖς, βελτίους δὲ τῶν ἄλλων εἰσὶν ἥ τε Ποσειδωνίου καὶ ἡ Ἐρατοσθένους·
αὕτη μὲν διὰ γεωμετρικῆς ἐφόδου δεικνύουσα τὸ μέγεθος αὐτῆς, ἡ δὲ Ποσειδωνίου ἐστὶν ἁπλουστέρα. ἑκάτερος δὲ αὐτῶν ὑποθέσεις τινὰς λαμβάνων διὰ
τῶν ἀκολούθων ταῖς ὑποθέσεσι ἐπὶ τὰς ἀποδείξεις παραγίνεται. ἐροῦμεν δὲ
περὶ προτέρας τῆς Ποσειδωνίου.

Φησὶν οὖν ὑπὸ τῷ αὐτῷ μεσημβρινῷ [1] κεῖσθαι Ῥόδον καὶ Ἀλεξάνδρειαν.
... καὶ τὸ διάστημα τὸ μεταξὺ τῶν πόλεων πεντακισχιλίων σταδίων εἶναι
δοκεῖ· καὶ ὑποκείσθω οὕτως ἔχειν ... ἑξῆς ὁ Ποσειδώνιος ἴσον ὄντα τὸν
ζῳδιακὸν τοῖς μεσημβρινοῖς ... εἰς ὀκτὼ καὶ τεσσαράκοντα καὶ ὀκτὼ μέρη
διαιρεῖ, ἕκαστον τῶν δωδεκατημορίων αὐτοῦ εἰς τέσσαρα τέμνων. ἂν τοίνυν
καὶ ὁ διὰ Ῥόδου καὶ Ἀλεξανδρείας μεσημβρινὸς εἰς τὰ αὐτὰ τῷ ζῳδιακῷ
τεσσαράκοντα καὶ ὀκτὼ μέρη διαιρεθῇ, ἴσα γίνεται αὐτοῦ τὰ τμήματα τοῖς
προειρημένοις τοῦ ζῳδιακοῦ τμήμασιν ... τούτων οὕτως ἐχόντων ἑξῆς φησι
ὁ Ποσειδώνιος, ὅτι ὁ Κάνωβος καλούμενος ἀστὴρ λαμπρότατός ἐστι πρὸς
μεσημβρίαν ὡς ἐπὶ τῷ πηδαλίῳ τῆς Ἀργοῦς. οὗτος ἐν Ἑλλάδι οὐδ᾽ ὅλως
ὁρᾶται, ὅθεν οὐδ᾽ ὁ Ἄρατος ἐν τοῖς Φαινομένοις μιμνήσκεται αὐτοῦ. ἀπὸ
δὲ τῶν ἀρκτικῶν ὡς πρὸς μεσημβρίαν ἰοῦσιν ἀρχὴν τοῦ ὁρᾶσθαι ἐν Ῥόδῳ
λαμβάνει καὶ ὀφθεὶς ἐπὶ τοῦ ὁρίζοντος εὐθέως κατὰ τὴν στροφὴν τοῦ κόσμου
καταδύεται. ὁπόταν δὲ τοὺς ἀπὸ Ῥόδου πεντακισχιλίους σταδίους διαπλεύ-
σαντες ἐν Ἀλεξανδρείᾳ γενώμεθα, εὑρίσκεται ὁ ἀστὴρ οὗτος ἐν Ἀλεξανδρείᾳ
ὕψος ἀπέχων τοῦ ὁρίζοντος, ἐπειδὰν ἀκριβῶς μεσουρανήσῃ, τέταρτον ζῳδίου,
ὅ ἐστι τεσσαρακοστὸν ὄγδοον τοῦ ζῳδιακοῦ· ἀνάγκη τοίνυν καὶ τὸ ὑπερκεί-
μενον τοῦ αὐτοῦ μεσημβρινοῦ τμῆμα τοῦ διαστήματος τοῦ μεταξὺ Ῥόδου καὶ
Ἀλεξανδρείας τεσσαρακοστὸν ὄγδοον μέρος αὐτοῦ εἶναι διὰ τὸ καὶ τὸν ὁρίζοντα
τῶν Ῥοδίων τοῦ ὁρίζοντος τῶν Ἀλεξανδρέων ἀφίστασθαι τεσσαρακοστὸν
ὄγδοον τοῦ ζῳδιακοῦ κύκλου. ἐπεὶ οὖν τὸ τούτῳ τῷ τμήματι ὑποκείμενον μέρος
τῆς γῆς πεντακισχιλίων σταδίων εἶναι δοκεῖ, καὶ τὰ τοῖς ἄλλοις τμήμασι
ὑποκείμενα πεντακισχιλίων σταδίων ἐστί. καὶ οὕτως ὁ μέγιστος τῆς γῆς
κύκλος εὑρίσκεται μυριάδων τεσσάρων καὶ εἴκοσιν, ἐὰν ἐῶσιν οἱ ἀπὸ Ῥόδου
εἰς Ἀλεξάνδρειαν πεντακισχίλιοι· εἰ δὲ μή, πρὸς λόγον τοῦ διαστήματος.
καὶ ἡ μὲν τοῦ Ποσειδωνίου ἔφοδος περὶ τοῦ κατὰ τὴν γῆν μεγέθους τοιαύτη.

---

[1] Meridian.

1176—As a philosopher of nature—his Φυσικὸς λόγος is repeatedly cited by Diog. Laërt.—Posid. appears to have been a vitalist: distinguishing, as Zeno and Chrysippus did, an active and a passive element in nature, Pos. seems to have spoken of a *vital force* (*vis vitalis*, ζωτικὴ δύναμις), which he found everywhere in the cosmos. We find traces of the theory in several writers who, on other points too, were influenced by Posidonius [1].

Cic., *De n.d.* II 33, 83: **Vitalism**

Quod si ea quae a terra stirpibus continentur arte naturae vivunt et vigent, profecto ipsa terra eadem vi continetur arte naturae, quippe quae gravidata seminibus omnia pariat et fundat ex sese, stirpes amplexa alat et augeat ipsaque alatur vicissim a superis externisque naturis; eiusdemque exspirationibus et aer alitur et aether et omnia supera. Ita si terra natura tenetur et viget, eadem ratio in reliquo mundo est; stirpes enim terrae inhaerent, animantes autem adspiratione aeris sustinentur; ipseque aer nobiscum videt nobiscum audit nobiscum sonat, nihil enim eorum sine eo fieri potest; quin etiam movetur nobiscum, quacumque enim imus, qua movemur, videtur quasi locum dare et cedere.

The term *vis vitalis* occurs in the same book, ch. 9, § 24, where he is speaking of heat as the source of life: *ex quo intellegi debet eam caloris naturam vim habere in se vitalem per omnem mundum pertinentem.* Cleanthes, who is cited, did speak of heat as a source of life, but the term *vis vitalis* does not occur in the Ancient Stoa.[2]

b. Seneca, *Nat. quaest.* V 5-6 (speaking of the cause of the winds):

An hoc existimas nobis quidem datas vires quibus nos moveremus, aera autem relictum inertem et inagitabilem esse, cum aqua motum suum habeat etiam ventis quiescentibus? Nec enim aliter animalia ederet; muscum quoque innasci aquis et herbosa quaedam videmus summo innatantia; est ergo aliquid in aqua vitale.

De aqua dico? ignis, qui omnia consumit, quaedam creat et, quod videri non potest simile veri, tamen verum est animalia igne generari. Habet ergo aliquam vim talem aer et ideo modo spissat se, modo expandit et purgat et alias contrahit diducit ac differt. Hoc ergo interest inter aera et ventum quod inter lacum et flumen.

---

[1] In the following passages the name of Posidonius is not mentioned; but there is some converging evidence for attributing the vis vitalis theory to him. G. Luck, *Der Akademiker Antiochos* (Noctes Romanae 7), Bern 1953, ascribes the theory to Antiochus of Ascalon, including Cic., *De n.d.* 2, 33.

[2] That it was used in medical literature, is shown by Crönert in *Gnomon* 1930, p. 155 ff.

c. Diodorus Siculus, who used Posid.'s historical and geographical works a great deal, speaks of the ζωτική δύναμις of the sun.

Diod. II 51, 3:

Δοκεῖ γὰρ ἡ συνεγγίζουσα χώρα τῇ μεσημβρίᾳ τὴν ἀφ' ἡλίου δύναμιν ζωτικωτάτην οὖσαν πολλὴν ἐμπνεῖσθαι καὶ διὰ τοῦτο πολλῶν καὶ ποικίλων, ἔτι δὲ καλῶν ζῴων φύσεις γεννᾶν.

d. Plutarchus, in the final chapter of the *De facie in orbe lunae* (945c) attributes the origin of new souls to the vital force of the moon:

Χρόνῳ δὲ κἀκείνας[1] κατεδέξατο εἰς αὑτὴν ἡ σελήνη καὶ κατεκόσμησεν, εἶτα τὸν νοῦν αὖθις ἐπισπείραντος τοῦ ἡλίου, τῷ ζωτικῷ δεχομένη, νέας ποιεῖ ψυχάς· ἡ δὲ γῆ τρίτον σῶμα παρέσχεν.

Cp. *Aquane an ignis sit utilior*, c. 13 (p. 958e): Τοῦ δὲ πυρὸς ἅπασα μὲν αἴσθησις, οἷον τὸ ζωτικὸν ἐνεργαζομένου, μετείληφεν.

Also *Quaest. conv.* VII 4, 3 (p. 703A) where he says: Nothing more resembles a living being than does fire, which moves and feeds by itself and, by its shining, makes everything clear. Μάλιστα δὲ ταῖς σβέσεσιν αὐτοῦ καὶ φθοραῖς ἐμφαίνεται δύναμις οὐκ ἀμοιροῦσα ζωτικῆς ἀρχῆς.

Reinhardt, *Pos.* p. 242 f.; *Kosmos u. Symp.* p. 320, 329; Pohlenz, *Stoa* II p. 107. On Posid.' vitalism as opposed to atomism, our nr. **1181**.

1177—The cosmos is a body forming an organical unity, of which all Symphyia the parts are naturally connected (συμφυῆ) and therefore interacting and (συμπαθῆ).
sympatheia

a. Cleomedes, *De motu circ.* I 1, 4, p. 8 Ziegler:

There is no void within the universe.

Δῆλον δὲ ἐκ τῶν φαινομένων. Εἰ γὰρ μὴ δι' ὅλου συμφυὴς ὑπῆρχεν ἡ τῶν ὅλων οὐσία, οὔτ' ἂν ὑπὸ φύσεως οἷόν τ' ἦν συνέχεσθαι καὶ διοικεῖσθαι τὸν κόσμον, οὔτε τῶν μερῶν αὐτοῦ συμπάθειά τις ἂν ἦν πρὸς ἄλληλα, οὔτε, μὴ ὑφ' ἑνὸς τόπου συνεχομένου αὐτοῦ καὶ τοῦ πνεύματος μὴ δι' ὅλου ὄντος συμφυοῦς, οἷόν τ' ἂν ἦν ἡμῖν ὁρᾶν ἢ ἀκούειν. Μεταξὺ γὰρ ὄντων κενωμάτων ἐνεποδίζοντο ἂν ὑπ' αὐτῶν αἱ αἰσθήσεις.

Cp. Cic., *De n.d.* II 83, cited above (**1176a**). The term συμφυΐα is used by Sextus Emp., *Adv. math.* VII 129.

See further Reinhardt, *Kosmos u. Symp.*, p. 92 ff.; W. Theiler, *Die Vorbereitung des Neuplatonismus*, pp. 72 ff., 112 ff.

b Sextus Emp., *Adv. math.* IX (= *Ag. the phys.* I) 78-80:

Τῶν τε σωμάτων τὰ μέν ἐστιν ἡνωμένα, τὰ δὲ ἐξ συναπτομένων, τὰ δὲ ἐκ

---

[1] I.e.: souls like those of Tityos and Typhon, foolish and arrogant and full of confusing passions.

διεστώτων. ἡνωμένα μὲν οὖν ἐστι τὰ ὑπὸ μιᾶς ἕξεως κρατούμενα καθάπερ φυτὰ
καὶ ζῷα, ἐκ συναπτομένων δὲ τὰ ἔκ τε παρακειμένων καὶ πρὸς ἕν τι κεφάλαιον
νευόντων συνεστῶτα ὡς ἁλύσεις καὶ πυργίσκοι καὶ νῆες, ἐκ διεστώτων δὲ τὰ
ἐκ διεζευγμένων καὶ [ἐκ] κεχωρισμένων καὶ καθ' αὑτὰ ὑποκειμένων συγκείμενα
ὡς στρατιαὶ καὶ ποιμναὶ καὶ χοροί. ἐπεὶ οὖν καὶ ὁ κόσμος σῶμά ἐστιν, ἤτοι
ἡνωμένον ἐστὶ σῶμα ἢ ἐκ συναπτομένων ἢ ἐκ διεστώτων. οὔτε δὲ ἐκ συναπτομένων οὔτε ἐκ διεστώτων, ὡς δείκνυμεν ἐκ τῶν περὶ αὐτὸν συμπαθειῶν.
κατὰ γὰρ τὰς τῆς σελήνης αὐξήσεις καὶ φθίσεις πολλὰ τῶν τε ἐπιγείων ζῴων
καὶ θαλασσίων φθίνει τε καὶ αὔξεται, ἀμπώτεις τε καὶ πλημμυρίδες περί τινα
μέρη τῆς θαλάσσης γίνονται. ὡσαύτως δὲ καὶ κατά τινας τῶν ἀστέρων ἐπιτολὰς
καὶ δύσεις μεταβολαὶ τοῦ περιέχοντος καὶ παμποίκιλοι περὶ τὸν ἀέρα τροπαὶ
συμβαίνουσιν, ὁτὲ μὲν ἐπὶ τὸ κρεῖττον, ὁτὲ δὲ λοιμικῶς. ἐξ ὧν συμφανὲς ὅτι
ἡνωμένον τι σῶμα καθέστηκεν ὁ κόσμος. ἐπὶ μὲν γὰρ τῶν ἐκ συναπτομένων ἢ
διεστώτων οὐ συμπάσχει τὰ μέρη ἀλλήλοις, εἴγε ἐν στρατιᾷ πάντων, εἰ τύχοι,
διαφθαρέντων τῶν στρατιωτῶν οὐδὲν κατὰ διάδοσιν πάσχειν φαίνεται ὁ περι-
σωθείς· ἐπὶ δὲ τῶν ἡνωμένων συμπάθειά τις ἐστιν, εἴγε δακτύλου τεμνομένου
τὸ ὅλον συνδιατίθεται σῶμα. ἡνωμένον τοίνυν ἐστὶ σῶμα καὶ ὁ κόσμος.

The same doctrine is found in Cic., *De n.d.* II 7, 19. The author speaks of *tanta
rerum consentiens conspirans continuata cognatio.*
Cp. also *De div.* II 14, 33, and Plinius, *N.H.* II 109, 112 ff. Certainly the notion
of cosmic sympathy did not originate with Posid. We dealt with it earlier as a
Chrysippean doctrine (our nr. **913**). But Reinhardt seems to be right in holding
that, in Posid.' system, the doctrine took a very important place, and, moreover,
a special character. [1]

1178—After Panaetius, who maintained that the world is indestruc-
tible, Posid. returned to the ekpyrosis theory.

The genera-
tion and the
destruction
of the world

   a. Diog. L. VII 142:

Περὶ δὴ οὖν τῆς γενέσεως καὶ τῆς φθορᾶς τοῦ κόσμου φησὶ Ζήνων μὲν
ἐν τῷ Περὶ ὅλου, Χρύσιππος δ' ἐν τῷ πρώτῳ τῶν Φυσικῶν καὶ Ποσειδώνιος
ἐν πρώτῳ Περὶ κόσμου.

---

[1] *Kosmos u. Symp.*, p. 52 ff.: "Als kosmischer, erklärender Begriff erscheint
die Sympathie zuerst bei Cicero, bei Strabo und bei Philo; bei den ersten beiden
ausschliesslich an Stellen wo sie nachweislich aus Poseidonios schöpfen. Daraus
folgt: erst Poseidonios hat die "Sympathie" aus der Beschränktheit astrologischer
Gleichungen einerseits, aus medizinischen, prognostischen und mirabilienartigen
einzelnen Beobachtungen andererseits zu einem physikalischen, das ganze Weltbild
ganz und gar durchdringenden .. Begriff erhoben; ... er erst hat den Weltzu-
sammenhang als Sympathie geschaut."—
Edelstein, however, holds that the doctrine of sympathy did not take a particularly important place in Posid.' philosophy (*Am. Journal of Philol.* 1936, p. 324).

b. Cp. Arius Did. ap. Stob., *Ecl.* I, p. 177 f.:

Ποσειδώνιος δὲ φθορὰς καὶ γενέσεις τέτταρας εἶναί φησιν ἐκ τῶν ὄντων εἰς τὰ ὄντα γινομένας. Τὴν μὲν γὰρ ἐκ τῶν οὐκ ὄντων καὶ τὴν εἰς οὐκ ὄντα, καθάπερ εἴπομεν πρόσθεν, ἀπέγνωσαν ἀνύπαρκτον οὖσαν. Τῶν δ' εἰς ὄντα γινομένων μεταβόλων τὴν μὲν εἶναι κατὰ διαίρεσιν, τὴν δὲ κατ' ἀλλοίωσιν, τὴν δὲ κατὰ σύγχυσιν, τὴν δ' ἐξ ὅλων, λεγομένην δὲ κατ' ἀνάλυσιν. Τούτων δὲ τὴν κατ' ἀλλοίωσιν περὶ τὴν οὐσίαν γίνεσθαι, τὰς δ' ἄλλας τρεῖς περὶ τοὺς ποιοὺς λεγομένους τοὺς ἐπὶ τῆς οὐσίας γινομένους. Ἀκολούθως δὲ τούτοις καὶ τὰς γενέσεις συμβαίνειν. Τὴν γὰρ οὐσίαν οὔτ' αὔξεσθαι οὔτε μειοῦσθαι κατὰ πρόσθεσιν ἢ ἀφαίρεσιν, ἀλλὰ μόνον ἀλλοιοῦσθαι, καθάπερ ἐπ' ἀριθμῶν καὶ μέτρων συμβαίνειν. Ἐπὶ δὲ τῶν ἰδίως ποιῶν, οἷον Δίωνος καὶ Θέωνος, καὶ αὐξήσεις καὶ μειώσεις γίνεσθαι. Διὸ καὶ παραμένειν τὴν ἑκάστου ποιότητα ἀπὸ τῆς γενέσεως μέχρι τῆς ἀναιρέσεως, ὡς ἐπὶ τῶν ἀναίρεσιν ἐπιδεχομένων ζῴων καὶ φυτῶν καὶ τῶν τούτοις παραπλησίων.

The passage is discussed by Edelstein in the above-mentioned article, p. 293 ff. Cp. also Philo, *De aetern. mundi* II, 497 M., cited there (n. 37).

The sun　**1179—a.** Of his theory of the sun, the following account is given by Diog. L. VII 144:

Εἶναι δὲ τὸν μὲν ἥλιον εἰλικρινὲς πῦρ, καθά φησι Ποσειδώνιος ἐν τῷ ἑβδόμῳ Περὶ μετεώρων· καὶ μείζονα τῆς γῆς, ὡς ὁ αὐτὸς ἐν τῷ ἕκτῳ τοῦ Φυσικοῦ λόγου· ἀλλὰ καὶ σφαιροειδῆ, ὡς οἱ περὶ αὐτὸν τοῦτόν φασιν, ἀναλόγως τῷ κόσμῳ. πῦρ μὲν οὖν εἶναι, ὅτι τὰ πυρὸς πάντα ποιεῖ. μείζω δὲ τῆς γῆς τῷ πᾶσαν ὑπ' αὐτοῦ φωτίζεσθαι, ἀλλὰ καὶ τὸν οὐρανόν. καὶ τὸ τὴν γῆν δὲ κωνοειδῆ σκιὰν ἀποτελεῖν τὸ μείζονα εἶναι σημαίνει. πάντοθεν δὲ βλέπεσθαι διὰ τὸ μέγεθος.

By Cleomedes, *De motu circ.* I 11, 65 (p. 118 Ziegler) we know that P. wrote a special treatise on the size of the sun. Hultsch, in the *Abh. d. Gött. Ges.* 1897, nr. 5, tried to reconstruct his methods.

b. Cleomedes, *De motu circ.* II 1, 84-85 (p. 152-154 Ziegler) is generally attributed to Posid.

After having dealt with the size of the sun and its distance from the earth, the author continues as follows.

Description **of its force**　Ἀλλ' εἰ καὶ μὴ τούτοις ἐπιστῆσαι οἷός τ' ἐγένετο μηδ' ἀνευρεῖν ταῦτα, ὧν μείζων ἡ ζήτησις ἦν ἀνθρώπου ἡδονὴν τετιμηκότος, αὐτῇ γε τῇ δυνάμει τοῦ ἡλίου ἐπιστῆσαι αὐτὸν ἐχρῆν καὶ πρῶτον μὲν ἐνθυμηθῆναι, διότι πάντα τὸν κόσμον φωτίζει σχεδὸν ἀπειρομεγέθη ὄντα, ἔπειτα, ὅτι οὕτω διακαίει τὴν γῆν, ὡς ἔνια μέρη αὐτῆς ὑπὸ φλογμοῦ ἀοίκητα εἶναι, καὶ ὑπὸ πολλῆς τῆς

δυνάμεως αὐτὸς ἔμπνουν παρέχεται τὴν γῆν, ὡς καὶ καρποφορεῖν αὐτὴν καὶ
ζωογονεῖν· καὶ ὅτι αὐτός ἐστιν αἴτιος τοῦ καὶ τὰ ζῷα ὑφεστάναι καὶ τοὺς
καρποὺς τρέφεσθαι καὶ αὔξεσθαι καὶ τελεσφορεῖσθαι· καὶ διότι μὴ μόνον
τὰς ἡμέρας καὶ νύκτας, ἀλλὰ καὶ θέρος καὶ χειμῶνα καὶ τὰς ἄλλας ὥρας αὐτός
ἐστιν ὁ ποιῶν, καὶ μὴν καὶ τοῦ μέλανας εἶναι καὶ λευκοὺς ἀνθρώπους καὶ
ξανθοὺς καὶ κατὰ τὰς ἄλλας ἰδέας διαφέροντας αὐτὸς αἴτιος γίνεται παρὰ τὸ
πῶς ἀποπέμπειν τὰς ἀκτῖνας ἐπὶ τὰ κλίματα τῆς γῆς· καὶ ὅτι οὐκ ἄλλη τις
εἰ μὴ ἡ τοῦ ἡλίου δύναμις τοὺς μὲν καθύγρους καὶ πληθύνοντας ποταμοῖς
παρέχεται τῶν ἐπὶ γῆς τόπων, τοὺς δὲ ξηροὺς καὶ ἀνύδρους, καὶ τοὺς μὲν
ἀκάρπους, τοὺς δὲ καρποφορεῖν ἱκανούς, καὶ τοὺς μὲν δριμεῖς καὶ δυσώδεις,
ὡς τοὺς τῶν Ἰχθυοφάγων, τοὺς δὲ εὐώδεις καὶ ἀρωματοφόρους, ὡς τοὺς περὶ
τὴν Ἀραβίαν, καὶ τοὺς μὲν τοιούσδε καρπούς, τοὺς δὲ τοιούσδε ἐκφέρειν δυναμένους.

See on this passage: Reinhardt, *Posid.* p. 205 ff.; Pohlenz, *Stoa* I p. 223.

1180—The moon is mixed with air and, for this very reason, has great **The moon**
influence on the earth.

    a. Diog. L. VII 145:

Τὴν δὲ σελήνην ἐκ ποτίμων ὑδάτων, ἀερομιγῆ τυγχάνουσαν καὶ πρόσγειον
οὖσαν, ὡς ὁ Ποσειδώνιος ἐν τῷ ἕκτῳ τοῦ Φυσικοῦ λόγου.

That Chrysippus held the same theory, appears in Arius Didymus's *Epit.* ap.
Stob., *Ecl.* I 185, l. 19 W.

    b. Cp. Cleomedes, *De motu circ.* II 4, 99 (p. 180 Ziegler):

Καὶ μὴν καὶ τὸ οἰκεῖον αὐτῆς σῶμα ἀερομιγὲς καὶ ζοφωδέστερόν ἐστι διὰ
τὸ μὴ εἶναι ἐν τῷ εἰλικρινεῖ τοῦ αἰθέρος, καθάπερ τὰ λοιπὰ τῶν ἄστρων,
ἀλλὰ κατὰ τὴν συναφὴν τῶν δύο στοιχείων, ὡς εἴρηται. —

Καὶ τὴν συμπάθειαν τὴν πρὸς τὰ ἐπίγεια αὐτὴ παρὰ τὰ ἄλλα τῶν ἄστρων
ἐξαίρετον ἔχει δι' αὐτὸ τὸ προσγειοτέρα εἶναι.

Cp. also Plut., *De facie in orbe lunae* c. 5, p. 921 f.; c. 29, the beginning. Reinhardt,
Poseid., p. 201 f.; Pohlenz, *Stoa* I, p. 223.

1181—**a.** In Sextus Emp., *Adv. math.* IX (= *Ag. the phys.* I) 81-85, the   **Four kinds**
divinity of the cosmos is proved by the following argument.   **of natural
bodies**

Ἀλλ' ἐπεὶ τῶν ἡνωμένων σωμάτων τὰ μὲν ὑπὸ ψιλῆς ἕξεως συνέχεται, τὰ δὲ
ὑπὸ φύσεως, τὰ δὲ ὑπὸ ψυχῆς, καὶ ἕξεως μὲν ὡς λίθοι καὶ ξύλα, φύσεως δὲ
καθάπερ τὰ φυτά, ψυχῆς δὲ τὰ ζῷα, πάντως δὴ καὶ ὁ κόσμος ὑπό τινος τούτων
διακρατεῖται. καὶ ὑπὸ μὲν ψιλῆς ἕξεως οὐκ ἂν συνέχοιτο. τὰ γὰρ ὑπὸ ἕξεως
κρατούμενα οὐδεμίαν ἀξιόλογον μεταβολήν τε καὶ τροπὴν ἀναδέχεται, καθάπερ

ξύλα καὶ λίθοι, ἀλλὰ μόνον ἐξ αὐτῶν πάσχει τὴν κατὰ ἄνεσιν καὶ τὴν κατὰ συμπιεσμὸν διάθεσιν. ὁ δὲ κόσμος ἀξιολόγους ἀναδέχεται μεταβολάς, ὁτὲ μὲν κρυμαλέου τοῦ περιέχοντος γινομένου, ὁτὲ δὲ ἀλεεινοῦ, καὶ ὁτὲ μὲν αὐχμώδους, ὁτὲ δὲ νοτεροῦ, ὁτὲ δὲ ἄλλως πως κατὰ τὰς τῶν οὐρανίων κινήσεις ἑτεροιουμένου. οὐ τοίνυν ὑπὸ ψιλῆς ἕξεως ὁ κόσμος συνέχεται. εἰ δὲ μὴ ὑπὸ ταύτης, πάντως ὑπὸ φύσεως· καὶ γὰρ τὰ ὑπὸ ψυχῆς διακρατούμενα πολὺ πρότερον ὑπὸ φύσεως συνείχετο. ἀνάγκη ἄρα ὑπὸ τῆς ἀρίστης αὐτὸν φύσεως συνέχεσθαι, ἐπεὶ καὶ περιέχει τὰς πάντων φύσεις. ἡ δέ γε τὰς πάντων περιέχουσα φύσεις καὶ τὰς λογικὰς περιέσχηκεν. ἀλλὰ καὶ ἡ τὰς λογικὰς περιέχουσα φύσεις πάντως ἔστι λογική· οὐ γὰρ οἷόν τε τὸ ὅλον τοῦ μέρους χεῖρον εἶναι. ἀλλ᾽ εἰ ἀρίστη ἐστὶ φύσις ἡ τὸν κόσμον διοικοῦσα, νοερά τε ἔσται καὶ σπουδαία καὶ ἀθάνατος. τοιαύτη δὲ τυγχάνουσα θεός ἐστιν.

The passage is cited and analysed by Reinhardt, *Kosmos u. Symp.*, p. 47 ff. In order to distinguish what does and what does not belong to Posid. in particular, the following remarks must be made.

1. The *hierarchy of three or four uniting forces*, forming the unity of natural bodies,—ἕξις, φύσις, ψυχή and ψυχὴ λογική or νοῦς—, was certainly known to Chrysippus. The doctrine is found e.g. in Philo, *Leg. alleg.* II 22, cited by V. Arnim, SVF II *458*, as illustrating Chrys.'s doctrine, and again in *Quod Deus sit immut.* 35 (SVF II ib.):

Τῶν γὰρ σωμάτων τὰ μὲν ἐνεδήσατο ἕξει, τὰ δὲ φύσει, τὰ δὲ ψυχῇ, τὰ δὲ καὶ λογικῇ ψυχῇ. Λίθων μὲν οὖν καὶ ξύλων, ἃ δὴ τῆς συμφυΐας ἀπέσπασται, δεσμὸν κραταιότατον ἕξιν εἰργάζετο. — Τὴν δε φύσιν ἀπένειμε τοῖς φυτοῖς. — (41) Ψυχὴν δὲ φύσεως τρισὶ διαλλάττουσαν ὁ ποιῶν ἐποίει αἰσθήσει, φαντασίᾳ, ὁρμῇ. — Τοσούτοις μὲν δὴ ζῷα προὔχει φυτῶν. ἴδωμεν δὲ τίνι τῶν ἄλλων ζῴων ὑπερβέβληκεν ἄνθρωπος. Ἐξαίρετον οὗτος τοίνυν γέρας ἔλαχε διάνοιαν, ᾗ τὰς ἁπάντων φύσεις, σωμάτων τε ὁμοῦ καὶ πραγμάτων εἴωθε καταλαμβάνειν.

Now this is the function of νοῦς, which is "the sight of soul", and as such τῶν ἐν ἡμῖν τὸ κρατιστεῦον.

Cp. Plut., *Stoic. repugn.* 43, p. 1053 F (SVF II 449), where Chrysippus is cited (on ἕξις).

The distinction between ἕξις, φύσις, ψυχή is also found in Clem. Alex., *Strom.* II p. 173 St., and in Galenus (SVF II 714-716).

2. In this, the theory of the *vital force of the elements*, as was illustrated under **1176**, seems to have been peculiar to Posid.

In Sen., *Nat. quaest.* II 2, a survey is given of various kinds of bodies. In this passage, *composite* bodies are opposed to *united* ones, i.e. such as are one by their own (organical) force. II 2, 4:

Quare istud? Si quando dixero unum, memineris me non ad numerum referre, sed ad naturam corporis nulla ope externa sed unitate sua cohaerentis: ex hac nota corporum aer est.

A description of this organical force of air is given in II 6, again in V 5, cited under **1176b**, and in VI 16.

Cp. also the passage of Sextus, cited under **1177b**.

Reinhardt, who deals with the question in *Kosmos und Symp.*, p. 34-54, concludes (p. 43) that the notion of unity, expounded in the above-cited passage of Seneca, is based on the organical character of the element, and that this conception of the element, which stands opposite to that of atomism, was peculiar to Posid.

It is, as is evident, closely connected with the idea of cosmic sympathy, which might be called its dynamical expression.

b. The following passage of Nemesius of Emesa, in which man is described as communicating with the three kinds of being, and thus as being placed ἐν μεθορίοις between God and the world (qualified as νοητή and αἰσθητὴ οὐσία), may contain some traces of Posidonian doctrine.

A trace of this doctrine in Nemesius

Nemesius, *De natura hominis* I, P. Gr. t. 40, col. 505B-507A:

Γνώριμον δὲ ὅτι καὶ τοῖς ἀψύχοις κοινωνεῖ, καὶ τῆς τῶν ἀλόγων ζῴων μετέχει ζωῆς, καὶ τῆς τῶν λογικῶν μετείληφε νοήσεως. Κοινωνεῖ γὰρ τοῖς μὲν ἀψύχοις κατὰ τὸ σῶμα καὶ τὴν ἀπὸ τῶν τεσσάρων στοιχείων κρᾶσιν· τοῖς δὲ φυτοῖς κατά τε ταῦτα καὶ τὴν θρεπτικὴν καὶ σπερματικὴν δύναμιν· τοῖς δὲ ἀλόγοις καὶ ἐν τούτοις μέν, ἐξ ἐπιμέτρου δὲ κατά τε τὴν καθ' ὁρμὴν κίνησιν καὶ κατὰ τὴν ὄρεξιν καὶ τὸν θυμὸν καὶ τὴν αἰσθητικὴν καὶ ἀναπνευστικὴν δύναμιν. — Συνάπτεται δὲ διὰ τοῦ λογικοῦ ταῖς ἀσωμάτοις καὶ νοεραῖς φύσεσι, λογιζόμενος καὶ νοῶν καὶ κρίνων ἕκαστα, καὶ τὰς ἀρετὰς μεταδιώκων, καὶ τῶν ἀρετῶν τὸν κολοφῶνα τὴν εὐσέβειαν ἀσπαζόμενος. Δι' ὃ καὶ ὥσπερ ἐν μεθορίοις ἐστὶ νοητῆς καὶ αἰσθητῆς οὐσίας, συναπτόμενος κατὰ μὲν τὸ σῶμα καὶ τὰς σωματικὰς δυνάμεις τοῖς ἀλόγοις ζῴοις τε καὶ τοῖς ἀψύχοις, κατὰ δὲ τὸ λογικὸν τοῖς ἀσωμάτοις οὐσίαις, ὡς εἴρηται πρότερον. Ὁ γὰρ Δημιουργὸς ἐκ τοῦ κατ' ὀλίγον ἔοικεν ἐπισυνάπτειν ἀλλήλαις τὰς διαφόρους φύσεις, ὥστε μίαν εἶναι καὶ συγγενῆ τὴν πᾶσαν κτίσιν.

See on this passage W. Jaeger, *Nemesios vom Emesa*, p. 98 ff.

1182—A trace of Posidonius' vitalism and his doctrine of the unity of the cosmos may be found in the following passage of Nemesius, where first the magnet, next certain intermediate forms between plants and animals (so-called ζωόφυτα) are mentioned as connecting links between the above mentioned groups.

Connecting links between the four groups

a. Between anorganic and organic nature. Nemesius, *De nat. hom.* I, P. Gr. t. 40, col. 508C-509A:

The magnet

Διαλλάττει μὲν γὰρ καὶ λίθος, λίθου δυνάμει τινί, ἀλλ' ἡ μαγνῆτις λίθος ἐξεληλυθέναι δοκεῖ τὴν τῶν ἄλλων λίθων φύσιν τε καὶ δύναμιν. ἐν τῷ προφανῶς ἕλκειν πρὸς ἑαυτὴν καὶ κατέχειν τὸν σίδηρον, ὥσπερ τροφὴν αὐτὸν ποιήσασθαι βουλομένη, καὶ μὴ μόνον ἐφ' ἑνὸς σιδήρου τοῦτο ποιεῖν, ἀλλὰ καὶ ἄλλον δι' ἄλλου κατέχειν τῷ μεταδιδόναι τοῖς ἐχομένοις πᾶσι τῆς δυνάμεως ἑαυτῆς.

In the same sense the magnet is mentioned by H. Lotze, *Mikrokosmos*, Leipzig 1896, I[5] p. 64.

Zoophyta

b. Between plants and animals. Ib., col. 509A-B:

Τὰς γὰρ πίννας καὶ τὰς ἀκαλύφας ὥσπερ αἰσθητικὰ δένδρα κατεσκεύασεν. ἐρρίζωσε μὲν γὰρ αὐτὰς ἐν τῇ θαλάσσῃ δίκην φυτῶν, καὶ ὥσπερ ξύλα τὰ ὄστρακα περιέθηκε καὶ ἔστησεν ὥσπερ φυτά. αἴσθησιν δ' αὐταῖς ἐνέθηκε τὴν ἁπτικήν, τὴν κοινὴν πάντων ζῴων αἴσθησιν, ὡς κοινωνεῖν τοῖς μὲν φυτοῖς κατὰ τὸ ἐρριζῶσθαι καὶ ἑστάναι, τοῖς δὲ ζῴοις κατὰ τὴν ἁφὴν [καὶ τὸ αἰσθάνεσθαι]. Τὸν γοῦν σπόγγον, καίτοι προσπεφυκότα ταῖς πέτραις καὶ συστέλλεσθαι καὶ ἀνοίγεσθαι ἢ μᾶλλον ἐκτείνεσθαι [καὶ ἀμύνεσθαι], ὅταν προσιόντος αἴσθηταί τινος, Ἀριστοτέλης ἱστόρησε. Διὸ τὰ τοιαῦτα πάντα ζωόφυτα καλεῖν ἔθος ἔχουσιν οἱ παλαιοὶ τῶν σοφῶν.

Cp. Aristot., *Hist. an.* 588 b 20, 487 b 9 (on the sponges); 588 b 15, 548 a 5 (on the πίνναι and ἀκαλῆφαι).

„Intelligent animals"

c. Between non-rational animals and man: ib., col. 509C-512A:

Πάλιν δὲ μεταβαίνων ἀπὸ τῶν ἀλόγων ἐπὶ τὸ λογικὸν ζῷον, τὸν ἄνθρωπον, οὐδὲ τοῦτο ἀθρόως κατεσκεύασεν, ἀλλὰ πρότερον καὶ τοῖς ἄλλοις ζῴοις φυσικάς τινας συνέσεις καὶ μηχανὰς καὶ πανουργίας πρὸς σωτηρίαν ἐνέθηκεν, ὡς ἐγγὺς λογικῶν αὐτὰ φαίνεσθαι, καὶ οὕτω τὸ ἀληθῶς λογικὸν ζῷον τὸν ἄνθρωπον προεβάλετο.

Conclusion

d. Thus, the whole creation was unified to an harmonious organism. Ib., col. 512B:

Καὶ οὕτω πᾶσι πάντα μουσικῶς συνήρμοσε καὶ συνέδησε καὶ εἰς ἓν συνήγαγε τά τε νοητὰ καὶ τὰ ὁρατὰ διὰ μέσου τῆς τῶν ἀνθρώπων γενέσεως.

Concerning the doctrine of intermediate forms, cp. Strabo VII 5, 8 (Posid. F 93 *F.Gr.Hist.*), where is spoken of an asphalt mine which, when trenched, fills itself up (τμηθὲν ἐκπληροῦται πάλιν τῷ χρόνῳ). The same is reported by Strabo V 2, 6 about the iron mines of Elba, about the ledges of rocks in Rhodos, the marble-rock in Paros and the salt-rock in India.
Cp. Theiler, *Vorb. d. Neupl.* p. 74.

Animal instinct distinguished from human reason

1183—The following passage in which a remarkable analysis is given of the difference between animal instinct and human reason, probably goes back to Posidonius.

Seneca, *Epist.* 121, 19-23:

Quid est, quare pavonem, quare anserem gallina non fugiat, at tanto minorem et ne notum quidem sibi accipitrem? quare pulli faelem timeant, canem non timeant? apparet illis inesse nocituri scientiam non experimento collectam: nam antequam possint experisci, cavent. deinde ne hoc casu existimes fieri, nec metuunt alia quam debent nec umquam obliviscuntur huius tutelae et diligentiae: aequalis est illis a pernicioso fuga. praeterea non fiunt timidiora vivendo. ex quo quidem apparet non usu illa in hoc pervenire, sed naturali amore salutis suae. et tardum est et varium, quod usus docet; quicquid natura tradit, et aequale omnibus est et statim. —

(21) Naturales ad utilia impetus, naturales a contrariis aspernationes sunt: sine ulla cogitatione, quae hoc dictet, sine consilio fit, quidquid natura praecepit. non vides, quanta sit subtilitas apibus ad fingenda domicilia, quanta dividui laboris obeundi undique concordia? non vides, quam nulli mortalium imitabilis illa aranei textura, quanto operis sit fila disponere, alia in rectum inmissa firmamenti loco, alia in orbem currentia ex denso rara, quae minora animalia, in quorum perniciem illa tenduntur, velut retibus implicata teneantur? nascitur ars ista, non discitur. itaque nullum est animal altero doctius: videbis araneorum pares telas, par in favis angulorum omnium foramen. incertum est et inaequabile, quidquid ars tradit; ex aequo venit, quod natura distribuit.

On the attribution to Posid., see Reinhardt, *Posid.* p. 356-365; Pohlenz, *Grundfragen* p. 5 ff.; *Stoa* I p. 227.

1184—Two important conclusions from the psychophysical unity which is man.

a. Man's moral character is in accordance with his physical constitution, and the latter is greatly influenced by the climate.

Galenus, *De plac. Hipp. et Plat.* p. 442 M.; F. Gr. Hist. II, F 102: **Climatic influence on man**

Συνάπτει δὲ εἰκότως τοῖς λόγοις τούτοις ὁ Ποσειδώνιος τὰ κατὰ τὴν φυσιογνωμονίαν φαινόμενα· καὶ γὰρ τῶν ζῴων καὶ τῶν ἀνθρώπων, ὅσα μὲν εὐρύστερνά τε καὶ θερμότερα, θυμικώτερα πάνθ' ὑπάρχειν φύσει, ὅσα δὲ πλατυΐσχιά τε καὶ ψυχρότερα, δειλότερα. καὶ κατὰ τὰς χώρας δὲ οὐ σμικρῷ τινι διενηνοχέναι τοῖς ἤθεσι τοὺς ἀνθρώπους εἰς δειλίαν καὶ τόλμαν ἤτοι φιλήδονόν τε καὶ φιλόπονον, ὡς τῶν παθητικῶν κινήσεων τῆς ψυχῆς ἐπομένων ἀεὶ τῇ διαθέσει τοῦ σώματος, ἣν ἐκ τῆς κατὰ τὸ περιέχον κράσεως οὐ κατὰ ὀλίγον ἀλλοιοῦσθαι.

b. The soul itself is not merely rational (as was held by Chrysippus), but contains an irrational part—or rather, has irrational functions. **Man's soul partly irrational**
Galenus, o.c., p. 460 f. M., accepts Plato's tripartition of psychical "forces", with Posid. and against Chrysippus:

Οὐδὲν γὰρ μᾶλλον τρία μόρια ἢ τρεῖς εἶναι δυνάμεις δείκνυσιν ὁ λόγος· ὅτι μέντοι γε τρία τὰ σύμπαντά ἐστιν εἴτε μόρια ψυχῆς εἴτε δυνάμεις, ὑφ' ὧν ὁ βίος ἡμῶν διοικεῖται, βιαστικῶς τε καὶ ἀναντιρρήτως ἀποδείκνυται. ὥστε καὶ ἐκ τῶν νῦν λεχθησομένων ἡ μὲν τοῦ Χρυσίππου διαβληθήσεται δόξα, κατασκευασθήσεται δὲ τὸ κοινὸν Ἀριστοτέλει καὶ Πλάτωνι καὶ Ποσειδωνίῳ δόγμα, τὸ καθ' ἑτέραν μὲν ἡμᾶς δύναμιν λογίζεσθαι, καθ' ἑτέραν δὲ θυμοῦσθαι, κατὰ ἄλλην δὲ ἐπιθυμεῖν.

Cp. also p. 501:

Ὁ δὲ Ἀριστοτέλης τε καὶ ὁ Ποσειδώνιος εἴδη μὲν ἢ μέρη ψυχῆς οὐκ ὀνομάζουσιν, δυνάμεις δὲ εἶναί φασι μιᾶς οὐσίας ἐκ τῆς καρδίας ὁρμωμένης· ὁ δὲ Χρύσιππος ὥσπερ εἰς μίαν οὐσίαν, οὕτω καὶ εἰς δύναμιν μίαν ἄγει καὶ τὸν θυμὸν καὶ τὴν ἐπιθυμίαν.

1185—Against Chrysippus's rational monism [1] Posid. defends
(1) that the πάθη are non-rational;
(2) that they are as such not unnatural.

The
πάθη
are
irrational

a. First argument: if the too violent ὁρμή is a too violent συγκατάθεσις and if the assent is caused by the greatness of its object, how is it that the wise man is not led into πάθη by such objects as are gréatly approved by him?

Chrysippus said: — ἀρρωστήματα γίνεσθαι κατὰ τὴν ψυχὴν οὐχ ἁπλῶς τῷ ψευδῶς ὑπειληφέναι περί τινων ὡς ἀγαθῶν ἢ κακῶν, ἀλλὰ τῷ μέγιστα νομίζειν αὐτά (Galenus, o.c., p. 369, 10 M.).

Posid. replies (Galenus o.c., p. 370, 2 M.):

Τοιούτων δὲ ὑπὸ τοῦ Χρυσίππου λεγομένων διαπορήσειεν ἄν τις πρῶτον μέν, πῶς οἱ σοφοὶ μέγιστα καὶ ἀνυπέρβλητα νομίζοντες εἶναι ἀγαθὰ τὰ καλὰ πάντα οὐκ ἐμπαθῶς κινοῦνται ὑπ' αὐτῶν ἐπιθυμοῦντές τε ὧν ὀρέγονται καὶ περιχαρεῖς γινόμενοι ἐπὶ τοῖς αὐτοῖς, ὅταν τύχωσιν αὐτῶν.

b. Secondly: fall into passions not only those who are involved in advanced moral badness, but all those who are "fools" (in the Stoic sense); and this not only in proportion to the object. And often men of the same weakness react differently in receiving a similar presentation, and even the same man may show different reactions at different moments.

Not in proportion to the
object

Galenus, o.c., p. 371, 9 - 372, 9 M.:

Εἶτα ἐφεξῆς καὶ τάδε γράφει (sc. ὁ Ποσειδώνιος)· οὐ μόνον δὲ οἱ ἐπὶ πλέον ἐρρυηκυῖαν ἔχοντες τὴν κακίαν καὶ ἐν ταῖς εὐεμπτωσίαις ὄντες ἐμπίπτουσιν εἰς τὰ πάθη, ἀλλὰ πάντες οἱ ἄφρονες, ἕως ἂν ἔχωσιν τὴν κακίαν, καὶ εἰς μεγάλα πάθη καὶ εἰς μίκρα ἐμπίπτουσι. καὶ τούτων ἑξῆς τάδε· τὸ δὲ ὑπολαμβάνειν

---

[1] Zeno's definition of πάθος and Chrysippus's interprétation of it are cited under the nrs. **1051** ff.; Cleanthes, **1054**.

κατὰ ἀξίαν εἶναι τῶν συμβεβηκότων οὕτως κεκινῆσθαι, ὥστε ἀποστρέφεσθαι τὸν λόγον, μέγα δὲ πάθος ἐμφαίνειν, οὐ καλῶς ὑπολαμβάνειν ἐστί. γίνεται δὲ καὶ διὰ σύμμετρον καὶ μικρόν. ἐχόμενα δὲ τούτων ὁ Ποσειδώνιος καὶ τάδε γράφει· δυοῖν τε τὴν αὐτὴν ἀσθένειαν ἐχόντων καὶ τὴν ὁμοίαν λαμβανόντων φαντασίαν ἀγαθοῦ ἢ κακοῦ ὁ μὲν ἐν πάθει γίνεται, ὁ δὲ οὔ, καὶ ὁ μὲν ἧττον, ὁ δὲ μᾶλλον, καὶ ἐνίοτε ὁ ἀσθενέστερος μεῖζον ὑπολαμβάνων τὸ προσπεπτωκὸς οὐ κινεῖται καὶ ὁ αὐτὸς ἐπὶ τοῖς αὐτοῖς ὁτὲ μὲν ἐν πάθει γίνεται, ἔστιν ὁτὲ δὲ οὔ, καὶ ὁτὲ μὲν μᾶλλον, ὁτὲ δὲ ἧττον.

Changed by time

c. Thirdly: that passions are not judgments appears from the fact that they are changed by time.

Now, Zeno was aware of this fact, as appears in his definition of λύπη. And Chrysippus, too, was aware of it.

Galenus, o.c., p. 391, 5-11 ; p. 397, 12-398, 4 M.:

Ὁ γοῦν ὅρος οὗτος, φησίν (sc. ὁ Ποσειδώνιος), ὁ τῆς λύπης, ὥσπερ οὖν καὶ ἄλλοι πολλοὶ τῶν παθῶν ὑπό τε Ζήνωνος εἰρημένοι καὶ πρὸς τοῦ Χρυσίππου γεγραμμένοι, σαφῶς ἐξελέγχουσι τὴν γνώμην αὐτοῦ. δόξαν γὰρ εἶναι πρόσφατον τοῦ κακὸν αὐτῷ παρεῖναί φησι τὴν λύπην. ἐν ᾧ καὶ συντομώτερον ἐνίοτε λέγοντες ὧδέ πως προφέρονται· λύπη ἐστὶ δόξα πρόσφατος κακοῦ παρουσίας. —

Προσχρῆται δὲ εἰς τοῦτο μάρτυρι καὶ αὐτῷ τῷ Χρυσίππῳ κατὰ τὸ δεύτερον Περὶ παθῶν ὧδέ πως γράφοντι· περὶ δὲ τῆς λύπης, [καὶ] ὡς ἂν ἐμπλησθέντες τινὲς ὁμοίως φαίνονται ἀφίστασθαι, καθάπερ καὶ ἐπὶ Ἀχιλλέως ταῦτα λέγει ὁ ποιητὴς πενθοῦντος τὸν Πάτροκλον·

"ἀλλ' ὅτε δὴ κλαίων τε κυλινδόμενός τ' ἐκορέσθη
καὶ οἱ ἀπὸ πραπίδων ἦλθ' ἵμερος ἠδ' ἀπὸ γυίων",

ἐπὶ τὸ παρακαλεῖν ὥρμησε τὸν Πρίαμον τὴν τῆς λύπης ἀλογίαν αὐτῷ παριστάς.

d. Chrysippus compares the man who is liable to passions with persons of weak health, Posid. considers him as a normal man.

The πάθη are not unnatural

Galenus, o.c., p. 408, 4-15 M.:

Ὁποία δέ τίς ἐστιν ἡ τῶν φαύλων ψυχὴ κατά τε τὰ πάθη καὶ πρὸ τῶν παθῶν, οὐκέθ' ὁμοίως ἐξηγοῦνται. Χρύσιππος μὲν γὰρ ἀνάλογον ἔχειν αὐτήν φησι τοῖς ἐπιτηδείοις σώμασιν εἰς πυρετοὺς ἐμπίπτειν ἢ διαρροίας ἤ τι τοιοῦτον ἕτερον ἐπὶ σμικρᾷ καὶ τυχούσῃ προφάσει. καὶ μέμφεταί γε ὁ Ποσειδώνιος αὐτοῦ τὴν εἰκόνα· χρῆναι γάρ φησιν οὐ τούτοις, ἀλλὰ τοῖς ἁπλῶς ὑγιαίνουσι σώμασιν εἰκάσαι τὴν τῶν φαύλων ψυχήν· εἴτε γὰρ ἐπὶ μεγάλοις αἰτίοις εἴτε ἐπὶ σκιμροῖς πυρέττοιεν, οὐδὲν διαφέρειν ὡς πρὸς τὸ πάσχειν τε αὐτὰ καὶ εἰς πάθος ἐσάγεσθαι καθ' ὁτιοῦν, ἀλλὰ τῷ τὰ μὲν εὐέμπτωτα εἶναι, τὰ δὲ δύσπτωτα διαφέρειν ἀλλήλων.

1186—A consequence of this psychological view of man is that, according to Posid., wickedness does not come from without (as was held by Chrys.), but has its roots in the soul itself.

Galenus, *Quod animi mores corporis temperamenta sequantur*, Scr. min. II, p. 78, 8 sqq. Müller:

Οὐ τοίνυν οὐδὲ Ποσειδωνίῳ δοκεῖ τὴν κακίαν ἔξωθεν ἐπεισιέναι τοῖς ἀνθρώποις οὐδεμίαν ἔχουσαν ἰδίαν ῥίζαν ‹ἐν› ταῖς ψυχαῖς ἡμῶν, ὅθεν ὁρμωμένη βλαστάνει τε καὶ αὐξάνεται, ἀλλ' αὐτὸ τοὐναντίον· καὶ γὰρ οὖν καὶ τῆς κακίας ἐν ἡμῖν αὐτοῖς σπέρμα· καὶ δεόμεθα πάντες οὐχ οὕτω τοῦ φεύγειν τοὺς πονηροὺς ὡς τοῦ διώκειν τοὺς καθαρίσοντάς τε καὶ κωλύσοντας ἡμῶν τὴν αὔξησιν τῆς κακίας.

1187—The paedagogical consequences.

    a. Galenus, *De plac. Hippocr. et Plat.*, p. 445, 8-15 M.:

Posid. praises Plato for his prescriptions about giving motion to infants.

Γέγραφεν οἷον ἐπιτομήν τινα κατὰ τὸ πρῶτον αὐτοῦ Περὶ παθῶν σύγγραμμα τῶν ὑπὸ Πλάτωνος εἰρημένων, ὡς χρὴ τρέφεσθαι καὶ παιδεύεσθαι τοὺς παῖδας ὑπὲρ τοῦ τὸ παθητικόν τε καὶ ἄλογον τῆς ψυχῆς σύμμετρον ἀποφαίνεσθαι ταῖς κινήσεσι καὶ τοῖς τοῦ λόγου προστάγμασιν εὐπειθές. Αὕτη γὰρ ἀρίστη παίδων παιδεία, παρασκευὴ τοῦ παθητικοῦ τῆς ψυχῆς, ὡς ἂν ἐπιτηδειοτάτη ᾖ πρὸς τὴν ἀρχὴν τοῦ λογιστικοῦ.

    b. Ib., p. 452, 10 - 453, 2 M.:

Καὶ τοὺς τρόπους δέ, φησί, τῆς ἀσκήσεως ἡ τῶν παθῶν αἰτία γνωρισθεῖσα διωρίσατο. τοὺς μὲν γὰρ ἐν τοιοῖσδε ῥυθμοῖς ἅμα καὶ ἁρμονίαις καὶ ἐπιτηδεύμασι, τοὺς δὲ ἐν τοιοῖσδε διαιτᾶσθαι κελεύσομεν, ὥσπερ ὁ Πλάτων ἡμᾶς ἐδίδαξε, τοὺς μὲν ἀμβλεῖς καὶ νωθροὺς καὶ ἀθύμους ἔν τε τοῖς ὀρθοῖς ῥυθμοῖς καὶ ταῖς κινούσαις ἰσχυρῶς τὴν ψυχὴν ἁρμονίαις καὶ τοῖς τοιούτοις ἐπιτηδεύμασι τρέφοντες, τοὺς δὲ θυμικωτέρους καὶ μανικώτερον ἄττοντας ἐν ταῖς ἐναντίαις.

    c. The πάθη then, being as such not unnatural, should be "formed" and educated, not extirpated. The same view, founded on the same anthropological principles (ἕξις, φύσις, ψυχὴ ἄλογος and λογική, all being present in man), is found in Plutarch, *De virtute morali* 12. The author concludes (451c):

Μέτεστιν οὖν αὐτῷ καὶ τοῦ ἀλόγου, καὶ σύμφυτον ἔχει τὴν τοῦ πάθους ἀρχήν, οὐκ ἐπεισόδιον, ἀλλὰ ἀναγκαίαν οὖσαν, οὐδὲ ἀναιρετέαν παντάπασιν, ἀλλὰ θεραπείας καὶ παιδαγωγίας δεομένην.

1188—a. The true cause of passions then is *that men do not follow the daimon in themselves*, which is of the same nature as the Ruler of the Universe. Text ap. Gal., p. 448 M., cited above, nr. **1055**.

The true cause of passions and the end of life

b. The author concludes that Posid., then, differed from Chrysippus in his explanation of the "end".

Galenus, p. 449, 8 - 450, 2 M.:

Ἐν τούτοις φανερῶς ὁ Ποσειδώνιος ἐδίδαξε, πηλίκον ἁμαρτάνουσιν οἱ περὶ τὸν Χρύσιππον οὐ μόνον ἐν τοῖς περὶ τῶν παθῶν λογισμοῖς, ἀλλὰ καὶ τοῖς περὶ τοῦ τέλους. οὐ γάρ, ὡς ἐκεῖνοι λέγουσιν, ἀλλὰ ὡς ὁ Πλάτων ἐδίδαξε, τὸ τῇ φύσει ζῆν ὁμολογουμένως ἐστίν. ὄντος γὰρ ἐν ἡμῖν τοῦ μὲν βελτίονος τῆς ψυχῆς μέρους, τοῦ δὲ χείρονος ὁ μὲν τῷ βελτίονι συνεπόμενος ὁμολογουμένως ἂν λέγοιτο τῇ φύσει ζῆν, ὁ δὲ τῷ χείρονι μᾶλλον ἑπόμενος ἀνομολογουμένως· ἔστι δὲ οὗτος μὲν ὁ κατὰ πάθος ζῶν, ἐκεῖνος δὲ ὁ κατὰ λόγον.

c. He criticized the telos formulae of Diogenes, Antipater and Archedemus (our nr. **1144**).

Chrysippus' successors criticized by Posid.

Galenus, ib., p. 450, 5-12 M. (citing Posid.):

"Ἃ (sc. Chrysippus' theory) δὴ παρέντες ἔνιοι τὸ ὁμολογουμένως ζῆν συστέλλουσιν εἰς τὸ πᾶν τὸ ἐνδεχόμενον ποιεῖν ἕνεκα τῶν πρώτων κατὰ φύσιν ὅμοιον αὐτὸ ποιοῦντες τῷ σκοπὸν ἐκτίθεσθαι τὴν ἡδονὴν ἢ τὴν ἀοχλησίαν ἢ ἄλλο τι τοιοῦτον. ἔστι δὲ μάχην ἐμφαῖνον κατὰ αὐτὴν τὴν ἐκφοράν, καλὸν δὲ καὶ εὐδαιμονικὸν οὐδέν, παρέπεται γὰρ κατὰ τὸ ἀναγκαῖον τῷ τέλει, τέλος δὲ οὐκ ἔστιν.

d. He concludes that, when the end is rightly understood, all difficulties can be solved, and there is no need of Chrysippus's "liberal" explanation (see our nr. **1004**, the end), which in fact is a simple tautology.

Galenus, ib., p. 450, 12 - 451, 2 (Posid. is still cited):

Chrysippus' formula rebuked

Ἀλλὰ καὶ τούτου (sc. τοῦ τέλους) διαληφθέντος ὀρθῶς ἔξεστι μὲν αὐτῷ χρῆσθαι πρὸς τὸ διακόπτειν τὰς ἀπορίας, ἃς οἱ σοφισταὶ προτείνουσι, μὴ μέντοι γε τῷ κατὰ ἐμπειρίαν τῶν κατὰ τὴν ὅλην φύσιν συμβαινόντων ζῆν, ὅπερ ἰσοδυναμεῖ τῷ ὁμολογουμένως εἰπεῖν ζῆν, ἡνίκα μὴ τοῦτο μικροπρεπῶς συντείνει εἰς τὸ τῶν ἀδιαφόρων τυγχάνειν.

1189—Solution of preceding difficulties.

a. Now it is evident why wise men—also *relatively* wise men [1]—do

---

[1] That the προκόπτοντες were recognized as such by Posid., may be inferred from Diog. L. VII 91.

Difficulties explained not fall into passion by attaining the object striven after or by expecting bad things.

Galenus, *De plac. Hipp. et Plat.*, p. 454, 12-15 M.:

Καὶ μὴν οἱ προκόπτοντες μεγάλα κακὰ δοκοῦντες ἑαυτοῖς παρεῖναι ἢ ἐπιφέρεσθαι οὐ λυποῦνται· φέρονται γὰρ οὐ κατὰ τὸ ἄλογον τῆς ψυχῆς οὕτως, ἀλλὰ κατὰ τὸ λογικόν.

b. How it is that passions are soothed by time.

Galenus, ib., p. 454, 15 - 455, 16 M.:

Εἶτα ἐφεξῆς οὗτος, δια τί τὰ χρονίζοντα τῶν παθῶν ἡσυχέστερά τε καὶ ἀσθενέστερα γίνεται, τὴν αἰτίαν ἀποδίδωσιν, ὑπὲρ ἧς ὁ Χρύσιππος ἐν τῷ δευτέρῳ Περὶ παθῶν ἀπορεῖν ὡμολόγησεν. εἴρηται δὲ περὶ αὐτῆς ὑφ' ἡμῶν ἐπὶ τῇ τελευτῇ τοῦ τετάρτου καὶ νῦν δὲ εἰρήσεται διὰ βραχέων οἷον ἐπιτομή τις τῆς Ποσειδωνίου ῥήσεως μακρᾶς ὑπαρχούσης. τὸ τοίνυν παθητικὸν τῆς ψυχῆς ἐν τῷ χρόνῳ τοῦτο μὲν ἐμπίπλαται τῶν οἰκείων ἐπιθυμιῶν, τοῦτο δὲ κάμνει ταῖς πολυχρονίοις κινήσεσιν, ὥστε διὰ ἄμφω καθησυχάσαντος αὐτοῦ καὶ μέτρι'α κινομένου κρατεῖν ὁ λογισμὸς ἤδη δύναται, ὥσπερ καὶ εἰ ἵππου τινὸς ἐκφόρου τὸν ἐπιβάτην ἐξενεγκόντος βιαίως, εἶτα κάμνοντός τε ἅμα τῷ δρόμῳ καὶ προσέτι καὶ ἐμπλησθέντος ὧν ἐπεθύμησεν αὖθις ὁ ἡνίοχος ἐγκρατὴς κατασταίη. φαίνεται γὰρ τοῦτο πολλάκις γινόμενον καὶ οἵ γε παιδεύοντες τὰ νέα τῶν ζῴων ἐπιτρέψαντες αὐτοῖς κάμνειν τε ἅμα καὶ ἐμπλησθῆναι κατὰ τὰς ἐκφόρους κινήσεις ὕστερον ἐπιτίθενται.

Virtues **1190**—Since there are rational and irrational forces in man, there is a real moral struggle in us, there is a virtue of ἐγκράτεια and σωφροσύνη [1].

a. Galenus, *De plac. Hipp. et Plat.* p. 467, 3 - 468, 5 M.:

Ἡ μὲν γὰρ ἄλογος ἐν ἡμῖν δύναμις ἐφ' ἕκαστον τῶν ἐπιθυμουμένων ἕλκει τὸν δεόμενον, ὁ δὲ λογισμὸς ἀντισπᾷ καὶ κατέχει τὴν οὐκ ἐν καιρῷ φοράν. καὶ μάχη γε πολλάκις ἑκατέρων ἰσχυρὰ γίνεται πρὸς ἄλληλα φανερῶς ἐπιδεικνυμένη διττὴν εἶναι φύσιν ἐν ἡμῖν τῶν στασιαζουσῶν ἀλλήλαις δυνάμεων. εἴπερ γὰρ ἦν μία μόνη, καθάπερ ἐν τοῖς παισίν, οὐδὲν ἂν ἐκώλυεν ἀκαίρως ἡμᾶς ἀπολαύειν τῶν ἐπιθυμουμένων, ὥσπερ γε καὶ εἰ μόνος ὁ λογισμὸς ἦν πρὸς οὐδὲν ἀνθέλκειν τε καὶ στασιάζειν εἰθισμένος, οὐδὲν ἂν ἦν πρᾶγμα διψῶντα μὴ πίνειν ἢ πεινῶντα μὴ ἐσθίειν οὐδὲ ἐγκρατὴς οὐδὲ σώφρων ἂν ὁ μὴ πίνων ὠνομάζετο, καθάπερ οὐδὲ ὁ μὴ βαδίζων, εἰ μὴ βούλοιτο. νυνὶ δέ, ἐπεὶ διτταί τινές εἰσιν αἱ τὸν ἄνθρωπον ἐπισπώμεναι δυνάμεις, ἔστι δὲ ἄλογος ἡ τοῦ πόματος

---

[1]   The following passage of Gal. is not a quotation from Posid., but it expresses his thought fairly well.

ἐπιθυμοῦσα, ἡ δὲ κατέχουσα ταύτην λογική, σωφροσύνης ἐν τῷ τοιούτῳ καὶ ἐγκρατείας ἡ γένεσις. ἀλλὰ τοῦτο μὲν ἡμῖν οὐ σμικρὸν ἐν παρέργῳ δειχθὲν εἰς τὸν περὶ τῶν ἀρετῶν λόγον μνημονευέσθω, μήτε ἐγκράτειαν εἶναί τι μήτε σωφροσύνην ἀναιρεθείσης τῷ λόγῳ τῆς ἐπιθυμητικῆς δυνάμεως.

b. Not every virtue should be defined as ἐπιστήμη, as was done by Chrysippus.

Galenus, ib., p. 446, 13 M.:

῞Επεται δὲ εὐθὺς τοῖσδε καὶ ὁ περὶ τῶν ἀρετῶν λόγος αὐτοῦ ἐλέγχων τὸ σφάλμα διττόν, εἴτε ἐπιστήμας τις ἁπάσας αὐτὰς εἴτε δυνάμεις ὑπολάβοι. τῶν μὲν γὰρ ἀλόγων τῆς ψυχῆς μερῶν ἀλόγους ἀνάγκη καὶ τὰς ἀρετὰς εἶναι, τοῦ λογιστικοῦ δὲ μόνου λογικήν. ὥστε εὐλόγως ἐκείνων μὲν αἱ ἀρεταὶ δυνάμεις εἰσίν, ἐπιστήμη δὲ μόνου τοῦ λογιστικοῦ.

c. Like Panaetius, Posid. considered virtue not as self-sufficient. Our nr. **1165a**.

1191—a. Posid. seems to have divided ethics into three main parts: (1) a prescriptive part, including suasion, consolation and exhortation; (2) an aetiological part; (3) a phenomenology of virtues, called *ethology*.

Division of ethics

Seneca, *Ep.* 95, 65:

Posidonius non tantum praeceptionem, nihil enim nos hoc verbo uti prohibet, sed etiam suasionem et consolationem et exhortationem necessariam iudicat. His adicit causarum inquisitionem, aetiologian quam quare nos dicere non audeamus, cum grammatici, custodes Latini sermonis, suo iure ita appellent, non video. ait utilem futuram et descriptionem cuiusque virtutis: hanc Posidonius ethologian vocat, quidam characterismon appellant, signa cuiusque virtutis ac vitii et notas reddentem, quibus inter se similia discriminentur.

b. Doubtless the aetiological part was concerned with the πάθη.

Galenus, *De plac.* 448, 9-11 M:

Νομίζω γὰρ καὶ τὴν περὶ ἀγαθῶν καὶ κακῶν καὶ τὴν περὶ τελῶν καὶ τὴν περὶ ἀρετῶν ἐκ τῆς περὶ παθῶν ὀρθῶς διασκέψεως ἠρτῆσθαι.

c. Diog. Laërt. VII 91, 129 mentions a *Protrepticus* of Posid. According to the same author, VII 124, 129, he wrote also a Π. καθήκοντος or Π. καθηκόντων.

Ethical treatises

Cic., *ad Att.* XVI 11, 4 says that Posidonius discussed the conflict of the *honestum* and the *utile*; but, according to *De off.* III 2, 7-8, he touched the subject only briefly.

The soul
and its im-
mortality

1192—a. Posid. opposed Epicurus's doctrine of mortality of the soul. Achilles Tat., *Isag. in Arat. Phaen.* c. 13, p. 41 M.:

Ποσειδώνιος δὲ ἀγνοεῖν τοὺς Ἐπικουρείους ἔφη ὡς οὐ τὰ σώματα τὰς ψυχὰς συνέχει, ἀλλ' αἱ ψυχαὶ τὰ σώματα, ὥσπερ καὶ ἡ κόλλα καὶ ἑαυτὴν καὶ τὰ ἐκτὸς κρατεῖ.

Other
evidence

The same argument is found in Sextus, *Adv. math.* IX (= *Ag. the phys.* I) 72. It is preceded by a remark on the fiery nature of soul, and followed by the statement that souls "having quitted the sphere of the sun, inhabit the region below the moon". Cp. Diodorus II 51, 3 (cited above, nr. **1176c**) on the ζωτικὴ δύναμις of the sun, and Diog. L. VII 157, where Posid. is mentioned with other Stoics who taught that soul is πνεῦμα ἔνθερμον. Cic., *Tusc.* I 18, 42, concludes (against Panaetius) that, if this be so, the soul must necessarily seek higher regions. With Plutarch, lastly, in the final chapters of the *De facie in orbe lunae* (28-30), we find the doctrine that *noûs* originates from the sun and finally returns to it, while *psyche*, sprung from the moon which is of a mixed nature, is dissolved into the substance of the moon, like bodies into earth. Since, in these chapters, we find certain hardly dubitable Posidonian features (in c. 30 the ζωτικὴ δύναμις of the moon is mentioned [1], in 29 its mixed character [2]), while in general the tenor is similar to that of the above mentioned passages of Sextus and of Cic., *Tusc.* I 19, 43, it is certainly not arbitrary to say that, for an essential part, Posid. is behind them. (For the moment I wish to make abstraction of the distinction between ψυχή and νοῦς made by Plutarch).

Sextus concludes (§ 74) that, since souls are permanent, they are *daemons*, and this he uses as a proof of the existence of gods.

Now we know by an important text of Galenus, cited under nr. **1055**, that Posid. spoke of the "daemon within us" which is of the same nature as the Ruler of the universe. —

After this short account we may proceed to cite our texts.

Sextus

b. Sextus Emp., *Adv. math.* IX (= *Ag. the phys.* I) 71-74:

Καὶ γὰρ οὐδὲ τὰς ψυχὰς ἔνεστιν ὑπονοῆσαι κάτω φερομένας· λεπτομερεῖς γὰρ οὖσαι καὶ οὐχ ἧττον πυρώδεις ἢ πνευματώδεις εἰς τοὺς ἄνω μᾶλλον τόπους κουφοφοροῦσιν. καὶ καθ' αὑτὰς δὲ διαμένουσι καὶ οὐχ, ὡς ἔλεγεν ὁ Ἐπίκουρος, ἀπολυθεῖσαι τῶν σωμάτων καπνοῦ δίκην σκίδνανται. οὐδὲ γὰρ πρότερον τὸ σῶμα διακρατητικὸν ἦν αὐτῶν, ἀλλ' αὐταὶ τῷ σώματι συμμονῆς ἦσαν αἴτιαι, πολὺ δὲ πρότερον καὶ ἑαυταῖς. ἔκσκηνοι γοῦν ἡλίου γενόμεναι τὸν ὑπὸ σελήνην οἰκοῦσι τόπον, ἐνθάδε τε διὰ τὴν εἰλικρίνειαν τοῦ ἀέρος πλείονα πρὸς διαμονὴν λαμβάνουσι χρόνον, τροφῇ τε χρῶνται οἰκείᾳ τῇ ἀπὸ γῆς ἀναθυμιάσει ὡς καὶ τὰ λοιπὰ ἄστρα, τὸ διαλῦσόν τε αὐτὰς ἐν ἐκείνοις τοῖς τόποις οὐκ ἔχουσιν. εἰ οὖν διαμένουσιν αἱ ψυχαί, δαίμοσιν αἱ αὐταὶ γίνονται· εἰ δὲ δαίμονές εἰσι, ῥητέον καὶ θεοὺς ὑπάρχειν.

Jones, *Posid. and solar eschatology*, in *Class. Philol.* 1936, p. 115, argues that, since the argument of soul holding the body together occurs in Aristotle's *De*

---

[1] See above, nr. **1176d**.
[2] See above, nr. **1180**.

Anima 411 b 6, there is no sufficient ground to see Posid. behind this passage of Sextus. The essential point is, however, that the *setting* of the argument in Sextus is similar to that of Ach. Tatius (both opposing it to Epicureanism, and both speaking of κρατεῖν-διακρατητικόν), while both the preceding and the following paragraphs point to that kind of spiritualizing Stoicism which may be expected of Posid. Cp. S. Blankert, *Seneca, Ep. 90,* p. 202.

c. Cp. Cic., *Tusc.* I 18, 42 - 19, 43:   **Cicero**

Is autem animus, qui si est horum quattuor generum, ex quibus omnia constare dicuntur, ex inflammata anima [1] constat, ut potissimum videri video Panaetio, superiora capessat necesse est. Nihil enim habent haec duo genera [2] proni et supera semper petunt. Ita, sive dissipantur, procul a terris id evenit, sive permanent et conservant habitum suum, hoc etiam magis necesse est ferantur ad caelum et ab is perrumpatur et dividatur crassus hoc et concretus aër, qui est terrae proximus. Calidior est enim vel potius ardentior animus quam est hic aër, quem modo dixi crassum et concretum; quod ex eo sciri potest, quia corpora nostra terreno principiorum genere confecta ardore animi concalescunt. Accedit ut eo facilius animus evadat ex hoc aëre, quem saepe iam appello, eumque perrumpat, quod nihil est animo velocius, nulla est celeritas quae possit cum animi celeritate contendere. Qui si permanet incorruptus suique similis, necesse est ita feratur, ut penetret et dividat omne caelum hoc, in quo nubes imbres ventique coguntur, quod et umidum et caliginosum est propter exhalationes terrae. Quam regionem cum superavit animus naturamque sui similem contigit et adgnovit, iunctis ex anima tenui [3] et ex ardore solis temperato ignibus insistit et finem altius se ecferendi facit. Cum enim sui similem et levitatem et calorem adeptus <est>, tamquam paribus exanimatus ponderibus nullam in partem movetur, eaque ei demum naturalis est sedes, cum ad sui simile penetravit; in quo nulla re egens aletur et sustentabitur isdem rebus, quibus astra sustentantur et aluntur [4].

In this passage Posid.'s doctrine of the soul as πνεῦμα ἔνθερμον is explained in this sense that, first, soul proves to be of the same (viz. intermediate) nature as the moon, and secondly, that being purified it may ascend to higher regions. Elsewhere, Cic. speaks of *mens* (νοῦς) which, according to Aristotle in II. φιλοσοφίας, consisted of aether.

---

[1]　πνεῦμα ἔνθερμον; cp. Diog. L. VII 157.
[2]　Sc. ignis et aër, which are implied in *inflammata anima.* Cp. the mixed character of the moon: our nr. **1180**.
[3]　i.e. *aether.*
[4]　On the doctrine that νοῦς (*mens*) is of the substance of the stars: our nr. **431d** (vol. II). Cp. also *Tusc.* I 10, 22.

Jones, *Posid. and Cicero's Tusc. Disp.* I 17-81, in *Class. Philol.* 1923, p. 202-228, tried to prove that the greater part of *Tusc.* I either *cannot* belong to Posid., or does not contain sufficient indications to attribute it to him. Generally, in this as well as in his two other articles on Posid. in which he criticizes i.a. Reinhardt's views, he does not take sufficiently into account that Posid. was greatly influenced by Plato, and that, therefore, we cannot conclude from the fact that a thought is platonic (e.g. the superiority of νοῦς to ψυχή, as will be found with Plutarch), that *ergo* it is not Posidonian. Again, the *setting* of this Platonism should be carefully observed.

Moreover, Jones is certainly wrong when saying (p. 227) that in *Tusc.* I 43 there is not any further ascent of the soul than to the sublunary sphere [1], and opposing it on this very point to the *Somnium Scipionis*, where the soul is said to ascend to the Milky Way. Essentially the same doctrine is found here. It will be illustrated further by Plutarch's last chapters of the *De facie*.

Plutarch   **d.**   In the following passage of Plutarch a distinction is made between ψυχή and νοῦς. The passage contains a similar view, but is more explicit than Cicero's in the above-cited text.

Plutarchus, *De facie in orbe lunae*, cc. 28-30:

(28) Νοῦς γὰρ ψυχῆς ὅσῳ ψυχὴ σώματος ἄμεινόν ἐστι καὶ θειότερον. —
Τριῶν δὲ τούτων συμπαγέντων τὸ μὲν σῶμα ἡ γῆ, τὴν δὲ ψυχὴν ἡ σελήνη, τὸν δὲ νοῦν ὁ ἥλιος παρέσχεν εἰς τὴν γένεσιν [2], . . ὥσπερ αὖ τῇ σελήνῃ τὸ φέγγος [3]. —

Συντυγχάνει δὲ οὕτως κατὰ φύσιν ἑκάτερον. Πᾶσαν ψυχήν, ἄνουν τε καὶ σὺν νῷ, σώματος ἐκπεσοῦσαν, εἱμαρμένον ἐστὶ τῷ μεταξὺ γῆς καὶ σελήνης χωρίῳ πλανηθῆναι χρόνον οὐκ ἴσον.

Follows a description of the different destinies of the souls, according to their merit. Next, at the beginning of c. 29, he speaks of the "mixed" substance of the moon. Now, in the moon there are βάθη καὶ κοιλώματα (what is called *its face*), the largest of which is called Ἑκάτης μυχός. It is here that the souls do penance or receive satisfaction for what they suffered or did, *after having become daemons*.

(944c) Καλοῦσι δ' αὐτῶν τὸ μὲν μέγιστον Ἑκάτης μυχόν, ὅπου καὶ δίκας διδόασιν αἱ ψυχαὶ καὶ λαμβάνουσιν, ὧν ἂν ἤδη γεγενημέναι δαίμονες [4] ἢ πάθωσιν ἢ δράσωσιν.

Next (30), Plutarch speaks of the duties of the daemons in the world and towards man. Some of them migrate to better regions.

(944e) Τυγχάνουσι δὲ οἱ μὲν πρότερον, οἱ δὲ ὕστερον, ὅταν ὁ νοῦς ἀποκριθῇ τῆς ψυχῆς· ἀποκρίνεται δ' ἔρωτι τῆς περὶ τὸν ἥλιον εἰκόνος, δι' ἧς ἐπιλάμπει

---

[1]   *quam regionem cum superavit animus* —
[2]   Cp. the expression ἔκσκηνοι γοῦν ἡλίου γενόμεναι ap. Sext. 73 (under **1192b**).
[3]   Noûs is given to man by the sun as light is given to the moon. Cp. the function of noûs in the text of Philo, cited under **1181**, sub. 1.
[4]   Cp. Sextus, § 74 (under **b**), and Galenus, *De plac. Hipp. et Plat.*, p. 448 M, cited under nr. **1055**.

τὸ ἐφετὸν καὶ καλὸν καὶ θεῖον καὶ μακάριον, οὗ πᾶσα φύσις, ἄλλη δ' ἄλλως, ὀρέγεται. Καὶ γὰρ αὐτὴν τὴν σελήνην ἔρωτι τοῦ ἡλίου περιπολεῖν ἀεί, καὶ συγγίνεσθαι ὀρεγομένην, ἀπ' αὐτοῦ τὸ γονιμώτατον ** (5) Λείπεται δὲ ἡ τῆς ψυχῆς φύσις ἐπὶ τὴν σελήνην, οἷον ἴχνη τινὰ βίου καὶ ὀνείρατα διαφυλάττουσα· καὶ περὶ ταύτης ὀρθῶς ἡγοῦ λελέχθαι τό,

"Ψυχὴ δ' ἠΰτ' ὄνειρος ἀποπταμένη πεπότηται." [1]

οὐδὲ γὰρ εὐθὺς οὐδὲ τοῦ σώματος ἀπαλλαγεῖσα, τοῦτο πέπονθεν, ἀλλὰ ὕστερον, ὅταν ἔρημος καὶ μόνη τοῦ νοῦ ἀπαλλαττομένη γένηται. (6) Καὶ Ὅμηρος ὢν εἶπε πάντων μάλιστα δὴ κατὰ θεὸν εἰπεῖν ἔοικε περὶ τῶν καθ' Ἅιδου

"Τὸν δὲ μετ' εἰσενόησα βίην Ἡρακληείην,
εἴδωλον· αὐτὸς δὲ μετ' ἀθανάτοισι θεοῖσιν." [2]

αὐτός τε γὰρ ἕκαστος ἡμῶν οὐ θυμός ἐστιν, οὐδὲ φόβος, οὐδ' ἐπιθυμία, καθάπερ οὐδὲ σάρκες οὐδὲ ὑγρότητες, ἀλλ' ᾧ διανοούμεθα καὶ φρονοῦμεν, * ἥ τε ψυχὴ τυπουμένη μὲν ὑπὸ τοῦ νοῦ, τυποῦσα δὲ τὸ σῶμα καὶ περιπτύσσουσα πανταχόθεν ἐκμάττεται τὸ εἶδος· ὥστε κἂν πολὺν χρόνον χωρὶς ἑκατέρου γένηται, διατηροῦσα τὴν ὁμοιότητα καὶ τὸν τύπον, εἴδωλον ὀρθῶς ὀνομάζεται. (7) Τούτων δὲ ἡ σελήνη, καθάπερ εἴρηται, στοιχεῖόν ἐστιν· ἀναλύονται γὰρ εἰς ταύτην, ὥσπερ εἰς τὴν γῆν τὰ σώματα τῶν νεκρῶν.

Noûs then, being born from the sun, returns to the sun; soul, being of a mixed nature, to the moon, and body, consisting of the grossest matter, to earth.

The passage is striking by its marked spiritualism. The question must be asked whether or not this sharp distinction between noûs and psychè goes back to Posid. Verbeke, *La doctrine du pneuma*, p. 129 f., observes that Plutarch's psychology does not correspond exactly with that of Posid. So did Pohlenz, *Gott. Gel. Anz.* 1926, p. 305.

Reinhardt, *Kosmos u. Symp.* p. 320-323, 348-353, defends the Posidonian origin of the whole theory, pointing out its closed and systematical character. "Von der Sonne geht das Werden aus (τὴν ἀρχὴν ἐνδίδωσι τῆς γενέσεως); die Sonne ist zugleich das "Herz der Welt", zugleich der "Nus der Welt".—Der Nus kann nur vom Nus ausgehen, der Nus des Menschen nur vom "Nus des Kosmos" " [3].

On *Tusc.* I, compared with this eschatology, Reinhardt, o.c., p. 363. Jones opposes Reinhardt in *Class. Philol.* 1936, p. 113-135, but his criticism is liable to the above-made objections.

Pohlenz, *Stoa* I, p. 229 f., appears to be convinced by Reinhardt's arguments. See also Blankert, *Seneca Ep.* 90, p. 229. Parallel passages concerning noûs: our nr. **1195**.

1193—a. That Posid. adopted the view of the Ancient Academy as Intermediate to the intermediate position of the soul (cp. Xenocrates, our nr. **759**, place of the soul vol. II), appears from the following passage.

---

[1] *Odyssea* λ 222.   [2] *Od.* λ 601 f.   [3] p. 351, 352.

Plutarchus, *De procr. animae in Tim.* 22, p. 1023b:

Ὅμοια δὲ τούτοις ἔστιν ἀντειπεῖν καὶ τοῖς περὶ Ποσειδώνιον· οὐ γὰρ μακρὰν τῆς ὕλης ἀπέστησαν· ἀλλὰ δεξάμενοι τὴν τῶν περάτων οὐσίαν περὶ τὰ σώματα λέγεσθαι μεριστὴν καὶ ταῦτα τῷ νοητῷ μίξαντες ἀπεφήναντο τὴν ψυχὴν ἰδέαν εἶναι τοῦ πάντη διαστατοῦ κατ' ἀριθμὸν συνεστῶσαν ἁρμονίαν περιέχοντα· τά τε γὰρ μαθηματικὰ τῶν πρώτων νοητῶν μεταξὺ καὶ τῶν αἰσθητῶν τετάχθαι, τῆς τε ψυχῆς, τῶν νοητῶν τὸ ἀΐδιον καὶ τῶν αἰσθητῶν τὸ παθητικὸν ἐχούσης, προσῆκον ἐν μέσῳ τὴν οὐσίαν ὑπάρχειν.

On this passage: R. M. Jones, *The Platonism of Plutarch*, Chicago 1916, pp. 73 ff.;

A. E. Taylor, *A commentary on Plato's Tim.* 1928, p. 118 f.

Ph. Merlan, *Beiträge zur Geschichte des antiken Platonismus. Poseidonios über die Weltseele in Platons Timaios*, Philologus 89 (NF 43), 1934, p. 198 ff.

P. Thévenaz, *L'âme du monde, le devenir et la matière chez Plutarque*, Paris 1938, p. 65-67.

G. Verbeke, *La doctrine du pneuma*, pp. 117-120.

Ph. Merlan, *From Platonism to Neoplatonism*, The Hague 1953, p. 31 ff.

C. J. de Vogel, *A la recherche des étapes précises entre le Platonisme et le Néoplat.*, Mnemosyne 1954, p. 111-122.

The essential point is that, according to this view, soul, being an intermediate body, is, though not identified, yet essentially connected with a mathematical principle (τὸ πάντη διαστατόν means: space).

spiritualism   **b.**   The following words of Posid. are the expression of a strongly "dualistic" or spiritualistic conception of man.

Seneca, *Ep.* 92, 10:

Prima ars hominis est ipsa virtus: huic committitur inutilis caro et fluida, receptandis tantum cibis habilis, ut ait Posidonius.

Immortality presupposed in Posid.'s theory of mantic   **1194—a.**   Posidonius's explanation of what is called *natural mantic* is based on this view of soul and its immortality.

Cic., *De div.* I 30, 63-64:

Cum ergo est somno sevocatus animus a societate et a contagione corporis, tum meminit praeteritorum, praesentia cernit, futura providet; iacet enim corpus dormientis ut mortui, viget autem et vivit animus. quod multo magis faciet post mortem, cum omnino corpore excesserit. itaque adpropinquante morte multo est divinior. nam et id ipsum vident qui sunt morbo gravi et mortifero adfecti, instare mortem; itaque is occurrunt plerumque imagines mortuorum tumque vel maxume laudi student eosque qui secus quam decuit vixerunt peccatorum suorum tum maxume paenitet. divinare autem morientes illo etiam exemplo confirmat Posidonius quod adfert, Rhodium quendam morientem sex aequales nominasse et dixisse qui primus eorum, qui secundus, qui deinde deinceps moriturus esset. Sed tribus modis censet deorum adpulsu homines somniare, uno quod provideat animus ipse per sese, quippe qui deorum cognatione teneatur, altero quod plenus aër sit immortalium animorum, in quibus tamquam insignitae notae veritatis appareant, tertio quod ipsi di cum dormientibus conloquantur.

First, the *quod plenus aër sit immortalium animorum* comes from the same theory as that which we found in Plutarch's *De facie* 28-30. It is the ψυχή, ἄνους τε καὶ σὺν νῷ, σώματος ἐκπεσοῦσα, which "roams" between the earth and the moon. And, first of all, there are the pre-existing souls coming from the sun and passing through the sublunary sphere before being bound in a body.

Secondly, these souls prove to possess certain innate notions of truth—, which certainly means, that its νοῦς comes from a higher region [1].

Cp. also Seneca, *Ep.* 90, 28, 105 and Aug., *Civ. Dei* VII 6 C. The passages are discussed by Blankert, o.c., p. 204 ff.

b. Having reported Posidonius's defense of "technical mantic", which is essentially based on *sympatheia*, i.e. the connexion of everything with everything in nature, the author concludes: *Also in that of technical mantic*

Cic., *De div.* I 57, 131:

Quid est igitur cur, cum domus sit omnium una eaque communis cumque animi hominum semper fuerint futurique sint, cur ii quid ex quoque eveniat et quid quamque rem significet perspicere non possint?

The passage must be interpreted in this sense that, by its *pre-existence and post-existence* (*cum animi hominum semper fuerint futurique sint*), the soul has certain "innate notions of truth", which enable man to understand *quid ex quoque eveniat*, etc.

It might seem perhaps to us that, to this purpose, the possession of innate notions of truth is not necessary or even helpful. Yet, it is clear that the argument *cumque animi* does not refer to the explanation of natural but to that of technical mantic.

1195—There is some converging evidence for the thesis that Posid. called the higher intellectual functions of man noûs, and that he derived it from regions superior to those of what he called psychè. Doubtless, the above cited passages from *De div.* I must be reckoned to this evidence. Moreover Pohlenz (St. II, p. 116) points to the following texts.

---

[1] Verbeke, *La doctrine du pneuma*, p. 125, explains the passage in this sense that, according to the Ancient Stoic theory, the τυπώσεις in the psychical pneuma could be *seen* in these souls delivered from the body.

This explanation, evidently, is possible in the case of those souls which, having left the body, are on the way to higher spheres. It does not apply, however, to those who, coming from the sun, are on the way to the earth.

The doctrine
of νοῦς
with Posid.

a. Strabo X 3, 9 (speaking of ekstasis being effected by music):

Καὶ τοῦθ' ἡ φύσις οὕτως ὑπαγορεύει. ἥ τε γὰρ ἄνεσις τὸν νοῦν ἀπάγει ἀπὸ τῶν ἀνθρωπικῶν ἀσχολημάτων, * τὸν δὲ ὄντως νοῦν τρέπει πρὸς τὸ θεῖον· ὅ τε ἐνθουσιασμὸς ἐπίπνευσίν τινα θείαν ἔχειν δοκεῖ καὶ τῷ μαντικῷ γένει πλησιάζειν.

It is at least probable that Strabo, who used Posid.' works continually, took these ideas from him.

b. Cp. Sextus Emp., *Adv. math.* VII (= *Ag. the log.* I) 129, explaining Heraclitus' words that not the senses, but *logos*, or τὸ κοινόν is the criterium of truth:

Τοῦτον δὴ τὸν θεῖον λόγον καθ' Ἡράκλειτον δι' ἀναπνοῆς σπάσαντες νοεροὶ γινόμεθα, καὶ ἐν μὲν ὕπνοις ληθαῖοι, κατὰ δὲ ἔγερσιν πάλιν ἔμφρονες. ἐν γὰρ τοῖς ὕπνοις μυσάντων τῶν αἰσθητικῶν πόρων χωρίζεται τῆς πρὸς τὸ περιέχον συμφυΐας ὁ ἐν ἡμῖν νοῦς, μόνης τῆς κατὰ ἀναπνοὴν προσφύσεως σῳζομένης οἱονεί τινος ῥίζης, χωρισθείς τε ἀποβάλλει ἣν πρότερον εἶχε μνημονικὴν δύναμιν· ἐν δὲ ἐγρηγορόσι πάλιν διὰ τῶν αἰσθητικῶν πόρων ὥσπερ διά τινων θυρίδων προκύψας καὶ τῷ περιέχοντι συμβαλὼν λογικὴν ἐνδύεται δύναμιν.

It is on the ground of these texts that by modern writers Posid. is usually represented as a mystic. The point is denied by Edelstein who, in his important article of 1936 [1], tried to make a reconstruction of Posid. exclusively on the ground of texts in which his name is mentioned. E. even denies that Posid. held the immortality of the soul. It may be clear by the preceding pages that E.'s method is defective.

Posid.'s
conception
of God

1196—a. At first sight, Posid.'s conception of God might seem to be hardly separable from that of other Stoics.

Diog. L. VII 138-139; 148:

Τὸν δὴ κόσμον διοικεῖσθαι κατὰ νοῦν καὶ πρόνοιαν, καθά φησι Χρύσιππός τ' ἐν τῷ πέμπτῳ Περὶ προνοίας καὶ Ποσειδώνιος ἐν τῷ τρίτῳ Περὶ θεῶν, εἰς ἅπαν αὐτοῦ μέρος διήκοντος τοῦ νοῦ, καθάπερ ἐφ' ἡμῶν τῆς ψυχῆς· ἀλλ' ἤδη δι' ὧν μὲν μᾶλλον, δι' ὧν δὲ ἧττον. δι' ὧν μὲν γὰρ ὡς ἕξις κεχώρηκεν, ὡς διὰ τῶν ὀστῶν καὶ τῶν νεύρων· δι' ὧν δὲ ὡς νοῦς, ὡς διὰ τοῦ ἡγεμονικοῦ. οὕτω δὴ καὶ τὸν ὅλον κόσμον ζῷον ὄντα καὶ ἔμψυχον καὶ λογικόν, ἔχειν ἡγεμονικὸν μὲν τὸν αἰθέρα, καθά φησιν Ἀντίπατρος ὁ Τύριος ἐν τῷ ὀγδόῳ Περὶ κόσμου. Χρύσιππος δ' ἐν τῷ πρώτῳ Περὶ προνοίας καὶ Ποσειδώνιος ἐν τῷ Περὶ θεῶν τὸν οὐρανόν φασι τὸ ἡγεμονικὸν τοῦ κόσμου, Κλεάνθης δὲ τὸν ἥλιον. —

---

[1] L. Edelstein, *The philosophical System of Posidonius*, in *American Journ. of Philol.* 57 (1936), p. 286-325.

Οὐσίαν δὲ θεοῦ Ζήνων μέν φησι τὸν ὅλον κόσμον καὶ τὸν οὐρανόν, ὁμοίως δὲ καὶ Χρύσιππος ἐν τῷ πρώτῳ Περὶ θεῶν καὶ Ποσειδώνιος ἐν πρώτῳ Περὶ θεῶν.

b. The following definition of God, explicitly attributed to Posid., does not bring us much further with regard to the question whether Posid. was a mere pantheist, or, if not, in what respects he differed from other Stoics, e.g. Chrysippus.

Commenta Lucani ad v. 578, ed. H. Usener, p. 305:

Θεός ἐστι πνεῦμα νοερὸν διῆκον δι' ἁπάσης οὐσίας.

c. We find another apparently pantheistic definition of God in Strabo's description of Moses's teaching, which certainly goes back to Posid.

Strabo XVI 2, 35:

Ἔφη γὰρ ἐκεῖνος (sc. ὁ Μωυσῆς) καὶ ἐδίδασκεν, ὡς οὐκ ὀρθῶς φρονοῖεν οἱ Αἰγύπτιοι θηρίοις εἰκάζοντες καὶ βοσκήμασι τὸ θεῖον [οὐδ' οἱ Λίβυες], οὐκ εὖ δ' οὐδ' οἱ Ἕλληνες ἀνθρωπομόρφους τυποῦντες· εἴη γὰρ ἓν τοῦτο μόνον θεὸς τὸ περιέχον ἡμᾶς ἅπαντας καὶ γῆν καὶ θάλατταν, ὃ καλοῦμεν οὐρανὸν καὶ κόσμον καὶ τὴν τῶν ὄντων φύσιν. τούτου δὴ τίς ἂν εἰκόνα πλάττειν θαρρήσειεν νοῦν ἔχων ὁμοίαν τινὶ τῶν παρ' ἡμῖν; ἀλλ' ἐᾶν δεῖν πᾶσαν ξοανοποιίαν, τέμενος δ' ἀφορίσαντας καὶ σηκὸν ἀξιόλογον τιμᾶν ἕδους χωρίς.

Blankert, *Seneca Ep. 90*, p. 228 ff., compares Sextus, *M.* IX 102 f., where it is argued that, lastly, every power which is in a part springs from the hegemonikón; much more then the whole, which contains all rational animals, must be rational itself. Blankert concludes that, since in this passage—be it or be it not "Posidonian" —the argument tends more to the ἡγεμονικόν than to the All, Strabo's definition, too, admits of a not merely pantheistic interpretation.

d. The following definition explicitly attributed to Posid., enables us to distinguish between the Ancient Stoic conception (cp. our nr. **918**) and Posid.'s conception of God.

Doxogr. Gr., p. 324 a 4:

Πρῶτον μὲν γὰρ εἶναι τὸν Δία, δεύτερον δὲ τὴν φύσιν, τρίτην δὲ τὴν εἱμαρμένην.

We may conclude that the identification, as it is expressed in Diog. L. VII 135 **Hierarchical** (the end): Ἕν τ' εἶναι θεὸν καὶ νοῦν καὶ εἱμαρμένην καὶ Δία—appears not to be Posido- **view of the** nean. **spiritual**

Posid., as might be expected from the evidence adduced in the preceding numbers, **forces in the** appears to have held a hierarchical view of the universe and of the (immanent) **universe** spiritual forces by which it is governed and "held together": *first* is the Noûs or ἡγεμονικόν, which is in the proper sense *God*; divine, but in a lower degree, is φύσις;

and last comes εἰμαρμένη, which may have been conceived like Plato's ἀνάγκη in the *Timaeus*.

Cp. Blankert, o.c., p. 206 ff., on Philo, *Spec. leg.* I 66.
See also Verbeke, *La doctrine du pneuma*, p. 120.
On εἰμαρμένη, Edelstein, o.c., p. 301.

From all this it may be clear that to consider Posid. as a forerunner of Neoplatonism is not an unfounded opinion.

On his influence on Plotinus and later Neoplatonists, as well as on later Stoics, see W. Theiler, *Die Vorbereitung des Neuplatonismus*, Berlin 1930, p. 61-109. Also R. E. Witt, *Plotinus and Posidonius*, in *Class. Quart.* 1930, p. 198-207.

4—THE FOURTH ACADEMY: PHILO AND ANTIOCHUS

Philo of Larisa

1197—a. Philo was the successor of Clitomachus, Carneades's successor in the Academy.

Euseb., *Praep. ev.* XIV 8, 15:

Διάδοχος δ' αὐτοῦ (sc. Καρνεάδου) τῆς διατριβῆς καθίσταται Κλειτόμαχος, μεθ' ὃν Φίλων.

Admired by Cicero

b. A. 88 he came to Rome, where Cicero heard him with great enthusiasm.

Cicero, *Brutus* 89, 306 (Cicero is speaking to Brutus):

Eodemque tempore, cum princeps Academiae Philo cum Atheniensium optumatibus Mithridatico bello domo profugisset Romamque venisset, totum ei me tradidi admirabili quodam ad philosophiam studio concitatus; in quo hoc etiam commorabar attentius — etsi rerum ipsarum varietas et magnitudo summa me delectatione retinebat.

Cp. also *Tusc.* II 3, 9.

He did not return to dogmatism

c. Cic., *Ac. pr.* (*Lucullus*) 4, 11 speaks of "two books of Philo", in which (according to *Ac. post.* 4, 13) he "denied that there are two Academies"; i.e. he considered the New Academy as being a legitimate continuation of the Old, while his pupil Antiochus denied this and desired to return to dogmatism.

Cic., *Ac. post.* 4, 13 (Cic. speaks to Varro):

Quamquam Antiochi magister Philo, magnus vir ut tu existimas ipse, negaret in libris, quod coram etiam ex ipso audiebamus, duas Academias esse, erroremque eorum qui ita putarent coarguit.

"Est", inquit (sc. Varro) "ut dicis; sed ignorare .te non arbitror quae contra Philonis Antiochus scripserit."

d. Cp. Cic., *Ac. pr.* (*Lucullus*) 6, 18:

(Lucullus, a pupil and friend of Antiochus, speaks.)

Philo autem dum nova quaedam commovet . . . in id ipsum se induit quod timebat. cum enim ita negaret quicquam esse quod comprehendi posset (id enim volumus esse ἀκατάλημπτον), si illud esset, sicut Zeno definiret, tale visum (iam enim hoc pro φαντασία verbum satis hesterno sermone trivimus) — visum igitur impressum effictumque ex eo unde esset quale esse non posset ex eo unde non esset [1] (id nos a Zenone definitum rectissime dicimus; qui enim potest quicquam conprehendi, ut plane confidas perceptum id cognitumque esse, quod est tale quale vel falsum esse possit?) — hoc cum infirmat tollitque Philo, iudicium tollit incogniti et cogniti; ex quo efficitur nihil posse conprehendi. ita inprudens eo quo minime volt revolvitur. Quare omnis oratio contra Academiam suscipitur a nobis, ut retineamus eam definitionem quam Philo voluit evertere; quam nisi optinemus, percipi nihil posse concedimus.

Philo, then, rejected the cataleptic presentation as a criterion of truth and therefore, in fact, fell into scepticism, though he did not intend this. Denying that there was any real difference between the Old and the New Academy, Philo probably maintained that Carneades's "empirical certitude" (see above, nr. **1116b**) did not differ essentially from Plato's or the Early Academic view of truth. In this, he was contradicted by Antiochus, who maintained the validity of sense-perception, and thus, went back essentially to Stoicism, not to classical Platonism. See Lucullus in the next par. of the *Ac. pr.* (19):

Meo autem iudicio ita est maxima in sensibus veritas, si et sani sunt ac valentes et omnia removentur quae obstant et impediunt.

Cp. also Sextus, *P.* I 235.

1198—Antiochus, then, who was Philo's disciple for quite a long time (see Cicero's *Lucullus* 22, 69), abandoned scepticism and went back to the Old Academy, or at least pretended to do so.

Antiochus of Ascalon

He seems to have left Athens with Philo in 88 B.C., and is found with Lucullus at Alexandria in 87/86, where the conflict with Philo arose when he received the above-mentioned two books, in which was written "that there are not two Academies".

a. Cic., *Ac. pr.* (*Lucullus*) 4, 11-12:

At ille (sc. Lucullus) "Cum Alexandriae pro quaestore" inquit "essem, fuit Antiochus mecum, et erat iam antea Alexandriae familiaris Antiochi

---

[1] *Visum igitur — ex eo unde non esset*: a translation of Zeno's definition of φαντασία καταληπτική cited under nr. **984b**.

Heraclitus Tyrius, qui et Clitomachum multos annos et Philonem audierat, homo sane in ista philosophia, quae nunc prope dimissa revocatur, probatus et nobilis; cum quo et Antiochum saepe disputantem audiebam — sed utrumque leniter; et quidem isti libri duo Philonis, de quibus heri dictum a Catulo est, tum erant allati Alexandriam tumque primum in Antiochi manus venerant; et homo natura lenissumus (nihil enim poterat fieri illo mitius) stomachari tamen coepit. —

Nec se tenuit quin contra suum doctorem librum etiam ederet, qui Sosus inscribitur.

b. He seems to have known Lucullus in Rome and to have lived in his house.

Plutarchus, *Luc.* 42:

Καὶ ὅλως ἑστία καὶ πρυτανεῖον Ἑλληνικὸν ὁ οἶκος ἦν αὐτοῦ τοῖς ἀφικνουμένοις εἰς Ῥώμην. φιλοσοφίαν δὲ πᾶσαν μὲν ἠσπάζετο καὶ πρὸς πᾶσαν εὐμενὴς ἦν καὶ οἰκεῖος, ἴδιον δὲ τῆς Ἀκαδημίας ἐξ ἀρχῆς ἔρωτα καὶ ζῆλον ἔσχεν, οὐ τῆς νέας λεγομένης, καίπερ ἀνθούσης τότε τοῖς Καρνεάδου λόγοις διὰ Φίλωνος, ἀλλὰ τῆς παλαιᾶς, πιθανὸν ἄνδρα καὶ δεινὸν εἰπεῖν τότε προστάτην ἐχούσης τὸν Ἀσκαλωνίτην Ἀντίοχον, ὃν πάσῃ σπουδῇ ποιησάμενος φίλον ὁ Λούκουλλος καὶ συμβιωτὴν ἀντέταττε τοῖς Φίλωνος ἀκροαταῖς, ὧν καὶ Κικέρων ἦν.

c. In 79, Cicero heard him during 6 months at Athens.

Cicero, *Brutus* 91, 315:

Cum venissem Athenas, sex menses cum Antiocho veteris Academiae nobilissumo et prudentissumo philosopho fui studiumque philosophiae nunquam intermissum a primaque adulescentia cultum et semper auctum hoc rursus summo auctore et doctore renovavi.

Cp. Plut., *Cic.* 4, where it is said that Cicero was charmed by the fluency and grace of Antiochus' diction, but disapproved of his innovations in doctrine.

Varro, too, belonged to the pupils and admirers of Antiochus.

Cicero makes him expound Antiochus' doctrine in the *Acad. post.* §§ 15-42, as he had it done by Lucullus in the *Prior Acad.*, 11-60, and by M. Pupius Piso Calpurnianus in *De finibus* V 9-74.

These are our direct sources concerning Antiochus' doctrine. Parts of *De finibus* IV also must be traced back to him (probably to another work than that which is followed in *De fin.* V).

De fin. II 33 ff. contain a summary of his views. So do the first chapters of S. Augustine's *De civ. Dei*, in which Varro is followed.

See the work of A. Lueder, *Die philosophische Persönlichkeit des Antiochos von Askalon*, Göttingen, 1940; also G. Luck, *Der Akademiker Antiochos* (Noctes Romanae 7), Bern 1953 (a collection of the fragments, preceded by some introductory chapters).

1199—Together with Posidonius, who was a platonizing and aristote- The founder of a philosophy of synthesis
lizing Stoic, Antiochus must be considered as the founder of that philoso-
phy of synthesis, which prevailed during the first centuries A.D.

Antiochus did not see any essential difference between Plato and
Aristotle, between the Academics (Speusippus, Xenocrates, etc. *until*
Arcesilas) and Peripatetics (eliminating Strato as *totum dissedentem a
suis*). Moreover, Stoicism was judged by him not to be a new doctrine,
but a correction of the Academy of Polemo and Crates, to which he
adhered essentially.

a.   Cic., *Acad. post.* I 4, 17-18:

Platonis autem auctoritate, qui varius et multiplex et copiosus fuit,
una et consentiens duobus vocabulis philosophiae forma instituta est
Academicorum et Peripateticorum, qui rebus congruentes nominibus
differebant. —

Nihil enim inter Peripateticos et illam veterem Academiam differebat.
abundantia quadam ingenii praestabat, ut mihi quidem videtur, Aristoteles, sed idem fons erat utrisque et eadem rerum expetendarum fugien-
darumque partitio.

b.   Ib., 9, 34-35:

Speusippus autem et Xenocrates, qui primi Platonis rationem auctori-
tatemque susceperant, et post eos Polemo et Crates unaque Crantor in
Academia congregati diligenter ea quae a superioribus acceperant tue-
bantur. Iam Polemonem audiverant assidue Zeno et Arcesilas, sed Zeno,
cum Arcesilam anteiret aetate valdeque subtiliter dissereret et peracute
moveretur, corrigere conatus est disciplinam.

1200—Did Antiochus, who wished to restore the authority of the Old Did he reintroduce the Platonic ideas?
Academy, or did he not, reintroduce the Platonic Ideas in their transcen-
dent sense?

Theiler, *Vorbereitung des Neupl.* pp. 40 ff., thinks he did, and therefore should
be called "the ἀρχηγέτης of the Academic schooltradition which ends in Neoplatonism". Witt [1], who is followed in this by A. Lueder, opposes him, arguing that,
as appears in Cic., *Ac. pr.* 10, 30, Antiochus was essentially a Stoic in his theory of
knowledge and not a transcendentalist. Albinus, on the contrary, went back to
the Early Academy, for this very reason, that Antiochus' philosophy was essentially
alien to Platonic metaphysics. Luck, *Antiochos*, p. 28 ff., adheres to Theiler's view.

---

[1]   R. E. Witt, *Albinus and the history of middle Platonism*, Cambridge 1937, p.
27, 57/8, 68.

a. The "third part of philosophy" (i.e. the theory of knowledge) is expounded by Varro, who follows Antiochus, as follows.

Cic., *Acad. post.* 8, 30-33:

Tertia deinde philosophiae pars, quae erat in ratione et in disserendo, sic tractabatur ab utrisque [1]. Quamquam oriretur a sensibus, tamen non esse iudicium veritatis in sensibus [2]. mentem volebant rerum esse iudicem, solam censebant idoneam cui crederetur, quia sola cerneret id quod semper esset simplex et unius modi et tale quale esset (hanc illi ἰδέαν appellabant, iam a Platone ita nominatam, nos recte speciem possumus dicere). sensus autem omnis hebetes et tardos esse arbitrabantur nec percipere ullo modo res eas quae subjectae sensibus viderentur, quod essent aut ita parvae ut sub sensum cadere non possent, aut ita mobiles et concitatae ut nihil umquam unum esset <et> constans, ne idem quidem, quia continenter laberentur et fluerent omnia. itaque hanc omnem partem rerum opinabilem appellabant; scientiam autem nusquam esse censebant nisi in animi notionibus [3] atque rationibus [4]. qua de causa definitiones rerum probabant et has ad omnia de quibus disceptabatur adhibebant; verborum etiam explicatio [5] probabatur, id est qua de causa quaeque essent ita nominata, quam ἐτυμολογίαν appellabant; post argumentis quibusdam et quasi rerum notis ducibus utebantur ad probandum et ad concludendum id quod explanari volebant. in qua tradebatur omnis dialecticae disciplina, id est, orationis ratione conclusae [6]; huic quasi ex altera parte oratoria vis dicendi adhibebatur, explicatrix orationis perpetuae ad persuadendum accommodatae. Haec forma erat illis prima, a Platone tradita.

The whole of this description bears a synthetic character, with a strong element of Stoicism in it. The formula *id quod semper esset simplex et eius modi et tale quale esset* may sound rather Platonic. Yet, the passage of the *Acad. pr.*, to be cited sub **c**, will not allow us to attribute a transcendental conception of the ideas to Antiochus.

b. *Acad. post.* 9, 33:

Aristoteles igitur primus species quas paulo ante dixi labefactavit, quas mirifice Plato erat amplexatus, ut in iis quiddam divinum esse

---

[1] Sc. Academics and Peripatetics.
[2] Cp. our nr. **985**.
[3] ἐννοίαις.
[4] Intelligible forms or definitions (λόγοις).
[5] He means: the derivation of words. This too is a Stoic feature in the description.
[6] "In a logical form".

diceret. Theophrastus autem, vir et oratione suavis et ita moratus ut prae se probitatem quandam et ingenuitatem ferat, vehementius etiam fregit quodam modo auctoritatem veteris disciplinae; spoliavit enim virtutem suo decore imbecillamque reddidit, quod negavit in ea sola positum esse beate vivere.

The question is, whether we may infer from this passage that by Antiochus, who wished to restore the authority of the Old Academy, Aristotle's criticism of Plato's Ideas, too, was considered as a destruction of the *vetus disciplina*. This is what Theiler thinks, who (in *Gnomon* 1939, p. 105) uses the passage as an argument against Witt. Much depends, evidently, on the sense of the word *mirifice*, which by Theiler is apparently interpreted as "in a wonderful way". I think it rather means "very strongly" (θαυμαστῶς ὡς); and the author thought that Aristotle was right in criticizing Plato's transcendentalism.

On the contrary, he rebuked Theophr. for having deprived virtue of its self-sufficiency. On both points Antiochus rather takes the Stoic point of view.

c. Cic., *Acad. pr.* (*Lucullus*) 10, 30:

Sequitur disputatio copiosa illa quidem, sed paulo abstrusior — habet enim aliquantum a physicis, ut verear ne maiorem largiar ei qui contra dicturus est libertatem et licentiam; nam quid eum facturum putem de abditis rebus et obscuris, qui lucem eripere conetur? — sed disputari poterat subtiliter quanto quasi artificio natura fabricata esset primum animal omne, deinde hominem maxime, quae vis esset in sensibus, quem ad modum prima visa nos pellerent, deinde adpetitio ab his pulsa sequeretur, tum ut sensus ad res percipiendas intenderemus. Mens enim ipsa, quae sensuum fons est atque etiam ipsa sensus est [1], naturalem vim habet, quam intendit ad ea quibus movetur. itaque alia visa sic arripit, ut iis statim utatur, alia quasi recondit, e quibus memoria oritur; cetera autem similitudinibus construit, ex quibus efficiuntur notitiae rerum, quas Graeci tum ἐννοίας, tum προλήμψεις vocant; eo cum accessit ratio argumentique conclusio rerumque innumerabilium multitudo, tum et perceptio eorum omnium apparet et eadem ratio perfecta his gradibus ad sapientiam pervenit.

The theory here expounded is purely Stoic, and certainly, even though we may hesitate to qualify it as mere sensualism, does not tend to a renewal of classical Platonism.

Cp. what is said of Antiochus in *Acad. pr.* 43, 132: *Erat quidem si perpauca mutavisset germanissimus Stoicus.*

---

[1] Hence, Witt (o.c., p. 68) says: "We must not forget, that for Antiochus *mens* and *sensus* mean the same thing".

Cp. however *De fin.* V, 13, 36, where, next to the sensus, *mens* is mentioned as *princeps pars animi*, which is said to possess two kinds of virtues, (1) innate intellectual gifts, (2) moral virtues depending on volition. On this passage: A. Lueder, o.c., p. 42 ff.

Ethics

1201—a.   In explaining the telos formula (vivere secundum naturam) Antiochus, starting from οἰκείωσις, first stresses the *progress* from the πρώτη ὁρμή to selfconsciousness, next the *difference between the species* of living beings.

The telos
formula
explained

Cic., *De fin.* V 9, 24-26:

Omne animal se ipsum diligit ac, simul ut ortum est, id agit, ut se conservet, quod hic ei primus ad omnem vitam tuendam appetitus a natura datur, se ut conservet atque ita sit affectum, ut optime secundum naturam affectum esse possit. Hanc initio institutionem confusam habet et incertam, ut tantum modo se tueatur, qualecumque sit, sed nec quid sit nec quid possit, nec quid ipsius natura sit, intellegit. Cum autem processit paulum et, quatenus quidque se attingat ad seque pertineat, perspicere coepit, tum sensim incipit progredi seseque agnoscere et intellegere. quam ob causam habeat eum quem diximus animi appetitum coeptatque et ea quae naturae sentit apta appetere et propulsare contraria. Ergo omni animali illud quod appetit positum est in eo quod naturae est accommodatum. Ita finis bonorum exsistit secundum naturam vivere sic affectum, ut optime affici possit ad naturamque accommodatissime.

Quoniam autem sua cuiusque animantis natura est, necesse est finem quoque omnium hunc esse, ut natura expleatur (nihil enim prohibet quaedam esse et inter se animalibus reliquis et cum bestiis homini communia, quoniam omnium est natura communis), sed extrema illa et summa quae quaerimus inter animalium genera distincta et dispertita sint et sua cuique propria et ad id apta quod cuiusque natura desideret. —

Ex quo intellegi debet homini id esse in bonis ultimum, secundum naturam vivere, quod ita interpretemur: vivere ex hominis natura undique perfecta et nihil requirente.

b.   In c. 12, the author proceeds to describe the nature of man: man consists of body and soul, both of which must be brought to perfection. He concludes:

Cic., *De fin.* V 13, 37-38:

Ea enim vita expetitur, quae sit animi corporisque expleta virtutibus, in eoque summum bonum poni necesse est, quandoquidem id tale esse debet, ut rerum expetendarum sit extremum. —

(38) Quibus expositis facilis est coniectura ea maxime esse expetenda ex nostris, quae plurimum habent dignitatis, ut optimae cuiusque partis,

quae per se expetatur, virtus sit expetenda maxime. Ita fiet ut animi virtus corporis virtuti anteponatur animique virtutes non voluntarias vincant virtutes voluntariae, quae quidem proprie virtutes appellantur multumque excellunt, propterea quod ex ratione gignuntur, qua nihil est in homine divinius.

c. Thus, for man there is a gradual ascent, from the πρώτη ὁρμή to the full development both of the body and of the mind.

Man's end the perfection of his whole being

Cic., *De fin.* V 14, 40:

Sic extitit extremum omnium appetendorum atque ductum a prima commendatione naturae multis gradibus adscendit, ut ad summum perveniret, quod cumulatur ex integritate corporis et ex mentis ratione perfecta.

This is what Antiochus called *tota natura* (ib. 15, 41), a conception which agrees essentially with the Aristotelian view of man. He appears to have opposed this to Chrysippus' one-sided conception of man.

1202—Self-knowledge means: to know the whole of our nature.

Self-knowledge

Cic., *De fin.* V 16, 44:

Intrandum est igitur in rerum naturam et penitus quid ea postulet pervidendum; aliter enim nosmet ipsos nosse non possumus. Quod praeceptum quia maius erat quam ut ab homine videretur, idcirco adsignatum est deo. Iubet igitur nos Pythius Apollo noscere nosmet ipsos. Cognitio autem haec est una nostri, ut vim corporis animique norimus sequamurque eam vitam quae rebus iis perfruatur.

1203—a. Since the perfection of the whole is desirable to us, the perfection of each part of our nature is also desirable to us for its own sake.

The perfection of the parts also desirable for their own sake

Cic., *De fin.* V 17, 46:

Nunc autem aliud iam argumentandi sequamur genus, ut non solum quia nos diligamus, sed quia cuiusque partis naturae et in corpore et in animo sua quaeque vis sit, idcirco in his rebus summe nostra sponte moveamur. Atque ut a corpore ordiar, videsne, ut, si quae in membris prava aut delibitata aut inminuta sint, occultent homines? ut etiam contendant et elaborent, si efficere possint, ut aut non appareat corporis vitium aut quam minimum appareat? multosque etiam dolores curationis causa perferant, ut, si ipse usus membrorum non modo non maior, verum etiam minor futurus sit, eorum tamen species ad naturam revertatur? Etenim, cum omnes natura totos se expetendos putent, nec id ob aliam rem, sed propter ipsos, necesse est eius etiam partis propter se expeti, quod universum propter se expetatur.

Health, strength and beauty desirable for their own sake

b. Therefore, health, strength and beauty are desirable for their own sake.

Ib., 47:

Quid? in motu et in statu corporis nihil inest, quod animadvertendum esse ipsa natura iudicet? quem ad modum quis ambulet, sedeat, qui ductus oris, qui vultus in quoque sit? nihilne est in his rebus quod dignum libero aut indignum esse ducamus? Nonne odio dignos multos putamus, qui quodam motu aut statu videntur naturae legem et modum contempsisse? Et quoniam haec deducuntur de corpore, quid est cur non recte pulchritudo etiam ipsa propter se expetenda ducatur? Nam si pravitatem imminutionemque corporis propter se fugiendam putamus, cur non etiam, ac fortasse magis, propter se formae dignitatem sequamur? Et si turpitudinem fugimus in statu et motu corporis, quid est cur pulchritudinem non sequamur? Atque etiam valetudinem, vires, vacuitatem doloris non propter utilitatem solum, sed etiam ipsas propter se expetemus. Quoniam enim natura suis omnibus expleri partibus vult, hunc statum corporis per se ipsum expetit qui est maxime e natura, quae tota perturbatur, si aut aegrum corpus est aut dolet aut caret viribus.

Man's task of realizing his endowments

1204—a. Both the striving for knowledge and social activities are natural to man. So is the germ of virtue, which must be developed by our personal energy.

Cic., *De fin.* V 21, 59-60:

Natura igitur corpus quidem hominis sic et genuit et formavit, ut alia in primo ortu perficeret, alia progrediente aetate fingeret neque sane multum adiumentis externis et adventiciis uteretur; animum autem reliquis rebus ita perfecit, ut corpus; sensibus enim ornavit ad res percipiendas idoneis, ut nihil aut non multum adiumento ullo ad suam confirmationem indigeret; quod autem in homine praestantissimum atque optimum est, id deseruit. Etsi dedit talem mentem, quae omnem virtutem accipere posset, ingenuitque sine doctrina notitias parvas rerum maximarum et quasi instituit docere et induxit in ea quae inerant tamquam elementa virtutis. Sed virtutem ipsam inchoavit, nihil amplius. Itaque nostrum est (quod nostrum dico, artis est) ad ea principia quae accepimus consequentia exquirere, quoad sit id quod volumus effectum; quod quidem pluris est haud paulo magisque ipsum propter se expetendum quam aut sensus aut corporis ea quae diximus, quibus tantum praestat mentis excellens perfectio, ut vix cogitari possit quid intersit. Itaque omnis honos, omnis admiratio, omne studium ad virtutem et ad eas actiones quae virtuti sunt consentaneae refertur, eaque omnia quae aut ita in animis sunt, aut ita geruntur uno nomine honesta dicuntur.

b. In this, man is helped first of all by the *ars vivendi*:

Cic., *De fin.* IV 7, 16:

Omnis natura vult esse conservatrix sui, ut et salva sit, et in genere conservetur suo. Ad hanc rem aiunt artis quoque requisitas, quae naturam adiuvarent; in quibus ea numeretur in primis, quae est vivendi ars, ut tueatur quod a natura datum sit, quod desit acquirat. Idemque diviserunt naturam hominis in animum et corpus. Cumque eorum utrumque per se expetendum esse dixissent, virtutes quoque utriusque eorum per se expetendas esse dicebant, et, cum animum infinita quadam laude anteponerent corpori, virtutes quoque animi bonis corporis anteponebant.

In § 76 of the same book he calls this art *prudentia*, saying: Omnibus enim artibus volumus attributam esse eam quae communis appellatur prudentia, quam omnes qui cuique artificio praesunt debent habere.

1205—The leading virtue is justice, which is rooted in the natural affection of man towards man (*caritas generis humani*).

Cic., *De fin.* V 23, 65:

In omni autem honesto, de quo loquimur, nihil est tam illustre nec quod latius pateat quam coniunctio inter homines hominum et quasi quaedam societas et communicatio utilitatum et ipsa caritas generis humani, quae nata a primo satu, quod a procreatoribus nati diliguntur et tota domus coniugio et stirpe coniungitur, serpit sensim foras, cognationibus primum, tum affinitatibus, deinde amicitiis, post vicinitatibus, tum civibus et iis qui publice socii atque amici sunt, deinde totius complexu gentis humanae; quae animi affectio, suum cuique tribuens atque hanc quam dico societatem coniunctionis humanae munifice et aeque tuens, iustitia dicitur, cui sunt adiunctae pietas, bonitas, liberalitas, benignitas, comitas, quaeque sunt generis eiusdem. Atque haec ita iustitiae propria sunt, ut sint virtutum reliquarum communia.

The terms *carus* and *caritas* are also repeatedly used in § 37 of the same book:
Nam cui proposita sit conservatio sui, necesse est huic partes quoque sui caras esse carioresque quo perfectiores sint. —

Ars vivendi

Caritas generis humani

Quo cognito, dubitari non potest quin, cum ipsi homines sibi sint per se et sua sponte cari, partes quoque et corporis et animi . . . sua caritate colantur et per se ipsae appetantur.

The *societas generis humani* and its *conciliatio* is repeatedly spoken of by Cicero in *De officiis*, especially in the last chapters of the first book (§§ 149, the end; 153; 157-160). See also III 5, 21 and 6, 26-32. In this, both Cicero and Antiochus were doubtless influenced by Panaetius. See above, our nrs. **1159** and **1162**, and the passages cited under **1159b**. Cp. also H. F. Reynders, *Societas generis humani bij Cicero*, diss. Utrecht 1954, p. 62-65.

A precise description of Antiochus's place in the history of philosophy is given by A. Lueder, o.c., p. 59-75; a new collection of the fragments by G. Luck, Bern 1953, (Noctes Romanae 7); See also Pohlenz, *Stoa* I, pp. 248-256, and *Grundfr.*, pp. 47-81.

5—SENECA

1206—With the later Stoics, moral philosophy becomes not only the essential part, but almost the whole of philosophy. Logic and "physics"— Seneca speaks of *naturales quaestiones*—have their function, but a subordinate one. As to the so-called *artes liberales*, admitted by Posidonius as a part of philosophy, Seneca does not even acknowledge the name and excludes them from philosophy, for this very reason that they are auxiliary sciences.

Auxiliary sciences not a part of philosophy

a. Seneca, *Ep*. 88, 23-25:

Solae autem liberales sunt, immo, ut dicam verius, liberae, quibus curae virtus est. "quemadmodum" inquit "est aliqua pars philosophiae naturalis, est aliqua moralis, est aliqua rationalis, sic et haec quoque liberalium artium turba locum sibi in philosophia vindicat. cum ventum est ad naturales quaestiones, geometriae testimonio statur: ergo eius quam adiuvat pars est." multa adiuvant nos nec ideo partes nostri sunt. immo si partes essent, non adiuvarent: cibus adiutorium corporis, nec tamen pars est. aliquid nobis praestat geometriae ministerium: sic philosophiae necessaria est, quomodo ipsi faber. sed nec hic geometriae pars est nec illa philosophiae.

The science of good and bad is the object of philosophy only

b. Ib., 28:

Una re consummatur animus, scientia bonorum ac malorum inmutabili, <quae soli philosophiae conpetit:> nihil autem ulla ars alia de bonis ac malis quaerit.

c. Liberal studies do not even make any real contribution to moral development.

Ib., 31-32:

"Cum dicatis" inquit "sine liberalibus studiis ad virtutem non per-
veniri, quemadmodum negatis illa nihil conferre virtuti?" quia nec sine
cibo ad virtutem pervenitur, cibus tamen ad virtutem non pertinet.
ligna navi nihil conferunt, quamvis non fiat navis nisi ex lignis: non est,
inquam, cur aliquid putes eius adiutorio fieri, sine quo non potest fieri.
potest quidem etiam illud dici, sine liberalibus studiis veniri ad sapientiam
posse. quamvis enim virtus discenda sit, tamen non per haec discitur.
quid est autem, quare existimem non futurum sapientem eum, qui
litteras nescit, cum sapientia non sit in litteris?

1207—The true aim of philosophy is: to form man's character and
enable him to stand firm against all blows of Fortune.

The aim of philosophy and how to reach it

Sen., *Ep.* 104, 21-24:

Si velis vitiis exui, longe a vitiorum exemplis recedendum est. avarus,
corruptor, saevos, fraudulentus, multum nocituri, si prope a te fuissent,
intra te sunt. ad meliores transi: cum Catonibus vive, cum Laelio, cum
Tuberone. quod si convivere etiam Graecis iuvat, cum Socrate, cum
Zenone versare: alter te docebit mori, si necesse erit, alter antequam
necesse erit. vive cum Chrysippo, cum Posidonio. hi tibi tradent huma-
norum divinorumque notitiam, hi iubebunt in opere esse nec tantum
scite loqui et in oblectationem audientium verba iactare, sed animum
indurare et adversus minas erigere. unus est enim huius vitae fluctuantis
et turbidae portus eventura contemnere, stare fidenter ac paratum tela
fortunae adverso pectore excipere, non latitantem nec tergiversantem.
magnanimos nos natura produxit et ut quibusdam animalibus ferum
dedit, quibusdam subdolum, quibusdam pavidum, ita nobis gloriosum
et excelsum spiritum, quaerentem ubi honestissime, non ubi tutissime
vivat, simillimum mundo, quem quantum mortalium passibus licet,
sequitur aemulaturque: profert se, laudari et aspici credit. ‹dominus›
omnium est, supra omnia est: itaque nulli se rei summittat, nihil illi
videatur grave, nihil quod virum incurvet. "terribiles visu formae letumque labosque" [1]: minime quidem si quis rectis oculis intueri illa possit
et tenebras perrumpere. multa per noctem habita terrori dies vertit ad
risum. "terribiles visu formae letumque labosque": egregie Vergilius
noster non re dixit terribiles esse, sed visu, id est videri, non esse.

1208—Asked by Lucilius whether the paraenetic part of philosophy

---

[1] Verg., *Aen.* VI 277.

is sufficient to attain perfect wisdom, Seneca, however, replies that there is a theoretical and a practical part of philosophy.

Theoretical and practical philosophy

Sen., *Ep.* 95, 10-14:

Philosophia autem et contemplativa est et activa: spectat simul agitque. erras enim, si tibi illam putas tantum terrestres operas promittere: altius spirat. totum, inquit, mundum scrutor nec me intra contubernium mortale contineo suadere vobis ac dissuadere contenta. magna me vocant supraque vos posita. —

Sequitur ergo ut, cum contemplativa sit, habeat decreta sua. quid? quod facienda quoque nemo rite obibit nisi is, cui ratio erit tradita, qua in quaque re omne officiorum numeros exequi possit, quos non servabit, qui in rem praesentem praecepta acceperit, non in omnem. inbecilla sunt per se et, ut ita dicam, sine radice, quae partibus dantur. decreta sunt, quae muniant, quae securitatem nostram tranquillitatemque tueantur, quae totam vitam totamque rerum naturam simul contineant. hoc interest inter decreta philosophiae et praecepta, quod inter elementa et membra: haec ex illis dependent, illa et horum causae sunt et omnium. "antiqua" inquit "sapientia nihil aliud quam facienda ac vitanda praecepit, et tunc longe meliores erant viri: postquam docti prodierunt, boni desunt. simplex enim illa et aperta virtus in obscuram et sollertem scientiam versa est docemurque disputare, non vivere". fuit sine dubio ut dicitis, vetus illa sapientia cum maxime nascens rudis non minus quam ceterae artes, quarum in processu subtilitas crevit. sed ne opus quidem adhuc erat remediis diligentibus. nondum in tantum nequitia surrexerat nec tam late se sparserat. poterant vitiis simplicibus obstare remedia simplicia. nunc necesse est tanto operosiora esse munimenta, quanto vehementiora sunt, quibus petimur.

1209—Pointing to the example of Socrates, he admonishes people to despise the *ineptiae poetarum* concerning the Gods, and rather to honour virtue and those who profess it than to listen to those who perform some vulgar rites of the so-called *mysteria*.

The cult of virtue is the true religion

Sen., *De vita beata* 26, 7 - 27, 1:

Sed quamquam ista me nihil laedant, vestra tamen vos moneo causa: suspicite virtutem, credite iis, qui illam diu secuti magnum quiddam ipsos et quod in dies maius appareat sequi clamant, et ipsam ut deos ac professores eius ut antistites colite et, quotiens mentio sacrarum litterarum intervenerit, favete linguis. hoc verbum non, ut plerique existimant, a favore trahitur, sed imperat silentium, ut rite peragi possit sacrum nulla voce mala opstrepente: quod multo magis necessarium est imperari vobis, ut, quotiens aliquid ex illo proferetur oraculo, intenti et compressa voce audiatis. cum sistrum aliquis concutiens ex imperio mentitur, cum aliquis secandi lacertos suos artifex brachia atque umeros suspensa manu cruentat, cum aliqua genibus per viam repens ululat laurumque linteatus senex et medio lucernam die praeferens conclamat iratum aliquem deorum, concurritis et auditis ac divinum esse eum, invicem mutum alentes stuporem, adfirmatis.

Ecce Socrates ex illo carcere, quem intrando purgavit omnique honestiorem curia reddidit, proclamat: "qui iste furor, quae ista inimica dis hominibusque natura est infamare virtutes et malignis sermonibus sancta violare? si potestis, bonos laudate, si minus, transite; quod si vobis exercere taetram istam licentiam placet, alter in alterum incursitate: nam cum in caelum insanitis, non dico sacrilegium facitis, sed operam perditis."

Cp. *Ep.* 95, 47-50, on the true manner of venerating the gods. Also *Superst.*, fr. 30-44.

1210—The greatest thing in life is: to stand firm against the blows of Fortune and to dominate our passions.

The greatest thing in life

Sen., *Nat. quaest.* III, Praef. 10-14:

Quid praecipuum in rebus humanis est? Non classibus maria complesse nec in Rubri maris litore signa fixisse nec, deficiente ad iniurias terra, errasse in oceano ignota quaerentem, sed animo omne vidisse et, qua maior nulla victoria est, vitia domuisse. Innumerabiles sunt qui populos, qui urbes habuerunt in potestate; paucissimi qui se.

Quid est praecipuum? Erigere animum supra minas et promissa fortunae; nihil dignum putare quod speres. Quid enim habet quod concupiscas? qui a divinorum conversatione quotiens ad humana recideris, non aliter caligabis quam quorum oculi in densam umbram ex claro sole redierunt.

Quid est praecipuum? Posse laeto animo adversa tolerare; quicquid acciderit, sic ferre, quasi tibi volueris accidere. Debuisses enim velle, si scisses omnia ex decreto dei fieri: flere, queri et gemere desciscere est.

Quid est praecipuum? Animus contra calamitates fortis et contumax, luxuriae non aversus tantum sed infestus, nec avidus periculi nec fugax, qui sciat fortunam non expectare sed facere et adversus utramque intrepidus inconfususque prodire, nec illius tumultu nec huius fulgore percussus.

Quid est praecipuum? Non admittere in animo mala consilia, puras ad caelum manus tollere, nullum bonum petere quod, ut ad te transeat, aliquis dare debet aliquis amittere, optare, quod sine adversario optatur, bonam mentem; cetera magno aestimata mortalibus, etiamsi quis domum casus attulerit, sic intueri quasi exitura qua venerint.

Happiness

1211—It is in this state of mind that happiness consists.

Sen., *Ep*. 92, 2-3:

(The first point is, that Reason must prevail.)

Si de hoc inter nos convenit, sequitur ut de illo quoque conveniat, in hoc uno positam esse beatam vitam, ut in nobis ratio perfecta sit. haec enim sola non submittit animum, stat contra fortunam: in quolibet rerum habitu securos servat. id autem unum bonum est, quod numquam defringitur. is est, inquam, beatus quem nulla res minorem facit. tenet summa, et ne ulli quidem nisi sibi innixus. nam qui aliquo auxilio susti- netur, potest cadere. si aliter est, incipient multum in nobis valere non nostra. quis autem vult constare fortunam aut quis se prudens ob aliena miratur? quid est beata vita? securitas et perpetua tranquillitas. hanc dabit animi magnitudo, dabit constantia bene iudicati tenax. ad haec quomodo pervenitur? si veritas tota perspecta est. si servatus est in rebus agendis ordo, modus, decor, innoxia voluntas ac benigna, intenta rationi nec umquam ab illa recedens, amabilis simul mirabilisque.

1212—Hence, no addition can be made to virtue: it is perfect in itself.

Virtue cannot increase

a. Sen., *Ep*. 66, 9:

Omnis in modo est virtus. modo certa mensura est: constantia non habet, quo procedat, non magis quam fiducia aut veritas aut fides. quid accedere perfecto potest? nihil, aut perfectum non erat, cui accessit: ergo ne virtuti quidem, cui si quid adici potest, defuit. honestum quoque nullam accessionem recipit. honestum est enim propter ista, quae rettuli. quid porro? decorum et iustum et legitimum non eiusdem esse formae putas, certis terminis conprensum? crescere posse imperfectae rei sig- num est.

Against Antipater

b. Sen., *Ep*. 92, 5:

Antipater quoque inter magnos sectae huius auctores aliquid se tribuere dicit externis, sed exiguum admodum. vides autem quale sit die non esse contentum, nisi aliquis igniculus adluxerit. quod potest in hac claritate solis habere scintilla momentum?

1213—In spite of his admiration for Posidonius, which is expressed
for instance in *Ep*. 90, 20, concerning the doctrine of the πάθη Seneca
follows essentially Chrysippus. Vid. *De ira* I 8, 2-3, cited above (nr.
1056a) in illustration of Chrysippus's doctrine of the ἡγεμονικόν
πως ἔχον:
Affectus et ratio in melius peiusque mutatio animi est.

On the psychology of the emotions: *De ira* II 1-4. On προπάθειαι further literature is mentioned in Pohlenz, *St*. II, p. 154.

1214—It is only consistent, then, that Seneca opposes Aristotle's
doctrine that Reason must be helped by feelings. [1]

a. Sen., *De ira* I 9, 2-10, 2; 11, 1:   **Seneca
                                                              opposes**
Ira, inquit Aristoteles, necessaria est, nec quicquam sine illa expugnari **Aristotle**
potest, nisi illa implet animum et spiritum accendit; utendum autem illa
est non ut duce sed ut milite. quod est falsum: nam si exaudit rationem
sequiturque qua ducitur, iam non est ira, cuius proprium est contumacia;
si vero repugnat et non ubi iussa est quiescit, sed libidine ferociaque pro-
vehitur, tam inutilis animi minister est quam miles, qui signum receptui
neglegit. itaque si modum adhiberi sibi patitur, alio nomine appellanda
est, desit ira esse, quam effrenatam indomitamque intellego; si non
patitur, perniciosa est nec inter auxilia numeranda: ita aut ira non est
aut inutilis est. nam si quis poenam exigit non ipsius poenae avidus sed
quia oportet, non est adnumerandus iratis. hic erit utilis miles qui scit
parere consilio; adfectus quidem tam mali ministri quam duces sunt.

(10, 1) Ideo numquam adsumet ratio in adiutorium inprovidos et
violentos impetus, aput quos nihil ipsa auctoritatis habeat, quos numquam comprimere possit, nisi pares illis similisque opposuerit [ut irae
metum, inertiae iram, timori cupiditatem]. apsit hoc a virtute malum,
ut umquam ratio ad vitia confugiat!

(11, 1) Sed adversus hostes, inquit, necessaria est ira. nusquam
minus: ubi non effusos esse oportet impetus sed temperatos et oboedientes.

b. Ib. 17, 1-2:
Aristoteles ait affectus quosdam, si quis illis bene utatur, pro armis
esse. quod verum foret, si velut bellica instrumenta sumi deponique

---

[1] On ὀργή with Aristotle, see our nr. **572** (*EN* 1108 a 3-9).—In general, concerning the relation between φρόνησις and ὄρεξις in Aristotle's Ethics, see the excellent article of D. J. Allan in *Proceedings of the XIth Internat. Congress of Phil.*,
Brussels 1953, p. 123 f.

possent induentis arbitrio. haec arma, quae Aristoteles virtuti dat, ipsa per se pugnant, non expectant manum, et habent, non habentur. nil aliis instrumentis opus est, satis nos instruxit ratione natura. hoc dedit telum firmum, perpetuum, obsequens, nec anceps, nec quod in dominum remitti posset. non ad providendum tantum, sed ad res gerendas satis est per se ipsa ratio; etenim quid est stultius quam hanc ab iracundia petere praesidium, rem stabilem ab incerta, fidelem ab infida, sanam ab aegra?

Sapientia

1215—*Sapientia*, then, is *mens perfecta*. It is *constantia*, called ὁμολογία by Zeno.

a. Seneca stresses the element of the will in it.

Sen., *Ep.* 20, 5:
Quid est sapientia? Semper idem velle atque idem nolle. —
Non potest enim cuiquam idem semper placere nisi rectum.

On the part of the will in Seneca's moral philosophy, see our next number.

b. The wise man is not liable to any offence.

Sen., *De constantia sap.* 3, 5:

Hoc igitur dico, sapientem nulli esse iniuriae obnoxium; itaque non refert, quam multa in illum coiciantur tela, cum sit nulli penetrabilis. quomodo quorundam lapidum inexpugnabilis ferro duritia est nec secari adamas aut caedi vel deteri potest sed incurrentia ultro retundit, quemadmodum quaedam non possunt igne consumi sed flamma circumfusa rigorem suum habitumque conservant, quemadmodum proiecti quidam in altum scopuli mare frangunt nec ipsi ulla saevitiae vestigia tot verberati saeculis ostentant: ita sapientis animus solidus est et id roboris collegit, ut tam tutus sit ab iniuria quam illa quae rettuli.

c. He is equal to the gods.

Sen., *Ep.* 31, 8:

His state of mind and life is described as *aequalitas ac tenor vitae per omnia consonans sibi*. The author continues:

Quod non potest esse, nisi rerum scientia contingit et ars, per quam humana ac divina noscantur. hoc est summum bonum. quod si occupas, incipis deorum socius esse, non supplex.

The part of the will in moral progress

1216—More than has been done by any Greek philosopher, the part of the will in moral progress was emphasized by Seneca.

a. Sen., *Ep.* 71, 36 f.:

Plus quam profligavimus restat, sed magna pars est profectus velle proficere. huius rei conscius mihi sum: volo, et mente tota volo. te quoque instinctum esse et magno ad pulcherrima properare impetu video. properemus: ita demum vita beneficium erit. alioqui mora est, et quidem turpis inter foeda versantibus. id agamus, ut nostrum omne tempus sit. non erit autem, nisi prius nos nostri esse coeperimus. quando continget contemnere utramque fortunam, quando continget omnibus oppressis adfectibus et sub arbitrium suum adductis hanc vocem emittere, "vici"? quem vicerim, quaeris? non Persas nec extrema Medorum nec si quid ultra Dahas bellicosum iacet, sed avaritiam, sed ambitionem, sed metum mortis, qui victores gentium vicit.

b. Cp. *Ep.* 80, 4:
Quid tibi opus est ut sis bonus? — Velle.

To will cannot be learned

c. Now willing does not depend on the intellect in such a sense that it could be learned by teaching.

Sen., *Ep.* 81, 13:

Velle non discitur.

On this important point s. Pohlenz, *Nachr. d. Gött. Ges. d. Wiss.*, phil.-hist. Kl. 1941, p. 241 ff.; *Hell. Mensch*, p. 210, 304; *Stoa* I, p. 319 f.

1217—Seneca lays great emphasis on the inner character of moral action. Cp. our nr. **1035a** (on the notion of κατόρθωμα).

Inner character of moral action

a. Sen., *De benef.* I 6, 1:

Quid est ergo beneficium? Benevola actio tribuens gaudium capiensque tribuendo in id, quod facit, prona et sponte sua parata. Itaque non, quid fiat aut quid detur, refert, sed qua mente, quia beneficium non in eo, quod fit aut datur, consistit, sed in ipso dantis aut facientis animo.

b. The principle is extended to all moral action.

De benef. IV 14, 1:

Non dicam pudicam, quae amatorem ut incenderet reppulit, quae aut legem aut virum timuit; ut ait Ovidius:

Quae, quia non licuit, non dedit, illa dedit.

Non immerito in numerum peccantium refertur, quae pudicitiam timori praestitit, non sibi. Eodem modo, qui beneficium ut reciperet dedit, non dedit.

c. As to *beneficium*, Seneca is quite categorical on the point that it is not concerned with gain.

Ib. 14, 2-4:

Ergo et nos beneficium damus animalibus, quae aut usui aut alimento futura nutrimus? beneficium damus arbustis, quae colimus, ne siccitate aut inmoti et neglecti soli duritia laborent? Nemo ad agrum colendum ex aequo et bono venit nec ad ullam rem, cuius extra ipsam fructus est; ad beneficium dandum non adducit cogitatio avara nec sordida, sed humana, liberalis, cupiens dare, etiam cum dederit, et augere novis ac recentibus vetera, unum habens propositum, quanto ei cui praestat bono futura sit; alioqui humile est, sine laude, sine gloria, prodesse, quia expedit. Quid magnifici est se amare, sibi parcere, sibi adquirere? ab omnibus istis vera beneficii dandi cupido avocat, ad detrimentum iniecta manu trahit et utilitates relinquit ipso bene faciendi opere laetissima.

Shorter at the end of chapter 13: *Non est beneficium quod in quaestum mittitur. "Hoc dabo et hoc recipiam" auctio est.*

Conscience 1218—Our good or bad conscience is, in the last instance, the reward or punishment of virtue and of vice.

a. The bad conscience.

Sen., *De clem.* I 13, 3:

(The cruel man must persevere in cruelty).

O miserabilem illum, sibi certe! nam ceteris misereri eius nefas sit, qui caedibus ac rapinis potentiam exercuit, qui suspecta sibi cuncta reddidit tam externa quam domestica, cum arma metuat ad arma confugiens, non amicorum fidei credens, non pietati liberorum; qui, ubi circumspexit, quaeque fecit quaeque facturus est, et conscientiam suam plenam sceleribus ac tormentis adaperuit, saepe mortem timet, saepius optat, invisior sibi quam servientibus.

b. The good conscience.

Sen., *De benef.* II 33, 3:

Sic beneficii fructus primus ille est conscientiae: hunc percipit qui, quo voluit, munus suum pertulit; secundus est et tertius et famae et eorum, quae praestari in vicem possunt.

c. Cp. *De benef.* IV 12, 4:

Quom interrogaveris quid reddat, respondebo: bonam conscientiam.

Quid reddat beneficium? dic tu mihi quid reddat iustitia, quid innocentia, quid magnitudo animi, quid pudicitia, quid temperantia; si quicquam praeter ipsas, ipsas non petis.

Cp. also *Ep.* 23, 7, and *De Clem.* I 1, 1.

d. In contrast to Epicurus, Seneca infers from the fact of conscience that man is naturally inclined to virtue.

Sen., *Ep.* 97, 15:

Illic dissentiamus cum Epicuro, ubi dicit nihil iustum esse natura et crimina vitanda esse, quia vitari metus non posse: hic consentiamus mala facinora conscientia flagellari et plurimum illi tormentorum esse eo, quod perpetua illam sollicitudo urget ac verberat, quod sponsoribus securitatis suae non potest credere. hoc enim ipsum argumentum est, Epicure, natura nos a scelere abhorrere, quod nulli non etiam inter tuta timor est. multos fortuna liberat poena, metu neminem. quare nisi quia infixa nobis eius rei aversatio est, quam natura damnavit?

On the importance of the notion of conscience in Seneca's moral philosophy, see Pohlenz, *Stoa* I, p. 317.

1219—Seneca speaks of the habit of daily examining one's conscience. **Daily examination of the conscience**

Sen., *De ira* III 36:

Omnes sensus perducendi sunt ad firmitatem; natura patientes sunt, si animus illos desit corrumpere, qui cotidie ad rationem reddendam vocandus est. faciebat hoc Sextius, ut consummato die, cum se ad nocturnam quietem recepisset, interrogaret animum suum: "quod hodie malum tuum sanasti? cui vitio obstitisti? qua parte melior es?" desinet ira et moderatior erit, quae sciet sibi cotidie ad iudicem esse veniendum. quicquam ergo pulchrius hac consuetudine excutiendi totum diem? qualis ille somnus post recognitionem sui sequitur quam tranquillus, quam altus ac liber, cum aut laudatus est animus aut admonitus et speculator sui censorque secretus cognovit de moribus suis! utor hac potestate et cotidie aput me causam dico. cum sublatum e conspectu lumen est et conticuit uxor moris iam mei conscia, totum diem meum scrutor factaque ac dicta mea remetior; nihil mihi ipse abscondo, nihil transeo. quare enim quicquam ex erroribus meis timeam, cum possim dicere: "vide ne istud amplius facias, nunc tibi ignosco. in illa disputatione pugnacius locutus es: noli postea congredi cum imperitis; nolunt discere, qui numquam didicerunt. illum liberius admonuisti quam debebas, itaque non emendasti sed offendisti: de cetero vide, non tantum an verum

sit quod dicis, sed an ille cui dicitur veri patiens sit; admoneri bonus
gaudet, pessimus quisque rectorem asperrime patitur.

Cp. *Carmen aureum* 40, cited sub **26g**, and the preceding remark. Sextius, of
whom a word will be said in Ch. XXIV, § 5, on this point at least followed a
Pythagorean tradition.

Seneca as a „directeur de conscience"

1220—In his *Letters to Lucilius* we see Seneca at work on the task
of giving directions for personal life.

a.   On using one's time well.

Sen., *Ep.* I 1, 1-2:

Ita fac, mi Lucili, vindica te tibi, et tempus, quod adhuc aut aufere-
batur aut subripiebatur aut excidebat, collige et serva. persuade tibi
hoc sic esse, ut scribo: quaedam tempora eripiuntur nobis, quaedam
subducuntur, quaedam effluunt. turpissima tamen est iactura, quae per
neglegentiam fit. et si volueris attendere, maxima pars vitae elabitur
male agentibus, magna nihil agentibus, tota vita aliud agentibus. quem
mihi dabis, qui aliquod pretium tempori ponat, qui diem aestimet, qui
intellegat se cotidie mori? in hoc enim fallimur, quod mortem prospicimus:
magna pars eius iam praeterit. quicquid aetatis retro est, mors tenet.
fac ergo, mi Lucili, quod facere te scribis, omnes horas complectere.

b.   On avoiding eccentricity.

Sen., *Ep.* 5, 1-2:

Quod pertinaciter studes et omnibus omissis hoc unum agis, ut te
meliorem cotidie facias, et probo et gaudeo, nec tantum hortor ut per-
severes, sed etiam rogo. illud autem te admoneo, ne eorum more, qui
non proficere sed conspici cupiunt, facias aliqua, quae in habitu tuo aut
genere vitae notabilia sint. asperum cultum et intonsum caput et ne-
glegentiorem barbam et indictum argento odium et cubile humi positum,
et quicquid aliud ambitio nempe perversa via sequitur, evita. satis ipsum
nomen philosophiae, etiam si modeste tractetur, invidiosum est: quid si
nos hominum consuetudini coeperimus excerpere? intus omnia dissi-
milia sint, frons populo nostra conveniat.

c.   The danger of consorting with the crowd.

Sen., *Ep.* 7, 1-2:

Quid tibi vitandum praecipue existimem, quaeris? turbam. nondum
illi tuto committeris. ego certe confitebor inbecillitatem meam: numquam
mores, quos extuli, refero. aliquid ex eo quod composui turbatur; aliquid

ex iis quae fugavi redit. quod aegris evenit, quos longa inbecillitas usque eo adfecit, ut nusquam sine offensa proferantur, hoc accidit nobis, quorum animi ex longo morbo reficiuntur. inimica est multorum conversatio: nemo non aliquod nobis vitium aut commendat aut imprimit aut nescientibus adlinit. utique quo maior est populus, cui miscemur, hoc periculi plus est. nihil vero tam damnosum bonis moribus quam in aliquo spectaculo desidere. tunc enim per voluptatem facilius vitia subrepunt.

See also *Ep.* 71, 36 f., cited sub nr. **1216a**.

1221—Seneca made a sharp distinction between God, as the cause of the universe, and the universe, which is His work.

God, the cause of the universe

a. Sen., *Ep.* 65, 12-14:

(Aristotle and Plato introduced different causes.)

Sed nos nunc primam et generalem quaerimus causam. haec simplex esse debet. nam et materia simplex est. quaerimus, quid sit causa? ratio scilicet faciens, id est deus. ista enim, quaecumque rettulisti, non sunt multae et singulae causae, sed ex una pendent, ex ea, quae faciet. formam dicis causam esse? hanc imponit artifex operi: pars causae est, non causa. exemplar quoque non est causa, sed instrumentum causae necessarium. sic necessarium est exemplar artifici, quomodo scalprum, quomodo lima: sine his procedere ars non potest. non tamen hae partes artis aut causae sunt. "propositum" inquit "artificis, propter quod ad faciendum aliquid accedit, causa est." ut sit causa, non est efficiens causa, sed superveniens. hae autem innumerabiles sunt: nos de causa generali quaerimus. illud vero non pro solita ipsis subtilitate dixerunt, totum mundum et consummatum opus causam esse. multum enim interest inter opus et causam operis.

b. Cp. *Nat. quaest.* VII 30, 3-4:

In Seneca's opinion, comets should be explained not as *fortuiti ignes*, but as *intexti mundo*, quos (deus) non frequenter educit sed in occulto movet. He continues:

Quam multa praeter hos per secretum eunt numquam humanis oculis orientia! Neque enim omnia deus homini ‹pate›fecit. Quota pars operis tanti nobis committitur? Ipse qui ista tractat, qui condidit, qui totum hoc fundavit deditque circa se, maiorque est pars sui operis ac melior, effugit oculos; cogitatione visendus est.

c. Cp. also *Nat. quaest.* I, Praef. 13:

Quid est deus? Mens universi. Quid est deus? Quod vides totum et quod non vides totum. Sic demum magnitudo illi sua redditur, qua nihil maius cogitari potest, si solus est omnia, si opus suum et intra et extra tenet.

Was Seneca a religious man?

1222—Seneca often speaks of God. Yet, if it is true that the feeling of utter dependence is essential in religion, he was not a religious man: in his opinion, the wise man—not even in the absolute sense, but what the Stoics called the "advanced" man—is equal to God and has nothing to ask from Him.

   a. Sen., *Ep.* 41, 1 and 4:

Facis rem optimam et tibi salutarem, si, ut scribis, perseveras ire ad bonam mentem, quam stultum est optare, cum possis a te impetrare. non sunt ad caelum elevandae manus nec exorandus aedituus, ut nos ad aurem simulacri, quasi magis exaudiri possimus, admittat: prope est a te deus, tecum est, intus est. —

Si hominem videris interritum periculis, intactum cupiditatibus, inter adversa felicem, in mediis tempestatibus placidum, ex superiore loco homines videntem, ex aequo deos: non subibit te veneratio eius? non dices: "iste res maior est altiorque quam ut credi similis huic, in quo est, corpusculo possit"? vis isto divina descendit.

   b. Cp. also *Ep.* 31, 8, cited under **1215c**, and *Ep.* 73, 12-13:

Plura Iuppiter habet, quae praestet hominibus, sed inter duos bonos non est melior qui locupletior, non magis quam inter duos, quibus par scientia regendi gubernaculum est, meliorem dixeris cui maius speciosiusque navigium est. Iuppiter quo antecedit virum bonum? diutius bonus est: sapiens nihilo se minoris existimat, quod virtutes eius spatio breviore cluduntur.

   c. In the following passage may be seen that, finally, Seneca's "advanced man" is alone with himself.

Sen., *De benef.* VII 1, 7:

Si animus fortuita contempsit, si se supra metus sustulit nec avida spe infinita conplectitur, sed didicit a se petere divitias; si deorum hominumque formidinem eiecit et scit non multum esse ab homine timendum, a deo nihil; si contemptor omnium, quibus torquetur vita, dum ornatur, eo perductus est, ut illi liqueat mortem nullius mali materiam esse, multorum finem; si animum virtuti consecravit et, quacumque vocat illa, planum putat; si sociale animal et in commune genitus

mundum ut unam omnium domum spectat et conscientiam suam dis
aperuit semperque tamquam in publico vivit se magis veritus quam
alios: subductus ille tempestatibus in solido ac sereno stetit consumma-
vitque scientiam utilem ac necessariam.

1223—a. In several passages Seneca spoke of after-life in the same Did Seneca
believe in
sense as Cicero did in the *Somnium Scipionis*. Some of these were cited in immortality?
our nr. **960**. The author seems to have been rather strongly impressed
by Posidonius and his spiritualistic tendency.

b. On the other hand, it should be noticed that, repeatedly, in the
same works in which the above-mentioned passages occur, he also admits
the possibility that death is the end of everything.

Thus, *Ad Marciam* 19, 4-6:
Cogita nullis defunctum malis adfici, illa, quae nobis inferos faciunt
terribiles, fabulas esse, nullas inminere mortuis tenebras nec carcerem
nec flumina igne flagrantia nec Oblivionem amnem nec tribunalia et reos
et in illa libertate tam laxa ullos iterum tyrannos: luserunt ista poetae
et vanis nos agitavere terroribus. mors dolorum omnium exolutio est et
finis, ultra quem mala nostra non exeunt, quae nos in illam tranquilli-
tatem, in qua antequam nasceremur iacuimus, reponit. si mortuorum
aliquis miseretur, et non natorum misereatur. mors nec bonum nec malum
est. id enim potest aut bonum aut malum esse, quod aliquid est; quod
vero ipsum nihil est et omnia in nihilum redigit, nulli nos fortunae tradit;
mala enim bonaque circa aliquam versantur materiam. non potest id
fortuna tenere, quod natura dimisit, nec potest miser esse qui nullus est.

The *magna et aeterna pax* which waits for us after this life according to the
present passage, turns out to be of a rather negative character.

c. Both the positive and the negative views occur in
Ad Polyb. 9, 2.
The author advises Polybius to argue with himself on his brother's death
in this way:
"Si illius nomine doleo, necesse est alterutrum ex his duobus esse
iudicem: nam si nullus defunctis sensus superest, evasit omnia frater
meus vitae incommoda et in eum restitutus est locum, in quo fuerat
antequam nasceretur, et expers omnis mali nihil timet, nihil cupit, nihil
patitur: quis iste furor est pro eo me numquam dolere desinere, qui numquam doliturus est? si est aliquis defunctis sensus, nunc animus fratris
mei velut ex diutino carcere emissus, tandem sui iuris et arbitrii, gestit

et rerum naturae spectaculo fruitur et humana omnia ex loco superiore despicit, divina vero, quorum rationem tam diu frustra quaesierat, propius intuetur. quid itaque eius desiderio maceror, qui aut beatus aut nullus est? beatum deflere invidia est, nullum dementia."

Also in *Ep.* 65, 24 and in *De prov.* 6, 6 both possibilities are admitted: *Mors quid est?* — *Aut finis aut transitus.*

Cp. also *Ep.* 57,8 f. (more positive); *Ep.* 71, 16; *Ep.* 36, 10-11.

On ending one's life artificially

1224—Seneca speaks repeatedly of the εὔλογος ἐξαγωγή. E.g.:

a. Sen., *Ep.* 58, 32-36:

Potest frugalitas producere senectutem, quam ut non puto concupiscendam, ita ne recusandam quidem. iucundum est secum esse quam diutissime, cum quis se dignum quo frueretur effecit. itaque de isto feremus sententiam, an oporteat fastidire senectutis extrema et finem non opperiri, sed manu facere. prope est a timente, qui fatum segnis expectat, sicut ille ultra modum deditus vino est, qui amphoram exiccat et faecem quoque exorbet. de hoc tamen quaeremus, pars summa vitae utrum [ea] faex sit an liquidissimum ac purissimum quiddam, si modo mens sine iniuria est et integri sensus animum iuvant nec defectum et praemortuum corpus est. plurimum enim refert, vitam aliquis extendat an mortem. at si inutile ministeriis corpus est, quidni oporteat educere animum laborantem? et fortasse paulo ante quam debet, faciendum est, ne cum fieri debebit, facere non possis. —

Non relinquam senectutem, si me totum mihi reservabit, totum autem ab illa parte meliore; at si coeperit concutere mentem, si partes eius convellere, si mihi non vitam reliquerit, sed animam, prosiliam ex aedificio putri ac ruenti. morbum morte non fugiam, dumtaxat sanabilem nec officientem animo. non adferam mihi manus propter dolorem: sic mori vinci est. hunc tamen si sciero perpetuo mihi esse patiendum, exibo, non propter ipsum, sed quia inpedimento mihi futurus est ad omne, propter quod vivitur. inbecillus est et ignavus, qui propter dolorem moritur, stultus, qui doloris causa vivit.

b. *Ep.* 24, 24-25:

Etiam cum ratio suadet finire se, non temere nec cum procursu capiendus est impetus. vir fortis ac sapiens non fugere debet e vita, sed exire. et ante omnia ille quoque vitetur affectus, qui multos occupavit, libido moriendi.

Seneca's death

1225—Seneca's death is reported by Tacitus, *Ann.* XV 62-64.

6—MUSONIUS RUFUS AND EPICTETUS

1226—Musonius, Epictetus' master, lived at Rome under Nero. **Musonius**
In 65 A.D. he was banished to Gyaros.   **Rufus**

a. Tacitus, *Ann.* XV 71:

Verginium ‹Flavum et Musonium› Rufum claritudo nominis expulit;
nam Verginius studia iuvenum eloquentia, Musonius praeceptis sapientiae
fovebat.

b. C. Plinius speaks of him and his son-in-law Artemidorus in a
tone of high admiration.

Plinius, *Epist.* III (ad Julium Genitorem), 11, 5 Müller:

Nam et C. Musonium, socerum eius, quantum licitum est per aetatem,
cum admiratione dilexi et Artemidorum ipsum iam tum, cum in Syria
tribunus militarem, arta familiaritate complexus sum idque primum
nonnullius indolis dedi specimen, quod virum aut sapientem, aut proxi-
mum simillimumque sapienti intelligere sum visus. Nam ex omnibus,
qui nunc se philosophos vocant, vix unum aut alterum invenies tanta
sinceritate, tanta veritate. Mitto qua patientia corporis hiemes iuxta
et aestates ferat, ut nullis laboribus cedat, ut nihil in cibo aut potu
voluptatibus tribuat, ut oculos animumque contineat. Sunt haec magna,
sed in alio; in hoc vero minima, si ceteris virtutibus comparentur, quibus
meruit ut a C. Musonio ex omnibus omnium ordinum assectatoribus
gener assumeretur.

More than Seneca, Musonius seems to have been a man of character.

c. The following passage shows us Musonius as a missionary in the
army.

Tac., *Hist.* III 81:

Miscuerat se legatis Musonius Rufus, equestris ordinis, studium philosophiae et placita Stoicorum aemulatus, coeptabatque permixtus mani-
pulis bona pacis ac belli discrimina disserens armatos monere. Id plerisque
ludibrio, pluribus taedio; nec deerant, qui propellerent proculcarentque, ni
admonitu modestissimi cuiusque et aliis minitantibus omisisset intem-
pestivam sapientiam.

1227—After Panaetius and Posidonius, who were learned men and   **Musonius**
did not address themselves to the masses, Musonius was the first among **affinity with**   **and his**
Stoics to take up the rôle of a popular preacher and of a spiritual adviser, **Cynicism**   **older**

joining with the older Cynics in their view of the moral task of man, his training and the essential equality of the sexes. From this he drew not only the conclusion for education, but he maintained also that in the field of sex ethics men and women are equal.

a.   Man and his moral task.

Musonius II, p. 6, 5-12 Hense:

Πάντες, ἔφη, φύσει πεφύκαμεν οὕτως, ὥστε ζῆν ἀναμαρτήτως καὶ καλῶς, οὐχ ὁ μὲν ἡμῶν ὁ δ' οὔ· καὶ τούτου μέγα τεκμήριον ὅτι πᾶσιν ὁμοίως οἱ νομοθέται καὶ προστάττουσιν ἃ χρὴ ποιεῖν καὶ ἀπαγορεύουσιν ἃ μὴ χρή, οὐχ ὑπεξαιρούμενοι οὐδένα τῶν ἀπειθούντων ἢ τῶν ἁμαρτανόντων ὥστε ἀτιμώρητον εἶναι, οὐ νέον, οὐ πρεσβύτην, οὐκ ἰσχυρόν, οὐκ ἀσθενῆ οὐχ ὅντινα οὖν.

b.   Therefore, men and women equally must practice philosophy.

III, p. 8, 15 - 9, 16 H.:

'Επεὶ δ' ἐπύθετό τις αὐτοῦ, εἰ καὶ γυναιξὶ φιλοσοφητέον, οὕτω πως ἤρξατο διδάσκειν ὡς φιλοσοφητέον αὐταῖς. Λόγον μέν, ἔφη, τὸν αὐτὸν εἰλήφασι παρὰ θεῶν αἱ γυναῖκες τοῖς ἀνδράσιν, ᾧ τε χρώμεθα πρὸς ἀλλήλους καὶ καθ' ὃν διανοούμεθα περὶ ἑκάστου πράγματος, <εἰ> ἀγαθὸν ἢ κακόν ἐστιν, καὶ καλὸν ἢ αἰσχρόν. ὁμοίως δὲ καὶ αἰσθήσεις τὰς αὐτὰς ἔχει τὸ θῆλυ τῷ ἄρρενι, ὁρᾶν, ἀκούειν, ὀσφραίνεσθαι καὶ τὰ ἄλλα. ὁμοίως δὲ καὶ μέρη σώματος τὰ αὐτὰ ὑπάρχει ἑκατέρῳ, καὶ οὐδὲν θατέρῳ πλέον. ἔτι δ' ὄρεξις καὶ οἰκείωσις φύσει πρὸς ἀρετὴν οὐ μόνον γίνεται τοῖς ἀνδράσι, ἀλλὰ καὶ γυναιξίν· οὐδὲν γὰρ ἧττον αὐταί γε τῶν ἀνδρῶν τοῖς μὲν καλοῖς καὶ δικαίοις ἔργοις ἀρέσκεσθαι πεφύκασι, τὰ δ' ἐναντία τούτων προβάλλεσθαι. τούτων δὲ ταύτῃ ἐχόντων, διὰ τί ποτ' οὖν τοῖς μὲν ἀνδράσι προσήκοι ἂν ζητεῖν καὶ σκοπεῖν ὅπως βιώσονται καλῶς, ὅπερ τὸ φιλοσοφεῖν ἐστι, γυναικὶ δὲ οὔ; πότερον ὅτι ἄνδρας μὲν προσήκει ἀγαθοὺς εἶναι, γυναῖκας δὲ οὔ;

c.   In what sense philosophy is required for everybody.

IV, p. 19, 8-14 H.:

Καὶ οὐ τοῦτο βούλομαι λέγειν, ὅτι τρανότητα περὶ λόγους καὶ δεινότητά τινα περιττὴν χρὴ προσεῖναι ταῖς γυναιξίν, εἴπερ φιλοσοφήσουσιν ὡς γυναῖκες· οὐδὲ γὰρ ἐπ' ἀνδρῶν ἐγὼ πάνυ τι τοῦτο ἐπαινῶ· ἀλλ' ὅτι ἤθους χρηστότητα καὶ καλοκἀγαθίαν τρόπου κτητέον ταῖς γυναιξίν· ἐπειδὴ καὶ φιλοσοφία καλοκἀγαθίας ἐστὶν ἐπιτήδευσις καὶ οὐδὲν ἕτερον.

Double askesis   **1228**—Since man consists of body and soul, a double training is needed, as was taught by the older Cynics (cp. our nr. **244**).

Musonius VI, p. 24, 8 - 25, 6 H.:

Πῶς οὖν καὶ τίνα τρόπον τούτοις ἀσκητέον; ἐπεὶ τὸν ἄνθρωπον οὔτε ψυχὴν μόνον εἶναι συμβέβηκεν οὔτε σῶμα μόνον, ἀλλά τι σύνθετον ἐκ τοῖν δυοῖν τούτοιν, ἀνάγκη τὸν ἀσκοῦντα ἀμφοῖν ἐπιμελεῖσθαι, τοῦ μὲν κρείττονος μᾶλλον, ὥσπερ ἄξιον, τουτέστι τῆς ψυχῆς· καὶ θατέρου δέ, εἴ γε μέλλει μηδὲν ἐνδεῶς ἔχειν τοῦ ἀνθρώπου μέρος. δεῖ γὰρ δὴ καὶ τὸ σῶμα παρεσκευάσθαι καλῶς πρὸς τὰ σώματος ἔργα τὸ τοῦ φιλοσοφοῦντος, ὅτι πολλάκις αἱ ἀρεταὶ καταχρῶνται τούτῳ ὄντι ὀργάνῳ ἀναγκαίῳ πρὸς τὰς τοῦ βίου πράξεις. τῆς οὖν ἀσκήσεως ἡ μέν τις ἰδία τῆς ψυχῆς μόνης γίνοιτ' ἂν ὀρθῶς, ἡ δέ τις κοινὴ ταύτης τε καὶ τοῦ σώματος.

1229—a. Musonius summarizes his sex ethics in the following lines. **Sex ethics**
Musonius XII, p. 63, 17 - 64, 9 H.:

Χρὴ δὲ τοὺς μὴ τρυφῶντας ἢ μὴ κακοὺς μόνα μὲν ἀφροδίσια νομίζειν δίκαια τὰ ἐν γάμῳ καὶ ἐπὶ γενέσει παίδων συντελούμενα, ὅτι καὶ νόμιμά ἐστιν· τὰ δέ γε ἡδονὴν θηρώμενα ψιλὴν ἄδικα καὶ παράνομα, κἂν ἐν γάμῳ ᾖ συμπλοκαὶ δὲ ἄλλαι αἱ μὲν κατὰ μοιχείαν παρανομώταται, καὶ μετριώτεραι τούτων οὐδὲν αἱ πρὸς ἄρρενας τοῖς ἄρρεσιν, ὅτι παρὰ φύσιν τὸ τόλμημα· ὅσαι δὲ μοιχείας ἐκτὸς συνουσίαι πρὸς θηλείας εἰσὶν ἐστερημέναι τοῦ γίνεσθαι κατὰ νόμον, καὶ αὗται πᾶσαι αἰσχραί, αἵ γε πράττονται δι' ἀκολασίαν.

b. Some people think that sexual intercourse with his bondswoman is allowed to a master on the ground of his proprietary right. To this Musonius opposes the following reply.

Musonius XII, p. 66, 6 - 67, 2 H.:

Πρὸς τοῦτο δὲ ἁπλοῦς μοι ὁ λόγος· εἰ γάρ τῳ δοκεῖ μὴ αἰσχρὸν μηδ' ἄτοπον εἶναι δούλη δεσπότην πλησιάζειν τῇ ἑαυτοῦ, καὶ μάλιστα εἰ τύχοι οὖσα χήρα, λογισάσθω ποῖόν τι καταφαίνεται αὐτῷ, εἰ δέσποινα δούλῳ πλησιάζοι. οὐ γὰρ ἂν δόξειεν εἶναι ἀνεκτόν, οὐ μόνον εἰ κεκτημένη ἄνδρα νόμιμον ἡ γυνὴ προσοῖτο δοῦλον, ἀλλ' εἰ καὶ ἄνανδρος οὖσα τοῦτο πράττοι; καίτοι τοὺς ἄνδρας οὐ δήπου τῶν γυναικῶν ἀξιώσει τις εἶναι χείρονας, οὐδ' ἧττον δύνασθαι τὰς ἐπιθυμίας παιδαγωγεῖν τὰς ἑαυτῶν, τοὺς ἰσχυροτέρους τὴν γνώμην τῶν ἀσθενεστέρων, τοὺς ἄρχοντας τῶν ἀρχομένων. πολὺ γὰρ κρείττονας εἶναι προσήκει τοὺς ἄνδρας, εἴπερ καὶ προεστάναι ἀξιοῦνται τῶν γυναικῶν. ἂν μέντοι ἀκρατέστεροι φαίνωνται ὄντες, . . * καὶ κακίονες. ὅτι δ' ἀκρασίας ἔργον καὶ οὐδενὸς ἄλλου ἐστὶ τὸ δεσπότην δούλῃ πλησιάζειν, τί δεῖ καὶ λέγειν; γνώριμον γάρ.

In his work on Musonius [1], p. 81-89, Dr. A. C. van Geytenbeek, dealing with

---

* ἔσονται suppl. Hense.
[1] *Musonius Rufus en de Griekse diatribe.* Diss. Utrecht 1948.

these remarkable passages, rightly points out the fact that in his moral approach
to these things Musonius differs profoundly from the older Cynics, who stressed
the facility of satifying one's sexual needs, without adding any moral condition.
Cp. Xenophon, *Symp.* 4, 38, where Antisthenes says, explaining to Socrates how
he feels so rich, having so little money:

Ἢν δέ ποτε καὶ ἀφροδισιάσαι τὸ σῶμά μου δεηθῇ, οὕτω μοι τὸ παρὸν ἀρκεῖ, ὥστε
αἷς ἂν προσέλθω ἀσπάζονταί με διὰ τὸ μηδένα ἄλλον αὐταῖς ἐθέλειν προσιέναι.

Likewise, Diogenes says in Dio Chrysostomus' 6th discourse, 16-17, that what
men go to the most trouble to obtain and what they spend the most money on,
is found by him the easiest and most inexpensive of all things to procure: "ἀπανταχοῦ
(γὰρ) παρεῖναι αὐτῷ τὴν Ἀφροδίτην προῖκα." — Cp. also the third century Cynic
Cercidas, *Meliamb.* III 23-33 Knox, who speaks of "Aphrodite of the market",
whom you can have for an obol.

Marriage   **1230—a.** The main purpose of marriage.

Musonius XIII A, p. 67-68 H.:

Βίου καὶ γενέσεως παίδων κοινωνίαν κεφάλαιον εἶναι γάμου. Τὸν γὰρ
γαμοῦντα, ἔφη, καὶ τὴν γαμουμένην ἐπὶ τούτῳ συνιέναι χρὴ ἑκάτερον θατέρῳ,
ὥσθ' ἅμα μὲν ἀλλήλοις βιοῦν, ἅμα δὲ <παιδο>ποιεῖσθαι, καὶ κοινὰ δὲ ἡγεῖσθαι
πάντα καὶ μηδὲν ἴδιον, μηδ' αὐτὸ τὸ σῶμα. μεγάλη μὲν γὰρ γένεσις ἀνθρώπου, ἣν
ἀποτελεῖ τοῦτο τὸ ζεῦγος. ἀλλ' οὔπω τοῦτο ἱκανὸν τῷ γαμοῦντι, ὃ δὴ καὶ δίχα
γάμου γένοιτ' ἂν συμπλεκομένων ἄλλως, ὥσπερ καὶ τὰ ζῷα συμπλέκεται αὐτοῖς.
δεῖ δὲ ἐν γάμῳ πάντως συμβίωσίν τε εἶναι καὶ κηδεμονίαν ἀνδρὸς καὶ γυναικὸς
περὶ ἀλλήλους, καὶ ἐρρωμένους καὶ νοσοῦντας καὶ ἐν παντὶ καιρῷ, ἧς ἐφιέμενος
ἑκάτερος ὥσπερ καὶ παιδοποιίας εἰσὶν ἐπὶ γάμον. ὅπου μὲν οὖν ἡ κηδεμονία αὕτη
τέλειός ἐστι, καὶ τελέως αὐτὴν οἱ συνόντες ἀλλήλοις παρέχονται, ἁμιλλώμενοι
νικᾶν ὁ ἕτερος τὸν ἕτερον, οὗτος μὲν οὖν ὁ γάμος ᾗ προσήκει ἔχει καὶ ἀξιοζή-
λωτός ἐστι· καλὴ γὰρ ἡ τοιαύτη κοινωνία· ὅπου δὲ ἑκάτερος σκοπεῖ τὸ ἑαυτοῦ
μόνον ἀμελῶν θατέρου, ἢ καὶ νὴ Δί' ὁ ἕτερος οὕτως ἔχει, καὶ οἰκίαν μὲν οἰκεῖ
τὴν αὐτήν, τῇ δὲ γνώμῃ βλέπει ἔξω, μὴ βουλόμενος τῷ ὁμόζυγι συντείνειν τε καὶ
συμπνεῖν, ἐνταῦθ' ἀνάγκη φθείρεσθαι μὲν τὴν κοινωνίαν, φαύλως δὲ ἔχειν τὰ
πράγματα τοῖς συνοικοῦσιν, καὶ ἢ διαλύονται τέλεον ἀπ' ἀλλήλων ἢ τὴν συμμο-
νὴν χείρω ἐρημίας ἔχουσιν.

Dudley, *History of Cynicism*, p. 196 n. 1, remarks that Musonius in his whole
attitude to women appears to be largely influenced by the old Roman tradition.

Children   **b.** The beauty of having a large family.

XV A, p. 79, 1-2:

Ἄξιον δὲ νοῆσαι ποῖόν τι καὶ θεάμά ἐστιν ἀνὴρ πολύπαις ἢ γυνὴ σὺν ἀθρόοις
ὁρώμενοι τοῖς ἑαυτῶν παισίν· οὔτε γὰρ πομπὴν πεμπομένην θεοῖς οὕτω καλὴν
θεάσαιτ' ἄν τις οὔτε χορείαν ἐπὶ ἱεροῖς κόσμῳ χορευόντων οὕτως ἀξιοθέατον, ὡς
χορὸν παίδων πολλῶν προηγουμένων ἐν πόλει πατρὸς τοῦ ἑαυτῶν ἢ μητρός,

‹καὶ› χειραγωγούντων τοὺς γονεῖς ἢ τρόπον ἕτερον περιεπόντων κηδεμονικῶς. τί μὲν τούτου κάλλιον τοῦ θεάματος; τί δὲ τῶν γονέων τούτων ζηλωτότερον, ἄλλως τε κἂν ἐπιεικεῖς ὦσι; τίσι δ' ἂν ἄλλοις οὕτω προθύμως ἢ συνεύξαιτό τις ἀγαθὰ παρὰ θεῶν, ἢ συμπράξειεν αὐτοῖς εἰς ὅ τι δέοιντο;

1231—Musonius' pupil Epictetus was a Phrygian slave, living at Rome under Nero. As a freedman, he settled in Nicopolis (Actium) under Domitianus and had his school there. His works were edited by his pupil Arrianus.

Epictetus

a. Suidas:

Epaphroditus' slave

Ἐπίκτητος· Ἱεραπόλεως τῆς Φρυγίας, φιλόσοφος, δοῦλος Ἐπαφροδίτου, τῶν σωματοφυλάκων τοῦ βασιλέως Νέρωνος. πηρωθεὶς δὲ τὸ σκέλος ὑπὸ ῥεύματος ἐν Νικοπόλει τῆς νέας Ἠπείρου ᾤκησε, καὶ διατείνας μέχρι Μάρκου Ἀντωνίνου. ἔγραψε πολλά.

That he lived till the reign of Marcus Aurelius is hardly possible.

b. His lameness was frequently said to have been caused by the brutality of a master. E.g. Celsus ap. Orig., *C. Celsum* VII 53:

Οὐκοῦν (sc. εἴχετε) Ἐπίκτητον, ὃς τοῦ δεσπότου στρεβλοῦντος αὐτοῦ τὸ σκέλος, ὑπομειδιῶν ἀνεκπλήκτως ἔλεγε "κατάσσεις" καὶ κατάξαντος "οὐκ ἔλεγον", εἶπεν, "ὅτι κατάσσεις;"

c. That he heard Musonius while yet in Epaphroditus' service, appears from the following passage.

Epict., *Diss.* I 9, 27-31:

Ἐμέ τις ἠξίωκεν ὑπὲρ αὐτοῦ γράψαι εἰς τὴν Ῥώμην ὡς ἐδόκει τοῖς πολλοῖς ἠτυχηκὼς καὶ πρότερον μὲν ἐπιφανὴς ὢν καὶ πλούσιος, ὕστερον δ' ἐκπεπτωκὼς ἁπάντων καὶ διάγων ἐνταῦθα. κἀγὼ ἔγραψα ὑπὲρ αὐτοῦ ταπεινῶς. ὁ δ' ἀναγνοὺς τὴν ἐπιστολὴν ἀπέδωκέν μοι αὐτὴν καὶ ἔφη ὅτι "Ἐγὼ βοηθηθῆναί τι ὑπὸ σοῦ ἤθελον, οὐχὶ ἐλεηθῆναι· κακὸν δέ μοι οὐθέν ἐστιν". οὕτως καὶ Ῥοῦφος πειράζων μ' εἰώθει λέγειν "Συμβήσεταί σοι τοῦτο καὶ τοῦτο ὑπὸ τοῦ δεσπότου". κἀμοῦ πρὸς αὐτὸν ἀποκριναμένου ὅτι "Ἀνθρώπινα" "Τί οὖν ἔτι ἐκεῖνον παρακαλῶ παρὰ σοῦ αὐτὰ λαβεῖν δυνάμενος"; τῷ γὰρ ὄντι, ὃ ἐξ αὐτοῦ τις ἔχει, περισσὸς καὶ μάταιος παρ' ἄλλου λαμβάνων.

We shall find the note of interior freedom to be the dominating motive of Epictetus' philosophy.

d. The fame of his wisdom and character resounds in an undated but fairly early inscription from Pisidia, edited by J. R. S. Sterrett,

Papers of the American School of Class. Stud. at Athens, 1884-5, 3, 315 f., and discussed by Kaibel in Hermes XXIII (1888), p. 542 ff.

Schenkl, *Epict. ed. maior*, test. XIX:

ὦ ξ[ένε], Ἐπ]ίκτατος δούλας ἀπὸ ματρὸς ἐτέχθη,
αἰε[τὸς] ἀνθρώπων, σοφίᾳ ἐπὶ κυδα[λί]μα φρήν.
ὃν [τί] χρή με λέγειν; θ[ε]ῖος γένετ'. αἴθε δὲ καὶ νῦν
τοιοῦτός τις ἀνὴρ ὄφελος μέγα καὶ μέγα χάρμα
πάντων εὐξαμένων δούλας ἀπὸ ματρὸς ἐτέχθη.

τὰ ἐφ' ἡμῖν καὶ τὰ οὐκ ἐφ' ἡμῖν
1232—First principles of his philosophy: the distinction between what is and what is not in our power.

a. *Encheiridion* I 1-3:

Τῶν ὄντων τὰ μέν ἐστιν ἐφ' ἡμῖν, τὰ δὲ οὐκ ἐφ' ἡμῖν. ἐφ' ἡμῖν μὲν ὑπόληψις, ὁρμή, ὄρεξις, ἔκκλισις καὶ ἑνὶ λόγῳ ὅσα ἡμέτερα ἔργα· οὐκ ἐφ' ἡμῖν
δὲ τὸ σῶμα, ἡ κτῆσις, δόξαι, ἀρχαὶ καὶ ἑνὶ λόγῳ ὅσα οὐχ ἡμέτερα ἔργα. καὶ
τὰ μὲν ἐφ' ἡμῖν ἐστι φύσει ἐλεύθερα, ἀκώλυτα, ἀπαραπόδιστα, τὰ δὲ οὐκ ἐφ'
ἡμῖν ἀσθενῆ, δοῦλα, κωλυτά, ἀλλότρια. μέμνησο οὖν, ὅτι, ἐὰν τὰ φύσει δοῦλα
ἐλεύθερα οἰηθῇς καὶ τὰ ἀλλότρια ἴδια, ἐμποδισθήσῃ, πενθήσεις, ταραχθήσῃ,
μέμψῃ καὶ θεοὺς καὶ ἀνθρώπους, ἐὰν δὲ τὸ σὸν μόνον οἰηθῇς σὸν εἶναι, τὸ δὲ
ἀλλότριον, ὥσπερ ἐστίν, ἀλλότριον, οὐδείς σε ἀναγκάσει οὐδέποτε, οὐδείς σε
κωλύσει, οὐ μέμψῃ οὐδένα, οὐκ ἐγκαλέσεις τινί, ἄκων πράξεις οὐδὲ ἕν, οὐδείς
σε βλάψει, ἐχθρὸν οὐχ ἕξεις, οὐδὲ γὰρ βλαβερόν τι πείσει.

b. *Diss.* II 6, 24:

τὰ σὰ καὶ τὰ οὐ σά
Μόνον ἐκείνης τῆς διαιρέσεως μέμνησο, καθ' ἣν διορίζεται τὰ σὰ καὶ οὐ
τὰ σά. μή ποτ' ἀντιποιήσῃ τινὸς τῶν ἀλλοτρίων.

Only the first are of real value
1233—Only things that are "ours" are of real value. Therefore, watch over your sense-impressions. It is your freedom that depends on it.

a. *Diss.* IV 3, 1-8:

Ἐκεῖνο πρόχειρον ἔχε, ὅταν τινὸς ἀπολείπῃ τῶν ἐκτός, τί ἀντ' αὐτοῦ περι-
ποιῇ· κἂν ᾖ πλείονος ἄξιον, μηδέποτ' εἴπῃς ὅτι "ἐζημίωμαι"· οὐδ' <ἂν> ἀντὶ
ὄνου ἵππον, οὐδ' ἀντὶ προβάτου βοῦν, οὐδ' ἀντὶ κέρματος πρᾶξιν καλήν,
οὐδ' ἀντὶ ψυχρολογίας ἡσυχίαν οἵαν δεῖ, οὐδ' ἀντὶ αἰσχρολογίας αἰδῶ. τούτων
μεμνημένος πανταχοῦ διασώσεις τὸ σαυτοῦ πρόσωπον οἷον ἔχειν σε δεῖ. εἰ
δὲ μή, σκόπει, ὅτι ἀπόλλυνται οἱ χρόνοι εἰκῇ καὶ ὅσα νῦν προσέχεις σεαυτῷ,
μέλλεις ἐκχεῖν ἅπαντα ταῦτα καὶ ἀνατρέπειν. ὀλίγου δὲ χρεία ἐστὶ πρὸς τὴν
ἀπώλειαν τὴν πάντων καὶ ἀνατροπήν, μικρᾶς ἀποστροφῆς τοῦ λόγου. ἵνα ὁ

κυβερνήτης ἀνατρέψῃ τὸ πλοῖον, οὐ χρείαν ἔχει τῆς αὐτῆς παρασκευῆς, ὅσης
εἰς τὸ σῶσαι· ἀλλὰ μικρὸν πρὸς τὸν ἄνεμον ἂν ἐπιστρέψῃ, ἀπώλετο· κἂν μὴ
αὐτὸς ἑκών, ὑποπαρενθυμηθῇ δ', ἀπώλετο. τοιοῦτόν ἐστί τι καὶ ἐνθάδε· μικρὸν
ἂν ἀπονυστάξῃς, ἀπῆλθεν πάντα τὰ μέχρι νῦν συνειλεγμένα. πρόσεχε οὖν ταῖς
φαντασίαις, ἐπαγρύπνει. οὐ γὰρ μικρὸν τὸ τηρούμενον, ἀλλ' αἰδὼς καὶ πίστις
καὶ εὐστάθεια, ἀπάθεια, ἀλυπία, ἀφοβία, ἀταραξία, ἁπλῶς ἐλευθερία.

b. *Ench.* 1, 5:

Εὐθὺς οὖν πάσῃ φαντασίᾳ τραχείᾳ μελέτα ἐπιλέγειν ὅτι "φαντασία εἶ καὶ
οὐ πάντως τὸ φαινόμενον". ἔπειτα ἐξέταζε αὐτὴν καὶ δοκίμαζε τοῖς κανόσι
τούτοις οἷς ἔχεις, πρώτῳ δὲ τούτῳ καὶ μάλιστα, πότερον περὶ τὰ ἐφ' ἡμῖν
ἐστιν ἢ περὶ τὰ οὐκ ἐφ' ἡμῖν· κἂν περί τι τῶν οὐκ ἐφ' ἡμῖν ᾖ, πρόχειρον ἔστω
τὸ διότι "οὐδὲν πρὸς ἐμέ".

1234—The free man does not revolt against the order of things given
to him, but obeys God of his own free will.

Inner
freedom

a. *Diss.* IV 3, 8-12:

Τίνων μέλλεις ταῦτα[1] πωλεῖν; βλέπε, πόσου ἀξίων. — 'Αλλ' οὐ τεύξομαι
τοιούτου τινὸς ἀντ' αὐτοῦ. — Βλέπε καὶ τυγχάνων πάλιν ἐκείνου, τί ἀντ'
αὐτοῦ λαμβάνεις. "ἐγὼ εὐκοσμίαν, ἐκεῖνος δημαρχίαν· ἐκεῖνος στρατηγίαν,
ἐγὼ αἰδῶ. ἀλλ' οὐ κραυγάζω, ὅπου ἀπρεπές· ἀλλ' οὐκ ἀναστήσομαι, ὅπου μὴ
δεῖ. ἐλεύθερος γάρ εἰμι καὶ φίλος τοῦ θεοῦ, ἵν' ἑκὼν πείθωμαι αὐτῷ. τῶν δ'
ἄλλων οὐδενὸς ἀντιποιεῖσθαί με δεῖ, οὐ σώματος, οὐ κτήσεως, οὐκ ἀρχῆς,
οὐ φήμης, ἁπλῶς οὐδενός· οὐδὲ γὰρ ἐκεῖνος βούλεταί μ' ἀντιποιεῖσθαι αὐτῶν.
εἰ γὰρ ἤθελεν, ἀγαθὰ πεποιήκει αὐτὰ ἂν ἐμοί. νῦν δ' οὐ πεποίηκεν· διὰ τοῦτο
οὐδὲν δύναμαι παραβῆναι τῶν ἐντολῶν." τήρει τὸ ἀγαθὸν τὸ σαυτοῦ ἐν παντί,
τῶν δ' ἄλλων κατὰ τὸ διδόμενον μέχρι τοῦ εὐλογιστεῖν ἐν αὐτοῖς, τούτῳ
μόνῳ ἀρκούμενος. εἰ δὲ μή, δυστυχήσεις, ἀτυχήσεις, κωλυθήσῃ, ἐμποδισθήσῃ,
οὗτοί εἰσιν οἱ ἐκεῖθεν ἀπεσταλμένοι νόμοι, ταῦτα τὰ διατάγματα· τούτων
ἐξηγητὴν δεῖ γενέσθαι, τούτοις ὑποτεταγμένον, οὐ τοῖς Μασουρίου καὶ Κασσίου[2].

b. Cp. *Ench.* 8:

Μὴ ζήτει τὰ γινόμενα γίνεσθαι ὡς θέλεις, ἀλλὰ θέλε τὰ γινόμενα ὡς γίνεται
καὶ εὑρήσεις.

The term εὔροια βίου was used by Zeno, who defined εὐδαιμονία by it.

---

[1] The things mentioned in the preceding sentence: αἰδὼς καὶ πίστις κτλ., ἁπλῶς
ἐλευθερία.
[2] Two well-known jurists of the first century.

The applica-
tion of these
principles

1235—In the *diatribes*, we see Epictetus continuously at work on the application of these principles.

a. *Diss.* I 29, 5-8:

Λοιπὸν ὅταν ἀπειλῇ ὁ τύραννος καὶ μὴ καλῇ ¹, λέγω "τίνι ἀπειλεῖ;" ἂν λέγει "δήσω σε", φημὶ ὅτι "ταῖς χερσὶν ἀπειλεῖ καὶ τοῖς ποσίν." ἂν λέγῃ "τραχη-λοκοπήσω σε", λέγω "τῷ τραχήλῳ ἀπειλεῖ". ἂν λέγῃ "εἰς φυλακήν σε βαλῶ", "ὅλῳ τῷ σαρκιδίῳ"· κἂν ἐξορισμὸν ἀπειλῇ, τὸ αὐτό. — σοὶ οὖν οὐδὲν ἀπειλεῖ· — εἰ πέπονθα ὅτι ταῦτα οὐδέν ἐστι πρὸς ἐμέ, οὐδέν· εἰ δὲ φοβοῦμαί τι τούτων, ἐμοὶ ἀπειλεῖ. τίνα λοιπὸν δέδοικα; τὸν τίνων ὄντα κύριον; τῶν ἐπ' ἐμοί; οὐδὲ εἷς ἐστιν. τῶν οὐκ ἐπ' ἐμοί; καὶ τί μοι αὐτῶν μέλει;

b. *Diss.* II 6, 20-27:

"Τῇ κεφαλῇ κινδυνεύω ἐπὶ Καίσαρος". ἐγὼ δ' οὐ κινδυνεύω, ὃς οἰκῶ ἐν Νικοπόλει, ὅπου σεισμοὶ τοσοῦτοι; σὺ δ' αὐτὸς ὅταν διαπλέῃς τὸν Ἀδρίαν, τί κινδυνεύεις; οὐ τῇ κεφαλῇ; "ἀλλὰ καὶ τῇ ὑπολήψει κινδυνεύω." τῇ σῇ; πῶς; τίς γάρ σε ἀναγκάσαι δύναται ὑπολαβεῖν τι ὧν οὐ θέλεις; ἀλλὰ τῇ ἀλλοτρίᾳ; καὶ ποῖός ἐστι κίνδυνος σὸς ἄλλους τὰ ψεύδη ὑπολαβεῖν; "ἀλλ' ἐξορισθῆναι κινδυνεύω." τί ἐστιν ἐξορισθῆναι; ἀλλαχοῦ εἶναι ἢ ἐν Ῥώμῃ; "ναί. τί οὖν; ἂν εἰς Γύαρα πεμφθῶ;" ἂν σοι ποιῇ, ἀπελεύσῃ· εἰ δὲ μή, ἔχεις ποῦ ἀντὶ Γυάρων ἀπέλθῃς, ὅπου κἀκεῖνος ἐλεύσεται, ἄν τε θέλῃ ἄν τε μή, ὁ πέμπων σε εἰς Γύαρα. τί λοιπὸν ὡς ἐπὶ μεγάλα ἀνέρχῃ; μικρότερά ἐστι τῆς παρασκευῆς, ἵν' εἴπῃ νέος εὐφυὴς ὅτι "οὐκ ἦν τοσούτου τοσούτων μὲν ἀκηκοέναι, τοσαῦτα δὲ γε-γραφέναι, τοσούτῳ δὲ χρόνῳ παρακεκαθικέναι γεροντίῳ οὐ πολλοῦ ἀξίῳ." μόνον ἐκείνης τῆς διαιρέσεως μέμνησο, καθ' ἣν διορίζεται τὰ σὰ καὶ οὐ τὰ σά. μή ποτ' ἀντιποιήσῃ τινὸς τῶν ἀλλοτρίων. βῆμα καὶ φυλακὴ τόπος ἐστὶν ἑκάτερον, ὁ μὲν ὑψηλός, ὁ δὲ ταπεινός· ἡ προαίρεσις δὲ ἴση, ἂν ἴσην αὐτὴν ἐν ἑκατέρῳ φυλάξαι θέλῃς, δύναται φυλαχθῆναι. καὶ τότ' ἐσόμεθα ζηλωταὶ Σωκράτους, ὅταν ἐν φυλακῇ δυνώμεθα παιᾶνας γράφειν. μέχρι δὲ νῦν ὡς ἔχομεν, ὅρα εἰ ἠνεσχόμεθ' ἂν ἐν τῇ φυλακῇ ἄλλου τινὸς ἡμῖν λέγοντος "θέλεις ἀναγνῶ σοι παιᾶνας;" "τί μοι πράγματα παρέχεις; οὐκ οἶδας τὰ ἔχοντά με κακά; ἐν τούτοις γάρ μοι ἔστιν —" ἐν τίσιν οὖν; "ἀποθνῄσκειν μέλλω". ἄνθρωποι δ' ἄλλοι ἀθάνατοι ἔσονται;

προαίρεσις

1236—A certain moral purpose, then, a deliberate choice, is the specific quality of man. On this his liberty depends.

a. *Diss.* I 29, 1-4 (lines preceding the quotation of **1235a**):

Οὐσία τοῦ ἀγαθοῦ προαίρεσις ποιά, τοῦ κακοῦ προαίρεσις ποιά. τί οὖν τὰ

---

¹ μὴ codd., με Wolf.

ἐκτός; ὕλαι τῇ προαιρέσει, περὶ ἃς ἀναστρεφομένη τεύξεται τοῦ ἰδίου ἀγαθοῦ ἢ κακοῦ. πῶς τοῦ ἀγαθοῦ τεύξεται; ἂν τὰς ὕλας μὴ θαυμάσῃ. τὰ γὰρ περὶ τῶν ὑλῶν δόγματα ὀρθὰ μὲν ὄντα ἀγαθὴν ποιεῖ τὴν προαίρεσιν, στρεβλὰ δὲ καὶ διεστραμμένα κακήν. τοῦτον τὸν νόμον ὁ θεὸς τέθεικεν καὶ φησίν "εἴ τι ἀγαθὸν θέλεις, παρὰ σεαυτοῦ λάβε". σὺ λέγεις "οὔ· ἀλλὰ παρ' ἄλλου". μή, ἀλλὰ παρὰ σεαυτοῦ.

b. By prohairesis man maintains his inner liberty against all violence.

Ib., 9-12:

Ὑμεῖς οὖν οἱ φιλόσοφοι διδάσκετε καταφρονεῖν τῶν βασιλέων; — Μὴ γένοιτο. τίς ἡμῶν διδάσκει ἀντιποιεῖσθαι πρὸς αὐτούς, ὧν ἐκεῖνοι ἔχουσιν ἐξουσίαν; τὸ σωμάτιον λάβε, τὴν κτῆσιν λάβε, τὴν φήμην λάβε, τοὺς περὶ ἐμὲ λάβε. ἄν τινας τούτων ἀναπείθω ἀντιποιεῖσθαι, τῷ ὄντι ἐγκαλείτω μοι. "ναί· ἀλλὰ καὶ τῶν δογμάτων ἄρχειν θέλω." καὶ τίς σοι ταύτην τὴν ἐξουσίαν δέδωκεν; ποῦ δύνασαι νικῆσαι δόγμα ἀλλότριον; "προσάγων", φησίν, "αὐτῷ φόβον νικήσω." ἀγνοεῖς ὅτι αὐτὸ αὐτὸ ἐνίκησεν, οὐχ ὑπ' ἄλλου ἐνικήθη· προαίρεσιν δὲ οὐδὲν ἄλλο νικῆσαι δύναται, πλὴν αὐτὴ ἑαυτήν.

c. The divine law that the better must always prevail over the worse.

Ib. 13-18:

Διὰ τοῦτο καὶ ὁ τοῦ θεοῦ νόμος κράτιστός ἐστι καὶ δικαιότατος· τὸ κρεῖσσον ἀεὶ περιγινέσθω τοῦ χείρονος. "κρείττονές εἰσιν οἱ δέκα τοῦ ἑνός." πρὸς τί; πρὸς τὸ δῆσαι, πρὸς τὸ ἀποκτεῖναι, πρὸς τὸ ἀπαγαγεῖν ὅπου θέλουσιν, πρὸς τὸ ἀφελέσθαι τὰ ὄντα. νικῶσιν τοίνυν οἱ δέκα τὸν ἕνα ἐν τούτῳ, ἐν ᾧ κρείσσονές εἰσιν. ἐν τίνι οὖν χείρονές εἰσιν; ἂν ὁ μὲν ἔχῃ δόγματα ὀρθά, οἱ δὲ μή. τί οὖν; ἐν τούτῳ δύνανται νικῆσαι; πόθεν; εἰ δὲ ἱστάμεθα ἐπὶ ζυγοῦ, οὐκ ἔδει τὸν βαρύτερον καθελκύσαι;

Σωκράτης οὖν ἵνα πάθῃ ταῦτα ὑπ' Ἀθηναίων; — Ἀνδράποδον, τί λέγεις τὸ Σωκράτης; ὡς ἔχει τὸ πρᾶγμα λέγε· ἵν' οὖν τὸ Σωκράτους σωμάτιον ἀπαχθῇ καὶ συρῇ ὑπὸ τῶν ἰσχυροτέρων εἰς δεσμωτήριον καὶ κώνειόν τις δῷ τῷ σωματίῳ τῷ Σωκράτους κἀκεῖνο ἀποψυγῇ; ταῦτά σοι φαίνεται θαυμαστά, ταῦτα ἄδικα, ἐπὶ τούτοις ἐγκαλεῖς τῷ θεῷ; οὐδὲν οὖν εἶχε Σωκράτης ἀντὶ τούτων; ποῦ ἦν ἡ οὐσία αὐτῷ τοῦ ἀγαθοῦ; τίνι προσσχῶμεν; σοὶ ἢ αὐτῷ; καὶ τί λέγει ἐκεῖνος; "ἐμὲ δ' Ἄνυτος καὶ Μέλητος ἀποκτεῖναι μὲν δύνανται, βλάψαι δ' οὔ". καὶ πάλιν "εἰ ταύτῃ τῷ θεῷ φίλον, ταύτῃ γινέσθω".

d. Cp. also *Diss.* II 10, 1:

Σκέψαι τίς εἶ. τὸ πρῶτον ἄνθρωπος, τοῦτο δ' ἔστιν οὐδὲν ἔχων κυριώτερον προαιρέσεως, ἀλλὰ ταύτῃ τὰ ἄλλα ὑποτεταγμένα, αὐτὴν δ' ἀδούλευτον καὶ ἀνυπότακτον.

The greater part of this diatribe will be cited later (s. nr. **1242**).

Thus, the notion of *prohairesis* becomes a basic principle of Epictetus' philosophy. The term, frequently used by Aristotle, does not occur in the early Stoa, where the "knowledge of good and bad" is said to be decisive. Pohlenz, *St.* I 332 f., discusses the subject and remarks that, by this notion, Epict. comes nearer to voluntarism than Chrysippus did, yet, in principle, keeps Chrysippus' intellectualism, by defining "choice" as a judgment.

Intellectual character of Epictetus' ethics

1237—Epictetus' ethics have a rather strong intellectual character: our judgment is decisive.

a. *Diss.* III 9, 1-2:

Εἰσελθόντος δέ τινος πρὸς αὐτόν, ὃς εἰς ῾Ρώμην ἀνῄει δίκην ἔχων περὶ τιμῆς τῆς αὐτοῦ, πυθόμενος τὴν αἰτίαν, δι' ἣν ἄνεισιν, ἐπερωτήσαντος ἐκείνου, τίνα γνώμην ἔχει περὶ τοῦ πράγματος, Εἴ μου πυνθάνῃ, τί πράξεις ἐν ῾Ρώμῃ, φησίν, πότερον κατορθώσεις ἢ ἀποτεύξῃ, θεώρημα πρὸς τοῦτο οὐκ ἔχω· εἰ δὲ πυνθάνῃ, πῶς πράξεις, τοῦτο εἰπεῖν, ὅτι, εἰ μὲν ὀρθὰ δόγματα ἔχεις, καλῶς, εἰ δὲ φαῦλα, κακῶς. παντὶ γὰρ αἴτιον τοῦ πράσσειν τι δόγμα.

b. Cp. *Ench.* 5:

Ταράσσει τοὺς ἀνθρώπους οὐ τὰ πράγματα, ἀλλὰ τὰ περὶ τῶν πραγμάτων δόγματα· οἷον ὁ θάνατος οὐδὲν δεινόν (ἐπεὶ καὶ Σωκράτει ἂν ἐφαίνετο), ἀλλὰ τὸ δόγμα τὸ περὶ τοῦ θανάτου, διότι δεινόν, ἐκεῖνο τὸ δεινόν ἐστιν. ὅταν οὖν ἐμποδιζώμεθα ἢ ταρασσώμεθα ἢ λυπώμεθα, μηδέποτε ἄλλον αἰτιώμεθα, ἀλλ' ἑαυτούς, τοῦτ' ἔστι τὰ ἑαυτῶν δόγματα.

Prohairesis a dogma

c. Prohairesis itself is a judgment. *Diss.* I 17, 26:

Πάλιν οὖν τὸ σὸν δόγμα σε ἠνάγκασεν, τοῦτ' ἔστι προαίρεσιν προαίρεσις.

1238—Epictetus accepts the consequence that Medea killed her own children by an erroneous judgment.

Medea

a. *Diss.* I 28, 6-8:

"Οὐ δύναται οὖν τις δοκεῖν μέν, ὅτι συμφέρει αὐτῷ, μὴ αἱρεῖσθαι δ' αὐτό;" οὐ δύναται. πῶς ἡ λέγουσα

καὶ μανθάνω μὲν οἷα δρᾶν μέλλω κακά,
θυμὸς δὲ κρείσσων τῶν ἐμῶν βουλευμάτων; [1]

ὅτι αὐτὸ τοῦτο, τῷ θυμῷ χαρίσασθαι καὶ τιμωρήσασθαι τὸν ἄνδρα, συμφορώτερον ἡγεῖται τοῦ σῶσαι τὰ τέκνα. "ναί· ἀλλ' ἐξηπάτηται." δεῖξον αὐτῇ ἐναργῶς

---

[1] Eur., *Med.* 1078 f.

ὅτι ἐξηπάτηται καὶ οὐ ποιήσει· μέχρι δ' ἂν οὗ μὴ δεικνύῃς, τίνι ἔχει ἀκολουθῆσαι ἢ τῷ φαινομένῳ; — οὐδενί.

I.e. in the question of the πάθη, Epictetus follows Chrysippus, not Posidonius.

b. Medea, therefore, ought rather to be pitied than condemned.

Ib. 9:

Τί οὖν χαλεπαίνεις αὐτῇ, ὅτι πεπλάνηται <ἡ> ταλαίπωρος περὶ τῶν μεγίστων καὶ ἔχις ἀντὶ ἀνθρώπου γέγονεν; οὐχὶ δ', εἴπερ ἄρα, μᾶλλον ἐλεεῖς, ὡς τοὺς τυφλοὺς ἐλεοῦμεν, ὡς τοὺς χωλούς, οὕτως τοὺς τὰ κυριώτατα τετυφλωμένους καὶ ἀποκεχωλωμένους;

c. In general, this point of view should bring us to lenience towards those who go astray on the most important matters.

Ib. 10:

Ὅστις οὖν τούτου μέμνηται καθαρῶς ὅτι ἀνθρώπῳ μέτρον πάσης πράξεως τὸ φαινόμενον (λοιπὸν ἢ καλῶς φαίνεται ἢ κακῶς· εἰ καλῶς, ἀνέγκλητός ἐστιν· εἰ κακῶς, αὐτὸς ἐζημίωται· οὐ δύναται γὰρ ἄλλος μὲν εἶναι ὁ πεπλανημένος, ἄλλος δὲ ὁ βλαπτόμενος), οὐδενὶ ὀργισθήσεται, οὐδενὶ χαλεπανεῖ, οὐδένα λοιδορήσει, οὐδένα μέμψεται, οὐ μισήσει, οὐ προσκόψει οὐδενί.

Also II 22, 36.

1239—To be a man of character, you must either labour to improve your own governing principle—i.e. opt for the inner man—, or be interested in externals. You cannot do both. *The dilemma*

a. *Diss.* III 15, 13:

Ἕνα σε δεῖ ἄνθρωπον εἶναι ἢ ἀγαθὸν ἢ κακόν· ἢ τὸ ἡγεμονικόν σε δεῖ ἐξεργάζεσθαι τὸ σαυτοῦ ἢ τὰ ἐκτός· ἢ περὶ τὰ ἔσω φιλοπονεῖν ἢ περὶ τὰ ἔξω· τοῦτ' ἔστι φιλοσόφου στάσιν ἔχειν ἢ ἰδιώτου.

b. *Ench.* 13:

Εἰ προκόψαι θέλεις, ὑπόμεινον ἕνεκα τῶν ἐκτὸς ἀνόητος δόξας καὶ ἠλίθιος, μηδὲν βούλου δοκεῖν ἐπίστασθαι· κἂν δόξῃς τις εἶναί τισιν, ἀπίστει σεαυτῷ. ἴσθι γὰρ ὅτι ῥᾴδιον τὴν προαίρεσιν τὴν σεαυτοῦ κατὰ φύσιν ἔχουσαν φυλάξαι καὶ τὰ ἐκτός, ἀλλὰ τοῦ ἑτέρου ἐπιμελούμενον τοῦ ἑτέρου ἀμελῆσαι πᾶσα ἀνάγκη.

1240—The cardinal virtues in Epictetus' ethical system are: *aidoos* and *pistis*. *Aidoos*

a. Epict., fr. 14 (Stob. III 6, 57). Against Epicurus.

Τί ποτ' οὖν ἡ ψυχὴ ἐπὶ μὲν τοῖς τοῦ σώματος ἀγαθοῖς μικροτέροις οὖσι χαίρει καὶ γαληνιᾷ, ὥς φησιν Ἐπίκουρος, ἐπὶ δὲ τοῖς αὐτῆς ἀγαθοῖς μεγίστοις οὖσιν οὐχ ἥδεται; καίτοι καὶ δέδωκέ μοι ἡ φύσις αἰδῶ καὶ πολλὰ ὑπερυθριῶ, ὅταν τι ὑπολάβω αἰσχρὸν λέγειν. τοῦτό με τὸ κίνημα οὐκ ἐᾷ τὴν ἡδονὴν θέσθαι ἀγαθὸν καὶ τέλος τοῦ βίου.

b. Cp. *Diss.* III 7, 27: Aidoos is peculiar to mankind.

Πεφύκαμεν δὲ πῶς; ὡς ἐλεύθεροι, ὡς γενναῖοι, ὡς αἰδήμονες. ποῖον γὰρ ἄλλο ζῷον ἐρυθριᾷ; ποῖον αἰσχροῦ φαντασίαν λαμβάνει;

Pistis **1241**—Pistis the basis of human society.

a. *Diss.* II 4, 1:

Λέγοντος αὐτοῦ ὅτι "Ὁ ἄνθρωπος πρὸς πίστιν γέγονεν καὶ τοῦτο ὁ ἀνατρέπων ἀνατρέπει τὸ ἴδιον τοῦ ἀνθρώπου" ἐπεισῆλθέν τις τῶν δοκούντων φιλολόγων, ὃς κατείληπτό ποτε μοιχὸς ἐν τῇ πόλει. ὁ δ᾽ ,,Ἀλλ᾽ ἄν'', φησίν, ,,ἀφέντες τοῦτο τὸ πιστόν, πρὸς ὃ πεφύκαμεν, ἐπιβουλεύωμεν τῇ γυναικὶ τοῦ γείτονος, τί ποιοῦμεν; τί γὰρ ἄλλο ἢ ἀπόλλυμεν καὶ ἀναιροῦμεν;" τίνα; ,,τὸν πιστόν, τὸν αἰδήμονα, τὸν ὅσιον.'' ταῦτα μόνα; γειτνίασιν δ᾽ οὐκ ἀναιροῦμεν, φιλίαν δ᾽ οὔ, πόλιν δ᾽ οὔ; εἰς τίνα δὲ χώραν αὐτοὺς κατατάσσομεν; ὡς τίνι σοι χρῶμαι, ἄνθρωπε; ὡς γείτονι, ὡς φίλῳ; ποίῳ τινί; ὡς πολίτῃ; τί σοι πιστεύσω;

b. He who loses his natural sense of fidelity, suffers a loss in his moral personality.

Diss. II 10, 21 f.:

(The man who lost his nose has suffered an injury.)

Ψυχῆς οὖν δύναμις οὐκ ἔστιν οὐδεμία, ἣν ὁ μὲν κτησάμενος ὠφελεῖται, ὁ δ᾽ ἀποβαλὼν ζημιοῦται; — Ποίαν καὶ λέγεις; — Οὐδὲν ἔχομεν αἰδῆμον φύσει; — Ἔχομεν. — Ὁ τοῦτο ἀπολλύων οὐ ζημιοῦται, οὐδενὸς στερίσκεται, οὐδὲν ἀποβάλλει τῶν πρὸς αὐτόν; οὐκ ἔχομεν φύσει τι πιστόν, φύσει στερκτικόν, φύσει ὠφελητικόν, ἀλλήλων φύσει ἀνεκτικόν; ὅστις οὖν εἰς ταῦτα περιορᾷ ζημιούμενον ἑαυτόν, οὗτος ἦ ἀβλαβὴς καὶ ἀζήμιος;

Cp. also *Ench.* 24, 4-5.

The example of Socrates **c.** Socrates, for instance, did not fear death. What he wished to preserve was: his moral personality.

Diss. IV 1, 160-161:

Ἐπὶ Λέοντα δ᾽ ὑπὸ τῶν τυράννων πεμφθείς [1], ὅτι αἰσχρὸν ἡγεῖτο, οὐδ᾽ ἐπεβουλεύσατο εἰδὼς ὅτι ἀποθανεῖν δεήσει, ἂν οὕτως τύχῃ. καὶ τί αὐτῷ διέφερεν; ἄλλο γάρ τι σῴζειν ἤθελεν· οὐ τὸ σαρκίδιον, ἀλλὰ τὸν πιστόν, τὸν αἰδήμονα. ταῦτα ἀπαρεγχείρητα, ἀνυπότακτα.

---

[1] Plato, *Apol.* 32c.

1242—On the whole, Epictetus' view of man is displayed fairly com- Man in his
pletely in the following passage.

Man in his
different
aspects

In this, prohairesis is mentioned as the first characteristic of man; next, man
is considered successively as a part of the cosmos—and a leading part, able to
understand the Divine administration of the world—; as a citizen—i.e., not a detached unit, but organically connected with the whole—; as a son—obedient to
his Father, honouring Him and cooperating with Him as much as he can—; and
finally as a brother.

Diss. II 10, 1-14:

Σκέψαι τίς εἶ. τὸ πρῶτον ἄνθρωπος, τοῦτο δ' ἔστιν οὐδὲν ἔχων κυριώτερον
προαιρέσεως, ἀλλὰ ταύτῃ τὰ ἄλλα ὑποτεταγμένα, αὐτὴν δ' ἀδούλευτον καὶ ἀνυπότακτον [1]. σκόπει οὖν, τίνων κεχώρισαι κατὰ λόγον. κεχώρισαι θηρίων, κεχώρισαι προβάτων. ἐπὶ τούτοις πολίτης εἶ τοῦ κόσμου καὶ μέρος αὐτοῦ, οὐχ
ἓν τῶν ὑπηρετικῶν, ἀλλὰ τῶν προηγουμένων· παρακολουθητικὸς γὰρ εἶ τῇ
θείᾳ διοικήσει καὶ τοῦ ἑξῆς ἐπιλογιστικός. τίς οὖν ἐπαγγελία πολίτου; μηδὲν
ἔχειν ἰδίᾳ συμφέρον, περὶ μηδενὸς βουλεύεσθαι ὡς ἀπόλυτον, ἀλλ' ὥσπερ
ἄν, εἰ ἡ χεὶρ ἢ ὁ πούς λογισμὸν εἶχον καὶ παρηκολούθουν τῇ φυσικῇ κατασκευῇ, οὐδέποτ' ἂν ἄλλως ὥρμησαν ἢ ὠρέχθησαν ἢ ἐπανενεγκόντες ἐπὶ τὸ
ὅλον. διὰ τοῦτο καλῶς λέγουσιν οἱ φιλόσοφοι ὅτι, εἰ προῄδει ὁ καλὸς καὶ ἀγαθὸς
τὰ ἐσόμενα, συνήργει ἂν καὶ τῷ νοσεῖν καὶ τῷ ἀποθνήσκειν καὶ τῷ πηροῦσθαι,
αἰσθανόμενός γε, ὅτι ἀπὸ τῆς τῶν ὅλων διατάξεως τοῦτο ἀπονέμεται, κυριώτερον
δὲ τὸ ὅλον τοῦ μέρους καὶ ἡ πόλις τοῦ πολίτου. νῦν δ' ὅτι οὐ προγιγνώσκομεν,
καθήκει τῶν πρὸς ἐκλογὴν εὐφυεστέρων ἔχεσθαι, ὅτι καὶ πρὸς τοῦτο γεγόναμεν.
Μετὰ τοῦτο μέμνησο, ὅτι υἱὸς εἶ. τίς τούτου τοῦ προσώπου ἐπαγγελία;
πάντα τὰ αὐτοῦ ἡγεῖσθαι τοῦ πατρός, πάντα ὑπακούειν, μηδέποτε ψέξαι
πρός τινα μήδε βλαβερόν τι αὐτῷ εἰπεῖν ἢ πρᾶξαι, ἐξίστασθαι ἐν πᾶσιν καὶ
παραχωρεῖν συνεργοῦντα κατὰ δύναμιν. μετὰ τοῦτο ἴσθι ὅτι καὶ ἀδελφὸς εἶ.
καὶ πρὸς τοῦτο δὲ τὸ πρόσωπον ὀφείλεται παραχώρησις, εὐπείθεια, εὐφημία,
μηδέποτ' ἀντιποιήσασθαί τινος πρὸς [ἑ]αὐτὸν τῶν ἀπροαιρέτων, ἀλλ' ἡδέως
ἐκεῖνα προίεσθαι, ἵν' ἐν τοῖς προαιρετικοῖς πλέον ἔχῃς. ὅρα γὰρ οἷόν ἐστιν ἀντὶ
θιδράκος, ἂν οὕτως τύχῃ, καὶ καθέδρας αὐτὸν εὐγνωμοσύνην κτήσασθαι, ὅσῃ
ἡ πλεονεξία. μετὰ ταῦτα εἰ βουλευτὴς πόλεώς τινος, ὅτι βουλευτής· εἰ νέος, ὅτι
νέος· εἰ πρεσβύτης, ὅτι πρεσβύτης· εἰ πατήρ, ὅτι πατήρ. ἀεὶ γὰρ ἕκαστον τῶν
τοιούτων ὀνομάτων εἰς ἐπιλογισμὸν ἐρχόμενον ὑπογράφει τὰ οἰκεῖα ἔργα.
ἐὰν δ' ἀπελθὼν ψέγῃς σου τὸν ἀδελφόν, λέγω σοι "ἐπελάθου τίς εἶ καὶ τί σοι
ὄνομα". εἶτα εἰ μὲν χαλκεὺς ὢν ἐχρῶ τῇ σφύρᾳ ἄλλως, ἐπιλελησμένος ἂν ἦς τοῦ
χαλκέως· εἰ δὲ τοῦ ἀδελφοῦ ἐπελάθου καὶ ἀντὶ ἀδελφοῦ ἐχθρὸς ἐγένου, οὐδὲν

---

[1]   This sentence has been already cited under **1236d**.

ἀντ' οὐδενὸς ἠλλάχθαι φανεῖ σεαυτῷ; εἰ δ' ἀντὶ ἀνθρώπου, ἡμέρου ζῴου καὶ
κοινωνικοῦ, θηρίον γέγονας βλαβερόν, ἐπίβουλον, δηκτικόν, οὐδὲν ἀπολώλεκας;
ἀλλὰ δεῖ σε κέρμα ἀπολέσαι, ἵνα ζημιωθῇς, ἄλλου δ' οὐδενὸς ἀπώλεια ζημιοῖ
τὸν ἄνθρωπον;

Natural love of one's neighbour   **1243**—Indeed, Epictetus calls man a ἡμερον ζῷον καὶ φιλάλληλον (*Diss.*
IV 1, 126; 5, 10, 17), i.e.: he knows a natural love of one's neighbour.
Cp. the *caritas* in Cicero's *De off.* and in Antiochus of Ascalon [1].
Epictetus repeatedly used the term ἀδελφός.

ἀδελφός   **a.** *Diss.* I 13, 3-5:

Somebody asks how it is possible to bear with persons refusing us some small
service or with servants not heeding our wishes. Epict. replies:

Ἀνδράποδον, οὐκ ἀνέξῃ τοῦ ἀδελφοῦ τοῦ σαυτοῦ, ὃς ἔχει τὸν Δία πρόγονον,
ὥσπερ υἱὸς ἐκ τῶν αὐτῶν σπερμάτων γέγονεν καὶ τῆς αὐτῆς ἄνωθεν καταβολῆς,
ἀλλ' εἰ ἕν τινι τοιαύτῃ χώρᾳ κατετάγης ὑπερεχούσῃ, εὐθὺς τύραννον καταστή-
σεις σεαυτόν; οὐ μεμνήσῃ τί εἶ καὶ τίνων ἄρχεις; ὅτι συγγενῶν, ὅτι ἀδελφῶν
φύσει, ὅτι τοῦ Διὸς ἀπογόνων;—Ἀλλ' ὠνὴν αὐτῶν ἔχω, ἐκεῖνοι δ' ἐμοῦ οὐκ
ἔχουσιν. — Ὁρᾷς ποῦ βλέπεις; ὅτι εἰς τὴν γῆν, ὅτι εἰς τὸ βάραθρον, ὅτι εἰς
τοὺς ταλαιπώρους τούτους νόμους τοὺς τῶν νεκρῶν, εἰς δὲ τοὺς τῶν θεῶν οὐ
βλέπεις;

b. To the tyrant who is going to chain his leg, the philosopher says:
Diss. I 19, 9:

"Πόθεν σύ; ἐμὲ ὁ Ζεὺς ἐλεύθερον ἀφῆκεν. ἢ δοκεῖς ὅτι ἔμελλεν τὸν ἴδιον
υἱὸν ἐᾶν καταδουλοῦσθαι; τοῦ νεκροῦ δέ μου κύριος εἶ, λάβε αὐτόν."

Also in *Diss.* III 22, 41 Epictetus calls the body τὸ φύσει νεκρόν, ἡ γῆ, ὁ πηλός.

Man is a part of God   **1244**—Man—i.e., the inner man—is a fragment of God and should be
aware of that in all his actions.

a. *Diss.* II 8, 11-12; 18-19:

Other things are ἔργα θεῶν, but not of primary importance, nor are they portions
of Divinity,—

Σὺ δὲ προηγούμενον εἶ, σὺ ἀπόσπασμα εἶ τοῦ θεοῦ· ἔχεις τι ἐν σεαυτῷ μέρος
ἐκείνου. τί οὖν ἀγνοεῖς σου τὴν συγγένειαν; τί οὐκ οἶδας πόθεν ἐλήλυθας;
οὐ θέλεις μεμνῆσθαι, ὅταν ἐσθίῃς, τίς ὢν ἐσθίεις καὶ τίνα τρέφεις; ὅταν συν-
ουσίᾳ χρῇ, τίς ὢν χρῇ; ὅταν ὁμιλίᾳ; ὅταν γυμνάζῃ, ὅταν διαλέγῃ, οὐκ οἶδας

---

[1] Above nr. **1205**.

ὅτι θεὸν τρέφεις, θεὸν γυμνάζεις; θεὸν περιφέρεις, τάλας, καὶ ἀγνοεῖς.—Ἀλλ᾽ εἰ μὲν τὸ ἄγαλμα ἦς τὸ Φειδίου, ἡ Ἀθηνᾶ ἢ ὁ Ζεύς, ἐμέμνησο ἂν καὶ σαυτοῦ καὶ τοῦ τεχνίτου καὶ εἴ τινα αἴσθησιν εἶχες, ἐπειρῶ ἂν μηδὲν [ἂν] ἀνάξιον ποιεῖν τοῦ κατασκευάσαντος μηδὲ σεαυτοῦ μηδ᾽ ἐν ἀπρεπεῖ σχήματι φαίνεσθαι τοῖς ὁρῶσι· νῦν δέ σε ὅτι ὁ Ζεὺς πεποίηκεν, διὰ τοῦτο ἀμελεῖς οἷόν τινα δείξεις σεαυτόν;

b. The fact that a part of God is in us, is a pledge of liberty.

Diss. I 17, 27:

Εἰ γὰρ τὸ ἴδιον μέρος, ὃ ἡμῖν ἔδωκεν ἀποσπάσας ὁ θεός, ὑπ᾽ αὐτοῦ ἢ ὑπ᾽ ἄλλου τινὸς κωλυτὸν ἢ ἀναγκαστὸν κατεσκευάκει, οὐκέτι ἂν ἦν θεὸς οὐδ᾽ ἐπεμελεῖτο ἡμῶν ὃν δεῖ τρόπον.

Also I 14, 6.

1245—He who wishes to live as a free and happy man, must surrender himself entirely to God.

Complete
acceptance
of the will
of God

a. *Diss.* IV 1, 91-94; 97-104; 131:

Οὕτως ποιοῦσι καὶ τῶν ὁδοιπόρων οἱ ἀσφαλέστεροι. ἀκήκοεν ὅτι λῃστεύεται ἡ ὁδός· μόνος οὐ τολμᾷ καθεῖναι, ἀλλὰ περιέμεινεν συνοδίαν ἢ πρεσβευτοῦ ἢ ταμίου ἢ ἀνθυπάτου καὶ προσκατατάξας ἑαυτὸν παρέρχεται ἀσφαλῶς. οὕτως καὶ ἐν τῷ κόσμῳ ποιεῖ ὁ φρόνιμος. ''πολλὰ λῃστήρια, τύραννοι, χειμῶνες, ἀπορίαι, ἀποβολαὶ τῶν φιλτάτων. ποῦ τις καταφύγῃ; πῶς ἀλῄστευτος παρέλθῃ; ποίαν συνοδίαν περιμείνας ἀσφαλῶς διέλθῃ; τίνι προσκατατάξας ἑαυτόν; τῷ δεῖνι, τῷ πλουσίῳ, τῷ ὑπατικῷ. καὶ τί μοι ὄφελος; αὐτὸς ἐκδύεται, οἰμώζει, πενθεῖ. τί δ᾽ ἂν ὁ συνοδοιπόρος αὐτὸς ἐπ᾽ ἐμὲ στραφεὶς λῃστής μου γένηται; τί ποιήσω;—

Οὐκ ἔστιν εὑρεῖν ἀσφαλῆ σύνοδον, πιστόν, ἰσχυρόν, ἀνεπιβούλευτον;'' οὕτως ἐφίστησιν καὶ ἐννοεῖ, ὅτι, ἐὰν τῷ θεῷ προσκατατάξῃ ἑαυτόν, διελεύσεται ἀσφαλῶς. Πῶς λέγεις προσκατατάξαι;—''Ἵν᾽, ὃ ἂν ἐκεῖνος θέλῃ, καὶ αὐτὸς θέλῃ καί, ὃ ἂν ἐκεῖνος μὴ θέλῃ, τοῦτο μηδ᾽ αὐτὸς θέλῃ.—Πῶς οὖν τοῦτο γένηται;—Πῶς γὰρ ἄλλως ἢ ἐπισκεψαμένῳ τὰς ὁρμὰς τοῦ θεοῦ καὶ τὴν διοίκησιν; τί μοι δέδωκεν ἐμὸν καὶ αὐτεξούσιον, τί αὐτῷ κατέλιπεν; τὰ προαιρετικά μοι δέδωκεν, ἐπ᾽ ἐμοὶ πεποίηκεν, ἀνεμπόδιστα, ἀκώλυτα. τὸ σῶμα τὸ πήλινον πῶς ἐδύνατο ἀκώλυτον ποιῆσαι; ὑπέταξεν οὖν τῇ τῶν ὅλων περιόδῳ, τὴν κτῆσιν, τὰ σκεύη, τὴν οἰκίαν, τὰ τέκνα, τὴν γυναῖκα. τί οὖν θεομαχῶ; τί θέλω τὰ μὴ θελητά; τὰ μὴ δοθέντα μοι ἐξ ἅπαντος ἔχειν; ἀλλὰ πῶς; ὡς δέδοται καὶ ἐφ᾽ ὅσον δύναται. ἀλλ᾽ ὁ δοὺς ἀφαιρεῖται. τί οὖν ἀντιτείνω; οὐ λέγω ὅτι ἠλίθιος ἔσομαι τὸν ἰσχυρότερον βιαζόμενος, ἀλλ᾽ ἔτι πρότερον ἄδικος.

πόθεν γὰρ ἔχων αὐτὰ ἦλθον; ὁ πατήρ μου αὐτὰ ἔδωκεν. ἐκείνῳ δὲ τίς; τὸν ἥλιον δὲ τίς πεποίηκε, τοὺς καρποὺς δὲ τίς, τὰς δ' ὥρας τίς, τὴν δὲ πρὸς ἀλλήλους συμπλοκὴν καὶ κοινωνίαν τίς;

Εἶτα σύμπαντα εἰληφὼς παρ' ἄλλου καὶ αὐτὸν σεαυτόν, ἀγανακτεῖς καὶ μέμφη τὸν δόντα, ἄν σού τι ἀφέληται; τίς ὢν καὶ ἐπὶ τί ἐληλυθώς; οὐχὶ ἐκεῖνός σε εἰσήγαγεν; οὐχὶ τὸ φῶς ἐκεῖνός σοι ἔδειξεν; οὐ συνεργοὺς δέδωκεν; οὐ καὶ αἰσθήσεις; οὐ λόγον; ὡς τίνα δ' εἰσήγαγεν; οὐχ ὡς θνητόν; οὐχ ὡς μετὰ ὀλίγου σαρκιδίου ζήσοντα ἐπὶ γῆς καὶ θεασόμενον τὴν διοίκησιν αὐτοῦ καὶ συμπομπεύσοντα αὐτῷ καὶ συνεορτάσοντα πρὸς ὀλίγον;

(131)—Αὕτη ἡ ὁδὸς ἐπ' ἐλευθερίαν ἄγει, αὕτη μόνη ἀπαλλαγὴ δουλείας, [μόνη] τὸ δυνηθῆναί ποτ' εἰπεῖν ἐξ ὅλης ψυχῆς τὸ

> ἄγου δέ μ', ὦ Ζεῦ, καὶ σύ γ' ἡ Πεπρωμένη,
> ὅποι ποθ' ὑμῖν εἰμι διατεταγμένος. [1]

b. Speaking for himself Epictetus says: I have been set free by God; I shall attach myself to Him; my will is one with His will.

Diss. IV 7, 17; 19-20:

Ἠλευθέρωμαι ὑπὸ τοῦ θεοῦ, ἔγνωκα αὐτοῦ τὰς ἐντολάς, οὐκέτι οὐδεὶς δουλαγωγῆσαί με δύναται. —

Τίνα οὖν ἔτι φοβηθῆναι δύναμαι; τοὺς ἐπὶ τοῦ κοιτῶνος; μὴ τί ποιήσωσιν; ἀποκλείσωσί με; ἄν με εὕρωσι θέλοντα εἰσελθεῖν, ἀποκλεισάτωσαν. — Τί οὖν ἔρχῃ ἐπὶ θύρας; — "Οτι καθήκειν ἐμαυτῷ δοκῶ μενούσης τῆς παιδιᾶς συμπαίζειν. — Πῶς οὖν οὐκ ἀποκλείῃ; — "Οτι ἂν μή τίς με δέχηται, οὐ θέλω εἰσελθεῖν, ἀλλ' ἀεὶ μᾶλλον ἐκεῖνο θέλω τὸ γινόμενον. κρεῖττον γὰρ ἡγοῦμαι ὃ ὁ θεὸς θέλει ἢ ὃ ἐγώ. προσκείσομαι διάκονος καὶ ἀκόλουθος ἐκείνῳ, συνορμῶ, συνορέγομαι, ἁπλῶς συνθέλω. ἀποκλεισμὸς ἐμοὶ οὐ γίνεται, ἀλλὰ τοῖς βιαζομένοις.

c. The punishment of not accepting things as they are. You must generously yield all things received and give them gladly back to the Giver.

Diss. I 12, 21-25:

Τίς οὖν ἡ κόλασις τοῖς οὐ προσδεχομένοις; τὸ οὕτως ἔχειν, ὡς ἔχουσιν. δυσαρεστεῖ τις τῷ μόνος εἶναι; ἔστω ἐν ἐρημίᾳ. δυσαρεστεῖ τις τοῖς γονεῦσιν; ἔστω κακὸς υἱὸς καὶ πενθείτω. δυσαρεστεῖ τοῖς τέκνοις; ἔστω κακὸς πατήρ. "βάλε αὐτὸν εἰς φυλακήν." ποίαν φυλακήν; ὅπου νῦν ἐστιν· ἄκων γάρ ἐστιν· ὅπου δέ τις ἄκων ἐστιν, ἐκεῖνο φυλακὴ αὐτῷ ἐστιν, καθὸ καὶ Σωκράτης οὐκ

---

[1] These lines are of Kleanthes (SVF I 527). Above, nr. **943c**.

ἦν ἐν φυλακῇ, ἑκὼν γὰρ ἦν. "σκέλος οὖν μοι γενέσθαι πεπηρωμένον." ἀνδράποδον, εἶτα δι' ἓν σκελύδριον τῷ κόσμῳ ἐγκαλεῖς; οὐκ ἐπιδώσεις αὐτὸ τοῖς
ὅλοις; οὐκ ἀποστήσῃ; οὐ χαίρων παραχωρήσεις τῷ δεδωκότι; ἀγανακτήσεις
δὲ καὶ δυσαρεστήσεις τοῖς ὑπὸ τοῦ Διός διατεταγμένοις, ἃ ἐκεῖνος μετὰ τῶν
Μοιρῶν παρουσῶν καὶ ἐπικλωθουσῶν σου τὴν γένεσιν ὥρισεν καὶ διέταξεν;

d. Do, as they say, some foolish thing for your freedom: give
yourself up completely to the Divine Will.

Diss. II 16, 41-43:

Ἄνθρωπε, τὸ λεγόμενον τοῦτο ἀπονοήθητι ἤδη ὑπὲρ εὐροίας, ὑπὲρ ἐλευθερίας,
ὑπὲρ μεγαλοψυχίας. ἀνάτεινόν ποτε τὸν τράχηλον ὡς ἀπηλλαγμένος δουλείας,
τόλμησον ἀναβλέψας πρὸς τὸν θεὸν εἰπεῖν ὅτι "χρῶ μοι λοιπὸν εἰς ὃ ἂν θέλῃς·
ὁμογνωμονῶ σοι, [ἴ]σός εἰμι· οὐδὲν παραιτοῦμαι τῶν σοὶ δοκούντων· ὅπου
θέλεις, ἄγε· ἣν θέλεις ἐσθῆτα περίθες. ἄρχειν με θέλεις, ἰδιωτεύειν, μένειν,
φεύγειν, πένεσθαι, πλουτεῖν; ἐγώ σοι ὑπὲρ ἁπάντων τούτων πρὸς τοὺς ἀνθρώπους ἀπολογήσομαι· δείξω τὴν ἑκάστου φύσιν οἵα ἐστίν."

1246—Epictetus, who sees the ideal of inner freedom realized by the   The calling
Cynic, is convinced that man cannot reach this, and ought not to try   of the Cynic
without the help of God. This is his first word to the man who asked
him what kind of person the Cynic ought to be.

a. *Diss.* III 22, 1-9:

Πυθομένου δὲ τῶν γνωρίμων τινὸς αὐτοῦ, ὃς ἐφαίνετο ἐπιρρεπῶς ἔχων πρὸς
τὸ κυνίσαι, Ποῖόν τινα εἶναι δεῖ τὸν κυνίζοντα καὶ τίς ἡ πρόληψις ἡ τοῦ πράγματος, Σκεψόμεθα κατὰ σχολήν. τοσοῦτον δ' ἔχω σοι εἰπεῖν, ὅτι ὁ δίχα θεοῦ
τηλικούτῳ πράγματι ἐπιβαλλόμενος θεοχόλωτός ἐστι καὶ οὐδὲν ἄλλο ἢ δημοσίᾳ
θέλει ἀσχημονεῖν. οὐδὲ γὰρ ἐν οἰκίᾳ καλῶς οἰκουμένῃ παρελθών τις αὐτὸς
ἑαυτῷ λέγει "ἐμὲ δεῖ οἰκονόμον εἶναι"· εἰ δὲ μή, ἐπιστραφεὶς ὁ κύριος καὶ
ἰδὼν αὐτὸν σοβαρῶς διατασσόμενον, ἑλκύσας ἔτεμεν. οὕτως γίνεται καὶ ἐν
τῇ μεγάλῃ ταύτῃ πόλει. ἔστι γάρ τις καὶ ἐνθάδ' οἰκοδεσπότης ἕκαστα ὁ διατάσ-
σων. "σὺ ἥλιος εἶ· δύνασαι περιερχόμενος ἐνιαυτὸν ποιεῖν καὶ ὥρας καὶ τοὺς
καρποὺς αὔξειν καὶ τρέφειν καὶ ἀνέμους κινεῖν καὶ ἀνιέναι καὶ τὰ σώματα τῶν
ἀνθρώπων θερμαίνειν συμμέτρως· ὕπαγε, περιέρχου καὶ οὕτως διακίνει ἀπὸ
τῶν μεγίστων ἐπὶ τὰ μικρότατα. σὺ μοσχάριον εἶ· ὅταν ἐπιφανῇ λέων, τὰ σαυτοῦ
πρᾶσσε· εἰ δὲ μή, οἰμώξεις. σὺ ταῦρος εἶ· προσελθὼν μάχου· σοὶ γὰρ τοῦτο
ἐπιβάλλει καὶ πρέπει καὶ δύνασαι αὐτὸ ποιεῖν. σὺ δύνασαι ἡγεῖσθαι τοῦ στρα-
τεύματος ἐπὶ Ἴλιον· ἴσθι Ἀγαμέμνων. σὺ δύνασαι τῷ Ἕκτορι μονομαχῆσαι·
ἴσθι Ἀχιλλεύς." εἰ δὲ Θερσίτης παρελθὼν ἀντεποιεῖτο τῆς ἀρχῆς, ἢ οὐκ ἂν

ἔτυχεν ἢ τυχὼν ἂν ἠσχημόνησεν ἐν πλείοσι μάρτυσι. Καὶ σὺ[μ] βούλευσαι περὶ πράγματος ἐπιμελῶς· οὐκ ἔστιν οἷον δοκεῖ σοι.

b. The Cynic is sent by God to the world and he has to serve Him without reserve.

Ib. 56-57:

Κυνικῷ δὲ Καῖσαρ τί ἐστιν ἢ ἀνθύπατος ἢ ἄλλος ἢ ὁ καταπεπομφὼς αὐτὸν καὶ ᾧ λατρεύει, ὁ Ζεύς; ἄλλον τινὰ ἐπικαλεῖται ἢ ἐκεῖνον; οὐ πέπεισται δ', ὅ τι ἂν πάσχῃ τούτων, ὅτι ἐκεῖνος αὐτὸν γυμνάζει; ἀλλ' ὁ μὲν Ἡρακλῆς ὑπὸ Εὐρυσθέως γυμναζόμενος οὐκ ἐνόμιζεν ἄθλιος εἶναι, ἀλλ' ἀόκνως ἐπετέλει πάντα τὰ προσταττόμενα· οὗτος δ' ὑπὸ τοῦ Διὸς ἀθλούμενος καὶ γυμναζόμενος μέλλει κεκραγέναι καὶ ἀγανακτεῖν, ἄξιος φορεῖν τὸ σκῆπτρον τὸ Διογένους;

Life is a campaign **1247**—Life is a campaign: you have to perform the duties assigned to you by the commanding officer.

a. *Diss.* III 24, 31-32:

(To a man who sits down, complaining of events and circumstances).

Ταῦτα ἤκουες παρὰ τοῖς φιλοσόφοις, ταῦτ' ἐμάνθανες; οὐκ οἶσθ', ὅτι στρατεία τὸ χρῆμά ἐστιν; τὸν μὲν δεῖ φυλάττειν, τὸν δὲ κατασκοπήσοντα ἐξιέναι, τὸν δὲ καὶ πολεμήσοντα· οὐχ οἷόν τ' εἶναι πάντας ἐν τῷ αὐτῷ οὐδ' ἄμεινον. σὺ δ' ἀφεὶς ἐκτελεῖν τὰ προστάγματα τοῦ στρατηγοῦ ἐγκαλεῖς, ὅταν τί σοι προσταχθῇ τραχύτερον, καὶ οὐ παρακολουθεῖς, οἷον ἀποφαίνεις, ὅσον ἐπὶ σοί, τὸ στράτευμα, ὅτι ἄν σε πάντες μιμήσωνται, οὐ τάφρον σκάψει τις, οὐ χάρακα περιβαλεῖ, οὐκ ἀγρυπνήσει, οὐ κινδυνεύσει, ἀλλὰ ἄχρηστος δόξει στρατεύεσθαι.

The metaphor of the drama of life **b.** Cp. *Ench.* 17:

Μέμνησο, ὅτι ὑποκριτὴς εἶ δράματος, οἷον ἂν θέλῃ ὁ διδάσκαλος· ἂν βραχύ, βραχέος· ἂν μακρόν, μακροῦ· ἂν πτωχὸν ὑποκρίνασθαί σε θέλῃ, ἵνα καὶ τοῦτον εὐφυῶς ὑποκρίνῃ· ἂν χωλόν, ἂν ἄρχοντα, ἂν ἰδιώτην. σὸν γὰρ τοῦτ' ἔστι, τὸ δοθὲν ὑποκρίνασθαι πρόσωπον καλῶς· ἐκλέξασθαι δ' αὐτὸ ἄλλου.

The same metaphor is found with the second century Cynic Favorinus. See Dudley, *History of Cynicism*, p. 200.

Death **1248**—Death is a natural redivision of the elements by Him who governs the universe, who has given life to us and may take it from us.

a. *Diss.* IV 10, 16:

Ὅ με σὺ ἐγέννησας, <χάριν ἔχω·> χάριν ἔχω, ὧν ἔδωκας· ἐφ' ὅσον ἐχρησάμην τοῖς σοῖς, ἀρκεῖ μοι. πάλιν αὐτὰ ἀπόλαβε καὶ κατάταξον εἰς ἣν θέλεις χώραν. σὰ γὰρ ἦν πάντα, σύ μοι αὐτὰ δέδωκας.

b. God supplies us with everything we need for living. As soon as He does not, this is a sign for retiring: He does not need us any longer.

Diss. III 13, 14-15:

Ὅταν δὲ μὴ παρέχῃ τἀναγκαῖα, τὸ ἀνακλητικὸν σημαίνει, τὴν θύραν ἤνοιξεν καὶ λέγει σοι "ἔρχου". ποῦ; εἰς οὐδὲν δεινόν, ἀλλ' ὅθεν ἐγένου, εἰς τὰ φίλα καὶ συγγενῆ, εἰς τὰ στοιχεῖα. ὅσον ἦν ἐν σοὶ πυρ<ός>, εἰς πῦρ ἄπεισιν, ὅσον ἦν γηδίου, εἰς γῆδιον, ὅσον πνευματίου, εἰς πνευμάτιον, ὅσον ὑδατίου, εἰς ὑδάτιον. οὐδεὶς ᾍδης οὐδ' Ἀχέρων οὐδὲ Κωκυτὸς οὐδὲ Πυριφλεγέθων, ἀλλὰ πάντα θεῶν μεστὰ καὶ δαιμόνων [1].

c. Cp. also III 24, 95-101:

Διὰ τοῦτο ὁ καλὸς καὶ ἀγαθὸς μεμνημένος τίς τ' ἐστὶ καὶ πόθεν ἐλήλυθεν καὶ ὑπὸ τίνος γέγονεν, πρὸς μόνῳ τούτῳ ἐστίν, πῶς τὴν αὑτοῦ χώραν ἐκπληρώσῃ εὐτάκτως καὶ εὐπειθῶς τῷ θεῷ. "ἔτι μ' εἶναι θέλεις; ὡς ἐλεύθερος, ὡς γενναῖος, ὡς σὺ ἠθέλησας· σὺ γάρ με ἀκώλυτον ἐποίησας ἐν τοῖς ἐμοῖς. ἀλλ' οὐκέτι μου χρείαν ἔχεις; καλῶς σοι γένοιτο· καὶ μέχρι νῦν διὰ σὲ ἔμενον, δι' ἄλλον οὐδένα, καὶ νῦν σοι πειθόμενος ἀπέρχομαι." "πῶς ἀπέρχῃ;" "πάλιν ὡς σὺ ἠθέλησας ὡς ἐλεύθερος, ὡς ὑπηρέτης σός, ὡς ᾐσθημένος σου τῶν προσταγμάτων καὶ ἀπαγορευμάτων. μέχρι δ' ἂν οὗ διατρίβω ἐν τοῖς σοῖς, τίνα με θέλεις εἶναι; ἄρχοντα ἢ ἰδιώτην, βουλευτὴν ἢ δημότην, στρατιώτην ἢ στρατηγόν, παιδευτὴν ἢ οἰκοδεσπότην; ἣν ἂν χώραν καὶ τάξιν ἐγχειρίσῃς, ὡς λέγει ὁ Σωκράτης, μυριάκις ἀποθανοῦμαι πρότερον ἢ ταύτην ἐγκαταλείψω. ποῦ δέ μ' εἶναι θέλεις; ἐν Ῥώμῃ ἢ ἐν Ἀθήναις ἢ ἐν Θήβαις ἢ ἐν Γυάροις; μόνον ἐκεῖ μου μέμνησο. ἄν μ' ἐκεῖ πέμπῃς, ὅπου κατὰ φύσιν διεξαγωγὴ οὐκ ἔστιν ἀνθρώπων, οὐ σοὶ ἀπειθῶν ἔξειμι, ἀλλ' ὡς σοῦ μοι σημαίνοντος τὸ ἀνακλητικόν· οὐκ ἀπολείπω σε· μὴ γένοιτο· ἀλλ' αἰσθάνομαι, ὅτι μου χρείαν οὐκ ἔχεις."

Parallel passages: III 26, 29; I 29, 28 f. See also above, our nrs. **1234, 1242, 1245**.

On the whole, there is a real grandeur in the fierce spiritualism of this little man with his lame leg and his entire surrender to the divine Will.

7—LATER CYNICS

1249—The kind of popular sermons, called *diatribes*, found in The diatribe Epictetus, originated with Bion of Borysthenes, a Cynic of the first half of the 3rd century. Of Bion's diatribes fragments are preserved in the remains of Teles' works, handed down to us by Stobaeus.

---

[1] A quotation of Thales; see our nr. **9c**.

Definition   **a.** The genre is defined by the rhetor Hermogenes, *Rhet. Graec.* III, p. 406 W.:

Διατριβή ἐστι βραχέος διανοήματος ἠθικὴ ἔκθεσις.

Bion.
Happiness
depends on
ourselves

b. Circumstances being immutable, happiness or unhappiness depends on our approach to them.

Bion in Teles, p. 4-5 Hense:

Εἰ λάβοι, φησὶ ὁ Βίων, φωνὴν τὰ πράγματα, ὃν τρόπον καὶ ἡμεῖς, καὶ δύναιτο δικαιολογεῖσθαι, οὖν ἂν εἴποι, φησίν, ἡ Πενία . . . πρὸς τὸν ἐγκαλοῦντα ''τί μοι μάχῃ; μὴ καλοῦ τινος δι' ἐμὲ στερίσκῃ; μὴ σωφροσύνης; μὴ δικαιοσύνης; μὴ ἀνδρείας; ἀλλὰ μὴ τῶν ἀναγκαίων ἐνδεὴς εἶ; ἢ οὐ μεσταὶ μὲν αἱ ὁδοὶ λαχάνων, πλήρεις δὲ αἱ κρῆναι ὕδατος; οὐκ εὐνάς σοι τοσαύτας παρέχω ὁπόσῃ γῇ; καὶ στρωμνὰς φύλλα; ἢ εὐφραίνεσθαι μετ' ἐμοῦ οὐκ ἔστιν; ἢ οὐχ ὁρᾷς γράδια φυστὴν φαγόντα τερετίζοντα; ἢ οὐκ ὄψον ἀδάπανον καὶ ἀτρύφερον παρασκευάζω σοι τὴν πεῖναν; —

Εἰ ταῦτα λέγοι ἡ Πενία, τί ἂν ἔχοις ἀντειπεῖν; ἐγὼ μὲν γὰρ ἂν δοκῶ ἄφωνος γενέσθαι. ἀλλ' ἡμεῖς πάντα μᾶλλον αἰτιώμεθα ἢ τὴν ἑαυτῶν δυστροπίαν καὶ κακοδαιμονίαν, τὸ γῆρας, τὴν πενίαν, τὸν ἀπαντήσαντα, τὴν ἡμέραν, τὴν ὥραν, τὸν τόπον. διό φησιν ὁ Διογένης φωνῆς ἀκηκοέναι κακίας ἑαυτὴν αἰτιωμένης,

οὔτις ἐμοὶ τῶνδ' ἄλλος ἐπαίτιος, ἀλλ' ἐγὼ αὐτή. [1]

Cp. Epictetus, nr. **1245**.

c. Bion, ib., p. 6-7 H.:

Ὁ δὲ Βίων, ὥσπερ τῶν θηρίων, φησί, παρὰ τὴν λῆψιν ἡ δῆξις γίνεται, κἂν μέσου τοῦ ὄφεωσ ἐπιλαμβάνῃ, δηχθήσῃ, ἐὰν τοῦ τραχήλου, οὐδὲν πείσῃ· οὕτω καὶ τῶν πραγμάτων, φησί, παρὰ τὴν ὑπόληψιν ἡ ὀδύνη γίνεται, καὶ ἐὰν μὲν οὕτως ὑπολάβῃς περὶ αὐτῶν, ὡς ἂν κρατῇς, οὐκ ὀδυνήσῃ, ἐὰν δὲ ὡς ἑτέρως, ἀνιάσῃ, οὐχ ὑπὸ τῶν πραγμάτων ἀλλ' ὑπὸ τῶν ἰδίων τρόπων καὶ τῆς ψευδοῦς δόξης. διὸ δεῖ μὴ τὰ πράγματα πειρᾶσθαι μετατιθέναι, ἀλλ' αὐτὸν παρασκευάσαι πρὸς ταῦτά πως ἔχοντα, ὅπερ ποιοῦσιν οἱ ναυτικοί· οὐ γὰρ τοὺς ἀνέμους καὶ τὴν θάλατταν πειρῶνται μετατιθέναι, ἀλλὰ παρασκευάζουσιν αὑτοὺς δυναμένους πρὸς ἐκεῖνα στρέφεσθαι. εὐδία, γαλήνη· ταῖς κώπαις πλέουσι· κατὰ ναῦν ἄνεμος· ἐπῆραν τὰ ἄρμενα. ἀντιπέπνευκεν· ἐστείλαντο, μεθείλαντο. καὶ σὺ πρὸς τὰ παρόντα χρῶ. γέρων γέγονας· μὴ ζήτει τὰ τοῦ νέου. ἀσθενὴς πάλιν· μὴ ζήτει τὰ τοῦ ἰσχυροῦ. — Ἄπορος πάλιν γέγονας· μὴ ζήτει τὴν τοῦ εὐπόρου δίαιταν.

---

[1] The verse is probably not a literal quotation, but a free Homeric reminiscence of such a line as Iliad A 335: οὔτι μοι ὔμμες ἐπαίτιοι, ἀλλ' Ἀγαμέμνων.

d. As to Teles, he was a Megarian schoolmaster in the second half of the 3rd **Teles** century. His own work was less interesting than what he quoted. Dudley, *History of Cynicism*, p. 84-87.

1250—a. After a period of silence, there is a revival of Cynicism in the first **Cynicism** cent. B.C. *Meleager of Gadara*, author of satires and of a collection of epigrams, **in the first** lived in the first half of the first Century, for the greater part at Tyrus, later on Cos. **cent. B.C.** Dudley, p. 121 f.

b. From the same period dates the so-called *Wiener Diogenes Papyrus*, which contains a number of anecdotes. It was first published by Wessely in *Festschrift Th. Gomperz*, Wien 1902, p. 68-72 (*Neues über Diogenes den Kyniker*); next by W. Crönert, *Kolotes u. Menedemos*, Leipzig 1906, (*Studien zur Palaeographie u. Papyruskunde*, herausgeg. von C. Wessely, Bd. VI), p. 49-52. K. von Fritz, *Quellenuntersuchungen zu Leben u. Philosophie des Diogenes von Sinope*. Philologus, Suppl. Bd. 18, 2, Leipzig 1926, p. 60-63; R. Höistad, *Cynic Hero and Cynic King*, Uppsala 1948, p. 147.

c. The so-called *Letters of the Cynics* (sc. of Antisthenes, Diogenes and Crates) date from the Augustan age and later. See von Fritz, o.c. p. 63-71; Dudley, p. 123 f.

1251—The first Cynic who is somewhat better known to us in the first **Demetrius** cent. A.D. is Demetrius, a well-known figure in Rome under Caligula and Nero, banished by Vespasianus in 71. Seneca admired him as a rare example of wisdom.

a. Seneca, *De benef.* VII 8, 2 - 9, 1; 10, 6:

Haec universa habere de quibus loqueris, abominabitur (sapiens). Non referam tibi Socratem, Chrysippum, Zenonem et ceteros magnos quidem viros, maiores quidem quia in laudem vetustorum invidia non obstat. Paulo ante Demetrium rettuli, quem mihi videtur rerum natura nostris tulisse temporibus, ut ostenderet nec illum a nobis corrumpi nec nos ab illo corripi posse, virum exactae, licet neget ipse, sapientiae firmaeque in iis, quae proposuit, constantiae, eloquentiae vero eius quae res fortissimas deceat, non concinnatae nec in verba sollicitae, sed ingenti animo, prout inpetus tulit, res suas prosequentis. Huic non dubito quin providentia et talem vitam et talem dicendi facultatem dederit, ne aut exemplum saeculo nostro aut convicium deesset. Demetrio si res nostras aliquis deorum possidendas velit tradere sub lege certa, ne liceat donare, adfirmaverim repudiaturum dicturumque: "Ego vero me ad istud inextricabile pondus non adligo nec in altam faecem rerum hunc expeditum hominem demitto. Quid ad me defers populorum omnium mala? quae ne daturus quidem acciperem, quoniam multa video, quae me donare non deceat." —

(10, 6) "Dimitte me et illis divitiis meis redde; ego regnum sapientiae novi, magnum, securum; ego sic omnia habeo, ut omnium sint."

b. Seneca, *Ep.* 62, 3:

Demetrium, virorum optimum, mecum circumfero et relictis conchyliatis cum illo seminudo loquor, illum admiror. quidni admirer? vidi nihil ei deesse. contemnere aliquis omnia potest, omnia habere nemo potest. brevissima ad divitias per contemptum divitiarum via est. Demetrius autem noster sic vivit, non tamquam contempserit omnia, sed tamquam aliis habenda permiserit.

Epictetus seems to have disliked him: he mentions him only once. On the association of Demetrius with Paetus Thrasea and his circle, see Dudley, o.c. p. 128 ff.

Epictetus' ideal of the Cynic

1252—Both Musonius and Epictetus had, as we pointed out, a strong affinity with older Cynics. Epictetus, however, in his diatribe "On the calling of the Cynic" warns against the vulgar kind of Cynicism: the essential thing is not wearing a rough cloak, having a hard bed and taking a wallet and a staff, but purity of the hegemonikón (III 22, 9: Πρῶτον οὖν τὸ ἡγεμονικόν σε δεῖ τὸ σαυτοῦ καθαρὸν ποιῆσαι) and a detachment from outward matters.   Next, he must know that he has a divine mission.

The Cynic has been sent by God to men

a. Epict., *Diss.* III 22, 23-27; 30:

Εἰδέναι δεῖ, ὅτι ἄγγελος ἀπὸ τοῦ Διὸς ἀπέσταλται καὶ πρὸς τοὺς ἀνθρώπους περὶ ἀγαθῶν καὶ κακῶν ὑποδείξων αὐτοῖς, ὅτι πεπλάνηνται καὶ ἀλλαχοῦ ζητοῦσι τὴν οὐσίαν τοῦ ἀγαθοῦ καὶ τοῦ κακοῦ, ὅπου οὐκ ἔστιν, ὅπου δ' ἔστιν οὐκ ἐνθυμοῦνται, καὶ ὡς ὁ Διογένης ἀπαχθεὶς πρὸς Φίλιππον μετὰ τὴν ἐν Χαιρωνείᾳ μάχην κατάσκοπος εἶναι [1]. τῷ γὰρ ὄντι κατάσκοπός ἐστιν ὁ Κύνικος τοῦ τίνα ἐστὶ τοῖς ἀνθρώποις φίλα καὶ τίνα πολέμια. καὶ δεῖ αὐτὸν ἀκριβῶς κατασκεψάμενον ἐλθόντ' ἀπαγγεῖλαι τἀληθῆ μήθ' ὑπὸ φόβου ἐκπλαγέντα, ὥστε τοὺς μὴ ὄντας πολεμίους δεῖξαι, μήτε τινὰ ἄλλον τρόπον ὑπὸ τῶν φαντασιῶν παραταραχθέντα ἢ συγχυθέντα.

Δεῖ οὖν αὐτὸν δύνασθαι ἀνατεινάμενον, ἂν οὕτως τύχῃ, καὶ ἐπὶ σκηνὴν τραγικὴν ἀνερχόμενον λέγειν τὸ τοῦ Σωκράτους "ἰὼ ἄνθρωποι, ποῖ φέρεσθε; τί ποιεῖτε, ὦ ταλαίπωροι; ὡς τυφλοὶ ἄνω καὶ κάτω κυλίεσθε· ἄλλην ὁδὸν ἀπέρχεσθε τὴν οὖσαν ἀπολελοιπότες, ἀλλαχοῦ ζητεῖτε τὸ εὔρουν καὶ τὸ εὐδαιμονικόν, ὅπου οὐκ ἔστιν, οὐδ' ἄλλου δεικνύοντος πιστεύετε. τί αὐτὸ ἔξω ζητεῖτε; ἐν σώματι οὐκ ἔστιν. εἰ ἀπιστεῖτε, ἴδετε Μύρωνα, ἴδετε 'Οφέλλιον. ἐν κτήσει οὐκ ἔστιν. εἰ δ' ἀπιστεῖτε, ἴδετε Κροῖσον, ἴδετε τοὺς νῦν πλουσίους, ὅσης οἰμωγῆς ὁ βίος αὐτῶν μεστός ἐστιν. ἐν ἀρχῇ οὐκ ἔστιν. εἰ δὲ μή γε, ἔδει τοὺς δὶς καὶ τρὶς ὑπάτους εὐδαίμονας εἶναι· οὐκ εἰσὶ δέ.

(30) — ἐν βασιλείᾳ οὐκ ἔστιν. εἰ δὲ μή, Νέρων ἂν εὐδαίμων ἐγένετο καὶ Σαρδανάπαλλος. ἀλλ' οὐδ' 'Αγαμέμνων εὐδαίμων ἦν καίτοι κομψότερος ὢν Σαρδαναπάλλου καὶ Νέρωνος.

---

[1] Cp. Diog. Laërt. VI 43.

b.   He has been sent to show in practice that it is possible to be free and happy without any externals.

Ib., 45-48:

Καὶ πῶς ἐνδέχεται μηδὲν ἔχοντα, γυμνόν, ἄοικον, ἀνέστιον, αὐχμῶντα, ἄδουλον, ἄπολιν διεξάγειν εὐρόως; ἰδοῦ ἀπέσταλκεν ὑμῖν ὁ θεὸς τὸν δείξοντα ἔργῳ, ὅτι ἐνδέχεται. "Ἰδετέ με, ἄοικός εἰμι, ἄπολις, ἀκτήμων, ἄδουλος· χαμαὶ κοιμῶμαι. οὐ γυνή, οὐ παιδία, οὐ πραιτωρίδιον, ἀλλὰ γῆ μόνον καὶ οὐρανὸς καὶ ἓν τριβωνάριον, καὶ τί μοι λείπει[ν]; οὐκ εἰμι ἄλυπος, οὐκ εἰμι ἄφοβος, οὐκ εἰμι ἐλεύθερος;

1253—Dio Chrysostomus or Dio of Prusa.   Dio of Prusa

Dio of Prusa, a famous sophist and Hellenist in his native city, came to Rome under Domitianus with the most brilliant prospects. But, by the downfall of his friend Flavius Sabinus, he was driven into exile and lost all his property. In his Or. 13, 1 ff., he relates how he was brought to philosophy by these events.

His Orations 6, 8, 9 and 10 are the exposition of a radical Cynicism, with a strong emphasis on ἀναίδεια, αὐτάρκεια and ἄσκησις.

Recalled by Nerva, he returned to Prusa, to be loaded with honours by his own and neighbouring states. He was in high favour with Trajanus. The orations I-IV, Περὶ βασιλείας, were delivered before this emperor in Rome, at the beginning of his reign.

Under this number, we quote some passages in which Dio expounds the old Cynic ideal of παιδεία, the example of which was found in Heracles.

a.   Dio, *Or.* 32, 3 (To the people of Alexandria):   The Cynic
                                                                 ideal of
Νῦν μὲν γὰρ ἁμαρτάνετε τὸ Ἀθηναίων ποτὲ ἁμάρτημα. τοῦ γὰρ Ἀπόλλωνος   Paideia
εἰπόντος, εἰ θέλουσιν ἄνδρας ἀγαθοὺς ἐν τῇ πόλει γενέσθαι, τὸ κάλλιστον
ἐμβάλλειν τοῖς ὠσὶ τῶν παίδων, οἱ δὲ τρήσαντες τὸ ἕτερον χρυσίον ἐνέβαλον,
οὐ συνέντες τοῦ θεοῦ. τοῦτο μὲν γὰρ κόραις μᾶλλον ἔπρεπε καὶ παισὶ Λυδῶν
ἢ Φρυγῶν· Ἑλλήνων δὲ παισί, καὶ ταῦτα θεοῦ προστάξαντος, οὐκ ἄλλο ἥρμοζεν
ἢ παιδεία καὶ λόγος, ὧν οἱ τυχόντες εἰκότως [ἂν] ἄνδρες ἀγαθοὶ γίγνονται καὶ
σωτῆρες τῶν πόλεων.

b.   Cp. Dio, *Or.* 1, 61. Heracles, the "educated" king.

Ἦν δὲ καὶ πεπαιδευμένος ἁπλῶς, οὐ πολυτρόπως οὐδὲ περιττῶς σοφίσμασι καὶ πανουργήμασιν ἀνθρώπων κακοδαιμόνων.

c.   Dio, *Or.* 32, 15-16. Paideia is a gift of the Gods, a help against human folly.

Διὰ γὰρ ἀνθρώπων ἄνοιαν καὶ τρυφὴν καὶ φιλοτιμίαν δυσχερὴς ὁ βίος καὶ μέστος ἀπάτης, πονηρίας, λύπης, μυρίων ἄλλων κακῶν. τούτων δὲ ἓν ἴαμα καὶ φάρμακον ἐποίησαν οἱ θεοὶ παιδείαν καὶ λόγον, ᾧ διὰ βίου μέν τις χρώμενος καὶ συνεχῶς ἦλθέ ποτε πρὸς τέλος ὑγιὲς καὶ εὔδαιμον· — οἱ δὲ διὰ παντὸς ἄπειροι τοῦ φαρμάκου τούτου καὶ μηδέποτε σωφρονοῦντι λόγῳ τὰς ἀκοὰς ὑπέχοντες ὁλοκλήρως ἄθλιοι μηδεμίαν σκέπην μηδὲ προβολὴν ἔχοντες ἀπὸ τῶν παθῶν.

Höistad, o.c., p. 164, concludes that Dio's Or. 32 expounds a genuine Cynic paideia, with its roots in classical Cynicism.

On Dio as a source of our knowledge of older Cynicism see also K. von Fritz, *Diogenes von Sinope*, p. 71-90.

The Cynic King

1254—The following passage shows us the classical Cynic ideal of the king.

a. Dio, *Or*. 1, 14:

Οὐδείς ποτε πονηρὸς καὶ ἀκόλαστος καὶ φιλοχρήματος οὔτε αὐτὸς ἑαυτοῦ γενέσθαι δυνατὸς ἄρχων οὐδ' ἐγκρατὴς οὔτε τῶν ἄλλων οὐδενός, οὐδ' ἔσται ποτὲ ἐκεῖνος βασιλεύς, οὐδ' ἂν πάντες φῶσιν Ἕλληνες καὶ βάρβαροι καὶ ἄνδρες καὶ γυναῖκες, καὶ μὴ μόνον ἄνθρωποι θαυμάζωσιν αὐτὸν καὶ ὑπακούωσιν, ἀλλ' οἵ τε ὄρνιθες πετόμενοι καὶ τὰ θηρία ἐν τοῖς ὄρεσι μηδὲν ἧττον τῶν ἀνθρώπων συγχωρῇ τε καὶ ποιῇ τὸ προσταττόμενον.

b. In the second part of the 3rd discourse, however, Dio's description of the basileus is strongly influenced by the Stoic conception of Zeus-basileus, who is the Governor of the universe. Virtue and vice are considered from the religious point of view. And also the belief in daemons comes in as an essential point.

Dio, *Or*. 3, 51-54:

Τοιοῦτος δ' ὢν πρῶτον μέν ἐστι θεοφιλής, ἅτε τῆς μεγίστης τυγχάνων παρὰ θεῶν τιμῆς καὶ πίστεως. καὶ πρῶτόν γε καὶ μάλιστα θεραπεύσει τὸ θεῖον, οὐχ ὁμολογῶν μόνον, ἀλλὰ καὶ πεπεισμένος εἶναι θεούς, ἵνα δὴ καὶ αὐτὸς ἔχῃ τοὺς κατ' ἀξίαν ἄρχοντας. ἡγεῖται δὲ τοῖς ἄλλοις ἀνθρώποις συμφέρειν τὴν αὐτοῦ πρόνοιαν οὕτως ὡς αὐτῷ τὴν ἐκείνων ἀρχήν. καὶ μὴν ἐκεῖνο ἑαυτῷ συνειδὼς ὡς οὔποτε δῶρον δέξεται παρὰ κακῶν ἀνδρῶν, οὐδὲ τοὺς θεοὺς ἀναθήμασιν οὐδὲ θυσίαις οἴεται χαίρειν τῶν ἀδίκων [ἀνδρῶν], παρὰ μόνων δὲ τῶν ἀγαθῶν προσίεσθαι τὰ δεδομένα. τοιγαροῦν θεραπεύειν ἀφθόνως αὐτοὺς σπουδάσει καὶ τούτοις· ἐκείνοις γε μὴν οὐδέποτε παύσεται τιμῶν, τοῖς καλοῖς ἔργοις καὶ ταῖς δικαίαις πράξεσιν. ἕκαστόν γε μὴν τῶν θεῶν ἱλάσκεται κατὰ [τὴν τοῦ θεοῦ] δύναμιν. ἡγεῖται δὲ τὴν μὲν ἀρετὴν ὁσιότητα, τὴν δὲ κακίαν πᾶσαν ἀσέβειαν. εἶναι γὰρ ἐναγεῖς καὶ ἀλιτηρίους οὐ μόνον τοὺς τὰ ἱερὰ συλῶντας ἢ λέγοντάς τι βλάσφημον περὶ τῶν θεῶν, ἀλλὰ πολὺ μᾶλλον τούς τε δειλοὺς καὶ ἀδίκους καὶ ἀκρατεῖς καὶ ἀνοήτους καὶ καθόλου τοὺς ἐναντίον τι πράττοντας τῇ τε δυνάμει καὶ βουλήσει τῶν θεῶν. οὐ μόνον δὲ ἡγεῖται θεούς, ἀλλὰ καὶ δαίμονας καὶ ἥρωας ἀγαθοὺς τὰς τῶν ἀγαθῶν ἀνδρῶν ψυχὰς μεταβαλούσας ἐκ τῆς θνητῆς φύσεως· τοῦτο δὲ βεβαιοῖ τὸ δόγμα οὐχ ἥκιστα χαριζόμενος αὐτῷ.

On this passage: Höistad o.c., p. 190 ff.

c. More than once the basileus is represented as a solitary, poor and suffering figure, as Heracles often was in ancient Cynic literature.

Dio, *Or.* 9, 8-9 (On Diogenes attending the Isthmian games):

Τινὲς μὲν οὖν αὐτὸν ἐθαύμαζον ὡς σοφώτατον πάντων, τισὶ δὲ μαίνεσθαι ἐδόκει, πολλοὶ δὲ κατεφρόνουν ὡς πτωχοῦ τε καὶ οὐδενὸς ἀξίου, τινὲς δ' ἐλοι-δόρουν, οἱ δὲ προπηλακίζειν ἐπεχείρουν, ὀστᾶ ῥιπτοῦντες πρὸ τῶν ποδῶν, ὥσπερ τοῖς κυσίν, οἱ δὲ καὶ τοῦ τρίβωνος ἥπτοντο προσιόντες, πολλοὶ δὲ οὐκ εἴων, ἀλλ' ἠγανάκτουν, καθάπερ Ὅμηρός φησι τὸν Ὀδυσσέα προσπαίζειν τοὺς μνηστῆρας, κἀκεῖνον πρὸς ὀλίγας ἡμέρας ἐνεγκεῖν τὴν ἀκολασίαν αὐτῶν καὶ τὴν ὕβριν· ὁ δὲ ὅμοιος ἦν ἐν ἅπαντι· τῷ ὄντι γὰρ ἐῴκει βασιλεῖ καὶ δεσπότῃ, πτωχοῦ στολὴν ἔχοντι, κἄπειτα ἐν ἀνδραπόδοις τε καὶ δούλοις αὐτοῦ στρε-φομένῳ τρυφῶσι καὶ ἀγνοοῦσιν ὅστις ἐστί, καὶ ῥᾳδίως φέροντι μεθύοντας ἀνθρώ-πους καὶ μαινομένους ὑπὸ ἀγνοίας καὶ ἀμαθίας.

Cp. also Dio, *Or.* 1, 61-62; *Or.* 47, 4; and Epictetus, *Diss.* III, 26, 32: Heracles, the ruler of all the land and sea, who introduced justice and righteousness every-where, ταῦτα ἐποίει καὶ γυμνὸς καὶ μόνος. Cp. Höistad, *Eine Hellenistische Parallele zu 2 Cor.* 6, 3 ff., Uppsala 1944.

1255—In his Seventh or Euboean discourse, Dio is to us a most precious witness about the life of the working classes in this period.

On the life of the working classes

He says that, on the whole, the poor are not at a disadvantage in comparison with the rich on account of their poverty, so far as living a seemly and natural life is concerned. On the contrary, as to hospitality, the poor are usually much more liberal than the rich.

a. Dio, *Or.* 7, 82:

Καὶ δῆτα καὶ τὸ τοῦ Εὐριπίδου [1] σκοπῶν, εἰ κατ' ἀλήθειαν ἀπόρως αὐτοῖς ἔχει τὰ πρὸς τοὺς ξένους, ὡς μήτε ὑποδέξασθαί ποτε δύνασθαι μήτε ἐπαρκέσαι δεομένῳ τινί, οὐδαμῇ πω τοιοῦτον εὑρίσκω τὸ τῆς ξενίας, ἀλλὰ καὶ πῦρ ἐναύον-τας προθυμότερον τῶν πλουσίων καὶ ὁδῶν ἀπροφασίστους ἡγεμόνας· ἐπεί τοι τὰ τοιαῦτα καὶ αἰσχύνοιντο ἄν· πολλάκις δὲ καὶ μεταδιδόντας ὧν ἔχουσιν ἑτοιμότερον· οὐ γὰρ δὴ ναυαγῷ τις δώσει ἐκείνων οὔτε τὸ τῆς γυναικὸς ἁλουργὲς

[1] The reference is to *Electra* 424 f., where the farmer says:
Ἔστιν δὲ δὴ τοσαῦτά γ' ἐν δόμοις ἔτι,
ὥσθ' ἕν γ' ἐπ' ἦμαρ τούσδε πληρῶσαι βορᾶς.

ἢ τὸ τῆς θυγατρὸς οὔτε πολὺ ἧττον τούτου φόρημα, τῶν χλαινῶν τινα ἢ χιτώνων, μυρία ἔχοντες, ἀλλ᾽ οὐδὲ τῶν οἰκετῶν οὐδενὸς ἱμάτιον.

b. For the poor in cities, however, it may be difficult to find a living.

Ib., 105-106:

Μήποτε σπάνια ᾖ τὰ ἐν ταῖς πόλεσιν ἔργα τοῖς τοιούτοις, ἀφορμῆς τε ἔξωθεν προσδεόμενα, ὅταν οἰκεῖν τε μισθοῦ δέῃ [1] καὶ τἄλλ᾽ ἔχειν ὠνουμένους, οὐ μόνον ἱμάτια καὶ σκεύη καὶ σῖτον, ἀλλὰ καὶ ξύλα, τῆς γε καθ᾽ ἡμέραν χρείας ἕνεκα τοῦ πυρός, κἂν φρυγάνων δέῃ ποτὲ ἢ φύλλων ἢ ἄλλου ὁτουοῦν τῶν πάνυ φαύλων, δίχα δὲ ὕδατος τὰ ἄλλα σύμπαντα ἀναγκάζωνται λαμβάνειν τιμὴν κατατιθέντες, ἅτε πάντων κατακλειομένων καὶ μηδενὸς ἐν μέσῳ φαινομένου, πλήν γε οἶμαι τῶν ἐπὶ πράσει, πολλῶν καὶ τιμίων. τάχα γὰρ φανεῖται χαλεπὸν τοιούτῳ βίῳ διαρκεῖν μηδὲν ἄλλο κτῆμα ἔξω τοῦ σώματος κεκτημένους, ἄλλως τε ὅταν μὴ τὸ τυχὸν ἔργον μηδὲ πάνθ᾽ ὁμοίως συμβουλεύωμεν αὐτοῖς, ὅθεν ἔστι κερδᾶναι.

c. Dio urges people to undertake any honest occupation without hesitation, and pay no heed to the sneers of idle objectors.

Ib. 114-115:

. . . θαρροῦντας ἐπιχειρεῖν κελεύομεν (sc. every kind of honest occupations), μηδὲν φροντίζοντας τῶν ἄλλως τὰ τοιαῦτα προφερόντων, οἷον εἰώθασι λοιδορούμενοι προφέρειν πολλάκις οὐ μόνον τὰς αὑτῶν ἐργασίας, αἷς οὐδὲν ἄτοπον πρόσεστιν, ἀλλὰ καὶ τῶν γονέων, ἄν τινος ἔριθος ἡ μήτηρ ἢ τρυγήτρια ἐξελθοῦσά ποτε ἢ μισθοῦ τιτθεύσῃ παῖδα τῶν ὀρφανῶν ἢ πλουσίων ἢ ὁ πατὴρ διδάξῃ γράμματα ἢ παιδαγωγήσῃ· μηδὲν οὖν τοιοῦτον αἰσχυνομένους ὁμόσε ἰέναι. οὐ γὰρ ἄλλως αὐτὰ ἐροῦσιν, ἂν λέγωσιν, ἢ ὡς σημεῖα πενίας, πενίαν αὐτὴν λοιδοροῦντες δῆλον ὅτι καὶ προφέροντες ὡς κακὸν δή τι καὶ δυστυχές, οὐ τῶν ἔργων οὐδέν. ὥστε ἐπειδὴ οὔ φαμεν χεῖρον οὐδὲ δυστυχέστερον πλούτου πενίαν, οὐδὲ πολλοῖς ἴσως ἀξυμφορώτερον, οὐδὲ τὸ ὄνειδος τοῦ ὀνείδους μᾶλλόν τι βαρυντέον τοῦτ᾽ ἐκείνου.

This passage shows a striking difference from the traditional view, e.g. Cicero's distinction between "vulgar" and "liberal" occupations, *De off.* I, ch. 42.

1256—In the second century, there were numerous Cynics, both in Rome and Alexandria, in Asia and Greece. The κυνικὸς βίος did not imply adherence to a theoretically developed system of philosophy.

The vulgar kind of Cynics
Of the kind of charlatans found among them a vivid picture is given in Lucianus' *Fugitivi*.

---

[1] Gen. pretii.

a. Lucianus, *Fugitivi* 3-4; 16:

While, on Olympus, Zeus and Apollo are discussing the death of Peregrinus, who burnt himself to death near Olympia, Philosophy enters in great trouble, weeping and complaining of how she has been treated on earth. Zeus speaks:

Τί, ὦ θύγατερ, δακρύεις; ἢ τί ἀπολιποῦσα τὸν βίον ἐλήλυθας; ἆρα μὴ οἱ ἰδιῶται αὖθις ἐπιβεβουλεύκασί σοι ὡς τὸ πρόσθεν, ὅτε τὸν Σωκράτην ἀπέκτειναν ὑπὸ Ἀνύτου κατηγορηθέντα, εἶτα φεύγεις διὰ τοῦτο αὐτούς;

ΦΙΛΟΣΟΦΙΑ. Οὐδὲν τοιοῦτον, ὦ πάτερ, ἀλλ᾽ ἐκεῖνοι μὲν ὁ πολὺς λεὼς ἐπήνουν καὶ διὰ τιμῆς ἦγον αἰδούμενοι καὶ θαυμάζοντές με καὶ μονονουχὶ προσκυνοῦντες, εἰ καὶ μὴ σφόδρα συνίεσαν ὧν λέγοιμι. οἱ δὲ πῶς ἂν εἴποιμι, οἱ συνήθεις καὶ φίλοι φάσκοντες εἶναι καὶ τοὔνομα τοὐμὸν ὑποδυόμενοι, ἐκεῖνοί με τὰ δεινότατα εἰργάσαντο.

ΖΕΥΣ. Οἱ φιλόσοφοι ἐπιβουλήν τινα ἐπιβεβουλεύκασί σοι;

ΦΙΛ. Οὐδαμῶς, ὦ πάτερ, οἵ γε συνηδίκηνταί μοι καὶ αὐτοί.

ΖΕΥΣ. Πρὸς τίνων οὖν ἠδίκησαι, εἰ μήτε τοὺς ἰδιώτας μήτε τοὺς φιλοσόφους αἰτιᾷ;

ΦΙΛ. Εἰσί τινες, ὦ Ζεῦ, ἐν μεταιχμίῳ τῶν τε πολλῶν καὶ τῶν φιλοσοφούντων, τὸ μὲν σχῆμα καὶ βλέμμα καὶ βάδισμα ἡμῖν ὅμοιοι καὶ κατὰ τὰ αὐτὰ ἐσταλμένοι· ἀξιοῦσι γοῦν ὑπ᾽ ἐμοὶ τάττεσθαι καὶ τοὔνομα τὸ ἡμέτερον ἐπιγράφονται, μαθηταὶ καὶ ὁμιληταὶ καὶ θιασῶται ἡμῶν εἶναι λέγοντες· ὁ βίος δὲ παμμίαρος αὐτῶν, ἀμαθίας καὶ θράσους καὶ ἀσελγείας ἀνάπλεως, ὕβρις οὐ μικρὰ καθ᾽ ἡμῶν· ὑπὸ τούτων, ὦ πάτερ, ἠδικημένη πέφευγα.

These vulgar and ignorant people take advantage of the profound respect which the average man usually shows towards the philosopher.

Τοιγαροῦν ἐμπέπλησται πᾶσα ἡ πόλις τῆς τοιαύτης ῥᾳδιουργίας, καὶ μάλιστα τῶν Διογένην καὶ Ἀντισθένην καὶ Κράτητα ἐπιγραφομένων καὶ ὑπὸ τῷ κυνὶ ταττομένων, οἳ τὸ μὲν χρήσιμον ὁπόσον ἔνεστι τῇ φύσει τῶν κυνῶν, οἷον τὸ φυλακτικὸν ἢ οἰκουρικὸν ἢ φιλοδέσποτον ἢ μνημονικὸν οὐδαμῶς ἐζηλώκασιν, ὑλακὴν δὲ καὶ λιχνείαν καὶ ἁρπαγὴν καὶ ἀφροδίσια συχνὰ καὶ κολακείαν καὶ τὸ σαίνειν τὸν διδόντα καὶ περὶ τραπέζας ἔχειν, ταῦτα ἀκριβῶς ἐκπεπονήκασιν.

b. As to Peregrinus, we have sufficient evidence to conclude that Lucianus **Peregrinus** presents a distorted picture. Gellius visited the man frequently and calls him *virum gravem atque constantem* (*N.A.* 8, 3). His death by fire was to be an example of endurance, like that of the Brahmani.

Literature:
J. Bernays, *Lukian u. die Kyniker*, Berlin 1879.
M. Caster, *Lucien et la pensée religieuse de son temps*, Paris 1937.
   On Peregrinus:
H. M. Hornsby, *The Cynicism of Peregrinus Proteus*, in *Hermathena* 1933.
Dudley, *History of Cynicism*, pp. 170-182.

Demonax.
His life and
character
1257—Lucianus describes the life and character of Demonax as follows.

a. Lucianus, *Demonax* 3:

Ἦν δὲ τὸ μὲν γένος Κύπριος, οὐ τῶν ἀφανῶν ὅσα εἰς ἀξίωμα πολιτικὸν καὶ κτῆσιν. οὐ μὴν ἀλλὰ καὶ πάντων τούτων ὑπεράνω γενόμενος καὶ ἀξιώσας ἑαυτὸν τῶν καλλίστων πρὸς φιλοσοφίαν ὥρμησεν οὐκ Ἀγαθοβούλου [1] μὰ Δί' οὐδὲ Δημητρίου πρὸ αὐτοῦ οὐδὲ Ἐπικτήτου ἐπεγειράντων, ἀλλὰ πᾶσι μὲν συνεγένετο τούτοις καὶ ἔτι Τιμοκράτει τῷ Ἡρακλεώτῃ, σοφῷ ἀνδρὶ φωνήν τε καὶ γνώμην μάλιστα κεκοσμημένῳ. ἀλλ' ὅ γε Δημῶναξ οὐχ ὑπὸ τούτων τινός, ὡς ἔφην, παρακληθείς, ἀλλ' ὑπ' οἰκείας πρὸς τὰ καλὰ ὁρμῆς καὶ ἐμφύτου πρὸς φιλοσοφίαν ἔρωτος ἐκ παίδων εὐθὺς κεκινημένος ὑπερεῖδε μὲν τῶν ἀνθρωπείων ἀγαθῶν ἁπάντων, ὅλον δὲ παραδοὺς ἑαυτὸν ἐλευθερίᾳ καὶ παρρησίᾳ διετέλεσεν αὐτός τε ὀρθῷ καὶ ὑγιεῖ καὶ ἀνεπιλήπτῳ βίῳ χρώμενος καὶ τοῖς ὁρῶσι καὶ ἀκούουσι παράδειγμα παρέχων τὴν ἑαυτοῦ γνώμην καὶ τὴν ἐν τῷ φιλοσοφεῖν ἀλήθειαν.

b. He was gentle in his behaviour towards other people.

Ib. 7:

Οὐδεπώποτε γοῦν ὤφθη κεκραγὼς ἢ ὑπερδιατεινόμενος ἢ ἀγανακτῶν, οὐδ' εἰ ἐπιτιμᾶν τῳ δέοι, ἀλλὰ τῶν μὲν ἁμαρτημάτων καθήπτετο, τοῖς δὲ ἁμαρτάνουσι συνεγίγνωσκε, καὶ τὸ παράδειγμα παρὰ τῶν ἰατρῶν ἠξίου λαμβάνειν τὰ μὲν νοσήματα ἰωμένων, ὀργῇ δὲ πρὸς τοὺς νοσοῦντας οὐ χρωμένων· ἡγεῖτο γὰρ ἀνθρώπου μὲν εἶναι τὸ ἁμαρτάνειν, θεοῦ δὲ ἢ ἀνδρὸς ἰσοθέου τὰ πταισθέντα ἐπανορθοῦν.

c. He calmed the excited, comforted the suffering and made peace between those who quarrelled.

Ib. 8-9:

Καὶ τοὺς μὲν εὐτυχεῖν δοκοῦντας αὐτῶν ὑπεμίμνησκεν ὡς ἐπ' ὀλιγοχρονίοις τοῖς δοκοῦσιν ἀγαθοῖς ἐπαιρομένους, τοὺς δὲ ἢ πενίαν ὀδυρομένους ἢ φυγὴν δυσχεραίνοντας ἢ γῆρας ἢ νόσον αἰτιωμένους σὺν γέλωτι παρεμυθεῖτο, οὐχ ὁρῶντας ὅτι μετὰ μικρὸν αὐτοῖς παύσεται μὲν τὰ ἀνιῶντα, λήθη δέ τις ἀγαθῶν καὶ κακῶν καὶ ἐλευθερία μακρὰ πάντας ἐν ὀλίγῳ καταλήψεται. ἔμελε δ' αὐτῷ καὶ ἀδελφοὺς στασιάζοντας διαλλάττειν καὶ γυναιξὶ πρὸς τοὺς γεγαμηκότας εἰρήνην πρυτανεύειν.

---

[1] Agathoboulos must have been a prominent Cynic in the first half of the second century. He is mentioned as the teacher both of Demonax and of Peregrinus.

d. He did all these things gracefully and with humour.

Ib. 10:

Καὶ πάντα ταῦτα μετὰ Χαρίτων καὶ Ἀφροδίτης αὐτῆς ἔπραττέ τε καὶ ἔλεγεν, ὡς ἀεί, τὸ κωμικὸν ἐκεῖνο, τὴν πειθὼ τοῖς χείλεσιν αὐτοῦ ἐπικαθῆσθαι.

1258—a. Lucianus, *Demonax* 21:

Περεγρίνου δὲ τοῦ Πρωτέως [1] ἐπιτιμῶντος αὐτῷ ὅτι ἐγέλα τὰ πολλὰ καὶ τοῖς ἀνθρώποις προσέπαιζε, καὶ λέγοντος, "Δημῶναξ, οὐ κυνᾷς", ἀπεκρίνατο, "Περεγρῖνε, οὐκ ἀνθρωπίζεις."

Demonax and Peregrinus

b. Ib. 28:

Ἰδὼν δέ ποτε δύο τινὰς φιλοσόφους κομιδῇ ἀπαιδεύτως ἐν ζητήσει ἐρίζοντας καὶ τὸν μὲν ἄτοπα ἐρωτῶντα, τὸν δὲ οὐδὲν πρὸς λόγον ἀποκρινόμενον, "οὐ δοκεῖ ὑμῖν", ἔφη, "ὦ φίλοι, ὁ μὲν ἕτερος τούτων τράγον ἀμέλγειν, ὁ δὲ αὐτῷ κόσκινον ὑποτιθέναι;"

Demonax on a philosophi-cal dispute

1259—During the last years of his life and after his death, at Athens he was worshipped as a saint.

a. Lucianus, *Demonax* 63:

Ἐβίω δὲ ἔτη ὀλίγου δέοντα τῶν ἑκατὸν ἄνοσος, ἄλυπος, οὐδένα ἐνοχλήσας τι ἢ αἰτήσας, φίλοις χρήσιμος, ἐχθρὸν οὐδένα οὐδεπώποτε ἐσχηκώς· καὶ τοσοῦτον ἔρωτα ἔσχον πρὸς αὐτὸν Ἀθηναῖοί τε αὐτοὶ καὶ ἅπασα ἡ Ἑλλάς, ὥστε παριόντι ὑπεξανίστασθαι μὲν τοὺς ἄρχοντας, σιωπὴν δὲ γίγνεσθαι παρὰ πάντων. τὸ τελευταῖον δὲ ἤδη ὑπέργηρως ὢν ἄκλητος εἰς ἣν τύχοι παριὼν οἰκίαν ἐδείπνει καὶ ἐκάθευδε, τῶν ἐνοικούντων θεοῦ τινα ἐπιφάνειαν ἡγουμένων τὸ πρᾶγμα καί τινα ἀγαθὸν δαίμονα εἰσεληλυθέναι αὐτοῖς ἐς τὴν οἰκίαν. παριόντα δὲ αἱ ἀρτοπώλιδες ἀνθεῖλκον πρὸς αὐτὰς ἑκάστη ἀξιοῦσα παρ' αὐτῆς λαμβάνειν τῶν ἄρτων, καὶ τοῦτο εὐτυχίαν ἑαυτῆς ἡ δεδωκυῖα ᾤετο. καὶ μὴν καὶ οἱ παῖδες ὀπώρας προσέφερον αὐτῷ πατέρα ὀνομάζοντες.

Demonax in old age

b. Ib. 65:

Ὅτε δὲ συνῆκεν οὐκέθ' οἷός τε ὢν αὑτῷ ἐπικουρεῖν, . . . πάντων ἀποσχόμενος ἀπῆλθε τοῦ βίου φαιδρὸς καὶ οἷος ἀεὶ τοῖς ἐντυγχάνουσιν ἐφαίνετο.

His death

c. Ib. 67:

Οἱ μέντοι Ἀθηναῖοι καὶ ἔθαψαν αὐτὸν δημοσίᾳ μεγαλοπρεπῶς καὶ ἐπὶ πολὺ ἐπένθησαν καὶ τὸν θᾶκον τὸν λίθινον, ἐφ' οὗ εἰώθει ὁπότε κάμνοι ἀναπαύεσθαι, προσεκύνουν καὶ ἐστεφάνουν ἐς τιμὴν τοῦ ἀνδρός, ἡγούμενοι ἱερὸν εἶναι καὶ τὸν λίθον ἐφ' οὗ ἐκαθέζετο.

A kind of saint worship

---

[1] Peregrinus called himself by this name after the Homeric Proteus: ἅπαντα γὰρ δόξης ἕνεκα γενόμενος καὶ μυρίας τροπὰς τραπόμενος τὰ τελευταῖα ταῦτα καὶ πῦρ ἐγένετο (Lucian., *De morte Peregrini* 1).

1260—Other second century Cynics.

Oenomaus of Gadara
a. *Oenomaus of Gadara* probably lived under Hadrian. Julian cites his work κατὰ τῶν χρηστηρίων. Eusebius, *Praep. ev.*, quotes passages of his Γοήτων φωρά (*The Charlatans exposed*). His criticism of oracles is most interesting. Dudley, p. 162-170.

Favorinus
b. Of *Favorinus*, who lived in Rome under Hadrian and for some time was exiled, a speech Περὶ φυγῆς has been found on papyrus (P. Vat. 11). He is influenced by Epictetus and by Dio. The Orations 37 and 64 under Dio's name have been ascribed to Favorinus with great probability. Dudley, p. 199 f.; B. Häsle, *Favorin über die Verbannung*, Thesis Berlin 1935.

Maximus of Tyrus
c. *Maximus of Tyrus*, second half of the second century, in his 36th discourse discusses the question as to whether the Cynic life is a προηγμένον and decides the point in the affirmative. In his Διαλέξεις Plato is frequently cited. We shall have a word to say of him in dealing with Prae-neoplatonism.

Influence on Christian authors
d. Of ecclesiastical authors, *S. Gregory of Nazianzus* had great sympathy for Cynicism. His works show a strong influence by the diatribe. The same can be said of the sermons of *Asterius*, bishop of Amasea (Pontus), c. 400 (Migne, P. Gr. 40).

See: A. Bretz, *Studien u. Texte zu Asterios von Amasea*, Leipzig 1914, in Harnack & Schmidt, Texte u. Untersuchungen XL. Bd., p. 46-55. Dudley, p. 207.

Sallustius
1261—The last Cynic was Sallustius, second half of the fifth century.

He came from Syria, was taught rhetoric and sophistic at Emesa, and later studied philosophy at Athens and Alexandria. He lived in a very ascetic style.

Suidas s.v. Σαλούστιος (III):

Δαμάσκιός φησι· Οὗτος εἰς ᾿Αλεξάνδρειαν ἧκεν ᾿Αθήνηθεν σὺν ᾿Ισιδώρῳ τῷ φιλοσόφῳ [1]. Παράδοξος δὲ ὁ τρόπος Σαλουστίου πᾶσιν ἀνθρώποις, τὰ μὲν φιλοσοφοῦντος ἐπὶ τὸ καρτερώτερον, τὰ δὲ παίζοντος ἐπὶ τὸ γελοιότερον· ἑκάτερον, οἶμαι, πέρα τοῦ μετρίου.

See further: Asmus, *Der Kyniker Sallustios bei Damascios*, in *Neue Jahrb.* XXV (1910), pp. 504-522.
Dudley, 207 ff.

8—MARCUS AURELIUS

Marcus Aurelius. His Stoicism and his individual problems
1262—The emperor Marcus Aurelius has left us the book of his Meditations, written during his campaign in Dacia.

Like Epictetus, Marcus is dominated by the idea of the freedom of the inner man. In his view of man, however, *social obligations* are the most prominent feature and receive a very strong emphasis. They are rooted in the Stoic view of the universe, in which we find Posidonius' idea of the organical Whole united with a certain spiritualism: νοῦς or νοερὰ ψυχή, which is related to νοῦς.

The love of our fellow-men is the natural and most binding consequence of this principle. Marcus' personal problems are here: (1) in the moral obligation

---

[1] Probably Marinus' successor in the School of Proclus is meant. If this is true, Sall. the Cynic cannot be identified with Julian's friend, the author of the Π. θεῶν καὶ κόσμου (infra, nr. **1454f**).

of loving men and being kind to them, while on the other hand, in practice, they are usually not lovable, and even very irritating; (2) in the very keen sense of the transience and futility of all things, and on the other hand, the importance of our task in the community.

a. Marc. Aur. II 1:

Man and his
social task

Ἕωθεν προλέγειν ἑαυτῷ· συντεύξομαι περιέργῳ, ἀχαρίστῳ, ὑβριστῇ, δολερῷ, βασκάνῳ, ἀκοινωνήτῳ· πάντα ταῦτα συμβέβηκεν ἐκείνοις παρὰ τὴν ἄγνοιαν τῶν ἀγαθῶν καὶ κακῶν. ἐγὼ δὲ τεθεωρηκὼς τὴν φύσιν τοῦ ἀγαθοῦ ὅτι καλὸν καὶ τοῦ κακοῦ ὅτι αἰσχρὸν καὶ τὴν αὐτοῦ τοῦ ἁμαρτάνοντος φύσιν ὅτι μοι συγγενής οὐχὶ αἵματος ἢ σπέρματος τοῦ αὐτοῦ, ἀλλὰ νοῦ καὶ θείας ἀπομοίρας μέτοχος, οὔτε βλαβῆναι ὑπό τινος αὐτῶν δύναμαι· αἰσχρῷ γάρ με οὐδεὶς περιβαλεῖ· οὔτε ὀργίζεσθαι τῷ συγγενεῖ δύναμαι οὔτε ἀπέχθεσθαι αὐτῷ. γεγόναμεν γὰρ πρὸς συνεργίαν, ὡς πόδες, ὡς χεῖρες, ὡς βλέφαρα, ὡς οἱ στοῖχοι τῶν ἄνω καὶ κάτω ὀδόντων. τὸ οὖν ἀντιπράσσειν ἀλλήλοις παρὰ φύσιν· ἀντιπρακτικὸν δὲ τὸ ἀγανακτεῖν καὶ ἀποστρέφεσθαι.

b. Ib. VII 55:

Μὴ περιβλέπου ἀλλότρια ἡγεμονικά, ἀλλ' ἐκεῖ βλέπε κατ' εὐθύ, ἐπὶ τί σε ἡ φύσις ὁδηγεῖ ἥ τε τοῦ ὅλου διὰ τῶν συμβαινόντων σοι καὶ ἡ σὴ διὰ τῶν πρακτέων ὑπὸ σοῦ. πρακτέον δὲ ἑκάστῳ τὸ ἑξῆς τῇ κατασκευῇ· κατεσκεύασται δὲ τὰ μὲν λοιπὰ τῶν λογικῶν ἕνεκεν καὶ ἐπὶ παντὸς ἄλλου τὰ χείρω τῶν κρειττόνων ἕνεκεν, τὰ δὲ λογικὰ ἀλλήλων ἕνεκεν. τὸ μὲν οὖν προηγούμενον ἐν τῇ τοῦ ἀνθρώπου κατασκευῇ τὸ κοινωνικόν ἐστι· δεύτερον δὲ τὸ ἀνένδοτον πρὸς τὰς σωματικὰς πείσεις· λογικῆς γὰρ καὶ νοερᾶς κινήσεως ἴδιον περιορίζειν ἑαυτὴν καὶ μήποτε ἡττᾶσθαι μήτε αἰσθητικῆς μήτε ὁρμητικῆς κινήσεως· ζωώδεις γὰρ ἑκάτεραι, ἡ δὲ νοερὰ ἐθέλει πρωτιστεύειν καὶ μὴ κατακρατεῖσθαι ὑπ' ἐκείνων.

c. Ib. VIII 7:

Ἀρκεῖται πᾶσα φύσις ἑαυτῇ εὐοδούσῃ· φύσις δὲ λογικὴ εὐοδεῖ ἐν μὲν φαντασίαις μήτε ψευδεῖ μήτε ἀδήλῳ συγκατατιθεμένη, τὰς ὁρμὰς δὲ ἐπὶ τὰ κοινωνικὰ ἔργα μόνα ἀπευθύνουσα, τὰς ὀρέξεις δὲ καὶ τὰς ἐκκλίσεις τῶν ἐφ' ἡμῖν μόνων πεποιημένη, τὸ δὲ ὑπὸ τῆς κοινῆς φύσεως ἀπονεμόμενον πᾶν ἀσπαζομένη. μέρος γὰρ αὐτῆς ἐστιν, ὡς ἡ τοῦ φύλλου φύσις τῆς τοῦ φυτοῦ φύσεως· πλὴν ὅτι ἐκεῖ μὲν ἡ τοῦ φύλλου φύσις μέρος ἐστὶ φύσεως καὶ ἀναισθήτου καὶ ἀλόγου καὶ ἐμποδίζεσθαι δυναμένης, ἡ δὲ τοῦ ἀνθρώπου φύσις μέρος ἐστὶν ἀνεμποδίστου φύσεως καὶ νοερᾶς καὶ δικαίας.

d. That indeed he found some difficulty in enduring the characters of his fellow-men, may be seen in a sentence such as the following.

V 10, 4:

Μετὰ τοῦτο[1] ἔπιθι ἐπὶ τὰ τῶν συμβιούντων ἤθη, ὧν μόλις ἐστὶ καὶ τοῦ χαριεστάτου ἀνασχέσθαι, ἵνα μὴ λέγω, ὅτι καὶ ἑαυτόν τις μόγις ὑπομένει.

e. Or also in V 33, 6:

Περιμενεῖς ἵλεως τὴν εἴτε σβέσιν εἴτε μετάστασιν. ἕως δὲ ἐκείνης ὁ καιρὸς ἐφίσταται, τί ἀρκεῖ; τί δ᾽ ἄλλο ἢ θεοὺς μὲν σέβειν καὶ εὐφημεῖν, ἀνθρώπους δὲ εὖ ποιεῖν καὶ ἀνέχεσθαι αὐτῶν καὶ ἀπέχεσθαι[2]; —

Independence of the hegemonikon

1263—The hegemonikón cannot be disturbed by anything, unless it be disturbed by itself.

a. Marc. Aur. VII 16, 4:

Ἀπροσδεές ἐστιν, ὅσον ἐφ᾽ ἑαυτῷ, τὸ ἡγεμονικόν, ἐὰν μὴ ἑαυτῷ ἔνδειαν ποιῇ, κατὰ ταὐτὰ δὲ καὶ ἀτάραχον καὶ ἀνεμπόδιστον, ἐὰν μὴ ἑαυτὸ ταράσσῃ καὶ ἐμποδίζῃ.

b. The hegemonikón can make itself whatever it wills.

Ib. VI 8:

Τὸ ἡγεμονικόν ἐστι τὸ ἑαυτὸ ἐγεῖρον καὶ τρέπον καὶ ποιοῦν μὲν ἑαυτό, οἷον ἂν καὶ θέλῃ, ποιοῦν δὲ ἑαυτῷ φαίνεσθαι πᾶν τὸ συμβαῖνον, οἷον αὐτὸ θέλει.

It is Chrysippus' theory of the hegemonikon πῶς ἔχον that recurs here. It is also found at the end of III 7, where it is said that the one thing we have to mind throughout our lives is: τὸ τὴν διάνοιαν ἔν τινι ἀνοικείῳ νοεροῦ <καὶ> πολιτικοῦ ζῴου τροπῇ γενέσθαι.

c. Cp. V 36, 4: All depends on the inner man.

Ἐγενόμην ποτὲ ὁπουδήποτε καταλειφθεὶς εὔμοιρος ἄνθρωπος· τὸ δὲ εὔμοιρος, ἀγαθὴν μοῖραν σεαυτῷ ἀπονείμας· ἀγαθαὶ δὲ μοῖραι ἀγαθαὶ τροπαὶ ψυχῆς, ἀγαθαὶ ὁρμαί, ἀγαθαὶ πράξεις.

External things cannot hurt us

1264—Outward events, as such, cannot hurt us.

a. Marc. Aurel. VIII 47, 1-3:

Εἰ μὲν διά τι τῶν ἐκτὸς λυπῇ, οὐκ ἐκεῖνό σοι ἐνοχλεῖ, ἀλλὰ τὸ σὸν περὶ αὐτοῦ κρῖμα. τοῦτο δὲ ἤδη ἐξαλεῖψαι ἐπὶ σοί ἐστιν. εἰ δὲ λυπεῖ σέ τι τῶν ἐν τῇ σῇ διαθέσει, τίς ὁ κωλύων διορθῶσαι τὸ δόγμα;

b. Ib., VII 14:

Ὃ θέλει, ἔξωθεν προσπιπτέτω τοῖς παθεῖν ἐκ τῆς προσπτώσεως ταύτης

---

[1] I.e.: after having realized, first, how mysterious all things are and how difficult to understand; next, how transitory and how worthless.

[2] Cp. Epictetus, fr. X Schenkl (= 179 Schw.): according to Favorinus Epict. used to say one should remember these two words: ἀνέχου and ἀπέχου (Gellius, N.A. 17, 19, 6).

δυναμένοις. ἐκεῖνα γάρ, ἐὰν θελήσῃ, μέμψεται τὰ παθόντα, ἐγὼ δέ, ἐὰν μὴ ὑπολάβω, ὅτι κακὸν τὸ συμβεβηκός, οὔπω βέβλαμμαι. ἔξεστι δέ μοι μὴ ὑπολαβεῖν.

c.   IV 7:

Ἆρον τὴν ὑπόληψιν, ἦρται τὸ βέβλαμμαι. ἆρον τὸ βέβλαμμαι, ἦρται ἡ βλάβη.

1265—That which is hidden within us makes the man.   Nous alone
is really ours

a.   X 38:

Μέμνησο ὅτι τὸ νευροσπαστοῦν ἐστιν ἐκεῖνο τὸ ἔνδον ἐγκεκρυμμένον· ἐκεῖνο ῥητορεία, ἐκεῖνο ζωή, ἐκεῖνο, εἰ δεῖ εἰπεῖν, ἄνθρωπος. μηδέποτε συμπεριφαντάζου τὸ περικείμενον ἀγγειῶδες καὶ τὰ ὀργάνια ταῦτα τὰ περιπεπλασμένα. ὅμοια γάρ ἐστι σκεπάρνῳ, μόνον διαφέροντα, καθότι προσφυῆ ἐστιν. ἐπεί τοι οὐ μᾶλλόν τι τούτων ὄφελός ἐστι τῶν μορίων χωρὶς τῆς κινούσης καὶ ἰσχούσης αὐτὰ αἰτίας, ἢ τῆς κερκίδος τῇ ὑφαντρίᾳ καὶ τοῦ καλάμου τῷ γράφοντι καὶ τοῦ μαστιγίου τῷ ἡνιόχῳ.

b.   Cp. XII 3, 1-2:   Σῶμα, ψυχή,
νοῦς

Τρία ἐστίν, ἐξ ὧν συνέστηκας· σωμάτιον, πνευμάτιον, νοῦς. τούτων τἆλλα μέχρι τοῦ ἐπιμελεῖσθαι δεῖν σά ἐστι· τὸ δὲ τρίτον μόνον κυρίως σόν.

The tripartition σῶμα, ψυχή, νοῦς also occurs in III 16, where it is explained as follows: σώματος αἰσθήσεις, ψυχῆς ὁρμαί, νοῦ δόγματα.
Now the first two, man shares with animals. As to the third, it is peculiar to man,—but not only to good men. See further under **1266**.
The distinction between ψυχή and νοῦς was apparently not made by Epictetus. Marcus is congenial to Posidonius, both on this point and on that of cosmic sympathy.

c.   God sees only the spiritual man.

XII 2:

Ὁ θεὸς πάντα τὰ ἡγεμονικὰ γυμνὰ τῶν ὑλικῶν ἀγγείων καὶ φλοιῶν καὶ καθαρμάτων ὁρᾷ· μόνῳ γὰρ τῷ ἑαυτοῦ νοερῷ μόνων ἅπτεται τῶν ἐξ ἑαυτοῦ εἰς ταῦτα ἐρρυηκότων καὶ ἀπωχετευμένων. ἐὰν δὲ καὶ σὺ τοῦτο ἐθίσῃς ποιεῖν, τὸν πολὺν περισπασμὸν σεαυτοῦ περιαιρήσεις. ὁ γὰρ μὴ τὰ περικείμενα κρεάδια ὁρῶν ἢ πού γε ἐσθῆτα καὶ οἰκίαν καὶ δόξαν καὶ τὴν τοιαύτην περιβολὴν καὶ σκηνὴν θεώμενος ἀσχολήσεται;

1266—What is peculiar to the *good* man.

a.   Marcus Aurelius III 16, 2-4:   Keep the
divine genius
within you
pure

Τὸ δὲ νοῦν ἡγεμόνα ἔχειν ἐπὶ τὰ φαινόμενα καθήκοντα καὶ τῶν θεοὺς μὴ νομιζόντων καὶ τῶν τὴν πατρίδα ἐγκαταλειπόντων καὶ τῶν . . . * ποιούντων,

---

*   ὁτιοῦν suppl. Gataker, ποῖ' οὐ Bury.

ἐπειδὰν κλείσωσι τὰς θύρας. εἰ οὖν τὰ λοιπὰ κοινά ἐστι πρὸς τὰ εἰρημένα, λοιπὸν τὸ ἴδιόν ἐστι τοῦ ἀγαθοῦ φιλεῖν μὲν καὶ ἀσπάζεσθαι τὰ συμβαίνοντα καὶ συγκλωθόμενα αὐτῷ· τὸν δὲ ἔνδον ἐν τῷ στήθει ἱδρυμένον δαίμονα μὴ φύρειν μηδὲ θορυβεῖν ὄχλῳ φαντασιῶν, ἀλλὰ ἵλεων διατηρεῖν, κοσμίως ἑπόμενον θεῷ, μήτε φθεγγόμενόν τι παρὰ τὰ ἀληθῆ μήτε ἐνεργοῦντα παρὰ τὰ δίκαια. εἰ δὲ ἀπιστοῦσιν αὐτῷ πάντες ἄνθρωποι, ὅτι ἁπλῶς καὶ αἰδημόνως καὶ εὐθύμως βιοῖ, οὔτε χαλεπαίνει τινὶ τούτων οὔτε παρατρέπεται τῆς ὁδοῦ τῆς ἀγούσης ἐπὶ τὸ τέλος τοῦ βίου, ἐφ᾽ ὃ δεῖ ἐλθεῖν καθαρόν, ἡσύχιον, εὔλυτον, ἀβιάστως τῇ ἑαυτοῦ μοίρᾳ συνηρμοσμένον.

Also in II 17 he speaks of τηρεῖν τὸν ἔνδον δαίμονα ἀνύβριστον καὶ ἀσινῆ. See **1275b**. In III 4, 4 he calls it "that which is enthroned within (us)", and hence, calls the good man "a kind of priest and minister of the gods", χρώμενος καὶ τῷ ἔνδον ἱδρυμένῳ αὐτῷ, ὃ παρέχεται τὸν ἄνθρωπον ἄχραντον ἡδονῶν, κτλ. See under **c**.

b. As a specific feature of the good man the fact that he gladly accepts everything that happens is always mentioned.

IV 33:

Τί οὖν ἐστι, περὶ ὃ δεῖ σπουδὴν εἰσφέρεσθαι; ἐν τοῦτο, διάνοια δικαία καὶ πράξεις κοινωνικαὶ καὶ λόγος, οἷος μηδέποτε διαψεύσασθαι, καὶ διάθεσις ἀσπαζομένη πᾶν τὸ συμβαῖνον, ὡς ἀναγκαῖον, ὡς γνώριμον, ὡς ἀπ᾽ ἀρχῆς τοιαύτης καὶ πηγῆς ῥέον.

c. Thus, the good man is depicted as follows.

III 4, 4:

Ὁ γάρ τοι ἀνὴρ ὁ τοιοῦτος οὐκ ἔτι ὑπερτιθέμενος τὸ ὡς ἐν ἀρίστοις ἤδη εἶναι ἱερεύς τις καὶ ὑπουργὸς θεῶν χρώμενος καὶ τῷ ἔνδον ἱδρυμένῳ αὐτοῦ, ὃ παρέχεται τὸν ἄνθρωπον ἄχραντον ἡδονῶν, ἄτρωτον ὑπὸ παντὸς πόνου, πάσης ὕβρεως ἀνέπαφον, πάσης ἀναίσθητον πονηρίας, ἀθλητὴν ἄθλου τοῦ μεγίστου, τοῦ ὑπὸ μηδενὸς πάθους καταβληθῆναι, δικαιοσύνῃ βεβαμμένον εἰς βάθος, ἀσπαζόμενον μὲν ἐξ ὅλης τῆς ψυχῆς τὰ συμβαίνοντα καὶ ἀπονεμόμενα πάντα, μὴ πολλάκις δὲ μηδὲ χωρὶς μεγάλης καὶ κοινωφελοῦς ἀνάγκης φαντα-ζόμενον, τί ποτε ἄλλος λέγει ἢ πράσσει ἢ διανοεῖται.

Obedience to Nature   **1267**—Obedience to nature, that gives all and may take all back again.

a. Marc. Aur. X 14:

Τῇ πάντα διδούσῃ καὶ ἀπολαμβανούσῃ φύσει ὁ πεπαιδευμένος καὶ αἰδήμων λέγει "δὸς ὃ θέλεις, ἀπόλαβε ὃ θέλεις". λέγει δὲ τοῦτο οὐ καταθρασυνόμενος, ἀλλὰ πειθαρχῶν μόνον καὶ εὐνοῶν αὐτῇ.

Everyone has his function in   **b.** Willingly or unwillingly, we all co-operate in one mighty scheme, governed by a rational Power.

Ib. VI 42:

the scheme
of the
universe

Πάντες εἰς ἓν ἀποτέλεσμα συνεργοῦμεν, οἱ μὲν εἰδότως καὶ παρακολουθητικῶς, οἱ δὲ ἀνεπιστάτως, ὥσπερ καὶ τοὺς καθεύδοντας, οἶμαι, ὁ Ἡράκλειτος ἐργάτας εἶναι λέγει καὶ συνεργοὺς τῶν ἐν τῷ κόσμῳ γινομένων. ἄλλος δὲ κατ' ἄλλο συνεργεῖ, ἐκ περιουσίας δὲ [1] καὶ ὁ μεμφόμενος καὶ ὁ ἀντιβαίνειν πειρώμενος καὶ ἀναιρεῖν τὰ γινόμενα· καὶ γὰρ τοῦ τοιούτου ἔχρῃζεν ὁ κόσμος. λοιπὸν οὖν σύνες, εἰς τίνας ἑαυτὸν κατατάσσεις· ἐκεῖνος μὲν γὰρ πάντως σοι καλῶς χρήσεται ὁ τὰ ὅλα διοικῶν καὶ παραδέξεταί σε εἰς μέρος τι τῶν συνεργῶν καὶ συνεργητικῶν. ἀλλὰ σὺ μὴ τοιοῦτον μέρος γένῃ, οἷος ὁ εὐτελὴς καὶ γελοῖος στίχος ἐν τῷ δράματι, οὗ Χρύσιππος μέμνηται [2].

In V 32, the end, he speaks of "the Logos who governs the Whole according to appointed cycles through all eternity" (τὸν δι' ὅλης τῆς οὐσίας διήκοντα λόγον καὶ διὰ παντὸς τοῦ αἰῶνος κατὰ περιόδους τεταγμένας οἰκονομοῦντα τὸ πᾶν.)

1268—The Logos, who governs the universe, is good.

The Logos
is good

    a.   Marc. Aur. VI 1:

Ἡ τῶν ὅλων οὐσία [3] εὐπειθὴς καὶ εὐτρεπής· ὁ δὲ ταύτην διοικῶν λόγος οὐδεμίαν ἐν ἑαυτῷ αἰτίαν ἔχει τοῦ κακοποιεῖν· κακίαν γὰρ οὐκ ἔχει οὐδέ τι κακῶς ποιεῖ οὐδὲ βλάπτεταί τι ὑπ' ἐκείνου. πάντα δὲ κατ' ἐκεῖνον γίνεται καὶ περαίνεται.

    b.   The Logos is "social": He coordinates and subordinates and gives and „social" everything its due.

Ib. V 30:

Ὁ τοῦ ὅλου νοῦς κοινωνικός. πεποίηκε γοῦν τὰ χείρω τῶν κρειττόνων ἕνεκεν καὶ τὰ κρείττω ἀλλήλοις συνήρμοσεν. ὁρᾷς, πῶς ὑπέταξε, συνέταξε καὶ τὸ κατ' ἀξίαν ἀπένειμεν ἑκάστοις καὶ τὰ κρατιστεύοντα εἰς ὁμόνοιαν ἀλλήλων συνήγαγεν.

1269—Repeatedly Marcus posits the dilemma of either atomism or rational World-order. In the first case, life would be senseless, in the latter we can gladly and confidently accept it.

Either
atomism or
rational
world-order

Marc. Aur. VI 10:

Ἤτοι κυκεὼν καὶ ἀντεμπλοκὴ καὶ σκεδασμός, ἢ ἕνωσις καὶ τάξις καὶ πρόνοια. εἰ μὲν οὖν τὰ πρότερα, τί καὶ ἐπιθυμῶ εἰκαίῳ συγκρίματι καὶ φυρμῷ τοιούτῳ ἐνδιατρίβειν; τί δέ μοι καὶ μέλει ἄλλου τινὸς ἢ τοῦ ὅπως ποτὲ αἶα

---

[1] Farquharson: "not in the main intention of his acts, but unwillingly and "as an extra"." Cp. the draught-dog of Cleanthes (above, **944b**).

[2] See Plut., *De comm. not.* 14, p. 1065d (SVF II 1181).

[3] He means apparently the passive aspect of the universe, as opposed to the Logos. Sometimes, Stoics speak of *matter*. Cp. our nrs. **899, 900**.

γίνεσθαι[1]; τί δὲ καὶ ταράσσομαι; ἥξει γὰρ ἐπ' ἐμὲ ὁ σκεδασμός, ὅ τι ἂν ποιῶ. εἰ δὲ θάτερά ἐστιν, σέβω καὶ εὐσταθῶ καὶ θαρρῶ τῷ διοικοῦντι.

The same alternative in XI 18, 2:

Ἄνωθεν δὲ ἔπιθι ἀπὸ τοῦ "εἰ μὴ ἄτομοι, φύσις ἡ τὰ ὅλα διοικοῦσα"· εἰ τοῦτο, τὰ χείρονα τῶν κρειττόνων ἕνεκεν, ταῦτα δὲ ἀλλήλων.

Also in IX 28:

Τὸ δ' ὅλον· εἴτε θεός, εὖ ἔχει πάντα, εἴτε τὸ εἰκῇ, μὴ καὶ σὺ εἰκῇ.

b. In the following passage he mentions three possibilities.

XII 14, 1-4:

Ἤτοι ἀνάγκη εἱμαρμένης καὶ ἀπαράβατος τάξις ἢ πρόνοια ἱλάσιμος ἢ φυρμὸς εἰκαιότητος ἀπροστάτητος. εἰ μὲν οὖν ἀπαράβατος ἀνάγκη, τί ἀντιτείνεις; εἰ δὲ πρόνοια ἐπιδεχομένη τὸ ἱλάσκεσθαι, ἄξιον σαυτὸν ποίησον τῆς ἐκ τοῦ θείου βοηθείας. εἰ δὲ φυρμὸς ἀνηγεμόνευτος, ἀσμένιζε, ὅτι ἐν τοιούτῳ τῷ κλύδωνι αὐτὸς ἔχεις ἐν σαυτῷ τινα νοῦν ἡγεμονικόν.

The first two possibilities evidently are compatible with a rational world-order. As to the last, Marcus does not admit this as a true possibility. He makes a firm choice of the first, in favour of the existence of Gods and of Providence.

The Gods and Providence

c. Cp. II 11, 2-3:

Τὸ δὲ ἐξ ἀνθρώπων ἀπελθεῖν, εἰ μὲν θεοί εἰσιν, οὐδὲν δεινόν· κακῷ γάρ σε οὐκ ἂν περιβάλοιεν· εἰ δὲ ἤτοι οὐκ εἰσὶν ἢ οὐ μέλει αὐτοῖς τῶν ἀνθρωπείων, τί μοι ζῆν ἐν κόσμῳ κενῷ θεῶν ἢ προνοίας κενῷ; ἀλλὰ καὶ εἰσὶ καὶ μέλει αὐτοῖς τῶν ἀνθρωπείων.

How to explain imperfection in the universe

1270—Imperfection in the universe explained as chips and shavings in a carpenter's shop.

Marc. Aur. VIII 50:

Σίκυος πικρός· ἄφες. βάτοι ἐν τῇ ὁδῷ· ἔκκλινον. ἀρκεῖ, μὴ προσεπείπῃς "τί δὲ καὶ ἐγένετο ταῦτα ἐν τῷ κόσμῳ;" ἐπεὶ καταγελασθήσῃ ὑπὸ ἀνθρώπου φυσιολόγου, ὡς ἂν καὶ ὑπὸ τέκτονος καὶ σκυτέως γελασθείης καταγινώσκων ὅτι ἐν τῷ ἐργαστηρίῳ ξέσματα καὶ περιτμήματα τῶν κατασκευαζομένων ὁρᾷς. καίτοι ἐκεῖνοί γε ἔχουσι ποῦ αὐτὰ ῥίψωσιν· ἡ δὲ τῶν ὅλων φύσιν ἔξω οὐδὲν ἔχει, ἀλλὰ τὸ θαυμαστὸν τῆς τέχνης ταύτης ἐστίν, ὅτι περιορίσασα ἑαυτὴν πᾶν τὸ ἔνδον διαφθείρεσθαι καὶ γηράσκειν καὶ ἄχρηστον εἶναι δοκοῦν εἰς ἑαυτὴν μεταβάλλει καὶ ὅτι πάλιν ἄλλα νεαρὰ ἐκ τούτων αὐτῶν ποιεῖ, ἵνα μήτε οὐσίας ἔξωθεν χρῄζῃ μήτε, ὅπου ἐκβάλῃ τὰ σαπρότερα, προσδέηται. ἀρκεῖται οὖν καὶ χώρᾳ τῇ ἑαυτῆς καὶ ὕλῃ τῇ ἑαυτῆς καὶ τέχνῃ τῇ ἰδίᾳ.

Unity of the cosmos

1271—The organical unity of the cosmos.

a. One substance, one soul, one Spirit (νοερὰ ψυχή) that governs the whole.

---

[1] Hom., Il. 7, 99.

Marc. Aur. XII 30:

Ἕν φῶς ἡλίου, κἂν διείργηται τοίχοις, ὄρεσιν, ἄλλοις μυρίοις. μία οὐσία [1] κοινή, κἂν διείργηται ἰδίως ποιοῖς σώμασι μυρίοις. μία ψυχή, κἂν φύσεσι διείργηται μυρίαις καὶ ἰδίαις περιγραφαῖς. μία νοερὰ ψυχή, κἂν διακεκρίσθαι δοκῇ. τὰ μὲν οὖν ἄλλα μέρη τῶν εἰρημένων, οἷον πνεύματα, καὶ ὑποκείμενα ἀναίσθητα καὶ ἀνοικείωτα ἀλλήλοις· καίτοι κἀκεῖνα τὸ νοοῦν συνέχει καὶ τὸ ἐπὶ τὰ αὐτὰ βρῖθον. διάνοια δὲ ἰδίως ἐπὶ τὸ ὁμόφυλον τείνεται καὶ συνίσταται καὶ οὐ διείργεται τὸ κοινωνικὸν πάθος.

b. Interdependence of all things in the universe.

VI 38:

Πολλάκις ἐνθυμοῦ τὴν ἐπισύνδεσιν πάντων τῶν ἐν τῷ κόσμῳ καὶ σχέσιν πρὸς ἄλληλα. τρόπον γάρ τινα πάντα ἀλλήλοις ἐπιπέπλεκται καὶ πάντα κατὰ τοῦτο φίλα ἀλλήλοις ἐστίν· καὶ γὰρ ἄλλῳ ἄλλο ἑξῆς ἐστι ταῦτα διὰ τὴν τονικὴν κίνησιν καὶ σύμπνοιαν καὶ τὴν ἕνωσιν τῆς οὐσίας.

See also VII 9.

c. What is advantageous to the whole, can never be injurious to the part.

X 6:

Εἴτε ἄτομοι εἴτε φύσις, πρῶτον κείσθω, ὅτι μέρος εἰμὶ τοῦ ὅλου ὑπὸ φύσεως διοικουμένου· ἔπειτα ὅτι ἔχω πως οἰκείως πρὸς τὰ ὁμογενῆ μέρη. τούτων γὰρ μεμνημένος, καθότι μὲν μέρος εἰμί, οὐδενὶ δυσαρεστήσω τῶν ἐκ τοῦ ὅλου ἀπονεμομένων· οὐδὲν γὰρ βλαβερὸν τῷ μέρει, ὃ τῷ ὅλῳ συμφέρει. οὐ γὰρ ἔχει τι τὸ ὅλον, ὃ μὴ συμφέρει ἑαυτῷ· πασῶν μὲν φύσεων κοινὸν ἐχουσῶν τοῦτο, τῆς δὲ τοῦ κόσμου προσειληφυίας τὸ μηδὲ ὑπό τινος ἔξωθεν αἰτίας ἀναγκάζεσθαι βλαβερόν τι ἑαυτῇ γεννᾶν. κατὰ μὲν δὴ τὸ μεμνῆσθαι, ὅτι μέρος εἰμὶ ὅλου τοῦ τοιούτου, εὐαρεστήσω παντὶ τῷ ἀποβαίνοντι. καθόσον δὲ ἔχω πως οἰκείως πρὸς τὰ ὁμογενῆ μέρη, οὐδὲν πράξω ἀκοινώνητον, μᾶλλον δὲ στοχάσομαι τῶν ὁμογενῶν καὶ πρὸς τὸ κοινῇ συμφέρον πᾶσαν ὁρμὴν ἐμαυτοῦ ἄξω καὶ ἀπὸ τοὐναντίου ἀπάξω. τούτων δὲ οὕτω περαινομένων ἀνάγκη τὸν βίον εὐροεῖν, ὡς ἂν καὶ πολίτου βίον εὔρουν ἐπινοήσειας προϊόντος διὰ πράξεων τοῖς πολίταις λυσιτελῶν καί, ὅπερ ἂν ἡ πόλις ἀπονέμῃ, τοῦτο ἀσπαζομένου.

d. Your personal health contributes to the health of the universe and the wellfare of Zeus.

V 8, 8-9, 12-13:

Τοιοῦτόν τί σοι δοκείτω ἄνυσις καὶ συντέλεια τῶν τῇ κοινῇ φύσει δοκούντων,

---

[1] οὐσία is here again used in the sense of ὕλη, as we found it in VI 1 (**1268a**).

οἷον ἡ σὴ ὑγίεια. καὶ οὕτως ἀσπάζου πᾶν τὸ γινόμενον, κἂν ἀπηνέστερον δοκῇ, διὰ τὸ ἐκεῖσε ἄγειν, ἐπὶ τὴν τοῦ κόσμου ὑγίειαν καὶ τὴν τοῦ Διὸς εὐοδίαν καὶ εὐπραγίαν. —

Οὐκοῦν κατὰ δυὸ λόγους στέργειν χρὴ τὸ συμβαῖνόν σοι· καθ᾽ ἕνα μέν, ὅτι σοὶ ἐγίνετο καὶ σοὶ συνετάττετο καὶ πρὸς σέ πως εἶχεν ἄνωθεν ἐκ τῶν πρεσβυτάτων αἰτίων συγκλωθόμενον. καθ᾽ ἕτερον δέ, ὅτι τῷ τὸ ὅλον διοικοῦντι τῆς εὐοδίας καὶ τῆς συντελείας καὶ νὴ Δία τῆς συμμονῆς αὐτῆς καὶ τὸ ἰδίᾳ εἰς ἕκαστον ἧκον αἴτιόν ἐστι. πηροῦται γὰρ τὸ ὁλόκληρον, ἐὰν καὶ ὁτιοῦν διακόψῃς τῆς συναφείας καὶ συνεχείας ὥσπερ τῶν μορίων, οὕτω δὲ καὶ τῶν αἰτίων· διακόπτεις δέ, ὅσον ἐπὶ σοί, ὅταν δυσαρεστῇς, καὶ τρόπον τινὰ ἀναιρεῖς.

Μέλος, not μέρος

1272—a. You are an organical part of the whole, therefore: μέλος, not μέρος.

VII 13:

Οἷόν ἐστιν ἐν ἡνωμένοις τὰ μέλη τοῦ σώματος, τοῦτον ἔχει τὸν λόγον ἐν διεστῶσι τὰ λογικὰ πρὸς μίαν τινὰ συνεργίαν κατεσκευασμένα. μᾶλλον δέ σοι ἡ τούτου νόησις προσπεσεῖται, ἐὰν πρὸς ἑαυτὸν πολλάκις λέγῃς ὅτι "μέλος εἰμὶ τοῦ ἐκ τῶν λογικῶν συστήματος"· ἐὰν δὲ διὰ τοῦ ῥῶ στοιχείου μέρος εἶναι ἑαυτὸν λέγῃς, οὔπω ἀπὸ καρδίας φιλεῖς τοὺς ἀνθρώπους, οὔπω σε καταληπτικῶς εὐφραίνει τὸ εὐεργετεῖν· ἔτι, εἰ ὡς πρέπον αὐτὸ ψίλον ποιεῖς, οὔπω ὡς ἑαυτὸν εὖ ποιῶν.

b. Cp. X 1, 3, where the kosmos is called the τέλειον ζῷον [1].

(He speaks to his soul.)

Συμπείσεις σεαυτήν, ὅτι πάντα, ἅ σοι πάρεστι, παρὰ τῶν θεῶν πάρεστι καὶ πάντα σοι εὖ ἔχει καὶ εὖ ἕξει, ὅσα φίλον αὐτοῖς καὶ ὅσα μέλλουσι δώσειν ἐπὶ σωτηρίᾳ τοῦ τελείου ζῴου, τοῦ ἀγαθοῦ καὶ δικαίου καὶ καλοῦ καὶ γεννῶντος πάντα καὶ συνέχοντος καὶ περιέχοντος καὶ περιλαμβάνοντος διαλυόμενα εἰς γένεσιν ἑτέρων ὁμοίων;

The kosmos renews itself

1273—The universe continually renews itself.

a. VII 23, 25:

(23) Ἡ τῶν ὅλων φύσις ἐκ τῆς ὅλης οὐσίας ὡς κηροῦ νῦν μὲν ἱππάριον ἔπλασε, συγχέασα δὲ τοῦτο εἰς δενδρύφιον συνεχρήσατο τῇ ὕλῃ αὐτοῦ, εἶτα εἰς ἀνθρωπάριον, εἶτα εἰς ἄλλο τι· ἕκαστον δὲ τούτων πρὸς ὀλίγιστον ὑπέστη, δεινὸν δὲ οὐδὲν τὸ διαλυθῆναι τῷ κιβωτίῳ, ὥσπερ οὐδὲ τὸ συμπαγῆναι.

---

[1] Plato, *Tim.* 30b-d; 37d.

(25) Πάντα, ὅσα ὁρᾷς, ὅσον οὔπω μεταβαλεῖ ἡ τὰ ὅλα διοικοῦσα φύσις καὶ ἄλλα ἐκ τῆς οὐσίας αὐτῶν ποιήσει καὶ πάλιν ἄλλα ἐκ τῆς ἐκείνων οὐσίας, ἵνα ἀεὶ νεαρὸς ᾖ ὁ κόσμος.

Cp. also VIII 50, l. 10 (nr. **1270**).

b. V 23:

The stream
of things

Πολλάκις ἐνθυμοῦ τὸ τάχος τῆς παραφορᾶς καὶ ὑπεξαγωγῆς τῶν ὄντων καὶ γινομένων. ἥ τε γὰρ οὐσία οἷον ποταμὸς ἐν διηνεκεῖ ῥύσει καὶ αἱ ἐνέργειαι ἐν συνεχέσι μεταβολαῖς καὶ τὰ αἴτια ἐν μυρίαις τροπαῖς καὶ σχεδὸν οὐδὲν ἑστὼς * καὶ τὸ πάρεγγυς· τὸ δὲ ἄπειρον τοῦ τε παρῳχηκότος καὶ μέλλοντος ἀχανές, ᾧ πάντα ἐναφανίζεται. πῶς οὖν οὐ μωρὸς ὁ ἐν τούτοις φυσώμενος ἢ σπώμενος ἢ σχετλιάζων ὡς ἔν τινι χρόνῳ καὶ ἐπὶ μάκρον ἐνοχλήσαντι;

Cp. also IV 43.

c. Human life is futile compared with eternity.

Human life
compared
with
eternity

IV 50, the end:

Βλέπε γὰρ ὀπίσω τὸ ἀχανὲς τοῦ αἰῶνος καὶ τὸ πρόσω ἄλλο ἄπειρον. ἐν δὴ τούτῳ τί διαφέρει ὁ τριήμερος τοῦ τριγερηνίου;

That the duration of life is of no importance, is a thought frequently expressed in the Emperor's Meditations, e.g. VII 49 (**1274b**).

1274—Things are ever the same, and nothing new can be expected.

Things are
always the
same

a. VI 37:

Ὁ τὰ νῦν ἰδὼν πάντα ἑώρακεν, ὅσα τε ἐξ ἀϊδίου ἐγένετο καὶ ὅσα εἰς τὸ ἄπειρον ἔσται· πάντα γὰρ ὁμογενῆ καὶ ὁμοειδῆ.

With a reminiscence of Heraclitus' ὁδὸς ἄνω κάτω he says in VI 46:

Πάντα γὰρ ἄνω κάτω τὰ αὐτὰ καὶ ἐκ τῶν αὐτῶν. Μέχρι τίνος οὖν;

b. VII 49: The man of 40 years has seen everything:

Τὰ προγεγονότα ἀναθεωρεῖν, τὰς τοσαύτας τῶν ἡγεμονιῶν μεταβολάς. ἔξεστι καὶ τὰ ἐσόμενα προεφορᾶν. ὁμοειδῆ γὰρ πάντως ἔσται καὶ οὐχ οἷόν τ' ἐκβῆναι τοῦ ῥυθμοῦ τῶν νῦν γινομένων· ὅθεν καὶ ἴσον τὸ τεσσαράκοντα ἔτεσιν ἱστορῆσαι τὸν ἀνθρώπινον βίον τῷ ἐπὶ ἔτη μύρια. τί γὰρ πλέον ὄψει;

c. VIII 6:

Ἡ τῶν ὅλων φύσις τοῦτο ἔργον ἔχει, τὰ ὧδε ὄντα ἐκεῖ μετατιθέναι, μεταβάλλειν, αἴρειν ἔνθεν καὶ ἐκεῖ φέρειν. πάντα τροπαί, οὐχ ὥστε φοβηθῆναι, μή τι καινόν· πάντα συνήθη· ἀλλὰ καὶ ἴσαι αἱ ἀπονεμήσεις.

---

* To the following words Schenkl noticed: „vix sana haec; exspectes καὶ ἔτι πάρεγγυς τό τε ἄπειρον τοῦ παρῳχηκότος καὶ <τὸ τοῦ> (sic iam Morus) μέλλοντος ἀχανές."

1275—Vanity of human life.—Yet, man has a great moral task.

a. V 33, 1-3:

Ὅσον οὐδέπω σποδὸς ἢ σκελετὸς καὶ ἤτοι ὄνομα ἢ οὐδὲ ὄνομα· τὸ δὲ ὄνομα
ψόφος καὶ ἀπήχημα. τὰ δὲ ἐν τῷ βίῳ πολυτίμητα κενὰ καὶ σαπρὰ καὶ μικρὰ
καὶ κυνίδια διαδακνόμενα καὶ παιδία φιλόνεικα, γελῶντα, εἶτα εὐθὺς κλαίοντα.
πίστις δὲ καὶ αἰδὼς καὶ δίκη καὶ ἀλήθεια

προς Ὄλυμπον ἀπὸ χθόνος εὐρυοδείης [1].

b. II 17:

Τοῦ ἀνθρωπίνου βίου ὁ μὲν χρόνος στιγμή, ἡ δὲ οὐσία ῥέουσα, ἡ δὲ αἴσθησις
ἀμυδρά, ἡ δὲ ὅλου τοῦ σώματος σύγκρισις εὔσηπτος, ἡ δὲ ψυχὴ ῥόμβος, ἡ δὲ
τύχη δυστέκμαρτον, ἡ δὲ φήμη ἄκριτον· συνελόντι δὲ εἰπεῖν, πάντα τὰ μὲν
τοῦ σώματος ποταμός, τὰ δὲ τῆς ψυχῆς ὄνειρος καὶ τῦφος, ὁ δὲ βίος πόλεμος
καὶ ξένου ἐπιδημία, ἡ δὲ ὑστεροφημία λήθη. τί οὖν τὸ παραπέμψαι δυνάμενον;
ἓν καὶ μόνον φιλοσοφία. τοῦτο δὲ ἐν τῷ τηρεῖν τὸν ἔνδον δαίμονα ἀνύβριστον
καὶ ἀσινῆ, ἡδονῶν καὶ πόνων κρείσσονα, μηδὲν εἰκῆ ποιοῦντα μηδὲ διεψευσμένως
καὶ μεθ' ὑποκρίσεως, ἀνενδεῆ τοῦ ἄλλον ποιῆσαί τι ἢ μὴ ποιῆσαι· ἔτι δὲ τὰ
συμβαίνοντα καὶ ἀπονεμόμενα δεχόμενον ὡς ἐκεῖθέν ποθεν ἐρχόμενα, ὅθεν
αὐτὸς ἦλθεν· ἐπὶ πᾶσι δὲ τὸν θάνατον ἵλεῳ τῇ γνώμῃ περιμένοντα ὡς οὐδὲν
ἄλλο ἢ λύσιν τῶν στοιχείων, ἐξ ὧν ἕκαστον ζῷον συγκρίνεται. εἰ δὲ αὐτοῖς
τοῖς στοιχείοις μηδὲν δεινὸν ἐν τῷ ἕκαστον διηνεκῶς εἰς ἕτερον μεταβάλλειν,
διὰ τί ὑπίδηταί τις τὴν πάντων μεταβολὴν καὶ διάλυσιν; κατὰ φύσιν γάρ·
οὐδὲν δὲ κακὸν κατὰ φύσιν.

One manuscript bears the subscription: Written at *Carnuntum* (Haimburg in
Hungary).

1276—**a.** Military achievements *sub specie aeternitatis*.

X 10:

Ἀράχνιον μυῖαν θηράσαν μέγα φρονεῖ, ἄλλος δὲ λαγίδιον, ἄλλος δὲ ὑποχῇ
ἀφύην, ἄλλος δὲ συΐδια, ἄλλος δὲ ἄρκτους, ἄλλος Σαρμάτας. οὗτοι γὰρ οὐ
λῃσταί, ἐὰν τὰ δόγματα ἐξετάζῃς;

b. The emperor challenges himself to his social task.

Simplicity
and love of
God and man

VI 30:

Ὅρα, μὴ ἀποκαισαρωθῇς, μὴ βαφῇς· γίνεται γάρ. τήρησον οὖν σεαυτὸν
ἁπλοῦν, ἀγαθόν, ἀκέραιον, σεμνόν, ἄκομψον, τοῦ δικαίου φίλον, θεοσεβῆ, εὐμενῆ,
φιλόστοργον, ἐρρωμένον πρὸς τὰ πρέποντα ἔργα. ἀγώνισαι, ἵνα τοιοῦτος συμμεί-

---

[1] Hesiod, *Erga* 197.

νης, οἷόν σε ἠθέλησε ποιῆσαι φιλοσοφία, αἰδοῦ θεούς, σῷζε ἀνθρώπους. βραχὺς ὁ βίος· εἷς κάρπος τῆς ἐπιγείου ζωῆς διάθεσις ὁσία καὶ πράξεις κοινωνικαί.

Cp. also VII 31:

Φαίδρυνον σεαυτὸν ἁπλότητι καὶ αἰδοῖ καὶ τῇ πρὸς τὸ ἀνὰ μέσον ἀρετῆς καὶ κακίας ἀδιαφορίᾳ. φίλησον τὸ ἀνθρώπινον γένος. ἀκολούθησον θεῷ. ἐκεῖνος¹ μέν φησιν, ὅτι "πάντα νομιστί, ἐτεῇ δὲ μόνα τὰ στοιχεῖα". ἀρκεῖ δὲ μεμνῆσθαι, ὅτι τὰ πάντα νομιστὶ ἔχει· ἤδη λίαν ὀλίγα.

1277—Having thus lived a social life, in the service of God and our fellow-men, we can leave it graciously. **The end of life**

a.　XII 36:

Ἄνθρωπε, ἐπολιτεύσω ἐν τῇ μεγάλῃ ταύτῃ πόλει· τί σοι διαφέρει, εἰ πέντε ἔτεσιν <ἢ τρισίν>; τὸ γὰρ κατὰ τοὺς νόμους ἴσον ἑκάστῳ. τί οὖν δεινόν, εἰ τῆς πόλεως ἀποπέμπει σε οὐ τύραννος οὐδὲ δικαστὴς ἄδικος, ἀλλ' ἡ φύσις ἡ εἰσαγαγοῦσα; οἷον εἰ κωμῳδὸν ἀπολύοι τῆς σκηνῆς ὁ παραλαβὼν στρατηγός² "ἀλλ' οὐκ εἶπον τὰ πέντε μέρη, ἀλλὰ τὰ τρία." καλῶς εἶπας· ἐν μέντοι τῷ βίῳ τὰ τρία ὅλον τὸ δρᾶμά ἐστι. τὸ γὰρ τέλειον ἐκεῖνος ὁρίζει ὁ τότε μὲν τῆς συγκρίσεως, νῦν δὲ τῆς διαλύσεως αἴτιος· σὺ δὲ ἀναίτιος ἀμφοτέρων. ἄπιθι οὖν ἵλεως· καὶ γὰρ ὁ ἀπολύων ἵλεως.

The term ἵλεως is repeatedly used by Marcus when speaking of death. E.g. II 17, cited above (nr. **1275b**), and V 33, 5 (**1262e**).

b.　Cp. also IV 48, the end:

Τὸ γὰρ ὅλον, κατιδεῖν ἀεὶ τὰ ἀνθρώπινα ὡς ἐφήμερα καὶ εὐτελῆ καὶ ἐχθὲς μὲν μυξάριον, αὔριον δὲ τάριχος ἢ τέφρα. τὸ ἀκαριαῖον οὖν τοῦτο τοῦ χρόνου κατὰ φύσιν διελθεῖν καὶ ἵλεων καταλῦσαι, ὡς ἂν εἰ ἡ ἐλαία πέπειρος γενομένη ἔπιπτεν εὐφημοῦσα τὴν ἐνεγκοῦσαν καὶ χάριν εἰδυῖα τῷ φύσαντι δένδρῳ.

---

¹ He means Democritus. Cp. above (Vol. I), nr. **142a**.
² στρατηγός - praetor.

BOOK VI

THE THEOLOGICAL AND THEOSOPHICAL SCHOOLS

TWENTY-FOURTH CHAPTER

PRAE-NEOPLATONISM

By Prae-neoplatonism—a term used by W. Theiler, *Die Vorbereitung des Neu-platonismus*, Berlin 1930—we mean that kind of philosophy of synthesis which appears in various forms from the first century B.C. onward. As far as it synthetizes the three great positive systems—Plato, Aristotle and the Stoa—, we found a beginning of it with Antiochus of Ascalon; as far as it is inclined towards a more or less hierarchical conception of the universe, we found a (probable) beginning of it with Posidonius, and further back in the Early Academy. In the first and second century of our era Platonism, explained in a metaphysical-religious sense, prevailed. More or less clearly we find the conception of a hierarchy of being in very different circles, and hence in rather different forms.

1—THE REVIVAL OF PYTHAGOREANISM IN THE FIRST CENTURY B.C. TILL THE SECOND CENTURY OF OUR ERA

Of the school of Pythagoras hardly any traces are found between Aristoxenus and the first century B.C. Since the first part of this century, however, a stream of Pythagorean pseudepigrapha bursts forth [1]. Varro mentions Pythagoreans frequently; he knows Ocellus and Archytas. Cicero mentions P. Nigidius Figulus as the man who restored Pythagoreanism in Rome.

1278—a. Cicero, *Timaeus* I 1:

Multa sunt a nobis et in Academicis conscripta contra physicos et saepe ⟨cum⟩ P. Nigidio Carneadeo more et modo disputata. fuit enim vir ille cum ceteris artibus, quae quidem dignae libero essent, ornatus omnibus, tum acer investigator et diligens earum rerum quae a natura involutae videntur; denique sic iudico, post illos nobiles Pythagoreos,

---

[1] A list of writings is found in Zeller III 2⁴, p. 116 ff. Nearly ninety are known to us either by fragments or by titles.

quorum disciplina exstincta est quodam modo, cum aliquot saecla in Italia Siciliaque viguisset, hunc exstitisse qui illam renovaret.

b. Gellius, *N.A.* IV 9, 1 cites Nigidius as a man of great learning:
Nigidius Figulus, homo, ut ego arbitror, iuxta M. Varronem doctissimus.

1279—Our oldest testimony of the revival of Pythagoreanism is Alexander Polyhistor's account of what he found ἐν Πυθαγορικοῖς ὑπομνή-μασιν, preserved in Diog. Laërt. VIII 25-35.

Alex.
Polyhistor
ap. Diog. L.

Alexander Polyhistor lived in Rome, ± 80-40 B.C. The doctrine described in his account was dated by Zeller[1] as little earlier than the first century B.C. Though the first part of it (c. 25) is clearly postplatonic, M. Wellmann argued in *Hermes* 54 (1919), p. 225 ff., that the whole document is of early Pythagorean origin. He was followed by Kranz, who added our passage to the section of *Anonymous Pythagoreans* in Diel's *Vorsokratiker*, 5th and 6th edition, 58 B. Also W. Wiersma (*Das Referat des Alexandros Polyhistor über die Pythag. Phil.* in *Mnemosyne* 1941, p. 97-112), though he makes an exception for the first part of c. 25, argues that the greater part of the account goes back to fifth century theories and therefore may be safely used as a source of ancient Pythagoreanism.

Against this A. J. Festugière (*Les "Mémoires pythagoriques" cités par Alexandre Polyhistor* in *Revue des Et. grecques* 1945, p. 1-65) shows:

(1) that Diog. L. VIII 24-35 contains an ἐπιτομή of the kind which does not occur before the Hellenistic age, the scheme of which is determined by Plato's *Timaeus*;

(2) that the first section (c. 25, first part, on First principles) can be the oldest, but not older than Speusippus (always eager to bring his theories under the flag of early Pythagoreanism).

(3) The section *De mundo* (25-27) contains an aether theory in an eclectic form, and a theory of the equilibrium of opposites which, indeed, goes back to Alcmaeon and Sicilian physicians, but is here probably taken from the dialogues of Plato.

(4) Of the last section (*De anima*) which contains the theory of a double pneuma, the physician Diocles of Carystos is the main source.

(5) The whole account was perhaps put together in the 2nd century from which may date the expression εἱμαρμένη in c. 27 (sub **d**).

In any case it cannot serve as a source of early Pythagoreanism.—Though Festugière's arguments must be corrected or completed on certain points of detail (see below, under **a** and **b**), his results are mainly right.

a. Diog. Laërt. VIII 25:

The monad
the principle
of all things

Ἀρχὴν μὲν ἁπάντων μονάδα· ἐκ δὲ τῆς μονάδος ἀόριστον δυάδα ὡς ἂν ὕλην τῇ μονάδι αἰτίῳ ὄντι ὑποστῆναι· ἐκ δὲ τῆς μονάδος καὶ τῆς ἀορίστου δυάδος τοὺς ἀριθμούς· ἐκ δὲ τῶν ἀριθμῶν τὰ σημεῖα· ἐκ δὲ τούτων τὰς γραμμάς, ἐξ ὧν τὰ ἐπίπεδα σχήματα· ἐκ δὲ τῶν ἐπιπέδων τὰ στερεὰ σχήματα· ἐκ δὲ τούτων τὰ αἰσθητὰ σώματα· ὧν καὶ τὰ στοιχεῖα εἶναι τέτταρα, πῦρ, ὕδωρ,

---

[1] *Ph. d. Gr.* III 2⁴, p. 107 f., 113.

γῆν, ἀέρα· μεταβάλλειν δὲ καὶ τρέπεσθαι δι᾽ ὅλων, καὶ γίνεσθαι ἐξ αὐτῶν κόσμον ἔμψυχον, νοερόν, σφαιροειδῆ, μέσην περιέχοντα τὴν γῆν καὶ αὐτὴν σφαιροειδῆ καὶ περιοικουμένην.

To the first sentence of this passage three remarks must be made. (1) That in fact the earliest Pythagoreans were not monists, but dualists, and, moreover, did not use by preference the term ἕν or μονάς to indicate their first principle in the left side of their συστοιχία may be seen in our nr. **42**. (2) Aristotle says in *Metaph.* A 6, 987 b 26 f. that, instead of the Pythagorean ἄπειρον which is one, Plato posited the undefined dyad. We must infer from this that, wherever the δυὰς ἀόριστος appears as a second principle, we have not to do with early Pythagorean doctrine. (3) As may be seen in our nr. **364**, Plato, at least in his later years, called his first Principle the One. He also assumed a second principle, which he called either by the Pythagorean term ἄπειρον (*Phil.* 24-25, our nr. **347**), or by his own denominations τὸ μέγα καὶ μικρόν or ἀόριστος δυάς (see the description in *Phil.* 24a-25b; cp. that of Hermodorus and of Sextus; above, nr. **371**). This second principle, however, far from being derived directly from the One, forms the antipole of the scale of being. One wonders how Plato could have traced it back to the First Principle. It seems that on this point Alexander's account shows a later, unplatonic conception. Cp. ps.-Archytas (infra, nr. **1281**) and Moderatus (**1285**).[1]

As to the derivation of mathematical figures from the One, see above, nr. **372**, and the passages cited in n. 2, p. 280. Also Sextus Emp., *Math.* X, 278 ff.

The doctrine that the elements interchange and turn into one another is Stoic Heracliteism. We shall find it also in Occelus and in Philo, who views the Logos as "mediating" between the opposites. Cp. Alexander's account under **b**.

Festugière's statement that the doctrine is found in *Tim.* 54b, is only partly correct: Plato says that the four elements only *seemed* to blend into each other, but that in fact one of them does not change into anything else.

An equilibrium of opposites

b. Ib. 26 (the same passage continued):

Ἰσόμοιρά τ᾽ εἶναι ἐν τῷ κόσμῳ φῶς καὶ σκότος, καὶ θερμὸν καὶ ψυχρόν, καὶ ξηρὸν καὶ ὑγρόν· ὧν κατ᾽ ἐπικράτειαν θερμοῦ μὲν θέρος γίνεσθαι, ψυχροῦ δὲ χειμῶνα, ξηροῦ δ᾽ ἔαρ, καὶ ὑγροῦ φθινόπωρον. ἐὰν δὲ ἰσομοιρῇ, τὰ κάλλιστα εἶναι τοῦ ἔτους, οὗ τὸ μὲν θάλλον ἔαρ ὑγιεινόν, τὸ δὲ φθίνον φθινόπωρον νοσερόν.

Cp. infra, Philo, nr. **1306 b, c**.—Doubtless, the doctrine of the opposite qualities and their equilibrium is found in Plato, as Festugière pointed out (e.g. *Symp.* 186d, 188a; *Tim.* 81e sqq.), and our author *may* have borrowed it there, though it goes back to Alcmaeon.

Mortal beings fed by air, immortal beings by aether

c. Ib. 26-27:

Τόν τε περὶ τὴν γῆν ἀέρα ἄσειστον καὶ νοσερὸν καὶ τὰ ἐν αὐτῷ πάντα θνητά· τὸν δὲ ἀνωτάτω ἀεικίνητόν τ᾽ εἶναι καὶ καθαρὸν καὶ ὑγιᾶ καὶ πάντα τὰ ἐν αὐτῷ ἀθάνατα καὶ διὰ τοῦτο θεῖα. ἥλιόν τε καὶ σελήνην καὶ τοὺς ἄλλους ἀστέρας εἶναι θεούς· ἐπικρατεῖν γὰρ τὸ θερμὸν ἐν αὐτοῖς, ὅπερ ἐστὶ ζωῆς αἴτιον.

What stands here comes partly from Plato, partly from Aristotle.

(1) The aether theory, as it occurs here, shows Plato's view in *Tim.* 58d, where

---

[1] The present author reconsidered this question in a paper read to the Sorbonne, May 2nd 1958, which will be published shortly in the *Revue de Phil.* (jan. 1959).

the aether is not yet a fifth element, but is known as the purest air. Cp. *Cratylus* 410 b, where αἰθήρ is derived from ἀεὶ θεῖ (later in Arist., *De caelo* I 3, 270 b 22).

(2) The aether feeds immortal beings, see above, nr. **431**. We shall find the point again in Philo and Plutarchus.

(3) As to the doctrine that heat is the cause of life, see for instance Aristotle's account of the genesis of living beings in *De generatione anim.* II 3, 736 b 33-737 a 6, where it is supposed that the "vital heat" in animals is something analogous to the aether, because it generates living beings.

d. Ib. 27 (continued):   God and man

Καὶ ἀνθρώποις εἶναι πρὸς θεοὺς συγγένειαν, κατὰ τὸ μετέχειν ἄνθρωπον θερμοῦ· διὸ καὶ προνοεῖσθαι τὸν θεὸν ἡμῶν, εἱμαρμένην τε τῶν ὅλων καὶ κατὰ Providence μέρος αἰτίαν εἶναι τῆς διοικήσεως.

Here, Alexander's Pythagoreans share Stoic pantheism: their God is not transcendent, but by his reason man is of the substance of God, i.e. of the fiery pneuma that penetrates the universe.

The formula that εἱμαρμένη is the cause of things being ordered, both as a whole and in particular, indicates that for these so-called Pythagoreans the relation of πρόνοια and εἱμαρμένη—much discussed in the second century after Christ, and later by Plotinus and those who follow him—was already a problem. In fact, we see that Varro (ap. Cic., *Acad. post.* 7, 29), speaking of the providence of God, calls it *prudentiam quandam procurantem caelestia maxime, deinde in terris ea quae pertineant ad homines; quam interdum eandem necessitatem appellant.*

Varro, who follows Antiochus (see above, nr. **1200**), though he says that πρόνοια (prudentia) is especially concerned with celestial things, still identifies it with εἱμαρμένη. As soon as platonic transcendence comes in, the distinction between the one and the other becomes necessary. We find it in Philo and ps.-Plutarchus' *De fato* (infra, nr. **1321**); with Celsus who opposes the view that God's providence is concerned with the preservation of the whole and not with details, to the Christian conception of an all-embracing Providence. See also Apuleius, infra, nr. **1331b**.

For Plotinus and later Neoplatonists the question of πρόνοια and εἱμαρμένη becomes quite an important problem. See Plotinus, *Enn.* III 1-3; also Proclus, *Elementa* 120 and Dodds's commentary on it (p. 263).

e. Ib. 32:   Souls or daemons in the air

Εἶναί τε πάντα τὸν ἀέρα ψυχῶν ἔμπλεων· καὶ ταύτας δαίμονάς τε καὶ ἥρωας ὀνομάζεσθαι· καὶ ὑπὸ τούτων πέμπεσθαι ἀνθρώποις τούς τ' ὀνείρους καὶ τὰ σημεῖα νόσου τε καὶ ὑγιείας, καὶ οὐ μόνον ἀνθρώποις, ἀλλὰ καὶ προβάτοις καὶ τοῖς ἄλλοις κτήνεσιν· εἴς τε τούτους γίνεσθαι τούς τε καθαρμοὺς καὶ ἀποτροπιασμοὺς μαντικήν τε πᾶσαν καὶ κληδόνας καὶ τὰ ὅμοια.

Also in Ocellus 3, 3; Ecphantus ap. Stob., IV 7, 64, p. 272, 2 H.; *Carmen Aur.* V 3. Timaeus Locr. says that God gave to daemons the rule over the world (infra, nrs. **1280c**, **1283**).

Cp. Philo, our nrs. **1304** and **1306**, Plutarchus, nrs. **1318-1320**, and such later Platonists as Albinus, Maximus of Tyrus and Apuleius. Nicomachus, *Theol. arithm.* p. 43 f. connects Greek demonology with the Persian and Jewish belief in angels. Cp. what St. Paul says of evil spirits in the air (*Eph.* 6, 12).

See also supra, nr. **1192**.

Harmony

f. Ib., 33:

Purification and abstinence

Τὴν τ' ἀρετὴν ἁρμονίαν εἶναι καὶ τὴν ὑγίειαν καὶ τὸ ἀγαθὸν ἅπαν καὶ τὸν θεόν· διὸ καὶ καθ' ἁρμονίαν συνεστάναι τὰ ὅλα. φιλίαν τ' εἶναι ἐναρμόνιον ἰσότητα.—Τὴν δ' ἁγνείαν εἶναι διὰ καθαρμῶν καὶ λουτρῶν καὶ περιρραντηρίων καὶ διὰ τοῦ καθαρεύειν ἀπό τε κήδους καὶ λεχοῦς καὶ μιάσματος παντὸς καὶ ἀπέχεσθαι βρωτῶν θνησειδίων τε κρεῶν καὶ τριγλῶν καὶ μελανούρων καὶ ᾠῶν καὶ τῶν ᾠοτόκων ζῴων καὶ κυάμων καὶ τῶν ἄλλων ὧν παρακελεύονται καὶ οἱ τὰς τελετὰς ἐν τοῖς ἱεροῖς ἐπιτελοῦντες.

These things bring us back to the ancient Orphic-Pythagorean sphere. Supra, nrs. **24, 29** and **33**.

Zeller l.l. was probably right in thinking that the doctrine here expounded did not originate from Rome, where Nigidius Figulus is said to have first restored Pythagoreanism, but from Alexandria, where it is known to Arius Didymus in the first century B.C.

One or two generations later Philo is strongly influenced by it.

Ocellus

1280—Ocellus, whose work Περὶ τοῦ παντὸς φύσεως is cited by Censorinus [1] and by Philo [2], shows mainly Peripatetic influence.

The universe is imperishable

a. Ocellus I 2, 7, 9 (Harder 2-3, 9, 11):

Δοκεῖ γάρ μοι τὸ πᾶν ἀνώλεθρον εἶναι καὶ ἀγένητον· ἀεί τε γὰρ ἦν καὶ ἔσται· εἰ γὰρ ἔγχρονον, οὐκ ἂν ἔτι ἦν· οὕτως οὖν ἀνώλεθρόν τε καὶ ἀγένητον τὸ πᾶν. οὔτε γὰρ εἰ γενόμενόν τις αὐτὸ δοξάζοι, εὕροιτο ἂν <ἐξ ὅτου γένοιτο, οὔτε εἰ φθαρτόν, εὕροιτο ἂν> εἰς ὃ φθαρείη καὶ διαλυθείη.— τὸ δέ γε ὅλον καὶ τὸ πᾶν ὀνομάζω τὸν σύμπαντα κόσμον· δι' αὐτὸ γὰρ τοῦτο καὶ τῆς προσηγορίας ἔτυχε ταύτης, ἐκ τῶν ἁπάντων διακοσμηθείς. σύστημα γάρ ἐστι τῆς τῶν ὅλων φύσεως αὐτοτελὲς καὶ τέλειον [3]. — ὁ δέ γε κόσμος αἴτιός ἐστι τοῖς ἄλλοις καὶ τοῦ εἶναι καὶ τοῦ σῴζεσθαι καὶ τοῦ αὐτοτελῆ εἶναι· αὐτὸς ἄρα ἐξ ἑαυτοῦ ἀΐδιός ἐστι καὶ αὐτοτελὴς καὶ διαμένων τὸν πάντα αἰῶνα, καὶ δι' αὐτὸ τοῦτο [τοῖς ἄλλοις] παραίτιος γινόμενος τῆς διαμονῆς τῶν ὅλων.

On coming-to-be

b. Ocellus II 3-6 (Harder 20-24):

Ἐν ᾧ δὲ μέρει τοῦ κόσμου φύσις τε καὶ γένεσις ἔχουσι τὴν δυναστείαν, τρία δεῖ ταῦτα ὑπεῖναι· πρῶτον μὲν τὸ πρὸς ἀφὴν ὑφιζόμενον σῶμα πᾶσι τοῖς εἰς γένεσιν ἐρχομένοις· τοῦτο δ' ἂν εἴη πανδεχὲς καὶ ἐκμαγεῖον αὐτῆς τῆς γενέσεως, οὕτως ἔχον πρὸς τὰ ἐξ αὐτοῦ γινόμενα ὡς ὕδωρ πρὸς χυλὸν καὶ σιγὴ πρὸς ψόφον καὶ σκότος πρὸς φῶς καὶ ὕλη πρὸς τεχνητόν. — δυνάμει

---

[1] Ap. Varro, R.r. II 1, 3.
[2] *De aeternitate mundi* 12.
[3] This definition of the cosmos is Stoic (S.V.F. II fr. 527 Chrysippus). Cp. also Plato, *Tim.* 33d.

μὲν οὖν πάντα ἐν τούτῳ πρὸ τῆς γενέσεως, συντελείᾳ δὲ γενόμενα καὶ λαβόντα φύσιν. ἐν οὖν δεῖ τοῦτο πρῶτον ὑπεῖναι πρὸς τὸ γίνεσθαι γένεσιν. δεύτερον δὲ τὰς ἐναντιότητας, ἵνα μεταβολαὶ καὶ ἀλλοιώσεις ἐπιτελῶνται πάθος καὶ διάθεσιν ἐπιδεχομένης τῆς ὕλης, καὶ ἵνα αἱ δυνάμεις ἀντιπαθεῖς οὖσαι μήτε κρατῶσιν εἰς τέλος αὐταὶ αὐτῶν μήτε κρατῶνται ὑπ' αὐτῶν· τυγχάνουσι δ' αὗται τό τε θερμὸν καὶ ψυχρὸν καὶ ξηρὸν καὶ ὑγρόν. τρίτον δὲ αἱ οὐσίαι ὧν αἱ δυνάμεις εἰσὶν αὗται, πῦρ καὶ ὕδωρ καὶ ἀὴρ καὶ γῆ· διαφέρουσι δὲ αὗται τῶν δυνάμεων· αἱ μὲν γὰρ οὐσίαι ἐν τόπῳ φθείρονται ἐξ ἀλλήλων, αἱ δὲ δυνάμεις οὔτε φθείρονται οὔτε γίνονται, λόγοι γὰρ ἀσώματοι τυγχάνουσι τούτων. τῶν δὲ τεσσάρων τὸ μὲν θερμὸν καὶ ψυχρὸν ὡς αἴτια καὶ ποιητικά, τὸ δὲ ξηρὸν καὶ ὑγρὸν ὡς ὕλη καὶ παθητικά. πρώτως δὲ ὕλη τὸ πανδεχές, κοινὸν γὰρ ὑπόκειται πᾶσιν· ὥστε πρῶτον μὲν τὸ δυνάμει σῶμα αἰσθητὸν ἀρχή, δεύτερον δὲ αἱ ἐναντιώσεις, οἷον θερμότης καὶ ψυχρότης καὶ ὑγρότης καὶ ξηρότης, τρίτον δὲ πῦρ καὶ ὕδωρ καὶ γῆ καὶ ἀήρ· ταῦτα γὰρ μεταβάλλουσιν εἰς ἄλληλα, αἱ δὲ ἐναντιώσεις οὐ μεταβάλλουσιν.

The last sentence (off ὥστε) is a quotation from Aristotle, *De gen. et corr.* II 1, 329 a 32-b3, of which the whole passage is a paraphrastic explanation. As Diels, *Dox.* 188, and Harder, *Ocellus Lucanus* p. 97 ff., suppose, the author probably used a younger peripatetic commentary on *De gen. et corr.* II.

c. Ocellus III 3 (Harder 40):

gods-men-daemons

The author distinguishes three "parts" of the cosmos, and a special kind of beings in each of them.

Ἐπεὶ οὖν καθ' ἑκάστην ἀποτομὴν ὑπερέχον τι γένος ἐντέτακται τῶν ἄλλων, ἐν μὲν οὐρανῷ τὸ τῶν θεῶν, ἐν δὲ γῇ ἄνθρωπος, ἐν δὲ τῷ μεταρσίῳ τόπῳ δαίμονες, ἀνάγκη τὸ γένος τῶν ἀνθρώπων ἀΐδιον εἶναι, εἴπερ ἀληθῶς ὁ λόγος συμβιβάζει μὴ μόνον τὰ·μέρη συνυπάρχειν τῷ κόσμῳ, ἀλλὰ καὶ τὰ <ἐμ>περιεχόμενα τοῖς μέρεσιν.

The tripartition οὐρανός, γῆ, μετάρσιον is found in Seneca, *Nat. qu.* II 1, 1 (*caelestia, sublimia, terrena*), probably due to Posidonius. Cp. also Cic., *De natura deorum* II 99-101; Plut., *De facie i.o.l.*, supra, nr. **1192**, infra, **1319**; *De fato* 571b, and further the passages and authors mentioned under **1279e**.

1281—Ps.-Archytas, Περὶ ἀρχᾶν, ap. Stob., *Ecl.* I, p. 278 ff. W., **Ps.-Archytas** follows Aristotle in assuming three principles in nature: a ὑποκείμενον which is ἀόριστον, the form (μορφή) and an efficient cause (ἁ αἰτία). That he calls the ὑποκείμενον or ὕλη "the substance" (ἁ ὠσία or ἁ ἐστώ), is Stoic [1].

Remarkable is also the dualism of this author: the definite and the indefinite principle are opposed as the good and the bad one, and hence two λόγοι are assumed, the one opposed to the other.

---

[1] Above, **900a**.

Two principles and a moving cause

a. Ps.-Archytas, Π. ἀρχᾶν, ap. Stob. *Ecl.* I, p. 278 ff. W.:

Ἀνάγκα [καὶ] δύο ἀρχὰς εἶμεν τῶν ὄντων, μίαν μὲν τὰν συστοιχίαν ἔχοισαν τῶν τεταγμένων καὶ ὁριστῶν, ἑτέραν δὲ τὰν συστοιχίαν ἔχοισαν τῶν ἀτάκτων καὶ ἀορίστων. —

Ἀλλ᾿ ἐπείπερ ἀρχαὶ δύο κατὰ γένος ἀντιδιαιρεόμεναι τὰ πράγματα τυγχάνοντι τῷ τὰν μὲν εἶμεν ἀγαθοποιόν, τὰν δ᾿ εἶμεν κακοποιόν, ἀνάγκα καὶ δύο λόγως εἶμεν, τὸν μὲν ἕνα τᾶς ἀγαθοποιῶ φύσιος, τὸν δ᾿ ἕνα τᾶς κακοποιῶ. Διὰ τοῦτο καὶ τὰ τέχνᾳ καὶ τὰ φύσι γινόμενα δύο τούτων πράτων μετείληφε, τᾶς τε μορφῶς καὶ τᾶς ὠσίας. Καὶ ἁ μὲν μορφώ ἐντι ἁ αἰτία τῶ τόδε τι εἶμεν· ἁ δὲ ὠσία τὸ ὑποκείμενον, παραδεχόμενον τὰν μορφώ.

Οὔτε δὲ τᾷ ὠσίᾳ οἷόν τέ ἐντι μορφῶς μετεῖμεν αὐτᾷ ἐξ αὐτᾶς, οὔτε μὰν τὰν μορφώ γενέσθαι περὶ τὰν ὠσίαν, ἀλλ᾿ ἀνάγκα ἀτέραν τινὰ εἶμεν αἰτίαν, τὰν κινάσοισαν τὰν ἐστὼ τῶν πραγμάτων ἐπὶ τὰν μορφώ· ταύταν δὲ τὰν πράταν τᾷ δυνάμι καὶ καθυπερτάταν εἶμεν τᾶν ἀλλᾶν· ὀνομάζεσθαι δ᾿ αὐτὰν ποθάκει [1] θεόν· ὥστε τρεῖς ἀρχὰς εἶμεν ἤδη, τόν τε θεὸν καὶ τὰν ἐστὼ τῶν πραγμάτων καὶ τὰν μορφώ. Καὶ τὸν μὲν θεὸν τὸν τεχνίταν καὶ τὸν κινέοντα, τὰν δ᾿ ἐστὼ τὰν ὕλαν καὶ τὸ κινεόμενον, τὰν δὲ μορφώ τὰν τέχναν καὶ ποθ᾿ ἂν κινέεται ὑπὸ τῶ κινέοντος ἁ ἐστώ.

The moving cause that harmonizes the opposites is also called Harmony,— and τὸ πράτως κινέον!

b. Syrianus says that Archytas called his First Principle αἰτία πρὸ αἰτίας.

Syrianus in Ar. *Metaph.* XIV, the beginning (Mullach II, p. 117):

Αἰτία πρὸ αἰτίας

Ὅλως δὲ οὐδὲ ἀπὸ τῶν ὡσανεὶ ἀντικειμένων οἱ ἄνδρες ἤρχοντο, ἀλλὰ καὶ τῶν δύο στοιχείων τὸ ἐπέκεινα ᾔδεσαν, ὡς μαρτυρεῖ Φιλόλαος τὸν θεὸν λέγων πέρας καὶ ἀπειρίαν ὑποστῆσαι, διὰ μὲν τοῦ πέρατος τὴν τῷ ἑνὶ συγγενεστέραν ἐνδεικνύμενος πᾶσαν συστοιχίαν, διὰ δὲ τῆς ἀπειρίας τὴν ταύτης ὑφειμένην, καὶ ἔτι πρὸ τῶν δύο ἀρχῶν τὴν ἑνιαίαν αἰτίαν καὶ πάντων ἐξῃρημένην προέταττον ἣν Ἀρχαίνετος (Ἀρχύτας) μὲν "αἰτίαν πρὸ αἰτίας" εἶναί φησι, Φιλόλαος δὲ τῶν πάντων ἀρχὰν εἶναι διισχυρίζεται.

Here the ps. Archytas shows the beginning of that extreme transcendentalism which posits the First Principle as an ἄρρητον beyond the Νοητόν, as will be rather generally found in the Platonism of the first centuries of our era.

1282—Onatus, another writer of this group, transposes this view into a defence of polytheism.

Onatus' defence of polytheism

Onatus, Περὶ Θεοῦ καὶ θείου (Mullach II p. 113):

Ὁ μὲν θεὸς τὰ τῶν ἄλλων ζῴων ἐπαΐει, οὔτε ὁρατὸς ὢν οὔτε ἐπάϊστος,

---

[1] ποθάκει = προσήκει.

εἰ μή τισι πάγχυ ὀλίγοις τῶν ἀνθρώπων. Αὐτὸς μὲν γὰρ ὁ θεὸς ἐντι νόος καὶ ψυχὰ καὶ τὸ ἀγεμονικὸν τῶ σύμπαντος κόσμω. —

Ὁ μὲν ὦν θεὸς αὐτὸς οὔτε ὁρατὸς οὔτε αἰσθητός, ἀλλὰ λόγω μόνον καὶ νόω θεωρατός· τὰ δὲ ἔργα αὐτῶ καὶ ταὶ πράξιες ἐναργέες τε καὶ αἰσθηταί ἐντι πάντεσιν ἀνθρώποις. Δοκέει δέ μοι καὶ μὴ εἷς εἶμεν θεός, ἀλλ' εἷς μὲν ὁ μέγιστος καὶ καθυπέρτερος καὶ ὁ κρατέων τῶ παντός, τοὶ δ' ἄλλοι πολλοὶ διαφέροντες κατὰ δύναμιν· βασιλεύειν δὲ πάντων αὐτῶν ὁ καὶ κράτει καὶ μεγέθει καὶ ἀρετᾷ μάζων. οὗτος δέ κα εἴη θεὸς ὁ περιέχων τὸν σύμπαντα κόσμον, τοὶ δ' ἄλλοι θεοὶ οἱ θέοντές ἐντι κατ' οὐρανὸν σὺν τᾷ τῶ παντὸς περιαγήσι, κατὰ λόγον ὁπαδέοντες τῶ πράτῳ καὶ νοατῷ. Τοὶ δὲ λέγοντες ἕνα θεὸν εἶμεν ἀλλὰ μὴ πολλώς, ἁμαρτάνοντι. Τὸ γὰρ μέγιστον ἀξίωμα τᾶς θείας ὑπεροχᾶς οὐ συνθεωρεῦντι. Λέγω δὴ τὸ ἄρχεν καὶ καθαγέεσθαι τῶν ὁμοίων, καὶ κράτιστον καὶ καθυπέρτερον εἶμεν τῶν ἄλλων. Τοὶ δ' ἄλλοι θεοὶ ποτὶ τὸν πρᾶτον θεὸν καὶ νοατὸν οὕτως ἔχοντι, ὥσπερ χορευταὶ ποτὶ κορυφαῖον, καὶ στρατιῶται ποτὶ στραταγόν, καὶ λοχῖται καὶ συντεταγμένοι ποτὶ ταξιάρχαν καὶ λοχαγέταν, ἔχοντες φύσιν ἕπεσθαι καὶ ἐπακολουθὲν τῶ καλῶς καθαγεομένῳ. — Θεὸς μὲν ὦν ἐντι, καθάπερ ἐν ἀρχᾷ τῶ λόγω εἶπον, αὐτὸς ἀρχὰ καὶ πρᾶτον· θεῖος δὲ ὁ κόσμος καὶ τὰ ἐν αὐτῷ δινεύμενα πάντα. Ὡς ὁμοίως δὲ καὶ δαίμων ἐντὶ ἁ ψυχά, αὐτὰ γὰρ ἄρχει καὶ κινεῖ τὸ διόλω ζῶον. Δαιμόνιον δὲ τὸ σῶμα καὶ τὰ τούτω δὲ πάντα.

In the second century a similar defence of polytheism was opposed by Celsus to the Christian doctrine of one God. See Origenes, *Contra Celsum*, e.g. V 6 and 26. Cp. also Philostratus, *Life of Apollonius of Tyana* III 32, 2; 35, 3.

1283—Daemons are usually placed in the intermediate sphere between Gods and man. Thus

Timaeus Locrus, *De anima mundi* 12 (the end), Mullach II p. 46:

Those who live a life of obedience to Reason live a happy life; but hardness and disobedience is followed by punishment hereafter and reincarnation.

Ἄπαντα δὲ ταῦτα ἐν δευτέρᾳ περιόδῳ ἁ Νέμεσις συνδιέκρινε σὺν δαίμοσι παλαμναίοις χθονίοις τε, τοῖς ἐπόπταις τῶν ἀνθρωπίνων, οἷς ὁ πάντων ἀγεμὼν θεὸς ἐπέτρεψε διοίκησιν κόσμω συμπεπληρωμένω ἐκ θεῶν τε καὶ ἀνθρώπων τῶν τε ἄλλων ζῴων, ὅσα δεδαμιούργαται ποτ' εἰκόνα τὰν ἀρίσταν εἴδεος ἀγεννάτω καὶ αἰωνίω καὶ νοατῷ.

The administration of the world is confided to daemons

1284—In Rome Quintus Sextius founded a school of philosophy, which flourished under Augustus and claimed to be Pythagorean but in fact was eclectic. Seneca knows the works of the elder Sextius and cites him often with great esteem.

Q. Sextius

a.   Seneca, *Epist*. 59, 7:

Sextium ecce cum maxime lego, virum acrem, Graecis verbis, Romanis moribus philosophantem.

b.   Seneca, *Epist*. 64, 2:

Lectus est deinde liber Quinti Sextii patris, magni, si quid mihi credis, viri et, licet neget, Stoici. Quantus in illo, di boni, vigor est, quantum animi! hoc non in omnibus philosophis invenies: quorundam scripta clarum habentium nomen exanguia sunt. instituunt, disputant, cavillantur, non faciunt animum, quia non habent: cum legeris Sextium, dices: "vivit, viget, liber est, supra hominem est, dimittit me plenum ingentis fiduciae."

c.   Seneca, *Epist*. 73, 12:

Solebat Sextius dicere Iovem plus non posse quam bonum virum.

d.   In Seneca's days the school was almost forgotten.

Seneca, *Nat. quaest*. VII 32, 2:

Pythagorica illa invidiosa turbae schola praeceptorem non invenit; Sextiorum nova et Romani roboris secta inter initia sua, cum magno impetu coepisset, extincta est.

1285—In the first and second century of our era only a few Neopythagoreans are known to us by name.

Moderatus of Gades
Moderatus of Gades lived under Nero or the Flavians. His 11 [1] books Πυθαγορικῶν σχολῶν are mentioned by Eusebius, *Praep. ev.* VI 19, 8. According to Porphyrius' account he used Pythagorean number theory as a means to explain Plato's metaphysical principles.

Plato's metaphysical principles explained by numbers
a.   Porphyrius, *Vita Pythag*. 48-51:

'Η δὲ περὶ τῶν ἀριθμῶν πραγματεία, ὡς ἄλλοι τε φασὶν καὶ Μοδέρατος ὁ ἐκ Γαδείρων πάνυ συνετῶς ἐν ἕνδεκα βιβλίοις συναγαγὼν τὸ ἀρέσκον τοῖς ἀνδράσι διὰ τοῦτο ἐσπουδάσθη. μὴ δυνάμενοι γάρ, φησί, τὰ πρῶτα εἴδη καὶ τὰς πρώτας ἀρχὰς σαφῶς τῷ λόγῳ παραδοῦναι διά τε τὸ δυσπερινόητον αὐτῶν καὶ δυσέξοιστον, παρεγένοντο ἐπὶ τοὺς ἀριθμοὺς εὐσήμου διδασκαλίας χάριν μιμησάμενοι τοὺς γεωμέτρας καὶ τοὺς γραμματιστάς. ὡς γὰρ οὗτοι, τὰς δυνάμεις τῶν στοιχείων καὶ αὐτὰ ταῦτα βουλόμενοι παραδοῦναι·, παρεγένοντο

---

[1]   According to another reading 10 books (Bücheler, Rhein. Mus. XXXVII p. 335).

ἐπὶ τοὺς χαρακτῆρας, τούτους λέγοντες ὡς πρὸς τὴν πρώτην διδασκαλίαν
στοιχεῖα εἶναι, ὕστερον μέντοι διδάσκουσιν ὅτι οὐχ οὗτοι στοιχεῖά εἰσιν οἱ
χαρακτῆρες, ἀλλὰ διὰ τούτων ἔννοια γίνεται τῶν πρὸς ἀλήθειαν στοιχείων· καὶ οἱ
γεωμέτραι μὴ ἰσχύοντες τὰ ἀσώματα εἴδη λόγῳ παραστῆσαι παραγίνονται ἐπὶ
τὰς διαγραφὰς τῶν σχημάτων, λέγοντες εἶναι τρίγωνον τόδε, οὐ τοῦτο βουλόμενοι τρίγωνον εἶναι τὸ ὑπὸ τὴν ὄψιν ὑποπῖπτον, ἀλλὰ τὸ τοιοῦτο, καὶ διὰ
τούτου τὴν ἔννοιαν τοῦ τριγώνου παριστᾶσι. καὶ ἐπὶ τῶν πρώτων οὖν λόγων
καὶ εἰδῶν τὸ αὐτὸ ἐποίησαν οἱ Πυθαγόρειοι, μὴ ἰσχύοντες λόγῳ παραδιδόναι
τὰ ἀσώματα εἴδη καὶ τὰς πρώτας ἀρχάς, παρεγένοντο ἐπὶ τὴν διὰ τῶν ἀριθμῶν
δήλωσιν. καὶ οὕτως τὸν μὲν τῆς ἑνότητος λόγον καὶ τὸν τῆς ταυτότητος καὶ
ἰσότητος καὶ τὸ αἴτιον τῆς συμπνοίας καὶ τῆς συμπαθείας τῶν ὅλων καὶ τῆς
σωτηρίας τοῦ κατὰ ταὐτὰ καὶ ὡσαύτως ἔχοντος ἓν προσηγόρευσαν. καὶ γὰρ
τὸ ἐν τοῖς κατὰ μέρος ἓν τοιοῦτον ὑπάρχει ἡνωμένον τοῖς μέρεσι καὶ σύμπνουν
κατὰ μετουσίαν τοῦ πρώτου αἰτίου. τὸν δὲ τῆς ἑτερότητος καὶ ἀνισότητος καὶ
παντὸς τοῦ μεριστοῦ καὶ ἐν μεταβολῇ καὶ ἄλλοτε ἄλλως ἔχοντος δυοειδῆ λόγον
καὶ δυάδα προσηγόρευσαν· τοιαύτη γὰρ κἂν τοῖς κατὰ μέρος ἡ τῶν δύο φύσις.
καὶ οὗτοι οἱ λόγοι οὐ κατὰ τούτους μὲν εἰσί, κατὰ δὲ τοὺς λοιποὺς οὐκ ἔτι,
ἀλλ' ἔστιν ἰδεῖν καὶ τοὺς ἄλλους φιλοσόφους δυνάμεις τινὰς ἀπολιπόντας
ἐνοποιοὺς καὶ διακρατητικὰς τῶν ὅλων οὔσας, καὶ εἰσί τινες καὶ παρ' ἐκείνοις
λόγοι ἰσότητος καὶ ἀνομοιότητος καὶ ἑτερότητος. τούτους οὖν τοὺς λόγους
εὐσήμου χάριν διδασκαλίας τῷ τοῦ ἑνὸς ὀνόματι προσαγορεύουσιν καὶ τῷ τῆς
δυάδος· οὐ διαφέρει δέ γε τοῖς αὐτοῖς ἢ δυοειδὲς ἢ ἀνισοειδὲς εἰπεῖν ἢ ἑτεροειδές.
ὁμοίως δὲ ἐπὶ τῶν ἄλλων ἀριθμῶν ὁ αὐτὸς λόγος· πᾶς γὰρ κατά τινων δυνάμεων
τέτακται. πάλιν γὰρ ἔστι τι ἐν τῇ φύσει τῶν πραγμάτων ἔχον ἀρχὴν καὶ μέσον
καὶ τελευτήν. κατὰ τοῦ τοιούτου εἴδους καὶ κατὰ τῆς τοιαύτης φύσεως τὸν τρία
ἀριθμὸν κατηγόρησαν. διὸ καὶ πᾶν τὸ μεσότητι προσκεχρημένον τριοειδὲς
εἶναι φασίν. [οὕτως δὲ καὶ πᾶν τὸ τέλειον προσηγόρευσαν.] καὶ εἴ τί ἐστι τέλειον, τοῦτό φασιν ἐκείνῃ τῇ ἀρχῇ προσκεχρῆσθαι καὶ κατ' ἐκείνην κεκοσμῆσθαι.
ἢν ἄλλως μὴ δυνάμενοι ὀνομάσαι τῷ τῆς τριάδος ὀνόματι ἐπ' αὐτῆς ἐχρήσαντο·
καὶ εἰς ἔννοιαν αὐτῆς βουλόμενοι εἰσαγαγεῖν ἡμᾶς διὰ τοῦ εἴδους τούτου ταύτῃ
εἰσήγαγον. καὶ ἐπὶ τῶν ἄλλων δ' ἀριθμῶν ὁ αὐτὸς λόγος. οὗτοι οὖν οἱ λόγοι
καθ' οὓς οἱ ῥηθέντες ἀριθμοὶ ἐτάγησαν.

b. We have another account of Moderatus' theory by Simplicius,
who cites a passage of Porphyrius' Περὶ ὕλης.

Simplicius, *Phys.*, p. 230, 41 - 231, 25 Diels:

Pythagoreans were the first to conceive ὕλη as something that is distinguished
by mass and distance and division (ὄγκῳ καὶ διαστάσει καὶ μερισμῷ) [1], not measur-

---

[1] This description of the ἄπειρον is certainly not of early Pythagorean origin,
but comes from Plato's description of τὰ ἄλλα in *Parm.* 164b-165e (our nr. **334**).

The Neo-
platonic
hierarchy
of being able by ordinary measures, but only capable of being defined by means of εἰδητικὰ μέτρα [1]. After them Plato conceived it in this way, as Moderatus says.

Οὗτος γὰρ κατὰ τοὺς Πυθαγορείους τὸ μὲν πρῶτον ἓν ὑπὲρ τὸ εἶναι καὶ πᾶσαν οὐσίαν ἀποφαίνεται, τὸ δὲ δεύτερον ἕν, ὅπερ ἐστὶ τὸ ὄντως ὂν καὶ νοητόν, τὰ εἴδη φησὶν εἶναι, τὸ δὲ τρίτον, ὅπερ ἐστὶ τὸ ψυχικόν, μετέχειν τοῦ ἑνὸς καὶ τῶν εἰδῶν, τὴν δὲ ἀπὸ τούτου τελευταίαν φύσιν τὴν τῶν αἰσθητῶν οὖσαν μηδὲ μετέχειν, ἀλλὰ κατ' ἔμφασιν ἐκείνων [2] κεκοσμῆσθαι, τῆς ἐν αὐτοῖς ὕλης τοῦ μὴ ὄντος πρώτως ἐν τῷ ποσῷ ὄντος οὔσης [3] σκίασμα καὶ ἔτι μᾶλλον ὑποβεβηκυίας καὶ ἀπὸ τούτου. καὶ ταῦτα δὲ ὁ Πορφύριος ἐν τῷ δευτέρῳ Περὶ ὕλης τὰ τοῦ Μοδεράτου παρατιθέμενος γέγραφεν ὅτι "βουληθεὶς ὁ ἑνιαῖος λόγος, ὥς πού φησιν ὁ Πλάτων, τὴν γένεσιν ἀφ' ἑαυτοῦ τῶν ὄντων συστήσασθαι, κατὰ στέρησιν αὐτοῦ ἐχώρησε τὴν ποσότητα πάντων αὐτὴν στερήσας τῶν αὐτοῦ λόγων καὶ εἰδῶν. τοῦτο δὲ ποσότητα ἐκάλεσεν ἄμορφον καὶ ἀδιαίρετον καὶ ἀσχημάτιστον, ἐπιδεχομένην μέντοι μορφὴν σχῆμα διαίρεσιν ποιότητα πᾶν τὸ τοιοῦτον. ἐπὶ ταύτης ἔοικε, φησί, τῆς ποσότητος ὁ Πλάτων τὰ πλείω ὀνόματα κατηγορῆσαι "πανδεχῆ" καὶ ἀνείδεον λέγων καὶ "ἀόρατον" καὶ "ἀπορώτατα τοῦ νοητοῦ μετειληφέναι" αὐτὴν καὶ "λογισμῷ νόθῳ μόλις ληπτήν" καὶ πᾶν τὸ τούτοις ἐμφερές. αὕτη δὲ ἡ ποσότης, φησί, καὶ τοῦτο τὸ εἶδος τὸ κατὰ στέρησιν τοῦ ἑνιαίου λόγου νοούμενον τοῦ πάντας τοὺς λόγους τῶν ὄντων ἐν ἑαυτῷ περιειληφότος παραδείγματά ἐστι τῆς τῶν σωμάτων ὕλης, ἣν καὶ αὐτὴν ποσὸν καὶ τοὺς Πυθαγορείους καὶ τὸν Πλάτωνα καλεῖν ἔλεγεν, οὐ τὸ ὡς εἶδος ποσόν, ἀλλὰ τὸ κατὰ στέρησιν καὶ παράλυσιν καὶ ἔκτασιν καὶ διασπασμὸν καὶ διὰ τὴν ἀπὸ τοῦ ὄντος παράλλαξιν, δι' ἃ καὶ κακὸν δοκεῖ ἡ ὕλη ὡς τὸ ἀγαθὸν ἀποφεύγουσα. καὶ καταλαμβάνεται ὑπ' αὐτοῦ καὶ ἐξελθεῖν τῶν ὅρων οὐ συγχωρεῖται, τῆς μὲν ἐκτάσεως τὸν τοῦ εἰδητικοῦ μεγέθους λόγον ἐπιδεχομένης καὶ τούτῳ ὁριζομένης, τοῦ δὲ διασπασμοῦ τῇ ἀριθμητικῇ διακρίσει εἰδοποιουμένου".

A Neo-
pythagorean
interpreta-
tion of
Plato's
Parmenides In Simplicius' account of Moderatus' doctrine we see for the first time the four stages of the Neoplatonic hierarchy of being clearly outlined. Dodds [4] recognized it as a Neopythagorean interpretation of Plato's *Parmenides*, of which he finds an earlier trace in a correction made by the Neopythagorean Eudorus of Alexandria (± 25 A.D.) in a passage of Aristotle. The text of Ar., *Metaph.* A 988 a 10-11 is: τὰ γὰρ εἴδη τοῦ τί ἐστιν αἴτια τοῖς ἄλλοις, τοῖς δ' εἴδεσιν τὸ ἕν. Alexander in *Metaph.* p. 58, l. 31-59, l. 8, says that Eudorus and Euarmostus read: τοῖς δ' εἴδεσιν τὸ ἓν καὶ

---

[1] This formula again is neither directly Pythagorean nor directly Platonic. The term and the wording ὁρίζεσθαι δυνάμενα ὑπὸ τῶν εἰδητικῶν μέτρων presupposes Aristotle as well as Plato.

[2] Sensible things are a *reflection* of the Ideas. We shall find this later in Plotinus.

[3] The term ποσόν or ποσότης to indicate multiplicity in the intelligible world is Neopythagorean. Theon of Smyrna e.g. defines number as τὸ ἐν νοητοῖς ποσόν (Dodds in *Class. Qu.* 1928, p. 138).

[4] *The Parmenides of Plato and the origin of the Neoplatonic "One"*, in *Class. Quart.* 1928, p. 129-142.

τῇ ὕλῃ. Dodds thinks there is not an omission here in our MSS, but Eudorus changed the text of Aristotle in the sense of Neopythagorean monism, which derived the ἄπειρον directly from the one. See above, nr. **1279b** and the footnote to the explanation given there.

1286—Moderatus seems to have conceived the soul as a kind of mathematical harmony, while "Timaeus Locrus" applied this notion to the genesis of beings, as "a mean" and "a bond".

Stob., *Ecl.* I p. 364, l. 19-25 W.:

The soul a harmony

Ἔτι τοίνυν τὴν ἁρμονίαν ἴδωμεν, οὐ τὴν ἐν σώμασιν ἐνιδρυμένην, ἀλλ' ἥτις ἐστὶ μαθηματική. Ταύτην τοίνυν, ὡς μὲν ἁπλῶς εἰπεῖν, τὴν τὰ διαφέροντα ὁπωσοῦν σύμμετρα καὶ προσήγορα ἀπεργαζομένην ἀναφέρει εἰς τὴν ψυχὴν Μοδέρατος· τὴν δ' ὡς ἐν οὐσίαις καὶ ζωαῖς καὶ γενέσει πάντων μεσότητα καὶ σύνδεσιν ὁ Τίμαιος αὐτῇ ἀνατίθησι.

Cp. "Timaeus"

We shall find that Philo conceived the Logos exactly in this sense. Infra, nr. **1306ab**.

1287—Apollonius of Tyana, too, lived in the first cent. A.D.

a. Suidas:

Apollonius of Tyana

Ἀπολλώνιος Τυανεύς, φιλόσοφος. — ἤκμαζε μὲν ἐπὶ Κλαυδίου καὶ Γαίου καὶ Νέρωνος καὶ μέχρι Νέρβα, ἐφ' οὗ καὶ μετήλλαξεν. ἐσιώπησε δὲ κατὰ Πυθαγόραν πέντε ἔτη. εἶτα ἀπῆρεν εἰς Αἴγυπτον, ἔπειτα εἰς Βαβυλῶνα πρὸς τοὺς μάγους κἀκεῖθεν ἐπὶ τοὺς Ἄραβας, καὶ συνῆξεν ἐκ πάντων τὰ μυρία καὶ περὶ αὐτοῦ θρυλούμενα μαγγανεύματα. συνέταξε δὲ τοσαῦτα· Τελετὰς ἢ περὶ θυσιῶν, Διαθήκην, Χρησμούς, Ἐπιστολάς, Πυθαγόρου βίον.

In the third century Philostratus wrote a kind of saint's life of Apollonius, as an example of the perfectus sapiens in Pythagorean style. The story abounds with miracles, but the author takes great pains to explain that they are not produced by magic art, but spring from a superior wisdom and intimate connection with God (or the gods) [1]. Dio Cassius mentions Apoll., LXXVII 18. His life of Pythagoras is cited by Porphyrius, *V.P.* 2, and by Iamblichus, *V.P.* 254. Of his books Π. θυσιῶν a fragment is preserved by Eusebius. See under **b**.

b. Apollonius ap. Euseb., *Praep. ev.* IV 13:

The true worship of God

Οὕτως τοίνυν μάλιστα ἄν τις, οἶμαι, τὴν προσήκουσαν ἐπιμέλειαν ποιοῖτο τοῦ θείου, τυγχάνοι τε αὐτόθεν ἵλεώ τε καὶ εὐμενοῦς αὐτοῦ παρ' ὅντινα οὖν μόνος ἀνθρώπων, εἰ Θεῷ μὲν ὃν δὴ πρῶτον ἔφαμεν, ἑνί τε ὄντι κεχωρισμένῳ πάντων, μεθ' ὃν γνωρίζεσθαι τοὺς λοιποὺς ἀναγκαῖον, μὴ θύοι τι τὴν ἀρχήν, μήτε ἀνάπτοι πῦρ, μήτε καθόλου τι τῶν αἰσθητῶν ἐπονομάζοι· (δεῖται γὰρ οὐδενὸς οὐδὲ παρὰ τῶν κρειττόνων ἤπερ ἡμεῖς ἐσμέν· οὐδ' ἔστιν ὃ τὴν ἀρχὴν ἀνίησι γῆ φυτόν, ἢ τρέφει ζῷον, ἢ ἀήρ, ᾧ μὴ πρόσεστί γέ τι μίασμα·) μόνῳ

---

[1] Philostr. I 2; V 12; VIII 7, 9.

δέ χρῷτο πρὸς αὐτὸν αἰεὶ τῷ κρείττονι λόγῳ, λέγω δὲ τῷ μὴ διὰ στόματος ἰόντι, καὶ παρὰ τοῦ καλλίστου τῶν ὄντων διὰ τοῦ καλλίστου τῶν ἐν ἡμῖν αἰτοίη τἀγαθά· νοῦς δέ ἐστιν οὗτος ὀργάνου μὴ δεόμενος.

Cp. Philostr., *Apoll.* III 4, VI 19.

Nicomachus   **1288**—Nicomachus of Gerasa elaborated the early Pythagorean theory of number as a cosmic principle.

a. Nicomachus, *Arithm. introd.* I 3, 3-6, p. 6-8 Hoche.

Of the mathematical sciences arithmetic is concerned with absolute quantity, music with relative quantity; two other sciences deal with size, geometry with the part that is at rest, astronomy with that which moves. These sciences are **Mathematics** indispensable for the knowledge of things and a condition of wisdom.

a condition
of wisdom   Οὐκ ἄρα τούτων ἄνευ δυνατὸν τὰ τοῦ ὄντος εἴδη ἀκριβῶσαι οὐδ' ἄρα τὴν ἐν τοῖς οὖσιν ἀλήθειαν εὑρεῖν, ἧς ἐπιστήμη σοφία, φαίνεται δέ, ὅτι οὐδ' ὀρθῶς φιλοσοφεῖν· ὅπερ γὰρ ζωγραφίη συμβάλλεται τέχναις βαναύσοις πρὸς θεωρίης ὀρθότητα, τοῦτό τοι γραμμαὶ καὶ ἀριθμοὶ καὶ ἁρμονικὰ διαστήματα καὶ κύκλων περιπολήσιες πρὸς λόγων σοφῶν μαθήσιας συνεργίην ἔχουσιν, 'Ανδροκύδης[1] φησὶν ὁ Πυθαγορικός. ἀλλὰ καὶ 'Αρχύτας ὁ Ταραντῖνος[2] ἀρχόμενος τοῦ ἁρμονικοῦ τὸ αὐτὸ οὕτω πως λέγει· καλῶς μοι δοκοῦντι περὶ τὰ μαθήματα δια-γνώμεναι καὶ οὐδὲν ἄτοπον αὐτοὺς ὀρθῶς, οἷα ἐντί, περὶ ἑκάστου φρονέειν. περὶ γὰρ τᾶς τῶν ὅλων φύσιος καλῶς διαγνόντες ἔμελλον καὶ περὶ τῶν κατὰ μέρος, οἷα ἐντί, καλῶς ὀψεῖσθαι· —

Καὶ Πλάτων δὲ ἐπὶ τέλει τοῦ τρισκαιδεκάτου τῶν Νόμων[3], ὅπερ τινὲς φιλόσοφον ἐπιγράφουσιν, ὅτι ἐν αὐτῷ περισκοπεῖ καὶ διορίζεται, ποταπὸν χρὴ τὸν ὄντως φιλόσοφον εἶναι, ἀνακεφαλαιούμενος τὰ διὰ πλειόνων προ-διαλεχθέντα καὶ προδιαβεβαιωθέντα ἐπιφέρει· ἅπαν διάγραμμα ἀριθμοῦ τε σύστημα καὶ ἁρμονίας σύστασιν ἅπασαν τῆς τε τῶν ἄστρων φορᾶς τὴν ἀνα-λογίαν μίαν ἀναφανῆναι δεῖ τῷ κατὰ τρόπον μανθάνοντι, φανήσεται δ' ἄν, ὃ λέγομεν, ὀρθῶς τις εἰς ἓν βλέπων πάντα μανθάνῃ[4]· δεσμὸς γὰρ ἁπάντων τούτων εἰς ἀναφανήσεται· εἰ δέ τις ἄλλως μεταχειριεῖται φιλοσοφίαν τύχην δεῖ καλεῖν συνεργόν· οὐ γὰρ ἄνευ τούτων ἡ ὁδός ποτε, ἀλλ' οὗτος ὁ τρόπος, ταῦτα τὰ μαθήματα εἴτε χαλεπὰ εἴτε ῥᾴδια, ταύτῃ ἰτέον, ἀμελεῖν δὲ οὐ δεῖ. τὸν δὲ ταῦτα πάντα οὕτω λαβόντα, ὡς ἐγὼ λέγω, τοῦτον ἐγὼ καλῶ σοφώτατον καὶ διισχυρίζομαι παίζων τε καὶ σπουδάζων. δῆλον γάρ, ὅτι κλίμαξί τισι καὶ

---

[1] Androcydes is also mentioned in the *Theol. Arithm.*, p. 40 Ast.
[2] The same passage is quoted by Porphyrius, *In Ptolem. Harm.*, p. 236.
[3] The reference is to *Epinomis* 991d ff.
[4] I follow the reading proposed by d'Ooge.

γεφύραις ἔοικε ταῦτα τὰ μαθήματα διαβιβάζοντα τὴν διάνοιαν ἡμῶν ἀπὸ τῶν αἰσθητῶν καὶ δοξαστῶν ἐπὶ τὰ νοητὰ καὶ ἐπιστημονικὰ καὶ ἀπὸ τῶν συντρόφων ἡμῖν καὶ ἐκ βρεφῶν ὄντων συνήθων ὑλικῶν καὶ σωματικῶν ἐπὶ τὰ ἀσυνήθη τε καὶ ἑτερόφυλα πρὸς τὰς αἰσθήσεις, τῇ δὲ ἀϋλίᾳ καὶ ἀϊδιότητι συγγενέστερα ταῖς ἡμετέραις ψυχαῖς καὶ πολὺ πρότερον τῷ ἐν αὐταῖς νοητικῷ.

b. Nicomachus, ib., I 6, 1; p. 12 Hoche: **Number pre-existing in the mind of God**

Πάντα τὰ κατὰ τεχνικὴν διέξοδον ὑπὸ φύσεως ἐν τῷ κόσμῳ διατεταγμένα κατὰ μέρος τε καὶ ὅλα φαίνεται κατ' ἀριθμὸν ὑπὸ τῆς προνοίας καὶ τοῦ τὰ ὅλα δημιουργήσαντος νοῦ διακεκρίσθαι τε καὶ κεκοσμῆσθαι βεβαιουμένου τοῦ παραδείγματος οἷον λόγον προχαράγματος ἐκ τοῦ ἐπέχειν τὸν ἀριθμὸν προϋποστάντα ἐν τῇ τοῦ κοσμοποιοῦ θεοῦ διανοίᾳ, νοητὸν αὐτὸν μόνον καὶ παντάπασιν ἄϋλον, οὐσίαν μέντοι τὴν ὄντως τὴν ἀΐδιον, ἵνα πρὸς αὐτὸν ὡς λόγον τεχνικὸν ἀποτελεσθῇ τὰ σύμπαντα ταῦτα, χρόνος, κίνησις, οὐρανός, ἄστρα, ἐξελιγμοὶ παντοῖοι.

Cp. infra, **1293b** and **c** (Philo); **1326b** (Albinus) and our notes there.

c. Nicomachus, *Arithm. theol.* epitome ap. Phot., *Bibl.*, cod. 187, p. 143, 22 Bekker: **The μονὰς ἀρσενόθηλυς**

Λέγει δὲ τὴν μονάδα ἄλλα τε οὐκ ὀλίγα τῶν πλασμάτων τῇ περὶ αὐτὴν ἀληθείᾳ, καὶ τοῖς προσοῦσι φυσικοῖς ἰδιώμασι καταμιγνύς, καὶ ὡς νοῦς τε εἴη, εἶτα καὶ ἀρσενόθηλυς, καὶ θεός, καὶ ὕλη δέ πως, πάντα χρήματα μιγνύς ὡς ἀληθῶς, καὶ πανδοχεὺς λοιπὸν καὶ χωρητικὴ καὶ χάος, σύγχυσις, σύγκρασις, ἀλαμπία, σκοτωδία, χάσμα, τάρταρος.

On the μονὰς ἀρσενόθηλυς see Festugière, *Le dieu inconnu et la gnose*, p. 43 ff. Infra **1340a**: the Νοῦς ἀρρενόθηλυς appears in *Corp. Herm.* I 9. See n. 2 there. That the first Principle *is* at once ὕλη—not only that ὕλη *derives* from it—, is not yet in Alexander Polyhistor's account of Pythagorean doctrine ap. Diog. L. VIII 25. But it is found in the Stoa (above nr. **900**). In spite of Festugière's comments, oriental influence is probable.

On σύγχυσις, χάσμα, etc.: Festugière, o.c., p. 51 ff. Cp. also *Theol. arithm.* ed. Ast. p. 6:

Ὡσαύτως δὲ χάος αὐτὴν φασι τὸ παρ' Ἡσιόδῳ πρωτόγονον, ἐξ οὗ τὰ λοιπὰ ὡς ἐκ μονάδος· ἡ αὐτὴ σύγχυσίς τε καὶ σύγκρασις, ἀλαμπία τε καὶ σκοτωδία στερήσει διαρθρώσεως καὶ διακρίσεως τῶν ἑξῆς ἁπάντων ἐπινοεῖται.

2—PHILO OF ALEXANDRIA

1289—With Philo a new element comes into the history of philosophy, namely Revelation. Since, however, Philo was an Alexandrian Jew of Hellenistic culture, bred in the Greek philosophy of his age, the question arises as to what prevails in his thought: either Revelation in Scripture or Greek philosophy.

I. Heinemann, H. Leisegang, E. R. Goodenough and others (see Biblogr.) think that with Philo Hellenism prevails. A different outlook was given recently by H. A. Wolfson, *Philo* (Cambridge Mass., 1948). Here Philo is represented as the father of that religious philosophy which, during the Middle Ages, subordinated philosophy to theology and, according to the author, is found not only in Western scholastic philosophy, but also with the Jewish and Arabic philosophers of that age. He therefore qualifies Philo as one of the greatest thinkers of mankind and attributes to him a perfectly clear and consistent system.

Important objections to this view were raised by I. Heinemann, *Philo als Vater der mittelalterlichen Philosophie?* in: *Theologische Zeitschrift*, (Basel) 1950, p. 99-116. See also H. Chadwick in *Class. Review* 1949, p. 24 f., and Leisegang's characteristic of Philo in Pauly-Wissowa XX 1 (1941).

Philo, in fact, accepted Revelation. His idea of God and creation is, as will be seen in the following texts, on essential points determined by it. This is, of course, important; but it does not yet make Philo a great philosopher. Moreover, it cannot be held that he made a clear distinction between natural Reason and Revelation, such as was made later by St. Thomas Aquinas. The climate of Philo's thought is highly syncretistic (see in particular our nrs. **1294** and **1303**): he read Scripture in the Septuagint version and understood its terms, often in an amazing way, in the sense of Greek philosophy, i.e. of that synthetical philosophy of his age, in which both Platonism and Stoicism prevailed.

a. Eusebius, *Hist. eccl.* II 4, 2:

Κατὰ δὴ τοῦτον (sc. τὸν Γάϊον) Φίλων ἐγνωρίζετο ¹ πλείστοις ἀνὴρ οὐ μόνον τῶν ἡμετέρων, ἀλλὰ καὶ τῶν ἀπὸ τῆς ἔξωθεν ὁρμωμένων παιδείας ἐπισημότατος. τὸ μὲν οὖν γένος ἀνέκαθεν Ἑβραῖος ἦν, τῶν ἐπ' Ἀλεξανδρείας ἐν τέλει διαφανῶν οὐδενὸς χείρων ², περὶ δὲ τὰ θεῖα καὶ πάτρια μαθήματα ὅσον τε καὶ ὁπηλίκον εἰσενήνεκται πόνον, ἔργῳ πᾶσι δῆλος ³, καὶ περὶ τὰ φιλόσοφα δὲ καὶ ἐλευθέρια τῆς ἔξωθεν παιδείας οἷός τις ἦν, οὐδὲν δεῖ λέγειν, ὅτε μάλιστα τὴν κατὰ Πλάτωνα καὶ Πυθαγόραν ἐζηλωκὼς ἀγωγήν ⁴, διενεγκεῖν ἅπαντας τοὺς καθ' ἑαυτὸν ἱστορεῖται.

b. In his treatise on the value of preliminary studies (§ 74 ff.), taking the story of Abraham, Hagar and Sarah as an allegory, he calls the ἐγκύκλια (grammar, geometry and musical theory) "the handmaids", while Philosophy is "the mistress" or "the lawful wife".

---

¹ Philo was an ambassador of Alexandria to the emperor Gaius (Caligula) 39 A.D.

² His brother Alabarches was, according to Josephus, *Antiqu.* XX 3, the wealthiest man of Alexandria.

³ Ph.'s three books Νόμων ἱερῶν ἀλληγορίαι and fifteen other works are commentaries on the Pentateuch or parts of it. In the books *De somniis* the theories of Chrysippus and Posidonius are illustrated by biblical instances. The *Quaestiones et solutiones in Genesim et Exodum* preserved in an Armenian translation, are a part of another allegorical commentary on the Pentateuch.

⁴ In fact Ph.'s Platonism shows all the features of first century-Pythagoreanism. The author is particularly interested in number speculations

Philo, *De congressu eruditionis gratia* 79-80 (C.W. III, p. 87 f.): His appre-
ciation of
philosophy

Καὶ μὴν ὥσπερ τὰ ἐγκύκλια συμβάλλεται πρὸς φιλοσοφίας ἀνάληψιν, οὕτω καὶ φιλοσοφία πρὸς σοφίας κτῆσιν. ἔστι γὰρ φιλοσοφία ἐπιτήδευσις σοφίας, σοφία δ' ἐπιστήμη θείων καὶ ἀνθρωπίνων καὶ τῶν τούτων αἰτίων [1]. γένοιτ' ἂν οὖν ὥσπερ ἡ ἐγκύκλιος μουσικὴ φιλοσοφίας, οὕτω καὶ φιλοσοφία δούλη σοφίας. φιλοσοφία δὲ ἐγκράτειαν μὲν γαστρός, ἐγκράτειαν δὲ τῶν μετὰ γαστέρα, ἐγκράτειαν δὲ καὶ γλώττης ἀναδιδάσκει. ταῦτα λέγεται μὲν εἶναι δι' αὐτὰ αἱρετά, σεμνότερα δὲ φαίνοιτ' <ἂν>, εἰ θεοῦ τιμῆς καὶ ἀρεσκείας ἕνεκα ἐπιτηδεύοιτο [2]. μεμνῆσθαι οὖν δεῖ τῆς κυρίας, ὁπότε μέλλοιμεν αὐτῆς <τὰς> θεραπαινίδας μνᾶσθαι· καὶ λεγώμεθα μὲν ἄνδρες εἶναι τούτων, ὑπαρχέτω δ' ἡμῖν ἐκείνη πρὸς ἀλήθειαν γυνή, μὴ λεγέσθω.

It would be certainly as erroneous to conclude from this passage that Philo proclaimed Philosophy to be "the mistress", and such in opposition to Scripture, as to say that here he is ranking "theology" above philosophy. He does not oppose Scripture or theology to philosophy at all. Where he corrects the Stoa, he does so by "true philosophy". And this is what he attributes to Moses. Cp. **1290a**.

c. The following passage shows how he speaks later of his philosophical studies.

Philo, *De special. legibus* III 1, 1-4 (C.W. V, p. 150 f.):

Ἦν ποτε χρόνος, ὅτε φιλοσοφία σχολάζων καὶ θεωρία τοῦ κόσμου καὶ τῶν ἐν αὐτῷ τὸν καλὸν καὶ περιπόθητον καὶ μακάριον ὄντως νοῦν ἐκαρπούμην, θείοις ἀεὶ λόγοις συγγινόμενος καὶ δόγμασιν, ὧν ἀπλήστως καὶ ἀκορέστως ἔχων ἐνευφραινόμην, οὐδὲν ταπεινὸν φρονῶν ἢ χαμαίζηλον οὐδὲ περὶ δόξαν ἢ πλοῦτον ἢ τὰς σώματος εὐπαθείας ἰλυσπώμενος, ἀλλ' ἄνω μετάρσιος ἐδόκουν ἀεὶ φέρεσθαι κατά τινα τῆς ψυχῆς ἐπιθειασμὸν καὶ συμπεριπολεῖν ἡλίῳ καὶ σελήνῃ καὶ σύμπαντι οὐρανῷ τε καὶ κόσμῳ. τότε δὴ τότε διακύπτων ἄνωθεν ἀπ' αἰθέρος καὶ τείνων ὥσπερ ἀπὸ σκοπιᾶς τὸ τῆς διανοίας ὄμμα κατεθεώμην τὰς ἀμυθήτους θεωρίας τῶν ἐπὶ γῆς ἁπάντων καὶ εὐδαιμόνιζον ἐμαυτὸν ὡς ἀνὰ κράτος ἐκπεφευγότα τὰς ἐν τῷ θνητῷ βίῳ κῆρας. ἐφήδρευε δ' ἄρα μοι τὸ κακῶν ἀργαλεώτατον, ὁ μισόκαλος φθόνος, ὃς ἐξαπιναίως ἐπιπεσὼν οὐ πρότερον ἐπαύσατο καθέλκων πρὸς βίαν ἤ με καταβαλεῖν εἰς μέγα πέλαγος τῶν ἐν πολιτείᾳ φροντίδων, ἐν ᾧ φορούμενος οὐδ' ὅσον ἀνανήξασθαι δύναμαι. στένων δ' ὅμως ἀντέχω τὸν ἐκ πρώτης ἡλικίας ἐνιδρυμένον τῇ ψυχῇ παιδείας ἵμερον ἔχων, ὃς ἔλεόν μου καὶ οἶκτον ἀεὶ λαμβάνων ἀνεγείρει καὶ ἀνακουφίζει. διὰ τοῦτον ἔστιν ὅτε τὴν κεφαλὴν ἐπαίρω καὶ τοῖς τῆς ψυχῆς ὄμμασιν ἀμυδρῶς μὲν — τὸ γὰρ ὀξυδερκὲς αὐτῶν ἡ τῶν ἀλλοκότων πραγμάτων ἀχλὺς ἐπεσκίασεν —

---

[1] This is a Stoic definition of philosophy. See above, **897b, 1215c**.
[2] Here Philo is correcting the Stoa.

ἀλλ' ἀναγκαίως γοῦν περιβλέπομαι τὰν κύκλῳ καθαρᾶς καὶ ἀμιγοῦς κακῶν
ζωῆς σπάσαι γλιχόμενος.

1290—In the very beginning of his treatise *On the Creation* Ph.
rebukes those who hold that the world is without beginning and is ever-
lasting. To their view he opposes Moses' doctrine of creation.

God and
the world

a. Philo, *De opif. mundi* 2, 7-9; C.W. I, p. 2-3.

Τινὲς γὰρ τὸν κόσμον μᾶλλον ἢ τὸν κοσμοποιὸν θαυμάσαντες τὸν μὲν ἀγένητόν
τε καὶ ἀίδιον ἀπεφήναντο, τοῦ δὲ θεοῦ πολλὴν ἀπραξίαν ἀνάγνως κατεψεύσαντο,
δέον ἔμπαλιν τοῦ μὲν τὰς δυνάμεις ὡς ποιητοῦ καὶ πατρὸς καταπλαγῆναι,
τὸν δὲ μὴ πλέον ἀποσεμνῦναι τοῦ μετρίου [1]. Μωυσῆς δὲ καὶ φιλοσοφίας ἐπ'
αὐτὴν φθάσας ἀκρότητα καὶ χρησμοῖς τὰ πολλὰ καὶ συνεκτικώτατα τῶν τῆς
φύσεως ἀναδιδαχθεὶς [2] ἔγνω δή, ὅτι ἀναγκαιότατόν ἐστιν ἐν τοῖς οὖσι τὸ μὲν
εἶναι δραστήριον αἴτιον, τὸ δὲ παθητόν [3], καὶ ὅτι τὸ μὲν δραστήριον ὁ τῶν ὅλων
νοῦς ἐστιν εἰλικρινέστατος καὶ ἀκραιφνέστατος, κρείττων ἢ ἀρετὴ καὶ κρείττων
ἢ ἐπιστήμη καὶ κρείττων ἢ αὐτὸ τὸ ἀγαθὸν καὶ αὐτὸ τὸ καλόν [4], τὸ δὲ παθητὸν
ἄψυχον καὶ ἀκίνητον ἐξ ἑαυτοῦ, κινηθὲν δὲ καὶ σχηματισθὲν καὶ ψυχωθὲν ὑπὸ τοῦ
νοῦ μετέβαλεν εἰς τὸ τελειότατον ἔργον, τόνδε τὸν κόσμον [5]· ὃν οἱ φάσκοντες
ὡς ἔστιν ἀγένητος λελήθασι τὸ ὠφελιμώτατον καὶ ἀναγκαιότατον τῶν εἰς
εὐσέβειαν ὑποτεμνόμενοι τὴν πρόνοιαν.

Providence

b. By the doctrine of Creation that of Providence is established
at the same time.

---

[1] By the last words, Ph. certainly alludes more to Aristotle's doctrine of the
ἀφθαρσία τοῦ κόσμου than to Plato's description in the *Timaeus*, where in the Greek
sense a κόσμος is "made" or "produced" by the Demiurge.
[2] The wording of this sentence shows that for Philo "philosophy" and Revelation are not opposed the one to the other; with Moses, personal insight and divine
instruction work together.
[3] This distinction between an active and a passive principle in Nature reminds
one of Stoic doctrine, as reported by Diog. Laert. VII 134 (supra, nr. **899a**),
though in calling the δραστήριον αἴτιον Νοῦς Philo speaks the language of Plato
in the *Philebus* and *Timaeus* (supra, nrs. **347e** and **349**).
[4] Philo stresses the transcendence of God as strongly as possible and declines
to call him αὐτὸ τὸ Ἀγαθόν (Plato's term in *Resp.* VI 508-509; supra, nr. **292**) or
αὐτὸ τὸ καλόν (*Symp.* 211d; supra, nr. **273**).
[5] The παθητόν, by being set in motion, shaped and quickened by the divine
Mind, is transformed into "the most perfect masterpiece", namely the world.
Here, Philo follows Plato and does not exclude some vague pre-existence of "matter". However, in *De conf. lingu.* 27, 136 (C.W. II p. 254, l. 24) he says that both
χώρα and τόπος were created coincidently with the existing things: καὶ χώραν
καὶ τόπον αὐτὸς τοῖς σώμασι συγγεγέννηκε. Cp. Plato, *Tim.* 49e-52a (supra, nrs.
356b-e); Wolfson I, p. 300-309. See also Philo, *Leg. alleg.* II 1 (infra, nr. **1279**).

Ib. 2, 10-11:

Τοῦ μὲν γὰρ γεγονότος ἐπιμελεῖσθαι τὸν πατέρα καὶ ποιητὴν αἱρεῖ λόγος·
καὶ γὰρ πατὴρ ἐκγόνων καὶ δημιουργὸς τῶν δημιουργηθέντων στοχάζεται
τῆς διαμονῆς καὶ ὅσα μὲν ἐπιζήμια καὶ βλαβερὰ μηχανῇ πάσῃ διωθεῖται,
τὰ δὲ ὅσα ὠφέλιμα καὶ λυσιτελῆ κατὰ πάντα τρόπον ἐκπορίζειν ἐπιποθεῖ·
πρὸς δὲ τὸ μὴ γεγονὸς οἰκείωσις¹ οὐδεμία τῷ μὴ πεποιηκότι. ἀπεριμάχητον
δὲ δόγμα καὶ ἀνωφελὲς ἀναρχίαν ὡς ἐν πόλει κατασκευάζον τῷδε τῷ κόσμῳ
τὸν ἔφορον ἢ βραβευτὴν ἢ δικαστὴν οὐκ ἔχοντι, ὑφ' οὗ πάντ' οἰκονομεῖσθαι
καὶ πρυτανεύεσθαι θέμις.

The rule of Providence over the cosmos and over human life according to Philo
is one of the main points of Moses' teaching. Together with the doctrine of God's
existence and His unity, it is also the leading idea of Philo's own thought: at the
same time a religious and a philosophical doctrine.

Cp. *De opif. mundi* 61, 170-172.

1291—God from eternity was alone and anything besides Him must **God is**
have been brought into being by Him. **unique**

Philo, *Leg. alleg.* II 1, 1-3 (C.W. I, p. 90):

"Καὶ εἶπε κύριος ὁ θεός· Οὐ καλὸν εἶναι τὸν ἄνθρωπον μόνον, ποιήσωμεν
αὐτῷ βοηθὸν κατ' αὐτόν" (*Gen.* 2, 18). διὰ τί τὸν ἄνθρωπον, ὦ προφῆτα,
οὐκ ἔστι καλὸν εἶναι μόνον; ὅτι, φησί, καλόν ἐστι τὸν μόνον εἶναι μόνον·
5 μόνος δὲ καὶ καθ' αὑτὸν εἷς ὢν ὁ θεός, οὐδὲν δὲ ὅμοιον θεῷ· ὥστ' ἐπεὶ τὸ μόνον
εἶναι τὸν ὄντα καλόν ἐστι — καὶ γὰρ περὶ μόνον αὐτὸν τὸ καλόν —, οὐκ ἂν εἴη
καλὸν τὸ εἶναι τὸν ἄνθρωπον μόνον. τὸ δὲ μόνον εἶναι τὸν θεὸν ἔστι μὲν ἐκδέξ-
ασθαι καὶ οὕτως, ὅτι οὔτε πρὸ γενέσεως ἦν τι σὺν τῷ θεῷ οὔτε κόσμου γενομένου συντάττεταί τι αὐτῷ· χρῄζει γὰρ οὐδενὸς τὸ παράπαν. ἀμείνων δὲ ἥδε
ἡ ἐκδοχή· ὁ θεὸς μόνος ἐστὶ καὶ ἕν, οὐ σύγκριμα, φύσις ἁπλῆ, ἡμῶν δ' ἕκαστος
καὶ τῶν ἄλλων ὅσα γέγονε πολλά· οἷον ἐγὼ πολλά εἰμι, ψυχὴ σῶμα, καὶ ψυχῆς
ἄλογον λογικόν, πάλιν σώματος θερμὸν ψυχρὸν βαρὺ κοῦφον ξηρὸν ὑγρόν·
ὁ δὲ θεὸς οὐ σύγκριμα οὐδὲ ἐκ πολλῶν συνεστώς, ἀλλ' ἀμιγὴς ἄλλῳ· ὁ γὰρ ἂν
15 προσκριθῇ θεῷ, ἢ κρεῖσσόν ἐστιν αὐτοῦ ἢ ἔλασσον ἢ ἴσον αὐτῷ· οὔτε δὲ ἴσον
οὔτε κρεῖσσόν ἐστι θεοῦ, ἔλασσόν γὲ μὴν οὐδὲν αὐτῷ προσκρίνεται· εἰ δὲ μή,
καὶ αὐτὸς ἐλαττωθήσεται· εἰ δὲ τοῦτο, καὶ φθαρτὸς ἔσται, ὅπερ οὐδὲ θέμις
νοῆσαι. τέτακται οὖν ὁ θεὸς κατὰ τὸ ἓν καὶ τὴν μονάδα, μᾶλλον δὲ ἡ μονὰς
20 κατὰ τὸν ἕνα θεόν· πᾶς γὰρ ἀριθμὸς νεώτερος κόσμου, ὡς καὶ χρόνος, ὁ δὲ θεὸς
πρεσβύτερος κόσμου καὶ δημιουργός.

---

¹ For the sense of this Stoic term see supra, under nr. **999b**.

God alone is really 1292—God alone has veritable being. Hence, His virtue alone is real virtue.

Philo, *Quod deterius potiori insidiari soleat* 44, 160 (C.W. I, p. 294, l. 19):

Τῶν γὰρ ἀρετῶν ἡ μὲν θεοῦ πρὸς ἀλήθειάν ἐστι κατὰ τὸ εἶναι συνεστῶσα, ἐπεὶ καὶ ὁ θεὸς μόνος ἐν τῷ εἶναι ὑφέστηκεν· οὗ χάριν ἀναγκαίως ἐρεῖ περὶ αὐτοῦ· "ἐγώ εἰμι ὁ ὤν" (*Exod.* 3, 14), ὡς τῶν μετ' αὐτὸν οὐκ ὄντων κατὰ τὸ εἶναι, δόξῃ δὲ μόνον ὑφεστάναι νομιζομένων· ἡ δὲ Μωυσέως σκηνὴ συμβολικῶς οὖσα ἀνθρώπου ἀρετὴ κλήσεως, οὐχ ὑπάρξεως, ἀξιωθήσεται, μίμημα καὶ ἀπεικόνισμα τῆς θείας ἐκείνης ὑπάρχουσα.

Creation of the intelligible world 1293—First, God created the intelligible world, as a perfect and God-like pattern for the creation of material things.

a. Philo, *De opif. mundi* 4, 16 (C.W. I, p. 4-5):

Προλαβὼν γὰρ ὁ θεὸς ἅτε θεὸς ὅτι μίμημα καλὸν οὐκ ἄν ποτε γένοιτο δίχα καλοῦ παραδείγματος οὐδέ τι τῶν αἰσθητῶν ἀνυπαίτιον, ὃ μὴ πρὸς ἀρχέτυπον καὶ νοητὴν ἰδέαν ἀπεικονίσθη, βουληθεὶς τὸν ὁρατὸν κόσμον τουτονὶ δημιουργῆσαι προεξετύπου τὸν νοητόν, ἵνα χρώμενος ἀσωμάτῳ καὶ θεοειδεστάτῳ παραδείγματι τὸν σωματικὸν ἀπεργάσηται, πρεσβυτέρου νεώτερον ἀπεικόνισμα, τοσαῦτα περιέξοντα αἰσθητὰ γένη ὅσαπερ ἐν ἐκείνῳ νοητά.

The intelligible World is in the divine Mind **b.** The intelligible world has no other location than the divine Mind. Ib., 4, 17 - 5, 20 (C.W. I, p. 5-6):

Τὸν δ' ἐκ τῶν ἰδεῶν συνεστῶτα κόσμον ἐν τόπῳ τινὶ λέγειν ἢ ὑπονοεῖν οὐ θεμιτόν· ᾗ δὲ συνέστηκεν, εἰσόμεθα παρακολουθήσαντες εἰκόνι τινὶ τῶν παρ' ἡμῖν. ἐπειδὰν πόλις κτίζηται κατὰ πολλὴν φιλοτιμίαν βασιλέως ἤ τινος ἡγεμόνος αὐτοκρατοῦς ἐξουσίας μεταποιουμένου καὶ ἅμα τὸ φρόνημα λαμπροῦ τὴν εὐτυχίαν συνεπικοσμοῦντος, παρελθὼν ἔστιν ὅτε τις τῶν ἀπὸ παιδείας ἀνὴρ ἀρχιτεκτονικὸς καὶ τὴν εὐκρασίαν καὶ εὐκαιρίαν τοῦ τόπου θεασάμενος δια-γράφει πρῶτον ἐν ἑαυτῷ τὰ τῆς μελλούσης ἀποτελεῖσθαι πόλεως μέρη σχεδὸν ἅπαντα, ἱερὰ γυμνάσια πρυτανεῖα ἀγορὰς λιμένας νεωσοίκους στενωπούς, τειχῶν κατασκευάς, ἱδρύσεις οἰκιῶν καὶ δημοσίων ἄλλων οἰκοδομημάτων· εἶθ' ὥσπερ ἐν κηρῷ τῇ ἑαυτοῦ ψυχῇ τοὺς ἑκάστων δεξάμενος τύπους ἀγαλματοφορεῖ νοητὴν πόλιν, ἧς ἀνακινήσας τὰ εἴδωλα μνήμῃ τῇ συμφύτῳ καὶ τοὺς χαρακ-τῆρας ἔτι μᾶλλον ἐνσφραγισάμενος, οἷα δημιουργὸς ἀγαθός, ἀποβλέπων εἰς τὸ παράδειγμα τὴν ἐκ λίθων καὶ ξύλων ἄρχεται κατασκευάζειν, ἑκάστη τῶν ἀσωμάτων ἰδεῶν τὰς σωματικὰς ἐξομοιῶν οὐσίας. τὰ παραπλήσια δὴ καὶ περὶ θεοῦ δοξαστέον, ὡς ἄρα τὴν μεγαλόπολιν κτίζειν διανοηθεὶς ἐνενόησε πρότερον τοὺς τύπους αὐτῆς, ἐξ ὧν κόσμον νοητὸν συστησάμενος ἀπετέλει καὶ τὸν αἰσθητὸν παραδείγματι χρώμενος ἐκείνῳ. καθάπερ οὖν ἡ ἐν τῷ ἀρχιτεκτονικῷ προδιατυπωθεῖσα πόλις χώραν ἐκτὸς οὐκ εἶχεν, ἀλλ' ἐνεσφράγιστο τῇ τοῦ τεχνίτου ψυχῇ, τὸν αὐτὸν τρόπον οὐδ' ὁ ἐκ τῶν ἰδεῶν κόσμος ἄλλον ἂν ἔχοι τόπον ἢ τὸν θεῖον λόγον τὸν ταῦτα διακοσμήσαντα.

c. To put it in a simpler form, it *is* nothing else than the Word of God, when already engaged in the act of creation.   *It is the divine Mind or Logos*

Ib. 6, 24 (C.W. I, p. 7):

Εἰ δέ τις ἐθελήσειε γυμνοτέροις χρήσασθαι τοῖς ὀνόμασιν, οὐδὲν ἂν ἕτερον εἴποι τὸν νοητὸν κόσμον εἶναι ἢ θεοῦ λόγον ἤδη κοσμοποιοῦντος· οὐδὲ γὰρ ἡ νοητὴ πόλις ἕτερόν τί ἐστιν ἢ ὁ τοῦ ἀρχιτέκτονος λογισμὸς ἤδη τὴν [νοητὴν] πόλιν κτίζειν διανοουμένου.

d. That such is really Moses' doctrine and not his own interpretation is concluded by Philo from *Genesis* I 27.   *This doctrine inferred from Gen. I 27*

Philo, *De opif. mundi* 6, 25 (C.W. I, p. 7-8):

Τὸ δὲ δόγμα τοῦτο Μωυσέως ἐστίν, οὐκ ἐμόν· τὴν γοῦν ἀνθρώπου γένεσιν ἀναγράφων ἐν τοῖς ἔπειτα διαρρήδην ὁμολογεῖ, ὡς ἄρα κατ' εἰκόνα θεοῦ διετυπώθη (*Gen.* I, 27). εἰ δὲ τὸ μέρος εἰκὼν εἰκόνος [δῆλον ὅτι] καὶ τὸ ὅλον εἶδος, σύμπας οὗτος ὁ αἰσθητὸς κόσμος, εἰ μείζων τῆς ἀνθρωπίνης ἐστίν, μίμημα θείας εἰκόνος, δῆλον ὅτι καὶ ἡ ἀρχέτυπος σφραγίς, ὅν φαμεν νοητὸν εἶναι κόσμον, αὐτὸς ἂν εἴη [τὸ παράδειγμα, ἀρχέτυπος ἰδέα τῶν ἰδεῶν] ὁ θεοῦ λόγος.

1294—In *De special. legibus* I 6, 45-48 (C.W. V, p. 11-12) Ph. identifies the Platonic Ideas with the scriptural *powers* of God.   *The Ideas identified with the Powers of God*

In *Exod.* 33, 13 Moses prays God: "Reveal Thyself to me", and again, on having been answered that such knowledge is impossible to man, he prays (v. 18): "I beseech Thee that I may at least see the glory that surrounds Thee"; and this he explains as "the powers that keep guard around God".

Ἱκετεύω δὲ τὴν γοῦν περὶ σὲ δόξαν θεάσασθαι (*Exod.* 33, 18)· δόξαν δὲ σὴν εἶναι νομίζω τὰς περὶ σὲ δορυφορούσας δυνάμεις. —

Ὁ δὲ ἀμείβεται καί φησιν· "ἃς ἐπιζητεῖς δυνάμεις εἰσὶν ἀόρατοι καὶ νοηταὶ πάντως ἐμοῦ τοῦ ἀοράτου καὶ νοητοῦ· λέγω δὲ νοητὰς οὐχὶ τὰς ἤδη ὑπὸ νοῦ καταλαμβανομένας [1], ἀλλ' ὅτι εἰ καταλαμβάνεσθαι οἷαί τε εἶεν, οὐκ ἂν αἴσθησις

---

[1] Modern interpreters seem to find difficulties in the formula τὰς ἤδη ὑπὸ νοῦ καταλαμβανομένας and suggest that the text is corrupt (Heinemann, Colson). I think it is correct and means simply: "By intelligible I do not mean those which are actually apprehended by mind", i.e. not directly all our "notions" or "concepts".

αὐτὰς ἀλλ' ἀκραιφνέστατος νοῦς καταλαμβάνοι. πεφυκυῖαι δ' ἀκατάληπτοι κατὰ
τὴν οὐσίαν ὅμως παραφαίνουσιν ἐκμαγεῖόν τι καὶ ἀπεικόνισμα τῆς ἑαυτῶν
ἐνεργείας· οἷαι αἱ παρ' ὑμῖν σφραγῖδες — ὅταν <γὰρ> προσενεχθῇ κηρὸς ἤ
τις ὁμοιότροπος ὕλη, μυρίους ὅσους τύπους ἐναπομάττονται, μηδὲν ἀκρωτη-
ριασθεῖσαι μέρος, ἀλλ' ἐν ὁμοίῳ μένουσαι —, τοιαύτας ὑποληπτέον καὶ τὰς
περὶ ἐμὲ δυνάμεις περιποιούσας ἀποίοις ποιότητας καὶ μορφὰς ἀμόρφοις καὶ
μηδὲν τῆς ἀϊδίου φύσεως μήτ' ἀλλαττομένας μήτε μειουμένας. ὀνομάζουσι
δ' αὐτὰς οὐκ ἀπὸ σκοποῦ τινες τῶν παρ' ὑμῖν ἰδέας, ἐπειδὴ ἕκαστα τῶν ὄντων
εἰδοποιοῦσι τὰ ἄτακτα τάττουσαι καὶ τὰ ἄπειρα καὶ ἀόριστα καὶ ἀσχημάτιστα
περατοῦσαι καὶ περιορίζουσαι καὶ σχηματίζουσαι καὶ συνόλως τὸ χεῖρον εἰς
τὸ ἄμεινον μεθαρμοζόμεναι.

The identification of the *glory* of God with the *powers* that stand around Him
was suggested to Philo by the Septuagint translation of the Hebrew expression
Jahweh sabaoth by κύριος τῶν δυνάμεων in such well-known verses as Ps. 24, 9-10.

Creation of the intelligible world

1295—First, then, God created an intelligible heaven and earth.

a. *De opif. mundi*, 7, 29 (C.W. I, p. 9):

Πρῶτον οὖν ὁ ποιῶν ἐποίησεν οὐρανὸν ἀσώματον καὶ γῆν ἀόρατον καὶ ἀέρος
ἰδέαν καὶ κενοῦ· ὧν τὸ μὲν ἐπεφήμισε σκότος, ἐπειδὴ μέλας ὁ ἀὴρ τῇ φύσει,
τὴν δ' ἄβυσσον, πολύβυθον γὰρ τό γε κενὸν καὶ ἀχανές· εἶθ' ὕδατος ἀσώματον
οὐσίαν καὶ πνεύματος καὶ ἐπὶ πᾶσιν ἑβδόμου φωτός, ὃ πάλιν ἀσώματον ἦν καὶ
νοητὸν ἡλίου παράδειγμα καὶ πάντων ὅσα φωσφόρα ἄστρα κατὰ τὸν οὐρανὸν
ἔμελλε συνίστασθαι.

b. The invisible Light was an image of the Divine Logos.

Ib., 8, 31 (C.W. I, p. 9):

Τὸ δὲ ἀόρατον καὶ νοητὸν φῶς ἐκεῖνο θείου λόγου γέγονεν εἰκών.

The creation of man

1296—After all the rest, man is created in the image of God and in
His likeness.

a. *De opif. mundi* 23, 69 (C.W. I, p. 23):

Μετὰ δὴ τἄλλα πάντα, καθάπερ ἐλέχθη, τὸν ἄνθρωπόν φησι γεγενῆσθαι
κατ' εἰκόνα θεοῦ καὶ καθ' ὁμοίωσιν (*Gen.* 1, 26)· πάνυ καλῶς, ἐμφερέστερον
γὰρ οὐδὲν γηγενὲς ἀνθρώπου θεῷ, τὴν δ' ἐμφέρειαν μηδεὶς εἰκαζέτω σώματος
χαρακτῆρι· οὔτε γὰρ ἀνθρωπόμορφος ὁ θεὸς οὔτε θεοειδὲς τὸ ἀνθρώπειον
σῶμα. ἡ δὲ εἰκὼν λέλεκται κατὰ τὸν τῆς ψυχῆς ἡγεμόνα νοῦν. πρὸς γὰρ ἕνα
τὸν τῶν ὅλων ἐκεῖνον ὡς ἂν ἀρχέτυπον ὁ ἐν ἑκάστῳ τῶν κατὰ μέρος ἀπεικονίσθη,
τρόπον τινὰ θεὸς ὢν τοῦ φέροντος καὶ ἀγαλματοφοροῦντος αὐτόν· ὃν γὰρ ἔχει

λόγον ὁ μέγας ἡγεμὼν ἐν ἅπαντι τῷ κόσμῳ, τοῦτον ὡς ἔοικε καὶ ὁ ἀνθρώπινος νοῦς ἐν ἀνθρώπῳ.

Here again Ph. follows Plato's pattern in the *Timaeus*, where first the worldsoul was created, next the world and the heavenly bodies, and only after these the soul of man.

b. Man thus created in God's image, however, is not the concrete composed by soul and body, but an "intelligible" man, an "idea" or "type" or "seal". *The spiritual man is created after God's image*

Ib. 46, 134 (C.W. I, p. 46):

Μετὰ δὲ ταῦτά φησιν ὅτι "ἔπλασεν ὁ θεὸς τὸν ἄνθρωπον χοῦν λαβὼν ἀπὸ τῆς γῆς, καὶ ἐνεφύσησεν εἰς τὸ πρόσωπον αὐτοῦ πνοὴν ζωῆς" (*Gen.* 2, 7). ἐναργέστατα καὶ διὰ τούτου παρίστησι ὅτι διαφορὰ παμμεγέθης ἐστὶ τοῦ τε νῦν πλασθέντος ἀνθρώπου καὶ τοῦ κατὰ τὴν εἰκόνα θεοῦ γεγονότος πρότερον· ὁ μὲν διαπλασθεὶς αἰσθητὸς ἤδη μετέχων ποιότητος, ἐκ σώματος καὶ ψυχῆς συνεστώς, ἀνὴρ ἢ γυνή, φύσει θνητός· ὁ δὲ κατὰ τὴν εἰκόνα ἰδέα τις ἢ γένος ἢ σφραγίς, νοητός, ἀσώματος, οὔτ' ἄρρεν οὔτε θῆλυ, ἄφθαρτος φύσει.

c. The concrete and individual man is composite, half material half spiritual, half mortal half immortal.

Ib. 46, 135 (C.W. I, p. 46-47):

Τοῦ δ' αἰσθητοῦ καὶ ἐπὶ μέρους ἀνθρώπου τὴν κατασκευὴν σύνθετον εἶναί φησιν ἔκ τε γεώδους οὐσίας καὶ πνεύματος θείου· γεγενῆσθαι γὰρ τὸ μὲν σῶμα χοῦν τοῦ τεχνίτου λαβόντος καὶ μορφὴν ἀνθρωπίνην ἐξ αὐτοῦ διαπλάσαντος, τὴν δὲ ψυχὴν ἀπ' οὐδενὸς γενητοῦ τὸ παράπαν, ἀλλ' ἐκ τοῦ πατρὸς καὶ ἡγεμόνος τῶν πάντων· ὃ γὰρ ἐνεφύσησεν, οὐδὲν ἦν ἕτερον ἢ πνεῦμα θεῖον ἀπὸ τῆς μακαρίας καὶ εὐδαίμονος φύσεως ἐκείνης ἀποικίαν τὴν ἐνθάδε στειλάμενον ἐπ' ὠφελείᾳ τοῦ γένους ἡμῶν, ἵν' εἰ καὶ θνητόν ἐστι κατὰ τὴν ὁρατὴν μερίδα, κατὰ γοῦν τὴν ἀόρατον ἀθανατίζηται. διὸ καὶ κυρίως ἄν τις εἴποι τὸν ἄνθρωπον θνητῆς καὶ ἀθανάτου φύσεως εἶναι μεθόριον ἑκατέρας ὅσον ἀναγκαῖόν ἐστι μετέχοντα καὶ γεγενῆσθαι θνητὸν ὁμοῦ καὶ ἀθάνατον, θνητὸν μὲν κατὰ τὸ σῶμα, κατὰ δὲ τὴν διάνοιαν ἀθάνατον.

1297—The problem of evil is dealt with by Ph. after the creation of the *spiritual* man; for vice and virtue have their dwelling-place in mind and reason. Ph. solves it in the same way as Plato did: since God cannot be the Creator of any kind of evil, he ascribes vice in man to subordinate fellow-workers of the Creator. *The problem of evil*

a. Philo, *De opif. mundi* 24, 72-75 (C.W. I, p. 24-25):

Ἀπορήσειε δ' ἄν τις οὐκ ἀπὸ σκοποῦ, τί δήποτε τὴν ἀνθρώπου μόνου γένεσιν οὐχ ἑνὶ δημιουργῷ καθάπερ τἆλλα ἀνέθηκεν, ἀλλ' ὡσανεὶ πλείοσιν· εἰσάγει γὰρ τὸν πατέρα τῶν ὅλων ταυτὶ λέγοντα· "ποιήσωμεν ἄνθρωπον κατ' εἰκόνα ἡμετέραν καὶ καθ' ὁμοίωσιν". μὴ γὰρ χρεῖός ἐστιν, εἴποιμ' ἄν, οὑτινοσοῦν, ᾧ 1 πάντα ὑπήκοα; ἢ τὸν μὲν οὐρανὸν ἡνίκα ἐποίει καὶ τὴν γῆν καὶ τὴν θάλατταν, οὐδενὸς ἐδεήθη τοῦ συνεργήσοντος, ἄνθρωπον δὲ βραχὺ ζῷον οὕτως καὶ ἐπίκηρον οὐχ οἷός τε ἦν δίχα συμπράξεως ἑτέρων αὐτὸς ἀφ' ἑαυτοῦ κατασκευάσασθαι; τὴν μὲν οὖν ἀληθεστάτην αἰτίαν θεὸν ἀνάγκη μόνον εἰδέναι, τὴν δ' εἰκότι στοχασμῷ πιθανὴν καὶ εὔλογον εἶναι δοκοῦσαν οὐκ ἀποκρυπτέον. ἔστι 2 δὲ ἥδε. τῶν ὄντων τὰ μὲν οὔτ' ἀρετῆς οὔτε κακίας μετέχει, ὥσπερ φυτὰ καὶ ζῷα ἄλογα, τὰ μὲν ὅτι ἄψυχά τέ ἐστι καὶ ἀφαντάστῳ φύσει διοικεῖται, τὰ δ' ὅτι νοῦν καὶ λόγον ἐκτέτμηται· κακίας δὲ καὶ ἀρετῆς ὡς ἂν οἶκος νοῦς καὶ λόγος, 1 ᾧ πεφύκασιν ἐνδιαιτᾶσθαι· τὰ δ' αὖ μόνης κεκοινώνηκεν ἀρετῆς ἀμέτοχα πάσης ὄντα κακίας, ὥσπερ οἱ ἀστέρες· οὗτοι γὰρ ζῷά τε εἶναι λέγονται καὶ ζῷα νοερά, μᾶλλον δὲ νοῦς αὐτὸς ἕκαστος, ὅλος δι' ὅλων σπουδαῖος καὶ παντὸς ἀνεπίδεκτος κακοῦ· τὰ δὲ τῆς μικτῆς ἐστι φύσεως, ὥσπερ ἄνθρωπος, ὃς ἐπι- 5 δέχεται τἀναντία, φρόνησιν καὶ ἀφροσύνην, σωφροσύνην καὶ ἀκολασίαν, ἀνδρείαν καὶ δειλίαν, δικαιοσύνην καὶ ἀδικίαν, καὶ συνελόντι φράσαι ἀγαθὰ καὶ κακά, καλὰ καὶ αἰσχρά, ἀρετὴν καὶ κακίαν. τῷ δὴ πάντων πατρὶ θεῷ τὰ μὲν σπουδαῖα δι' αὑτοῦ μόνου ποιεῖν οἰκειότατον ἦν ἕνεκα τῆς πρὸς αὐτὸν συγγενείας, τὰ δὲ 1 ἀδιάφορα οὐκ ἀλλότριον, ἐπειδὴ καὶ ταῦτα τῆς ἔχθρας αὐτῷ κακίας ἀμοιρεῖ, τὰ δὲ μικτὰ τῇ μὲν οἰκεῖον τῇ δ' ἀνοίκειον, οἰκεῖον μὲν ἕνεκα τῆς ἀνακεκραμένης βελτίονος ἰδέας, ἀνοίκειον δ' ἕνεκα τῆς ἐναντίας καὶ χείρονος. διὰ τοῦτ' ἐπὶ μόνης τῆς ἀνθρώπου γενέσεώς φησιν ὅτι εἶπεν ὁ θεὸς "ποιήσωμεν", ὅπερ ἐμφαίνει συμπαράληψιν ἑτέρων ὡς ἂν συνεργῶν, ἵνα ταῖς μὲν ἀνεπιλήπτοις 2 βουλαῖς τε καὶ πράξεσιν ἀνθρώπου κατορθοῦντος ἐπιγράφηται θεὸς ὁ πάντων ἡγεμών, ταῖς δ' ἐναντίαις ἕτεροι τῶν ὑπηκόων· ἔδει γὰρ ἀναίτιον εἶναι κακοῦ τὸν πατέρα τοῖς ἐκγόνοις· κακὸν δ' ἡ κακία καὶ αἱ κατὰ κακίαν ἐνέργειαι.

b. Cp. Philo, *De fuga et inventione* 13, 67-68 (C.W. III, p. 124):

Τὰ μὲν γὰρ πρεσβύτερα ἀγαθά, οἷς ἡ ψυχὴ τρέφεται, ἀνέθηκε θεῷ, τὰ δὲ νεώτερα ὅσα ἐκ φυγῆς ἁμαρτημάτων περιγίνεται, θεράποντι θεοῦ. διὰ τοῦτ', οἶμαι, καὶ ἡνίκα τὰ τῆς κοσμοποιίας ἐφιλοσόφει, πάντα τἆλλα εἰπὼν ὑπὸ θεοῦ 2 γενέσθαι μόνον τὸν ἄνθρωπον ὡς ἂν μετὰ συνεργῶν ἑτέρων ἐδήλωσε διαπλασθέντα.

In Plato's *Timaeus* 41d-42e only the soul of man is made by the Demiurge and by Him alone, while the body is made by the "created gods", i.e. the astral Spirits (supra, nrs. **353-354**).

1298—Nevertheless, the soul of man is said by Ph. to be a copy of the The soul a
copy of the
Logos
Divine Logos and therefore, in the first man at least, perfect.

Philo, *De opif. mundi* 48, 139 (C.W. I, p. 48-49):

Ὅτι δὲ καὶ τὴν ψυχὴν ἄριστος ἦν, φανερόν· οὐδενὶ γὰρ ἑτέρῳ παραδείγματι
τῶν ἐν γενέσει πρὸς τὴν κατασκευὴν αὐτῆς ἔοικε χρήσασθαι, μόνῳ δ᾽ ὡς εἶπον τῷ
ἑαυτοῦ λόγῳ. διὸ φησιν ἀπεικόνισμα καὶ μίμημα γεγενῆσθαι τούτου τὸν ἄνθρωπον ἐμπνευσθέντα εἰς τὸ πρόσωπον, ἔνθα τῶν αἰσθήσεων ὁ τόπος, αἷς τὸ μὲν
σῶμα ἐψύχωσεν ὁ δημιουργός, τὸν δὲ βασιλέα λογισμὸν ἐνιδρυσάμενος τῷ
ἡγεμονικῷ παρέδωκε δορυφορεῖσθαι πρὸς τὰς χρωμάτων καὶ φωνῶν χυλῶν
τε αὖ καὶ ἀτμῶν καὶ τῶν παραπλησίων ἀντιλήψεις, ἃς ἄνευ αἰσθήσεως δι᾽
αὐτοῦ μόνου καταλαβεῖν οὐχ οἷός τε ἦν. ἀνάγκη δὲ παγκάλου παραδείγματος
πάγκαλον εἶναι τὸ μίμημα. θεοῦ δὲ λόγος καὶ αὐτοῦ κάλλους, ὅπερ ἐστὶν ἐν
τῇ φύσει κάλλος, ἀμείνων, οὐ κοσμούμενος κάλλει, κόσμος δ᾽ αὐτός, εἰ δεῖ
τάληθὲς εἰπεῖν, εὐπρεπέστατος ἐκείνου.

1299—The term *Logos* is used by Philo in different meanings. The term
Logos used
in different
senses

    a.   First, he knows a *transcendent Logos*, which is the divine Mind,
whose powers are infinite, as is said for instance in *De sacrif. Abelis et
Caini* 15, 59 (C.W. I, p. 226):

Ἀπερίγραφος γὰρ ὁ θεός, ἀπερίγραφοι δὲ αἱ δυνάμεις αὐτοῦ.

    b.   The Ideas, which God conceived as the pattern of the world to 1. The Logos
uncreated
and eternal
be created, are therefore said to have their place *within* the *Divine Logos*
(*Opif.* 5, 20; supra, **1293b** the end), whose boundless powers are only
limited by the capacity of the creation.

Philo, *Opif.* 6, 23 (C.W. I, p. 7):

— μόνῳ δὲ αὐτῷ χρησάμενος ὁ θεὸς ἔγνω δεῖν εὐεργετεῖν ἀταμιεύτοις καὶ
πλουσίαις χάρισι.
— Ἀλλ᾽ οὐ πρὸς τὸ μέγεθος εὐεργετεῖ τῶν ἑαυτοῦ χαρίτων — ἀπερίγραφοι
γὰρ αὗταί γε καὶ ἀτελεύτητοι —, πρὸς δὲ τὰς τῶν εὐεργετουμένων δυνάμεις·
οὐ γὰρ ὡς πέφυκεν ὁ θεὸς εὖ ποιεῖν, οὕτως καὶ τὸ γινόμενον εὖ πάσχειν, ἐπεὶ
τοῦ μὲν αἱ δυνάμεις ὑπερβάλλουσι, τὸ δ᾽ ἀσθενέστερον ὂν ἢ ὥστε δέξασθαι
τὸ μέγεθος αὐτῶν ἀπεῖπεν ἄν, εἰ μὴ διεμετρήσατο σταθμησάμενος εὐαρμόστως
ἑκάστῳ τὸ ἐπιβάλλον.

In this sense then the Logos is uncreated and eternal.

Wolfson I, p. 210 and 223, described it rightly by saying that, before God
conceived the κόσμος τῶν ἰδεῶν which served as a pattern of the things of the
world to be created, there existed from eternity an infinite variety of Ideas in the
Mind of God. The limited κόσμος τῶν ἰδεῶν however, conceived "at a certain

moment" by God when He is going to create the world, is according to Wolfson's account still uncreated, but not eternal. It should be noticed, however, that Ph. explains even creation as an act of the divine Mind *before time comes in*; χρόνος γὰρ οὐκ ἦν πρὸ κόσμου (*Opif.* 7, 26).

Therefore, also his κόσμος τῶν ἰδεῶν before the creation must certainly be considered as eternal.

2. The transcendent Logos created   **1300—a.** The κόσμος νοητός, then, is created by God to an existence, as it seems, outside His thoughts.

Philo, *Opif.* 7, 29 (supra, **1295a**).

b. This creation is explained by Ph. explicitly as not being an event in time.

but not in time   Philo, *Opif.* 7, 26 (C.W. I, p. 8):

Φησὶ δ' ὡς "ἐν ἀρχῇ ἐποίησεν ὁ θεὸς τὸν οὐρανὸν καὶ τὴν γῆν", τὴν ἀρχὴν παραλαμβάνων οὐχ ὡς οἴονταί τινες τὴν κατὰ χρόνον· χρόνος γὰρ οὐκ ἦν πρὸ κόσμου, ἀλλ' ἢ σὺν αὐτῷ γέγονεν ἢ μετ' αὐτόν· ἐπεὶ γὰρ διάστημα τῆς τοῦ κόσμου κινήσεώς [1] ἐστιν ὁ χρόνος, προτέρα δὲ τοῦ κινουμένου κίνησις οὐκ ἂν γένοιτο, ἀλλ' ἀναγκαῖον αὐτὴν ἢ ὕστερον ἢ ἅμα συνίστασθαι, ἀναγκαῖον ἄρα καὶ τὸν χρόνον ἢ ἰσήλικα κόσμου γεγονέναι ἢ νεώτερον ἐκείνου· πρεσβύτερον δ' ἀποφαίνεσθαι τολμᾶν ἀφιλόσοφον.

Also the "created Logos" in Philo's sense must therefore be regarded as eternal.

The Logos described as rays of light   **c.** The created κόσμος νοητός is also described as myriads of rays of light poured forth by God as "the archetypal Light".

Philo, *De cherubim* 28, 97 (C.W. I, p. 193-194):

(God is His own light).

Ὁ γὰρ τοῦ ὄντος ὀφθαλμὸς φωτὸς ἑτέρου πρὸς κατάληψιν οὐ δεῖται, αὐτὸς δ' ὢν ἀρχέτυπος αὐγὴ μυρίας ἀκτῖνας ἐκβάλλει, ὧν οὐδεμία ἐστὶν αἰσθητή, νοηταὶ δ' ἅπασαι· παρὸ καὶ μόνος ὁ νοητὸς θεὸς αὐταῖς χρῆται, τῶν δὲ γενέσεως μεμοιραμένων οὐδείς· αἰσθητὸν γὰρ τὸ γενόμενον, αἰσθήσει δὲ ἀκατάληπτος ἡ νοητὴ φύσις.

Three centuries later the great Athanasius will use the simile of rays of light poured forth by God to illustrate that the Word or "Son" is of the substance of the Father and therefore uncreated (*Or. c. Arianos* I 28, II 33, II 34, III 4, III 5, III 13 (the end), III 36, IV 10). The fact that Philo did not distinguish between "generation" and "creation" gave rise to theological difficulties; for the "created" (transcendent) Logos is called by him God, but in the sense of a δεύτερος θεός subordinate to the πρῶτος Θεός. See our next nr.

Intermediate place of the created Logos   **1301**—The created Logos occupies an intermediate place between God and the world.

---

[1] This is Chrysippus' definition of time (Stob. Ecl. I, p. 106, 5 W.; SVF II 509 ff.).

a. Philo, *Leg. alleg.* III 61, 175 - 62, 177 (C.W. I, p. 151 f.):

Ὁ λόγος δὲ τοῦ θεοῦ ὑπεράνω παντός ἐστι τοῦ κόσμου καὶ πρεσβύτατος καὶ γενικώτατος τῶν ὅσα γέγονεν. —

Ὁ δὲ Ἰακὼβ καὶ τὸν λόγον ὑπερκύψας ὑπ' αὐτοῦ φησι τρέφεσθαι τοῦ θεοῦ, λέγει δ' οὕτως· "ὁ θεός, ᾧ εὐηρέστησαν οἱ πατέρες μου Ἀβραὰμ καὶ Ἰσαάκ, ὁ θεὸς ὁ τρέφων με ἐκ νεότητος ἕως τῆς ἡμέρας ταύτης, ὁ ἄγγελος ὁ ῥυόμενός με ἐκ πάντων τῶν κακῶν, εὐλογήσαι τὰ παιδία ταῦτα" (*Gen.* 48, 15, 16). ὡραῖος οὗτος ὁ τρόπος· τροφέα τὸν θεόν, οὐχὶ λόγον, ἡγεῖται, τὸν δὲ ἄγγελον, ὅς ἐστι λόγος, ὥσπερ ἰατρὸν κακῶν· φυσικώτατα· ἀρέσκει γὰρ αὐτῷ τὰ μὲν προηγούμενα ἀγαθὰ αὐτοπροσώπως αὐτὸν τὸν ὄντα διδόναι, τὰ δεύτερα δὲ τοὺς ἀγγέλους καὶ λόγους αὐτοῦ· δεύτερα δ' ἐστὶν ὅσα περιέχει κακῶν ἀπαλλαγήν.

Cp. also *Leg. alleg.* II 21, 86:
Τὸ δὲ γενικώτατόν ἐστιν ὁ θεός, καὶ δεύτερος ὁ Θεοῦ Λόγος.

b. The created Logos is called *God* by Philo, but without the article.

Philo, *De somniis* I 39, 227-229 (C.W. III, p. 253 f.):

The angel of Jahweh spoke to Jacob in his dream:

"Ἐγώ εἰμι ὁ θεὸς ὁ ὀφθείς σοι ἐν τόπῳ θεοῦ" (*Gen.* 31, 13) [1]. πάγκαλόν γε αὔχημα ψυχῇ, τὸ ἀξιοῦν θεὸν ἐπιφαίνεσθαι καὶ ἐνομιλεῖν αὐτῇ. μὴ παρέλθῃς δὲ τὸ εἰρημένον, ἀλλὰ ἀκριβῶς ἐξέτασον, εἰ τῷ ὄντι δύο εἰσὶ θεοί· λέγεται γὰρ ὅτι "ἐγώ εἰμι ὁ θεὸς ὁ ὀφθείς σοι", οὐκ ἐν τόπῳ ἐμῷ, ἀλλ' "ἐν τόπῳ θεοῦ", ὡς ἂν ἑτέρου. τί οὖν χρὴ λέγειν; ὁ μὲν ἀληθείᾳ θεὸς εἷς ἐστιν, οἱ δ' ἐν καταχρήσει λεγόμενοι πλείους. διὸ καὶ ὁ ἱερὸς λόγος ἐν τῷ παρόντι τὸν μὲν ἀληθείᾳ διὰ τοῦ ἄρθρου μεμήνυκεν εἰπών· "ἐγώ εἰμι ὁ θεός", τὸν δ' ἐν καταχρήσει χωρὶς ἄρθρου φάσκων· "ὁ ὀφθείς σοι ἐν τόπῳ", οὐ τοῦ θεοῦ, ἀλλ' αὐτὸ μόνον "θεοῦ". καλεῖ δὲ θεὸν τὸν πρεσβύτατον αὐτοῦ νυνὶ λόγον.

> It is called Θεός, but not ὁ Θεός

c. He is also called *the elder Son of God*, while the visible world is called His younger Son.

> Also „the elder Son of God"

Philo, *Quod Deus sit immutabilis* 6, 31 (C. W. II, p. 63):

Ὁ μὲν γὰρ κόσμος οὗτος νεώτερος υἱὸς θεοῦ, ἅτε αἰσθητὸς ὤν· τὸν γὰρ πρεσβύτερον [οὐδένα εἶπε] — νοητὸς δ' ἐκεῖνος — πρεσβείων ἀξιώσας παρ' ἑαυτῷ καταμένειν διενοήθη.

1302—The Ideas, after having served as patterns on which God modelled the world, were introduced by Him into the world to act within

> 3. The Logos as the Law immanent in nature

[1] The formula of the Septuagint version ἐν τόπῳ θεοῦ is a translation of the Hebrew word *Bethel*.

Sensible things bear an impress of „the archetypal seal" as the immutable laws of nature. See above, nr. **1293d**, where the κόσμος αἰσθητός is called "a copy of a divine image", sc. of the created but transcendent κόσμος νοητός, which in this very passage is also called "the archetypal seal".

a. Philo, *De fuga et inventione* 2, 12 (C.W. III, p. 112):

Γέγονέ τε γὰρ ὁ κόσμος καὶ πάντως ὑπ' αἰτίου τινὸς γέγονεν· ὁ δὲ τοῦ ποιοῦντος λόγος αὐτός ἐστιν ἡ σφραγίς, ᾗ τῶν ὄντων ἕκαστον μεμόρφωται· παρὸ καὶ τέλειον τοῖς γινομένοις ἐξ ἀρχῆς παρακολουθεῖ τὸ εἶδος, ἅτε ἐκμαγεῖον καὶ εἰκὼν τελείου λόγου.

Cp. later, in Athanasius, *Or. c. Arianos* II 79:
Αὐτὴ ἡ δημιουργὸς καὶ ἀληθινὴ Σοφία, ἧς τύπος ἐστὶν ἡ ἐν κόσμῳ ἐκχυθεῖσα σοφία . . . ἡ ἐγκτιζομένη τοῖς ἔργοις (i.e. in things created).

b. Cp. *De mutatione nominum* 23, 135 (C.W. III, p.179), where "the seal of the universe, the archetypal Idea" appears on a level with "the world-order, the chain of destiny, the correspondence and sequence of all things".

Εἱμαρμένη Tamar says: "To whomsoever these things belong, of him I bear a child".

Τίνος ὁ δακτύλιος, ἡ πίστις [1], ἡ τῶν ὅλων σφραγίς, ἡ ἀρχέτυπος ἰδέα, ᾗ τὰ πάντ' ἀνείδεα ὄντα καὶ ἄποια σημειωθέντα ἐτυπώθη; τίνος δὲ καὶ <ὁ> ὁρμίσκος, ἡ [ὁ κόσμος] εἱμαρμένη, ἀκολουθία καὶ ἀναλογία τῶν συμπάντων εἰρμὸν ἔχουσα ἀδιάλυτον;

Cp. what has been said above of the Stoic notion of εἱμαρμένη and of cosmic sympathy.

The immutable laws of nature **c.** The immutable laws of nature are mentioned e.g. in *De opif. mundi* 19, 61 (C.W. I, p. 20):

Εἰς τοσαύτας καὶ οὕτως ἀναγκαίας διατείνουσιν ὠφελείας αἱ τῶν κατ' οὐρανὸν φύσεις τε καὶ κινήσεις ἀστέρων· εἰς πόσα δ' ἄλλα φαίην ἂν ἔγωγε τῶν ἡμῖν μὲν ἀδηλουμένων — οὐ γὰρ πάντα τῷ θνητῷ γένει γνώριμα — πρὸς δὲ τὴν τοῦ ὅλου συνεργούντων διαμονήν, ἃ θεσμοῖς καὶ νόμοις, οὓς ὥρισεν ὁ θεὸς ἀκινήτους ἐν τῷ παντί, συμβαίνει πάντη τε καὶ πάντως ἐπιτελεῖσθαι.

Cp. also *De special. legibus* IV 14, 232 (C.W. V, p. 263):
Πάντα ἰσότης τά τε κατ' οὐρανὸν καὶ τὰ ἐπὶ γῆς εὖ διετάξατο νόμοις καὶ θεσμοῖς ἀκινήτοις.

The cyclical motion of the Logos **d.** Even the Stoic idea of the cyclical motion of the universal order appears in Philo, *Quod Deus sit immutabilis* 36, 176 (C.W. II, p. 92):

---

[1] "The pledge of faith".

Χορεύει γὰρ ἐν κύκλῳ λόγος ὁ θεῖος, ὃν οἱ πολλοὶ τῶν ἀνθρώπων ὀνομάζουσι τύχην· εἶτα ἀεὶ ῥέων κατὰ πόλεις καὶ ἔθνη καὶ χώρας τὰ ἄλλων ἄλλοις καὶ πᾶσι τὰ πάντων ἐπινέμει, χρόνοις αὐτὸ μόνον ἀλλάττων τὰ παρ' ἑκάστοις, ἵνα ὡς μία πόλις ἡ οἰκουμένη πᾶσα τὴν ἀρίστην πολιτειῶν ἄγῃ δημοκρατίαν.

e. Ph. also calls "the divine Logos", which is the active element of Λόγος σπερ-
knowledge, both of the intellect and of the senses, σπερματικὸς καὶ ματικὸς καὶ
τεχνικός.   τεχνικός

Philo, *Quis rerum divinarum heres sit* 24, 119 (C.W. III, p. 28):

Ὁ γὰρ διοιγνὺς τὴν μήτραν ἑκάστων, τοῦ μὲν νοῦ πρὸς τὰς νοητὰς καταλήψεις, τοῦ δὲ λόγου πρὸς τὰς διὰ φωνῆς ἐνεργείας, τῶν δὲ αἰσθήσεων πρὸς τὰς
ἀπὸ τῶν ὑποκειμένων ἐγγινομένας φαντασίας, τοῦ δὲ σώματος πρὸς τὰς οἰκείους αὐτῷ σχέσεις τε καὶ κινήσεις ἀόρατος καὶ σπερματικὸς καὶ τεχνικὸς
θεῖός ἐστι λόγος.

In the *Legatio ad Gaium* 8, 55 (C.W. VI, p. 166) he speaks of λόγοι σπερματικοί.

1303—Ph., however, never identifies the immanent law of nature The imma-
with God. He definitely opposed the Stoic identification of God with nent law of
Εἱμαρμένη and those astrological beliefs which rather generally were identified
connected with it.   with God

a. Philo, *De migratione Abr.* 32, 179-181 (C.W. II, p. 303):

Οὗτοι (sc. οἱ Χαλδαῖοι) τὸν φαινόμενον τοῦτον κόσμον ἐν τοῖς οὖσιν ὑπετό-
πησαν εἶναι μόνον, ἢ θεὸν ὄντα αὐτὸν ἢ ἐν αὐτῷ θεὸν περιέχοντα, τὴν τῶν
ὅλων ψυχήν· εἱμαρμένην τε καὶ ἀνάγκην θεοπλαστήσαντες ἀσεβείας πολλῆς
κατέπλησαν τὸν ἀνθρώπινον βίον, ἀναδιδάξαντες ὡς δίχα τῶν φαινομένων
οὐδενός ἐστιν οὐδὲν αἴτιον τὸ παράπαν, ἀλλ' ἡλίου καὶ σελήνης καὶ τῶν ἄλλων
ἀστέρων αἱ περίοδοι τά τε ἀγαθὰ καὶ τὰ ἐναντία ἑκάστῳ τῶν ὄντων ἀπονέ-
μουσι. Μωυσῆς μέντοι τῇ μὲν ἐν τοῖς μέρεσι κοινωνίᾳ καὶ συμπαθείᾳ τοῦ
παντὸς ἔοικε συνεπιγράφεσθαι, ἕνα καὶ γενητὸν ἀποφηνάμενος τὸν κόσμον
εἶναι . . . , τῇ δὲ περὶ θεοῦ δόξῃ διαφέρεσθαι· μήτε γὰρ τὸν κόσμον μήτε τὴν
τοῦ κόσμου ψυχὴν τὸν πρῶτον εἶναι θεὸν μηδὲ τοὺς ἀστέρας ἢ τὰς χορείας
αὐτῶν τὰ πρεσβύτατα τῶν συμβαινόντων ἀνθρώποις αἴτια, ἀλλὰ συνέχεσθαι
μὲν τόδε τὸ πᾶν ἀοράτοις δυνάμεσιν, ἃς ἀπὸ γῆς ἐσχάτων ἄχρις οὐρανοῦ
περάτων ὁ δημιουργὸς ἀπέτεινε, τοῦ μὴ ἀνεθῆναι τὰ δεθέντα καλῶς προμη-
θούμενος· δεσμοὶ γὰρ αἱ δυνάμεις τοῦ παντὸς ἄρρηκτοι.

According to this passage the established world-order is maintained by spiritual
beings, called "the powers". And these powers are, as Ph. says repeatedly, governed
or conducted by the divine Logos.

b. Thus, the divine Logos is represented as the charioteer, conducting the powers, but commanded by God, who is seated in the chariot and gives directions to the charioteer.

The charioteer conducting the powers

Philo, *De fuga et inventione* 19, 101 (C.W. III, p. 132):

Ὁ δ᾽ ὑπεράνω τούτων λόγος θεῖος εἰς ὁρατὴν οὐκ ἦλθεν ἰδέαν, ἅτε μηδενὶ τῶν κατ᾽ αἴσθησιν ἐμφερὴς ὤν, ἀλλ᾽ αὐτὸς εἰκὼν ὑπάρχων θεοῦ, τῶν νοητῶν ἅπαξ ἁπάντων ὁ πρεσβύτατος, ὁ ἐγγυτάτω, μηδενὸς ὄντος μεθορίου διαστήματος, τοῦ μόνου, ὃ ἔστιν ἀψευδῶς, ἐφιδρυμένος. λέγεται γάρ· "λαλήσω σοι ἄνωθεν τοῦ ἱλαστηρίου, ἀνὰ μέσον τῶν δυεῖν Χερουβίμ" (*Exod.* 25, 21), ὥστ᾽ ἡνίοχον μὲν εἶναι τῶν δυνάμεων τὸν λόγον, ἔποχον δὲ τὸν λαλοῦντα, ἐπικελευόμενον τῷ ἡνιόχῳ τὰ πρὸς ὀρθὴν τοῦ παντὸς ἡνιόχησιν.

It can hardly be said, as is done by Wolfson, that it is the immanent Logos who is represented here as the charioteer. It is rather the Powers that represent the immanent world-order; and they are governed by the *transcendent* Logos, "who did not take a visible form". The transcendent Logos, however, is itself an *image* of God, though nearest to Him (τῶν νοητῶν πρεσβύτατος). It occupies, as we saw above, an intermediate place.

c. Again, in another passage, commenting on the beginning of the 23rd psalm ("The Lord is my shepherd; I shall not want"), Ph. represents the Logos as the Shepherd, set by God over the flock of the elements and all living beings (including the heavenly bodies), "like some viceroy of a great king".

The Shepherd of the flock

Philo, *De agricultura* 12, 51 (C.W. II, p. 105-106):

Τοῦτο μέντοι τὸ ᾆσμα παντὶ φιλοθέῳ μελετᾶν ἐμπρεπές, τῷ δὲ δὴ κόσμῳ καὶ διαφερόντως· καθάπερ γάρ τινα ποίμνην γῆν καὶ ὕδωρ καὶ ἀέρα καὶ πῦρ καὶ ὅσα ἐν τούτοις φυτά τε αὖ καὶ ζῷα, τὰ μὲν θνητὰ τὰ δὲ θεῖα, ἔτι δὲ οὐρανοῦ φύσιν καὶ ἡλίου καὶ σελήνης περιόδους καὶ τῶν ἄλλων ἀστέρων τροπάς τε αὖ καὶ χορείας ἐναρμονίους ὁ ποιμὴν καὶ βασιλεὺς θεὸς ἄγει κατὰ δίκην καὶ νόμον, προστησάμενος τὸν ὀρθὸν αὐτοῦ λόγον καὶ πρωτόγονον υἱόν, ὃς τὴν ἐπιμέλειαν τῆς ἱερᾶς ταύτης ἀγέλης οἷά τις μεγάλου βασιλέως ὕπαρχος διαδέξεται· καὶ γὰρ εἴρηταί που· "'Ἰδοὺ ἐγώ εἰμι, ἀποστέλλω ἄγγελόν μου εἰς πρόσωπόν σου τοῦ φυλάξαι σε ἐν τῇ ὁδῷ" (*Exod.* 23, 20).

Here again the Logos, called ὀρθὸς Λόγος of God and His Firstborn Son, is certainly not the immanent order of the universe, but the transcendent Logos, who occupies the intermediate position of a satrap of the great King. But cp. **1306.**

That for a Platonist of those days the idea of God as the ἀγωγεύς or κορυφαῖος of the heavenly bodies is quite familiar, may be seen in Maximus Tyrius 41, 2 (Hobein), who calls God:

Τὸν οὐρανοῦ ἁρμοστήν, τὸν ἡλίου καὶ σελήνης ἀγωγέα, τὸν κορυφαῖον τῆς τῶν ἄστρων περιφορᾶς καὶ δινήσεως καὶ χορείας καὶ δρόμου.

The simile of the κορυφαῖος was used first, so far as we can see, by the author of the pseudo-Aristotelian treatise Περὶ κόσμου, Arist., Bekker 399a 12-21 (Didot vol. III p. 638, l. 44-51). In his 6th ch. he gives an ample description of the work of Providence. Here, too, we find the Lord and Governor of the universe compared with the Persian kings [1], a simile by which the author wishes to illustrate that it would not suit the Lord of the universe to exercise a direct and all-embracing providence, "enduring the trouble of an animal which works and toils itself" (p. 636, 40-43) [2] or of a slave. It suits Him to have His place ἐπὶ τῆς ἀνωτάτω χώρας, τὴν δὲ δύναμιν διὰ τοῦ σύμπαντος κόσμου διήκουσαν ἥλιόν τε κινεῖν καὶ σελήνην, καὶ τὸν πάντα οὐρανὸν περιάγειν, αἴτιόν τε γίνεσθαι τοῖς ἐπὶ τῆς γῆς σωτηρίας (p. 637, 50-54) [3].

Thus, we shall find in Plotinus the idea of providence exercised from a distance, and distinguished from direct providence, which is exercised only by soul coming into contact with a body. Below, nrs. **1376** and **1426**.

To Philo's view of the universe, cp. also Plotinus' view of the sensible world as being full of δυνάμεις. Below, nr. **1428e, f**.

1304—Elsewhere, spiritual beings—"souls" or "spirits"—floating in the air between heaven and earth, are identified by Ph. with the daemons of philosophy (cp. above, our nr. **431a**) and with the angels in the books of Moses.

    a. Philo, *De gigantibus* 2, 6-9 and 3, 12 (C.W. II, p. 43 f.):   **The angels**

Οὓς ἄλλοι φιλόσοφοι δαίμονας, ἀγγέλους Μωυσῆς εἴωθεν ὀνομάζειν· ψυχαὶ δ' εἰσὶ κατὰ τὸν ἀέρα πετόμεναι. καὶ μηδεὶς ὑπολάβῃ μῦθον εἶναι τὸ εἰρημένον· ἀνάγκη γὰρ ὅλον δι' ὅλων τὸν κόσμον ἐψυχῶσθαι, τῶν πρώτων καὶ στοιχειωδῶν μερῶν ἑκάστου τὰ οἰκεῖα καὶ πρόσφορα ζῷα περιέχοντος, γῆς μὲν τὰ χερσαῖα, θαλάττης δὲ καὶ ποταμῶν τὰ ἔνυδρα, πυρὸς δὲ τὰ πυρίγονα — λόγος δ' ἔχει ταῦτα κατὰ Μακεδονίαν μάλιστα γίνεσθαι —, οὐρανοῦ δὲ τοὺς ἀστέρας. καὶ γὰρ οὗτοι ψυχαὶ ὅλαι δι' ὅλων ἀκήρατοί τε καὶ θεῖαι, παρὸ καὶ κύκλῳ κινοῦνται τὴν συγγενεστάτην νῷ κίνησιν· νοῦς γὰρ ἕκαστος αὐτῶν ἀκραιφνέστατος. ἔστιν οὖν ἀναγκαῖον καὶ τὸν ἀέρα ζῴων πεπληρῶσθαι· ταῦτα δὲ ἡμῖν ἐστιν ἀόρατα, ὅτιπερ καὶ αὐτὸς οὐχ ὁρατὸς αἰσθήσει. ἀλλ' οὐ παρ' ὅσον ἀδύνατος ἡ ὄψις ψυχῶν φαντασιωθῆναι τύπους, διὰ τοῦτ' οὔκ εἰσιν ἐν ἀέρι ψυχαί, κατα-λαμβάνεσθαι δ' αὐτὰς ἀναγκαῖον ὑπὸ νοῦ, ἵνα πρὸς τῶν ὁμοίων τὸ ὅμοιον θεωρῆται. — Τῶν οὖν ψυχῶν αἱ μὲν πρὸς σώματα κατέβησαν, αἱ δὲ οὐδενὶ τῶν γῆς μορίων ἠξίωσάν ποτε συνενεχθῆναι. ταύταις ἀφιερωθείσαις καὶ τῆς τοῦ πατρὸς θεραπείας περιεχομέναις ὑπηρέτισι καὶ διακόνοις ὁ δημιουργὸς εἴωθε χρῆσθαι πρὸς τὴν τῶν θνητῶν ἐπιστασίαν.

---

[1] For this very reason Festugière (*Le Dieu Cosmique* p. 479) dates the treatise at the beginning of our era. It might be even earlier and come from the school of Posidonius.

[2] Bekker 397b, 20-23.

[3] Bekker 398b, 6-10.

b. Cp. Philo, *De somniis* I 134-135, where the Jacob's ladder (*Genesis* 28, 12-13) is identified with the air, which up to the Moon is said to be full of souls without body (C.W. III, p. 234).

Κλῖμαξ τοίνυν ἐν μὲν τῷ κόσμῳ συμβολικῶς λέγεται ὁ ἀήρ, οὗ βάσις μέν ἐστι γῆ, κορυφὴ δ' οὐρανός· ἀπὸ γὰρ τῆς σεληνιακῆς σφαίρας, ἣν ἐσχάτην μὲν τῶν κατ' οὐρανὸν κύκλων, πρώτην δὲ τῶν πρὸς ἡμᾶς ἀναγράφουσιν οἱ φροντισταὶ τῶν μετεώρων, ἄχρι γῆς ἐσχάτης ὁ ἀὴρ πάντη ταθεὶς ἔφθακεν. οὗτος δ' ἐστὶ ψυχῶν ἀσωμάτων οἶκος, ἐπειδὴ πάντα τῷ ποιητῇ τὰ τοῦ κόσμου μέρη καλὸν ἔδοξεν εἶναι ζῴων ἀναπληρῶσαι. διὰ τοῦτο γῆ μὲν τὰ χερσαῖα ἐγκατεσκεύαζε, θαλάτταις δὲ καὶ ποταμοῖς τὰ ἔνυδρα, οὐρανῷ δὲ τοὺς ἀστέρας — καὶ γὰρ ἕκαστος τούτων οὐ μόνον ζῷον, ἀλλὰ καὶ νοῦς ὅλος δι' ὅλων ὁ καθαρώτατος εἶναι λέγεται· — ὥστε καὶ ἐν τῷ λοιπῷ τμήματι τοῦ παντός, ἀέρι, ζῷα γέγονεν. εἰ δὲ μὴ αἰσθήσει καταληπτά, τί τοῦτο; καὶ ψυχὴ γὰρ ἀόρατον.

See also **1306c**.

We shall find the theme again in Plutarch, *De defectu oraculorum* and *De facie in orbe lunae* (infra, nrs. **1318** and **1319**).

The idea of spiritual Powers ruling the forces of Nature or identified with them is seen e.g. in the N.T., *Joh.* 5, 4 (the angel of the pond of Bethesda), and is found in many of the Christian Fathers. J. H. Newman is quite familiar with it, as appears for instance in his Sermon on *The Powers of Nature* (*Parochial and Plain Sermons* II 29), where he says: "I do not pretend to say that we are told in Scripture what Matter is; but I affirm that, as our souls move our bodies, . . . so there are spiritual Intelligences which move those wonderful and vast portions of the natural world which seem to be inanimate" (p. 361).

The Logos the instrumental cause of creation

1305—Sometimes the Logos is called the instrumental cause of creation, or the ὄργανον δι' οὗ God created the world.

a. Philo, *De cherubim* 35, 126-127 (C.W. I, p. 200):

Φέρε γάρ, εἴ τις ἀνέροιτο, οἰκία καὶ πόλις πᾶσα ἵνα κατασκευασθῇ, τίνα συνελθεῖν δεῖ; ἆρ' οὐ δημιουργὸν καὶ λίθους καὶ ξύλα καὶ ὄργανα; τί οὖν ἐστι δημιουργὸς πλὴν τὸ αἴτιον ὑφ' οὗ; τί δὲ λίθοι καὶ ξύλα πλὴν ἡ ὕλη, ἐξ ἧς ἡ κατασκευή; τί δὲ τὰ ὄργανα πλὴν τὰ δι' ὧν; τίνος δὲ ἕνεκα πλὴν σκέπης καὶ ἀσφαλείας, τὸ δι' ὃ τοῦτό ἐστι; μετελθὼν οὖν ἀπὸ τῶν ἐν μέρει κατασκευῶν ἴδε τὴν μεγίστην οἰκίαν ἢ πόλιν, τόνδε τὸν κόσμον· εὑρήσεις γὰρ αἴτιον μὲν αὐτοῦ τὸν θεὸν ὑφ' οὗ γέγονεν, ὕλην δὲ τὰ τέσσαρα στοιχεῖα ἐξ ὧν συνεκράθη, ὄργανον δὲ λόγον θεοῦ δι' οὗ κατεσκευάσθη, τῆς δὲ κατασκευῆς αἰτίαν τὴν ἀγαθότητα τοῦ δημιουργοῦ.

To the four Aristotelian causes (above, nrs. **393-394**) apparently the later Stoa added one or two others. Seneca, *Ep.* 65, 8 speaks of five causes:

Quinque ergo causae sunt, ut Plato dicit: *id ex quo, id a quo, id in quo, id ad quod, id propter quod.*

Cp. Simpl., *In Arist. Phys.* 184, l. 11, citing Porphyry:

Τετραχῶς οὖν ἡ ἀρχὴ κατὰ τὸν Ἀριστοτέλην· ἢ γὰρ τὸ ἐξ οὗ ὡς ἡ ὕλη ἢ τὸ καθ' ὃ ὡς τὸ εἶδος ἢ τὸ ὑφ' οὗ ὡς τὸ ποιοῦν ἢ τὸ δι' ὃ ὡς τὸ τέλος. Κατὰ δὲ Πλάτωνα καὶ τὸ πρὸς ὃ ὡς τὸ παράδειγμα καὶ τὸ δι' οὗ ὡς τὸ ὀργανικόν.

b. Philo, *De special. legibus* I 81 (C.W. V, p. 21):

Λόγος δ' ἐστὶν εἰκὼν θεοῦ, δι' οὗ σύμπας ὁ κόσμος ἐδημιουργεῖτο.

Here also the Logos is doubtless the transcendent but created Logos.

1306—We find the *immanent* Logos for instance in the following passages, where it is firstly described as δεσμὸς ἄρρηκτος, as were the "powers" above (**1291a**). **The Logos a bond of the universe**

a. Philo, *De plantatione* 2, 8-9 (C.W. II, p. 135):

Οὐδὲν τῶν ἐν ὕλαις κραταιὸν οὕτως, ὡς τὸν κόσμον ἀχθοφορεῖν ἰσχῦσαι, λόγος δὲ ὁ ἀΐδιος θεοῦ τοῦ αἰωνίου τὸ ὀχυρώτατον καὶ βεβαιότατον ἔρεισμα τῶν ὅλων ἐστίν. οὗτος ἀπὸ τῶν μέσων ἐπὶ τὰ πέρατα καὶ ἀπὸ τῶν ἄκρων ἐπὶ τὰ μέσα ταθεὶς δολιχεύει τὸν τῆς φύσεως δρόμον ἀήττητον συνάγων τὰ μέρη πάντα καὶ σφίγγων· δεσμὸν γὰρ αὐτὸν ἄρρηκτον τοῦ παντὸς ὁ γεννήσας ἐποίει πατήρ.

We can only conclude that the totality of the spiritual beings called the Powers or angels, are sometimes spoken of as the Logos.

b. To the Logos Philo attributes the function of harmonizing opposites. He therefore says that it "mediates" and "arbitrates", or he speaks of μεσίται and διαιτηταὶ λόγοι. **The Logos is a „mediator" and arbiter**

Philo, *Quaestiones in Exodum* II 68:

Ὁ τοῦ θεοῦ λόγος μέσος ὢν οὐδὲν ἐν τῇ φύσει καταλείπει κενόν, τὰ ὅλα πληρῶν, καὶ μεσιτεύει καὶ διαιτᾷ τοῖς παρ' ἑκάτερα διεστάναι δοκοῦσι, φιλίαν καὶ ὁμόνοιαν ἐργαζόμενος· ἀεὶ γὰρ κοινωνίας αἴτιος καὶ δημιουργὸς εἰρήνης.

c. Man needs λόγοι acting on our behalf as mediators (μεσίται) and arbiters (διαιτηταί). This is what the angels serve for. **The angels are called μεσίται καὶ διαιτηταὶ λόγοι**

Philo, *De somniis* I 141-142 (C.W. III, p. 235):

Pure souls that never have felt any craving for the things of earth, act as God's servants [1] and messengers.

Ταύτας δαίμονας μὲν οἱ ἄλλοι φιλόσοφοι, ὁ δὲ ἱερὸς λόγος ἀγγέλους εἴωθε καλεῖν προσφυεστέρῳ χρώμενος ὀνόματι· καὶ γὰρ τὰς τοῦ πατρὸς ἐπικελεύσεις τοῖς ἐγγόνοις καὶ τὰς τῶν ἐγγόνων χρείας τῷ πατρὶ διαγγέλλουσι. παρὸ καὶ

---

[1] Here again Philo uses the term ὕπαρχοι τοῦ πανηγεμόνος, "*satraps* of the great Ruler", as he said of the *transcendent* Logos (**1291c**).

ἀνερχομένους αὐτοὺς καὶ κατιόντας εἰσήγαγεν, οὐκ ἐπειδὴ τῶν μηνυσόντων
ὁ πάντη ἐφθακὼς θεὸς δεῖται, ἀλλ' ὅτι τοῖς ἐπικήροις ἡμῖν συνέφερε μεσίταις
καὶ διαιτηταῖς λόγοις χρῆσθαι διὰ τὸ τεθηπέναι καὶ πεφρικέναι τὸν παμπρύ-
τανιν καὶ τὸ μέγιστον ἀρχῆς αὐτοῦ κράτος.

The Logos
πρωτόγονος
is said to be
immanent

    d. Indeed, after having declared that the Λόγος πρεσβύτατος is
transcendent (**1301a**), Philo goes on without any difficulty to say that
ὁ πρωτόγονος θεῖος Λόγος is *within* the cosmos.

    Philo, *De somniis* I 215 (C.W. III, p. 251):

    Ἕν μὲν ὅδε ὁ κόσμος, ἐν ᾧ καὶ ἀρχιερεὺς ὁ πρωτόγονος αὐτοῦ θεῖος λόγος,
ἕτερον δὲ λογικὴ ψυχή, ἧς ἱερεὺς ὁ πρὸς ἀλήθειαν ἄνθρωπος, οὗ μίμημα αἰσθητὸν
ὁ τὰς πατρίους εὐχὰς καὶ θυσίας ἐπιτελῶν ἐστιν, ᾧ τὸν εἰρημένον ἐπιτέτραπται
χιτῶνα ἐνδύεσθαι, τοῦ παντὸς ἀντίμιμον ὄντα οὐρανοῦ, ἵνα συνιερουργῇ καὶ
ὁ κόσμος ἀνθρώπῳ καὶ τῷ παντὶ ἄνθρωπος.

    The immanent Logos is not essentially distinguished from the transcendent one,
as it is distinguished on the other hand from the soul of man.

The twofold
Logos in the
cosmos and
in man

    1307—Summarizing, Ph. speaks of a twofold Logos, both in the cosmos
and in man.

    De vita Mosis II 13, 127 (C.W. IV, p. 229 f.):

    Διπλοῦν δὲ τὸ λογεῖον οὐκ ἀπὸ σκοποῦ· διττὸς γὰρ ὁ λόγος ἔν τε τῷ παντὶ
καὶ ἐν ἀνθρώπου φύσει· κατὰ μὲν τὸ πᾶν ὅ τε περὶ τῶν ἀσωμάτων καὶ παραδειγματικῶν ἰδεῶν, ἐξ ὧν ὁ νοητὸς ἐπάγη κόσμος, καὶ ὁ περὶ τῶν ὁρατῶν,
ἃ δὴ μιμήματα καὶ ἀπεικονίσματα τῶν ἰδεῶν ἐκείνων ἐστίν, ἐξ ὧν ὁ αἰσθητὸς
οὗτος ἀπετελεῖτο· ἐν ἀνθρώπῳ δ' ὁ μέν ἐστιν ἐνδιάθετος, ὁ δὲ προφορικός,
<καὶ ὁ μὲν> οἷά τις πηγή, ὁ δὲ γεγωνὸς ἀπ' ἐκείνου ῥέων· καὶ τοῦ μέν ἐστι χώρα
τὸ ἡγεμονικόν, τοῦ δὲ κατὰ προφορὰν γλῶττα καὶ στόμα καὶ ἡ ἄλλη πᾶσα
φωνῆς ὀργανοποιία.

    The distinction between λόγος ἐνδιάθετος and λόγος προφορικός is Stoic [1].

Man as a
cosmopolites
stands under
the law of
nature

    1308—The first man was placed in the universe, and therefore under
the same law as the universe itself.

    Philo, *De opif. mundi* 49, 142 - 50, 143 (C.W. I, p. 50):

    Τὸν δ' ἀρχηγέτην ἐκεῖνον οὐ μόνον πρῶτον ἄνθρωπον ἀλλὰ καὶ μόνον
κοσμοπολίτην λέγοντες ἀψευδέστατα ἐροῦμεν· ἦν γὰρ οἶκος αὐτῷ καὶ πόλις
ὁ κόσμος, μηδεμιᾶς χειροποιήτου κατασκευῆς δεδημιουργημένης ἐκ λίθων
καὶ ξύλων ὕλης, ᾧ καθάπερ ἐν πατρίδι μετὰ πάσης ἀσφαλείας ἐνδιητᾶτο. —

---

[1] Above, nr. **965**.

Ἐπεὶ δὲ πᾶσα πόλις εὔνομος ἔχει πολιτείαν, ἀναγκαίως συνέβαινε τῷ κοσμοπολίτῃ χρῆσθαι πολιτείᾳ ᾗ καὶ σύμπας ὁ κόσμος· αὕτη δέ ἐστιν ὁ τῆς φύσεως ὀρθὸς λόγος, ὃς κυριωτέρᾳ κλήσει προσονομάζεται θεσμός, νόμος θεῖος ὤν, καθ᾽ ὃν τὰ προσήκοντα καὶ ἐπιβάλλοντα ἑκάστοις ἀπενεμήθη.

It is a curious sign of Ph.'s syncretistic spirit, that he identifies the ὀρθὸς λόγος of Stoicism with the divine Law of Scripture.

1309—Ph. himself is so much penetrated by the thought of the divine Law, that he regarded pious and virtuous men such as the patriarchs almost as an incarnation of it, before special laws were written.

a.   Philo, *De Abr.* 1, 4-6 (C.W. IV, p. 2):

The patriarchs an incarnation of the Divine Law of nature

Οὗτοι δέ εἰσιν ἀνδρῶν οἱ ἀνεπιλήπτως καὶ καλῶς βιώσαντες, ὧν τὰς ἀρετὰς
5 ἐν ταῖς ἱερωτάταις ἐστηλιτεῦσθαι γραφαῖς συμβέβηκεν, οὐ πρὸς τὸν ἐκείνων ἔπαινον αὐτὸ μόνον, ἀλλὰ καὶ ὑπὲρ τοῦ τοὺς ἐντυγχάνοντας προτρέψασθαι καὶ ἐπὶ τὸν ὅμοιον ζῆλον ἀγαγεῖν. οἱ γὰρ ἔμψυχοι καὶ λογικοὶ νόμοι ἄνδρες ἐκεῖνοι γεγόνασιν, οὓς δυοῖν χάριν ἐσέμνυνεν· ἑνὸς μὲν βουλόμενος ἐπιδεῖξαι,
10 ὅτι τὰ τεθειμένα διατάγματα τῆς φύσεως οὐκ ἀπάδει, δευτέρου δὲ ὅτι οὐ πολὺς πόνος τοῖς ἐθέλουσι κατὰ τοὺς κειμένους νόμους ζῆν, ὁπότε καὶ ἀγράφῳ τῇ νομοθεσίᾳ, πρίν τι τὴν ἀρχὴν ἀναγραφῆναι τῶν ἐν μέρει, ῥᾳδίως καὶ εὐπετῶς ἐχρήσαντο οἱ πρῶτοι· ὡς δεόντως ἄν τινα φάναι, τοὺς τεθέντας νόμους μηδὲν ἄλλ᾽ ἢ ὑπομνήματα εἶναι βίου τῶν παλαιῶν, ἀρχαιολογοῦντας ἔργα καὶ λόγους,
15 οἷς ἐχρήσαντο. ἐκεῖνοι γὰρ οὔτε γνώριμοι καὶ φοιτηταὶ γενόμενοί τινων οὔτε παρὰ διδασκάλοις ἃ χρὴ πράττειν καὶ λέγειν ἀναδιδαχθέντες, αὐτήκοοι δὲ καὶ αὐτομαθεῖς, ἀκολουθίαν φύσεως ἀσπασάμενοι, τὴν φύσιν αὐτήν, ὅπερ ἐστὶ πρὸς ἀλήθειαν, πρεσβύτατον θεσμὸν εἶναι ὑπολαβόντες ἅπαντα τὸν βίον ηὐνομήθησαν, ὑπαίτιον μὲν οὐδὲν γνώμαις ἑκουσίοις ἐργασάμενοι, περὶ δὲ τῶν ἐκ
20 τύχης ποτνιώμενοι τὸν θεὸν καὶ λιταῖς καὶ ἱκεσίαις ἐξευμενιζόμενοι πρὸς ὁλοκλήρου μετουσίαν ζωῆς δι᾽ ἀμφοτέρων κατορθουμένης τῶν τε ἐκ προνοίας καὶ τῶν ἄνευ ἑκουσίου γνώμης.

b.   Thus, Ph. describes the tenor of Moses' life in the terms of Stoic philosophy.

De vita Mosis, I 48 (C.W. IV, p. 131):

Ἐν ᾧ δὲ ἔμελλε δικάζειν (sc. ὁ Θεὸς αὐτόν), τοὺς ἀρετῆς ἄθλους Μωυσῆς διήθλει τὸν ἀλείπτην ἔχων ἐν ἑαυτῷ λογισμὸν ἀστεῖον, ὑφ᾽ οὗ γυμναζόμενος πρὸς τοὺς ἀρίστους βίους, τόν τε θεωρητικὸν καὶ πρακτικόν, ἐπονεῖτο φιλο-
30 σοφίας ἀνελίττων ἀεὶ δόγματα καὶ τῇ ψυχῇ διαγινώσκων εὐτρόχως καὶ μνήμῃ παρακατατιθέμενος εἰς τὸ ἄληστον αὐτὰ καὶ τὰς οἰκείας αὐτίκα πράξεις ἐφαρμόττων ἐπαινετὰς πάσας, ἐφιέμενος οὐ τοῦ δοκεῖν ἀλλὰ τῆς ἀληθείας, διὰ τὸ

προκεῖσθαι σκοπὸν ἕνα τὸν ὀρθὸν τῆς φύσεως λόγον, ὃς μόνος ἐστὶν ἀρετῶν ἀρχή τε καὶ πηγή.

Enthusiasm

1310—To the Stoic notion of the divine Law practised by virtuous men Ph. adds his idea of *enthusiasm*, a kind of extasy, by which the prophet is characterized.

   a. *De vita Mosis* II 23, 191 (C.W. IV, p. 245):

   Τὸ ἐνθουσιῶδες —, καθ' ὃ μάλιστα καὶ κυρίως νενόμισται προφήτης. 2

beyond reason

   b. Ph. describes this "enthusiasm" as a kind of sober intoxication, happening to the mind of him who contemplates the intelligible truth and beauty of the Ideas. *De opif. mundi* 23, 70-71 (C.W. I, p. 23 f.):

   The mind of man first investigates the earthly elements.

   Καὶ πάλιν πτηνὸς ἀρθεὶς καὶ τὸν ἀέρα καὶ τὰ τούτου παθήματα κατασκε- 1
ψάμενος ἀνωτέρω φέρεται πρὸς αἰθέρα καὶ τὰς οὐρανοῦ περιόδους, πλανήτων
τε καὶ ἀπλανῶν χορείαις συμπεριποληθεὶς κατὰ τοὺς μουσικῆς τελείας νόμους,
ἑπόμενος ἔρωτι σοφίας ποδηγετοῦντι, πᾶσαν τὴν αἰσθητὴν οὐσίαν ὑπερκύψας, 2
ἐνταῦθα ἐφίεται τῆς νοητῆς· καὶ ὧν εἶδεν ἐνταῦθα αἰσθητῶν ἐν ἐκείνῃ τὰ παραδείγματα καὶ τὰς ἰδέας θεασάμενος, ὑπερβάλλοντα κάλλη, μέθῃ νηφαλίῳ
κατασχεθεὶς ὥσπερ οἱ κορυβαντιῶντες ἐνθουσιᾷ, ἑτέρου γεμισθεὶς ἱμέρου καὶ
πόθου βελτίονος, ὑφ' οὗ πρὸς τὴν ἄκραν ἀψῖδα παραπεμφθεὶς τῶν νοητῶν ἐπ' 5
αὐτὸν ἰέναι δοκεῖ τὸν μέγαν βασιλέα· γλιχομένου δ' ἰδεῖν, ἀθρόου φωτὸς ἄκρατοι
καὶ ἀμιγεῖς αὐγαὶ χειμάρρου τρόπον ἐκχέονται, ὡς ταῖς μαρμαρυγαῖς τὸ τῆς
διανοίας ὄμμα σκοτοδινιᾶν.

The prerogative of the heir of divine things

   c. This kind of extasy, then, by which the mind, surpassing reason, comes to the knowledge of God, is the prerogative of "the heir of divine things".

   Philo, *Quis rerum divinarum heres sit* 14, 68-70 (C.W. III, p. 16 f.):

   Τίς οὖν γενήσεται κληρονόμος; οὐχ ὁ μένων ἐν τῇ τοῦ σώματος εἱρκτῇ 1
λογισμὸς καθ' ἑκούσιον γνώμην, ἀλλ' ὁ λυθεὶς τῶν δεσμῶν καὶ ἐλευθερωθεὶς
καὶ ἔξω τειχῶν προεληλυθὼς καὶ καταλελοιπώς, εἰ οἷόν τε τοῦτο εἰπεῖν,
αὐτὸς ἑαυτόν. "ὃς γὰρ ἐξελεύσεται ἐκ σοῦ" φησίν, "οὗτος κληρονομήσει σε
(*Gen.* 15, 4)". πόθος οὖν εἴ τις εἰσέρχεταί σε, ψυχή, τῶν θείων ἀγαθῶν κλη- 1
ρονομῆσαι, μὴ μόνον "γῆν", τὸ σῶμα, καὶ "συγγένειαν", ‹τὴν› αἴσθησιν, καὶ
"οἶκον πατρός" (*Gen.* 12, I), τὸν λόγον, καταλίπῃς, ἀλλὰ καὶ σαυτὴν ἀπόδραθι
καὶ ἔκστηθι σεαυτῆς, ὥσπερ οἱ κατεχόμενοι καὶ κορυβαντιῶντες βακχευθεῖσα
καὶ θεοφορηθεῖσα κατά τινα προφητικὸν ἐπιθειασμόν· ἐνθουσιώσης γὰρ καὶ
οὐκέτ' οὔσης ἐν ἑαυτῇ διανοίας, ἀλλ' ἔρωτι οὐρανίῳ σεσοβημένης κἀκμεμη- 2

νυίας καὶ ὑπὸ τοῦ ὄντως ὄντος ἡγμένης καὶ ἄνω πρὸς αὐτὸ εἱλκυσμένης, προϊούσης ἀληθείας καὶ τὰν ποσὶν ἀναστελλούσης, ἵνα κατὰ λεωφόρου βαίνοι τῆς ὁδοῦ, κλῆρος οὗτος.

d. Philo also uses the term ἔκστασις (*Heres* 249 ff.), of which he distinguishes four kinds, the fourth and best being the ἔνθεος κατοκωχή τε καὶ μανία ᾗ τὸ προφητικὸν γένος χρῆται. The prophet, being divinely inspired, does not speak his own word. Yet, the inspiration is not detached from his moral character. *Not detached from moral qualities*

Heres 52, 259 (C.W. III, p. 59):

Προφήτης γὰρ ἴδιον μὲν οὐδὲν ἀποφθέγγεται, ἀλλότρια δὲ πάντα ὑπηχοῦντος ἑτέρου· φαύλῳ δὲ οὐ θέμις ἑρμηνεῖ γενέσθαι θεοῦ, ὥστε κυρίως μοχθηρὸς οὐδεὶς ἐνθουσιᾷ, μόνῳ δὲ σοφῷ ταῦτ᾽ ἐφαρμόττει, ἐπεὶ καὶ μόνος ὄργανον θεοῦ ἐστιν ἠχεῖον, κρουόμενον καὶ πληττόμενον ἀοράτως ὑπ᾽ αὐτοῦ.

The terms φαῦλος and σοφός in this passage are again a sign of the syncretistic climate of Ph.'s thought.

1311—By his allegorical interpretation of Scripture Ph. inaugurates a long period in the history of exegesis. *Allegorical interpretation*

The method itself is not new: as we have seen above, it was much practised in the Stoa (nr. **924a**); but it can be traced back at least to the second half of the fifth century. See the articles of J. Tate in *Class. Rev.* XLI p. 214; *Class. Quart.* XXIII p. 41, 142; XXIV p. 1; XXVIII p. 105; H. Leisegang in *Philol. Wochenschrift* LII p. 265 ff.; J. Heinemann in *Mnemos.* 1949, and again J. Tate in *Eranos* 1953.
The method, applied by Greek philosophers to Homer and Hesiod, was by Philo applied to Scripture, as was done before him to a certain extent in Talmudic literature.
Lit.: I. Heinemann, *Altjüdische Allegoristik*, 1936.
Wolfson, *Philo* I, p. 133 f.

a. The following passage reveals Ph.'s attitude towards those things in Greek mythology and the classical poets which are shocking to the moral and religious sense of a later generation. *Its function with relation to Greek mythology*

Philo, *De providentia* II 40:

Blasphemiam includit de diis, sed est indicium inclusae physiologiae; cuius non licet apud illos, quorum capita minime sunt uncta, patefacere mysteria.

In other words: "blasphemies" (i.e. such strange things about the gods, as abound in Homer and Hesiod) are an indication that such passages of the poets contain a doctrine on nature ("physiologia"), which can only be understood by the initiated.—Ph. means that the Gods of Greek mythology must be understood either as powers of nature or as moral powers. Such was also Varro's conviction.

b. Cp. Varro's description of the *tria genera theologiae*, cited by Augustinus, *De civ. Dei* VI, 5 (the beginning):

Mythicon appellant, quo maxime utuntur poetae; physicon, quo philosophi; civile, quo populi. Primum, inquit, quod dixi, in eo sunt multa contra dignitatem et naturam immortalium ficta. In hoc . . . omnia diis adtribuuntur, quae non modo in hominem, sed etiam quae in contemptissimum hominem cadere possunt. —

Secundum genus est, inquit, quod demonstravi, de quo multos libros philosophi reliquerunt; in quibus est, dii qui sint, ubi, quod genus, quale est: a quodam tempore an a sempiterno fuerint dii; ex igni sint, ut credit Heraclitus, an ex numeris, ut Pythagoras, an ex atomis, ut ait Epicurus. Sic alia quae facilius intra parietes in schola quam extra in foro ferre possunt aures.

c. We find it also defined by Euseb., *Praep. ev.* III 1, 3:

Ἡ παλαιὰ φυσιολογία καὶ παρ' Ἕλλησι καὶ βαρβάροις λόγος ἦν φυσικὸς ἐγκεκρυμμένος μύθοις, τὰ πολλὰ δι' αἰνιγμάτων καὶ ὑπονοιῶν ἐπίκρυφος καὶ μυστηριώδης θεολογία. — Τοῦτο δὴ τὸ συμβολικὸν εἶδος.

Why Philo applies the method to Scripture — Philo applied the method to Scripture, not because he regarded the books of Moses as being of the same level as Greek mythology. Doubtless, Scripture was in his eyes divinely inspired. That he seeks a "hidden truth" behind its words, is not because he found some kind of blasphemy in it, but because he wished to bring it into the sphere of mystery.

3—PLUTARCHUS

General character of his philosophy — Plutarchus of Chaeronea is the greatest representative of Platonism in the first and early second century. Like Philo he may be called a preparer of Neoplatonism, 1° by a marked transcendentalism in his conception of God, 2° by ranking Νοῦς higher than ψυχή, 3° in general, by his religious attitude and by making a sort of philosophical synthesis in which certain Aristotelian and Stoic elements are introduced into a theologically interpreted Platonism.

Plutarchus' idea of God is expressed most clearly in two of his writings, the treatise *De E apud Delphos* and *De Iside et Osiride*. His thoughts on Providence are expounded in *De sera numinis vindicta*, while his ideas of the afterworld are displayed in three great myths, placed at the end of the *De sera vindicta, De facie in orbe lunae* and *De genio Socratis*.

Also his demonology is interesting. It is known to us by different works, but chiefly by a long passage in *De defectu oraculorum*.

Plutarchus lived from the middle of the first century till about 125. He must have been in Rome towards the end of Vespasian's reign [1] and again under Domitian, shortly after 90 [2]. Usually he lived at Chaeronea, where he had a kind of informal School.

1312—As was done in those days by Neopythagorean interpreters, Plut. applies to God expressions which by Plato were used of the Ideas or the νοητά.

a. Plut., *De E apud Delphos* 17-18 (391F-392B):

Plutarchus with a circle of friends are engaged in a conversation on the sense of the letter E on the wall of the temple of Apollo at Delphi. Six explanations have been proposed, when Ammonius begins to speak as follows:

Οὔτ' ... ἀριθμὸν οὔτε τάξιν οὔτε σύνδεσμον οὔτ' ἄλλο τῶν ἐλλιπῶν μορίων οὐδὲν οἶμαι τὸ γράμμα σημαίνειν· ἀλλ' ἔστιν αὐτοτελὴς τοῦ θεοῦ προσαγόρευσις καὶ προσφώνησις, ἅμα τῷ ῥήματι τὸν φθεγγόμενον εἰς ἔννοιαν καθιστᾶσα τῆς τοῦ θεοῦ δυνάμεως. Ὁ μὲν γὰρ θεὸς ἕκαστον ἡμῶν ἐνταῦθα προσιόντα οἷον ἀσπαζόμενος προσαγορεύει τὸ "Γνῶθι σαυτόν", ὃ δὴ τοῦ χαῖρε οὐδὲν μεῖόν ἐστι. Ἡμεῖς δὲ πάλιν ἀμειβόμενοι τὸν θεόν, "Εἶ" φαμέν, ὡς ἀληθῆ καὶ ἀψευδῆ καὶ μόνην μόνῳ προσήκουσαν τὴν τοῦ εἶναι προσαγόρευσιν ἀποδιδόντες.

God alone has true being

Ἡμῖν μὲν γὰρ ὄντως τοῦ εἶναι μέτεστιν οὐδέν, ἀλλὰ πᾶσα θνητὴ φύσις ἐν μέσῳ γενέσεως καὶ φθορᾶς γενομένη φάσμα παρέχει καὶ δόκησιν ἀμυδρὰν καὶ ἀβέβαιον αὑτῆς· ἂν δὲ τὴν διάνοιαν ἐπερείσῃς λαβέσθαι βουλόμενος, ὥσπερ ἡ σφοδρὰ περίδραξις ὕδατος τῷ πιέζειν εἰς ταὐτὸ καὶ συνάγειν διαρρέον ἀπόλλυσι τὸ περιλαμβανόμενον, οὕτω τῶν παθητῶν καὶ μεταβλητῶν ἑκάστου τὴν ἄγαν ἐνάργειαν ὁ λόγος διώκων ἀποσφάλλεται, τῇ μὲν εἰς τὸ γιγνόμενον αὐτοῦ, τῇ δ' εἰς τὸ φθειρόμενον, οὐδενὸς λαβέσθαι μένοντος οὐδὲ ὄντως ὄντος δυνάμενος.

b. Ib., c. 19 (392E-F):

Sensible things are continually changing and, therefore, *are* not in the full sense; God alone, who is always the Same, *is*.

Τί οὖν ὄντως ὄν ἐστι; Τὸ ἀΐδιον καὶ ἀγένητον καὶ ἄφθαρτον, ᾧ χρόνος μεταβολὴν οὐδὲ εἷς ἐπάγει. Κινητὸν γάρ τι, καὶ κινουμένη συμφανταζόμενον ὕλῃ, καὶ ῥέον ἀεὶ καὶ μὴ στέγον, ὥσπερ ἀγγεῖον φθορᾶς καὶ γενέσεως, ὁ χρόνος· οὗ γε δὴ τὸ μὲν ἔπειτα καὶ τὸ πρότερον, καὶ τὸ ἔσται λεγόμενον καὶ τὸ γέγονεν, αὐτόθεν ἐξομολόγησίς ἐστι τοῦ μὴ ὄντος· τὸ γὰρ ἐν τῷ εἶναι τὸ μηδέπω γεγονὸς ἢ πεπαυμένον ἤδη τοῦ εἶναι λέγειν, ὡς ἔστιν, εὔηθες καὶ ἄτοπον.

True being is beyond time and motion

---

[1]   *Vita Demosth.* II 2; cp. *De curios.* 15, 522 D.
[2]   *Quaest. conv.* VIII 7, 1.

God alone is truly one

c. Ib., c. 20 (393AB):

'Αλλ' ἔστιν ὁ θεός, εἰ χρὴ φάναι, καὶ ἔστι κατ' οὐδένα χρόνον, ἀλλὰ κατὰ τὸν αἰῶνα τὸν ἀκίνητον καὶ ἄχρονον καὶ ἀνέγκλιτον καὶ οὗ πρότερον οὐδέν ἐστιν 1◦ οὐδ' ὕστερον οὐδὲ μέλλον οὐδὲ παρῳχημένον οὐδὲ πρεσβύτερον οὐδὲ νεώτερον· ἀλλ' εἷς ὢν ἑνὶ τῷ νῦν τὸ ἀεὶ πεπλήρωκε, καὶ μόνον ἐστὶ τὸ κατὰ τοῦτον ὄντως ὄν, οὐ γεγονὸς οὐδ' ἐσόμενον οὐδ' ἀρξάμενον οὐδὲ παυσόμενον. Οὕτως οὖν αὐτὸν δεῖ σεβομένους ἀσπάζεσθαι καὶ προσαγορεύειν, "εἶ", ἢ καὶ νὴ Δία, ὡς 1. ἔνιοι τῶν παλαιῶν, "Εἶ ἕν". Οὐ γὰρ πολλὰ τὸ θεῖόν ἐστιν, ὡς ἡμῶν ἕκαστος ἐκ μυρίων διαφορῶν ἐν πάθεσι γινομένων, ἄθροισμα παντοδαπὸν καὶ πανηγυρικῶς μεμιγμένον· ἀλλ' ἓν εἶναι δεῖ τὸ ὄν, ὥσπερ ὂν τὸ ἕν. Ἡ δ' ἑτερότης διαφορᾷ τοῦ ὄντος εἰς γένεσιν ἐξίσταται τοῦ μὴ ὄντος. 2◦

1313—Thus, Plut. seems to make the distance between God and the world as great as possible. In *De Iside et Osiride* he calls Him as the First Principle ἀμιγὴς καὶ ἀπαθής (c. 54), even "as far as possible removed from the earth and from all things that are subject to destruction and death" (c. 78). He also identifies Him ("Osiris") with τὸ 'Αγαθόν (in Plato's sense) and says that "Isis" (which means: the receptive principle, χώρα or ὕλη) is longing for it (c. 53).

The highest Principle identified with God

a. Plut., *De Iside et Osiride* c. 53 (372 EF):

Ἡ γὰρ Ἶσίς ἐστι μὲν τὸ τῆς φύσεως θῆλυ καὶ δεκτικὸν ἁπάσης γενέσεως, καθὸ τιθηνὴ καὶ πανδεχὴς ὑπὸ τοῦ Πλάτωνος [1], ὑπὸ δὲ τῶν πολλῶν μυριώνυμος 2◦ κέκληται διὰ τὸ πάσας ὑπὸ τοῦ λόγου τρεπομένη μορφὰς δέχεσθαι καὶ ἰδέας. Ἔχει δὲ σύμφυτον ἔρωτα τοῦ πρώτου καὶ κυριωτάτου πάντων, ὃ τἀγαθῷ ταὐτόν ἐστι, κἀκεῖνο ποθεῖ καὶ διώκει [2]· τὴν δ' ἐκ τοῦ κακοῦ φεύγει καὶ διωθεῖται μοῖραν, ἀμφοῖν μὲν οὖσα χώρα καὶ ὕλη, ῥέπουσα δ' ἀεὶ πρὸς τὸ βέλτιον 2. ἐξ ἑαυτῆς, καὶ παρέχουσα γεννᾶν ἐκείνῳ καὶ κατασπείρειν εἰς ἑαυτὴν ἀπορροίας καὶ ὁμοιότητας, αἷς χαίρει καὶ γέγηθε κυϊσκομένη καὶ ὑποπιμπλαμένη τῶν 1 γενέσεων. Εἰκὼν γάρ ἐστιν οὐσίας <ἡ> ἐν ὕλῃ γένεσις καὶ μίμημα τοῦ ὄντος τὸ γινόμενον.

b. Osiris cannot be the cause of evil and disorder in the world. Another power, therefore, subordinate to Him, must be introduced to account for evil. Plutarch identifies him with Typhon, while Horus is the symbol of the visible world.

---

[1]　Above, nr. **356**.
[2]　The idea of Matter longing for its Form as a τέλος which is always an ἀγαθόν is Aristotelian. Cp. our nrs. **490b** and **514**.

De Iside et Osiride 54 (373 AB):

He is
eternal and
imperishable

"Οθεν οὐκ ἀπὸ τρόπου μυθολογοῦσι τὴν Ὀσίριδος ψυχὴν ἀίδιον εἶναι καὶ
ἄφθαρτον, τὸ δὲ σῶμα πολλάκις διασπᾶν καὶ ἀφανίζειν τὸν Τυφῶνα· τὴν δ'
Ἶσιν πλανωμένην καὶ ζητεῖν καὶ συναρμόττειν πάλιν. Τὸ γὰρ ὂν καὶ νοητὸν
καὶ ἀγαθὸν φθορᾶς καὶ μεταβολῆς κρεῖττόν ἐστιν· ἃς δ' ἀπ' αὐτοῦ τὸ αἰσθητὸν
καὶ σωματικὸν εἰκόνας ἐκμάττεται, καὶ λόγους καὶ εἴδη καὶ ὁμοιότητας ἀνα-
λαμβάνει, καθάπερ ἐν κηρῷ σφραγῖδες οὐκ ἀεὶ διαμένουσιν, ἀλλὰ καταλαμβάνει
τὸ ἄτακτον αὐτὰς καὶ ταραχῶδες ἐνταῦθα τῆς ἄνω χώρας ἀπεληλαμένον καὶ
μαχόμενον πρὸς τὸν Ὧρον, ὃν ἡ Ἶσις εἰκόνα τοῦ νοητοῦ κόσμου [1] αἰσθητὸν ὄντα
γεννᾷ. Διὸ καὶ δίκην φεύγειν λέγεται νοθείας ὑπὸ Τυφῶνος, ὡς οὐκ ὢν καθαρὸς
οὐδὲ εἰλικρινής, οἷος ὁ πατὴρ λόγος αὐτὸς καθ' ἑαυτόν, ἀμιγὴς καὶ ἀπαθής [2],
ἀλλὰ νενοθευμένος τῇ ὕλῃ διὰ τὸ σωματικόν.

According to this passage, Osiris is identified with "the Logos in itself". Plut.
evidently knows also lower and derived forms of "logos". His thought resembles
in this very much that of Philo. He does not, however, distinguish the supreme
God (Osiris) from the κόσμος νοητός, as Philo did by introducing the "created"
κόσμος νοητός which then becomes a δεύτερος θεός, but identifies Osiris directly
with the Intelligible world, of which Horus, being the κόσμος αἰσθητός, becomes an
εἰκών and a μίμημα. E. de Faye [3] was mistaken when he wrote that Plut. interposed
Horus as a δεύτερος θεός between the supreme God and man, *Horus* being called
λόγος αὐτὸς καθ' ἑαυτὸν ἀμιγὴς καὶ ἀπαθής. This is not what Plutarchus wrote.
    Meanwhile, Plut. did know intermediate powers between the supreme God
and man: the daemons. In this too his thought is very much like Philo's and that
of the early Fathers of the Christian Church.

the Logos in
itself

c. Plut. opposed those who identified Osiris with Dis or Plouton.

Osiris
separated
from the
material
world

De Iside et Osiride, c. 78 (382 EF):

Καὶ τοῦτο ὅπερ οἱ νῦν ἱερεῖς ἀφοσιούμενοι καὶ παρακαλυπτόμενοι μετ'
εὐλαβείας ὑποδηλοῦσιν, ὡς ὁ θεὸς οὗτος ἄρχει καὶ βασιλεύει τῶν τεθνηκότων,
οὐχ ἕτερος ὢν τοῦ καλουμένου παρ' Ἕλλησιν Ἅιδου καὶ Πλούτωνος, ἀγνοούμενον ὅπως ἀληθές ἐστι, διαταράττει τοὺς πολλοὺς ὑπονοοῦντας ἐν γῇ καὶ ὑπὸ
γῆν τὸν ἱερὸν καὶ ὅσιον ὡς ἀληθῶς Ὄσιριν οἰκεῖν, ὅπου τὰ σώματα κρύπτεται
τῶν τέλος ἔχειν δοκούντων. Ὁ δ' ἔστι μὲν αὐτὸς ἀπωτάτω τῆς γῆς ἄχραντος
καὶ ἀμίαντος καὶ καθαρὸς οὐσίας ἀπάσης φθορὰν δεχομένης καὶ θάνατον.

1314—Plut. follows Plato in stating that neither ἄψυχα σώματα nor an
ὕλη ἄποιος could be the cause or ἀρχή of things. But, since Osiris is the

Dualism

---

[1] Horus is called an εἰκὼν τοῦ νοητοῦ κόσμου. The term κόσμος νοητός is used here
by Plutarch as a current expression. Though it is first found in Philo, it is improbable that he introduced the term, as Wolfson thinks he did.
[2] Osiris then is called καθαρὸς καὶ εἰλικρινής, Λόγος αὐτὸς καθ' ἑαυτόν, ἀμιγὴς καὶ
ἀπαθής.
[3] *Origène*, Vol. II, *L'ambiance philosophique*, Paris 1927, p. 135 ff.

cause of good things only, another (living) principle must be admitted in Nature.

a. Plut., *De Iside et Osiride* 45 (369 B-D):

Διὸ καὶ παμπάλαιος αὕτη κάτεισιν ἐκ θεολόγων καὶ νομοθετῶν εἴς τε ποιητὰς καὶ φιλοσόφους δόξα, τὴν ἀρχὴν ἀδέσποτον ἔχουσα, τὴν δὲ πίστιν ἰσχυρὰν καὶ δυσεξάλειπτον, οὐκ ἐν λόγοις μόνον οὐδὲ ἐν φήμαις, ἀλλὰ ἔν τε τελεταῖς ἔν τε θυσίαις, καὶ βαρβάροις καὶ ῞Ελλησι πολλαχοῦ περιφερομένη, ὡς οὔτ᾽ ἄνουν καὶ ἄλογον καὶ ἀκυβέρνητον αἰωρεῖται τῷ αὐτομάτῳ τὸ πᾶν, οὔτε εἷς ἐστιν ὁ κρατῶν καὶ κατευθύνων ὥσπερ οἴαξιν ἤ τισι πειθηνίοις χαλινοῖς [1] λόγος, ἀλλὰ πολλὰ καὶ μεμιγμένα κακοῖς καὶ ἀγαθοῖς· μᾶλλον δὲ μηδέν, ὡς ἁπλῶς εἰπεῖν, ἄκρατον ἐνταῦθα τῆς φύσεως φερούσης, οὐ δυεῖν πίθων εἷς ταμίας [2], ὥσπερ νάματα τὰ πράγματα καπηλικῶς διανέμων ἀνακεράννυσιν ἡμῖν· ἀλλ᾽ ἀπὸ δυεῖν ἐναντίων ἀρχῶν, καὶ δυεῖν ἀντιπάλων δυνάμεων, τῆς μὲν ἐπὶ τὰ δεξιὰ καὶ κατ᾽ εὐθεῖαν ὑφηγουμένης, τῆς δ᾽ ἔμπαλιν ἀναστρεφούσης καὶ ἀνακλώσης, ὅ τε βίος μικτός, ὅ τε κόσμος, εἰ καὶ μὴ πᾶς, ἀλλ᾽ ὁ περίγειος οὗτος καὶ μετὰ σελήνην, ἀνώμαλος καὶ ποικίλος γέγονε, καὶ μεταβολὰς πάσας δεχόμενος. Εἰ γὰρ οὐθὲν ἀναιτίως πέφυκε γενέσθαι, αἰτίαν δὲ κακοῦ τἀγαθὸν οὐκ ἂν παράσχοι, δεῖ γένεσιν ἰδίαν καὶ ἀρχήν, ὥσπερ ἀγαθοῦ καὶ κακοῦ, τὴν φύσιν ἔχειν.

b. In the next chapter Plut. speaks of the Persian Mazdeists and explains the doctrine of Zarathustra in such a way, that Ahriman (as a daemon) is subordinated to the God Ahura Mazda.

De Iside et Osiride, c. 46 (369 EF):

Καὶ δοκεῖ τοῦτο τοῖς πλείστοις καὶ σοφωτάτοις. Νομίζουσι γὰρ οἱ μὲν θεοὺς εἶναι δύο, καθάπερ ἀντιτέχνους, τὸν μὲν ἀγαθῶν, τὸν δὲ φαύλων δημιουργόν. Οἱ δὲ τὸν μὲν ἀμείνονα θεόν, τὸν δὲ ἕτερον δαίμονα καλοῦσιν· ὥσπερ Ζωροάστρης ὁ μάγος, ὃν πεντακισχιλίοις ἔτεσι τῶν Τρωικῶν γεγονέναι πρεσβύτερον ἱστοροῦσιν. Οὗτος οὖν ἐκάλει τὸν μὲν ῾Ωρομάζην, τὸν δ᾽ Ἀρειμάνιον· καὶ προσαπεφαίνετο τὸν μὲν ἐοικέναι φωτὶ μάλιστα τῶν αἰσθητῶν, τὸν δ᾽ ἔμπαλιν σκότῳ καὶ ἀγνοίᾳ, μέσον δ᾽ ἀμφοῖν τὸν Μίθρην εἶναι. Διὸ καὶ Μίθρην Πέρσαι τὸν Μεσίτην ὀνομάζουσιν. — Καὶ γὰρ τῶν φυτῶν νομίζουσι τὰ μὲν τοῦ ἀγαθοῦ θεοῦ, τὰ δὲ τοῦ κακοῦ δαίμονος εἶναι· καὶ τῶν ζῴων, ὥσπερ κύνας καὶ ὄρνιθας καὶ χερσαίους ἐχίνους, τοῦ ἀγαθοῦ· τοῦ δὲ φαύλου τοὺς ἐνύδρους εἶναι·—

See on the whole passage Th. Hopfner's Commentary, vol. II, p. 201 ff.

---

[1] Cp. Sophocles, fr. 785 Nauck.
[2] Cp. Hom., *Ilias* 24, 527 f. and Plato, *Resp.* 379d.

c. He finds the essence of this doctrine also with the Chaldaeans, in Greek official religion and in philosophy, especially with the Pythagoreans and in Plato.

De Iside et Osiride, c. 48 (370 C-371 A):

Χαλδαῖοι δὲ τῶν πλανητῶν, οὓς θεοὺς γενεθλίους * καλοῦσι, δύο μὲν ἀγαθουργούς, δύο δὲ κακοποιούς, μέσους δὲ τοὺς τρεῖς ἀποφαίνουσι καὶ κοινούς. Τὰ δὲ Ἑλλήνων πᾶσί που δῆλα, τὴν μὲν ἀγαθὴν Διὸς Ὀλυμπίου μερίδα, τὴν δ᾽ ἀποτρόπαιον Ἅιδου ποιουμένων. Ἐκ δ᾽ Ἀφροδίτης καὶ Ἄρεως Ἁρμονίαν γεγονέναι μυθολογοῦνται· ὧν ὁ μὲν ἀπηνὴς καὶ φιλόνεικος, ἡ δὲ μειλίχιος καὶ γενέθλιος. Σκόπει δὲ τοὺς φιλοσόφους τούτοις συμφερομένους. Ἡράκλειτος μὲν γὰρ ἄντικρυς πόλεμον ὀνομάζει πατέρα καὶ βασιλέα καὶ κύριον πάντων [1]. — Ἐμπεδοκλῆς δὲ τὴν μὲν ἀγαθουργὸν ἀρχὴν φιλότητα καὶ φιλίαν [2] —, τὴν δὲ χείρονα νεῖκος οὐλόμενον καὶ δῆριν αἱματόεσσαν. Οἱ μὲν Πυθαγορικοὶ διὰ πλειόνων ὀνομάτων κατηγοροῦσι, τοῦ μὲν ἀγαθοῦ τὸ ἕν, τὸ πεπερασμένον, τὸ μένον, τὸ εὐθύ, τὸ περισσόν, τὸ τετράγωνον, <τὸ ἴσον>, τὸ δεξιόν, τὸ λαμπρόν· τοῦ δὲ κακοῦ τὴν δυάδα, τὸ ἄπειρον, τὸ φερόμενον, τὸ καμπύλον, τὸ ἄρτιον, τὸ ἑτερόμηκες, τὸ ἄνισον, τὸ ἀριστερόν, τὸ σκοτεινόν· ὥστε ταύτας ἀρχὰς γενέσεως ὑποκειμένας [3]. Ἀναξαγόρας δὲ νοῦν καὶ ἄπειρον [4]· Ἀριστοτέλης δὲ τὸ μὲν εἶδος τὸ δὲ στέρησιν [5]· Πλάτων δὲ πολλαχοῦ μὲν οἷον ἐπηλυγαζόμενος καὶ παρακαλυπτόμενος, τῶν ἐναντίων ἀρχῶν τὴν μὲν ταὐτὸν ὀνομάζει, τὴν δὲ θάτερον [6]. Ἐν δὲ τοῖς Νόμοις ἤδη πρεσβύτερος ὢν οὐ δι᾽ αἰνιγμῶν οὐδὲ συμβολικῶς, ἀλλὰ κυρίοις ὀνόμασιν, οὐ μιᾷ ψυχῇ φησι κινεῖσθαι τὸν κόσμον, ἀλλὰ πλείοσιν ἴσως, δυεῖν δὲ πάντως οὐκ ἐλάττοσιν· ὧν τὴν μὲν ἀγαθουργὸν εἶναι, τὴν δ᾽ ἐναντίαν ταύτῃ καὶ τῶν ἐναντίων δημιουργόν [7]· ἀπολείπει δὲ καὶ τρίτην τινὰ μεταξὺ φύσιν, οὐκ ἄψυχον οὐδ᾽ ἄλογον οὐδ᾽ ἀκίνητον ἐξ αὑτῆς, ὥσπερ ἔνιοι νομίζουσιν, ἀλλ᾽ ἀνακειμένην ἀμφοῖν ἐκείναις, ἐφιεμένην δὲ τῆς ἀμείνονος ἀεί, καὶ ποθοῦσαν καὶ διώκουσαν, ὡς τὰ ἐπιόντα δηλώσει τοῦ λόγου, τὴν Αἰγυπτίων θεολογίαν μάλιστα ταύτῃ τῇ φιλοσοφίᾳ συνοικειοῦντος.

d. Thus, "Osiris" and "Typhon" are present both in the world and in the soul of man.

De Iside et Osiride 49 (371 AB):

Μεμειγμένη γὰρ ἡ τοῦδε τοῦ κόσμου γένεσις καὶ σύστασις ἐξ ἐναντίων, οὐ

Osiris and Typhon in the world and in the soul of man

---

* οὓς θεοὺς γενεθλίους corr. Wyttenbach; τοὺς θεοὺς γενέσθαι οὓς codd.
[1] Above, nr. **53**.   [2] Our nr. **107**.
[3] Above, nr. **42**.
[4] The opposition is somewhat strange here. Cp. our nrs. **124a** and **127**.
[5] Above (vol. II), nrs. **478, 480**.
[6] *Tim.* 35ab, our nr. **350**.
[7] *Leg.* X 896e, our nr. **390**.

μὴν ἰσοσθενῶν, δυνάμεων, ἀλλὰ τῆς βελτίονος τὸ κράτος ἐστίν· ἀπολέσθαι δὲ
τὴν φαύλην παντάπασιν ἀδύνατον, πολλὴν μὲν ἐμπεφυκυῖαν τῷ σώματι, πολλὴν
δὲ τῇ ψυχῇ τοῦ παντός, καὶ πρὸς τὴν βελτίονα ἀεὶ δυσμαχοῦσαν. Ἐν μὲν οὖν
τῇ ψυχῇ νοῦς καὶ λόγος ὁ τῶν ἀρίστων πάντων ἡγεμὼν καὶ κύριος Ὄσιρίς
ἐστιν. ἐν δὲ γῇ καὶ πνεύμασι καὶ ὕδασι καὶ οὐρανῷ καὶ ἄστροις τὸ τεταγμένον
καὶ καθεστηκὸς καὶ ὑγιαῖνον, ὥραις καὶ κράσεσι καὶ περιόδοις, Ὀσίριδος
ἀπορροὴ καὶ εἰκὼν ἐμφαινομένη· Τυφὼν δέ, τῆς ψυχῆς τὸ παθητικὸν καὶ τιτα-
νικὸν ⌊καὶ ἄλογον καὶ ἔμπληκτον· τοῦ δὲ σωματικοῦ τὸ ἐπίκηρον * καὶ νοσῶδες
καὶ ταρακτικὸν ἀωρίαις καὶ δυσκρασίαις καὶ κρύψεσι ἡλίου καὶ ἀφανισμοῖς
σελήνης, οἷον ἐκδρομαὶ καὶ ἀφηνιασμοὶ ** Τυφῶνος.

1315—Plutarch defends divine Providence against the objections that
by the lateness of the Divine punishment sinners are encouraged in their
wickedness, while those who suffer are discouraged.

a.   It is hard, nay impossible, to man to judge the methods of Divine
Providence. Even human laws often seem absurd.

Plut., *De sera numinis vindicta* 4 (549 E-550 C):

Πρῶτον οὖν ὥσπερ ἀφ᾽ ἑστίας ἀρχόμενοι πατρῴας, τῆς πρὸς τὸ θεῖον εὐλαβείας τῶν ἐν Ἀκαδημίᾳ φιλοσόφων, τὸ μὲν ὡς εἰδότες τι περὶ τούτων λέγειν
ἀφοσιωσόμεθα. Πλέον γάρ ἐστι τοῦ περὶ μουσικῶν ἀμούσους καὶ πολεμικῶν
ἀστρατεύτους διαλέγεσθαι τὸ τὰ θεῖα καὶ τὰ δαιμόνια πράγματα διασκοπεῖν,
ἀνθρώπους ὄντας, οἷον ἀτέχνους τεχνιτῶν διάνοιαν ἀπὸ δόξης καὶ ὑπονοίας
κατὰ τὸ εἰκὸς μετιόντας. Οὐ γὰρ ἰατροῦ μὲν ἰδιώτην ὄντα συμβαλεῖν λογισμόν,
ὡς πρότερον οὐκ ἔτεμεν ἀλλ᾽ ὕστερον, οὐδὲ χθὲς ἔκαυσεν ⁺ ἀλλὰ σήμερον, ἔργον
ἐστί· περὶ θεῶν δὲ θνητὸν ῥάδιον ἢ βέβαιον εἰπεῖν ἄλλο, πλὴν ὅτι τὸν καιρὸν
εἰδὼς ἄριστα τῆς περὶ τὴν κακίαν ἰατρείας, ὡς φάρμακον ἑκάστῳ προσφέρει
τὴν κόλασιν οὔτε μεγέθους μέτρον κοινὸν οὔτε χρόνον ἕνα καὶ τὸν αὐτὸν ἐπὶ
πάντων ἔχουσαν. Ὅτι γὰρ ἡ περὶ τὴν ψυχὴν ἰατρεία, δίκη δὲ καὶ δικαιοσύνη
προσαγορευομένη, πασῶν ἐστι τεχνῶν μεγίστη, πρὸς μυρίοις ἑτέροις καὶ
Πίνδαρος ἐμαρτύρησεν [1], ἀριστοτέχναν ἀνακαλούμενος τὸν ἄρχοντα καὶ κύριον
ἁπάντων θεόν, ὡς δὴ δίκης ὄντα δημιουργόν, ᾗ προσήκει τὸ πότε καὶ πῶς καὶ
μέχρι πόσου κολαστέον ἕκαστον τῶν πονηρῶν ὁρίζειν. Καὶ ταύτης φησὶ τῆς τέχνης
ὁ Πλάτων [2] υἱὸν ὄντα τοῦ Διὸς γεγονέναι τὸν Μίνω μαθητήν, ὡς οὐ δυνατὸν
ἐν τοῖς δικαίοις κατορθοῦν οὐδ᾽ αἰσθάνεσθαι τοῦ κατορθοῦντος τὸν μὴ μαθόντα

---

*   ἐπίκηρον is a correction of Xylander. Mss. ἐπίκλητον.
** ἀφηνιασμοί Markland; ἀφανισμοί Mss.
⁺   Corr. Klostermann. Two mss read ἔλυσεν, others ἔλουσεν.
[1] Fr. 57.   [2] *Leg.* 624a; cp. *Minos* 319d.

μηδὲ κτησάμενον τὴν ἐπιστήμην. Οὐδὲ γὰρ οὓς ἄνθρωποι νόμους τίθενται τὸ
εὔλογον ἁπλῶς ἔχουσι καὶ πάντοτε φαινόμενον, ἀλλ' ἔνια καὶ δοκεῖ κομιδῇ
γελοῖα τῶν προσταγμάτων· οἷον ἐν Λακεδαίμονι κηρύττουσιν οἱ ἔφοροι παριόντες
εὐθὺς εἰς τὴν ἀρχὴν μὴ τρέφειν μύστακα καὶ πείθεσθαι τοῖς νόμοις, ὡς μὴ
χαλεποὶ ὦσιν αὐτοῖς· Ῥωμαῖοι δέ, οὓς ἂν εἰς ἐλευθερίαν ἀφαιρῶνται, κάρφος
αὐτῶν λεπτὸν ἐπιβάλλουσι τοῖς σώμασιν· ὅταν δὲ διαθήκας γράφωσιν, ἑτέρους
μὲν ἀπολείπουσι κληρονόμους, ἑτέροις δὲ πωλοῦσι τὰς οὐσίας [1]. ὃ δοκεῖ παρά-
λογον εἶναι. Παραλογώτατον δὲ τὸ τοῦ Σόλωνος, ἄτιμον εἶναι τὸν ἐν στάσει
πόλεως μηδετέρᾳ μερίδι προσθέμενον μηδὲ συστασιάσαντα [2]. Καὶ ὅλως πολλὰς
ἄν τις ἐξείποι νόμων ἀτοπίας μήτε τὸν λόγον ἔχων τοῦ νομοθέτου μήτε τὴν
αἰτίαν συνιεὶς ἑκάστου τῶν γραφομένων. Τί δὴ θαυμαστόν, εἰ τῶν ἀνθρωπίνων
οὕτως ἡμῖν ὄντων δυσθεωρήτων οὐκ εὔπορόν ἐστι τὸ περὶ τῶν θεῶν εἰπεῖν,
ᾧτινι λόγῳ τοὺς μὲν ὕστερον, τοὺς δὲ πρότερον τῶν ἁμαρτανόντων κολάζουσιν;

b.　God is for man an example of order and of long-suffering.

Ib., c. 5　(550 C-F):

Ἀλλὰ σκοπεῖτε πρῶτον, ὅτι κατὰ Πλάτωνα πάντων καλῶν ὁ θεὸς ἑαυτὸν
ἐν μέσῳ παράδειγμα θέμενος [3], τὴν ἀνθρωπίνην ἀρετήν, ἐξομοίωσιν οὖσαν
ἀμωσγέπως πρὸς αὐτόν, ἐνδίδωσι τοῖς ἕπεσθαι θεῷ δυναμένοις. Καὶ γὰρ ἡ
πάντων φύσις ἄτακτος οὖσα, ταύτην ἔσχε τὴν ἀρχὴν τοῦ μεταβαλεῖν καὶ
γενέσθαι κόσμος, ὁμοιότητι καὶ μεθέξει τινὶ τῆς περὶ τὸ θεῖον ἰδέας καὶ ἀρετῆς.
Καὶ τὴν ὄψιν αὐτὸς οὗτος ἀνὴρ ἀνάψαι φησὶ τὴν φύσιν ἐν ἡμῖν, ὅπως ὑπὸ θέας
τῶν ἐν οὐρανῷ φερομένων καὶ θαύματος ἀσπάζεσθαι καὶ ἀγαπᾶν ἐθιζομένη τὸ
εὔσχημον ἡ ψυχὴ καὶ τεταγμένον, ἀπεχθάνηται τοῖς ἀναρμόστοις καὶ πλανητοῖς
πάθεσι καὶ φεύγῃ τὸ εἰκῇ καὶ ὡς ἔτυχεν, ὡς κακίας καὶ πλημμελείας ἁπάσης
γένεσιν [4]. Οὐ γάρ ἐστιν ὅτι μεῖζον ἄνθρωπος ἀπολαύειν θεοῦ πέφυκεν ἢ τὸ μιμήσει καὶ διώξει τῶν ἐν ἐκείνῳ καλῶν καὶ ἀγαθῶν εἰς ἀρετὴν καθίστασθαι. Διὸ
καὶ τοῖς πονηροῖς ἐν χρόνῳ καὶ σχολαίως τὴν δίκην ἐπιτίθησιν, οὐκ αὐτός τινα
τοῦ ταχὺ κολάζειν ἁμαρτίαν δεδιὼς ἢ μετάνοιαν, ἀλλ' ἡμῶν τὸ περὶ τὰς τιμωρίας
θηριῶδες καὶ λάβρον ἀφαιρῶν καὶ διδάσκων μὴ σὺν ὀργῇ μηδ' ὅτε μάλιστα
φλέγεται καὶ σφαδᾳζει

Πηδῶν ὁ θυμὸς τῶν φρενῶν ἀνωτέρω [5],

καθάπερ δίψαν ἢ πεῖναν ἀποπιμπλάντας, ἐπιπηδᾶν τοῖς λελυπηκόσιν, ἀλλὰ
μιμουμένους τὴν ἐκείνου πραότητα καὶ τὴν μέλλησιν, ἐν τάξει καὶ ἐμμελείᾳ τὸν
ἥκιστα μετανοίᾳ προσοισόμενον χρόνον ἔχοντας σύμβουλον, ἅπτεσθαι τῆς δίκης.

---

[1]　Cp. Gai *Inst.* II 103.　　[2]　Cp. Plut. *Solon* c. 20.
[3]　E.g. *Leg.* IV 715e-716c (see vol. I, nr. **374b**) and *Theaet.* 176b (the ὁμοίωσις
τῷ θεῷ). Vol. I, nr. **318**. For τοῖς ἕπεσθαι δυναμένοις cp. *Phaedr.* 247a: ἕπεται δὲ ὁ
ἀεὶ ἐθέλων τε καὶ δυνάμενος (our nr. **272**), and 253a.
[4]　*Tim.* 47bc (our nr. **355**).　　[5]　Fragm. Trag. Adesp. 390

God an
example
for man

**His long-
suffering**

c.   God cares for the souls of sinners and gives them time to repent.

Ib. c. 6 (551 C-E):

Δεύτερον τοίνυν τοῦτο διανοηθῶμεν, ὡς αἱ μὲν δικαιώσεις αἱ παρ' ἀνθρώπων μόνον ἔχουσαι τὸ ἀντιλυποῦν [καὶ] ἐν τῷ κακῶς τὸν δεδρακότα παθεῖν
ἵστανται, περαιτέρω δ' οὐκ ἐξικνοῦνται· διὸ τοῖς ἁμαρτήμασι κυνὸς δίκην
ἐφυλακτοῦσαι κατακολουθοῦσι καὶ τὰς πράξεις ἐκ ποδὸς ἐπιδιώκουσι· τὸν
θεὸν δ' εἰκός, ἧς ἂν ἐφάπτηται τῇ δίκῃ ψυχῆς νοσούσης, τά τε πάθη διορᾶν,
εἴ πῄ τι καμπτόμενα πρὸς μετάνοιαν ἐνδίδωσι, καὶ χρόνον γε οἷς οὐκ ἄκρατος
οὐδ' ἄτρεπτος ἡ κακία πέφυκε προσιζάνειν. Ἅτε γὰρ εἰδὼς ὅσην μοῖραν ἀρετῆς
ἀπ' αὐτοῦ φερόμεναι πρὸς γένεσιν αἱ ψυχαὶ βαδίζουσι, καὶ τὸ γενναῖον ὡς
ἰσχυρὸν αὐταῖς καὶ οὐκ ἐξίτηλον ἐμπέφυκεν, ἐξανθεῖ δὲ παρὰ φύσιν τὴν κακίαν
ὑπὸ τροφῆς καὶ ὁμιλίας φαύλης φθειρόμενον, εἶτα θεραπευθὲν ἐνίοις καλῶς
ἀπολαμβάνει τὴν προσήκουσαν ἕξιν, οὐ πᾶσι κατεπείγει τὴν τιμωρίαν ὁμοίως·
ἀλλὰ τὸ μὲν ἀνήκεστον εὐθὺς ἐξεῖλε τοῦ βίου καὶ ἀπέκοψεν, ὡς ἑτέροις γε πάντως
βλαβερόν, αὐτῷ τε βλαβερώτατον, ἀεὶ συνεῖναι μετὰ πονηρίας· οἷς δ' ὑπ'
ἀγνοίας τοῦ καλοῦ μᾶλλον ἢ προαιρέσει τοῦ αἰσχροῦ τὸ ἁμαρτητικὸν εἰκὸς
ἐγγεγονέναι, δίδωσι μεταβαλέσθαι χρόνον. Ἐὰν δ' ἐπιμένωσι, καὶ τούτοις
ἀπέδωκε τὴν δίκην· οὐ γάρ που δέδιε, μὴ διαφύγωσι.

1316—Reply to those who say that it is senseless to visit the sins
of the fathers upon the children and grandchildren.

a.   Plut., *De sera numinis vindicta* 19 (561 C-562 A):

Ὁ γὰρ Βίων τὸν θεὸν κολάζοντα τοὺς παῖδας τῶν πονηρῶν γελοιότερον
εἶναί φησιν ἰατροῦ διὰ νόσον πάππου καὶ πατρὸς ἔκγονον ἢ παῖδα φαρμα-
κεύοντος. Ἔστι δὲ πῇ μὲν ἀνόμοια τὰ πράγματα, πῇ δ' ἐοικότα καὶ ὅμοια.
Νόσου μὲν γὰρ ἄλλος ἄλλον οὐ παύει θεραπευόμενος, οὐδὲ βέλτιόν τις ἔσχε
τῶν ὀφθαλμιώντων ἢ πυρεττόντων ἰδὼν ἄλλον ὑπαλειφόμενον ἢ καταπλατ-
τόμενον· αἱ δὲ τιμωρίαι τῶν πονηρῶν διὰ τοῦτο δείκνυνται πᾶσιν, ὅτι δίκης
κατὰ λόγον περαινομένης ἔργον ἐστὶν ἑτέρους δι' ἑτέρων κολαζομένων ἐπισχεῖν.
Ἡ δὲ προσέοικε τῷ ζητουμένῳ τὸ παραβαλλόμενον ὑπὸ τοῦ Βίωνος ἔλαθεν
αὐτόν· ἤδη γὰρ ἀνδρὸς εἰς νόσημα μοχθηρὸν οὐ μὴν ἀνίατον ἐμπεσόντος, εἶτ'
ἀκρασίᾳ καὶ μαλακίᾳ προεμένου τῷ πάθει τὸ σῶμα καὶ διαφθαρέντος, υἱὸν
οὐ δοκοῦντα νοσεῖν, ἀλλὰ μόνον ἐπιτηδείως ἔχοντα πρὸς τὴν αὐτὴν νόσον,
ἰατρὸς ἢ οἰκεῖος ἢ ἀλείπτης καταμαθὼν ἢ δεσπότης χρηστός, ἐμβαλὼν εἰς
δίαιταν αὐστηρὰν καὶ ἀφελὼν ὄψα καὶ πέμματα καὶ πότους καὶ γύναια, φαρ-
μακείαις δὲ χρησάμενος ἐνδελεχέσι καὶ διαπονήσας [τὸ σῶμα] γυμνασίοις,
ἐσκέδασε καὶ ἀπέπεμψε μεγάλου πάθους σπέρμα μικρόν, οὐκ ἐάσας εἰς μέγεθος
προελθεῖν. Ἡ γὰρ οὐχ οὕτω παρακελευόμεθα, προσέχειν ἀξιοῦντες ἑαυτοῖς
καὶ παραφυλάττεσθαι καὶ μὴ παραμελεῖν ὅσοι γεγόνασιν ἐκ πατέρων ἢ μη-

τέρων νοσηματικῶν, ἀλλ' εὐθὺς ἐξωθεῖν τὴν ἐγκεκραμένην ἀρχὴν εὐκίνητον οὖσαν καὶ ἀκροσφαλῆ προκαταλαμβάνοντας; Πάνυ μὲν οὖν, ἔφασαν. Οὐ τοίνυν ἄτοπον, εἶπον, ἀλλ' ἀναγκαῖον, οὐδὲ γελοῖον, ἀλλ' ὠφέλιμον πρᾶγμα ποιοῦμεν, ἐπιληπτικῶν παισὶ καὶ μελαγχολικῶν καὶ ποδαγρικῶν γυμνάσια καὶ διαίτας καὶ φάρμακα προσάγοντες οὐ νοσοῦσιν ἀλλ' ἕνεκα τοῦ μὴ νοσῆσαι. Τὸ γὰρ ἐκ πονηροῦ σώματος γινόμενον σῶμα τιμωρίας μὲν οὐδεμιᾶς, ἰατρείας δὲ καὶ φυλακῆς ἄξιόν ἐστιν· ἣν εἴ τις, ὅτι τὰς ἡδονὰς ἀφαιρεῖ, καὶ δηγμὸν ἐπάγει καὶ πόνον, τιμωρίαν ὑπὸ δειλίας καὶ μαλακίας ἀποκαλεῖ, χαίρειν ἐατέον. Ἆρ' οὖν σῶμα μὲν ἔκγονον φαύλου σώματος ἄξιόν ἐστι θεραπεύειν καὶ φυλάττειν, κακίας δὲ ὁμοιότητα συγγενικὴν ἐν νέῳ βλαστάνουσαν ἤθει καὶ ἀναφυομένην ἐᾶν δεῖ καὶ περιμένειν καὶ μέλλειν ἄχρις ἂν ἐκχυθεῖσα τοῖς πάθεσιν ἐμφανὴς γένηται

> ''κακόφρονά τ' ἀμφάνῃ πραπίδων
> καρπόν'',

ὡς φησι Πίνδαρος; [1]

b. Often men do not show their true nature directly. But God, who knows their hidden dispositions, often prevents their wickedness from bursting out.

Ib., c. 20-21 (562 C-E):

Οὐ γὰρ ἅμα γίγνεται καὶ φαίνεται τῶν πονηρῶν ἕκαστος· ἀλλ' ἔχει μὲν ἐξ ἀρχῆς τὴν κακίαν, χρῆται δὲ καιροῦ καὶ δυνάμεως ἐπιλαβόμενος τῷ κλέπτειν ὁ κλέπτης καὶ τῷ παρανομεῖν ὁ τυραννικός. 'Αλλ' ὁ θεὸς οὔτ' ἀγνοεῖ δήπου τὴν ἑκάστου διάθεσιν καὶ φύσιν, ἅτε δὴ ψυχῆς μᾶλλον ἢ σώματος αἰσθάνεσθαι πεφυκώς, οὔτ' ἀναμένει τὴν βίαν ἐν χερσὶ γενομένην καὶ τὴν ἀναίδειαν ἐν φωνῇ καὶ τὴν ἀκολασίαν ἐν αἰδοίοις κολάζειν. Οὐ γὰρ ἀμύνεται τὸν ἀδικήσαντα κακῶς παθών, οὐδ' ὀργίζεται τῷ ἁρπάσαντι βιασθείς, οὐδὲ μισεῖ τὸν μοιχὸν ὑβρισθείς, ἀλλ' ἰατρείας ἕνεκα τὸν μοιχικὸν καὶ τὸν πλεονεκτικὸν καὶ ἀδικητικὸν κολάζει πολλάκις, ὥσπερ ἐπιληψίαν τὴν κακίαν πρὶν ἢ καταλαβεῖν ἀναιρῶν.

'Ημεῖς δ' ἀρτίως μὲν ἠγανακτοῦμεν, ὡς ὀψὲ καὶ βραδέως τῶν πονηρῶν δίκην διδόντων· νῦν δὲ ὅτι καὶ πρὶν ἀδικεῖν ἐνίους τὴν ἕξιν αὐτῶν κολούει καὶ τὴν διάθεσιν, ἐγκαλοῦμεν, ἀγνοοῦντες ὅτε τοῦ γενομένου πολλάκις τὸ μέλλον καὶ τὸ λανθάνον τοῦ προδήλου χεῖρόν ἐστι καὶ φοβερώτερον· οὐ δυνάμενοι δὲ συλλογίζεσθαι τὰς αἰτίας, δι' ἃς ἐνίους μὲν καὶ ἀδικήσαντας ἐᾶν βέλτιόν ἐστιν, ἐνίους δὲ καὶ διανοουμένους προκαταλαμβάνειν· ὥσπερ ἀμέλει καὶ φάρμακα ἐνίοις μὲν οὐχ ἁρμόζει νοσοῦσιν, ἐνίοις δὲ λυσιτελεῖ καὶ μὴ νοσοῦσιν ἐπισφαλέστερον ἐκείνων ἔχουσιν.

1317—The treatise ends by the story of Thespesius of Soli, a man who

Often God
prevents sin
from
bursting out

The story of
Thespesius

---

[1] Fr. 211.

lived in evil throughout his life, till one day he fell down from a height and broke his neck, but on the third day came back to life, after a vision of the life hereafter. Here is his account of the punishment of sinners.

Plut., *De sera numinis vindicta* 30 (566 E-567 D):

Μετὰ δὲ ταῦτα πρὸς τὴν θέαν τῶν κολαζομένων ἐτρέποντο. Καὶ τὰ μὲν πρῶτα δυσχερεῖς καὶ οἰκτρὰς εἶχον ὄψεις μόνον· ἐπεὶ δὲ καὶ φίλοις καὶ οἰκείοις καὶ συνήθεσιν Θεσπέσιος οὐκ ἂν προσδοκήσας κολαζομένοις ἐνετύγχανε, οἳ καὶ δεινὰ παθήματα καὶ τιμωρίας ἀσχήμονας καὶ ἀλγεινὰς ὑπομένοντες ᾠκτίζοντο πρὸς ἐκεῖνον καὶ ἀνεκλαίοντο· τέλος δὲ τὸν πατέρα τὸν ἑαυτοῦ κατεῖδεν ἔκ τινος βαράθρου στιγμάτων καὶ οὐλῶν μεστὸν ἀναδυόμενον, ὀρέγοντα τὰς χεῖρας αὐτῷ καὶ σιωπᾶν οὐκ ἐώμενον, ἀλλ' ὁμολογεῖν ἀναγκαζόμενον ὑπὸ τῶν ἐφεστώτων ταῖς τιμωρίαις, ὅτι περὶ ξένους τινὰς μιαρὸς γενόμενος χρυσίον ἔχοντας, φαρμάκοις διαφθείρας καὶ ἐκεῖ διαλαθὼν ἅπαντας, ἐνταῦθ' ἐξελεγχθείς, τὰ μὲν ἤδη πέπονθε, τὰ δ' ἄγεται πεισόμενος. Ἱκετεύειν μὲν [οὖν] ἢ παραιτεῖσθαι περὶ τοῦ πατρὸς οὐκ ἐτόλμα δι' ἔκπληξιν καὶ δέος· ὑποστρέψαι δὲ καὶ φυγεῖν βουλόμενος οὐκ ἔτι τὸν πρᾶον ἐκεῖνον ἑώρα καὶ οἰκεῖον ξεναγόν, ἀλλ' ὑφ' ἑτέρων τινῶν φοβερῶν τὴν ὄψιν εἰς τὸ πρόσθεν ὠθούμενος, ὡς ἀνάγκην οὖσαν οὕτω διεξελθεῖν, ἐθεᾶτο τῶν μὲν γνωρίμως πονηρῶν γενομένων καὶ κολασθέντων αὐτόθι τὴν σκιὰν οὐκέτ' εἶναι χαλεπῶς οὐδ' ὁμοίως τριβομένην, ἅτε δὴ περὶ τὸ ἄλογον καὶ παθητικὸν ἐπίπονον οὖσαν· ὅσοι δὲ πρόσχημα καὶ δόξαν ἀρετῆς περιβαλόμενοι διεβίωσαν κακίᾳ λανθανούσῃ, τούτους ἐπιπόνως καὶ ὀδυνηρῶς ἠνάγκαζον ἕτεροι περιεστῶτες ἐκτρέπεσθαι τὰ ἐντὸς ἔξω τῆς ψυχῆς, ἰλυσπωμένους παρὰ φύσιν καὶ ἀνακαμπτομένους, ὥσπερ αἱ θαλάττιαι σκολόπενδραι καταπιοῦσαι τὸ ἄγκιστρον, ἐκτρέπουσιν ἑαυτάς· ἐνίους δ' ἀναδέροντες αὐτῶν καὶ ἀναπτύσσοντες ἀπεδείκνυσαν ὑπούλους καὶ ποικίλους, ἐν τῷ λογιστικῷ καὶ κυρίῳ τὴν μοχθηρίαν ἔχοντας. Ἄλλας δ' ἔφη ψυχὰς ἰδεῖν, ὥσπερ τὰς ἐχίδνας περιπεπλεγμένας σύνδυο καὶ σύντρεις καὶ πλείονας, ἀλλήλας ἐσθιούσας ὑπὸ μνησικακίας καὶ κακοθυμίας ὧν ἔπαθον ἐν τῷ ζῆν ἢ ἔδρασαν. Εἶναι δὲ καὶ λίμνας παρ' ἀλλήλας, τὴν μὲν χρυσοῦ περιζέοντος, τὴν δὲ μολίβδου ψυχροτάτην, ἄλλην δὲ τραχεῖαν σιδήρου· καί τινας ἐφεστάναι δαίμονας ὥσπερ οἱ χαλκεῖς ὀργάνοις ἀναλαμβάνοντας καὶ καθιέντας ἐν μέρει τὰς ψυχὰς τῶν δι' ἀπληστίαν καὶ πλεονεξίαν πονηρῶν. Ἐν μὲν γὰρ τῷ χρυσῷ διαπύρους καὶ διαφανεῖς ὑπὸ τοῦ φλέγεσθαι γενομένας ἐνέβαλλον εἰς τὴν τοῦ μολίβδου βάπτοντες. ἐκπαγείσας δ' αὐτόθι καὶ γενομένας σκληρὰς ὥσπερ αἱ χάλαζαι, πάλιν εἰς τὴν τοῦ σιδήρου μεθίστασαν· ἐνταῦθα δὲ μέλαιναί τε δεινῶς ἐγίνοντο, καὶ περικλώμεναι διὰ σκληρότητα καὶ συντριβόμεναι τὰ εἴδη μετέβαλλον· εἶθ' οὕτω πάλιν εἰς τὸν χρυσὸν ἐκομίζοντο, δεινάς, ὡς ἔλεγεν, ἐν ταῖς μεταβολαῖς ἀλγηδόνας ὑπομένουσαι.

The framework of the story and its general tendency reminds us strongly of the myth of Er in Plato's *Resp.* X. Many of the details, however are of Plutarch's invention. The myth is amply discussed by G. Méautis, *Plutarque, Des délais de la justice divine*, Lausanne 1935, p. 57 ff.

1318—a. On admitting demons as intermediate powers between God and man.

Demonology

Plut. *De defectu oraculorum* 10, 414 F-415 C; 12, the end (416 C):

Εὖ μὲν οὖν λέγουσι καὶ οἱ λέγοντες, ὅτι Πλάτων τὸ ταῖς γεννωμέναις ποιότησιν ὑποκείμενον στοιχεῖον ἐξευρών, ὃ νῦν ὕλην καὶ φύσιν καλοῦσιν, πολλῶν ἀπήλλαξε καὶ μεγάλων ἀποριῶν τοὺς φιλοσόφους· ἐμοὶ δὲ δοκοῦσι πλείονας λῦσαι καὶ μείζονας ἀπορίας οἱ τὸ τῶν δαιμόνων γένος ἐν μέσῳ * θεῶν καὶ ἀνθρώπων, καὶ τρόπον τινὰ τὴν κοινωνίαν ἡμῶν συνάγον εἰς ταὐτὸ καὶ συνάπτον ἐξευρόντες· εἴτε μάγων τῶν περὶ Ζωροάστρην ὁ λόγος οὗτός ἐστιν, εἴτε Θράκιος ἀπ' Ὀρφέως εἴτ' Αἰγύπτιος ἢ Φρύγιος, ὡς τεκμαιρόμεθα ταῖς ἑκατέρωθι τελεταῖς ἀναμεμιγμένα πολλὰ θνητὰ καὶ πένθιμα τῶν ὀργιαζομένων καὶ δρωμένων ἱερῶν ὁρῶντες. Ἑλλήνων δ' Ὅμηρος μὲν ἔτι φαίνεται κοινῶς ἀμφοτέροις χρώμενος τοῖς ὀνόμασι καὶ τοὺς θεοὺς ἔστιν ὅτε δαίμονας προσαγορεύων [1]. Ἡσίοδος δὲ καθαρῶς καὶ διωρισμένως πρῶτος ἐξέθηκε τῶν λογικῶν τέσσαρα γένη, θεοὺς εἶτα δαίμονας εἶθ' ἥρωας, τὸ δ' ἐπὶ πᾶσιν ἀνθρώπους, ἐξ ὧν ἔοικε ποιεῖν τὴν μεταβολήν, τοῦ μὲν χρυσοῦ γένους εἰς δαίμονας πολλοὺς κἀγαθούς, τῶν δ' ἡμιθέων εἰς ἥρωας ἀποκριθέντων [2]. Ἕτεροι δὲ μεταβολὴν τοῖς τε σώμασιν ὁμοίως ποιοῦσι καὶ ταῖς ψυχαῖς, ὥσπερ [γὰρ] ἐκ γῆς ὕδωρ, ἐκ δὲ ὕδατος ἀήρ, ἐκ δ' ἀέρος πῦρ γεννώμενον ὁρᾶται, τῆς οὐσίας ἄνω φερομένης· οὕτως ἐκ μὲν ἀνθρώπων εἰς ἥρωας, ἐκ δὲ ἡρώων εἰς δαίμονας αἱ βελτίονες ψυχαὶ τὴν μεταβολὴν λαμβάνουσιν [3]. Ἐκ δὲ δαιμόνων ὀλίγαι μὲν ἐν χρόνῳ πολλῷ δι' ἀρετῆς καθαρθεῖσαι παντάπασι θειότητος μετέσχον· ἐνίαις δὲ συμβαίνει μὴ κρατεῖν ἑαυτῶν, ἀλλ' ὑφιεμέναις καὶ ἀναδυομέναις πάλιν σώμασι θνητοῖς, ἀλαμπῆ καὶ ἀμυδρὰν ζωὴν ὥσπερ ἀναθυμίασιν ἴσχειν.

As to the lifetime of these beings, different views are put forward. The essential point, however, is that their existence must be admitted.

Καὶ γὰρ ἂν πλείων ὁ χρόνος ᾖ, κἂν ἐλάττων κἂν τεταγμένος κἂν ἄτακτος, ἐν ᾧ μεταλλάττει δαίμονος ψυχὴ καὶ ἥρωος βίος, οὐδὲν ἧττον ἐφ' ᾧ βούλεται δεδείξεται μετὰ μαρτύρων σοφῶν καὶ παλαιῶν, ὅτι φύσεις εἰσί τινες ὥσπερ

---

* ἐν μέσῳ θέντες Eus.

[1] E.g. *Ilias* III 420, where Aphrodite is called a δαίμων.

[2] Hes. *Erga* 159 f. was explained by Plato in this sense (*Resp.* V 468e-469b; *Crat.* 397e-398c). Cp. O. Reverdin, *La religion de la cité platonicienne*, p. 128 ff.

[3] Flacelière in his commentary on the *De def. orac.* thinks of *Epinomis* 984d. But there the argument is different. Cp. our nr. **431a** (vol. II) and the literature cited there. Also G. Soury, *La démonologie de Plutarque*, p. 24 f.

ἐν μεθορίῳ θεῶν καὶ ἀνθρώπων, δεχόμεναι πάθη θνητὰ καὶ μεταβολὰς ἀναγκαίας, οὓς δαίμονας ὀρθῶς ἔχει κατὰ νόμον πατέρων ἡγουμένους καὶ ὀνομάζοντας σέβεσθαι.

b. Plutarchus mentions Xenocrates as a source of these theories. The moon is described as a mixed body which parallels the demons.

De def. orac. 13, 416 D-F:

Παράδειγμα δὲ τῷ λόγῳ Ξενοκράτης μέν, ὁ Πλάτωνος ἑταῖρος, ἐποιήσατο τὸ τῶν τριγώνων, θείῳ μὲν ἀπεικάσας τὸ ἰσόπλευρον, θνητῷ δὲ τὸ σκαληνόν, τὸ δ' ἰσοσκελὲς δαιμονίῳ· τὸ μὲν γὰρ ἴσον πάντη, τὸ δ' ἄνισον πάντη· τὸ δ' πῇ μὲν ἴσον, πῇ δ' ἄνισον, ὥσπερ ἡ δαιμόνων φύσις ἔχουσα καὶ πάθος θνητοῦ καὶ θεοῦ δύναμιν. Ἡ δὲ φύσις αἰσθητὰς εἰκόνας ἐξέθηκε καὶ ὁμοιότητας ὁρωμένας, θεῶν μὲν ἥλιον καὶ ἄστρα, θνητῶν δὲ σέλα καὶ κομήτας καὶ διάττοντας. Ὡς Εὐριπίδης εἴκασεν, ἐν οἷς εἶπεν·

> Ὁ δ' ἄρτι θάλλων σάρκα, διοπετὴς ὅπως
> ἀστὴρ ἀπέσβη, πνεῦμ' ἀφεὶς εἰς αἰθέρα. [1]

Μικτὸν δὲ σῶμα καὶ μίμημα δαιμόνιον ὄντως τὴν σελήνην, τῷ τῇ τούτου τοῦ γένους συνᾴδειν περιφορᾷ, φθίσεις φαινομένας δεχομένην καὶ αὐξήσεις καὶ μεταβολάς, ὁρῶντες οἱ μὲν ἄστρον γεῶδες, οἱ δ' ὀλυμπίαν γῆν [2], οἱ δὲ χθονίας ὁμοῦ καὶ οὐρανίας κλῆρον Ἑκάτης προσεῖπον. Ὥσπερ οὖν εἰ τὸν ἀέρα τις ἀνέλοι καὶ ἀποσπάσειε τὸν μεταξὺ γῆς καὶ σελήνης, τὴν ἑνότητα διαλύσει καὶ τὴν κοινωνίαν τοῦ παντὸς ἐν μέσῳ κενῆς καὶ ἀσυνδέτου χώρας γενομένης, οὕτως οἱ δαιμόνων γένος μὴ ἀπολείποντες, ἀνεπίμικτα τὰ τῶν θεῶν καὶ ἀνθρώπων ποιοῦσι καὶ ἀσυνάλλακτα, τὴν ἑρμηνευτικήν, ὡς Πλάτων ἔλεγεν [3], καὶ διακονικὴν ἀναιροῦντες φύσιν, ἢ πάντα φύρειν ἅμα καὶ ταράττειν ἀναγκάζουσιν ἡμᾶς τοῖς ἀνθρωπίνοις πάθεσι καὶ πράγμασι τὸν θεὸν ἐμβιβάζοντας, καὶ κατασπῶντας ἐπὶ τὰς χρείας, ὥσπερ αἱ Θετταλαὶ λέγονται τὴν σελήνην.

On "the air between the earth and the moon" as the dwelling-place of "souls" or daemons, cp. Philo, above, our nr. **1304**. There, the "souls" or angels are also introduced as spirits serving God (ὑπηρετίδες καὶ διάκονοι).

c. The function of the demons on earth.

Ib., c. 13, 417 AB:

Ἡμεῖς δὲ μήτε μαντείας τινὰς ἀθειάστους εἶναι λέγοντας, ἢ τελετὰς καὶ ὀργιασμοὺς ἀμελουμένους ὑπὸ θεῶν, ἀκούωμεν· μήτ' αὖ πάλιν τὸν θεὸν ἐν τούτοις ἀναστρέφεσθαι καὶ παρεῖναι καὶ συμπραγματεύεσθαι δοξάζωμεν, ἀλλ'

---

[1] Fr. 971 Nauck.
[2] The expression γῆν ὀλυμπίαν is also used in the *De facie*, 935c. Cp. also *De facie* 943e: οἷον ἄστρου σύγκραμα καὶ γῆς οὖσαν (sc. τ. σελήνην).
[3] *Symp.* 202e: Ἑρμηνεῦον (πᾶν τὸ δαιμόνιον) καὶ διαπορθμεῦον θεοῖς τὰ παρ' ἀνθρώπων καὶ ἀνθρώποις τὰ παρὰ θεῶν.

οἷς δίκαιόν ἐστι ταῦτα λειτουργοῖς θεῶν ἀνατιθέντες ὥσπερ ὑπηρέταις καὶ γραμματεῦσι, δαίμονας νομίζωμεν ἐπισκόπους θείων + ἱερῶν καὶ μυστηρίων ὀργιαστάς· ἄλλους δὲ τῶν ὑπερηφάνων καὶ μεγάλων τιμωροὺς ἀδικιῶν περιπολεῖν.

Cp. infra, *De facie* c. 30, under nr. **1319c**.

d. Older traces of the doctrine.

De def. orac. 17, 419 A:

Πρὸς ταῦτα τοῦ Ἡρακλέωνος σιωπῇ διανοουμένου τι πρὸς αὐτόν, "'Ἀλλὰ φαύλους μέν," ἔφη, "δαίμονας οὐκ Ἐμπεδοκλῆς μόνον, ὦ Ἡρακλέων, ἀπέλιπεν, ἀλλὰ καὶ Πλάτων καὶ Ξενοκράτης καὶ Χρύσιππος· ἔτι δὲ Δημόκριτος, εὐχόμενος εὐλόγχων εἰδώλων τυγχάνειν, δῆλος ἦν ἕτερα δυστράπελα καὶ μοχθηρὰς γινώσκων ἔχοντα προαιρέσεις τινὰς καὶ ὁρμάς." —

As to Empedocles, cp. fr. 115 Diels (our nr. **116a**); Democritus fr. 166 Diels (Gr. Ph. **143d**). Plato, *Symp.* 202e is cited in n. 3 on this page. For Xenocrates, see Heinze, *Xenocr.* p. 89 ff.; for Chrysippus, Von Arnim, *SVF* II nr. 1104.

1319—In the myth of the *De facie*, which we cited above when dealing with Posidonius (nr. **1192d**), is found the tripartition of man into body, soul and spirit.

a. Plut., *De facie in orbe lunae* 28, 943 AB:

Noûs is superior to soul

Τὸν ἄνθρωπον οἱ πολλοὶ σύνθετον μὲν ὀρθῶς, ἐκ δυοῖν δὲ μόνων σύνθετον οὐκ ὀρθῶς ἡγοῦνται· μόριον γὰρ εἶναί πως ψυχῆς οἴονται τὸν νοῦν, οὐδὲν ἧττον ἐκείνων ἁμαρτάνοντες, οἷς ἡ ψυχὴ δοκεῖ μόριον εἶναι τοῦ σώματος· νοῦς γὰρ ψυχῆς ὅσῳ ψυχὴ σώματος ἄμεινόν ἐστι καὶ θειότερον· ποιεῖ δὲ ἡ μὲν ψυχῆς <καὶ σώματος μῖξις αἴσθησιν, ἡ δὲ νοῦ καὶ ψυχῆς> * σύνοδος λόγον, ὧν τὸ μὲν ἡδονῆς ἀρχὴ καὶ πόνου, τὸ δ' ἀρετῆς καὶ κακίας. Τριῶν δὲ τούτων συμπαγέντων, τὸ μὲν σῶμα ἡ γῆ, τὴν δὲ ψυχὴν ἡ σελήνη, τὸν δὲ νοῦν ὁ ἥλιος παρέσχεν εἰς τὴν γένεσιν, ... ** ὥσπερ αὖ τῇ σελήνῃ τὸ φέγγος. Ὃν δ' ἀποθνήσκομεν θάνατον, ὁ μὲν ἐκ τριῶν δύο ποιεῖ τὸν ἄνθρωπον, ὁ δὲ ἓν ἐκ δυοῖν· καὶ ὁ μέν ἐστιν ἐν τῇ τῆς Δήμητρος, ... *** ἐν αὐτῇ τελεῖν, καὶ τοὺς νεκροὺς Ἀθηναῖοι Δημητρείους ὠνόμαζον τὸ παλαιόν· ὁ δ' ἐν τῇ σελήνῃ τῆς Περσεφόνης [1].

The moon the abode of souls

b. The moon is the place where souls are punished for their sins, while on another side of it are the Elysian fields.

+ θείων Reiske, followed by Flacelière; θεῶν codd.
* Suppl. Pohlenz. ** Lacuna of 7 letters.
*** Lacuna of 22 letters, filled by Cherniss as follows: <διὸ τελευτᾶν λέγεται τὸν βίον αὐτῇ τελεῖν. Before τῆς Δήμητρος Madvig supplied γῆ.
[1] Kore or Persephone, according to the myth (**942d**), should not be placed in the same regions as Demeter, but the latter rules the earth, while Persephone governs the moon.

Ib., c. 29, 944 BC:

Ἐκφοβεῖ δ' αὐτὰς (sc. τὰς τῶν κολαζομένων ψυχάς) καὶ τὸ καλούμενον πρόσωπον, ὅταν ἐγγὺς γένωνται, βλοσυρόν τι καὶ φρικῶδες ὁρώμενον. Ἔστι δ' οὐ τοιοῦτον· ἀλλ' ὥσπερ ἡ παρ' ἡμῖν ἔχει γῆ κόλπους βαθεῖς καὶ μεγάλους, ἕνα μὲν ἐνταῦθα διὰ στηλῶν Ἡρακλείων ἀναχεόμενον εἴσω πρὸς ἡμᾶς, ἔξω δὲ τὸν Κάσπιον καὶ τοὺς περὶ τὴν Ἐρυθρὰν θάλατταν, οὕτω βάθη ταῦτα τῆς σελήνης ἐστὶ καὶ κοιλώματα· καλοῦσι δ' αὐτῶν τὸ μὲν μέγιστον Ἑκάτης μυχόν, ὅπου καὶ δίκας διδόασιν αἱ ψυχαὶ καὶ λαμβάνουσιν, ὧν ἂν ἤδη γεγενημέναι δαίμονες ἢ πάθωσιν ἢ δράσωσι· τὰ δὲ δύο, μακρά *· περαιοῦνται γὰρ αἱ ψυχαὶ δι' αὐτῶν, νῦν μὲν εἰς τὰ πρὸς οὐρανὸν τῆς σελήνης, νῦν δὲ πάλιν εἰς τὰ πρὸς γῆν· ὀνομάζεσθαι δὲ τὰ μὲν πρὸς οὐρανὸν τῆς σελήνης Ἠλύσιον πεδίον, τὰ δ' ἐνταῦθα Φερσεφόνης οὐκ ἀντίχθονος [1].

In this chapter again Xenocrates, and to a certain extent Plato, are mentioned as the authors of the theory that the moon has a "mixed" nature, intermediate between the earth and the fiery nature of the sun, Xenocrates holding that both the stars and the sun are of a fiery nature, while Plato held that no body is visible unless it is mixed up with a certain, however small, part of earth.

The function of daemons on the earth   **c.**   Here again the function of the daemons on earth is mentioned.

Ib., c. 30, 944 CD:

Οὐκ ἀεὶ δὲ διατρίβουσιν ἐπ' αὐτὴν οἱ δαίμονες, ἀλλὰ χρηστηρίων δεῦρο κατίασιν ἐπιμελησόμενοι, καὶ ταῖς ἀνωτάτω συμπάρεισι καὶ συνοργιάζουσι τῶν τελετῶν, κολασταί τε γίνονται καὶ φύλακες ἀδικημάτων, καὶ σωτῆρες ἔν τε πολέμοις καὶ κατὰ θάλατταν ἐπιλάμπουσιν· ὅ τι ἂν μὴ καλῶς περὶ ταῦτα πράξωσιν, ἀλλὰ ὑπ' ὀργῆς ἢ πρὸς ἄδικον χάριν ἢ φθόνῳ, δίκην τίνουσιν· ὠθοῦνται γὰρ αὖθις ἐπὶ γῆν συρρηγνύμενοι σώμασιν ἀνθρωπίνοις.

The myth is discussed by R. M. Jones, *The Platonism of Plutarch*, p. 49-56. Recent literature:

W. Hamilton, *Class. Quart.* 28 (1934), p. 25 ff.

Also G. Soury, *Mort et initiation*. Sur quelques sources de Plutarque, *De facie* 943 CD, in *Revue des Et. grecques* 53 (1940), p. 51-58.

1320—Another account of daemons and their genesis is found in the story of Timarchus.

Plut., *De genio Socratis* 22, 591 C-F:

Timarchus was a young friend and disciple of Socrates who, after the master's death, went to the oracle of Trophonius to inquire about the daimonion. He stayed

---

* τὰ δὲ δύο μακρά ‹τὰς Πύλας› Cherniss.

[1] P. Rainguard in his commentary on the *De facie* thinks that the Persephone of the moon is distinguished from another Persephone in the Antichthon. Perhaps the text is not sound and should be read without the negation. Zuntz (in Rhein. Mus. 1953, p. 233) suggested οὖδος ἀντιχθόνιος.

in the cave for two days and in his dreams saw a vision of the world hereafter.
Over him he saw isles flooded by a soft light, beneath a dark and wide gap (μέγα
χάσμα), whence wailings and lamentations were heard. A voice gave him the
following explanation.

"Αἱ μὲν γὰρ ἄλλαι νῆσοι θεοὺς ἔχουσι· σελήνη δὲ δαιμόνων ἐπιχθονίων
οὖσα φεύγει τὴν Στύγα μικρὸν ὑπερφέρουσα· λαμβάνεται δὲ ἅπαξ ἐν μέτροις
δευτέροις ἑκατὸν ἑβδομήκοντα ἑπτά· καὶ τῆς Στυγὸς ἐπιφερομένης αἱ ψυχαὶ
βοῶσι δειμαίνουσαι· πολλὰς γὰρ ὁ "Αιδης ἀφαρπάζει περιολισθανούσας· ἄλλας
δ' ἀνακομίζεται κάτωθεν ἡ σελήνη προσνηχομένας, αἷς εἰς καιρὸν ἡ τῆς γενέσεως
τελευτὴ ἐνέπεσε, πλὴν ὅσαι μιαραὶ καὶ ἀκάθαρτοι· ταύτας δ' ἀστράπτουσα
καὶ μυκωμένη φοβερὸν οὐκ ἐᾷ πελάζειν, ἀλλὰ θρηνοῦσαι τὸν ἑαυτῶν πότμον
ἀποσφαλλόμεναι φέρονται κάτω πάλιν ἐπ' ἄλλην γένεσιν, ὡς ὁρᾷς." "'Αλλ'
οὐδὲν ὁρῶ", τὸν Τίμαρχον εἰπεῖν, "ἢ πολλοὺς ἀστέρας περὶ τὸ χάσμα παλλομένους,
ἑτέρους δὲ καταδυομένους εἰς αὐτό, τοὺς δὲ ἄττοντας αὖ κάτωθεν." "Αὐτοὺς
ἄρα", φάναι, "τοὺς δαίμονας ὁρῶν ἀγνοεῖς. "Εχει γὰρ ὧδε· ψυχὴ πᾶσα νοῦ μετ-
έσχεν· ἄλογος δὲ καὶ ἄνους οὐκ ἔστιν· ἀλλ' ὅσον ἂν αὐτῆς σαρκὶ μιχθῇ καὶ πάθεσιν,
ἀλλοιούμενον τρέπεται καθ' ἡδονὰς καὶ ἀλγηδόνας εἰς τὸ ἄλογον. Μίγνυται δ'
οὐ πᾶσα τὸν αὐτὸν τρόπον· ἀλλ' αἱ μὲν ὅλαι κατέδυσαν εἰς σῶμα, καὶ δι' ὅλων
ἀναταραχθεῖσαι τὸ σύμπαν ὑπὸ παθῶν διαφέρονται κατὰ τὸν βίον· αἱ δὲ πῇ
μὲν ἀνεκράθησαν, πῇ δ' ἔλιπον ἔξω τὸ καθαρώτατον, οὐκ ἐπισπώμενον, ἀλλ'
οἷον ἀκρόπλουν ἐπιψαῦον ἐκ κεφαλῆς τοῦ ἀνθρώπου, καθάπερ ἐν βυθῷ δεδυκότος
ἄρτημα κορυφαῖον, ὀρθουμένης περὶ αὐτὸ τῆς ψυχῆς ἀνέχον ὅσον ὑπακούει
καὶ οὐ κρατεῖται τοῖς πάθεσιν. Τὸ μὲν οὖν ὑποβρύχιον ἐν τῷ σώματι φερόμενον
ψυχὴ λέγεται. τὸ δὲ φθορᾶς λειφθὲν οἱ πολλοὶ Νοῦν καλοῦντες ἐντὸς εἶναι
νομίζουσιν αὐτῶν *, ὥσπερ ἐν τοῖς ἐσόπτροις τὰ φαινόμενα κατ' ἀνταύγειαν·
οἱ δ' ὀρθῶς ὑπονοοῦντες, ὡς ἐκτὸς ὄντα Δαίμονα προσαγορεύουσι. Τοὺς μὲν
οὖν ἀποσβέννυσθαι δοκοῦντας ἀστέρας, ὦ Τίμαρχε," φάναι, "τὰς εἰς σῶμα κατα-
δυομένας ὅλας ψυχὰς ὁρᾶν νόμιζε· τοὺς δὲ οἷον ἀναλάμποντας πάλιν καὶ ἀνα-
φαινομένους κάτωθεν, ἀχλύν τινα καὶ ζόφον ὥσπερ πηλὸν ἀποσειομένους,
τὰς ἐκ τῶν σωμάτων ἐπαναπλεούσας μετὰ τὸν θάνατον· οἱ δ' ἄνω διαφερό-
μενοι δαίμονές εἰσι τῶν νοῦν ἔχειν λεγομένων ἀνθρώπων."

Here, then, it is the higher part of man, Noûs, which is called Daemon. Cp. the
above-cited passage of Philo in De gigantibus 2, 8 (our nr. **1292a**) where it is said
that each of the "souls" or angels is νοῦς ἀκραιφνέστατος.

Literature on the myth:

W. Hamilton, *The myth in Plutarch's De genio, Class. Quart.* 28 (1934), p. 175 ff.
Also G. Méautis, *Recherches sur le Pythagorisme*, Neuchâtel 1922.
R. M. Jones, *The Platonism of Plutarch*, Chicago 1916, p. 57 ff.
Heinze, *Xenocr.* 130 f., tried to prove that Posidonius is the source of the myth;
R. Hirzel, *Der Dialog* II p. 160, attributed it to Dicaearchus.
Jones, following Rohde, thinks that Heracl. Ponticus is the source.

---

* αὐτῶν Bernardakis.

1321—Summarizing, we find in Plutarch the following hierarchy:

Νοῦς→ψυχή→σῶμα (nrs. **1319a, 1320**)

God (τὸ Πρῶτον, τὸ Νοητόν, τὸ Ἀγαθόν (nrs. **1312, 1313**)→

the daemons (bodiless Souls or Spirits) as intermediate powers)→

man (nrs. **1319b, c; 1320**).

Jones, *The Platonism of Plutarch* p. 11, noticed that Plut. did not carry the doctrine of the transcendence of God to the same extent as Neoplatonists "or even certain other Platonists or Neopythagoreans": he did not place God above the Νοῦς or νοητόν, or call Him ἄποιος (as Philo did, *Leg. Alleg.* I 51 [1]; cp. Albinus, Εἰσαγωγή 10), or make the Demiurge a second God.—We might reply that in such texts as cited under **1312f.** the distinction between τὸ Πρῶτον (νοητόν) and further νοητά is very near at least, and even that it appears in the following passage of the Περὶ εἱμαρμένης, where the δεύτεροι θεοί are clearly νοητά ranked under the Πρῶτον νοητόν which is God.

The treatise Περὶ εἱμαρμένης (*De fato*) is not of Plutarch, but (as Ziegler says [2]) could be so as to the contents.

a. [Plut.] *De fato* 9, 572 F-573 B:

Ἔστιν οὖν πρόνοια, ἡ μὲν ἀνωτάτω καὶ πρώτη, τοῦ πρώτου θεοῦ νόησις, εἴτε καὶ βούλησις οὖσα εὐεργέτις ἁπάντων, καθ' ἣν πρώτως ἕκαστα τῶν θείων διὰ παντὸς ἄριστά τε καὶ κάλλιστα κεκόσμηται. Ἡ δὲ δευτέρα, δευτέρων θεῶν τῶν κατ' οὐρανὸν ἰόντων, καθ' ἣν τά τε θνητὰ γίνεται τεταγμένως καὶ ὅσα πρὸς διαμονὴν καὶ σωτηρίαν ἑκάστων τῶν γενῶν. Τρίτη δ' ἂν εἰκότι ῥηθείη πρόνοιά τε καὶ προμήθεια τῶν ὅσοι περὶ γῆν δαίμονες τεταγμένοι τῶν ἀνθρωπίνων πράξεων φύλακές τε καὶ ἐπίσκοποί εἰσι. Τριττῆς τοίνυν τῆς προνοίας θεωρουμένης, κυριώτατα δὲ καὶ μάλιστα τῆς πρώτης λεγομένης, οὐκ ἂν ὀκνήσαιμεν εἰπεῖν, εἰ καὶ φιλοσόφοις ἀνδράσι τἀναντία λέγειν δόξαιμεν, ὡς πάντα μὲν καθ' εἱμαρμένην καὶ κατὰ πρόνοιαν, οὐ μὴν καὶ κατὰ φύσιν· ἀλλ' ἔνια μὲν κατὰ πρόνοιαν καὶ ἄλλα γε κατ' ἄλλην, ἔνια δὲ καθ' εἱμαρμένην. Καὶ ἡ μὲν εἱμαρμένη πάντως κατὰ πρόνοιαν, ἡ δὲ πρόνοια οὐδαμῶς καθ' εἱμαρμένην (ἔστω δ' ὁ λόγος τὰ νῦν περὶ τῆς πρώτης καὶ ἀνωτάτω)· τὸ μὲν <γὰρ> κατά τι ὕστερον ἐκείνου, καθ' ὅ τι ἂν καὶ λέγηται· οἷον τὸ κατὰ νόμον τοῦ νόμου, καὶ τὸ κατὰ φύσιν τῆς φύσεως· οὕτω δὲ καὶ τὸ καθ' εἱμαρμένην τῆς εἱμαρμένης νεώτερον ἂν εἴη. Ἡ δ' ἀνωτάτω πρόνοια πρεσβύτατον ἁπάντων, πλὴν οὗπέρ ἐστιν εἴτε βούλησις εἴτε νόησις εἴτε καὶ ἑκάτερον. Ἔστι δ' ὡς πρότερον εἴρηται τοῦ πάντων πατρός τε καὶ δημιουργοῦ.

Follow quotations from the *Timaeus*: 29d, 41d, 42d. At the end of the chapter *Leg.* 875c is cited, where Plato says that Knowledge and Insight (ἐπιστήμη and νοῦς) are superior to any (written) law or τάξις, "for it is not suitable that Noûs should be subjected to anything."

---

[1] C.W. I p. 73.
[2] Pauly-Wissowa, *RE* XXI 1, col. 725 f.

b. Ib. 10, 574 B:

Τριττῆς γὰρ οὔσης τῆς προνοίας ἡ μέν, ἅτε γεννήσασα τὴν εἱμαρμένην, τρόπον τινὰ αὐτὴν περιλαμβάνει· ἡ δὲ συγγεννηθεῖσα τῇ εἱμαρμένῃ πάντως 5 αὐτῇ συμπεριλαμβάνεται· ἡ δὲ ὡς ὕστερον τῆς εἱμαρμένης γενομένη κατὰ τὰ αὐτὰ δὴ ἐμπεριέχεται ὑπ' αὐτῆς, καθ'ἃ καὶ τὸ ἐφ' ἡμῖν καὶ ἡ τύχη εἴρηται.

Philo, too, distinguished between God and εἱμαρμένη (supra, nr. ·1303a).
Cp. also Origenes, *Contra Celsum* IV 99, V 14. The doctrine Celsus opposed to the Christian view of Providence was that the providence of God only aims at the perfection and preservation of the whole, while on earth His power is legated to the daemons, who act as secondary causes in a field where God himself cannot intermeddle. See our comment on **1279d** (supra) and the passages cited there.

1322—Ethics are most systematically dealt with by Plutarch in the treatise *De virtute morali* (Π. ἠθικῆς ἀρετῆς). In this writing Aristotelian influence prevails. Elsewhere, much of Plato's thought and also Stoic elements may be found in Plutarch's ethics.

His moral attitude is first of all characterized by what he calls himself φιλανθρωπία: love of our fellow-creatures (animals included).

a. Love of one's fellow-men the sum of virtues.   φιλανθρωπία

Plut., *Consolatio ad Apollonium* 34, p. 120 A:

Οὗτος δ' ἐπὶ τῆς εὐανθεστάτης ἡλικίας προαπεφοίτησεν ὁλόκληρος ἡμίθεος, 5 ζηλωτὸς καὶ περίβλεπτος πᾶσι τοῖς συνήθεσιν αὐτῷ· φιλοπάτωρ γενόμενος καὶ φιλομήτωρ καὶ φιλοίκειος καὶ φιλόσοφος, τὸ δὲ σύμπαν εἰπεῖν, φιλάνθρωπος.

b. Τὸ φιλάνθρωπον καὶ φιλόκαλον is that which honours a man.

Plut., *An seni respubl. gerenda sit* 1, p. 783 D:

(Not tyranny) πολιτεία δὲ δημοκρατικὴ καὶ νόμιμος ἀνδρὸς εἰθισμένου παρ-5 έχειν αὐτὸν οὐχ ἧττον ἀρχόμενον ὠφελίμως ἢ ἄρχοντα, καλὸν ἐντάφιον ὡς ἀληθῶς τὴν ἀπὸ τοῦ βίου δόξαν τῷ θανάτῳ προστίθησι· τοῦτο γὰρ "ἔσχατον δύεται κατὰ γᾶς", ὥς φησι Σιμωνίδης [1], πλὴν ὧν προαποθνήσκει τὸ φιλάν-●θρωπον καὶ φιλόκαλον, καὶ προαπαυδᾷ τῆς τῶν ἀναγκαίων ἐπιθυμίας ὁ τῶν καλῶν ζῆλος, ὡς τὰ πρακτικὰ μέρη καὶ θεῖα τῆς ψυχῆς ἐξιτηλότερα τῶν παθη-τικῶν καὶ σωματικῶν ἐχούσης· ὅπερ οὐδὲ λέγειν καλόν· οὐδ' ἀποδέχεσθαι [δεῖ] τῶν λεγόντων ὡς κερδαίνοντες μόνον οὐ κοπιῶμεν·—

c. Cp. Plut., *Cons. ad uxorem* 2, p. 608 D:

5 Αὐτὴ δὲ (sc. the little daughter he lost and who was particularly dear to him) ... θαυμαστὴν ἔσχεν εὐκολίαν καὶ πρᾳότητα, καὶ τὸ ἀντιφιλοῦν καὶ χαριζόμενον αὐτῆς, ἡδονὴν ἅμα καὶ κατανόησιν τοῦ φιλανθρώπου παρεῖχεν·—

---

[1] Fr. 59 Diehl.

1323—Besides the passages where the term φιλανθρωπία or τὸ φιλάνθρωπον is explicitly used, there is quite a number of passages where the
matter itself is described with practical details.

a.   The true statesman is φιλάνθρωπος, says Plut. (*An seni gerenda
sit resp.* 26, p. 796 E). And here are the details.

Plut., *Praecepta gerendae reipubl.* 32, p. 824 D:

Λείπεται δὴ τῷ πολιτικῷ μόνον ἐκ τῶν ὑποκειμένων ἔργων, ὃ μηδενὸς
ἔλαττόν ἐστι τῶν ἀγαθῶν, ὁμόνοιαν ἐμποιεῖν καὶ φιλίαν πρὸς ἀλλήλους ἀεὶ 5
τοῖς συνοικοῦσιν, ἔριδας δὲ καὶ διχοφροσύνας καὶ δυσμένειαν ἐξαιρεῖν ἅπασαν,
ὥσπερ ἐν φίλων διαφοραῖς, τὸ μᾶλλον οἰόμενον ἀδικεῖσθαι μέρος ἐξομιλοῦντα
πρότερον καὶ συναδικεῖσθαι δοκοῦντα καὶ συναγανακτεῖν, εἶτα οὕτως ἐπιχει- 1
ροῦντα πραΰνειν καὶ διδάσκειν ὅτι τῶν βιάζεσθαι καὶ νικᾶν ἐριζόντων οἱ
παρέντες οὐκ ἐπιεικείᾳ καὶ ἤθει μόνον, ἀλλὰ καὶ φρονήματι καὶ μεγέθει ψυχῆς
διαφέρουσι, καὶ μικρὸν ὑφιέμενοι νικῶσιν ἐν τοῖς καλλίστοις καὶ μεγίστοις·
ἔπειτα καὶ καθ᾽ ἕνα καὶ κοινῇ διδάσκοντα καὶ φράζοντα τὴν τῶν Ἑλληνικῶν 1
πραγμάτων ἀσθένειαν, ἧς ἐναπολαῦσαι ἄμεινόν ἐστι τοῖς εὖ φρονοῦσι, καὶ μεθ᾽
ἡσυχίας καὶ ὁμονοίας καταβιῶναι, μηδὲν ἐν μέσῳ τῆς τύχης ἄθλον ὑπολελοι-
πυίας. —

And, if a στάσις has arisen,—

Οὐδενὸς ἧττον τῷ πολιτικῷ προσήκει ταῦτ᾽ ἰᾶσθαι καὶ προκαταλαμβάνειν, 5
ὅπως τὰ μὲν οὐδὲ ὅλως ἔσται, τὰ δὲ παύσεται ταχέως, τὰ δ᾽ οὐ λήψεται μέγεθος,
οὐδὲ ἅψεται τῶν δημοσίων, ἀλλ᾽ ἐν αὐτοῖς μενεῖ τοῖς διαφερομένοις, αὐτόν
τε προσέχοντα καὶ φράζοντα τοῖς ἄλλοις, ὡς ἴδια κοινῶν καὶ μικρὰ μεγάλων 1
αἴτια καθίσταται, παροφθέντα καὶ μὴ τυχόντα θεραπείας ἐν ἀρχῇ μηδὲ παρ-
ηγορίας.

b.   He rebukes Cato for his brutish treatment of slaves.

Plut., *Cato maior* 5 (p. 338 F-339 A):

Πλὴν τὸ τοῖς οἰκέταις ὡς ὑποζυγίοις ἀποχρησάμενον ἐπὶ γήρως ἐλαύνειν
καὶ πιπράσκειν ἀτενοῦς ἄγαν ἤθους ἐγὼ τίθεμαι καὶ μηδὲν ἀνθρώπῳ πρὸς 2
ἄνθρωπον οἰόμενου κοινώνημα τῆς χρείας πλέον ὑπάρχειν. Καίτοι τὴν χρηστότητα τῆς δικαιοσύνης πλατύτερον τόπον ὁρῶμεν ἐπιλαμβανούσαν· νόμῳ μὲν
γὰρ καὶ τῷ δικαίῳ πρὸς ἀνθρώπους μόνον χρῆσθαι πεφύκαμεν, πρὸς εὐεργεσίας
δὲ καὶ χάριτας ἔστιν ὅτε καὶ μέχρι τῶν ἀλόγων ζῴων ὥσπερ ἐκ πηγῆς πλουσίας 2
ἀπορρεῖ τῆς ἡμερότητος. Καὶ γὰρ ἵππων ἀπειρηκότων ὑπὸ πόνου τροφαὶ καὶ
κυνῶν οὐ σκυλακεῖαι μόνον, ἀλλὰ καὶ γηροκομίαι τῷ χρηστῷ προσήκουσιν.

c. Very characteristic is the following passage.

Pericles 38, p. 173 BC:

"Ἤδη δὲ πρὸς τῷ τελευτᾶν ὄντος αὐτοῦ περικαθήμενοι τῶν πολιτῶν οἱ βέλτιστοι καὶ τῶν φίλων οἱ περιόντες λόγον ἐποιοῦντο τῆς ἀρετῆς καὶ τῆς δυνάμεως, ὅση γένοιτο, καὶ τὰς πράξεις ἀνεμετροῦντο καὶ τῶν τροπαίων τὸ πλῆθος· ἐννέα γὰρ ἦν ἃ στρατηγῶν καὶ νικῶν ἔστησεν ὑπὲρ τῆς πόλεως. Ταῦτα ὡς οὐκέτι συνιέντος, ἀλλὰ καθῃρημένου τὴν αἴσθησιν αὐτοῦ διελέγοντο πρὸς ἀλλήλους· ὁ δὲ πᾶσιν ἐτύγχανε τὸν νοῦν προσεσχηκὼς καὶ φθεγξάμενος εἰς μέσον ἔφη θαυμάζειν, ὅτι ταῦτα μὲν ἐπαινοῦσιν αὐτοῦ καὶ μνημονεύουσιν, ἃ καὶ πρὸς τύχην ἐστὶ κοινὰ καὶ γέγονεν ἤδη πολλοῖς στρατηγοῖς, τὸ δὲ κάλλιστον καὶ μέγιστον οὐ λέγουσιν· "Οὐδεὶς γάρ," ἔφη, "δι' ἐμὲ τῶν ὄντων Ἀθηναίων μέλαν ἱμάτιον περιεβάλετο."

R. Hirzel, who wrote an excellent chapter on Plutarch's "philanthropia", says: "Wer überhaupt durch die Schriften Plutarchs in seinen Freundes- und Familienkreis hineinblickt, hat den Eindruck in ein Heiligtum der Philanthropie zu blicken" (*Plutarch* p. 29).

The same author noticed the difference between *humanitas* as "erhöhtes menschliches Selbstgefühl" and *philanthropia*: the latter can also be said of the Gods and of animals, and, in fact, is often used so, while humanitas can only be predicated of man [1].

1324—Plut.'s attitude towards women and marriage bears strongly the stamp of φιλανθρωπία.

Women and marriage

a. Plut., *De fraterno amore* 21, op. 491 D-F:

A man must care for his brothers, their friends and relatives, but his brother's wife he should venerate and honour as the most holy thing of all.

Ἐπιμέλεια δὲ καλὴ μὲν αὐτῶν τῶν ἀδελφῶν, ἔτι δὲ καλλίων πενθεροῖς καὶ γαμβροῖς τοῖς ἐκείνων εὔνουν ἀεὶ παρέχειν εἰς ἅπαντα καὶ πρόθυμον ἑαυτόν, οἰκέτας τε φιλοδεσπότους ἀσπάζεσθαι, καὶ φιλοφρονεῖσθαι, καὶ χάριν ἔχειν ἰατροῖς θεραπεύσασιν αὐτοὺς καὶ φίλοις πιστοῖς καὶ προθύμως συνδιενεγκοῦσιν ἀποδημίαν ἢ στρατείαν· γυναῖκα δ' ἀδελφοῦ γαμετὴν ὡς ἁπάντων ἱερῶν ἁγιώτατον προσορῶντα καὶ σεβόμενον, * τιμᾶν τὸν ἄνδρα καὶ εὐφημεῖν, ἀμελουμένη δὲ συναγανακτεῖν, χαλεπαίνουσαν δὲ πραΰνειν· ἂν δ' ἁμάρτῃ τι τῶν μετρίων, συνδιαλλάττειν καὶ συμπαρακαλεῖν τὸν ἄνδρα· κἂν αὐτῷ τις ἰδίᾳ γένηται διαφορὰ πρὸς τὸν ἀδελφόν, αἰτιᾶσθαι παρ' ἐκείνῃ καὶ διαλύεσθαι τὴν μέμψιν· ἀγαμίαν δ' ἀδελφοῦ καὶ ἀπαιδίαν μάλιστα δυσχεραίνειν, καὶ παρακαλοῦντα καὶ λοιδοροῦντα, συνελαύνειν πανταχόθεν εἰς γάμον καὶ συνειργνύναι νομίμοις κηδεύμασι· κτησαμένου δὲ παῖδας ἐμφανέστερον χρῆσθαι τῇ τε πρὸς αὐτὸν εὐνοίᾳ καὶ τῇ πρὸς τὴν γυναῖκα τιμῇ.

---

[1] R. Hirzel, *Plutarch* p. 24.

* <ἂν μὲν φιλοστόργως πρὸς αὐτὴν ἔχῃ> Pohlenz.

b. *Cato Maior* 20, p. 347 F:

Plut. praises Cato as περὶ γυναῖκα χρηστὸς ἀνήρ and illustrates this by the following description.

Τὸν δὲ τύπτοντα γαμετὴν ἢ παῖδα τοῖς ἁγιωτάτοις ἔλεγεν ἱεροῖς προσφέρειν τὰς χεῖρας. Ἐν ἐπαίνῳ δὲ μείζονι τίθεσθαι τὸ γαμέτην ἀγαθὸν ἢ τὸ μέγαν εἶναι συγκλητικόν· ἐπεὶ καὶ Σωκράτους οὐδὲν ἄλλο θαυμάζειν τοῦ παλαιοῦ πλὴν ὅτι γυναικὶ χαλεπῇ καὶ παισὶν ἀποπλήκτοις χρώμενος ἐπιεικῶς καὶ πρᾴως διετέλεσε. Γενομένου δὲ τοῦ παιδὸς οὐδὲν ἦν ἔργον οὕτως ἀναγκαῖον, εἰ μή τι δημόσιον, ὡς μὴ παρεῖναι τῇ γυναικὶ λουούσῃ τὸ βρέφος καὶ σπαργανούσῃ.

The coniugalia praecepta   **c.** Sexual love is not stable unless it is fed and established by personal affection.

Plut., *Coniugalia praecepta* 4 (138 F):

Ὥσπερ τὸ πῦρ ἐξάπτεται μὲν εὐχερῶς ἐν ἀχύροις [καὶ θρυαλλίδι] καὶ θριξὶ λαγώαις, σβέννυται δὲ τάχιον, ἂν μή τινος ἑτέρου δυναμένου στέγειν ἅμα καὶ τρέφειν ἐπιλάβηται, οὕτω τὸν ἀπὸ σώματος καὶ ὥρας ὀξὺν ἔρωτα τῶν νεογάμων 2 ἀναφλεγόμενον, δεῖ μὴ διαρκῆ μηδὲ βέβαιον νομίζειν, ἂν μὴ περὶ τὸ ἦθος ἱδρυθείς, καὶ τοῦ φρονοῦντος ἁψάμενος ἔμψυχον λάβῃ διάθεσιν.

d. A man should share his spiritual life with his wife.

Ib. 48 (145 BC):

Καὶ σὺ μὲν ὥραν ἔχων ἤδη φιλοσοφεῖν, τοῖς μετ᾽ ἀποδείξεως καὶ κατασκευῆς λεγομένοις ἐπικόσμει τὸ ἦθος, ἐντυγχάνων [καὶ πλησιάζων] τοῖς 5 ὠφελοῦσι· τῇ δὲ γυναικὶ πανταχόθεν τὸ χρήσιμον συνάγων, ὥσπερ αἱ μέλιτται, καὶ φέρων αὐτὸς ἐν σεαυτῷ, μεταδίδου καὶ προσδιαλέγου φίλους αὐτῇ ποιῶν καὶ συνήθεις τῶν λόγων τοὺς ἀρίστους· "Πατὴρ" μὲν γὰρ "ἐσσὶ" αὐτῇ

καὶ πότνια μήτηρ,   1

ἠδὲ κασίγνητος. [1]

Οὐχ ἧττον δὲ σεμνὸν ἀκοῦσαι γαμετῆς λεγούσης· "Ἄνερ, ἀτὰρ σύ μοί ἐσσι καθηγητὴς καὶ φιλόσοφος καὶ διδάσκαλος τῶν καλλίστων καὶ θειοτάτων." Τὰ δὲ τοιαῦτα μαθήματα πρῶτον ἀφίστησι τῶν ἀτόπων τὰς γυναῖκας· αἰσχυν- 1 θήσεται γὰρ ὀρχεῖσθαι γυνὴ γεωμετρεῖν μανθάνουσα, καὶ φαρμάκων ἐπῳδὰς οὐ προσδέξεται, τοῖς Πλάτωνος ἐπᾳδομένη λόγοις καὶ τοῖς Ξενοφῶντος· ἂν δέ τις ἐπαγγέλληται καθαιρεῖν τὴν σελήνην, γελάσεται τὴν ἀμαθίαν καὶ τὴν ἐβελτηρίαν τῶν ταῦτα πειθομένων γυναικῶν.

---

[1] An adaptation of the well-known words of Andromache to Hector, *Iliad* VI 429.

4—MIDDLE PLATONISM: ALBINUS, APULEIUS, MAXIMUS OF TYRUS

In the second century Platonism is concentrated in at least three **Platonism** centres: (1) Athens. Here *Calvisius Taurus* (mentioned by Gellius I 26) **in the 2nd century** was the head of the Academy under Hadrian and Antoninus. He was probably succeeded by *Atticus*, under Marcus Aurelius. (2) Pergamum, where *Gaius* was heard by Galenus [1], and Smyrna where Albinus had his School [2]. Also *Theon* belongs to this group and probably the author of the anonymous commentary on the Theaetetus. (3) Alexandria. Probably *Celsus* lived here, and in any case *Ammonius Saccas*, the teacher of Plotinus. Maximus of Tyrus engaged in philosophy at Rome. Also Nigrinus (known to us by Lucianus' portrait) lived there. [3]

1325—The Academy of the second century appears to have been **Atticus** hostile towards Aristotle. Of Atticus, we have long fragments in Eusebius' *Praeparatio*, where he opposes the habit of introducing Aristotelian elements into Platonism, a habit which (as we saw) dates from the first century B.C. (Antiochus of Ascalon, who was followed by Arius Didymus) and was practised for instance by Albinus.

a.　Euseb., *Praep. ev.* XI 1, 2 - 2, 3 (p. 509a-d):

Atticus, opposing the infiltration of Aristotelian doctrine into Platonism, himself ascribes the Stoic tripartition of philosophy to Plato.　　　　　　　**His view of Plato**

a　Θήσω δὲ τὰ ἀρέσκοντα Πλάτωνι ἀπὸ τῶν τὰ αὐτοῦ πρεσβευόντων, ὧν Ἀττικὸς διαφανὴς ἀνὴρ τῶν Πλατωνικῶν φιλοσόφων ὧδέ πη τὰ δοκοῦντα τῷ ἀνδρὶ διέξεισιν, ἐν οἷς ἵσταται πρὸς τοὺς διὰ τῶν Ἀριστοτέλους τὰ Πλάτωνος ὑπισχνουμένους.

b　Τριχῇ τοίνυν διαιρουμένης τῆς ἐντελοῦς φιλοσοφίας, εἴς τε τὸν ἠθικὸν καλούμενον τόπον, καὶ τὸν φυσικόν, καὶ ἔτι τὸν λογικόν, καὶ τοῦ μὲν πρώτου κατασκευάζοντος ἡμῶν ἕκαστον καλὸν καὶ ἀγαθόν, καὶ τοὺς οἴκους ὅλους εἰς c τὸ ἄριστον ἐπανορθοῦντος, ἤδη δὲ καὶ δῆμον σύμπαντα πολιτείᾳ τῇ διαφερούσῃ καὶ νόμοις τοῖς ἀκριβεστάτοις κοσμοῦντος, τοῦ δευτέρου δὲ πρὸς τὴν περὶ τῶν θείων γνῶσιν διήκοντος, αὐτῶν τε τῶν πρώτων, καὶ τῶν αἰτίων, καὶ τῶν ἄλλων, ὅσα ἐκ τούτων γίνεται, ἃ δὴ περὶ φύσεως ἱστορίαν ὁ Πλάτων ὠνόμακεν· εἰς δὲ τὴν περὶ τούτων ἀμφοτέρων διάκρισίν τε καὶ εὕρεσιν τοῦ τρίτου παραλαμβανομένου· ὅτι μὲν Πλάτων πρῶτος καὶ μάλιστα συναγείρας εἰς ἓν πάντα τὰ τῆς φιλοσοφίας μέρη, τέως ἐσκεδασμένα καὶ διερριμμένα ὥσπερ τὰ τοῦ

---

[1]　V, 41 K.
[2]　Galenus, ib.
[3]　Luc., *Nigr.* 18.

Πενθέως μέλη, καθάπερ εἶπέ τις, σῶμά τι καὶ ζῷον ὁλόκληρον ἀπέφηνε τὴν
φιλοσοφίαν, δῆλα παντὶ λεγόμενα.

I.e. Atticus interprets Plato's philosophy as an organic and complete system.

b. Euseb., *Praep. ev.* XV 3, 1 - 4, 2; 4, 5 (794a-d, 795c):

Atticus opposes the Peripatetic doctrine that virtue is not sufficient for happiness.

The telos 　Τοῦ τε Πλάτωνος ... τέλος εὐδαιμονίας τὴν ἀρετὴν ἀποφαινομένου, τὴν
ἑτέραν ὁδεύσας ὁ Ἀριστοτέλης οὐκ ἄλλως εὐδαίμονά τινά φησιν ἔσεσθαι
ἢ καὶ διὰ τῆς τοῦ σώματος εὐπαθείας καὶ τῆς τῶν ἐκτὸς περιουσίας, ὧν ἄνευ
μηδὲ τὴν ἀρετὴν ὠφελεῖν. Πρὸς ὃν ὅπως ἔστησαν διεψευσμένην αὐτοῦ τὴν
ὑπόληψιν ἀπελέγχοντες οἱ Πλάτωνος γνώριμοι πάρεστι μαθεῖν διὰ τούτων·

　Τῆς γὰρ συμπάσης φιλοσοφίας κοινῇ γνώμῃ τῶν φιλοσοφησάντων τὴν
ἀνθρωπίνην εὐδαιμονίαν ὑπισχνουμένης, τριχῇ δὲ διαιρουμένης κατὰ τὴν
τῶν ὅλων ποιητικὴν διανέμησιν, τοσοῦτον ἀποδέων ἐν τούτοις τοῦ διδάσκειν
τι τῶν Πλάτωνος ὁ Περιπατητικὸς ὀφθήσεται, ὥστε πλειόνων ὄντων οἷ
διαφέρονται Πλάτωνι, μάλιστα ἐναντιούμενος αὐτὸς φανεῖται. Καὶ πρῶτόν
γε ἀπὸ τοῦ κοινοῦ καὶ μεγίστου καὶ κυριωτάτου τὴν πρὸς Πλάτωνα παραλλαγὴν ἐποιήσατο, μὴ τηρήσας τὸ μέτρον τῆς εὐδαιμονίας μηδὲ τὴν ἀρετὴν
αὐτάρκη πρὸς τοῦτο συγχωρήσας, ἀλλ' ἀπολισθὼν τῆς δυνάμεως τῆς κατὰ
τὴν ἀρετὴν καὶ ἡγησάμενος αὐτῇ προσδεῖν τῶν ἐκ τῆς τύχης, ἵνα μετὰ τούτων
ἕλη τὴν εὐδαιμονίαν· εἰ δ' ἐφ' ἑαυτῆς ληφθείη, ὡς ἀδύνατον καὶ οὐκ ἐφικτὸν
τῆς εὐδαιμονίας μεμψάμενος. — Καὶ μεθ' ἕτερα ἐπιλέγει· Τούτων τοίνυν
οὕτως ἐχόντων, καὶ πειρωμένου τοῦ Πλάτωνος ἕλκειν τὰς τῶν νέων ψυχὰς
ἄνω που πρὸς τὸ θεῖον, καὶ τοῦτον τὸν τρόπον προσοικειοῦντος μὲν τῇ ἀρετῇ
καὶ τῷ καλῷ, τῶν δὲ ἄλλων ἁπάντων ἀναπείθοντος ὑπερφρονεῖν, φράσον ἡμῖν,
ὦ Περιπατητικέ, πῶς ἐκδιδάξεις ταῦτα; Πῶς ὁδηγήσεις ἐπ' αὐτὰ τοὺς φιλο-
πλάτωνας; Ποῦ σοι τῆς αἱρέσεως τοσοῦτον ὕψος λόγων, ὥστε τὸ τῶν Ἀλωάδων
φρόνημα κτήσασθαι καὶ τὴν εἰς οὐρανὸν ὁδὸν ζητεῖν;

c. Euseb., *Praep. ev.* XV 5, 1-3 (798c-799a):

Providence Again, Atticus opposes Aristotle who denies the universal providence of God.

Πάλιν Μωσέως καὶ τῶν παρ' Ἑβραίοις προφητῶν, οὐ μὴν ἀλλὰ καὶ Πλάτωνος
ἐν τούτοις συμφώνως, τὸν περὶ τῆς τῶν ὅλων προνοίας λόγον εὐκρινῶς διατεθει-
μένων, ὁ Ἀριστοτέλης μέχρι σελήνης στήσας τὸ θεῖον τὰ λοιπὰ τοῦ κόσμου
μέρη περιγράφει τῆς τοῦ Θεοῦ διοικήσεως· ἐφ' οἷς καὶ ἀπελέγχεται πρὸς τοῦ
δηλωθέντος, ὧδέ πη διεξιόντος·

　Ὄντος δ' ἔτι μεγίστου καὶ κυριωτάτου τῶν εἰς εὐδαιμονίαν συντελούντων
τοῦ περὶ τῆς προνοίας πείσματος, ὃ δὴ καὶ μάλιστα τὸν ἀνθρώπινον βίον ὀρθοῖ,
εἴ γε μὴ μέλλομεν ἀγνοεῖν

Πότερον δίκα τεῖχος ὕψιον
ἢ σκολιαῖς ἀπάταις ἀναβαίνει
ἐπιχθονίων γένος ἀνδρῶν· [1]

ὁ μὲν Πλάτων εἰς Θεὸν καὶ ἐκ Θεοῦ πάντα ἀνάπτει. Φησὶ γὰρ [2] αὐτόν, ἀρχήν τε
καὶ μέσα καὶ τελευτὴν τῶν ὄντων ἁπάντων ἔχοντα, εὐθείᾳ περαίνειν περιπο-
ρευόμενον. Καὶ αὖ πάλιν φησὶν [3] αὐτὸν ἀγαθὸν εἶναι, ἀγαθῷ δὲ μηδένα φθόνον
ἐγγίγνεσθαι περὶ μηδενός. Τούτου δὲ ἐκτὸς ὄντα, πάντα ὅτι μάλιστα ἀγαθὰ
ποιεῖν, εἰς τάξιν ἄγοντα ἐκ τῆς ἀταξίας. Πάντων δὲ ἐπιμελούμενον καὶ πάντα
κατὰ δύναμιν κοσμοῦντα πεφροντικέναι καὶ τῶν ἀνθρώπων. — Καὶ μετὰ βραχέα·
Καὶ ὁ μὲν Πλάτων οὕτως. Ὁ δὲ τὴν δαιμονίαν ταύτην φύσιν ἐκποδὼν ποιούμενος, καὶ τήν γε εἰσαῦθις ἐλπίδα τῆς ψυχῆς ἀποτέμνων, τήν τε ἐν τῷ παρόντι
πρὸς τῶν κρειττόνων εὐλάβειαν ἀφαιρούμενος, τίνα πρὸς Πλάτωνα ἔχει κοινωνίαν; Ἢ πῶς ἂν ἐφ' ἃ βούλεται Πλάτων παρακαλέσαι, καὶ πιστώσαιτο τὰ
εἰρημένα;

d.   Euseb. Ib. 6, 1-3 (801b-802a):   Creation

Πάλιν Μωσέως γενητὸν εἶναι τὸν κόσμον ὁρισαμένου, ποιητήν τε καὶ δημιουργὸν τοῖς ὅλοις τὸν Θεὸν ἐπιστήσαντος, τοῦ τε Πλάτωνος τὰ ἴσα Μωσεῖ
φιλοσοφοῦντος, τὴν ἐναντίαν κἂν τούτῳ ὁ Ἀριστοτέλης ὁδεύσας ἀπελέγχεται
πρὸς τοῦ δηλωθέντος συγγραφέως, ὧδε πρὸς ῥῆμα γράφοντος· Πρῶτον δὴ
περὶ γενέσεως κόσμου σκοπῶν καὶ τὸ τῆς προνοίας τὸ μέγα τοῦτο καὶ πολυω-
φελὲς δόγμα πάντα ζητεῖν ἀναγκαῖον ἡγούμενος, καὶ λογισάμενος ὅτι τῷ μὴ
γενομένῳ οὔτε τινὸς ποιητοῦ οὔτε τινὸς κηδεμόνος πρὸς τὸ γενέσθαι καλῶς
χρεία, ἵνα μὴ ἀποστερήσῃ τὸν κόσμον τῆς προνοίας ἀφεῖλε τὸ ἀγένητον αὐτοῦ.
Παραιτούμεθα δὲ νῦν μὴ ἐμποδὼν ἡμῖν τοὺς ἀπὸ τῆς αὐτῆς ἑστίας εἶναι, οἷς
ἀρέσκει καὶ κατὰ Πλάτωνα τὸν κόσμον ἀγένητον εἶναι. Δίκαιοι γάρ εἰσιν ἡμῖν
συγγνώμην νέμειν, εἰ περὶ τῶν δοκούντων Πλάτωνι πιστεύομεν οἷς αὐτὸς
Ἕλλην ὢν πρὸς Ἕλληνας ἡμᾶς σαφεῖ τε καὶ τρανῷ τῷ στόματι διείλεκται.
Παραλαβὼν γάρ, φησίν [4], ὁ θεὸς πᾶν ὅσον ἦν ὁρατόν, οὐχ ἡσυχίαν ἄγον πλημμελῶς δὲ καὶ ἀτάκτως κινούμενον, εἰς τάξιν ἤγαγεν ἐκ τῆς ἀταξίας, ἡγησάμενος
τοῦτο ἐκείνου πάντως ἄμεινον. Ἔτι δὲ καὶ μᾶλλον ὅτι μὴ δι' αἰνιγμάτων, μηδ'
ἐπὶ τοῦ σαφοῦς χρείᾳ τὴν γένεσιν παρεδέξατο, δηλοῖ δι' ὧν ὁ πατὴρ αὐτῷ τῶν
πάντων διείλεκται περὶ τούτου μετὰ τὴν τῶν ὅλων δημιουργίαν. Ἐπειδὴ γάρ,
φησί [5], γεγένησθε (λέγει δὲ πρὸς τοὺς θεούς), ἀθάνατοι μὲν οὐκ ἐστὲ οὐδ'
ἄλυτοι τὸ πάμπαν, οὔτε μὲν δὴ λυθήσεσθέ γε, τῆς ἐμῆς βουλήσεως τυχόντες.

---

[1]   Pindarus, Fr. incert. 129 Boeckh.
[2]   Plato, Leg. IV 715e.
[3]   *Tim.* 29e.
[4]   *Tim.* 30a.
[5]   *Tim.* 41b.

The
immortality
of the soul

e. Euseb., ib. 9, 1-3 (p. 808d-809c):

Finally Atticus maintains the immortality of the soul as the keystone
of Plato's philosophy as opposed to Aristotle.

'Υπὲρ δὲ τῆς ψυχῆς τί καὶ λέγοιμεν ἄν; Δῆλα γὰρ ταῦτα οὐ μόνον τοῖς
φιλοσοφοῦσιν ἀλλ' ἤδη σχεδὸν καὶ τοῖς ἰδιώταις ἄπασιν, ὅτι Πλάτων μὲν
ἀθάνατον τὴν ψυχὴν ἀπολείπει, καὶ πολλοὺς ὑπὲρ τούτου λόγους πεποίηται,
ποικίλως καὶ παντοίως ἀποδεικνὺς ὅτι ἐστὶν ἀθάνατος ἡ ψυχή. Πολλὴ δὲ καὶ
τοῖς ἐσπουδακόσι περὶ τὰ Πλάτωνος ἡ φιλοτιμία γέγονε, συναγωνιζομένοις
τῷ τε δόγματι καὶ τῷ Πλάτωνι. Σχεδὸν γὰρ τὸ συνέχον τὴν πᾶσαν αἵρεσιν
τἀνδρὸς τοῦτό ἐστιν. 'Ή τε γὰρ τῶν ἠθικῶν δογμάτων ὑπόθεσις ἐπηκολούθησε
τῇ τῆς ψυχῆς ἀθανασίᾳ, τὸ μέγα καὶ λαμπρὸν καὶ νεανικὸν τῆς ἀρετῆς διὰ τὸ
τῆς ψυχῆς θεῖον σῶσαι δυνηθείσης· τά τε τῆς φύσεως πράγματα πάντα κατὰ
τὴν τῆς ψυχῆς διοίκησιν ἔσχε τὸ καλῶς διοικεῖσθαι δύνασθαι. Ψυχὴ γὰρ πᾶσα,
φησί [1], παντὸς ἐπιμελεῖται τοῦ ἀψύχου, πάντα δὲ οὐρανὸν περιπολεῖ, ἄλλοτ'
ἐν ἄλλοις εἴδεσι γινομένη. 'Αλλὰ μὴν καὶ τὰ τῆς ἐπιστήμης καὶ τῆς σοφίας
εἰς τὴν ἀθανασίαν τῆς ψυχῆς ἀνῆπται τῷ Πλάτωνι. Πᾶσαι γὰρ αἱ μαθήσεις
ἀναμνήσεις· καὶ οὐκ ἄλλως οἴεται δύνασθαι σῴζεσθαι καὶ ζήτησιν καὶ μάθησιν, ἐξ
ὧν ἐπιστήμη γίνεται. Εἰ δὲ μή ἐστιν ἡ ψυχὴ ἀθάνατος, οὐδὲ ἀνάμνησις· εἰ δὲ μὴ
τοῦτο, οὐδὲ μάθησις. Πάντων οὖν τῶν Πλάτωνος δογμάτων ἀτεχνῶς ἐξηρτη-
μένων καὶ ἐκκρεμαμένων τῆς κατὰ τὴν ψυχὴν θειότητός τε καὶ ἀθανασίας,
ὁ μὴ συγχωρῶν τοῦτο τὴν πᾶσαν ἀνατρέπει φιλοσοφίαν Πλάτωνος. Τίς οὖν
ἐστιν ὁ πρῶτος ἐγχειρήσας ἀντιτάξασθαι ἀποδείξεσι, καὶ τὴν ψυχὴν ἀφελέσθαι
τῆς ἀθανασίας καὶ τῆς ἄλλης πάσης δυνάμεως; Τίς δ' ἕτερος πρὸ 'Αριστοτέλους;

Albinus

1326—Albinus [2] must have been a Platonist of great authority in
his time [3]. His work is usually referred to under the title of *Didaskalikos*,
but the older MSS give the title *Epitome* [4]. The author expounds the
doctrine of the ἀρχαί as follows.

The ἀρχαί

a. First there is ὕλη.

Albinus, *Epitome* 8, 2:

ὕλη described

Ταύτην τοίνυν ἐκμαγεῖόν τε καὶ πανδεχὲς καὶ τιθήνην καὶ μητέρα καὶ χώραν

---

[1]   *Phaedr.* 246b.
[2]   The name Alkinoos, which is read in all the MSS, is due to a palaeographical
error, as was shown by Freudenthal, *Hellenistische Studien* III (1879), p. 322 ff.
[3]   Testimonia are cited by P. Louis, *Albinos, Epitome* (Thèse compl., Paris
1945) p. XIII f. Cp. also E. R. Witt, *Albinus and the History of Middle Platonism*,
Cambridge 1937, p. 107 ff.
[4]   P. Louis, o.c., p. XII. The full title is: 'Επιτομὴ τῶν Πλάτωνος δογμάτων.

ὀνομάζει καὶ ὑποκείμενον ἁπτόν τε μετ' ἀναισθησίας καὶ νόθῳ λογισμῷ ληπτόν·
ἰδιότητα δ' ἔχειν τοιαύτην, ὥστε πᾶσαν γένεσιν ὑποδέχεσθαι τιθήνης λόγον
ἐπέχουσαν τῷ φέρειν αὐτὰς καὶ ἀναδέχεσθαι μὲν αὐτὴν πάντα τὰ εἴδη, αὐτὴν
δὲ καθ' αὐτὴν ἄμορφόν τε ὑπάρχειν καὶ ἄποιον καὶ ἀνείδεον, ἀναματτομένην
δὲ τὰ τοιαῦτα καὶ ἐκτυπουμένην καθάπερ ἐκμαγεῖον καὶ σχηματιζομένην ὑπὸ
τούτων, μηδὲν ἴδιον σχῆμα ἔχουσαν μηδὲ ποιότητα.

Cp. *Tim.* 50b-52b. The term ὑποκείμενον is not used by Plato. The terms ἄμορφον
καὶ ἄποιον are not found in any of the dialogues either, but something very similar
is found at the end of the Hermodorus passage (above, **371a**).

b. The two other ἀρχαί. The ἰδέα defined.

Albinus 9, 1-2:

The ἰδέαι

'Ἀρχικὸν δὲ λόγον ἐπεχούσης τῆς ὕλης, ἔτι καὶ ἄλλας ἀρχὰς παραλαμβάνει
τήν τε παραδειγματικήν, τουτέστι τὴν τῶν ἰδεῶν, καὶ τὴν τοῦ πατρός τε καὶ
αἰτίου πάντων θεοῦ. Ἔστι δὲ ἡ ἰδέα ὡς μὲν πρὸς θεὸν νόησις αὐτοῦ, ὡς δὲ πρὸς
ἡμᾶς νοητὸν πρῶτον, ὡς δὲ πρὸς τὴν ὕλην μέτρον, ὡς δὲ πρὸς τὸν αἰσθητὸν
κόσμον παράδειγμα, ὡς δὲ πρὸς αὐτὴν ἐξεταζομένη οὐσία. —

(2) Ὁρίζονται δὲ τὴν ἰδέαν παράδειγμα τῶν κατὰ φύσιν αἰώνιον. Οὔτε
γὰρ τοῖς πλείστοις τῶν ἀπὸ Πλάτωνος ἀρέσκει τῶν τεχνικῶν εἶναι ἰδέας,
οἷον ἀσπίδος ἢ λύρας, οὔτε μὴν τῶν παρὰ φύσιν, οἷον πυρετοῦ καὶ χολέρας,
οὔτε τῶν κατὰ μέρος, οἷον Σωκράτους καὶ Πλάτωνος, ἀλλ' οὐδὲ τῶν
εὐτελῶν τινος, οἷον ῥύπου καὶ κάρφους, οὔτε τῶν πρός τι, οἷον μείζονος καὶ
ὑπερέχοντος· εἶναι γὰρ τὰς ἰδέας νοήσεις θεοῦ αἰωνίους τε καὶ αὐτοτελεῖς.

We found this conception of the Ideas also in Philo (our nr. **1293**), and
certainly he was not the first to introduce it. That the Stoics, in their allegorising
of the Gods of mythology, explained Athena as ἡ τοῦ Διὸς σύνεσις, and identified
this with Πρόνοια [1], is certainly not the same, but it must be noted here. For Varro
(according to Augustinus, *De civ.* VII 28) explained "Minerva" as "exempla rerum
quas Plato appellat ideas", and Seneca in *Epist.* 65, 7, probably using Arius Didymus,
says: *Haec exemplaria rerum omnium Deus intra se habet numerosque universorum
quae agenda sunt et modos mente complexus est, plenus his figuris est quas Plato
ideas appellat, immortales, immutabiles, infatigabiles.*

Surely this betrays (as Witt [2] has well seen), that in the first century B.C. a
doxographical account existed according to which the exemplaric Forms of Plato
were explained as eternal and immutable thoughts of a divine Mind. Our oldest
explicit trace of this conception goes back to the IVth century. It is found in Alki-
mos' account of Plato's doctrine ap. Diog. Laërt. III 12-13:

Ἔστι δὲ τῶν εἰδῶν ἓν ἕκαστον ἀΐδιόν τε καὶ νόημα καὶ πρὸς τούτοις ἀπαθές.

The matter is discussed by W. Theiler, *Vorbereitung des Neuplatonismus*, p. 33 ff.
(cp. our nr. **1200**); Witt, *Albinus* 70-77; C. J. de Vogel, *A la recherche des étapes
précises entre Platon et le Néoplatonisme*, in *Mnemosyne* 1954, p. 118 ff.

On Plato, *Soph.* 249a as the source of this conception, see: C. J. de Vogel in
Actes du XIe Congrès International de Philosophie, Bruxelles 1953, Vol. XII, p. 61-67.

---

[1] Thus, Cornutus, p. 35, 7 Lang.
[2] *Albinus*, p. 75.

The third
ἀρχή
is almost
ἄρρητον

1327—The third Principle is above human understanding.

a. Albinus X 1:

Ἑξῆς δὲ περὶ τῆς τρίτης ἀρχῆς ποιητέον τὸν λόγον, ἣν μικροῦ δεῖν καὶ ἄρρητον ἡγεῖται ὁ Πλάτων· ἐπαχθείημεν δ' ἂν περὶ αὐτῆς τοῦτον τὸν τρόπον. Εἰ ἔστι νοητά, ταῦτα δὲ οὔτε αἰσθητά ἐστιν οὔτε μέτοχα τῶν αἰσθητῶν, ἀλλὰ πρώτων τινῶν τῶν νοητῶν, ἔστι πρῶτα νοητὰ ἁπλᾶ, ὡς καὶ πρῶτα αἰσθητά· τὸ δ' ἡγούμενον, τὸ ἄρα λῆγον [1]. Ἄνθρωποι μὲν δὴ ἅτε τοῦ τῆς αἰσθήσεως πάθους ἐμπιπλάμενοι, ὥστε καὶ ὁπότε νοεῖν προαιροῖντο τὸ νοητόν, ἐμφαντα-ζόμενον ἔχειν τὸ αἰσθητόν, ὡς καὶ μέγεθος συνεπινοεῖν καὶ σχῆμα καὶ χρῶμα πολλάκις, οὐ καθαρῶς τὰ νοητὰ νοοῦσι, θεοὶ δὲ ἀπηλλαγμένως τῶν αἰσθητῶν εἰλικρινῶς τε καὶ ἀμιγῶς.

Νοῦς
ἀκίνητος

b. It is the Cause which is above the continually active Noûs. Albinus X 2:

Ἐπεὶ δὲ ψυχῆς νοῦς ἀμείνων, νοῦ δὲ τοῦ ἐν δυνάμει ὁ κατ' ἐνέργειαν πάντα νοῶν καὶ ἅμα καὶ ἀεί, τούτου δὲ καλλίων ὁ αἴτιος τούτου καὶ ὅπερ ἂν ἔτι ἀνω-τέρω τούτων ὑφέστηκεν, οὗτος ἂν εἴη ὁ πρῶτος θεός, αἴτιος ὑπάρχων τοῦ ἀεὶ ἐνεργεῖν τῷ νῷ τοῦ σύμπαντος οὐρανοῦ. Ἐνεργεῖ δὲ ἀκίνητος, αὐτὸς ὢν εἰς τοῦτον ὡς καὶ ὁ ἥλιος εἰς τὴν ὅρασιν, ὅταν αὐτῷ προσβλέπῃ, καὶ ὡς τὸ ὀρεκτὸν κινεῖ τὴν ὄρεξιν ἀκίνητον ὑπάρχον· οὕτω γε δὴ καὶ οὗτος ὁ νοῦς κινήσει τὸν νοῦν τοῦ σύμπαντος οὐρανοῦ.

The
hierarchy
of being

Thus, the Cause of the always active νοῦς τοῦ σύμπαντος οὐρανοῦ is itself Νοῦς, and we have the following hierarchy:

1. ὁ (πρῶτος) Νοῦς ἀκίνητος (First Principle).
2. ὁ Νοῦς τοῦ σύμπαντος οὐρανοῦ (ἀεὶ ἐνεργῶν)
3. ὁ ἐν δυνάμει νοῦς which is (according to the next §) a "power" of the ψυχή τοῦ κόσμου.

Next follow the stars ("visible gods", ch. 14), and finally the earth with its elements, governed by δαίμονες in each of them (ch. 15).

Λόγος
ἄληπτος

c. The first Principle is also called λόγος ἄληπτος. Albinus IV 2:

Διττὸς δ' ἐστὶν ὁ λόγος· ὁ μὲν γάρ ἐστι παντελῶς ἄληπτός τε καὶ ἀτρεκής, ὁ δὲ κατὰ τὴν τῶν πραγμάτων γνῶσιν ἀδιάψευστος, τούτων δὲ ὁ μὲν πρότερος θεῷ δυνατός, ἀνθρώπῳ δὲ ἀδύνατος, ὁ δὲ δεύτερος καὶ ἀνθρώπῳ δυνατός.

d. As it was done by Aristotle, the first Νοῦς is conceived as ἑαυτὸν νοῶν, just as in Plato it is called good and conceived as the Cause of order, i.e. as Δημιουργός in the sense of the *Timaeus*.

---

[1] Albinus uses the technical terminology of Stoic logic: si antecedens, ergo consequens.

Ἑαυτὸν νοεῖ

Albinus X 3:

Ἐπεὶ δὲ ὁ πρῶτος νοῦς κάλλιστος, δεῖ καὶ κάλλιστον αὐτῷ νοητὸν ὑποκεῖσθαι, οὐδὲν δὲ αὐτοῦ κάλλιον· ἑαυτὸν ἂν οὖν καὶ τὰ ἑαυτοῦ νοήματα ἀεὶ νοοίη, καὶ αὕτη ἡ ἐνέργεια αὐτοῦ ἰδέα ὑπάρχει. Καὶ μὴν ὁ πρῶτος θεὸς ἀίδιός ἐστιν, ἄρρητος, αὐτοτελής, τουτέστιν ἀπροσδεής, ἀειτελής, τουτέστιν ἀεὶ τέλειος, παντελής, τουτέστι πάντη τέλειος· θειότης, οὐσιότης, ἀλήθεια, συμμετρία, ἀγαθόν. Λέγω δὲ οὐχ ὡς χωρίζων ταῦτα, ἀλλ᾽ ὡς κατὰ πάντα ἑνὸς νοουμένου.

Καὶ ἀγαθὸν μέν ἐστι, διότι πάντα εἰς δύναμιν εὐεργετεῖ, παντὸς ἀγαθοῦ αἴτιος ὤν· καλὸν δέ, ὅτι αὐτὸς τῇ ἑαυτοῦ φύσει τέλειόν ἐστι καὶ σύμμετρον· ἀλήθεια δέ, διότι πάσης ἀληθείας ἀρχὴ ὑπάρχει, ὡς ὁ ἥλιος παντὸς φωτός· πατὴρ δέ ἐστι τῷ αἴτιος εἶναι πάντων καὶ κοσμεῖν τὸν οὐράνιον νοῦν καὶ τὴν ψυχὴν τοῦ κόσμου πρὸς ἑαυτὸν καὶ πρὸς τὰς ἑαυτοῦ νοήσεις. Κατὰ γὰρ τὴν ἑαυτοῦ βούλησιν ἐμπέπληκε πάντα ἑαυτοῦ, τὴν ψυχὴν τοῦ κόσμου ἐπεγείρας καὶ εἰς ἑαυτὸν ἐπιστρέψας, τοῦ νοῦ αὐτῆς αἴτιος ὑπάρχων· ὃς κοσμηθεὶς ὑπὸ τοῦ πατρὸς διακοσμεῖ σύμπασαν φύσιν ἐν τῷδε τῷ κόσμῳ.

Αἴτιος παντὸς ἀγαθοῦ

e.   Again it is called ἄρρητος and beyond any attribute or quality.

Albinus X 4:

ἄρρητος

Ἄρρητος δ᾽ ἐστὶ καὶ νῷ μόνῳ ληπτός, ὡς εἴρηται, ἐπεὶ οὔτε γένος ἐστὶν οὔτε εἶδος οὔτε διαφορά, ἀλλ᾽ οὐδὲ συμβέβηκέ τι αὐτῷ, οὔτε κακόν (οὐ γὰρ θέμις τοῦτο εἰπεῖν), οὔτε ἀγαθόν (κατὰ μετοχὴν γὰρ τινος ἔσται οὗτος καὶ μάλιστα ἀγαθότητος), οὔτε ἀδιάφορον (οὐδὲ γὰρ τοῦτο κατὰ ἔννοιαν αὐτοῦ), οὔτε ποιόν (οὐ γὰρ ποιωθέν ἐστι καὶ ὑπὸ ποιότητος τοιοῦτον ἀποτετελεσμένον), οὔτε ἄποιον (οὐ γὰρ ἐστέρηται τοῦ ποιὸν εἶναι ἐπιβάλλοντός τινος αὐτῷ ποιοῦ)· οὔτε μέρος τινός, οὔτε ὡς ὅλον ἔχον τινὰ μέρη, οὔτε ὥστε ταὐτόν τινι εἶναι ἢ ἕτερον· οὐδὲν γὰρ αὐτῷ συμβέβηκε, καθ᾽ ὃ δύναται τῶν ἄλλων χωρισθῆναι· οὔτε κινεῖ οὔτε κινεῖται.

1328—Again, the First Νοῦς is identified with the Demiurge.

Identified with the Δημιουργός

Albinus XII 1:

Ἐπεὶ γὰρ τῶν κατὰ φύσιν αἰσθητῶν καὶ κατὰ μέρος ὡρισμένα τινὰ δεῖ παραδείγματα εἶναι τὰς ἰδέας, ὧν καὶ τὰς ἐπιστήμας γίνεσθαι καὶ τοὺς ὅρους, — — ἀναγκαῖον καὶ τὸ κάλλιστον κατασκεύασμα τὸν κόσμον ὑπὸ τοῦ θεοῦ δεδημιουργῆσθαι πρός τινα ἰδέαν κόσμου ἀποβλέποντος, παράδειγμα ὑπάρχουσαν τοῦδε τοῦ κόσμου ὡς ἂν ἀπεικονισμένου ἀπ᾽ ἐκείνης, πρὸς ἣν ἀφομοιωθέντα ὑπὸ τοῦ δημιουργοῦ αὐτὸν ἀπειργάσθαι κατὰ θαυμασιωτάτην πρόνοιαν καὶ δίαιταν ἐλθόντος ἐπὶ τὸ δημιουργεῖν τὸν κόσμον, διότι ἀγαθὸς ἦν.

1329—a.   The seven planets and the fixed stars are "visible gods".
Albinus XIV 7 (the end):

Πάντες δὲ οὗτοι (sc. οἱ ἀστέρες) νοερὰ ζῷα καὶ θεοὶ καὶ σφαιρικὰ τοῖς σχήμασιν.

b.   Albinus XV 1-2:

(1) Εἰσὶ δὲ καὶ ἄλλοι δαίμονες, οὓς καὶ καλοίη ἄν τις γενητοὺς θεούς,
καθ᾽ ἕκαστον τῶν στοιχείων, οἱ μὲν ὁρατοί, οἱ δὲ ἀόρατοι, ἔν τε αἰθέρι καὶ πυρὶ
ἀέρι τε καὶ ὕδατι, ὡς μηδὲν κόσμου μέρος ψυχῆς ἄμοιρον εἶναι μηδὲ ζῴου
κρείττονος θνητῆς φύσεως· τούτοις δὲ ὑποτέτακται τὰ ὑπὸ σελήνην πάντα
καὶ τὰ ἐπίγεια.

(2) Ὁ μὲν γὰρ θεὸς τοῦ τε παντὸς ὑπάρχει ποιητὴς αὐτὸς καὶ τῶν θεῶν
τε καὶ δαιμόνων, ὁ δὴ πᾶν λύσιν οὐκ ἔχει κατὰ τὴν ἐκείνου βούλησιν· τῶν δὲ
ἄλλων οἱ ἐκείνου παῖδες ἡγοῦνται, κατὰ τὴν ἐκείνου ἐντολὴν καὶ μίμησιν πράτ-
τοντες ὅσα πράττουσιν, ἀφ᾽ ὧν κληδόνες καὶ ὀττεῖαι καὶ ὀνείρατα καὶ χρησμοὶ
καὶ ὅσα κατὰ μαντείαν ὑπὸ θνητῶν τεχνιτεύεται.

1330—Maximus of Tyrus in his diatribe Τίς ὁ Θεὸς κατὰ Πλάτωνα
expounds a very similar doctrine.

a.   It is a matter of general agreement that there is one supreme
God and many subordinate gods.

Maximus Tyr. XI 5a-b (Hobein):

Ἐν τοσούτῳ δὴ πολέμῳ καὶ στάσει καὶ διαφωνίᾳ ἕνα ἴδοις ἂν ἐν πάσῃ
γῇ ὁμόφωνον νόμον καὶ λόγον, ὅτι θεὸς εἷς πάντων βασιλεὺς καὶ πατήρ, καὶ
θεοὶ πολλοί, θεοῦ παῖδες, συνάρχοντες θεοῦ. Ταῦτα καὶ ὁ Ἕλλην λέγει, καὶ ὁ
βάρβαρος λέγει, καὶ ὁ ἠπειρώτης, καὶ ὁ θαλάττιος καὶ <ὁ σοφὸς καὶ ὁ> ἄσοφος.

b.   God cannot be placed in the stream of changing things.

Maximus Tyr. XI 8 h-i:

Λείπεται δὴ ὥσπερ εἰς ἀκρόπολιν ἀναβιβασαμένους τῷ λόγῳ τὸν θεὸν
ἱδρῦσαι κατὰ τὸν νοῦν αὐτὸν τὸν ἀρχηγικώτατον. Ἀλλὰ καὶ ἐνταῦθα διφυῆ
ὁρῶ· τοῦ γὰρ νοῦ ὁ μὲν νοεῖν πέφυκεν, καὶ μὴ νοῶν· ὁ δὲ καὶ πέφυκε, καὶ
νοεῖ· ἀλλὰ καὶ οὗτος οὔπω τέλειος, ἂν μὴ προσθῇς αὐτῷ τὸ καὶ νοεῖν ἀεί,
καὶ πάντα νοεῖν, καὶ μὴ ἄλλοτε ἄλλα· ὥστε εἴη ἂν ἐντελέστατος, ὁ νοῶν ἀεί,
καὶ πάντα, καὶ ἅμα.

c.   This Noûs is the Father and the Creator of the universe, invisible,
intangible, unspeakable.

Ib., 9 c d:

Τοῦτον μὲν δὴ ὁ ἐξ Ἀκαδημίας ἡμῖν ἄγγελος δίδωσι πατέρα καὶ γεννητὴν τοῦ ξύμπαντος· τούτου ὄνομα μὲν οὐ λέγει, οὐ γὰρ οἶδεν· οὐδὲ χρόαν λέγει, οὐ γὰρ εἶδεν· οὐδὲ μέγεθος λέγει, οὐ γὰρ ἥψατο. —

Τὸ δὲ θεῖον αὐτὸ ἀόρατον ὀφθαλμοῖς, ἄρρητον φωνῇ, ἀναφὲς σαρκί, ἀπευθὲς ἀκοῇ, μόνῳ δὲ τῷ τῆς ψυχῆς καλλίστῳ καὶ καθαρωτάτῳ καὶ νοερωτάτῳ καὶ κουφοτάτῳ καὶ πρεσβυτάτῳ ὁρατὸν δι᾽ ὁμοιότητα, καὶ ἀκουστὸν διὰ συγγένειαν, ὅλον ἀθρόον ἀθρόᾳ συνέσει παραγινόμενον.

d. All beauty streams from Him as from an eternally flowing source. Ib., 11 b-d:

Εἰ δὲ καὶ νῦν ἤδη μαθεῖν ἐρᾷς τὴν ἐκείνου φύσιν, πῶς τις αὐτὴν διηγήσεται; Καλὸν μὲν γὰρ εἶναι τὸν θεόν, καὶ τῶν καλῶν τὸ φανότατον· ἀλλ᾽ οὐ σῶμα καλόν, ἀλλ᾽ ὅθεν καὶ τῷ σώματι ἐπιρρεῖ τὸ κάλλος· οὐδὲ λειμῶνα καλόν, ἀλλ᾽ ὁπόθεν καὶ ὁ λειμὼν καλός· καὶ ποταμοῦ κάλλος, καὶ θαλάττης, καὶ οὐρανοῦ, καὶ τῶν ἐν οὐρανῷ θεῶν, πᾶν τὸ κάλλος τοῦτο ἐκεῖθεν ῥεῖ, ὃν ἐκ πηγῆς ἀενάου καὶ ἀκηράτου. Καθόσον δ᾽ αὐτοῦ μετέσχεν ἕκαστα, καλὰ καὶ ἑδραῖα καὶ σῳζόμενα, καὶ καθόσον αὐτοῦ ἀπολείπεται, αἰσχρὰ καὶ διαλυόμενα καὶ φθειρόμενα. Εἰ μὲν ταῦτα ἱκανά, ἑώρακας τὸν θεόν· εἰ δὲ μή, πῶς τις αὐτὸν αἰνίξηται;

e. At the end of this diatribe Maximus described the intermediate powers between God and man.

Ib., XI 12 a-e:

Εἰ δὲ ἐξασθενεῖς πρὸς τὴν τοῦ πατρὸς καὶ δημιουργοῦ θέαν, ἀρκεῖ σοι τὰ ἔργα ἐν τῷ παρόντι ὁρᾶν, καὶ προσκυνεῖν τὰ ἔγγονα πολλὰ καὶ παντοδαπὰ ὄντα, οὐχ ὅσα Βοιώτιος ποιητὴς λέγει [1]· οὐ γὰρ τρισμύριοι μόνον θεοὶ θεοῦ παῖδες καὶ φίλοι, ἀλλ᾽ ἄληπτοι ἀριθμῷ· τοῦτο μὲν κατ᾽ οὐρανὸν αἱ ἀστέρων φύσεις, τοῦτο δ᾽ αὖ κατ᾽ αἰθέρα αἱ δαιμόνων οὐσίαι. Βούλομαι δέ σοι δεῖξαι τὸ λεγόμενον σαφεστέρᾳ εἰκόνι. Ἐννόει μεγάλην ἀρχήν, καὶ βασιλείαν ἐρρωμένην, πρὸς μίαν ψυχὴν βασιλέως τοῦ ἀρίστου καὶ πρεσβυτάτου συμπάντων νενευκότων ἑκόντων. ὅρον δὲ τῆς ἀρχῆς οὐχ Ἅλυν ποταμόν, οὐδὲ Ἑλλήσποντον, οὐδὲ τὴν Μαιῶτιν, οὐδὲ τὰς ἐπὶ τῷ ὠκεανῷ ἠϊόνας· ἀλλὰ οὐρανὸν καὶ γῆν, τὸν μὲν ὑψοῦ, τὴν δ᾽ ἔνερθεν· οὐρανὸν μὲν οἷον τεῖχός τι ἐληλαμένον ἐν κύκλῳ, ἄρρηκτον, πάντα χρήματα ἐν ἑαυτῷ στέγον, γῆν δὲ οἷον φρουρὰν καὶ δεσμοὺς ἀλιτρῶν σωμάτων· βασιλέα δὲ αὐτὸν δὴ τὸν μέγαν ἀτρεμοῦντα, ὥσπερ νόμον, παρέχοντα τοῖς πειθομένοις σωτηρίαν ὑπάρχουσαν ἐν αὐτῷ· καὶ κοινωνοὺς τῆς ἀρχῆς πολλοὺς μὲν ὁρατοὺς θεούς, πολλοὺς δὲ ἀφανεῖς, τοὺς μὲν περὶ τὰ πρόθυρα αὐτὰ εἰλουμένους, οἷον εἰσαγγελέας τινὰς καὶ βασιλεῖ συγγενεστάτους, ὁμοτραπέζους αὐτοῦ καὶ συνεστίους, τοὺς δὲ τούτων ὑπηρέτας, τοὺς δ᾽ ἔτι τούτων καταδεεστέρους. Διαδοχὴν ὁρᾷς καὶ τάξιν ἀρχῆς καταβαίνουσαν ἐκ τοῦ θεοῦ μεχρὶ γῆς.

The inferior gods and daemons

---

[1] The reference is to Hes., *Erga* 252.

Apuleius

1331—Also Apuleius explains Plato's doctrine in this sense.

a. Apuleius, *De Platone* I 11:

Speaking of the fixed stars and planets he says:

Hos astrorum ignes sphaeris adfixos perpetuis atque indefessis cursibus labi. et hos animalis deos dicit esse, sphaerarum vero ingenium ex igni coalitum et fabricatum. iam ipsa animantium genera in quattuor species dividuntur, quarum una est ex natura ignis eiusmodi, qualem solem ac lunam videmus ceterasque siderum stellas, alterum ex aëria qualitate — hanc etiam daemonum dicit —, tertium ex aqua terraque coalescere et mortale genus corporum ex eo dividi terrenum atque terrestre — sic enim πεζόν et χερσαῖον censui[t] nuncupanda — terrenumque esse arborum ceterarumque frugum, quae humi fixae vitam trahunt, terrestria vero,

Three kinds of Gods quae alit ac sustinet tellus. deorum trinas nuncupat species, quarum est prima unus et solus summus ille, ultramundanus, incorporeus, quem patrem et architectum huius divini orbis superius ostendimus; aliud genus est, quale astra habent ceteraque numina, quos caelicolas nominamus; tertium habent, quos medioximos Romani veteres appellant, quod [est] sui ratione, sed <et> loco * et potestate diis summis sunt minores, natura hominum profecto maiores.

b. There is a double providence: that of the First, transcendent God, and next that of the caelicolae and daemones subordinated to Him.

A double providence Apuleius, ib. 12:

Sed omnia, quae naturaliter et propterea recte feruntur, providentiae custodia gubernantur nec ullius mali causa deo poterit adscribi. quare nec omnia ad fati sortem arbitratur esse referenda. ita enim definit: providentiam esse divinam sententiam, conservatricem prosperitatis eius, cuius causa tale suscepit officium; divinam legem esse fatum, per quod inevitabiles cogitationes dei atque incepta complentur. unde si quid providentia geritur, id agitur et fato, et quod fato terminatur, providentia debet susceptum videri. et primam quidem providentiam esse summi exsuperantissimique deorum omnium, qui non solum deos caelicolas ordinavit, quos ad tutelam et decus per omnia mundi membra dispersit, sed natura etiam mortales eos, qui praestarent sapientia ceteris terrenis animantibus, ad aevitatem temporis [s] e<di>dit fundatisque legibus reliquarum dispositionem ac tutelam rerum, quas cotidie fieri necesse est, diis ceteris tradidit. unde susceptam providentiam dii secundae providentiae ita naviter retinent, ut omnia, etiam quae caelitus mortali-

---

* Or rather: et sui ratione et loco ?

bus exhibentur, inmutabilem ordinationis paternae statum teneant.
daemonas vero, quos Genios et Lares possumus nuncupare, ministros
deorum arbitra[n]tur custodesque hominum et interpretes, si quid a
diis velint. nec sane omnia referenda esse ad vim fati puta[n]t, sed esse
aliquid in nobis, et in fortuna esse nonnihil.

c. Cp. Apuleius, *De deo Socratis* 6:

Divinae
mediae
potestates

Ceterum sunt quaedam divinae mediae potestates inter summum
aethera et infimas terras in isto intersitae aëris spatio, per quas et desi-
deria nostra et merita ad deos commeant. hos Graeci nomine δαίμονας
nuncupant, inter ‹terricolas› caelicolasque vectores hinc precum, inde
donorum, qui ultro citro portant hinc petitiones, inde suppetias, ceu
quidam utri[u]sque interpretes et salutigeri. per hos eosdem, ut Plato in
Symposio autumat, cuncta denuntiata et magorum varia miracula omnesque praesagiorum species reguntur. eorum quippe de numero praediti
curant singuli * [eorum], proinde ut est cuique tributa provincia, vel
somniis conformandis vel extis fissiculandis vel praepetibus gubernandis
vel oscinibus erudiendis vel vatibus inspirandis vel fulminibus iaculandis
vel nubibus coruscandis ceterisque adeo, per quae futura dinoscimus.
quae cuncta caelestium voluntate et numine et auctoritate sed daemonum
obsequio et opera et ministerio fieri arbitrandum est.

5—GNOSIS AND HERMETICS

1332—a. Gnosticism or gnosis was a wide-spread religious movement,
inspired by Oriental myths and influenced by mystery religions, partly
also connected with Christianity. It flourished in Egypt in the second
century, is found in Palestine in the days of the Apostles (Simon Magus)
and got new forces when in the third century the Persian Mani connected
it with Zoroastrian dualism. In Egypt Basilides (c. 130) and Valentinus
(about ten years younger) were Christian gnostics of Greek culture.
Especially in the form the latter gave it gnosticism, though always
too mythological and fantastic to be considered as philosophy, shows
an affinity with the Platonism of the first and second century.

The variety
of gnostic
systems

b. The following features should be noted.

1. A very transcendent conception of God.

General cha-
racteristics
of gnosis

All gnostics, except Marcion who is more a biblical theologian, place God beyond
reason. He is the ἄγνωστος θεός, by Valentinus called Βυθός and said to exist together with Σιγή.
Cp. Albinus (ἄρρητος: above, nr. **1327**).

---

* Scaliger corr. singula.

2. A rather strong dualism of Spirit versus Matter.

Not all gnostic systems, however, were dualistic in the sense of Zoroaster and Mani. In Valentinian gnosis evil springs from the spiritual world (called pleroma) and thus is neither an eternal nor an independent principle.

3. A hierarchy of spiritual and semi-spiritual beings is placed between the supreme God and the visible world.

Valentinus populates his pleroma with a whole series of spiritual beings. The last of them, Sophia, leaves the pleroma and, vexed by passions, creates the Demiurge, a "psychic" being, placed in a middle sphere. By the Demiurge the visible world is created, and the earthy part of man, not after the example of the spiritual world, as it is with Plato, but in ignorance of it.

Normally man, as a son of the Demiurge, is a ψυχικός. But a part of mankind by some special gift from above is endowed with spirit. These are called πνευματικοί. They are akin to the spiritual world by nature and therefore can never perish. Others are so entangled in matter that they cannot be saved. These are called ὑλικοί. As to the middle group, they are αὐτεξούσιοι: it depends on their own will whether they will be saved or not.

Other gnostic sects regarded the Demiurge as a bad spirit and man as either πνευματικός or ὑλικός.

4. A return of the spiritual part of man to the spiritual world.

According to Valentinus, who was deeply influenced by Christianity, the return is worked by redemption: Christ is sent forth from the pleroma and, after having healed Sophia from her passions, brings gnosis to man, as far as he is turned to the spiritual world, be it by nature (in the case of the πνευματικοί) or by choice (in the case of the ψυχικοί).

According to other gnostics the return is either a result of inner illumination (the "coming back to oneself") or of magic (the journey of the soul through the astral spheres, in which the knowledge of magic formulas is essential).

Prae-neo-platonism

In its general outline Valentinian metaphysics, in spite of its mythological appearance, is a kind of prae-neoplatonism.

Sources

c. Till lately gnostic systems were mainly known to us by the criticism of ecclesiastical authors who polemized against them. Thus, Clement of Alexandria and Origenes preserved to us some fragments of Basilides and of Valentinus and his direct followers; Irenaeus in the first chapters of his *Adversus haereses* gives an outline of Valentinian metaphysics; Tertullianus is our main source for Marcion. Various other forms of gnosis are described in the works of Irenaeus, Hippolytus and Epiphanius. St. Augustine, who belonged to the Manichaean sect for 9 years, speaks of it repeatedly in his *Confessions* and wrote a special treatise *Contra Faustum Manichaeum.*

A few gnostic writings were (long before the newly found manuscripts mentioned below) preserved in Coptic: *Pistis Sophia*, the *books of Jeû* and another book without title. These works, however, date from the second half of the third century, which is for Egyptian gnosis a time of decay.

Valentinus and Valentinians

d. As to Valentinus, *Irenaeus' testimony* is proved by recent studies to be of the greatest value.

W. Förster, *Von Valentin zu Herakleon*, Giessen 1928.

F. M. M. Sagnard, *La gnose valentinienne et le témoignage de St. Irénée*, Paris 1947.

Of Valentinus' direct disciples Ptolemaeus and Heracleon important texts are preserved.

The *fragments of Heracleon*, for the greater part cited by Origenes in Joh. t. I-XX, were collected by Hilgenfeld, *Ketzergeschichte des Urchristentums*, Leipzig 1870, p. 472-498.

Discussed by E. de Faye, *Gnostiques et gnosticisme*, Paris 1925, p. 77-102.

Ptolemaeus' *Letter to Flora*, preserved by Epiphanius, *C. haer.* 33, 3-7, was edited by Harnack in *Lietzmann's Kleine Texte*, Bonn 1904. New edition by G. Quispel (*Sources chrétiennes*) Paris 1949.

The letter deals with Mosaic Law and is not primarily concerned with metaphysics.

Another important source for Valentinianism are the *Excerpta ex Theodoto*. The text is found in:

W. Völker, *Quellen zur Geschichte der christlichen Gnosis*, Tüb. 1932.

R. P. Casey, *Excerpta ex Theodoto*, London 1934.

New edition by F. Sagnard in *Sources chrétiennes*, Paris 1948.

e. W. Bousset, *Hauptprobleme der Gnosis*, Göttingen 1907. **General works on gnosis**
Derives all kinds of gnosis from Irano-Babylonian syncretism.

E. de Faye, *Gnostiques et gnosticisme*, ²Paris 1925.

Still a very interesting study, though the author's explanations are sometimes rather artificial.

H. Leisegang, *Die Gnosis*, Leipzig 1924.

Explains gnosis as a Greek form of thinking, going back to mythical and mystical elements in pre-Socratic philosophy.

H. Jonas, *Gnosis u. spätantiker Geist.* Teil I: *Die mythologische Gnosis*, Göttingen 1934; Teil II 1: *Von der Mythologie zur mystischen Philosophie*, 1954.

The author represents a kind of pangnosticism, including Philo, Origenes and Plotinus.

In fact, Origenes opposed gnosticism very sharply by his theory of free will (see especially *De principiis* III 1, 8), while Plotinus criticizes their view of the cosmos and of the origin of evil, but most of all detests their irrationalism (*Enn.* II 9).

f. In 1930 Manichaean manuscripts were found in Medinet Madi (Egypt). **Finds of new manuscripts**
Part of them—a collection of sermons, a kind of dogmatic and half a psalter—are already edited.

Recently (1946) a whole gnostic library was found in Nag Hammadi (Egypt): 13 papyrus codices, containing 48 gnostic books written in Coptic, translated from the Greek.

Communications of J. Doresse, H. C. Puech and Togo Mina, read in the *Institut de France*, Académie des Inscriptions et Belles Lettres, the 20th Febr. 1948, published in the *Comptes-Rendus de L'Académie des Inscr. et Belles-Lettres*, 1948.

Togo Mina and J. Doresse in *Vigiliae Christianae* 1948, p. 129-160; 1949, p. 129-141;

G. Quispel, ib. 1953, p. 193.

H. C. Puech, *Les Nouveaux écrits gnostiques*, in: *Coptic Studies in honour of Walter Crum*, The Byzantine Institute, Boston (Mass.) 1950, p. 91-154.

See also G. Quispel, *Gnosis als Weltreligion*, Zürich 1951.

These books belonged to the sect of the Sethians, in their days regarded as Christian heretics. In fact they were rather far from the Christian Church, which is founded on the appearance of Christ in history, while gnostics were not interested in history at all. They prove to have had relations with Palestine and with the Hermetics of Alexandria (see our next paragraph). Three of the books mentioned by Porphyrius as being in the hands of the Egyptian gnostics against whom Plotinus wrote his anti-gnostic treatise, were found at Nag Hammadi.

The pleroma described by Valentinus

1333—The pleroma or spiritual world according to Valentinus.

a. Irenaeus, *Adv. haereses* I 1, 1-2:

Λέγουσιν [1] γάρ τινα εἶναι ἐν ἀοράτοις καὶ ἀκατονομάστοις ὑψώμασι τέλειον Αἰῶνα προόντα [2]· τοῦτον δὲ καὶ προαρχὴν καὶ προπάτορα καὶ Βυθὸν [3] καλοῦσιν. ὑπάρχοντα δ' αὐτὸν ἀχώρητον καὶ ἀόρατον, ἀΐδιόν τε καὶ ἀγέννητον, ἐν ἡσυχίᾳ καὶ ἠρεμίᾳ πολλῇ γεγονέναι ἐν ἀπείροις αἰῶσι χρόνων. συνυπάρχειν δ' αὐτῷ καὶ Ἔννοιαν [4], ἣν δὴ καὶ Χάριν, καὶ Σιγὴν ὀνομάζουσι· καὶ ἐννοηθῆναί ποτε ἀφ' ἑαυτοῦ προβαλέσθαι τὸν Βυθὸν τοῦτον, ἀρχὴν τῶν πάντων καὶ καθάπερ σπέρμα, τὴν προβολὴν ταύτην, ἣν προβαλέσθαι ἐνενοήθη, καὶ καθέσθαι ὡς ἐν μήτρᾳ τῇ συνυπαρχούσῃ ἑαυτῷ Σιγῇ. ταύτην δὲ ὑποδεξαμένην τὸ σπέρμα τοῦτο καὶ ἐγκύμονα γενομένην, ἀποκυῆσαι Νοῦν, ὅμοιόν τε καὶ ἴσον τῷ προβαλόντι, καὶ μόνον χωροῦντα τὸ μέγεθος τοῦ Πατρός· τὸν δὲ Νοῦν τοῦτον καὶ Μονογενῆ καλοῦσι, καὶ Πατέρα, καὶ Ἀρχὴν τῶν πάντων· συμπροβεβλῆσθαι δὲ αὐτῷ Ἀλήθειαν· καὶ εἶναι ταύτην πρῶτον καὶ ἀρχέγονον Πυθαγορικὴν τετρακτύν, ἣν καὶ ῥίζαν τῶν πάντων καλοῦσιν· ἔστι γὰρ Βυθὸς καὶ Σιγή, ἔπειτα Νοῦς καὶ Ἀλήθεια. Αἰσθόμενόν τε τὸν Μονογενῆ τοῦτον ἐφ' οἷς προεβλήθη, προβαλεῖν καὶ αὐτὸν Λόγον καὶ Ζωήν, πατέρα πάντων τῶν μετ' αὐτὸν ἐσομένων, καὶ ἀρχὴν καὶ μόρφωσιν παντὸς τοῦ πληρώματος. Ἐκ δὴ τοῦ Λόγου καὶ τῆς Ζωῆς προβεβλῆσθαι κατὰ συζυγίαν Ἄνθρωπον καὶ Ἐκκλησίαν· καὶ εἶναι ταύτην ἀρχέγονον Ὀγδοάδα, ῥίζαν καὶ ὑπόστασιν τῶν πάντων, τέτρασιν ὀνόμασι παρ' αὐτοῖς καλουμένων Βυθῷ, καὶ Νῷ καὶ Λόγῳ, καὶ Ἀνθρώπῳ· εἶναι γὰρ αὐτῶν ἕκαστον ἀρρενόθηλυν. —

Τούτους δὲ τοὺς Αἰῶνας εἰς δόξαν τοῦ Πατρὸς προβεβλημένους, βουληθέντας καὶ αὐτοὺς διὰ τοῦ ἰδίου δοξάσαι τὸν Πατέρα, προβαλεῖν προβολὰς ἐν συζυγίᾳ·

---

[1] Sc. Valentinians. Irenaeus is not speaking here of Valentinus alone.

[2] Cp. Tertull. *Adv. Valentinianos* 7: Substantialiter quidem αἰῶνα τέλειον appellant, personaliter vero προαρχήν et τὴν ἀρχήν, etiam Bython.

[3] The names Προαρχή and Προπάτωρ were frequently used by Valentinus' immediate followers who changed the doctrine in the sense of Christian monotheism. He himself appears to have spoken of Βυθός.

[4] The nomination Ἔννοια to indicate the female aspect of the First Principle is found in other gnostic sects, e.g. with Simon Magus and his Helena. Valentinus coupled Βυθός with Σιγή. Cp. Iren. I 11.

τὸν μὲν Λόγον καὶ τὴν Ζωήν, μετὰ τὸ προβαλέσθαι τὸν Ἄνθρωπον καὶ τὴν
Ἐκκλησίαν, ἄλλους δέκα Αἰῶνας. —

Τὸν δὲ Ἄνθρωπον καὶ αὐτὸν προβαλεῖν μετὰ τῆς Ἐκκλησίας Αἰῶνας δώδεκα.

The last couple of aeons was called Thelètos and Sophia.

b. Irenaeus, ib. I 2, 1:

Νοῦς
only knows
Βυθός

Τὸν μὲν οὖν Προπάτορα αὐτῶν γινώσκεσθαι μόνῳ λέγουσι τῷ ἐξ αὐτοῦ
γεγονότι Μονογενεῖ, τουτέστι τῷ Νῷ· τοῖς δὲ λοιποῖς πᾶσιν ἀόρατον καὶ
ἀκατάληπτον ὑπάρχειν· μόνος δὲ ὁ Νοῦς κατ' αὐτοὺς ἐτέρπετο θεωρῶν τὸν
Πατέρα, καὶ τὸ μέγεθος τὸ ἀμέτρητον αὐτοῦ κατανοῶν ἠγάλλετο· καὶ διενοεῖτο
καὶ τοῖς λοιποῖς αἰῶσιν ἀνακοινώσασθαι τὸ μέγεθος τοῦ Πατρός, ἡλίκος τε καὶ
ὅσος ὑπῆρχε, καὶ ὡς ἦν ἄναρχός τε καὶ ἀχώρητος, καὶ οὐ καταληπτὸς ἰδεῖν·
κατέσχε δ' αὐτὸν ἡ Σιγὴ βουλήσει τοῦ Πατρός, διὰ τὸ θέλειν πάντος αὐτοὺς
εἰς ἔννοιαν καὶ πόθον ζητήσεως τοῦ προειρημένου Προπάτορος αὐτῶν ἀγαγεῖν.
Καὶ οἱ μὲν λοιποὶ ὁμοίως Αἰῶνες ἡσυχῇ πως ἐπεπόθουν τὸν προβολέα τοῦ
σπέρματος αὐτῶν ἰδεῖν, καὶ τὴν ἄναρχον ῥίζαν ἱστορῆσαι· —

Bythos
separated
from the
other aeons

c. Valentinus separated his First Principle from the rest of the
pleroma, as the pleroma again was separated from inferior being, which
is generated by Sophia (called "the Mother") after her leaving the
spiritual world.

Irenaeus, ib. I 11, 1:

Ὅρους τε δύο ὑπέθετο, ἕνα μὲν μεταξὺ τοῦ Βυθοῦ καὶ τοῦ λοιποῦ πληρώματος, διορίζοντα τοὺς γεννητοὺς Αἰῶνας ἀπὸ τοῦ ἀγεννήτου Πατρός· ἕτερον
δὲ τὸν ἀφορίζοντα αὐτῷ [αὐτῶν] τὴν Μητέρα ἀπὸ τοῦ πληρώματος.

1334—The thirtieth aeon by ὕβρις separates himself from the spiritual
world and gets entangled in passions.

The
ὕβρις
of Sophia

a. Irenaeus, ib. I 2, 2:

Προήλατο δὲ πολὺ ὁ τελευταῖος καὶ νεώτατος τῆς δωδεκάδος, τῆς ὑπὸ τοῦ
Ἀνθρώπου καὶ τῆς Ἐκκλησίας, προβεβλημένος Αἰών, τουτέστιν ἡ Σοφία,
καὶ ἔπαθε πάθος ἄνευ τῆς ἐπιπλοκῆς τοῦ ζυγοῦ τοῦ Θελητοῦ· ὃ ἐνήρξατο μὲν ἐν
τοῖς περὶ τὸν Νοῦν καὶ τὴν Ἀλήθειαν, ἀπέσκηψε [1] δ' εἰς τοῦτον τὸν παρατρα-
πέντα, πρόφασιν μὲν ἀγάπης, τόλμης δέ, διὰ τὸ μὴ κεκοινωνῆσθαι τῷ Πατρὶ
τῷ τελείῳ, καθὼς καὶ ὁ Νοῦς. Τὸ δὲ πάθος εἶναι ζήτησιν τοῦ Πατρός· ἤθελε
γάρ, ὡς λέγουσι, τὸ μέγεθος αὐτοῦ καταλαβεῖν· —

---

[1] ἀπέσκηψε is a medical term, used of the determination of humours to a certain
part of the body. Thus Tertull., *Adv. Val.* 9, explains: In hunc autem, id est in
Sophiam, derivarat, ut solent vitia in corpore alibi connata in aliud membrum
perniciem suam efflare. Cp. Galenus, *De methodo medendi*, II 9.

She meets "Ορος

b. Finally she meets Horos. Irenaeus ib.:

Ἔπειτα μὴ δυνηθῆναι, διὰ τὸ ἀδυνάτῳ ἐπιβαλεῖν πράγματι, καὶ ἐν πολλῷ πάνυ ἀγῶνι γενόμενον, διά τε τὸ μέγεθος τοῦ βάθους, καὶ τὸ ἀνεξιχνίαστον τοῦ Πατρός, καὶ τὴν πρὸς αὐτὸν στοργήν, ἐκτεινόμενον ἀεὶ ἐπὶ τὸ πρόσθεν, ὑπὸ τῆς γλυκύτητος αὐτοῦ τελευταῖον ἂν καταπεπόσθαι, καὶ ἀναλελύσθαι εἰς τὴν ὅλην οὐσίαν, εἰ μὴ τῇ στηριζούσῃ καὶ ἐκτὸς τοῦ ἀρρήτου μεγέθους φυλασσούσῃ τὰ ὅλα συνέτυχε δυνάμει. Ταύτην δὲ τὴν δύναμιν καὶ "Ορον καλοῦσιν, ὑφ' ἧς ἐπεσχῆσθαι καὶ ἐστηρίχθαι, καὶ μόγις ἐπιστρέψαντα εἰς ἑαυτόν, καὶ πεισθέντα ὅτι ἀκατάληπτός ἐστιν ὁ Πατήρ, ἀποθέσθαι τὴν προτέραν ἐνθύμησιν σὺν τῷ ἐπιγινομένῳ πάθει ἐκ τοῦ ἐκπλήκτου ἐκείνου θαύματος.

c. How the Demiurge is brought forth by Sophia.

The demiurge brought forth by Sophia

Irenaeus, ib. I 11, 1:

Καὶ τὸν Χριστὸν δὲ οὐκ ἀπὸ τῶν ἐν τῷ πληρώματι Αἰώνων προβεβλῆσθαι, ἀλλὰ ὑπὸ τῆς μητρός, ἔξω γενομένης, κατὰ τὴν γνώμην [1] τῶν κρειττόνων ἀποκεκυῆσθαι μετὰ σκιᾶς τινος. Καὶ τοῦτον μέν, ἅτε ἄρρενα ὑπάρχοντα, ἀποκόψαντα ἀφ' ἑαυτοῦ τὴν σκιάν, ἀναδραμεῖν εἰς τὸ πλήρωμα. Τὴν δὲ μητέρα ὑπολειφθεῖσαν μετὰ τῆς σκιᾶς, κεκενωμένην τε τῆς πνευματικῆς ὑποστάσεως, ἕτερον υἱὸν προενέγκασθαι· καὶ τοῦτον εἶναι τὸν Δημιουργόν, ὃν καὶ παντοκράτορα λέγει τῶν ὑποκειμένων.

d. How both ψυχή and ὕλη arise from the passions of Sophia.

Irenaeus, ib. I 4, 1-2:

Μὴ δυνηθεῖσαν δὲ διοδεῦσαι τὸν "Ορον, διὰ τὸ συμπεπλέχθαι τῷ πάθει, καὶ μόνην ἀπολειφθεῖσαν ἔξω, παντὶ μέρει τοῦ πάθους ὑποπεσεῖν πολυμεροῦς καὶ πολυποικίλου ὑπάρχοντος, καὶ παθεῖν, λύπην μέν, ὅτι οὐ κατέλαβε [2]· φόβον δέ, μὴ καθάπερ αὐτὴν τὸ φῶς, οὕτω καὶ τὸ ζῆν ἐπιλίπῃ· ἀπορίαν τε ἐπὶ τούτοις· ἐν ἀγνοίᾳ δὲ τὰ πάντα. — Ἐπισυμβεβηκέναι δ' αὐτῇ καὶ ἑτέραν διάθεσιν, τὴν τῆς ἐπιστροφῆς ἐπὶ τὸν ζωοποιήσαντα.

The elements arise from her passions

Ταύτην σύστασιν καὶ οὐσίαν τῆς ὕλης γεγενῆσθαι λέγουσιν, ἐξ ἧς ὅδε ὁ κόσμος συνέστηκεν. Ἐκ μὲν γὰρ τῆς ἐπιστροφῆς τὴν τοῦ κόσμου καὶ τοῦ δημιουργοῦ πᾶσαν ψυχὴν τὴν γένεσιν εἰληφέναι, ἐκ δὲ τοῦ φόβου καὶ τῆς λύπης τὰ λοιπὰ τὴν ἀρχὴν ἐσχηκέναι· ἀπὸ γὰρ τῶν δακρύων αὐτῆς γεγονέναι πᾶσαν ἔνυγρον οὐσίαν· ἀπὸ δὲ τοῦ γέλωτος, τὴν φωτεινήν· ἀπὸ δὲ τῆς λύπης καὶ τῆς ἐκπλήξεως, τὰ σωματικὰ τοῦ κόσμου στοιχεῖα.

---

[1] She brings forth Christ in remembrance of the higher world. Perhaps μνήμην should be read instead of γνώμην.

[2] sc. τὸν Πατέρα.

e. The Demiurge creates the world without knowing the archetypal Ideas.

Irenaeus, ib. I 5, 3:

Οὐρανὸν ‹γὰρ› πεποιηκέναι μὴ εἰδότα τὸν οὐρανόν· καὶ ἄνθρωπον πεπλακέναι, μὴ εἰδότα τὸν ἄνθρωπον· γῆν δὲ δεδειχέναι, μὴ ἐπιστάμενον. τὴν γῆν· καὶ ἐπὶ πάντων οὕτως λέγουσιν ἡγνοηκέναι αὐτῶν τὰς ἰδέας ὧν ἐποίει, καὶ αὐτὴν τὴν μητέρα· αὐτὸν δὲ μόνον ᾠῆσθαι πάντα εἶναι.

1335—a. Three kinds of beings: πνευματικοί, ψυχικοί, ὑλικοί.

Irenaeus, ib. I 6, 1:

Τριῶν οὖν ὄντων, τὸ μὲν ὑλικόν, ὃ καὶ ἀριστερὸν καλοῦσι, κατὰ ἀνάγκην ἀπόλλυσθαι λέγουσιν, ἅτε μηδεμίαν ἐπιδέξασθαι πνοὴν ἀφθαρσίας δυνάμενον· τὸ δὲ ψυχικόν, ὃ καὶ δεξιὸν προσαγορεύουσιν, ἅτε μέσον ὂν τοῦ τε πνευματικοῦ καὶ ὑλικοῦ, ἐκεῖσε χωρεῖν, ὅπου ἂν καὶ τὴν πρόσκλισιν ποιήσηται· τὸ δὲ πνευματικὸν ἐκπεπέμφθαι, ὅπως ἐνθάδε τῷ ψυχικῷ συζυγὲν μορφωθῇ, συμπαιδευθὲν αὐτῷ ἐν τῇ ἀναστροφῇ. Καὶ τοῦτ᾽ εἶναι λέγουσι τὸ ἅλας, καὶ τὸ φῶς τοῦ κόσμου· ἔδει γὰρ τῶν ψυχικῶν [τῷ ψυχικῷ] καὶ αἰσθητῶν παιδευμάτων. Δι᾽ ὧν καὶ κόσμον κατεσκευάσθαι λέγουσι, καὶ τὸν Σωτῆρα δὲ ἐπὶ τοῦτο παραγεγονέναι τὸ ψυχικόν, ἐπεὶ καὶ αὐτεξούσιόν ἐστιν, ὅπως αὐτὸ σώσῃ.

b. The πνευματικοί are imperishable by nature.

Irenaeus, ib. I 6, 2:

Ὡς γὰρ τὸ χοϊκὸν ἀδύνατον σωτηρίας μετασχεῖν (οὐ γὰρ εἶναι λέγουσιν αὐτοὶ δεκτικὸν αὐτῆς), οὕτως πάλιν τὸ πνευματικὸν θέλουσιν οἱ αὐτοὶ εἶναι ἀδύνατον φθορὰν καταδέξασθαι, κἂν ὁποίαις συγκαταγένωνται πράξεσιν. Ὃν γὰρ τρόπον χρυσὸς ἐν βορβόρῳ κατατεθεὶς οὐκ ἀποβάλλει τὴν καλλονὴν αὐτοῦ, ἀλλὰ τὴν ἰδίαν φύσιν διαφυλάττει, τοῦ βορβόρου μηδὲν ἀδικῆσαι δυναμένου τὸν χρυσόν, οὕτω δὲ καὶ αὐτοὺς λέγουσι, κἂν ἐν ὁποίαις ὑλικαῖς πράξεσι καταγένωνται, μηδὲν αὐτοὺς παραβλάπτεσθαι, μηδὲ ἀποβάλλειν τὴν πνευματικὴν ὑπόστασιν.

c. Clem. Alex., *Excerpta ex Theodoto* 56:

Κατὰ τοῦτο πατὴρ ἡμῶν ὁ Ἀδάμ "ὁ πρῶτος [δ᾽] ἄνθρωπος ἐκ γῆς χοϊκός". — Διὰ τοῦτο πολλοὶ μὲν οἱ ὑλικοί, οὐ πολλοὶ δὲ ψυχικοί· σπάνιοι δὲ οἱ πνευματικοί.

Cp. *Asclepius* 22: Sunt autem non multi aut admodum pauci, ita ut numerari etiam in mundo possint, religiosi [1].

---

[1] *Corpus Hermeticum*, ed. Nock et Festugière II p. 323.

A Valentinian psalm

1336—a. Valentinus expressed his vision of the hierarchy of being in the following psalm.

Philosophoumena VI 11, p. 300 f Cruice:

'Αέρος πάντα βλέπω κρεμάμενα,
πάντα δ' ὀχούμενα πνεύματι νοῶ,
σάρκα μὲν ἐκ ψυχῆς κρεμαμένην,
ψυχὴν δ' ἀέρος ἐξεχομένην,
ἀέρα δ' ἐξ αἴθρης κρεμάμενον,
ἐκ δὲ βυθοῦ καρποὺς φερομένους,
ἐκ μήτρας δὲ βρέφος φερόμενον.

The hierarchy of being

The author of the *Philosophoumena* explains:

Οὕτως ταῦτα νοῶν· σάρξ ἐστιν ἡ ὕλη κατ' αὐτούς, ἥτις κρέμαται ἐκ τῆς ψυχῆς τοῦ δημιουργοῦ. ψυχὴ δὲ ἀέρος ἐξέχεται, τουτέστιν ὁ Δημιουργὸς τοῦ πνεύματος ἔξω πληρώματος. 'Αὴρ δὲ αἴθρης ἐξέχεται, τουτέστιν ἡ ἔξω Σοφία τοῦ ἐντὸς ὅρου καὶ παντὸς πληρώματος. 'Εκ δὲ Βυθοῦ καρποὶ φέρονται ἡ ἐκ τοῦ Πατρὸς πᾶσα προβολὴ τῶν Αἰώνων γενομένη.

b. A clear summary of Valentinus' doctrine is found in Hippolytus, *Ref.* X 13. What follows in chapter 14 on Basilides' doctrine is much less clear. It seems, however, that Basilides taught a similar conception of metaphysics: under the

Basilides

unknown God he placed a double Noûs, which he separated from the "psychic" sphere by a μεθόριον πνεῦμα. The sphere of "soul" was divided into two stages, (1) aether, inhabited by the aether-soul, (2) air, with the air-soul. Next follows the spiritual man in the visible world,—the non-spiritual man being not considered as a man at all! Thus, redemption is for "mankind" as a whole!

See on Basilides: G. Quispel, *L'homme gnostique* in: *Eranos Jahrbuch*, Zürich 1949, p. 89-139.

Oracula chaldaica

c. A similar conception is found in the Chaldaic oracles.
Oracula Chaldaica, Kroll [1] p. 14; p. 28:

Δυὰς παρὰ τῷδε [2] κάθηται·
ἀμφότερον γὰρ ἔχει, νῷ μὲν κατέχειν τὰ νοητά,
αἴσθησιν δ' ἐπάγειν κόσμοις [3].—

Μετὰ δὴ πατρικὰς διανοίας
ψυχὴ ἐγὼ ναίω θέρμη ψυχοῦσα τὰ πάντα.

The double Noûs is also found in Arnobius II 25 (Marchesi p. 95):
Haecine est anima docta illa quam dicitis, immortalis perfecta divina, post Deum principem rerum et post geminas mentes locum optinens quartum.

---

[1] W. Kroll, *De oraculis Chaldaicis*, Bresl. philol. Abh. VII 1895.
[2] Sc. the supreme God or τέλειος Πατήρ.
[3] Cp. the Hermetic treatise *Asclepius* 32, where the all-embracing Intellect which is nearest to the supreme God is called *omnis sensus* (= ὁ πᾶς νοῦς), while the world-Spirit (νοῦς ἐγκόσμιος) is indicated by the term *sensus mondanus*.

1337—In Valentinus, as in other gnostics, we find the same kind of **Demonology** demonology which we found in other authors of the first and second century.

a. The human heart inhabited by many evil spirits.

Clem. Alex., *Strom*. II 20, 114, 3 (St. II, p. 175):

God alone is good, and He alone can make the heart of man pure.   **The heart a dwelling-place of demons**

Πολλὰ γὰρ ἐνοικοῦντα αὐτῇ πνεύματα οὐκ ἐᾷ καθαρεύειν, ἕκαστον δ' αὐτῶν τὰ ἴδια ἐκτελεῖ ἔργα πολλαχῶς ἐνυβριζόντων ἐπιθυμίαις οὐ προσηκούσαις. καί μοι δοκεῖ ὅμοιόν τι πάσχειν τῷ πανδοχείῳ ἡ καρδία· καὶ γὰρ ἐκεῖνο κατατιτρᾶταί τε καὶ ὀρύττεται καὶ πολλάκις κόπρου πίμπλαται ἀνθρώπων ἀσελγῶς ἐμμενόντων καὶ μηδεμίαν πρόνοιαν ποιουμένων τοῦ χωρίου, καθάπερ ἀλλοτρίου καθεστῶτος. τὸν τρόπον τοῦτον καὶ ἡ καρδία, μέχρι μὴ προνοίας τυγχάνει, ἀκάθαρτος [οὖσα], πολλῶν οὖσα δαιμόνων οἰκητήριον.

b. Irenaeus, *Adv. haereses* I 5, 4:

The "hylic substance" springs from the passions of the Mother: like the Demiurge arose from her ἐπιστροφή, so from her sorrow "the evil spirits" are said to have arisen.   **The evil spirits**

Ἐκ δὲ τῆς λύπης τὰ πνευματικὰ τῆς πονηρίας διδάσκουσι γεγονέναι· ὅθεν τὸν Διάβολον τὴν γένεσιν ἐσχηκέναι, ὃν καὶ κοσμοκράτορα καλοῦσι, καὶ τὰ δαιμόνια, καὶ τοὺς ἀγγέλους, καὶ πᾶσαν τὴν πνευματικὴν τῆς πονηρίας ὑπόστασιν.

c. There are also good spirits or "angels". Jesus, who comes from the pleroma, takes them with him for the redemption of man, — at least: the spiritual man, called "the seed".

Clem. Alex., *Excerpta ex Theodoto* 35:   **Good spirits or Angels**

Ὁ Ἰησοῦς, "τὸ Φῶς" ἡμῶν, ὡς λέγει ὁ Ἀπόστολος, "ἑαυτὸν κενώσας" [1] (τουτέστιν· ἐκτὸς τοῦ Ὅρου γενόμενος, κατὰ Θεόδοτον), ἐπεὶ '"Ἄγγελος" ἦν τοῦ πληρώματος, τοὺς Ἀγγέλους τοῦ διαφέροντος σπέρματος συνεξήγαγεν ἑαυτῷ. Καὶ αὐτὸς μὲν τὴν λύτρωσιν, ὡς ἀπὸ πληρώματος προελθών, εἶχεν· τοὺς δὲ Ἀγγέλους εἰς διόρθωσιν τοῦ σπέρματος ἤγαγεν.

1338—The Corpus Hermeticum is a collection of religious works of different **The Corpus** form and inspiration: dialogues, letters, popular treatises, revelations. Sometimes **Hermeticum** Hermes is speaking to his pupil Asclepius, sometimes the Noûs is introduced speaking to Hermes. In some of the Hermetic writings (V, VIII, IX) the deity is conceived (with Stoicism) as penetrating the cosmos; in others the cosmos is viewed as radically bad (VI, VII, XIII) and God is the unknown God of Gnosticism: He must be found by flying from the world. Sometimes contradictory ideas are found in the same treatise, e.g. in X that the cosmos is good (c. 14) and that it is not good (c. 10).

---

[1] *Philipp.* 2, 7: ἀλλ' ἑαυτὸν ἐκένωσε μορφὴν δούλου λαβών.

Poimandres
and
Asclepius

Two important writings of the Corpus, the *Poimandres* (I) and the *Asclepius*, are gnostic writings: the explanation of the universe is dualistic, in the *Poimandres* Eros is considered as the fundamental evil; mention is made of the return of the separated self to its origin.

In both treatises the part of mythology is less important than it is in nearly all other gnostic writings. In the *Poimandres*, the first Principle is called Noûs. In Him the archetypal Ideas are seen as "innumerable Powers". A second Noῦς δημιουργός is generated by Him. Man is a spiritual being as created by the first Noῦς, but of a lower nature as far as united with matter.

The text of the *Asclepius* is only preserved in Latin. It is found in vol. II of the edition of Nock and Festugière [1]. Also in vol. III of the works of Apuleius, ed. P. Thomas, Leipzig 1908, p. 36-81.

1339—a. *Corp. Herm.* I 1 (*Poimandres*), 4-5.

Hermes' first vision: Light and darkness

The Noûs appears to Hermes and reveals to him the nature of things. He calls himself ὁ Ποιμάνδρης. Hermes' first vision.

Εὐθέως πάντα μοι ἤνοικτο ῥοπῇ, καὶ ὁρῶ θέαν ἀόριστον, φῶς δὲ πάντα γεγενημένα, εὔδιόν τε καὶ ἱλαρόν, καὶ ἠράσθην ἰδών. καὶ μετ' ὀλίγον σκότος κατωφερὲς ἦν, ἐν μέρει γεγενημένον [2], φοβερόν τε καὶ στυγνόν, σκολιῶς ἐσπειραμένον, ὡς <ὄφει> [3] εἰκάσαι με· εἶτα μεταβαλλόμενον τὸ σκότος εἰς ὑγράν τινα φύσιν, ἀφάτως τεταραγμένην καὶ καπνὸν ἀποδιδοῦσαν, ὡς ἀπὸ πυρός, καί τινα ἦχον ἀποτελοῦσαν ἀνεκλάλητον γοώδη· εἶτα βοὴ ἐξ αὐτῆς ἀσυνάρθρως ἐξεπέμπετο, ὡς εἰκάσαι φωνῇ πυρός [4], ἐκ δὲ φωτὸς ... λόγος ἅγιος ἐπέβη τῇ φύσει, καὶ πῦρ ἄκρατον ἐξεπήδησεν ἐκ τῆς ὑγρᾶς φύσεως ἄνω εἰς ὕψος· κοῦφον δὲ ἦν καὶ ὀξύ, δραστικὸν δὲ ἅμα, καὶ ὁ ἀὴρ ἐλαφρὸς ὢν ἠκολούθησε τῷ πνεύματι, ἀναβαίνοντος αὐτοῦ μέχρι τοῦ πυρὸς ἀπὸ γῆς καὶ ὕδατος, ὡς δοκεῖν κρέμασθαι αὐτὸν ἀπ' αὐτοῦ· γῆ δὲ καὶ ὕδωρ ἔμενε καθ' ἑαυτὰ συμμεμιγμένα, ὡς μὴ θεωρεῖσθαι <τὴν γῆν> ἀπὸ τοῦ ὕδατος· κινούμενα δὲ ἦν διὰ τὸν ἐπιφερόμενον πνευματικὸν λόγον εἰς ἀκοήν.

The Light is Noûs

b. The vision explained. *Corp. Herm.* I 1, 6:

Ὁ δὲ Ποιμάνδρης ἐμοί, Ἐνόησας, φησί, τὴν θέαν ταύτην ὅ τι καὶ βούλεται;

---

[1] Corpus Hermeticum t. II, Paris 1945, pp. 296-355.

[2] Festugière translates in C.H. I (1945): "il y avait une obscurité se portant vers le bas, *survenue à son tour*." But in *Le Dieu inconnu et la Gnose* (1954) p. 41 ff. he suggests that the expression means that Matter is split off from the substance of God (the Light), like Moderatus said that God "separated quantity (i.e. matter) from Himself"—αὐτοῦ ἐχώρισε τὴν ποσότητα (supra, nr. **1285b**)—and Iamblichus, *De mysteriis* VIII 3, p. 264, 13 ff. P. says that God "made matter exist" (ὕλην παρήγαγεν ὁ θεός) by splitting off materiality from the divine Substance (ἀπὸ τῆς οὐσιότητος ὑποσχισθείσης ὑλότητος).—This interpretation of ἐν μέρει γεγενημένον seems doubtful. The vision of Hermes rather makes the impression of dualism.

[3] Obscurity is represented as a dragon e.g. in *Pistis Sophia* c. 126 (p. 207 Schmidt) and with several other gnostics.

[4] The brutal cry of Chaos is opposed to the articulated word of the Logos.

καὶ Γνώσομαι, ἔφην ἐγώ. — Τὸ φῶς ἐκεῖνο, ἔφη, ἐγὼ Νοῦς ὁ σὸς θεός, ὁ πρὸ φύσεως ὑγρᾶς τῆς ἐκ σκότους φανείσης· ὁ δὲ ἐκ Νοὸς φωτεινὸς Λόγος υἱὸς θεοῦ. — Τί οὖν; φημί. — Οὕτω γνῶθι· τὸ ἐν σοὶ βλέπον καὶ ἀκοῦον, λόγος κυρίου, ὁ δὲ νοῦς πατὴρ θεός. οὐ γὰρ διίστανται ἀπ' ἀλλήλων· ἕνωσις γὰρ τούτων ἐστὶν ἡ ζωή.

c. Second vision: the Light consists of innumerable powers.

Corp. Herm. I 1, 7-8:

Εἰπόντος ταῦτα ἐπὶ πλείονα χρόνον ἀντώπησέ μοι, ὥστε μὲν τρέμειν αὐτοῦ τὴν ἰδέαν· ἀνανεύσαντος δέ, θεωρῶ ἐν τῷ νοΐ μου τὸ φῶς ἐν δυνάμεσιν ἀναριθμήτοις ὄν, καὶ κόσμον ἀπεριόριστον γεγενημένον, καὶ περιίσχεσθαι τὸ πῦρ δυνάμει μεγίστῃ, καὶ στάσιν ἐσχηκέναι κρατούμενον· ταῦτα δὲ ἐγὼ διενοήθην ὁρῶν διὰ τὸν τοῦ Ποιμάνδρου λόγον.

Ὡς δὲ ἐν ἐκπλήξει μου ὄντος, φησὶ πάλιν ἐμοί· Εἶδες ἐν τῷ νῷ τὸ ἀρχέτυπον εἶδος, τὸ προάρχον [1] τῆς ἀρχῆς τῆς ἀπεράντου· ταῦτα ὁ Ποιμάνδρης ἐμοί. — Τὰ οὖν, ἐγώ φημι, στοιχεῖα τῆς φύσεως πόθεν ὑπέστη; — πάλιν ἐκεῖνος πρὸς ταῦτα· Ἐκ βουλῆς θεοῦ, ἥτις λαβοῦσα τὸν Λόγον καὶ ἰδοῦσα τὸν καλὸν κόσμον ἐμιμήσατο, κοσμοποιηθεῖσα διὰ τῶν ἑαυτῆς στοιχείων καὶ γεννημάτων ψυχῶν.

1340—By the first Noûs or Light a second Noûs is generated: the δημιουργός.

a. *Corp. Herm.* I 1, 9:

Ὁ δὲ Νοῦς ὁ θεός, ἀρρενόθηλυς [2] ὤν, ζωὴ καὶ φῶς ὑπάρχων, ἀπεκύησε λόγῳ ἕτερον Νοῦν δημιουργόν, ὃς θεὸς τοῦ πυρὸς καὶ πνεύματος ὤν, ἐδημιούργησε διοικητάς τινας [3] ἑπτά, ἐν κύκλοις περιέχοντας τὸν αἰσθητὸν κόσμον, καὶ ἡ διοίκησις αὐτῶν εἱμαρμένη καλεῖται.

(margin: In the Light there are innumerable powers)

(margin: The second Noûs)

---

[1] Cp. Valentinus ap. Iren. I 1, 1: προαρχὴν καὶ προπάτορα, of the first God (Βυθός) who is the Father of Noûs (above, **1333a**).

[2] That the supreme God is bisexual is a current idea in Indian theosophy and in all kinds of Oriental gnosis. Festugière, *Le Dieu inconnu et la gnose* p. 43 ff. points to Greek precedents: there is the Orphic fragment 21a Kern—Ζεὺς ἄρσην γένετο, Ζεὺς ἄμβροτος ἔπλετο νύμφη—preserved in ps.-Aristot., Π. κόσμου 401 a 25; next Diog. Babyl. fr. 33 (SVF III), where Ζεὺς ἄρρην, Ζεὺς θῆλυς is spoken of as a well-known expression. Later it is found in Nicomachus of Gerasa and Iamblichus. Festugière concludes that it is Pythagorean doctrine of the third century B.C., since Pythagoreans are found to have been monists as early as the second century at least (see above, nr. **1279a**).—Evidently this possibility does not exclude oriental influence at all. Cp. Valentinus (supra, **1333a**). The Asclepius says of the Father of all things: *hic ergo, solus ut omnia, utraque sexus fecunditate plenissimus* (C.H. II p. 321, 9-10).

[3] Ἡ διοίκησις τοῦ κόσμου is a Stoic term. E.g. SVF III p. 17, 7; cp. Philo V 252, 4 C.W. The planets are called "governors" e.g. by Bardesanes, *The books of the Laws* (*Patrol. Syriaca* II 567 f.).

b. The Logos leaves the elements and unites with the Νοῦς δημιουργός.

Corp. Herm. I 1, 10:

Ἐπήδησεν εὐθὺς ἐκ τῶν κατωφερῶν στοιχείων [τοῦ θεοῦ] ὁ τοῦ θεοῦ Λόγος εἰς τὸ καθαρὸν τῆς φύσεως δημιούργημα, καὶ ἡνώθη τῷ δημιουργῷ Νῷ (ὁμοούσιος γὰρ ἦν), καὶ κατελείφθη [τὰ] ἄλογα τὰ κατωφερῆ τῆς φύσεως στοιχεῖα, ὡς εἶναι ὕλην μόνην [1]. Ὁ δὲ δημιουργὸς Νοῦς σὺν τῷ Λόγῳ, ὁ περιίσχων τοὺς κύκλους καὶ δινῶν ῥοίζῳ, ἔστρεψε τὰ ἑαυτοῦ δημιουργήματα καὶ εἴασε στρέφεσθαι ἀπ' ἀρχῆς ἀορίστου εἰς ἀπέραντον τέλος· ἄρχεται γάρ, οὗ λήγει· ἡ δὲ τούτων περιφορά, καθὼς ἠθέλησεν ὁ Νοῦς, ἐκ τῶν κατωφερῶν στοιχείων ζῷα ἤνεγκεν ἄλογα (οὐ γὰρ ἐπεῖχε τὸν Λόγον), ἀὴρ δὲ πετεινὰ ἤνεγκε, καὶ τὸ ὕδωρ νηκτά· διακεχώρισται δὲ ἀπ' ἀλλήλων ἥ τε γῆ καὶ τὸ ὕδωρ, καθὼς ἠθέλησεν ὁ Νοῦς, καὶ <ἡ γῆ> ἐξήνεγκεν ἀπ' αὐτῆς ἃ εἶχε ζῷα τετράποδα <καὶ> ἑρπετά, θηρία ἄγρια καὶ ἥμερα.

The archetypal man

1341—The archetypal man is created by the first Noûs.

a. *Corp. Herm.* I 1, 12:

Ὁ δὲ πάντων πατὴρ ὁ Νοῦς, ὢν ζωὴ καὶ φῶς, ἀπεκύησεν Ἄνθρωπον αὐτῷ ἴσον, οὗ ἠράσθη ὡς ἰδίου τόκου· περικαλλὴς γάρ, τὴν τοῦ πατρὸς εἰκόνα ἔχων· ὄντως γὰρ καὶ ὁ θεὸς ἠράσθη τῆς ἰδίας μορφῆς, παρέδωκε τὰ ἑαυτοῦ πάντα δημιουργήματα.

How he comes to be a double being

b. He becomes a double being by attaching himself to Matter.

Corp. Herm. I 1, 14-15:

Καὶ ὁ τοῦ τῶν θνητῶν κόσμου καὶ τῶν ἀλόγων ζῴων ἔχων πᾶσαν ἐξουσίαν διὰ τῆς ἁρμονίας [2] παρέκυψεν, ἀναρρήξας τὸ κύτος [3], καὶ ἔδειξε τῇ κατωφερεῖ φύσει τὴν καλὴν τοῦ θεοῦ μορφήν, ὃν ἰδοῦσα ἀκόρεστον κάλλος <καὶ> πᾶσαν ἐνέργειαν ἐν ἑαυτῷ ἔχοντα τῶν διοικητόρων τήν τε μορφὴν τοῦ θεοῦ ἐμειδίασεν ἔρωτι, ὡς ἄτε τῆς καλλίστης μορφῆς τοῦ Ἀνθρώπου τὸ εἶδος ἐν τῷ ὕδατι ἰδοῦσα καὶ τὸ σκίασμα ἐπὶ τῆς γῆς. ὁ δὲ ἰδὼν τὴν ὁμοίαν αὐτῷ μορφὴν ἐν αὐτῇ οὖσαν ἐν τῷ ὕδατι, ἐφίλησε καὶ ἠβουλήθη αὐτοῦ οἰκεῖν· ἅμα δὲ τῇ βουλῇ ἐγένετο ἐνέργεια, καὶ ᾤκησε τὴν ἄλογον μορφήν· ἡ δὲ φύσις λαβοῦσα τὸν ἐρώμενον περιεπλάκη ὅλη καὶ ἐμίγησαν· ἐρώμενοι γὰρ ἦσαν.

---

[1] Likewise, according to Valentinus Jesus returns to the pleroma and leaves his Mother, and she, "bereft of the spiritual substance", brought forth the Demiurge (above, nr. **1334c**).

[2] The "composite framework" of the heavenly spheres (Nock).

[3] Κύτος of the starry vault of heaven, also ap. Vettius Valens 172, 32 Kr.

Καὶ διὰ τοῦτο παρὰ πάντα τὰ ἐπὶ γῆς ζῷα διπλοῦς ἐστιν ὁ ἄνθρωπος, θνητὸς μὲν διὰ τὸ σῶμα, ἀθάνατος δὲ διὰ τὸν οὐσιώδη ἄνθρωπον.

1342—The man who comes to know himself returns to the Light. — The return of the spiritual man

a. *Corp. Herm.* I 1, 21:

Κατὰ τί δὲ "ὁ νοήσας ἑαυτὸν εἰς αὐτὸν χωρεῖ", ὅπερ ἔχει ὁ τοῦ θεοῦ λόγος; — φημὶ ἐγώ· Ὅτι ἐκ φωτὸς καὶ ζωῆς συνέστηκεν ὁ πατὴρ τῶν ὅλων, ἐξ οὗ γέγονεν ὁ Ἄνθρωπος. — Εὖ φὴς λαλῶν· φῶς καὶ ζωή ἐστιν ὁ θεὸς καὶ πατήρ, ἐξ οὗ ἐγένετο ὁ Ἄνθρωπος. ἐὰν οὖν μάθῃς αὐτὸν ἐκ ζωῆς καὶ φωτὸς ὄντα καὶ ὅτι ἐκ τούτων τυγχάνεις, εἰς ζωὴν πάλιν χωρήσεις. ταῦτα ὁ Ποιμάνδρης εἶπεν.

b. His ascent through the celestial spheres and his return to God. — His ascent through the spheres
Corp. Herm. I 1, 25-26:

Καὶ οὕτως ὁρμᾷ λοιπὸν ἄνω διὰ τῆς ἁρμονίας, καὶ τῇ πρώτῃ ζώνῃ δίδωσι τὴν αὐξητικὴν ἐνέργειαν καὶ τὴν μειωτικήν, καὶ τῇ δευτέρᾳ τὴν μηχανὴν τῶν κακῶν, δόλον ἀνενέργητον, καὶ τῇ τρίτῃ τὴν ἐπιθυμητικὴν ἀπάτην ἀνενέργητον, καὶ τῇ τετάρτῃ τὴν ἀρχοντικὴν προφανίαν ἀπλεονέκτητον, καὶ τῇ πέμπτῃ τὸ θράσος τὸ ἀνόσιον καὶ τῆς τόλμης τὴν προπέτειαν, καὶ τῇ ἕκτῃ τὰς ἀφορμὰς τὰς κακὰς τοῦ πλούτου ἀνενεργήτους, καὶ τῇ ἑβδόμῃ ζώνῃ τὸ ἐνεδρεῦον ψεῦδος. καὶ τότε γυμνωθεὶς ἀπὸ τῶν τῆς ἁρμονίας ἐνεργημάτων[1] γίνεται ἐπὶ τὴν ὀγδοατικὴν φύσιν[2], τὴν ἰδίαν δύναμιν ἔχων, καὶ ὑμνεῖ σὺν τοῖς οὖσι τὸν πατέρα· συγχαίρουσι δὲ οἱ παρόντες τῇ τούτου παρουσίᾳ, καὶ ὁμοιωθεὶς τοῖς συνοῦσιν ἀκούει καί τινων δυνάμεων ὑπὲρ τὴν ὀγδοατικὴν φύσιν φωνῇ τινι ἡδείᾳ ὑμνουσῶν τὸν θεόν· καὶ τότε τάξει ἀνέρχονται πρὸς τὸν πατέρα, καὶ αὐτοὶ εἰς δυνάμεις ἑαυτοὺς παραδιδόασι, καὶ δυνάμεις γενόμενοι ἐν θεῷ γίνονται.

See on this passage Festugière, *Les doctrines de l'âme*, p. 130-152.
On the δυνάμεις ib., 153-174.
Similar ideas are found in Numenius, Porphyrius and many others. See our nr. **1356** and the note under **b.**

1343—*Corp. Herm.* I 1, 31: — The final hymn of the Poimandres

Ἅγιος ὁ θεὸς καὶ πατὴρ τῶν ὅλων.
Ἅγιος ὁ θεός, οὗ ἡ βουλὴ τελεῖται ἀπὸ τῶν ἰδίων δυνάμεων.

---

[1] Cp. Plotinus, *Enn.* I 6, 7: ἕως ἄν τις παρελθὼν ἐν τῇ ἀναβάσει πᾶν ὅσον ἀλλότριον τοῦ θεοῦ αὐτῷ μόνῳ αὐτὸ μόνον ἴδῃ εἰλικρινές, ἁπλοῦν καθαρόν, ἀφ' οὗ πάντα ἐξήρτηται. See also Cumont, *Les religions orientales dans le paganisme romain*, Paris ⁴1929, p. 282 f., n. 69, and W. Bousset, *Hauptprobleme der Gnosis*, p. 361-369.
[2] The ogdoas is also mentioned in C.H. XIII 15. Cp. Clem. Alex., *Exc. ex Theod.* 63, 1.

Ἅγιος ὁ θεός, ὃς γνωσθῆναι βούλεται καὶ γινώσκεται τοῖς ἰδίοις.

Ἅγιος εἶ, ὁ λόγῳ συστησάμενος τὰ ὄντα.

Ἅγιος εἶ, οὗ πᾶσα φύσις εἰκὼν ἔφυ.

Ἅγιος εἶ, ὃν ἡ φύσις οὐκ ἐμόρφωσεν.

Ἅγιος εἶ, ὁ πάσης δυνάμεως ἰσχυρότερος.

Ἅγιος εἶ, ὁ πάσης ὑπεροχῆς μείζων.

Ἅγιος εἶ, ὁ κρείττων τῶν ἐπαίνων.

Here we see an idea of God which is very near to Philo's, e.g. God's will is fulfilled by His own Powers (cp. above, nr. **1294, 1303b**); by the Logos He constituted all that is (**1305**); nature is an image of Him (**1302a**); He is stronger than all Powers (**1303b**). "He is known, or makes himself known, by those who belong to Him" is a gnostic feature. Cp. Hippolytus, *Ref.* V 8, p. 156 Duncker-Schneidewin (on the Naassene sect): ὁ Ἀδάμας, φησί, λέγει πρὸς τοὺς ἰδίους ἀνθρώπους.

An expression like πάσης ὑπεροχῆς μείζων foreshadows Proclus, e.g. *El. theol.* 122 (p. 108, 3 Dodds), 124 (p. 110, 17), 151 (p. 132, 29).

The soul of man is drawn down by the body **1344**—In X, which is a summary of the teaching of Hermes (called Κλείς) the "fall" of soul by its incorporation in a body is spoken of as a necessity.

Corp. Herm. I 10, 15:

Οὐ γὰρ ἀγνοεῖ τὸν ἄνθρωπον ὁ θεός, ἀλλὰ καὶ πάνυ γνωρίζει καὶ θέλει γνωρίζεσθαι. τοῦτο μόνον σωτήριον ἀνθρώπῳ ἐστίν, ἡ γνῶσις τοῦ θεοῦ. αὕτη εἰς τὸν Ὄλυμπον ἀνάβασις· οὕτω μόνως ἀγαθὴ ψυχή, καὶ οὐδέποτε ἀγαθὴ ‹ἀεί›, κακὴ δὲ γίνεται· κατ' ἀνάγκην γίνεται. — πῶς τοῦτο λέγεις, ὦ Τρισμέγιστε; — Ψυχὴν παιδὸς θέασαι, ὦ τέκνον, αὐτὴν διάλυσιν αὐτῆς μηδέπω ἐπιδεχομένην, τοῦ σώματος αὐτῆς * ἔτι ὀλίγον ὄγκωτο καὶ * μηδέπω τὸ πᾶν ὠγκωμένου, πῶς καλὴν μὲν βλέπειν πανταχοῦ, μηδέποτε δὲ τεθολωμένην ὑπὸ τῶν τοῦ σώματος παθῶν, ἔτι σχεδὸν ἠρτημένην τῆς τοῦ κόσμου ψυχῆς· ὅταν δὲ ὀγκωθῇ τὸ σῶμα καὶ κατασπάσῃ αὐτὴν εἰς τοὺς τοῦ σώματος ὄγκους, διαλύσασα δὲ ἑαυτὴν ἐγγεννᾷ λήθην, καὶ τοῦ καλοῦ καὶ ἀγαθοῦ οὐ μεταλαμβάνει· ἡ δὲ λήθη κακία γίνεται.

What is said of the oblivion of the spiritual world as the source of evil recalls words of Plotinus in *Enn.* I 8, 4. Plotinus, however, does not go so far as to call it a *necessity* to be pulled down by the body (see *Enn.* I 8, 5, the end: κρατεῖν γὰρ αὐτῆς . . . τῷ μὴ ἐνύλῳ ἐν αὐτοῖς ὄντι). He says that the body is not bad in the primary sense (I 8, 4, the beginning); but it does trouble the soul by its irregular motion and may bring it to ἀμετρία. Also 8, 8: Γενομένη γὰρ κυρία τοῦ εἰς αὐτὴν ἐμφασθέντος φθείρει αὐτό, κτλ.

Cp. Porph. Ἀφορμαί 29, 2 (p. 14, 18 M.): the body brings the soul to complete obscurity and stupidity (πεσούσῃ δὲ εἰς σώματα, . . . ἄγνοια ἕπεται τοῦ ὄντος τελεία καὶ σκότωσις καὶ νηπιότης).

6—NUMENIUS

1345—a.   Suidas s.v. Νουμήνιος (test. 1 Leemans):   Numenius
                                                                         of Apamea

'Απαμεὺς ἀπὸ Συρίας, φιλόσοφος Πυθαγόρειος· οὗτός ἐστιν ὁ τὴν τοῦ Πλάτωνος
ἐξελέγξας διάνοιαν, ὡς ἐκ τῶν Μωσαϊκῶν τὰ περὶ θεοῦ καὶ κόσμου γενέσεως
ἀποσυλήσασαν, καὶ διὰ τοῦτό φησι· τί γάρ ἐστι Πλάτων .ἢ Μωσῆς
ἀττικίζων;

The name Νουμήνιος is probably the Greek transcription of a Phoenician, in
any case of a Semitic name. It is found in Phoenician inscriptions (C.I.S., I, nr.
117 and 118). See H. Puech in *Mélanges Bidez* (1934) p. 754.

b.   Cp. Clem. Alex., *Strom.* I 22, p. 93 St. (Fr. 10 L.):

Νουμήνιος ὁ Πυθαγορικὸς φιλόσοφος ἄντικρυς γράφει· Τί γάρ ἐστι Πλάτων
ἢ Μωυσῆς ἀττικίζων;

c. Numenius lived in the second century. He was a Pythagorean in the
sense of that age. His philosophy is full of the metaphysics of Plato, which he
explains with philosophical arguments, but seeking confirmation in old religious
traditions, both in Greece and in the Orient. He has a preference for the books
of Moses and knows even the rabbine tradition (see Orig., *C.Celsum* I 15; IV 51).
Lydus (*De mensibus* p. 109, 25 Wünsch) says, Num. called the God of the temple
in Jerusalem πατέρα πάντων τῶν θεῶν.

Num. is cited frequently by Neoplatonic writers; also by Origenes. Porphyry,
V. Plot. 17, tells he was read in the school of Plotinus.

Plotinus' friend and pupil Amelius wrote a book on the difference between
Plotinus' doctrine and that of Numenius (Porph., *V. Plot.* 17).

Of Num.' work Περὶ τἀγαθοῦ important fragments are preserved in Eusebius,   The
Praep. ev. XI and XV, of his work against the scepticism of the Academy (Π. τῆς   fragments
τῶν 'Ακαδημαϊκῶν πρὸς Πλάτωνα διαστάσεως) in *Praep. ev.* XIV. His books Π.
ἀφθαρσίας ψυχῆς are cited by Orig., *C. Celsum* V 57.

A new edition of the fragments of Numenius (after Thedinga, Bonn 1875) was   Editions
given by E. A. Leemans, Bruxelles 1937. It is preceded by a study on "The philosopher Numenius of Apamea". Though by no means neglecting the Oriental
elements in Numenius' thought, Leemans stresses the fact that N. is a philosopher
trained in Greek dialectic and shows himself so in every fragment.

W. Bousset (in a review of J. Kroll's *Lehren des Hermes Trismegistos* in *Gött.*   Literature
gelehrte Anz. 1914, p. 716) classed Num. among Greek gnostics. Cp. also E. Norden,
Agnostos Theos, Berlin 1923, p. 72 f.

Similarly H. C. Puech in *Mélanges Bidez*, Bruxelles 1934, pp. 745-778. See infra
under nr. **1349c** and **1350f**.

That Numenius' work Π. ἀφθαρσίας ψυχῆς is the source of Macrobius in *Somn.*
Scip. I 2 and 12, was argued by Fr. Cumont in *Revue des Etudes grecques* 1919,
p. 119 f.; *Revue de Philol.* 1920, p. 231 n. 1; *Les religions orientales dans le paganisme*
romain, ⁴Paris 1929, p. 301, and by Leemans, o.c., p. 43-64.

Festugière deals with Num. in *Les doctrines de l'âme*, Paris 1953, p. 42-47, and
in *Le Dieu inconnu et la gnose*, Paris 1954, p. 123-132. He considers Num. as a Platonist of the same kind as Albinus. and his school.

Numenius' method

1346—a. Euseb., *Praep. ev.* IX 7, p. 411 B (fr. 9 a L.):

Καὶ αὐτοῦ δὲ τοῦ Πυθαγορικοῦ φιλοσόφου, τοῦ Νουμηνίου λέγω, ἀπὸ τοῦ πρώτου Περὶ τἀγαθοῦ τάδε παραθήσομαι·

Εἰς δὲ τοῦτο δεήσει εἰπόντα καὶ σημηνάμενον ταῖς μαρτυρίαις ταῖς Πλάτωνος ἀναχωρήσασθαι καὶ ξυνδήσασθαι τοῖς λόγοις τοῦ Πυθαγόρου, ἐπικαλέσασθαι δὲ τὰ ἔθνη τὰ εὐδοκιμοῦντα, προσφερόμενον αὐτῶν τὰς τελετὰς καὶ τὰ δόγματα τάς τε ἱδρύσεις συντελουμένας Πλάτωνι ὁμολογουμένως, ὁπόσας Βραχμᾶνες καὶ Ἰουδαῖοι καὶ Μάγοι καὶ Αἰγύπτιοι διέθεντο.

b. Cp. Origenes, *C. Celsum* I 15 (fr. 9 b L.):

Πόσῳ δὲ βελτίων Κέλσου καὶ διὰ πολλῶν δείξας εἶναι ἐλλογιμώτατος καὶ πλείονα βασανίσας δόγματα, καὶ ἀπὸ πλειόνων συναγαγὼν ἃ ἐφαντάσθη εἶναι ἀληθῆ ὁ Πυθαγόρειος Νουμήνιος, ὅστις ἐν τῷ πρώτῳ περὶ τἀγαθοῦ λέγων περὶ τῶν ἐθνῶν, ὅσα περὶ τοῦ θεοῦ ὡς ἀσωμάτου διείληφεν, ἐγκατέταξεν αὐτοῖς καὶ τοὺς Ἰουδαίους, οὐκ ὀκνήσας ἐν τῇ συγγραφῇ αὐτοῦ χρήσασθαι καὶ λόγοις προφητικοῖς καὶ τροπολογῆσαι αὐτούς· —

Dialectical arguments

1347—Though he seeks confirmation by authorities, Num. begins by philosophical arguments.

a. Eusebius, *Praep. ev.* XV 17, p. 819 A (fr. 12 L.):

Ἀλλὰ τί δή ἐστι τὸ ὄν; ἆρα ταυτὶ τὰ στοιχεῖα τὰ τέτταρα, ἡ γῆ καὶ τὸ πῦρ καὶ αἱ ἄλλαι δύο μεταξὺ φύσεις; Ἆρα οὖν δὴ τὰ ὄντα ταῦτά ἐστιν, ἤτοι ξυλ- b λήβδην ἢ καθ' ἕν γέ τι αὐτῶν;

— Καὶ πῶς, ἅ γέ ἐστι καὶ γενητὰ καὶ παλινάγρετα, εἴ γε ἔστιν ὁρᾶν αὐτὰ ἐξ ἀλλήλων γιγνόμενα καὶ ἐπαλλασσόμενα καὶ μήτε στοιχεῖα ὑπάρχοντα μήτε συλλαβάς;

— Σῶμα μὲν ταυτὶ οὕτως οὐκ ἂν εἴη τὸ ὄν. Ἀλλ' ἆρα ταυτὶ μὲν οὔ, ἡ δὲ 5 ὕλη δύναται εἶναι ὄν;

— Ἀλλὰ καὶ αὐτὴν παντὸς μᾶλλον ἀδύνατον, ἀρρωστίᾳ τοῦ μένειν· ποταμὸς γὰρ ἡ ὕλη ῥοώδης καὶ ὀξύρροπος, βάθος καὶ πλάτος καὶ μῆκος ἀόριστος καὶ ἀνήνυτος.

b. Eusebius, ib. 819 C (fr. 13 L.):

Καὶ μετὰ βραχέα ἐπιλέγει· ὥστε καλῶς ὁ λόγος εἴρηκε φάς, εἰ ἔστιν ἄπειρος c ἡ ὕλη, ἀόριστον εἶναι αὐτήν· εἰ δὲ ἀόριστος, ἄλογος· εἰ δὲ ἄλογος, ἄγνωστος. Ἄγνωστον δέ γε οὖσαν αὐτὴν ἀναγκαῖον εἶναι ἄτακτον, ὡς τεταγμένα γνωσ- 5 θῆναι πάνυ δήπουθεν ἂν εἴη ῥᾴδια· τὸ δὲ ἄτακτον οὐχ ἕστηκεν, ὅ τι δὲ μὴ ἕστηκεν, οὐκ ἂν εἴη ὄν. —

Οὐκ οὖν φημι τὴν ὕλην οὔτε αὐτὴν οὔτε τὰ σώματα εἶναι ὄν.

— Τί οὖν δή; Ἦ ἔχομεν παρὰ ταῦτα ἄλλο τι ἐν τῇ φύσει τῇ τῶν ὅλων;

— Ναί· τοῦτο οὐδὲν εἰπεῖν ποικίλον, εἰ τόδε πρῶτον μὲν ἐν ἡμῖν αὐτοῖς ἅμα πειραθείημεν διαλεγόμενοι· *** Ἐπεὶ δὲ τὰ σώματά ἐστι φύσει τεθνηκότα καὶ νεκρὰ καὶ πεφορημένα καὶ οὐδ' ἐν ταὐτῷ μένοντα, ἆρ' οὐχὶ τοῦ καθέξοντος αὐτοῖς ἔδει;

— Παντὸς μᾶλλον.

— Εἰ μὴ τύχοι δὴ τούτου, ἄρα μείνειεν ἄν;

— Παντὸς ἧττον.

— Τί οὖν ἐστι τὸ κατασχῆσον; Εἰ μὲν δὴ καὶ τοῦτο εἴη σῶμα, Διὸς σωτῆρος δοκεῖ ἂν ἐμοὶ δεηθῆναι αὐτὸ παραλυόμενον καὶ σκιδνάμενον· εἰ μέντοι χρὴ αὐτὸ ἀπηλλάχθαι τῆς τῶν σωμάτων πάθης, ἵνα κἀκείνοις κεκυημένοις τὴν φθορὰν ἀμύνειν δύνηται καὶ κατέχῃ, ἐμοὶ μὲν οὐ δοκεῖ ἄλλο τι εἶναι ἢ μόνον γε τὸ ἀσώματον· αὕτη γὰρ δὴ φύσεως πασῶν μόνη ἔστηκε καὶ ἔστιν ἀραρυῖα καὶ οὐδὲν σωματική. Οὔτε γοῦν γίγνεται οὔτε αὔξεται οὔτε κίνησιν κινεῖται ἄλλην οὐδεμίαν, καὶ διὰ ταῦτα καλῶς δίκαιον ἐφάνη πρεσβεῦσαι τὸ ἀσώματον.

1348—Euseb., *Praep. ev.* XI 21, p. 543 B (fr. 11 L.):

Πάλιν δὲ καὶ ὁ Νουμήνιος ἐν τοῖς περὶ τἀγαθοῦ, τὴν τοῦ Πλάτωνος διάνοιαν διερμηνεύων, τοῦτον διέξεισι τὸν τρόπον· Τὰ μὲν οὖν σώματα λαβεῖν ὑμῖν ἔξεστι σημαινομένοις ἔκ τε ὁμοίων ἀπό τε τῶν ἐν τοῖς παρακειμένοις γνωρισμάτων ἐνόντων· τἀγαθὸν δὲ οὐδενὸς ἐκ παρακειμένου οὐδ' αὖ ἀπὸ ὁμοίου αἰσθητοῦ ἐστι λαβεῖν μηχανή τις οὐδεμία· ἀλλὰ δεήσει, οἷον εἴ τις ἐπὶ σκοπῇ καθήμενος ναῦν ἁλιάδα βραχεῖάν τινα τούτων τῶν ἐπακτρίδων τῶν μόνων μίαν μόνην ἔρημον μεταξὺ κυμίοις ἐχομένην ὀξὺ δεδορκώς, μιᾷ βολῇ κατεῖδε [τὴν ναῦν], οὕτως δεῖ τινα ἀπελθόντα πόρρω ἀπὸ τῶν αἰσθητῶν ὁμιλῆσαι τῷ ἀγαθῷ μόνῳ μόνον, ἔνθα μήτε τις ἄνθρωπος μήτε τι ζῷον ἕτερον, μηδὲ σῶμα μέγα μηδὲ σμικρόν, ἀλλά τις ἄφατος καὶ ἀδιήγητος ἀτεχνῶς ἐρημία θεσπέσιος, ἔνθα τοῦ ἀγαθοῦ ἤδη διατριβαί τε καὶ ἀγλαΐαι, αὐτὸ δὲ ἐν εἰρήνῃ ἐν εὐμενείᾳ τε, ἤρεμον τὸ ἡγεμονικόν, ἵλεων ἐποχούμενον ἐπὶ τῇ οὐσίᾳ. Εἰ δέ τις πρὸς τοῖς αἰσθητοῖς λιπαρῶν τὸ ἀγαθὸν ἐφιπτάμενον φαντάζεται, κἄπειτα τρυφῶν οἴοιτο τῷ ἀγαθῷ ἐντετυχηκέναι, τοῦ παντὸς ἁμαρτάνει. Τῷ γὰρ ὄντι οὐ ῥᾳδίας, θείας δὲ πρὸς αὐτὸ δεῖ μεθόδου· καὶ ἔστι κράτιστον, τῶν αἰσθητῶν ἀμελήσαντι νεανιευσαμένῳ πρὸς τὰ μαθήματα, τοὺς ἀριθμοὺς θεασαμένῳ, οὕτως ἐκμελετῆσαι μάθημα, τί ἐστι τὸ ὄν.

1349—a. Euseb., *Praep. ev.* XI 17, p. 536 D (fr. 20 L.):

Ὁ δὲ Νουμήνιος τὰ Πλάτωνος πρεσβεύων, ἐν τοῖς Περὶ τἀγαθοῦ τάδε καὶ αὐτὸς περὶ τοῦ δευτέρου αἰτίου λέγων διερμηνεύει· Τὸν μέλλοντα δὲ συνήσειν θεοῦ περὶ πρώτου καὶ δευτέρου χρὴ πρότερον διελέσθαι ἕκαστα ἐν τάξει καὶ ἐν

εὐθημοσύνη τινί· κἄπειτα ἐπὰν δοκῇ ἤδη εὖ ἔχειν, τότε καὶ δεῖ ἐπιχειρεῖν p
εἰπεῖν κοσμίως, ἄλλως δὲ μή. Ἢ τῷ πρωϊαίτερον πρὶν τὰ πρῶτα γενέσθαι
ἁπτομένῳ σποδὸς ὁ θησαυρὸς γίγνεσθαι λέγεται. Μὴ δὴ πάθωμεν ἡμεῖς ταὐτόν·
θεὸν δὲ προκαλεσάμενοι ἑαυτοῦ γνώμονα γενόμενον τῷ λόγῳ δεῖξαι θησαυρὸν 5
φροντίδων, ἀρχώμεθα οὕτως. Εὐκτέον μὲν ἤδη, διελέσθαι δὲ δεῖ. Ὁ θεὸς ὁ
μὲν πρῶτος ἐν ἑαυτῷ ὤν ἐστιν ἁπλοῦς διὰ τὸ ἑαυτῷ συγγιγνόμενος διόλου μή
ποτε εἶναι διαιρετός· ὁ θεὸς μέντοι ὁ δεύτερος καὶ τρίτος ἐστὶν εἷς. συμφερό- k
μενος δὲ τῇ ὕλῃ δυάδι οὔσῃ ἑνοῖ μὲν αὐτήν, σχίζεται δὲ ὑπ' αὐτῆς, ἐπιθυμητικὸν
ἦθος ἐχούσης καὶ ῥεούσης. Τῷ οὖν μὴ εἶναι πρὸς τῷ νοητῷ (ἦν γὰρ ἂν πρὸς
ἑαυτῷ) διὰ τὸ τὴν ὕλην βλέπειν, ταύτης ἐπιμελούμενος ἀπερίοπτος ἑαυτοῦ
γίγνεται. Καὶ ἅπτεται τοῦ αἰσθητοῦ καὶ περιέπει ἀνάγει τε ἔτι εἰς τὸ ἴδιον 5
ἦθος ἐπορεξάμενος τῆς ὕλης.

According to this description Numenius' first God is absolutely one—Plato's
Ἕν or Ἀγαθόν—, the second is Noûs adhering to Himself, the third is Noûs turned
to Matter. The First principle is not called Noûs. This might *seem* to be a difference
from Albinus and an analogy to gnosticism, but in fact it is not. For in fr. 25 (below,
1350a) the first God is called Noûs. Cp. Albinus who, though calling his First
principle ἄρρητος and ἄληπτος, qualified it as Νοῦς ἀκίνητος (supra, nr. **1327**).

When Numenius, as will appear in the following text, separates the demiurgic
function from the First principle, he differs from Albinus by a greater logical consistency (cp. nr. **1328**), but is hardly further removed from Plato.

The first God
is an
ἀργὸς
βασιλεύς,
the second
God is the
Demiurge

b. Euseb., ib. 537 B (fr. 21 L.):

Καὶ μεθ' ἕτερά φησι·

Καὶ γὰρ οὔτε δημιουργεῖν ἐστι χρεὼν τὸν πρῶτον, καὶ τοῦ δημιουργοῦντος
θεοῦ χρὴ εἶναι νομίζεσθαι πατέρα τὸν πρῶτον θεόν.

Εἰ μὲν οὖν περὶ τοῦ δημιουργικοῦ ζητοῦμεν, φάσκοντες δεῖν τὸν πρότερον 1
ὑπάρξαντα οὕτως ἂν ποιεῖν ἔχειν διαφερόντως, ἐοικυῖα ἡ πρόσοδος αὕτη γεγο- c
νυῖα ἂν εἴη τοῦ λόγου· εἰ δὲ περὶ τοῦ δημιουργοῦ μή ἐστιν ὁ λόγος, ζητοῦμεν
δὲ περὶ τοῦ πρώτου, ἀφοσιοῦμαί τε τὰ λεχθέντα, καὶ ἔστω μὲν ἐκεῖνα ἄρρητα,
μέτειμι δὲ ἑλεῖν τὸν λόγον ἑτέρωθεν θηράσας. Πρὸ μέντοι τοῦ λόγου τῆς ἁλώ-
σεως διομολογησόμεθα ἡμῖν αὐτοῖς ὁμολογίαν οὐκ ἀμφισβητήσιμον ἀκοῦσαι, 5
τὸν μὲν πρῶτον θεὸν ἀργὸν εἶναι ἔργων ξυμπάντων καὶ βασιλέα, τὸν δημιουργικὸν
δὲ θεὸν ἡγεμονεύειν, δι' οὐρανοῦ ἰόντα.

That Numenius' second God is essentially the same as the transcendent Logos
in Philo, appears from the nrs. **1301**, **1303** and **1305** supra. A similar conception of a
second God who is Noûs, is found in the Chaldaic oracles. See Kroll, *Orac. Chald.* p. 14:

Πάντα γὰρ ἐξετέλεσσε Πατὴρ καὶ Νῷ παρέδωκε
δευτέρῳ, ὃν πρῶτον κληΐζετε πᾶν γένος ἀνδρῶν.

See also the following text of Numenius.

c. Euseb., *Praep. ev.* XI 18, p. 538 B (fr. 22 L.):

Νουμήνιος ἐπάκουσον οἷα περὶ τοῦ δευτέρου αἰτίου θεολογεῖ· Ὥσπερ δὲ

c πάλιν λόγος ἐστὶ γεωργῷ πρὸς τὸν φυτεύοντα ἀναφερόμενος, τὸν αὐτὸν λόγον
μάλιστά ἐστιν ὁ πρῶτος θεὸς πρὸς τὸν δημιουργόν. Ὁ μέν γε ὢν σπέρμα πάσης
ψυχῆς σπείρει εἰς τὰ μεταλαγχάνοντα αὐτοῦ χρήματα ξύμπαντα· ὁ νομοθέτης δὲ
5 φυτεύει καὶ διανέμει καὶ μεταφυτεύει εἰς ἡμᾶς ἑκάστους τὰ ἐκεῖθεν προκατα-
βεβλημένα.

In fact, the relation between the First and the Second God as here described
is rather that of the ὄργανον δι' οὗ (Philo, nr. **1305**) than that of the demiurge of
the gnostics. The latter is not conceived as a spirit (Νοῦς), but always as generated
outside the spiritual world (or pleroma). He created the visible world in ignorance
of the archetypal Ideas. Such a view is as far from Num. as it was from Philo and
will be found to be from Plotinus.

H. C. Puech, o.c., did not see this when ranking Num. with gnostics because of
his separating the demiurgic function from the First Principle and attributing
it to a second.

1350—The difference between Numenius' second God and the gnostic
demiurge will be seen more clearly in the following fragments. Even the
first God is not quite so "gnostic" as it might appear above.

*The first
God called
Noûs*

   a. Euseb., *Praep. ev.* XI 22, p. 544 A (fr. 25 L.):

Ἐν δὲ τῷ πέμπτῳ ταῦτά φησιν· Εἰ δ' ἐστὶ μὲν νοητὸν ἡ οὐσία καὶ ἡ ἰδέα,
ταύτης δ' ὡμολογήθη πρεσβύτερον καὶ αἴτιον εἶναι ὁ νοῦς, αὐτὸς οὗτος μόνος
5 ηὕρηται ὢν τὸ ἀγαθόν. Καὶ γὰρ εἰ ὁ μὲν δημιουργὸς θεός ἐστι γενέσεως, ἀρκεῖ
τὸ ἀγαθὸν οὐσίας εἶναι ἀρχή.

Ἀνάλογον δὲ τούτῳ μὲν ὁ δημιουργὸς θεός, ὢν αὐτοῦ μιμητής, τῇ δὲ οὐσίᾳ
ἡ γένεσις, <ἡ> εἰκὼν αὐτῆς ἐστι καὶ μίμημα. Εἴπερ δὲ ὁ δημιουργὸς ὁ τῆς
b γενέσεώς ἐστιν ἀγαθός, ἦ που ἔσται καὶ ὁ τῆς οὐσίας δημιουργὸς αὐτοάγαθον,
σύμφυτον τῇ οὐσίᾳ. ὁ γὰρ δεύτερος διττὸς ὤν, αὐτοποιεῖ τήν τε ἰδέαν ἑαυτοῦ
καὶ τὸν κόσμον, δημιουργὸς ὤν· ἔπειτα θεωρητικὸς ὅλως.

5 Συλλελογισμένων δ' ἡμῶν ὀνόματα τεσσάρων πραγμάτων, τέσσαρα ἔστω
ταῦτα· ὁ μὲν πρῶτος θεὸς αὐτοάγαθον· ὁ δὲ τούτου μιμητὴς δημιουργὸς
ἀγαθός, ἡ δ' οὐσία μία μὲν ἡ τοῦ πρώτου, ἑτέρα δὲ ἡ τοῦ δευτέρου· ἧς μίμημα
ὁ καλὸς κόσμος, κεκαλλωπισμένος μετουσίᾳ τοῦ καλοῦ.

This view of the Demiurge and of the cosmos is certainly not gnostic, but rather such
as Plotinus considered the relation between Noûs and cosmos to be. (What Plotinus
rejected in Numenius' theory was the element of mythology in it, when there is
question of a Father, a son, and a grandson. Cp. Porphyrius' testimony, below,
nr. **1363a**).

   b. Also what follows in the above-cited fr. 21 **(1349a)** after the
words that the God who is Demiurge governs, δι' οὐρανοῦ ἰόντα, shows
that Num. is far from the gnostic view of man and matter.

Euseb., *Praep. ev.* XI 18, 537 C (fr. 21 L., l. 19):

Διὰ δὲ τούτου καὶ ὁ στόλος ἡμῖν ἐστιν, κάτω τοῦ νοῦ πεμπομένου ἐν διεξόδῳ
πᾶσι τοῖς κοινωνῆσαι συντεταγμένοις.

Βλέποντος μὲν οὖν καὶ ἐπεστραμμένου πρὸς ἡμῶν ἕκαστον τοῦ θεοῦ συμβαίνει d
ζῆν τε καὶ βιώσκεσθαι τότε τὰ σώματα, κηδεύοντος τοῦ θεοῦ τοῖς ἀκροβολισμοῖς·
μεταστρέφοντος δὲ εἰς τὴν ἑαυτοῦ περιωπὴν τοῦ θεοῦ ταῦτα μὲν ἀποσβέννυσθαι,
τὸν δὲ νοῦν ζῆν βίου ἐπαυρόμενον εὐδαίμονος.   5

Here Num. shows a remarkable difference from Plotinus. The latter is concerned
with the soul's either looking or not looking to the superior sphere of being (Noûs)
and says that in the first case soul is creative, in the second not. Num. however
speaks of God the Demiurge (Noûs) as looking to man and by His looking keeping
the body alive. He may have learned this from "Moses", not from Plato.

c.   Again, the first God is called Noûs in the following fragment.

Euseb., *Praep. ev.* XI 18, p. 539 B (fr. 26 L.):

Ἐπὶ τούτοις καὶ ἐν τῷ ἕκτῳ προστίθησι ταῦτα· Ἐπειδὴ ᾔδει ὁ Πλάτων
παρὰ τοῖς ἀνθρώποις τὸν μὲν δημιουργὸν γιγνωσκόμενον μόνον, τὸν μέντοι c
πρῶτον νοῦν, ὅστις καλεῖται αὐτὸ ὄν, παντάπασιν ἀγνοούμενον παρ' αὐτοῖς,
διὰ τοῦτο οὕτως εἶπεν, ὥσπερ ἄν τις [οὕτω]λέγῃ· ὦ ἄνθρωποι, ὃν τοπάζετε
ὑμεῖς νοῦν, οὐκ ἔστι πρῶτος, ἀλλ' ἕτερος πρὸ τούτου νοῦς πρεσβύτερος καὶ
θειότερος.   5

**The function
of the
Demiurge
described**   **1351**—The following description of the function of the Demiurge is
in its essence purely Platonic[1]. It is only put in a more dramatic
setting.

Euseb., ib. p. 539 C (fr. 27 L.):

Κυβερνήτης μέν που ἐν μέσῳ πελάγει φορούμενος ὑπὲρ πηδαλίων ὑψίζυγος
τοῖς οἴαξι διιθύνει τὴν ναῦν ἐφεζόμενος, ὄμματα δ' αὐτοῦ καὶ νοῦς εὐθὺ τοῦ d
αἰθέρος ξυντέταται πρὸς τὰ μετάρσια, καὶ ἡ ὁδὸς αὐτῷ ἄνω δι' οὐρανοῦ ἄπεισι,
πλέοντι κάτω κατὰ τὴν θάλατταν· οὕτω καὶ ὁ δημιουργὸς τὴν ὕλην, τοῦ μήτε
διακροῦσαι μήτε ἀποπλαγχθῆναι αὐτήν, ἁρμονίᾳ ξυνδησάμενος, αὐτὸς μὲν ὑπὲρ
ταύτης ἵδρυται, οἷον ὑπὲρ νεὼς ἐπὶ θαλάττης, τῆς ὕλης· τὴν ἁρμονίαν δὲ ἰθύνει, 5
ταῖς ἰδέαις οἰακίζων, βλέπει τε ἀντὶ τοῦ οὐρανοῦ εἰς τὸν ἄνω θεὸν προσαγόμενον
αὐτοῦ τὰ ὄμματα, λαμβάνει τε τὸ μὲν κριτικὸν ἀπὸ τῆς θεωρίας, τὸ δὲ ὁρμητικὸν
ἀπὸ τῆς ἐφέσεως.

---

[1]   Cp. Plato, *Tim.* 28ab, 29a: The Demiurge created the world looking to that
which is always unchanging and using it as a pattern of the world to be made.

1352—Proclus describes Numenius' theory of the three gods not quite correctly.

a. Proclus, *in Tim.* I p. 303, 27 Diehl (Test. 24 L.):

Νουμήνιος μὲν γὰρ τρεῖς ἀνυμνήσας θεοὺς πατέρα μὲν καλεῖ τὸν πρῶτον, ποιητὴν δὲ τὸν δεύτερον, ποίημα δὲ τὸν τρίτον· ὁ γὰρ κόσμος κατ' αὐτὸν ὁ τρίτος ἐστὶ θεός. ὥστε ὁ κατ' αὐτὸν δημιουργὸς διττός, ὅ τε πρῶτος θεὸς καὶ ὁ δεύτερος, τὸ δὲ δημιουργούμενον ὁ τρίτος· Ἄμεινον γὰρ οὕτω λέγειν ἢ ὡς ἐκεῖνος λέγει προστραγῳδῶν, πάππον, ἔγγονον, ἀπόγονον [1].

It is not correct to say that according to Num. the Demiurge was double, "namely, the First and the second God". Cp. above, **1349a**. That *the cosmos* was called by Num. the third God, is not correct either. This appears most clearly in the following passage of Proclus.

b. Proclus, *in Tim.* III p. 103, 28 D (Test. 25 L.):

Νουμήνιος δὲ τὸν μὲν πρῶτον (sc. νοῦν) κατὰ τὸ ὅ ἐστι ζῷον τάττει καί φησιν ἐν προσχρήσει τοῦ δευτέρου νοεῖν, τὸν δὲ δεύτερον κατὰ τὸν νοῦν, καὶ τοῦτον αὖ ἐν προσχρήσει τοῦ τρίτου δημιουργεῖν, τὸν δὲ τρίτον κατὰ τὸ διανοούμενον.

This passage proves two things: (1) Proclus understood Numenius' First God not as the Ἕν of Plotinus or the Unknown God of the Gnostics, but as the intelligible World conceived as a Noûs or living being (τὸ ὅ ἐστι ζῷον = αὐτὸ τὸ ζῷον). See my interpretation of Plato, *Soph.* 249 a and *Tim.* 31b in: *Proceedings of the XIth international Congress of Phil.*, Brussels 1953, vol. XII, p. 61-67, and the text of Aristotle, *De anima* I 2, 404b, 16-21, cited in Gr. Ph. I, nr. **372**).

(2) Since the third God of Num. was ranked κατὰ τὸ διανοούμενον, the term appears to have meant not the visible world, but the conception of it in the mind of the Demiurge. Thus, the second God was the demiurgic Intellect in its active aspect (the Demiurge thinking the world), while the third means the same Intellect viewed in its passive sense (the world as thought by the Demiurge). Cp. fr. 20 (nr. **1349a**). The passage is explained in this sense by Festugière, *Le Dieu inconnu et la gnose*, p. 123 f.

1353—Numenius does not join the monistic trend of the Neopythagorean school which derived the δυὰς ἀόριστος of Plato's later doctrine from the One (see above, **1279a**).

a. Chalcidius, *in Timaeum* c. 295 f. (test. 30 L.):

Nunc iam Pythagoricum dogma recenseatur. Numenius ex Pythagorae magisterio Stoicorum hoc de initiis [2] dogma refellens Pythagorae dogmate cui concinere dicit dogma Platonicum [3], ait Pythagoram deum

---

[1] Cp. *Tim.* 50 d: Καὶ δὴ καὶ προσεικάσαι πρέπει τὸ μὲν δεχόμενον μητρί, τὸ δ' ὅθεν πατρί, τὴν δὲ μεταξὺ τούτων φύσιν ἐκγόνῳ.

[2] de initiis-περὶ ἀρχῶν.

[3] That in fact the doctrine of ἕν and ἀόριστος δυάς as first principles was a Platonic and not an originally Pythagorean doctrine, has been shown above (see **1279a**).

quidem singularitatis <nomine> [1] nominasse, silvam vero duitatis [2]. quam duitatem indeterminatam quidem minime genitam [3], limitatam vero generatam esse dicere [4].

Num. opposes both those Pythagoreans who wisli to derive the infinite principle from the Ἕν, and those Stoics who admit that matter is defined and limited and has a *propria natura* [5].

(296) Igitur Pythagoras quoque, inquit, fluidam [6] et sine qualitate silvam esse censet, nec tamen, ut Stoici, naturae mediae, interque bonorum malorumque viciniam, quod genus illi appellant indifferens [7], sed plane noxiam. Deum quippe esse, ut etiam Platoni videtur, initium et causam bonorum, silvam malorum.

Mixed character of the cosmos

b. Chalcidius, ib. 296 (continued):

At vero quod ex specie silvaque sit [8] indifferens. Non ergo silvam sed mundum ex speciei bonitate silvaeque malitia temperatum [9], denique ex providentia et necessitate progenitum [10] veterum theologorum scitis haberi.

Matter the source of evil

c. Numenius, therefore stresses the necessity of evil. Chalcidius, ib. 297:

Ait (Pythagoras) existente providentia mala quoque necessario substitisse, propterea quod silva sit, et eadem sit malitia praedita. Quod si mundus ex silva, certe factus est de existente olim natura maligna [11];

---

[1] We have no reason to admit that *Pythagoras* called God τὸ Ἕν, but Pythagoreans did, from the second century B.C.

[2] silva—ὕλη; duitatis—δυάς.

[3] duitatem indeterminatam e.q.s.—τὴν ἀόριστον δυάδα εἶναι ἀγένητον.

[4] limitatam vero generatam esse—τὸν δὲ κόσμον γενητόν.
Thus, Atticus taught (according to Proclus, *in Tim.* I p. 283, 27 D) τὸ μὲν πλημμελῶς καὶ ἀτάκτως κινούμενον (*Tim.* 30a) εἶναι ἀγένητον, τὸν δὲ κόσμον ἀπὸ χρόνου γενητόν. Cp. C. Bäumker, *Das Problem der Materie in der griech. Phil.*, München 1890, p. 143 ff.

[5] This is, however, not exact. Stoics always called ὕλη ἄποιος, but they did call it οὐσία and σῶμα (above, nrs. **899-902**).

[6] This, again, is Plato's doctrine in *Phil.* 24 ff. and according to Hermodorus. See **347a b, 371a**, l. 11 f.: ἔστι γὰρ μᾶλλον εἶναι μεῖζον καὶ ἔλαττον εἰς ἄπειρον φερόμενα.—ὥστε ἄστατον καὶ ἄμορφον καὶ ἄπειρον ... τὸ τοιοῦτον λέγεσθαι.

[7] ἀδιάφορον. Above, nrs. **1012b, 1018**.

[8] "what is composed from form and matter", sc. the cosmos.

[9] That, in fact, according to the *Timaeus* the cosmos can hardly be called a composite or "mixture" of form and matter, may be seen in the passages cited under nr. **356** (particularly *Tim.* 51e-52b).

[10] *Tim.* 68e: Διὸ δὴ χρὴ δυ' αἰτίας εἴδη διορίζεσθαι, τὸ μὲν ἀναγκαῖον, τὸ δὲ θεῖον, e.q.s.

[11] Here Numenius' dualism is certainly stronger than Plato's.

proptereaque Numenius laudat Heraclitum [1] reprehendentem Homerum, qui optaverit interitum ac vastitatem malis vitae, quod non intellegeret mundum sibi deleri placere, siquidem silva quae malorum fons est, exterminaretur.

d. Numenius identifies "the bad worldsoul" of *Leg.* 896e [2] with "matter" and divides the soul of man into a passive and a rational part, the first of which is connected with matter.

Chalcidius, ib. (297 continued):

Platonemque idem Numenius laudat, quod duas mundi animas au- tumet, unam benificentissimam, malignam alteram, scilicet silvam. Quae licet incondite fluctuet, tamen quia intimo proprioque motu movetur, vivat et anima convegetetur necesse est, lege eorum omnium quae genuino motu moventur. Quae quidem etiam patibilis animae partis, in qua est aliquid corpulentum mortaleque et corporis simile, auctrix est et patrona, sicut rationabilis animae pars auctore utitur ratione ac Deo.

The bad worldsoul and the soul of man

Porph. says that Num. did not "divide" the soul of man into a "passive" and a rational part, but spoke of *two souls* in man. See **1354a**.

e. Matter moves πλημμελῶς καὶ ἀτάκτως (Plato, *Tim.* 30a), and though the Demiurge brought· it from ἀταξία to τάξις (ib.), the mixture is *confusa*, says Chalcidius following Num., *nec ex providentiae consultis salubribus.* Hence

Chalcidius, ib. 298:

Ergo iuxta Pythagoram silvae anima neque sine ulla est substantia, ut plerique arbitrantur, et adversatur providentiae, consulta eius impugnare gestiens malitiae suae viribus.

Matter is not merely στέρησις, but positively bad

The term *malitia* is certainly stronger than what is said either by Plato or by Aristotle on ὕλη resisting the Demiurge (Plato, *Politicus* 273b [3]; cp. what is said of the nature of the ἕτερον in *Tim.* 35a [4]) and on the ἀναγκαῖον in *Tim.* 68e) or resisting Form (Arist., *De gen. anim.* IV 4, 770b, 17 [5].

Plotinus, *Enn.* I 8, maintains strictly the στέρησις character of ὕλη [6]. The soul turns bad if it turns away from Νοῦς, thus getting filled with ἀοριστία (c. 4 at the end).

---

[1] See our nr. **53b** (Arist., *Eth. Eud.* VII 1, 1235a, 25).
[2] Our nr. **390**. For the identification, cp. **388**.
[3] The Cause of θόρυβοι and ταραχή in the cosmos is: τὸ σωματοειδὲς τῆς συγκράσεως, τὸ τῆς πάλαι ποτὲ φύσεως σύντροφον, ὅτι πολλῆς ἦν μετέχον ἀταξίας πρὶν εἰς τὸν νῦν κόσμον ἀφικέσθαι.
[4] τὴν θατέρου φύσιν δύσμεικτον οὖσαν εἰς ταὐτὸν συναρμόττων βίᾳ (supra, nr. **350**).
[5] ὅταν μὴ κρατήσῃ τὴν κατὰ τὴν ὕλην ἡ κατὰ τὸ εἶδος φύσις (Above, nr. **496b**).
[6] See in particular the cc. 3-5 and 11-12; below, nr. **1410**.

Two souls
in man

1354—a. Porphyrius, Π. τῶν τῆς ψυχῆς δυνάμεων, ap. Stob. I p. 350, 25 W. (Test. 36 L.):

᾿Άλλοι δέ, ὧν καὶ Νουμήνιος, οὐ τρία μέρη ψυχῆς μιᾶς ἢ δύο γε, τὸ λογικὸν καὶ ἄλογον, ἀλλὰ δύο ψυχὰς ἔχειν ἡμᾶς οἴονται, ὥσπερ καὶ ἄλλα, τὴν μὲν λογικήν, τὴν δὲ ἄλογον.

b. Cp. Iamblichus, Π. ψυχῆς, ap. Stob. I p. 374, 21 W. (Test. 35 L.):

῎Ηδη τοίνυν καὶ ἐν αὐτοῖς τοῖς Πλατωνικοῖς πολλοὶ διαστασιάζουσιν, οἱ μὲν εἰς μίαν σύνταξιν καὶ μίαν ἰδέαν τὰ εἴδη καὶ τὰ μόρια τῆς ζωῆς καὶ τὰ ἐνεργήματα συνάγοντες, ὥσπερ Πλωτῖνός τε καὶ Πορφύριος· οἱ δὲ εἰς μάχην ταῦτα κατατείνοντες, ὥσπερ Νουμήνιος· οἱ δὲ ἐκ μαχομένων αὐτὰ συναρμόζοντες, ὥσπερ οἱ περὶ ᾿Αττικὸν καὶ Πλούταρχον.

To be bound
in a body is
always evil

1355—Since "matter" is bad, the κάθοδος τῶν ψυχῶν and their embodiment is considered by Num. as always an evil.

a. Iambl., Π. διαφορᾶς καθόδου τῶν ψυχῶν, ap. Stob. I p. 380, 14 W. (Test. 40 L.):

Some people, Iambl. says, consider the κάθοδος τῶν ψυχῶν as not always evil: it may serve for different purposes, e.g. for the σωτηρία and κάθαρσις of others, or also for the training and correction of one's own character.

<Τινὲς δὲ τῶν νεωτέρων οὐχ οὕτως> διακρίνουσιν, οὐκ ἔχοντες δὲ σκοπὸν τῆς διαφορότητος εἰς ταὐτὸ συγχέουσι τὰς ἐνσωματώσεις τῶν ὅλων, κακάς τε εἶναι πάσας διισχυρίζονται καὶ διαφερόντως οἱ περὶ Κρόνιόν τε καὶ Νουμήνιον.

The soul
reunited
with its
ἀρχαί

b. The soul delivered from the body is unified with its ἀρχαί.

Iambl., Π. ψυχῆς, ap. Stob. I p. 458, 3 W. (Test. 34 L.):

῎Ενωσιν μὲν οὖν καὶ ταὐτότητα ἀδιάκριτον τῆς ψυχῆς πρὸς τὰς ἑαυτῆς ἀρχὰς πρεσβεύειν φαίνεται Νουμήνιος.

What is meant by this return of the soul to its "origins", will appear more clearly in the next fragment. Certainly the plural is not used without reason. Cp. also the final chapters of Plut., De facie, cited above (nrs. **1192d** and **1319**).

The ascent
of the soul
after death

1356—Numenius' ideas on the ascent of the soul after death and its abode hereafter are found in a fragment of his comments on the myth of Er cited by Proclus.

a. Proclus, In rempubl. II, p. 128, 26 Kroll (Test. 42 L.):

Νουμήνιος μὲν γὰρ τὸ κέντρον εἶναί φησιν τοῦτον (sc. τὸν τόπον) τοῦ τε κόσμου παντὸς καὶ τῆς γῆς, ὡς μεταξὺ μὲν ὂν τοῦ οὐρανοῦ, μεταξὺ δὲ καὶ p. τῆς γῆς· ἐν ᾧ καθῆσθαι τοὺς δικαστὰς καὶ παραπέμπειν τὰς μὲν εἰς οὐρανὸν τῶν ψυχῶν, τὰς δὲ εἰς τὸν ὑπὸ γῆς τόπον καὶ τοὺς ἐκεῖ ποταμούς· οὐρανὸν μὲν

5 τὴν ἀπλανῆ λέγων καὶ ἐν ταύτῃ δύο χάσματα, τὸν αἰγόκερω καὶ τὸν καρκίνον,
τοῦτον μὲν καθόδου χάσμα τῆς εἰς γένεσιν, ἀνόδου δὲ ἐκεῖνον, ποταμοὺς δὲ ὑπὸ γῆς
τὰς πλανωμένας (ἀνάγει γὰρ εἰς ταύτας τοὺς ποταμοὺς καὶ αὐτὸν τὸν Τάρταρον)·
καὶ ἄλλην πολλὴν ἐπεισάγων τερατολογίαν, πηδήσεις τε ψυχῶν ἀπὸ τῶν τρο-
● πικῶν ἐπὶ τὰ ἰσημερινὰ καὶ ἀπὸ τούτων εἰς τὰ τροπικὰ καὶ μεταβάσεις, ἃς
αὐτὸς πηδῶν ἐπὶ τὰ πράγματα μεταφέρει, καὶ συρράπτων τὰ Πλατωνικὰ
ῥήματα τοῖς γενεθλιαλογικοῖς καὶ ταῦτα τοῖς τελεστικοῖς· μαρτυρόμενος τῶν
δύο χασμάτων καὶ τὴν Ὁμήρου ποίησιν οὐ μόνον λέγουσαν (Ὀδ., ν, 110-112)
5 "τὰς μὲν πρὸς βορέαο καταίβατας ἀνθρώποισιν" ὁδούς, ἐπείπερ ὁ καρκίνος εἰς
* αἰγόκερον προσελθὼν ἀποτελεῖ· τὰς δὲ πρὸς νότον [εἶναι θειοτέρας], δι' ὧν
οὐκ ἔστιν ἀνδράσιν [εἰσελθε]ῖν, ἀθανάτων δὲ μόνον ὁδοὺς αὐτὰς ὑπάρχειν·
● ὁ γὰρ αἰγόκερως ἀνάγων τὰς ψυχὰς λύει μὲν αὐτῶν τὴν ἐν ἀνδράσι ζωήν,
μόνην δὲ τὴν ἀθάνατον εἰσδέχεται καὶ θείαν· οὐ ταῦτα δ' οὖν μόνον, ἀλλὰ καὶ
ἡλίου πύλας ὑμνοῦσαν καὶ δῆμον ὀνείρων (Ὀδ., ω, 12), τὰ μὲν δύο τροπικὰ
ζῴδια πύλας ἡλίου προσαγορεύσασαν, δῆμον δὲ ὀνείρων, ὥς φησιν ἐκεῖνος,
5 τὸν γαλαξίαν. Καὶ γὰρ τὸν Πυθαγόραν δι' ἀπορρήτων Ἅιδην τὸν γαλαξίαν
καὶ τόπον ψυχῶν ἀποκαλεῖν, ὡς ἐκεῖ συνωθουμένων· διὸ παρά τισιν ἔθνεσιν
● γάλα σπένδεσθαι τοῖς θεοῖς τοῖς τῶν ψυχῶν καθαρταῖς, καὶ τῶν πεσουσῶν εἰς
γένεσιν εἶναι γάλα τὴν πρώτην τροφήν. Τὸν δὲ δὴ Πλάτωνα διὰ μὲν τῶν
χασμάτων, ὡς εἴρηται, δηλοῦν τὰς δύο πύλας, διὰ δὲ τοῦ φωτός, ὃ δὴ σύνδεσμον
5 εἶναι τοῦ οὐρανοῦ, τὸν γαλαξίαν· εἰς ὃν ἀνιέναι δι' ἡμερῶν δυοκαίδεκα τὰς ψυχὰς
ἀπὸ τοῦ τόπου τῶν δικαστῶν.

There are also fragments of Num. in Porph., *De antro nympharum* c. 21 and 28.
Similar ideas are found in Macrob., *In somn. Scip.* I 12, 1-3. On the whole question:
Leemans, p. 43-64; test. 43-47.
The conception of the Milky Way as the abode of souls before their descent
goes back to Heraclides Ponticus (above, **775**). Thus,

b. Macrobius, *In somn. Scip.* I 11, 11 (p. 529 Eyss.) (Test. 47 L.):

7 Animae beatae ab omni cuiuscumque contagione corporis liberae caelum possident; quae vero appetentiam corporis et huius, quam in terris
● vitam vocamus ab illa specula altissima et perpetua luce despiciens
desiderio latenti cogitaverit, pondere ipso terrenae cogitationis paulatim
in inferiora delabitur. Nec subito a perfecta incorporalitate luteum corpus
5 induitur, sed sensim per tacita detrimenta et longiorem simplicis et
absolutissimae puritatis recessum in quaedam siderei corporis incrementa
turgescit: in singulis enim sphaeris, quae caelo subiectae sunt, aetheria
obvolutione vestitur, ut per eas gradatim societati huius indumenti
● testei concilietur, et ideo totidem mortibus, quot sphaeras transit, ad
hanc pervenit, quae in terris vita vocitatur.

The descent of the soul from the Milky Way

Then, the descent of the soul is described. The tropica signa, Capricornus et Cancer, are mentioned.

Capricornus et Cancer

(12) — hominum una, altera deorum vocatur: hominum Cancer, quia per hunc in inferiora descensus est, Capricornus deorum, quia per illum animae in propriae inmortalitatis sedem et in deorum numerum revertuntur.

At the Lion the soul leaves the Milky way and first participates of matter.

The Lion

Ergo descensurae cum adhuc in Cancro sunt, quoniam illic positae p necdum lacteum reliquerunt, adhuc in numero sunt deorum. Cum vero ad Leonem labendo pervenerint, illic condicionis futurae auspicantur exordium, et quia in Leone sunt rudimenta nascendi et quaedam humanae naturae tirocinia[1]. —

Ibique a puncto suo, quod est monas, venit (anima) in dyadem, quae est prima protractio[2]. —

Anima ergo cum trahitur ad corpus, in hanc prima sui productione silvestrem tumultum[3], id est ὕλην influentem, sibi incipit experiri.

The acquisition of earthly powers

Now begins the descent of the soul through the planetary spheres. In each of them she acquires one of the powers of an earthly being.

Hoc ergo primo pondere de zodiaco et lacteo ad subiectas usque sphaeras anima delapsa, dum et per illas labitur, in singulis non solum, ut iam diximus, luminosi corporis amicitur accessu, sed et singulos motus, quos in exercitio est habitura, producit; in Saturni ratiocinationem et intelligentiam, quod λογιστικόν et θεωρητικόν vocant; in Iovis vim agendi, quod πρακτικόν dicitur; in Martis animositatis ardorem, quod θυμικόν nuncupatur; in solis sentiendi opinandique naturam, quod αἰσθητικόν et φανταστικόν appellant; desiderii vero motum, quod ἐπιθυμητικόν vocatur, in Veneris; pronuntiandi et interpretandi quae sentiat, quod ἑρμηνευτικόν dicitur, in orbe Mercurii; φυτικόν vero, id est naturam plantandi et augendi corpora, in ingressu globi lunaris exercet. et est haec, sicut a divinis ultima, ita in nostris terrenis omnibus prima: corpus enim hoc, sicut faex rerum divinarum est, ita animalis est prima

---

[1] See the explanation under the text.

[2] Since Plato and the Early Academy, length was derived from the ideal number 2. See the passages in Aristotle's *Metaph.* cited in *Gr. Ph.* I, p. 280, n. 2; in particular *Metaph.* N 3, 1090b 21.

[3] *Silvestrem tumultum* - Doubtless a reminiscence of *Tim.* 43b-d, where the disorder resulting from the soul's being bound in a body is described as a θόρυβος caused by a violent stream, and as a violent and perpetual motion. For further explanation, see under the text.

4 substantia. et haec est differentia inter terrena corpora et supera, caeli dico et siderum aliorumque elementorum, quod illa quidem sursum arcessita sunt ad animae sedem et immortalitatem ex ipsa natura 5 regionis et sublimitatis imitatione meruerunt: ad haec vero terrena corpora anima ipsa deducitur, et ideo mori creditur, cum in caducam regionem et in sedem mortalitatis includitur.

These ideas are evidently connected with Chaldaic astrology. Since they are also found in the gnostic writings of the *Corpus Hermeticum* (above, **1342b**), in the *Chaldaic Oracles* (Kroll, p. 51, n. 2), in Servius *in Verg. Aen.* (VI 714; XI 51), in Arnobius (*Adv. nationes* II 16-28), and took a great place in the Mithras cult [1], we must admit that they were by no means confined to Num., Porphyrius and their followers and go back to a much earlier date [2].

As to the "first influx of matter" mentioned by Macrob., this refers to the πνευματικόν or αἰθέριον σῶμα, also called ὄχημα, repeatedly mentioned by Porphyrius (e.g. *Sententiae* 29, p. 13 Mommert) and Proclus (e.g. *in Tim.* I 147, III 234 Diehl). It is opposed to the σῶμα γήϊνον ἐκ τῶν τεττάρων στοιχείων φυραθέν (Procl., ib. I 5 D.).

Cp. Verbeke, *La doctrine du Pneuma*, p. 364 ff.

---

[1] Here the Lion was a high degree of initiation. See Vermaseren, *De Mithras-dienst in Rome*, Nijmegen 1951, p. 128 ff. Cp. Orig., *C. Celsum* II p. 92 K. and Cumont, *Les religions orientales*, p. 282 n. 69; M. J. Vermaseren, *Corpus inscr. et monum. religionis Mithriacae*, Hagae Comitis 1956, the numbers mentioned in the General index s.v. lion as a grade.

[2] On Hellenistic astrology and astrological Hermetism, see A. J. Festugière, *La Révélation d'Hermès Trismégiste* I, *L'Astrologie et les sciences occultes*, especially pp. 89-123. Further literature is mentioned there (p. 89 n. 1).

PLOTINUS, THE FOUNDER OF NEOPLATONISM

1—LIFE AND WORKS

1357—Plotinus' life and personality are mainly known to us by the Vita of Porphyrius.

He was silent about his birth and origin

a. Porphyrius, *Vita Plot.* 1, 1-9 Henry-Schwyzer:

Πλωτῖνος ὁ καθ' ἡμᾶς γεγονὼς φιλόσοφος ἐῴκει μὲν αἰσχυνομένῳ ὅτι ἐν σώματι εἴη. Ἀπὸ δὲ τῆς τοιαύτης διαθέσεως οὔτε περὶ τοῦ γένους αὐτοῦ διηγεῖσθαι ἠνείχετο οὔτε περὶ τῶν γονέων οὔτε περὶ τῆς πατρίδος. Ζωγράφου δὲ ἀνασχέσθαι ἢ πλάστου τοσοῦτον ἀπηξίου ὥστε καὶ λέγειν πρὸς Ἀμέλιον δεόμενον εἰκόνα αὐτοῦ γενέσθαι ἐπιτρέψαι· οὐ γὰρ ἀρκεῖ φέρειν ὃ ἡ φύσις εἴδωλον ἡμῖν περιτέθεικεν, ἀλλὰ καὶ εἰδώλου εἴδωλον συγχωρεῖν αὐτὸν ἀξιοῦν πολυχρονιώτερον καταλιπεῖν ὡς δή τι τῶν ἀξιοθεάτων ἔργων;

Eunapius, *Vit. soph.* p. 6 Boiss., and Suidas say that he was born at Lycopolis in Egypt.

The year of his death

b. Ib., 2, 23, 25-27, 29-31, 34-43 H.-S.:

Μέλλων δὲ τελευτᾶν ... φήσας πειρᾶσθαι τὸ ἐν ἡμῖν θεῖον ἀνάγειν πρὸς τὸ ἐν τῷ παντὶ θεῖον, ... ἀφῆκε τὸ πνεῦμα ἔτη γεγονός, ὡς ὁ Εὐστόχιος ἔλεγεν, ἕξ τε καὶ ἑξήκοντα, τοῦ δευτέρου ἔτους τῆς Κλαυδίου βασιλείας πληρουμένου. [1]—

Ἀναψηφίζουσι δὲ ἡμῖν ἀπὸ τοῦ δευτέρου ἔτους τῆς Κλαυδίου βασιλείας εἰς τοὐπίσω ἔτη ἕξ τε καὶ ἑξήκοντα ὁ χρόνος αὐτῷ τῆς γενέσεως εἰς τὸ τρισκαιδέκατον ἔτος τῆς Σεβήρου βασιλείας πίπτει [2]. Οὔτε δὲ τὸν μῆνα δεδήλωκέ τινι καθ' ὃν γεγένηται, οὔτε τὴν γενέθλιον ἡμέραν, ἐπεὶ οὐδὲ θύειν ἢ ἑστιᾶν τινα τοῖς αὐτοῦ γενεθλίοις ἠξίου, καίπερ ἐν τοῖς Πλάτωνος καὶ Σωκράτους παραδεδομένοις γενεθλίοις θύων τε καὶ ἑστιῶν τοὺς ἑταίρους [3], ὅτε καὶ λόγον ἔδει τῶν ἑταίρων τοὺς δυνατοὺς ἐπὶ τῶν συνελθόντων ἀναγνῶναι.

1358—**a.** Porph., *Vita* 3, 6-24 H.-S.:

Εἰκοστὸν δὲ καὶ ὄγδοον ἔτος αὐτὸν ἄγοντα ὁρμῆσαι ἐπὶ φιλοσοφίαν καὶ τοῖς

---

[1] I.e. A.D. 270.
[2] A.D. 203/4.
[3] Cp. supra, nr. **815**.

τότε κατὰ τὴν Ἀλεξάνδρειαν εὐδοκιμοῦσι συσταθέντα κατιέναι ἐκ τῆς ἀκροά-
σεως αὐτῶν κατηφῆ καὶ λύπης πλήρη, ὡς καί τινι τῶν φίλων διηγεῖσθαι ἃ **His master**
πάσχοι· τὸν δὲ συνέντα αὐτοῦ τῆς ψυχῆς τὸ βούλημα ἀπενέγκαι πρὸς Ἀμμώνιον, **Ammonius**
οὗ μηδέπω πεπείρατο. Τὸν δὲ εἰσελθόντα καὶ ἀκούσαντα φάναι πρὸς τὸν ἑταῖρον·
"τοῦτον ἐζήτουν". Καὶ ἀπ' ἐκείνης τῆς ἡμέρας συνεχῶς τῷ Ἀμμωνίῳ παραμέ-
νοντα τοσαύτην ἕξιν ἐν φιλοσοφίᾳ κτήσασθαι, ὡς καὶ τῆς παρὰ τοῖς Πέρσαις
ἐπιτηδευομένης πεῖραν λαβεῖν σπεῦσαι καὶ τῆς παρ' Ἰνδοῖς κατορθουμένης.
Γορδιανοῦ δὲ τοῦ βασιλέως ἐπὶ τοὺς Πέρσας παριέναι μέλλοντος δοὺς ἑαυτὸν **Gordianus'**
τῷ στρατοπέδῳ συνεισῄει ἔτος ἤδη τριακοστὸν ἄγων καὶ ἔννατον. Ἕνδεκα **expedition**
γὰρ ὅλων ἐτῶν παραμένων τῷ Ἀμμωνίῳ συνεσχόλασε. Τοῦ δὲ Γορδιανοῦ περὶ **to Persia**
τὴν Μεσοποταμίαν ἀναιρεθέντος μόλις φεύγων εἰς τὴν Ἀντιόχειαν διεσώθη.
Καὶ Φιλίππου τὴν βασιλείαν κρατήσαντος τεσσαράκοντα γεγονὼς ἔτη εἰς **Arrival at**
τὴν Ῥώμην ἄνεισιν. **Rome**

On Ammonius see:
M. Dehaut, *Vie et doctrine d'Ammonius Sakkas* (Mémoires de l'Acad. Royale
de Belgique IX, Bruxelles 1836).
K. H. E. de Jong, *Plotinus of Ammonius Sakkas?*, Leiden 1941.
H. Dörrie, *Ammonius, der Lehrer Plotins*, in: Hermes 83 (1955), p. 439-477.

    b. Ib., l. 32-38 H.-S.: **His teaching**

Πλωτῖνος δὲ ἄχρι μὲν πολλοῦ γράφων οὐδὲν διετέλεσεν, ἐκ δὲ τῆς Ἀμμωνίου
συνουσίας ποιούμενος τὰς διατριβάς· καὶ οὕτως ὅλων ἐτῶν δέκα διετέλεσε,
συνὼν μέν τισι, γράφων δὲ οὐδέν. Ἦν δὲ ἡ διατριβή, ὡς ἂν αὐτοῦ ζητεῖν
προτρεπομένου τοὺς συνόντας, ἀταξίας πλήρης καὶ πολλῆς φλυαρίας, ὡς
Ἀμέλιος ἡμῖν διηγεῖτο.

    c. Amelius stayed with P. for 24 years and kept records of his **His pupil**
lectures. **Amelius**

Ib., l. 38-42, 46 f.:

Προσῆλθε δὲ αὐτῷ ὁ Ἀμέλιος τρίτον ἔτος ἄγοντι ἐν τῇ Ῥώμῃ κατὰ τὸ
τρίτον ἔτος τῆς Φιλίππου βασιλείας καὶ ἄχρι τοῦ πρώτου ἔτους τῆς Κλαυδίου
βασιλείας παραμείνας ἔτη ὅλα συγγέγονεν εἴκοσι καὶ τέσσαρα, ... σχόλια δὲ
ἐκ τῶν συνουσιῶν ποιούμενος ἑκατόν που βιβλία συνέταξε τῶν σχολίων. —

    d. Porphyry himself came to P. when the latter was 59 years of age. He **Porphyry**
stayed with him for six years, then went to Sicily for reasons of health. In the
cc. 4-6 he gives a chronological list of Plotinus' works.

1359—Among P.'s pupils at Rome quite a number of intellectuals **The senator**
are mentioned; several of them were senators. **Rogatianus**

Porph., *Vita* 7, 29-46 H.-S.:

Ἠκροῶντο δὲ αὐτοῦ καὶ τῶν ἀπὸ τῆς συγκλήτου οὐκ ὀλίγοι ὧν ἔργον ἐν φιλοσοφίᾳ μάλιστα ἐποίουν Μάρκελλος Ὀρρόντιος καὶ Σαβινίλλος. Ἦν δὲ 3 καὶ Ῥογατιανὸς ἐκ τῆς συγκλήτου, ὃς εἰς τοσοῦτον ἀποστροφῆς τοῦ βίου τούτου προκεχωρήκει ὡς πάσης μὲν κτήσεως ἀποστῆναι, πάντα δὲ οἰκέτην ἀποπέμψασθαι, ἀποστῆναι δὲ καὶ τοῦ ἀξιώματος· καὶ πραίτωρ προιέναι 3 μέλλων παρόντων τῶν ὑπηρετῶν μήτε προελθεῖν μήτε φροντίσαι τῆς λειτουργίας, ἀλλὰ μηδὲ οἰκίαν ἑαυτοῦ ἑλέσθαι κατοικεῖν, ἀλλὰ πρός τινας τῶν φίλων καὶ συνήθων φοιτῶντα ἐκεῖ τε δειπνεῖν κἀκεῖ καθεύδειν, σιτεῖσθαι δὲ παρὰ μίαν· ἀφ' ἧς δὴ ἀποστάσεως καὶ ἀφροντιστίας τοῦ βίου ποδαγρῶντα μὲν 4 οὕτως, ὡς καὶ δίφρῳ βαστάζεσθαι, ἀναρρωσθῆναι, τὰς χεῖρας δὲ ἐκτεῖναι μὴ οἷόν τε ὄντα χρῆσθαι ταύταις πολὺ μᾶλλον εὐμαρῶς ἢ οἱ τὰς τέχνας διὰ τῶν χειρῶν μετιόντες. Τοῦτον ἀπεδέχετο ὁ Πλωτῖνος καὶ ἐν τοῖς μάλιστα ἐπαινῶν διετέλει εἰς ἀγαθὸν παράδειγμα τοῖς φιλοσοφοῦσι προβαλλόμενος. 4

1360—The following chapter gives us a view of Plotinus' domestic life.

a. Porph., *Vita* 9, l. 1, 5-22:

Women pupils　Ἔσχε δὲ καὶ γυναῖκας σφόδρα προσκειμένας. —

Πολλοὶ δὲ καὶ ἄνδρες καὶ γυναῖκες ἀποθνήσκειν μέλλοντες τῶν εὐγενεσ- 5 **His care of** τάτων φέροντες τὰ ἑαυτῶν τέκνα, ἄρρενάς τε ὁμοῦ καὶ θηλείας, ἐκείνῳ παρε**orphans** δίδοσαν μετὰ τῆς ἄλλης οὐσίας ὡς ἱερῷ τινι καὶ θείῳ φύλακι. Διὸ καὶ ἐπεπλήρωτο αὐτῷ ἡ οἰκία παίδων καὶ παρθένων. Ἐν τούτοις δὲ ἦν καὶ Ποτάμων, οὗ τῆς 1 παιδεύσεως φροντίζων πολλάκις ἓν καὶ μεταποιοῦντος [1] ἠκροάσατο. Ἠνείχετο δὲ καὶ τοὺς λογισμούς, ἀναφερόντων τῶν ἐκείνοις παραμενόντων, καὶ τῆς ἀκριβείας ἐπεμελεῖτο λέγων, ἕως ἂν μὴ φιλοσοφῶσιν, ἔχειν αὐτοὺς δεῖν τὰς κτήσεις καὶ τὰς προσόδους ἀνεπάφους τε καὶ σῳζομένας. Καὶ ὅμως τοσούτοις ἐπαρκῶν τὰς εἰς τὸν βίον φροντίδας τε καὶ ἐπιμελείας τὴν πρὸς τὸν νοῦν τάσιν οὐδέποτ' ἂν ἐγρηγορότως ἐχάλασεν.

Arbiter in Ἦν δὲ καὶ πρᾶος καὶ πᾶσιν ἐκκείμενος τοῖς ὁπωσοῦν πρὸς αὐτὸν συνήθειαν **quarrels** ἐσχηκόσι. Διὸ εἴκοσι καὶ ἓξ ἐτῶν ὅλων ἐν τῇ Ῥώμῃ διατρίψας καὶ πλείστοις 2 διαιτήσας τὰς πρὸς ἀλλήλους ἀμφισβητήσεις οὐδένα τῶν πολιτικῶν ἐχθρόν ποτε ἔσχε.

His insight into human character　**b.** Ib., 11:

Περιῆν δὲ αὐτῷ τοσαύτη περιουσία ἠθῶν κατανοήσεως, ὡς κλοπῆς ποτε γεγονυίας πολυτελοῦς περιδεραίου Χιόνης, ἥτις αὐτῷ συνῴκει μετὰ τῶν τέκνων σεμνῶς τὴν χηρείαν διεξάγουσα, καὶ ὑπ' ὄψιν τοῦ Πλωτίνου τῶν οἰκείων συνηγμένων ἐμβλέψας ἅπασιν· "οὗτος", ἔφη, "ἐστὶν ὁ κεκλοφώς", δείξας ἕνα τινά. 5 Μαστιζόμενος δὲ ἐκεῖνος καὶ ἐπιπλεῖον ἀρνούμενος τὰ πρῶτα ὕστερον ὡμολόγησε

---

[1] The text is explained by H.-S.: *etiam cum unum idemque retractabat*. Wyttenbach corrected it elegantly by reading ἂν καὶ μέ<τ>ρα ποιοῦντος.

καὶ φέρων τὸ κλαπὲν ἀπέδωκε. Προεῖπε δ' ἂν καὶ τῶν συνόντων παίδων περὶ
ἑκάστου οἷος ἀποβήσεται· ὡς καὶ περὶ τοῦ Πολέμωνος οἷος ἔσται, ὅτι ἐρωτικὸς
ἔσται καὶ ὀλιγοχρόνιος, ὅπερ καὶ ἀπέβη.

Καί ποτε ἐμοῦ Πορφυρίου ᾔσθετο ἐξάγειν ἐμαυτὸν διανοουμένου τοῦ βίου·
καὶ ἐξαίφνης ἐπιστάς μοι ἐν τῷ οἴκῳ διατρίβοντι καὶ εἰπὼν μὴ εἶναι ταύτην
τὴν προθυμίαν ἐκ νοερᾶς καταστάσεως, ἀλλ' ἐκ μελαγχολικῆς τινος νόσου,
ἀποδημῆσαι ἐκέλευσε. Πεισθεὶς δὲ αὐτῷ ἐγὼ εἰς τὴν Σικελίαν ἀφικόμην
Πρόβον τινὰ ἀκούων ἐλλόγιμον ἄνδρα περὶ τὸ Λιλύβαιον διατρίβειν· καὶ αὐτός
τε τῆς τοιαύτης προθυμίας ἀπεσχόμην τοῦ τε παρεῖναι ἄχρι θανάτου τῷ
Πλωτίνῳ ἐνεποδίσθην.

Platonopolis

1361—His project of founding a city.

Ib., 12:

Ἐτίμησαν δὲ τὸν Πλωτῖνον μάλιστα καὶ ἐσέφθησαν Γαλιῆνός τε ὁ αὐτοκρά-
τωρ καὶ ἡ τούτου γυνὴ Σαλωνίνα. Ὁ δὲ τῇ φιλίᾳ τῇ τούτων καταχρώμενος
φιλοσόφων τινὰ πόλιν κατὰ τὴν Καμπανίαν γεγενῆσθαι λεγομένην, ἄλλως
δὲ κατηριπωμένην, ἠξίου ἀνεγείρειν καὶ τὴν πέριξ χώραν χαρίσασθαι οἰκισθείσῃ
τῇ πόλει, νόμοις δὲ χρῆσθαι τοὺς κατοικεῖν μέλλοντας τοῖς Πλάτωνος καὶ τὴν
προσηγορίαν αὐτῇ Πλατωνόπολιν θέσθαι, ἐκεῖ τε αὐτὸς μετὰ τῶν ἑταίρων
ἀναχωρήσειν ὑπισχνεῖτο. Καὶ ἐγένετ' ἂν τὸ βούλημα ἐκ τοῦ ῥᾴστου τῷ φιλοσόφῳ, εἰ μή τινες τῶν συνόντων τῷ βασιλεῖ φθονοῦντες ἢ νεμεσῶντες ἢ δι'
ἄλλην μοχθηρὰν αἰτίαν ἐνεπόδισαν.

1362—His way of writing and teaching.

Porphyry
his corrector

a. Porph., *Vita* 7, 49-51; 8, 1-8 H.-S.:

Ἔσχε δὲ καὶ ἐμὲ Πορφύριον Τύριον ὄντα ἐν τοῖς μάλιστα ἑταῖρον, ὃν καὶ
διορθοῦν αὐτοῦ τὰ συγγράμματα ἠξίου.

(8). Γράψας γὰρ ἐκεῖνος δὶς τὸ γραφὲν μεταλαβεῖν οὐδέποτ' ἂν ἠνέσχετο,
ἀλλ' οὐδὲ ἅπαξ γοῦν ἀναγνῶναι καὶ διελθεῖν διὰ τὸ τὴν ὅρασιν μὴ ὑπηρετεῖσθαι
αὐτῷ πρὸς τὴν ἀνάγνωσιν. Ἔγραφε δὲ οὔτε εἰς κάλλος ἀποτυπούμενος τὰ
γράμματα οὔτε εὐσήμως τὰς συλλαβὰς διαιρῶν οὔτε τῆς ὀρθογραφίας φροντίζων, ἀλλὰ μόνον τοῦ νοῦ ἐχόμενος, καί, ὃ πάντες ἐθαυμάζομεν, ἐκεῖνο ποιῶν
ἄχρι τελευτῆς διετέλεσε.

His way of
writing

b. The works of other philosophers were read in his school and
commented on in a personal style.

Other
philosophers
read in his
school

Ib., 14, 10-18 H.-S.:

Ἐν δὲ ταῖς συνουσίαις ἀνεγινώσκετο μὲν αὐτῷ τὰ ὑπομνήματα, εἴτε Σεβήρου εἴη, εἴτε Κρονίου ἢ Νουμηνίου ἢ Γαίου ἢ 'Αττικοῦ, κἂν τοῖς Περιπατητικοῖς τά τε 'Ασπασίου καὶ 'Αλεξάνδρου 'Αδράστου τε καὶ τῶν ἐμπεσόντων. 'Ελέγετο δὲ ἐκ τούτων οὐδὲν καθάπαξ, ἀλλ' ἴδιος ἦν καὶ ἐξηλλαγμένος ἐν τῇ θεωρίᾳ καὶ τὸν 'Αμμωνίου φέρων νοῦν ἐν ταῖς ἐξετάσεσιν. 'Επληροῦτο δὲ ταχέως καὶ δι' ὀλίγων δοὺς νοῦν βαθέος θεωρήματος ἀνίστατο.

Longinus about P. and Amelius

1363—Longinus' judgment about Plotinus and Amelius.

a. Porph., *Vita* 20, 68-81 H.-S.:

Longinus, passing in review the writers of his time, mentions Plotinus and Amelius as the most able authors he knows.

Οἱ δὲ καὶ πλήθει προβλημάτων ἃ μετεχειρίσαντο τὴν σπουδὴν τοῦ γράφειν ἀποδειξάμενοι καὶ τρόπῳ θεωρίας ἰδίῳ χρησάμενοι Πλωτῖνός εἰσι καὶ Γεντιλια- 7 νὸς 'Αμέλιος· ὃς μὲν τὰς Πυθαγορείους ἀρχὰς καὶ Πλατωνικάς, ὡς ἐδόκει, πρὸς σαφεστέραν τῶν πρὸ αὐτοῦ καταστησάμενος ἐξήγησιν· οὐδὲ γὰρ οὐδὲν ἐγγύς τι τὰ Νουμηνίου καὶ Κρονίου καὶ Μοδεράτου καὶ Θρασύλλου τοῖς Πλωτίνου 7 περὶ τῶν αὐτῶν συγγράμμασιν εἰς ἀκρίβειαν· ὁ δὲ 'Αμέλιος κατ' ἴχνη μὲν τούτου βαδίζειν προαιρούμενος καὶ τὰ πολλὰ μὲν τῶν αὐτῶν δογμάτων ἐχόμενος, τῇ δὲ ἐξεργασίᾳ πολὺς ὢν καὶ τῇ τῆς ἑρμηνείας περιβολῇ πρὸς τὸν ἐναντίον ἐκείνῳ ζῆλον ὑπαγόμενος· ὧν καὶ μόνων ἡμεῖς ἄξιον εἶναι νομίζομεν ἐπισκοπεῖ- 8 σθαι τὰ συγγράμματα.

b. Ib., 19, 34-41 H.-S.:

Again, in a letter to Porphyrius, Longinus wrote as follows.

Τοῦτο γὰρ οὖν καὶ παρόντι σοι καὶ μακρὰν ἀπόντι καὶ περὶ τὴν Τύρον διατρί- 3 βοντι τυγχάνω δήπουθεν ἐπεσταλκὼς ὅτι τῶν μὲν ὑποθέσεων οὐ πάνυ με τὰς πολλὰς προσίεσθαι συμβέβηκε· τὸν δὲ τύπον τῆς γραφῆς καὶ τῶν ἐννοιῶν τἀνδρὸς τὴν πυκνότητα καὶ τὸ φιλόσοφον τῆς τῶν ζητημάτων διαθέσεως ὑπερβαλλόντως ἄγαμαι καὶ φιλῶ καὶ μετὰ τῶν ἐλλογιμωτάτων ἄγειν τὰ τούτου 4 βιβλία φαίην ἂν δεῖν τοὺς ζητητικούς.

2—THE THEORY OF THE THREE HYPOSTASES

The monistic principle

1364—All things must be reduced to one single Cause, which works by itself and as a whole, not by its parts.

a. Plot., *Enn.* VI 5, 9, 1-10 Br.:

Καὶ τοίνυν εἰ πάντα γενόμενα ἤδη τὰ στοιχεῖα τῷ λόγῳ τις εἰς ἓν σφαιρικὸν σχῆμα ἄγοι, οὐ πολλοὺς φατέον τὴν σφαῖραν ποιεῖν κατὰ μέρη ἄλλον ἄλλῃ ἀποτεμνόμενον αὐτῷ εἰς τὸ ποιεῖν μέρος, ἀλλ' ἓν εἶναι τὸ αἴτιον τῆς ποιήσεως

ὅλῳ ἑαυτῷ ποιοῦν οὐ μέρους αὐτοῦ ἄλλου ἄλλο ποιοῦντος· οὕτω γὰρ ἂν πάλιν
πολλοὶ εἶεν, εἰ μὴ εἰς ἓν ἀμερὲς ἀναφέροις τὴν ποίησιν, μᾶλλον δ' εἰ μὴ ἐν
ἀμερὲς τὸ ποιοῦν τὴν σφαῖραν εἴη οὐκ αὐτοῦ χυθέντος εἰς τὴν σφαῖραν τοῦ
ποιοῦντος, ἀλλὰ τῆς σφαίρας ὅλης εἰς τὸ ποιοῦν ἀνηρτημένης.

Cp. VI 5, 5, where the many νοητά are represented as many centres (not in a
flat surface, but in a sphere), which can be reduced to one.

b. The First Principle contains everything within itself.

Enn. VI 8, 18, 1-3 Br.:

Καὶ σὺ ζητῶν μηδὲν ἔξω ζήτει αὐτοῦ, ἀλλ' εἴσω πάντα τὰ μετ' αὐτόν· —
Τὸ γὰρ ἔξω αὐτός ἐστι, περίληψις πάντων καὶ μέτρον.

c. *Enn.* VI 8, 21, 19-22 Br.:

Τὸ δὲ συνέχειν ἑαυτὸν οὕτω ληπτέον νοεῖν, εἴ τις ὀρθῶς αὐτὸ φθέγγοιτο,
ὡς τὰ μὲν ἄλλα πάντα ὅσα ἐστὶ παρὰ τούτου ἀνέχεται· μετουσίᾳ γάρ τινι
αὐτοῦ ἔστι, καὶ εἰς τοῦτον ἡ ἀναγωγὴ πάντων· —

d. Every multitude must be traced back to a principle which is
absolutely one.

Enn. V 3, 16, 12-16 Br.:

Οὐ γὰρ ἐκ πολλοῦ πολύ, ἀλλὰ τὸ πολὺ τοῦτο ἐξ οὗ πολλοῦ· εἰ γὰρ καὶ αὐτὸ
πολύ, οὐκ ἀρχὴ τοῦτο, ἀλλ' ἄλλο πρὸ τούτου. Συστῆναι οὖν δεῖ εἰς ἓν ὄντως
παντὸς πλήθους ἔξω καὶ ἁπλότητος ἡστινοσοῦν, εἴπερ ὄντως ἁπλοῦν.

1365—Many intelligible forms *must* spring from the First Principle, **The neces-**
like the sensible world *must* spring from Soul, every nature producing **sity of**
by necessity what comes "after" it. **"creation"**

a. *Enn.* IV 8, 6, 1-16 Br.:

Εἴπερ οὖν δεῖ μὴ ἓν μόνον εἶναι — ἐκέκρυπτο γὰρ ἂν πάντα μορφὴν ἐν
ἐκείνῳ οὐκ ἔχοντα, οὐδ' ἂν ὑπῆρχέ τι τῶν ὄντων στάντος ἐν αὐτῷ ἐκείνου,
οὐδ' ἂν τὸ πλῆθος ἦν ἂν τῶν ὄντων τούτων τῶν ἀπὸ τοῦ ἑνὸς γεννηθέντων
μὴ τῶν μετ' αὐτὸ τὴν πρόοδον λαβόντων, ἃ ψυχῶν εἴληχε τάξιν· τὸν αὐτὸν
τρόπον οὐδὲ ψυχὰς ἔδει μόνον εἶναι μὴ τῶν δι' αὐτὰς γενομένων φανέντων,
εἴπερ ἑκάστῃ φύσει τοῦτο ἔνεστι τὸ μετ' αὐτὴν ποιεῖν καὶ ἐξελίττεσθαι οἷον
σπέρματος ἔκ τινος ἀμεροῦς ἀρχῆς εἰς τέλος τὸ αἰσθητὸν ἰούσῃ, μένοντος
μὲν ἀεὶ τοῦ προτέρου ἐν τῇ οἰκείᾳ ἕδρᾳ, τοῦ δὲ μετ' αὐτὸ οἷον γεννωμένου
ἐκ δυνάμεως ἀφάτου, ὅση ἦν ἐν ἐκείνῳ, ἣν οὐκ ἔδει στῆσαι οἷον περιγράψαντα
φθόνῳ, χωρεῖν δὲ ἀεί, ἕως εἰς ἔσχατον μέχρι τοῦ δυνατοῦ τὰ πάντα ἥκῃ
αἰτίᾳ δυνάμεως ἀπλέτου ἐπὶ πάντα παρ' αὐτῆς πεμπούσης καὶ οὐδὲν περιιδεῖν
ἄμοιρον αὐτῆς δυναμένης.

b. *Enn.* IV 3, 17, 12-16 Br.:

Ἔστι γάρ τι οἷον κέντρον, ἐπὶ δὲ τούτῳ κύκλος ἀπ' αὐτοῦ ἐκλάμπων, ἐπὶ δὲ τούτοις ἄλλος, φῶς ἐκ φωτός· ἔξωθεν δὲ τούτων οὐκέτι φωτὸς κύκλος ἄλλος, ἀλλὰ δεόμενος οὗτος, οἰκείου φωτὸς ἀπορίᾳ, αὐγῆς ἀλλοτρίας.

The first circle of light, radiating from the centre, is Noûs (Cp. V 3, 12, l. 40-48). The second circle is Soul, ἔξωθεν περὶ τοῦτον (sc. τὸν Νοῦν) χορεύουσα, as it is said in I 8, 2, l. 23 f.
The light of soul at its utmost confines turns into darkness, and soul merely by its presence forms this darkness. This is the origin of the sensible world (texts under **c** and **d**).

c. *Enn.* IV 3, 9, 23-30; 34-36:

Τῆς δὴ στάσεως αὐτῆς (sc. τῆς ψυχῆς) ἐν αὐτῇ τῇ στάσει οἱονεὶ ῥωννυμένης οἷον πολὺ φῶς ἐκλάμψαν ἐπ' ἄκροις τοῖς ἐσχάτοις τοῦ πυρὸς σκότος ἐγίγνετο, 2 ὅπερ ἰδοῦσα ἡ ψυχή, ἐπείπερ ὑπέστη, ἐμόρφωσεν αὐτό. Οὐ γὰρ ἦν θεμιτὸν γειτονοῦντι αὐτῇ λόγου ἄμοιρον εἶναι, οἷον ἐδέχετο τὸ λεγόμενον, ἀμυδρὸν ἐν ἀμυδρῷ τῷ γενομένῳ. Γενόμενος δὴ οἷον οἶκός τις καλὸς καὶ ποικίλος οὐκ ἀπετμήθη τοῦ πεποιηκότος· ... ἔμψυχος τῷ τοιούτῳ τρόπῳ, ἔχων ψυχὴν 3 οὐχ αὑτοῦ, ἀλλ' αὑτῷ, κρατούμενος οὐ κρατῶν, καὶ ἐχόμενος ἀλλ' οὐκ ἔχων. 3

d. *Enn.* V 9, 9, 8-15:

Ὡς γὰρ ὄντος λόγου ζῴου τινός, οὔσης δὲ καὶ ὕλης τῆς τὸν λόγον τὸν σπερματικὸν δεξαμένης, ἀνάγκη ζῷον γενέσθαι, τὸν αὐτὸν τρόπον καὶ φύσεως 1 νοερᾶς καὶ παντοδυνάμου οὔσης καὶ οὐδενὸς διείργοντος, μηδενὸς ὄντος μεταξὺ τούτου καὶ τοῦ δέξασθαι δυναμένου, ἀνάγκη τὸ μὲν κοσμηθῆναι, τὸ δὲ κοσμῆσαι. Καὶ τὸ μὲν κοσμηθὲν ἔχει τὸ εἶδος μεμερισμένον, ἀλλαχοῦ ἄνθρωπον καὶ ἀλλαχοῦ ἥλιον· τὸ δὲ ἐν ἑνὶ πάντα. 1

Creation explained

1366—*How* was it that anything sprang from the First Principle? — P. answers: The First Principle remains in itself and turned to itself. By its fullness it overflows (ἐξερρύη) and shines around (περιλάμπει — περίλαμψις).

Which means: "creation" is an *eternal relation*; it is *not an act of the will*. There is "love" of the created Spirit and Soul for its Creator; not the reverse.

Enn. V 1, 6, 4-54:

Πῶς ἐξ ἑνὸς τοιούτου ὄντος, οἷον λέγομεν τὸ ἓν εἶναι, ὑπόστασιν ἔσχεν ὁτιοῦν εἴτε πλῆθος εἴτε δυὰς εἴτε ἀριθμός, ἀλλ' οὐκ ἔμεινεν ἐκεῖνο ἐφ' ἑαυτοῦ, 5 **abundance** τοσοῦτον δὲ πλῆθος ἐ ξ ε ρ ρ ύ η, ὃ ὁρᾶται μὲν ἐν τοῖς οὖσιν, ἀνάγειν δὲ αὐτὸ πρὸς ἐκεῖνο ἀξιοῦμεν; Ὧδε οὖν λεγέσθω θεὸν αὐτὸν ἐπικαλεσαμένοις οὐ

λόγῳ γεγωνῷ, ἀλλὰ τῇ ψυχῇ ἐκτείνασιν ἑαυτοὺς εἰς εὐχὴν πρὸς ἐκεῖνον,
εὔχεσθαι τὸν τρόπον τοῦτον δυναμένους μόνους πρὸς μόνον. Δεῖ τοίνυν θεατὴν
ἐκείνου ἐν τῷ εἴσω οἷον νεῷ ἐφ᾽ ἑαυτοῦ ὄντος, μένοντος ἡσύχου ἐπέκεινα ἁπάντων,
τὰ οἷον πρὸς τὰ ἔξω ἤδη ἀγάλματα ἑστῶτα, μᾶλλον δὲ ἄγαλμα τὸ πρῶτον ἐκφανὲν θεᾶσθαι πεφηνὸς τοῦτον τὸν τρόπον· παντὶ τῷ κινουμένῳ δεῖ τι εἶναι,
πρὸς ὃ κινεῖται· μὴ ὄντος δὲ ἐκείνῳ μηδενὸς μὴ τιθώμεθα αὐτὸ κινεῖσθαι, ἀλλ᾽
εἴ τι μετ᾽ αὐτὸ γίνεται, ἐπιστραφέντος ἀεὶ ἐκείνου πρὸς αὐτὸ ἀναγκαῖόν ἐστι
γεγονέναι. (Ἐκποδὼν δὲ ἡμῖν ἔστω γένεσις ἡ ἐν χρόνῳ τὸν λόγον περὶ τῶν ἀεὶ
ὄντων ποιουμένοις· τῷ δὲ λόγῳ τὴν γένεσιν προσάπτοντας αὐτοῖς αἰτίας καὶ
τάξεως ἀποδόσει)· τὸ γοῦν γινόμενον ἐκεῖθεν οὐ κινηθέντος φατέον γίνεσθαι·
εἰ γὰρ κινηθέντος αὐτοῦ τι γίνοιτο, τρίτον ἀπ᾽ ἐκείνου τὸ γινόμενον μετὰ τὴν
κίνησιν ἂν γίνοιτο καὶ οὐ δεύτερον. Δεῖ οὖν ἀκινήτου ὄντος, εἴ τι δεύτερον μετ᾽
αὐτό, οὐ προσνεύσαντος οὐδὲ βουληθέντος οὐδὲ ὅλως κινηθέντος ὑποστῆναι
αὐτό. Πῶς οὖν; Καὶ τί δεῖ νοῆσαι περὶ ἐκεῖνο μένον; Π ε ρ ί λ α μ ψ ι ν ἐξ   *radiation*
αὐτοῦ μέν, ἐξ αὐτοῦ δὲ μένοντος, οἷον ἡλίου τὸ περὶ αὐτὸν λαμπρὸν φῶς περιθέον,
ἐξ αὐτοῦ ἀεὶ γεννώμενον μένοντος. Καὶ πάντα τὰ ὄντα ἕως μένει ἐκ τῆς αὐτῶν
οὐσίας ἀναγκαίαν τὴν περὶ αὐτὰ πρὸς τὸ ἔξω αὐτῶν ἐκ τῆς παρούσης δυνάμεως
δίδωσιν αὐτῶν ἐξηρτημένην ὑπόστασιν, εἰκόνα οὖσαν οἷον ἀρχετύπων ὧν ἐξέφυ,
πῦρ μὲν τὴν παρ᾽ αὐτοῦ θερμότητα· καὶ χιὼν οὐκ εἴσω μόνον τὸ ψυχρὸν κατέχει·
μάλιστα δὲ ὅσα εὐώδη μαρτυρεῖ τούτῳ· ἕως γὰρ ἔστι, πρόεισί τι ἐξ αὐτῶν περὶ
αὐτά, ὧν ἀπολαύει ὑποστάντων ὅ τι πλησίον. Καὶ πάντα δὲ ὅσα ἤδη τέλεια
γεννᾷ· τὸ δὴ ἀεὶ τέλειον ἀεὶ καὶ ἀΐδιον γεννᾷ· καὶ ἔλαττον δὲ ἑαυτοῦ γεννᾷ.
Τί οὖν χρὴ περὶ τοῦ τελειοτάτου λέγειν; Μηδὲν ἀπ᾽ αὐτοῦ ἢ τὰ μέγιστα μετ᾽
αὐτό. Μέγιστον δὲ μετ᾽ αὐτὸ νοῦς καὶ δεύτερον· καὶ γὰρ ὁρᾷ ὁ νοῦς ἐκεῖνο καὶ
δεῖται αὐτοῦ μόνου· ἐκεῖνο δὲ τούτου οὐδέν· καὶ τὸ γεννώμενον ἀπὸ κρείττονος
νοῦ νοῦν εἶναι, καὶ κρείττων ἁπάντων νοῦς, ὅτι τἆλλα μετ᾽ αὐτόν· οἷον καὶ ἡ
ψυχὴ λόγος νοῦ καὶ ἐνέργειά τις, ὥσπερ αὐτὸς ἐκείνου. Ἀλλὰ ψυχῆς μὲν ἀμυδρὸς
ὁ λόγος· ὡς γὰρ εἴδωλον νοῦ, ταύτῃ καὶ εἰς νοῦν βλέπειν δεῖ· νοῦς δὲ ὡσαύτως
πρὸς ἐκεῖνο, ἵνα ᾖ νοῦς. Ὁρᾷ δὲ αὐτὸ οὐ χωρισθείς, ἀλλ᾽ ὅτι μετ᾽ αὐτὸ καὶ
μεταξὺ οὐδέν, ὡς οὐδὲ ψυχῆς καὶ νοῦ. Ποθεῖ δὲ πᾶν τὸ γεννῆσαν <τὸ γεγεννη-
μένον> καὶ τοῦτο ἀγαπᾷ, καὶ μάλιστα ὅταν ὦσι μόνοι τὸ γεννῆσαν καὶ τὸ γε-
γεννημένον· ὅταν δὲ καὶ τὸ ἄριστον ᾖ τὸ γεννῆσαν, ἐξ ἀνάγκης σύνεστιν αὐτῷ,
ὡς τῇ ἑτερότητι μόνον κεχωρίσθαι.

1367—Enn. VI 9, 9, 1-13.   An eternal
relation

The soul dances as it were round the First Principle.

Ἐν δὲ ταύτῃ τῇ χορείᾳ καθορᾷ πηγὴν μὲν ζωῆς, πηγὴν δὲ νοῦ, ἀρχὴν ὄντος,
ἀγαθοῦ αἰτίαν, ῥίζαν ψυχῆς· οὐκ ἐκχεομένων ἀπ᾽ αὐτοῦ ἐκείνων, εἶτ᾽ ἐλατ-
τούντων· οὐ γὰρ ὄγκος· ἢ φθαρτὰ ἂν ἦν τὰ γεννώμενα. Νῦν δέ ἐστιν ἀΐδια,

ὅτι ἡ ἀρχὴ αὐτῶν ὡσαύτως μένει οὐ μεμερισμένη εἰς αὐτά, ἀλλ' ὅλη μένουσα. 5
Διὸ κἀκεῖνα μένει· οἷον εἰ μένοντος ἡλίου καὶ τὸ φῶς μένει. Οὐ γὰρ ἀποτετμήμεθα οὐδὲ χωρὶς ἐσμέν, εἰ καὶ παρεμπεσοῦσα ἡ σώματος φύσις πρὸς αὐτὴν
ἡμᾶς εἵλκυσεν, ἀλλ' ἐμπνέομεν καὶ σῳζόμεθα οὐ δόντος, εἶτα ἀποστάντος   1
ἐκείνου, ἀλλ' ἀεὶ χορηγοῦντος ἕως ἂν ᾖ ὅπερ ἐστί. Μᾶλλον μέντοι ἐσμὲν νεύσαντες
πρὸς αὐτὸ καὶ τὸ εὖ ἐνταῦθα, τὸ <δὲ> πόρρω εἶναι μόνον καὶ ἧττον εἶναι· —

Creation is not by deliberation or providence

1368—The First Principle is beyond thinking and intelligence. It is
something like eternal waking, not distinct from its subject. All things
spring from it, but evidently not by any kind of deliberation or by any
act of conscious providence.

    a. *Enn.* VI 8, 16, 31-38 Br.:

Εἰ οὖν μὴ γέγονε, ἀλλ' ἦν ἀεὶ ἡ ἐνέργεια αὐτοῦ καὶ οἷον ἐγρήγορσις οὐκ ἄλλου
ὄντος τοῦ ἐγρηγορότος, ἐγρήγορσις καὶ ὑπερνόησις ἀεὶ οὖσα, ἔστιν οὕτως, 3
ὡς ἐγρηγόρησεν. Ἡ δὲ ἐγρήγορσίς ἐστιν ἐπέκεινα οὐσίας καὶ νοῦ καὶ ζωῆς
ἔμφρονος· ταῦτα δὲ αὐτός ἐστι. Αὐτὸς ἄρα ἐστὶν ἐνέργεια ὑπὲρ νοῦν καὶ
φρόνησιν καὶ ζωήν· ἐξ αὐτοῦ δὲ ταῦτα καὶ οὐ παρ' ἄλλου.

    b. Ib., 17, 1-12 Br.:

Ἔτι δὲ καὶ ὧδε· ἕκαστά φαμεν τὰ ἐν τῷ παντὶ καὶ τόδε τὸ πᾶν οὕτως
ἔχειν, ὡς ἂν ἔσχεν, ὡς ἡ τοῦ ποιοῦντος προαίρεσις ἠθέλησε, καὶ ὡς ἂν προθέ-
μενος, καὶ προϊδὼν ἐν λογισμοῖς κατὰ πρόνοιαν οὕτως εἰργάσατο· ἀεὶ δὲ οὕτως
ἐχόντων καὶ ἀεὶ οὕτως γιγνομένων, οὕτω τοι καὶ ἀεὶ ἐν τοῖς ποιοῦσι κεῖσθαι 5
τοὺς λόγους ἐν μείζονι εὐθημοσύνῃ ἑστῶτας· ὥστε ἐπέκεινα προνοίας τἀκεῖ
εἶναι καὶ ἐπέκεινα προαιρέσεως καὶ πάντα ἀεὶ νοερῶς ἑστηκότα εἶναι, ὅσα
ἐν τῷ ὄντι. Ὥστε τὴν οὕτω διάθεσιν εἴ τις ὀνομάζοι πρόνοιαν, οὕτω νοείτω,   1
ὅτι ἐστὶ πρὸ τοῦδε νοῦς τοῦ παντὸς ἑστώς, ἀφ' οὗ καὶ καθ' ὃν τὸ πᾶν τόδε.

    Cp. below, the nrs. **1426**, **1429**.

    1369—The sensible universe does not come into being by deliberation
either. As we saw above (**1365c, d**), an "image" of the intelligible Form
appears in the ὕλη by the mere "neighbourhood" of the intelligible being.

How sensible things arise

    a. *Enn.* V 8, 7, 1-16 Br.:

Τοῦτο δὴ τὸ πᾶν, ἐπείπερ συγχωροῦμεν παρ' ἄλλου αὐτὸ εἶναι καὶ τοιοῦτον
εἶναι, ἆρα οἰώμεθα τὸν ποιητὴν αὐτοῦ ἐπινοῆσαι παρ' αὑτῷ γῆν καὶ ταύτην
ἐν μέσῳ δεῖν στῆναι, εἶτα ὕδωρ καὶ ἐπὶ τῇ γῇ τοῦτο καὶ τὰ ἄλλα ἐν τάξει μέχρι
τοῦ οὐρανοῦ, εἶτα ζῷα πάντα καὶ τούτοις μορφὰς τοιαύτας ἑκάστῳ, ὅσαι νῦν 5
εἰσι, καὶ τὰ ἔνδον ἑκάστοις σπλάγχνα καὶ τὰ ἔξω μέρη, εἶτα διατιθέντα ἕκαστα

παρ' αὐτῷ οὕτως ἐπιχειρεῖν τῷ ἔργῳ; Ἀλλ' οὔτε ἡ ἐπίνοια δυνατὴ ἡ τοιαύτη·
πόθεν γὰρ ἐπῆλθεν οὐπώποτε ἑωρακότι; Οὔτε ἐξ ἄλλου λαβόντι δυνατὸν ἦν
ἐργάσασθαι, ὅπως νῦν οἱ δημιουργοὶ ποιοῦσι χερσὶ καὶ ὀργάνοις χρώμενοι·
ὕστερον γὰρ καὶ χεῖρες καὶ πόδες. Λείπεται τοίνυν εἶναι μὲν πάντα ἐν ἄλλῳ,
οὐδενὸς δὲ μεταξὺ ὄντος τῇ <τοῦ> ἐν τῷ ὄντι πρὸς ἄλλο γειτονείᾳ οἷον ἐξαίφνης
ἀναφανῆναι ἴνδαλμα καὶ εἰκόνα ἐκείνου εἴτε αὐτόθεν εἴτε ψυχῆς διακονησαμένης
(διαφέρει γὰρ οὐδὲν ἐν τῷ παρόντι) ἢ ψυχῆς τινος.

b. Everything here has its archetypon in the intelligible world or
Noûs.

Noûs con-
tains the
archetypa of
all sensible
things

Enn. V 8, 7, 16-18 Br.:

Ἀλλ' οὖν ἐκεῖθεν ἦν σύμπαντα ταῦτα, καὶ καλλιόνως ἐκεῖ· τὰ γὰρ τῇδε
μέμικται, καὶ οὐκ ἐκεῖνα μέμικται.

c. *Enn.* V 9, 5, 17-23; 26-29 Br.:

Τὸ γὰρ πρῶτον ἕκαστον οὐ τὸ αἰσθητόν· τὸ γὰρ ἐν αὐτοῖς εἶδος ἐπὶ ὕλῃ
εἴδωλον ὄντος, πᾶν τε εἶδος ἐν ἄλλῳ παρ' ἄλλου εἰς ἐκεῖνο ἔρχεται καὶ ἐστιν
εἰκὼν ἐκείνου. Εἰ δὲ καὶ ποιητὴν δεῖ εἶναι τοῦδε τοῦ παντός, οὐ τὰ ἐν τῷ
μήπω ὄντι οὗτος νοήσει, ἵνα αὐτὸ ποιῇ. Πρὸ τοῦ κόσμου ἄρα δεῖ εἶναι ἐκεῖνα,
οὐ τύπους ἀφ' ἑτέρων, ἀλλὰ καὶ ἀρχέτυπα καὶ πρῶτα καὶ νοῦ οὐσίαν. — Ὁ
νοῦς ἄρα τὰ ὄντα ὄντως, οὐχ οἷά ἐστιν ἄλλοθι νοῶν· οὐ γὰρ ἔστιν οὔτε πρὸ
αὐτοῦ οὔτε μετ' αὐτόν· ἀλλὰ οἷον νομοθέτης πρῶτος, μᾶλλον δὲ νόμος αὐτὸς
τοῦ εἶναι.

Cp. also **1376**, **1426**.

1370—a. A summary of the theory of the three hypostases.

The three
hypostases

Enn. V 2, 1, 1-22 Br.:

Τὸ ἓν πάντα καὶ οὐδὲ ἕν· ἀρχὴ γὰρ πάντων οὐ πάντα, ἀλλ' ἐκεῖνο πάντα·
ἐκεῖ γὰρ οἷον ἀνέδραμε· μᾶλλον δὲ οὔπω ἔστιν, ἀλλ' ἔσται. — Πῶς οὖν ἐξ
ἁπλοῦ ἑνὸς οὐδεμιᾶς ἐν ταὐτῷ φαινομένης ποικιλίας, οὐ διπλόης ὁτουοῦν; —
Ἦ ὅτι οὐδὲν ἦν ἐν αὐτῷ, διὰ τοῦτο ἐξ αὐτοῦ πάντα, καὶ ἵνα τὸ ὂν ᾖ, διὰ τοῦτο
αὐτὸ οὐκ ὄν, γεννητὴς δὲ αὐτοῦ· καὶ πρώτη οἷον γέννησις αὕτη· ὂν γὰρ τέλειον
τῷ μηδὲν ζητεῖν μηδὲ ἔχειν μηδὲ δεῖσθαι οἷον ὑπερερρύη καὶ τὸ ὑπερπλῆρες
αὐτοῦ πεποίηκεν ἄλλο· τὸ δὲ γενόμενον εἰς αὐτὸ ἐπεστράφη καὶ ἐπληρώθη καὶ
ἐγένετο πρὸς αὐτὸ βλέπον καὶ νοῦς οὕτως. Καὶ ἡ μὲν πρὸς ἐκεῖνο στάσις αὐτοῦ
τὸ ὂν ἐποίησεν, ἡ δὲ πρὸς αὐτὸ θέα τὸν νοῦν. Ἐπεὶ οὖν ἔστη πρὸς αὐτό, ἵνα ἴδῃ,
ὁμοῦ νοῦς γίνεται καὶ ὄν.

Οὕτως οὖν ὢν οἷον ἐκεῖνος τὰ ὅμοια ποιεῖ δύναμιν προχέας πολλήν· εἶδος δὲ καὶ τοῦτο αὐτοῦ, ὥσπερ τὸ πρὸ αὐτοῦ πρότερον προέχεε. Καὶ αὕτη ἐκ τῆς οὐσίας ἐνέργεια ψυχὴ τοῦτο μένοντος ἐκείνου γενομένη· καὶ γὰρ ὁ νοῦς μένοντος τοῦ πρὸ αὐτοῦ ἐγένετο. — Ἡ δὲ οὐ μένουσα ποιεῖ, ἀλλὰ κινηθεῖσα ἐγέννα εἴδωλον. Ἐκεῖ μὲν οὖν βλέπουσα, ὅθεν ἐγένετο, πληροῦται, προελθοῦσα δὲ εἰς κίνησιν ἄλλην καὶ ἐναντίαν γεννᾷ εἴδωλον αὑτῆς αἴσθησιν καὶ φύσιν τὴν ἐν 2 τοῖς φυτοῖς. — Οὐδὲν δὲ τοῦ πρὸ αὐτοῦ ἀπήρτηται οὐδ' ἀποτέτμηται· —

b. It is illustrated by the following simile.

Enn. V 6, 4, 16-22 Br.:

Καὶ οὖν ἀπεικαστέον τὸ μὲν φωτί, τὸ δὲ ἐφεξῆς ἡλίῳ, τὸ δὲ τρίτον τῷ σελήνης ἄστρῳ κομιζομένῳ τὸ φῶς παρ' ἡλίου. Ψυχὴ μὲν γὰρ ἐπακτὸν νοῦν ἔχει ἐπιχρωννύντα αὐτὴν νοερὰν οὖσαν, νοῦς δ' ἐν αὐτῷ οἰκεῖον ἔχει οὐ φῶς ὢν μόνον, ἀλλ' ὅ ἐστι πεφωτισμένον ἐν τῇ αὑτοῦ οὐσίᾳ, τὸ δὲ παρέχον τούτῳ 2 τὸ φῶς οὐκ ἄλλο ὂν φῶς ἐστιν ἁπλοῦν παρέχον τὴν δύναμιν ἐκείνῳ τοῦ εἶναι ὃ ἔστι.

c. The One, Noûs and Soul—these three principles must be assumed. No more than these and no less.

For the One *must* be distinguished as the absolute Principle from Noûs which is all, and Noûs from Soul which is nearest to ὕλη. But neither the First nor the second Principle could be doubled, e.g. by saying that the one is potential, the other in act; for the One is beyond this distinction, and Noûs is always "act". Nor is it allowed to place Logos as another hypostasis between Noûs and Soul; for Soul depends on Noûs directly. There could be nothing between.

There are three and no more than three hypostases

Enn. II 9, 1, l. 1-33, 57-63; c. 2, l. 1-2:

Ἐπειδὴ τοίνυν ἐφάνη ἡμῖν ἡ τοῦ ἀγαθοῦ ἁπλῆ φύσις καὶ πρώτη — πᾶν γὰρ τὸ οὐ πρῶτον οὐχ ἁπλοῦν — καὶ οὐδὲν ἔχον ἐν ἑαυτῷ, ἀλλὰ ἕν τι, καὶ τοῦ ἑνὸς λεγομένου ἡ φύσις ἡ αὐτή — καὶ γὰρ αὕτη οὐκ ἄλλο, εἶτα ἕν, οὐδὲ τοῦτο ἄλλο, εἶτα ἀγαθόν —, ὅταν λέγωμεν τὸ ἕν, καὶ ὅταν λέγωμεν τἀγαθόν, ταύτην δεῖ 5 νομίζειν τὴν φύσιν καὶ μίαν λέγειν οὐ κατηγοροῦντας ἐκείνης οὐδέν, δηλοῦντας δὲ ἡμῖν αὐτοῖς ὡς οἷόν τε. Καὶ τὸ πρῶτον δὲ οὕτως, ὅτι ἁπλούστατον, καὶ τὸ αὔταρκες, ὅτι οὐκ ἐκ πλειόνων· οὕτω γὰρ ἀναρτηθήσεται εἰς τὰ ἐξ ὧν· καὶ οὐκ ἐν ἄλλῳ, ὅτι πᾶν τὸ ἐν ἄλλῳ καὶ παρ' ἄλλου. Εἰ οὖν μηδὲ παρ' ἄλλου 1 μηδὲ ἐν ἄλλῳ μηδὲ σύνθεσις μηδεμία, ἀνάγκη μηδὲν ὑπὲρ αὐτὸ εἶναι. Οὐ τοίνυν δεῖ ἐφ' ἑτέρας ἀρχὰς ἰέναι, ἀλλὰ τοῦτο προστησαμένους, εἶτα νοῦν μετ' αὐτὸ καὶ τὸ νοοῦν πρώτως, εἶτα ψυχὴν μετὰ νοῦν — αὕτη γὰρ τάξις κατὰ φύσιν — 1 μήτε πλείω τούτων τίθεσθαι ἐν τῷ νοητῷ, μήτε ἐλάττω. Εἴτε γὰρ ἐλάττω, ἢ ψυχὴν καὶ νοῦν ταὐτὸν φήσουσιν, ἢ νοῦν καὶ τὸ πρῶτον· ἀλλ' ὅτι ἕτερα ἀλλήλων, ἐδείχθη πολλαχῇ. Λοιπὸν δὲ ἐπισκέψασθαι ἐν τῷ παρόντι, εἰ πλείω τῶν τριῶν τούτων, τίνες ἂν οὖν εἶεν φύσεις παρ' αὐτάς. Τῆς τέ γὰρ λεχθείσης οὕτως ἔχειν ἀρχῆς τῆς πάντων οὐδεὶς ἂν εὕροι ἁπλουστέραν οὐδ' ἐπαναβεβηκυῖαν ἡντινοῦν. Οὐ γὰρ δὴ τὴν μὲν δυνάμει, τὴν δὲ ἐνεργείᾳ φήσουσι· γελοῖον γὰρ ἐν τοῖς ἐνεργείᾳ οὖσι καὶ ἀΰλοις τὸ δυνάμει καὶ ἐνεργείᾳ διαιρουμένους φύσεις ποιεῖσθαι πλείους. 'Αλλ' οὐδὲ ἐν τοῖς μετὰ ταῦτα· οὐδ' ἐπινοεῖν τὸν μέν τινα νοῦν ἐν ἡσυχίᾳ τινί, τὸν δὲ οἷον κινούμενον. Τίς γὰρ ἂν ἡσυχία νοῦ καὶ τίς κίνησις καὶ προφορὰ ἂν εἴη ἢ τίς ἀργία καὶ τοῦ ἑτέρου τί ἔργον; "Εστι γὰρ ὡς ἔστι νοῦς ἀεὶ ὡσαύτως ἐνεργείᾳ κείμενος ἑστώσῃ· κίνησις δὲ πρὸς αὐτὸν καὶ περὶ αὐτὸν ψυχῆς ἤδη ἔργον καὶ λόγος ἀπ' αὐτοῦ εἰς ψυχὴν ψυχὴν νοερὰν ποιῶν, οὐκ ἄλλην τινὰ μεταξὺ νοῦ καὶ ψυχῆς φύσιν. — Τὸν δὲ λόγον ὅταν τις ἀπὸ τοῦ νοῦ ποιῇ, εἶτα ἀπὸ τούτου γίνεσθαι ἐν ψυχῇ ἄλλον ἀπ' αὐτοῦ τοῦ λόγου, ἵνα μεταξὺ ψυχῆς καὶ νοῦ ᾖ οὗτος, ἀποστερήσει τὴν ψυχὴν τοῦ νοεῖν, εἰ μὴ παρὰ τοῦ νοῦ κομιεῖται, ἀλλὰ παρὰ ἄλλου τοῦ μεταξὺ τὸν λόγον· καὶ εἴδωλον λόγου, ἀλλ' οὐ λόγον ἕξει, καὶ ὅλως οὐκ εἰδήσει νοῦν οὐδὲ ὅλως νοήσει. —

(2) Οὐ τοίνυν οὔτε πλείω τούτων οὔτε ἐπινοίας περιττὰς ἐν ἐκείνοις ... θετέον.

Thus, P. maintains his doctrine of the three hypostases against Valentinian gnostics, who first double the First Principle and next introduce a whole series of other spiritual beings to populate their pleroma (above, nr. **1333**).

3—SOUL: ITS ΜΕΣΗ ΤΑΞΙΣ

Since for Plotinus soul is, by its self-reflection, the true starting-point of man's ascent to the Source of all things, or (as he says in V 1, 1) "to the Father", we begin our more detailed exposition by considering soul.

1371—Soul is the cause of the unity of bodies. Therefore, it must be itself a unity, though not an absolute one.

a. *Enn.* VI 2, 5, 1-10 Br.:

Πρῶτον δὲ τοῦτο ἐνθυμητέον ὡς, ἐπειδὴ τὰ σώματα, οἷον τῶν ζῴων καὶ τῶν φυτῶν, ἕκαστον αὐτῶν πολλά ἐστι καὶ χρώμασι καὶ σχήμασι καὶ μεγέθεσι καὶ εἴδεσι μερῶν καὶ ἄλλο ἄλλοθι, ἔρχεται δὲ τὰ πάντα ἐξ ἑνός, ἢ παντάπασιν ἐξ ἑνὸς ἢ ἕξει πάντῃ παντὸς ἑνός· ἢ μᾶλλον μὲν ἑνὸς ἢ οἷον τὸ ἐξ αὐτοῦ, ὥστε καὶ μᾶλλον ὄντος ἢ τὸ γενόμενον· ὅσῳ γὰρ πρὸς ἓν ἡ ἀπόστασις, τόσῳ καὶ πρὸς ὄν. 'Επεὶ οὖν ἐξ ἑνός μέν, οὐχ οὕτω δὲ ἑνός, ὡς πάντῃ ἓν ἢ αὐτοέν (οὐ γὰρ ἂν διεστηκὸς πλῆθος ἐποίει) λείπεται εἶναι ἐκ πλήθους ἑνός. Τὸ δὲ ποιοῦν ἦν ψυχή· τοῦτο ἄρα πλῆθος ἕν.

Soul is
plurality-
unity

b. It is, therefore, both μεριστή and ἀμέριστος [1], but essentially the latter, since it belongs to the θεία φύσις, as is said in IV 7, 10.

Enn. IV 2, 1, 62-76 Br.:

'Η δ' ὁμοῦ μεριστή τε καὶ ἀμέριστος φύσις, ἣν δὴ ψυχὴν εἶναί φαμεν, οὐχ οὕτως ὡς τὸ συνεχὲς μία, μέρος ἄλλο, τὸ δ' ἄλλο ἔχουσα· ἀλλὰ μεριστὴ μέν, ὅτι ἐν πᾶσι μέρεσι τοῦ ἐν ᾧ ἔστιν, ἀμέριστος δέ, ὅτι ὅλη ἐν πᾶσι καὶ ἐν ὁτῳοῦν 6 αὐτῶν ὅλη. Καὶ ὁ τοῦτο κατιδὼν τὸ μέγεθος τῆς ψυχῆς καὶ τὴν δύναμιν αὐτῆς εἴσεται, ὡς θεῖον τὸ χρῆμα αὐτῆς καὶ θαυμαστὸν καὶ τῶν ὑπὲρ τὰ χρήματα φύσεων. Μέγεθος οὐκ ἔχουσα παντὶ μεγέθει σύνεστι καὶ ὡδὶ οὖσα ὡδὶ πάλιν αὖ ἐστιν 7 οὐκ ἄλλῳ, ἀλλὰ τῷ αὐτῷ· ὥστε μεμερίσθαι καὶ μὴ μεμερίσθαι αὖ, μᾶλλον δὲ μὴ μεμερίσθαι αὐτὴν μηδὲ μεμερισμένην γεγονέναι· μένει γὰρ μεθ' ἑαυτῆς ὅλη, περὶ δὲ τὰ σώματά ἐστι μεμερισμένη τῶν σωμάτων τῷ οἰκείῳ μεριστῷ οὐ δυναμένων αὐτὴν ἀμερίστως δέξασθαι· ὥστε εἶναι τῶν σωμάτων πάθημα 7 τὸν μερισμόν, οὐκ αὐτῆς.

P. speaks repeatedly of the relation of μεριστόν and ἀμέριστον in the soul. His most explicit and definite view of it is found in IV 3, 19.

c. Since it is essentially indivisible, soul cannot be the entelechy of the body. It belongs to "true being" in the Platonic sense of the term.

Soul is not the entelechy of the body

Enn. IV 7, 8⁵, l. 35-51:

Πῶς δ' ἂν καὶ ἀμερὴς οὖσα μεριστοῦ τοῦ σώματος ἐντελέχεια γένοιτο 3 μεριστή; Ἥ τε αὐτὴ ψυχὴ ἐξ ἄλλου ζῴου ἄλλου γίνεται· πῶς οὖν ἡ τοῦ προτέρου τοῦ ἐφεξῆς ἂν γένοιτο, εἰ ἦν ἐντελέχεια ἑνός; Φαίνεται δὲ τοῦτο ἐκ τῶν μεταβαλλόντων ζῴων εἰς ἄλλα ζῷα. Οὐκ ἄρα τῷ εἶδος εἶναί τινος τὸ 4 εἶναι ἔχει, ἀλλ' ἔστιν οὐσία οὐ παρὰ τοῦ ἐν σώματι ἱδρῦσθαι τὸ εἶναι λαμβάνουσα, ἀλλ' οὖσα πρὶν καὶ τοῦδε γενέσθαι οἷον ζῴου, οὗ τὸ σῶμα τὴν ψυχὴν γεννήσει. Τίς οὖν οὐσία αὐτῆς; Εἰ δὲ μήτε σῶμα, μήτε πάθος σώματος, πρᾶξις δὲ καὶ ποίησις, καὶ πολλὰ καὶ ἐν αὐτῇ καὶ ἐξ αὐτῆς, οὐσία παρὰ τὰ 4 σώματα οὖσα ποία τίς ἐστιν; Ἢ δῆλον ὅτι ἣν φαμεν ὄντως οὐσίαν εἶναι. Τὸ μὲν γὰρ γένεσις, ἀλλ' οὐκ οὐσία, πᾶν τὸ σωματικὸν εἶναι λέγοιτ' ἄν, γινόμενον καὶ ἀπολλύμενον, ὄντως δὲ οὐδέποτε ὄν [2], μεταλήψει δὲ τοῦ ὄντος σωζόμενον, καθ' ὅσον ἂν αὐτοῦ μεταλαμβάνῃ. 5

Against the Aristotelian definition of soul as the entelechy of an organical body (above, nr. **636**) P. uses also the following interesting argument: in that case *sleep would be impossible,* for the entelechy is always present and thus soul would not have any opportunity of withdrawing ἄνω! (l. 9-11).

---

[1] The terms are Plato's in *Tim.* 35a. See Gr. Phil. I, nr. **350**.
[2] Cp. Plato, *Ph.* 79a-80b, *Phaedr.* 245 c-e; *Tim.* 27d-28a; *Phil.* 59 ab.

1372—This twofold nature of soul is due to its intermediate position: on the outskirts of the νοητόν, quite close to sensible nature.

a. *Enn.* IV 8, 7, 1-14 Br.:

Its
μέση τάξις

Διττῆς δὲ φύσεως ταύτης οὔσης, τῆς μὲν νοητῆς, τῆς δὲ αἰσθητῆς, ἄμεινον μὲν ψυχῇ ἐν τῷ νοητῷ εἶναι, ἀνάγκη γε μὴν ἔχει καὶ τοῦ αἰσθητοῦ μεταλαμβάνειν τοιαύτην φύσιν ἐχούσῃ, καὶ οὐκ ἀγανακτητέον αὐτήν, εἰ μὴ πάντα ἐστὶ τὸ
5 κρεῖττον, μέσην τάξιν ἐν τοῖς οὖσιν ἐπισχοῦσαν, θείας μὲν μοίρας οὖσαν, ἐν ἐσχάτῳ δὲ τοῦ νοητοῦ οὖσαν, ὡς ὅμορον οὖσαν τῇ αἰσθητῇ φύσει διδόναι μέν τι τούτῳ τῶν παρ' αὐτῆς, ἀντιλαμβάνειν δὲ καὶ παρ' αὐτοῦ, εἰ μὴ μετὰ τοῦ αὐτῆς ἀσφαλοῦς διακοσμοῖ, προθυμίᾳ δὲ πλείονι εἰς τὸ εἴσω δύοιτο μὴ μείνασα ὅλη μεθ' ὅλης, ἄλλως τε καὶ δυνατὸν <ὂν> αὐτῇ πάλιν ἐξαναδῦναι, ἱστορίαν ὧν ἐνταῦθα εἶδέ τε καὶ ἔπαθε προσλαβούσῃ καὶ μαθούσῃ, οἷον ἄρα ἐστὶν ἐκεῖ εἶναι καὶ τῇ παραθέσει τῶν οἷον ἐναντίων σαφέστερον τὰ ἀμείνω μαθούσῃ.

About the question of "how soul can exercise providence in safety for itself", see our next numbers.

As to the intermediate place of soul, we found the idea fairly emphatically in Nemesius of Emesa and traced it back to Posidonius; supra, nr. **1181b**, cp. **1193**. Plotinus, too, knows "intermediate stages" between anorganic and organic nature, between plants and animals, between animals and man. See *Enn.* IV 22-27, on the soul of the earth. In his opinion not only the rational soul of man is eternal, but also the vegetative soul; the soul of animals as well as the soul of plants (*Enn.* IV 7, 14). Cp. above, **1182**.

As to man and his μέση τάξις, we found that the idea comes from the Early Academy (above, nr. **1193**). Later, it plays an important part in the philosophy of Marsilio Ficino. See also below, **1430a**.

b. *Enn.* VI 2, 22, 28-35 Br.:

double
aspect of
soul

Ψυχῆς δὲ ἐνεργούσης ὡς γένους ἢ εἴδους αἱ ἄλλαι ψυχαὶ ὡς εἴδη· καὶ τούτων αἱ ἐνέργειαι διτταί. Ἡ μὲν γὰρ πρὸς τὸ ἄνω νοῦς, ἡ δὲ πρὸς τὸ κάτω αἱ ἄλλαι δυνάμεις κατὰ λόγον· ἡ δὲ ἐσχάτη ὕλης ἤδη ἐφαπτομένη καὶ μορφοῦσα καὶ τὸ κάτω αὐτῆς τὸ ἄλλο πᾶν οὐ κωλύει εἶναι ἄνω. Ἥ καὶ τὸ κάτω λεγόμενον αὐτῆς ἴνδαλμά ἐστιν αὐτῆς, οὐκ ἀποτετμημένον δέ, ἀλλ' ὡς τὰ ἐν τοῖς κατόπτροις,
5 ἕως ἂν τὸ ἀρχέτυπον παρῇ ἔξω.

1373—Soul is at different distances from Noûs: first, there is universal soul (l. 21 ff., τὴν μὲν ἐκ παντός); next, the worldsoul, (l. 26 ff., τῆς μὲν οὖν —) which is the lower part of the first (τῆς κατωτάτω τῆς ψυχῆς τοῦ παντός); then, there is a lower soul of man (l. 28 ff., τοῦ δὲ ἡμῶν κάτω), and finally a higher soul of man (l. 30 ff., τῆς δὲ ἄλλης ψυχῆς —).

a. *Enn.* IV 3, 4, l. 21-37 Br.:

Souls of
different
kinds

Καὶ τὴν μὲν τοῦ παντὸς ἀεὶ ὑπερέχειν τῷ μηδὲ εἶναι αὐτῇ τὸ κατελθεῖν μηδὲ τὸ κάτω μηδὲ ἐπιστροφὴν ‹πρὸς› τὰ τῇδε, τὰς δ' ἡμετέρας ‹οὐκ ἀεὶ› τῷ τε εἶναι ἀφωρισμένον αὐταῖς τὸ μέρος ἐν τῷδε καὶ τῇ ἐπιστροφῇ τοῦ προσδεο- μένου φροντίσεως, τῆς μὲν οὖν ἐοικυίας τῇ ἐν φυτῷ μεγάλῳ ψυχῇ, ἣ ἀπόνως τὸ φυτὸν καὶ ἀψόφως διοικεῖ, τῆς κατωτάτω τῆς ψυχῆς τοῦ παντός, τοῦ δὲ ἡμῶν κάτω, οἷον εἰ εὐλαὶ ἐν σαπέντι μέρει τοῦ φυτοῦ γίνοιντο — οὕτω γὰρ τὸ σῶμα τὸ ἔμψυχον ἐν τῷ παντί· τῆς δὲ ἄλλης ψυχῆς τῆς ὁμοειδοῦς τῶν ἄνω τῆς ὅλης, οἷον εἴ τις γεωργὸς ἐν φροντίδι τῶν ἐν τῷ φυτῷ εὐλῶν γίνοιτο καὶ ταῖς μερίμναις πρὸς τῷ φυτῷ γίνοιτο, ἢ εἴ τις ὑγιαίνοντα μὲν καὶ μετὰ τῶν ἄλλων τῶν ὑγιαινόντων ὄντα πρὸς ἐκείνοις εἶναι λέγοι, πρὸς οἷς ἐστιν ἢ πράττων ἢ θεωρίαις ἑαυτὸν παρέχων, νοσήσαντος δὲ καὶ πρὸς ταῖς τοῦ σώματος θερα- πείαις ὄντος πρὸς τῷ σώματι εἶναι καὶ τοῦ σώματος γεγονέναι.

On the distinction between a "Soul of the universe" which is transcendent, and a soul of the visible world which is δεθεῖσα σώματι, cp. the following passages.

III 5, c. 2 l. 14 ff. and c. 3 l. 27 ff., where Ἀφροδίτη ἡ οὐρανία is opposed to another who belongs to "this world".

II 1, 5, l. 7 ff.: ἀπὸ δὲ τῆς οὐρανίας ἴνδαλμα αὐτῆς ἰὸν καὶ οἷον ἀπορρέον ἀπὸ τῶν ἄνω τὰ ἐπὶ γῆς ζῷα ποιεῖν.

II 3, 9, l. 31 ff.: καὶ πᾶς ὁ κόσμος δὲ ὁ μὲν τὸ ἐκ σώματος καὶ ψυχῆς τινος δεθείσης σώματι, ὁ δὲ ἡ τοῦ παντὸς ψυχὴ ἡ μὴ ἐν σώματι, ἐλλάμπουσα δὲ ἴχνη τῇ ἐν σώματι.

II 3, 17, l. 15 ff.: Νοῦς δὴ ψυχῇ δίδωσι τῇ τοῦ παντὸς (τοὺς λόγους), ψυχὴ δὲ παρ' αὐτῆς ἡ μετὰ Νοῦν τῇ μετ' αὐτὴν ἐλλάμπουσα καὶ τυποῦσα, ἡ δὲ ὡσπερεὶ ἐπιταχθεῖσα ἤδη ποιεῖ.

II 3, 18 l. 12: τὸ ἐξ αὐτῆς ἴνδαλμα.

b. Universal soul is more creative than particular souls, because the first is nearer to Noûs.

Universal soul and particular souls

Enn. IV 3, 6, l. 21-34 Br.:

Τῶν γὰρ ἐκεῖ νενευκότων ἡ δύναμις μείζων. Σῴζουσαι γὰρ αὐτὰς ἐπ' ἀσφαλοῦς ἐκ τοῦ ῥάστου ποιοῦσι . . . ἡ δὲ δύναμις ἐκ τοῦ ἄνω μένει. Μένουσα οὖν ἐν αὑτῇ ποιεῖ προσιόντων, αἱ δὲ αὐταὶ προῆλθον. Ἀπέστησαν οὖν εἰς βάθος. Ἡ πολὺ αὐτῶν καθελκυσθὲν συνεφειλκύσατο καὶ αὐτὰς ταῖς γνώμαις εἰς τὸ κάτω ἰέναι. Τὸ γὰρ δευτέρας καὶ τρίτας[1] τῷ ἐγγύθεν καὶ τῷ πορρώτερον ὑπονοητέον εἰρῆσθαι, ὥσπερ καὶ παρ' ἡμῖν οὐχ ὁμοίως πάσαις ψυχαῖς ὑπάρχει τὰ πρὸς τὰ ἐκεῖ, ἀλλ' οἱ μὲν ἑνοῖντο ἄν, οἱ δὲ ἐπιβάλλοιεν ἂν ἐγγὺς ἐφιέμενοι, τοῖς δὲ ἧττον ἂν ἔχοι τοῦτο, καθ' ὃ ταῖς δυνάμεσιν οὐ ταῖς αὐταῖς ἐνεργοῦσιν, ἀλλ' οἱ μὲν τῇ πρώτῃ, οἱ δὲ τῇ μετ' ἐκείνην, οἱ δὲ τῇ τρίτῃ, ἁπάντων τὰς πάσας ἐχόντων.

c. Our own soul is not a part of the world-soul (as it might seem to be suggested in *Philebus* 30a).

---

[1] *Tim.* 41d: δεύτερα καὶ τρίτα.

Enn. IV 3, 7, 1-12:

Individual
souls not a
part of the
world-soul

Ταῦτα μὲν οὖν ταύτῃ. Ἀλλὰ τὸ ἐν Φιλήβῳ λεχθὲν παρέχον ὑπόνοιαν μοίρας τῆς τοῦ παντὸς τὰς ἄλλας εἶναι; Βούλεται δὲ ὁ λόγος οὐ τοῦτο, ὅ τις οἴεται, ἀλλ' ὅπερ ἦν χρήσιμον αὐτῷ τότε, καὶ τὸν οὐρανὸν ἔμψυχον εἶναι. Τοῦτο οὖν
5 πιστοῦται λέγων, ὡς ἄτοπον τὸν οὐρανὸν ἄψυχον λέγειν ἡμῶν, οἳ μέρος σώματος ἔχομεν τοῦ παντός, ψυχὴν ἐχόντων. Πῶς γὰρ ἂν τὸ μέρος ἔσχεν ἀψύχου τοῦ παντὸς ὄντος; Δῆλον δὲ μάλιστα τὸ τῆς γνώμης αὐτοῦ ἐν Τιμαίῳ ποιεῖ, οὗ γενομένης τῆς ψυχῆς τοῦ παντὸς ὕστερον τὰς ἄλλας ποιεῖ ἐκ τοῦ αὐτοῦ μιγνύων κρατῆρος, ἀφ' οὗ καὶ ἡ τῶν ὅλων, ὁμοειδῆ ποιῶν καὶ τὴν ἄλλην, τὴν δὲ διαφορὰν δευτέροις καὶ τρίτοις διδούς [1].

On the difference between Universal Soul and our individual souls cp. also IV 8, 7, l. 17-32: Universal soul cannot come into direct contact with things here, individual souls can.

1374—To the question "how is there a plurality of souls" P. answers: Because there is a plurality in Noûs.

a.　*Enn.* IV 8, 3, l. 6-13 Br.:

Ὄντος τοίνυν παντὸς νοῦ ἐν τῷ τῆς νοήσεως τόπῳ ὅλου τε καὶ παντός, ὃν δὴ κόσμον νοητὸν τιθέμεθα, ὄντων δὲ καὶ τῶν ἐν τούτῳ περιεχομένων νοερῶν δυνάμεων καὶ νόων τῶν καθέκαστα — οὐ γὰρ εἷς νοῦς μόνος, ἀλλ' εἷς καὶ πολλοί — πολλὰς ἔδει καὶ ψυχὰς καὶ μίαν εἶναι, καὶ ἐκ τῆς μιᾶς τὰς πολλὰς διαφόρους, ὥσπερ ἐκ γένους ἑνὸς εἴδη τὰ μὲν ἀμείνω, τὰ δὲ χείρω, καὶ τὰ μὲν νοερώτερα, τὰ δ' ἧττον ἐνεργείᾳ τοιαῦτα.

b.　In Noûs there is a plurality of intelligible Forms, because it contains the (intelligible) principle of ἑτερότης; and this plurality ends in infinity. So it is with soul.

Enn. VI 2, 22, l. 7-23 Br.:

Ὁ δὴ νοῦς οὗτος, ὃν φαμὲν καθορᾶν, οὐκ ἀπαλλαγεὶς τοῦ πρὸ αὐτοῦ ἐξ αὐτοῦ ὤν, ἅτε ὢν ἐξ ἑνὸς πολλὰ καὶ τὴν τοῦ θατέρου φύσιν συνοῦσαν ἔχων, εἰς πολλὰ γίνεται. Εἷς δὲ νοῦς τὰ πολλὰ ὢν καὶ τοὺς πολλοὺς νοῦς ποιεῖ ἐξ ἀνάγκης τῆς τοιαύτης. Ὅλως δὲ οὐκ ἔστι τὸ ἓν ἀριθμῷ λαβεῖν καὶ ἄτομον· ὅ τι γὰρ ἂν λάβῃς, εἶδος· ἄνευ γὰρ ὕλης. Διὸ καὶ τοῦτο αἰνιττόμενος ὁ Πλάτων εἰς ἄπειρά φησι κατακερματίζεσθαι τὴν οὐσίαν [2]. Ἕως μὲν γὰρ εἰς ἄλλο εἶδος,
5 οἷον ἐκ γένους, οὔπω ἄπειρον· περατοῦται γὰρ τοῖς γεννηθεῖσιν εἴδεσι· τὸ δ' ἔσχατον εἶδος ὃ μὴ διαιρεῖται εἰς εἴδη, μᾶλλον ἄπειρον. Καὶ τοῦτό ἐστι τὸ

---

[1] The passage referred to is again *Tim.* 41d.
[2] P. thinks of *Parm.* 144b.

τότε δὲ ἤδη εἰς τὸ ἄπειρον μεθέντα ἐᾶν χαίρειν[1]. Ἀλλ' ὅσον μὲν ἐπ' αὐτοῖς, ἄπειρα· τῷ δὲ ἑνὶ περιληφθέντα εἰς ἀριθμὸν ἔρχεται ἤδη. Νοῦς μὲν οὖν ἔχει τὸ μεθ' ἑαυτὸν ψυχήν, ὥστε ἐν ἀριθμῷ εἶναι καὶ ψυχὴν μέχρι τοῦ ἐσχάτου αὐτῆς, τὸ δὲ ἔσχατον αὐτῆς ἤδη ἄπειρον παντάπασι.

Thus, the plurality of souls is explained by P. not by the presence of ὕλη nor of bodies, as was done by Aristotle. According to P., plurality originates in the intelligible world itself and by an intelligible principle.

c. The same question is asked in the following passage. In his answer the author stresses the fact that this plurality in the world of Spirit and of soul does not exclude unity.

Plurality not opposed to unity

Enn. VI 4, 4, l. 18 f.; 23-26; 32-46 Br.:

Ἀλλὰ πῶς ψυχαὶ πολλαὶ καὶ νοῖ πολλοῖ καὶ τὸ ὂν καὶ τὰ ὄντα; — Τὸ ὂν πολλὰ συγχωροῦμεν εἶναι ἑτερότητι, οὐ τόπῳ. Ὁμοῦ γὰρ πᾶν τὸ ὄν, κἂν πολὺ οὕτως ᾖ· ἐὸν γὰρ ἐόντι πελάζει[2] καὶ πᾶν ὁμοῦ[3] καὶ νοῦς πολὺς ἑτερότητι, οὐ τόπῳ, ὁμοῦ δὲ πᾶς. — Ἐπεί, ὅτι οὐ συνδιείληπται τοῖς μέρεσιν, ἀλλ' ὅλη πανταχοῦ, φανερὸν ποιεῖ τὸ ἓν καὶ τὸ ἀμέριστον ὄντως τῆς φύσεως. Οὔτ' οὖν τὸ μίαν εἶναι τὰς πολλὰς ἀναιρεῖ, ὥσπερ οὐδὲ τὸ ὂν τὰ ὄντα, οὔτε μάχεται τὸ πλῆθος ἐκεῖ τῷ ἑνί, οὔτε τῷ πλήθει συμπληροῦν δεῖ ζωῆς τὰ σώματα, οὔτε διὰ τὸ μέγεθος τοῦ σώματος δεῖ νομίζειν τὸ πλῆθος τῶν ψυχῶν γίνεσθαι, ἀλλὰ πρὸ τῶν σωμάτων εἶναι καὶ πολλὰς καὶ μίαν. Ἐν γὰρ τῷ ὅλῳ αἱ πολλαὶ ἤδη οὐ δυνάμει, ἀλλ' ἐνεργείᾳ ἑκάστη· οὔτε γὰρ ἡ μία ἡ ὅλη κωλύει τὰς πολλὰς ἐν αὐτῇ εἶναι, οὔτε αἱ πολλαὶ τὴν μίαν. Διέστησαν γὰρ οὐ διεστῶσαι καὶ πάρεισιν ἀλλήλαις οὐκ ἀλλοτριωθεῖσαι· οὐ γὰρ πέρασίν εἰσι διωρισμέναι, ὥσπερ οὐδὲ ἐπιστῆμαι αἱ πολλαὶ ἐν ψυχῇ μιᾷ. καὶ ἔστιν ἡ μία τοιαύτη, ὥστε ἔχειν ἐν ἑαυτῇ πάσας. Οὕτως ἐστὶν ἄπειρος ἡ τοιαύτη φύσις.

1375—The function of soul is not only thinking,—for in this case it would not differ from Noûs. Soul has a particular task with regard to what comes after it: the task of ordering and governing.

a. *Enn.* IV 8, 3, l. 21-31 Br.:

The function of soul

Ψυχῆς δὲ ἔργον τῆς λογικωτέρας νοεῖν μέν, οὐ τὸ νοεῖν δὲ μόνον· τί γὰρ ἂν καὶ νοῦ διαφέροι; Προσλαβοῦσα γὰρ τῷ νοερὰ εἶναι καὶ ἄλλο, καθ' ὃ τὴν οἰκείαν ἔσχεν ὑπόστασιν, νοῦς οὐκ ἔμεινεν, ἔχει τε ἔργον καὶ αὐτή, εἴπερ καὶ πᾶν, ὃ ἂν ᾖ τῶν ὄντων. Βλέπουσα δὲ πρὸς μὲν τὸ πρὸ ἑαυτῆς νοεῖ, εἰς δὲ ἑαυτὴν σῴζει ἑαυτήν, εἰς δὲ τὸ μετ' αὐτὴν κοσμεῖ τε καὶ διοικεῖ καὶ ἄρχει αὐτοῦ· ὅτι μηδὲ

---

[1]   *Phil.* 16e.
[2]   Parmenides, fr. 8, l. 25 (*Gr. Ph.* I, nr. **83**).
[3]   Anaxagoras, fr. 1 (*Gr. Ph.* I, nr. **124a**).

οἷόν τε ἦν στῆναι τὰ πάντα ἐν τῷ νοητῷ, δυναμένου ἐφεξῆς καὶ ἄλλου γενέσθαι ἐλάττονος μέν, ἀναγκαίου δὲ εἶναι, εἴπερ καὶ τὸ πρὸ αὐτοῦ.

b. Cp. *Enn.* IV 7, 13, l. 2-13 Br. :

Its difference from Noûs

Ὅσος μὲν νοῦς μόνος, ἀπαθὴς ἐν τοῖς ζωὴν μόνον νοερὰν ἔχων ἐκεῖ ἀεὶ μένει· οὐ γὰρ ἔνι ὁρμὴ οὐδ' ὄρεξις· ὁ δ' ἂν ὄρεξιν προσλάβῃ ἐφεξῆς ἐκείνῳ τῷ νῷ ὄν, τῇ προσθήκῃ τῆς ὀρέξεως οἷον πρόεισιν ἤδη ἐπὶ πλέον καὶ κοσμεῖν ὀρεγόμενον καθ' ἃ ἐν νῷ εἶδεν, ὥσπερ κυοῦν ἀπ' αὐτῶν καὶ ὠδῖνον γεννῆσαι, ποιεῖν σπεύδει καὶ δημιουργεῖν. Καὶ τῇ σπουδῇ ταύτῃ περὶ τὸ αἰσθητὸν τεταμένη, μετὰ μὲν πάσης τῆς τῶν ὅλων ψυχῆς ὑπερέχουσα τοῦ διοικουμένου εἰς τὸ ἔξω καὶ τοῦ παντὸς συνεπιμελουμένη, μέρος δὲ διοικεῖν βουληθεῖσα μονουμένη καὶ ἐν ἐκείνῳ γιγνομένη, ἐν ᾧ ἔστιν, οὐχ ὅλη οὐδὲ πᾶσα τοῦ σώματος γενομένη, ἀλλά τι καὶ ἔξω σώματος ἔχουσα.

c. Individual souls may exercise their task of providence while staying "yonder" with universal Soul and turned to this. So long they are safe. But as soon as a soul attaches itself to a part, it loses its contact with the spiritual world. To such souls the body becomes a prison. They can free themselves only by noûs; for they always keep some higher principle within themselves.

Enn. IV 8, 4, l. 1-23, 28-35 Br. :

The body not necessarily a prison

Τὰς δὴ καθέκαστα ψυχὰς ὀρέξει μὲν νοερᾷ χρωμένας ἐν τῇ ἐξ οὗ ἐγένοντο πρὸς αὐτὸ ἐπιστροφῇ, δύναμιν δὲ καὶ εἰς τὸ ἐπὶ τάδε ἐχούσας, οἷά περ φῶς ἐξηρτημένον μὲν κατὰ τὰ ἄνω ἡλίου, τῷ δὲ μετ' αὐτὸ οὐ φθονοῦν τῆς χορηγίας, ἀπήμονας μὲν εἶναι <δεῖ> μετὰ τῆς ὅλης μενούσας ἐν τῷ νοητῷ, ἐν οὐρανῷ δὲ μετὰ τῆς ὅλης συνδιοικεῖν ἐκείνῃ, οἷα οἱ βασιλεῖς τῷ πάντων κρατοῦντι συνόντες συνδιοικοῦσιν ἐκείνῳ οὐ καταβαίνοντες οὐδ' αὐτοὶ ἀπὸ τῶν βασιλείων τόπων· καὶ γὰρ εἰσιν ὁμοῦ ἐν τῷ αὐτῷ τότε.

Μεταβάλλουσαι δὲ ἐκ τοῦ ὅλου εἰς τὸ μέρος τε εἶναι καὶ ἑαυτῶν[1] καὶ οἷον κάμνουσαι τῷ σὺν ἄλλῳ εἶναι ἀναχωροῦσιν εἰς τὸ αὐτῶν ἑκάστη. Ὅταν δὴ τοῦτο διὰ χρόνων ποιῇ φεύγουσα τὸ πᾶν καὶ τῇ διακρίσει ἀποστᾶσα καὶ μὴ πρὸς τὸ νοητὸν βλέπῃ, μέρος γενομένη μονοῦταί τε καὶ ἀσθενεῖ καὶ πολυπραγμονεῖ καὶ πρὸς μέρος βλέπει καὶ τῷ ἀπὸ τοῦ ὅλου χωρισμῷ ἑνός τινος ἐπιβᾶσα καὶ τὸ ἄλλο πᾶν φυγοῦσα, ἐλθοῦσα καὶ στραφεῖσα εἰς τὸ ἓν ἐκεῖνο πληττόμενον ὑπὸ τῶν ὅλων καὶ πάντων τοῦ τε ὅλου ἀπέστη, καὶ τὸ καθέκαστον μετὰ περιστάσεως διοικεῖ ἐφαπτομένη ἤδη καὶ θεραπεύουσα τὰ ἔξωθεν καὶ

---

[1] Cp. V 1, 1, where the question of "What it is that made the souls forget God their Father" is answered by these words: "The beginning of evil was for them recklessness, becoming, the first difference and *the will to be of themselves*" (τὸ βουληθῆναι ἑαυτῶν εἶναι).

παροῦσα καὶ δῦσα αὐτοῦ πολὺ εἰς τὸ εἴσω. Ἔνθα καὶ συμβαίνει αὐτῇ τὸ λεγόμενον πτερορρυῆσαι [1] καὶ ἐν δεσμοῖς τοῖς τοῦ σώματος γενέσθαι ... ἐπιστρα-
φεῖσα δὲ πρὸς νόησιν λύεσθαί τε ἐκ τῶν δεσμῶν καὶ ἀναβαίνειν, ὅταν ἀρχὴν
λάβῃ ἐξ ἀναμνήσεως θεᾶσθαι τὰ ὄντα. Ἔχει γὰρ ἀεὶ οὐδὲν ἧττον ὑπερέχον τι. 3

Γίγνονται οὖν οἷον ἀμφίβιοι ἐξ ἀνάγκης τόν τε ἐκεῖ βίον τόν τε ἐνταῦθα παρὰ
μέρος βιοῦσαι, πλεῖον μὲν τὸν ἐκεῖ, αἱ δύνανται πλέον τῷ νῷ συνεῖναι, τὸν δὲ
ἐνθάδε πλεῖον, αἷς τὸ ἐναντίον ἢ φύσει ἢ τύχαις ὑπῆρξεν. 3

P.'s theory about the "providence" exercised by Soul in general and by the
particular souls is expounded in a preceding chapter of the same treatise, which is
cited below (**1376**).

Two kinds
of providence

1376—P. distinguishes two kinds of "providence": general providence,
which works indirectly, by orders, and direct providence, working by
contact. The first is the way in which Universal soul, which is transcendent, cares for the cosmos as a whole; the latter is the kind of care of
particular bodies taken by particular souls.

 a. *Enn.* IV 8, 2, l. 27-39 Br.:

Διττὴ γὰρ ἐπιμέλεια παντός, τοῦ μὲν καθόλου κελεύσει κοσμοῦσα ἀπράγμονι
ἐπιστασίᾳ βασιλικῇ, τοῦ δὲ καθέκαστα ἤδη αὐτουργῷ τινι ποιήσει συναφῇ 3
τῇ πρὸς τὸ πραττόμενον τὸ πρᾶττον τοῦ πραττομένου τῆς φύσεως ἀναπιμπλᾶσα.
Τῆς δὲ θείας ψυχῆς τοῦτον τὸν τρόπον τὸν οὐρανὸν ἅπαντα διοικεῖν ἀεὶ λεγομένης,
ὑπερεχούσης μὲν τῷ κρείττονι, δύναμιν δὲ τὴν ἐσχάτην εἰς τὸ εἴσω πεμπούσης,
αἰτίαν μὲν ὁ θεὸς οὐκ ἂν ἔτι λέγοιτο ἔχειν τοῦ τὴν ψυχὴν τοῦ παντὸς ἐν χείρονι 3
πεποιηκέναι, ἥ τε ψυχὴ οὐκ ἀπεστέρηται τοῦ κατὰ φύσιν ἐξ ἀιδίου τοῦτ'
ἔχουσα καὶ ἕξουσα ἀεί, ὃ μὴ οἷόν τε παρὰ φύσιν αὐτῇ εἶναι· ὅπερ διηνεκῶς
αὐτῇ ἀεὶ ὑπάρχει οὔποτε ἀρξάμενον.

Providence
exercised by
star-souls

 b. Star-souls exercise the same kind of providence as Universal soul.
Ib., l. 39-48 Br.:

Τάς τε τῶν ἀστέρων ψυχὰς τὸν αὐτὸν τρόπον πρὸς τὸ σῶμα ἔχειν λέγων, 4
ὥσπερ τὸ πᾶν — ἐντίθησι γὰρ καὶ τούτων τὰ σώματα εἰς τὰς τῆς ψυχῆς περι-
φοράς — ἀποσῴζοι ἂν καὶ τὴν περὶ τούτους πρέπουσαν εὐδαιμονίαν. Δύο γὰρ
ὄντων δι' ἃ δυσχεραίνεται ἡ ψυχῆς πρὸς σώματα κοινωνία, ὅτι τε ἐμπόδιον
πρὸς τὰς νοήσεις γίγνεται, καὶ ὅτι ἡδονῶν καὶ ἐπιθυμιῶν καὶ λυπῶν πίμπλησιν 4
αὐτήν, οὐδέτερον τούτων ἂν γένοιτο ψυχῇ, ἥτις μὴ εἰς τὸ εἴσω ἔδυ τοῦ σώματος,
μηδέ τινός ἐστι, μηδὲ ἐκείνου ἐγένετο, ἀλλ' ἐκεῖνο αὐτῆς.

Star-souls are, like the All-soul, ἀπαθεῖς: they have neither desires (ἐπιθυμίαι)
nor πάθη. Cp. IV 4, 42, l. 23 ff.:

---

[1] *Phaedr.* 246c, 248c.

Ἐπεὶ καὶ τοῖς ἄστροις, καθ' ὅσον μὲν μέρη, τὰ πάθη, ἀπαθῆ μέντοι αὐτὰ τῷ τε τὰς προαιρέσεις καὶ αὐτοῖς ἀπαθεῖς εἶναι.

c. Soul (i.e. Universal soul or All-soul) "illuminates darkness" (i.e. creates the sensible world) κατὰ λόγους, i.e. according to spiritual principles [1]. But this act of creation, again, is an act of nature, all conscious deliberation and will being excluded.

Soul works κατὰ λόγους

Enn. IV 3, 10, l. 10-22 Br.:

Ἐκοσμεῖτο δὲ κατὰ λόγον ψυχῆς δυνάμει ἐχούσης ἐν αὐτῇ δι' ὅλης δύναμιν κατὰ λόγους κοσμεῖν· οἷα καὶ οἱ ἐν σπέρμασι λόγοι πλάττουσι καὶ μορφοῦσι τὰ ζῷα οἷον μικρούς τινας κόσμους. Ὅ τι γὰρ ἂν ἐφάψηται ψυχῆς, οὕτω ποιεῖται ὡς ἔχει φύσεως ψυχῆς ἡ οὐσία· ἡ δὲ ποιεῖ οὐκ ἐπακτῷ γνώμῃ οὐδὲ βουλὴν ἢ σκέψιν ἀναμείνασα· οὕτω γὰρ ἂν οὐ κατὰ φύσιν, ἀλλὰ κατ' ἐπακτὸν τέχνην ἂν ποιοῖ. Τέχνη γὰρ ὑστέρα αὐτῆς καὶ μιμεῖται ἀμυδρὰ καὶ ἀσθενῆ ποιοῦσα μιμήματα, παίγνια ἄττα καὶ οὐ πολλοῦ ἄξια, μηχαναῖς πολλαῖς εἰς εἰδώλων φύσιν προσχρωμένη. Ἡ δὲ οὐσίας δυνάμει κυρία σωμάτων εἰς τὸ γενέσθαι τε καὶ οὕτως ἔχειν ὡς αὐτὴ ἄγει, οὐ δυναμένων τῶν ἐξ ἀρχῆς ἐναντιοῦσθαι τῇ αὐτῆς βουλήσει.

it is κυρία σωμάτων

d. Soul, then, is not so much a reasoning power as a never-failing reasonable power. As φρόνησις it is opposed to φύσις, which does not possess any intelligence.

Enn. IV 4, 13, l. 1-8, 17-22 Br.:

Ἀλλὰ τί διοίσει τῆς λεγομένης φύσεως ἡ τοιαύτη φρόνησις; Ἢ ὅτι ἡ μὲν φρόνησις πρῶτον, ἡ δὲ φύσις ἔσχατον· ἴνδαλμα γὰρ φρονήσεως ἡ φύσις καὶ ψυχῆς ἔσχατον ὂν ἔσχατον καὶ τὸν ἐν αὐτῇ ἐλλαμπόμενον λόγον ἔχει, οἷον εἰ ἐν κηρῷ βαθεῖ διικνοῖτο εἰς ἔσχατον ἐπὶ θάτερα ἐν τῇ ἐπιφανείᾳ τύπος, ἐναργοῦς μὲν ὄντος τοῦ ἄνω, ἴχνους δὲ ἀσθενοῦς ὄντος τοῦ κάτω. Ὅθεν οὐδὲ οἶδε, μόνον δὲ ποιεῖ. — Νοῦς μὲν οὖν ἔχει, ψυχὴ δὲ ἡ τοῦ παντὸς ἐκομίσατο εἰς ἀεὶ καὶ τοῦτό ἐστιν αὐτῇ τὸ ζῆν καὶ τὸ φαινόμενον ἀεὶ σύνεσις νοούσης· τὸ δὲ ἐξ αὐτῆς ἐμφαντασθὲν εἰς ὕλην φύσις, ἐν ᾗ ἴσταται τὰ ὄντα, ἢ καὶ πρὸ τούτου, καὶ ἔστιν ἔσχατα ταῦτα τοῦ νοητοῦ· ἤδη γὰρ τὸ ἐντεῦθεν τὰ μιμήματα.

"Thinking" opposed to "nature"

1377—The soul which enters into a body is not necessarily harmed

Direct providence may be exercised without harm

---

[1] λόγοι means for P.: *spiritual principles with regard to creation.* Thus, in V 9, 3, l. 31 f.: Νοῦς procures λ. for soul. Cp. IV 7, 4-5 (against the Stoic doctrine that soul is a body): the notion of πνεῦμα ἔννουν presupposes a λόγος; V 9, 5, l. 23 ff. (against the Stoic conception of λ. σπερματικοί): Εἰ δὲ λόγους φήσουσιν ἀρκεῖν, ἀιδίους δῆλον· εἰ δὲ ἀιδίους καὶ ἀπαθεῖς, ἐν νῷ δεῖ εἶναι καὶ τοιούτῳ καὶ προτέρῳ ἕξεως καὶ φύσεως καὶ ψυχῆς· δυνάμει γὰρ ταῦτα.

by the contact: if it withdraws directly, it does not get entangled with evil.

a. *Enn.* IV 8, 5, l. 24-30 Br.:

Οὕτω τοι καίπερ οὖσα θεῖον καὶ ἐκ τῶν τόπων τῶν ἄνω ἐντὸς γίνεται τοῦ σώματος καὶ θεὸς οὖσα ὁ ὕστερος ῥοπῇ αὐτεξουσίῳ καὶ αἰτίᾳ δυνάμεως καὶ τοῦ 2 μετ' αὐτὴν κοσμήσεως ὡδὶ ἔρχεται· κἂν μὲν θᾶττον φύγῃ, οὐδὲν βέβλαπται γνῶσιν κακοῦ προσλαβοῦσα καὶ φύσιν κακίας γνοῦσα τάς τε δυνάμεις ἀγαγοῦσα αὐτῆς εἰς τὸ φανερόν. 3

b. That indeed soul in itself belongs to the θεία or νοητὴ φύσις, will be found if one considers a pure soul: here πάθη and ἐπιθυμίαι will appear to be προσθῆκαι.

Soul and its προσθῆκαι *Enn.* IV 7, 10, l. 7-16 Br.:

Λάβωμεν δὲ ψυχὴν μὴ τὴν ἐν σώματι ἐπιθυμίας ἀλόγους καὶ θυμοὺς προσλαβοῦσαν καὶ πάθη ἄλλα ἀναδεξαμένην, ἀλλὰ τὴν ταῦτα ἀποτριψαμένην καὶ καθ' ὅσον οἷόν τε μὴ κοινωνοῦσαν τῷ σώματι. Ἥτις καὶ δῆλον ποιεῖ, ὡς προσθῆκαι 1 τὰ κακὰ τῇ ψυχῇ καὶ ἄλλοθεν, καθηραμένη δὲ αὐτῇ ἐνυπάρχει τὰ ἄριστα, φρόνησις καὶ ἡ ἄλλη ἀρετή, οἰκεῖα ὄντα. Εἰ οὖν τοιοῦτον ἡ ψυχή, ὅταν ἐφ' ἑαυτὴν ἀνέλθῃ, πῶς οὐ τῆς φύσεως ἐκείνης, οἵαν φαμὲν τὴν τοῦ θείου καὶ ἀϊδίου 1 παντὸς εἶναι;

c. The pure soul strips easily the additional qualities due to its incarnation, viz. in the dissolution of the compositum; others may keep them quite a long time.

Enn. IV 7, 14, l. 8-14 Br.:

Εἰ δὲ τὴν ἀνθρώπου ψυχὴν τριμερῆ οὖσαν τῷ συνθέτῳ λυθήσεσθαι <φήσουσι>, καὶ ἡμεῖς φήσομεν τὰς μὲν καθαρὰς ἀπαλλαττομένας τὸ προσπλασθὲν ἐν τῇ 1 γενέσει ἀφήσειν, τὰς δὲ τούτῳ συνέσεσθαι ἐπὶ πλεῖστον· ἀφειμένον δὲ τὸ χεῖρον οὐδὲ αὐτὸ ἀπολεῖσθαι, ἕως ἂν ᾖ ὅθεν ἔχει τὴν ἀρχήν. Οὐδὲν γὰρ ἐκ τοῦ ὄντος ἀπολεῖται.

Cp. below, nr. **1414**.

1378—Both perception and memory are "additions". For perception is effected by means of the body (soul using the organs of the body as its instruments). And as to μνήμη, νοῦς being eternal cannot be its subject, for it does not know a succession in time. Soul, then, must be the subject, the body being only an impediment for memory. But by what function? P. answers: by the φανταστικόν. And the φάντασμα is a result of perception.

The higher soul, therefore, strips the remembrances of the lower soul (III 3, cc. 25-32).

a. The compositum may be said to be the subject of perception, but in this sense only that soul has the leading part, while the body is the instrument employed by the soul.

Enn. IV 3, 26, l. 1-8 Br.:

Εἰ μὲν οὖν τὸ συναμφότερόν ἐστιν ἐν ταῖς αἰσθήσεσι ταῖς κατ᾽ ἐνέργειαν, δεῖ τὸ αἰσθάνεσθαι τοιοῦτον εἶναι — διὸ καὶ κοινὸν λέγεται — οἷον τὸ τρυπᾶν καὶ τὸ ὑφαίνειν, ἵνα κατὰ μὲν τὸν τεχνίτην ἡ ψυχὴ ᾖ ἐν τῷ αἰσθάνεσθαι, κατὰ
5 δὲ τὸ ὄργανον τὸ σῶμα, τοῦ μὲν σώματος πάσχοντος καὶ ὑπηρετοῦντος, τῆς δὲ ψυχῆς παραδεχομένης τὴν τύπωσιν τὴν τοῦ σώματος, ἢ τὴν διὰ τοῦ σώματος, ἢ τὴν κρίσιν, ἣν ἐποιήσατο ἐκ τοῦ παθήματος τοῦ σώματος· —

See further below, nr. **1415** f.

Perception belongs to the compositum

b. Memory, however, cannot be in this sense a κοινὸν ἔργον, for the body appears to be a cause of oblivion, not of memory.

Ib., l. 50-56:

Τὸ δὲ τῆς μνήμης καὶ τὸ σῶμα ἐμπόδιον ἔχει· ἐπεὶ καὶ νῦν προστιθεμένων
τινῶν λήθη, ἐν δ᾽ ἀφαιρέσει καὶ καθάρσει ἀνακύπτει πολλάκις ἡ μνήμη. Μονῆς δὲ οὔσης αὐτῆς ἀνάγκη τὴν τοῦ σώματος φύσιν κινουμένην καὶ ῥέουσαν λήθης αἰτίαν, ἀλλ᾽ οὐ μνήμης εἶναι· διὸ καὶ ὁ τῆς λήθης ποταμὸς οὕτως ἂν ὑπονοοῖτο.
5 Ψυχῆς μὲν δὴ ἔστω τὸ πάθημα τοῦτο.

Memory belongs to soul

c. But by what faculty of soul do we remember?—Not by the same as that by which we perceive.

Enn. IV 3, 27, l. 23-25; 29, l. 19-32 Br.:

Ἡ δὲ δὴ μόνη γενομένη τί μνημονεύσει; Ἢ πρότερον σκεπτέον τίνι δυνάμει
5 ψυχῆς τὸ μνημονεύειν παραγίνεται.
(29.) Ἀλλὰ πάλιν αὖ, εἰ ἄλλο ἑκάτερον δεήσει εἶναι, καὶ ἄλλο μνημονεύσει ὧν
10 ἡ αἴσθησις ᾔσθετο πρότερον, κἀκεῖνο δεῖ αἰσθέσθαι οὗπερ μελλήσει μνημο-
νεύειν. Ἢ οὐδὲν κωλύσει τῷ μνημονεύσοντι τὸ αἴσθημα φάντασμα εἶναι, καὶ τῷ φανταστικῷ ἄλλῳ ὄντι τὴν μνήμην καὶ κατοχὴν ὑπάρχειν· τοῦτο γάρ ἐστιν,
15 εἰς ὃ λήγει ἡ αἴσθησις, καὶ μηκέτι οὔσης τούτῳ πάρεστι τὸ ὅραμα. Εἰ οὖν παρὰ τούτῳ τοῦ ἀπόντος ἤδη ἡ φαντασία, μνημονεύει ἤδη, κἂν ἐπ᾽ ὀλίγον παρῇ.
Ὧ δὲ εἰ μὲν ἐπ᾽ ὀλίγον παραμένοι, ὀλίγη ἡ μνήμη, ἐπὶ πολὺ δὲ μᾶλλον μνημονικοὶ τῆς δυνάμεως ταύτης οὔσης ἰσχυροτέρας, ὡς μὴ ῥᾳδίως τρεπομένης ἀφεῖσθαι
20 ἀποσεισθεῖσαν τὴν μνήμην. Τοῦ φανταστικοῦ ἄρα ἡ μνήμη, καὶ τὸ μνημονεύειν τῶν τοιούτων ἔσται.

By what faculty of soul do we remember?

1379—As soon as it is in the intelligible world, the soul has lost its remembrance of things here and lives in eternity.

a. *Enn.* IV 4, 1, l. 1-6, 10-17 Br.:

Τί οὖν ἐρεῖ, καὶ τίνων τὴν μνήμην ἕξει ψυχὴ ἐν τῷ νοητῷ καὶ ἐπὶ τῆς οὐσίας ἐκείνης γενομένη; Ἢ ἀκόλουθον εἰπεῖν ἐκεῖνα θεωρεῖν καὶ περὶ ἐκεῖνα ἐνεργεῖν, ἐν οἷς ἔστιν, ἢ μηδὲ ἐκεῖ εἶναι. Τῶν οὖν ἐνταῦθα οὐδέν, οἷον ὅτι ἐφιλοσόφησε, καὶ δὴ καὶ ὅτι ἐνταῦθα οὖσα ἐθεᾶτο τὰ ἐκεῖ. — Οὐκ ἂν εἴη ἐν τῷ νοητῷ καθαρῶς 5 ὄντα μνήμην ἔχειν τῶν τῇδέ ποτε αὐτῷ τινι γεγενημένων. Εἰ δὲ καί, ὥσπερ ι δοκεῖ, ἄχρονος πᾶσα ἡ νόησις, ἐν αἰῶνι, ἀλλ' οὐκ ἐν χρόνῳ ὄντων τῶν ἐκεῖ, ἀδύνατον μνήμην εἶναι ἐκεῖ οὐχ ὅτι τῶν ἐνταῦθα, ἀλλὰ καὶ ὅλως ὁτουοῦν. Ἀλλ' ἔστιν ἕκαστον παρόν.

b. Will the soul in its life yonder remain conscious of its own individuality?

Enn. IV 4, 2, l. 1-14, 30-32 Br.:

Ἀλλὰ ταῦτα μὲν ταύτῃ. Ἑαυτοῦ δὲ πῶς; Ἢ οὐδὲ ἑαυτοῦ ἕξει τὴν μνήμην, οὐδ' ὅτι αὐτὸς ὁ θεωρῶν, οἷον Σωκράτης, ἢ ὅτι νοῦς ἢ ψυχή. Πρὸς δὴ ταῦτά τις ἀναμνησθήτω, ὡς ὅταν καὶ ἐνταῦθα θεωρῇ καὶ μάλιστα ἐναργῶς, οὐκ ἐπιστρέφει πρὸς ἑαυτὸν τότε τῇ νοήσει, ἀλλ' ἔχει μὲν ἑαυτόν, ἡ δὲ ἐνέργεια 5 πρὸς ἐκεῖνο, κἀκεῖνο γίνεται οἷον ὕλην ἑαυτὸν παρασχών, εἰδοποιούμενος δὲ κατὰ τὸ ὁρώμενον καὶ δυνάμει ὢν τότε αὐτός. Τότε οὖν αὐτός ἐστιν ἐνεργείᾳ, ὅταν μηδὲν νοῇ· ἤ, εἰ μὲν αὐτός, κενός ἐστι παντός. Εἰ δέ ἐστιν αὐτὸς τοιοῦτος οἷος πάντα εἶναι, ὅταν αὐτὸν νοῇ, πάντα ὁμοῦ νοεῖ· ὥστε ι τῇ μὲν εἰς ἑαυτὸν ὁ τοιοῦτος ἐπιβολῇ καὶ ἐνεργείᾳ ἑαυτὸν ὁρῶν τὰ πάντα ἐμπεριεχόμενα ἔχει, τῇ δὲ πρὸς τὰ πάντα ἐμπεριεχόμενον ἑαυτόν. — Οὕτως οὖν ἔχουσα οὐκ ἂν μεταβάλλοι, ἀλλὰ ἔχοι ἂν ἀτρέπτως πρὸς νόησιν ὁμοῦ 3 ἔχουσα τὴν συναίσθησιν αὐτῆς, ὡς ἓν ἅμα τῷ νοητῷ ταὐτὸν γενομένη.

1380—The individual existence of soul in the intelligible world is explained by P.'s theory of the plurality in Noûs (above, **1374**). In answer to the question concerning what is called immortality of the soul it is clearly expressed in the following passage.

Enn. IV 3, 5, l. 1-14 Br.:

Ἀλλὰ πῶς ἔτι ἡ μὲν σή, ἡ δὲ τοῦδε, ἡ δὲ ἄλλου ἔσται; ἆρ' οὖν τοῦδε μὲν κατὰ τὸ κάτω, οὐ τοῦδε δέ, ἀλλ' ἐκείνου κατὰ τὸ ἄνω; Ἀλλ' οὕτως γε Σωκράτης μὲν ἔσται ὅταν ἐν σώματι ᾖ ἡ Σωκράτους ψυχή· ἀπολεῖται δέ, ὅταν μάλιστα γένηται ἐν τῷ ἀρίστῳ. Ἢ ἀπολεῖται οὐδὲν τῶν ὄντων· ἐπεὶ κἀκεῖ 5 οἱ νόες οὐκ ἀπολοῦνται, ὅτι μή εἰσι σωματικῶς μεμερισμένοι, [εἰς ἕν] ἀλλὰ μένει ἕκαστον ἐν ἑτερότητι ἔχον τὸ αὐτὸ ὃ ἔστιν εἶναι. Οὕτω τοίνυν καὶ <αἱ> ψυχαὶ ἐφεξῆς καθ᾽ ἕκαστον νοῦν ἐξηρτημέναι, λόγοι νῶν οὖσαι καὶ ἐξειλιγμέναι μᾶλλον ἢ ἐκεῖνοι, οἷον πολὺ ἐξ ὀλίγου γενόμεναι, συναφεῖς τῷ ὀλίγῳ οὖσαι ἀμερεστέρῳ ἐκείνων ἑκάστῳ μερίζεσθαι ἤδη θελήσασαι καὶ οὐ δυνάμεναι εἰς πᾶν μερισμοῦ ἰέναι τὸ ταὐτὸν καὶ ἕτερον σῴζουσαι μένει τε ἑκάστη ἕν, καὶ ὁμοῦ ἓν πᾶσαι.

1381—In V 1 P. leads the way of ascent to "the Father" (above, **1375c**, n. 1) by the self-reflection of the soul.

a. *Enn.* V 1, 2:

Self-reflection
of the soul

Ἐνθυμείσθω τοίνυν πρῶτον ἐκεῖνο πᾶσα ψυχή, ὡς αὐτὴ μὲν ζῷα ἐποίησε πάντα ἐμπνεύσασα αὐτοῖς ζωήν, ἅ τε γῆ τρέφει ἅ τε θάλασσα ἅ τε ἐν ἀέρι ἅ τε ἐν οὐρανῷ ἄστρα θεῖα, αὐτὴ δὲ ἥλιον, αὐτὴ δὲ τὸν μέγαν τοῦτον οὐρανόν, καὶ αὐτὴ ἐκόσμησεν, αὐτὴ δὲ ἐν τάξει περιάγει φύσις οὖσα ἑτέρα ὧν κοσμεῖ καὶ ὧν κινεῖ καὶ ἃ ζῆν ποιεῖ· καὶ τούτων ἀνάγκη εἶναι τιμιωτέραν, γιγνομένων <μὲν> τούτων καὶ φθειρομένων, ὅταν αὐτὰ ψυχὴ ἀπολείπῃ ἢ χορηγεῖ τὸ ζῆν, αὐτὴ δὲ οὖσα ἀεὶ τῷ μὴ ἀπολείπειν ἑαυτήν. Τίς δὲ <ὁ> τρόπος τῆς χορηγίας τοῦ ζῆν ἔν τε τῷ σύμπαντι ἔν τε τοῖς ἑκάστοις, ὧδε λογιζέσθω. Σκοπείσθω δὴ τὴν μεγάλην ψυχὴν ἄλλη ψυχὴ οὐ σμικρὰ ἀξία τοῦ σκοπεῖν γενομένη ἀπαλλαγεῖσα ἀπάτης καὶ τῶν γεγοητευκότων τὰς ἄλλας ἡσύχῳ τῇ καταστάσει. Ἥσυχον δὲ αὐτῇ ἔστω μὴ μόνον τὸ περικείμενον σῶμα καὶ ὁ τοῦ σώματος κλύδων, ἀλλὰ καὶ πᾶν τὸ περιέχον· ἥσυχος μὲν γῆ, ἥσυχος δὲ θάλασσα καὶ ἀὴρ καὶ αὐτὸς οὐρανὸς ἀμείνων. Νοείτω δὲ πάντοθεν εἰς αὐτὸν ἑστῶτα ψυχὴν ἔξωθεν οἷον εἰσρέουσαν καὶ εἰσχυθεῖσαν καὶ πάντοθεν εἰσιοῦσαν καὶ εἰσλάμπουσαν· οἷον σκοτεινὸν νέφος ἡλίου βολαὶ φωτίσασαι λάμπειν ποιοῦσι χρυσοειδῆ ὄψιν διδοῦσαι, οὕτω τοι καὶ ψυχὴ ἐλθοῦσα εἰς σῶμα οὐρανοῦ ἔδωκε μὲν ζωήν, ἔδωκε δὲ ἀθανασίαν, ἤγειρε δὲ κείμενον. Ὁ δὲ κινηθεὶς κίνησιν ἀίδιον ὑπὸ ψυχῆς ἐμφρόνως ἀγούσης ζῷον εὔδαιμον ἐγένετο, ἔσχε τε ἀξίαν οὐρανὸς ψυχῆς εἰσοικισθείσης ὢν πρὸ ψυχῆς σῶμα νεκρόν, γῆ καὶ ὕδωρ, μᾶλλον δὲ σκότος ὕλης καὶ μὴ ὂν καὶ "ὃ στυγέουσιν οἱ θεοί" [1], φησί τις. Γένοιτο δ᾽ ἂν φανερωτέρα αὐτῆς καὶ ἐναργεστέρα ἡ δύναμις καὶ ἡ φύσις, εἴ τις ἐνταῦθα διανοηθείη, ὅπως περιέχει καὶ ἄγει ταῖς αὑτῆς βουλήσεσι τὸν οὐρανόν [2]. Παντὶ μὲν γὰρ τῷ μεγέθει τούτῳ, ὅσος ἐστίν, ἔδωκεν ἑαυτὴν καὶ πᾶν διάστημα καὶ μέγα καὶ μικρὸν ἐψύχωται ἄλλου μὲν ἄλλῃ κειμένου τοῦ σώματος καὶ τοῦ μὲν ὡδί, τοῦ δὲ ὡδὶ ὄντος, καὶ τῶν μὲν ἐξ ἐναντίας, τῶν δὲ ἄλλην ἀπάρτησιν ἀπ᾽ ἀλλήλων ἐχόντων. Ἀλλ᾽ οὐχ ἡ ψυχὴ οὕτως, οὐδὲ μέρει ἑαυτῆς ἑκάστῳ κατακερματισθεῖσα

---

[1] *Ilias* 21, 165.
[2] The subject is dealt with in *Enn.* II 2.

μορίῳ [ψυχῆς] ζῆν ποιεῖ, ἀλλὰ πάντα ζῇ τῇ ὅλῃ, καὶ πάρεστι πᾶσα πανταχοῦ τῷ γεννήσαντι πατρὶ [1] ὁμοιουμένη καὶ κατὰ τὸ ἓν καὶ κατὰ τὸ πάντη. Καὶ πολὺς ὢν ὁ οὐρανὸς καὶ ἄλλος ἄλλῃ ἕν ἐστι τῇ ταύτης δυνάμει καὶ θεός ἐστι διὰ ταύτην ὁ κόσμος ὅδε. Ἔστι δὲ καὶ ἥλιος θεός, ὅτι ἔμψυχος, καὶ τὰ ἄλλα ἄστρα, καὶ ἡμεῖς, εἴπερ τι, διὰ τοῦτο· "νέκυες γὰρ κοπρίων ἐκβλητότεροι." [2] Τὴν δὴ θεοῖς [3] αἰτίαν τοῦ θεοῖς εἶναι ἀνάγκη πρεσβυτέραν [θεὸν] αὐτῶν εἶναι· ὁμοειδὴς δὲ καὶ ἡ ἡμετέρα, καὶ ὅταν ἄνευ τῶν προσελθόντων σκοπῆς λαβὼν κεκαθαρμένην, εὑρήσεις τὸ αὐτὸ τίμιον, ὃ ἦν ψυχή, καὶ τιμιώτερον παντὸς τοῦ ὃ ἂν σωματικὸν ᾖ. Γῆ γὰρ πάντα· κἂν πῦρ δὲ ᾖ, τί ἂν εἴη τὸ καῖον αὐτοῦ; Καὶ ὅσα ἐκ τούτων σύνθετα κἂν ὕδωρ αὐτοῖς προσθῇς κἂν ἀέρα. Εἰ δ' ὅτι ἔμψυχον διωκτὸν ἔσται, τί παρείς τις ἑαυτὸν ἄλλον διώκει; Τὴν δὲ ἐν ἄλλῳ ψυχὴν ἀγάμενος σεαυτὸν ἄγασαι.

It is an image of Noûs

b. Ib., c. 3:

Οὕτω δὴ τιμίου καὶ θείου ὄντος χρήματος τῆς ψυχῆς, πιστεύσας ἤδη τῷ τοιούτῳ θεὸν μετιέναι μετὰ τοιαύτης αἰτίας ἀνάβαινε πρὸς ἐκεῖνον· πάντως που οὐ πόρρω ἐπιβαλεῖς· οὐδὲ πολλὰ τὰ μεταξύ. Λάμβανε τοίνυν τοῦ θείου τούτου θειότερον τὸ ψυχῆς πρὸς τὸ ἄνω γειτόνημα, μεθ' ὃ καὶ ἀφ' οὗ ἡ ψυχή· καίπερ γὰρ οὖσα χρῆμα οἷον ἔδειξεν ὁ λόγος, εἰκών τίς ἐστι νοῦ· οἷον λόγος ὁ ἐν προφορᾷ λόγου τοῦ ἐν ψυχῇ, οὕτω τοι καὶ αὐτὴ λόγος νοῦ καὶ ἡ πᾶσα ἐνέργεια καθ' ἣν προΐεται ζωὴν εἰς ἄλλου ὑπόστασιν [4]· οἷον πυρὸς τὸ μὲν ἡ συνοῦσα θερμότης, ἡ δὲ ἣν παρέχει. Δεῖ δὲ λαβεῖν ἐκεῖ οὐκ ἐκρέουσαν, ἀλλὰ μένουσαν μὲν τὴν ἐν αὐτῷ, τὴν δὲ ἄλλην ὑφισταμένην [5]. Οὖσα οὖν ἀπὸ νοῦ νοερά ἐστι, καὶ ἐν λογισμοῖς ὁ νοῦς αὐτῆς καὶ ἡ τελείωσις ἀπ' αὐτοῦ πάλιν οἷον πατρὸς ἐκθρέψαντος, ὃν οὐ τέλειον ὡς πρὸς αὐτὸν ἐγέννησεν. Ἥ τε οὖν ὑπόστασις αὐτῇ ἀπὸ νοῦ ὅ τε ἐνεργείᾳ λόγος νοῦ αὐτῇ ὁρωμένου. Ὅταν γὰρ ἐνίδῃ εἰς νοῦν, ἔνδοθεν ἔχει καὶ οἰκεῖα ἃ νοεῖ καὶ ἐνεργεῖ. Καὶ ταύτας μόνας δεῖ λέγειν ἐνεργείας ψυχῆς, ὅσα νοερῶς καὶ ὅσα οἴκοθεν· τὰ δὲ χείρω ἄλλοθεν καὶ πάθη ψυχῆς τῆς τοιαύτης. Νοῦς οὖν ἐπὶ μᾶλλον θειοτέραν ποιεῖ καὶ τῷ πατὴρ εἶναι καὶ τῷ παρεῖναι· οὐδὲν γὰρ μεταξὺ ἢ τὸ ἑτέροις εἶναι, ὡς ἐφεξῆς μέντοι καὶ ὡς τὸ δεχόμενον, τὸ δὲ ὡς εἶδος [6]· καλὴ δὲ καὶ ἡ νοῦ ὕλη νοοειδὴς οὖσα καὶ

---

[1] Sc. the Noûs.
[2] Heracl. fr. 96 Diels.
[3] Sc. the stars.
[4] Soul is "the λόγος of Noûs and its whole activity, according to which it sends forth life to make subsist other beings". Cp. **1376c**, n. 1, on the sense of λόγος.
[5] Part of Soul stays with Noûs, part of it comes to an existence of its own. Cp. above, **1373**.
[6] With regard to Noûs soul is "receptive", for it receives the "forms" from Noûs. Thus, the relation of Noûs to ψυχή is that of εἶδος to ὕλη, to speak in Aristo-

ἀπλῆ, οἷον δὴ ὁ νοῦς. Καὶ αὐτῷ μὲν τούτῳ δῆλον, ὅτι κρείττων ψυχῆς τοιᾶσδε
5 οὔσης.

4—NOÛS OR THE INTELLIGIBLE WORLD

1382—Noûs is a light springing from the original Light.

a. *Enn.* V 3, 12, l. 40-51 Br.:

Light from
Light

"Η κατὰ λόγον θησόμεθα τὴν μὲν ἀπ' αὐτοῦ οἷον ῥυεῖσαν ἐνέργειαν ὡς ἀπὸ
ἡλίου ‹φῶς›. Φῶς τι οὖν θησόμεθα καὶ πᾶσαν τὴν νοητὴν φύσιν, αὐτὸν δὲ ἐπ'
ἄκρῳ τῷ νοητῷ ἑστηκότα βασιλεύειν ἐπ' αὐτοῦ οὐκ ἐξώσαντα ἀπ' αὐτοῦ τὸ
ἐκφανέν. "Η ἄλλο φῶς πρὸ φωτὸς ποιήσομεν, ἐπιλάμπειν δὲ ἀεὶ μένον ἐπὶ
5 τοῦ νοητοῦ. Οὐδὲ γὰρ ἀποτέτμηται τὸ ἀπ' αὐτοῦ οὐδ' αὖ ταὐτὸν αὐτῷ οὐδὲ
τοιοῦτον οἷον μὴ οὐσία εἶναι, οὐδ' αὖ οἷον τυφλὸν εἶναι· ἀλλ' ὁρῶν καὶ γινῶσκον
ἑαυτὸ καὶ πρῶτον γινῶσκον. Τὸ δὲ ὥσπερ ἐπέκεινα νοῦ, οὕτως καὶ ἐπέκεινα
γνώσεως, οὐδὲν δεόμενον ὥσπερ οὐδενός, οὕτως οὐδὲ τοῦ γινώσκειν· ἀλλ'
0 ἔστιν ἐν δευτέρᾳ φύσει τὸ γινώσκειν.

b. Noûs is not the Good itself, but the direct image of it.
Enn. V 6, 4, l. 6 f.:

A direct
image of the
Good

"Ετι ἄλλο νοῦς τοῦ ἀγαθοῦ· ἀγαθοειδὴς γὰρ τῷ τὸ ἀγαθὸν νοεῖν.

Thus, in V 1, 6, l. 14 f. Noûs is called ἄγαλμα τὸ πρῶτον ἐκφανέν. Cp. also **1370b**.

c. The relation of the Good to Noûs is also explained in the following passage.

Enn. VI 7, 15, l. 10-24 Br.:

Multiplicity
begins in
Noûs

0 Τὸ μὲν γάρ ἐστιν ἀγαθόν, ὁ δὲ ἀγαθός ἐστιν ἐν τῷ θεωρεῖν τὸ ζῆν ἔχων·
θεωρεῖ δὲ ἀγαθοειδῆ ὄντα τὰ θεωρούμενα καὶ αὐτά, ἃ ἐκτήσατο, ὅτε ἐθεώρει
τὴν τοῦ ἀγαθοῦ φύσιν. "Ηλθε δὲ εἰς αὐτὸν οὐχ ὡς ἐκεῖ ἦν, ἀλλ' ὡς αὐτὸς ἔσχεν.
5 Ἀρχὴ γὰρ ἐκεῖνος καὶ ἐξ ἐκείνου ἐν τούτῳ καὶ οὗτος ὁ ποιήσας ταῦτα ἐξ ἐκείνου.
Οὐ γὰρ ἦν θέμις βλέποντα εἰς ἐκεῖνον μηδὲν νοεῖν οὐδ' αὖ τὰ ἐν ἐκείνῳ· οὐ γὰρ
ἂν αὐτὸς ἐγέννα. Δύναμιν οὖν εἰς τὸ γεννᾶν εἶχε παρ' ἐκείνου καὶ τῶν αὐτοῦ
0 πληροῦσθαι γεννημάτων διδόντος ἐκείνου ἃ μὴ εἶχεν αὐτός. Ἀλλ' ἐξ ἑνὸς
αὐτοῦ πολλὰ τούτῳ· ἣν γὰρ ἐκομίζετο δύναμιν ἀδυνατῶν ἔχειν συνέθραυε καὶ
πολλὰ ἐποίησε τὴν μίαν, ἵν' οὕτω δύναιτο κατὰ μέρος φέρειν. "Ο τι οὖν ἐγέννα,
ἀγαθοῦ ἐκ δυνάμεως ἦν καὶ ἀγοθοειδὲς ἦν καὶ αὐτὸς ἀγαθὸς ἐξ ἀγαθοειδῶν,
ἀγαθὸν ποικίλον.

---

telian terms. Yet, the tendency of the passage is more Platonical: what the author
means is not that soul is potentially noûs, but that soul receives "forms" from noûs,
by a downward motion going from noûs to soul.

The second God

d. Noûs, therefore, is a God, but not the highest God.

Enn. V 5, 3, l. 1-21 Br.:

Μία τοίνυν φύσις αὕτη ἡμῖν [νοῦς], τὰ ὄντα πάντα [ἡ ἀλήθεια]· εἰ δέ, θεός τις μέγας· μᾶλλον δὲ οὐ τίς, ἀλλὰ πᾶς ἀξιοῖ ταῦτα εἶναι. Καὶ θεὸς αὕτη ἡ φύσις, καὶ θεὸς δεύτερος προφαίνων ἑαυτὸν πρὶν ὁρᾶν ἐκεῖνον· ὁ δὲ ὑπερκάθηται καὶ ὑπερίδρυται ἐπὶ καλῆς οὕτως οἷον κρηπῖδος, ἢ ἐξ αὐτοῦ ἐξήρτηται. 5 Ἔδει γὰρ ἐκεῖνον βαίνοντα μὴ ἐπ' ἀψύχου τινὸς μηδ' αὖ ἐπὶ ψυχῆς εὐθὺς βεβηκέναι, ἀλλ' εἶναι αὐτῷ κάλλος ἀμήχανον πρὸ αὐτοῦ προϊόν, οἷον πρὸ μεγάλου βασιλέως πρόεισι μὲν πρῶτα ἐν ταῖς προόδοις τὰ ἐλάττω, ἀεὶ δὲ τὰ μείζω καὶ τὰ σεμνότερα ἐπ' αὐτοῖς, καὶ τὰ περὶ βασιλέα ἤδη μᾶλλον βασιλικώτερα, εἶτα τὰ μετ' αὐτὸν τίμια· ἐφ' ἅπασι δὲ τούτοις βασιλεὺς προφαίνεται ἐξαίφνης αὐτὸς ὁ μέγας, οἱ δ' εὔχονται καὶ προσκυνοῦσιν, ὅσοι μὴ προαπῆλθον ἀρκεσθέντες τοῖς πρὸ τοῦ βασιλέως ὀφθεῖσιν. Ἐκεῖ μὲν οὖν ὁ βασιλεὺς ἄλλος, οἵ τε πρὸ αὐτοῦ προϊόντες ἄλλοι αὐτοῦ· ὁ δὲ ἐκεῖ βασιλεὺς οὐκ ἀλλοτρίων ἄρχων, ἀλλ' ἔχων τὴν δικαιοτάτην καὶ φύσει ἀρχὴν καὶ τὴν ἀληθῆ βασιλείαν, ἅτε τῆς ἀληθείας βασιλεὺς καὶ ὢν κατὰ φύσιν κύριος τοῦ αὐτοῦ ἀθρόου γεννήματος καὶ θείου συντάγματος, βασιλεὺς βασιλέων καὶ πατὴρ δικαιότερον ἂν κληθεὶς θεῶν. 2

For the notion of a δεύτερος θεός cp. Philo **1301b**, **1305a b**, **1306b**, **d**; Plut **1321**; Albinus **1327b**; Apuleius **1331**; Poimandres **1340**; Numenius **1349**.

Eternal spirit contains all eternal being

1383—Noûs is eternal and contains all spiritual being within itself.

a. *Enn.* V 1, 4, l. 10-29 Br.:

Πάντα γὰρ ἐν αὐτῷ τὰ ἀθάνατα περιέχει, νοῦν πάντα, θεὸν πάντα, ψυχὴν 1 πᾶσαν, ἑστῶτα ἀεί. Τί γὰρ ζητεῖ μεταβάλλειν εὖ ἔχων; Ποῖ δὲ μετελθεῖν πάντα παρ' αὐτῷ ἔχων; Ἀλλ' οὐδὲ αὔξην ζητεῖ τελειότατος ὤν¹. Διὸ καὶ τὰ παρ' αὐτῷ πάντα τέλεια, ἵνα πάντη ᾖ τέλειος οὐδὲν ἔχων ὅ τι μὴ τοιοῦτον, οὐδὲν <δ'> ἔχων ἐν αὐτῷ ὃ μὴ νοεῖ· νοεῖ δὲ οὐ ζητῶν, ἀλλ' ἔχων². Καὶ τὸ μακάριον αὐτῷ οὐκ ἐπίκτητον, ἀλλ' ἐν αἰῶνι πάντα, καὶ ὁ ὄντως αἰών, ὃν μιμεῖται χρόνος περιθέων ψυχὴν τὰ μὲν παριείς, τοῖς δὲ ἐπιβάλλων. Καὶ γὰρ ἄλλα καὶ ἄλλα αὖ περὶ ψυχήν· ποτὲ γὰρ Σωκράτης, ποτὲ δὲ ἵππος, ἕν τι ἀεὶ τῶν 2 ὄντων· ὁ δὲ νοῦς πάντα. Ἔχει οὖν ἐν αὐτῷ πάντα ἑστῶτα ἐν τῷ αὐτῷ, καὶ ἔστι μόνον, καὶ τὸ ἔστιν ἀεί, καὶ οὐδαμοῦ τὸ μέλλον· ἔστι γὰρ καὶ τότε· οὐδὲ τὸ παρεληλυθός· οὐ γάρ τι ἐκεῖ παρελήλυθεν, ἀλλ' ἐνέστηκεν ἀεὶ ἅτε τὰ αὐτὰ ὄντα οἷον ἀγαπῶντα ἑαυτὰ οὕτως ἔχοντα. Ἕκαστον δὲ αὐτῶν νοῦς καὶ ὄν 2 ἐστι καὶ τὸ σύμπαν πᾶς νοῦς καὶ πᾶν ὄν³, ὁ μὲν νοῦς κατὰ τὸ νοεῖν ὑφιστὰς

---

¹ These lines remind us strongly of Parm. fr. 8 (above, nr. **83**) l. 6 f. and 26 ff.

² I.e.: Noûs is not discursive thinking, but *intuitive* thinking, since it possesses its object within itself. Cp. nr. **1385**, l. 28 ff.

³ Cp. again Parm. fr. 8, l. 34 ff.

τὸ ὄν, τὸ δὲ ὄν τῷ νοεῖσθαι τῷ νῷ διδὸν τὸ νοεῖν καὶ τὸ εἶναι· τοῦ δὲ νοεῖν αἴτιον ἄλλο, ὃ καὶ τῷ ὄντι.

b. Cp. *Enn.* V 4, 2, l. 46-51 Br.:

Noûs is identic with its object

Οὐ γὰρ τῶν πραγμάτων ὁ νοῦς, ὥσπερ ἡ αἴσθησις τῶν αἰσθητῶν προόντων, ἀλλ' αὐτὸς ‹ὁ› νοῦς τὰ πράγματα, εἴπερ μὴ εἴδη αὐτῶν κομίζεται. Πόθεν γάρ; Ἀλλ' ἐνταῦθα μετὰ τῶν πραγμάτων καὶ ταὐτὸν αὐτοῖς καὶ ἕν· καὶ ἡ ἐπιστήμη δὲ ὅλη τῶν ἄνευ ὕλης τὰ πράγματα.

c. Noûs in the primary sense is ἐνέργεια and therefore being. *Enn.* V 3, 5, l. 29-48 Br.:

Why Noûs = the νοητόν

Ἀλλ' εἰ ἡ νόησις καὶ τὸ νοητὸν ἕν, πῶς διὰ τοῦτο τὸ νοοῦν νοήσει ἑαυτό; Ἡ μὲν γὰρ νόησις οἷον περιέξει τὸ νοητόν, ἢ ταὐτὸν τῷ νοητῷ ἔσται, οὔπω δὲ ὁ νοῦς δῆλος ἑαυτὸν νοῶν. — Ἀλλ' εἰ ἡ νόησις καὶ τὸ νοητὸν ταὐτόν — ἐνέργεια γάρ τις τὸ νοητόν· οὐ γὰρ δὴ δύναμις οὐδέ γε ζωῆς χωρὶς οὐδ' αὖ ἐπακτὸν τὸ ζῆν οὐδὲ τὸ νοεῖν ἄλλῳ ὄντι, οἷον λίθῳ ἢ ἀψύχῳ τινί, καὶ οὐσία ἡ πρώτη τὸ νοητόν· εἰ οὖν ἐνέργεια, καὶ ἡ πρώτη ἐνέργεια καὶ καλλίστη δὴ νόησις ἂν εἴη καὶ οὐσιώδης νόησις· καὶ γὰρ ἀληθεστάτη· νόησις δὲ τοιαύτη καὶ πρώτη οὖσα καὶ πρώτως νοῦς ἂν εἴη ὁ πρῶτος· οὐδὲ γὰρ ὁ νοῦς οὗτος δυνάμει οὐδ' ἕτερος μὲν αὐτός, ἡ δὲ νόησις ἄλλο· οὕτω γὰρ ἂν πάλιν τὸ οὐσιῶδες αὐτοῦ δυνάμει. Εἰ οὖν ἐνέργεια καὶ ἡ οὐσία αὐτοῦ ἐνέργεια, ἓν καὶ ταὐτὸν τῇ ἐνεργείᾳ ἂν εἴη· ἓν δὲ τῇ ἐνεργείᾳ τὸ ὄν καὶ τὸ νοητόν· ἓν ‹ἄρα› ἅμα πάντα ἔσται, νοῦς, νόησις, τὸ νοητόν. Εἰ οὖν ἡ νόησις αὐτοῦ τὸ νοητόν, τὸ δὲ νοητὸν αὐτός, αὐτὸς ἄρα ἑαυτὸν νοήσει· νοήσει γὰρ τῇ νοήσει, ὅπερ ἦν αὐτός, καὶ νοήσει τὸ νοητόν, ὅπερ ἦν αὐτός. Καθ' ἑκάτερον ἄρα ἑαυτὸν νοήσει, καθ' ὅ τι καὶ ἡ νόησις αὐτὸς ἦν, καὶ καθ' ὅ τι τὸ νοητὸν αὐτός, ὅπερ ἐνόει τῇ νοήσει, ὃ ἦν αὐτός.

d. Primary thinking must contain its object within itself. *Enn.* V 6, 1, l. 5-14 Br.:

Noûs = primary thinking

Μᾶλλον οὖν νοεῖ, ὅτι ἔχει, καὶ πρώτως νοεῖ, ὅτι τὸ νοοῦν δεῖ ἓν καὶ δύο εἶναι. Εἴτε γὰρ μὴ ἕν, ἄλλο τὸ νοοῦν, ἄλλο τὸ νοούμενον ἔσται — οὐκ ἂν οὖν πρώτως νοοῦν εἴη, ὅτι ἄλλου τὴν νόησιν λαμβάνον οὐ τὸ πρώτως νοοῦν ἔσται, ὅτι ὃ νοεῖ οὐκ ἔχει ὡς αὐτοῦ, ὥστε οὐδ' αὐτό· ἢ εἰ ἔχει ὡς αὐτό, ἵνα κυρίως νοῇ, τὰ δύο ἓν ἔσται· δεῖ ἄρα ἓν εἶναι ἄμφω — εἴτε ἓν μέν, μὴ δύο δὲ αὖ ἔσται, ὃ τι νοήσει οὐχ ἕξει· ὥστε οὐδὲ νοοῦν ἔσται. Ἁπλοῦν ἄρα καὶ οὐχ ἁπλοῦν δεῖ εἶναι.

1384—a. On the other hand: "being" is *living* being, and therefore is thinking.

"Being" is thinking

Enn. V 4, 2, l. 44-46 Br.:

Τὸ γὰρ ὄν οὐ νεκρὸν οὐδὲ οὐ ζωὴ οὐδὲ οὐ νοοῦν· νοῦς δὴ καὶ ὄν ταὐτόν.

b. Noûs is τὰ πρῶτα, i.e. Noûs is the intelligible universe: "everything is together" (speaking with Anaxagoras) within Noûs, as its eternal object.

Enn. V 9, 7, l. 8-17 Br.:

Ὁ νοῦς ... ἐστιν αὐτὰ τὰ πρῶτα, συνὼν αὐτῷ ἀεὶ καὶ ἐνέργεια ὑπάρχων καὶ οὐκ ἐπιβάλλων ὡς οὐκ ἔχων ἢ ἐπικτώμενος ἢ διεξοδεύων [1] οὐ προκεχει- ιⸯ ρισμένα· ψυχῆς γὰρ ταῦτα πάθη· ἀλλ' ἔστηκεν ἐν αὐτῷ ὁμοῦ πάντα ὤν [2], οὐ νοήσας, ἵν' ὑποστήσῃ ἕκαστα. Οὐ γάρ, ὅτε ἐνόησε θεόν, θεὸς ἐγένετο, οὐδέ, ὅτε ἐνόησε κίνησιν, κίνησις ἐγένετο. Ὅθεν καὶ τὸ λέγειν νοήσεις τὰ εἴδη, εἰ οὕτω λέγεται, ὡς, ἐπειδὴ ἐνόησε, τότε ἐγένετο ἢ ἔστι τόδε, οὐκ ὀρθῶς. Ταύτης ι, γὰρ τῆς νοήσεως πρότερον δεῖ τὸ νοούμενον εἶναι.

In this passage the author declares with a certain emphasis that the intelligible "things" are *not produced* by Noûs, as if they did not exist before being thought. Noûs *contains* the νοητά as its eternal object and in this sense the Ideas are the object of the divine Mind which is Noûs; but they are not just "thoughts" in the sense of conceptions or "ideas" that did not exist before being conceived. As will be confirmed in our next nrs., *P. maintains fairly emphatically the priority of being to thinking* (cp. **1385a**, the beginning, and **1386b**).

c. Intelligible being, therefore, must be contained in Noûs.

Enn. V 5, 2, l. 1-12 Br.:

Οὐ τοίνυν δεῖ οὔτε ἔξω τὰ νοητὰ ζητεῖν, οὔτε τύπους ἐν τῷ νῷ τῶν ὄντων λέγειν εἶναι, οὔτε τῆς ἀληθείας ἀποστεροῦντας αὐτὸν ἀγνωσίαν τε τῶν νοητῶν ποιεῖν καὶ ἀνυπαρξίαν καὶ ἔτι αὐτὸν τὸν νοῦν ἀναιρεῖν· ἀλλ' εἴπερ καὶ γνῶσιν δεῖ καὶ ἀλήθειαν εἰσάγειν καὶ τὰ ὄντα τηρεῖν καὶ γνῶσιν τοῦ τί ἕκαστόν ἐστιν, 5 ἀλλὰ μὴ τοῦ ποῖόν τι ἕκαστον, ἅτε εἴδωλον αὐτοῦ καὶ ἴχνος ἴσχοντας, ἀλλὰ μὴ αὐτὰ ἔχοντας καὶ συνόντας καὶ συγκραθέντας αὐτοῖς, τῷ ἀληθινῷ νῷ δοτέον τὰ πάντα. Οὕτω γὰρ ἂν καὶ εἰδείη, καὶ ἀληθινῶς εἰδείη, καὶ οὐδ' ἂν ἐπιλάθοιτο οὐδ' ἂν περιέλθοι ζητῶν, καὶ ἡ ἀλήθεια ἐν αὐτῷ καὶ ἕδρα ἔσται τοῖς οὖσι καὶ ιⸯ ζήσεται καὶ νοήσει.

1385—The identification of Noûs and being.

a. Thinking is the "act" of being and, therefore, can be identified with it.

Enn. V 9, 8, l. 8-17 Br.:

Εἰ μὲν οὖν προεπενοεῖτο ὁ νοῦς πρότερος τοῦ ὄντος, ἔδει τὸν νοῦν λέγειν

---

[1] διεξοδεύω means in the technical language of Carneades (above, nr. **1116b**) the first operation of contrôling a πιθανὴ φαντασία.

[2] The expression "ὁμοῦ πάντα" is probably a reminiscence of Anaxagoras, fr. 1 (above, nr. **124a**).

ἐνεργήσαντα καὶ νοήσαντα ἀποτελέσαι καὶ γεννῆσαι τὰ ὄντα· ἐπεὶ δὲ τὸ ὂν τοῦ νοῦ προεπινοεῖν ἀνάγκη, ἐγκεῖσθαι δεῖ τίθεσθαι ἐν τῷ νοοῦντι τὰ ὄντα, τὴν δὲ ἐνέργειαν καὶ τὴν νόησιν ἐπὶ τοῖς οὖσιν, οἷον ἐπὶ πυρὶ ἤδη τὴν τοῦ πυρὸς ἐνέργειαν, ἵν᾽ ἐνόντα τὸν νοῦν ἐφ᾽ ἑαυτοῖς ἔχῃ ἐνέργειαν αὐτῶν. Ἔστι δὲ καὶ τὸ ὂν ἐνέργεια· μία οὖν ἀμφοῖν ἐνέργεια, μᾶλλον δὲ τὰ ἄμφω ἕν. Μία μὲν οὖν φύσις τό τε ὂν ὅ τε νοῦς· —

b. The question of "How Noûs which is one produces the plurality of particular beings" is answered by P. by an enthusiastic description of the perfection of Noûs: Noûs is an organical living Being, and there is nothing failing in Him.

Enn. VI 2, 21, l. 1-38; 44-45; 51-59 Br.:

Noûs
described in
its fullness

Πῶς οὖν μένων αὐτὸς ἐν τῷ λόγῳ τὰ ἐν μέρει ποιεῖ; Τοῦτο δὲ ταὐτὸν ⟨τῷ⟩ πῶς ἐκ τῶν τεττάρων ἐκείνων τὰ λεγόμενα ἐφεξῆς. Ὅρα τοίνυν ἐν τούτῳ ⟨τῷ⟩ μεγάλῳ νῷ καὶ ἀμηχάνῳ, οὐ πολυλάλῳ ἀλλὰ πολύνῳ νῷ, τῷ πάντα νῷ καὶ ὅλῳ καὶ οὐ μέρει οὐδὲ τινὶ νῷ, ὅπως ἔνι τὰ πάντα ἐξ αὐτοῦ. Ἀριθμὸν δὴ πάντως ἔχει ἐν τούτοις οἷς ὁρᾷ, καὶ ἔστι δὲ ἓν καὶ πολλά, καὶ ταῦτα δὲ δυνάμεις καὶ θαυμασταὶ δυνάμεις, οὐκ ἀσθενεῖς, ἀλλ᾽ ἅτε καθαραὶ οὖσαι μέγισταί εἰσι καὶ οἷον σφριγῶσαι καὶ ἀληθῶς δυνάμεις, οὐ τὸ μέχρι τινὸς ἔχουσαι· ἄπειρον τοίνυν καὶ ἀπειρία καὶ τὸ μέγα. Τοῦτο τοίνυν τὸ μέγα σὺν τῷ ἐν αὐτῷ καλῷ τῆς οὐσίας καὶ τῇ περὶ αὐτὸ ἀγλαΐᾳ καὶ τῷ φωτὶ ὡς ἐν νῷ ὄντα ἰδὼν ὁρᾷς καὶ τὸ ποιὸν ἤδη ἐπανθοῦν, μετὰ δὲ τοῦ συνεχοῦς τῆς ἐνεργείας μέγεθος προφαινόμενον τῇ σῇ προσβολῇ ἐν ἡσύχῳ κείμενον. Ἑνὸς δὲ καὶ δύο ὄντων καὶ τριῶν, καὶ τὸ μέγεθος τριττὸν ὂν καὶ τὸ ποσὸν πᾶν. Τοῦ δὲ ποσοῦ ἐνορωμένου καὶ τοῦ ποιοῦ καὶ ἄμφω εἰς ἓν ἰόντων καὶ οἷον γινομένων καὶ σχῆμα ὅρα. Εἰσπίπτοντος δὲ τοῦ θατέρου καὶ διαιροῦντος καὶ τὸ ποσὸν καὶ τὸ ποιὸν σχημάτων τε διαφοραὶ καὶ ποιότητες ἄλλαι· καὶ ταυτότης μὲν συνοῦσα ἰσότητα ποιεῖ εἶναι, ἑτερότης δὲ ἀνισότητα ἐν ποσῷ, ἔν τε ἀριθμῷ ἔν τε μεγέθει, ἐξ ὧν καὶ κύκλους καὶ τετράγωνα καὶ τὰ ἐξ ἀνίσων σχήματα, ἀριθμούς τε ὁμοίους καὶ ἀνομοίους, περιττούς τε καὶ ἀρτίους. Ὅσα γὰρ ἔννους ζωὴ καὶ ἐνέργεια οὐκ ἀτελὴς οὐδὲν παραλείπει ὧν εὑρίσκομεν νῦν νοερὸν ἔργον ὄν, ἀλλὰ πάντα ἔχει ἐν τῇ αὐτῆς δυνάμει ὄντα αὐτὰ ἔχουσα καὶ ὡς ἂν νοῦς ἔχοι.

It is not
discursive
reasoning

Ἔχει δὲ νοῦς ὡς ἐν νοήσει· νοήσει δὲ οὐ τῇ ἐν διεξόδῳ· παραλέλειπται δὲ οὐδὲν τῶν ὅσα λόγοι, ἀλλ᾽ ἔστιν εἷς οἷον λόγος, μέγας, τέλειος, πάντας περιέχων, ἀπὸ τῶν πρώτων αὐτοῦ ἐπεξιών, μᾶλλον δὲ ἀεὶ ἐπεξελθών, ὥστε μηδέποτε τὸ ἐπεξιέναι ἀληθὲς εἶναι. Ὅλως γὰρ πανταχοῦ, ὅσα ἄν τις ἐκ λογισμοῦ λάβῃ ἐν τῇ φύσει ὄντα, ταῦτα εὑρήσει ἐν νῷ ἄνευ λογισμοῦ ὄντα, ὥστε νομίζειν τὸ ὂν νοῦν λελογισμένον οὕτω ποιῆσαι, οἷον καὶ ἐπὶ τῶν λόγων τῶν τὰ ζῷα ποιούντων· ὡς γὰρ ἂν ὁ ἀκριβέστατος λογισμὸς λογίσαιτο ὡς ἄριστα, οὕτως ἔχει πάντα ἐν τοῖς λόγοις πρὸ λογισμοῦ οὖσι. —

Σχημάτων δὴ πάντων ὀφθέντων ἐν τῷ ὄντι καὶ ποιότητος ἁπάσης ... καὶ ζωῆς ἐπιθεούσης, μᾶλλον δὲ συνούσης πανταχοῦ, πάντα ἐξ ἀνάγκης ζῷα ἐγίνετο, καὶ ἦν καὶ σώματα ὕλης καὶ ποιότητος οὐσῶν. Γενομένων δὲ πάντων ἀεὶ καὶ μενόντων καὶ ἐν τῷ εἶναι αἰῶνι περιληφθέντων, χωρὶς μὲν ἑκάστων ἃ ἔστιν ὄντων, ὁμοῦ δ' αὖ ἐν ἑνὶ ὄντων, ἡ πάντων ἐν ἑνὶ ὄντων οἷον συμπλοκὴ καὶ σύνθεσις νοῦς ἐστι· καὶ ἔχων μὲν τὰ ὄντα ἐν αὑτῷ ζῷόν ἐστι παντελὲς καὶ ὃ ἔστι ζῷον, τῷ δ' ἐξ αὑτοῦ ὄντι παρέχων ἑαυτὸν ὁρᾶσθαι νοητὸν γενόμενος ἐκείνῳ δίδωσιν ὀρθῶς λέγεσθαι.

a perfect living being

The expression ζῷον παντελές is used by Plato in *Tim.* 31b, apparently to indicate the intelligible παράδειγμα of the ζῷον ἔμψυχον ἔννουν which is the visible world. Cp. also Arist., *De anima* I 2, 404b 19 ff. (above, nr. **372**, with n. 1): αὐτὸ τὸ ζῷον.

That the παντελῶς ὄν of *Soph.* 249a must be understood in this sense, was expounded by me at Brussels 1953. See: *Actes du XIe Congrès international de Phil.*, vol. XII, p. 61-67.

1386—All things are contained in Noûs as an organical unity, "all together" and yet distinguished. Thus, Noûs is "the perfect living Being", containing all living beings.

The intelligible world a living being

a. *Enn.* VI 6, 7, l. 1-4, 7, 9-10, 15-19 Br.:

Ὅλως γὰρ δεῖ νοῆσαι τὰ πράγματα ἐν μιᾷ <φύσει> καὶ μίαν φύσιν πάντα ἔχουσαν καὶ οἷον περιλαβοῦσαν, οὐχ ὡς ἐν τοῖς αἰσθητοῖς ἕκαστον χωρίς, ἀλλαχοῦ ἥλιος καὶ ἄλλο ἄλλοθι, ἀλλ' ὁμοῦ ἐν ἑνὶ πάντα· αὕτη γὰρ νοῦ φύσις· — Ὁμοῦ δὲ πάντων ὄντων ἕκαστον αὖ χωρίς ἐστιν· — Κεχώρισται γὰρ ἤδη ἐν αὐτῷ ἀεί. — Τὸ δὴ παντελὲς ζῷον ἐκ πάντων ζῴων ὄν, μᾶλλον δὲ ἐν αὑτῷ τὰ πάντα ζῷα περιέχον καὶ ἓν ὂν τοσοῦτον, ὅσα τὰ πάντα, ὥσπερ καὶ τόδε τὸ πᾶν ἓν ὂν καὶ πᾶν τὸ ὁρατὸν περιέχον πάντα τὰ ἐν τῷ ὁρατῷ.

b. It contains Number and all Ideas, but in a different sense, Number being of primary importance and to be ranked with οὐσία, while "thinking" and "living being" are ranked after it.

Number is ranked first in the intelligible world

Enn. VI 6, 8, l. 1-7, 17-22 Br.:

Ἐπειδὴ τοίνυν καὶ ζῷον πρώτως ἐστὶ καὶ διὰ τοῦτο αὐτοζῷον καὶ νοῦς ἐστι καὶ οὐσία ἡ ὄντως καὶ φαμὲν ἔχειν καὶ ζῷα τὰ πάντα καὶ ἀριθμὸν τὸν σύμπαντα καὶ δίκαιον αὐτὸ καὶ καλὸν καὶ ὅσα ἄλλα τοιαῦτα (ἄλλως γὰρ αὐτοάνθρωπόν φαμεν καὶ ἀριθμὸν αὐτὸν καὶ δίκαιον αὐτό), σκεπτέον πῶς τούτων ἕκαστον καὶ τί ὂν εἰς ὅσον οἷόν τέ τι εὑρεῖν περὶ τούτων. —

Εἰ δὴ τὸ ὂν πρῶτον δεῖ λαβεῖν πρῶτον ὄν, εἶτα νοῦν, εἶτα τὸ ζῷον (τοῦτο

γὰρ ἤδη πάντα δοκεῖ περιέχειν) ὁ δὲ νοῦς δεύτερον (ἐνέργεια γὰρ τῆς οὐσίας),
οὔτ' ἂν κατὰ τὸ ζῷον ὁ ἀριθμὸς εἴη (ἤδη γὰρ καὶ πρὸ αὐτοῦ καὶ ἓν καὶ δύο ἦν)
οὔτε κατὰ τὸν νοῦν· πρὸ γὰρ αὐτοῦ ἡ οὐσία ἓν οὖσα καὶ πολλὰ ἦν.

1387—In what sense is Number before Being?

a. *Enn.* VI 6, 9, l. 11-29 Br.:

'Αλλ' εἰ τὸ ὂν ἓν ὄν ἐστι καὶ τὰ δύο δύο ὄντα ἐστί, προηγήσεται τοῦ τε ὄντος
τὸ ἓν καὶ ὁ ἀριθμὸς τῶν ὄντων. Ἆρ' οὖν τῇ ἐπινοίᾳ καὶ τῇ ἐπιβολῇ; ἢ καὶ τῇ
ὑποστάσει. Σκεπτέον δὲ ὧδε· ὅταν τις ἄνθρωπον ὄντα νοῇ καὶ καλὸν ἕν, ὕστερον
δήπου τὸ ἓν νοεῖ ἐφ' ἑκατέρῳ· καὶ δὴ καὶ ὅταν ἵππον καὶ κύνα· καὶ δὴ σαφῶς
τὰ δύο ἐνταῦθα ὕστερον. 'Αλλ' εἰ γεννῴη ἄνθρωπον καὶ γεννῴη ἵππον καὶ
κύνα ἢ ἐν αὐτῷ ὄντας προφέροι καὶ μὴ κατὰ τὸ ἐπελθὸν μήτε γεννῴη μήτε
προφέροι, ἆρ' οὐκ ἐρεῖ· "εἰς ἓν ἰτέον καὶ μετιτέον εἰς ἄλλο ἓν καὶ δύο ποιητέον
καὶ μετ' ἐμοῦ καὶ ἄλλο ποιητέον"; Καὶ μὴν οὐδὲ τὰ ὄντα, ὅτε ἐγένετο, ἠριθμήθη,
ἀλλ' ὅσα δεῖ γενέσθαι δῆλον ἦν, ὅτε ἔδει. Πᾶς ἄρα ὁ ἀριθμὸς ἦν πρὸ αὐτῶν τῶν
ὄντων. 'Αλλ' εἰ πρὸ τῶν ὄντων, οὐκ ἦν ὄντα. Ἢ ἦν ἐν τῷ ὄντι, οὐκ ἀριθμὸς ὢν
τοῦ ὄντος (ἓν γὰρ ἦν ἔτι τὸ ὄν) ἀλλ' ἡ τοῦ ἀριθμοῦ δύναμις ὑποστᾶσα ἐμέρισε
τὸ ὂν καὶ οἷον ὠδίνειν ἐποίησεν αὐτὸ τὸ πλῆθος· ἢ γὰρ ἡ οὐσία αὐτοῦ ἢ ἡ
ἐνέργεια ἀριθμὸς ἔσται καὶ τὸ ζῷον αὐτὸ καὶ ὁ νοῦς ἀριθμός.

b. Since Being springs from the One, it must be Number, and
Ideas may be called Numbers or units.

Ib., l. 29-42 Br.:

Ἆρ' οὖν τὸ μὲν ὂν ἀριθμὸς ἡνωμένος, τὰ δὲ ὄντα ἐξεληλιγμένος ἀριθμός, νοῦς
δὲ ἀριθμὸς ἐν ἑαυτῷ κινούμενος, τὸ δὲ ζῷον ἀριθμὸς περιέχων; Ἐπεὶ καὶ ἀπὸ
τοῦ ἑνὸς γενόμενον τὸ ὄν, ὡς ἦν ἓν ἐκεῖνο, δεῖ αὐτὸ οὕτως ἀριθμὸν εἶναι· διὸ
καὶ τὰ εἴδη ἔλεγον καὶ ἑνάδας καὶ ἀριθμούς. Καὶ οὗτός ἐστιν ὁ οὐσιώδης ἀριθμός·
ἄλλος δὲ ὁ μοναδικὸς λεγόμενος εἴδωλον τούτου [1]. Ὁ δὲ οὐσιώδης ὁ μὲν ἐπι-
θεωρούμενος τοῖς εἴδεσι καὶ συγγεννῶν αὐτά, πρώτως δὲ ὁ ἐν τῷ ὄντι καὶ μετὰ
τοῦ ὄντος καὶ πρὸ τῶν ὄντων. Βάσιν δὲ ἔχει τὰ ὄντα ἐν αὐτῷ καὶ πηγὴν καὶ
ῥίζαν καὶ ἀρχήν. Καὶ γὰρ τῷ ὄντι τὸ ἓν ἀρχὴ καὶ ἐπὶ τούτου ἐστὶν ὄν· σκεδασ-
θείη γὰρ ἄν· ἀλλ' οὐκ ἐπὶ τῷ ὄντι τὸ ἕν· ἤδη γὰρ ἂν εἴη ἓν πρὶν
τυχεῖν τοῦ ἑνός, καὶ ἤδη τὸ τυγχάνον τῆς δεκάδος δεκὰς πρὶν τυχεῖν τῆς
δεκάδος.

---

[1] "Ideal Number", as it is called by Aristotle (εἰδητικὸς ἀριθμός, *Metaph.* N 3,
1090b, 32-36; *Gr. Ph.*I nr. **363b**), by P. is named οὐσιώδης ἀριθμός, while "mathematical number" (μαθηματικὸς in Ar., l.c.) is named by him μοναδικὸς ἀριθμός.

True being
is immutable
and
ἀπαθής

1388—Immutability of the intelligible world.

Enn. VI 5, 3, l. 1-12:

Εἰ δὴ τὸ ὂν ὄντως τοῦτο καὶ ὡσαύτως ἔχει καὶ οὐκ ἐξίσταται αὐτὸ ἑαυτοῦ καὶ γένεσις περὶ αὐτὸ οὐδεμία οὐδ' ἐν τόπῳ ἐλέγετο εἶναι, ἀνάγκη αὐτὸ οὕτως ἔχον ἀεί τε σὺν αὐτῷ εἶναι, καὶ μὴ διεστάναι ἀφ' αὑτοῦ μηδὲ αὐτοῦ τὸ μὲν ὡδί, τὸ δὲ ὡδὶ εἶναι, μηδὲ προϊέναι τι ἀπ' αὐτοῦ· ἤδη γὰρ ἂν ἐν ἄλλῳ καὶ ἄλλῳ εἴη, καὶ ὅλως ἔν τινι εἴη, καὶ οὐκ ἐφ' ἑαυτοῦ οὐδ' ἀπαθές· πάθοι γὰρ ἄν, εἰ ἐν ἄλλῳ· εἰ δ' ἐν ἀπαθεῖ ἔσται, οὐκ ἐν ἄλλῳ. Εἰ οὖν μὴ ἀποστὰν ἑαυτοῦ μηδὲ μερισθὲν μηδὲ μεταβάλλον αὐτὸ μηδεμίαν μεταβολὴν ἐν πολλοῖς ἅμα εἴη ἓν ὅλον ἅμα ἑαυτῷ ὄν, τὸ αὐτὸ ὂν πανταχοῦ ἑαυτῷ τὸ ἐν πολλοῖς εἶναι ἂν ἔχοι· τοῦτο δέ ἐστιν ἐφ' ἑαυτοῦ ὂν μὴ αὖ ἐφ' ἑαυτοῦ εἶναι.

Cp. also **1375b**, the beginning.

1389—Noûs possesses two faculties: first, that of *thinking*, i.e. seeing what is within itself, secondly, that of seeing what is beyond it.

Double
function of
νοῦς

a. *Enn.* VI 7, 35, r. 19-30 Br :

Καὶ τὸν νοῦν τοίνυν <δεῖ> τὴν μὲν ἔχειν δύναμιν εἰς τὸ νοεῖν, ᾗ τὰ ἐν αὐτῷ βλέπει, τὴν δέ, ᾗ τὰ ἐπέκεινα αὐτοῦ ἐπιβολῇ τινι καὶ παραδοχῇ, καθ' ἣν καὶ πρότερον ἑώρα μόνον καὶ ὁρῶν ὕστερον καὶ νοῦν ἔσχε καὶ ἕν ἐστι· καὶ ἔστιν ἐκείνη μὲν ἡ θέα νοῦ ἔμφρονος, αὕτη δὲ νοῦς ἐρῶν. Ὅταν γὰρ ἄφρων γένηται μεθυσθεὶς τοῦ νέκταρος, τότε ἐρῶν γίνεται ἁπλωθεὶς εἰς εὐπάθειαν τῷ κόρῳ· καὶ ἔστιν αὐτῷ μεθύειν βέλτιον ἢ σεμνοτέρῳ εἶναι τοιαύτης μέθης.

Παρὰ μέρος δὲ ὁ νοῦς ἐκεῖνος ἄλλα, τὰ δὲ ἄλλοτε ἄλλα ὁρᾷ; Ἢ οὔ· ὁ δὲ λόγος διδάσκων γινόμενα ποιεῖ, ὁ δὲ ἔχει τὸ νοεῖν ἀεί, ἔχει δὲ καὶ τὸ μὴ νοεῖν, ἀλλὰ ἄλλως ἐκεῖνον βλέπειν.

b. Noûs sees the νοητά through the light of the One; but it (he) can also contemplate this Light itself. Just as our corporeal eye has light within itself, so Noûs finds the Light-itself deep down in His own heart.

Noûs finds
the Light of
the One
within itself

Enn. V 5, 7, l. 17-35 Br.:

Οὕτω τοίνυν καὶ ἡ τοῦ νοῦ ὄψις ὁρᾷ μὲν καὶ αὐτὴ δι' ἄλλου φωτὸς τὰ πεφωτισμένα ἐκείνῃ τῇ πρώτῃ φύσει καὶ ἐν ἐκείνοις ὄντως ὁρᾷ, νεύουσα μέντοι πρὸς τὴν τῶν καταλαμπομένων φύσιν ἧττον αὐτὸ ὁρᾷ. Εἰ δ' ἀφήσει τὰ ὁρώμενα καὶ δι' οὗ εἶδεν εἰς αὐτὸ βλέπει, φῶς ἂν καὶ φωτὸς ἀρχὴν ἂν βλέποι.

Ἀλλ' ἐπεὶ μὴ ὡς ἔξω ὂν δεῖ τὸν νοῦν τοῦτο τὸ φῶς βλέπειν, πάλιν ἐπὶ τὸν ὀφθαλμὸν ἰτέον, ὅς ποτε καὶ αὐτὸς οὐ τὸ ἔξω φῶς οὐδὲ τὸ ἀλλότριον εἴσεται, ἀλλὰ πρὸ τοῦ ἔξω οἰκεῖόν τι καὶ μᾶλλον στιλπνότερον ἐν ἀκαρεῖ θεᾶται, ἢ

νύκτωρ ἐν σκότῳ πρὸ αὐτοῦ ἐξ αὐτοῦ προπηδήσαντος ἢ ὅταν μηδὲν ἐθελήσας
τῶν ἄλλων βλέπειν προβάλληται πρὸ αὐτοῦ τὴν τῶν βλεφάρων φύσιν τὸ φῶς
ὅμως προφέρων, ἢ καὶ πιέσαντος τοῦ ἔχοντος τὸ ἐν αὐτῷ φῶς ἴδῃ· τότε γὰρ
οὐχ ὁρῶν ὁρᾷ καὶ μάλιστα τότε ὁρᾷ· φῶς γὰρ ὁρᾷ· τὰ δ' ἄλλα φωτοειδῆ μὲν
ἦν, φῶς δὲ οὐκ ἦν. Οὕτω δὴ καὶ νοῦς αὐτὸν ἀπὸ τῶν ἄλλων καλύψας καὶ συναγαγὼν εἰς τὸ εἴσω μηδὲν ὁρῶν θεάσεται οὐκ ἄλλο ἐν ἄλλῳ φῶς, ἀλλ' αὐτὸ
καθ' αὑτὸ μόνον καθαρὸν ἐφ' ἑαυτοῦ ἐξαίφνης φανέν.

c. The contemplation of the One. We must wait quietly till it
appears. It comes without coming. It is Noûs that must come. And
Noûs sees it with that part of itself which is not thinking.

The contemplation of the One

Enn. V 5, 8, l. 1-26 Br.:

Ὥστε ἀπορεῖν ὅθεν ἐφάνη, ἔξωθεν ἢ ἔνδον, καὶ ἀπελθόντος εἰπεῖν "ἔνδον
ἄρα ἦν καὶ οὐκ ἔνδον αὖ". Ἢ οὐ δεῖ ζητεῖν πόθεν· οὐ γάρ ἐστι τὸ πόθεν· οὔτε
γὰρ ἔρχεται οὔτε ἄπεισιν οὐδαμοῦ, ἀλλὰ φαίνεταί τε καὶ οὐ φαίνεται· διὸ οὐ
χρὴ διώκειν, ἀλλ' ἡσυχῇ μένειν, ἕως ἂν φανῇ, παρασκευάσαντα ἑαυτὸν θεατὴν
εἶναι, ὥσπερ ὀφθαλμὸς ἀνατολὰς ἡλίου περιμένει· ὁ δὲ ὑπερφανεὶς τοῦ ὁρίζοντος
(ἐξ ὠκεανοῦ φασιν οἱ ποιηταί) ἔδωκεν ἑαυτὸν θεάσασθαι τοῖς ὄμμασιν. —
Οὑτοσὶ δέ, ὃν μιμεῖται ὁ ἥλιος, ὑπερσχήσει πόθεν; Καὶ τί ὑπερβαλὼν φανήσεται;
— Ἢ αὐτὸν ὑπερσχὼν τὸν νοῦν τὸν θεώμενον· ἑστήξεται μὲν γὰρ ὁ νοῦς πρὸς
τὴν θέαν εἰς οὐδὲν ἄλλο ἢ πρὸς τὸ καλὸν βλέπων, ἐκεῖ ἑαυτὸν πᾶς τρέπων καὶ
διδούς, στὰς δὲ καὶ οἷον πληρωθεὶς μένους εἶδε μὲν τὰ πρῶτα καλλίω γενόμενον ἑαυτὸν καὶ ἐπιστίλβοντα, ὡς ἐγγὺς ὄντος αὐτοῦ. Ὁ δὲ οὐκ ᾔει, ὥς τις
προσεδόκα, ἀλλ' ἦλθεν ὡς οὐκ ἐλθών· ὤφθη γὰρ ὡς οὐκ ἐλθών, ἀλλὰ πρὸ
ἁπάντων παρών, πρὶν καὶ τὸν νοῦν ἐλθεῖν. Εἶναι δὲ <δεῖ> τὸν νοῦν τὸν ἐλθόντα
καὶ τοῦτον εἶναι καὶ τὸν ἀπιόντα, ὅτι μὴ οἶδε ποῦ μένειν δεῖ καὶ ποῦ ἐκεῖνος
μένει, ὅτι ἐν οὐδενί. Καὶ εἰ οἷόν τε ἦν καὶ αὐτῷ τῷ νῷ μένειν μηδαμοῦ — οὐχ
ὅτι ἐν τόπῳ· οὐδὲ γὰρ οὐδ' αὐτὸς ἐν τόπῳ, ἀλλ' ὅλως οὐδαμοῦ —, ἦν ἂν ἀεὶ
ἐκεῖνον βλέπων· καίτοι οὐδὲ βλέπων, ἀλλ' ἐν ἐκείνῳ ὢν καὶ οὐ δύο. Νῦν δέ,
ὅτι ἐστὶ νοῦς, οὕτω βλέπει, ὅτε βλέπει, τῷ ἑαυτοῦ μὴ νῷ. Θαῦμα δή, πῶς οὐκ
ἐλθὼν πάρεστι, καὶ πῶς οὐκ ὢν οὐδαμοῦ οὐκ ἔστιν ὅπου μὴ ἔστιν.

1390—Why Noûs is not the first, but the second principle. First, it
contains a duality.

a. *Enn.* VI 9, 2, l. 32-40 Br.:

Noûs not the first but the second principle

Ὅτι δὲ οὐχ οἷόν τε τὸν νοῦν τὸ πρῶτον εἶναι καὶ ἐκ τῶνδε δῆλον ἔσται·
τὸν νοῦν ἀνάγκη ἐν τῷ νοεῖν εἶναι καὶ τόν γε ἄριστον καὶ τὸν οὐ πρὸς τὰ ἔξω
βλέποντα νοεῖν τὸ πρὸ αὐτοῦ· εἰς ἑαυτὸν γὰρ ἐπιστρέφων εἰς ἀρχὴν ἐπιστρέφει.

Καὶ εἰ μὲν αὐτὸς τὸ νοοῦν καὶ τὸ νοούμενον, διπλοῦς ἔσται καὶ οὐχ ἁπλοῦς οὐδὲ τὸ ἕν· εἰ δὲ πρὸς τὸ ἕτερον βλέπει, πάντως πρὸς τὸ κρεῖττον καὶ πρὸ αὐτοῦ. Εἰ δὲ καὶ πρὸς αὐτὸν καὶ πρὸς τὸ κρεῖττον, καὶ οὕτω δεύτερον.

Cp. also III 8, 9, l. 5 f.: Καὶ οὗτος νοῦς καὶ νοητὸν ἅμα, ὥστε δύο ἅμα. Εἰ δὲ δύο, δεῖ τὸ πρὸ τοῦ δύο λαβεῖν.

b. It is the cause of beauty of the soul, is beautiful in itself—the One being beyond beauty—and as it were a vestibule of the Good.

Noûs is a vestibule of the Good

Enn. V 9, 2, l. 16-28 Br.:

Τί οὖν τὸ ποιῆσαν σῶμα καλόν; "Αλλως μὲν κάλλους παρουσία, ἄλλως δὲ ψυχή, ἣ ἔπλασέ τε καὶ μορφὴν τοιάνδε ἐνῆκε. Τί οὖν; Ψυχὴ παρ' αὐτῆς καλόν; "Η οὔ. Οὐ γὰρ <ἂν> ἡ μὲν ἦν φρόνιμός τε καὶ καλή, ἡ δὲ ἄφρων τε καὶ αἰσχρά. Φρονήσει ἄρα τὸ καλὸν περὶ ψυχήν. Καὶ τίς οὖν ὁ φρόνησιν δοὺς ψυχῇ; "Η νοῦς 2 ἐξ ἀνάγκης, νοῦς δὲ οὐ ποτὲ μὲν νοῦς, ποτὲ δὲ ἄνους [1], ὅ γε ἀληθινός. Παρ' αὐτοῦ ἄρα καλός. Καὶ πότερον δὲ ἐνταῦθα δεῖ στῆναι, ὡς πρῶτον, ἢ καὶ νοῦ ἐπέκεινα δεῖ ἰέναι; Νοῦς δὲ προέστηκε μὲν ἀρχῆς τῆς πρώτης ὡς πρὸς ἡμᾶς, ὥσπερ ἐν προθύροις τἀγαθοῦ ἀπαγγέλλων ἐν αὐτῷ τὰ πάντα, ὥσπερ ἐκείνου 2 τύπος μᾶλλον ἐν πλήθει, ἐκείνου πάντη μένοντος ἐν ἑνί [2].

Noûs is a universe, ergo not the One

c. Noûs is Being, and Being is the All. Therefore not the One.

Enn. VI 9, 2, l. 40-47 Br.:

Καὶ χρὴ τὸν νοῦν τοιοῦτον τίθεσθαι, οἷον παρεῖναι μὲν τῷ ἀγαθῷ καὶ τῷ 4 πρώτῳ καὶ βλέπειν εἰς ἐκεῖνον, συνεῖναι δὲ καὶ ἑαυτῷ νοεῖν τε καὶ ἑαυτὸν καὶ νοεῖν ἑαυτὸν ὄντα τὰ πάντα. Πολλοῦ ἄρα δεῖ τὸ ἓν εἶναι ποικίλον ὄντα. Οὐ τοίνυν οὐδὲ τὸ ἓν τὰ πάντα ἔσται, οὕτω γὰρ <ἂν> οὐκέτι ἓν εἴη· οὐδὲ νοῦς, καὶ γὰρ ἂν οὕτως εἴη τὰ πάντα τοῦ νοῦ τὰ πάντα ὄντος· οὐδὲ τὸ ὄν· τὸ γὰρ 4 ὂν τὰ πάντα.

d. Cp. *Enn.* III 8, 9, l. 39-44 Br.:

Οὐ γὰρ ἀρχὴ τὰ πάντα, ἀλλ' ἐξ ἀρχῆς τὰ πάντα· αὐτὴ δὲ οὐκέτι τὰ πάντα 4 οὐδέ τι τῶν πάντων, ἵνα γεννήσῃ τὰ πάντα, καὶ ἵνα μὴ πλῆθος ᾖ, ἀλλὰ τοῦ πλήθους ἀρχή· τοῦ γὰρ γεννηθέντος πανταχοῦ τὸ γεννῶν ἁπλούστερον. Εἰ οὖν τοῦτο νοῦν ἐγέννησεν, ἁπλούστερον νοῦ δεῖ αὐτὸ εἶναι.

1391—a. "Thought thinking itself" [3] cannot be the First Principle.

---

[1] Cp. Arist., *De an.* III 5, 430a 22-23: ἀλλ' οὐχ ὁτὲ μὲν νοεῖ, ὁτὲ δ' οὐ νοεῖ. Supra (vol. II), nr. **652.**

[2] Cp. Plato, *Tim.* 37d: μένοντος αἰῶνος ἐν ἑνί.

[3] Νόησις νοήσεως, as Aristotle said of the Prime Mover (*Metaph.* Λ 9; supra, nr. **516b**) is a formula which might have been used by Plot., but in fact does not occur in a passage such as V 3, 5 (cited under **1383c**).

Enn. VI 7, 40, l. 43-46; 51-54 Br.:

Εἰ δέ τις καὶ τοῦτο (sc. τὸ ῞Εν ἢ τὸ ᾽Αγαθόν) ἅμα νοοῦν καὶ νοούμενον ποιοῖ
καὶ οὐσίαν καὶ νόησιν συνοῦσαν τῇ οὐσίᾳ, καὶ οὕτως αὐτὸ νοοῦν θέλοι ποιεῖν,
ἄλλου δεήσεται καὶ τούτου πρὸ αὐτοῦ· —
᾽Ωι δὲ μήτε τι ἄλλο πρὸ αὐτοῦ μήτε τι σύνεστιν αὐτῷ ἐξ ἄλλου, τί καὶ νοήσει
ἢ πῶς ἑαυτό; τί γὰρ ἐζήτει; ἢ τί ἐπόθει;

b. Thinking is given to divine but not absolute natures.

Enn. VI 7, 41, l. 1-7 Br.:

Κινδυνεύει γὰρ βοήθεια τὸ νοεῖν δεδόσθαι ταῖς φύσεσι ταῖς θειοτέραις μέν,
ἐλάττοσι δὲ οὔσαις, καὶ οἷον αὐταῖς τυφλαῖς οὔσαις ὄμμα. ῾Ο δ᾽ ὀφθαλμὸς τί
ἂν δέοιτο τὸ ὂν ὁρᾶν φῶς αὐτὸς ὤν; ῾Ο δ᾽ ἂν δέηται δι᾽ ὀφθαλμοῦ, σκότον ἔχον
5 παρ᾽ αὐτῷ φῶς ζητεῖ. Εἰ οὖν φῶς τὸ νοεῖν, τὸ δὲ φῶς φῶς οὐ ζητεῖ, οὐκ ἂν
ἐκείνη ἡ αὐγὴ φῶς μὴ ζητοῦσα ζητήσειε νοεῖν, οὐδὲ προσθήσει αὐτῇ τὸ νοεῖν.

5—THE ONE OR THE GOOD

1392—a. The One is the First Principle, for it is simple and not
composite.

Enn. VI 9, 2, l. 29-32 Br.:

῞Ολως δὲ τὸ μὲν ἓν πρῶτον, ὁ δὲ νοῦς καὶ τὰ εἴδη καὶ τὸ ὂν οὐ πρῶτα. Εἶδός
τε γὰρ ἕκαστον ἐκ πολλῶν καὶ σύνθετον καὶ ὕστερον· ἐξ ὧν γὰρ ἕκαστόν ἐστι,
πρότερα ἐκεῖνα.

It is before
Being and
has no form

b. It is before Noûs, for it does not belong to Being. It has neither
Form not property, not even that it is a Cause.

Enn. VI 9, 3, l. 36-51 Br.:

Οὐδὲ νοῦς τοίνυν, ἀλλὰ πρὸ νοῦ· τί γὰρ τῶν ὄντων ἐστὶν ὁ νοῦς· ἐκεῖνο δὲ
οὔ τι, ἀλλὰ πρὸ ἑκάστου, οὐδὲ ὄν· καὶ γὰρ τὸ ὂν οἷον μορφὴν τὴν τοῦ ὄντος
ἔχει, ἄμορφον δὲ ἐκεῖνο καὶ μορφῆς νοητῆς. Γεννητικὴ γὰρ ἡ τοῦ ἑνὸς φύσις
10 οὖσα τῶν πάντων οὐδέν ἐστιν αὐτῶν. Οὔτε οὖν τι οὔτε ποιὸν οὔτε ποσὸν οὔτε
νοῦς οὔτε ψυχή· οὐδὲ κινούμενον οὐδ᾽ αὖ ἑστώς, οὐκ ἐν τόπῳ, οὐκ ἐν χρόνῳ,
ἀλλὰ τὸ καθ᾽ αὐτὸ μονοειδές, μᾶλλον δὲ ἀνείδεον πρὸ εἴδους ὂν παντός, πρὸ
κινήσεως, πρὸ στάσεως· ταῦτα γὰρ περὶ τὸ ὄν, ἃ πολλὰ αὐτὸ ποιεῖ. Διὰ τί
15 οὖν, εἰ μὴ κινούμενον, οὐχ ἑστώς; ῞Οτι περὶ μὲν τὸ ὂν τούτων θάτερον ἢ ἀμφότερα ἀνάγκη, τό τε ἑστὼς στάσει ἑστὼς καὶ οὐ ταὐτὸν τῇ στάσει· ὥστε
συμβήσεται αὐτῷ καὶ οὐκέτι ἁπλοῦν μένει. ᾽Επεὶ καὶ τὸ αἴτιον λέγειν οὐ κατη-
20 γορεῖν ἐστι συμβεβηκός τι αὐτῷ [1], ἀλλ᾽ ἡμῖν, ὅτι ἔχομέν τι παρ᾽ αὐτοῦ ἐκείνου
ὄντος ἐν αὐτῷ.

---

[1] συμβεβηκός is used by P. in the sense of "property".

c. It is called one neither as a predicate nor as a numeric unit.

Enn. VI 9, 5, l. 24-26, 29-46 Br.:

not a
predicate

not a
numerical
unit

Τὸ δὴ πρὸ τοῦ ἐν τοῖς οὖσι τιμιωτάτου (εἴπερ δεῖ τι πρὸ νοῦ εἶναι ἐν μὲν 2
εἶναι βουλομένου, οὐκ ὄντος δὲ ἕν, ἑνοειδοῦς δέ), — τὸ δὴ πρὸ τούτου θαῦμα τὸ
ἕν, ὃ μὴ ὄν ἐστιν, ἵνα μὴ καὶ ἐνταῦθα κατ' ἄλλου τὸ ἕν, ᾧ ὄνομα μὲν κατ' 3
ἀλήθειαν οὐδὲν προσῆκον, εἴπερ δὲ δεῖ ὀνομάσαι, κοινῶς ἂν λεχθείη προση-
κόντως ἕν, οὐχ ὡς ἄλλο, εἶτα ἕν, χαλεπὸν μὲν γνωσθῆναι διὰ τοῦτο, γιγνωσκόμενον δὲ μᾶλλον τῷ ἀπ' αὐτοῦ γεννήματι, τῇ οὐσίᾳ· καὶ <γὰρ> ἄγει εἰς
οὐσίαν νοῦν, καὶ αὐτοῦ ἡ φύσις τοιαύτη, ὡς πηγὴν τῶν ἀρίστων εἶναι καὶ 3
δύναμιν γεννῶσαν τὰ ὄντα μένουσαν ἐν ἑαυτῇ καὶ οὐκ ἐλαττουμένην οὐδ' ἐν
τοῖς γινομένοις ὑπ' αὐτῆς οὖσαν, ὅτι καὶ πρὸ τούτων, <ἣν> ὀνομάζομεν ἓν ἐξ
ἀνάγκης τῷ σημαίνειν ἀλλήλοις αὐτὴν τῷ ὀνόματι εἰς ἔννοιαν ἀμέριστον ἄγοντες 4
καὶ τὴν ψυχὴν ἑνοῦν θέλοντες, οὐχ οὕτως ἓν λέγοντες καὶ ἀμερές, ὡς σημεῖον
ἢ μονάδα λέγοντες· τὸ γὰρ οὕτως ἓν ποσοῦ ἀρχή, ὃ οὐκ ἂν ὑπέστη μὴ προούσης
οὐσίας καὶ τοῦ πρὸ οὐσίας· οὔκουν δεῖ ἐνταῦθα βάλλειν τὴν διάνοιαν, ἀλλὰ
ταῦτα ὁμοιῶσαι ἐκείνοις ἐν ἀναλογίαις τῷ ἁπλῷ καὶ τῇ φυγῇ τοῦ πλήθους καὶ 4
τοῦ μερισμοῦ.

d. No relation to anything should be attributed to it. It is what
it is, and even the "is" cannot be applied to it.

no relation
to anything,
no
"ἔστιν"
or
"πέφυκεν"

Enn. VI 8, 8, l. 12-16 Br.:

Δεῖ δὲ ὅλως πρὸς οὐδὲν αὐτὸν λέγειν· ἔστι γὰρ ὅπερ ἔστι καὶ πρὸ αὐτῶν·
ἐπεὶ καὶ τὸ ἔστιν ἀφαιροῦμεν, ὥστε καὶ τὸ πρὸς τὰ ὄντα ὁπωσοῦν· οὐδὲ δὴ 1
τὸ ὡς πέφυκεν· ὕστερον γὰρ καὶ τοῦτο.

1393—a. The One *is* its οὐσία and its ἐνέργεια.

The One is
its essence

Enn. VI 8, 12, l. 1-15, 22-25 Br.:

Τί οὖν; Οὐκ ἔστιν ὃ ἔστι; Τοῦ δὲ εἶναι ὃ ἔστιν ἢ τοῦ ἐπέκεινα εἶναι ἄρά γε
κύριος αὐτός; Πάλιν γὰρ ἡ ψυχὴ οὐδέν τι πεισθεῖσα τοῖς εἰρημένοις ἄπορός
ἐστι. Λεκτέον τοίνυν πρὸς ταῦτα ὧδε, ὡς ἕκαστος μὲν ἡμῶν κατὰ μὲν τὸ σῶμα
πόρρω ἂν εἴη οὐσίας, κατὰ δὲ τὴν ψυχὴν καὶ ὃ μάλιστά ἐσμεν μετέχομεν οὐσίας 5
καὶ ἐσμέν τις οὐσία. Τοῦτο δὲ ἔστιν οἷον σύνθετόν τι ἐκ διαφορᾶς καὶ οὐσίας·
οὔκουν κυρίως οὐσία οὐδ' αὐτοουσία· διὸ οὐδὲ κύριοι τῆς αὐτῶν οὐσίας. Ἄλλο
γάρ πως ἡ οὐσία καὶ ἡμεῖς ἄλλο, καὶ κύριοι οὐχ ἡμεῖς τῆς αὐτῶν οὐσίας, ἀλλ' 1
ἡ οὐσία αὐτὴ ἡμῶν, εἴπερ αὕτη καὶ τὴν διαφορὰν προστίθησιν. Ἀλλ' ἐπειδὴ
ὅπερ κύριον ἡμῶν ἡμεῖς πως ἐσμέν, οὕτω τοι οὐδὲν ἧττον καὶ ἐνταῦθα λεγοίμεθα
ἂν αὐτῶν κύριοι· ὃ δέ γε παντελῶς ἐστιν ὃ ἔστιν καὶ οὐκ ἄλλο μὲν αὐτό, ἄλλο
δὲ ἡ οὐσία αὐτοῦ, ἐνταῦθα ὅπερ ἔστι τοῦτο ἐστί. — 1

Εἰ μὲν οὖν ἐστί τις ἐνέργεια ἐν αὐτῷ καὶ ἐν τῇ ἐνεργείᾳ αὐτὸν θησόμεθα, **and its activity**
οὐδ' ἂν διὰ τοῦτο εἴη ἂν ἕτερον αὐτοῦ καὶ οὐκ αὐτὸς αὐτοῦ κύριος, ἀφ' οὗ ἡ
5 ἐνέργεια, ὅτι μὴ ἕτερον ἐνέργεια καὶ αὐτός.

b. But, if activities are attributed to it, then also will; and if activity is its essence, the same must be said of its will.

Enn. VI 8, 13, l. 5-8; 27-33 Br.: **it is its will**

5 Εἰ γὰρ δοίημεν ἐνεργείας αὐτῷ, τὰς δὲ ἐνεργείας αὐτοῦ οἷον βουλήσει αὐτοῦ
(οὐ γὰρ ἀβουλῶν ἐνεργεῖ) αἱ δὲ ἐνέργειαι ἢ οἷον οὐσία αὐτοῦ, ἡ βούλησις αὐτοῦ
καὶ ἡ οὐσία ταὐτὸν ἔσται. —

Καὶ σύνεστιν αὐτοῦ τῇ οἷον οὐσίᾳ ἡ θέλησις τοῦ οἷον τοιοῦτον εἶναι, καὶ οὐκ
ἔστιν αὐτὸν λαβεῖν ἄνευ τοῦ θέλειν ἑαυτῷ ὅπερ ἔστι, καὶ σύνδρομος αὐτὸς
10 ἑαυτῷ θέλων αὐτὸς εἶναι καὶ τοῦτο ὤν, ὅπερ θέλει, καὶ ἡ θέλησις καὶ αὐτὸς
ἕν, καὶ τούτῳ οὐχ ἧττον ἕν, ὅτι μὴ ἄλλο αὐτός,. ὅπερ ἔτυχεν, ἄλλο δὲ τὸ ὡς
ἐβουλήθη ἄν. Τί γὰρ ἂν καὶ ἠθέλησεν ἢ τοῦτο, ὃ ἔστι;

P. speaks of βούλησις or θέλημα of the One, not to ascribe some kind of "providence" to it—for, as we shall see, this he denies—but to refute those opponents who argue that, if the One is not by a reasonable will, it is τύχη or αὐτομάτῳ or ἀνάγκη. P. replies: the One is by a reasonable Will, but not by any will anterior to or distinct from itself. It is beyond τύχη and αὐτόματον, and evidently it is beyond ἀνάγκη. See further **d.**
On the influence of Plotinus' theory of the first Principle on the Christian reflection on God: under **d.**

c. Likewise "good" does not belong to it as an attribute. **and its goodness**

Enn. V 5, 13, l. 1-11 Br.:

Ἔδει δὲ καὶ τἀγαθὸν αὐτὸν ὄντα καὶ μὴ ἀγαθὸν μὴ ἔχειν ἐν ἑαυτῷ μηδέν,
ἐπεὶ μηδὲ ἀγαθόν. Ὁ γὰρ ἕξει, ἢ ἀγαθὸν ἔχει ἢ οὐκ ἀγαθόν· ἀλλ' οὔτε ἐν τῷ
ἀγαθῷ τῷ κυρίως καὶ πρώτως ἀγαθῷ τὸ μὴ ἀγαθόν, οὔτε τὸ ἀγαθὸν ἔχει τὸ
5 ἀγαθόν. Εἰ οὖν μήτε τὸ οὐκ ἀγαθὸν μήτε τὸ ἀγαθὸν ἔχει, οὐδὲν ἔχει· εἰ οὖν
οὐδὲν ἔχει, μόνον καὶ ἔρημον τῶν ἄλλων ἐστίν. Εἰ οὖν τὰ ἄλλα ἢ ἀγαθά ἐστι
καὶ οὐ τἀγαθὸν ἢ οὐκ ἀγαθά ἐστιν, οὐδέτερα δὲ τούτων ἔχει, οὐδὲν ἔχων τῷ
μηδὲν ἔχειν ἐστὶ τὸ ἀγαθόν. Εἰ δ' ἄρα τις ὁτιοῦν αὐτῷ προστίθησιν, ἢ οὐσίαν
10 ἢ νοῦν ἢ καλόν, τῇ προσθήκῃ ἀφαιρεῖται αὐτοῦ τἀγαθὸν εἶναι.

d. Since it is the Father of Reason, Cause and causal Essence, it is its own ground, depending on nothing but itself.

Enn. VI 8, 14, l. 38 f., 42 f. Br.: **It is causa sui**

Λόγου ὢν καὶ αἰτίας καὶ οὐσίας αἰτιώδους πατήρ, ... αἴτιον ἑαυτοῦ καὶ
παρ' αὐτοῦ καὶ δι' αὐτὸν αὐτός· καὶ γὰρ πρώτως αὐτὸς καὶ ὑπερόντως αὐτός.

How much Christian reflection on God owes to the thought of P., may be seen e.g. in the following chapters of Thomas Aquinas.

S. Th. I 3, a. 3: Deus est idem quod sua essentia vel natura;

S. Th. I 19, a. 1, ad 3*m*: Voluntas Dei est eius essentia;

Ib.: Objectum divinae voluntatis est bonitas sua, quae est eius essentia;

S. Th. I 19, a. 3: Deus bonitatem suam ex necessitate vult.

S. Th. I 59, a. 2: Ibi solum est idem essentia et voluntas, ubi totaliter bonum continetur in essentia volentis, sc. in Deo.

S. Th. I 40, a. 1, ad 1*m*: Quia vero divina simplicitas excludit compositionem subjecti et accidentis, sequitur quod quidquid attribuitur Deo, est eius essentia.

St. Thomas evidently did not read Plotinus, but he was influenced by Neoplatonism through the medium of St. Augustine on the one hand and Dionysius Areopagita on the other.

Dionysius' exuberant language, full of expressions like ὑπερουσιώδης θειότης and ὑπέρθειος, is somewhat foreshadowed by P.'s language in the above passage.

1394—In what sense is the One "the Good".

The One is the Good:　　**a.** Not as a predicate. In that sense P. declares that the One is beyond the Good.

not as a predicate

Enn. VI 9, 6, l. 40-42 Br.:

'Αλλ' ἔστιν ὑπεράγαθον καὶ αὐτὸ οὐχ ἑαυτῷ, τοῖς δ' ἄλλοις ἀγαθόν, εἴ τι αὐτοῦ δύναται μεταλαμβάνειν·

Cp. V 5, 13, cited above (**1393c**).

The Good is not a primary genus　　**b.** Not as a primary genus; for the Good itself is not predicated of anything. And "good" as a quality is of secondary order.

Enn. VI 2, 17, l. 1-22 Br.:

In this treatise P. deals with the theory of the supreme kinds in Plato's *Sophistes* 250a-255 (*Gr. Ph.* I, nr. **341**). Like Plato he considers στάσις and κίνησις, ταὐτόν and ἕτερον as coequal with the ὄν, excluding all other concepts from the rank of first genera. In contradistinction to Aristotle, he confines their use strictly to the intelligible world, and deals with the supreme kinds of the κόσμος αἰσθητός in his next treatise.

'Αλλὰ τὸ καλὸν καὶ τὸ ἀγαθὸν καὶ αἱ ἀρεταὶ διὰ τί οὐκ ἐν τοῖς πρώτοις, ἐπιστήμη, νοῦς; Ἦ τὸ μὲν ἀγαθόν, εἰ τὸ πρῶτον, ἣν δὴ λέγομεν τὴν τοῦ ἀγαθοῦ φύσιν, καθ' ἧς οὐδὲν κατηγορεῖται, ἀλλ' ἡμεῖς μὴ ἔχοντες ἄλλως σημῆναι οὕτω λέγομεν, γένος οὐδενὸς ἂν εἴη. Οὐ γὰρ κατ' ἄλλων λέγεται ἢ ἣν ἂν καθ' 5 ὧν λέγεται ἕκαστον ἐκεῖνο λεγόμενον. Καὶ πρὸ οὐσίας δὲ ἐκεῖνο, οὐκ ἐν οὐσίᾳ. Εἰ δ' ὡς ποιὸν τὸ ἀγαθόν, ὅλως τὸ ποιὸν οὐκ ἐν τοῖς πρώτοις. Τί οὖν; ἡ τοῦ ὄντος φύσις οὐκ ἀγαθόν; Ἦ πρῶτον μὲν ἄλλως καὶ οὐκ ἐκείνως ὡς τὸ πρῶτον· καὶ ἔστιν ἀγαθὸν οὐχ ὡς ποιόν, ἀλλ' ἐν αὐτῷ. 'Αλλὰ καὶ τὰ ἄλλα ἔφαμεν γένη 10 ἐν αὐτῷ, καὶ διότι κοινόν τι ἦν ἕκαστον καὶ ἐν πολλοῖς ἑωρᾶτο, γένος. Εἰ οὖν καὶ τὸ ἀγαθὸν ὁρᾶται ἐφ' ἑκάστῳ μέρει τῆς οὐσίας ἢ τοῦ ὄντος ἢ ἐπὶ τοῖς πλείστοις, διὰ τί οὐ γένος καὶ ἐν τοῖς πρώτοις; Ἦ ἐν ἅπασι τοῖς μέρεσιν οὐ 15

ταὐτόν, ἀλλὰ πρώτως καὶ δευτέρως καὶ ὑστέρως· ἢ γὰρ ὅτι θάτερον παρὰ
θατέρου, τὸ ὕστερον παρὰ τοῦ προτέρου, ἢ ὅτι παρ' ἑνὸς πάντα τοῦ ἐπέκεινα,
ἄλλα ἄλλως κατὰ φύσιν τὴν αὐτῶν μεταλαμβάνει. Εἰ δὲ δὴ καὶ γένος ἐθέλοι
τις θέσθαι, ὕστερον· ὕστερον γὰρ τῆς οὐσίας καὶ τοῦ τί ἐστι τὸ εἶναι αὐτὸ
ἀγαθόν, κἂν ἀεὶ συνῇ, ἐκεῖνα δὲ ἦν τοῦ ὄντος ᾗ ὂν καὶ εἰς τὴν οὐσίαν.

c.   Can the Good be defined as the ἐφετόν, as Aristotle did in *Eth.
Nic.* I 1 (the beginning)? P. answers this question in the negative:
the First Principle is the Good, not because it is desirable, but it is desirable because it is the Good.—There is a hierarchy of goods, the Good
itself being at the top, as the absolute Cause of all.

Enn. VI 7, 25, l. 16-24:

Is it the
ἐφετόν?

Ἐφετὸν μὲν οὖν δεῖ τὸ ἀγαθὸν εἶναι, οὐ μέντοι τῷ ἐφετὸν εἶναι ἀγαθὸν γίνεσθαι, ἀλλὰ τῷ ἀγαθὸν εἶναι ἐφετὸν γίνεσθαι.

Ἆρ' οὖν τῷ μὲν ἐσχάτῳ ἐν τοῖς οὖσι τὸ πρὸ αὐτοῦ, καὶ ἀεὶ ἡ ἀνάβασις τὸ

The hier-
archy of
ἀγαθά

ὑπὲρ ἕκαστον διδοῦσα ἀγαθὸν εἶναι τῷ ὑπ' αὐτῷ, εἰ ἡ ἀνάβασις οὐκ ἐξίσταιτο
τοῦ ἀνὰ λόγον, ἀλλὰ ἐπὶ μεῖζον ἀεὶ προχωροῖ; Τότε δὲ στήσεται ἐπ' ἐσχάτῳ,
μεθ' ὃ οὐδὲν ἔστιν εἰς τὸ ἄνω λαβεῖν, καὶ τοῦτο τὸ πρῶτον καὶ τὸ ὄντως καὶ τὸ
μάλιστα κυρίως ἔσται, καὶ αἴτιον δὲ καὶ τοῖς ἄλλοις.

1395—Trying to define the Good positively, P. describes it as the Light
by which the intelligible world becomes desirable and soul is awakened
and gets wings.

a.   *Enn.* VI 7, 21, l. 2-7, 11-17; c. 22, l. 1-21:

What makes
the
νοητά
a good?

Ὧδε τοίνυν τετολμήσθω· εἶναι μὲν τὸν νοῦν καὶ τὴν ζωὴν ἐκείνην ἀγαθοειδῆ,
ἔφεσιν δὲ εἶναι καὶ τούτων, καθ' ὅσον ἀγαθοειδῆ· ἀγαθοειδῆ δὲ λέγω τῷ τὴν
μὲν τἀγαθοῦ εἶναι ἐνέργειαν, μᾶλλον δὲ ἐκ τἀγαθοῦ ἐνέργειαν, τὸν δὲ ἤδη
ὁρισθεῖσαν ἐνέργειαν· εἶναι δ' αὐτὰ μεστὰ μὲν ἀγλαΐας καὶ διώκεσθαι μὲν
ὑπὸ ψυχῆς, ὡς ἐκεῖθεν καὶ πρὸς ἐκεῖνα αὖ. — Γίνεται δὲ πρὸς αὐτὰ ἔρως
ὁ σύντονος οὐχ ὅταν ᾖ ἅπερ ἐστίν, ἀλλ' ὅταν ἐκεῖθεν ἤδη ὂν ἅπερ ἐστὶν ἄλλο
προσλάβῃ. Οἷον γὰρ ἐπὶ τῶν σωμάτων φωτὸς ἐμμεμιγμένου ὅμως δεῖ φωτὸς
ἄλλου, ἵνα καὶ φανείη τὸ ἐν αὐτοῖς φῶς, οὕτω τοι δεῖ καὶ ἐπὶ τῶν ἐκεῖ καίπερ
πολὺ φῶς ἐχόντων φωτὸς κρείττονος ἄλλου, ἵνα κἀκεῖνα καὶ ὑπ' αὐτῶν καὶ
ὑπ' ἄλλου ὀφθῇ.

(22) Ὅταν οὖν τὸ φῶς τοῦτό τις ἴδῃ, τότε δὴ καὶ κινεῖται ἐπ' αὐτὰ καὶ

The light of
the Good
makes Noῦs
desirable

τοῦ φωτὸς τοῦ ἐπιθέοντος ἐπ' αὐτοῖς γλιχόμενος εὐφραίνεται, ὥσπερ καὶ τῶν
ἐνταῦθα σωμάτων οὐ τῶν ὑποκειμένων ἐστὶν ὁ ἔρως, ἀλλὰ τοῦ ἐμφανταζομένου
κάλλους ἐπ' αὐτοῖς. Ἔστι γὰρ ἕκαστον ὃ ἔστιν ἐφ' αὑτοῦ· ἐφετὸν δὲ γίνεται

ἐπιχρώσαντος αὐτὸ τοῦ ἀγαθοῦ, ὥσπερ χάριτας δόντος αὐτοῖς καὶ εἰς τὰ ἐφιέμενα ἔρωτας. Καὶ τοίνυν ψυχὴ λαβοῦσα εἰς αὐτὴν τὴν ἐκεῖθεν ἀπορροὴν κινεῖται καὶ ἀναβακχεύεται καὶ οἴστρων πίμπλαται καὶ ἔρως γίνεται. Πρὸ τοῦ δὲ οὐδὲ πρὸς τὸν νοῦν κινεῖται, καίπερ καλὸν ὄντα· ἀργόν τε γὰρ τὸ κάλλος αὐτοῦ, 10 πρὶν τοῦ ἀγαθοῦ φῶς λάβῃ, ὑπτία τε ἀναπέπτωκεν ἡ ψυχὴ παρ' αὑτῆς καὶ πρὸς πᾶν ἀργῶς ἔχει καὶ παρόντος νοῦ ἐστι πρὸς αὐτὸν νωθής. Ἐπειδὰν δὲ ἥκῃ εἰς αὐτὴν ὥσπερ θερμασία ἐκεῖθεν, ῥώννυταί τε καὶ ἐγείρεται καὶ ὄντως πτεροῦται καὶ πρὸς τὸ παρακείμενον καὶ πλησίον καίπερ ἐπτοημένη ὅμως 15 πρὸς ἄλλο οἷον τῇ μνήμῃ μεῖζον κουφίζεται. Καὶ ἕως τί ἐστιν ἀνωτέρω τοῦ παρόντος, αἴρεται φύσει ἄνω αἰρομένη ὑπὸ τοῦ δόντος τὸν ἔρωτα. Καὶ νοῦν μὲν ὑπεραίρει, οὐ δύναται δὲ ὑπὲρ τὸ ἀγαθὸν δραμεῖν, ὅτι μηδέν ἐστι τὸ ὑπερ- 20 κείμενον.

The light by which the νοητά are seen   b. Again, P. says repeatedly that the One is the Light by which noûs sees the νοητά. Cp. above, nrs. **1382a** and **1389b**. In the following passage he describes the difference between discursive thinking or reasoning, and direct contemplation, "when the soul suddenly gets light" and by this sudden illumination sees that Light itself which is her true τέλος.

Enn. V 3, 17, l. 23-38:

The light itself is seen   Δεῖ τὴν διάνοιαν, ἵνα τι εἴπῃ, ἄλλο καὶ ἄλλο λαβεῖν· οὕτω γὰρ καὶ διέξοδος· ἐν δὲ πάντῃ ἁπλῷ διέξοδος τίς ἐστιν; Ἀλλ' ἀρκεῖ κἂν νοερῶς ἐφάψασθαι· 2 ἐφαψάμενον δέ, ὅτε ἐφάπτεται, πάντῃ μηδὲν μήτε δύνασθαι μήτε σχολὴν ἄγειν λέγειν, ὕστερον δὲ περὶ αὐτοῦ συλλογίζεσθαι. Τότε δὲ χρὴ ἑωρακέναι πιστεύειν, ὅταν ἡ ψυχὴ ἐξαίφνης φῶς λάβῃ· τοῦτο γὰρ παρ' αὐτοῦ καὶ αὐτός· καὶ τότε χρὴ νομίζειν παρεῖναι, ὅταν ὥσπερ θεὸς ἄλλος εἰς οἶκον καλοῦντός τινος ἐλθὼν 3 φωτίσῃ· ἢ μηδ' ἐλθὼν οὐκ ἐφώτισεν. Οὕτω τοι καὶ ψυχὴ ἀφώτιστος ἀθέατος ἐκείνου· φωτισθεῖσα δὲ ἔχει, ὃ ἐζήτει, καὶ τοῦτο τὸ τέλος τἀληθινὸν ψυχῇ, ἐφάψασθαι φωτὸς ἐκείνου καὶ αὐτῷ αὐτὸ θεάσασθαι, οὐκ ἄλλῳ φωτί, ἀλλ' 3 αὐτῷ, δι' οὗ καὶ ὁρᾷ. Δι' οὗ γὰρ ἐφωτίσθη, τοῦτό ἐστιν, ὃ δεῖ θεάσασθαι· οὐδὲ γὰρ ἥλιον διὰ φωτὸς ἄλλου. Πῶς ἂν οὖν τοῦτο γένοιτο; Ἄφελε πάντα.

The Good is anterior to Beauty   **1396—a.**   The Good is ranked higher than Beauty.

Enn. V 5, 12, l. 9-19, 31-38:

Καὶ τοῦ μὲν καλοῦ ἤδη οἷον εἰδόσι καὶ ἐγρηγορόσιν ἡ ἀντίληψις καὶ τὸ θάμβος 1 καὶ τοῦ ἔρωτος ἡ ἔγερσις, τὸ δ' ἀγαθὸν ἅτε πάλαι παρὸν εἰς ἔφεσιν σύμφυτον καὶ κοιμωμένοις πάρεστι καὶ οὐ θαμβεῖ ποτε ἰδόντας, ὅτι σύνεστιν ἀεὶ καὶ οὐ ποτὲ ἡ ἀνάμνησις· οὐ μὴν ὁρῶσιν αὐτό, ὅτι κοιμωμένοις πάρεστι. Τοῦ δὲ καλοῦ ὁ ἔρως, ὅταν παρῇ, ὀδύνας δίδωσιν, ὅτι δεῖ ἰδόντας ἐφίεσθαι. Δεύτερος <οὖν> ὢν 1

οὗτος ὁ ἔρως καὶ ἤδη συνιέντων μᾶλλον δεύτερον μηνύει τὸ καλὸν εἶναι· ἡ δὲ
ἀρχαιοτέρα τούτου καὶ ἀναίσθητος ἔφεσις ἀρχαιότερόν φησι καὶ τἀγαθὸν εἶναι
9 καὶ πρότερον τούτου. —

Καὶ ... τὸ μὲν ἀγαθὸν αὐτὸ οὐ δεῖται τοῦ καλοῦ, τὸ δὲ καλὸν ἐκείνου.
Καὶ ἔστι δὲ τὸ μὲν ἤπιον καὶ προσηνὲς καὶ ἀβρότερον καί, ὡς ἐθέλει τις, παρὸν
5 αὐτῷ· τὸ δὲ θάμβος ἔχει καὶ ἔκπληξιν καὶ συμμιγῆ τῷ ἀλγύνοντι τὴν ἡδονήν.
Καὶ γὰρ αὖ καὶ ἕλκει ἀπὸ τοῦ ἀγαθοῦ τοὺς οὐκ εἰδότας, ὥσπερ ἀπὸ πατρὸς
τὸ ἐρώμενον· νεώτερον γάρ· τὸ δὲ πρεσβύτερον οὐ χρόνῳ. ἀλλὰ τῷ ἀληθεῖ,
ὃ καὶ τὴν δύναμιν προτέραν ἔχει.

b.   Yet, it is the source of Beauty, and as such ἐράσμιον.

Enn. VI 7, 32, l. 1-10, 14-17, 19-20, 23-34:

Ποῦ οὖν ὁ ποιήσας τὸ τοσοῦτον κάλλος καὶ τὴν τοσαύτην ζωὴν καὶ γεννήσας
οὐσίαν; Ὁρᾷς τὸ ἐπ' αὐτοῖς ἅπασι ποικίλοις οὖσιν εἴδεσι κάλλος; καλὸν μὲν
ὡδὶ μένειν· ἀλλ' ἐν καλῷ ὄντα δεῖ βλέπειν, ὅθεν ταῦτα καὶ ὅθεν καλά. Δεῖ δ'
5 αὐτὸν εἶναι τούτων μηδὲ ἕν· τί γὰρ αὐτῶν ἔσται μέρος τε ἔσται. Οὐ τοίνυν οὐδὲ
τοιαύτη μορφὴ οὐδέ τις δύναμις οὐδ' αὖ πᾶσαι αἱ γεγενημέναι καὶ οὖσαι ἐνταῦθα, ἀλλὰ δεῖ ὑπὲρ πάσας εἶναι δυνάμεις καὶ ὑπὲρ πάσας μορφάς. Ἀρχὴ
0 δὲ τὸ ἀνείδεον, οὐ τὸ μορφῆς δεόμενον, ἀλλ' ἀφ' οὗ πᾶσα μορφὴ νοερά. —
Πάντα δὲ ποιεῖν δυνάμενον τί ἂν μέγεθος ἔχοι; Ἢ ἄπειρον ἂν εἴη, ἀλλ' εἰ
5 ἄπειρον, μέγεθος ἂν ἔχοι οὐδέν· καὶ γὰρ μέγεθος ἐν τοῖς ὑστάτοις· καὶ δεῖ,
εἰ καὶ τοῦτο ποιήσει, αὐτὸν μὴ ἔχειν. — Τὸ δὲ μέγα αὐτοῦ τὸ μηδὲν αὐτοῦ εἶναι
0 δυνατώτερον παρισοῦσθαί τε μηδὲν δύνασθαι· — Οὐ τοίνυν αὖ οὐδὲ σχῆμα.
Καὶ μήν, ὅτου ἂν ποθεινοῦ ὄντος μήτε σχῆμα μήτε μορφὴν ἔχῃς λαβεῖν, ποθεινό-
5 τατον καὶ ἐρασμιώτατον ἂν εἴη, καὶ ὁ ἔρως ἂν ἄμετρος εἴη· οὐ γὰρ ὥρισται
ἐνταῦθα ὁ ἔρως, ὅτι μηδὲ τὸ ἐρώμενον, ἀλλ' ἄπειρος ἂν εἴη ὁ τούτου ἔρως, ὥστε
καὶ τὸ κάλλος αὐτοῦ ἄλλον τρόπον καὶ κάλλος ὑπὲρ κάλλος. Οὐδὲν γὰρ ὂν τί
0 κάλλος; Ἐράσμιον δὲ ὂν τὸ γεννῶν ἂν εἴη τὸ κάλλος. Δύναμις οὖν <ὂν> παντὸς
καλοῦ ἄνθος ἐστὶ κάλλους καλλοποιόν· καὶ γὰρ γεννᾷ αὐτὸ καὶ κάλλιον ποιεῖ τῇ
παρ' αὐτοῦ περιουσίᾳ τοῦ κάλλους, ὥστε ἀρχὴ κάλλους καὶ πέρας κάλλους.

1397—The First Principle is not only beyond providence, i.e. the care
of all those things that are not Itself. Aristotle too denied this to his
First Principle, defining it as νόησις νοήσεως [1].

P. went further: he placed the One beyond any kind of thought.

a.   *Enn.* VI 7, 37, l. 1-10:

Οἱ μὲν οὖν νόησιν αὐτῷ δόντες τῶν μὲν ἐλαττόνων καὶ τῶν ἐξ αὐτοῦ οὐκ

---

[1]   *Gr. Ph.* II, nr. **516.**

ἔδοσαν· καίτοι καὶ τοῦτο ἄτοπον τὰ ἄλλα, φασί τινες, μὴ εἰδέναι· ἀλλ' οὖν
ἐκεῖνοι ἄλλο τιμιώτερον αὐτοῦ οὐχ εὑρόντες τὴν νόησιν αὐτῷ αὐτοῦ εἶναι
ἔδοσαν, ὥσπερ τῇ νοήσει σεμνοτέρου αὐτοῦ ἐσομένου καὶ τοῦ νοεῖν κρείττονος 5
ἢ κατ' αὐτὸν ὅ ἐστιν ὄντος, ἀλλ' οὐκ αὐτοῦ σεμνύνοντος τὴν νόησιν. Τίνι γὰρ τὸ
τίμιον ἕξει, τῇ νοήσει ἢ αὐτῷ; Εἰ μὲν τῇ νοήσει, αὐτῷ οὐ τίμιον ἢ ἧττον, εἰ δὲ
αὐτῷ, πρὸ τῆς νοήσεώς ἐστι τέλειος καὶ οὐ τῇ νοήσει τελειούμενος.   1

Cp. above, nr. **1391**.

b. As we found above (nr. **1386b**), a deliberate choice and care of
things is by P. not even attributed to Noûs. What is usually called "providence" is explained by him by the existence of an eternal and intelligible order of things: πάντα ἀεὶ νοερῶς ἑστηκότα εἶναι ὅσα ἐν τῷ ὄντι (VI
8, 17). Since, however, this whole order depends directly on the One,
there is at least an analogy between the First Principle and Noûs; in
the author's words: this order "testifies τὸν οἷον ἐν ἑνὶ νοῦν οὐ νοῦν ὄντα".

P. admits an analogy between the One and Noûs

Enn. VI 8, 18, l. 8-22:

Ὥσπερ ἂν οὖν κύκλος ἐφαπτόμενος κέντρου ὁμολογοῖτο ἂν τὴν δύναμιν
παρὰ τοῦ κέντρου ἔχειν, καὶ οἷον κεντροειδής, ἢ γραμμαὶ ἐν κύκλῳ πρὸς κέντρον 1
ἓν συνιοῦσαι τὸ πέρας αὐτῶν τὸ πρὸς τὸ κέντρον ποιοῦσι τοιοῦτον εἶναι οἷον
τὸ πρὸς ὃ ἠνέχθησαν καὶ ἀφ' οὗ οἷον ἐξέφυσαν, μείζονος ὄντος ἢ κατὰ ταύτας
τὰς γραμμὰς καὶ τὰ πέρατα αὐτῶν (καὶ ἔστι μὲν οἷον ἐκεῖνο, ἀμυδρὰ δὲ καὶ
οἷον ἴχνη ἐκείνου τοῦ ὃ δύναται αὐτὰ καὶ τὰς γραμμὰς δυναμένου, αἳ πανταχοῦ 1
ἔχουσιν αὐτό, καὶ ἐμφαίνεται διὰ τῶν γραμμῶν, οἷόν ἐστιν ἐκεῖνο, οἷον ἐξελιχθὲν
οὐκ ἐξεληλιγμένον), οὕτω τοι καὶ τὸν νοῦν καὶ τὸ ὂν χρὴ λαμβάνειν, γενόμενον
ἐξ ἐκείνου καὶ οἷον ἐκχυθὲν καὶ ἐξελιχθὲν καὶ ἐξηρτημένον ἐκ τῆς αὐτοῦ νοερᾶς 2
φύσεως μαρτυρεῖν τὸν οἷον ἐν ἑνὶ νοῦν οὐ νοῦν ὄντα· ἐν γάρ.

For P.' frequent use of the simile of the centre of a circle or a sphere, see above,
1364a, b and **1365b**. Besides in the passages cited there, the simile occurs in V 1,
11, l. 10-15. Cp. VI 9, 8, where soul is said to turn in a circle round the One as its
centre; and I 8, 2, l. 23 ff.: soul "dances" in a circle round Noûs and through it
sees God.

ἐνέργεια without οὐσία

1398—a. P. does not hesitate to call the One ἐνέργεια, though he
does not call it "being".

Enn. VI 8, 20, l. 9-11:

Οὐδὲ γὰρ φοβητέον ἐνέργειαν τὴν πρώτην τίθεσθαι ἄνευ οὐσίας, ἀλλ' αὐτὸ
τοῦτο τὴν οἷον ὑπόστασιν θετέον.

It is infinite Power

b. After having explained that the One is not indivisible in the
sense of a quantitative minimum, P. declares that it is a dynamical
maximum.

Enn. VI 9, 6, l. 6-12:

Τὸ δὲ οὔτε ἐν ἄλλῳ οὔτε ἐν μεριστῷ οὔτε οὕτως ἀμερές, ὡς τὸ σμικρότατον·
μέγιστον γὰρ ἁπάντων οὐ μεγέθει, ἀλλὰ δυνάμει, ὥστε καὶ τὸ ἀμέγεθες δυνάμει·
ἐπεὶ καὶ τὰ μετ' αὐτὸ ὄντα ταῖς δυνάμεσιν ἀμέριστα καὶ ἀμερῆ, οὐ τοῖς ὄγκοις.
Ληπτέον δὲ καὶ ἄπειρον αὐτὸ οὐ τῷ ἀδιεξιτήτῳ ἢ τοῦ μεγέθους ἢ τοῦ ἀριθμοῦ,
ἀλλὰ τῷ ἀπεριλήπτῳ τῆς δυνάμεως.

P. speaks of δυνάμεις in the One in the sense of *potentia activa*: as the Source of
all intelligible Being, the First Principle is δύναμις ἄπειρος. Cp. VI 7, 14, l. 11 ff.:
Also in Noûs there must be infinity, to explain the infinite variety of being within
it. And IV 3, 8, l. 35 ff.: Soul is an ἄπειρον, because its δύναμις is infinite.

In VI 6, 1 P. asks the question "Whether plurality is apostasy of the One, and
infinity absolute apostasy, because it is innumerable plurality". He answers
(ch. 3) by saying that in the realm of being plurality is always *unified* plurality
and in so far good; and likewise infinity in the sphere of *being* is always determined.

Ἀλλ' ἡ ἀπειρία πῶς; — Ἡ γὰρ οὖσα ἐν τοῖς οὖσιν ἤδη ὥρισται, ἢ εἰ μὴ ὥρισται, οὐκ
ἐν τοῖς οὖσιν, ἀλλ' ἐν τοῖς γινομένοις ἴσως, ὡς καὶ τῷ χρόνῳ.

c. "Could it then have made itself different from what it is?" **Its liberty**
By this question P. replies to such problems as "Whether the Good can
cause evil" and "if not, how it can be called free".

He answers that these questions are senseless, since the First Principle *is* its
Will and its Goodness. By a higher form of liberty it cannot otherwise but be willing
Itself (cp. VI 8, 13, l. 27 ff.; above, nr. **1393b**). It is *beyond opposites* [1], beyond the
alternative of acting in this or that way.

Enn. VI 8, 21, l. 1-7:

Ἐδύνατο οὖν ἄλλο τι ποιεῖν ἑαυτὸν ἢ ὃ ἐποίησεν; Ἢ οὕτω καὶ τὸ ἀγαθὸν
ποιεῖν ἀναιρήσομεν, ὅτι μὴ ἂν κακοποιοῖ. Οὐ γὰρ οὕτω τὸ δύνασθαι ἐκεῖ, ὡς
καὶ τὰ ἀντικείμενα, ἀλλ' ὡς ἀστεμφεῖ καὶ ἀμετακινήτῳ δυνάμει, ἢ μάλιστα
δύναμίς ἐστιν, ὅταν μὴ ἐξίστηται τοῦ ἕν· καὶ γὰρ τὸ τὰ ἀντικείμενα δύνασθαι
ἀδυναμίας ἐστὶ τοῦ ἐπὶ τοῦ ἀρίστου μένειν.

Cp. the passages of Thomas Aquinas cited under **1393c**.

d. That it "contains itself", should be taken in this sense, that
everything depends on it (*Enn.* VI 8, 21, l. 19 ff., cited above, nr. **1364c**).
In the same sense P. could call the First Principle δύναμις τῶν πάντων:
it is like an ever-streaming source of life, which in itself stays what it is.

Enn. III 8, 10, l. 1-19: **the ever-
streaming
source**

[It is οὐδὲν τῶν πάντων, ἀλλὰ πρὸ τῶν πάντων.]

Τί δὴ ὄν; Δύναμις τῶν πάντων· ἧς μὴ οὔσης οὐδ' ἂν τὰ πάντα, οὐδ' ἂν νοῦς
ζωὴ ἡ πρώτη καὶ πᾶσα. Τὸ δὲ ὑπὲρ τὴν ζωὴν αἴτιον ζωῆς· οὐ γὰρ ἡ τῆς ζωῆς
ἐνέργεια τὰ πάντα οὖσα πρώτη, ἀλλ' ὥσπερ προχυθεῖσα αὐτὴ οἷον ἐκ πηγῆς.

---

[1] Nicolaus Cusanus' idea of the *coincidentia oppositorum* in God is rooted here.

Νόησον γὰρ πηγὴν ἀρχὴν ἄλλην οὐκ ἔχουσαν, δοῦσαν δὲ ποταμοῖς πᾶσιν 5
αὐτήν, οὐκ ἀναλωθεῖσαν τοῖς ποταμοῖς, ἀλλὰ μένουσαν αὐτὴν ἡσύχως, τοὺς δὲ
ἐξ αὐτῆς προεληλυθότας πρὶν ἄλλον ἄλλη ῥεῖν ὁμοῦ συνιόντας ἔτι, ἤδη δὲ οἷον
ἑκάστους εἰδότας οἷ ἀφήσουσιν αὐτῶν τὰ ῥεύματα· ἢ ζωὴν φυτοῦ μεγίστου διὰ 1
παντὸς ἐλθοῦσαν ἀρχῆς μενούσης καὶ οὐ σκεδασθείσης περὶ πᾶν αὐτῆς οἷον
ἐν ῥίζῃ ἱδρυμένης. Αὕτη τοίνυν παρέσχε μὲν τὴν πᾶσαν ζωὴν τῷ φυτῷ τὴν
πολλήν, ἔμεινε δὲ αὐτὴ οὐ πολλὴ οὖσα, ἀλλ' ἀρχὴ τῆς πολλῆς. Καὶ θαῦμα οὐδέν.

Ἦ καὶ θαῦμα, πῶς τὸ πλῆθος τῆς ζωῆς ἐξ οὐ πλήθους ἦν, καὶ οὐκ ἦν τὸ 1
πλῆθος, εἰ μὴ πρὸ τοῦ πλήθους ἦν ὃ μὴ πλῆθος ἦν. Οὐ γὰρ μερίζεται εἰς τὸ πᾶν
ἡ ἀρχή· μερισθεῖσα γὰρ ἀπώλεσεν ἂν καὶ τὸ πᾶν, καὶ οὐδ' ἂν ἔτι γένοιτο μὴ
μενούσης τῆς ἀρχῆς ἐφ' ἑαυτῆς ἑτέρας οὔσης.

1399—Since it is beyond being and beyond reason, it is known by
direct presence, by those only who are able to see it and have left all
other things behind them.

It is known
by
παρουσία

    a. *Enn.* VI 9, 4, l. 1-26, 30-34:

Γίνεται δὲ ἡ ἀπορία μάλιστα, ὅτι μηδὲ κατ' ἐπιστήμην ἡ σύνεσις ἐκείνου
μηδὲ κατὰ νόησιν, ὥσπερ τὰ ἄλλα νοητά, ἀλλὰ κατὰ παρουσίαν ἐπιστήμης
κρείττονα. Πάσχει δὲ ἡ ψυχὴ τοῦ ἓν εἶναι τὴν ἀπόστασιν καὶ οὐ πάντη ἐστὶν
ἕν, ὅταν ἐπιστήμην τοῦ λαμβάνῃ· λόγος γὰρ ἡ ἐπιστήμη, πολλὰ δὲ ὁ λόγος. 5
Παρέρχεται οὖν τὸ ἓν εἰς ἀριθμὸν καὶ πλῆθος πεσοῦσα. Ὑπὲρ ἐπιστήμην τοίνυν
δεῖ δραμεῖν καὶ μηδαμῇ ἐκβαίνειν τοῦ ἓν εἶναι, ἀλλ' ἀποστῆναι δεῖ καὶ ἐπιστήμης καὶ ἐπιστητῶν καὶ παντὸς ἄλλου καὶ καλοῦ θεάματος. Πᾶν γὰρ καλὸν
ὕστερον ἐκείνου καὶ παρ' ἐκείνου, ὥσπερ πᾶν φῶς μεθημερινὸν παρ' ἡλίου. Διὸ 1
οὐδὲ ῥητὸν οὐδὲ γραπτόν φησιν[1]. Ἀλλὰ λέγομεν καὶ γράφομεν πέμποντες
εἰς αὐτὸ καὶ ἀνεγείροντες ἐκ τῶν λόγων ἐπὶ τὴν θέαν ὥσπερ ὁδὸν δεικνύντες τῷ
τι θεάσασθαι βουλομένῳ. Μέχρι μὲν γὰρ τῆς ὁδοῦ καὶ τῆς πορείας ἡ δίδαξις, 1
ἡ δὲ θέα αὐτοῦ ἔργον ἤδη τοῦ ἰδεῖν βεβουλημένου. Εἰ δὲ μὴ ἦλθέ τις ἐπὶ τὸ
θέαμα, μηδὲ σύνεσιν ἔσχεν ἡ ψυχὴ τῆς ἐκεῖ ἀγλαΐας μηδὲ ἔπαθε μηδὲ ἔσχεν
ἐν ἑαυτῇ οἷον ἐρωτικὸν πάθημα ἐκ τοῦ ἰδεῖν ἐραστοῦ ἐν ᾧ ἐρᾷ ἀναπαυσαμένου,
δεξάμενος <μὲν> φῶς ἀληθινὸν καὶ πᾶσαν τὴν ψυχὴν περιφωτίσας διὰ τὸ 2
ἐγγυτέρω γεγονέναι, ἀναβεβηκὼς δὲ ἔτι ὀπισθοβαρὴς ὑπάρχων, ἃ ἐμπόδια
ἦν τῇ θέᾳ, καὶ οὐ μόνος ἀναβεβηκώς, ἀλλ' ἔχων τὸ διεῖργον ἀπ' αὐτοῦ, ἢ μήπω
εἰς ἓν συναχθείς — οὐ γὰρ δὴ ἄπεστιν οὐδενὸς ἐκεῖνο καὶ πάντων δέ, ὥστε παρὸν
μὴ παρεῖναι ἀλλ' ἢ τοῖς δέχεσθαι δυναμένοις καὶ παρεσκευασμένοις — ... 2
εἰ οὖν μήπω ἐστὶν ἐκεῖ, ἀλλὰ διὰ ταῦτά ἐστιν ἔξω, ἢ δι' ἔνδειαν τοῦ παιδαγω-
γοῦντος λόγου καὶ πίστιν περὶ αὐτοῦ παρεχομένου, δι' ἐκεῖνα μὲν αὐτὸν ἐν
αἰτίᾳ τιθέσθω, καὶ πειράσθω ἀποστὰς πάντων μόνος εἶναι.

---

[1] Plato, *Ep.* VII 341c (supra, nr. **262**).

b. Those who think that things exist and are held together by chance and corporeal necessity, are unable to understand anything concerning the One.

Enn. VI 9, 5, l. 1-9:

Ὅστις οἴεται τὰ ὄντα τύχη καὶ τῷ αὐτομάτῳ διοικεῖσθαι καὶ σωματικαῖς συνέχεσθαι αἰτίαις, οὗτος πόρρω ἀπελήλαται καὶ θεοῦ καὶ ἐννοίας ἑνός, καὶ ὁ λόγος οὐ πρὸς τούτους, ἀλλὰ πρὸς τοὺς ἄλλην φύσιν παρὰ τὰ σώματα τιθεμένους
5 καὶ ἀνιόντας ἐπὶ ψυχήν. Καὶ δεῖ δὴ τούτους φύσιν ψυχῆς κατανενοηκέναι τά τε ἄλλα καὶ ὡς παρὰ νοῦ ἐστι καὶ λόγου παρὰ τούτου κοινωνήσασα ἀρετὴν ἴσχει· μετὰ δὲ ταῦτα νοῦν λαβεῖν ἕτερον τοῦ λογιζομένου καὶ λογιστικοῦ καλουμένου.

P., as so often, polemizes against the Stoa.

c. *Enn.* VI 9, 7, l. 1-9, 12-16:

Εἰ δ’ ὅτι μηδὲν τούτων ἐστίν, ἀοριστεῖς τῇ γνώμῃ, στῆσον σαυτὸν εἰς ταῦτα, καὶ ἀπὸ τούτων θεῶ· θεῶ δὲ μὴ ἔξω ῥίπτων τὴν διάνοιαν. Οὐ γὰρ κεῖταί που ἐρημῶσαν αὐτοῦ τὰ ἄλλα, ἀλλ’ ἔστι τῷ δυναμένῳ θιγεῖν ἐκεῖνο παρόν, τῷ δ’
5 ἀδυνατοῦντι οὐ πάρεστιν. Ὥσπερ δὲ ἐπὶ τῶν ἄλλων οὐκ ἔστι τι νοεῖν ἄλλο νοοῦντα καὶ πρὸς ἄλλῳ ὄντα, ἀλλὰ δεῖ μηδὲν προσάπτειν τῷ νοουμένῳ, ἵνα ᾖ αὐτὸ τὸ νοούμενον, οὕτω δεῖ καὶ ἐνταῦθα συνιέναι, ὡς οὐκ ἔστιν ἄλλου ἔχοντα
9 ἐν τῇ ψυχῇ τύπον ἐκεῖνο νοῆσαι, . . . ἀλλ’ ὥσπερ περὶ τῆς ὕλης λέγεται, ὡς ἄρα ἄποιον εἶναι δεῖ πάντων, εἰ μέλλει δέχεσθαι τοὺς πάντων τύπους, οὕτω καὶ πολὺ μᾶλλον ἀνείδεον τὴν ψυχὴν γίνεσθαι, εἰ μέλλει μηδὲν ἐμπόδιον ἐγκαθήμενον
5 ἔσεσθαι πρὸς πλήρωσιν καὶ ἔλλαμψιν αὐτῇ τῆς φύσεως τῆς πρώτης.

d. *Enn.* VI 8, 21, l. 25-28:

Ὅταν αὐτὸν εἴπης ἢ ἐννοηθῇς, τὰ ἄλλα πάντα ἄφες. Ἀφελὼν <οὖν> πάντα, καταλιπὼν δὲ μόνον αὐτόν, μή τι προσθῇς ζήτει, ἀλλὰ μή τί πω οὐκ ἀφῄρηκας ἀπ’ αὐτοῦ ἐν γνώμῃ τῇ σῇ.

1400—a. The soul is always around It, but she does not always look at It. If only she does, she reaches her true goal. For the true life and full development of the spirit are "yonder".

Enn. VI 9, 8, l. 36-45; c. 9, l. 13-22:

Καὶ ἀεὶ μὲν περὶ αὐτό, οὐκ ἀεὶ δὲ εἰς αὐτὸ βλέπομεν, ἀλλ’ οἷον χορὸς ἐξᾴδων καίπερ ἔχων περὶ τὸν κορυφαῖον τραπείη ἂν εἰς τὸ ἔξω τῆς θέας, ὅταν δὲ
0 ἐπιστρέψῃ, ᾄδει τε καλῶς καὶ ὄντως περὶ αὐτὸν ἔχει· οὕτω καὶ ἡμεῖς ἀεὶ μὲν περὶ αὐτό, καὶ ὅταν μή, λύσις ἡμῖν παντελὴς ἔσται καὶ οὐκέτι ἐσόμεθα· οὐκ ἀεὶ δὲ εἰς αὐτό, ἀλλ’ ὅταν εἰς αὐτὸ ἴδωμεν, τότε ἡμῖν τέλος καὶ ἀνάπαυλα
5 καὶ τὸ μὴ ἀπᾴδειν χορεύουσιν ὄντως περὶ αὐτὸ χορείαν ἔνθεον. —

Ἐνταῦθα καὶ ἀναπαύεται ψυχὴ κακῶν ἔξω εἰς τὸν τῶν κακῶν καθαρὸν τόπον

ἀναδραμοῦσα· καὶ νοεῖ ἐνταῦθα, καὶ ἀπαθὴς ἐνταῦθα· καὶ τὸ ἀληθῶς ζῆν ἐν-
ταῦθα· τὸ γὰρ νῦν καὶ τὸ ἄνευ θεοῦ ἴχνος ζωῆς ἐκείνην μιμούμενον, τὸ δὲ ἐκεῖ 1
ζῆν ἐνέργεια μὲν νοῦ [1], ἐνεργείᾳ δὲ καὶ γεννᾷ θεοὺς ἐν ἡσύχῳ τῇ πρὸς ἐκεῖνο
ἐπαφῇ, γεννᾷ δὲ κάλλος, γεννᾷ δικαιοσύνην, ἀρετὴν γεννᾷ [2]· ταῦτα γὰρ κύει ψυχὴ
πληρωθεῖσα θεοῦ καὶ τοῦτο αὐτῇ ἀρχὴ καὶ τέλος· ἀρχὴ μέν, ὅτι ἐκεῖθεν, 2
τέλος δέ, ὅτι τὸ ἀγαθὸν ἐκεῖ, καὶ ἐκεῖ γενομένη γίνεται αὐτὴ ὅπερ ἦν.

Perfect happiness

b. *Enn.* VI 7, 34, 1. 8-27; 32-38:

῞Οταν δὲ τούτου εὐτυχήσῃ ἡ ψυχὴ καὶ ἥκῃ πρὸς αὐτήν, μᾶλλον δὲ παρὸν φανῇ,
ὅταν ἐκείνη ἐκνεύσῃ τῶν παρόντων, καὶ παρασκευάσασα αὑτὴν ὡς ὅτι μάλιστα 1
καλὴν καὶ εἰς ὁμοιότητα ἐλθοῦσα· ἡ δὲ παρασκευὴ καὶ ἡ κόσμησις δήλη που
τοῖς παρασκευαζομένοις· ἰδοῦσα δὲ ἐν αὑτῇ ἐξαίφνης φανέντα (μεταξὺ γὰρ
οὐδὲν οὐδ' ἔτι δύο, ἀλλ' ἓν ἄμφω· οὐ γὰρ ἂν διακρίναις ἔτι, ἕως πάρεστι·
μίμησις δὲ τούτου καὶ οἱ ἐνταῦθα ἐρασταὶ καὶ ἐρώμενοι συγκρῖναι θέλοντες) 1
οὔτε σώματος ἔτι αἰσθάνεται, ὅτι ἐστὶν ἐν αὐτῷ, οὔτε ἑαυτὴν ἄλλο τι λέγει,
οὐκ ἄνθρωπον, οὐ ζῷον, οὐκ ὄν, οὐδὲ πᾶν· ἀνώμαλος γὰρ ἡ τούτων πως θέα,
καὶ οὔτε σχολὴν ἄγει πρὸς αὐτὰ οὔτε θέλει, ἀλλὰ καὶ αὐτὸ ζητήσασα ἐκείνῳ
παρόντι ἀπαντᾷ κἀκεῖνο ἀντ' αὐτῆς βλέπει· τίς δὲ οὖσα βλέπει, οὐδὲ τοῦτο 2
σχολάζει ὁρᾶν. ῎Ενθα δὴ οὐδὲν πάντων ἂν τούτου ἀλλάξαιτο, οὐδ' εἴ τις αὐτῇ
πάντα τὸν οὐρανὸν ἐπιτρέποι, ὡς οὐκ ὄντος ἄλλου ἔτι ἀμείνονος οὐδὲ μᾶλλον
ἀγαθοῦ· οὔτε γὰρ ἀνωτέρω τρέχει τά τε ἄλλα πάντα κατιούσης, κἂν ᾖ ἄνω·
ὥστε τότε ἔχει καὶ τὸ κρίνειν καλῶς καὶ γινώσκειν, ὅτι τοῦτό ἐστιν οὗ ἐφίετο, 2
καὶ τίθεσθαι, ὅτι μηδέν ἐστι κρεῖττον αὐτοῦ. —

᾿Αλλὰ καὶ τὰ ἄλλα πάντα, οἷς πρὶν ἥδετο, ἀρχαῖς ἢ δυνάμεσιν ἢ πλούτοις ἢ
κάλλεσιν ἢ ἐπιστήμαις, ταῦτα ὑπεριδοῦσα λέγει οὐκ ἂν εἰποῦσα μὴ κρείττοσι
συντυχοῦσα τούτων· οὐδὲ φοβεῖται, μή τι πάθῃ, μετ' ἐκείνου οὖσα οὐδ' ὅλως 3
ἰδοῦσα· εἰ δὲ καὶ τὰ ἄλλα τὰ περὶ αὐτὴν φθείροιτο, εὖ μάλα καὶ βούλεται,
ἵνα πρὸς τούτῳ ᾖ μόνον· εἰς τόσον ἥκει εὐπαθείας.

The light only

c. *Enn.* VI 7, 36, 1. 15-21:

῎Ενθα δὴ ἐάσας τις πᾶν μάθημα καὶ μέχρι τούτου παιδαγωγηθεὶς καὶ ἐν
καλῷ ἱδρυθείς, ἐν ᾧ μέν ἐστι, μέχρι τούτου νοεῖ, ἐξενεχθεὶς δὲ τῷ αὐτῷ τοῦ νοῦ
οἷον κύματι καὶ ὑψοῦ ὑπ' αὐτοῦ οἷον οἰδήσαντος ἀρθεὶς εἰσεῖδεν ἐξαίφνης [3]
οὐκ ἰδὼν ὅπως, ἀλλ' ἡ θέα πλήσασα φωτὸς τὰ ὄμματα οὐ δι' αὐτοῦ πεποίηκεν
ἄλλο ὁρᾶν, ἀλλ' αὐτὸ τὸ φῶς τὸ ὅραμα ἦν.

---

[1] Aristotle, speaking of the διαγωγή of the Prime Mover, attributes life to it, because life is ἡ νοῦ ἐνέργεια (*Metaph.* Λ 7, 1072b 26; above, nr. **516a**). It is certainly this passage which P. has in his mind, when applying the definition to the life of Soul in contemplating the One, not to the One itself.

[2] In this whole passage P. is inspired by Plato, *Symp.* 211d-212a (above, nr. **273**).

[3] Plato, *Symp.* 210 c.

6—THE SENSIBLE WORLD

1401—Creation, as we saw above (nrs. **1365-1369**), is a necessary and eternal process, which reaches its final term (τέλος) in the αἰσθητόν.

a. *Enn.* IV 8, 6, l. 1-16:

The text was cited above, nr. **1365a**.

The αἰσθητόν is the end of the creative power of Divine Nature

b. Ib., l. 16-28:

Therefore, matter, too, must participate of the nature of the good. For "that which gives existence as it were by grace" could not stop before coming to it. This is proved by the beauty found in sensible things.

Matter, too, must partake of goodness

Οὐ γὰρ δὴ ἦν ὁ ἐκώλυεν ὁτιοῦν ἔμμοιρον εἶναι φύσεως ἀγαθοῦ, καθ' ὅσον ἕκαστον οἷόν τε ἦν μεταλαμβάνειν. Εἴτ' οὖν ἦν ἀεὶ ἡ τῆς ὕλης φύσις, οὐχ οἷόν τε
10 ἦν αὐτὴν μὴ μετασχεῖν οὖσαν τοῦ πᾶσι τὸ ἀγαθὸν καθ' ὅσον δύναται ἕκαστον χορηγοῦντος· εἴτ' ἐπηκολούθησεν ἐξ ἀνάγκης ἡ γένεσις αὐτῆς τοῖς πρὸ αὐτῆς αἰτίοις, οὐδ' ὡς ἔδει χωρὶς εἶναι, ἀδυναμίᾳ πρὶν εἰς αὐτὴν ἐλθεῖν στάντος τοῦ καὶ τὸ εἶναι οἷον ἐν χάριτι δόντος. Δεῖξις οὖν τῶν ἀρίστων ἐν νοητοῖς τὸ ἐν
15 αἰσθητῷ κάλλιστον, τῆς τε δυνάμεως τῆς τε ἀγαθότητος αὐτῶν, καὶ συνέχεται πάντα εἰς ἀεὶ τά τε νοητῶς τά τε αἰσθητῶς ὄντα, τὰ μὲν παρ' αὐτῶν ὄντα, τὰ δὲ μετοχῇ τούτων τὸ εἶναι εἰς ἀεὶ λαβόντα, μιμούμενα τὴν νοητὴν καθ' ὅσον δύναται φύσιν.

c. In the following passage the spiritual man, detached from sense-perception, describes how he sees the relation between Noûs ("the God") and the sensible world. In the form of a theogony he qualifies this world as "the last-born son" of "the God", the only one who did not stay with Him (cp. above: Philo, nr. **1301c**). This world is beautiful, since it is an image of "the Father"; and for the same reason it must be eternal and created eternally,—i.e. not by deliberation nor by an act of the will.

The created world „the youngest Son of God"

Enn. V 8, 12, l. 2-25:

Ἰδὼν δὴ (sc. ὁ νοῦς), — τί ἀπαγγέλλει; Ἢ θεὸν ἑωρακέναι τόκον ὠδίνοντα καλὸν καὶ πάντα δὴ ἐν αὐτῷ γεγεννηκότα καὶ ἄλυπον ἔχοντα τὴν ὠδῖνα ἐν αὐτῷ· ἡσθεὶς
5 γὰρ οἷς ἐγέννα καὶ ἀγασθεὶς τῶν τόκων κατέσχε πάντα παρ' αὐτῷ τὴν αὐτοῦ καὶ τὴν αὐτῶν ἀγλαΐαν ἀσμενίσας· ὁ δὲ καλῶν ὄντων καὶ καλλιόνων τῶν εἰς τὸ εἴσω μεμενηκότων μόνος ἐκ τῶν ἄλλων παῖς ἐξεφάνη εἰς τὸ ἔξω. Ἀφ' οὗ καὶ
10 ὑστάτου παιδὸς ὄντος ἔστιν ἰδεῖν οἷον ἐξ εἰκόνος τινὸς αὐτοῦ, ὅσος ὁ πατὴρ ἐκεῖνος καὶ οἱ μείναντες παρὰ τῷ πατρὶ ἀδελφοί. Ὁ δὲ οὔ φησι μάτην ἐλθεῖν παρὰ τοῦ πατρός· εἶναι γὰρ δὴ αὐτοῦ ἄλλον κόσμον γεγονότα καλόν, ὡς εἰκόνα καλοῦ· μηδὲ γὰρ εἶναι θεμιτὸν εἰκόνα καλὴν μὴ εἶναι μήτε καλοῦ μήτε

οὐσίας. Μιμεῖται δὴ τὸ ἀρχέτυπον πανταχῇ· καὶ γὰρ ζωὴν ἔχει καὶ τὸ τῆς 1
οὐσίας, ὡς μίμημα, καὶ τὸ κάλλος εἶναι, ὡς ἐκεῖθεν· ἔχει δὲ καὶ τὸ ἀεὶ αὐτοῦ,
ὡς εἰκών· ἢ ποτὲ μὲν ἕξει εἰκόνα, ποτὲ δὲ οὔ, οὐ τέχνῃ γενομένης τῆς εἰκόνος;
Πᾶσα δὲ φύσει εἰκών ἐστιν, ὅσον ἂν τὸ ἀρχέτυπον μένῃ. Διὸ οὐκ ὀρθῶς, οἱ
φθείρουσι τοῦ νοητοῦ μένοντος καὶ γεννῶσιν οὕτως, ὡς ποτὲ βουλευσαμένου τοῦ 2
ποιοῦντος ποιεῖν. Ὅστις γὰρ τρόπος ποιήσεως τοιαύτης οὐκ ἐθέλουσι συνιέναι
οὐδ' ἴσασιν, ὅτι, ὅσον ἐκεῖνο ἐλλάμπει, οὐ μήποτε τὰ ἄλλα ἐλλείπῃ, ἀλλ' ἐξ
οὗ ἔστι καὶ ταῦτα ἔστιν· ἦν δ' ἀεὶ καὶ ἔσται.

<table>
<tr><td>Mixed
character of
this world</td><td>**1402—a.**　This world is of a mixed character, and here is the source
of difficulties.</td></tr>
</table>

Enn. II 3, 9, l. 42-47:

Τὰ δὲ δυσχερῆ διὰ τὴν μῖξιν. Μεμιγμένη γὰρ οὖν δὴ ἡ τοῦδε τοῦ παντὸς
φύσις, καὶ εἴ τις τὴν ψυχὴν τὴν χωριστὴν αὐτοῦ χωρίσειε, τὸ λοιπὸν οὐ μέγα.
Θεὸς μὲν οὖν ἐκείνης συναριθμουμένης, τὸ δὲ λοιπὸν **δ α ί μ ω ν**, φησί, **μ έ γ α ς** 4
καὶ τὰ πάθη τὰ ἐν αὐτῷ δαιμόνια. [1]

<table>
<tr><td>How it
arises from
soul as a
perpetual
image</td><td>**b.**　It is an εἰκὼν ἀεὶ εἰκονιζόμενος, a reality of the third degree.</td></tr>
</table>

Enn. II 3, 18, l. 8-22:

Εἰ δὴ ταῦτα ὀρθῶς εἴρηται, δεῖ τὴν τοῦ παντὸς ψυχὴν θεωρεῖν μὲν τὰ ἄριστα
ἀεὶ ἱεμένην πρὸς τὴν νοητὴν φύσιν καὶ τὸν θεόν, πληρουμένης δὲ αὐτῆς καὶ 1
πεπληρωμένης οἷον ἀπομεστουμένης αὐτῆς τὸ ἐξ αὐτῆς ἴνδαλμα καὶ τὸ ἔσχατον
αὐτῆς πρὸς τὸ κάτω τὸ ποιοῦν τοῦτο εἶναι [2]. Ποιητὴς οὖν ἔσχατος οὗτος· ἐπὶ δ'
αὐτῷ τῆς ψυχῆς τὸ πρώτως πληρούμενον παρὰ νοῦ· ἐπὶ πᾶσι δὲ νοῦς δημιουργός, ὃς καὶ τῇ ψυχῇ τῇ μετ' αὐτὸν δίδωσιν ὧν ἴχνη ἐν τῇ τρίτῃ. Εἰκότως 1
οὖν λέγεται οὗτος ὁ κόσμος εἰκὼν ἀεὶ εἰκονιζόμενος, ἑστηκότων μὲν τοῦ πρώτου
καὶ δευτέρου, τοῦ δὲ τρίτου ἑστηκότος μὲν καὶ αὐτοῦ, ἀλλ' ἐν τῇ ὕλῃ καὶ κατὰ
συμβεβηκὸς κινουμένου. Ἕως γὰρ ἂν ᾖ νοῦς καὶ ψυχή, ῥεύσονται οἱ λόγοι εἰς
τοῦτο τὸ εἶδος τῆς ψυχῆς, ὥσπερ, ἕως ἂν ᾖ ἥλιος, πάντα τὰ ἀπ' αὐτοῦ φῶτα. 2

c.　According to the following passage, the particular soul produces
the μὴ ὄν (i.e. ὕλη) as an εἴδωλον, which is quite indetermined and obscure.
Next, at a second glance, she illuminates it and forms it.

<table>
<tr><td>The
μὴ ὄν
is first
produced by
the particu-
lar Soul;
next it is
illuminated
by it</td><td>*Enn.* III 9, 3, l. 7-16:

Φωτίζεται μὲν οὖν ἡ μερικὴ (ψυχὴ) πρὸς τὸ πρὸ αὐτῆς φερομένη — ὄντι γὰρ
ἐντυγχάνει —, εἰς δὲ τὸ μετ' αὐτὴν εἰς τὸ μὴ ὄν. Τοῦτο δὲ ποιεῖ, ὅταν πρὸς αὐτήν·</td></tr>
</table>

---

[1]　It is of *Eros* that Plato says (*Symp.* 202d-e) that he is a "great daemon".
[2]　By this lowest form of soul, which is creative, the author means: φύσις. Cp.
below, nr. **1405.**

πρὸς αὐτὴν γὰρ βουλομένη * τὸ μετ’ αὐτὴν ποιεῖ εἴδωλον αὐτῆς, τὸ μὴ
ὄν, οἷον κενεμβατοῦσα καὶ ἀοριστοτέρα γινομένη· καὶ τοῦτο τὸ εἴδωλον τὸ
ἀόριστον πάντη σκοτεινόν· ἄλογον γὰρ καὶ ἀνόητον πάντη καὶ πολὺ τοῦ ὄντος
ἀποστατοῦν. Εἰς δὲ τὸ μεταξύ ἐστιν ἐν τῷ οἰκείῳ, πάλιν δὲ ἰδοῦσα οἷον δευτέρᾳ
προσβολῇ τὸ εἴδωλον ἐμόρφωσε καὶ ἡσθεῖσα ἔρχεται εἰς αὐτό.

1403—Opposing the gnostics—according to recent discoveries they
were a Christian sect of Sethians from Egypt—Plotinus states:

a. The sensible world is a clear and beautiful image of the intelligible. It is not equal to it, but it does resemble it.

Enn. II 9, 8, l. 8-20:

> Ἐπεὶ οὐδὲ τοῦ παντὸς τὴν διοίκησιν ὀρθῶς ἄν τις μέμψαιτο πρῶτον μὲν
> ἐνδεικνυμένην τῆς νοητῆς φύσεως τὸ μέγεθος. Εἰ γὰρ οὕτως εἰς τὸ ζῆν παρε-
> λήλυθεν, ὡς μὴ ζωὴν ἀδιάρθρωτον ἔχειν—ὁποῖα τὰ σμικρότερα τῶν ἐν αὐτῷ,
> ἃ τῇ πολλῇ ζωῇ τῇ ἐν αὐτῷ ἀεὶ νύκτωρ καὶ μεθ’ ἡμέραν γεννᾶται—ἀλλ’ ἔστι
> συνεχὴς καὶ ἐναργὴς καὶ πολλὴ καὶ πανταχοῦ ζωὴ σοφίαν ἀμήχανον ἐνδεικνυ-
> μένη, πῶς οὐκ ἄν τις ἄγαλμα ἐναργὲς καὶ καλὸν τῶν νοητῶν θεῶν[1] εἴποι;
> Εἰ δὲ μιμούμενον μή ἐστιν ἐκεῖνο, αὐτὸ τοῦτο κατὰ φύσιν ἔχει· οὐ γὰρ ἦν **
> ἔτι μιμούμενον. Τὸ δὲ ἀνομοίως μεμιμῆσθαι ψεῦδος· οὐδὲν γὰρ παραλέλειπται
> ὧν οἷόν τε ἦν καλὴν εἰκόνα φυσικὴν ἔχειν.

(margin) The sensible world is an ἄγαλμα resembling the intelligible

b. It has not been created by sin or a lapse of the soul.

Enn. II 9, 4, l. 1-11:

> Εἰ δὲ οἷον πτερορρυήσασαν[2] τὴν ψυχὴν φήσουσι πεποιηκέναι, οὐχ ἡ τοῦ
> παντὸς τοῦτο πάσχει· εἰ δὲ σφαλεῖσαν αὐτοὶ φήσουσι, τοῦ σφάλματος λεγέτωσαν
> τὴν αἰτίαν. Πότε δὲ ἐσφάλη; Εἰ μὲν γὰρ ἐξ ἀϊδίου, μένει κατὰ τὸν αὐτῶν λόγον
> ἐσφαλμένη· εἰ δὲ ἤρξατο, διὰ τί οὐ πρὸ τοῦ; Ἡμεῖς δὲ οὐ νεῦσίν φαμεν τὴν
> ποιοῦσαν, ἀλλὰ μᾶλλον μὴ νεῦσιν. Εἰ δὲ ἔνευσε, τῷ ἐπιλελῆσθαι δηλονότι τῶν
> ἐκεῖ· εἰ δὲ ἐπελάθετο, πῶς δημιουργεῖ; Πόθεν γὰρ ποιεῖ ἢ ἐξ ὧν εἶδεν ἐκεῖ;
> Εἰ δὲ ἐκείνων μεμνημένη ποιεῖ, οὐδὲ ὅλως ἔνευσεν, οὐδὲ γὰρ εἰ ἀμυδρῶς ἔχει.
> Οὐ μᾶλλον νεύει ἐκεῖ, ἵνα μὴ ἀμυδρῶς ἴδῃ;

(margin) It was not created by a lapse of the soul

c. Those who blame the sensible world do not understand that
there *must* be a hierarchy of being and that things belonging to a lower
stage are not evil because they are not as good as that which is "before"
them.

Enn. II 9, 13, l. 1-8:

> Ὁ ἄρα μεμφόμενος τῇ τοῦ κόσμου φύσει οὐκ οἶδεν ὅ τι ποιεῖ, οὐδ’ ὅπου τὸ

(margin) There is no reason for blaming it

---

* ⟨εἶναι⟩ suppl. Vitringa.   [1] Plato, *Tim.* 37c.
** ⟨ἄν⟩ suppl. Kirchhoff.   [2] Plato, *Phaedr.* 246c.

θράσος αὐτοῦ τοῦτο χωρεῖ. Τοῦτο δέ, ὅτι οὐκ ἴσασι τάξιν τῶν ἐφεξῆς πρώτων καὶ δευτέρων καὶ τρίτων καὶ ἀεὶ μέχρι τῶν ἐσχάτων, καὶ ὡς οὐ λοιδορητέον τοῖς χείροσι τῶν πρώτων, ἀλλὰ πρᾴως συγχωρητέον τῇ πάντων φύσει αὐτὸν θέοντα 5 πρὸς τὰ πρῶτα παυσάμενον τῆς τραγῳδίας τῶν φοβερῶν, ὡς οἴονται, ἐν ταῖς τοῦ κόσμου σφαίραις, αἳ δὴ πάντα μείλιχα τεύχουσιν [1] αὐτοῖς·—

d. By despising this world and the gods that are in it man makes himself evil. For you cannot honour the intelligible while despising the visible order which springs from it.

Despising this world makes evil men

Enn. II 9, 16, l. 1-9:

Οὐδ᾽ αὖ τῷ καταφρονῆσαι κόσμου καὶ θεῶν τῶν ἐν αὐτῷ καὶ τῶν ἄλλων καλῶν ἀγαθόν ἐστι γενέσθαι. Καὶ γὰρ πᾶς κακὸς καὶ πρὸ τοῦ καταφρονήσειεν ἂν θεῶν, καὶ μὴ πρότερον πᾶς κακὸς καταφρονήσας, καὶ εἰ τὰ ἄλλα μὴ πάντα κακὸς εἴη, αὐτῷ τούτῳ ἂν γεγονὼς εἴη. Καὶ γὰρ ἂν καὶ ἡ πρὸς τοὺς νοητοὺς 5 θεοὺς λεγομένη αὐτοῖς τιμὴ ἀσυμπαθὴς ἂν γένοιτο· ὁ γὰρ τὸ φιλεῖν πρὸς ὁτιοῦν ἔχων καὶ τὸ συγγενὲς πᾶν οὗ φιλεῖ ἀσπάζεται καὶ τοὺς παῖδας ὧν τὸν πατέρα ἀγαπᾷ· ψυχὴ δὲ πᾶσα πατρὸς ἐκείνου.

1404—Plotinus, as we saw above, says repeatedly that the world must be eternal and that creation is an eternal process. E.g. **1402b**: εἰκὼν ἀεὶ εἰκονιζόμενος, and **1403b**: πότε δὲ ἐσφάλη; e.q.s.

In the treatise Περὶ τοῦ κόσμου (II 1) the "immortality" of the cosmos is amply discussed. It is defended first of all by the argument that it would be absurd to admit that soul by its "wonderful power" should not *always* hold the world together.

The world is imperishable

a. *Enn.* II 1, 3, l. 1-5:

Πῶς οὖν ἡ ὕλη καὶ τὸ σῶμα τοῦ παντὸς συνεργὸν ἂν εἴη πρὸς τὴν τοῦ κόσμου ἀθανασίαν ἀεὶ ῥέον; Ἢ ὅτι, φαῖμεν ἄν, ‹ῥεῖ ἐν αὐτῷ›· ῥεῖ γὰρ οὐκ ἔξω. Εἰ οὖν ἐν αὐτῷ καὶ οὐκ ἀπ᾽ αὐτοῦ, μένον τὸ αὐτὸ οὔτ᾽ ἂν αὔξοιτο οὔτε φθίνοι· οὐ 5 τοίνυν οὐδὲ γηράσκει.

Soul holds it together eternally

b. *Enn.* II 1, 4, l. 14-20:

Τὸ δὲ δὴ μέγιστον, τὴν ψυχὴν ἐφεξῆς τοῖς ἀρίστοις κινουμένην δυνάμει θαυμαστῇ κειμένην, πῶς ἐκφεύξεταί τι αὐτὴν εἰς τὸ μὴ εἶναι τῶν ἅπαξ ἐν αὐτῇ 15 τεθέντων; Μὴ παντὸς δὲ δεσμοῦ οἴεσθαι κρείττονα εἶναι ἐκ θεοῦ ὡρμημένην, ἀνθρώπων ἀπείρων ἐστὶν αἰτίας τῆς συνεχούσης τὰ πάντα. Ἄτοπον γὰρ τὴν καὶ ὁποσονοῦν χρόνον δυνηθεῖσαν συνέχειν μὴ καὶ ἀεὶ ποιεῖν τοῦτο. 20

c. Thus, in opposing the gnostics, Plotinus argues that "the soul

---

[1] Pind. *Olymp.* I 48.

which stayed yonder" and is not a part of us, while we are not a part of it, gives to the cosmos whatever this world is able to accept of the intelligible; and, being illuminated from beyond eternally, she (i.e. universal soul) does so without end.

Enn. II 9, 2, l. 11 - 3, l. 15:

Ψυχὴ μείνασα, ἡ μὴ μέρος, μηδὲ ἧς ἡμεῖς ἔτι μέρος, ἔδωκε τῷ παντὶ σώματι αὐτῷ τε ἔχειν ὅσον δύναται παρ' αὐτῆς ἔχειν, μένει τε ἀπραγμόνως αὐτὴ οὐκ ἐκ διανοίας διοικοῦσα οὐδέ τι διορθουμένη, ἀλλὰ τῇ εἰς τὸ πρὸ αὐτῆς θέα κατα-
5 κοσμοῦσα δυνάμει θαυμαστῇ. Ὅσον γὰρ πρὸς αὐτῇ ἐστι, τόσῳ καλλίων καὶ δυνατωτέρα· κἀκεῖθεν ἔχουσα δίδωσι τῷ μετ' αὐτὴν καὶ ὥσπερ ἐλλάμπουσα ἀεὶ ἐλλάμπεται.

(3) Ἀεὶ οὖν ἐλλαμπομένη καὶ διηνεκὲς ἔχουσα τὸ φῶς δίδωσιν εἰς τὰ ἐφεξῆς, τὰ δ' ἀεὶ συνέχεται καὶ ἄρδεται τούτῳ τῷ φωτὶ καὶ ἀπολαύει τοῦ ζῆν καθ' ὅσον δύναται· ὥσπερ εἰ πυρὸς ἐν μέσῳ που κειμένου ἀλεαίνοιντο οἷς οἷόν τε.
5 Καίτοι τὸ πῦρ ἐστιν ἐν μέτρῳ· ὅταν δὲ δυνάμεις μὴ μετρηθεῖσαι μὴ ἐκ τῶν ὄντων ὦσιν ἀνηρημέναι, πῶς οἷόν τε εἶναι μέν, μηδὲν δὲ αὐτῶν μεταλαμβάνειν; Ἀλλ' ἀνάγκη ἕκαστον τὸ αὐτοῦ διδόναι καὶ ἄλλῳ, ἢ τὸ ἀγαθὸν οὐκ ἀγαθὸν ἔσται, ἢ ὁ νοῦς οὐ νοῦς, ἢ ψυχὴ μὴ τοῦτο, εἰ μή τι μετὰ τοῦ πρώτως ζῆν
10 ζωὴ καὶ δευτέρως ἕως ἔστι τὸ πρώτως. Ἀνάγκη τοίνυν ἐφεξῆς εἶναι πάντα ἀλλήλοις καὶ ἀεί, γενητὰ δὲ τὰ ἕτερα τῷ παρ' ἄλλων εἶναι. Οὐ τοίνυν ἐγένετο, ἀλλ' ἐγίνετο καὶ γενήσεται, ὅσα γενητὰ λέγεται· οὐδὲ φθαρήσεται, ἀλλ' ἢ
15 ὅσα ἔχει εἰς ἅ· ὃ δὲ μὴ ἔχει εἰς ὅ, οὐδὲ φθαρήσεται.

d. Cp. *Enn.* II 9, 12, l. 32 f.:

Τί γὰρ ἐλλάμπειν ἔδει, εἰ μὴ πάντως ἔδει;

1405—What is φύσις?

In *Enn.* IV, 4, 13, cited under **1376d**, we found φρόνησις opposed to φύσις, the latter being described as ψυχῆς ἔσχατον ὄν. Nature "produces" (ποιεῖ) without knowing.—It does not even possess imagination, which is a mean between νόησις and φύσις.

a. *Enn.* IV 4, 13, l. 7-15:

Οὐδὲ οἶδε, μόνον δὲ ποιεῖ· ὃ γὰρ ἔχει τῷ ἐφεξῆς διδοῦσα ἀπροαιρέτως τὴν δόσιν τῷ σωματικῷ καὶ ὑλικῷ ποίησιν ἔχει, οἷον καὶ τὸ θερμανθὲν τῷ ἐφεξῆς
10 ἀψαμένῳ δέδωκε τὸ αὐτοῦ εἶδος θερμὸν ἐλαττόνως ποιῆσαν. Διὰ τοῦτό τοι ἡ φύσις οὐδὲ φαντασίαν ἔχει· ἡ δὲ νόησις φαντασίας κρείττων· φαντασία δὲ μεταξὺ φύσεως τύπου καὶ νοήσεως. Ἡ μὲν γὰρ οὐδενὸς ἀντίληψιν οὐδὲ σύνεσιν
15 ἔχει, ἡ δὲ φαντασία σύνεσιν ἐπακτοῦ.

Margin notes:

Creation must be an eternal process

Why illuminating if not eternally?

φύσις, the lowest stage of soul

b. P. speaks again of φύσις in the treatise Περὶ θεωρίας (III 8). The productive power in nature, he explains here, is the logos in it. This logos is an εἶδος without ὕλη. It produces another logos, which "gives something" (of itself) to the ὑποκείμενον.

The stable element in nature, which is creative, is the logos

Enn. III 8, 2, l. 9-34:

'Αλλὰ γὰρ ἐχρῆν συννοοῦντας, ὡς καὶ ἐπὶ τῶν τὰς τέχνας τὰς τοιαύτας μετιόν- 1 των, ὅτι δεῖ τι ἐν αὐτοῖς μένειν, καθ' ὃ μένον διὰ χειρῶν ποιήσουσιν ἃ αὐτῶν ἔργα, ἐπὶ τὸ τοιοῦτον ἀνελθεῖν τῆς φύσεως καὶ αὐτοὺς καὶ συνεῖναι, ὡς μένειν δεῖ καὶ ἐνταῦθα τὴν δύναμιν τὴν οὐ διὰ χειρῶν ποιοῦσαν καὶ πᾶσαν μένειν. Οὐ γὰρ δὴ δεῖται τῶν μὲν ὡς μενόντων, τῶν δὲ ὡς κινουμένων — ἡ γὰρ ὕλη τὸ κινούμενον, αὐτῆς δὲ οὐδὲν κινούμενον — ἢ ἐκεῖνο οὐκ ἔσται τὸ κινοῦν πρώτως, οὐδὲ ἡ φύσις τοῦτο, ἀλλὰ τὸ ἀκίνητον τὸ ἐν τῷ ὅλῳ. Ὁ μὲν δὴ λόγος, φαίη ἄν τις, ἀκίνητος, αὕτη δὲ ἄλλη παρὰ τὸν λόγον καὶ κινουμένη. 'Αλλ' εἰ μὲν πᾶσαν 2 φήσουσι, καὶ ὁ λόγος· εἰ δέ τι αὐτῆς ἀκίνητον, τοῦτο καὶ ὁ λόγος. Καὶ γὰρ εἶδος αὐτὴν δεῖ εἶναι καὶ οὐκ ἐξ ὕλης καὶ εἴδους· τί γὰρ δεῖ αὐτῇ ὕλης θερμῆς ἢ ψυχρᾶς; Ἡ γὰρ ὑποκειμένη καὶ δημιουργουμένη ὕλη ἥκει τοῦτο φέρουσα, ἢ γίνεται τοιαύτη ἡ μὴ ποιότητα ἔχουσα λογωθεῖσα. Οὐ γὰρ πῦρ δεῖ προσελθεῖν, 2 ἵνα πῦρ ἡ ὕλη γένηται, ἀλλὰ λόγον· ὃ καὶ σημεῖον οὐ μικρὸν τοῦ ἐν τοῖς ζῴοις καὶ ἐν τοῖς φυτοῖς τοὺς λόγους εἶναι τοὺς ποιοῦντας καὶ τὴν φύσιν εἶναι λόγον, ὃς ποιεῖ λόγον ἄλλον γέννημα αὐτοῦ δόντα μέν τι τῷ ὑποκειμένῳ, μένοντα δ' αὐτόν. Ὁ μὲν οὖν λόγος ὁ κατὰ τὴν μορφὴν τὴν ὁρωμένην ἔσχατος ἤδη καὶ 3 νεκρὸς καὶ οὐκέτι ποιεῖν δύναται ἄλλον, ὁ δὲ ζωὴν ἔχων ὁ τοῦ ποιήσαντος τὴν μορφὴν ἀδελφὸς ὢν καὶ αὐτὸς τὴν αὐτὴν δύναμιν ἔχων ποιεῖ ἐν τῷ γενομένῳ.

c. This productive faculty may be called θεωρία, since it is productive without being practical.

In what sense this productive faculty may be called θεωρία

Enn. III 8, 3, l. 1-6; 12-22:

Πῶς οὖν ποιῶν καὶ οὕτω ποιῶν θεωρίας τινὸς ἂν ἐφάπτοιτο; Ἢ, εἰ μένων ποιεῖ καὶ ἐν αὑτῷ μένων καί ἐστι λόγος, εἴη ἂν αὐτὸς θεωρία. Ἡ μὲν γὰρ πρᾶξις γένοιτ' ἂν κατὰ λόγον ἑτέρα οὖσα δηλονότι τοῦ λόγου· ὁ μέντοι λόγος καὶ αὐτὸς ὁ συνὼν τῇ πράξει καὶ ἐπιστατῶν οὐκ ἂν εἴη πρᾶξις. Εἰ οὖν μὴ πρᾶξις 5 ἀλλὰ λόγος, θεωρία· — Πῶς δὲ αὕτη ἔχει θεωρίαν; Τὴν μὲν δὴ ἐκ λόγου οὐκ ἔχει· λέγω δ' ἐκ λόγου τὸ σκοπεῖσθαι περὶ τῶν ἐν αὐτῇ. Διὰ τί οὖν ζωή τις οὖσα καὶ λόγος καὶ δύναμις ποιοῦσα; ˀΑρ' ὅτι τὸ σκοπεῖσθαί ἐστι τὸ μήπω 1 ἔχειν; Ἡ δὲ ἔχει, καὶ διὰ τοῦτο ὅτι ἔχει καὶ ποιεῖ. Τὸ οὖν εἶναι αὐτῇ ὅ ἐστι τοῦτό ἐστι τὸ ποιεῖν αὐτῇ καὶ ὅσον ἐστὶ τοῦτό ἐστι τὸ ποιοῦν. Ἔστι δὲ θεωρία καὶ θεώρημα, λόγος γάρ. Τῷ οὖν εἶναι θεωρία καὶ θεώρημα καὶ λόγος τούτῳ καὶ ποιεῖ 2 ἢ ταῦτά ἐστιν. Ἡ ποίησις ἄρα θεωρία ἡμῖν ἀναπέφανται· ἔστι γὰρ ἀποτέλεσμα θεωρίας μενούσης θεωρίας οὐκ ἄλλο τι πραξάσης, ἀλλὰ τῷ εἶναι θεωρία ποιησάσης.

d. Nature produces without thinking or conscience. It is soul, but soul of the lowest degree.

Enn. III 8, 4, l. 15-25:

5 Τί οὖν ταῦτα βούλεται; Ὡς ἡ μὲν λεγομένη φύσις ψυχὴ οὖσα, γέννημα ψυχῆς προτέρας δυνατώτερον ζώσης, ἡσυχῆ ἐν ἑαυτῇ θεωρίαν ἔχουσα οὐ πρὸς τὸ ἄνω οὐδ' αὖ ἔτι πρὸς τὸ κάτω, στᾶσα δὲ ἐν ᾧ ἔστιν, ἐν τῇ αὑτῆς στάσει καὶ οἷον 10 συναισθήσει, τῇ συνέσει ταύτῃ καὶ συναισθήσει τὸ μετ' αὐτὴν εἶδεν ὡς οἷόν τε αὐτῇ καὶ οὐκέτι ἐζήτησεν ἄλλα θεώρημα ἀποτελέσασα ἀγλαὸν καὶ χαρίεν. Καὶ εἴτε τις βούλεται σύνεσίν τινα ἢ αἴσθησιν αὐτῇ διδόναι, οὐχ οἵαν λέγομεν ἐπὶ τῶν ἄλλων τὴν αἴσθησιν ἢ τὴν σύνεσιν, ἀλλ' οἷον εἴ τις τὴν τοῦ ὕπνου 15 τῇ * ἐγρηγορότος προσεικάσειε.

1406—Plotinus' theory of ὕλη is chiefly expounded in the treatise Περὶ τῶν δύο ὑλῶν (II 4), as it is named by Porphyry.

The ὕλη which is the ὑποκείμενον of the sensible world, is prefigured in the intelligible world. In other words: if there is ὕλη αἰσθητή, the existence of ὕλη νοητή must be assumed.

a. *Enn.* II 4, 3, l. 1-16:

Πρῶτον οὖν λεκτέον ὡς οὐ πανταχοῦ τὸ ἀόριστον ἀτιμαστέον, οὐδὲ ὃ ἂν ἄμορφον ᾖ τῇ ἑαυτοῦ ἐπινοίᾳ, εἰ μέλλοι παρέχειν αὐτὸ τοῖς πρὸ αὑτοῦ καὶ τοῖς ἀρίστοις· οἷόν τι καὶ ψυχὴ πρὸς νοῦν καὶ λόγον πέφυκε μορφουμένη παρὰ τούτων 5 καὶ εἰς εἶδος βέλτιον ἀγομένη· ἔν τε τοῖς νοητοῖς τὸ σύνθετον ἑτέρως, οὐχ ὡς τὰ σώματα· ἐπεὶ καὶ λόγοι σύνθετοι καὶ ἐνεργείᾳ δὲ σύνθετον ποιοῦσι τὴν ἐνεργοῦσαν εἰς εἶδος φύσιν. Εἰ δὲ καὶ πρὸς ἄλλο καὶ παρ' ἄλλου, καὶ μᾶλλον. Ἡ δὲ τῶν γιγνομένων ὕλη ἀεὶ ἄλλο καὶ ἄλλο εἶδος ἴσχει, τῶν δὲ ἀϊδίων ἡ αὐτὴ 10 ταὐτὸν ἀεί. Τάχα δὲ ἀνάπαλιν ἡ ἐνταῦθα. Ἐνταῦθα μὲν γὰρ παρὰ μέρος πάντα καὶ ἐν ἑκάστοτε· διὸ οὐδὲν ἐμμένει ἄλλου ἄλλο ἐξωθοῦντος· διὸ οὐ ταὐτὸν ἀεί. Ἐκεῖ δ' ἅμα πάντα· διὸ οὐκ ἔχει εἰς ὃ μεταβάλλοι, ἤδη γὰρ ἔχει πάντα. Οὐδέποτ' οὖν ἄμορφος οὔτε ἐκεῖ ἢ ἐκεῖ, ἐπεὶ οὐδ' ἡ ἐνταῦθα, ἀλλ' ἕτερον τρόπον ἑκατέρα.

ὕλη νοητή, its difference from ὕλη αἰσθητή

b. Ib., c. 4, l. 2-17:

Εἰ οὖν πολλὰ τὰ εἴδη, κοινὸν μέν τι ἐν αὐτοῖς ἀνάγκη εἶναι· καὶ δὴ καὶ ἴδιον, 5 ᾧ διαφέρει ἄλλο ἄλλου. Τοῦτο δὴ τὸ ἴδιον καὶ ἡ διαφορὰ ἡ χωρίζουσα ἡ οἰκεία ἐστὶ μορφή. Εἰ δὲ μορφή, ἔστι τὸ μορφούμενον, περὶ ὃ ἡ διαφορά. Ἔστιν ἄρα καὶ ὕλη ἡ τὴν μορφὴν δεχομένη καὶ ἀεὶ τὸ ὑποκείμενον. Ἔτι, εἰ κόσμος νοητὸς ἔστιν ἐκεῖ, μίμημα δὲ οὗτος ἐκείνου, οὗτος δὲ σύνθετος 10 καὶ ἐξ ὕλης, κἀκεῖ δεῖ ὕλην εἶναι. Ἢ πῶς προσερεῖς κόσμον μὴ εἰς εἶδος ἰδών; Πῶς δὲ εἶδος μὴ ἐφ' ᾧ τὸ εἶδος λαβών; Ἀμερὲς μὲν γὰρ παντελῶς πάντη αὐτό,

Arguments for assuming ὕλη νοητή

---

* τοῦ codd.; <τῇ> τοῦ Müller, Br.

μεριστὸν δὲ ὁπωσοῦν. Καὶ εἰ μὲν διασπασθέντα ἀπ' ἀλλήλων τὰ μέρη, ἡ τομὴ
καὶ ἡ διάσπασις ὕλης ἐστὶ πάθος· αὕτη γὰρ ἡ τμηθεῖσα· εἰ δὲ πολλὰ ὂν ἀμέριστόν
ἐστι, τὰ πολλὰ ἐν ἑνὶ ὄντα ἐν ὕλῃ ἐστὶ τῷ ἑνὶ αὐτὰ μορφαὶ αὐτοῦ ὄντα· τὸ γὰρ   1.
ἐν τοῦτο τὸ ποικίλον νόησον ποικίλον καὶ πολύμορφον.

c. In what sense intelligible things are composite.

Ib., c. 5, l. 1-9:

Εἰ δ', ὅτι ἀεὶ ἔχει ταῦτα καὶ ὁμοῦ, ἐν ἄμφω καὶ οὐχ ὕλη ἐκεῖνο, οὐδ' ἐνταῦθα ἔσται τῶν σωμάτων ὕλη, οὐδέποτε γὰρ ἄνευ μορφῆς, ἀλλ' ἀεὶ ὅλον σῶμα,
σύνθετον μὴν ὅμως. Καὶ νοῦς εὑρίσκει τὸ διττόν· οὗτος γὰρ διαιρεῖ, ἕως
εἰς ἁπλοῦν ἥκῃ μηκέτι αὐτὸ ἀναλύεσθαι δυνάμενον· ἕως δὲ δύναται, χωρεῖ 5

ὕλη
is darkness

αὐτοῦ εἰς τὸ βάθος. Τὸ δὲ βάθος ἑκάστου ἡ ὕλη· διὸ καὶ σκοτεινὴ πᾶσα, ὅτι
τὸ φῶς ὁ λόγος καὶ ὁ νοῦς λόγος. Διὸ τὸν ἐφ' ἑκάστου λόγον ὁρῶν τὸ κάτω
ὡς ὑπὸ τὸ φῶς σκοτεινὸν ἡγεῖται *. —

d. Again: the difference between intelligible and sensible ὕλη. The first is οὐσία.

Ib., c. 5, l. 12-23:

Again: difference between the two ὕλαι

Διάφορόν γε μὴν τὸ σκοτεινὸν τό τε ἐν τοῖς νοητοῖς τό τε ἐν τοῖς αἰσθητοῖς
ὑπάρχει διάφορός τε ἡ ὕλη, ὅσῳ καὶ τὸ εἶδος τὸ ἐπικείμενον ἀμφοῖν διάφορον·
ἡ μὲν γὰρ θεία λαβοῦσα τὸ ὁρίζον αὐτὴν ζωὴν ὡρισμένην καὶ νοερὰν ἔχει,   1.
ἡ δὲ ὡρισμένον μέν τι γίγνεται, οὐ μὴν ζῶν οὐδὲ νοοῦν, ἀλλὰ νεκρὸν κεκοσμημένον.
Καὶ ἡ μορφὴ δὲ εἴδωλον· ὥστε καὶ τὸ ὑποκείμενον εἴδωλον. Ἐκεῖ δὲ ἡ μορφὴ
ἀληθινόν· ὥστε καὶ τὸ ὑποκείμενον. Διὸ καὶ τοὺς λέγοντας οὐσίαν τὴν ὕλην,
εἰ περὶ ἐκείνης ἔλεγον, ὀρθῶς ἔδει ὑπολαμβάνειν λέγειν· τὸ γὰρ ὑποκείμενον   20

ὕλη νοητὴ
is substance

ἐκεῖ οὐσία, μᾶλλον δὲ μετὰ τοῦ ἐπ' αὐτῇ νοουμένη καὶ ὅλη οὖσα πεφωτισμένη
οὐσία.

e. Ib., c. 5, l. 24-37:

It is eternal

Πότερα δὲ ἀΐδιος ἡ νοητὴ ὁμοίως ζητητέον, ὡς ἄν τις καὶ τὰς ἰδέας ζητοῖ·
γενητὰ μὲν γὰρ τῷ ἀρχὴν ἔχειν, ἀγένητα δέ, ὅτι μὴ χρόνῳ τὴν ἀρχὴν ἔχει,   25

eternally produced by ἑτερότης

ἀλλ' ἀεὶ παρ' ἄλλου, οὐχ ὡς γινόμενα ἀεί, ὥσπερ ὁ ** κόσμος, ἀλλὰ ὄντα
ἀεί, ὥσπερ ὁ ἐκεῖ κόσμος. Καὶ γὰρ ἡ ἑτερότης ἡ ἐκεῖ ἀεί, ἡ τὴν ὕλην ποιεῖ·
ἀρχὴ γὰρ ὕλης αὕτη, καὶ ἡ κίνησις ἡ πρώτη· διὸ καὶ αὕτη ἑτερότης ἐλέγετο, 30
ὅτι ὁμοῦ ἐξέφυσαν κίνησις καὶ ἑτερότης· ἀόριστον δὲ καὶ ἡ κίνησις καὶ ἡ ἑτερότης
ἡ ἀπὸ τοῦ πρώτου, κἀκείνου πρὸς τὸ ὁρισθῆναι δεόμενα· ὁρίζεται δέ, ὅταν πρὸς
αὐτὸ ἐπιστραφῇ· πρὶν δὲ ἀόριστον ἡ ὕλη καὶ τὸ ἕτερον καὶ οὔπω ἀγαθόν, ἀλλ'   35
ἀφώτιστον ἐκείνου. Εἰ γὰρ παρ' ἐκείνου τὸ φῶς, τὸ δεχόμενον τὸ φῶς, πρὶν
δέξασθαι, φῶς οὐκ ἔχει ἀεί, ἀλλὰ ἄλλο ὂν ἔχει, εἴπερ τὸ φῶς παρ' ἄλλου.

---

* ἥγηται H.-S.   ** ⟨ἐνταῦθα⟩ suppl. Müller, Br.

1407—a. Why ὕλη αἰσθητή must be assumed.

Enn. II 4, 6, l. 1-10:

Why ὕλη αἰσθητή?

Περὶ δὴ τῆς τῶν σωμάτων ὑποδοχῆς ὧδε λεγέσθω. "Ὅτι μὲν οὖν δεῖ τι τοῖς σώμασιν ὑποκείμενον εἶναι ἄλλο ὂν παρ' αὐτά, ἥ τε εἰς ἄλληλα μεταβολὴ τῶν στοιχείων δηλοῖ. Οὐ γὰρ παντελὴς τοῦ μεταβάλλοντος ἡ φθορά· ἢ ἔσται τις
5 οὐσία εἰς τὸ μὴ ὂν ἀπολομένη· οὐδ' αὖ τὸ γενόμενον ἐκ τοῦ παντελῶς μὴ ὄντος εἰς τὸ ὂν ἐλήλυθεν, ἀλλ' ἔστιν εἴδους μεταβολὴ ἐξ εἴδους ἑτέρου. Μένει δὲ τὸ δεξάμενον τὸ εἶδος τοῦ γενομένου καὶ ἀποβαλὸν θάτερον. Τοῦτό τε οὖν δηλοῖ
10 καὶ ὅλως ἡ φθορά· συνθέτου γάρ· εἰ δὲ τοῦτο, ἐξ ὕλης καὶ εἴδους ἕκαστον.

b. Sensible matter is completely ἄποιος.

Ib., c. 8, l. 1-8, 11, 13-14:

It is completely ἄποιος

Τίς οὖν ἡ μία αὕτη καὶ συνεχὴς καὶ ἄποιος λεγομένη; Καὶ ὅτι μὲν μὴ σῶμα, εἴπερ ἄποιος, δῆλον· ἢ ποιότητα ἕξει. Λέγοντες δὲ πάντων αὐτὴν εἶναι τῶν αἰσθητῶν καὶ οὐ τινῶν μὲν ὕλην, πρὸς ἄλλα δὲ εἶδος οὖσαν — οἷον τὸν πηλὸν
5 ὕλην τῷ κεραμεύοντι, ἁπλῶς δὲ οὐχ ὕλην — οὐ δὴ οὕτως, ἀλλὰ πρὸς πάντα λέγοντες, οὐδὲν ἂν αὐτῇ προσάπτοιμεν τῇ αὐτῆς φύσει, ὅσα ἐπὶ τοῖς αἰσθητοῖς ὁρᾶται. — Οὐ τοίνυν οὐδὲ μέγεθος. — Δεῖ δὲ αὐτὴν μὴ σύνθετον εἶναι, ἀλλ' ἁπλοῦν καὶ ἕν τι τῇ αὐτῆς φύσει· οὕτω γὰρ πάντων ἔρημος.

c. How can it be the "receptacle", if it does not possess μέγεθος or ὄγκος?

How is it the ὑποδεχό-μενον without extension or mass?

Ib., c. 11, l. 1-7, 13-16, 17-19; 25-38, 40-43:

Καὶ τί δεῖ τινος ἄλλου πρὸς σύστασιν σωμάτων μετὰ μέγεθος καὶ ποιότητας ἀπάσας; Ἢ τοῦ ὑποδεξομένου πάντα. Οὔκουν ὁ ὄγκος· εἰ δὲ ὁ ὄγκος, μέγεθος δήπου· εἰ δὲ ἀμέγεθες, οὐδ' ὅπου δέξεται ἔχει. Ἀμέγεθες δὲ ὂν τί
5 ἂν συμβάλλοιτο, εἰ μήτε εἰς εἶδος καὶ τὸ ποιὸν μήτε εἰς τὴν διάστασιν καὶ τὸ μέγεθος, ὃ δὴ παρὰ τῆς ὕλης δοκεῖ, ὅπου ἂν ᾖ, ἔρχεσθαι εἰς τὰ σώματα; — Πρῶτον μὲν οὖν οὐκ ἀνάγκη τὸ ὑποδεχόμενον ὁτιοῦν ὄγκον εἶναι, ἐὰν μὴ
15 μέγεθος ἤδη αὐτῷ παρῇ· ἐπεὶ καὶ ἡ ψυχὴ πάντα δεχομένη ὁμοῦ ἔχει πάντα. — Ἡ δὲ ὕλη διὰ τοῦτο ἐν διαστήματι ἃ δέχεται λαμβάνει, ὅτι διαστήματός ἐστι δεκτική· —

Μέγεθος is not required as a substrate for Form.

It has only the appearance of ὄγκος

25 Οὐ τοίνυν ὄγκον δεῖ εἶναι τὸ δεξόμενον τὸ εἶδος, ἀλλ' ὁμοῦ τῷ γενέσθαι ὄγκον καὶ τὴν ἄλλην ποιότητα δέχεσθαι. Καὶ φάντασμα μὲν ἔχειν ὄγκου ὡς ἐπιτηδειότητα τούτου ὥσπερ πρώτην, κενὸν δὲ ὄγκον. "Ὅθεν τινὲς ταὐτὸν
40 τῷ κενῷ τὴν ὕλην εἰρήκασι. Φάντασμα δὲ ὄγκου λέγω, ὅτι καὶ ἡ ψυχὴ οὐδὲν ἔχουσα ὁρίσαι, ὅταν τῇ ὕλῃ προσομιλῇ, εἰς ἀοριστίαν χεῖ ἑαυτὴν οὔτε περιγρά-

It is great
and small φουσα οὔτε εἰς σημεῖον ἰέναι δυναμένη· ἤδη γὰρ ὁρίζει. Διὸ οὔτε μέγα λεκτέον
χωρὶς οὔτε σμικρὸν αὖ, ἀλλὰ μέγα καὶ μικρόν ¹· καὶ οὕτως ὄγκος καὶ ἀμέγεθες
οὕτως, ὅτι ὕλη ὄγκου καὶ συστελλόμενον ἐκ τοῦ μεγάλου ἐπὶ τὸ σμικρὸν καὶ ἐκ 35
τοῦ σμικροῦ ἐπὶ τὸ μέγα οἷον ὄγκον διατρέχει· καὶ ἡ ἀοριστία αὐτῆς ὁ τοιοῦτος
ὄγκος, ὑποδοχὴ μεγέθους ἐν αὐτῇ ². — Ἡ δὲ ἀόριστος οὖσα καὶ μήπω στᾶσα ³
παρ' αὐτῆς ἐπὶ πᾶν εἶδος φερομένη δεῦρο κἀκεῖσε καὶ πάντα εὐάγωγος οὖσα 40
πολλή τε γίνεται τῇ ἐπὶ πάντα ἀγωγῇ καὶ γενέσει καὶ ἔσχε τοῦτον τὸν τρόπον
φύσιν ὄγκου.

1408—Since the "essence" of ὕλη is indefiniteness (ἀοριστία), two
questions arise, namely

1) whether it must be distinguished from the Aristotelian notion of
στέρησις (see above, nrs. **476, 478, 480**),

2) in what sense it may be called ἄπειρον.

Is
ὕλη
= στέρησις? **a.** *Enn.* II 4, 14, l. 1-6, 22-30:

'Αλλ' ἐκεῖνο ζητητέον, πότερα στέρησις, ἢ περὶ αὐτῆς ἡ στέρησις. Ὁ τοίνυν
λέγων λόγος ὑποκειμένῳ μὲν ἐν ἄμφω, λόγῳ δὲ δύο, δίκαιος ἦν διδάσκειν καὶ
τὸν λόγον ἑκατέρου ὄντινα δεῖ ἀποδιδόναι, τῆς μὲν ὕλης ὃς ὁριεῖται αὐτὴν οὐδὲν
προσαπτόμενος τῆς στερήσεως, τῆς τε αὖ στερήσεως ὡσαύτως. 5

Εἰ μὲν οὖν οὐκ ὄν, ὅτι μὴ τὸ ὄν, ἀλλ' ἄλλο ὄν τί ἐστι, δύο οἱ λόγοι, ὁ μὲν τοῦ
ὑποκειμένου ἁπτόμενος, ὁ δὲ τῆς στερήσεως τὴν πρὸς τὰ ἄλλα σχέσιν δηλῶν.
Ἢ ὁ μὲν τῆς ὕλης πρὸς τὰ ἄλλα καὶ ὁ τοῦ ὑποκειμένου δὲ πρὸς τὰ ἄλλα, ὁ δὲ 2
τῆς στερήσεως εἰ τὸ ἀόριστον αὐτῆς δηλοῖ, τάχα ἂν αὐτὸς αὐτῆς ἐφάπτοιτο·
πλὴν ἕν γε ἑκατέρως τῷ ὑποκειμένῳ, λόγῳ δὲ δύο. Εἰ μέντοι τῷ ἀορίστῳ
εἶναι καὶ ἀπείρῳ εἶναι καὶ ἀποίῳ εἶναι τῇ ὕλῃ ταὐτόν, πῶς ἔτι δύο οἱ λόγοι;

b. Ὕλη = the ἄπειρον, but not in the sense of a property.

ὕλη =
the
ἄπειρον *Enn.* II 4, 15, l. 10-12, 17:

'Ανάγκη τοίνυν τὴν ὕλην τὸ ἄπειρον εἶναι, οὐχ οὕτω δὲ ἄπειρον, ὡς κατὰ
συμβεβηκὸς καὶ τῷ συμβεβηκέναι τὸ ἄπειρον αὐτῇ. — Αὐτὴ τοίνυν τὸ ἄπειρον.

c. The ἄπειρον, namely, is twofold, like ὕλη is. Only in this case the
archetypon, i.e. the ἄπειρον in the intelligible world, is less infinite than
its image in the sensible world. For (as P. says in VI 6, 3) the ἄπειρον
in the intelligible world is always determined. Cp. II 4, 3, l. 14 f.: οὐδέποτ'
οὖν ἄμορφος ἡ ἐκεῖ (ὕλη), nr. **1406a**, and **1406d**.

¹ Cp. Arist. on Plato in *Metaph.* A 6, 987b 20 (*Gr. Ph.* I, nr. **365a**).
² Cp. Plato, *Parm.* 164d (*Gr. Ph.* I, nr. **334**).
³ Cp. Hermodorus ap. Simpl., *Phys.* 248 (*Gr. Ph.* I, nr. **371a**, the end). ὥστε
ἄστατον καὶ ἄμορφον καὶ ἄπειρον, κτλ.

Enn. II 4, 15, l. 17-28:

The ἄπειρον as archetypon is less infinite

'Επεὶ καὶ ἐν τοῖς νοητοῖς ἡ ὕλη τὸ ἄπειρον καὶ εἴη ἂν γεννηθὲν ἐκ τῆς τοῦ
20 ἑνὸς ἀπειρίας ἢ δυνάμεως ἢ τοῦ ἀεί, οὐκ οὔσης ἐν ἐκείνῳ ἀπειρίας ἀλλὰ ποιοῦντος.
Πῶς οὖν ἐκεῖ καὶ ἐνταῦθα; Ἢ διττὸν καὶ τὸ ἄπειρον. Καὶ τί διαφέρει; Ὡς
ἀρχέτυπον καὶ εἴδωλον. Ἐλαττόνως οὖν ἄπειρον τοῦτο; Ἢ μᾶλλον· ὅσῳ γὰρ
εἴδωλον πεφευγὸς τὸ εἶναι τὸ ἀληθές, μᾶλλον ἄπειρον. Ἡ γὰρ ἀπειρία ἐν τῷ ἧττον
25 ὁρισθέντι μᾶλλον· τὸ γὰρ ἧττον ἐν τῷ ἀγαθῷ μᾶλλον ἐν τῷ κακῷ. Τὸ ἐκεῖ οὖν
μᾶλλον ὂν εἴδωλον ὡς ἄπειρον, τὸ δ' ἐνταῦθα ἧττον, ὅσῳ πέφευγε τὸ εἶναι
καὶ τὸ ἀληθές, εἰς δὲ εἰδώλου κατερρύη φύσιν, ἀληθεστέρως ἄπειρον.

d. That there is ἄπειρον in Noûs, because this is one and many,
is said by P. repeatedly, e.g. in *Enn.* VI 7, 14, l. 11 f.:

The ἄπειρον in the intelligible world

Καὶ τὸ ἄπειρον οὕτως ἐν νῷ, ὅτι αὐτὸς ἓν πολλά, οὐχ ὡς οἶκος εἷς, ἀλλ'
ὡς λόγος πολὺς ἐν αὐτῷ.

Cp. also VI 2, 21, l. 10 (above, nr. **1385b**) and III 8, 8, the end. As we saw above,
in II 4, 3 (nr. **1406a**) he reminds the reader that the ἄπειρον should not always be
despised. In VI 6 he begins his treatise Περὶ ἀριθμῶν by asking:
Ἆρ' ἐστὶ τὸ πλῆθος ἀπόστασις τοῦ ἑνός, καὶ ἡ ἀπειρία ἀπόστασις παντελὴς τῷ πλῆθος
ἀνάριθμον εἶναι, καὶ διὰ τοῦτο κακὸν ἡ ἀπειρία καὶ ἡμεῖς κακοί, ὅταν πλῆθος;
To this question he answers in c. 3 that in the intelligible world πλῆθος is always
determined, and even the ἄπειρον is so.

e. Thus, ὕλη (= the ἄπειρον) together with the intelligible world
is derived by P. from the First Principle, which he calls δύναμις τῶν
πάντων (III 8, 10, the beginning), and "the Father" who made the intelligible world; e.g. V 1, 5, l. 3 ff.:

It is derived directly from the First Principle

Τίς οὖν ὁ τοῦτον γεννήσας, ὁ ἁπλοῦς καὶ ὁ πρὸ τοῦ τοιούτου, ὁ αἴτιος τοῦ
5 καὶ εἶναι καὶ πολὺν εἶναι τοῦτον, ὁ τὸν ἀριθμὸν ποιῶν; Ὁ γὰρ ἀριθμὸς οὐ πρῶ-
τος· καὶ γὰρ πρὸ τῆς δυάδος τὸ ἕν, δεύτερον δὲ δυὰς καὶ παρὰ τοῦ ἑνὸς γεγενημένη ἐκεῖνο ὁριστὴν ἔχει, αὐτὴ δὲ ἀόριστον παρ' αὑτῆς.

Here again we find the indefinite Two directly engendered by the One. Cp. above,
nr. **1279a**, **1285b** and the explanations given there. Also **1288c**: on the μονὰς
ἀρσενόθηλυς, and **1340a** (*Corpus Herm.* I 9, where the Noûs is called ἀρρενόθηλυς).

By the derivation of ὕλη from the First Principle Plotinus' monism
is completed and a certain obscurity of classical Platonism corrected
and made precise.

Monism completed

1409—In III 6, second part (cc. 6-19), Plotinus deals with ὕλη as an
ἀσώματον, and as such ἀπαθής.

a. Ὕλη is ἀπαθής in quite another sense than intelligible Being is.
The latter is beyond πάθη, ὕλη is below. As non-being it is never really
"formed" by that which comes into it.

Enn. III 6, 6, l. 1-7; c. 7, l. 3-31, 37-43:

Τὴν μὲν δὴ οὐσίαν τὴν νοητὴν τὴν κατὰ τὸ εἶδος ἄπασαν τεταγμένην ὡς ἀπαθῆ δεῖ εἶναι δοκεῖν εἴρηται. Ἐπεὶ δὲ καὶ ἡ ὕλη ἕν τι τῶν ἀσωμάτων, εἰ καὶ ἄλλον τρόπον, σκεπτέον καὶ περὶ ταύτης τίνα τρόπον ἔχει, πότερα παθητή, 5 ὡς λέγεται, καὶ κατὰ πάντα τρεπτή [1], ἢ καὶ ταύτην δεῖ ἀπαθῆ εἶναι οἴεσθαι, καὶ τίς ὁ τρόπος τῆς ἀπαθείας. —

Ἔστι μὲν οὖν (ἡ ὕλη) ἀσώματος, ἐπείπερ τὸ σῶμα ὕστερον καὶ σύνθετον καὶ αὐτὴ μετ’ ἄλλου ποιεῖ σῶμα. Οὕτω γὰρ τοῦ ὀνόματος τετύχηκε τοῦ αὐτοῦ 5 κατὰ τὸ ἀσώματον, ὅτι ἑκάτερον τό τε ὂν ἥ τε ὕλη ἕτερα τῶν σωμάτων. Οὔτε δὲ ψυχὴ οὖσα οὔτε νοῦς οὔτε ζωὴ οὔτε εἶδος οὔτε λόγος οὔτε πέρας — ἀπειρία γάρ —

described as μὴ ὄν

οὔτε δύναμις — τί γὰρ καὶ ποιεῖ; — ἀλλὰ ταῦτα ὑπερεκπεσοῦσα πάντα οὐδὲ τὴν 10 τοῦ ὄντος προσηγορίαν ὀρθῶς ἂν δέχοιτο, μὴ ὂν δ’ ἂν εἰκότως λέγοιτο, καὶ οὐχ ὥσπερ κίνησις μὴ ὂν ἢ στάσις μὴ ὄν, ἀλλ’ ἀληθινῶς μὴ ὄν, εἴδωλον καὶ φάντασμα ὄγκου καὶ ὑποστάσεως ἔφεσις καὶ ἑστηκὸς οὐκ ἐν στάσει καὶ ἀόρατον καθ’ αὑτὸ καὶ φεῦγον τὸ βουλόμενον ἰδεῖν, καὶ ὅταν τις μὴ ἴδῃ γιγνόμενον, ἀτενίσαντι 15 δὲ οὐχ ὁρώμενον, καὶ τὰ ἐναντία ἀεὶ ἐφ’ ἑαυτοῦ φανταζόμενον, μικρὸν καὶ μέγα καὶ ἧττον καὶ μᾶλλον, ἐλλεῖπόν τε καὶ ὑπερέχον, εἴδωλον οὐ μένον οὐδ’ αὖ φεύγειν δυνάμενον· οὐδὲ γὰρ οὐδὲ τοῦτο ἰσχύει ἅτε μὴ ἰσχὺν παρὰ νοῦ λαβόν, ἀλλ’ ἐν

its deceptive character

ἐλλείψει τοῦ ὄντος παντὸς γενόμενον. Διὸ πᾶν ὃ ἂν ἐπαγγέλληται ψεύδεται, 20 κἂν μέγα φαντασθῇ, μικρόν ἐστι, κἂν μᾶλλον, ἧττόν ἐστι, καὶ τὸ ὂν αὐτοῦ ἐν φαντάσει οὐκ ὄν ἐστιν, οἷον παίγνιον φεῦγον· ὅθεν καὶ τὰ ἐν αὐτῷ ἐγγίγνεσθαι δοκοῦντα παίγνια, εἴδωλα ἐν εἰδώλῳ ἀτεχνῶς, ὡς ἐν κατόπτρῳ τὸ ἀλλαχοῦ 25 ἱδρυμένον, ἀλλαχοῦ φανταζόμενον· καὶ πιμπλάμενον, ὡς δοκεῖ, καὶ ἔχον οὐδὲν καὶ δοκοῦν τὰ πάντα [2]. Τὰ δὲ εἰσιόντα καὶ ἐξιόντα τῶν ὄντων μιμήματα [3] καὶ εἴδωλα εἰς εἴδωλον ἄμορφον καὶ διὰ τὸ ἄμορφον αὐτῆς ἐνορώμενα ποιεῖν μὲν δοκεῖ εἰς αὐτήν, ποιεῖ δὲ οὐδέν· ἀμενηνὰ γὰρ καὶ ἀσθενῆ καὶ ἀντερεῖδον οὐκ ἔχοντα. — 30

Κἀκ τούτων μαθεῖν ἔστι τὸ τῆς πείσεως ψεῦδος ψεύδους ὄντος τοῦ ἐνορωμένου καὶ οὐδαμῇ ἔχοντος ὁμοιότητα πρὸς τὸ ποιῆσαν. Ἀσθενὲς δὴ καὶ ψεῦδος ὂν καὶ εἰς ψεῦδος ἐμπῖπτον, οἷα ἐν ὀνείρῳ ἢ ὕδατι ἢ κατόπτρῳ, ἀπαθῆ αὐτὴν 40 εἴασεν ἐξ ἀνάγκης εἶναι· καίτοι ἕν γε τοῖς προειρημένοις ὁμοίωσις τοῖς ἐνορωμένοις ἐστὶ πρὸς τὰ ἐνορῶντα.

b. Matter is not affected by that which comes into it. Thus, it cannot be influenced by the good. This means that it is evil by nature—"evil" in the sense οι στέρησις (cp. Plato's doctrine of the ἄπειρον, above, vol. I, nr. **371**).

---

[1] This is the Stoic doctrine. Cp. SVF II 309.

[2] The whole description is clearly inspired by Plato, *Parm.* 164d-165c (*Gr. Ph.* I, **334**).

[3] Plato, *Tim.* 50c.

Enn. III 6, 11, l. 15-18, 36-45:   Its
ἀπάθεια

5 Τῇ δὲ ὕλῃ οὔτε τι πλέον εἰς τὴν αὐτῆς σύστασιν προσελθόντος ὁτουοῦν·
οὐ γὰρ γίγνεται τότε ὃ ἔστι προσελθόντος, οὔτε ἔλαττον ἀπελθόντος· μένει γὰρ
ὃ ἐξ ἀρχῆς ἦν. — Οὐ γὰρ ἐξίσταται ἑαυτῆς, ἀλλ' ὅτι μὲν ἀναγκαῖόν ἐστι μεταλαμβάνειν ἀμηγέπη μεταλαμβάνει ἕως ἂν ᾖ, τῷ δ' εἶναι ὃ ἔστι τρόπῳ μετα-
λήψεως τηροῦντι αὐτὴν οὐ βλάπτεται εἰς τὸ εἶναι παρὰ τοῦ οὕτω διδόντος,
καὶ κινδυνεύει διὰ τοῦτο οὐχ ἧττον εἶναι κακή, ὅτι ἀεὶ μένει τοῦτο ὅ ἐστι.
Μεταλαμβάνουσα γὰρ ὄντως καὶ ἀλλοιουμένη ὄντως ὑπὸ τοῦ ἀγαθοῦ οὐκ ἂν In this sense
it is evil
ἦν τὴν φύσιν κακή. Ὥστε εἴ τις τὴν ὕλην λέγει κακήν, οὕτως ἂν ἀληθεύοι, εἰ
5 τοῦ ἀγαθοῦ ἀπαθῆ λέγοι· τοῦτο δὲ ταὐτόν ἐστι τῷ ὅλως ἀπαθῆ εἶναι.

c. Cp. ib., c. 13, l. 29-34, 49-55:

"Υλη is the "receptacle"; but what comes into it are neither the Ideas themselves,
nor is the image produced in it a full reality.

Καὶ χώρα πάντων, καὶ οὐδενὸς ὅτου οὐχ * ὑποδοχή. Ἀλλὰ δεῖ καὶ εἰσιόντων The Forms
themselves
τὴν αὐτὴν μένειν καὶ ἐξιόντων ἀπαθῆ, ἵνα καὶ εἰσίῃ τι ἀεὶ εἰς αὐτὴν καὶ ἐξίῃ. do not come
into it
Εἴσεισι δὴ τὸ εἰσιὸν εἴδωλον ὂν καὶ εἰς οὐκ ἀληθινὸν οὐκ ἀληθές. Ἆρ' οὖν
ἀληθῶς; Καὶ πῶς, ᾧ μηδαμῶς θέμις ἀληθείας μετέχειν διὰ τὸ ψεῦδος εἶναι; —
Εἰ μὲν οὖν ἔστι τι ἐν τοῖς κατόπτροις, καὶ ἐν τῇ ὕλῃ οὕτω τὰ αἰσθητὰ ἔστω·
εἰ δὲ μὴ ἔστι, φαίνεται δὲ εἶναι, κἀκεῖ φατέον φαίνεσθαι ἐπὶ τῆς ὕλης αἰτιωμένους
τῆς φαντάσεως τὴν τῶν ὄντων ὑπόστασιν, ἧς τὰ μὲν ὄντα ὄντως ἀεὶ μεταλαμβάνει, τὰ δὲ μὴ ὄντα μὴ ὄντως, ἐπείπερ οὐ δεῖ οὕτως ἔχειν αὐτὰ ὡς εἶχεν ἂν
5 τοῦ ὄντως μὴ ὄντος, εἰ ἦν αὐτά.

1410—Thus, in a sense, matter is bad; namely, *sensible* matter, which
is formless and in complete lack of the good. P. deals with this problem
more amply in the treatise Πόθεν τὰ κακά (I 8).

a.   There is no evil in the intelligible world. Therefore, evil cannot
belong to the sphere of Being; it must be non-being, relative non-being,
and this not in the sense of ἕτερον, but either in the sense of an εἰκών
(which means an inferior degree of reality) or below this.

Enn. I 8, 2, l. 25-31; c. 3, l. 1-12.

After having spoken of the life of the Spirit (Noûs) and of Soul, which "dances
around Him" and sees God through Him, P. goes on:

5 Καὶ οὗτος θεῶν ἀπήμων καὶ μακάριος βίος καὶ τὸ κακὸν οὐδαμοῦ ἐνταῦθα
καὶ εἰ ἐνταῦθα ἔστη, κακὸν οὐδὲν ἂν ἦν, ἀλλὰ πρῶτον καὶ δεύτερα τἀγαθὰ
καὶ τρίτα· περὶ τὸν πάντων βασιλέα πάντα ἐστί, καὶ ἐκεῖνο αἴτιον

---

* ὅτου οὐχ corr. Kirchhoff; ὁτουοῦν codd., H.-S.

πάντων καλῶν, καὶ πάντα ἐστὶν ἐκείνου, καὶ δεύτερον περὶ τὰ δεύτερα καὶ τρίτον περὶ τὰ τρίτα[1].

No evil in the intelligible world

(3) Εἰ δὴ ταῦτά ἐστι τὰ ὄντα καὶ τὸ ἐπέκεινα τῶν ὄντων, οὐκ ἂν ἐν τοῖς οὖσι τὸ κακὸν ἐνείη, οὐδ' ἐν τῷ ἐπέκεινα τῶν ὄντων· ἀγαθὰ γὰρ ταῦτα. Λείπεται τοίνυν, εἴπερ ἔστιν, ἐν τοῖς μὴ οὖσιν εἶναι οἷον εἶδός τι[2] τοῦ μὴ ὄντος ὂν καὶ περί τι τῶν μεμιγμένων τῷ μὴ ὄντι ἢ ὁπωσοῦν κοινωνούντων τῷ μὴ ὄντι. 5

It must be a μὴ ὄν

Μὴ ὂν δὲ οὔτι τὸ παντελῶς μὴ ὄν, ἀλλ' ἕτερον μόνον τοῦ ὄντος· οὐχ οὕτω δὲ μὴ ὄν, ὡς κίνησις καὶ στάσις ἡ περὶ τὸ ὄν[3], ἀλλ' ὡς εἰκὼν τοῦ ὄντος ἢ καὶ ἔτι μᾶλλον μὴ ὄν. Τοῦτο δ' ἐστὶ τὸ αἰσθητὸν πᾶν καὶ ὅσα περὶ τὸ αἰσθητὸν πάθη ἢ ὕστερόν τι τούτων καὶ ὡς συμβεβηκὸς τούτοις ἢ ἀρχὴ τούτων ἢ ἕν τι τῶν 10 συμπληρούντων τοῦτο τοιοῦτον ὄν.

As will become clear in what follows, P. does not mean that the αἰσθητόν is μὴ ὄν as such or evil as such. But he does mean that it is evil "in a sense", namely *so far as it is defective*. It is, as he says below, evil *in a secondary sense*. See under **d**.

b. Evil defined as ἀμετρία, ἄπειρον, etc. It is essentially negative, and therefore never a substance.

Evil defined as αἰσθητά, etc.

Enn. I 8, 3, l. 12-24, 30-32, 35-40:

Ἤδη γὰρ ἄν τις εἰς ἔννοιαν ἥκοι αὐτοῦ οἷον ἀμετρίαν εἶναι πρὸς μέτρον καὶ ἄπειρον πρὸς πέρας καὶ ἀνείδεον πρὸς εἰδοποιητικὸν καὶ ἀεὶ ἐνδεὲς πρὸς αὔταρκες, ἀεὶ ἀόριστον, οὐδαμῇ ἑστώς[4], παμπαθές, ἀκόρητον, πενία παντελής· 15 καὶ οὐ συμβεβηκότα ταῦτα αὐτῷ, ἀλλ' οἷον οὐσία[5] αὐτοῦ ταῦτα, καὶ ὅ τι ἂν αὐτοῦ μέρος ἴδῃς, καὶ αὐτὸ πάντα ταῦτα· τὰ δ' ἄλλα, ὅσα ἂν αὐτοῦ μεταλάβῃ καὶ ὁμοιωθῇ, κακὰ μὲν γίνεσθαι, οὐχ ὅπερ δὲ κακὰ εἶναι.

Is there an evil in itself?

Τίνι οὖν ὑποστάσει ταῦτα πάρεστιν οὐχ ἕτερα ὄντα ἐκείνης, ἀλλ' ἐκείνη; Καὶ γὰρ 20 εἰ ἑτέρῳ συμβαίνει τὸ κακόν, δεῖ τι πρότερον αὐτὸ εἶναι, κἂν μὴ οὐσία τις ᾖ. Ὡς γὰρ ἀγαθὸν τὸ μὲν αὐτό, τὸ δὲ ὃ συμβέβηκεν, οὕτω καὶ κακὸν τὸ μὲν αὐτό, τὸ δὲ ἤδη κατ' ἐκεῖνο συμβεβηκὸς ἑτέρῳ. — Δεῖ οὖν εἶναί τι καὶ ἄπειρον καθ' 30 αὐτὸ καὶ ἀνείδεον αὖ αὐτὸ καὶ τὰ ἄλλα τὰ πρόσθεν, ἃ τὴν τοῦ κακοῦ ἐχαρακτήριζε φύσιν. — Τὴν δὴ ὑποκειμένην σχήμασι καὶ εἴδεσι καὶ μορφαῖς καὶ 35 μέτροις καὶ πέρασι καὶ ἀλλοτρίῳ κόσμῳ κοσμουμένην, μηδὲν παρ' αὐτῆς ἀγαθὸν ἔχουσαν, εἴδωλον δὲ ὡς πρὸς τὰ ὄντα, κακοῦ δὴ οὐσίαν, εἴ τις καὶ

---

[1] The quotation is from [Plato], *Epist.* II 312e.

[2] By the οἷον P. avoids to call the κακόν (which is completely negative) an εἶδος.

[3] Evil is not non-being in the sense in which Plato defined it in *Soph.* 256d-258e (above, nr. **342**).

[4] The definition recalls once more Hermodorus' description ap. Simpl., *Phys.* p. 248, l. 13-15 (our nr. **371a**, the end).

[5] Again, the οἷον indicates that the κακόν cannot be, properly speaking, a substance.

δύναται κακοῦ οὐσία εἶναι [1], ταύτην ἀνευρίσκει ὁ λόγος κακὸν εἶναι πρῶτον
₄₀ καὶ καθ' αὐτὸ κακόν.

c. Neither in the body nor in soul is evil primary. Since soul in Evil in body
itself is not bad, moreover, beyond πάθη, and cannot be the source of and soul
evil, it appears that only the lower soul is liable to this. The cause of it
is ὕλη, sc. lack of measure, from which springs vice.

Enn. I 8, 4, l. 1-2, 5-32:

In what
sense can
soul be bad?

Σωμάτων δὲ φύσις, καθόσον μετέχει ὕλης, κακὸν ἂν οὐ πρῶτον εἴη· —
₅ ψυχὴ δὲ καθ' ἑαυτὴν μὲν οὐ κακὴ οὐδ' αὖ πᾶσα κακή. Ἀλλὰ τίς ἡ κακή; Οἷόν
φησι [2] δουλωσάμενοι μὲν ᾧ πέφυκε κακία ψυχῆς ἐγγίνεσθαι, ὡς
τοῦ ἀλόγου τῆς ψυχῆς εἴδους τὸ κακὸν δεχομένου, ἀμετρίαν καὶ ὑπερβολὴν καὶ
₁₀ ἔλλειψιν [3], ἐξ ὧν καὶ ἀκολασία καὶ δειλία καὶ ἡ ἄλλη ψυχῆς κακία, ἀκούσια
παθήματα, δόξας ψευδεῖς ἐμποιοῦντα κακά τε νομίζειν καὶ ἀγαθὰ ἃ φεύγει τε
καὶ διώκει.

Ἀλλὰ τί τὸ πεποιηκὸς τὴν κακίαν ταύτην καὶ πῶς εἰς ἀρχὴν ἐκείνην καὶ αἰτίαν ἀμετρία
ἀνάξεις; Ἢ πρῶτον μὲν οὐκ ἔξω ὕλης οὐδὲ καθ' αὐτὴν ἡ ψυχὴ ἡ τοιαύτη. the cause
₁₅ Μέμικται οὖν ἀμετρίᾳ καὶ ἄμοιρος εἴδους τοῦ κοσμοῦντος καὶ εἰς μέτρον ἄγοντος· of evil
σώματι γὰρ ἐγκέκραται ὕλην ἔχοντι. Ἔπειτα δὲ καὶ τὸ λογιζόμενον εἰ βλάπτοιτο,
ὁρᾶν κωλύεται καὶ τοῖς πάθεσι καὶ τῷ ἐπισκοτεῖσθαι τῇ ὕλῃ καὶ πρὸς ὕλην
νενευκέναι καὶ ὅλως οὐ πρὸς οὐσίαν, ἀλλὰ πρὸς γένεσιν ὁρᾶν, ἧς ἀρχὴ ἡ ὕλης
₂₀ φύσις οὕτως οὖσα κακὴ ὡς καὶ τὸ μήπω ἐν αὐτῇ, μόνον δὲ βλέψαν εἰς αὐτήν,
ἀναπιμπλάναι κακοῦ ἑαυτῆς. Ἄμοιρος γὰρ παντελῶς οὖσα ἀγαθοῦ καὶ στέρησις
τούτου καὶ ἄκρατος ἔλλειψις ἐξομοιοῖ ἑαυτῇ πᾶν ὅ τι ἂν αὐτῆς προσάψηται
ὁπωσοῦν.

Ἡ μὲν οὖν τελεία καὶ πρὸς νοῦν νεύουσα ψυχὴ ἀεὶ καθαρὰ καὶ ὕλην ἀπέ-
₂₅ στραπται καὶ τὸ ἀόριστον ἅπαν καὶ τὸ ἄμετρον καὶ κακὸν οὔτε ὁρᾷ οὔτε πελάζει·
καθαρὰ οὖν μένει ὁρισθεῖσα νῷ παντελῶς. Ἡ δὲ μὴ μείνασα τοῦτο, ἀλλ' ἐξ
αὐτῆς προελθοῦσα τῷ μὴ τελείῳ μηδὲ πρώτῳ οἷον ἴνδαλμα ἐκείνης, τῷ ἐλλείμματι
₃₀ καθόσον ἐνέλιπεν ἀοριστίας πληρωθεῖσα σκότον ὁρᾷ καὶ ἔχει ἤδη ὕλην βλέπουσα
εἰς ὃ μὴ βλέπει, ὡς λεγόμεθα ὁρᾶν καὶ τὸ σκότος.

d. Complete ἔλλειψις means evil in itself. Now this is exactly
ὕλη, which—as we saw before—cannot participate in the good (nr.
1409b).

---

[1] Again: there is not, properly speaking, a "substance" of evil.
[2] Sc. Plato, *Phaedr.* 256 b.
[3] Cp. ὑπεροχὴ καὶ ἔλλειψις in Sext. Emp., *Adv. math.* X 275 (my nr. **371b**);
ὑπερβολή and ἔλλειψις are frequently used in Aristotle's *Ethics*. See nrs. **571b**,
572, 573.

Complete
ἔλλειψις
is evil in
itself

Enn. I 8, 5, l. 5-14; c. 8, l. 37-44:

῍Η οὐκ ἐν τῇ ὁπωσοῦν ἐλλείψει, ἀλλ᾽ ἐν τῇ παντελεῖ τὸ κακόν· τὸ γοῦν 5
ἐλλεῖπον ὀλίγῳ τοῦ ἀγαθοῦ οὐ κακόν, δύναται γὰρ καὶ τέλεον εἶναι ὡς πρὸς
φύσιν τὴν αὐτοῦ. ᾽Αλλ᾽ ὅταν παντελῶς ἐλλείπῃ, ὅπερ ἐστὶν ἡ ὕλη, τοῦτο τὸ
ὄντως κακὸν μηδεμίαν ἔχον ἀγαθοῦ μοῖραν. Οὐδὲ γὰρ τὸ εἶναι ἔχει ἡ ὕλη, ı
ἵνα ἀγαθοῦ ταύτῃ μετεῖχεν, ἀλλ᾽ ὁμώνυμον αὐτῇ τὸ εἶναι, ὡς ἀληθὲς εἶναι
λέγειν αὐτὸ μὴ εἶναι. ῾Η οὖν ἔλλειψις ἔχει μὲν τὸ μὴ ἀγαθὸν εἶναι, ἡ δὲ παντελὴς
τὸ κακόν· ἡ δὲ πλείων τὸ πεσεῖν εἰς τὸ κακὸν δύνασθαι καὶ ἤδη κακόν.

Vice, then, is evil in a secondary sense, and so are the ἔξω ψυχῆς κακά. Thus,
P. explains (c. 8, l. 37):

Vice is
secondary
evil

῎Εστω δὴ πρώτως μὲν τὸ ἄμετρον κακόν, τὸ δ᾽ ἐν ἀμετρίᾳ γενόμενον ἢ
ὁμοιώσει ἢ μεταλήψει τῷ συμβεβηκέναι αὐτῷ [1] δευτέρως κακόν· καὶ πρώτως 4
μὲν τὸ σκότος, τὸ δὲ ἐσκοτισμένον δευτέρως ὡσαύτως. Κακία δὴ ἄγνοια
οὖσα καὶ ἀμετρία περὶ ψυχὴν δευτέρως κακὸν καὶ οὐκ αὐτοκακόν· οὐδὲ γὰρ
ἀρετὴ πρῶτον ἀγαθόν, ἀλλ᾽ ὅ τι ὡμοίωται ἢ μετείληφεν αὐτοῦ.

e. Evil, then, lies in στέρησις and thus cannot be substantial. In
the soul it is a lack of goodness,—evidently not an absolute lack; for
then this would not be a soul at all.

Evil as
στέρησις

Enn. I 8, 11, l. 1-6, 8-9:

᾽Αλλ᾽ ἡ ἐναντία τῷ εἴδει παντὶ φύσις στέρησις· στέρησις δὲ ἀεὶ ἐν ἄλλῳ
καὶ ἐπ᾽ αὐτῆς οὐχ ὑπόστασις· ὥστε τὸ κακὸν εἰ ἐν στερήσει, ἐν τῷ ἐστερημένῳ
εἴδους τὸ κακὸν ἔσται· ὥστε καθ᾽ ἑαυτὸ οὐκ ἔσται. Εἰ οὖν ἐν τῇ ψυχῇ ἔσται
κακόν, ἡ στέρησις ἐν αὐτῇ τὸ κακὸν καὶ ἡ κακία ἔσται καὶ οὐδὲν ἔξω. — 5
Οὐδὲν οὖν δεῖ ἄλλοθι ζητεῖν τὸ κακόν, ἀλλὰ θέμενον ἐν ψυχῇ οὕτω θέσθαι
ἀπουσίαν ἀγαθοῦ εἶναι.

On moral evil or sin see also our next paragraph, nr. **1417**.

1411—To gnostics and gnosticism Plotinus opposes the following

Arguments
against
gnosticism

arguments (in *Enn.* II 9, Πρὸς τοὺς γνωστικούς):

1. Creation must be eternal (cc. 3, 8, 12, from l. 32).
2. It is impossible that a lapse of soul should be the cause of creation
(cc. 4 and 8).
3. In that case, the cause of evil would be transferred to the spiritual
world (c. 12, from l. 32).
4. The demiurge, as they represent him (viz. not as a spiritual being),
cannot have created the cosmos (c. 12, l. 1-3).

---

[1] τῷ συμβεβηκέναι αὐτῷ—having as an attribute.

5. Gnostics despise this world, which is a clear and beautiful image of the intelligible (cc. 5, 8, 16).

6. They deny that divine Providence extends to the cosmos (cc. 10-12, 15, 16, l. 16-32: they confine Providence to themselves).

7. Thus, they despise the gods that are here (cc. 9, 16, 18, l. 17-20).

8. They think of the Spiritual World not spiritually enough (cc. 6, 8, 14).

9. They blame unduly the connection of soul and body (cc. 6, 18, l. 1-17).

10. They do not care for virtue at all (cc. 15, 18, l. 27-35).

We saw some of these arguments in dealing with creation (nr. **1403**) and will find others when speaking of man and his life on earth. Two other passages deserve particular attention here.

P. reproaches gnostics with a lack of interest in moral questions (cp. above, our nr. **1335**; below, **1420d**) and confining the care of divine Providence to their own persons. To this he opposes his conviction that, if God cares for individual men, much more must He care for the whole of the cosmos and for the heavenly bodies. Therefore, he rebukes this Christian sect for not honouring the "gods that are here". But he also opposes to them the duty of honouring the νοητοὶ θεοί and *not to confine Divinity to one*; for "the great King" shows His greatness most of all in the plurality of the many gods. Cp. below, **1428a**.

Thus, in opposing these Christian gnostics, P. firmly maintains polytheism, and it is the presence of the many gods that makes him honour both the spiritual and the sensible universe.

a. *Enn.* II 9, 9, l. 26-54; 55-60:

> 'Αλλὰ χρὴ ὡς ἄριστον μὲν αὐτὸν πειρᾶσθαι γίνεσθαι, μὴ μόνον δὲ αὐτὸν * νομίζειν ἄριστον δύνασθαι γενέσθαι — οὕτω γὰρ οὔπω ἄριστος — ἀλλὰ καὶ ἀν-
> 0 θρώπους ἄλλους ἀρίστους, ἔτι καὶ δαίμονας ἀγαθοὺς εἶναι, πολὺ δὲ μᾶλλον θεοὺς τούς τε ἐν τῷδε ὄντας κἀκεῖ βλέποντας, πάντων δὲ μάλιστα τὸν ἡγεμόνα τοῦδε τοῦ παντός, ψυχὴν μακαριωτάτην· ἐντεῦθεν δὲ ἤδη καὶ τοὺς νοητοὺς ὑμνεῖν θεούς, ἐφ' ἅπασι δὲ ἤδη τὸν μέγαν τὸν ἐκεῖ βασιλέα καὶ ἐν τῷ πλήθει
> 5 μάλιστα τῶν θεῶν τὸ μέγα αὐτοῦ ἐνδεικνυμένους· οὐ γὰρ τὸ συστεῖλαι εἰς ἕν, ἀλλὰ τὸ δεῖξαι πολὺ τὸ θεῖον, ὅσον ἔδειξεν αὐτός, τοῦτό ἐστι δύναμιν θεοῦ εἰδότων, ὅταν μένων ὅς ἐστι πολλοὺς ποιῇ πάντας εἰς αὐτὸν ἀνηρτημένους καὶ δι' ἐκεῖνον καὶ παρ' ἐκείνου ὄντας.
>
> 0 Καὶ ὁ κόσμος δὲ ὅδε δι' ἐκεῖνόν ἐστι κἀκεῖ βλέπει, καὶ πᾶς καὶ θεῶν ἕκαστος καὶ τὰ ἐκείνου προφητεύει ἀνθρώποις καὶ χρῶσιν ἃ ἐκείνοις φίλα. Εἰ δὲ μὴ τοῦτό εἰσιν, ὃ ἐκεῖνός ἐστιν, αὐτὸ τοῦτο κατὰ φύσιν ἔχει. Εἰ δ' ὑπερορᾶν θέλεις καὶ σεμνύνεις σαυτὸν ὡς οὐ χείρων, πρῶτον μέν, ὅσῳ τις ἄριστος, πρὸς πάντας
> 5 εὐμενῶς ἔχει καὶ πρὸς ἀνθρώπους· ἔπειτα σεμνὸν [1] δεῖ εἰς μέτρον μετὰ οὐκ ἀγροικίας, ἐπὶ τοσοῦτον ἰόντα ἐφ' ὅσον ἡ φύσις δύναται ἡμῶν, ἀνιέναι, τοῖς δ'

Side notes:
P. defends polytheism against Chr. gnostics

These gnostics are arrogant

---

* αὐτὸν Kirchhoff, Br.
[1] H.-S. explain: cum μέτρον coniungendum.

ἄλλοις νομίζειν εἶναι χώραν παρὰ τῷ θεῷ καὶ μὴ αὐτὸν μόνον μετ' ἐκεῖνον τάξαντα ὥσπερ ὀνείρασι πέτεσθαι ἀποστεροῦντα ἑαυτὸν καθ' ὅσον ἐστὶ δυνατὸν ψυχῇ ἀνθρώπου θεῷ γενέσθαι· δύναται δὲ εἰς ὅσον νοῦς ἄγει· τὸ δ' ὑπὲρ νοῦν ἤδη ἐστὶν ἔξω νοῦ πεσεῖν. Πείθονται δὲ ἄνθρωποι ἀνόητοι τοῖς τοιούτοις τῶν λόγων ἐξαίφνης ἀκούοντες ὡς σὺ ἔσῃ βελτίων ἁπάντων οὐ μόνον ἀνθρώπων, ἀλλὰ καὶ θεῶν. — 50 54

To the doctrine of "salvation by faith" he opposes his way of the ascent of the soul by and through the spirit: "the soul of man may become god"—in a sense, by purification and meditation. Immediate salvation by faith seems to him an αὐθάδεια.

Their αὐθάδεια

(l. 55) Πολλὴ γὰρ ἐν ἀνθρώποις ἡ αὐθάδεια, καὶ ὁ πρότερον ταπεινὸς καὶ μέτριος καὶ ἰδιώτης ἀνὴρ εἰ ἀκούσειε· "σὺ εἶ θεοῦ παῖς, οἱ δ' ἄλλοι, οὓς ἐθαύμαζες, οὐ παῖδες οὐδ' <ἄστρα> * ἃ τιμῶσιν ἐκ πατέρων λαβόντες, σὺ δὲ κρείττων καὶ τοῦ οὐρανοῦ οὐδὲν πονήσας" — εἶτα καὶ συνεπηχῶσιν [1] ἄλλοι;

b. *Enn.* II 9, 18, l. 17-20.

Manifestly, P. would have greatly preferred to call the sun and the heavenly bodies his brothers than to call by this name many of the most undistinguished people.

Brother Sun and brothers stars

Ἦ ἀδελφοὺς μὲν καὶ τοὺς φαυλοτάτους ἀξιοῦσι προσεννέπειν, ἥλιον δὲ καὶ τοὺς ἐν τῷ οὐρανῷ ἀπαξιοῦσιν ἀδελφοὺς λέγειν οὐδὲ τὴν κόσμου ψυχὴν στόματι μαινομένῳ [2];

7—MAN AND HIS LIFE ON EARTH

What is man?

1412—To the question of "what is man" Plotinus answers that there is intelligible man, who has a more divine soul than concrete man.

a. *Enn.* VI 7, 4, l. 6-21:

Is "man here" (ὁ ἄνθρωπος οὗτος) = the soul? Or is he the soul using a body? Or the composite of both? [3]

Ἀρχὴ δὲ τῆς σκέψεως ἐντεῦθεν· ἆρα ὁ ἄνθρωπος οὗτος λόγος ἐστὶ ψυχῆς

---

* Add. Müller, Br.
[1] H.-S. explain: coniunctivus dubitativus.
[2] Heracl., fr. 92 D.
[3] The first thesis, that "man = the soul", is found ipsis verbis in the *Alcib. Mai.* 130c, a passage repeatedly cited or referred to by Plotinus (e.g. I 3, 3 and V 1, 10). "Socrates" in the *Alcib.* comes to this conclusion by the premiss that man is "soul using the body" (130a). To the author, this excludes the possibility of the third thesis: "man using the body" is essentially soul, which is superior to the body, not a composite of both. As to the last theory, this is held by Aristotle in *De anima*, a treatise belonging to the author's latest years. See the definition cited in our nr. **636** (vol. II) and its consequences (**637**). A comparison with the numbers **417a, c** and **422b** will show the difference of this later theory from that of Aristotle's early works.

ἕτερος τῆς τὸν ἄνθρωπον τοῦτον ποιούσης καὶ ζῆν αὐτὸν καὶ λογίζεσθαι παρε-
10 χομένης; Ἢ ἡ ψυχὴ ἡ τοιαύτη ὁ ἄνθρωπός ἐστιν; Ἢ ἡ τῷ σώματι τῷ τοιῷδε
ψυχὴ προσχρωμένη; Ἀλλ' εἰ μὲν ζῷον λογικὸν ὁ ἄνθρωπος, ζῷον δὲ τὸ ἐκ
ψυχῆς καὶ σώματος, οὐκ ἂν εἴη ὁ λόγος οὗτος τῇ ψυχῇ ὁ αὐτός. Ἀλλ' εἰ
τὸ ἐκ ψυχῆς λογικῆς καὶ σώματος ὁ λόγος τοῦ ἀνθρώπου, πῶς ἂν εἴη ὑπό-
15 στασις ἀίδιος, τούτου τοῦ λόγου τοῦ τοιούτου ἀνθρώπου γινομένου, ὅταν σῶμα
καὶ ψυχὴ συνέλθῃ; Ἔσται γὰρ ὁ λόγος οὗτος δηλωτικὸς τοῦ ἐσομένου, οὐχ
οἷος ὄν φαμεν αὐτοάνθρωπος, ἀλλὰ μᾶλλον ἐοικὼς ὅρῳ, καὶ τοιούτῳ οἵῳ μηδὲ
δηλωτικῷ τοῦ τί ἦν εἶναι. Οὐδὲ γὰρ εἴδους ἐστὶ τοῦ ἐνύλου, ἀλλὰ τὸ συναμ-
20 φότερον δηλῶν, ὃ ἔστιν ἤδη· εἰ δὲ τοῦτο, οὔπω εὕρηται ὁ ἄνθρωπος· ἦν γὰρ
ὁ κατὰ τὸν λόγον [1].

b. Ib., c. 5, l. 11-18, 21-25:

P. opposes the Aristotelian thesis that man is a composite. Surely, in a sense, he
says, this is man; but not man in the primary sense. It is only an εἰκών of the first
man, which is intelligible.

Ἡ δὲ ψυχὴ ἡ τοιαύτη ἡ ἐγγενομένη τῇ τοιαύτῃ ὕλῃ, ἅτε οὖσα τοῦτο, οἷον
οὕτω διακειμένη καὶ ἄνευ τοῦ σώματος, ἄνθρωπος, ἐν σώματι δὲ μορφώσασα
15 καθ' αὑτὴν καὶ ἄλλο εἴδωλον ἀνθρώπου ὅσον ἐδέχετο τὸ σῶμα ποιήσασα,
ὥσπερ καὶ τούτου αὖ ποιήσει ὁ ζωγράφος ἔτι ἐλάττω ἄνθρωπόν τινα, τὴν
μορφὴν ἔχει καὶ τοὺς λόγους ἢ τὰ ἤθη, τὰς διαθέσεις, τὰς δυνάμεις, ἀμυδρὰ
21 πάντα, ὅτι μὴ οὗτος πρῶτος· — ὁ δὲ ἐπὶ τούτῳ ἄνθρωπος ψυχῆς ἤδη θειο-
τέρας, ἐχούσης βελτίω ἄνθρωπον καὶ αἰσθήσεις ἐναργεστέρας. Καὶ εἴη ἂν ὁ
Πλάτων τοῦτον ὁρισάμενος, προσθεὶς δὲ τὸ χρωμένην σώματι, ὅτι ἐποχεῖται
25 τῇ ἥτις προσχρῆται πρώτως σώματι, ἡ δὲ δευτέρως.

c. Enn. VI 7, 9, l. 6-10.

Man here
differs from
man yonder

Man here differs from man yonder in that the first is λογικός (i.e. has the faculty
of discursive reasoning), while the latter is πρὸ τοῦ λογίζεσθαι. For in Noûs, as was
said before, is intuitive thinking and knowledge, while the faculty of λογίζεσθαι
is proper to soul.

. . . ὁ ἄνθρωπος ὁ ἐνταῦθα οὐ τοιοῦτός ἐστιν οἷος ἐκεῖνος, ὥστε καὶ τὰ ἄλλα
ζῷα οὐχ οἷα τὰ ἐνταῦθα κἀκεῖ, ἀλλὰ μειζόνως δεῖ ἐκεῖνα λαμβάνειν· εἶτα
οὐδὲ τὸ λογικὸν ἐκεῖ· ὧδε γὰρ ἴσως λογικός, ἐκεῖ δὲ ὁ πρὸ τοῦ λογίζεσθαι.

d. Enn. VI 4, 14, l. 16-31.

Pre-existing
man and man
in a body

Before being born in a body, man pre-existed as pure soul with Noûs, connected
with universal Being (sc. the intelligible world). To this spiritual man that we were,
another quite different kind of man was added; and thus we became the συνάμφω. And sometimes even the latter man prevails, as though the first were not present.

---

[1] Above, nr. **541**.

Ἡμεῖς δέ — τίνες δὲ ἡμεῖς; ᾿Αρα ἐκεῖνο ἢ τὸ πελάζον καὶ τὸ γινόμενον ἐν χρόνῳ; ῍Η καὶ πρὸ τοῦ ταύτην τὴν γένεσιν γενέσθαι ἦμεν ἐκεῖ ἄνθρωποι ἄλλοι
ὄντες καί τινες καὶ θεοί, ψυχαὶ καθαραὶ καὶ νοῦς συνημμένος τῇ ἁπάσῃ οὐσίᾳ,
μέρη ὄντες τοῦ νοητοῦ οὐκ ἀφωρισμένα οὐδ᾽ ἀποτετμημένα, ἀλλ᾽ ὄντες τοῦ ὅλου· 20
οὐδὲ γὰρ οὐδὲ νῦν ἀποτετμήμεθα. ᾿Αλλὰ γὰρ νῦν ἐκείνῳ τῷ ἀνθρώπῳ προσε-
λήλυθεν ἄνθρωπος ἄλλος εἶναι θέλων καὶ εὑρὼν ἡμᾶς· ἦμεν γὰρ τοῦ παντὸς
οὐκ ἔξω· περιέθηκεν ἑαυτὸν ἡμῖν καὶ προσέθηκεν ἑαυτὸν ἐκείνῳ τῷ ἀνθρώπῳ
τῷ ὃς ἦν ἕκαστος ἡμῶν τότε (οἷον εἰ φωνῆς οὔσης μιᾶς καὶ λόγου ἑνὸς ἄλλος 25
ἄλλοθεν παραθεὶς τὸ οὖς ἀκούσειε καὶ δέξαιτο καὶ γένοιτο κατ᾽ ἐνέργειαν ἀκοή
τις ἔχουσα τὸ ἐνεργοῦν εἰς αὐτὴν παρόν) καὶ γεγενήμεθα τὸ συνάμφω, καὶ οὐ
θάτερον, ὃ πρότερον ἦμεν, καὶ θάτερόν ποτε, ὃ ὕστερον προσεθέμεθα ἀργή- 30
σαντος τοῦ προτέρου ἐκείνου καὶ ἄλλον τρόπον οὐ παρόντος.

**Man in a
body**

e. *Enn.* VI 4, 15, l. 18-40.

Man in a body is good as long as the divine soul prevails in him. The body
brings disturbance (cp. Plato in *Tim.* 43b, c and the whole passage of 69c ff. and
86b-88c. Supra, nrs. **357-361**).

Ἡ μὲν δὴ ἐκ τοῦ θείου ψυχὴ ἥσυχος ἦν κατὰ τὸ ἦθος τὸ ἑαυτῆς ἐφ᾽ ἑαυτῆς
βεβῶσα, τὸ δὲ ὑπ᾽ ἀσθενείας θορυβούμενον καὶ ῥέον τε αὐτὸ καὶ πληγαῖς κρουό- 20
μενον ταῖς ἔξω πρῶτον αὐτό, <εἶτα> εἰς τὸ κοινὸν τοῦ ζῴου ἐφθέγγετο, καὶ
τὴν αὐτοῦ ταραχὴν ἐδίδου τῷ ὅλῳ· οἷον <ἐν> ἐκκλησίᾳ δημογερόντων καθημένων
ἐφ᾽ ἡσύχῳ συννοίᾳ δῆμος ἄτακτος τροφῆς δεόμενος καὶ ἄλλα ἃ δὴ πάσχει
αἰτιώμενος τὴν πᾶσαν ἐκκλησίαν εἰς θόρυβον ἀσχήμονα <ἂν> ἐμβάλλοι. Ὅταν 25
μὲν οὖν ἡσυχίαν ἀγόντων τῶν τοιούτων ἀπό του φρονοῦντος ἥκῃ εἰς αὐτοὺς
λόγος, κατέστη εἰς τάξιν μετρίαν τὸ πλῆθος, καὶ οὐ κεκράτηκε τὸ χεῖρον·
εἰ δὲ μή, κρατεῖ τὸ χεῖρον ἡσυχίαν ἄγοντος τοῦ βελτίονος, ὅτι μὴ ἠδυνήθη 30
τὸ θορυβοῦν δέξασθαι τὸν ἄνωθεν λόγον, καὶ τοῦτό ἐστι πόλεως καὶ ἐκκλησίας
κακία. Τοῦτο δὲ καὶ ἀνθρώπου κακία αὖ ἔχοντος δῆμον ἐν αὑτῷ ἡδονῶν καὶ
ἐπιθυμιῶν καὶ φόβων κρατησάντων συνδόντος ἑαυτὸν τοῦ τοιούτου ἀνθρώπου
δήμῳ τῷ τοιούτῳ· ὃς δ᾽ ἂν τοῦτον τὸν ὄχλον δουλώσηται καὶ ἀναδράμῃ εἰς 35
ἐκεῖνον, ὅς ποτε ἦν, κατ᾽ ἐκεῖνόν τε ζῇ καὶ ἔστιν ἐκεῖνος διδοὺς τῷ σώματι,
ὅσα δίδωσιν ὡς ἑτέρῳ ὄντι ἑαυτοῦ· ἄλλος δέ τις ὁτὲ μὲν οὕτως, ὁτὲ δὲ ἄλλως
ζῇ, μικτός τις ἐξ ἀγαθοῦ ἑαυτοῦ καὶ κακοῦ ἑτέρου γεγενημένος. 40

**The inner
man**

1413—Thus, P. declares that, beyond his connection with a body, man
has a higher soul, and this is his true self.

a. *Enn.* II 1, 5, l. 18-23.

In this passage the author distinguishes between a lower soul (the πάθη), which
is given to man by the heavenly bodies ("the gods in the heavens") and by the

heavens themselves [1], and a higher soul by which we are our true selves. It is, as will be explained in the passage to be quoted sub **b**, what Plato suggested in *Tim.* 41a-d and 69c [2].

Ἡμεῖς δὲ πλασθέντες ὑπὸ τῆς διδομένης παρὰ τῶν ἐν οὐρανῷ θεῶν ψυχῆς καὶ αὐτοῦ τοῦ οὐρανοῦ κατ' ἐκείνην καὶ σύνεσμεν τοῖς σώμασιν· ἡ γὰρ ἄλλη ψυχή, καθ' ἢν ἡμεῖς, τοῦ εὖ εἶναι, οὐ τοῦ εἶναι αἰτία [3]. Ἤδη γοῦν τοῦ σώματος ἔρχεται γενομένου μικρὰ ἐκ λογισμοῦ πρὸς τὸ εἶναι συνεκλαμβανομένη.

b. *Enn.* II 3, 9, 1. 6-30:

Ἔν τε Τιμαίῳ θεὸς μὲν ὁ ποιήσας τὴν ἀρχὴν τῆς ψυχῆς δίδωσιν, οἱ δὲ φερόμενοι θεοὶ τὰ δεινὰ καὶ ἀναγκαῖα πάθη, θυμοὺς καὶ ἐπιθυμίας καὶ ἡδονὰς καὶ λύπας αὖ, καὶ ψυχῆς ἄλλο εἶδος, ἀφ' οὗ τὰ παθήματα ταυτί [4]. Οὗτοι γὰρ οἱ λόγοι συνδέουσιν ἡμᾶς τοῖς ἄστροις παρ' αὐτῶν ψυχὴν κομιζομένους καὶ ὑποτάττουσι τῇ ἀνάγκῃ ἐνταῦθα ἰόντας· καὶ ἤθη τοίνυν παρ' αὐτῶν καὶ κατὰ τὰ ἤθη πράξεις καὶ πάθη ἀπὸ ἕξεως παθητικῆς οὔσης· ὥστε τί λοιπὸν ἡμεῖς; Ἥ ὅπερ ἐσμὲν κατ' ἀλήθειαν ἡμεῖς, οἷς καὶ κρατεῖν τῶν παθῶν ἔδωκεν ἡ φύσις. Καὶ γὰρ ὅμως ἐν τούτοις τοῖς κακοῖς διὰ τοῦ σώματος ἀπειλημμένοις ἀδέσποτον ἀρετὴν [5] θεὸς ἔδωκεν. Οὐ γὰρ ἐν ἡσύχῳ οὖσιν ἀρετῆς δεῖ ἡμῖν, ἀλλ' ὅταν κίνδυνος ἐν κακοῖς εἶναι ἀρετῆς οὐ παρούσης. Διὸ καὶ φεύγειν ἐντεῦθεν δεῖ [6] καὶ χωρίζειν αὐτοὺς ἀπὸ τῶν προσγεγενημένων [7] καὶ μὴ τὸ σύνθετον εἶναι σῶμα ἐψυχωμένον ἐν ᾧ κρατεῖ μᾶλλον ἡ σώματος φύσις ψυχῆς τι ἴχνος λαβοῦσα, ὡς τὴν ζωὴν τὴν κοινὴν μᾶλλον τοῦ σώματος εἶναι· πάντα γὰρ σωματικά, ὅσα ταύτης. Τῆς δὲ ἑτέρας τῆς ἔξω ἡ πρὸς τὸ ἄνω φορὰ καὶ τὸ καλὸν καὶ τὸ θεῖον ὧν οὐδεὶς κρατεῖ, ἀλλ' ἢ προσχρῆται, ἵν' ἦ ἐκεῖνο καὶ κατὰ τοῦτο ζῇ ἀναχωρήσας· ἢ ἔρημος ταύτης τῆς ψυχῆς γενόμενος ζῇ ἐν εἱμαρμένῃ [8], καὶ ἐνταῦθα τὰ ἄστρα αὐτῷ οὐ μόνον σημαίνει [9], ἀλλὰ γίνεται αὐτὸς οἷον μέρος καὶ τῷ ὅλῳ συνέπεται, οὗ μέρος [10].

---

[1] The "created gods" of *Tim.* 41a.   [2] Above, vol. I, nrs. **353** and **357a**.

[3] For the formula καθ' ἢν ἡμεῖς cp. the passages cited infra, sub **b** and **c**. τοῦ εὖ εἶναι, οὐ τοῦ εἶναι reminds us of a well-known expression used repeatedly by Aristotle. Above, vol. II, nrs. **420b, 566** (*E.N.* I 4, 1095a, 19), **608b, 610a**.

[4] *Tim.* 69c-d.   [5] *Rep.* 617e (above, nr. **306**, p. 215).

[6] Also Plotinus' treatise Π. ἀρετῶν (*Enn.* I, 2) is a comment on the χρὴ ἐνθένδε ἐκεῖσε φεύγειν of *Theaet.* 176a (supra, nr. **318**).

[7] τὰ προσγεγενημένα, also called the προσθῆκαι, are the cause of sin. Infra, **1417b**.

[8] εἱμαρμένη indicates physical necessity as opposed to πρόνοια. See our next paragraph.

[9] As we shall see later, P. does believe in the influence of the heavenly bodies on things on earth, but he opposes the popular view that this influence should result from a deliberate will. Hence he stresses the fact that, for man, the heavenly bodies are *a sign* of what is going to happen, not properly speaking the "cause" of it.

[10] Man who lives according to the lower soul becomes a part of the physical universe and thus is submitted to physical necessity, while the higher soul is beyond this.

c. *Enn.* I 1, 7, l. 14-24.

P. after having described the "perception of the soul" as a contemplation of "forms", which takes place ἀπαθῶς [1], continues as follows.

„We", i.e. our intellectual life

Ἀπὸ δὴ τούτων τῶν εἰδῶν, ἀφ᾽ ὧν ψυχὴ ἤδη παραδέχεται μόνη τὴν τοῦ 15 ζῴου ἡγεμονίαν, διάνοιαι δὴ καὶ δόξαι καὶ νοήσεις· ἔνθα δὴ ἡμεῖς μάλιστα. Τὰ δὲ πρὸ τούτων ἡμέτερα, ἡμεῖς δὴ τὸ ἐντεῦθεν ἄνω ἐφεστηκότες τῷ ζῴῳ. Κωλύσει δὲ οὐδὲν τὸ σύμπαν ζῷον λέγειν, μικτὸν μὲν τὰ κάτω, τὸ δὲ ἐντεῦθεν ὁ ἄνθρωπος ὁ ἀληθὴς σχεδόν· ἐκεῖνα δὲ τὸ λεοντῶδες καὶ τὸ ποικίλον ὅλως 20 θηρίον. Συνδρόμου γὰρ ὄντος τοῦ ἀνθρώπου τῇ λογικῇ ψυχῇ, ὅταν λογιζώμεθα, ἡμεῖς λογιζόμεθα τῷ τοὺς λογισμοὺς ψυχῆς εἶναι ἐνεργήματα.

Thus, the πάθη do not belong to "us".

d. *Enn.* I 1, 10, l. 1-11.

Sometimes, the κοινόν is called man, "the beast" being included. But the true man is the spiritual man, called ὁ ἔνδον ἄνθρωπος (I 1, 10, l. 15), or elsewhere ὁ ἔσω ἄνθρωπος (V 1, 10, l. 10).

Sometimes "the beast" is included

Ἀλλ᾽ εἰ ἡμεῖς ἡ ψυχή, πάσχομεν δὲ ταῦτα ἡμεῖς, ταῦτα ἂν εἴη πάσχουσα ἡ ψυχὴ καὶ αὖ ποιήσει ἃ ποιοῦμεν. Ἢ καὶ τὸ κοινὸν ἔφαμεν ἡμῶν εἶναι καὶ μάλιστα οὔπω κεχωρισμένων· ἐπεὶ καὶ ἃ πάσχει τὸ σῶμα ἡμῶν ἡμᾶς φαμεν πάσχειν. Διττὸν οὖν τὸ ἡμεῖς, ἢ συναριθμουμένου τοῦ θηρίου, ἢ τὸ ὑπὲρ τοῦτο 5 ἤδη· θηρίον δὲ ζωωθὲν τὸ σῶμα. Ὁ δ᾽ ἀληθὴς ἄνθρωπος ἄλλος ὁ καθαρὸς τούτων τὰς ἀρετὰς ἔχων τὰς ἐν νοήσει, αἳ δὴ ἐν αὐτῇ τῇ χωριζομένῃ ψυχῇ ἵδρυνται, χωριζομένῃ δὲ καὶ χωριστῇ ἔτι ἐνταῦθα οὔσῃ· ἐπεὶ καί, ὅταν αὐτὴ παντάπασιν 10 ἀποστῇ, καὶ ἡ ἀπ᾽ αὐτῆς ἐλλαμφθεῖσα ἀπελήλυθε συνεπομένη.

The πάθη

1414—To what do the πάθη belong: to the body, or to the soul, or to the compound? (I 1, 1). — To this question P. answers:

(1) If the soul is not identical with its essence, it would be a compound and hence might have πάθη. But, on the other hand, if it is identical with its essence, it is an εἶδος and as such ἀπαθής (I 1, 2).

(2) Moreover, soul which uses the body as an instrument must be above the πάθη (I 1, 3).

a. *Enn.* I 1, 1, l. 1-4; 2, l. 1-13; 3, l. 1-5.

Ἡδοναὶ καὶ λῦπαι φόβοι τε καὶ θάρρη ἐπιθυμίαι τε καὶ ἀποστροφαὶ καὶ τὸ ἀλγεῖν τίνος ἂν εἶεν; Ἢ γὰρ ψυχῆς, ἢ χρωμένης ψυχῆς σώματι, ἢ τρίτου τινὸς ἐξ ἀμφοῖν. —

(c. 2) Πρῶτον δὲ ψυχὴν ληπτέον πότερον ἄλλο μὲν ψυχή, ἄλλο δὲ ψυχῇ

---

[1] On πάθη and αἴσθησις see our next numbers.

εἶναι. Εἰ γὰρ τοῦτο, σύνθετόν τι ἡ ψυχὴ καὶ οὐκ ἄτοπον ἤδη δέχεσθαι αὐτὴν
καὶ αὐτῆς εἶναι τὰ πάθη τὰ τοιαῦτα, εἰ ἐπιτρέψει καὶ οὕτως ὁ λόγος, καὶ ὅλως
5 ἕξεις καὶ διαθέσεις χείρους καὶ βελτίους. Ἤ, εἰ ταὐτόν ἐστι ψυχὴ καὶ τὸ ψυχῇ
εἶναι, εἶδός τι ἂν εἴη ψυχὴ ἄδεκτον τούτων ἁπασῶν τῶν ἐνεργειῶν, ὧν ἐποιστικὸν
ἄλλῳ, ἑαυτῷ δὲ συμφυᾶ ἔχον τὴν ἐνέργειαν ἐν ἑαυτῷ, ἥντινα ἂν φήνῃ ὁ λόγος.
10 Οὕτω γὰρ καὶ τὸ ἀθάνατον ἀληθὲς λέγειν, εἴπερ δεῖ τὸ ἀθάνατον καὶ ἄφθαρτον
ἀπαθὲς εἶναι, ἄλλῳ ἑαυτοῦ πως διδόν, αὐτὸ δὲ παρ' ἄλλου μηδὲν ἢ ὅσον παρὰ
τῶν πρὸ αὐτοῦ ἔχειν, ὧν μὴ ἀποτέτμηται κρειττόνων ὄντων. —

(c. 3) Ἀλλὰ γὰρ ἐν σώματι θετέον ψυχήν, οὖσαν εἴτε πρὸ τούτου, εἴτ'
ἐν τούτῳ, ἐξ οὗ καὶ αὐτῆς ζῷον τὸ σύμπαν ἐκλήθη· Χρωμένη μὲν οὖν σώματι
οἷα ὀργάνῳ οὐκ ἀναγκάζεται δέξασθαι τὰ διὰ τοῦ σώματος παθήματα, ὥσπερ
5 οὐδὲ τὰ τῶν ὀργάνων παθήματα οἱ τεχνῖται.

b.   How is it that the compound feels pain? And where lies the
origin of pain and other feelings: in the soul, in the compound, or in the
body? (I 1, 5) — To these questions P. answers: the faculties of the soul,
ἐπιθυμητικόν and θυμικόν, make feelings possible by their presence in the
living being, but are themselves impassible. Subject of feelings is the
living being as such (c. 6), i.e. the compound.

Enn. I 1, 5, l. 8-35; 6, l. 1-4, 10-14:

**How do pain
and other
feelings
arise?**

Τὸ δὲ συναμφότερον οἷον λυπεῖσθαι πῶς; Ἆρα ὅτι τοῦ σώματος οὑτωσὶ
10 διατεθέντος καὶ μέχρις αἰσθήσεως διελθόντος τοῦ πάθους τῆς αἰσθήσεως εἰς
ψυχὴν τελευτώσης; Ἀλλ' ἡ αἴσθησις οὔπω δῆλον πῶς. Ἀλλ' ὅταν ἡ λύπη ἀρχὴν
ἀπὸ δόξης καὶ κρίσεως λάβῃ τοῦ κακόν τι παρεῖναι [1] ἢ αὐτῷ ἤ τινι τῶν
οἰκείων, εἶτ' ἐντεῦθεν τροπὴ λυπηρὰ ἐπὶ τὸ σῶμα καὶ ὅλως ἐπὶ πᾶν τὸ ζῷον
15 γένηται; Ἀλλὰ καὶ τὸ τῆς δόξης οὔπω δῆλον τίνος, τῆς ψυχῆς ἢ τοῦ συν-
αμφοτέρου· εἶτα ἡ μὲν δόξα ἡ περὶ τοῦ κακὸν τὸ τῆς λύπης οὐκ ἔχει πάθος·
καὶ γὰρ καὶ δυνατὸν τῆς δόξης παρούσης μὴ πάντως ἐπιγίνεσθαι τὸ λυπεῖσθαι,
20 μηδ' αὖ τὸ ὀργίζεσθαι δόξης τοῦ ὀλιγωρεῖσθαι γενομένης, μηδ' αὖ ἀγαθοῦ
δόξης κινεῖσθαι τὴν ὄρεξιν. Πῶς οὖν κοινὰ ταῦτα; Ἤ, ὅτι καὶ ἡ ἐπιθυμία
τοῦ ἐπιθυμητικοῦ καὶ ὁ θυμὸς τοῦ θυμικοῦ καὶ ὅλως τοῦ ὀρεκτικοῦ ἡ ἐπί
τι ἔκστασις [2]. Ἀλλ' οὕτως οὐκέτι κοινὰ ἔσται, ἀλλὰ τῆς ψυχῆς μόνης· ἢ
25 καὶ τοῦ σώματος, ὅτι δεῖ αἷμα καὶ χολὴν ζέσαι καί πως διατεθὲν τὸ σῶμα τὴν
ὄρεξιν κινῆσαι, οἷον ἐπὶ ἀφροδισίων. Ἡ δὲ τοῦ ἀγαθοῦ ὄρεξις μὴ κοινὸν πάθημα
ἀλλὰ ψυχῆς ἔστω, ὥσπερ καὶ ἄλλα, καὶ οὐ πάντα τοῦ κοινοῦ δίδωσί τις λόγος.
30 Ἀλλὰ ὀρεγομένου ἀφροδισίων τοῦ ἀνθρώπου ἔσται μὲν ὁ ἄνθρωπος ὁ ἐπιθυμῶν,

---

[1]   See above, Zeno's definition of λύπη, under nrs. **954** and **955**.
[2]   ἔκστασις is a common Greek word for displacement. The author may quite
well have used it here in the vague sense of "tendency".

ἔσται δὲ ἄλλως καὶ τὸ ἐπιθυμητικὸν ἐπιθυμοῦν. Καὶ πῶς; Ἆρα ἄρξει μὲν ὁ
ἄνθρωπος τῆς ἐπιθυμίας, ἐπακολουθήσει δὲ τὸ ἐπιθυμητικόν; Ἀλλὰ πῶς
ὅλως ἐπεθύμησεν ὁ ἄνθρωπος μὴ τοῦ ἐπιθυμητικοῦ κεκινημένου; Ἀλλ' ἄρξει τὸ
ἐπιθυμητικόν. Ἀλλὰ τοῦ σώματος μὴ πρότερον οὑτωσὶ διατεθέντος πόθεν ἄρξεται;
(c. 6) Ἀλλ' ἴσως βέλτιον εἰπεῖν καθόλου τῷ παρεῖναι τὰς δυνάμεις τὰ
ἔχοντα εἶναι τὰ ἐνεργοῦντα κατ' αὐτάς, αὐτὰς δὲ ἀκινήτους εἶναι χορηγούσας
τὸ δύνασθαι τοῖς ἔχουσιν. — Ἀλλ' εἰ ἡ αἴσθησις διὰ σώματος κίνησις οὖσα εἰς ιο
ψυχὴν τελευτᾷ, πῶς ἡ ψυχὴ οὐκ αἰσθήσεται; Ἢ τῆς δυνάμεως τῆς αἰσθητικῆς
παρούσης τῷ ταύτην παρεῖναι αἰσθήσεται. Τί αἰσθήσεται; Τὸ συναμφότερον;

c. But, P. objects, if the faculties of the soul are impassible, what
then is the part of the soul in having feelings? — Reply: Soul gives herself
to the compound (which is the living being) not as such, but in such a
way that she somehow illuminates the living body.

How soul is **Enn.** I 1, 6, l. 14-16; 7, l. 1-6:
related with
the body   Ἀλλ' εἰ ἡ δύναμις μὴ κινήσεται, πῶς ἔτι τὸ συναμφότερον μὴ συναριθμουμένης ψυχῆς μηδὲ τῆς ψυχικῆς δυνάμεως;

(c. 7) Ἢ τὸ συναμφότερον ἔστω τῆς ψυχῆς τῷ παρεῖναι οὐχ αὐτὴν δούσης
τῆς τοιαύτης εἰς τὸ συναμφότερον ἢ εἰς θάτερον, ἀλλὰ ποιούσης ἐκ τοῦ σώματος
τοῦ τοιούτου καί τινος οἷον φωτὸς τοῦ παρ' αὐτῆς [1] δοθέντος τὴν τοῦ ζῴου
φύσιν ἕτερόν τι, οὗ τὸ αἰσθάνεσθαι καὶ τὰ ἄλλα ὅσα ζῴου πάθη εἴρηται.   5

1415—How to explain perception, if soul is impassible.
What is The perception of the soul is not directly concerned with αἰσθητά, but
αἴσθησις? is impassibly a contemplation of τύποι in the living being which come
from the αἰσθητά. These τύποι, far from being material (as was taught
by the Stoa), are already νοητά.

It has not a. **Enn.** I 1, 7, l. 9-14:
to do with
sensible Τὴν δὲ τῆς ψυχῆς τοῦ αἰσθάνεσθαι δύναμιν οὐ τῶν αἰσθητῶν εἶναι δεῖ, τῶν ιο
impressions δὲ ἀπὸ τῆς αἰσθήσεως ἐγγιγνομένων τῷ ζῴῳ τύπων ἀντιληπτικὴν εἶναι μᾶλλον·
νοητὰ γὰρ ἤδη ταῦτα· ὡς τὴν αἴσθησιν τὴν ἔξω εἴδωλον εἶναι ταύτης, ἐκείνην
δὲ ἀληθεστέραν τῇ οὐσίᾳ οὖσαν εἰδῶν μόνων ἀπαθῶς εἶναι θεωρίαν.

b. Consequently discursive thinking, called διάνοια, which is a link
between outward things and the inner man, is a purely intellectual
function which has nothing to do with sense-impressions.

διάνοια **Enn.** I 1, 9, l. 15-23:
is purely
intellectual Διείλομεν δὴ τὰ κοινὰ καὶ τὰ ἴδια τῷ τὰ μὲν σωματικὰ καὶ οὐκ ἄνευ σώ- 15

[1] H.-S. explain: ratione ipsius.

ματος εἶναι, ὅσα δὲ οὐ δεῖται σώματος εἰς ἐνέργειαν, ταῦτα ἴδια ψυχῆς εἶναι,
καὶ τὴν διάνοιαν ἐπίκρισιν ποιουμένην τῶν ἀπὸ τῆς αἰσθήσεως τύπων εἴδη
20 ἤδη θεωρεῖν καὶ θεωρεῖν οἷον συναισθήσει, τήν γε κυρίως τῆς ψυχῆς τῆς
ἀληθοῦς διάνοιαν· νοήσεως γὰρ ἐνέργεια ἡ διάνοια ἡ ἀληθὴς καὶ τῶν ἔξω
πολλάκις πρὸς τἄνδον ὁμοιότης καὶ κοινωνία.

c.   Again, in the treatise Περὶ τῆς ἀπαθείας τῶν ἀσωμάτων P. begins
by stating that the so-called τυπώσεις do not have the character of πάθη
(as is usually thought), but are ἐνέργειαι [1].

Enn. III 6, 1, l. 1-11:

The so-called
τυπώσεις
are
ἐνέργειαι

Τὰς αἰσθήσεις οὐ πάθη λέγοντες εἶναι, ἐνεργείας δὲ περὶ παθήματα καὶ
κρίσεις, τῶν μὲν παθῶν περὶ ἄλλο γινομένων, οἷον τὸ σῶμα φέρε τὸ τοιόνδε,
τῆς δὲ κρίσεως περὶ τὴν ψυχήν, οὐ τῆς κρίσεως πάθους οὔσης — ἔδει γὰρ αὖ
5 ἄλλην κρίσιν γίνεσθαι καὶ ἐπαναβαίνειν ἀεὶ εἰς ἄπειρον — εἴχομεν οὐδὲν
ἧττον καὶ ἐνταῦθα ἀπορίαν, εἰ ἡ κρίσις ἢ κρίσις οὐδὲν ἔχει τοῦ κρινομένου. Ἤ, εἰ
τύπον ἔχοι, πέπονθεν. Ἦν δ᾽ ὅμως λέγειν καὶ περὶ τῶν καλουμένων τυπώ-
10 σεων, ὡς ὁ τρόπος ὅλως ἕτερος ἢ ὡς ὑπείληπται, ὁποῖος καὶ ἐπὶ τῶν νοήσεων
ἐνεργειῶν καὶ τούτων οὐσῶν γινώσκειν ἄνευ τοῦ παθεῖν τι δυναμένων· —

1416—Generally speaking, the so-called passive part of the soul is
not passive at all. Since soul is an εἶδος, she must be active.

a.   *Enn.* III 6, 4, l. 31-43:

Soul as an
εἶδος
must be
active

Ἀλλ᾽ ἔστι μὲν τοῦτο τὸ τῆς ψυχῆς μέρος τὸ παθητικὸν οὐ σῶμα μέν, εἶδος
δέ τι. Ἐν ὕλῃ μέντοι καὶ τὸ ἐπιθυμοῦν καὶ τό γε θρεπτικόν τε καὶ αὐξητικὸν
καὶ γεννητικόν, ὅ ἐστι ῥίζα καὶ ἀρχὴ τοῦ ἐπιθυμοῦντος καὶ παθητικοῦ εἴδους.
35 Εἴδει δὲ οὐδενὶ δεῖ παρεῖναι ταραχὴν ἢ ὅλως πάθος, ἀλλ᾽ ἑστηκέναι μὲν αὐτό,
τὴν δὲ ὕλην αὐτοῦ ἐν τῷ πάθει γίγνεσθαι, ὅταν γίγνηται, ἐκείνου τῇ παρουσίᾳ
κινοῦντος. Οὐ γὰρ δὴ τὸ φυτικόν, ὅταν φύῃ, φύεται, οὐδ᾽, ὅταν αὔξῃ, αὔξεται,
οὐδ᾽ ὅλως, ὅταν κινῇ, κινεῖται ἐκείνην τὴν κίνησιν ἣν κινεῖ, ἀλλ᾽ ἢ οὐδ᾽ ὅλως,
40 ἢ ἄλλος τρόπος κινήσεως ἢ ἐνεργείας. Αὐτὴν μὲν οὖν δεῖ τὴν τοῦ εἴδους φύσιν
ἐνέργειαν εἶναι καὶ τῇ παρουσίᾳ ποιεῖν, οἷον εἰ ἡ ἁρμονία ἐξ αὑτῆς τὰς χορδὰς
ἐκίνει.

b.   This whole conception is opposed by P. to Stoic materialism.
Perception, though the active rôle of the soul is maintained, must be
said to presuppose the body and hence is to be considered as belonging to
a kind of sleeping state of the soul. Her true awaking is: leaving the body
entirely.

---

[1]   Cp. Zeno's description of sense-impressions, above, nr. **984**.

Perception
is proper to
a sleeping
state of the
soul

Enn. III 6, 6, l. 65-76:

Ταῦτα μὲν οὖν εἴρηται πρὸς τοὺς ἐν τοῖς σώμασι τιθεμένους τὰ ὄντα τῇ 6
τῶν ὠθισμῶν μαρτυρίᾳ καὶ τοῖς διὰ τῆς αἰσθήσεως φαντάσμασι πίστιν τῆς
ἀληθείας λαμβάνοντας, οἳ παραπλήσιον τοῖς ὀνειρώττουσι ποιοῦσι ταῦτα
ἐνεργεῖν νομίζουσιν, ἃ ὁρῶσιν εἶναι ἐνύπνια ὄντα. Καὶ γὰρ τὸ τῆς αἰσθήσεως
ψυχῆς ἐστιν εὐδούσης· ὅσον γὰρ ἐν σώματι ψυχῆς, τοῦτο εὕδει· ἡ δ' ἀληθινὴ 7°
ἐγρήγορσις ἀληθινὴ ἀπὸ σώματος, οὐ μετὰ σώματος, ἀνάστασις ¹. Ἡ μὲν γὰρ
μετὰ σώματος μετάστασίς ἐστιν ἐξ ἄλλου εἰς ἄλλον ὕπνον, οἷον ἐξ ἑτέρων
δεμνίων· ἡ δ' ἀληθὴς ὅλως ἀπὸ τῶν σωμάτων, ἃ τῆς φύσεως ὄντα τῆς ἐναντίας
ψυχῇ τὸ ἐναντίον εἰς οὐσίαν ἔχει. 7°

1417—How can man, who is a spiritual being, sin?

Answer: Not by his higher soul which is divine, but by yielding
to what is inferior to it. Soul in itself is undisturbed.

Sin ascribed
to what is
inferior to
soul

a. *Enn.* I 1, 9, l. 1-13; 23-26:

Ἔσται τοίνυν ἐκείνης ἡμῖν τῆς ψυχῆς ἡ φύσις ἀπηλλαγμένη αἰτίας κακῶν,
ὅσα ἄνθρωπος ποιεῖ καὶ πάσχει· περὶ γὰρ τὸ ζῷον ταῦτα, τὸ κοινόν, καὶ κοινόν,
ὡς εἴρηται. Ἀλλ' εἰ δόξα τῆς ψυχῆς καὶ διάνοια, πῶς ἀναμάρτητος; Ψευδὴς
γὰρ δόξα καὶ πολλὰ κατ' αὐτὴν πράττεται τῶν κακῶν. Ἢ πράττεται μὲν τὰ 5
κακὰ ἡττωμένων ἡμῶν ὑπὸ τοῦ χείρονος — πολλὰ γὰρ ἡμεῖς — ἢ ἐπιθυμίας ἢ
θυμοῦ ἢ εἰδώλου κακοῦ· ἡ δὲ τῶν ψευδῶν λεγομένη διάνοια φαντασία οὖσα
οὐκ ἀνέμεινε τὴν τοῦ διανοητικοῦ κρίσιν, ἀλλ' ἐπράξαμεν τοῖς χείροσι πεισθέν- 1°
τες, ὥσπερ ἐπὶ τῆς αἰσθήσεως πρὶν τῷ διανοητικῷ ἐπικρῖναι ψευδῆ ὁρᾶν συμβαίνει τῇ κοινῇ αἰσθήσει. Ὁ δὲ νοῦς ἢ ἐφήψατο ἢ οὔ, ὥστε ἀναμάρτητος. —
Ἀτρεμήσει οὖν οὐδὲν ἧττον ἡ ψυχὴ πρὸς ἑαυτὴν καὶ ἐν ἑαυτῇ· αἱ δὲ τροπαὶ
καὶ ὁ θόρυβος ἐν ἡμῖν παρὰ τῶν συνηρτημένων καὶ τῶν τοῦ κοινοῦ, ὅ τι δήποτέ 2°
ἐστι τοῦτο, ὡς εἴρηται, παθημάτων.

These remarks are once more directed against the Stoics, who explained sin as
ψευδὴς δόξα (above, nrs. **1053** ff.) and considered πάθη as *perturbationes animi*
(cp. nr. **1060b**).

b. If soul is impeccable, why punishments here and hereafter?
To this question again P. answers, as was seen above (**1412e**), that at
his birth man was conjoined to another kind of soul, which is liable to
πάθη, and that hence the compound can sin.

Only the
soul with
προσθῆκαι
can sin

Enn. I 1, 12, l. 1-12, 17-21:

Ἀλλ' εἰ ἀναμάρτητος ἡ ψυχή, πῶς αἱ δίκαι; Ἀλλὰ γὰρ οὗτος ὁ λόγος
ἀσυμφωνεῖ παντὶ λόγῳ, ὅς φησιν αὐτὴν καὶ ἁμαρτάνειν καὶ κατορθοῦν καὶ
διδόναι δίκας καὶ ἐν Ἅιδου καὶ μετενσωματοῦσθαι. Προσθετέον μὲν οὖν ὅτῳ

---

¹ This is obviously directed against the Christian doctrine of resurrection.

τις βούλεται λόγῳ· τάχα δ' ἄν τις ἐξεύροι καὶ ὅπῃ μὴ μαχοῦνται. Ὁ μὲν γὰρ
τὸ ἀναμάρτητον διδοὺς τῇ ψυχῇ λόγος ἓν ἁπλοῦν πάντη ἐτίθετο τὸ αὐτὸ ψυχὴν
καὶ τὸ ψυχῇ εἶναι λέγων, ὁ δ' ἁμαρτεῖν διδοὺς συμπλέκει μὲν καὶ προστίθησιν
αὐτῇ καὶ ἄλλο ψυχῆς εἶδος τὸ τὰ δεινὰ ἔχον πάθη· σύνθετος οὖν καὶ τὸ ἐκ
πάντων ἡ ψυχὴ αὐτὴ γίνεται καὶ πάσχει δὴ κατὰ τὸ ὅλον καὶ ἁμαρτάνει τὸ
σύνθετον καὶ τοῦτό ἐστι τὸ διδὸν δίκην αὐτῷ, οὐκ ἐκεῖνο. — Ἄλλη οὖν ζωὴ
καὶ ἄλλαι ἐνέργειαι καὶ τὸ κολαζόμενον ἕτερον· ἡ δὲ ἀναχώρησις καὶ ὁ χωρισμὸς
οὐ μόνον τοῦδε τοῦ σώματος, ἀλλὰ καὶ ἅπαντος τοῦ προστεθέντος. Καὶ γὰρ
ἐν τῇ γενέσει ἡ προσθήκη· ἢ ὅλως ἡ γένεσις τοῦ ἄλλου ψυχῆς εἴδους.

1418—Man as a spiritual being is above the nexus of physical causality.
Hence P. leaves a large space to the free will of the individual man.

a. *Enn.* III 1, 8, l. 4-20:

Free will

Ψυχὴν δὴ δεῖ ἀρχὴν οὖσαν ἄλλην ἐπεισφέροντας εἰς τὰ ὄντα, οὐ μόνον τὴν
τοῦ παντός, ἀλλὰ καὶ τὴν ἑκάστου μετὰ ταύτης, ὡς ἀρχῆς οὐ σμικρᾶς οὔσης,
πλέκειν τὰ πάντα, οὐ γινομένης καὶ αὐτῆς, ὥσπερ τὰ ἄλλα, ἐκ σπερμάτων,
ἀλλὰ πρωτουργοῦ αἰτίας οὔσης. Ἄνευ μὲν οὖν σώματος οὖσα κυριωτάτη τε
αὐτῆς * καὶ ἐλευθέρα καὶ κοσμικῆς αἰτίας ἔξω· ἐνεχθεῖσα δὲ εἰς σῶμα οὐκέτι
πάντα κυρία, ὡς ἂν μεθ' ἑτέρων ταχθεῖσα. Τύχαι δὲ τὰ κύκλῳ πάντα, οἷς
συνέπεσεν ἐλθοῦσα εἰς μέσον, τὰ πολλὰ ἤγαγον, ὥστε τὰ μὲν ποιεῖν διὰ ταῦτα,
τὰ δὲ κρατοῦσαν αὐτὴν ταῦτα ὅπῃ ἐθέλει ἄγειν. Πλείω δὲ κρατεῖ ἡ ἀμείνων,
ἐλάττω δὲ ἡ χείρων. Ἡ γὰρ κράσει σώματός τι ἐνδιδοῦσα ἐπιθυμεῖν ἢ ὀργίζεσθαι
ἠνάγκασται ἢ πενίαις ταπεινὴ ἢ πλούτοις χαῦνος ἢ δυνάμεσι τύραννος· ἡ δὲ
καὶ ἐν τοῖς αὐτοῖς τούτοις ἀντέσχεν, ἡ ἀγαθὴ τὴν φύσιν, καὶ ἠλλοίωσεν αὐτὰ
μᾶλλον ἢ ἠλλοιώθη, ὥστε τὰ μὲν ἑτεροιῶσαι, τοῖς δὲ συγχωρῆσαι μὴ μετὰ
κάκης.

b. Ib., c. 9, l. 4-16:

Ὅταν μὲν οὖν ἀλλοιωθεῖσα παρὰ τῶν ἔξω ψυχὴ πράττῃ τι καὶ ὁρμᾷ οἷον
τυφλῇ τῇ φορᾷ χρωμένη, οὐχὶ ἑκούσιον τὴν πρᾶξιν οὐδὲ τὴν διάθεσιν λεκτέον·
καὶ ὅταν αὐτὴ παρ' αὑτῆς χείρων οὖσα οὐκ ὀρθαῖς πανταχοῦ οὐδὲ ἡγεμονούσαις
ταῖς ὁρμαῖς ᾖ χρωμένη. Λόγον δὲ ὅταν ἡγεμόνα καθαρὸν καὶ ἀπαθῆ τὸν οἰκεῖον
ἔχουσα ὁρμᾷ, ταύτην μόνην τὴν ὁρμὴν φατέον εἶναι ἐφ' ἡμῖν καὶ ἑκούσιον,
καὶ τοῦτο εἶναι τὸ ἡμέτερον ἔργον, ὃ μὴ ἄλλοθεν ἦλθεν, ἀλλ' ἔνδοθεν ἀπὸ
καθαρᾶς τῆς ψυχῆς, ἀπ' ἀρχῆς πρώτης ἡγουμένης καὶ κυρίας, ἀλλ' οὐ πλάνην
ἐξ ἀγνοίας παθούσης ἢ ἧτταν ἐκ βίας ἐπιθυμῶν, αἳ προσελθοῦσαι ἄγουσι καὶ
ἕλκουσι καὶ οὐκέτι ἔργα ἐῶσιν εἶναι, ἀλλὰ παθήματα παρ' ἡμῶν.

See further our next paragraph, the nrs. **1425, 1430** ff.

---

* αὑτῆς Br.

Virtue

1419—To the question of "what is virtue" P. answers that virtue is: the state of the soul which follows if she turns to what is congenial to her.

a. *Enn.* I 2, 4, l. 1-28.

In this treatise (Π. ἀρετῶν) P. inquires into the φυγὴ ἐνθένδε which is ὁμοίωσις θεῷ κατὰ τὸ δυνατόν according to *Theaet.* 176a, b.
When the soul has purified herself from the body and is concerned with things intelligible, this state may be called resemblance to God. Is then virtue = purification, or is it identical with the state of being purified?

Is virtue
κάθαρσις?

Ζητητέον δέ, εἰ ἡ κάθαρσις ταὐτὸν τῇ τοιαύτῃ ἀρετῇ, ἢ προηγεῖται μὲν ἡ κάθαρσις, ἕπεται δὲ ἡ ἀρετή, καὶ πότερον ἐν τῷ καθαίρεσθαι ἡ ἀρετὴ ἢ ἐν τῷ κεκαθάρθαι. Ἀτελεστέρα τῆς ἐν τῷ κεκαθάρθαι <ἡ ἐν τῷ καθαίρεσθαι· τὸ 5 γὰρ κεκαθάρθαι> οἷον τέλος ἤδη. Ἀλλὰ τὸ κεκαθάρθαι ἀφαίρεσις ἀλλοτρίου παντός, τὸ δὲ ἀγαθὸν ἕτερον αὐτοῦ. Ἤ, εἰ πρὸ τῆς ἀκαθαρσίας ἀγαθὸν ἦν, ἡ κάθαρσις ἀρκεῖ· ἀλλ' ἀρκέσει μὲν ἡ κάθαρσις, τὸ δὲ καταλειπόμενον ἔσται τὸ ἀγαθόν, οὐχ ἡ κάθαρσις. Καὶ τί τὸ καταλειπόμενόν ἐστι, ζητητέον· ἴσως γὰρ 10 οὐδὲ τὸ ἀγαθὸν ἦν ἡ φύσις ἡ καταλειπομένη· οὐ γὰρ ἂν ἐγένετο ἐν κακῷ. Ἆρ' οὖν ἀγαθοειδῆ λεκτέον; Ἤ οὐχ ἱκανὴν πρὸς τὸ μένειν ἐν τῷ ὄντως ἀγαθῷ· πέφυκε γὰρ ἐπ' ἄμφω. Τὸ οὖν ἀγαθὸν αὐτῆς τὸ συνεῖναι τῷ συγγενεῖ, τὸ δὲ κακὸν τὸ τοῖς ἐναντίοις. Δεῖ οὖν καθηραμένην συνεῖναι. Συνέσται δὲ ἐπιστρα- 15 φεῖσα. Ἆρ' οὖν μετὰ τὴν κάθαρσιν ἐπιστρέφεται; Ἤ μετὰ τὴν κάθαρσιν ἐπέστραπται. Τοῦτ' οὖν ἡ ἀρετὴ αὐτῆς; Ἤ τὸ γινόμενον αὐτῇ ἐκ τῆς ἐπιστροφῆς. Τί οὖν τοῦτο; Θέα καὶ τύπος τοῦ ὀφθέντος ἐντεθεὶς καὶ ἐνεργῶν, ὡς ἡ ὄψις περὶ τὸ ὁρώμενον. Οὐκ ἄρα εἶχεν αὐτὰ οὐδ' ἀναμιμνήσκεται; Ἤ εἶχεν οὐκ 20 ἐνεργοῦντα, ἀλλὰ ἀποκείμενα ἀφώτιστα· ἵνα δὲ φωτισθῇ καὶ τότε γνῷ αὐτὰ ἐνόντα, δεῖ προσβαλεῖν τῷ φωτίζοντι. Εἶχε δὲ οὐκ αὐτά, ἀλλὰ τύπους· δεῖ οὖν τὸν τύπον τοῖς ἀληθινοῖς, ὧν καὶ οἱ τύποι, ἐφαρμόσαι. Τάχα δὲ καὶ οὕτω λέγεται ἔχειν, ὅτι ὁ νοῦς οὐκ ἀλλότριος καὶ μάλιστα δὲ οὐκ ἀλλότριος, ὅταν πρὸς αὐτὸν 25 βλέπῃ· εἰ δὲ μή, καὶ παρὼν ἀλλότριος. Ἐπεὶ καὶ ταῖς ἐπιστήμαις· ἐὰν μηδ' ὅλως ἐνεργῶμεν κατ' αὐτάς, ἀλλότριαι.

Thus, just as Aristotle in *E.N.* I 1098a 7-18 defined εὐδαιμονία (above, vol. II, p. 143), P. defines virtue as *an activity of the soul.* But according to P. for this ἐνέργεια an "illumination" from beyond is needed. Cp. St. Augustine in *De magistro* XII 40; *De civ. Dei* l. X c. 2; *De Trin.* l. XII c. 15; *Retract.* l. I c. 8.

b. Cp. also the following passage of the treatise Περὶ τοῦ καλοῦ, in which the traditional "moral virtues" are described as a purification from the πάθη of the body and a preparation for that state of the soul in which she is brought back to Noûs, which for her is the source of beauty and resemblance to God.

Enn. I 6, 6, l. 1-3, 6-20:

Ἔστι γὰρ δή, ὡς ὁ παλαιὸς λόγος, καὶ ἡ σωφροσύνη καὶ ἡ ἀνδρία καὶ πᾶσα ἀρετὴ κάθαρσις καὶ ἡ φρόνησις αὐτή. — Τί γὰρ ἂν καὶ εἴη σωφροσύνη ἀληθὴς ἢ τὸ μὴ προσομιλεῖν ἡδοναῖς τοῦ σώματος, φεύγειν δὲ ὡς οὐ καθαρὰς οὐδὲ καθαροῦ; Ἡ δὲ ἀνδρία ἀφοβία θανάτου. Ὁ δέ ἐστιν ὁ θάνατος χωρὶς εἶναι τὴν ψυχὴν τοῦ σώματος. Οὐ φοβεῖται δὲ τοῦτο, ὃς ἀγαπᾷ μόνος γενέσθαι. Μεγαλοψυχία δὲ δὴ ὑπεροψία τῶν τῇδε. Ἡ δὲ φρόνησις νόησις ἐν ἀποστροφῇ τῶν κάτω, πρὸς δὲ τὰ ἄνω τὴν ψυχὴν ἄγουσα. Γίνεται οὖν ἡ ψυχὴ καθαρθεῖσα εἶδος καὶ λόγος καὶ πάντη ἀσώματος καὶ νοερὰ καὶ ὅλη τοῦ θείου, ὅθεν ἡ πηγὴ τοῦ καλοῦ καὶ τὰ συγγενῆ πάντα τοιαῦτα. Ψυχὴ οὖν ἀναχθεῖσα πρὸς νοῦν ἐπὶ τὸ μᾶλλόν ἐστι καλόν. Νοῦς δὲ καὶ τὰ παρὰ νοῦ τὸ κάλλος αὐτῇ οἰκεῖον καὶ οὐκ ἀλλότριον, ὅτι τότε ἐστὶν ὄντως μόνον ψυχή. Διὸ καὶ λέγεται ὀρθῶς τὸ ἀγαθὸν καὶ καλὸν τὴν ψυχὴν γίνεσθαι ὁμοιωθῆναι εἶναι θεῷ, ὅτι ἐκεῖθεν τὸ καλόν. —

κάθαρσις a condition to the ὁμοίωσις θεῷ

Thus, P. knows a higher and a lower virtue, the latter of which is the condition to the first, while the first is not implied in the latter. Below, **1420b**.

c. As long as soul is not entirely purified from the πάθη, she is demoniac, not divine.

Enn. I 2, 6, l. 3-7:

Εἰ μὲν οὖν τι τῶν τοιούτων ἀπροαίρετον γίνοιτο, θεὸς ἂν εἴη ὁ τοιοῦτος καὶ δαίμων διπλοῦς ὤν, μᾶλλον δὲ ἔχων σὺν αὐτῷ ἄλλον ἄλλην ἀρετὴν ἔχοντα· εἰ δὲ μηδέν, θεὸς μόνον· θεὸς δὲ τῶν ἑπομένων τῷ πρώτῳ [1].

d. In a later treatise P. qualifies (higher) virtue as "a ἕξις which causes the soul to be spiritualized" or even as "another kind of Noûs"; from which he concludes that that liberty of man which is called τὸ ἐφ' ἡμῖν lies not in action but in Noûs.

Enn. VI 8, 5, l. 34-37:

Εἰ οὖν οἷον νοῦς τις ἄλλος ἐστὶν ἡ ἀρετὴ καὶ ἕξις οἷον νοωθῆναι τὴν ψυχὴν ποιοῦσα, πάλιν αὖ ἥκει οὐκ ἐν πράξει τὸ ἐφ' ἡμῖν, ἀλλ' ἐν νῷ ἡσύχῳ τῶν πράξεων.

Virtue is a spiritualized state of the soul

e. In soul, the contemplation of intelligible being is called virtue; in Noûs itself it is not. Here it is "act" (ἐνέργεια) and essence.

Enn. I 2, 6, l. 12-18:

Ἡ σοφία μὲν καὶ φρόνησις ἐν θεωρίᾳ ὧν νοῦς ἔχει· νοῦς δὲ τῇ ἐπαφῇ. Διττὴ δὴ ἑκατέρα, ἡ μὲν ἐν νῷ οὖσα, ἡ δὲ ἐν ψυχῇ. Κἀκεῖ μὲν οὐκ ἀρετή, ἐν

What is „act" in Noûs, in soul becomes virtue

---

[1] For P.'s polytheism, see our preceding paragraph, nr. **1411**.

δὲ ψυχῇ ἀρετή. Ἐκεῖ οὖν τί; Ἐνέργεια αὐτοῦ καὶ ὅ ἐστιν· ἐνταῦθα δὲ τὸ ἐν ¦
ἄλλῳ ἐκεῖθεν ἀρετή. Οὐδὲ γὰρ αὐτοδικαιοσύνη καὶ ἑκάστη ἀρετή, ἀλλ' οἷον
παράδειγμα· τὸ δὲ ἀπ' αὐτῆς ἐν ψυχῇ ἀρετή.

1420—The distinction between a higher and a lower kind of virtue
must be made, because "moral virtue" (as it is called by Aristotle)
presupposes πλῆθος, while virtue in the higher sense does not.

Higher and lower virtue

a. *Enn.* I 2, 6, l. 19-27:

Δικαιοσύνη δὲ εἴπερ οἰκειοπραγία [1], ἆρα ἀεὶ ἐν πλήθει μερῶν; Ἢ ἡ μὲν ἐν ¦
πλήθει, ὅταν πολλὰ ᾖ τὰ μέρη, ἡ δὲ ὅλως οἰκειοπραγία, κἂν ἑνὸς ᾖ. Ἡ γοῦν
ἀληθὴς αὐτοδικαιοσύνη ἑνὸς πρὸς αὑτό *, ἐν ᾧ οὐκ ἄλλο, τὸ δὲ ἄλλο· ὥστε καὶ
τῇ ψυχῇ δικαιοσύνη ἡ μείζων τὸ πρὸς νοῦν ἐνεργεῖν, τὸ δὲ σωφρονεῖν ἡ εἴσω
πρὸς νοῦν στροφή, ἡ δὲ ἀνδρία ἀπάθεια καθ' ὁμοίωσιν τοῦ πρὸς ὃ βλέπει ¦
ἀπαθὲς ὂν τὴν φύσιν· αὕτη δὲ ἐξ ἀρετῆς, ἵνα μὴ συμπαθῇ τῷ χείρονι συνοίκῳ.

b. Virtues are linked the one with the other, as their examples
are in Noûs. Moreover, he who possesses the higher virtues always possesses the minor ones, at least potentially. On the other hand, the man
who possesses the minor virtues does not necessarily possess the higher
ones.

How far they are linked

Enn. I 2, 7, l. 1-12:

Ἀντακολουθοῦσι τοίνυν ἀλλήλαις καὶ αὖται αἱ ἀρεταὶ ἐν ψυχῇ, ὥσπερ κἀκεῖ
τὰ πρὸ τῆς ἀρετῆς αἱ ἐν νῷ ὥσπερ παραδείγματα. Καὶ γὰρ ἡ νόησις ἐκεῖ
ἐπιστήμη καὶ σοφία, τὸ δὲ πρὸς αὐτὸν ἡ σωφροσύνη, τὸ δὲ οἰκεῖον ἔργον ἡ
οἰκειοπραγία, τὸ δὲ οἷον ἀνδρία ἡ ἀϋλότης καὶ τὸ ἐφ' αὑτοῦ μένειν καθαρόν. 5
Ἐν ψυχῇ τοίνυν πρὸς νοῦν ἡ ὅρασις σοφία καὶ φρόνησις, ἀρεταὶ αὐτῆς· οὐ γὰρ
αὐτὴ ταῦτα, ὥσπερ ἐκεῖ. Καὶ τὰ ἄλλα ὡσαύτως ἀκολουθεῖ· καὶ τῇ καθάρσει
δέ, εἴπερ πᾶσαι καθάρσεις κατὰ τὸ κεκαθάρθαι, ἀνάγκη πάσας· ἢ οὐδεμία ¦
τελεία. Καὶ ὁ μὲν ἔχων τὰς μείζους καὶ τὰς ἐλάττους ἐξ ἀνάγκης δυνάμει, ὁ δὲ
τὰς ἐλάττους οὐκ ἀναγκαίως ἔχει ἐκείνας.

c. It is the task of dialectic to form man's natural aptitudes into
real virtue, both by arguments and by exercise.

Dialectic has to train man to virtue

Enn. I 3, 6, l. 14-24:

Πότερα δὲ ἔστι τὰ κάτω [2] εἶναι ἄνευ διαλεκτικῆς καὶ σοφίας; Ἢ ἀτελῶς καὶ ¦
ἐλλειπόντως. Ἔστι δὲ σοφὸν εἶναι καὶ διαλεκτικὸν οὕτως ἄνευ τούτων; Ἢ οὐδ' ἂν

---

* αὐτό Br.
[1] According to Plato's definition in *Resp.* IV 433d-e, 435b (our nrs. **284c, 285a**).
[2] The lower virtues.

γένοιτο, ἀλλὰ ἢ πρότερον ἢ ἅμα συναύξεται. Καὶ τάχα ἂν φυσικάς τις ἀρετὰς ἔχοι,
ἐξ ὧν αἱ τέλειαι σοφίας γενομένης *. Μετὰ τὰς φυσικὰς οὖν ἡ σοφία· εἶτα
τελειοῖ τὰ ἤθη. Ἡ τῶν φυσικῶν οὐσῶν συναύξεται ἤδη ἄμφω καὶ συντελειοῦται·
ἢ προλαβοῦσα ἡ ἑτέρα τὴν ἑτέραν ἐτελείωσεν· ὅλως γὰρ ἡ φυσικὴ ἀρετὴ καὶ
ὄμμα ἀτελὲς καὶ ἦθος ἔχει, καὶ αἱ ἀρχαὶ τὸ πλεῖστον ἀμφοτέραις, ἀφ' ὧν ἔχομεν.

d. How much P. is convinced that training in the lower virtues
is an indispensable condition for any higher spiritual life, may be seen
in his treatise against the gnostics, whom he blames not only for denying
providence, but also for their complete neglect of virtue "which is perfected by λόγος and ἄσκησις".

Enn. II 9, 15, l. 8-17, 26-40:

P. blames
gnostics for
their neglect
of virtue

Ὁ μὲν Ἐπίκουρος τὴν πρόνοιαν ἀνελὼν τὴν ἡδονὴν καὶ τὸ ἥδεσθαι, ὅπερ
ἦν λοιπόν, τοῦτο διώκειν παρακελεύεται· ὁ δὲ λόγος οὗτος ἔτι νεανικώτερον
τὸν τῆς προνοίας κύριον καὶ αὐτὴν τὴν πρόνοιαν μεμψάμενος καὶ πάντας
νόμους τοὺς ἐνταῦθα ἀτιμάσας καὶ τὴν ἀρετὴν τὴν ἐκ παντὸς τοῦ χρόνου
ἀνηυρημένην τό τε σωφρονεῖν τοῦτο ἐν γέλωτι θέμενος, ἵνα μηδὲν καλὸν
ἐνταῦθα δὴ ὀφθείη ὑπάρχον, ἀνεῖλε τό τε σωφρονεῖν καὶ τὴν ἐν τοῖς ἤθεσι
σύμφυτον δικαιοσύνην τὴν τελειουμένην ἐκ λόγου καὶ ἀσκήσεως καὶ ὅλως
καθ' ἃ σπουδαῖος ἄνθρωπος ἂν γένοιτο. — Οἷς δὲ ἀρετῆς μὴ μέτεστιν, οὐκ
ἂν εἶεν τὸ παράπαν κινηθέντες πρὸς ἐκεῖνα [1].

Μαρτυρεῖ δὲ αὐτοῖς καὶ τόδε τὸ μηδένα λόγον περὶ ἀρετῆς πεποιῆσθαι,
ἐκλελοιπέναι δὲ παντάπασι τὸν περὶ τούτων λόγον, καὶ μήτε τί ἐστιν εἰπεῖν
μήτε πόσα μήτε ὅσα τεθεώρηται πολλὰ καὶ καλὰ τοῖς τῶν παλαιῶν λόγοις,
μήτε ἐξ ὧν περιέσται καὶ κτήσεται, μήτε ὡς θεραπεύεται ψυχὴ μήτε ὡς καθαίρεται. Οὐ γὰρ δὴ τὸ εἰπεῖν "βλέπε πρὸς θεόν" προύργου τι ἐργάζεται,
ἐὰν μὴ καὶ πῶς ** βλέψει διδάξῃ. Τί γὰρ κωλύει, εἴποι τις ἄν, βλέπειν καὶ μηδεμιᾶς ἀπέχεσθαι ἡδονῆς, ἢ ἀκρατῆ θυμοῦ εἶναι μεμνημένον μὲν ὀνόματος τοῦ

Without
virtue the
cult of God
a meaning-
less dictum

θεός, συνεχόμενον δὲ ἅπασι πάθεσι, μηδὲν δὲ αὐτῶν πειρώμενον ἐξαιρεῖν;
Ἀρετὴ μὲν οὖν εἰς τέλος προϊοῦσα καὶ ἐν ψυχῇ ἐγγενομένη μετὰ φρονήσεως
θεὸν δείκνυσιν· ἄνευ δὲ ἀρετῆς ἀληθινῆς θεὸς λεγόμενος ὄνομά ἐστιν.

1421—Man can possess happiness, because he is able to have the per- Happiness
fect life, i.e. spiritual life. Since this is not a part of him, but his true
being, he may be said to be the cause of his own happiness, though the
deepest ground of it is transcendent. Moreover, he is αὐτάρκης, so far as
he does not strive after other things.

---

* <προς>γενομένης Müller, Br.
[1] ἐκεῖνα is Plotinus' usual term for the Intelligible World which is "God".
** καὶ πῶς transp. Volkmann, Br.; πῶς καὶ codd., H.-S.

Enn. I 4, 4, l. 1-23:

Εἰ μὲν οὖν τὴν τελείαν ζωὴν ἔχειν οἷός τε ἄνθρωπος, καὶ ἄνθρωπος ὁ ταύτην ἔχων τὴν ζωὴν εὐδαίμων. Εἰ δὲ μή, ἐν θεοῖς ἄν τις τὸ εὐδαιμονεῖν θεῖτο, εἰ ἐν ἐκείνοις μόνοις ἡ τοιαύτη ζωή. Ἐπειδὴ τοίνυν φαμὲν εἶναι καὶ ἐν ἀνθρώποις τὸ εὐδαιμονεῖν τοῦτο, σκεπτέον πῶς ἔστι τοῦτο. Λέγω δὲ ὧδε· ὅτι μὲν οὖν 5 ἔχει τελείαν ζωὴν ἄνθρωπος οὐ τὴν αἰσθητικὴν μόνον ἔχων, ἀλλὰ καὶ λογισμὸν καὶ νοῦν ἀληθινόν, δῆλον καὶ ἐξ ἄλλων. Ἀλλ᾽ ἆρά γε ὡς ἄλλος ὢν ἄλλο τοῦτο ἔχει; Ἢ οὐδ᾽ ἐστὶν ὅλως ἄνθρωπος μὴ οὐ καὶ τοῦτο ἢ δυνάμει ἢ ἐνεργείᾳ ἔχων, ὃν δὴ καὶ φαμὲν εὐδαίμονα εἶναι. Ἀλλ᾽ ὡς μέρος αὐτοῦ τοῦτο φήσομεν ἐν αὐτῷ τὸ εἶδος τῆς ζωῆς τὸ τέλειον εἶναι; Ἢ τὸν μὲν ἄλλον ἄνθρωπον μέρος τι τοῦτο ἔχειν δυνάμει ἔχοντα, τὸν δὲ εὐδαίμονα ἤδη, ὃς δὴ καὶ ἐνεργείᾳ ἐστὶ τοῦτο καὶ μεταβέβηκε πρὸς τὸ αὐτό, εἶναι τοῦτο· περικεῖσθαι δ᾽ αὐτῷ τὰ 1 ἄλλα ἤδη, ἃ δὴ οὐδὲ μέρη αὐτοῦ ἄν τις θεῖτο οὐκ ἐθέλοντι περικείμενα· ἦν δ᾽ ἂν αὐτοῦ κατὰ βούλησιν συνηρτημένα.

Τούτῳ τοίνυν τί ποτ᾽ ἐστὶ τὸ ἀγαθόν; Ἢ αὐτὸς αὑτῷ ὅπερ ἔχει· τὸ δὲ ἐπέκεινα αἴτιον τοῦ ἐν αὐτῷ καὶ ἄλλως ἀγαθόν, αὐτῷ παρὸν ἄλλως.

Μαρτύριον δὲ τοῦ τοῦτο εἶναι τὸ μὴ ἄλλο ζητεῖν τὸν οὕτως ἔχοντα. Τί γὰρ 2 ἂν καὶ ζητήσειε; Τῶν μὲν γὰρ χειρόνων οὐδέν, τῷ δὲ ἀρίστῳ σύνεστιν. Αὐτάρκης οὖν ὁ βίος τῷ οὕτως ζωὴν ἔχοντι.

1422—a. The Peripatetic arguments against the self-sufficiency of the spiritual life.

Arguments against self-sufficiency

Enn. I 4, 5, l. 1-5, 14-22:

Ἀλγηδόνες δ᾽ ἔτι καὶ νόσοι καὶ τὰ ἄλλως * κωλύοντα ἐνεργεῖν; Εἰ δὲ δὴ μηδ᾽ ἑαυτῷ παρακολουθοῖ[1]; Γένοιτο γὰρ ἂν καὶ ἐκ φαρμάκων καί τινων νόσων. Πῶς δὴ ἐν τούτοις ἅπασι τὸ ζῆν εὖ καὶ τὸ εὐδαιμονεῖν ἂν ἔχοι; Πενίας γὰρ καὶ ἀδοξίας ἐατέον. — Ἡδονῆς δὲ συναριθμουμένης τῷ εὐδαίμονι βίῳ, πῶς ἂν λυπηρὸν διὰ τύχας καὶ ὀδύνας ἔχων εὐδαίμων εἴη, ὅτῳ ταῦτα σπουδαίῳ 1 ὄντι γίγνοιτο; Ἀλλὰ θεοῖς μὲν ἡ τοιαύτη διάθεσις εὐδαίμων καὶ αὐτάρκης, ἀνθρώποις δὲ προσθήκην τοῦ χείρονος λαβοῦσι περὶ ὅλον χρὴ τὸ γενόμενον τὸ εὔδαιμον ζητεῖν, ἀλλὰ μὴ περὶ μέρος, ὅτι ἐκ θατέρου κακῶς ἔχοντος ἀναγκάζοιτο ἂν καὶ θάτερον τὸ κρεῖττον ** ἐμποδίζεσθαι πρὸς τὰ αὐτοῦ, ὅτι μὴ καὶ 2 τὰ τοῦ ἑτέρου καλῶς ἔχει.

b. To this Plotinus answers that, since happiness is not in outward things, the wise man will not seek for it there.

---

* ὅλως H.-S.; ἄλλως Br.

[1] παρακολουθεῖν and παρακολούθησις are Plotinian terms for (having) self-consciousness. See under **c.**

** τὸ κρεῖττον secl. Müller, Br.

Ib., c. 6, l. 1-13, 27-33:

Ἀλλ᾿ εἰ μὲν τὸ εὐδαιμονεῖν ἐν τῷ μὴ ἀλγεῖν μηδὲ νοσεῖν μηδὲ δυστυχεῖν μηδὲ συμφοραῖς μεγάλαις περιπίπτειν ἐδίδου ὁ λόγος, οὐκ ἦν τῶν ἐναντίων παρόντων εἶναι ὁντινοῦν εὐδαίμονα· εἰ δ᾿ ἐν τῇ τοῦ ἀληθινοῦ ἀγαθοῦ κτήσει
5 τοῦτό ἐστι κείμενον, τί δεῖ παρέντας τοῦτο καὶ οὐ * πρὸς τοῦτο βλέποντας κρίνειν τὸν εὐδαίμονα τὰ ἄλλα ζητεῖν, ἃ μὴ ἐν τῷ εὐδαιμονεῖν ἠρίθμηται; Εἰ μὲν γὰρ συμφόρησις ἦν ἀγαθῶν καὶ ἀναγκαίων ἢ καὶ οὐκ ἀναγκαίων, ἀλλ᾿ ἀγαθῶν καὶ τούτων λεγομένων, ἐχρῆν καὶ ταῦτα παρεῖναι ζητεῖν· εἰ δὲ τὸ τέλος ἕν τι
10 εἶναι ἀλλ᾿ οὐ πολλὰ δεῖ — οὕτω γὰρ ἂν οὐ τέλος, ἀλλὰ τέλη ἂν ζητοῖ — ἐκεῖνο χρὴ λαμβάνειν μόνον, ὃ ἔσχατόν τέ ἐστι καὶ τιμιώτατον καὶ ὃ ἡ ψυχὴ ζητεῖ ἐν αὑτῇ ἐγκολπίσασθαι. — Ἃ δὲ παρόντα μὲν οὐδὲν ἐπαγωγὸν ἔχει οὐδὲ προστίθησί τι πρὸς τὸ εὐδαιμονεῖν, ἀπόντα δὲ διὰ τὴν τῶν λυπούντων παρουσίαν ζητεῖ<ται>,
15 εὔλογον ἀναγκαῖα, ἀλλ᾿ οὐκ ἀγαθὰ φάσκειν εἶναι. Οὐδὲ συναριθμητέα τοίνυν τῷ τέλει, ἀλλὰ καὶ ἀπόντων αὐτῶν καὶ τῶν ἐναντίων παρόντων ἀκέραιον τὸ τέλος τηρητέον.

c. To those who say that even the spiritual man may lose his awareness and, as it seems, his faculty of thinking by illness or by drugs, P. answers: there is an activity of our spirit before we are aware of it. To this activity our consciousness is not of primary importance. Soul is like a mirror, reflecting the image of what happens in Noûs. The mirror may go to pieces, the life of the spirit goes on. It may be even purer if it is not reflected.

Enn. I 4, 10, l. 3-19, 21-33:

Αὐτὸς δὲ ὁ νοῦς διὰ τί οὐκ ἐνεργήσει καὶ ἡ ψυχὴ περὶ αὐτὸν ἡ πρὸ αἰσθήσεως
5 καὶ ὅλως ἀντιλήψεως; Δεῖ γὰρ τὸ πρὸ ἀντιλήψεως ἐνέργημα εἶναι, εἴπερ τὸ αὐτὸ τὸ νοεῖν καὶ εἶναι [1]. Καὶ ἔοικεν ἡ ἀντίληψις εἶναι καὶ γίνεσθαι ἀνακάμπτοντος τοῦ νοήματος καὶ τοῦ ἐνεργοῦντος τοῦ κατὰ τὸ ζῆν τῆς ψυχῆς οἷον ἀπωσθέντος πάλιν, ὥσπερ τὸ ἐν κατόπτρῳ περὶ τὸ λεῖον καὶ λαμπρὸν ἡσυχάζον.
10 Ὡς οὖν ἐν τοῖς τοιούτοις παρόντος μὲν τοῦ κατόπτρου ἐγένετο τὸ εἴδωλον, μὴ παρόντος δὲ ἢ μὴ οὕτως ἔχοντος ἐνεργείᾳ πάρεστιν οὗ τὸ εἴδωλον ἦν ἄν, οὕτω καὶ περὶ ψυχὴν ἡσυχίαν μὲν ἄγοντος τοῦ ἐν ἡμῖν τοιούτου, ᾧ ἐμφαίνεται τὰ τῆς διανοίας καὶ τοῦ νοῦ εἰκονίσματα, ἐνορᾶται ταῦτα καὶ οἷον αἰσθητῶς
15 γινώσκεται μετὰ τῆς προτέρας γνώσεως, ὅτι ὁ νοῦς καὶ ἡ διάνοια ἐνεργεῖ. Συγκλασθέντος δὲ τούτου διὰ τὴν τοῦ σώματος ταραττομένην ἁρμονίαν ἄνευ εἰδώλου ἡ διάνοια καὶ ὁ νοῦς νοεῖ καὶ ἄνευ φαντασίας ἡ νόησις τότε· — Πολλὰς
20 δ᾿ ἄν τις εὕροι καὶ ἐγρηγορότων καλὰς ἐνεργείας καὶ θεωρίας καὶ πράξεις, ὅτε θεωροῦμεν καὶ ὅτε πράττομεν, τὸ παρακολουθεῖν ἡμᾶς αὐταῖς οὐκ ἐχούσας.

---

* οὐ Br.; τὸ codd., H.-S.   [1] Parm., fr. 3 D.

Οὐ γὰρ τὸν ἀναγινώσκοντα ἀνάγκη παρακολουθεῖν ὅτι ἀναγινώσκει καὶ τότε 2⸴
μάλιστα, ὅτε μετὰ τοῦ συντόνου ἀναγινώσκοι· οὐδὲ ὁ ἀνδριζόμενος ὅτι ἀνδρίζεται καὶ κατὰ τὴν ἀνδρίαν ἐνεργεῖ ὅσῳ ἐνεργεῖ· καὶ ἄλλα μυρία· ὥστε τὰς
παρακολουθήσεις κινδυνεύειν ἀμυδροτέρας αὐτὰς τὰς ἐνεργείας αἷς παρακολου-
θοῦσι ποιεῖν, μόνας δὲ αὐτὰς οὔσας καθαρὰς τότε εἶναι καὶ μᾶλλον ἐνεργεῖν καὶ 3⸰
μᾶλλον ζῆν καὶ δὴ καὶ ἐν τῷ τοιούτῳ πάθει τῶν σπουδαίων γενομένων μᾶλλον
τὸ ζῆν εἶναι, οὐ κεχυμένον εἰς αἴσθησιν, ἀλλ' ἐν τῷ αὐτῷ ἐν ἑαυτῷ συνηγμένον.

The wise
man and his
happiness
1423—That man is not the compound, may be seen in the wise man:
his happiness is not of the living being as such, but of the soul, and even
exclusively of the higher soul.

a. *Enn.* I 4, 14, l. 1-31:

Τὸ δὲ μὴ συναμφότερον εἶναι τὸν ἄνθρωπον καὶ μάλιστα τὸν σπουδαῖον
μαρτυρεῖ καὶ ὁ χωρισμὸς ὁ ἀπὸ τοῦ σώματος καὶ ἡ τῶν λεγομένων ἀγαθῶν τοῦ
σώματος καταφρόνησις. Τὸ δὲ καθόσον ἀξιοῦν τὸ ζῷον τὴν εὐδαιμονίαν εἶναι
γελοῖον εὐζωίας τῆς εὐδαιμονίας οὔσης, ἢ περὶ ψυχὴν συνίσταται, ἐνεργείας 5
ταύτης οὔσης καὶ ψυχῆς οὐ πάσης — οὐ γὰρ δὴ τῆς φυτικῆς, ἵν' ἂν καὶ ἐφήψατο
σώματος· οὐ γὰρ δὴ τὸ εὐδαιμονεῖν τοῦτο ἦν σώματος μέγεθος καὶ εὐεξία —
οὐδ' αὖ ἐν τῷ αἰσθάνεσθαι εὖ, ἐπεὶ καὶ κινδυνεύσουσιν αἱ τούτων πλεονεξίαι
βαρύνασαι πρὸς αὐτὰς φέρειν τὸν ἄνθρωπον. Ἀντισηκώσεως δὲ οἷον ἐπὶ 1⸰
θάτερα πρὸς τὰ ἄριστα γενομένης μινύθειν * καὶ χείρω τὰ σώματα ποιεῖν,
ἵνα δεικνύοιτο οὗτος ὁ ἄνθρωπος ἄλλος ὢν ἢ τὰ ἔξω. Ὁ δὲ τῶν τῇδε ἄνθρωπος
ἔστω καὶ καλὸς καὶ μέγας καὶ πλούσιος καὶ πάντων ἀνθρώπων ἄρχων ὡς ἂν 15
ὢν τοῦδε τοῦ τόπου, καὶ οὐ φθονητέον αὐτῷ τῶν τοιούτων ἠπατημένῳ. Περὶ δὲ
σοφὸν ταῦτα ἴσως μὲν ἂν οὐδὲ τὴν ἀρχὴν γένοιτο, γενομένων δὲ ἐλαττώσει
αὐτός, εἴπερ αὐτοῦ κήδεται. Καὶ ἐλαττώσει μὲν καὶ μαρανεῖ ἀμελείᾳ τὰς τοῦ
σώματος πλεονεξίας, ἀρχὰς δὲ ἀποθήσεται. Σώματος δὲ ὑγίειαν φυλάττων οὐκ 2⸰
ἄπειρος νόσων εἶναι παντάπασι βουλήσεται· οὐδὲ μὴν οὐδὲ ἄπειρος εἶναι ἀλγη-
δόνων· ἀλλὰ καὶ μὴ γινομένων νέος ὢν μαθεῖν βουλήσεται, ἤδη δὲ ἐν γήρᾳ
ὢν οὔτε ταύτας οὔτε ἡδονὰς ἐνοχλεῖν οὐδέ τι τῶν τῇδε οὔτε προσηνὲς οὔτε
ἐναντίον, ἵνα μὴ πρὸς τὸ σῶμα βλέπῃ. Γινόμενος δ' ἐν ἀλγηδόσι τὴν πρὸς 25
ταύτας αὐτῷ πεπορισμένην δύναμιν ἀντιτάξει οὔτε προσθήκην ἐν ταῖς ἡδοναῖς
καὶ ὑγιείαις καὶ ἀπονίαις πρὸς τὸ εὐδαιμονεῖν λαμβάνων οὔτε ἀφαίρεσιν ἢ
ἐλάττωσιν ταύτης ἐν τοῖς ἐναντίοις τούτων. Τοῦ γὰρ ἐναντίου μὴ προστιθέντος 3⸰
τῷ αὐτῷ πῶς ἂν τὸ ἐναντίον ἀφαιροῖ;

b. Since he is above outward things, he will not be more happy
if he has them than if he has not.

---

* μινύθειν ⟨δεῖ⟩ Müller, Br.

Ib., c. 15, l. 1-8:

Ἀλλ' εἰ δύο εἶεν σοφοί, τῷ δὲ ἑτέρῳ παρείη ὅσα κατὰ φύσιν λέγεται, τῷ
δὲ τὰ ἐναντία, ἴσον φήσομεν τὸ εὐδαιμονεῖν αὐτοῖς παρεῖναι; Φήσομεν, εἴπερ
ἐπίσης σοφοί. Εἰ δὲ καλὸς τὸ σῶμα ὁ ἕτερος καὶ πάντα τὰ ἄλλα ὅσα μὴ πρὸς
5 σοφίαν μηδὲ ὅλως πρὸς ἀρετὴν καὶ τοῦ ἀρίστου θέαν καὶ τὸ ἄριστον εἶναι, τί
τοῦτο ἂν εἴη; Ἐπεὶ οὐδὲ αὐτὸς ὁ ταῦτα ἔχων σεμνυνεῖται ὡς μᾶλλον
εὐδαίμων τοῦ μὴ ἔχοντος. —

c. The wise man *must* be placed on this spiritual level. Otherwise
he would be just a decent man, who is of a mixed life and character and
not worthy of being called happy.

Ib., c. 16, l. 1-15:

Εἰ δέ τις μὴ ἐνταῦθα ἐν τῷ νῷ τούτῳ ἄρας θήσειε τὸν σπουδαῖον, κατάγοι
δὲ πρὸς τύχας καὶ ταύτας φοβήσεται περὶ αὐτὸν γενέσθαι, οὔτε σπουδαῖον
τηρήσει, οἷον ἀξιοῦμεν εἶναι, ἀλλ' ἐπιεικῆ ἄνθρωπον, καὶ μικτὸν ἐξ ἀγαθοῦ
5 καὶ κακοῦ διδοὺς μικτὸν βίον ἔκ τινος ἀγαθοῦ καὶ κακοῦ ἀποδώσει τῷ τοιούτῳ,
καὶ οὐ ῥάδιον γενέσθαι. Ὃς εἰ καὶ γένοιτο, οὐκ ἂν ὀνομάζεσθαι εὐδαίμων εἴη
ἄξιος οὐκ ἔχων τὸ μέγα οὔτε ἐν ἀξίᾳ σοφίας οὔτε ἐν καθαρότητι ἀγαθοῦ.
10 Οὐκ ἔστιν οὖν ἐν τῷ κοινῷ εὐδαιμόνως ζῆν. Ὀρθῶς γὰρ καὶ Πλάτων ἐκεῖθεν
ἄνωθεν τὸ ἀγαθὸν ἀξιοῖ λαμβάνειν καὶ πρὸς ἐκεῖνο βλέπειν τὸν μέλλοντα σοφὸν
καὶ εὐδαίμονα ἔσεσθαι καὶ ἐκείνῳ ὁμοιοῦσθαι καὶ κατ' ἐκεῖνο ζῆν. Τοῦτο οὖν
δεῖ ἔχειν μόνον πρὸς τὸ τέλος, τὰ δ' ἄλλα ὡς ἂν καὶ τόπους μεταβάλλοι οὐκ
15 ἐκ τῶν τόπων προσθήκην πρὸς τὸ εὐδαιμονεῖν ἔχων. —

1424—As we saw above (nr. **1411**, **1420d**), Plotinus rebuked gnostics
for despising the visible world, for denying that the care of Providence
extends to it, despising "the gods that are here", and also for blaming
unduly the connection of soul and body. Here follows the passage where
he speaks of the last point.

Enn. II 9, 18, l. 1-17:

Ἀλλ' ἴσως φήσουσιν ἐκείνους μὲν τοὺς λόγους [1] φεύγειν τὸ σῶμα ποιεῖν
πόρρωθεν μισοῦντας, τοὺς δὲ ἡμετέρους κατέχειν τὴν ψυχὴν πρὸς αὐτῷ. Τοῦτο
δὲ ὅμοιον ἂν εἴη, ὥσπερ ἂν εἰ δύο οἶκον καλὸν τὸν αὐτὸν οἰκούντων, τοῦ μὲν
5 ψέγοντος τὴν κατασκευὴν καὶ τὸν ποιήσαντα καὶ μένοντος οὐχ ἧττον ἐν αὐτῷ,
τοῦ δὲ μὴ ψέγοντος, ἀλλὰ τὸν ποιήσαντα τεχνικώτατα πεποιηκέναι λέγοντος,
τὸν δὲ χρόνον ἀναμένοντος ἕως ἂν ἥκῃ, ἐν ᾧ ἀπαλλάξεται, οὗ μηκέτι οἴκου
10 δεήσοιτο, ὁ δὲ σοφώτερος οἴοιτο εἶναι καὶ ἑτοιμότερος ἐξελθεῖν, ὅτι οἶδε λέγειν
ἐκ λίθων ἀψύχων τοὺς τοίχους καὶ ξύλων συνεστάναι καὶ πολλοῦ δεῖν τῆς

[1] Sc. their own theories.

ἀληθινῆς οἰκήσεως, ἀγνοῶν ὅτι τῷ μὴ φέρειν τὰ ἀναγκαῖα διαφέρει, εἴπερ καὶ μὴ ποιεῖται * δυσχεραίνειν ἀγαπῶν ἡσυχῇ τὸ κάλλος τῶν λίθων. Δεῖ δὲ μένειν μὲν ἐν οἴκοις σῶμα ἔχοντας κατασκευασθεῖσιν ὑπὸ ψυχῆς ἀδελφῆς ι; ἀγαθῆς πολλὴν δύναμιν εἰς τὸ δημιουργεῖν ἀπόνως ἐχούσης.

8—FATE AND PROVIDENCE, LOGOS AND THE "BOUNDLESS POWERS", TIME AND ETERNITY

1425—The doctrine of Fate, so important in later Antiquity, is discussed by P. in the treatise Π. εἰμαρμένης (*Enn.* III 1).

The Stoic ἓν καὶ πᾶν criticized

a. *Enn.* III 1, 4, l. 1-28.

After having dealt shortly with Democritean atomism, which makes everything determined by the mere mechanical motion of the atoms and thus destroys all personal life, reducing living beings to machines, P. criticizes the Stoic conception of the universe as ἓν καὶ πᾶν, which is at the same time ποιοῦν and πάσχον (above, nr. **899**). In this case too, human liberty is destroyed, and moreover the first and universal Principle would be the cause of evil.

Ἀλλ' ἆρα μία τις ψυχὴ διὰ παντὸς διήκουσα περαίνει τὰ πάντα ἑκάστου ταύτῃ κινουμένου ὡς μέρους, ᾗ τὸ ὅλον ἄγει, φερομένων δὲ ἐκεῖθεν τῶν αἰτίων ἀκολούθων ἀνάγκη τὴν τούτων ἐφεξῆς συνέχειαν καὶ συμπλοκὴν εἰμαρμένην; Οἷον εἰ φυτοῦ ἐκ ῥίζης τὴν ἀρχὴν ἔχοντος τὴν ἐντεῦθεν ἐπὶ πάντα διοίκησιν ** 5 αὐτοῦ τὰ μέρη καὶ πρὸς ἄλληλα συμπλοκήν, ποίησίν τε καὶ πεῖσιν, διοίκησιν μίαν καὶ οἷον εἰμαρμένην τοῦ φυτοῦ τις εἶναι λέγοι. Ἀλλὰ πρῶτον μὲν τοῦτο τὸ σφοδρὸν τῆς ἀνάγκης καὶ τῆς τοιαύτης εἰμαρμένης αὐτὸ τοῦτο τὴν εἰμαρ- 10 μένην καὶ τῶν αἰτίων τὸν εἰρμὸν καὶ τὴν συμπλοκὴν ἀναιρεῖ. Ὡς γὰρ ἐν τοῖς ἡμετέροις μέρεσι κατὰ τὸ ἡγεμονοῦν κινουμένοις ἄλογον τὸ καθ' εἰμαρμένην λέγειν κινεῖσθαι — οὐ γὰρ ἄλλο μὲν τὸ ἐνδεδωκὸς τὴν κίνησιν, ἄλλο δὲ τὸ παραδεξάμενον καὶ παρ' αὐτοῦ τῇ ὁρμῇ κεχρημένον, ἀλλ' ἐκεῖνό ἐστι πρῶτον τὸ 15 κινῆσαν τὸ σκέλος — τὸν αὐτὸν τρόπον εἰ καὶ ἐπὶ τοῦ παντὸς ἓν ἔσται τὸ πᾶν ποιοῦν καὶ πάσχον καὶ οὐκ ἄλλο παρ' ἄλλου κατ' αἰτίας τὴν ἀναγωγὴν ἀεὶ ἐφ' ἕτερον ἐχούσας, οὐ δὴ ἀληθὲς κατ' αἰτίας τὰ πάντα γίγνεσθαι, ἀλλ' ἓν ἔσται τὰ πάντα. Ὥστε οὔτε ἡμεῖς ἡμεῖς οὔτε τι ἡμέτερον ἔργον· οὐδὲ λογιζόμεθα 20 αὐτοί, ἀλλ' ἑτέρου λογισμοὶ τὰ ἡμέτερα βουλεύματα· οὐδὲ πράττομεν ἡμεῖς, ὥσπερ οὐδ' οἱ πόδες λακτίζουσιν, ἀλλ' ἡμεῖς διὰ μερῶν τῶν ἑαυτῶν. Ἀλλὰ γὰρ δεῖ καὶ ἕκαστον ἕκαστον εἶναι καὶ πράξεις ἡμετέρας καὶ διανοίας ὑπάρχειν 25 καὶ τὰς ἑκάστου καλάς τε καὶ αἰσχρὰς πράξεις παρ' αὐτοῦ ἑκάστου, ἀλλὰ μὴ τῷ παντὶ τὴν γοῦν τῶν αἰσχρῶν ποίησιν ἀνατιθέναι.

The influence of the heavenly bodies

b. Next, P. criticizes the doctrine of the influence of the heavenly bodies as it was usually conceived in his days.

---

* πρὸς ταῦτα corr. Br.; <προσ>ποιεῖται Dodds in Class. Qu. 16, 1922, p. 94.
** διήκουσαν Br.

As was said before, P. does not doubt of this influence itself (cp. IV 3, 12, l. 12-30 and IV 4, 26). He accepts it as a consequence of what is called by Stoics cosmic sympathy (above, nrs. **912** f., **935, 937, 1177**). What he rejects is: (1) the idea that the heavenly bodies, instead of being for man a· *sign* of things to come, *cause* these things directly and by deliberate will [1]; (2) that they are the cause of spiritual qualities, of the character of man and of those things which depend on our own will; (3) that they (being gods) would be the cause of evil.

Enn. III 1, 5, l. 1-24, 37-59; c. 6, l. 1-11:

Ἀλλ' ἴσως μὲν οὐχ οὕτως ἕκαστα περαίνεται, ἡ δὲ φορὰ διοικοῦσα πάντα καὶ ἡ τῶν ἄστρων κίνησις οὕτως ἕκαστα τίθησιν, ὡς ἂν πρὸς ἄλληλα στάσεως ἔχῃ μαρτυρίαις [2] καὶ ἀνατολαῖς, δύσεσί τε καὶ παραβολαῖς. Ἀπὸ τούτων γοῦν
5 μαντευόμενοι προλέγουσι περί τε τῶν ἐν τῷ παντὶ ἐσομένων περί τε ἑκάστου, ὅπως τε τύχης καὶ διανοίας οὐχ ἥκιστα ἕξει. Ὁρᾶν δὲ καὶ τὰ ἄλλα ζῷά τε καὶ φυτὰ ἀπὸ τῆς τούτων συμπαθείας αὐξόμενά τε καὶ μειούμενα καὶ τὰ ἄλλα
ο παρ' αὐτῶν πάσχοντα, τούς τε τόπους τοὺς ἐπὶ γῆς διαφέροντας ἀλλήλων εἶναι κατά τε τὴν πρὸς τὸ πᾶν σχέσιν καὶ πρὸς ἥλιον μάλιστα· ἀκολουθεῖν δὲ τοῖς τόποις οὐ μόνον τὰ ἄλλα φυτά τε καὶ ζῷα, ἀλλὰ καὶ ἀνθρώπων εἴδη τε καὶ μεγέθη καὶ χρόας καὶ θυμοὺς καὶ ἐπιθυμίας ἐπιτηδεύματά τε καὶ ἤθη. Κυρία
5 ἄρα ἡ τοῦ παντὸς πάντων φορά. Πρὸς δὴ ταῦτα πρῶτον μὲν ἐκεῖνο ῥητέον, ὅτι καὶ οὗτος ἕτερον τρόπον ἐκείνοις ἀνατίθησι τὰ ἡμέτερα, βουλὰς καὶ πάθη, κακίας τε καὶ ὁρμάς, ἡμῖν δὲ οὐδὲν διδοὺς λίθοις φερομένοις καταλείπει εἶναι, ἀλλ' οὐκ ἀνθρώποις ἔχουσι παρ' αὐτῶν καὶ ἐκ τῆς αὑτῶν φύσεως ἔργον. Ἀλλὰ
ο χρὴ διδόναι μὲν τὸ ἡμέτερον ἡμῖν, ἥκειν δὲ εἰς τὰ ἡμέτερα ἤδη τινὰ ὄντα καὶ οἰκεῖα ἡμῶν ἀπὸ τοῦ παντὸς ἄττα, καὶ διαιρούμενον, τίνα μὲν ἡμεῖς ἐργαζόμεθα, τίνα δὲ πάσχομεν ἐξ ἀνάγκης, μὴ πάντα ἐκείνοις ἀνατιθέναι. — Ἔτι δὲ καὶ ἐκ τῶνδε ἀκριβέστερον ἄν τις περὶ τούτων ἐπισκέψαιτο. Ἅ τις ἂν ἰδὼν εἰς τὴν τῶν
ο ἄστρων σχέσιν, ἣν εἶχον ὅτε ἕκαστος ἐγίνετο, προείποι, ταῦτά φασι καὶ γίνεσθαι παρ' αὐτῶν οὐ σημαινόντων μόνον, ἀλλὰ καὶ ποιούντων. Ὅταν τοίνυν περὶ εὐγενείας λέγωσιν ὡς ἐξ ἐνδόξων τῶν πατέρων καὶ μητέρων, πῶς ἔνι ποιεῖσθαι λέγειν ταῦτα, ἃ προϋπάρχει περὶ τοὺς γονεῖς πρὶν τὴν σχέσιν γενέσθαι ταύτην τῶν
5 ἄστρων ἀφ' ἧς προλέγουσι; Καὶ μὴν καὶ γονέων τύχας ἀπὸ τῶν παίδων τῆς γενέσεως καὶ παίδων διαθέσεις οἷαι ἔσονται καὶ ὁποίαις συνέσονται τύχαις ἀπὸ τῶν πατέρων περὶ τῶν οὔπω γεγονότων λέγουσι καὶ ἐξ ἀδελφῶν ἀδελφῶν θανάτους καὶ ἐκ γυναικῶν τὰ περὶ τοὺς ἄνδρας ἀνάπαλίν τε ἐκ τούτων ἐκεῖνα.
ο Πῶς ἂν οὖν ἡ ἑκάστου σχέσις ἐπὶ τῶν ἄστρων ποιοῖ, ἃ ἤδη ἐκ πατέρων οὕτως ἕξειν λέγεται; Ἢ γὰρ ἐκεῖνα τὰ πρότερα ἔσται τὰ ποιοῦντα, ἤ, εἰ μὴ ἐκεῖνα ποιεῖ, οὐδὲ ταῦτα. Καὶ μὴν καὶ ἡ ὁμοιότης ἐν τοῖς εἴδεσι πρὸς τοὺς γονέας

---

[1] The question of how cosmic laws function is dealt with amply in IV 4, 30-42, which will be cited below.

[2] H.-S. explain: positus stellarum. Br. reads, with Orelli: μεσουρανήσεσι.

οἴκοθέν φησι καὶ κάλλος καὶ αἶσχος ἰέναι, ἀλλ' οὐ παρὰ φορᾶς ἄστρων. Εὔλογόν 5
τε κατὰ τοὺς αὐτοὺς χρόνους καὶ ἄλλα * ἅμα ζῷά τε παντοδαπὰ καὶ ἀνθρώπους
ἅμα γίνεσθαι· οἷς ἅπασιν ἐχρῆν τὰ αὐτὰ εἶναι, οἷς ἡ αὐτὴ σχέσις. Πῶς οὖν
ἅμα μὲν ἀνθρώπους, ἅμα δὲ τὰ ἄλλα διὰ τῶν ** σχημάτων;

(6) Ἀλλὰ γὰρ γίγνεται μὲν ἕκαστα κατὰ τὰς αὐτῶν φύσεις, ἵππος μέν,
ὅτι ἐξ ἵππου, καὶ ἄνθρωπος, ὅτι ἐξ ἀνθρώπου, καὶ τοιόσδε, ὅτι ἐκ τοιοῦδε.
Ἔστω δὲ συνεργὸς καὶ ἡ τοῦ παντὸς φορὰ συγχωροῦσα τὸ πολὺ τοῖς γινομένοις,
ἔστωσαν δὲ πρὸς τὰ τοῦ σώματος πολλὰ σωματικῶς διδόντες, θερμότητας καὶ 5
ψύξεις καὶ σωμάτων κράσεις ἐπακολουθούσας, πῶς οὖν τὰ ἤθη καὶ τὰ ἐπιτηδεύ-
ματα καὶ μάλιστα ὅσα οὐ *** δοκεῖ κράσει σωμάτων δουλεύειν, οἷον γραμματικὸς
τίς καὶ γεωμετρικὸς καὶ κυβευτικὸς καὶ τῶνδε τίς εὑρετής; Πονηρία δὲ
ἤθους παρὰ **** θεῶν ὄντων πῶς ἂν δοθείη; 10

Stoic determinism rejected c. The Stoic conception of everything being determined by the universal law of Nature does not leave any liberty to man.

Enn. III 1, 7, l. 1-4, 12-24:

Λοιπὸν δὲ ἰδεῖν τὴν ἐπιπλέκουσαν καὶ οἷον συνείρουσαν ἀλλήλοις πάντα
καὶ τὸ πῶς ἐφ' ἑκάστου ἐπιφέρουσαν ἀρχὴν τιθεμένην μίαν, ἀφ' ἧς πάντα κατὰ
λόγους σπερματικοὺς περαίνεται. — Τοιαῦτα δὲ ὄντα ὡς ἀπὸ μιᾶς ἀρχῆς
ὡρμημένα ἡμῖν οὐδὲν καταλείπει, ἢ φέρεσθαι ὅπη ἂν ἐκεῖνα ὠθῇ. Αἵ τε γὰρ
φαντασίαι τοῖς προηγησαμένοις αἵ τε ὁρμαὶ κατὰ ταύτας ἔσονται, ὄνομά τε
μόνον τὸ ἐφ' ἡμῖν ἔσται· οὐ γὰρ ὅτι ὁρμῶμεν ἡμεῖς, ταύτῃ τι πλέον ἔσται τῆς 15
ὁρμῆς κατ' ἐκεῖνα γεννωμένης· τοιοῦτόν τε τὸ ἡμέτερον ἔσται, οἷον καὶ τὸ
τῶν ἄλλων ζῴων καὶ τὸ τῶν νηπίων καθ' ὁρμὰς τυφλὰς ἰόντων καὶ τὸ τῶν
μαινομένων· ὁρμῶσι γὰρ καὶ οὗτοι· καὶ νὴ Δία αἱ πυρὸς ὁρμαὶ καὶ πάντων ὅσα 20
δουλεύοντα τῇ αὐτῶν κατασκευῇ φέρεται κατὰ ταύτην. Τοῦτο δὲ καὶ πάντες
ὁρῶντες οὐκ ἀμφισβητοῦσιν, ἀλλὰ τῆς ὁρμῆς ταύτης ἄλλας αἰτίας ζητοῦντες
οὐχ ἵστανται ὡς ἐπ' ἀρχῆς ταύτης.

Soul an independent cause d. P.'s own solution—that Soul must be introduced into the system of the universe as an independent principle, free from physical necessity—is expounded in the cc. 8-9, cited above, sub **1418a**. P. concludes as follows.

Enn. III 1, 10, l. 1-11:

Τέλος δή φησιν ὁ λόγος πάντα μὲν σημαίνεσθαι καὶ γίνεσθαι κατ' αἰτίας
μὲν πάντα, διττὰς δὲ ταύτας· καὶ τὰ μὲν ὑπὸ ψυχῆς, τὰ δὲ δι' ἄλλας αἰτίας τὰς
κύκλῳ. Πραττούσας δὲ ψυχὰς ὅσα πράττουσι κατὰ μὲν λόγον ποιούσας ὀρθὸν

---

* ἄλλα om. H.-S. ** τῶν αὐτῶν Volkmann, Br.
*** ὅσα οὐ Orelli, Br.; οὐχ ὅσα codd., H.-S.
**** παρ' <ἀστέρων> Müller, Br.; H.-S. notice: ,,immo tacite supplendum''.

5 παρ' αὐτῶν πράττειν ὅταν πράττωσι, τὰ δ' ἄλλα ἐμποδιζομένας τὰ αὐτῶν
πράττειν, πάσχειν τε μᾶλλον ἢ πράττειν. Ὥστε τοῦ μὲν μὴ φρονεῖν ἄλλα αἴτια
εἶναι· καὶ ταῦτα ἴσως ὀρθὸν καθ' εἱμαρμένην λέγειν πράττειν, οἷς γε καὶ
10 δοκεῖ ἔξωθεν τὴν εἱμαρμένην αἴτιον εἶναι· τὰ δὲ ἄριστα παρ' ἡμῶν. Ταύτης γὰρ
καὶ τῆς φύσεώς ἐσμεν, ὅταν μόνοι ὦμεν. —

Cp. below, our nrs. **1430** and **1431**. See also Carneades' criticism of Stoic
εἱμαρμένη, above, nr. **1124**.

1426—As was said before (nr. **1376**), P. distinguished between indirect
providence, exercised from a distance by Universal soul, and direct **Providence**
providence, exercised by particular souls coming into contact with a
body. Emphasis is laid on this point, that Universal soul operates through
a reasonable power called Λόγος, which is natural, but not by deliberation,
which would mean that it were ἐπακτόν. The same or similar ideas are
expressed in the opening chapters of the treatises Περὶ προνοίας (III
2 and 3), which are among P.'s latest works. They were written against
those who either deny Providence or hold that the world was made by
a bad Demiurge. It is clear that P. is thinking in particular of gnostics.

a. Providence in detail, in the sense of deliberation before the **Deliberation**
work, is excluded; but also deliberation about the whole. *Providence* **excluded**
means only that the universe is κατὰ νοῦν. Nothing else. Creation is not in
time, and Noûs is the archetypon of sensible things not in the chronological order but eternally.

Enn. III 2, 1, l. 10-26:

Πρόνοιαν τοίνυν τὴν μὲν ἐφ' ἑκάστῳ, ἥ ἐστι λόγος πρὸ ἔργου ὅπως δεῖ
γενέσθαι ἢ μὴ γενέσθαι τι τῶν οὐ δεόντων πραχθῆναι ἢ ὅπως τι εἴη ἢ μὴ
εἴη ἡμῖν, ἀφείσθω· ἣν δὲ τοῦ παντὸς λέγομεν πρόνοιαν εἶναι, ταύτην ὑποθέμενοι
5 τὰ ἐφεξῆς συνάπτωμεν. Εἰ μὲν οὖν ἀπό τινος χρόνου πρότερον οὐκ ὄντα τὸν
κόσμον ἐλέγομεν γεγονέναι, τὴν αὐτὴν ἂν τῷ λόγῳ ἐτιθέμεθα, οἵαν καὶ ἐπὶ
τοῖς κατὰ μέρος ἐλέγομεν εἶναι, προόρασίν τινα καὶ λογισμὸν θεοῦ, ὡς ἂν
γένοιτο τόδε τὸ πᾶν, καὶ ὡς ἂν ἄριστα κατὰ τὸ δυνατὸν εἴη. Ἐπεὶ δὲ τὸ ἀεὶ
10 καὶ τὸ οὔποτε μὴ τῷ κόσμῳ τῷδέ φαμεν παρεῖναι, τὴν πρόνοιαν ὀρθῶς ἂν
καὶ ἀκολούθως λέγοιμεν τῷ παντὶ εἶναι τὸ κατὰ νοῦν αὐτὸν εἶναι, καὶ νοῦν πρὸ
αὐτοῦ εἶναι οὐχ ὡς χρόνῳ πρότερον ὄντα, ἀλλ' ὅτι παρὰ νοῦ ἐστι καὶ φύσει
15 πρότερος ἐκεῖνος καὶ αἴτιος τούτου ἀρχέτυπον οἷον καὶ παράδειγμα εἰκόνος
τούτου ὄντος καὶ δι' ἐκεῖνον ὄντος καὶ ὑποστάντος ἀεί. —

b. Our world came into being "by the necessity inherent in the **The "power"**
second nature". For this, which had an "immense power" in itself, **inherent in**
could not be the last of all things. **Noûs**

Enn. III 2, 2, l. 1-2, 8-15:

Ὑφίσταται γοῦν ἐκ τοῦ κόσμου τοῦ ἀληθινοῦ ἐκείνου καὶ ἑνὸς κόσμος οὗτος οὐχ εἷς ἀληθῶς. — Γέγονε δὲ οὐ λογισμῷ τοῦ δεῖν γενέσθαι, ἀλλὰ φύσεως δευτέρας ἀνάγκη· οὐ γὰρ ἦν τοιοῦτον ἐκεῖνο οἷον ἔσχατον εἶναι τῶν ὄντων. Πρῶτον γὰρ ἦν καὶ πολλὴν δύναμιν ἔχον καὶ πᾶσαν· καὶ ταύτην τοίνυν τὴν 10 τοῦ ποιεῖν ἄλλο ἄνευ τοῦ ζητεῖν ποιῆσαι. Ἤδη γὰρ ἂν αὐτόθεν οὐκ εἶχεν, εἰ ἐζήτει, οὐδ' ἂν ἦν ἐκ τῆς αὑτοῦ οὐσίας, ἀλλ' ἦν οἷον τεχνίτης ἀπ' αὑτοῦ τὸ ποιεῖν οὐκ ἔχων, ἀλλ' ἐπακτόν, ἐκ τοῦ μαθεῖν λαβὼν τοῦτο. 15

Similarly, in the ps. Aristotelian treatise Π. κόσμου, cited above (under **1303c**), we find the natural power of the Lord and Governor of the universe opposed to technical help and aid from others:

Οὐδὲν γὰρ ἐπιτεχνήσεως αὐτῷ δεῖ καὶ ὑπηρεσίας τῆς παρ' ἑτέρων, ὥσπερ τοῖς παρ' ἡμῖν ἄρχουσι τῆς πολυχειρίας διὰ τὴν ἀσθένειαν· ἀλλὰ τοῦτο ἦν τὸ θειότατον, τὸ μετὰ ῥαιστώνης καὶ ἁπλῆς κινήσεως παντοδαπὰς ἀποτελεῖν ἰδέας. — οὕτως οὖν καὶ ἡ θεία φύσις ἀπό τινος ἁπλῆς κινήσεως τοῦ πρώτου τὴν δύναμιν εἰς τὰ ξυνεχῆ δίδωσι, καὶ ἀπ' ἐκείνων πάλιν εἰς τὰ πορρωτέρω, μέχρι ἂν διὰ τοῦ παντὸς διεξέλθῃ.

Aristotle, Bekker 398b, 10-14, 19-22 (Didot, vol. III p. 638, l. 1-5, 11-14).

1427—With regard to creation both the terms δύναμις (or δυνάμεις) and λόγος (or λόγοι) are used.

The term Logos used with regard to creation
a. Noûs gives something of itself to ὕλη, and this is λόγος. It flows eternally from Noûs, containing the multiplicity and the opposites that are in the visible world, exactly as the λόγοι σπερματικοί contain in themselves the multiplicity and the opposites that are in individual living beings.

Enn. III 2, 2, l. 15-33:

Νοῦς τοίνυν δούς τι ἑαυτοῦ εἰς ὕλην ἀτρεμὴς καὶ ἥσυχος τὰ πάντα εἰργάζετο· 15 οὗτος δὲ ὁ λόγος ἐκ νοῦ ῥυείς. Τὸ γὰρ ἀπορρέον ἐκ νοῦ λόγος, καὶ ἀεὶ ἀπορρεῖ, ἕως ἂν ᾖ παρὼν ἐν τοῖς οὖσι νοῦς. Ὥσπερ δὲ ἐν λόγῳ τῷ ἐν τῷ σπέρματι ὁμοῦ πάντων καὶ ἐν τῷ αὐτῷ ὄντων καὶ οὐδενὸς οὐδενὶ μαχομένου οὐδὲ διαφερομένου 20 οὐδὲ ἐμποδίου ὄντος, γίνεταί τι ἤδη ἐν ὄγκῳ καὶ ἄλλο μέρος ἀλλαχοῦ καὶ δὴ καὶ ἐμποδίσειεν ἂν ἕτερον ἑτέρῳ καὶ ἀπαναλώσειεν ἄλλο ἄλλο, οὕτω δὴ καὶ ἐξ ἑνὸς νοῦ καὶ τοῦ ἀπ' αὐτοῦ λόγου ἀνέστη τόδε τὸ πᾶν καὶ διέστη καὶ ἐξ ἀνάγκης τὰ μὲν ἐγένετο φίλα καὶ προσηνῆ, τὰ δὲ ἐχθρὰ καὶ πολέμια, καὶ τὰ 25 μὲν ἑκόντα, τὰ δὲ καὶ ἄκοντα ἀλλήλοις ἐλυμήνατο καὶ φθειρόμενα θάτερα γένεσιν ἀλλήλοις εἰργάσατο, καὶ μίαν ἐπ' αὐτοῖς τοιαῦτα ποιοῦσι καὶ πάσχουσιν ὅμως ἁρμονίαν ἀνεστήσατο φθεγγομένων μὲν ἑκάστων τὰ αὑτῶν, τοῦ δὲ λόγου ἐπ' αὐτοῖς τὴν ἁρμονίαν καὶ μίαν τὴν σύνταξιν εἰς τὰ ὅλα ποιουμένου. Ἔστι γὰρ 30 τὸ πᾶν τόδε οὐχ ὥσπερ ἐκεῖ νοῦς καὶ λόγος, ἀλλὰ μετέχον νοῦ καὶ λόγου.

b. Similarly, Logos is explained in the following passage as a rational principle in life, coming forth from Noûs and Soul, without being identical with them, and containing in itself all opposites, uniting them into a harmonious whole.

Enn. III 2, 16, l. 12-54, 56-58:

Ἔστι τοίνυν οὗτος ὁ λόγος — τετολμήσθω γάρ· τάχα δ᾽ ἂν καὶ τύχοιμεν — ἔστι τοίνυν οὗτος οὐκ ἄκρατος νοῦς οὐδ᾽ αὐτονοῦς οὐδέ γε ψυχῆς καθαρᾶς τὸ
15 γένος, ἠρτημένος δὲ ἐκείνης καὶ οἷον ἔκλαμψις ἐξ ἀμφοῖν, νοῦ καὶ ψυχῆς καὶ ψυχῆς κατὰ νοῦν διακειμένης γεννησάντων τὸν λόγον τοῦτον ζωὴν λόγον τινὰ ἡσυχῇ ἔχουσαν. Πᾶσα δὲ ζωὴ ἐνέργεια, καὶ ἡ φαύλη· ἐνέργεια δὲ οὐχ ὡς τὸ πῦρ ἐνεργεῖ, ἀλλ᾽ ἡ ἐνέργεια αὐτῆς, κἂν μὴ αἴσθησίς τις παρῇ, κίνησίς τις οὐκ
20 εἰκῇ. Οἷς γοῦν ἂν παρῇ * καὶ μετάσχῃ ὁπωσοῦν ὁτιοῦν, εὐθὺς λελόγωται, τοῦτο δέ ἐστι μεμόρφωται, ὡς τῆς ἐνεργείας τῆς κατὰ τὴν ζωὴν μορφοῦν δυναμένης καὶ κινούσης οὕτως ὡς μορφοῦν. Ἡ τοίνυν ἐνέργεια αὐτῆς τεχνική, ὥσπερ ἂν ὁ ὀρχούμενος κινούμενος εἴη· ὁ γὰρ ὀρχηστὴς τῇ οὕτω τεχνικῇ ζωῇ ἔοικεν
25 αὐτὸς καὶ ἡ τέχνη αὐτὸν κινεῖ καὶ οὕτω κινεῖ, ὡς τῆς ζωῆς αὐτῆς τοιαύτης πως οὔσης. Ταῦτα μὲν οὖν εἰρήσθω τοῦ οἵαν δεῖ καὶ τὴν ἡντινοῦν ζωὴν ἡγεῖσθαι ἕνεκα. Ἥκων τοίνυν οὗτος ὁ λόγος ἐκ νοῦ ἑνὸς καὶ ζωῆς μιᾶς πλήρους ὄντος
30 ἑκατέρου οὐκ ἔστιν οὔτε ζωὴ μία οὔτε νοῦς τις εἷς οὔτε ἑκασταχοῦ πλήρης οὐδὲ διδοὺς ἑαυτὸν οἷς δίδωσιν ὅλον τε καὶ πάντα. Ἀντιθεὶς δὲ ἀλλήλοις τὰ μέρη καὶ ποιήσας ἐνδεᾶ πολέμου καὶ μάχης σύστασιν καὶ γένεσιν εἰργάσατο καὶ οὕτως ἐστὶν εἷς πᾶς, εἰ μὴ ἓν εἴη. Γενόμενον γὰρ ἑαυτῷ τοῖς μέρεσι πολέμιον
35 οὕτως ἕν ἐστι καὶ φίλον, ὥσπερ ἂν εἰ δράματος λόγος· εἷς ὁ τοῦ δράματος ἔχων ἐν αὐτῷ πολλὰς μάχας. Τὸ μὲν οὖν δρᾶμα τὰ μεμαχημένα οἷον εἰς μίαν ἁρμονίαν ἄγει σύμφωνον, οἷον διήγησιν τὴν πᾶσαν τῶν μαχομένων ποιούμενον **· ἐκεῖ δὲ ἐξ
40 ἑνὸς λόγου ἡ τῶν διαστάτων μάχη· ὥστε μᾶλλον ἄν τις τῇ ἁρμονίᾳ τῇ ἐκ μαχομένων εἰκάσειε καὶ ζητήσει διὰ τί τὰ μαχόμενα ἐν τοῖς λόγοις. Εἰ οὖν καὶ ἐνταῦθα ὀξὺ καὶ βαρὺ <σύμφωνα> *** ποιοῦσι λόγοι καὶ συνίασιν εἰς ἕν, ὄντες ἁρμονίας λόγοι, εἰς αὐτὴν τὴν ἁρμονίαν, ἄλλον λόγον μείζονα, ὄντες ἐλάττους αὐτοὶ καὶ μέρη,
45 ὁρῶμεν δὲ καὶ ἐν τῷ παντὶ τὰ ἐναντία, οἷον λευκὸν μέλαν, θερμὸν ψυχρόν, καὶ δὴ πτερωτὸν ἄπτερον, ἄπουν ὑπόπουν, λογικὸν ἄλογον, πάντα δὲ ζῴου ἑνὸς τοῦ σύμπαντος μέρη, καὶ τὸ πᾶν ὁμολογεῖ ἑαυτῷ τῶν μερῶν πολλαχοῦ μαχομένων, κατὰ λόγον δὲ τὸ πᾶν, ἀνάγκη καὶ τὸν ἕνα τοῦτον λόγον ἐξ ἐναντίων
50 λόγον εἶναι ἕνα, τὴν σύστασιν αὐτῶν καὶ οἷον οὐσίαν τῆς τοιαύτης ἐναντιώσεως φερούσης. Καὶ γὰρ εἰ μὴ πολὺς ἦν, οὐδ᾽ ἂν ἦν πᾶς, οὐδ᾽ ἂν λόγος· λόγος δὲ ὢν διάφορός τε πρὸς αὐτόν ἐστι καὶ ἡ μάλιστα διαφορὰ ἐναντίωσίς ἐστιν· — ὥστε ἄκρως ἕτερον ποιῶν καὶ τὰ ἐναντία ποιήσει ἐξ ἀνάγκης καὶ τέλεος ἔσται,
55 οὐκ εἰ διάφορα μόνον, ἀλλ᾽ εἰ καὶ ἐναντία ποιοῖ εἶναι ἑαυτόν.

---

*   H.-S. keep the reading of most codd.: ἐὰν μὴ παρῇ.
**   The reading ποιούμενος is defended by H.-S.   ***   Added by Br.

It should be noticed that also Philo of Alexandria spoke of Logos with regard to creation (above, **1293**), and that he too described it as the harmonizer of opposites (above, **1306b**). Yet, to say—as Bréhier did [1]—that P. simply reproduced the theory of Logos as it is found in Philo, would be misleading. In fact, there is a great difference between Philo's view and that of Plotinus. As shown above (**1299ff.**) Philo's doctrine was complicated: for him Logos was not only the Stoic notion of universal Law, immanent in nature; it was also the Platonic world of transcendent paradeigmata, the κόσμος νοητός (above, nr. **1293**). For Philo, the Logos *is* primarily *the divine Mind*, or what Plotinus called Noûs. For Plotinus it is not. He refuses explicitly to use the term in this sense. He does speak of δύναμις in Noûs (below, nr. **1428**); he does say that Noûs contains everything in its archetypal form (above, **1369c**); that all things are ὁμοῦ in Noûs and yet distinguished the one from the other, since every νοητόν is a δύναμις ἰδία (V 9, 6). But he does not say that Noûs as such is Logos. On the contrary, he excludes this. Thus, Plotinus marks clearly the difference between Plato's intelligible world and the Stoic conception of logos. Philo's use of the term could give rise to the Christian identification of Logos with the Son of God, that of Plotinus could not.

"Power" and "powers"

1428—As we saw above (**1426b**), the "second nature", i.e. Noûs, was said to possess πολλὴν δύναμιν καὶ πᾶσαν. Δύναμις is a term much used by Plotinus, not only with reference to the intelligible world.

The boundless Power in Noûs

a. In Noûs there is boundless power, because intelligible being does not contain matter, so that it would be limited by the extent of its mass (V 5, 12, l. 3-7). On the other hand, since it is the totality of being, it does contain πλῆθος. Therefore, Plotinus can speak of the "many different powers of the many gods that are in God the Creator", forming together "universal Power which is boundless" (δύναμις πᾶσα, εἰς ἄπειρον ἰοῦσα).

The following passage describes how to imagine and to invoke this Power.

Enn. V 8, 9, l. 7-37:

Ἔστω οὖν ἐν τῇ ψυχῇ φωτεινή τις φαντασία σφαίρας ἔχουσα πάντα ἐν αὐτῇ, εἴτε κινούμενα εἴτε ἑστηκότα, ἢ τὰ μὲν κινούμενα, τὰ δὲ ἑστηκότα. Φυλάττων δὲ ταύτην ἄλλην παρὰ σαυτῷ ἀφελὼν τὸν ὄγκον λαβέ· ἄφελε δὲ 10 καὶ τοὺς τόπους καὶ τὸ τῆς ὕλης ἐν σοὶ φάντασμα, καὶ μὴ πειρῶ αὐτῆς ἄλλην σμικροτέραν λαβεῖν τῷ ὄγκῳ, θεὸν δὲ καλέσας τὸν πεποιηκότα ἧς ἔχεις τὸ φάντασμα εὖξαι ἐλθεῖν. Ὁ δὲ ἥκοι τὸν αὑτοῦ κόσμον φέρων μετὰ πάντων τῶν ἐν αὑτῷ θεῶν εἷς ὢν καὶ πάντες καὶ ἕκαστος πάντες, συνόντες εἰς ἓν καὶ ταῖς 15 μὲν δυνάμεσιν ἄλλοι, τῇ δὲ μιᾷ ἐκείνῃ τῇ πολλῇ πάντες εἷς· μᾶλλον δὲ ὁ εἷς πάντες· οὐ γὰρ ἐπιλείπει αὐτός, ἢν πάντες ἐκεῖνοι γένωνται, ὁμοῦ δέ εἰσι καὶ

---

[1] Plotin, *Ennéades*, texte établi et traduit, vol. III, p. 19: "Nous retrouvons d'abord, dans presque tous ces détails, la théorie du logos sous la forme qu'elle a prise chez Philon d'Alexandrie".

20 ἕκαστος χωρὶς αὖ ἐν στάσει ἀδιαστάτῳ οὐ μορφὴν αἰσθητὴν οὐδεμίαν ἔχων·
ἤδη γὰρ ἂν ὁ μὲν ἄλλοθι, ὁ δέ που ἄλλοθι ἦν, καὶ ἕκαστος δὲ οὐ πᾶς ἐν αὐτῷ·
οὐδὲ μέρη ἄλλα ἔχων ἄλλοις ἢ αὐτῷ οὐδὲ ἕκαστον ὅλον δύναμις κερματισθεῖσα
καὶ τοσαύτη οὖσα, ὅσα τὰ μέρη μετρούμενα. Τὸ δέ ἐστι δύναμις πᾶσα, εἰς
25 ἄπειρον μὲν ἰοῦσα, εἰς ἄπειρον δὲ δυναμένη· καὶ οὕτως ἐστὶν ἐκεῖνος μέγας,
ὡς καὶ τὰ μέρη αὐτοῦ ἄπειρα γεγονέναι. Ποῦ γάρ τι ἔστιν εἰπεῖν, ὅπου μὴ
φθάνει; Μέγας μὲν οὖν καὶ ὅδε ὁ οὐρανὸς καὶ αἱ ἐν αὐτῷ πᾶσαι δυνάμεις ὁμοῦ,
30 ἀλλὰ μείζων ἂν ἦν καὶ ὁπόσος οὐδ' ἂν ἦν εἰπεῖν, εἰ μή τις αὐτῷ συνῆν σώματος
δύναμις μικρά· καίτοι γε μεγάλας ἄν τις φήσειε πυρὸς καὶ τῶν ἄλλων σωμάτων
τὰς δυνάμεις· ἀλλὰ ἤδη ἀπειρίᾳ δυνάμεως ἀληθινῆς φαντάζονται καίουσαι καὶ
φθείρουσαι καὶ θλίβουσαι καὶ πρὸς γένεσιν τῶν ζῴων ὑπουργοῦσαι. Ἀλλὰ ταῦτα
35 μὲν φθείρει, ὅτι καὶ φθείρεται, καὶ συγγεννᾷ, ὅτι καὶ αὐτὰ γίνεται· ἡ δὲ δύναμις
ἡ ἐκεῖ μόνον τὸ εἶναι ἔχει καὶ μόνον τὸ καλὸν εἶναι.

b. Also of the Ideas, which are "together" in Noûs, P. says that *The ideas are Powers* each of them is a particular Power.

Enn. V 9, 6, l. 1-9:

Νοῦς μὲν δὴ ἔστω τὰ ὄντα, καὶ πάντα ἐν αὐτῷ οὐχ ὡς ἐν τόπῳ ἔχων, ἀλλ'
ὡς αὑτὸν ἔχων καὶ ἓν ὢν αὐτοῖς. Πάντα δὲ ὁμοῦ ἐκεῖ καὶ οὐδὲν ἧττον διακε-
κριμένα. Ἐπεὶ καὶ ψυχὴ ὁμοῦ ἔχουσα πολλὰς ἐπιστήμας ἐν ἑαυτῇ οὐδὲν ἔχει
5 συγκεχυμένον καὶ ἑκάστη πράττει τὸ αὑτῆς, ὅταν δέῃ, οὐ συνεφέλκουσα τὰς
ἄλλας, νόημα δὲ ἕκαστον καθαρὸν ἐνεργεῖ ἐκ τῶν ἔνδον αὖ νοημάτων κειμένων.
Οὕτως οὖν καὶ πολὺ μᾶλλον ὁ νοῦς ἐστιν ὁμοῦ πάντα καὶ αὖ οὐχ ὁμοῦ, ὅτι
ἕκαστον δύναμις ἰδία.

Cp. Philo, above, nr. **1294**.

c. Since Noûs as "the second Nature" derives its Power from the *The Absolute Power of the* First Principle, we can hardly wonder that P., in describing this Principle, *First* speaks of the absoluteness (τὸ ἀπερίληπτον) of its power. *Principle*

The passage was cited under **1398b**.

d. In general, "every nature"—i.e. every spiritual or divine Nature, including Soul—must bring forth what comes after it ἐκ δυνάμεως ἀφάτου, *Soul, too,* as was in the First Principle (ὅση ἦν ἐν ἐκείνῳ). "For this Power should *has an* not be stopped, as by limitation from envy, but it should always go on, *unspeakable* until all its effects come to the utmost limits of what is possible, by an *Power* *immense power* (αἰτίᾳ δυνάμεως ἀπλέτου), which sends forth from itself (sc. all that is good) and cannot leave anything without a share in itself".

The passage was cited under **1365a**.

e. But for P., δύναμις is not confined to the spiritual world. As we said above (sub **a**, this nr.) he speaks also of the powers in the οὐρανός:

Μέγας μὲν οὖν καὶ ὅδε ὁ οὐρανὸς καὶ αἱ ἐν αὐτῷ πᾶσαι δυνάμεις, e.q.s. (V 8, 9, l. 33 ff.), and in describing the forces of the sensible universe he says that it contains a great variety of δυνάμεις.

Enn. IV 4, 36, l. 1-27:

Ποικιλώτατον γὰρ τὸ πᾶν καὶ λόγοι πάντες ἐν αὐτῷ καὶ δυνάμεις ἄπειροι καὶ ποικίλαι. Οἷον δή φασι καὶ ἐπ᾽ ἀνθρώπου ἄλλην μὲν δύναμιν ἔχειν ὀφθαλμὸν καὶ ὀστοῦν τόδε, τοδὶ δ᾽ ἄλλην, χειρὸς μὲν τοδὶ καὶ δακτύλου τοῦ ποδός, καὶ οὐδὲν μέρος εἶναι ὃ μὴ ἔχει καὶ οὐ τὴν αὐτὴν δὲ ἔχει — ἀγνοοῦμεν δὲ ἡμεῖς, 5 εἰ μή τις τὰ τοιαῦτα μεμάθηκεν —, οὕτω καὶ πολὺ μᾶλλον· μᾶλλον δέ, ‹ὅτι› ἴχνος ταῦτα ἐκείνων· ἐν τῷ παντὶ ἀδιήγητον δὴ καὶ θαυμαστὴν ποικιλίαν εἶναι δυνάμεων, καὶ δὴ καὶ ἐν τοῖς κατ᾽ οὐρανὸν φερομένοις. Οὐ γὰρ δή, ὥσπερ ἄψυχον οἰκίαν μεγάλην ἄλλως καὶ πολλὴν ἔκ τινων εὐαριθμήτων κατ᾽ εἶδος, 10 οἷον λίθων καὶ ξύλων, εἰ δὲ βούλει, καὶ ἄλλων τινῶν, εἰς κόσμον ἔδει αὐτὸ γεγονέναι, ἀλλ᾽ εἶναι αὐτὸ ἐγρηγορὸς πανταχῇ καὶ ζῶν ἄλλο ἄλλως καὶ μηδὲν δύνασθαι εἶναι, ὃ μή ἐστιν ‹ἐν› αὐτῷ.

Διὸ καὶ ἐνταῦθα λύοιτο ἂν ἡ ἀπορία ἡ πῶς ἐν ζῴῳ ἐμψύχῳ ἄψυχον· οὕτως 15 γὰρ ὁ λόγος φησὶν ἄλλο ἄλλως ζῆν ἐν τῷ ὅλῳ, ἡμᾶς δὲ τὸ μὴ αἰσθητῶς παρ᾽ αὐτοῦ κινούμενον ζῆν μὴ λέγειν· τὸ δέ ἐστιν ἕκαστον ζῶν λανθάνον, καὶ τὸ αἰσθητῶς ζῶν συγκείμενον ἐκ τῶν μὴ αἰσθητῶς μὲν ζώντων, θαυμαστὰς δὲ δυνάμεις εἰς τὸ ζῆν τῷ τοιούτῳ ζῴῳ παρεχομένων. Μὴ γὰρ ἂν κινηθῆναι ἐπὶ 20 τοσαῦτα ἄνθρωπον ἐκ πάντη ἀψύχων τῶν ἐν αὐτῷ δυνάμεων κινούμενον, μηδ᾽ αὖ τὸ πᾶν οὕτω ζῆν μὴ ἑκάστου τῶν ἐν αὐτῷ ζῶντος τὴν οἰκείαν ζωήν, κἂν προαίρεσις αὐτῷ μὴ παρῇ. Ποιεῖ γὰρ καὶ προαιρέσεως οὐ δεηθέν, ἅτε προαι- 25 ρέσεως ὂν προγενέστερον· διὸ καὶ πολλὰ δουλεύει αὐτῶν ταῖς δυνάμεσιν.

f. Not every part of the great living being which is the κόσμος αἰσθητός possesses life perceptible to us. Yet, as is said in the above-cited passage, imperceptibly these parts of the cosmos do live. They do not have προαίρεσις, no "choice" or conscious will. They need not even

be rational powers, as λόγος is, but may be ἄλογοι. Thus in the next chapter of IV 4 it is said that everything that was generated and formed in the universe has an ἄλογος δύναμις.

Enn. IV 4, 37, l. 11-26:

Ἔχειν μὲν οὖν ἕκαστον δύναμίν τινα ἄλογον φατέον ἐν τῷ παντὶ πλασθὲν καὶ μορφωθὲν καὶ μετειληφός πως ψυχῆς παρὰ τοῦ ὅλου ὄντος ἐμψύχου καὶ περιει- λημμένον ὑπὸ τοιούτου καὶ μόριον ὂν ἐμψύχου — οὐδὲν γὰρ ἐν αὐτῷ ὅ τι μὴ 15

μέρος —, ἄλλα δὲ ἄλλων πρὸς τὸ δρᾶν δυνατώτερα, καὶ τῶν ἐπὶ γῆς τὰ τῶν οὐρανίων μᾶλλον, ἅτε ἐναργεστέρᾳ φύσει χρώμενα, καὶ γίνεσθαι πολλὰ κατὰ τὰς δυνάμεις ταύτας, οὐ τῇ προαιρέσει ἀφ' ὧν δοκεῖ ἰέναι τὸ δρώμενον — ἔστι γὰρ καὶ ἐν τοῖς προαίρεσιν οὐκ ἔχουσιν —, οὐδὲ ἐπιστραφέντων τῇ δόσει τῆς δυνάμεως, κἂν ψυχῆς τι ἀπ' αὐτῶν ἴῃ. Γένοιτο γὰρ ἂν καὶ ζῷα ἐκ ζῴου οὐ τῆς προαιρέσεως ποιούσης οὐδ' αὖ ἐλαττουμένου οὐδ' αὖ παρακολουθοῦντος· αὐτὸ γὰρ <οὐκ> * ἦν ἡ προαίρεσις, εἰ ἔχοι, ἡ ποιοῦσα. Εἰ δὲ μὴ ἔχοι τι προαίρεσιν
5 ζῷον, ἔτι μᾶλλον τὸ μὴ παρακολουθεῖν. [1]

From all this may be concluded that for P., on the one hand, the "power" of the **Conclusion** spiritual world is more spiritual than λόγος is. Λόγος for P. is related to ὕλη, while the "powers" of the spiritual world are not. On the other hand, P. knows "powers" in the sensible universe, and these powers are not eternal. They may be ἄλογοι.

As to this view of the visible world as being full of "powers", cp. Philo, nr. **1303b, c**, and what is noticed there.

1429—The multiform variety of nature is for P. an argument in defence of Providence: things ought not to be the same; by their very variety **Excusatio** the world has a harmonious beauty, worked by the all-embracing Logos. **providentiae**

a. *Enn.* III 2, 11, l. 1-16:

Πότερα δὲ φυσικαῖς ἀνάγκαις οὕτως ἕκαστα καὶ ἀκολουθίαις καὶ ὅπῃ δυνατὸν καλῶς; Ἢ οὔ, ἀλλ' ὁ λόγος ταῦτα πάντα ποιεῖ ἄρχων καὶ οὕτω βούλεται καὶ τὰ λεγόμενα κακὰ αὐτὸς κατὰ λόγον ποιεῖ οὐ βουλόμενος πάντα ἀγαθὰ
5 εἶναι, ὥσπερ ἂν εἴ τις τεχνίτης οὐ πάντα τὰ ἐν τῷ ζῴῳ ὀφθαλμοὺς ποιεῖ· οὕτως οὐδ' ὁ λόγος πάντα θεοὺς εἰργάζετο, ἀλλὰ τὰ μὲν θεούς, τὰ δὲ δαίμονας, δευτέραν φύσιν, εἶτα ἀνθρώπους καὶ ζῷα ἐφεξῆς, οὐ φθόνῳ, ἀλλὰ λόγῳ ποικιλίαν νοερὰν ἔχοντι. Ἡμεῖς δέ, ὥσπερ οἱ ἄπειροι γραφικῆς τέχνης αἰτιῶνται, ὡς οὐ καλὰ τὰ χρώματα πανταχοῦ, ὁ δὲ ἄρα τὰ προσήκοντα ἀπέδωκεν ἑκάστῳ τόπῳ· καὶ αἱ πόλεις δὲ οὐκ ἐξ ἴσων καὶ εἰ εὐνομίᾳ ** χρῶνται, ἢ εἴ τις δρᾶμα μέμφοιτο, ὅτι μὴ πάντες ἥρωες ἐν αὐτῷ, ἀλλὰ καὶ οἰκέτης καί τις ἀγροῖκος καὶ φαύλως
5 φθεγγόμενος· τὸ δὲ οὐ καλόν ἐστιν, εἴ τις τοὺς χείρους ἐξέλοι, καὶ ἐκ τούτων συμπληρούμενον.

Many of the questions dealt with and many of the arguments used by the Stoics in their theodicy recur in this treatise of Plotinus.

b. The world was not made by deliberation; but its order is so **The world is** reasonable, that it might have been made so in the most perfect sense. **reasonable but not by**

Enn. III 2, 14, l. 1-6: **deliberation**

Ἔχει τοίνυν ἡ διάταξις οὕτω κατὰ νοῦν, ὡς ἄνευ λογισμοῦ εἶναι, οὕτω

---

* <οὐκ> add. Br.
[1] See above, ad **1422a**.
** καὶ εἰ εὐνομίᾳ Page, followed by H.-S.; καὶ αἱ εὐνομίαι codd.

δὲ εἶναι, ὡς, εἴ τις ἄριστα δύναιτο λογισμῷ χρῆσθαι, θαυμάσαι, ὅτι μὴ ἂν
ἄλλως εὗρε λογισμὸς ποιῆσαι, ὁποῖόν τι γινώσκεται καὶ ἐν ταῖς καθ' ἕκαστα
φύσεσι, γινομένων εἰς ἀεὶ νοερώτερον ἢ κατὰ λογισμοῦ διάταξιν.

   c. Evil men have their due place and function in the whole. Thus,
the beauty of the universe is not disturbed by their wickedness.

Wicked men
have their
due place in
the whole

Enn. III 2, 17, l. 64-89:

   Καὶ γὰρ ἐν τῷ ὅλῳ τὸ πρέπον καὶ τὸ καλόν, εἰ ἕκαστος οὗ δεῖ τετάξεται
φθεγγόμενος κακὰ ἐν τῷ σκότῳ καὶ τῷ ταρτάρῳ· ἐνταῦθα γὰρ καλὸν τὸ οὕτω
φθέγγεσθαι· καὶ τὸ ὅλον τοῦτο καλόν, οὐκ εἰ λίθος * εἴη ἕκαστος, ἀλλ' εἰ τὸν
φθόγγον τὸν αὑτοῦ εἰσφερόμενος συντελεῖ εἰς μίαν ἁρμονίαν ζωὴν καὶ αὐτὸς
φωνῶν, ἐλάττω δὲ καὶ χείρω καὶ ἀτελεστέραν· ὥσπερ οὐδ' ἐν σύριγγι φωνὴ
μία, ἀλλὰ καὶ ἐλάττων τις οὖσα καὶ ἀμυδρὰ πρὸς ἁρμονίαν τῆς πάσης σύριγγος
συντελεῖ, ὅτι μεμέρισται ἡ ἁρμονία εἰς οὐκ ἴσα μέρη καὶ ἄνισοι μὲν οἱ φθόγγοι
πάντες, ὁ δὲ τέλεος εἷς ἐκ πάντων. Καὶ δὴ καὶ ὁ λόγος ὁ πᾶς εἷς, μεμέρισται
δὲ οὐκ εἰς ἴσα· ὅθεν καὶ τοῦ παντὸς διάφοροι τόποι, βελτίους καὶ χείρους, καὶ
ψυχαὶ οὐκ ἴσαι ἐναρμόττουσιν οὕτω τοῖς οὐκ ἴσοις, καὶ οὕτω καὶ ἐνταῦθα
συμβαίνει καὶ τοὺς τόπους ἀνομοίους καὶ τὰς ψυχὰς οὐ τὰς αὐτάς, ἀλλ' ἀνίσους
οὔσας καὶ ἀνομοίους τοὺς τρόπους ἐχούσας, οἷον κατὰ σύριγγος ἢ τινος ἄλλου
ὀργάνου ἀνομοιότητας, ἐν τόποις τε πρὸς ἄλληλα διαφέρουσιν εἶναι <καὶ> καθ'
ἕκαστον τόπον τὰ αὐτῶν συμφώνως καὶ τοῖς τόποις καὶ τῷ ὅλῳ φθεγγομένας.
Καὶ τὸ κακῶς αὐταῖς ἐν καλῷ κατὰ τὸ πᾶν κείσεται καὶ τὸ παρὰ φύσιν τῷ
παντὶ κατὰ φύσιν καὶ οὐδὲν ἧττον φθόγγος ἐλάττων. Ἀλλ' οὐ χεῖρον πεποίηκε
τὸ ὅλον οὕτω φθεγγομένη, ὥσπερ οὐδὲ ὁ δήμιος πονηρὸς ὢν χείρω πεποίηκε
τὴν εὐνομουμένην πόλιν, εἰ δεῖ καὶ ἄλλῃ χρῆσθαι εἰκόνι. Δεῖ γὰρ καὶ τούτου ἐν
πόλει — δεῖ δὲ καὶ ἀνθρώπου τοιούτου πολλάκις — καὶ καλῶς καὶ οὗτος κεῖται.

The part of
man and his
free will

   1430—Within the framework of cosmic order man is placed as a
reasonable being, not the supreme, but for a large part free, and hence
responsible for his deeds.

   a. Man must execute his own affairs and fight his own victories.
He should not expect God to do this for him and in his place.

Enn. III 2, 8, l. 7-16, 36-52:

What about
injustice in
the world?

Θαυμάζεται δὲ ἐν ἀνθρώποις ἀδικία, ὅτι ἄνθρωπον ἀξιοῦσιν ἐν τῷ παντὶ
τὸ τίμιον εἶναι ὡς οὐδενὸς ὄντος σοφωτέρου. Τὸ δὲ κεῖται ** ἐν μέσῳ θεῶν καὶ
θηρίων καὶ ῥέπει ἐπ' ἄμφω καὶ ὁμοιοῦνται οἱ μὲν τῷ ἑτέρῳ, οἱ δὲ τῷ ἑτέρῳ,
οἱ δὲ μεταξὺ εἰσιν, οἱ πολλοί. Οἱ δὴ κακυνθέντες εἰς τὸ ἐγγὺς ζώων ἀλόγων

---

* H.-S. adopt Sleeman's suggestion, Λίνος (Class. Qu. 1926, p. 153), explaining:
nam imperitus quoque aliquantum affert ad harmoniam.

** The MSS reading Τὸ δὲ κεῖται ἄνθρωπος is maintained by H.-S.

καὶ θηρίων ἰέναι ἕλκουσι τοὺς μέσους καὶ βιάζονται· οἱ δὲ βελτίους μέν εἰσι
τῶν βιαζομένων, κρατοῦνταί γε μὴν ὑπὸ τῶν χειρόνων· ἢ εἰσι χείρους καὶ
5 αὐτοὶ καὶ οὐκ εἰσὶν ἀγαθοὶ οὐδὲ παρεσκεύασαν αὐτοὺς μὴ παθεῖν. — Ἔνθα οὐ
θεὸν ἔδει ὑπὲρ τῶν ἀπολέμων αὐτὸν μάχεσθαι· σώζεσθαι γὰρ ἐκ πολέμων φησὶ
δεῖν ὁ νόμος ἀνδριζομένους, ἀλλ᾽ οὐκ εὐχομένους· οὐδὲ γὰρ κομίζεσθαι καρποὺς
εὐχομένους ἀλλὰ γῆς ἐπιμελουμένους, οὐδέ γε ὑγιαίνειν μὴ ὑγιείας ἐπιμελου-
10 μένους· οὐδ᾽ ἀγανακτεῖν δέ, εἰ τοῖς φαύλοις πλείους γίνοιντο καρποὶ ἢ ὅλως
αὐτοῖς γεωργοῦσιν ἢ ἄμεινον. Ἔπειτα γελοῖον τὰ μὲν ἄλλα πάντα τὰ κατὰ
τὸν βίον γνώμῃ τῇ ἑαυτῶν πράττειν, κἂν μὴ ταύτῃ πράττωσιν, ἢ θεοῖς φίλα,
15 σώζεσθαι δὲ μόνον παρὰ θεῶν οὐδὲ ταῦτα ποιήσαντας, δι᾽ ὧν κελεύουσιν αὐτοὺς
οἱ θεοὶ σώζεσθαι. Καὶ τοίνυν οἱ θάνατοι αὐτοῖς βελτίους ἢ τὸ οὕτως ζῶντας
εἶναι, ὅπως ζῆν αὐτοὺς οὐκ ἐθέλουσιν οἱ ἐν τῷ παντὶ νόμοι· ὥστε τῶν ἐναντίων
γιγνομένων, εἰρήνης ἐν ἀνοίαις καὶ κακίαις πάσαις φυλαττομένης, ἀμελῶς ἂν
20 ἔσχε τὰ τῆς προνοίας ἐώσης κρατεῖν οὕτως τὰ χείρω. Ἄρχουσι δὲ οἱ κακοὶ
ἀρχομένων ἀνανδρίᾳ· τοῦτο γὰρ δίκαιον, οὐκ ἐκεῖνο.

About the μέση τάξις of man, above, nr. **1372a**.

b. Providence is not so, that nothing should be left to man. What
is left to him is: to perform his own task,—which means: *to be man*.

Enn. III 2, 9, l. 1-8:

Οὐ γὰρ δὴ οὕτως τὴν πρόνοιαν εἶναι δεῖ, ὥστε μηδὲν ἡμᾶς εἶναι· πάντα
δὲ οὔσης προνοίας καὶ μόνης αὐτῆς οὐδ᾽ ἂν εἴη· τίνος γὰρ ἂν ἔτι εἴη; Ἀλλὰ
μόνον ἂν εἴη τὸ θεῖον. Τοῦτο δὲ καὶ νῦν ἐστι· καὶ πρὸς ἄλλο δὲ ἐλήλυθεν,
οὐχ ἵνα ἀνέλῃ τὸ ἄλλο, ἀλλ᾽ ἐπιόντι οἷον ἀνθρώπῳ ἦν ἐπ᾽ αὐτῷ τηροῦσα τὸν
ἄνθρωπον ὄντα· τοῦτο δέ ἐστι νόμῳ προνοίας ζῶντα, ὁ δή ἐστι πράττοντα
ὅσα ὁ νόμος αὐτῆς λέγει.

To man the task is left of being man

c. The old Socratic principle of "Nobody sins willingly" does not
take away responsibility. Surely the laws of nature are fixed, but not
in such a sense that human liberty would be excluded. Man and his will
is an independent cause.

Enn. III 2, 10, l. 1-19:

Man is an independent principle

Ἀλλ᾽ εἰ ἄνθρωποι ἄκοντές εἰσι κακοὶ καὶ τοιοῦτοι οὐχ ἑκόντες, οὔτ᾽ ἄν τις
τοὺς ἀδικοῦντας αἰτιάσαιτο, οὔτε τοὺς πάσχοντας ὡς δι᾽ αὐτοὺς ταῦτα πάσχοντας. Εἰ δὲ δὴ καὶ ἀνάγκη οὕτω κακοὺς γίνεσθαι εἴτε ὑπὸ τῆς φορᾶς εἴτε
5 τῆς ἀρχῆς διδούσης τὸ ἀκόλουθον ἐντεῦθεν, φυσικῶς οὕτως. Εἰ δὲ δὴ ὁ λόγος
αὐτός ἐστιν ὁ ποιῶν, πῶς οὐκ ἄδικα οὕτως; Ἀλλὰ τὸ μὲν ἄκοντες, ὅτι ἁμαρτία
ἀκούσιον· τοῦτο δὲ οὐκ ἀναιρεῖ τὸ αὐτοὺς τοὺς πράττοντας παρ᾽ αὐτῶν εἶναι,
ἀλλ᾽ ὅτι αὐτοὶ ποιοῦσι, διὰ τοῦτο καὶ αὐτοὶ ἁμαρτάνουσιν· ἢ οὐδ᾽ ἂν ὅλως

ἥμαρτον μὴ αὐτοὶ οἱ ποιοῦντες ὄντες. Τὸ δὲ τῆς ἀνάγκης οὐκ ἔξωθεν, ἀλλ' ὅτι 10
πάντως. Τὸ δὲ τῆς φορᾶς οὐχ ὥστε μηδὲν ἐφ' ἡμῖν εἶναι· καὶ γὰρ εἰ ἔξωθεν τὸ
πᾶν, οὕτως ἂν ἦν, ὡς αὐτοὶ οἱ ποιοῦντες ἐβούλοντο· ὥστε οὐκ ἂν αὐτοῖς ἐναντία
ἐτίθεντο ἄνθρωποι οὐδ' ἂν ἀσεβεῖς, εἰ θεοὶ ἐποίουν. Νῦν δὲ παρ' αὐτῶν τοῦτο. 15
'Αρχῆς δὲ δοθείσης τὸ ἐφεξῆς περαίνεται συμπαραλαμβανομένων εἰς τὴν
ἀκολουθίαν καὶ τῶν ὅσαι εἰσὶν ἀρχαί· ἀρχαὶ δὲ καὶ ἄνθρωποι. Κινοῦνται γοῦν
πρὸς τὰ καλὰ οἰκείᾳ φύσει καὶ ἀρχὴ αὕτη αὐτεξούσιος.

d. Thus, in describing the laws of the universe in IV 4 (a description
which will be cited in our next nr.) P. says that man is only partly subject to these laws and compares him with a labourer in free service:
he does receive orders, but moderate ones; he is not a slave, in complete
possession of a master.

Man is only   *Enn.* IV 4, 34, 1. 1-7:
partly
subject to   'Ημᾶς δὲ διδόντας τὸ μέρος αὐτῶν εἰς τὸ πάσχειν, ὅσον ἦν ἡμέτερον ἐκείνου
the cosmic   τοῦ σώματος, μὴ τὸ πᾶν ἐκείνου νομίζοντας, μέτρια παρ' αὐτοῦ πάσχειν·
laws   ὥσπερ οἱ ἔμφρονες τῶν θητευόντων τὸ μέν τι τοῖς δεσπόζουσιν ὑπηρετοῦντες,
                 τὸ δ' αὐτῶν ὄντες, μετριωτέρων τῶν παρὰ τοῦ δεσπότου ἐπιταγμάτων διὰ 5
                 τοῦτο τυγχάνοντες, ἅτε μὴ ἀνδράποδα ὄντες μηδὲ τὸ πᾶν ἄλλου.

The laws of   **1431**—In connection with the question of "How the stars hear our
the universe   prayers" P. dealt amply with the problem of how cosmic forces work
in the long excursus of his Περὶ ψυχῆς ἀποριῶν Β' (IV 4), cc. 30-45.
Here too, his first care is to exclude deliberation.

a. He describes the motion of the universe as a dance in which
each dancer performs spontaneously those movements that are needed
for the order of the whole.

The cosmic   *Enn.* IV 4, 33, 1. 1-41:
dance
Τῆς δὴ φορᾶς τὸ εἰκῇ οὐκ ἐχούσης, ἀλλὰ λόγῳ τῷ κατὰ τὸ ζῷον φερομένης,
ἔδει καὶ συμφωνίαν τοῦ ποιοῦντος πρὸς τὸ πάσχον εἶναι καί τινα τάξιν εἰς
ἄλληλα καὶ πρὸς ἄλληλα συντάσσουσαν, ὥστε καθ' ἑκάστην σχέσιν τῆς φορᾶς
καὶ τῶν αὖ ὑπὸ τὴν φορὰν ἄλλην καὶ ἄλλην τὴν διάθεσιν εἶναι, οἷον μίαν ὄρχησιν 5
ἐν ποικίλῃ χορείᾳ ποιούντων· ἐπεὶ καὶ ἐν ταῖς παρ' ἡμῖν ὀρχήσεσι τὰ μὲν ἔξω
πρὸς τὴν ὄρχησιν καθ' ἕκαστον τῶν κινημάτων ὡς ἑτέρως μεταβαλλόντων τῶν
συντελούντων πρὸς τὴν ὄρχησιν, αὐλῶν τε καὶ ᾠδῶν καὶ τῶν ἄλλων τῶν συνηρ- 10
τημένων, τί ἄν τις λέγοι φανερῶν ὄντων; 'Αλλὰ τὰ μέρη τοῦ τὴν ὄρχησιν παρεχομένου καθ' ἕκαστον σχῆμα ἐξ ἀνάγκης οὐκ ἂν ὡσαύτως δύναιτο λέγειν τῶν
μελῶν τοῦ σώματος ταύτῃ συνεπομένων καὶ καμπτομένων, καὶ πιεζομένου μὲν
ἑτέρου, ἀνιεμένου δὲ ἄλλου, καὶ τοῦ μὲν πονοῦντος, τοῦ δὲ ἀναπνοήν τινα ἐν τῷ 15

διαφόρῳ σχηματισμῷ δεχομένου. Καὶ ἡ μὲν προαίρεσις τοῦ ὀρχουμένου πρὸς
ἄλλο βλέπει, τὰ δὲ πάσχει τῇ ὀρχήσει ἑπομένως καὶ ὑπουργεῖ τῇ ὀρχήσει καὶ
συναποτελεῖ τὴν πᾶσαν, ὥστε τὸν ἔμπειρον ὀρχήσεως εἰπεῖν ἄν, ὡς τῷ τοιούτῳ
σχηματισμῷ αἴρεται μὲν ὑψοῦ τοδὶ μέλος τοῦ σώματος, συγκάμπτεται δὲ τοδί,
τοδὶ δὲ ἀποκρύπτεται, ταπεινὸν δὲ ἄλλο γίνεται, οὐκ ἄλλως τοῦ ὀρχηστοῦ
προελομένου τοῦτο ποιεῖν, ἀλλ' ἐν τῇ τοῦ ὅλου σώματος ὀρχήσει θέσιν ταύτην
ἀναγκαίαν ἴσχοντος τοῦδε τοῦ μέρους τοῦ τὴν ὄρχησιν διαπεραίνοντος. Τοῦτον
τοίνυν τὸν τρόπον καὶ τὰ ἐν οὐρανῷ φατέον ποιεῖν, ὅσα ποιεῖ, τὰ δὲ καὶ σημαίνειν, μᾶλλον δὲ τὸν μὲν ὅλον κόσμον τὴν ὅλην αὐτοῦ ζωὴν ἐνεργεῖν κινοῦντα
ἐν αὐτῷ τὰ μέρη τὰ μεγάλα καὶ μετασχηματίζοντα ἀεί, τὰς δὲ σχέσεις τῶν
μερῶν πρὸς ἄλληλα καὶ πρὸς τὸ ὅλον καὶ τὰς διαφόρους αὐτῶν θέσεις ἑπόμενα
καὶ τὰ ἄλλα, ὡς ζῴου ἑνὸς κινουμένου, παρέχεσθαι, ὡδὶ μὲν ἴσχοντα κατὰ τὰς
ὡδὶ σχέσεις καὶ θέσεις καὶ σχηματισμούς, ὡδὶ δὲ κατὰ τὰς ὡδί, ὡς μὴ τοὺς
σχηματιζομένους τοὺς ποιοῦντας εἶναι, ἀλλὰ τὸν σχηματίζοντα, μηδ' αὖ τὸν
σχηματίζοντα ἄλλο ποιοῦντα ἄλλο ποιεῖν· οὐ γὰρ εἰς ἄλλο· ἀλλ' αὐτὸν πάντα
τὰ γινόμενα εἶναι, ἐκεῖ μὲν τὰ σχήματα, ἐνθαδὶ δὲ τὰ συνεπόμενα τοῖς σχήμασιν
ἀναγκαῖα παθήματα περὶ τὸ οὑτωσὶ κινούμενον ζῷον εἶναι, καὶ αὖ περὶ τὸ
οὑτωσὶ συγκείμενον καὶ συνεστὼς φύσει καὶ πάσχον καὶ δρῶν εἰς αὐτὸ ἀνάγκαις.

b. What is the power of the figures of this dance?—P. emphasizes
that the parts of the cosmos (e.g. the heavenly bodies) do not have any
will of their own. The whole living Being, which is the Universe, has but
one will, and the parts perform their motions in subordination to this.

Enn. IV 4, 35, l. 1-38:   The universe
is one
living being

Πῶς δὴ οὖν αὗται αἱ δυνάμεις; Σαφέστερον γὰρ πάλιν λεκτέον. Τί τὸ
τρίγωνον παρὰ τὸ τρίγωνον διάφορον ἔχει; Τί δὲ ὁδὶ πρὸς τονδί, καὶ κατὰ τί
τοδὶ ἐργάζεται καὶ μέχρι τίνος; Ἐπειδὴ οὔτε τοῖς σώμασιν αὐτῶν οὔτε ταῖς
προαιρέσεσιν ἀπέδομεν τὰς ποιήσεις· τοῖς μὲν σώμασιν, ὅτι μὴ μόνον σώματος
ἦν ποιήματα τὰ γινόμενα, ταῖς δὲ προαιρέσεσιν, ὅτι ἄτοπον ἦν <κατὰ> προαίρεσιν
θεοὺς ποιεῖν ἄτοπα. Εἰ δὲ μνημονεύοιμεν, ὅτι ζῷον ἓν ὑπεθέμεθα εἶναι, καὶ ὅτι
οὕτως ἔχον συμπαθὲς αὐτὸ ἑαυτῷ ἐξ ἀνάγκης ἔδει εἶναι, καὶ δὴ καὶ ὅτι κατὰ
λόγον ἡ διέξοδος τῆς ζωῆς σύμφωνος ἑαυτῇ ἅπασα, καὶ ὅτι τὸ εἰκῇ οὐκ ἔστιν
ἐν τῇ ζωῇ, ἀλλὰ μία ἁρμονία καὶ τάξις, καὶ οἱ σχηματισμοὶ κατὰ λόγον, καὶ
κατ' ἀριθμοὺς δὲ ἕκαστα καὶ τὰ χορεύοντα ζῴου μέρη, ἄμφω ἀνάγκη ὁμολογεῖν
τὴν ἐνέργειαν τοῦ παντὸς εἶναι, τά τε ἐν αὐτῷ γινόμενα σχήματα καὶ τὰ σχη-
ματιζόμενα μέρη αὐτοῦ καὶ τὰ τούτοις ἑπόμενα, καὶ οὕτω καὶ τοῦτον τὸν τρόπον
ζῆν τὸ πᾶν καὶ τὰς δυνάμεις εἰς τοῦτο συμβάλλειν, ὥσπερ καὶ ἔχουσαι ἐγένοντο
ὑπὸ τοῦ ἐν λόγοις πεποιηκότος· καὶ τὰ μὲν σχήματα οἷον λόγους εἶναι ἢ διαστάσεις ζῴου καὶ ῥυθμοὺς καὶ σχέσεις ζῴου κατὰ λόγον, τὰ δὲ διεστηκότα καὶ

ἐσχηματισμένα μέλη ἄλλα· καὶ εἶναι τοῦ ζῴου δυνάμεις χωρὶς τῆς προαιρέσεως ἄλλας τὰς ὡς ζῴου μέρη, ἐπεὶ τὸ τῆς προαιρέσεως αὐτοῖς ἔξω καὶ οὐ συντελοῦν πρὸς τοῦ ζῴου τοῦδε τὴν φύσιν. Μία γὰρ ἡ προαίρεσις ἑνὸς ζῴου, 2, αἱ δὲ δυνάμεις αἱ ἄλλαι αὐτοῦ πρὸς ἄλλο πολλαί. Ὅσαι δ᾽ ἐν αὐτῷ προαιρέσεις, πρὸς τὸ αὐτό, πρὸς ὃ καὶ ἡ τοῦ παντὸς ἡ μία. Ἐπιθυμία μὲν γὰρ ἄλλου πρὸς ἄλλο τῶν ἐν αὐτῷ· λαβεῖν γάρ τι τῶν ἑτέρων ἐθέλει μέρος τὸ ἄλλο μέρος ἐνδεὲς ὂν αὐτοῦ· καὶ θυμὸς πρὸς ἕτερον, ὅταν τι παραλυπῇ, καὶ ἡ αὔξησις παρ᾽ ἄλλου 30 καὶ ἡ γένεσις εἰς ἄλλο τῶν μερῶν. Τὸ δ᾽ ὅλον καὶ ἐν τούτοις μὲν ταῦτα ποιεῖ, αὐτὸ δὲ τὸ ἀγαθὸν ζητεῖ, μᾶλλον δὲ βλέπει. Τοῦτο τοίνυν καὶ ἡ ὀρθὴ προαίρεσις ἡ ὑπὲρ τὰ πάθη ζητεῖ καὶ εἰς τὸ αὐτὸ ταύτῃ συμβάλλει· ἐπεὶ καὶ τῶν παρ᾽ ἄλλῳ θητευόντων πολλὰ μὲν τῶν ἔργων αὐτοῖς βλέπει πρὸς τὰ ἐπιταχθέντα 35 ὑπὸ τοῦ δεσπότου, ἡ δὲ τοῦ ἀγαθοῦ ὄρεξις πρὸς τὸ αὐτό, πρὸς ὃ καὶ ὁ δεσπότης.

c. P. concludes from this that, since in the universe things happen by a kind of physical necessity, evil cannot be said to be produced by the will of the gods.

Evil not to be attributed to the will of the gods

Enn. IV 4, 39, l. 18-28:

Εἰ δὴ ταῦτα ὀρθῶς λέγεται, λύοιντο ἂν ἤδη αἱ ἀπορίαι, ἥ τε πρὸς τὸ κακῶν δόσιν παρὰ θεῶν γίνεσθαι τῷ μήτε προαιρέσεις εἶναι τὰς ποιούσας, φυσικαῖς 20 δὲ ἀνάγκαις γίνεσθαι ὅσα ἐκεῖθεν, ὡς μερῶν πρὸς μέρη, καὶ ἑπόμενα ἑνὸς ζωῇ, καὶ τῷ πολλὰ παρ᾽ αὐτῶν τοῖς γινομένοις προστιθέναι, καὶ τῷ τῶν διδομένων παρ᾽ ἑκάστων οὐ κακῶν ὄντων ἐν τῇ μίξει γίνεσθαι ἄλλο τι, καὶ τῷ μὴ ἕνεκα ἑκάστου ἀλλ᾽ ἕνεκα τοῦ ὅλου τὴν ζωὴν <εἶναι>, καὶ τὴν ὑποκειμένην δὲ 25 φύσιν ἄλλο λαβοῦσαν ἄλλο πάσχειν καὶ μηδὲ δύνασθαι κρατῆσαι τοῦ δοθέντος.

d. Thus, the effect of prayers is a mere mechanical reaction, due to the organical unity of the cosmos. The heavenly bodies do not need either perception or memory to "hear" our prayers and "act" on them; for what is called their influence is nothing but a reaction which happens automatically.

The effect of prayers an automatic process

The influence of the stars not due to will

Enn. IV 4, 41, l. 1-3; c. 42, l. 1-6:

Καὶ γίνεται τὸ κατὰ τὴν εὐχὴν συμπαθοῦς μέρους μέρει γενομένου, ὥσπερ ἐν μιᾷ νευρᾷ τεταμένῃ· κινηθεῖσα γὰρ ἐκ τοῦ κάτω καὶ ἄνω ἔχει τὴν κίνησιν.—

(42) Ὥστε οὔτε μνήμης διὰ τοῦτο δεήσει τοῖς ἄστροις, οὗπερ χάριν καὶ ταῦτα πεπραγμάτευται, οὔτε αἰσθήσεων ἀναπεμπομένων· οὐδὲ ἐπινεύσεις τοῦτον τὸν τρόπον εὐχαῖς, ὡς οἴονταί τινες, προαιρετικάς τινας, ἀλλὰ καὶ μετ᾽ εὐχῆς γίνεσθαί τι δοτέον καὶ εὐχῆς ἄνευ παρ᾽ αὐτῶν, ᾗ μέρη καὶ <αὐτὰ> ἑνός. 5

1432—In the same way the effect of magic art must be explained.

a. *Enn.* IV 4, 40, l. 1-6, 12-27, 27-33:

Τὰς δὲ γοητείας πῶς; Ἡ τῇ συμπαθείᾳ, καὶ τῷ πεφυκέναι συμφωνίαν εἶναι ὁμοίων καὶ ἐναντίωσιν ἀνομοίων, καὶ τῇ τῶν δυνάμεων τῶν πολλῶν ποικιλίᾳ εἰς ἓν ζῷον συντελούντων. Καὶ γὰρ μηδενὸς μηχανωμένου ἄλλου πολλὰ ἕλκεται
5 καὶ γοητεύεται· καὶ ἡ ἀληθινὴ μαγεία ἡ ἐν τῷ παντὶ φιλία καὶ τὸ νεῖκος αὖ.—

The sorcerer is the man who knows and makes use of the forces in the universe, which attract and repel one another.

Καὶ συνάπτουσι δὲ ἄλλην ψυχὴν ἄλλῃ, ὥσπερ ἂν εἰ φυτὰ διεστηκότα ἐξαψά-
15 μενοι πρὸς ἄλληλα· καὶ τοῖς σχήμασι δὲ προσχρῶνται δυνάμεις ἔχουσι, καὶ αὐτοὺς σχηματίζοντες ὡδὶ ἐπάγουσιν ἐπ' αὐτοὺς ἀψοφητὶ δυνάμεις ἐν ἑνὶ ὄντες εἰς ἕν· ἐπεὶ ἔξω γε τοῦ παντὸς εἴ τις ὑπόθοιτο τὸν τοιοῦτον, οὔτ' ἂν ἕλξειεν οὔτ' ἂν καταγάγοι ἐπαγωγαῖς ἢ καταδέσμοις· ἀλλὰ νῦν, ὅτι μὴ οἷον
20 ἀλλαχοῦ ἄγει, ἔχει ἄγειν εἰδὼς ὅπη τι ἐν τῷ ζῴῳ πρὸς ἄλλο ἄγεται. Πέφυκε δὲ καὶ ἐπῳδῆς τῷ μέλει καὶ τῇ τοιᾷδε ἠχῇ καὶ τῷ σχήματι τοῦ δρῶντος—ἕλκει γὰρ τὰ τοιαῦτα, οἷον τὰ ἐλεεινὰ σχήματα καὶ φθέγματα—ἄγεσθαι ἡ ψυχή· οὐ γὰρ ἡ προαίρεσις οὐδ' ὁ λόγος ὑπὸ μουσικῆς θέλγεται, ἀλλ' ἡ ἄλογος ψυχή,
25 καὶ οὐ θαυμάζεται ἡ γοητεία ἡ τοιαύτη· καίτοι φιλοῦσι κηλούμενοι, κἂν μὴ τοῦτο αἰτῶνται παρὰ τῶν τῇ μουσικῇ χρωμένων.

Thus, the influence of prayers is impersonal.

Καὶ τὰς ἄλλας δὲ εὐχὰς οὐ τῆς προαιρέσεως ἀκουούσης οἰητέον· οὐ γὰρ οἱ θελγόμενοι ταῖς ἐπῳδαῖς οὕτως, οὐδ' ὅταν γοητεύῃ ὄφις ἀνθρώπους, σύνεσιν
30 ὁ γοητευόμενος ἔχει, οὐδ' αἰσθάνεται, ἀλλὰ γινώσκει ἤδη παθὼν ὅτι πέπονθεν, ἀπαθὲς δ' αὐτὸ τὸ ἡγούμενόν ἐστιν. Ὧ δ' ηὔξατο, ἦλθέ τι πρὸς αὐτὸν ἐξ ἐκείνου ἢ πρὸς ἄλλον· ὁ δὲ ἥλιος ἢ ἄλλο ἄστρον οὐκ ἐπαΐει.

b. The magician is not necessarily a good man. For a wicked man too may draw from the source of the natural forces.

Enn. IV 4, 42, l. 14-19:

15 Εἰ δὲ κακὸς ὁ αἰτῶν, θαυμάζειν οὐ δεῖ· καὶ γὰρ ἐκ ποταμῶν ἀρύονται οἱ κακοὶ καὶ τὸ διδὸν αὐτὸ οὐκ οἶδεν ὃ δίδωσιν, ἀλλὰ δίδωσι μόνον. ἀλλ' ὅμως συντέτακται καὶ δέδοται τῇ φύσει τοῦ παντός. Ὥστε εἴ τις ἔλαβεν ἐκ τῶν πᾶσι κειμένων, οὐ δέον, ἕπεσθαι αὐτῷ ἀναγκαίῳ νόμῳ τὴν δίκην.

c. Since magic (as was said above, sub **a**) works through the ἄλογος ψυχή, it is evident that the higher soul of the spiritual man is beyond magic influence.

Enn. IV 4, 43, l. 1-7:

Ὁ δὲ σπουδαῖος πῶς ὑπὸ γοητείας καὶ φαρμάκων; Ἡ τῇ μὲν ψυχῇ ἀπαθὴς εἰς γοήτευσιν, καὶ οὐκ ἂν τὸ λογικὸν αὐτοῦ πάθοι, οὐδ' ἂν μεταδοξάσειε· τὸ δὲ

ὅσον τοῦ παντὸς ἐν αὐτῷ ἄλογον κατὰ τοῦτο πάθοι ἄν, μᾶλλον δὲ τοῦτο πάθοι
ἄν· ἀλλ' οὐκ ἔρωτας ἐκ φαρμάκων, εἴπερ τὸ ἐρᾶν ἐπινευούσης καὶ τῆς ψυχῆς 5
τῆς ἄλλης τῷ τῆς ἄλλης παθήματι.

On Plotinus' relation to magic see A. H. Armstrong, *Was P. a magician?* in
Phronesis I, 1, p. 73-79.

Time and eternity

1433—The problems of time and eternity are introduced by P. by
the statement that usually αἰών is considered as being related to the
ἀΐδιος φύσις, while χρόνος belongs to τὸ γιγνόμενον, but that, for the rest,
precision is difficult. He first considers αἰών.

a. Is eternity identical with intelligible being?—It is predicated
of it, but is not identical with it. Nor can it be identical with rest.

Is eternity = intelligible being?

Enn. III 7, 2, l. 1-27:

Τίνα οὖν ποτε χρὴ φάναι τὸν αἰῶνα εἶναι; Ἆρά γε τὴν νοητὴν αὐτὴν οὐσίαν,
ὥσπερ ἂν εἴ τις λέγοι τὸν χρόνον τὸν σύμπαντα οὐρανὸν καὶ κόσμον εἶναι;
Καὶ γὰρ αὖ καὶ ταύτην τὴν δόξαν ἔσχον τινές, φασί, περὶ τοῦ χρόνου. Ἐπεὶ
γὰρ σεμνότατόν τι τὸν αἰῶνα εἶναι φανταζόμεθα καὶ νοοῦμεν, σεμνότατον δὲ 5
τὸ τῆς νοητῆς φύσεως, καὶ οὐκ ἔστιν εἰπεῖν ὅτι σεμνότερον ὁποτερονοῦν — τοῦ δ'
ἐπέκεινα οὐδὲ τοῦτο κατηγορητέον — εἰς ταὐτὸν ἄν τις οὕτω συνάγοι. Καὶ γὰρ
αὖ ὅ τε κόσμος ὁ νοητὸς ὅ τε αἰὼν περιεκτικὰ ἄμφω καὶ τῶν αὐτῶν. Ἀλλ'
ὅταν τὸ ἕτερον ἐν θατέρῳ λέγωμεν, ἐν τῷ αἰῶνι * κεῖσθαι, καὶ ὅταν τὸ αἰώνιον 10
κατηγορῶμεν αὐτῶν — ἡ μὲν γάρ, φησι, τοῦ παραδείγματος φύσις ἐτύγχανεν
οὖσα αἰώνιος — ἄλλο τὸν αἰῶνα πάλιν αὖ λέγομεν, εἶναι μέντοι περὶ ἐκείνην ἢ
ἐν ἐκείνῃ ἢ παρεῖναι ἐκείνῃ φαμέν. Τὸ δὲ σεμνὸν ἑκάτερον εἶναι ταὐτότητα 15
οὐ δηλοῖ· ἴσως γὰρ ἂν καὶ τῷ ἑτέρῳ αὐτῶν παρὰ τοῦ ἑτέρου τὸ σεμνὸν γίνοιτο.
Ἥ τε περιοχὴ τῷ μὲν ὡς μερῶν ἔσται, τῷ δὲ αἰῶνι ὁμοῦ τὸ ὅλον οὐχ ὡς μέρος,
ἀλλ' ὅτι πάντα τὰ τοιαῦτα οἷα αἰώνια κατ' αὐτόν.

Ἀλλ' ἆρα κατὰ τὴν στάσιν φατέον τὴν ἐκεῖ τὸν αἰῶνα εἶναι, ὥσπερ ἐνταῦθα 20
τὸν χρόνον κατὰ τὴν κίνησίν φασιν; Ἀλλ' εἰκότως ἄν τις τὸν αἰῶνα ζητήσειε
πότερα ταὐτὸν τῇ στάσει λέγοντες ἢ οὐχ ἁπλῶς, ἀλλὰ τῇ στάσει τῇ περὶ τὴν
οὐσίαν. Εἰ μὲν γὰρ τῇ στάσει ταὐτόν, πρῶτον μὲν οὐκ ἐροῦμεν αἰώνιον τὴν στάσιν,
ὥσπερ οὐδὲ τὸν αἰῶνα αἰώνιον· τὸ γὰρ αἰώνιον τὸ μετέχον αἰῶνος. Ἔπειτα ἡ 25
κίνησις πῶς αἰώνιον;

b. Together with intelligible Being and on the same level, motion
and rest are given, identity and difference. These are the five supreme
genera of Plato's *Sophistes*, acknowledged as the five "categories" of the
intelligible world in P.'s second treatise Περὶ τῶν γενῶν τοῦ ὄντος (*Enn.*

---

* ἐν τῷ αἰῶνι del. Kirchhoff, Br.

VI 2). Uniting these five aspects of intelligible being and viewing them as one life, without end and always staying what it was, you see eternity,— not the "substrate" of the intelligible world, but as it were its radiance.

Enn. III 7, 3, l. 8-38:

Καὶ ὅ γε τὴν πολλὴν δύναμιν εἰσαθρήσας κατὰ μὲν τοδὶ τὸ οἷον ὑποκείμενον λέγει οὐσίαν, εἶτα κίνησιν τοῦτο, καθ᾽ ὃ ζωὴν ὁρᾷ, εἶτα στάσιν τὸ πάντη ὡσαύτως, θάτερον δὲ καὶ ταὐτόν, ᾗ ταῦτα ὁμοῦ ἕν. Οὕτω δὴ καὶ συνθεὶς πάλιν αὖ εἰς ἓν ὁμοῦ εἶναι ζωὴν μόνην, ἐν τούτοις τὴν ἑτερότητα συστείλας καὶ τῆς ἐνεργείας τὸ ἄπαυστον καὶ τὸ ταὐτὸν καὶ οὐδέποτε ἄλλο καὶ οὐκ ἐξ ἄλλου εἰς ἄλλο νόησιν ἢ ζωήν, ἀλλὰ τὸ ὡσαύτως καὶ ἀεὶ ἀδιαστάτως, ταῦτα πάντα ἰδὼν αἰῶνα εἶδεν ἰδὼν ζωὴν μένουσαν ἐν τῷ αὐτῷ ἀεὶ παρὸν τὸ πᾶν ἔχουσαν, ἀλλ᾽ οὐ νῦν μὲν τόδε, αὖθις δ᾽ ἕτερον, ἀλλ᾽ ἅμα τὰ πάντα, καὶ οὐ νῦν μὲν ἕτερα, αὖθις δ᾽ ἕτερα, ἀλλὰ τέλος ἀμερές, οἷον ἐν σημείῳ ὁμοῦ πάντων ὄντων καὶ οὔποτε εἰς ῥύσιν προϊόντων, ἀλλὰ μένοντος ἐν τῷ αὐτῷ ἐν αὑτῷ καὶ οὐ μὴ μεταβάλλοντος, ὄντος δὲ ἐν τῷ παρόντι ἀεί, ὅτι οὐδὲν αὐτοῦ παρῆλθεν οὐδ᾽ αὖ γενήσεται, ἀλλὰ τοῦτο ὅπερ ἔστι, τοῦτο καὶ ἀεὶ ὄντος· ὥστε εἶναι τὸν αἰῶνα οὐ τὸ ὑποκείμενον, ἀλλὰ τὸ ἐξ αὐτοῦ τοῦ ὑποκειμένου οἷον ἐκλάμπον κατὰ τὴν ἣν ἐπαγγέλλεται περὶ τοῦ μὴ μέλλοντος, ἀλλὰ ἤδη ὄντος, ταὐτότητα, ὡς ἄρα οὕτως καὶ οὐκ ἄλλως.

Τί γὰρ ἂν καὶ ὕστερον αὐτῷ γένοιτο, ὃ μὴ νῦν ἔστι; Μηδ᾽ αὖ ὕστερον ἐσομένου, ὃ μὴ ἔστιν ἤδη. Οὔτε γὰρ ἔστιν, ἀφ᾽ οὗ εἰς τὸ νῦν ἥξει· ἐκεῖνο γὰρ ἦν οὐκ ἄλλο, ἀλλὰ τοῦτο· οὔτε μέλλοντος ἔσεσθαι, ὃ μὴ νῦν ἔχει, ἐξ ἀνάγκης· οὔτε τὸ ἦν ἕξει περὶ αὐτό· τί γὰρ ἔστιν, ὃ ἦν αὐτῷ καὶ παρελήλυθεν; Οὔτε τὸ ἔσται· τί γὰρ ἔσται αὐτῷ;

Λείπεται δὴ ἐν τῷ εἶναι τοῦτο ὅπερ ἔστιν εἶναι. Ὁ οὖν μήτε ἦν, μήτε ἔσται, ἀλλ᾽ ἔστι μόνον, τοῦτο ἑστὼς ἔχον τὸ εἶναι τῷ μὴ μεταβάλλειν εἰς τὸ ἔσται μηδ᾽ αὖ μεταβεβληκέναι ἐστὶν ὁ αἰών.

Γίνεται τοίνυν ἡ περὶ τὸ ὂν ἐν τῷ εἶναι ζωὴ ὁμοῦ πᾶσα καὶ πλήρης ἀδιάστατος πανταχῇ τοῦτο, ὃ δὴ ζητοῦμεν, αἰών.

c. P. arrives at his final definition by adding to the notion of the "totality" of life the note of "nothing of it being lost".

Enn. III 7, 5, l. 22-30:

Εἰ δ᾽ ἐκ πολλῶν λέγομεν αὐτόν, οὐ δεῖ θαυμάζειν· πολλὰ γὰρ ἕκαστον τῶν ἐκεῖ διὰ δύναμιν ἄπειρον· ἐπεὶ καὶ τὸ ἄπειρον τὸ * μὴ ἂν ἐπιλείπειν, καὶ τοῦτο κυρίως, ὅτι μηδὲν αὑτοῦ ἀναλίσκει. Καὶ εἴ τις οὕτω τὸν αἰῶνα λέγοι ζωὴν ἄπειρον ἤδη τῷ πᾶσαν εἶναι καὶ μηδὲν ἀναλίσκειν αὑτῆς τῷ μὴ παρεληλυθέναι μηδ᾽ αὖ μέλλειν — ἤδη γὰρ οὐκ ἂν εἴη πᾶσα — ἐγγὺς ἂν εἴη τοῦ ὁρί-

Marginal notes:
- Eternity = total life in intelligible Being
- What is always and at the same time present
- This life in its fullness and indivisible
- Final definition of eternity

* τὸ codd., H.-S.; τῷ ed. princeps, Br.

ζεσθαι. Τὸ γὰρ ἑξῆς τῷ πᾶσαν εἶναι καὶ μηδὲν ἀναλίσκειν ἐξήγησις ἂν εἴη
τοῦ ἄπειρον ἤδη εἶναι.   30

1434—Time is not motion. Is it something which belongs to motion?
Is it the interval of motion, or of regular motion? Or is it the space
covered by a moving object?—In all these cases, time would be many,
not one, and its repetition will be a number, while its interval will be in
the space covered by the movement. And where then place the duration of rest?

**It is not
motion**   a. *Enn.* III 7, 8, l. 1-8, 23-44, 53-69:

Κίνησιν μὲν οὐχ οἷόν τε οὔτε τὰς συμπάσας λαμβάνοντι κινήσεις καὶ
οἷον μίαν ἐκ πασῶν ποιοῦντι, οὔτε τὴν τεταγμένην· ἐν χρόνῳ γὰρ ἡ κίνησις
ἑκατέρα ἡ λεγομένη. Εἰ δέ τις μὴ ἐν χρόνῳ, πολὺ μᾶλλον ἂν ἀπείη τοῦ χρόνος
εἶναι, ὡς ἄλλου ὄντος τοῦ ἐν ᾧ ἡ κίνησις, ἄλλου * τῆς κινήσεως αὐτῆς οὔσης.   5
Καὶ ἄλλων λεγομένων καὶ λεχθέντων ἂν ἀρκοῖ τοῦτο καὶ ὅτι κίνησις μὲν ἂν
καὶ παύσαιτο καὶ διαλίποι, χρόνος δὲ οὔ. ¹—

**Is it the
interval of
motion?**   Ἆρ᾽ οὖν κινήσεώς τι; Εἰ μὲν διάστημα, πρῶτον μὲν οὐ πάσης κινήσεως τὸ
αὐτό, οὐδὲ τῆς ὁμοειδοῦς· θᾶττον γὰρ καὶ βραδύτερον ἡ κίνησις καὶ ἡ ἐν τόπῳ.   25
Καὶ εἶεν ἂν ἄμφω μετρούμενα· αἱ διαστάσεις ἑνὶ ἑτέρῳ, ὃ δὴ ὀρθότερον ἄν τις
εἴποι χρόνον. Ποτέρας δὲ αὐτῶν τὸ διάστημα χρόνος, μᾶλλον δὲ τίνος αὐτῶν
ἀπείρων οὐσῶν; Εἰ δὲ τῆς τεταγμένης, οὐ πάσης μὲν οὐδὲ τῆς τοιαύτης· πολλαὶ
γὰρ αὗται· ὥστε καὶ πολλοὶ χρόνοι ἅμα ἔσονται. Εἰ δὲ τῆς τοῦ παντὸς διά-   30
στημα, εἰ μὲν τὸ ἐν αὐτῇ τῇ κινήσει διάστημα, τί ἂν ἄλλο ἢ ἡ κίνησις ἂν εἴη;
Τοσήδε μέντοι· τὸ δὲ τοσόνδε τοῦτο ἤτοι τῷ τόπῳ, ὅτι τοσόσδε ὂν διεξῆλθε,
μετρηθήσεται, καὶ τὸ διάστημα τοῦτο ἔσται· τοῦτο δὲ οὐ χρόνος, ἀλλὰ τόπος·
ἢ αὐτὴ ἡ κίνησις τῇ συνεχείᾳ αὐτῆς καὶ τῷ μὴ εὐθὺς πεπαῦσθαι, ἀλλ᾽ ἐπιλαμ-   35
βάνειν ἀεί, τὸ διάστημα ἕξει. Ἀλλὰ τοῦτο τὸ πολὺ τῆς κινήσεως ἂν εἴη· καὶ
εἰ μὲν εἰς αὐτήν τις βλέπων ἀποφανεῖται πολλήν, ὥσπερ ἂν εἴ τις πολὺ τὸ
θερμὸν λέγοι, οὐδ᾽ ἐνταῦθα χρόνος φανεῖται οὐδὲ προσπίπτει, ἀλλὰ κίνησις   40
πάλιν καὶ πάλιν, ὥσπερεὶ ὕδωρ ῥέον πάλιν καὶ πάλιν, καὶ τὸ ἐπ᾽ αὐτῷ διάστημα
θεωρούμενον. Καὶ τὸ μὲν πάλιν καὶ πάλιν ἔσται ἀριθμός, ὥσπερ δυὰς ἢ τριάς,
τὸ δὲ διάστημα τοῦ ὄγκου. — Εἰ δὲ τὸ διάστημα τῆς κινήσεως λέγοι τις χρόνον,
οὐ τὸ αὐτῆς τῆς κινήσεως, ἀλλὰ παρ᾽ ὃ αὐτὴ ἡ κίνησις τὴν παράτασιν ἔχοι οἷον   55
συμπαραθέουσα ἐκείνῳ, τί δὲ τοῦτό ἐστιν οὐκ εἴρηται. Δῆλον γάρ, ὅτι τοῦτ᾽
ἐστὶν ὁ χρόνος, ἐν ᾧ γέγονεν ἡ κίνησις. Τοῦτο δ᾽ ἦν ὁ ἐξ ἀρχῆς ἐζήτει ὁ λόγος,
τί ὤν ἐστι χρόνος· ἐπεὶ ὅμοιόν τε γίνεται καὶ ταὐτὸν οἷον εἴ τις ἐρωτηθεὶς τί

---

* ἀλλ᾽ οὐ H.-S.
¹ Cp. Aristotle, *Phys.* IV 10; above, nr. **508a**.

50 ἐστι χρόνος, λέγοι κινήσεως διάστημα ἐν χρόνῳ. Τί οὖν ἐστι τοῦτο τὸ διάστημα,
ὃ δὴ χρόνον καλεῖς τῆς κινήσεως τοῦ οἰκείου διαστήματος ἔξω τιθέμενος;
Καὶ γὰρ αὖ καὶ ἐν αὐτῇ ὁ τιθέμενος τῇ κινήσει τὸ διάστημα τὴν τῆς ἠρεμίας
55 διάστασιν ποῖ θήσεται, ἄπορος ἔσται. Ὅσον γὰρ κινεῖταί τι, τοσοῦτον ἂν σταίη
καὶ ἄλλο, καὶ εἴποις ἂν τόν χρόνον ἑκατέρου τὸν αὐτὸν εἶναι, ὡς ἄλλον δηλονότι
ἀμφοῖν ὄντα. Τί οὖν ἐστι καὶ τίνα φύσιν ἔχει τοῦτο τὸ διάστημα; Ἐπείπερ
τοπικὸν οὐχ οἷόν τε· ἐπεὶ καὶ τοῦτό γε ἔξωθέν ἐστιν.

b. Next, Aristotle's definition (above, nr. **510**) is considered.
Enn. III 7, 9, l. 1-28, 35-61, 71-76, 78-84:

Is it
ἀριθμός
or
μέτρον
κινήσεως?

Ἀριθμὸς δὲ κινήσεως ἢ μέτρον — βέλτιον γὰρ οὕτω συνεχοῦς οὔσης — πῶς,
σκεπτέον. Πρῶτον μὲν οὖν καὶ ἐνταῦθα τὸ πάσης ὁμοίως ἀπορητέον, ὥσπερ
καὶ ἐπὶ τοῦ διαστήματος τῆς κινήσεως, εἴ τις τῆς πάσης εἶναι ἐλέγετο. Πῶς γὰρ
5 ἄν τις ἀριθμήσειε τὴν ἄτακτον καὶ ἀνώμαλον; ἢ τίς ἀριθμὸς ἢ μέτρον ἢ κατὰ
τί τὸ μέτρον;
Εἰ δὲ τῷ αὐτῷ ἑκατέραν καὶ ὅλως πᾶσαν, ταχεῖαν, βραδεῖαν, ἔσται ὁ ἀριθμὸς
καὶ τὸ μέτρον τοιοῦτον, οἷον εἰ δεκὰς εἴη μετροῦσα καὶ ἵππους καὶ βοῦς, ἢ εἰ
10 τὸ αὐτὸ μέτρον καὶ ὑγρῶν καὶ ξηρῶν εἴη. Εἰ δὴ τοιοῦτον μέτρον, τίνων μέν
ἐστιν ὁ χρόνος εἴρηται, ὅτι κινήσεως, αὐτὸς δὲ ὅ ἐστιν οὔπω εἴρηται. Εἰ δὲ
ὥσπερ δεκάδος ληφθείσης καὶ ἄνευ ἵππων ἔστι νοεῖν τὸν ἀριθμόν, καὶ τὸ μέτρον
μέτρον ἐστὶ φύσιν ἔχον τινά, κἂν μήπω μετρῇ, οὕτω δεῖ ἔχειν καὶ τὸν χρόνον
15 μέτρον ὄντα· εἰ μὲν τοιοῦτόν ἐστιν ἐφ' ἑαυτοῦ οἷον ἀριθμός, τί ἂν τοῦδε τοῦ
ἀριθμοῦ τοῦ κατὰ τὴν δεκάδα ἢ ἄλλου ὁτουοῦν διαφέροι μοναδικοῦ; Εἰ δὲ συνεχὲς
μέτρον ἐστί, ποσόν τι ὂν μέτρον ἔσται, οἷον τὸ πηχυαῖον μέγεθος. Μέγεθος τοίνυν ἔσται, οἷον γραμμὴ συνθέουσα δηλονότι κινήσει. Ἀλλ' αὕτη συνθέουσα
20 πῶς μετρήσει τὸ ᾧ συνθεῖ; Τί γὰρ μᾶλλον ὁποτερονοῦν θάτερον; Καὶ βέλτιον
τίθεσθαι καὶ πιθανώτερον οὐκ ἐπὶ πάσης, ἀλλ' ᾗ συνθεῖ. Τοῦτο δὲ συνεχὲς δεῖ
εἶναι, ἢ ἐφέξει ἡ συνθέουσα. Ἀλλ' οὐκ ἔξωθεν δεῖ τὸ μετροῦν λαμβάνειν οὐδὲ
25 χωρίς, ἀλλὰ ὁμοῦ κίνησιν μεμετρημένην. Καὶ τί τὸ μετροῦν ἔσται; Ἡ μεμετρημένη μὲν ἡ κίνησις ἔσται, μεμετρηκὸς δὲ ἔσται μέγεθος. Καὶ ποῖον αὐτῶν
ὁ χρόνος ἔσται; Ἡ κίνησις ἡ μεμετρημένη, ἢ τὸ μέγεθος τὸ μετρῆσαν; —
35 Εἰ δὲ δὴ μεμετρημένη κίνησις ὁ χρόνος καὶ ὑπὸ τοῦ ποσοῦ μεμετρημένη, ὥσπερ
τὴν κίνησιν, εἰ ἔδει μεμετρῆσθαι, οὐχ ὑπ' αὐτῆς ἔδει μεμετρῆσθαι, ἀλλ' ἑτέρῳ,
οὕτως ἀνάγκη, εἴπερ μέτρον ἕξει ἄλλο ἡ κίνησις παρ' αὐτήν, καὶ διὰ τοῦτο
40 ἐδεήθημεν τοῦ συνεχοῦς μέτρου εἰς μέτρησιν αὐτῆς, τὸν αὐτὸν τρόπον δεῖ καὶ
τῷ μεγέθει αὐτῷ μέτρου, ἵν' ἡ κίνησις τοσοῦδε γεγενημένου τοῦ καθ' ὃ μετρεῖται ὅση, μετρηθῇ. Καὶ ὁ ἀριθμὸς τοῦ μεγέθους ἔσται τῇ κινήσει παρο-
μαρτοῦντος ἐκεῖνος ὁ χρόνος, ἀλλ' οὐ τὸ μέγεθος τὸ συνθέον τῇ κινήσει. Οὗτος
45 δὲ τίς ἂν εἴη ἢ ὁ μοναδικός; Ὃς ὅπως μετρήσει ἀπορεῖν ἀνάγκη. Ἐπεί, κἂν

τις ἐξεύρῃ ὅπως, οὐ χρόνον εὑρήσει μετροῦντα, ἀλλὰ τὸν τοσόνδε χρόνον·
τοῦτο δὲ οὐ ταὐτὸν χρόνῳ. Ἕτερον γὰρ εἰπεῖν χρόνον, ἕτερον δὲ τοσόνδε χρόνον·
πρὸ γὰρ τοῦ τοσόνδε δεῖ ὅ τί ποτ' ἐστὶν εἰπεῖν ἐκεῖνο, ὃ τοσόνδε ἐστίν. Ἀλλ' 50
ὁ ἀριθμὸς ὁ μετρήσας τὴν κίνησιν ἔξωθεν τῆς κινήσεως ὁ χρόνος, οἷον ἡ δεκὰς
ἐπὶ τῶν ἵππων οὐ μετὰ τῶν ἵππων λαμβανόμενος *. Τίς οὖν οὗτος ὁ ἀριθμὸς οὐκ
εἴρηται, ὃς πρὸ τοῦ μετρεῖν ἐστιν ὅπερ ἔστιν, ὥσπερ ἡ δεκάς.

Ἢ οὗτος, ὃς κατὰ τὸ πρότερον καὶ ὕστερον τῆς κινήσεως παραθέων ἐμέ- 55
τρησεν. Ἀλλ' οὗτος ὁ κατὰ τὸ πρότερον καὶ ὕστερον οὔπω δῆλος ὅστις ἐστίν.
Ἀλλ' οὖν κατὰ τὸ πρότερον καὶ ὕστερον μετρῶν εἴτε σημείῳ εἴθ' ὁτῳοῦν ἄλλῳ
πάντως κατὰ χρόνον μετρήσει. Ἔσται οὖν ὁ χρόνος οὗτος ὁ μετρῶν τὴν κίνησιν 60
τῷ προτέρῳ καὶ ὑστέρῳ ἐχόμενος τοῦ χρόνου καὶ ἐφαπτόμενος, ἵνα μετρῇ.—

Ἀλλ' οὖν διὰ τί ἀριθμοῦ μὲν γενομένου χρόνος ἔσται, κινήσεως δὲ οὔσης καὶ
τοῦ προτέρου πάντως ὑπάρχοντος περὶ αὐτὴν καὶ τοῦ ὑστέρου οὐκ ἔσται χρόνος;
Ὥσπερ ἂν εἴ τις λέγοι τὸ μέγεθος μὴ εἶναι ὅσον ἐστίν, εἰ μή τις τὸ ὅσον ἐστὶ
τοῦτο λάβοι. Ἀπείρου δὲ τοῦ χρόνου ὄντος καὶ λεγομένου πῶς ἂν περὶ αὐτὸν 75
ἀριθμὸς εἴη;—Διὰ τί δὲ οὐκ ἔσται πρὶν καὶ ψυχὴν τὴν μετροῦσαν εἶναι; [1]
Εἰ μή τις τὴν γένεσιν αὐτοῦ παρὰ ψυχῆς λέγοι γίνεσθαι. Ἐπεὶ διά γε τὸ μετρεῖν 80
οὐδαμῶς ἀναγκαῖον εἶναι **· ὑπάρχει γὰρ ὅσον ἐστί, κἂν μή τις μετρῇ. Τὸ δὲ
τῷ μεγέθει χρησάμενον πρὸς τὸ μετρῆσαι τὴν ψυχὴν ἄν τις λέγοι· τοῦτο δὲ τί
ἂν εἴη πρὸς ἔννοιαν χρόνου;

P.'s definition of time

c. P. now comes to his own explanation. He starts from his own
view of eternity as "total life which in its fullness is always present",
and states that "in soul was a non-quiet power": *this could not bear that
all intelligible Being was present to it directly and as a whole.* It asked
for a succession of acts. And thus its life, which is *a movement by which
soul passes from one state into the other*, is time, like the non-changing,
ever constant life of the intelligible World is eternity.

Enn. III 7, 11, l. 1-62:

Δεῖ δὴ ἀναγαγεῖν ἡμᾶς αὐτοὺς πάλιν εἰς ἐκείνην τὴν διάθεσιν ἣν ἐπὶ τοῦ
αἰῶνος ἐλέγομεν εἶναι, τὴν ἀτρεμῆ ἐκείνην καὶ ὁμοῦ πᾶσαν καὶ ἄπειρον ἤδη
ζωὴν καὶ ἀκλινῆ πάντη καὶ ἐν ἑνὶ καὶ πρὸς ἓν ἑστῶσαν. Χρόνος δὲ οὔπω ἦν, 5
ἢ ἐκείνοις γε οὐκ ἦν, γεννήσομεν δὲ χρόνον λόγῳ καὶ φύσει τοῦ ὑστέρου.
Τούτων δὴ οὖν ἡσυχίαν ἀγόντων ἐν αὐτοῖς, ὅπως δὴ πρῶτον ἐξέπεσε χρόνος,
τὰς μὲν Μούσας οὔπω τότε οὔσας οὐκ ἄν τις ἴσως καλοῖ εἰπεῖν τοῦτο· ἀλλ'

---

* λαμβανόμενος H.-S., who explain: congruit cum ἀριθμός. λαμβανομένη Br.
[1] Cp. Aristotle, *Phys.* IV 14; above, nr. **512**.
** ἀναγκαῖόν ἐστιν Volkmann, Br.

10 ἴσως εἴπερ ἦσαν καὶ αἱ Μοῦσαι τότε, αὐτὸν δ᾽ ἄν τις τάχα τὸν γενόμενον χρόνον,
ὅπως ἐστὶν ἐκφανεὶς καὶ γενόμενος. Λέγοι δ᾽ ἂν περὶ αὐτοῦ ὧδέ πως·
ὡς πρότερον, πρὶν τὸ πρότερον δὴ τοῦτο γεννῆσαι καὶ·τοῦ ὑστέρου δεηθῆναι,
σὺν αὐτῷ ἐν τῷ ὄντι ἀνεπαύετο χρόνος οὐκ ὤν, ἀλλ᾽ ἐν ἐκείνῳ καὶ αὐτὸς ἡσυχίαν
15 ἦγε. Φύσεως δὲ πολυπράγμονος καὶ ἄρχειν αὐτῆς βουλομένης καὶ εἶναι αὐτῆς
καὶ τὸ πλέον τοῦ παρόντος ζητεῖν ἑλομένης ἐκινήθη μὲν αὐτή, ἐκινήθη δὲ καὶ
αὐτός, καὶ εἰς τὸ ἔπειτα ἀεὶ καὶ τὸ ὕστερον καὶ οὐ ταὐτόν, ἀλλ᾽ ἕτερον εἶθ᾽
ἕτερον κινούμενοι μῆκός τι τῆς πορείας ποιησάμενοι αἰῶνος εἰκόνα τὸν χρόνον
20 εἰργάσμεθα[1]. Ἐπεὶ γὰρ ψυχῆς ἦν τις δύναμις οὐχ ἥσυχος,
τὸ δ᾽ ἐκεῖ ὁρώμενον ἀεὶ μεταφέρειν εἰς ἄλλο βουλομένης, τὸ μὲν ἀθρόον αὐτῇ πᾶν παρεῖναι οὐκ ἤθελεν·
ὥσπερ δ᾽ ἐκ σπέρματος ἡσύχου ἐξελίττων αὐτὸν ὁ λόγος διέξοδον εἰς πολύ,
25 ὡς οἴεται, ποιεῖ ἐμφανίζων * τὸ πολὺ τῷ μερισμῷ, καὶ ἀνθ᾽ ἑνὸς ἐν αὐτῷ οὐκ ἐν
αὐτῷ τὸ ἓν δαπανῶν εἰς μῆκος ἀσθενέστερον πρόεισιν, οὕτω δὴ καὶ αὐτὴ κόσμον
ποιοῦσα αἰσθητὸν μιμήσει ἐκείνου κινούμενον κίνησιν οὐ τὴν ἐκεῖ, ὁμοίαν δὲ
τῇ ἐκεῖ καὶ ἐθέλουσαν εἰκόνα ἐκείνης εἶναι, πρῶτον μὲν ἑαυτὴν ἐχρόνωσεν
30 ἀντὶ τοῦ αἰῶνος τοῦτον ποιήσασα· ἔπειτα δὲ καὶ τῷ γενομένῳ ἔδωκε δουλεύειν
χρόνῳ, ἐν χρόνῳ αὐτὸν πάντα ποιήσασα εἶναι, τὰς τούτου διεξόδους ἁπάσας ἐν
αὐτῷ περιλαβοῦσα· ἐν ἐκείνῃ γὰρ κινούμενος—οὐ γάρ τις αὐτοῦ τοῦδε τοῦ
παντὸς τόπος ἢ ψυχή—καὶ ἐν τῷ ἐκείνης αὖ ἐκινεῖτο χρόνῳ.
35 Τὴν γὰρ ἐνέργειαν αὐτῆς παρεχομένη ἄλλην μετ᾽ ἄλλην, εἶθ᾽ ἑτέραν πάλιν
ἐφεξῆς, ἐγέννα τε μετὰ τῆς ἐνεργείας τὸ ἐφεξῆς καὶ συμπροῄει μετὰ διανοίας
ἑτέρας μετ᾽ ἐκείνην τὸ μὴ πρότερον ὄν, ὅτι οὐδ᾽ ἡ διάνοια ἐνεργηθεῖσα ἦν
40 οὐδ᾽ ἡ νῦν ζωὴ ὁμοία τῇ πρὸ αὑτῆς. Ἅμα οὖν ζωὴ ἄλλη καὶ τὸ ἄλλη χρόνον
εἶχεν ἄλλον. Διάστασις οὖν ζωῆς χρόνον εἶχε καὶ τὸ πρόσω ἀεὶ τῆς ζωῆς
χρόνον ἔχει ἀεὶ καὶ ἡ παρελθοῦσα ζωὴ χρόνον ἔχει παρεληλυθότα. Εἰ οὖν
χρόνον τις λέγοι ψυχῆς ἐν κινήσει μεταβατικῇ ἐξ
ἄλλου εἰς ἄλλον βίον ζωὴν εἶναι, ἆρ᾽ ἂν δοκοῖ τι
45 λέγειν;

The life of soul in its transition from one state to the other

Εἰ γὰρ αἰών ἐστι ζωὴ ἐν στάσει καὶ τῷ αὐτῷ καὶ ὡσαύτως καὶ ἄπειρος ἤδη,
εἰκόνα δὲ δεῖ τοῦ αἰῶνος τὸν χρόνον εἶναι, ὥσπερ καὶ τόδε τὸ πᾶν ἔχει πρὸς
ἐκεῖνο, ἀντὶ μὲν ζωῆς τῆς ἐκεῖ ἄλλην δεῖ ζωὴν τὴν τῆσδε τῆς δυνάμεως τῆς
50 ψυχῆς ὥσπερ ὁμώνυμον λέγειν εἶναι καὶ ἀντὶ κινήσεως νοερᾶς ψυχῆς τινος
μέρους κίνησιν, ἀντὶ δὲ ταὐτότητος καὶ τοῦ ὡσαύτως καὶ μένοντος τὸ μὴ μένον
ἐν τῷ αὐτῷ, ἄλλο δὲ καὶ ἄλλο ἐνεργοῦν, ἀντὶ δὲ ἀδιαστάτου καὶ ἑνὸς εἴδωλον
τοῦ ἑνὸς τὸ ἐν συνεχείᾳ ἕν, ἀντὶ δὲ ἀπείρου ἤδη καὶ ὅλου τὸ εἰς ἄπειρον πρὸς τὸ

---

[1] Time was called "a moving likeness of eternity" by Plato in *Tim.* 37d (above, nr. **351**).

* ἀφανίζων codd., H.-S.; ἐμφανίζων conj. Schegk, Br.

ἐφεξῆς ἀεί, ἀντὶ δὲ ἀθρόου ὅλου τὸ κατὰ μέρος ἐσόμενον καὶ ἀεὶ ἐσόμενον ὅλον. 55
Οὕτω γὰρ μιμήσεται τὸ ἤδη ὅλον καὶ ἀθρόον καὶ ἄπειρον ἤδη, εἰ ἐθελήσει ἀεὶ
προσκτώμενον εἶναι ἐν τῷ εἶναι· καὶ γὰρ τὸ εἶναι οὕτω τὸ ἐκείνου μιμήσεται.

Time essentially connected with soul

Δ ε ῖ δ ὲ ο ὐ κ ἔ ξ ω θ ε ν τ ῆ ς ψ υ χ ῆ ς λ α μ β ά ν ε ι ν τ ὸ ν χ ρ ό -
ν ο ν, ὥ σ π ε ρ ο ὐ δ ὲ τ ὸ ν α ἰ ῶ ν α ἐ κ ε ῖ ἔ ξ ω τ ο ῦ ὄ ν τ ο ς, οὐδ' 60
αὖ παρακολούθημα οὐδ' ὕστερον, ὥσπερ οὐδ' ἐκεῖ, ἀλλ' ἐνορώμενον καὶ ἐνόντα
καὶ συνόντα, ὥσπερ κἀκεῖ ὁ αἰών.

Time a distentio

1435—a. Hence P. described time as a "distention of the soul", as
it was said by St. Augustine: it must be understood as "the length of
such a life (sc. of the soul), progressing silently in regular and equable
changes".

Enn. III 7, 12, l. 1-4:

Νοῆσαι δὲ δεῖ καὶ ἐντεῦθεν, ὡς ἡ φύσις αὕτη, χρόνος, τὸ τοιούτου μῆκος βίου
ἐν μεταβολαῖς προϊὸν ὁμαλαῖς τε καὶ ὁμοίαις ἀψοφητὶ προϊούσαις, συνεχὲς
τὸ τῆς ἐνεργείας ἔχον.

Augustinus, *Conf.* XI 23, 30 (the end) and 26, 33 (l. 24) defines time as a *distentio*.
He adds: "sed cuius rei nescio, et mirum si non ipsius animi". His way of posing
the problem and of illustrating it is original, but the idea itself of a *distentio* comes
from Plotinus.

Time was engendered together with the sensible universe

b. Supposing that this life of the soul should stop and that soul
should stay in Noûs,—there would be nothing but Noûs itself; no sensible
world, no time. Both of these are engendered together, as was said by
Plato (*Tim.* 38b).

Enn. III 7, 12, l. 4-25:

Εἰ δὴ πάλιν τῷ λόγῳ ἀναστρέψαι ποιήσαιμεν τὴν δύναμιν ταύτην καὶ παύ-
σαιμεν τοῦδε τοῦ βίου, ὃν νῦν ἔχει ἄπαυστον ὄντα καὶ οὔποτε λήξοντα, ὅτι ψυχῆς 5
τινος ἀεὶ οὔσης ἐστὶν ἐνέργεια, οὐ πρὸς αὐτὴν οὐδ' ἐν αὐτῇ, ἀλλ' ἐν ποιήσει καὶ
γενέσει—εἰ οὖν ὑποθοίμεθα μηκέτι ἐνεργοῦσαν, ἀλλὰ παυσαμένην ταύτην τὴν
ἐνέργειαν καὶ ἐπιστραφὲν καὶ τοῦτο τὸ μέρος τῆς ψυχῆς πρὸς τὸ ἐκεῖ καὶ τὸν 10
αἰῶνα καὶ ἐν ἡσυχίᾳ μένον, τί ἂν ἔτι μετὰ αἰῶνα εἴη; Τί δ' ἂν ἄλλο καὶ ἄλλο
πάντων ἐν ἑνὶ μεινάντων; Τί δ' ἂν ἔτι πρότερον; Τί δ' ἂν ὕστερον ἢ μέλλον *;
Ποῦ δ' ἂν ἔτι ψυχὴ ἐπιβάλλοι εἰς ἄλλο ἢ ἐν ᾧ ἔστι; Μᾶλλον δὲ οὐδὲ τούτῳ·
ἀφεστήκοι γὰρ ἂν πρότερον, ἵνα ἐπιβάλῃ. Ἐπεὶ οὐδ' ἂν ἡ σφαῖρα αὐτὴ εἴη, 15
ἢ οὐ πρώτως ὑπάρχει· [χρόνος] ** ἐν χρόνῳ γὰρ καὶ αὕτη καὶ ἔστι καὶ κινεῖ.αι,
κἂν στῇ, ἐκείνης ἐνεργούσης, ὅση ἡ στάσις αὐτῆς μετρήσομεν, ἕως ἐκείνη τοῦ
αἰῶνός ἐστιν ἔξω.

＊　μέλλον Page, H.-S.; μᾶλλον codd.
＊＊　χρόνος del. H.-S.

20   Εἰ οὖν ἀποστάσης ἐκείνης καὶ ἑνωθείσης ἀνῄρηται χρόνος, δῆλον ὅτι ἡ ταύτης ἀρχὴ πρὸς ταῦτα κινήσεως καὶ οὗτος ὁ βίος τὸν χρόνον γεννᾷ. Διὸ καὶ εἴρηται ἅμα τῷδε τῷ παντὶ γεγονέναι, ὅτι ψυχὴ αὐτὸν μετὰ τοῦδε τοῦ παντὸς ἐγέννησεν. Ἐν γὰρ τῇ τοιαύτῃ ἐνεργείᾳ καὶ τόδε γεγένηται τὸ πᾶν· καὶ ἡ μὲν χρόνος, τὸ δὲ ἐν χρόνῳ.

Thus, Augustinus in *Confess.* XI 30, 40 rebukes those people who ask questions such as: "What was God doing before He made the heavens and the earth" and "How did He come to the idea of making something, while He did not do so before?"—To this Aug. replies: "Videant itaque nullum tempus esse posse sine creatura et desinant istam vanitatem loqui. Extendantur etiam in ea, quae ante sunt, et intellegant te ante omnia tempora aeternum Creatorem omnium temporum neque ulla tempora tibi esse coaeterna nec ullam creaturam, etiamsi est aliqua supra tempora".

Cp. Thomas Aq., *S. th.* I, qu. 46, art. 3: "In principio creavit Deus coelum et terram" does not mean that things were created *in principio temporis*, but "quia simul cum tempore coelum et terra creata sunt".

LATER NEOPLATONISM

1—PORPHYRIUS

Neoplatonic succession

1436—Julianus mentions Plotinus, Porphyrius and Iamblichus in succession as carrying on the tradition of Plato.

Julianus, *Or.* VII 222B:

Speaking of the worship of Dionysos he says: the man in whom the multifarious character of life has not been perfected by divine frenzy for the god, whose nature is uniform and indivisible, runs the risk that his life may flow into many channels, and as it flows be torn to shreds. But these expressions should not be taken literally,—

ξυνιέτω δὲ τὰ λεγόμενα τρόπον ἄλλον, ὃν Πλάτων, ὃν Πλωτῖνος, ὃν Πορφύριος, ὃν ὁ δαιμόνιος Ἰάμβλιχος.

Porphyrius

1437—Porphyrius' life is partly known to us by what he tells us himself in his Life of Plotinus, partly by Eunapius.

a. Eunapius, *Vitae phil.* p. 455/6:

Πορφυρίῳ Τύρος μὲν ἦν πατρίς, ἡ πρώτη τῶν ἀρχαίων Φοινίκων πόλις, καὶ πατέρες δὲ οὐκ ἄσημοι. τυχὼν δὲ τῆς προσηκούσης παιδείας, ἀνά τε ἔδραμε τοσοῦτον καὶ ἐπέδωκεν, ὡς Λογγίνου μὲν ἦν ἀκροατής, καὶ ἐκόσμει τὸν διδάσκαλον ἐντὸς ὀλίγου χρόνου. Λογγῖνος δὲ κατὰ τὸν χρόνον ἐκεῖνον βιβλιοθήκη τις ἦν ἔμψυχος καὶ περιπατοῦν μουσεῖον. — Καὶ εἴ τις κατέγνω τινὸς τῶν παλαιῶν, οὐ τὸ δοξασθὲν ἐκράτει πρότερον, ἀλλ᾽ ἡ Λογγίνου πάντως ἐκράτει κρίσις. οὕτω δὲ ἀχθεὶς τὴν πρώτην παιδείαν καὶ ὑπὸ πάντων ἀποβλεπόμενος, τὴν μεγίστην Ῥώμην ἰδεῖν ἐπιθυμήσας ἵνα κατάσχῃ διὰ σοφίας τὴν πόλιν, ἐπειδὴ τάχιστα εἰς αὐτὴν ἀφίκετο καὶ τῷ μεγίστῳ Πλωτίνῳ συνῆλθεν εἰς ὁμιλίαν, πάντων ἐπελάθετο τῶν ἄλλων, καὶ προσέθετο φέρων ἑαυτὸν ἐκείνῳ.

b. Porph., *Vita Plot.* 4; l. 1-9:

Τῷ δεκάτῳ δὲ ἔτει τῆς Γαλιήνου βασιλείας [1] ἐγὼ Πορφύριος ἐκ τῆς Ἑλλάδος μετὰ Ἀντωνίου τοῦ Ῥοδίου γεγονὼς καταλαμβάνω μὲν τὸν Ἀμέλιον ὀκτωκαιδέκατον ἔτος ἔχοντα τῆς πρὸς Πλωτῖνον συνουσίας, μηδὲν δέ πω γράφειν τολμήσαντα πλὴν τῶν σχολίων ἃ οὐδέπω εἰς ἑκατὸν τὸ πλῆθος αὐτῷ

---

[1] A. 363.

συνῆκτο. ἦν δὲ ὁ Πλωτῖνος τῷ δεκάτῳ ἔτει τῆς Γαλιήνου βασιλείας ἀμφὶ τὰ
πεντήκοντα ἔτη καὶ ἐννέα. ἐγὼ δὲ Πορφύριος τὸ πρῶτον αὐτῷ συγγέγονα
αὐτὸς ὢν τότε ἐτῶν τριάκοντα.

Porph. stayed for five years with Plotinus, then was sent to Sicily for reasons
of health (above, nr. **1360b**: *V.P.* 11, l. 11 ff.). On his intimacy with the master
and his function as a corrector, above, nr. **1362a**.

c. Porph. came back to Rome after the death of Plotinus (Eunapius'
account is incorrect on this point) and settled there to teach his master's
philosophy. Eunapius praises him for the lucidity of his expositions
and for his learning.

Eunapius, *Vitae* 456/7:   His fame
as a teacher

Ὁ μὲν γὰρ Πλωτῖνος τῷ τε τῆς ψυχῆς οὐρανίῳ καὶ τῷ λοξῷ καὶ αἰνιγμα-
τώδει τῶν λόγων, βαρὺς ἐδόκει καὶ δυσήκοος· ὁ δὲ Πορφύριος, ὥσπερ Ἑρμαϊκή
τις σειρά [1] καὶ πρὸς ἀνθρώπους ἐπινεύουσα, διὰ ποικίλης παιδείας πάντα εἰς
τὸ εὔγνωστον καὶ καθαρὸν ἐξήγγειλεν. —

Ἔστι γοῦν ἀπορῆσαι καθ' ἑαυτὸν καὶ θαυμάσαι, τί πλεῖόν ἐστι τῶν ἐσπου- His learning
δασμένων· πότερον τὰ εἰς ὕλην ῥητορικὴν τείνοντα, ἢ τὰ εἰς γραμματικὴν
ἀκρίβειαν φέροντα, ἢ ὅσα τῶν ἀριθμῶν ἤρτηται, ἢ ὅσα νεύει πρὸς γεωμετρίαν,
ἢ ὅσα πρὸς μουσικὴν ῥέπει. τὰ δὲ εἰς φιλοσοφίαν, οὐδὲ τὰ περὶ λόγου καταληπτόν,
οὔτε τὸ ἠθικὸν ἐφικτὸν λόγῳ· τὸ δὲ φυσικὸν καὶ θεουργὸν τελεταῖς ἀφείσθω καὶ
μυστηρίοις· οὕτω παντομιγὲς πρὸς ἅπασαν ἀρετὴν ὁ ἀνὴρ αὐτὸς [2] χρῆμά τι γέγονεν.

d. He married the widow of a friend.

Eunapius, *Vitae* 457:   His
marriage

Γάμοις τε ὁμιλήσας φαίνεται, καὶ πρὸς Μάρκελλάν γε αὐτοῦ γυναῖκα γενομένην βιβλίον φέρεται, ἥν φησιν ἀγαγέσθαι καὶ ταῦτα οὖσαν πέντε μητέρα
τέκνων, οὐχ ἵνα παῖδας ἐξ αὐτῆς ποιήσηται, ἀλλ' ἵνα οἱ γεγονότες παιδείας
τύχωσιν· ἐκ φίλου γὰρ ἦν αὐτοῦ τῇ γυναικὶ τὰ τέκνα προϋπάρξαντα.

1438—Porph. is known to us first as the editor of the *Enneads*. He His works
also speaks of explicatory works of his own on Plotinus' writings.

Porph., *Vita Plot.* 26, l. 28-37 H.-S.:

After having enumerated the treatises of Plotinus as arranged by him in six
enneads he concludes:

---

[1] Probably a vague reminiscence of the χρυσῆ σειρά of *Iliad* VIII 19, which
played a part in Neoplatonic symbolism (cf. Kern, *Orph. fragm.* nr. 166) and may
have been connected by the author with Hermes by some strange error (a con-
fusion with Ἑρμαϊκὴ λύρα?).—Unless H. (ψυχοπομπός) was in fact represented with
a cord. But of such a representation so far as I know not a trace has been found.

[2] "the man himself"—as opposed to his fellow-disciples (συμφοιτηταί) who
are mentioned before as famous men and praised by Porph. for their ability.

Τὰ μὲν οὖν βιβλία εἰς ἓξ ἐννεάδας τοῦτον τὸν τρόπον κατετάξαμεν τέσσαρα καὶ πεντήκοντα ὄντα· καταβεβλήμεθα δὲ καὶ εἴς τινα αὐτῶν ὑπομνήματα 30 ἀτάκτως διὰ τοὺς ἐπείξαντας ἡμᾶς ἑταίρους γράφειν εἰς ἅπερ αὐτοὶ τὴν σαφή- νειαν αὐτοῖς γενέσθαι ἠξίουν. Ἀλλὰ μὴν καὶ τὰ κεφάλαια τῶν πάντων πλὴν τοῦ "Περὶ τοῦ καλοῦ" διὰ τὸ λεῖψαι ἡμῖν πεποιήμεθα κατὰ τὴν χρονικὴν ἔκδοσιν τῶν βιβλίων· ἀλλ' ἐν τούτῳ οὐ τὰ κεφάλαια μόνον καθ' ἕκαστον ἔκκειται τῶν 35 βιβλίων, ἀλλὰ καὶ ἐπιχειρήματα, ἃ ὡς κεφάλαια συναριθμεῖται.

What are the 'Αφορμαί The question has been raised whether the works mentioned here, either the three or one or two of them, were identical with the Ἀφορμαὶ πρὸς τὰ νοητά which are preserved to us (cited below as *Sententiae*). The Ἀφορμαί are a short description of Plotinus' doctrine, a kind of στοιχείωσις θεολογική in aphorisms, comparable with the *Enchiridion* of Epictetus in its relation to the *Diatribes*. Mommert seems to be right in stating that this work is probably neither identic with the ὑπομνήματα (commentaries of parts of the *Enneads*), nor with the κεφάλαια (which were sum- maries of *all* Plotinus's treatises except the Περὶ τοῦ καλοῦ), nor with the ἐπιχειρήματα (discussions or exppsitions of Plotinus's arguments in the *Enneads*, comparable with the "Notices" of Bréhier which precede the text of each of the treatises in his edition).

Character of Porph.'s teaching In his teaching of Plotinus' philosophy Porph. laid great emphasis on its moral implications. The purification from the πάθη, the ὁμοίωσις τῷ θεῷ, the moral and spiritual character of the true service of God, these are the leading principles, both of his letter to Marcella and of his four books *De abstinentia* (Περὶ ἀποχῆς ἐμψύχων).

1439—From the Ἀφορμαί we cite the chapter on virtues, which shows the author's interest in ethics. From a comparison with *Enn.* I 2 (above, nrs. **1419**, **1420**) will appear that Porph.'s classification of virtues is more elaborate than Plotinus's was.

Classifica- tion of virtues Porph., *Sent.* 32 (Stob. III 3, p. 89), 1-5:

Ἄλλαι αἱ ἀρεταὶ τοῦ πολιτικοῦ καὶ ἄλλαι αἱ τοῦ πρὸς θεωρίαν ἀνιόντος καὶ § 1 διὰ τοῦτο λεγομένου θεωρητικοῦ καὶ ἄλλαι αἱ τοῦ ἤδη τελείου θεωρητικοῦ καὶ ἤδη θεατοῦ καὶ ἄλλαι αἱ τοῦ νοῦ, καθὸ νοῦς καὶ ἀπὸ ψυχῆς καθαρός.

Αἱ μὲν τοῦ πολιτικοῦ ἐν μετριοπαθείᾳ κείμεναι, τῷ ἕπεσθαι καὶ ἀκολουθεῖν § 2 τῷ λογισμῷ τοῦ καθήκοντος κατὰ τὰς πράξεις. διὸ πρὸς κοινωνίαν βλέπουσαι τὴν ἀβλαβῆ τῶν πλησίον ἐκ τοῦ συναγελασμοῦ καὶ τῆς κοινωνίας πολιτικαὶ λέ- γονται. —

Αἱ δὲ τοῦ πρὸς θεωρίαν προκόπτοντος θεωρητικοῦ ἐν ἀποστάσει κεῖνται § 3 τῶν ἐντεῦθεν· διὸ καὶ καθάρσεις αὗται λέγονται, ἐν ἀποχῇ θεωρούμεναι τῶν μετὰ τοῦ σώματος πράξεων καὶ συμπαθειῶν τῶν πρὸς αὐτό. αὗται μὲν γὰρ τῆς ψυχῆς ἀφισταμένης πρὸς τὸ ὄντως ὄν, αἱ δὲ πολιτικαὶ τὸν θνητὸν ἄνθρωπον κατακοσμοῦσι, καὶ πρόδρομοί γε αἱ πολιτικαὶ τῶν καθάρσεων· δεῖ γὰρ κοσμη-

θέντα κατ᾽ αὐτὰς ἀποστῆναι τοῦ σὺν σώματι πράττειν τι προηγουμένως. —
Ἡ μὲν οὖν κατὰ τὰς πολιτικὰς ἀρετὰς διάθεσις ἐν μετριοπαθείᾳ θεωρεῖται
τέλος ἔχουσα τὸ ζῆν ὡς ἄνθρωπον κατὰ φύσιν, ἡ δὲ κατὰ τὰς θεωρητικὰς ἐν
ἀπαθείᾳ, ἧς τέλος ἡ πρὸς θεὸν ὁμοίωσις. —
Ἀλλ᾽ ἐπεὶ τὸ καθαίρειν τε καὶ κεκαθάρθαι ἀφαίρεσις ἦν παντὸς τοῦ ἀλλοτρίου,
τὸ ἀγαθὸν ἕτερον ἂν εἴη τοῦ καθήραντος· ὡς εἴγε πρὸ τῆς ἀκαθαρσίας ἀγαθὸν
ἦν τὸ καθαιρόμενον, ἡ κάθαρσις ἥρκει. ἀλλ᾽ ἀρκέσει μὲν ἡ κάθαρσις, τὸ δὲ
καταλειπόμενον ἔσται τὸ ἀγαθὸν καὶ οὐχ ἡ κάθαρσις. ἀλλ᾽ ἡ ψυχῆς φύσις οὐκ
ἦν ἀγαθόν, ἀλλ᾽ ἀγαθοῦ μετέχειν δυνάμενον καὶ ἀγαθοειδές. οὐ γὰρ ἂν
ἐγένετο ἐν κακῷ. τὸ οὖν ἀγαθὸν αὐτῇ ἐν τῷ συνεῖναι τῷ γεννήσαντι, κακία
δὲ τὸ τοῖς ὑστέροις. καὶ διπλῆ γε κακία· τό τε τούτοις συνεῖναι καὶ μετὰ
παθῶν ὑπερβολῆς. διὸ πᾶσαι αἱ πολιτικαὶ ἀρεταί, μιᾶς γοῦν αὐτὴν κακίας
ἀπαλλάττουσαι, ἀρεταὶ ἐκρίθησαν καὶ τίμιαι. αἱ δὲ καθαρτικαὶ τιμιώτεραι καὶ
τῆς ὡς ψυχῆς κακίας ἀπαλλάττουσαι· δεῖ τοίνυν καθηραμένην αὐτὴν συνεῖναι
τῷ γεννήσαντι. καὶ ἀρετὴ ἄρα αὐτῆς μετὰ τὴν ἐπιστροφὴν αὕτη, ἥπερ ἐστὶν ἐν
γνώσει καὶ εἰδήσει τοῦ ὄντος, οὐχ ὅτι οὐκ ἔχει παρ᾽ αὐτῇ ταύτην, ἀλλ᾽ ὅτι ἄνευ
τοῦ πρὸ αὐτῆς οὐχ ὁρᾷ τὰ αὐτῆς.

§ 4   Ἄλλο οὖν γένος τρίτον ἀρετῶν μετὰ τὰς καθαρτικὰς καὶ πολιτικάς, νοερῶς
τῆς ψυχῆς ἐνεργούσης. σοφία μὲν καὶ φρόνησις ἐν θεωρίᾳ ὧν νοῦς ἔχει, δικαιοσύνη δὲ οἰκειοπραγία ἐν τῇ πρὸς τὸν νοῦν ἀκολουθίᾳ καὶ τῷ πρὸς τὸν νοῦν
ἐνεργεῖν, σωφροσύνη δὲ ἡ εἴσω πρὸς νοῦν στροφή, ἡ δὲ ἀνδρεία ἀπάθεια καθ᾽
ὁμοίωσιν τοῦ πρὸς ὃ βλέπει, ἀπαθὲς ὂν τὴν φύσιν. καὶ ἀνταλοκουθοῦσί γε
αὗται ἀλλήλαις, ὥσπερ καὶ αἱ ἄλλαι.

§ 5   Τέταρτὸν δὲ εἶδος ἀρετῶν, τὸ τῶν παραδειγματικῶν, αἵπερ ἦσαν ἐν τῷ
νῷ, κρείττους οὖσαι τῶν ψυχικῶν καὶ τούτων παραδείγματα, ὧν αἱ τῆς ψυχῆς
ἦσαν ὁμοιώματα.

The distinction between πολιτικαί and καθαρτικαί ἀρεταί is added by Porph.
to Plotinus' theory. Moreover, Plotinus does not speak of "virtue" in Noûs:
the παράδειγμα of virtue is no virtue, he declared (*Enn.* I 2, 6, 1. 14-18; above,
nr. **1419e**).
The passage on κάθαρσις and virtue (§ 3, l. 11 ff.) is taken from *Enn.* I 2, 4,
l. 5-17 (above, nr. **1419b**), § 4 from I 2, 6, l. 20 ff. (above, **1420a**).

1440—We follow Porph. in his admonitions to his wife.

The letter to
Marcella

His first point is that ἡδονή and ῥαθυμία are opposed to the ascent to God and
that, hence, πόνος must be practised as a training for spiritual life. The life of
the philosopher must bear witness to his theory.—Follows a summary of the doctrine. The author admonishes his correspondent to find spiritual wealth within
herself and to exercise her mind. For the mind of the wise man is a temple of God,
and God is the only thing the wise man needs. Unless one is directed towards
Him, the soul becomes a dwelling-place of daemons.

a. Porph., *Ad Marc.* 7-11 (Nauck, *Porph. opusc. sel.* p. 278 l. 17-282 l. 4):

Praise of πόνος

Παντὸς γὰρ καλοῦ κτήματος πόνους δεῖ προηγεῖσθαι, καὶ πονεῖν ἀνάγκη τὸν τυχεῖν ἀρετῆς σπουδάζοντα. ἀκούεις δὲ καὶ τὸν Ἡρακλέα τούς τε Διοσκούρους καὶ τὸν Ἀσκληπιὸν τούς τε ἄλλους ὅσοι θεῶν παῖδες ἐγένοντο ὡς διὰ τῶν πόνων καὶ τῆς καρτερίας τὴν μακαρίαν εἰς θεοὺς ὁδὸν ἐξετέλεσαν. οὐ γὰρ ἐκ τῶν δι᾽ ἡδονῆς βεβιωκότων ἀνθρώπων αἱ εἰς θεὸν ἀναδρομαί, ἀλλ᾽ ἐκ τῶν τὰ μέγιστα τῶν συμβαινόντων γενναίως διενεγκεῖν μεμαθηκότων.—

Life must bear witness to theory

(8) Ἔχει δὲ οὐχ οὕτω παντάπασι δυσκαρτερήτως σοι τὰ παρόντα, εἰ παρεῖσα τὴν ἐκ τοῦ πάθους ἀλόγιστον ταραχὴν μὴ περὶ φαύλων ἡγήσῃ μεμυῆσθαι ὧν εἰς φιλοσοφίαν τὴν ὀρθὴν παρὰ τῶν θείων ἐτελέσθης λόγων· ὧν τὴν βεβαίαν ἀκρόασιν αἱ πράξεις ἐλέγχειν εἰώθασι. τὰ γὰρ ἔργα τῶν δογμάτων ἑκάστου φέρειν πέφυκε τὰς ἀποδείξεις· καὶ δεῖ οὕτως βιοῦν ὅστις ἐπίστευσεν, ἵνα καὶ αὐτὸς πιστὸς ᾖ μάρτυς περὶ ὧν λέγει τοῖς ἀκρωμένοις.

Τίνα οὖν ἦν ἄρα ἃ παρὰ τῶν σαφέστατ᾽ εἰδότων τὰ κατ᾽ ἀνθρώπους μεμαθήκαμεν; ἆρ᾽ οὐχ ὅτι μὲν σοὶ ἐγὼ οὐχ ὁ ἁπτὸς οὗτος καὶ τῇ αἰσθήσει ὑποπτωτός, ὁ δὲ ἐπὶ πλεῖστον ἀφεστηκὼς τοῦ σώματος, ὁ ἀχρώματος καὶ ἀσχημάτιστος, καὶ χερσὶ μὲν οὐδαμῶς ἐπαφητός, διανοίᾳ δὲ μόνῃ κρατητός;—

(9) Πρὸς δὲ τούτοις οὐχ ὅτι πᾶν πάθος ψυχῆς εἰς σωτηρίαν αὐτῆς πολεμιώτατον, καὶ ἀπαιδευσία μὲν τῶν παθῶν πάντων μήτηρ, τὸ δὲ πεπαιδεῦσθαι οὐκ ἐν πολυμαθείας ἀναλήψει, ἐν ἀπαλλάξει δὲ τῶν ψυχικῶν παθῶν ἐθεωρεῖτο; πάθη δὲ νοσημάτων ἀρχαί· ψυχῆς δὲ νόσημα κακία· κακία δὲ πᾶσα αἰσχρόν· τὸ δὲ αἰσχρὸν τῷ καλῷ ἐναντίον· καλοῦ δὲ ὄντος τοῦ θείου ἀμήχανον αὐτῷ σὺν κακίᾳ πελάζειν· καθαροῦ γὰρ μὴ καθαρὸν ἐφάπτεσθαι οὐδὲν ὁ Πλάτων φησὶ θεμιτὸν εἶναι. διὸ καὶ μέχρι τοῦ νῦν καθαρεύειν δεῖ τῶν παθῶν τε καὶ τῶν διὰ τὸ πάθος ἁμαρτημάτων.

Ἆρ᾽ οὖν οὐ τοιαῦτα ἦν οἷς μάλιστα συνήνεις, ὡς γράμματα θεῖα ἐνόντα παρὰ σαυτῇ διὰ τῆς τῶν λόγων ἐπιδείξεως ἀναγινώσκουσα; πῶς οὖν οὐκ ἄτοπον τὴν πεπεισμένην ἐν σοὶ εἶναι καὶ τὸ σῷζον καὶ τὸ σῳζόμενον καὶ τό γε ἀπολλύον καὶ <τὸ> ἀπολλύμενον τόν τε πλοῦτον καὶ τὴν πενίαν τόν τε πατέρα καὶ τὸν ἄνδρα καὶ τὸν τῶν ὄντως ἀγαθῶν καθηγεμόνα, κεχηνέναι πρὸς τὴν τοῦ ὑφηγητοῦ σκιάν, ὡς δὴ τὸν ὄντως ὑφηγητὴν μὴ ἐντὸς ἔχουσαν μηδὲ παρὰ σαυτῇ πάντα τὸν πλοῦτον;—

(10) Συνάγοις δ᾽ ἂν καὶ ἑνίζοις τὰς ἐμφύτους ἐννοίας καὶ διαρθροῦν συγκεχυμένας καὶ εἰς φῶς ἕλκειν ἐσκοτισμένας πειρωμένη. ἀφ᾽ ὧν ὁρμώμενος καὶ ὁ θεῖος Πλάτων ἀπὸ τῶν αἰσθητῶν ἐπὶ τὰ νοητὰ τὰς ἀνακλήσεις πεποίηται.—

(11) Λέγει δὲ ὁ λόγος πάντη μὲν καὶ πάντως παρεῖναι τὸ θεῖον, νεὼν δὲ τούτῳ παρ᾽ ἀνθρώποις καθιερῶσθαι τὴν διάνοιαν μάλιστα τοῦ σοφοῦ μόνην, τιμήν τε προσήκουσαν ἀπονέμεσθαι τῷ θεῷ ὑπὸ τοῦ μάλιστα τὸν θεὸν ἐγνω-

κότος· τοῦτον δὲ εἶναι εἰκότως μόνον τὸν σοφόν.—Θεὸς μὲν γὰρ δεῖται
οὐδενός, σοφὸς δὲ μόνου θεοῦ. οὐ γὰρ ἂν ἄλλος καλὸς κἀγαθὸς γένοιτο ἢ <ὁ>
νοῶν τό τε ἀγαθὸν καὶ καλόν, ὅπερ ἐξέχει τοῦ θείου· οὐδ' αὖ ἄλλος κακοδαίμων
ἄνθρωπος ἢ <ὁ> πονηρῶν δαιμόνων ἐνδιαίτημα τὴν ψυχὴν κατασκευάσας.
ἀνθρώπῳ δὲ σοφῷ θεὸς θεοῦ δίδωσιν ἐξουσίαν, καὶ καθαίρεται μὲν ἄνθρωπος
ἐννοίᾳ θεοῦ, δικαιοπραγίαν δὲ ἀπὸ θεοῦ ὁρμώμενος διώκει.

b. *Ad Marc.* 12 (Nauck p. 282 l. 5-19):

Think of God as being present at all your works and deeds. He is the cause of
all good things, while we ourselves are the cause of evil. Ask of Him only spiritual
blessings, which cannot be lost.

**God's
presence
in our life**

Πάσης πράξεως καὶ παντὸς ἔργου καὶ λόγου θεὸς ἐπόπτης παρέστω καὶ
ἔφορος. καὶ πάντων ὧν πράττομεν ἀγαθῶν τὸν θεὸν αἴτιον ἡγώμεθα· τῶν
δὲ κακῶν αἴτιοι ἡμεῖς ἐσμεν οἱ ἑλόμενοι, θεὸς δὲ ἀναίτιος [1]. ὅθεν καὶ εὐκτέον
θεῷ τὰ ἄξια θεοῦ. καὶ αἰτώμεθα ἃ μὴ λάβοιμεν ἂν παρ' ἑτέρου· καὶ ὧν ἡγεμόνες
οἱ μετ' ἀρετῆς πόνοι, ταῦτα εὐχώμεθα γενέσθαι μετὰ τοὺς πόνους· εὐχὴ γὰρ
ῥᾳθύμου μάταιος λόγος. ἃ δὲ κτησαμένη οὐ καθέξεις, μὴ αἰτοῦ παρὰ θεοῦ·
δῶρον γὰρ θεοῦ πᾶν ἀναφαίρετον· ὥστε οὐ δώσει ὃ μὴ καθέξεις. ὧν δὴ τοῦ
σώματος ἀπαλλαγεῖσα οὐ δεηθήσῃ, ἐκείνων καταφρόνει· καὶ ὧν ἂν ἀπαλλαγεῖσα
δεηθῇς, ταῦτά σοι ἀσκουμένῃ τὸν θεὸν παρακάλει γενέσθαι συλλήπτορα.
οὔκουν δεήσῃ οὐδενὸς ὧν καὶ ἡ τύχη δοῦσα πολλάκις πάλιν ἀφαιρεῖται.

c. Ib., 14-19 (Nauck p. 283-287):

Striving after pleasure is incompatible with the love of God. Do not speak lightly
about God. Virtue is the only way to serve Him.

**Love of
pleasure
excluded**

Ἀδύνατον τὸν αὐτὸν φιλόθεόν τε εἶναι καὶ φιλήδονον [καὶ φιλοσώματον].
ὁ γὰρ φιλήδονος καὶ φιλοσώματος, ὁ δὲ φιλοσώματος πάντως καὶ φιλοχρήματος,
ὁ δὲ φιλοχρήματος ἐξ ἀνάγκης ἄδικος, ὁ δε ἄδικος καὶ εἰς θεὸν καὶ εἰς πατέρας
ἀνόσιος καὶ εἰς τοὺς ἄλλους παράνομος, ὥστε κἂν ἑκατόμβας θύῃ καὶ μυρίοις
ἀναθήμασι τοὺς νεὼς ἀγάλλῃ, ἀσεβής ἐστι καὶ ἄθεος καὶ τῇ προαιρέσει ἱερό-
συλος. διὸ καὶ πάντα φιλοσώματον ὡς ἄθεον καὶ μιαρὸν ἐκτρέπεσθαι χρή. —

(15) Νόμιζε αἱρετώτερον εἶναι σιγᾶν ἢ λόγον εἰκῇ προέσθαι περὶ θεοῦ.
ἀξίαν σε ποιήσει θεοῦ τὸ μηδὲν ἀνάξιον θεοῦ μήτε λέγειν μήτε πράττειν μήτε
πάντως εἰδέναι ἀξιοῦν. ὁ δὲ ἄξιος ἄνθρωπος θεοῦ θεὸς ἂν εἴη. καὶ τιμήσεις μὲν
ἄριστα τὸν θεόν, ὅταν τῷ θεῷ τὴν σαυτῆς διάνοιαν ὁμοιώσῃς· ἡ δὲ ὁμοίωσις
ἔσται διὰ μόνης ἀρετῆς· μόνη γὰρ ἀρετὴ τὴν ψυχὴν ἄνω ἕλκει καὶ πρὸς τὸ
συγγενές. καὶ μέγα οὐδὲν ἄλλο μετὰ θεὸν ἢ ἀρετή.—

Οὐχ ἡ γλῶττα τοῦ σοφοῦ τίμιον παρὰ θεῷ, ἀλλὰ τὰ ἔργα. σοφὸς γὰρ ἀνὴρ
καὶ σιγῶν τὸν θεὸν τιμᾷ· ἄνθρωπος δὲ ἀμαθὴς καὶ εὐχόμενος καὶ θύων μιαίνει
τὸ θεῖον. μόνος οὖν ἱερεὺς ὁ σοφός, μόνος θεοφιλής, μόνος εἰδὼς εὔξασθαι.

**Virtue the
only way to
God**

---

[1] Plato, *Rep.* X 617e (*Gr. Ph.* I, p. 215).

καὶ ὁ σοφίαν ἀσκῶν ἐπιστήμην ἀσκεῖ τὴν περὶ θεοῦ, οὐ λιτανεύων ἀεὶ καὶ θύων, διὰ δὲ τῶν ἔργων τὴν πρὸς θεὸν ἀσκῶν εὐσέβειαν.

(18) Βωμοὶ δὲ θεοῦ ἱερουργούμενοι μὲν οὐδὲν βλάπτουσιν, ἀμελούμενοι δὲ οὐδὲν ὠφελοῦσιν. ὅστις δὲ τιμᾷ τὸν θεὸν ὡς προσδεόμενον, οὗτος λέληθεν ἑαυτὸν δοξάζων τοῦ θεοῦ κρείττων εἶναι. — (19) Οὔτε δάκρυα καὶ ἱκετεῖαι θεὸν ἐπιστρέφουσιν οὔτε θυηπολίαι θεὸν τιμῶσιν οὔτε ἀναθημάτων πλῆθος κοσμοῦσι θεόν, ἀλλὰ τὸ ἔνθεον φρόνημα καλῶς ἡδρασμένον συνάπτει θεῷ.

d. As soon as man forgets God his soul becomes a dwelling-place of evil spirits.

Religious and irreligious men Ib., 21-24 (Nauck p. 287-289):

Ὅπου δ' ἂν λήθη παρεισέλθῃ θεοῦ, τὸν κακὸν δαίμονα ἀνάγκη ἐνοικεῖν· 2 χώρημα γὰρ ἡ ψυχή, ὥσπερ μεμάθηκας, ἢ θεῶν ἢ δαιμόνων. καὶ θεῶν μὲν συνόντων πράξει τὰ ἀγαθὰ καὶ διὰ τῶν λόγων καὶ διὰ τῶν ἔργων· ὑποδεξαμένη δὲ [ψυχὴ] τὸν κακὸν σύνοικον διὰ πονηρίας πάντα ἐνεργεῖ. ὅταν οὖν ἴδῃς ἄνθρωπον τοῖς κακοῖς χαίροντα καὶ δρῶντα, γίνωσκε τοῦτον ἠρνῆσθαι μὲν τὸν θεὸν ἐν τῇ γνώμῃ, πονηροῦ δὲ δαίμονος ὄντα ἐνδιαίτημα.

Θεὸν οἱ μὲν εἶναι νομίζοντες καὶ διοικεῖν ἅπαντα τοῦτο γέρας ἐκτήσαντο διὰ τῆς γνώσεως καὶ τῆς βεβαίας πίστεως, τὸ μεμαθηκέναι ὅτι ὑπὸ θεοῦ προνοεῖται πάντα καὶ εἰσὶν ἄγγελοι θεῖοί τε καὶ ἀγαθοὶ δαίμονες ἐπόπται τῶν πραττομένων, οὓς καὶ λαθεῖν ἀμήχανον. καὶ δὴ τοῦτο οὕτως ἔχειν πεπεισμένοι φυλάττονται μὲν μὴ διαπίπτειν τοῖς κατὰ τὸν βίον, πρὸ ὄψεως ἔχοντες τὴν τῶν θεῶν ἀναπόδραστον ἐφόρασιν· εὐγνώμονα δὲ βίον κτησάμενοι μανθάνουσι θεοὺς γινώσκονταί τε γινωσκομένοις θεοῖς. οἱ δὲ μήτε εἶναι θεοὺς πιστεύσαντες μήτε 2 προνοίᾳ θεοῦ διοικεῖσθαι τὰ ὅλα, δίκης κόλασιν πεπόνθασι τὸ μήτε ἑαυτοῖς πιστεύειν μήθ' ἑτέροις ὅτι θεοὶ εἰσὶ καὶ οὐκ ἀλόγῳ φορᾷ διοικεῖται τὰ πάντα. εἰς κίνδυνον οὖν ἄφατον ἑαυτοὺς ἐμβαλόντες ἀλόγῳ ὁρμῇ καὶ εὐδιαπτώτῳ τοῖς κατὰ τὸν βίον ἐπιτίθενται καὶ πάντα δρῶσιν ἃ μὴ θέμις, ἀναιρεῖν πειρώμενοι τὴν περὶ θεοὺς ὑπόληψιν. καὶ δὴ τούτους μὲν ἀγνοίας ἕνεκα καὶ ἀπιστίας θεοὶ διαφεύγουσιν· αὐτοὶ δὲ θεοὺς καὶ τὴν ὀπαδὸν τῶν θεῶν δίκην οὔτε φυγεῖν οὔτε λαθεῖν δύνανται· βίον δὲ κακοδαίμονα καὶ πλανήτην ἑλόμενοι ἀγνοοῦντες θεοὺς γινώσκονται θεοῖς καὶ τῇ δίκῃ τῇ παρὰ θεῶν. κἂν θεοὺς τιμᾶν οἴωνται 2 καὶ πεπεῖσθαι εἶναι θεούς, ἀρετῆς δὲ ἀμελῶσι καὶ σοφίας, ἤρνηνται θεοὺς καὶ ἀτιμάζουσιν.

Their prayers (24) Εὐχὴ ἡ μὲν μετὰ φαύλων ἔργων ἀκάθαρτος καὶ διὰ τοῦτο ἀπρόσδεκτος 2 ὑπὸ θεοῦ· ἡ δὲ μετὰ καλῶν ἔργων καθαρά τε ὁμοῦ καὶ εὐπρόσδεκτος.

e. Porph. wishes to establish four principles concerning God.

Four principles Ad Marc. 24 (Nauck p. 289, l. 17-25):

Τέσσαρα στοιχεῖα μάλιστα κεκρατύνθω περὶ θεοῦ· πίστις, ἀλήθεια, ἔρως,

ἐλπίς. πιστεῦσαι γὰρ δεῖ ὅτι μόνη σωτηρία ἡ πρὸς τὸν θεὸν ἐπιστροφή, καὶ
πιστεύσαντα ὡς ἔνι μάλιστα σπουδάσαι τἀληθῆ γνῶναι περὶ αὐτοῦ, καὶ γνόντα
ἐρασθῆναι τοῦ γνωσθέντος, ἐρασθέντα δὲ ἐλπίσιν ἀγαθαῖς τρέφειν τὴν ψυχὴν
διὰ τοῦ βίου. ἐλπίσι γὰρ ἀγαθαῖς οἱ ἀγαθοὶ τῶν φαύλων ὑπερέχουσι. στοιχεῖα
μὲν οὖν ταῦτα καὶ τοσαῦτα κεκρατύνθω.

No doubt Porph. arrived at these four principles in defending the Neoplatonic
view of life and God against Christian doctrine. His master Plotinus neither began
by faith nor ended with hope.

f. Plotinus, as we found above (nr. **1410c**) excluded soul as the **The body not**
cause of evil. Sin is the consequence of yielding to things that are inferior **the cause of**
to soul, and the cause of this yielding is not soul itself, but its προσθῆκαι. **sin**
Porphyrius, though not of an essentially different opinion, expressed
himself in other terms.

Ad Marc. 28 (Nauck p. 292/3):

Μηδὲ αἰτιώμεθα τὴν σάρκα ὡς τῶν μεγάλων κακῶν αἰτίαν μηδ' εἰς τὰ
πράγματα τρέπωμεν τὰς δυσφορίας, ἐν δὲ τῇ ψυχῇ τὰς τούτων αἰτίας μᾶλλον
ζητῶμεν καὶ ἀπορρήξαντες πᾶσαν ματαίαν τῶν ἐφημέρων ὄρεξιν καὶ ἐλπίδα
ὅλοι γενώμεθα ἑαυτῶν. ἢ γὰρ διὰ φόβον τις κακοδαιμονεῖ ἢ δι' ἀόριστον καὶ
κενὴν ἐπιθυμίαν· ἅ τις χαλινῶν δύναται τὸν μακάριον ἑαυτῷ περιποιεῖσθαι
λογισμόν.

Evidently, in declaring that the cause of great sins should not be sought for
in the body but in "soul", Porph. took "soul" in a more comprehensive sense
than Plotinus did when he denied that soul could be the cause of sin. Cp. Iamblichus, below, nr. **1453**.

1441—Also in *De abstinentia* Porphyrius's first warning is against
the πάθη. Man should refrain from all sensations which could stimulate
them.

Porph., *De abst.* I 33-35:   **How to get**
                                                                  rid of the
33   Δύο πηγαὶ ἀνεῖνται πρὸς δεσμὸν τῆς ψυχῆς ἐνταῦθα, ἐξ ὧν ὥσπερ θανασίμων **πάθη**
πωμάτων ἐμπιμπλαμένη ἐν λήθῃ τῶν οἰκείων γίγνεται θεαμάτων, ἡδονή τε
καὶ λύπη· ὧν παρασκευαστικὴ μὲν ἡ αἴσθησις καὶ ἡ κατὰ τὴν αἴσθησιν ἀντίληψις αἵ τε συνομαρτοῦσαι ταῖς αἰσθήσεσι φαντασίαι τε καὶ δόξαι καὶ μνῆμαι,
ἐκ δὲ τούτων ἐγειρόμενα τὰ πάθη καὶ πᾶσα ἡ ἀλογία παχυνομένη κατάγει
τὴν ψυχὴν καὶ τοῦ οἰκείου περὶ τὸ ὂν ἀποστρέφει ἔρωτος. ἀποστατέον ἄρα εἰς
δύναμιν τούτων. αἱ δὲ ἀποστάσεις διὰ τῶν ἐκκλίσεων τῶν κατὰ τὰς αἰσθήσεις
παθῶν καὶ τῶν κατὰ τὰς ἀλογίας, αἱ δὲ αἰσθήσεις ἢ διὰ τῶν ὁρατῶν ἢ τῶν
ἀκουστῶν ἢ γευστῶν ἢ ὀσφραντῶν ἢ ἁπτῶν. οἷον γὰρ μητρόπολις ἡ αἴσθησις ἦν

τῆς ἐν ἡμῖν ἐκφύλου τῶν παθῶν ἀποικίας. φέρε γὰρ ἴδε καθ' ἑκάστην ὅσον τὸ
ὑπέκκαυμα εἰσρεῖ τῶν παθῶν εἰς ἡμᾶς, τοῦτο μὲν ἐκ τῆς κατὰ τὰς θέας ἵππων
τε ἀμίλλης καὶ ἀθλητῶν ἢ τῶν ἐκλελυγισμένων ὀρχήσεων, τοῦτο δὲ ἐκ τῆς
ἐπιβλέψεως τῆς πρὸς τὸ θῆλυ, αἱ δέλεαρ τοῦ ἀλογίστου παντοίαις ἐπιθέτοις
παγίσι χειροῦνται τὸ ἄλογον. κατὰ γὰρ πάντα τὰ τοιαῦτα ἐκβακχευομένη ὑπὸ 3
τῆς ἀλογίας ἀναπηδᾶν τε ποιεῖ καὶ ἐκβοᾶν καὶ κεκραγέναι, τῆς ἔξω ταραχῆς
ἀπὸ τῆς ἔνδον ἐκκαομένης, ἣν ἀνῆψεν ἡ αἴσθησις. αἱ δὲ διὰ τῶν ἀκοῶν ἐμπαθεῖς
οὖσαι κινήσεις ἔκ τε ποιῶν ψόφων καὶ ἤχων, αἰσχρορρημοσύνης τε καὶ λοιδορίας,
[ὡς] τοὺς μὲν πολλοὺς τέλεον τοῦ λογισμοῦ ἐκδεδυκότος φέρεσθαι ποιοῦσιν
οἰστρουμένους, τοὺς δ' αὖ θηλυνομένους παντοίας στροφὰς ἑλίττεσθαι. θυ-
μιαμάτων δὲ χρήσεις ἢ εὐώδεις πνοαί, αἵ τε τοὺς αὐτῶν ἔρωτας τοῖς ἐρασταῖς
ἐμπορευόμεναι, τίνα λελήθασιν, ὅσην τῆς ψυχῆς τὴν ἠλογίαν πιαίνουσιν; περὶ
γὰρ τῶν διὰ τῆς γεύσεως τί ἄν τις καὶ εἴποι παθημάτων, διπλοῦ μάλιστ' ἐνταῦθα
τοῦ δεσμοῦ συμπλεκομένου· τοῦ μὲν ὂν ἐκ τῆς γεύσεως τὰ πάθη πιαίνει, τοῦ δὲ
ὂν ἐκ τῆς ἐμφορήσεως τῶν ἀλλοτρίων σωμάτων βαρύν τε καὶ δυνατὸν ἐργαζόμεθα; φάρμακα γάρ, ὥς πού τις τῶν ἰατρῶν ἔφη, οὐ μόνα τὰ σκευαστὰ ὑπὸ
τῆς ἰατρικῆς, ἀλλὰ καὶ τὰ καθ' ἡμέραν εἰς τροφὴν παραλαμβανόμενα σιτία
τε καὶ ποτά· καὶ πολὺ μᾶλλον τὸ θανάσιμον ἐκ τούτων τῇ ψυχῇ ἀναδίδοται ἢ
ἐκ τῶν φαρμακειῶν εἰς διάλυσιν τοῦ σώματος κατασκευάζεται. αἱ δὲ ἀφαὶ
μόνον οὐ σωματοῦσαι τὴν ψυχὴν καὶ εἰς ἀνάρθρους ψόφους, οἷα δὴ σῶμα,
πολλάκις ἐκπίπτειν ἠρέθισαν. ἐξ ὧν αἱ μνῆμαι καὶ αἱ φαντασίαι αἵ τε δόξαι
ἀθροιζόμεναι ἑσμὸν τῶν παθῶν ἐγείρουσαι, φόβων, ἐπιθυμιῶν, ὀργῶν, ἐρώτων,
φίλτρων, λυπῶν, ζήλων, μεριμνῶν, νοσημάτων, τῶν ὁμοίων παθῶν πλήρη
ἀπέδειξαν. διὸ πολὺς μὲν ὁ ἀγὼν τούτων καθαρεῦσαι, πολὺς δὲ ὁ πόνος ἀπαλλα- 35
γῆναι αὐτῶν τῆς μελέτης, καὶ νύκτωρ καὶ μεθ' ἡμέραν τῆς κατὰ τὴν αἴσθησιν
ἀναγκαίας συμπλοκῆς ἡμῖν παρούσης. ὅθεν ὅση δύναμις ἀποστατέον τῶν τοιούτων χωρίων, ἐν οἷς καὶ μὴ βουλόμενόν ἐστιν περιπίπτειν τῷ πάθει.

1442—In the following passage Porph. gives a survey of the doctrine
of "some Platonists" about God, gods and daemons.

God, gods
and
daemons

    a. Porph., *De abst.* II 37-39:

Ὁ μὲν πρῶτος θεὸς ἀσώματός τε ὢν καὶ ἀκίνητος καὶ ἀμέριστος καὶ οὔτε 37
ἔν τινι ὢν οὔτ' ἐνδεδεμένος εἰς ἑαυτόν, χρῄζει οὐδενὸς τῶν ἔξωθεν, ὥσπερ
εἴρηται, οὐ μὴν οὐδ' ἡ τοῦ κόσμου ψυχὴ ἔχουσα μὲν τὸ τριχῇ διαστατὸν καὶ
αὐτοκίνητον ἐκ φύσεως, προαιρεῖσθαι δὲ πεφυκυῖα τὸ καλῶς καὶ εὐτάκτως
κινεῖσθαι καὶ κινεῖν τὸ σῶμα τοῦ κόσμου κατὰ τοὺς ἀρίστους λόγους. δέδεκται
δὲ τὸ σῶμα εἰς ἑαυτὴν καὶ περιείληφεν, καίπερ ἀσώματος οὖσα καὶ παντὸς
πάθους ἀμέτοχος. τοῖς δὲ λοιποῖς θεοῖς, τῷ τε κόσμῳ καὶ τοῖς ἀπλανέσι καὶ

πλανωμένοις, ἔκ τε ψυχῆς καὶ σώματος οὖσιν ὁρατοῖς θεοῖς, ἀντευχαριστητέον τὸν εἰρημένον τρόπον διὰ τῶν θυσιῶν τῶν ἀψύχων. λοιπὸν οὖν ἡμῖν ἐστὶ τὸ τῶν ἀοράτων πλῆθος, οὓς δαίμονας ἀδιαστόλως εἴρηκε Πλάτων. τούτων δὲ οἱ μὲν κατονομασθέντες ὑπὸ τῶν ἀνθρώπων παρ' ἑκάστοις τυγχάνουσι τιμῶν τ' ἰσοθέων καὶ τῆς ἄλλης θεραπείας, οἱ δὲ ὡς τὸ πολὺ μὲν οὐ πάνυ τι κατωνομάσθησαν, ὑπ' ἐνίων δὲ κατὰ κώμας ἤ τινας πόλεις ὀνόματός τε καὶ θρησκείας ἀφανῶς τυγχάνουσιν. τὸ δὲ ἄλλο πλῆθος οὕτω μὲν κοινῶς προσαγορεύεται τῷ τῶν δαιμόνων ὀνόματι, πεῖσμα δὲ περὶ πάντων τοιοῦτόν ἐστιν, ὡς ἄρα καὶ βλάπτοιεν <ἂν> εἰ χολωθεῖεν ἐπὶ τῷ παρορᾶσθαι καὶ μὴ τυγχάνειν τῆς νενομισμένης θεραπείας, καὶ πάλιν εὐεργετοῖεν ἂν τοὺς εὐχαῖς τε αὐτοὺς καὶ λιτα-
38 νείαις θυσίαις τε καὶ τοῖς ἀκολούθοις ἐξευμενιζομένους. συγκεχυμένης δὲ τῆς περὶ αὐτῶν ἐννοίας καὶ εἰς πολλὴν διαβολὴν χωρούσης ἀναγκαῖον διαστεῖλαι λόγῳ τὴν φύσιν αὐτῶν. ἴσως γὰρ ἀναγκαῖον φασὶν ὅθεν ἡ πλάνη γέγονεν τοῖς ἀνθρώποις περὶ αὐτῶν ἀναφαίνειν. διαιρετέον οὖν τὸν τρόπον τοῦτον. ὅσαι μὲν ψυχαὶ τῆς ὅλης ἐκπεφυκυῖαι μεγάλα μέρη διοικοῦσι τῶν ὑπὸ σελήνην τόπων, ἐπερειδόμεναι μὲν πνεύματι [1], κρατοῦσαι δὲ αὐτοῦ κατὰ λόγον, ταύτας δαίμονάς τε ἀγαθοὺς νομιστέον καὶ ἐπ' ὠφελείᾳ τῶν ἀρχομένων πάντα πραγματεύεσθαι, εἴτε τινῶν ἀφηγοῖντο ζώων, εἴτε καρπῶν ἀποτεταγμένων, εἴτε καὶ τῶν ἕνεκα τούτων, οἷον ὄμβρων, πνευμάτων μετρίων, εὐδίας, τῶν τε ἄλλων ἃ τούτοις συνεργεῖ, εὐκρασίας τε ὡρῶν τοῦ ἔτους, ἡμῖν αὖ τεχνῶν τε καὶ τῶν κατὰ μουσικὴν παιδείας τε συναπάσης ἰατρικῆς τε καὶ γυμναστικῆς ἤ τινος τούτοις ὁμοίας. τούτους γὰρ ἀδύνατόν ἐστι καὶ τὰς ὠφελείας ἐκπορίζειν καὶ πάλιν αὖ βλάβης ἐν τοῖς αὐτοῖς αἰτίους γίγνεσθαι. ἐν δὲ τούτοις ἀριθμητέον καὶ τοὺς πορθμεύοντας, ὥς φησι Πλάτων [2] καὶ διαγγέλλοντας τὰ παρ' ἀνθρώπων θεοῖς καὶ τὰ παρὰ θεῶν ἀνθρώποις, τὰς μὲν παρ' ἡμῶν εὐχὰς ὡς πρὸς δικαστὰς ἀναφέροντας τοὺς θεούς, τὰς δὲ ἐκείνων παραινέσεις καὶ νουθεσίας μετὰ μαντειῶν ἐκφέροντας ἡμῖν. ὅσαι δὲ ψυχαὶ τοῦ συνεχοῦς πνεύματος οὐ κρατοῦσιν, ἀλλ' ὡς τὸ πολὺ καὶ κρατοῦνται, δι' αὐτὸ τοῦτο ἄγονταί τε καὶ φέρονται λίαν, ὅταν αἱ τοῦ πνεύματος ὀργαί τε καὶ ἐπιθυμίαι τὴν ὁρμὴν λάβωσιν. αὗται δ' αἱ ψυχαὶ δαίμονες μὲν καὶ
39 αὗταί, κακοεργοὶ δ' ἂν εἰκότως λέγοιντο. καὶ εἰσὶν οἱ σύμπαντες οὗτοί τε καὶ οἱ τῆς ἐναντίας δυνάμεως ἀόρατοί τε καὶ τελέως ἀναίσθητοι αἰσθήσεσιν ἀνθρωπί-

Good and
evil
daemons

---

[1] By this πνεῦμα is meant the "ethereal" or shining body of light which, according to Porph., envelops the world-soul as well as individual souls (Proclus, *In rem publ.* II p. 196, 24 Kroll). Daemons who do not have a material body "rest on it" as upon a vehicle (ὄχημα), as it is called by Porph., *Sent.* 29, p. 13 Mommert. Cp. Procl., *In Tim.* I p. 5 Diehl: ὄχημα αἰθέριον ἀνάλογον τῷ οὐρανῷ. As will appear in the last lines of the present chapter and the beginning of the next, Porph. regards the pneumatical (or ethereal) body as liable to πάθη and perishable. The doctrine is referred to by Zeller, *Ph. d. Gr.* III 2, p. 727; Verbeke, *La doctrine du pneuma*, p. 363 ff.

[2] *Symp.* 202e.

ναις. οὐ γὰρ στερεὸν σῶμα περιβέβληνται οὐδὲ μορφὴν πάντες μίαν, ἀλλ’ ἐν σχήμασι πλείοσιν ἐκτυπούμεναι αἱ χαρακτηρίζουσαι τὸ πνεῦμα αὐτῶν μορφαὶ τοτὲ μὲν ἐπιφαίνονται, τοτὲ δὲ ἀφανεῖς εἰσιν· ἐνίοτε δὲ καὶ μεταβάλλουσι τὰς μορφὰς οἵ γε χείρους. τὸ δὲ πνεῦμα ᾗ μέν ἐστι σωματικόν, παθητικόν ἐστι καὶ φθαρτόν· τῷ δὲ ὑπὸ τῶν ψυχῶν οὕτως δεδέσθαι, ὥστε τὸ εἶδος αὐτῶν διαμένειν πλείω χρόνον, οὐ μήν ἐστιν αἰώνιον.

According to Proclus, *In Tim.* I, p. 152 Diehl, Porph. called the highest of the good daemons ἀρχάγγελοι. Cp. also the *Letter to Anebo* (in ps.-Iambl. *De mysteriis*, ed. Parthey, Berlin 1857), nr. 10, 16.

The work of evil daemons　　**b.** Porph., *De abst.* II 40:

Ἐν γὰρ δὴ καὶ τοῦτο τῆς μεγίστης βλάβης τῆς ἀπὸ τῶν κακοεργῶν δαιμόνων θετέον, ὅτι αὐτοὶ αἴτιοι γιγνόμενοι τῶν περὶ τὴν γῆν παθημάτων, οἷον λοιμῶν, ἀφοριῶν, σεισμῶν, αὐχμῶν καὶ τῶν ὁμοίων, ἀναπείθουσιν ἡμᾶς, ὡς ἄρα τούτων αἴτιοί εἰσιν οἵπερ καὶ τῶν ἐναντιωτάτων [τουτέστιν τῶν εὐφοριῶν], ἑαυτοὺς ἐξαιροῦντες τῆς αἰτίας καὶ αὐτὸ τοῦτο πραγματευόμενοι πρῶτον, τὸ λανθάνειν ἀδικοῦντες. τρέπουσίν τε μετὰ τοῦτο ἐπὶ λιτανείας ἡμᾶς καὶ θυσίας τῶν ἀγαθοεργῶν θεῶν ὡς ὠργισμένων. ταῦτα δὲ καὶ τὰ ὅμοια ποιοῦσιν μεταστῆσαι ἡμᾶς ἐθέλοντες ἀπὸ τῆς ὀρθῆς ἐννοίας τῶν θεῶν καὶ ἐφ’ ἑαυτοὺς ἐπιστρέψαι. —

By rousing desires and passions in men the evil daemons are also the cause of wars and quarrels.
Cp. also Proclus, *In Tim.* I p. 77, II p. 12 Diehl; Euseb., *Praep. ev.* IV 23; August., *De civ. Dei* X 19. August., *De civ. Dei* X 9 cites Porph. on "theurgy".

Precious offerings a moral danger　　**1443**—Those who introduced precious offerings actually introduced a host of evil habits and ideas.

a. Porph., *De abst.* II 60:

Ἀγνοοῦσιν δὲ οἱ τὴν πολυτέλειαν εἰσαγαγόντες εἰς τὰς θυσίας, ὅπως ἅμα ταύτῃ ἑσμὸν κακῶν εἰσήγαγον, δεισιδαιμονίαν, τρυφήν, ὑπόληψιν τοῦ δεκάζειν δύνασθαι τὸ θεῖον καὶ θυσίαις ἀκεῖσθαι τὴν ἀδικίαν. ἢ πόθεν οἱ μὲν τριττύας χρυσόκερως, οἱ δ’ ἑκατόμβας, Ὀλυμπιὰς δ’ ἡ Ἀλεξάνδρου μήτηρ πάντα χίλια ἔθυεν, ἅπαξ τῆς πολυτελείας ἐπὶ τὴν δεισιδαιμονίαν προαγούσης; ὅταν δὲ νέος θεοὺς χαίρειν πολυτελείαις γνῷ καί, ὡς φασιν, ταῖς τῶν βοῶν καὶ τῶν ἄλλων ζῴων θοίναις, πότ’ ἂν ἑκὼν σωφρονήσειεν; πῶς δὲ κεχαρισμένα θύειν ἡγούμενος τοῖς θεοῖς ταῦτα, οὐκ ἐξεῖναι ἀδικεῖν οἰήσεται αὐτῷ μέλλοντι διὰ τῶν θυσιῶν ἐξωνεῖσθαι τὴν ἁμαρτίαν; πεισθεὶς δὲ ὅτι τούτων χρείαν οὐκ ἔχουσιν οἱ θεοί, εἰς δὲ τὸ ἦθος ἀποβλέπουσι τῶν προσιόντων, μεγίστην θυσίαν λαμβάνοντες τὴν ὀρθὴν περὶ αὐτῶν τε καὶ τῶν πραγμάτων διάληψιν, πῶς οὐ σώφρων καὶ ὅσιος καὶ δίκαιος ἔσται;

b. Ib., 61:

Θεοῖς δὲ ἀρίστη μὲν ἀπαρχὴ νοῦς καθαρὸς καὶ ψυχὴ ἀπαθής, οἰκεῖον δὲ καὶ
τὸ μετρίων μὲν ἀπάρχεσθαι τῶν ἄλλων, μὴ παρέργως δέ, ἀλλὰ σὺν πάσῃ
προθυμίᾳ.

1444—Against the Stoics, who exclude animals from their civitas of Abstinence
rational beings and hold that, hence, man has no moral obligations to them, duty to the
Porph. defends that animals do have a share in reason, both προφορικός philosopher
and ἐνδιαθετός. Therefore, man should treat animals as kindred beings.

Porph. does not intend to impose abstinence from flesh on everybody,
but he does hold that the philosopher, who is an ἄνθρωπος λελογωμένος,
must follow a stricter rule than the mass.

Porph., *De abst.* IV 18 (the end).

Not everything that is allowed to simple or uncivilized people will suit more
distinguished persons.

Τοιοῦτον οὖν τι καὶ τὸ ἐπὶ τῆς διαίτης φαίνεται· καὶ οὐχ ἥτις τοῖς πολλοῖς
συγκεχώρηται, ταύτην ἄν τις καὶ τοῖς βελτίστοις συγχωρήσειεν. φιλοσοφῶν
δὲ ἀνὴρ μάλιστ' ἂν τοὺς ἱεροὺς ἑαυτῷ ὑπογράψειε νόμους, οὓς θεοί τε καὶ
ἄνθρωποι ἀφώρισαν θεοῖς ἑπόμενοι. οἱ δ' ἱεροὶ πεφήνασι νόμοι κατὰ ἔθνη
καὶ κατὰ πόλεις ἁγνείαν μὲν προστάττοντες, ἐμψύχων δὲ βρῶσιν ἀπαγορεύοντες
τοῖς ἱερεῦσιν, ἤδη <δὲ> καὶ εἰς πλῆθος πίνειν κωλύοντες, ἢ δι' εὐσέβειαν ἢ διά
τινας βλάβας ἐκ τῆς τροφῆς· ὥστε ἢ τοὺς ἱερέας μιμητέον ἢ πᾶσι πειστέον
τοῖς νομοθέταις. ἑκατέρως γὰρ πάντων ἀφεκτέον τὸν νόμιμόν τε τελείως καὶ
εὐσεβῆ· εἰ γὰρ κατὰ μέρος τινὲς δι' εὐσέβειάν τινων ἀπέχονται, ὁ πρὸς πάντα
εὐσεβὴς πάντων ἀφέξεται.

1445—**a.** Porph. wrote commentaries on several works of Aristotle. Other works
Extant are: his short introduction to the *Categories*, Εἰσαγωγὴ εἰς τὰς of Porph.
Ἀριστοτέλους Κατηγορίας, also called Περὶ τῶν πέντε φωνῶν, and two Εἰσαγωγή
Commentaries on the *Categories* (*Comment. in Arist.* IV 1). and Comm.
on the
Categ.

After Plotinus' sharp criticism of Aristotle's theory of the categories in *Enn.*
VI 1, Porph. restored this theory. His Εἰσαγωγή is a work of far-reaching influence:
in the Latin translation of Boëthius it was used in the Medieval schools and commented on by Medieval logicians. See e.g. Abaelard's *Dialectica* ed. by L. M. de
Rijk, Assen 1956.

b. The Πυθαγόρου βίος was probably a part of a history of philo- b. Life of
sophy down to Plato. Pythagoras

c. The letter to the Egyptian priest Anebo (Πρὸς Ἀνεβώ) recon- c. Letter to
structed from fragments in Euseb., Cyrillus and Augustinus by Thomas Anebo

Gale in his edition of ps.-Iambl., *De mysteriis* (1678). It was re-edited by Parthey, Berlin 1857. The letter contains a sharp criticism of Egyptian polytheism.

d. De antro nympharum

d. The *De antro nympharum*, a sample of the allegorical interpretation of a passage in the *Odyssea*.

In Homer's description of the grotto of the Nymphs on Ithaca (*Od.* XIII 102-112) Porph. finds a "hidden meaning", namely, an ancient "theological wisdom", identical with "true philosophy".

e. Against the Christians

e. Of his 15 books Κατὰ Χριστιανῶν only fragments are extant.

f. Technical treatises

f. Three works on technical subjects are nowadays attributed to Porph., namely: (1) a commentary on Ptolemaeus' *Harmonica*; (2) an introduction to Ptolemaeus' *Tetrabiblos*; (3) a treatise on embryology, Πρὸς Γαῦρον περὶ τοῦ πῶς ἐμψυχοῦται τὰ ἔμβρυα (formerly attributed to Galenus).

g. A collection of oracles

g. Eusebius, *Praep. ev.* IV 7 preserved a collection of oracles gathered by Porph., which bears witness to the interest he took in these "signs of the gods to men".

2—IAMBLICHUS AND HIS SCHOOL

Life and personality

1446—a. Eunapius, *Vitae phil.* p. 457/8:

Μετὰ τούτους ὀνομαστότατος ἐπιγίνεται φιλόσοφος Ἰάμβλιχος, ὃς ἦν καὶ κατὰ γένος μὲν ἐπιφανὴς καὶ τῶν ἁβρῶν καὶ τῶν εὐδαιμόνων· πατρὶς δὲ ἦν αὐτῷ Χαλκίς· κατὰ τὴν κοίλην Συρίαν προσαγορευομένην ἐστὶν ἡ πόλις. οὗτος Ἀνατολίῳ τῷ μετὰ Πορφύριον τὰ δεύτερα φερομένῳ συγγενόμενος, πολύ γε ἐπέδωκε καὶ εἰς ἄκρον φιλοσοφίας ἤλασεν· εἶτα μετ' Ἀνατόλιον Πορφυρίῳ προσθεὶς ἑαυτόν, οὐκ ἔστιν ὅτι καὶ Πορφυρίου διήνεγκεν, πλὴν ὅσον κατὰ τὴν συνθήκην καὶ δύναμιν τοῦ λόγου. οὔτε γὰρ εἰς Ἀφροδίτην αὐτοῦ καὶ χάριν τὰ λεγόμενα βέβαπται, οὔτε ἔχει λευκότητά τινα καὶ τῷ καθαρῷ καλλωπίζεται· οὐ μὴν οὐδὲ ἀσαφῆ παντελῶς τυγχάνει, οὐδὲ κατὰ τὴν λέξιν ἡμαρτημένα, ἀλλ' ὥσπερ ἔλεγε περὶ Ξενοκράτους ὁ Πλάτων, ταῖς Ἑρμαϊκαῖς οὐ τέθυται Χάρισιν. οὔκουν κατέχει τὸν ἀκροατὴν καὶ γοητεύει πρὸς τὴν ἀνάγνωσιν, ἀλλ' ἀποστρέφειν καὶ ἀποκναίειν τὴν ἀκοὴν ἔοικεν. δικαιοσύνην δὲ ἀσκήσας, εὐηκόϊας ἔτυχε θεῶν τοσαύτης, ὥστε πλῆθος μὲν ἦσαν οἱ ὁμιλοῦντες, πανταχόθεν δὲ ἐφοίτων οἱ παιδείας ἐπιθυμοῦντες. —

The names of Sopater, Aedesius, Eustathius and others are mentioned.

Καὶ γὰρ ἦν πρὸς ἅπαντας ἄφθονος. ὀλίγα μὲν οὖν χωρὶς τῶν ἑταίρων καὶ

ὁμιλητῶν ἔπραττεν ἐφ' ἑαυτοῦ, τὸ θεῖον σεβαζόμενος· τὰ δὲ πλεῖστα τοῖς
ἑταίροις συνῆν, τὴν μὲν δίαιταν ὢν εὔκολος καὶ ἀρχαῖος, τῇ δὲ παρὰ πότον
ὁμιλίᾳ τοὺς παρόντας καθηδύνων καὶ διαπιμπλὰς ὥσπερ νέκταρος.

b. Ib., 458:

Οἱ δέ, ἀλήκτως ἔχοντες καὶ ἀκορέστως τῆς ἀπολαύσεως, ἠνώχλουν αὐτῷ
συνεχῶς, καὶ προστησάμενοί γε τοὺς ἀξίους λόγου, πρὸς αὐτὸν ἔφασκον·
"τί δῆτα μόνος, ὦ διδάσκαλε θειότατε, καθ' ἑαυτόν τινα πράττεις, οὐ μεταδιδοὺς
τῆς τελεωτέρας σοφίας ἡμῖν; καίτοι γε ἐκφέρεται πρὸς ἡμᾶς λόγος ὑπὸ τῶν σῶν
ἀνδραπόδων, ὡς εὐχόμενος τοῖς θεοῖς μετεωρίζῃ μὲν ἀπὸ τῆς γῆς πλέον ἢ
δέκα πήχεις εἰκάζεσθαι· τὸ σῶμα δέ σοι καὶ ἡ ἐσθὴς εἰς χρυσοειδές τι κάλλος
ἀμείβεται, παυομένῳ δὲ τῆς εὐχῆς σῶμά τε γίνεται τῷ πρὶν εὔχεσθαι ὅμοιον,
καὶ κατελθὼν ἐπὶ τῆς γῆς τὴν πρὸς ἡμᾶς ποιῇ συνουσίαν." οὔ τι μάλα γελα-
σείων, ἐγέλασεν ἐπὶ τούτοις τοῖς λόγοις Ἰάμβλιχος. ἀλλ' εἰπὼν πρὸς αὐτούς,
ὡς "ὁ μὲν ἀπατήσας ὑμᾶς οὐκ ἦν ἄχαρις, ταῦτα δὲ οὐχ οὕτως ἔχει· τοῦ λοιποῦ
δὲ οὐδὲν χωρὶς ὑμῶν πεπράξεται."—

His fame
among his
disciples

In the following pages Eunapius tells two miracle-stories about Iamblichus,
which he heard from Chrysanthius, the pupil of Aedesius.

θεουργία

c. That Iambl. ranked θεουργία above θεωρία, is at least highly
probable. So is done in any case in the book *De mysteriis* II 11. For the
authenticity of this work see below (ad **1449c**).

Cf. also Olympiodorus, *In Phaed.*, p. 123, 3-6 Norvin:

"Ὅτι οἱ μὲν τὴν φιλοσοφίαν προτιμῶσιν, ὡς Πορφύριος καὶ Πλωτῖνος καὶ
ἄλλοι πολλοὶ φιλόσοφοι· οἱ δὲ τὴν ἱερατικήν, ὡς Ἰάμβλιχος καὶ Συριανὸς καὶ
Πρόκλος καὶ οἱ ἱερατικοὶ πάντες.

d. The emperor Julianus praises him as a great philosopher, not
inferior to Plato.

Julianus'
testimony

Julianus, *Or.* IV 146a:

—καὶ Πλάτωνα τὸν μέγαν καὶ μετὰ τοῦτον ἄνδρα τοῖς χρόνοις, οὔτι μὴν
τῇ φύσει καταδεέστερον· τὸν Χαλκιδέα φημί, τὸν Ἰάμβλιχον· ὃς ἡμᾶς τά τε
ἄλλα περὶ τὴν φιλοσοφίαν καὶ δὴ καὶ ταῦτα διὰ τῶν λόγων ἐμύησεν.—

Cp. also *Or.* VII 217b:

— οὐκέτι μαρτύρων παλαιῶν ἐν πᾶσι προσδεόμενοι, ἑπόμενοι δὲ νέοις ἴχνεσιν ἀνδρός,
ὃν ἐγὼ μετὰ τοὺς θεοὺς ἐξ ἴσης Ἀριστοτέλει καὶ Πλάτωνι ἄγαμαί τε τέθηπά τε.

1447—Iambl. calls himself a Pythagorean. He wrote a *Life of Pytha-*
goras, and also his *Protrepticus* is full of Pythagoreanism.

He is a
Pythagorean

a. He speaks of Pythagoras' doctrine as of θεῖα δόγματα, considering mathematics as a preparation for knowledge of the gods.

Iambl., *Protr.* 21, p. 110 Pistelli:

Γνῶσιν οὖν θεῶν διαφερόντως τοῦτο εἰσηγεῖται, ὡς πάντα δυναμένων αὐτῶν. διὰ τοῦτο δὴ οὖν περὶ θεῶν μηδὲν ἀπιστεῖν παραγγέλλει. πρόσκειται δὲ μηδὲ περὶ θείων δογμάτων, τῶν τῇ Πυθαγορικῇ φιλοσοφίᾳ δοκούντων· ταῦτα γὰρ ὑπὸ μαθημάτων καὶ ἐπιστήμονος θεωρίας ἠσφαλισμένα ἀληθῆ καὶ ἀδιάψευστα μόνα ὑπάρχει, ἀποδείξει παντοίᾳ καὶ συναναγκασμῷ ὠχυρωμένα. τὰ δὲ αὐτὰ ταῦτα δύναται καὶ πρὸς τὴν ἐπιστήμην τὴν περὶ θεῶν προτρέπειν· παραγγέλλει γὰρ ἐπιστήμην τοιαύτην κτήσασθαι, δι' ἧς οὐδενὶ ἀπιστήσομεν τῶν λεγομένων περὶ θεῶν καὶ περὶ θείων δογμάτων.

b. The study of mathematics prepares the mind for the "great mysteries" of philosophy.

Iambl., *Protr.* 2, p. 10 Pistelli:

Κοσμητέον ἱερὸν μὲν ἀναθήμασι, τὴν δὲ ψυχὴν μαθήμασιν, ὡς πρὸ τῶν μεγάλων μυστηρίων τὸ μικρὰ παραδοτέον, καὶ πρὸ φιλοσοφίας παιδείαν.

c. The doctrine of Pythagoras is a gift of the Gods, and divine grace is needed to take hold of it.

Iambl., *Vita Pythag.* 1:

Ἐπὶ πάσης μὲν φιλοσοφίας ὁρμῇ θεὸν δήπου παρακαλεῖν ἔθος ἅπασι τοῖς γε σώφροσιν, ἐπὶ δὲ τῇ τοῦ θείου Πυθαγόρου δικαίως ἐπωνύμῳ νομιζομένῃ πολὺ δήπου μᾶλλον ἁρμόττει τοῦτο ποιεῖν· ἐκ θεῶν γὰρ αὐτῆς παραδοθείσης τὸ κατ' ἀρχὰς οὐκ ἔνεστιν ἄλλως ἢ διὰ τῶν θεῶν ἀντιλαμβάνεσθαι.

It should be noticed here that three mathematical works on the name of Iambl. are extant, namely:

Περὶ τῆς κοινῆς μαθηματικῆς ἐπιστήμης (*De communi mathematica scientia*), Περὶ τῆς Νικομάχου ἀριθμητικῆς εἰσαγωγῆς (*In Nicomachi arithmeticam introductionem*) and Τὰ θεολογούμενα τῆς ἀριθμητικῆς (*Theologoumena arithmeticae*). The authenticity of the last work has been questioned.

1448—He explains the old Pythagorean precepts allegorically as an exhortation to the contemplation of the universe with the help of mathematics.

a. Iambl., *Protr.* 21, p. 116:

Τὸ δὲ ἀλεκτρυόνα τρέφε μέν, μὴ θῦε δέ· μήνῃ γὰρ καὶ ἡλίῳ καθιέρωται ¹ συμβουλεύει ἡμῖν ὑποτρέφειν καὶ σωματοποιεῖν καὶ μὴ παρορᾶν

---

¹ On the Pythagorean ἀκούσματα καὶ σύμβολα see *Gr. Ph.* I, nr. **29**.

ἀπολλύμενα καὶ διαφθειρόμενα τὰ τῆς τοῦ κόσμου ἑνώσεως καὶ ἀλληλουχίας συμπαθείας τε καὶ συμπνοίας μεγάλα τεκμήρια. ὥστε προτρέπει τῆς τοῦ παντὸς θεωρίας καὶ φιλοσοφίας ἀντιλαμβάνεσθαι. ἐπεὶ γὰρ ἀπόκρυφος φύσει ἡ περὶ τοῦ παντὸς ἀλήθεια, καὶ δυσθήρατος ἱκανῶς· ζητητέα δὲ ὅμως ἀνθρώπῳ καὶ ἐξιχνευτέα μάλιστα διὰ φιλοσοφίας. διὰ γὰρ ἄλλου τινὸς ἐπιτηδεύματος οὕτως ἀδύνατον· αὕτη δὲ μικρά τινα ἐναύσματα παρὰ τῆς φύσεως λαμβάνουσα καὶ ὡσανεὶ ἐφοδιαζομένη ζωπυρεῖ τε αὐτὰ καὶ μεγεθύνει καὶ ἐνεργέστερα διὰ τῶν παρ᾽ αὐτῆς μαθημάτων ἀπεργάζεται. φιλοσοφητέον ‹ἄρα› ἂν εἴη.

b. Ib., p. 118-119:

Τὸ δὲ ἐν ὁδῷ μὴ σχίζε δηλοῖ ὅτι ἓν μὲν τὸ ἀληθές, πολυσχιδὲς δὲ τὸ ψεῦδος· — Λέγει οὖν ὅτι αἱροῦ φιλοσοφίαν ἐκείνην καὶ τὴν ἐπὶ σοφίαν ὁδόν, ἐν ᾗ οὐ σχίσεις οὐδὲ ἀντιλεγόμενα δογματίσεις, ἀλλὰ ἑστῶτα καὶ τὰ αὐτὰ ἑαυτοῖς ἀποδείξει ἐπιστημονικῇ βεβαιωθέντα διὰ μαθημάτων καὶ θεωρίας, ὅ ἐστι Πυθαγορικῶς φιλοσοφεῖ. — Συμβουλεύει τοίνυν ἡμῖν τὸ παράγγελμα, ἐπειδὰν φιλοσοφῶμεν καὶ τὴν δηλουμένην ὁδὸν ἀνύωμεν, φεύγειν μὲν τὴν τῶν σωματικῶν πολυσχιδῶν ἐπιβολὴν καὶ ἀποδοχήν, προσοικειοῦσθαι δὲ τῇ τῶν ἀσωμάτων οὐσίᾳ τῇ οὐκ ἔστιν ὅτε οὐχὶ ἑαυτοῖς ὁμοίων διατελούντων διὰ τὴν ἐνυπάρχουσαν αὐτοῖς φύσει ἀλήθειαν καὶ ἀδιαπτωσίαν.

c. Philosophy promotes human sympathy and mutual love.

Ib., p. 123:

Τὸ δὲ καρδίαν μὴ τρῶγε σημαίνει τὸ μὴ δεῖν τὴν ἕνωσιν τοῦ παντὸς καὶ τὴν σύμπνοιαν διασπᾶν, καὶ ἔτι μᾶλλον τὸ μὴ ἴσθι βάσκανος, ἀλλὰ φιλάνθρωπος καὶ κοινωνικός. ἐκ δὲ τούτου φιλοσοφεῖν παραινεῖ· μόνη γὰρ αὕτη ἐπιστημῶν καὶ τεχνῶν οὔτε ἐπιλυπεῖται ἀγαθοῖς ἀλλοτρίοις οὔτε ἐπιχαίρει κακοῖς τοῖς πέλας ἅτε φύσει συγγενεῖς καὶ οἰκείους ὁμοιοπαθεῖς τε καὶ κοινῇ ὑποκειμένους τύχῃ ἀπροόρατόν τε τὸ μέλλον ἔχοντας τοὺς ἀνθρώπους πάντας ὁμαλῶς ἀποφαίνουσα· διόπερ συμπαθεῖς τε καὶ φιλαλλήλους παραγγέλλει εἶναι, κοινωνικόν τε ὡς ἀληθῶς καὶ λογικὸν ζῷον.

(margin: Phil. promotes human sympathy)

1449—Iamblichus first elaborated the theory of emanation by assuming intermediate stages between the three fundamental hypostases of Plotinus, as will be done afterwards by the Athenian School in a more systematical form.

a. He assumes another One between the Absolute One of Plotinus (which he calls ἄρρητον) and Noûs.

Damascius, *Dubitationes et solutiones* c. 43, I p. 86 Ruelle:

Μετὰ δὲ ταῦτα ἐκεῖνο προβαλλόμεθα εἰς ἐπίσκεψιν, πότερον δύο εἰσὶν αἱ

(margin: The ἕν placed after the ἄρρητος ἀρχή)

πρῶται ἀρχαὶ πρὸ τῆς νοητῆς πρώτης τριάδος, ἥ τε πάντη ἄρρητος καὶ ἡ ἀσύν-
τακτος πρὸς τὴν τριάδα, καθάπερ ἠξίωσεν ὁ μέγας Ἰάμβλιχος — ἢ ὡς οἱ
πλεῖστοι τῶν μετ᾽ αὐτὸν ἐδοκίμασαν, μετὰ τὴν ἄρρητον αἰτίαν καὶ μίαν εἶναι
τὴν πρώτην τριάδα τῶν νοητῶν.

The First
Principle
doubled

Apparently Iambl., who called the First Principle ἡ πάντη ἄρρητος ἀρχή or τὸ
πάντη ἄρρητον, wished to insert an intermediate stage between this absolute ἀρχή
of which nothing could be predicated, not even that it is one, and the intelligible
World which, according to Proclus' doctrine, is called by Damascius "the
intelligible Triad". Thus, the First Principle of Plotinus was doubled by
Iamblichus.

Damascius, taking the doctrine in this sense, concludes his c. 43 by stating:

Εἰ τοίνυν πρὸ μὲν τοῦ τριαδικοῦ τὸ μονοειδές, πρὸ δὲ τούτου τὸ πάντη ἄρρητον,
ὡς ἐλέγομεν, δῆλον τὸ συμβαῖνον.

b. In c. 45 Damasc. mentions another explanation, namely, that the
two First Principles beyond the intelligible World correspond with the
πέρας and the ἄπειρον of early Pythagoreanism, of which the first is the
unifying principle, while the latter is at the root of πλῆθος. After a slight
hesitation he rejects this more or less dualistic interpretation with regard
to Iamblichus.

Damascius, *Dub. et sol.* c. 45, I p. 88-89 R.:

Ἀλλὰ μὴν τὸ αὐτὸ καὶ ὧδε κατασκευάσειεν ἄν τις ἀπὸ τῶν κάτωθεν, οἷον
ἀπὸ τεκμηρίου· δύο γὰρ ἐν τοῖς οὖσιν ὁρῶντες ἀντιδιηρημένας συστοιχίας
ἀλλήλαις, τὴν μὲν κρείττω φασί, τὴν δὲ χείρω, τὴν μὲν ἑνοειδῆ, τὴν δὲ πληθοει-
δῆ, ἀπὸ τούτων ἀναπεμπόμεθα καὶ εἰς δύο ἀρχάς, εἴς τε ἓν καὶ πλῆθος, τὰ
ἀντιδιωρισμένα φημί, εἴτε ἄλλας ἃς βούλεταί τις ὑποτίθεσθαι· ἑκατέρας δ᾽
οὖν εἶναι ἀρχὴν ἰδιότροπον, ἅτε ἰδιοτρόπου, ἀφ᾽ ἧς ἑκατέρα τὸ κοινὸν ἔνεστιν,
οἷον τῇ μὲν ἑνοειδεῖ τὸ τοῦ ἑνὸς ἰδίωμα, τῇ δὲ πληθοειδεῖ τὸ τοῦ πλήθους ἴχνος. —
Ἆρα οὖν οὕτω θετέον δύο τὰς ἐπέκεινα τῶν νοητῶν τριάδων ἀρχάς, καὶ ὅλως
εἰπεῖν, τῶν ὄντων ἁπάντων, ὡς ἠξίωσεν ὁ Ἰάμβλιχος, ὅσον ἐμέ γε εἰδέναι,
μόνος ἀξιώσας τό γε τῶν πρὸ ἡμῶν ἁπάντων; ἢ τοῖς ἄλλοις ἅπασιν ἀκολουθητέον
τοῖς μετ᾽ αὐτόν;

Τὸ μὲν οὖν ἀληθέστατον θεὸς ἂν εἰδείη περὶ τῶν τηλικούτων· εἰ δὲ χρὴ τά
γε ἐμοὶ δοκοῦντα εἰπεῖν, οὔ μοι δοκεῖ ταῦτα ἐχυρὰ εἶναι πρὸς τὴν προκειμένην
ἀπόδειξιν.

Cp. Proclus, *Elem. th.* 92, below, nr. **1462** f.

The same
doctrine in
De myst.

c. The same doctrine transposed into religious terms is found
in the *Liber de mysteriis*, a work which is usually regarded as coming

from the School of Iamblichus but, after all, might be authentic [1].

[Iambl.], *De myst.* 8, 2:

Πρὸ τῶν ὄντως ὄντων καὶ τῶν ὅλων ἀρχῶν ἔστι θεὸς εἷς, πρότερος καὶ τοῦ πρώτου θεοῦ καὶ βασιλέως, ἀκίνητος ἐν μονότητι τῆς ἑαυτοῦ ἑνότητος μένων. οὔτε γὰρ νοητὸν αὐτῷ ἐπιπλέκεται οὔτε ἄλλο τι· παράδειγμα δὲ ἵδρυται τοῦ αὐτοπάτορος αὐτογόνου καὶ μονοπάτορος θεοῦ τοῦ ὄντως ἀγαθοῦ. μεῖζον γάρ τι καὶ πρῶτον καὶ πηγὴ τῶν πάντων καὶ πυθμὴν τῶν νοουμένων πρώτων ἰδεῶν ὄντων· ἀπὸ δὲ τοῦ ἑνὸς τούτου ὁ αὐτάρκης θεὸς ἑαυτὸν ἐξέλαμψε, διὸ καὶ αὐτοπάτωρ καὶ αὐτάρκης. ἀρχὴ γὰρ οὗτος καὶ θεὸς θεῶν, μονὰς ἐκ τοῦ ἑνός, προούσιος καὶ ἀρχὴ τῆς οὐσίας. ἀπ' αὐτοῦ γὰρ ἡ οὐσιότης καὶ ἡ οὐσία, διὸ καὶ οὐσιοπάτωρ καλεῖται· αὐτὸς γὰρ τὸ προόντως ὄν ἐστιν, τῶν νοητῶν ἀρχή, διὸ καὶ νοητάρχης προσαγορεύεται· αὗται μὲν οὖν εἰσὶν ἀρχαὶ πρεσβύταται πάντων, ἃς Ἑρμῆς πρὸ τῶν αἰθερίων καὶ ἐμπυρίων θεῶν προτάττει καὶ τῶν ἐπουρανίων.

Here the First and absolute Principle is called θεὸς εἷς, while the second "First" Principle is introduced as αὐτοπάτωρ αὐτόγονος and called ὁ ὄντως ἀγαθός. To maintain the absoluteness of the First, this "self-sufficient God" is said to have "radiated" Himself (ἑαυτὸν ἐξέλαμψε). He is μονὰς ἐκ τοῦ ἑνός, is beyond Being and the Source of Being.

1450—While Plotinus regarded Noûs as one-and-many, Iambl. doubles it by distinguishing Noûs that is one from Noûs that is many. He hypostasizes the first as τὸ ἀεὶ ὄν or αὐτὸ τὸ ὅπερ ὄν, which is a παράδειγμα τοῦ παντός and as such superior to the γένη τοῦ ὄντος and nearest to the One.

a. Proclus, *In Tim.* I p. 230, l. 5-8 Diehl:

The Noûs which is one above the Noûs which is many

᾿Αλλ' ὁ θεῖος ᾿Ιάμβλιχος ἐμβριθῶς διαμάχεται τῷ λόγῳ [2], τὸ ἀεὶ ὂν κρεῖττον καὶ τῶν γενῶν τοῦ ὄντος [3] καὶ τῶν ἰδεῶν ἀποφαινόμενος καὶ ἐπ' ἄκρῳ τῆς νοητῆς οὐσίας ἰδρύων αὐτὸ πρώτως μετέχον τοῦ ἑνός.

b. Cp. Proclus, ib. I p. 321, l. 26-30 D.:

῾Ο μὲν γὰρ θεῖος ᾿Ιάμβλιχος αὐτὸ τὸ ὅπερ ὄν, ὃ δὴ νοήσει μετὰ λόγου περιληπτόν ἐστιν, ἀφωρίσατο τὸ παράδειγμα τοῦ παντός, τὸ μὲν ἓν ἐπέκεινα τιθέμενος τοῦ παραδείγματος, τὸ δὲ ὅπερ ὄν αὐτῷ σύνδρομον ἀποφαίνων, ἑκάτερον δὲ νοήσει περιληπτὸν ἀποκαλῶν.

---

[1] The authenticity was defended by Rasche (*De Iamblichi libri qui inscribitur de Mysteriis auctore*, Münster 1911) and Geffcken (*Ausgang* p. 283 ff.) and is accepted by Dodds (Proclus, *The Elements of Theol.*, p. XIX n. 1).

[2] τῷ λόγῳ—the view that πᾶς ὁ νοητὸς κόσμος = τὸ ἀεὶ ὄν, as was held by Plotinus.

[3] The five genera of the *Sophistes*, accepted by Plot. as given together with the ὄν itself.

1451—Meanwhile, Iambl. describes the first Noûs as a Triad: πατήρ -
δύναμις - νοῦς, or also ὕπαρξις - δύναμις τῆς ὑπάρξεως - νόησις τῆς δυνάμεως
(or ἐνέργεια).

a. Damascius, *Dub. et sol.* c. 54, I p. 108 R.:

The two First Principles, as admitted by Iambl., are so related the one to the
other, as the Gods themselves, speaking with men, declare the relation between
the three ἀρχαί that are contained in the Third Principle (i.e. the first Noûs, which is
one) to be. This means: there is no ἑτερότης between these sub-principles, since
the five genera of being are not yet given in the first Noûs.

Δῆλον δὲ ὅτι οὔτε ὁμοταγεῖς εἰσιν ... οὔτε διωρισμέναι εἰσὶν ἀπ' ἀλλήλων,
... οὔτε ἑτερότης διαλαμβάνει αὐτάς, εἴπερ οὐδὲ ταὐτότης ἐν ἐκείνοις· ἀλλ'
ὡς οἱ θεοὶ καὶ αὐτοὶ μέντοι ἀνθρώποις διαλεγόμενοι οὕτως ἔχειν πρὸς ἀλλήλας
ἀπεφήναντο τὰς τρεῖς ἀρχὰς ὡς ἂν ἔχοι νοῦς καὶ δύναμις καὶ πατήρ, ἢ ὕπαρξις
καὶ δύναμις τῆς ὑπάρξεως καὶ νόησις τῆς δυνάμεως.

b. Apparently Iambl. admitted three intelligible Triads, viewing
each particular member of his first Triad as a new one. After these three
νοηταὶ τριάδες and—as it seems—after three others of νοεροὶ θεοί, he speaks
in the following passage of a νοερὰ ἑβδομάς, the third member of which
is identified with the Demiurge.

Proclus, *In Tim.* I, p. 308 f. Diehl:

Περὶ γὰρ τῆς ἐν Τιμαίῳ τοῦ Διὸς δημηγορίας [1] γράφων μετὰ τὰς νοητὰς 20
τριάδας καὶ τὰς τῶν νοερῶν θεῶν τρεῖς τριάδας ἐν τῇ νοερᾷ ἑβδομάδι τὴν
τρίτην ἐν τοῖς πατράσιν ἀπονέμει τῷ δημιουργῷ τάξιν· τρεῖς γὰρ εἶναι θεοὺς
τούτους καὶ παρὰ τοῖς Πυθαγορείοις ὑμνημένους, οἳ τοῦ μὲν ἑνὸς νοῦ, φησίν,
καὶ τὰς μονάδας ὅλας ἐν ἑαυτῷ περιέχοντος τὸ ἁπλοῦν καὶ ἀδιαίρετον καὶ 25
ἀγαθοειδὲς καὶ μένον ἐν ἑαυτῷ καὶ συνηνωμένον τοῖς νοητοῖς καὶ τὰ τοιαῦτα
γνωρίσματα τῆς ὑπεροχῆς παραδεδώκασι, τοῦ δὲ μέσου καὶ τὴν συμπλήρωσιν
συνάγοντος τῶν τριῶν καὶ τὸ τῆς ἐνεργείας ἀποπληρωτικὸν καὶ τὸ τῆς θείας 30
ζωῆς γεννητικὸν καὶ τὸ προϊὸν πάντη καὶ τὸ ἀγαθουργὸν κάλλιστα δείγματα p.
λέγουσι, τοῦ δὲ τρίτου καὶ δημιουργοῦντος τὰ ὅλα τὰς μονίμους προόδους καὶ
τὰς τῶν αἰτίων ὅλων ποιήσεις καὶ συνοχὰς τάς τε ἀφωρισμένας ὅλας τοῖς εἴδεσιν
αἰτίας καὶ τὰς προϊούσας πάσας δημιουργίας καὶ τὰ ὅμοια τούτοις τεκμήρια 5
κάλλιστα ἀναδιδάσκουσι. τὴν μὲν οὖν Ἰαμβλίχειον θεολογίαν ἀπὸ τούτων
ἄξιον κρίνειν, ὁποία τίς ἐστι περὶ τοῦ δημιουργοῦ τῶν ὅλων· καὶ πῶς γὰρ ἂν
ἦν ὅλον τὸ ἀεὶ ὂν ὁ δημιουργός, εἴπερ τὸ μὲν ἀεὶ ὂν ἤδη κατεδήσατο διὰ τῆς 10
ὁρικῆς ἀποδόσεως, τὸν δὲ δημιουργὸν εὑρεῖν τε ἔργον εἶναί φησι [2]
καὶ εὑρόντα εἰς ἅπαντας ἀδύνατον λέγειν; πῶς γὰρ ταῦτα ἀληθεύσει
περὶ τοῦ ὁρικῶς ἀποδοθέντος καὶ εἰς φῶς ἐξενεχθέντος πᾶσι τοῖς παροῦσι;

---

[1] Plato, *Tim.* 41a-d (supra, nr. **353**).   [2] Plato, ib. 28c (supra, nr. **349a**).

Apparently we have in this passage a contamination of two different conceptions: **Chaldaean influence**
(1) the hierarchical order of (a) three νοηταὶ τριάδες, (b) three other triads of νοεροὶ
θεοί (doubtless, in the Noûs which is many), (c) the νοερὰ ἑβδομάς, the third member
of which is said to be "the creator". (11) Three main principles, called "Gods",
the first of which is Noûs which is one, the second the "Generator of divine Life",
the third the Creator of the Universe. How these two different views should be
combined, does not become clear in this passage. Cp. Zeller III 2, p. 748 ff.

c. The introduction of the seven is due to Chaldaean influence, as
appears from the following text.

Damascius, *Dub. et sol.* c. 94, I p. 237 l. 11 R.:

Ὁ ἑπταχῇ προϊὼν ὅλος δημιουργὸς παρὰ τοῖς Χαλδαίοις.

Cp. Julianus, *Or.* V 172D, who speaks of "the God of the seven rays" of the
Chaldaeans. Doubtless here the seven planets are intended.
All this belongs to a polytheistic system, elaborated in conscious opposition
to the rising Christian faith and doctrine.
The above-cited line of Damascius suggests that the Demiurge himself was **The Demiur-**
conceived as a septifold being, unfolding the third member of the νοερὸς τριάς. **ge conceived**
Here the analogy with the Third Person of the Trinity of Christian doctrine, the **as sevenfold**
Holy Spirit with its sevenfold gifts, presents itself to the mind.

1452—In the realm of Soul, too, Iamblichus applies the triadic system, **The triadic**
deducing two other souls from the first which is one. **system applied to soul**

a. Proclus, *In Tim.* II p. 240, l. 4-6 D.:

Ὁ μὲν γὰρ θεῖος Ἰάμβλιχος ἄνω που μετεωροπολεῖ καὶ τἀφανῆ μεριμνᾷ,
τήν τε μίαν ψυχὴν καὶ τὰς ἀπ' αὐτῆς προελθούσας δύο.

b. Soul, evidently, does not depend directly on the first and absolute Noûs, but on the Noûs which is many. Iambl. also opposes those
who hold that this noûs is a ἕξις of the soul.

Proclus, ib. II, p. 313, l. 15 ff. D.:

Ἰάμβλιχος δὲ τὸν νοῦν τοῦτον πρεσβύτερον ἀκούει τῆς ψυχῆς, ἄνωθεν αὐτὴν
συνέχοντα καὶ τελειοῦντα, καὶ διαγωνίζεται πρὸς τοὺς ἢ αὐτόθι τῷ παντελεῖ
νῷ συνάπτοντας τὴν ψυχήν .... ἢ τὸν νοῦν ἕξιν ὑποτιθεμένους τῆς ψυχῆς.

1453—Iambl., who maintains that noûs is of a level superior to soul, **Soul is**
does not admit that soul contains a part which is ἀπαθές. If she sins, she **neither**
does so by προαίρεσις; and how then hold that she is ἀναμάρτητος? **ἀπαθής nor ἀναμάρτητος**

a. Proclus, ib. III, p. 333 f. Diehl:

Proclus is commenting here on *Tim.* 43a-44b, where Plato described the disorder
thrown into the soul when it is united to a body. By the strong and perpetual
commotion of the body the περίοδοι of the soul which is joined to it are violently

shaken: that of the ταὐτόν (see above, nr. **350**) is completely hampered, while that of the θάτερον is greatly disturbed. Proclus comments on this as follows.

Ἡ μὲν ταὐτοῦ περίοδος ἄρα πεπέδηται μόνον καὶ ἔοικε τοῖς δεσμώταις μὲν καὶ διὰ τοῦτο κωλυομένοις ἐνεργεῖν, μένουσι δὲ καὶ ἐν τοῖς δεδεμένοις ἀδιαστρόφοις. ἡ δὲ θατέρου διασέσεισται ψευδῶν ἀναπλησθεῖσα δογμάτων· ἡ γὰρ πρὸς τὴν ἀλογίαν γειτνίασις ποιεῖ καὶ αὐτὴν εἰσδέχεσθαί τι πάθος ἀπὸ τῶν ἐκτός. ἀπὸ δὴ τούτων ὁρμώμενοι παρρησιασόμεθα πρὸς Πλωτῖνον καὶ τὸν μέγαν Θεόδωρον [1] ἀπαθές τι φυλάττοντας ἐν ἡμῖν καὶ ἀεὶ νοοῦν· δύο γὰρ 30 κύκλους μόνον εἰς τὴν οὐσίαν τῆς ψυχῆς παραλαβὼν ὁ Πλάτων τὸν μὲν ἐπέδησε, τὸν δὲ διέσεισεν, οὐδὲ τὸν πεπεδημένον οὔτε τὸν διασεσεισμένον ἐνεργεῖν νοερῶς δυνατόν. ὀρθῶς ἄρα καὶ ὁ θεῖος Ἰάμβλιχος διαγωνίζεται πρὸς τοὺς ταῦτα οἰομένους· τί γὰρ τὸ ἁμαρτάνον ἐν ἡμῖν, ὅταν τῆς ἀλογίας κινησάσης πρὸς ἀκόλαστον φαντασίαν ἐπιδράμωμεν; ἆρ᾽ οὐχ ἡ προαίρεσις; καὶ πῶς οὐχ αὕτη; 5 κατὰ γὰρ ταύτην διαφέρομεν τῶν φαντασθέντων προπετῶς. εἰ δὲ προαίρεσις ἁμαρτάνει, πῶς ἀναμάρτητος ἡ ψυχή;

b. Cp. Stob., *Ecl.* I p. 365 Wachsmuth, where Iambl., Π. ψυχῆς, is cited as follows:

Ἴθι δὴ οὖν ἐπὶ τὴν καθ᾽ αὑτὴν ἀσώματον οὐσίαν ἐπανίωμεν, διακρίνοντες 5 καὶ ἐπ᾽ αὐτῆς ἐν τάξει τὰς περὶ ψυχῆς πάσας δόξας. Εἰσὶ δή τινες, οἳ πᾶσαν τὴν τοιαύτην οὐσίαν ὁμοιομερῆ καὶ τὴν αὐτὴν καὶ μίαν ἀποφαίνονται, ὡς καὶ ἐν ὁτῳοῦν αὐτῆς μέρει εἶναι τὰ ὅλα· οἵτινες καὶ ἐν τῇ μεριστῇ ψυχῇ τὸν νοητὸν κόσμον καὶ θεοὺς καὶ δαίμονας καὶ τἀγαθὸν καὶ πάντα τὰ πρεσβύτερα γένη 10 αὐτῆς ἐνιδρύουσι καὶ ἐν πᾶσιν ὡσαύτως πάντα εἶναι ἀποφαίνονται, οἰκείως μέντοι κατὰ τὴν αὐτῶν οὐσίαν ἐν ἑκάστοις. Καὶ ταύτης τῆς δόξης ἀναμφισβητήτως μέν ἐστι Νουμήνιος, οὐ πάντῃ δὲ ὁμολογουμένως Πλωτῖνος, ἀστάτως 15 δὲ ἐν αὐτῇ φέρεται Ἀμέλιος· Πορφύριος δὲ ἐνδοιάζει περὶ αὐτήν, πῇ μὲν διατεταμένως αὐτῆς ἀφιστάμενος, πῇ δὲ συνακολουθῶν αὐτῇ, ὡς παραδοθείσῃ ἄνωθεν. Κατὰ δὴ ταύτην νοῦ καὶ θεῶν καὶ τῶν κρειττόνων γενῶν οὐδὲν ἡ ψυχὴ 20 διενήνοχε κατά γε τὴν ὅλην οὐσίαν.

Ἀλλὰ μὴν ἥ γε πρὸς ταύτην ἀνθισταμένη δόξα χωρίζει μὲν τὴν ψυχήν, ὡς ἀπὸ νοῦ γενομένην δευτέραν καθ᾽ ἑτέραν ὑπόστασιν, τὸ δὲ μετὰ νοῦ αὐτῆς ἐξηγεῖται ὡς ἐξηρτημένον ἀπὸ τοῦ νοῦ, μετὰ τοῦ κατ᾽ ἰδίαν ὑφεστηκέναι 25 αὐτοτελῶς, χωρίζει δὲ αὐτὴν καὶ ἀπὸ τῶν κρειττόνων γενῶν ὅλων, ἴδιον δὲ αὐτῇ τῆς οὐσίας ὅρον ἀπονέμει ἤτοι τὸ μέσον τῶν μεριστῶν καὶ ἀμερίστων ‹τῶν τε σωματικῶν καὶ ἀ›σωμάτων γενῶν, ἢ τὸ πλήρωμα τῶν καθόλου λόγων, p. 3 ἢ τὴν μετὰ τὰς ἰδέας ὑπηρεσίαν τῆς δημιουργίας, ἢ ζωὴν παρ᾽ ἑαυτῆς ἔχουσαν τὸ ζῆν τὴν ἀπὸ τοῦ νοητοῦ προελθοῦσαν, ἢ τὴν αὖ τῶν γενῶν ὅλου τοῦ ὄντως

---

[1] Theodorus of Asine, a disciple of Iamblichus.

5 ὄντος πρόοδον εἰς ὑποδεεστέραν οὐσίαν. Περὶ δὴ ταύτας τὰς δόξας ὅ τε Πλάτων
αὐτὸς καὶ ὁ Πυθαγόρας, ὅ τε Ἀριστοτέλης καὶ ἀρχαῖοι πάντες, ὧν ὀνόματα
μεγάλα ἐπὶ σοφίᾳ ὑμνεῖται, τελέως ἐπιστρέφονται, εἴ τις αὐτῶν τὰς δόξας
10 ἀνιχνεύοι μετ᾽ ἐπιστάσεως.

Iambl., who calls himself a follower of Pythagoras, doubtless preferred the latter
party.

1454—a. *Aedesius* was Iamblichus' successor in the School of Per- The School
gamum.   of Iambl.

Eunapius, *Vitae* 461:

Ἐκδέχεται δὲ τὴν Ἰαμβλίχου διατριβὴν καὶ ὁμιλίαν ἐς τοὺς ἑταίρους Αἰδέσιος
ὁ ἐκ Καππαδοκίας.

b. Iamblichus' pupil *Sopater* came to great influence at the court
of Constantine.

Eunapius, ib. 462:   Sopater

Σώπατρος δὲ ὁ πάντων δεινότερος, διά τε φύσεως ὕψος καὶ ψυχῆς μέγεθος
οὐκ ἐνεγκὼν τοῖς ἄλλοις ἀνθρώποις ὁμιλεῖν, ἐπὶ τὰς βασιλικὰς αὐλὰς ἔδραμεν
ὀξύς, ὡς τὴν Κωνσταντίνου πρόφασίν τε καὶ φορὰν τυραννήσων καὶ μεταστή-
σων τῷ λόγῳ. καὶ ἐς τοσοῦτόν γε ἐξίκετο σοφίας καὶ δυνάμεως, ὡς ὁ μὲν
βασιλεὺς ἑαλώκει τε ὑπ᾽ αὐτῷ, καὶ δημοσίᾳ σύνεδρον εἶχεν, εἰς τὸν δέξιον καθί-
ζων τόπον, ὃ καὶ ἀκοῦσαι καὶ ἰδεῖν ἄπιστον.

But malicious people, "bursting with envy against a court so lately converted
to the study of philosophy" (ῥηγνύμενοι τῷ φθόνῳ πρὸς βασιλείαν ἄρτι φιλοσοφεῖν
μεταμανθάνουσαν) plotted against him and he was put to death.

c. *Maximus* and *Chrysanthius*, who both were pupils of Aedesius   Maximus,
and famous for their "theurgy", were the masters and friends of the   Chrysan-
emperor Julianus, who still heard Aedesius in his old age.   thius,
                                                                         Priscus

Eunapius, *Vitae* 474:

Τῆς δὲ ὁμιλίας αὐτοῦ (sc. Αἰδεσίου) προεστήκεσαν καὶ ἀνὰ τοὺς πρώτους
ἐφέροντο Μάξιμός τε, ὑπὲρ οὗ τάδε γράφεται, καὶ Χρυσάνθιος ὁ ἐκ Σάρδεων,
Πρίσκος τε ὁ Θεσπρωτὸς ἢ Μολοσσὸς Εὐσέβιός τε ὁ ἐκ Καρίας Μύνδου πόλεως.
καὶ συνουσίας ἀξιωθεὶς τῆς Αἰδεσίου, ὁ καὶ ἐν μειρακίῳ πρεσβύτης Ἰουλιανός,
τὴν μὲν ἀκμὴν καὶ τὸ θεοειδὲς τῆς ψυχῆς καταπλαγείς, οὐκ ἐβούλετο χωρίζεσθαι, ἀλλ᾽, ὥσπερ οἱ κατὰ τὸν μῦθον ὑπὸ τῆς διψάδος δηχθέντες, χανδὸν καὶ
ἀμυστὶ τῶν μαθημάτων ἕλκειν ἐβούλετο, καὶ δῶρά γε ἐπὶ τούτοις βασιλικὰ
διέπεμπεν· ὁ δὲ οὐδὲ ταῦτα προσίετο καὶ μετακαλέσας τὸν νεανίσκον, εἶπεν·
"ἀλλὰ σὺ μὲν καὶ τὴν ψυχὴν τὴν ἐμὴν οὐκ ἀγνοεῖς, τηλικαύταις ἀκοαῖς ἀκροώ-

μενος, τὸ δὲ ὄργανον αὐτῆς συνορᾷς ὅπως διάκειται, τῆς γομφώσεως καὶ
πήξεως διαλυομένης εἰς τὸ συντιθέν· σὺ δέ, εἴ τι καὶ δρᾶν βούλει, τέκνον σοφίας
ἐπήρατον (τοιαῦτα γάρ σου τὰ τῆς ψυχῆς ἰνδάλματα καταμανθάνω), πρὸς τοὺς
ἐμοὺς παῖδας πορευθεὶς ὄντας γνησίους, ἐκεῖθεν ῥύδην ἐμφοροῦ σοφίας ἁπάσης
καὶ μαθημάτων· κἂν τύχῃς τῶν μυστηρίων, αἰσχυνθήσῃ πάντως ὅτι ἐγένου καὶ
ἐκλήθης ἄνθρωπος.''

With these words Aedesius sends the young Julian to his above-mentioned
fellow-pupils. At the time Maximus was at Ephesus and Julian went to see
him there. The emperor mentions him repeatedly in his writings. Three of his
letters (8, 12 and 59) are addressed to him. *Priscus* too became his friend and adviser.
He accompanied the emperor to Persia. Julian's letters 1, 2 and 5 are addressed
to him.

Theodorus
of Asine

d. *Theodorus of Asine* was an immediate disciple both of Porphyrius
and of Iamblichus. Proclus cites his commentaries frequently (see e.g.
above, **1453a**).

Dexippus

e. *Dexippus*, a disciple of Iamblichus, wrote a work on the *Categories*
of Aristotle which survives (*Comment. in Arist.* IV 2).

Sallustius

f. *Sallustius*, another friend of Julian, is the author of the little
book *De diis et mundo* (ed. Orelli 1821, included in Mullach, *Fr. phil.*
Gr. III).

3—PROCLUS

The School
of Athens

1455—At the beginning of the 5th century we find Neoplatonism
taught at Athens by one Plutarchus, who is succeeded by Syrianus.
Both of them were the masters of Proclus, a Lycian who came from
Alexandria to Athens to study philosophy.

The School
of
Alexandria

In those days the Neoplatonic school of Alexandria flourished under the guidance of *Hypatia*, who is frequently mentioned and praised in the letters of her
disciple Synezius. Apparently Proclus came to Alexandria a few years later. He
first studied rhetoric and later, converted to philosophy on a journey to Byzantium,
became the pupil of *Olympiodorus* and of the mathematician Hero. Having left
Alexandria for Athens, he came first into contact with Syrianus, who introduced
him to the aged master Plutarchus.

Proclus,
disciple
of Plut. and
Syrianus

a. Marinus, *Proclus* cc. 10-12:

Τούτοις (sc. Olympiodorus and Hero) οὖν ἐν Ἀλεξανδρείᾳ συσχολάσας, καὶ
καθόσον αὐτοὶ δυνάμεως εἶχον τῆς συνουσίας αὐτῶν ἀπονάμενος, ἐπειδὴ ἐν
τῇ συναναγνώσει τινὸς ἔδοξεν αὐτῷ οὐκέτι ἀξίως τῆς τοῦ φιλοσόφου διανοίας
φέρεσθαι ἐν ταῖς ἐξηγήσεσιν, ὑπεριδὼν ἐκείνων τῶν διδασκαλείων, ἅμα δὲ
καὶ μεμνημένος τῆς ἐν τῷ Βυζαντίῳ θείας ὄψεως καὶ παρακελεύσεως, ἐπὶ τὰς

Ἀθήνας ἀνήγετο σὺν πομπῇ τινὶ πάντων τῶν λογίων καὶ τῶν φιλοσοφίας ἐφόρων θεῶν τε καὶ δαιμόνων ἀγαθῶν. — (11) Ὑπερφρονήσας δὲ κἀνταῦθα τῶν ῥητορικῶν διατριβῶν, καίτοι περιμάχητος τοῖς ῥητορικοῖς γενόμενος, ὡς δὴ καὶ ἐπ' αὐτὸ τοῦτο ἥκων, ἐντυγχάνει πρώτῳ τῶν φιλοσόφων Συριανῷ τῷ Φιλοξένου. — (12) Παραλαβὼν δὲ αὐτὸν ὁ Συριανὸς προσάγει τῷ μεγάλῳ Πλουτάρχῳ τῷ Νεστορίου. Ὁ δὲ νέον μὲν ἰδὼν καὶ οὐδὲ ὅλον εἰκοστὸν ἔτος ἄγοντα, ἀκούσας δὲ αὐτοῦ τὴν αἵρεσιν καὶ τὴν πολλὴν ἔφεσιν τοῦ ἐν φιλοσοφίᾳ βίου, σφόδρα ἤσθη ἐπ' αὐτῷ, ὥστε καὶ ἑτοίμως ἑαυτὸν ἐπιδοῦναι αὐτῷ τῶν φιλοσόφων διατριβῶν, καὶ ταῦτα κωλυόμενος ὑπὸ τῆς ἡλικίας· μάλα γὰρ ἦν ἤδη πρεσβύτης. Ἀναγινώσκει οὖν παρὰ τούτῳ Ἀριστοτέλους μὲν τὰ Περὶ ψυχῆς, Πλάτωνος δὲ τὸν Φαίδωνα. Προύτρεπε δὲ αὐτὸν ὁ μέγας καὶ ἀπογράφεσθαι τὰ λεγόμενα, τῇ φιλοτιμίᾳ τοῦ νέου ὀργάνῳ χρώμενος, καὶ φάσκων ὅτι συμπληρωθέντων αὐτῷ τῶν σχολίων ἔσται καὶ Πρόκλου ὑπομνήματα φερόμενα εἰς τὸν Φαίδωνα. Καὶ ἄλλως δὲ ἔχαιρε τῷ νεανίσκῳ πεῖραν αὐτοῦ λαβὼν τῆς πρὸς τὰ καλὰ ἐπιτηδειότητος καὶ τέκνον αὐτὸν συνεχῶς ἀπεκάλει καὶ ὁμοέστιον ἐποιεῖτο. — Δύο δὲ μόνα σχεδὸν ἔτη ἐπεβίω αὐτῷ ἐπιδημήσαντι ὁ πρεσβύτης, καὶ τελευτῶν τῷ διαδόχῳ Συριανῷ τὸν νέον συνίστα, οἷα καὶ τὸν ἔγγονον Ἀρχιάδαν. ὁ δὲ παραλαβὼν αὐτὸν οὐ μόνον ἔτι περὶ τοὺς λόγους μειζόνως ὠφέλει, ἀλλὰ καὶ σύνοικον τοῦ λοιποῦ καὶ τοῦ φιλοσόφου βίου κοινωνὸν εἶχεν, τοιοῦτον αὐτὸν εὑρὼν οἷον πάλαι ἐζήτει ἀκροατὴν ἔχειν καὶ διάδοχον δεκτικὸν ὄντα τῶν ἐκείνῳ παμπόλλων μαθημάτων καὶ θείων δογμάτων.

b. With Syrianus P. studied the complete works of Aristotle, and after these Plato's writings. He wrote his commentary on the *Timaeus* when he was 28.

Marinus, ib. c. 13:

Ἐν ἔτεσι γοῦν οὔτε δύο ὅλοις πάσας αὐτῷ τὰς Ἀριστοτέλους συνανέγνω πραγματείας, λογικὰς ἠθικὰς πολιτικὰς φυσικάς, καὶ τὴν ὑπὲρ ταύτας θεολογικὴν ἐπιστήμην. Ἀχθέντα δὲ διὰ τούτων ἱκανῶς, ὥσπερ διὰ τινῶν προτελείων καὶ μικρῶν μυστηρίων, εἰς τὴν Πλάτωνος ἦγε μυσταγωγίαν, ἐν τάξει καὶ οὐχ ὑπερβάθμιον πόδα, κατὰ τὸ λόγιον, τείνοντα, καὶ τὰς παρ' ἐκείνῳ θείας ὄντως τελετὰς ἐποπτεύειν ἐποίει, τοῖς τῆς ψυχῆς ἀνεπιθολώτοις ὄμμασι καὶ τῇ τοῦ νοῦ ἀχράντῳ περιωπῇ. Ὁ δὲ ἀγρύπνῳ τε τῇ ἀσκήσει καὶ ἐπιμελείᾳ χρώμενος νύκτωρ τε καὶ μεθ' ἡμέραν, καὶ τὰ λεγόμενα συνοπτικῶς καὶ μετ' ἐπικρίσεως ἀπογραφόμενος, τοσοῦτον ἐν οὐ πολλῷ χρόνῳ ἐπεδίδου, ὥστε ὄγδοον καὶ εἰκοστὸν ἔτος ἄγων, ἄλλα τε πολλὰ συνέγραψε, καὶ τὰ εἰς Τίμαιον, γλαφυρὰ ὄντως καὶ ἐπιστήμης γέμοντα ὑπομνήματα.

Syrianus himself wrote commentaries on many of the works of Aristotle. His **Syrianus** commentary on *Metaph.* ΒΓΜΝ is extant (Usener, schol. in Arist. p. 837-944).

Proclus speaks of his master with a profound veneration, calling him a teacher "filled with divine truth", who "came to earth as the benefactor of banished souls ... and fount of salvation both to his own and to future generations" (*In Parm.* 618, 3 ff., transl. by Dodds). For the text, see under **1472a**.

No doubt Syrianus' doctrine has a considerable part in those theories which are commonly regarded as characteristic of Proclus (Dodds, *The Elements*, p. XXIII f.).

Fasting and abstinence

1456—The following passages of Marinus are revealing as to Proclus' attitude towards the forms and practices of religion.

a. He not only abstained from animal food, but fasted on all the days prescribed by different religions. To these he added some private days of fasting.

Marinus, *Proclus* c. 19:

Τὰς δὲ ἀπὸ σίτων καὶ ποτῶν ἀναγκαίας ἡδονάς, ἀπαλλαγὰς πόνων ἐποιεῖτο, ἵνα μὴ ἐνοχλοῖτο ὑπ' αὐτῶν· βραχέα γὰρ τούτων προσεφέρετο. Τὰ πολλὰ δὲ τὴν τῶν ἐμψύχων ἀποχὴν ἠσπάζετο· εἰ δέ ποτε καιρός τις ἰσχυρότερος ἐπὶ τὴν τούτων χρῆσιν ἐκάλει, μόνον ἀπεγεύετο, καὶ τοῦτο ὁσίας χάριν. τὰς δὲ Μητρῳακὰς παρὰ Ῥωμαίοις ἢ καὶ πρότερόν ποτε παρὰ Φρυξὶ σπουδασθείσας καστείας ἑκάστου μηνὸς ἥγνευεν, καὶ τὰς παρ' Αἰγυπτίοις δὲ ἀποφράδας ἐφύλαττε μᾶλλον ἢ αὐτοὶ ἐκεῖνοι, καὶ ἰδικώτερον δέ τινας ἐνήστευεν ἡμέρας ἐξ ἐπιφανείας [1].

b. He is praised for his θεουργικὴ ἀρετή and his θεουργικὰ ἐνεργήματα.

Marinus, ib. c. 28 f.:

θεουργία

... ἐκ τῆς περὶ τὰ τοιαῦτα σχολῆς ἀρετὴν ἔτι μείζονα καὶ τελεωτέραν (sc. τῆς θεωρητικῆς) ἐπορίσατο τὴν θεουργικήν, καὶ οὐκ ἔτι μέχρι τῆς θεωρητικῆς ἔστατο. —

(29) Καὶ πολλὰ ἄν τις ἔχοι λέγειν μηκύνειν ἐθέλων, καὶ τὰ τοῦ εὐδαίμονος ἐκείνου θεουργικὰ ἐνεργήματα ἀφηγούμενος.

Marinus then proceeds to report the story of how Proclus by his prayer restored to health the daughter of Plutarchus who was seriously ill.

c. Marinus also says that Proclus practised a cult of the dead in its most extensive form.

Cult of the dead

Marinus, ib. c. 36:

Οὐδένα γὰρ καιρὸν τῆς εἰωθυίας αὐτῶν θεραπείας παραλέλοιπεν, ἑκάστου δὲ ἔτους κατά τινας ὡρισμένας ἡμέρας, καὶ τὰ τῶν Ἀττικῶν ἡρώων περινοστῶν, τά τε τῶν φιλοσοφησάντων μνήματα καὶ τῶν ἄλλων τῶν φίλων καὶ γνωρίμων αὐτῷ γεγονότων, ἔδρα τὰ νενομισμένα, οὐ δι' ἑτέρου ἀλλ' αὐτὸς ἐνεργῶν· μετὰ δὲ τὴν περὶ ἕκαστον θεραπείαν, ἀπιὼν εἰς τὴν Ἀκαδημίαν, τὰς τῶν

---

[1] sc. τῆς σελήνης.

προγόνων καὶ ὅλως τὰς ὁμογνίους ψυχὰς ἀφορισμένως ἐν τόπῳ τινὶ ἐξιλεοῦτο·
κοινῇ δὲ πάλιν ταῖς τῶν φιλοσοφησάντων ἁπάντων ψυχαῖς ἐν ἑτέρῳ μέρει
ἐχεῖτο· καὶ ἐπὶ πᾶσι τούτοις ὁ εὐαγέστατος τρίτον ἄλλον περιγράψας τόπον,
πάσαις ἐν αὐτῷ ταῖς τῶν ἀποιχομένων ἀνθρώπων ψυχαῖς ἀφωσιοῦτο.

Th. Whittaker, *The Neoplatonists* p. 159, observes that in these things Proclus
anticipated the idea of Comte's *Religion of Humanity* with a remarkable closeness.

1457—Proclus' works fall into five groups.   **Works**
1. His commentaries, mainly on Plato, of which the following survive: on the
Republic, the *Parmenides*, the *Timaeus*, and *Alcib. I*. Of that on the *Cratylus* we
possess excerpts.
2. The *Theologia Platonica* (not edited since 1618). It was translated into Latin
by Ficino, and into English by Thomas Taylor (1816).
3. A group of lost works on religious symbols (Π. τῶν μυθικῶν συμβόλων), on
theurgy (Π. ἀγωγῆς), against the Christians, on Cybele and on Hecate. These are
represented for us only by the fragment Περὶ τῆς καθ' Ἕλληνας ἱερατικῆς τέχνης
(*de sacrificio et magia*), translated into Latin by Ficino, now published in Greek
by Bidez (*Catalogue des Mss alchimiques grecs*, VI, 148 ff.).
4. Three essays, translated into Latin by William of Morbecca (13th century):
De decem dubitationibus circa providentiam, De providentia et fato, and *De malorum
subsistentia*. This Latin translation is printed in the *Procli philosophi platonici
opera inedita* ed. V. Cousin, Paris, ²1864. A few other essays are lost.
5. Two systematic manuals: the Στοιχείωσις θεολογική (*Elementa theologiae*),
edited by E. R. Dodds, Oxford 1933, and the Στοιχείωσις φυσική (*Institutio physica*),
ed. A. Ritzenfeld, Leipzig 1912.
Both works have the logical form of propositions followed by a proof. The *Inst.
phys.* is almost exclusively based on Aristotle's *Physics*, while the *Elem.* are a compendium of Neoplatonic metaphysics. Proclus follows the footsteps of Iambl. and   **The
character of**
Theodorus of Asine in applying the triadic system to Plotinus' doctrine of Noûs. **the Elementa**
Moreover, he follows Iambl. (and probably Syrianus) in admitting unparticipated
terms, and hence introducing another First Principle between the First and Being
(or Noûs), and in doubling Noûs into an unparticipated and a participated one;
finally in assigning to Soul a humbler cosmic status than it had in Plotinus' theory.
His doctrine of the henads, which might seem to us rather characteristic of
Proclus, was in fact at least prepared by Syrianus and, in a sense, by Neopythagoreans (see Dodds, *Elem.* p. 257 f.). Thus, in the *Elements* at least, Proclus is (as
was said by Dodds) more a systematizer than an innovator.
In the nrs. **1458-1469** we shall follow the line of argument in the *Elements*.

1458—a. Proclus first establishes the priority of the one to the many **The One and**
by the following propositions. (The first is cited with the argument). **the many**
Proclus, *Elem. theol.*, prop. 1-6:

1. Πᾶν πλῆθος μετέχει πῃ τοῦ ἑνός.

Εἰ γὰρ μηδαμῇ μετέχοι, οὔτε τὸ ὅλον ἓν ἔσται οὔθ' ἕκαστον τῶν πολλῶν ἐξ
ὧν τὸ πλῆθος, ἀλλ' ἔσται καὶ ἐκείνων ἕκαστον πλῆθος, καὶ τοῦτο εἰς ἄπειρον,
καὶ τῶν ἀπείρων τούτων ἕκαστον ἔσται πάλιν πλῆθος ἄπειρον. μηδενὸς γὰρ
ἑνὸς μηδαμῇ μετέχον μήτε καθ' ὅλον ἑαυτὸ μήτε καθ' ἕκαστον τῶν ἐν αὐτῷ,

πάντη ἄπειρον ἔσται καὶ κατὰ πᾶν. τῶν γὰρ πολλῶν ἕκαστον, ὅπερ ἂν λάβῃς, ἤτοι ἓν ἔσται ἢ οὐχ ἕν· καὶ εἰ οὐχ ἕν, ἤτοι πολλὰ ἢ οὐδέν. ἀλλ᾽ εἰ μὲν ἕκαστον οὐδέν, καὶ τὸ ἐκ τούτων οὐδέν· εἰ δὲ πολλά, ἐξ ἀπειράκις ἀπείρων ἕκαστον. ταῦτα δὲ ἀδύνατα. οὔτε γὰρ ἐξ ἀπειράκις ἀπείρων ἐστί τι τῶν ὄντων (τοῦ γὰρ ἀπείρου πλέον οὐκ ἔστι, τὸ δὲ ἐκ πάντων ἑκάστου πλέον) οὔτε ἐκ τοῦ μηδενὸς συντίθεσθαί τι δυνατόν. πᾶν ἄρα πλῆθος μετέχει πη τοῦ ἑνός.

2. Πᾶν τὸ μετέχον τοῦ ἑνὸς καὶ ἕν ἐστι καὶ οὐχ ἕν.

3. Πᾶν τὸ γινόμενον ἓν μεθέξει τοῦ ἑνὸς γίνεται ἕν.

4. Πᾶν τὸ ἡνωμένον ἕτερόν ἐστι τοῦ αὐτοενός.

5. Πᾶν πλῆθος δεύτερόν ἐστι τοῦ ἑνός.

6. Πᾶν πλῆθος ἢ ἐξ ἡνωμένων ἐστὶν ἢ ἐξ ἑνάδων.

The hierarchy of causes　　**b.**　Next, the priority of cause to effect, of participated good to the primal Good, of the self-sufficient to what is not self-sufficient; the inferiority of all that is self-sufficient to the absolute Good, and the dependence of all that exists on one single Cause.

Ib., prop. 7-11:

7. Πᾶν τὸ παρακτικὸν ἄλλου κρεῖττόν ἐστι τῆς τοῦ παραγομένου φύσεως. Ἤτοι γὰρ κρεῖττόν ἐστιν ἢ χεῖρον ἢ ἴσον.

Ἔστω πρότερον ἴσον. τὸ τοίνυν ἀπὸ τούτου παραγόμενον ἢ δύναμιν ἔχει καὶ αὐτὸ παρακτικὴν ἄλλου τινὸς ἢ ἄγονον ὑπάρχει παντελῶς. ἀλλ᾽ εἰ μὲν ἄγονον εἴη, κατ᾽ αὐτὸ τοῦτο τοῦ παράγοντος ἠλάττωται, καὶ ἔστιν ἄνισον ἐκείνῳ, γονίμῳ ὄντι καὶ δύναμιν ἔχοντι τοῦ ποιεῖν, ἀδρανὲς ὄν. εἰ δὲ καὶ αὐτὸ παρακτικόν ἐστιν ἄλλων, ἢ καὶ αὐτὸ ἴσον ἑαυτῷ παράγει, καὶ τοῦτο ὡσαύτως ἐπὶ πάντων, καὶ ἔσται τὰ ὄντα πάντα ἴσα ἀλλήλοις καὶ οὐδὲν ἄλλο ἄλλου κρεῖττον, ἀεὶ τοῦ παράγοντος ἴσον ἑαυτῷ τὸ ἐφεξῆς ὑφιστάντος· ἢ ἄνισον, καὶ οὐκέτ᾽ ἂν ἴσον εἴη τῷ αὐτὸ παράγοντι· δυνάμεων γὰρ ἴσων ἐστὶ τὸ τὰ ἴσα ποιεῖν· τὰ δ᾽ ἐκ τούτων ἄνισα ἀλλήλοις, εἴπερ τὸ μὲν παράγον τῷ πρὸ αὐτοῦ ἴσον, αὐτῷ δὲ τὸ μετ᾽ αὐτὸ ἄνισον. οὐκ ἄρα ἴσον εἶναι δεῖ τῷ παράγοντι τὸ παραγόμενον.

Ἀλλὰ μὴν οὐδ᾽ ἔλαττον ἔσται ποτὲ τὸ παράγον. εἰ γὰρ αὐτὸ τὴν οὐσίαν τῷ παραγομένῳ δίδωσιν, αὐτὸ καὶ τὴν δύναμιν αὐτῷ χορηγεῖ κατὰ τὴν οὐσίαν. εἰ δὲ αὐτὸ παρακτικόν ἐστι τῆς δυνάμεως τῷ μετ᾽ αὐτὸ πάσης, κἂν ἑαυτῷ δύναιτο ποιεῖν τοιοῦτον, οἷον ἐκεῖνο. εἰ δὲ τοῦτο, καὶ ποιήσειεν ἂν ἑαυτὸ δυνατώτερον. οὔτε γὰρ τὸ μὴ δύνασθαι κωλύει, παρούσης τῆς ποιητικῆς δυνάμεως· οὔτε τὸ μὴ βούλεσθαι, πάντα γὰρ τοῦ ἀγαθοῦ ὀρέγεται κατὰ φύσιν· ὥστε εἰ ἄλλο δύναται τελειότερον ἀπεργάσασθαι, κἂν ἑαυτὸ πρὸ τοῦ μετ᾽ αὐτὸ τελειώσειεν.

Οὔτε ἴσον ἄρα τῷ παράγοντι τὸ παραγόμενόν ἐστιν οὔτε κρεῖττον. πάντη ἄρα τὸ παράγον κρεῖττον τῆς τοῦ παραγομένου φύσεως.

8. Πάντων τῶν ὁπωσοῦν τοῦ ἀγαθοῦ μετεχόντων ἡγεῖται τὸ πρώτως ἀγαθὸν καὶ ὃ μηδέν ἐστιν ἄλλο ἢ ἀγαθόν.

9. Πᾶν τὸ αὔταρκες ἢ κατ' οὐσίαν ἢ κατ' ἐνέργειαν κρεῖττόν ἐστι τοῦ μὴ αὐτάρκους ἀλλ' εἰς ἄλλην οὐσίαν ἀνηρτημένου τὴν τῆς τελειότητος αἰτίαν.

10. Πᾶν τὸ αὔταρκες τοῦ ἁπλῶς ἀγαθοῦ καταδεέστερόν ἐστι.

11. Πάντα τὰ ὄντα πρόεισιν ἀπὸ μιᾶς αἰτίας, τῆς πρώτης.

1459—a. Things existing are divided into three groups: the unmoved, the selfmoved and the extrinsically moved. **The grades of reality**

Proclus, *Elem.*, prop. 14:

Πᾶν τὸ ὂν ἢ ἀκίνητόν ἐστιν ἢ κινούμενον· καὶ εἰ κινούμενον, ἢ ὑφ' ἑαυτοῦ ἢ ὑπ' ἄλλου· καὶ εἰ μὲν ὑφ' ἑαυτοῦ, αὐτοκίνητόν ἐστιν· εἰ δὲ ὑπ' ἄλλου, ἑτεροκίνητον. πᾶν ἄρα ἢ ἀκίνητόν ἐστιν ἢ αὐτοκίνητον ἢ ἑτεροκίνητον.

Ἀνάγκη γὰρ τῶν ἑτεροκινήτων ὄντων εἶναι καὶ τὸ ἀκίνητον, καὶ μεταξὺ τούτων τὸ αὐτοκίνητον.

b. All that is capable of reverting upon itself is incorporeal.

Ib., 15:

Πᾶν τὸ πρὸς ἑαυτὸ ἐπιστρεπτικὸν ἀσώματόν ἐστιν.

Οὐδὲν γὰρ τῶν σωμάτων πρὸς ἑαυτὸ πέφυκεν ἐπιστρέφειν. εἰ γὰρ τὸ ἐπι-στρέφον πρός τι συνάπτεται ἐκείνῳ πρὸς ὃ ἐπιστρέφει, δῆλον δὴ ὅτι καὶ τὰ μέρη τοῦ σώματος πάντα πρὸς πάντα συνάψει τοῦ πρὸς ἑαυτὸ ἐπιστραφέντος· τοῦτο γὰρ ἦν τὸ πρὸς ἑαυτὸ ἐπιστρέψαι, ὅταν ἓν γένηται ἄμφω, τό τε ἐπιστραφὲν καὶ πρὸς ὃ ἐπεστράφη. ἀδύνατον δὲ ἐπὶ σώματος τοῦτο, καὶ ὅλως τῶν μεριστῶν πάντων· οὐ γὰρ ὅλον ὅλῳ συνάπτεται ἑαυτῷ τὸ μεριστὸν διὰ τὸν τῶν μερῶν χωρισμόν, ἄλλων ἀλλαχοῦ κειμένων. οὐδὲν ἄρα σῶμα πρὸς ἑαυτὸ πέφυκεν ἐπιστρέφειν, ὡς ὅλον ἐπεστράφθαι πρὸς ὅλον. εἴ τι ἄρα πρὸς ἑαυτὸ ἐπιστρεπτικόν ἐστιν, ἀσώματόν ἐστι καὶ ἀμερές.

c. To this he adds: it has as such an existence separable from the body, and next: all that is self-moving belongs to it.

Ib., 16 and 17:

16. Πᾶν τὸ πρὸς ἑαυτὸ ἐπιστρεπτικὸν χωριστὴν οὐσίαν ἔχει παντὸς σώματος.

17. Πᾶν τὸ ἑαυτὸ κινοῦν πρώτως πρὸς ἑαυτό ἐστιν ἐπιστρεπτικόν.

d. The four stages.

Ib., 20:

Πάντων σωμάτων ἐπέκεινά ἐστιν ἡ ψυχῆς οὐσία, καὶ πασῶν ψυχῶν ἐπέκεινα ἡ νοερὰ φύσις, καὶ πασῶν τῶν νοερῶν ὑποστάσεων ἐπέκεινα τὸ Ἕν.

Argument: Body is moved by Soul; Soul as αὐτοκίνητον is inferior to Νοῦς which is ἀκίνητον; and Νοῦς which is ἀκίνητον but not one, is ranked under the One.

e. It should be observed here, that Proclus explicitly assigns a certain degree of being to the body: since it participates of being, body is *in a sense* an ὄν.

Ib., 87:

Πᾶν μὲν τὸ αἰώνιον ὄν ἐστιν, οὐ πᾶν δὲ τὸ ὂν αἰώνιον.

Καὶ γὰρ τοῖς γενητοῖς ὑπάρχει πως τοῦ ὄντος μέθεξις, καθ' ὅσον οὐκ ἔστι ταῦτα τὸ μηδαμῶς ὄν, εἰ δὲ μὴ ἔστι τὸ γινόμενον οὐδαμῶς ὄν, ἔστι πως ὄν. τὸ δὲ αἰώνιον οὐδαμῇ τοῖς γενητοῖς ὑπάρχει.

Procession and reversion

1460—In speaking of procession Proclus also speaks of reversion. For he sees procession (= emanation) as a cyclical movement, reverting to its source.

Proclus, *Elem.*, 31-33:

31. Πᾶν τὸ προϊὸν ἀπό τινος κατ' οὐσίαν ἐπιστρέφεται πρὸς ἐκεῖνο ἀφ' οὗ πρόεισιν.

Εἰ γὰρ προέρχοιτο μέν, μὴ ἐπιστρέφοι δὲ πρὸς τὸ αἴτιον τῆς προόδου ταύτης, οὐκ ἂν ὀρέγοιτο τῆς αἰτίας· πᾶν γὰρ τὸ ὀρεγόμενον ἐπέστραπται πρὸς τὸ ὀρεκτόν. ἀλλὰ μὴν πᾶν τοῦ ἀγαθοῦ ἐφίεται, καὶ ἡ ἐκείνου τεῦξις διὰ τῆς προσεχοῦς αἰτίας ἑκάστοις· ὀρέγεται ἄρα καὶ τῆς ἑαυτῶν αἰτίας ἕκαστα. δι' οὗ γὰρ τὸ εἶναι ἑκάστῳ, διὰ τούτου καὶ τὸ εὖ· δι' οὗ δὲ τὸ εὖ, πρὸς τοῦτο ἡ ὄρεξις πρῶτον· πρὸς ὃ δὲ πρῶτον ἡ ὄρεξις, πρὸς τοῦτο ἡ ἐπιστροφή.

32. Πᾶσα ἐπιστροφὴ δι' ὁμοιότητος ἀποτελεῖται τῶν ἐπιστρεφομένων πρὸς ὃ ἐπιστρέφεται.

Τὸ γὰρ ἐπιστρεφόμενον πᾶν πρὸς πᾶν συνάπτεσθαι σπεύδει καὶ ὀρέγεται τῆς πρὸς αὐτὸ κοινωνίας καὶ συνδέσεως. συνδεῖ δὲ πάντα ἡ ὁμοιότης, ὥσπερ διακρίνει ἡ ἀνομοιότης καὶ διίστησιν. εἰ οὖν ἡ ἐπιστροφὴ κοινωνία τίς ἐστι καὶ συναφή, πᾶσα δὲ κοινωνία καὶ συναφὴ πᾶσα δι' ὁμοιότητος, πᾶσα ἄρα ἐπιστροφὴ δι' ὁμοιότητος ἀποτελοῖτο ἄν.

33. Πᾶν τὸ προϊὸν ἀπό τινος καὶ ἐπιστρέφον κυκλικὴν ἔχει τὴν ἐνέργειαν.

Εἰ γάρ, ἀφ' οὗ πρόεισιν, εἰς τοῦτο ἐπιστρέφει, συνάπτει τῇ ἀρχῇ τὸ τέλος, καὶ ἔστι μία καὶ συνεχὴς ἡ κίνησις, τῆς μὲν ἀπὸ τοῦ μένοντος, τῆς δὲ πρὸς τὸ μεῖναν γινομένης· ὅθεν δὴ πάντα κύκλῳ πρόεισιν ἀπὸ τῶν αἰτίων ἐπὶ τὰ αἴτια. μείζους δὲ κύκλοι καὶ ἐλάττους, τῶν μὲν ἐπιστροφῶν πρὸς τὰ ὑπερκείμενα προσεχῶς γινομένων, τῶν δὲ πρὸς τὰ ἀνωτέρω καὶ μέχρι τῆς πάντων ἀρχῆς· ἀπὸ γὰρ ἐκείνης πάντα καὶ πρὸς ἐκείνην.

That which is causa sui

1461—The doctrine of αὐθυπόστατα or self-constituted principles.

a. All that proceeds from another cause is subordinate to principles which get their substance from themselves and have a self-constituted existence.

Proclus, *Elem.* 40:

Πάντων τῶν ἀφ' ἑτέρας αἰτίας προϊόντων ἡγεῖται τὰ παρ' ἑαυτῶν ὑφιστάμενα καὶ τὴν οὐσίαν αὐθυπόστατον κεκτημένα.

Εἰ γὰρ πᾶν τὸ αὔταρκες ἢ κατ' οὐσίαν ἢ κατ' ἐνέργειαν κρεῖττον τοῦ εἰς ἄλλην αἰτίαν ἀνηρτημένου· τὸ δὲ ἑαυτὸ παράγον, ἑαυτῷ τοῦ εἶναι παρεκτικὸν ὑπάρχον, αὔταρκες πρὸς οὐσίαν, τὸ δὲ ἀπ' ἄλλου μόνον παραγόμενον οὐκ αὔταρκες· τῷ δὲ ἀγαθῷ συγγενέστερον τὸ αὔταρκες· τὰ δὲ συγγενέστερα καὶ ὁμοιότερα ταῖς αἰτίαις πρὸ τῶν ἀνομοίων ὑφέστηκεν ἐκ τῆς αἰτίας· τὰ ἄρα παρ' ἑαυτῶν παραγόμενα καὶ αὐθυπόστατα πρεσβύτερά ἐστι τῶν ἀφ' ἑτέρου μόνον εἰς τὸ εἶναι προελθόντων.

b. All that has its existence in another is produced entirely from another, but all that exists in itself is self-constituted.

Ib., 41:

Πᾶν μὲν τὸ ἐν ἄλλῳ ὂν ἀπ' ἄλλου μόνον παράγεται· πᾶν δὲ τὸ ἐν ἑαυτῷ ὂν αὐθυπόστατόν ἐστι.

Τὸ μὲν γὰρ ἐν ἄλλῳ ὂν καὶ ὑποκειμένου δεόμενον ἑαυτοῦ γεννητικὸν οὐκ ἄν ποτε εἴη· τὸ γὰρ γεννᾶν ἑαυτὸ πεφυκὸς ἕδρας ἄλλης οὐ δεῖται, συνεχόμενον ὑφ' ἑαυτοῦ καὶ σωζόμενον ἐν ἑαυτῷ τοῦ ὑποκειμένου χωρίς. τὸ δὲ ἐν ἑαυτῷ μένειν καὶ ἱδρῦσθαι δυνάμενον ἑαυτοῦ παρακτικόν ἐστιν, αὐτὸ εἰς ἑαυτὸ προϊόν, καὶ ἑαυτοῦ συνεκτικὸν ὑπάρχον, καὶ οὕτως ἐν ἑαυτῷ ὄν, ὡς ἐν αἰτίῳ τὸ αἰτιατόν.

c. All that is self-constituted is capable of reversion to itself.

Ib., 42:

Πᾶν τὸ αὐθυπόστατον πρὸς ἑαυτό ἐστιν ἐπιστρεπτικόν.

Εἰ γὰρ ἀφ' ἑαυτοῦ πρόεισι, καὶ τὴν ἐπιστροφὴν ποιήσεται πρὸς ἑαυτό· ἀφ' οὗ γὰρ ἡ πρόοδος ἑκάστοις, εἰς τοῦτο καὶ ἡ τῇ προόδῳ σύστοιχος ἐπιστροφή. εἰ γὰρ πρόεισιν ἀφ' ἑαυτοῦ μόνον, μὴ ἐπιστρέφοιτο δὲ προϊὸν εἰς ἑαυτό, οὐκ ἄν ποτε τοῦ οἰκείου ἀγαθοῦ ὀρέγοιτο καὶ ὃ δύναται ἑαυτῷ παρέχειν. δύναται δὲ πᾶν τὸ αἴτιον τῷ ἀπ' αὐτοῦ διδόναι μετὰ τῆς οὐσίας, ἧς δίδωσι, καὶ τὸ εὖ τῆς οὐσίας, ἧς δίδωσι, συζυγές· ὥστε καὶ αὐτὸ ἑαυτῷ. τοῦτο ἄρα τὸ οἰκεῖον τῷ αὐθυποστάτῳ ἀγαθόν. τούτου δὲ οὐκ ὀρέξεται τὸ ἀνεπίστροφον πρὸς ἑαυτό· μὴ ὀρεγόμενον δέ, οὐδ' ἂν τύχοι, καὶ μὴ τυγχάνον, ἀτελὲς ἂν εἴη καὶ οὐκ αὔταρκες. ἀλλ' εἴπερ τῳ ἄλλῳ, προσήκει καὶ τῷ αὐθυποστάτῳ αὐτάρκει καὶ τελείῳ εἶναι. καὶ τεύξεται ἄρα τοῦ οἰκείου καὶ ὀρέξεται καὶ πρὸς ἑαυτὸ στραφήσεται.

d.　Also the reversed proposition is valid.

Ib., 43:

Πᾶν τὸ πρὸς ἑαυτὸ ἐπιστρεπτικὸν αὐθυπόστατόν ἐστιν.

Εἰ γὰρ ἐπέστραπται πρὸς ἑαυτὸ κατὰ φύσιν καὶ ἔστι τέλειον ἐν τῇ πρὸς ἑαυτὸ ἐπιστροφῇ, καὶ τὴν οὐσίαν ἂν παρ᾽ ἑαυτοῦ ἔχοι· πρὸς ὃ γὰρ ἡ κατὰ φύσιν ἐπιστροφή, ἀπὸ τούτου καὶ ἡ πρόοδος ἡ κατ᾽ οὐσίαν ἑκάστοις. εἰ οὖν ἑαυτῷ τὸ εὖ εἶναι παρέχει, καὶ τὸ εἶναι δήπου ἑαυτῷ παρέξει, καὶ ἔσται τῆς ἑαυτοῦ κύριον ὑποστάσεως. αὐθυπόστατον ἄρα ἐστὶ τὸ πρὸς ἑαυτὸ δυνάμενον ἐπιστρέφειν.

e.　All that is self-constituted is without temporal origin; is imperishable; is eternal, and transcends the things which are measured by time.

Ib., 45, 46, 49, 51:

45.　Πᾶν τὸ αὐθυπόστατον ἀγένητόν ἐστιν.

Εἰ γὰρ γενητόν, διότι μὲν γενητόν, ἀτελὲς ἔσται καθ᾽ ἑαυτὸ καὶ τῆς ἀπ᾽ ἄλλου τελειώσεως ἐνδεές· διότι δὲ αὐτὸ ἑαυτὸ παράγει, τέλειον καὶ αὔταρκες.

46.　Πᾶν τὸ αὐθυπόστατον ἄφθαρτόν ἐστιν.

Εἰ γὰρ φθαρήσεται, ἀπολείψει ἑαυτὸ καὶ ἔσται ἑαυτοῦ χωρίς. ἀλλὰ τοῦτο ἀδύνατον.

49.　Πᾶν τὸ αὐθυπόστατον ἀίδιόν ἐστι.

Δύο γὰρ εἰσι τρόποι, καθ᾽ οὓς ἀνάγκη τι μὴ ἀίδιον εἶναι, ὅ τε ἀπὸ τῆς συνθέσεως καὶ ὁ ἀπὸ τῶν ἐν ἄλλῳ ὄντων. τὸ δὲ αὐθυπόστατον οὔτε σύνθετόν ἐστιν, ἀλλ᾽ ἁπλοῦν· οὔτε ἐν ἄλλῳ, ἀλλ᾽ ἐν ἑαυτῷ. ἀίδιον ἄρα ἐστίν.

51.　Πᾶν τὸ αὐθυπόστατον ἐξήρηται τῶν ὑπὸ χρόνου μετρουμένων κατὰ τὴν οὐσίαν.

Εἰ γὰρ ἀγένητόν ἐστι τὸ αὐθυπόστατον, οὐκ ἂν ὑπὸ χρόνου κατὰ τὸ εἶναι μετροῖτο· γένεσις γὰρ περὶ τὴν ὑπὸ χρόνου μετρουμένην φύσιν ἐστίν. οὐδὲν ἄρα τῶν αὐθυποστάτων ἐν χρόνῳ ὑφέστηκεν.

Finite and infinite

1462—a.　What always is, is infinite in potency.

Proclus. *Elem.* 84:

Πᾶν τὸ ἀεὶ ὂν ἀπειροδύναμόν ἐστιν.

b.　True being is infinite, neither in number nor in size, but only in potency.

Ib., 86:

Πᾶν τὸ ὄντως ὂν ἄπειρόν ἐστιν οὔτε κατὰ τὸ πλῆθος οὔτε κατὰ τὸ μέγεθος, ἀλλὰ κατὰ τὴν δύναμιν μόνην.

c. True being is composed of πέρας and ἄπειρον.

Ib., 89:

Πᾶν τὸ ὄντως ὂν ἐκ πέρατός ἐστι καὶ ἀπείρου.

Εἰ γὰρ ἀπειροδύναμόν ἐστι, δῆλον ὅτι ἄπειρόν ἐστι, καὶ ταύτῃ ἐκ τοῦ ἀπείρου ὑφέστηκεν. εἰ δὲ ἀμερὲς καὶ ἑνοειδές, ταύτῃ πέρατος μετείληφε· τὸ γὰρ ἑνὸς μετασχὸν πεπέρασται. ἀλλὰ μὴν ἀμερὲς ἅμα καὶ ἀπειροδύναμόν ἐστιν. ἐκ πέρατος ἄρα ἐστὶ καὶ ἀπείρου πᾶν τὸ ὄντως ὄν.

d. Beyond Being there is the πρῶτον πέρας and πρώτη ἀπειρία.

Ib., 90:

Πάντων τῶν ἐκ πέρατος καὶ ἀπειρίας ὑποστάντων προϋπάρχει καθ' αὑτὰ τὸ πρῶτον πέρας καὶ ἡ πρώτη ἀπειρία.

Εἰ γὰρ τῶν τινὸς ὄντων τὰ ἐφ' ἑαυτῶν ὄντα προϋφέστηκεν ὡς κοινὰ πάντων καὶ ἀρχηγικὰ αἴτια καὶ μὴ τινῶν, ἀλλὰ πάντων ἁπλῶς, δεῖ πρὸ τοῦ ἐξ ἀμφοῖν εἶναι τὸ πρῶτον πέρας καὶ τὸ πρώτως ἄπειρον. τὸ γὰρ ἐν τῷ μικτῷ πέρας ἀπειρίας ἐστὶ μετειληφὸς καὶ τὸ ἄπειρον πέρατος· τὸ δὲ πρῶτον ἑκάστου οὐκ ἄλλο ἐστὶν ἢ ὅ ἐστιν· οὐκ ἄρα δεῖ περατοειδὲς εἶναι τὸ πρώτως ἄπειρον καὶ ἀπειροειδὲς τὸ πρῶτον πέρας· πρὸ τοῦ μικτοῦ ἄρα ταῦτα πρώτως.

Cp. Proclus, *In Parm.* II, p. 764, l. 28-30 Cousin: πλῆθος καὶ ἓν οὐ μόνον οὐσιῶδές ἐστιν, ἀλλὰ καὶ ὑπὲρ οὐσίαν.

e. Finite potencies arise from infinite potency.

Ib., 91:

Πᾶσα δύναμις ἢ πεπερασμένη ἐστὶν ἢ ἄπειρος· ἀλλ' ἡ μὲν πεπερασμένη πᾶσα ἐκ τῆς ἀπείρου δυνάμεως ὑφέστηκεν, ἡ δὲ ἄπειρος δύναμις ἐκ τῆς πρώτης ἀπειρίας.

f. All infinite potencies depend on the first Infinity, called αὐτο-απειρία. This is not the very First Principle but, as it were, its reverse which is placed between the Ἕν (called τὸ αὐτόπερας in *Theol. Plat.* 132) and ὄν.

Ib., 92:

Πᾶν τὸ πλῆθος τῶν ἀπείρων δυνάμεων μιᾶς ἐξῆπται τῆς πρώτης ἀπειρίας, ἥτις οὐχ ὡς μετεχομένη δύναμίς ἐστιν, οὐδὲ ἐν τοῖς δυναμένοις ὑφέστηκεν, ἀλλὰ καθ' αὑτήν, οὐ τινὸς οὖσα δύναμις τοῦ μετέχοντος, ἀλλὰ πάντων αἰτία τῶν ὄντων.

Εἰ γὰρ καὶ τὸ ὂν αὐτὸ τὸ πρῶτον ἔχει δύναμιν, ἀλλ' οὐκ ἔστιν ἡ αὐτοδύναμις. ἔχει γὰρ καὶ πέρας· ἡ δὲ πρώτη δύναμις ἀπειρία ἐστίν. αἱ γὰρ ἄπειροι δυνάμεις διὰ μετουσίαν ἀπειρίας ἄπειροι· ἡ οὖν αὐτοαπειρία πρὸ πασῶν ἔσται δυνάμεων,

δι' ἣν καὶ τὸ ὂν ἀπειροδύναμον καὶ πάντα μετέσχεν ἀπειρίας. οὔτε γὰρ τὸ
πρῶτον ἡ ἀπειρία (μέτρον γὰρ πάντων ἐκεῖνο, τἀγαθὸν ὑπάρχον καὶ ἕν) οὔτε
τὸ ὂν (ἄπειρον γὰρ τοῦτο, ἀλλ' οὐκ ἀπειρία)· μεταξὺ ἄρα τοῦ πρώτου καὶ τοῦ
ὄντος ἡ ἀπειρία, πάντων αἰτία τῶν ἀπειροδυνάμων καὶ αἰτία πάσης τῆς ἐν τοῖς
οὖσιν ἀπειρίας.

This is the explanation of Iamblichus' doubled ἀρχή we found in Damascius
c. 45, cited above, **1449b**. The Christian author who calls himself Dionysius Aɪeo-
pagita unites the two ἀρχαί of Proclus and Damascius in the God-over-all, who
is at the same time the Limit of all things and Infinitude. *De div. nom.* 5, 10:

Ὁ προὼν (Θεὸς) . . . πέρας πάντων καὶ ἀπειρία, πάσης ἀπειρίας καὶ πέρατος ὑπερ-
οχικῶς ἐξῃρημένος τῶν ὡς ἀντικειμένων.

Of unparti-
cipated
terms

1463—At the head of each series is an unparticipated term which
has no cause other than itself, and as such is ἀγένητος.

a. Proclus, *Elem.* 99:

Πᾶν ἀμέθεκτον, ᾗ ἀμέθεκτόν ἐστι, ταύτῃ ἀπ' ἄλλης αἰτίας οὐχ ὑφίσταται, ἀλλ'·
αὐτὸ ἀρχή ἐστι καὶ αἰτία τῶν μετεχομένων πάντων· καὶ οὕτως ἀρχὴ πᾶσα καθ'
ἑκάστην σειρὰν ἀγένητος. —

b. Yet, these ἀρχαί are not absolute principles: they depend on
the First Principle of all things.

Ib., 100:

Πᾶσα μὲν σειρὰ τῶν ὅλων εἰς ἀμέθεκτον ἀρχὴν καὶ αἰτίαν ἀνατείνεται,
πάντα δὲ τὰ ἀμέθεκτα τῆς μιᾶς ἐξέχεται τῶν πάντων ἀρχῆς. —

In general, Proclus starts from the principle that "the main task of knowledge
is to find intermediate stages" (or, as he says, "mean terms") and "to produce
fine workmanship as to the grades of the procession of beings". *In Tim.* III 153,
l. 13-15 Diehl:

Καὶ ὅλως τοῦτο καὶ μέγιστόν ἐστι τῆς ἐπιστήμης ἔργον, ὁ τὰς μεσότητας καὶ τὰς
προόδους τῶν ὄντων λεπτουργεῖν.

c. Thus, at the head of the intelligible World there is unparticipated
Noûs, unparticipated Life, and unparticipated Being, the "Noûs" of
Plotinus being conceived as a triad of which ὂν is first, Life second and
Noûs last.

Ib., 101:

Πάντων τῶν νοῦ μετεχόντων ἡγεῖται ὁ ἀμέθεκτος νοῦς, καὶ τῶν τῆς ζωῆς
ἡ ζωή, καὶ τῶν τοῦ ὄντος τὸ ὄν· αὐτῶν δὲ τούτων τὸ μὲν ὂν πρὸ τῆς ζωῆς,
ἡ δὲ ζωὴ πρὸ τοῦ νοῦ.

Διότι μὲν γὰρ ἐν ἑκάστῃ τάξει τῶν ὄντων πρὸ τῶν μετεχομένων ἐστὶ τὰ ἀμέθεκτα, δεῖ πρὸ τῶν νοερῶν εἶναι τὸν νοῦν καὶ πρὸ τῶν ζώντων τὴν ζωὴν καὶ πρὸ τῶν ὄντων τὸ ὄν. διότι δὲ προηγεῖται τὸ τῶν πλειόνων αἴτιον ἢ τὸ τῶν ἐλαττόνων, ἐν ἐκείνοις τὸ μὲν ὂν ἔσται πρώτιστον· πᾶσι γὰρ πάρεστιν, οἷς ζωὴ καὶ νοῦς (ζῶν γὰρ πᾶν καὶ νοήσεως μετέχον ἔστιν ἐξ ἀνάγκης), οὐκ ἔμπαλιν δέ (οὐ γὰρ τὰ ὄντα πάντα ζῇ καὶ νοεῖ). δευτέρα δὲ ἡ ζωή· πᾶσι γάρ, οἷς νοῦ μέτεστι, καὶ ζωῆς μέτεστιν, οὐκ ἔμπαλιν δέ· πολλὰ γὰρ ζῇ μέν, γνώσεως δὲ ἄμοιρα ἀπολείπεται. τρίτος δὲ ὁ νοῦς· πᾶν γὰρ τὸ γνωστικὸν ὁπωσοῦν καὶ ζῇ καὶ ἔστιν. εἰ οὖν πλειόνων αἴτιον τὸ ὄν, ἐλαττόνων δὲ ἡ ζωή, καὶ ἔτι ἐλαττόνων ὁ νοῦς, πρώτιστον τὸ ὄν, εἶτα ζωή, εἶτα νοῦς.

In the *Elements* the members of this fundamental Triad are not subdivided into new triads, as we know was already done by Iamblichus and Theodorus of Asine. That Pr. himself made such subdivisions, appears in his later work the *Theol. Plat.* III, 14.

1464—The doctrine of divine Henads or Gods.

a. Proclus supposing that there is a plurality of gods, begins by positing that this plurality must have the character of a unity.

Elem., 113:

Πᾶς ὁ θεῖος ἀριθμὸς ἑνιαῖός ἐστιν.

Εἰ γὰρ ὁ θεῖος ἀριθμὸς αἰτίαν ἔχει προηγουμένην τὸ ἕν, ὡς ὁ νοερὸς τὸν νοῦν καὶ ὁ ψυχικὸς τὴν ψυχήν, καὶ ἔστιν ἀνάλογον τὸ πλῆθος πανταχοῦ πρὸς τὴν αἰτίαν, δῆλον δὴ ὅτι καὶ ὁ θεῖος ἀριθμὸς ἑνιαῖός ἐστιν, εἴπερ τὸ ἓν θεός· τοῦτο δέ, εἴπερ τἀγαθὸν καὶ ἓν ταὐτόν· καὶ γὰρ τἀγαθὸν καὶ θεὸς ταὐτόν (οὗ γὰρ μηδέν ἐστιν ἐπέκεινα καὶ οὗ πάντα ἐφίεται, θεὸς τοῦτο· καὶ ἀφ' οὗ τὰ πάντα καὶ πρὸς ὅ, τοῦτο δὲ τἀγαθόν). εἰ ἄρα ἔστι πλῆθος θεῶν, ἑνιαῖόν ἐστι τὸ πλῆθος. ἀλλὰ μὴν ὅτι ἔστι, δῆλον, εἴπερ πᾶν αἴτιον ἀρχικὸν οἰκείου πλήθους ἡγεῖται καὶ ὁμοίου πρὸς αὐτὸ καὶ συγγενοῦς.

b. Every god is a self-complete henad, and every self-complete henad is a god.

Ib., 114:

Πᾶς θεὸς ἑνάς ἐστιν αὐτοτελής, καὶ πᾶσα αὐτοτελὴς ἑνὰς θεός.

Εἰ γὰρ τῶν ἑνάδων διττὸς ὁ ἀριθμός, ὡς δέδεικται πρότερον, καὶ αἱ μὲν αὐτοτελεῖς εἰσιν αἱ δὲ ἐλλάμψεις ἀπ' ἐκείνων, τῷ δὲ ἑνὶ καὶ τἀγαθῷ συγγενὴς καὶ ὁμοφυὴς ὁ θεῖος ἀριθμός, ἑνάδες εἰσὶν αὐτοτελεῖς οἱ θεοί.

Καὶ ἔμπαλιν, εἰ ἔστιν αὐτοτελὴς ἑνάς, θεός ἐστι. καὶ γὰρ ὡς ἑνὰς τῷ ἑνὶ καὶ ὡς αὐτοτελὴς τἀγαθῷ συγγενεστάτη διαφερόντως ἐστί, καὶ κατ' ἄμφω τῆς θείας ἰδιότητος μετέχει, καὶ ἔστι θεός. εἰ δὲ ἦν ἑνὰς μὲν οὐκ αὐτοτελὴς δέ, ἢ αὐτοτελὴς μὲν ἡ ὑπόστασις οὐκέτι δὲ ἑνάς, εἰς ἑτέραν ἂν ἐτάττετο τάξιν διὰ τὴν τῆς ἰδιότητος ἐξαλλαγήν.

c. Every god is above Being, Life and Noûs: for these are not henads, but unified groups.

Ib., 115:

Πᾶς θεὸς ὑπερούσιός ἐστι καὶ ὑπέρζωος καὶ ὑπέρνους.

Εἰ γὰρ ἑνάς ἐστιν ἕκαστος αὐτοτελής, ἕκαστον δὲ τούτων οὐχὶ ἑνὰς ἀλλ᾽ ἡνωμένον, δῆλον δὴ ὅτι πάντων ἐστὶν ἐπέκεινα τῶν εἰρημένων ἅπας θεός, οὐσίας καὶ ζωῆς καὶ νοῦ. εἰ γὰρ διέστηκε μὲν ταῦτα ἀλλήλων, πάντα δέ ἐστιν ἐν πᾶσιν, ἕκαστον τὰ πάντα ὂν ἓν ἂν οὐκ ἂν εἴη μόνον.

Ἔτι δέ, εἰ τὸ πρῶτον ὑπερούσιον, ἅπας δὲ θεὸς τῆς τοῦ πρώτου σειρᾶς ἐστιν ἢ θεός, ὑπερούσιος ἕκαστος ἂν εἴη.

d. The First Principle differs from the other henads in that the First is not participable, while the others are.

Ib., 116:

Πᾶς θεὸς μεθεκτός ἐστι, πλὴν τοῦ ἑνός.

e. Every god is a measure of things existing.

Ib., 117:

Πᾶς θεὸς μέτρον ἐστὶ τῶν ὄντων.

Εἰ γάρ ἐστιν ἑνιαῖος ἅπας θεός, τὰ πλήθη πάντα τῶν ὄντων ἀφορίζει καὶ μετρεῖ. πάντα μὲν γὰρ τὰ πλήθη, τῇ ἑαυτῶν φύσει ἀόριστα ὄντα, διὰ τὸ ἓν ὁρίζεται· τὸ δὲ ἑνιαῖον μετρεῖν καὶ περατοῦν, οἷς ἂν παρῇ, βούλεται, καὶ περιάγειν εἰς ὅρον τὸ μὴ τοιοῦτον κατὰ τὴν αὑτοῦ δύναμιν.

f. The attributes of the Gods.

Ib., 118, 119:

Πᾶν ὅ τι περ ἂν ἐν τοῖς θεοῖς ᾖ, κατὰ τὴν αὐτῶν ἰδιότητα προϋφέστηκεν ἐν αὐτοῖς, καὶ ἔστιν ἡ ἰδιότης αὐτῶν ἑνιαία καὶ ὑπερούσιος· ἑνιαίως ἄρα καὶ ὑπερουσίως πάντα ἐν αὐτοῖς.—

119. Πᾶς θεὸς κατὰ τὴν ὑπερούσιον ἀγαθότητα ὑφέστηκε, καὶ ἔστιν ἀγαθὸς οὔτε καθ᾽ ἕξιν οὔτε κατ᾽ οὐσίαν (καὶ γὰρ αἱ ἕξεις καὶ αἱ οὐσίαι δευτέραν καὶ πολλοστὴν ἔλαχον τάξιν ἀπὸ τῶν θεῶν), ἀλλ᾽ ὑπερουσίως.—

g. Their providence.

Ib., 120:

Πᾶς θεὸς ἐν τῇ ἑαυτοῦ ὑπάρξει τὸ προνοεῖν τῶν ὅλων κέκτηται· καὶ τὸ πρώτως προνοεῖν ἐν τοῖς θεοῖς.—

h. Their goodness, power and knowledge.

Ib,. 121:

Πᾶν τὸ θεῖον ὕπαρξιν μὲν ἔχει τὴν ἀγαθότητα, δύναμιν δὲ ἑνιαίαν καὶ γνῶσιν κρύφιον καὶ ἄληπτον πᾶσιν ὁμοῦ τοῖς δευτέροις. —

i. How the gods may be known by secondary beings.

Ib., 123:

Πᾶν τὸ θεῖον αὐτὸ μὲν διὰ τὴν ὑπερούσιον ἕνωσιν ἄρρητόν ἐστι καὶ ἄγνωστον πᾶσι τοῖς δευτέροις, ἀπὸ δὲ τῶν μετεχόντων ληπτόν ἐστι καὶ γνωστόν· διὸ μόνον τὸ πρῶτον παντελῶς ἄγνωστον, ἅτε ἀμέθεκτον ὄν. —

j. On divine knowledge.

Ib., 124:

Πᾶς θεὸς ἀμερίστως μὲν τὰ μεριστὰ γινώσκει, ἀχρόνως δὲ τὰ ἔγχρονα, τὰ δὲ μὴ ἀναγκαῖα ἀναγκαίως, καὶ τὰ μεταβλητὰ ἀμεταβλήτως, καὶ ὅλως πάντα κρειττόνως ἢ κατὰ τὴν αὐτῶν τάξιν. —

k. A god is more universal as he is nearer to the One.

Ib., 126:

Πᾶς θεὸς ὁλικώτερος μέν ἐστιν ὁ τοῦ ἑνὸς ἐγγυτέρω, μερικώτερος δὲ ὁ πορρώτερον. —

1465—a. Grades of participation in the Divine.

Proclus, *Elem.* 128, 129, 138, 139:

128. Πᾶς θεός, ὑπὸ μὲν τῶν ἐγγυτέρω μετεχόμενος, ἀμέσως μετέχεται· ὑπὸ δὲ τῶν πορρωτέρω, διὰ μέσων ἢ ἐλαττόνων ἢ πλειόνων τινῶν. —

129. Πᾶν μὲν σῶμα θεῖον διὰ ψυχῆς ἐστι θεῖον τῆς ἐκθεουμένης, πᾶσα δὲ ψυχὴ θεία διὰ τοῦ θείου νοῦ, πᾶς δὲ νοῦς [θεῖος] κατὰ μέθεξιν τῆς θείας ἑνάδος· καὶ ἡ μὲν ἑνὰς αὐτόθεν θεός, ὁ δὲ νοῦς θειότατον, ἡ δὲ ψυχὴ θεία, τὸ δὲ σῶμα θεοειδές. —

138. Πάντων τῶν μετεχόντων τῆς θείας ἰδιότητος καὶ ἐκθεουμένων πρώτιστόν ἐστι καὶ ἀκρότατον τὸ ὄν. —

139. Πάντα τὰ μετέχοντα τῶν θείων ἑνάδων, ἀρχόμενα ἀπὸ τοῦ ὄντος, εἰς τὴν σωματικὴν τελευτᾷ φύσιν· τὸ γὰρ πρῶτόν ἐστι τῶν μετεχόντων τὸ ὄν, ἔσχατον δὲ τὸ σῶμα (καὶ γὰρ σώματα θεῖα εἶναί φαμεν). —

b. All inferior principles retreat before the presence of the gods.

Ib., 143:

143. Πάντα τὰ καταδεέστερα τῇ παρουσίᾳ τῶν θεῶν ὑπεξίσταται· κἂν ἐπιτήδειον ᾖ τὸ μετέχον, πᾶν μὲν τὸ ἀλλότριον τοῦ θείου φωτὸς ἐκποδὼν γίνεται, καταλάμπεται δὲ πάντα ἀθρόως ὑπὸ τῶν θεῶν.

c. The procession of things existent and all cosmic orders of existent things extend as far as do the orders of the gods.

Ib., 144:

Πάντα τὰ ὄντα καὶ πᾶσαι τῶν ὄντων αἱ διακοσμήσεις ἐπὶ τοσοῦτον προεληλύθασιν, ἐφ' ὅσον καὶ αἱ τῶν θεῶν διατάξεις.

Principles of divine procession

1466—a. Divine procession is a circular motion: without beginning and without end.

Proclus, *Elem.* 146:

Πασῶν τῶν θείων προόδων τὰ τέλη πρὸς τὰς ἑαυτῶν ἀρχὰς ὁμοιοῦται, κύκλον ἄναρχον καὶ ἀτελεύτητον σώζοντα διὰ τῆς πρὸς τὰς ἀρχὰς ἐπιστροφῆς. —

b. The manifold of divine henads must be limited in number, for it stands nearest to the One.

Ib., 149:

Πᾶν τὸ πλῆθος τῶν θείων ἑνάδων πεπερασμένον ἐστὶ κατὰ ἀριθμόν.

Εἰ γὰρ ἐγγυτάτω τοῦ ἑνός ἐστιν, οὐκ ἂν ἄπειρον ὑπάρχοι· οὐ γὰρ συμφυὲς τῷ ἑνὶ τὸ ἄπειρον, ἀλλὰ ἀλλότριον.

Cp. above, **1462 f.**

Πέρας and ἄπειρον

c. Πέρας and ἄπειρον are maintained as the two fundamental principles from which every order of gods is derived.

Ib., 159:

Πᾶσα τάξις θεῶν ἐκ τῶν πρώτων ἐστὶν ἀρχῶν, πέρατος καὶ ἀπειρίας· ἀλλ' ἡ μὲν πρὸς τῆς τοῦ πέρατος αἰτίας μᾶλλον, ἡ δὲ πρὸς τῆς ἀπειρίας. —

Grades of participation

d. There are νοεραὶ ἑνάδες, participated by Νοῦς, ὑπερκόσμιοι ἑνάδες, participated by Soul, and ἐγκόσμιοι ἑνάδες participated by sensible bodies. And since according to Proclus Being is above Νοῦς and νοηταὶ ἑνάδες above those which are called νοεραί, he ranks the νοηταὶ ἑνάδες directly after the Ἕν and regards them as participated by supreme Being which is the ἀμεθέκτως ὄν.

Ib., 163-165:

163. Πᾶν τὸ πλῆθος τῶν ἑνάδων τὸ μετεχόμενον ὑπὸ τοῦ ἀμεθέκτου νοῦ νοερόν ἐστιν.

Ὡς γὰρ ἔχει νοῦς πρὸς τὸ ὄντως ὄν, οὕτως αἱ ἑνάδες αὗται πρὸς τὰς ἑνάδας τὰς νοητὰς ἔχουσιν. ᾗπερ οὖν καὶ ἐκεῖναι, καταλάμπουσαι τὸ ὄν, νοηταί εἰσι, ταύτῃ καὶ αὗται, καταλάμπουσαι τὸν θεῖον καὶ ἀμέθεκτον νοῦν, νοεραί εἰσιν, ἀλλ' οὐχ οὕτω νοεραὶ ὡς ἐν νῷ ὑφεστηκυῖαι, ἀλλ' ὡς κατ' αἰτίαν τοῦ νοῦ προϋπάρχουσαι καὶ ἀπογεννῶσαι τὸν νοῦν.

164. Πᾶν τὸ πλῆθος τῶν ἑνάδων τὸ μετεχόμενον ὑπὸ τῆς ἀμεθέκτου πάσης ψυχῆς ὑπερκόσμιόν ἐστι.

Διότι γὰρ ἡ ἀμέθεκτος ψυχὴ πρώτως ὑπὲρ τὸν κόσμον ἐστί, καὶ οἱ μετεχόμενοι ὑπ' αὐτῆς θεοὶ ὑπερκόσμιοί εἰσιν, ἀνὰ λόγον ὄντες πρὸς τοὺς νοεροὺς καὶ νοητούς, ὃν ἔχει ψυχὴ πρὸς νοῦν καὶ νοῦς πρὸς τὸ ὄντως ὄν. ὡς οὖν ψυχὴ πᾶσα εἰς νοῦς ἀνήρτηται καὶ νοῦς εἰς τὸ νοητὸν ἐπέστραπται, οὕτω δὴ καὶ οἱ ὑπερκόσμιοι θεοὶ τῶν νοερῶν ἐξέχονται, καθάπερ δὴ καὶ οὗτοι τῶν νοητῶν.

165. Πᾶν τὸ πλῆθος τῶν ἑνάδων τῶν μετεχομένων ὑπό τινος αἰσθητοῦ σώματος ἐγκόσμιόν ἐστιν.

'Ελλάμπει γὰρ εἴς τι τῶν τοῦ κόσμου μερῶν διὰ μέσων τοῦ νοῦ καὶ τῆς ψυχῆς. οὔτε γὰρ νοῦς ἄνευ ψυχῆς πάρεστί τινι τῶν ἐγκοσμίων σωμάτων οὔτε θεότης ἀμέσως συνάπτεται ψυχῇ (διὰ γὰρ τῶν ὁμοίων αἱ μεθέξεις) · καὶ αὐτὸς ὁ νοῦς κατὰ τὸ νοητὸν τὸ ἑαυτοῦ καὶ τὸ ἀκρότατον μετέχει τῆς ἑνάδος. ἐγκόσμιοι οὖν αἱ ἑνάδες ὡς συμπληροῦσαι τὸν ὅλον κόσμον καὶ ὡς ἐκθεωτικαὶ τῶν ἐμφανῶν σωμάτων.

Dodds, *Elements* p. 282, gives the following scheme of participation, according to Proclus in the above-cited propositions.

τὸ Ἕν — ἑνάδες νοηταί — ἑνάδες νοεραί — ἑνάδες ὑπερκόσμιοι — ἑνάδες ἐγκόσμιοι

τὸ ἀμεθέκτως ὄν   μεθέκτως ὄν   μεθέκτως ὄν   μεθέκτως ὄν

θεῖος Νοῦς ἀμέθεκτος   θ. Νοῦς μεθεκτός   θ. Νοῦς μεθεκτός

θεία ψυχὴ ἀμέθεκτος   θ. ψυχὴ μεθεκτή

θεῖον σῶμα

1467—a. Participated and unparticipated Noûs.

Noûs

Proclus, *Elem.* 166:

Πᾶς νοῦς ἢ ἀμέθεκτός ἐστιν ἢ μεθεκτός· καὶ εἰ μεθεκτός, ἢ ὑπὸ τῶν ὑπερκοσμίων ψυχῶν μετεχόμενος ἢ ὑπὸ τῶν ἐγκοσμίων.

Παντὸς μὲν γὰρ τοῦ πλήθους τῶν νόων ὁ ἀμέθεκτος ἡγεῖται, πρωτίστην ἔχων ὕπαρξιν· τῶν δὲ μετεχομένων οἱ μὲν τὴν ὑπερκόσμιον καὶ ἀμέθεκτον ἐλλάμπουσι ψυχήν, οἱ δὲ τὴν ἐγκόσμιον. οὔτε γὰρ ἀπὸ τοῦ ἀμεθέκτου τὸ πλῆθος εὐθὺς τὸ ἐγκόσμιον, εἴπερ αἱ πρόοδοι διὰ τῶν ὁμοίων, ὁμοιότερον δὲ τῷ ἀμεθέκτῳ τὸ χωριστὸν τοῦ κόσμου μᾶλλον ἢ τὸ διῃρημένον περὶ αὐτόν· οὔτε μόνον τὸ ὑπερκόσμιον ὑπέστη πλῆθος, ἀλλ' εἰσὶ καὶ ἐγκόσμιοι, εἴπερ καὶ θεῶν ἐγκοσμίων πλῆθος, καὶ αὐτὸς ὁ κόσμος ἔμψυχος ἅμα καὶ ἔννους ἐστί, καὶ ἡ μέθεξις ταῖς ἐγκοσμίοις ψυχαῖς τῶν ὑπερκοσμίων νόων διὰ μέσων ἐστὶ τῶν ἐγκοσμίων νόων.

b. Every noûs knows itself by intuitive knowledge. The first Noûs knows itself only; subsequent intelligence knows both itself and what is prior to it.

Ib., 167:

Πᾶς νοῦς ἑαυτὸν νοεῖ· ἀλλ' ὁ μὲν πρώτιστος ἑαυτὸν μόνον, καὶ ἓν κατ' ἀριθμὸν ἐν τούτῳ νοῦς καὶ νοητόν· ἕκαστος δὲ τῶν ἐφεξῆς ἑαυτὸν ἅμα καὶ τὰ πρὸ αὐτοῦ, καὶ νοητόν ἐστι τούτῳ τὸ μὲν ὅ ἐστι, τὸ δὲ ἀφ' οὗ ἐστιν. —

c. The first Noûs has absolute knowledge, subsequent intelligences have not.

Ib., 170:

Πᾶς νοῦς πάντα ἅμα νοεῖ· ἀλλ' ὁ μὲν ἀμέθεκτος ἁπλῶς πάντα, τῶν δὲ μετ' ἐκεῖνον ἕκαστος καθ' ἓν πάντα. —

d. Noûs and the Ideas.

Ib., 177:

Πᾶς νοῦς πλήρωμα ὢν εἰδῶν, ὁ μὲν ὁλικωτέρων, ὁ δὲ μερικωτέρων ἐστὶ περιεκτικὸς εἰδῶν· καὶ οἱ μὲν ἀνωτέρω νόες ὁλικώτερον ἔχουσιν ὅσα μερικώτερον οἱ μετ' αὐτούς, οἱ δὲ κατωτέρω μερικώτερον ὅσα ὁλικώτερον οἱ πρὸ αὐτῶν. —

e. Divine and not-divine Noûs.

Ib., 182-183:

182. Πᾶς θεῖος νοῦς μετεχόμενος ὑπὸ ψυχῶν μετέχεται θείων. —

183. Πᾶς νοῦς μετεχόμενος μέν, νοερὸς δὲ μόνον ὤν, μετέχεται ὑπὸ ψυχῶν οὔτε θείων οὔτε νοῦ καὶ ἀνοίας ἐν μεταβολῇ γινομένων. —

Soul   **1468—a.** Different kinds of souls.

Proclus, *Elem.* 184, 185:

184. Πᾶσα ψυχὴ ἢ θεία ἐστίν, ἢ μεταβάλλουσα ἀπὸ νοῦ εἰς ἄνοιαν, ἢ μεταξὺ τούτων ἀεὶ μὲν νοοῦσα, καταδεεστέρα δὲ τῶν θείων ψυχῶν. —

185. Πᾶσαι μὲν αἱ θεῖαι ψυχαὶ θεοί εἰσι ψυχικῶς, πᾶσαι δὲ αἱ τοῦ νοεροῦ μετέχουσαι νοῦ θεῶν ὀπαδοὶ ἀεί, πᾶσαι δὲ αἱ μεταβολῆς δεκτικαὶ θεῶν ὀπαδοὶ ποτέ. —

b. Their common nature.

Ib., 186-187:

186. Πᾶσα ψυχὴ ἀσώματός ἐστιν οὐσία καὶ χωριστὴ σώματος.

187. Πᾶσα ψυχὴ ἀνώλεθρός ἐστι καὶ ἄφθαρτος.

c. Soul is both a principle of life and a living being.

Ib., 188, 189:

188. Πᾶσα ψυχὴ καὶ ζωή ἐστι καὶ ζῶν.

Ὧ γὰρ ἂν παραγένηται ψυχή, τοῦτο ζῇ ἐξ ἀνάγκης· καὶ τὸ ψυχῆς ἐστερη-μένον ζωῆς εὐθὺς ἄμοιρον ἀπολείπεται.

Εἰ οὖν ζωὴν ἐπιφέρει τοῖς ἐμψύχοις, ἢ ζωή ἐστιν ἢ ζῶν μόνον ἢ τὸ συνάμφω, ζωὴ ἅμα καὶ ζῶν. —

Εἰ δὲ ζωὴ μόνον ἐστίν, οὐκέτι μεθέξει τῆς νοερᾶς ζωῆς. τὸ γὰρ ζωῆς μετέχον ζῶν ἐστι καὶ οὐ ζωὴ μόνον· ζωὴ γὰρ μόνον ἡ πρώτη καὶ ἀμέθεκτος, ἡ δὲ μετ' ἐκείνην ζῶν ἅμα καὶ ζωή· ψυχὴ δὲ οὐκ ἔστιν ἡ ἀμέθεκτος ζωή, ἅμα ἄρα ζωή ἐστι καὶ ζῶν ἡ ψυχή.

189. Πᾶσα ψυχὴ αὐτόζως ἐστίν.

Εἰ γὰρ ἐπιστρεπτικὴ πρὸς ἑαυτήν, τὸ δὲ πρὸς ἑαυτὸ ἐπιστρεπτικὸν πᾶν αὐθυπόστατον, καὶ ἡ ψυχὴ ἄρα αὐθυπόστατος καὶ ἑαυτὴν ὑφίστησιν.

d. Participated soul has eternal existence, but a temporal activity. She both shares eternal being and is the first of things that come to be.

Ib., 191, 192:

191. Πᾶσα ψυχὴ μεθεκτὴ τὴν μὲν οὐσίαν αἰώνιον ἔχει, τὴν δὲ ἐνέργειαν κατὰ χρόνον. —

192. Πᾶσα ψυχὴ μεθεκτὴ τῶν τε ἀεὶ ὄντων ἐστὶ καὶ πρώτη τῶν γενητῶν. —

e. She possesses all the Forms which Noûs possesses primarily.

Ib., 194:

Πᾶσα ψυχὴ πάντα ἔχει τὰ εἴδη, ἃ ὁ νοῦς πρώτως ἔχει.

Εἰ γὰρ ἀπὸ νοῦ πρόεισι καὶ νοῦς ὑποστάτης ψυχῆς, καὶ αὐτῷ τῷ εἶναι ἀκίνητος ὢν πάντα ὁ νοῦς παράγει, δώσει καὶ τῇ ψυχῇ τῇ ὑφισταμένῃ τῶν ἐν αὐτῷ πάντων οὐσιώδεις λόγους.

1469—a. Soul in the world has periodical motion and cyclic re-instatements.

The periodical motion of soul

Proclus, *Elem.* 199:

Πᾶσα ψυχὴ ἐγκόσμιος περιόδοις χρῆται τῆς οἰκείας ζωῆς καὶ ἀποκατα-στάσεσιν.

Εἰ γὰρ ὑπὸ χρόνου μετρεῖται καὶ μεταβατικῶς ἐνεργεῖ, καὶ ἔστιν αὐτῆς ἰδία κίνησις, πᾶν δὲ τὸ κινούμενον καὶ χρόνου μετέχον, ἀΐδιον ὄν, χρῆται περιόδοις καὶ περιοδικῶς ἀνακυκλεῖται καὶ ἀποκαθίσταται ἀπὸ τῶν αὐτῶν ἐπὶ τὰ αὐτά, δῆλον ὅτι καὶ πᾶσα ψυχὴ ἐγκόσμιος, κίνησιν ἔχουσα καὶ ἐνεργοῦσα κατὰ χρόνον, περιόδους τε τῶν κινήσεων ἕξει καὶ ἀποκαταστάσεις· πᾶσα γὰρ περίοδος τῶν ἀϊδίων ἀποκαταστατική ἐστιν.

b. Each soul has a periodic alternation of ascents and descents, and this movement is unceasing.

Ib., 206:

Πᾶσα ψυχὴ μερικὴ κατιέναι τε εἰς γένεσιν ἐπ' ἄπειρον καὶ ἀνιέναι δύναται ἀπὸ γενέσεως εἰς τὸ ὄν.

Εἰ γὰρ ποτὲ μὲν ἕπεται θεοῖς, ποτὲ δὲ ἀποπίπτει τῆς πρὸς τὸ θεῖον ἀνατάσεως, νοῦ τε καὶ ἀνοίας μετέχει, δῆλον δὴ ὅτι παρὰ μέρος ἔν τε τῇ γενέσει γίνεται καὶ ἐν τοῖς θεοῖς ἔστιν. οὐδὲ γὰρ <τὸν ἄπειρον οὖσα χρόνον ἐν σώμασιν ἐνύλοις ἔπειτα ἕτερον τοιοῦτον χρόνον ἔσται ἐν τοῖς θεοῖς, οὐδὲ> τὸν ἄπειρον οὖσα χρόνον ἐν τοῖς θεοῖς αὖθις ὅλον τὸν ἐφεξῆς χρόνον ἔσται ἐν τοῖς σώμασι· τὸ γὰρ ἀρχὴν χρονικὴν μὴ ἔχον οὐδὲ τελευτήν ποτε ἕξει, καὶ τὸ μηδεμίαν ἔχον τελευτὴν ἀνάγκη μηδὲ ἀρχὴν ἔχειν. λείπεται ἄρα περιόδους ἑκάστην ποιεῖσθαι ἀνόδων τε ἐκ τῆς γενέσεως καὶ τῶν εἰς γένεσιν καθόδων, καὶ τοῦτο ἄπαυστον εἶναι διὰ τὸν ἄπειρον χρόνον. ἑκάστη ἄρα ψυχὴ μερικὴ κατιέναι τε ἐπ' ἄπειρον δύναται καὶ ἀνιέναι, καὶ τοῦτο οὐ μὴ παύσεται περὶ ἁπάσας τὸ πάθημα γινόμενον.

On Proclus' rejection of the possibility of eternal punishment, below, nr. **1474b**. Cp. Sallustius c. 20, where the author says that souls cannot leave the body once for all and "remain for ever and ever in idleness" (τὸν ἅπαντα αἰῶνα μένειν ἐν ἀργείᾳ).

c. Particular souls have an ὄχημα which is immaterial and impas-

The vehicle of soul sible. It acquires increasingly material vestures in descending.

Ib., 208, 209:

208. Πάσης μερικῆς ψυχῆς τὸ ὄχημα ἄϋλόν ἐστι καὶ ἀδιαίρετον κατ' οὐσίαν καὶ ἀπαθές. —

209. Πάσης μερικῆς ψυχῆς τὸ ὄχημα κάτεισι μὲν προσθέσει χιτώνων ἐνυλοτέρων, συ<να>νάγεται δὲ τῇ ψυχῇ δι' ἀφαιρέσεως παντὸς τοῦ ἐνύλου καὶ τῆς εἰς τὸ οἰκεῖον εἶδος ἀναδρομῆς, ἀνάλογον τῇ χρωμένῃ ψυχῇ· καὶ γὰρ ἐκείνη κάτεισι μὲν ἀλόγους προσλαβοῦσα ζωάς, ἄνεισι δὲ ἀποσκευασαμένη πάσας τὰς γενεσιουργοὺς δυνάμεις, ἃς ἐν τῇ καθόδῳ περιεβάλλετο, καὶ γενομένη καθαρὰ καὶ γυμνὴ τῶν τοιούτων πασῶν δυνάμεων ὅσαι πρὸς τὴν τῆς γενέσεως χρείαν ὑπηρετοῦσι.

On the doctrine of the immaterial vehicle of soul and its προσθῆκαι more explicit information is found in the Commentary on the *Timaeus*, a passage of which will be cited below (**1474a**).

Soul descends entire **d.** When a soul descends into temporal existence, she descends entire. There is not a part of her which stays "yonder".

Ib., 211:

Πᾶσα μερικὴ ψυχὴ κατιοῦσα εἰς γένεσιν ὅλη κάτεισι. καὶ οὐ τὸ μὲν αὐτῆς ἄνω μένει, τὸ δὲ κάτεισιν.—

Cp. *In Tim.* III p. 333 f. Diehl, cited above (**1453a**). On this point as on many others Proclus joins Iamblichus.

1470—As Plotinus did when speaking of the ἄπειρον in the intelligible **The cause** World (above, nr. **1408b-e**) and in maintaining the existence of ὕλη **of evil** νοητή (above, ib.), Pr. denies that "matter" taken in the sense of the πρώτως ἄπειρον should be evil. For it springs from the First Cause, which is also called [1] "the Cause of the mixture".

a.   Proclus, *De malorum subsistentia*, p. 235/6 Cousin:

Si autem et ex se infinitum materiam dicendum, ex Deo materia sive τὸ prime infinitum. Substantialem enim infinitatem ex una causa dependentem divinitus exgenerari dicendum, et maxime eam quae cum fine facere mixturam non potentem: etenim subsistentiae ipsorum et mixtionis Deus causa; haec quidem igitur et corporis, qua corpus, naturam in unam causam ducere, scilicet Deum; ipse enim est qui mixtum genuit. Neque ergo corpus malum, neque materia: haec enim sunt Dei γεννήματα hoc quidem ut mixtura, haec autem ut infinitum.

In this passage Pr. does not differ from Plotinus, as was pointed out above, except in so far as the conditional form of the first sentence marks a certain reserve as to calling the πρώτως ἄπειρον "matter". "If this is matter", Pr. says, *"then* matter is generated by God"; and in this he joins Plotinus. But cp. *Theol. Plat.* p. 137-138, where he says that Being τὴν μὲν ὕπαρξιν ἐκ τοῦ πέρατος κομίζεται, τὴν δὲ δύναμιν ἐκ τοῦ ἀπείρου· that, therefore, Being certainly μετέχει τῆς ἀπειρίας, but that it would be against the spirit of Platonism to call this ἄπειρον "matter" and thus to introduce a formless and undetermined nature into intelligible Being.

Theol. Plat. III c. 9, the end: **The**
Εἰ δὲ ἄμορφόν τινα καὶ ἀνείδεον φύσιν καὶ ἀόριστον ἐπὶ τὴν νοητὴν οὐσίαν ἀναπέμπουσι,   **πρώτως**
τῆς Πλατωνικῆς ἁμαρτάνειν μοι δοκοῦσι διανοίας. Οὐ γάρ ἐστιν ὕλη τοῦ πέρατος τὸ   **ἄπειρον**
ἄπειρον, ἀλλὰ δύναμις, οὐδὲ εἶδος τοῦ ἀπείρου τὸ πέρας, ἀλλὰ ὕπαρξις.—   **should not**
                                                                              be called
b.   To the question of Πόθεν τὰ κακά Pr. answers that there is   **ὕλη**
not just one cause of evil.
                                                                              There is not
                                                                              one cause of
Proclus, *De malorum subs.* p. 250, 5-8 Cousin: **evil**

Unam quidem itaque secundum se malorum causam nullatenus ponendum. Si enim bonorum causa una, malorum multa et non unum.

---

[1] In Plato's *Philebus*, 23c.

c. *Malum* in the sense of *privatio* is perfectly negative and therefore could not be the cause of anything at all.

χαχόν in the sense of στέρησις cannot be a cause at all

Proclus, ib., p. 240, 16-26 C.:

Si igitur malum quidem contrarium bono et dissidet ad ipsam, privatio autem neque oppugnat sui ipsius habitui, neque facere aliquid nata est cuius et esse tale debile omnino et non mansivum, ut illorum sermo, quomodo utique adhuc τὸ malificum ad ipsam reducemus, a qua remotum est omne facere? Species enim est hoc et potentia; haec autem informis et debilis, sed non potentia, magis autem absentia potentiae.

By this argument Pr. opposes Plotinus' doctrine of *Enn.* I 8, 11 (above, **1410d**), in a sense at least. What he rejects is not so much the view of matter as στέρησις, but that matter so defined could "work". This could, however, hardly be meant by Plotinus. In fact, the essential point where Pr. differs from Plotinus is not so much matter, but soul (as was stated above).

d. Therefore, if souls are drawn towards an inferior level, it is by their own desires and their own inclinations, i.e. by themselves and not by matter.

The soul itself is the cause of evil

Ib., p. 233, 16-23 C.:

Quomodo autem rursum habebit facere τὸ ἄποιον secundum se? Verum autem et adducit ad se ipsam materia animas, aut a se ipsis illae ducuntur et separatae fiunt potentia et impotentia sui ipsarum; si quidem itaque a se ipsis ducuntur, hoc erat ipsis malum qui ad deterius impetus et appetitus, sed non materia.

Cp. above, **1453a**.

Fate and Providence

1471—As Plotinus was, Pr. is much concerned with the problems of Fate and Providence. "Fate" for him is, so to say, the lower aspect of Providence, as it is seen by us. If we had a complete knowledge of reality, that which appears to us as mechanical necessity would be seen as a part of Providence.

a. Proclus, *De prov. et fato*, p. 148, l. 27-38; p. 149 l. 17-24 Cousin:

Primum quidem est Providentiam et Fatum non hac differre qua scripsisti (hoc quidem connexam consequentiam, hanc autem necessitatem huius causam), sed ambo quidem causas mundi et eorum quae in mundo fiunt esse, praeexistere autem Providentiam Fato et omnia quidem quaecumque fiunt secundum Fatum multo prius a Providentia fieri; contrarium autem non iam verum esse: summa enim totorum a Providentia recta esse diviniora Fato.—

Diffugiunt multa fatum, providentiam autem nihil; et ... desuper
providentia fatum gubernans, quod ipsa produxit, separavit ipsius
ἐπιστασίαν usque ad ab altero mobilia [1] aut ad sortita in ab altero mobilibus
prima subsistentia.

Which means that Providence, as we found before, works from a distance, leaving
the details of the sensible world to secondary causes, partly to ἑτεροκίνητα, partly
to divine beings placed in this world (the ἐγκόσμιοι ἑνάδες). Cp. above, ad **1279d**,
1331b, etc. On the function of angels and daemons, see our next nrs.

b. Proclus, ib., p. 156, 23 - 157, 1:

Fate sub-
ordinated to

Providentiam itaque non est tibi difficile videre quam dicimus. Si **Providence**
enim fontem bonorum, primum quidem divinam ipsam causam deter-
minans recte dices (unde enim aliunde omnibus bona quam divinitus? Ita
ut bonorum quidem, ait Plato [2], nullum alium causandum quam Deum);
deinde, omnibus superstantem intellectualibusque et sensibilibus, su-
periorem esse Fato; et quae quidem sub Fato entia et sub Providentia
perseverare, τὸ connecti quidem a Fato habentia, bonificari autem a
Providentia, ut et connexio finem habeat Bonum, et Providentia Fati
in se ipsa; quae autem rursum sub Providentia non adhuc omnia indigere
et Fato, sed intellectualia ab hoc exempta esse.

In all this, again, Pr. did not essentially differ from Plotinus; but he did give a
personal form to these conceptions.

1472—The four groups of henads or Gods we found in *Elem.* 163 ff.
(above, **1466d**) reappear in the prayer which, at the beginning of his
commentary on the *Parmenides*, is addressed by Pr. to all the gods and
goddesses. In this prayer they are followed by the choirs of angels, by
the good daemons, and finally by heroes.

Gods -
angels -
daemons -
heroes

a. Proclus, *In Parm.* p. 617, 1 - 618, 1 Cousin:

Εὔχομαι τοῖς θεοῖς πᾶσι καὶ πάσαις ποδηγῆσαί μου τὸν νοῦν εἰς τὴν προκειμένην θεωρίαν, καὶ φῶς ἐν ἐμοὶ στιλπνὸν τῆς ἀληθείας ἀνάψαντας ἀναπλῶσαι
τὴν ἐμὴν διάνοιαν ἐπ' αὐτὴν τὴν τῶν ὄντων ἐπιστήμην, ἀνοῖξαί τε τὰς τῆς
ψυχῆς τῆς ἐμῆς πύλας εἰς ὑποδοχὴν τῆς ἐνθέου τοῦ Πλάτωνος ὑφηγήσεως·
καὶ ὁρμήσαντάς μου τὴν γνῶσιν εἰς τὸ φανότατον τοῦ ὄντος παῦσαί με τῆς
πολλῆς δοξοσοφίας καὶ τῆς περὶ τὰ μὴ ὄντα πλάνης τῇ περὶ τὰ ὄντα νοερωτάτῃ
διατριβῇ, παρ' ὧν μόνων τὸ τῆς ψυχῆς ὄμμα τρέφεταί τε καὶ ἄρδεται [3], καθάπερ
φησὶ ὁ ἐν τῷ Φαίδρῳ Σωκράτης· ἐνδοῦναί τέ μοι νοῦν μὲν τέλειον τοὺς νοητοὺς
θεούς, δύναμιν δ' ἀναγωγὸν τοὺς νοερούς, ἐνέργειαν δὲ ἄλυτον καὶ ἀφειμένην

---

[1] I.e. ἑτεροκίνητα.   [2] *Rep.* 379c.
[3] Plato, *Phaedr.* 251 b: ἡ τοῦ πτεροῦ φύσις ἄρδεται. Cf. 246 e: τὸ τῆς ψυχῆς
πτέρωμα, cited by Proclus in his Commentary on the *First Alcib.*, p. 324 Cousin.

τῶν ὑλικῶν γνώσεων τοὺς ὑπὲρ τὸν οὐρανὸν τῶν ὅλων ἡγεμόνας [1], ζωὴν δὲ
ἐπτερωμένην τοὺς τὸν κόσμον λαχόντας [2], ἔκφανσιν δὲ τῶν θείων ἀληθῆ τοὺς
ἀγγελικοὺς χορούς, ἀποπλήρωσιν δὲ τῆς παρὰ θεῶν ἐπιπνοίας τοὺς ἀγαθοὺς
δαίμονας, μεγαλόφρονα δὲ καὶ σεμνὴν καὶ ὑψηλὴν κατάστασιν τοὺς ἥρωας·
πάντα δὴ ἁπλῶς τὰ θεῖα γένη παρασκευὴν ἐνθεῖναί μοι τελείαν εἰς τὴν μετουσίαν
τῆς ἐποπτικωτάτης τοῦ Πλάτωνος καὶ μυστικωτάτης θεωρίας. —

It is in the following lines that Pr. speaks of his master Syrianus as ὁ τῷ Πλάτωνι
μὲν συμβακχεύσας ὡς ἀληθῶς καὶ ὁ μεστὸς καταστὰς τῆς θείας ἀληθείας, as τῶν θείων
τούτων λόγων ὄντως ἱεροφάντης and as a saviour of mankind (σωτηρίας ἀρχηγὸν
τοῖς γε νῦν οὖσι ἀνθρώποις καὶ τοῖς εἰσαῦθις γενησομένοις).
The passage was referred to above, under **1455b**.

b. The functions of angels, daemons and heroes are described in
the following passage.

The functions of angels, daemons and heroes

Proclus, *In Tim.* III p. 165, l. 5-8, 11-30 Diehl:

Πᾶν γὰρ τὸ δαιμόνιον τὴν μεταξὺ χώραν ἀναπληροῖ θεῶν τε καὶ ἀνθρώπων. 5
διότι δὴ παντελὴς ἀπόστασίς ἐστι τῶν τε ἡμετέρων καὶ τῶν θείων πραγμάτων,
... διὰ δὴ τοῦτο καὶ τριάς ἐστιν ἡ συνάπτουσα τὰ ἡμέτερα τοῖς θεοῖς, ἀνὰ λόγον 11
προελθοῦσα ταῖς τρισὶν ἀρχικαῖς αἰτίαις, εἰ καὶ πᾶσαν δαιμόνιον αὐτὸς εἴωθε
καλεῖν· τὸ μὲν γὰρ ἀγγελικὸν πρὸς τὸ νοητὸν τὸ πρώτως ἐκφανὲν ἀπὸ τῆς
ἀρρήτου καὶ ἀποκεκρυμμένης τῶν ὄντων πηγῆς ἀναλογίαν ἀποσῴζει, διὸ καὶ 15
αὐτὸ τοὺς θεοὺς ἐκφαίνει καὶ τὸ κρύφιον αὐτῶν ἐξαγγέλλει. τὸ δὲ δαιμόνιον πρὸς
τὴν ζωὴν τὴν ἄπειρον, διὸ πανταχοῦ πρόεισι κατὰ πολλὰς τάξεις καὶ πολυειδές
ἐστι καὶ πολύμορφον. τὸ δὲ ἡρωϊκὸν κατὰ τὸν νοῦν καὶ τὴν ἐπιστροφήν, διὸ 20
καὶ αὐτὸ καθάρσεώς ἐστιν ἔφορον καὶ ζωῆς μεγαλουργοῦ καὶ ὑψηλῆς χορηγόν.
ἔτι δὲ τὸ μὲν ἀγγελικὸν κατὰ τὴν νοερὰν τοῦ δημιουργοῦ προέρχεται ζωήν, διὸ
καὶ αὐτὸ νοερόν ἐστι κατὰ τὴν οὐσίαν καὶ ἑρμηνεύει καὶ διαπορθμεύει τὸν
θεῖον νοῦν εἰς τὰ δεύτερα. τὸ δὲ δαιμόνιον κατὰ τὴν δημιουργικὴν τῶν ὅλων 25
πρόνοιαν καὶ τὴν φύσιν κατευθύνει καὶ τὴν τάξιν ὀρθῶς συμπληροῖ τοῦ παντὸς
κόσμου. τὸ δὲ ἡρωϊκὸν κατὰ τὴν ἐπιστρεπτικὴν αὖ τούτων πάντων προμήθειαν,
διὸ καὶ τοῦτο τὸ γένος ὑψηλόν ἐστι καὶ ἀναγωγὸν τῶν ψυχῶν καὶ ἁδρότητος 30
αἴτιον. —

c. Cp. *Theol. Plat.* VI 4, p. 352:

Ἅπαντες [3] γὰρ ἡγεμόνες εἰσὶ καὶ ἄρχοντες ἐν τῷ παντί. καὶ πολλῶν μὲν
ἀγγέλων τάξεις περιχορεύουσιν αὐτοῖς. πολλοί τε δαιμόνων ἀριθμοί, πολλαὶ
δὲ ἡρώων ἀγέλαι, παμπληθεῖς δὲ ψυχαὶ μερικαί.

Cp. also *In Tim.* III 153, 11-15 and *In Remp.* I 91, 11 ff.

---

[1] The ἑνάδες ὑπερκόσμιοι of *Elem.* 164.
[2] The ἑνάδες ἐγκόσμιοι of *Elem.* 165 (above, **1466d**).
[3] In the preceding lines the author spoke of the heavenly bodies.

1473—a. That Providence is not only general (as e.g. Celsus opposed to Christian doctrine) but extends to individuals, is explicitly asserted by Proclus.

Proclus, *In Rempubl.* II p. 103, l. 5-6 Kroll:

Καὶ οὐ τὰ ὅλα προνοεῖται μόνον, ἀλλὰ καὶ τὰ καθ' ἕκαστα, θεῶν ὄντων καὶ δαιμόνων ὑπουργούντων τοῖς θεοῖς.

b. In commenting on *Resp.* 617d-e (above, nr. **307**) he maintains the importance of the free will of man against ἀνάγκη.

Proclus, *In Rempubl.* II p. 275, l. 14-19 Kr.:

Τόνδε γὰρ ἑλόμενοι τὸν βίον συνεσόμεθα αὐτῷ ἐξ ἀνάγκης· ἁπλῶς δὲ οὐκ ἐξ ἀνάγκης· ἐνεδέχετο γὰρ καὶ ἄλλον βίον ζῆν, ἀλλὰ πρὸ τῆς αἱρέσεως, μετὰ δὲ τὴν αἵρεσιν ἀδύνατον. καὶ οὕτως ἔοικεν καὶ πᾶν τὸ ἐνδεχόμενον[1] εἰς ἀναγκαίαν μεταπίπτειν δύναμιν διὰ τῆς ἀκολουθίας, καὶ τῶν ἐνδεχομένων ἀναγκαίως ἐνδεχομένοις ἄλλοις ἑπομένων.

1474—As we found above (**1469c**) Pr.—apparently following Syrianus—asserted that every particular soul has an immaterial body which is immortal. He assumes that this body (θεῖον σῶμα or ὄχημα) in descending is increased by another, semi-spiritual body (πνευματικὸν σῶμα) which is not eternal but πολυχρόνιον and survives the material body. The theory is expounded in the following passage.

a. Proclus, *In Tim.* III p. 236, 31 - 237, 9 Diehl:

To questions concerning punishments, purification, reincarnations, possibly in animals (ἄλογα), Pr. replies:

Μήποτε οὖν κάλλιον οὕτω λέγειν, ὥσπερ ὁ ἡμέτερος διδάσκαλος[2], τὰς μὲν
37 ἀκρότητας τῆς ἀλόγου ζωῆς τὸ πνεῦμα περιέχειν καὶ εἶναι ταύτας μετὰ τοῦ ὀχήματος ἀϊδίους ὡς ἀπὸ τοῦ δημιουργοῦ παρηγμένας[3], ταύτας δὲ ἐκτεινομένας καὶ μεριζομένας ποιεῖν τὴν ζωὴν ταύτην, ἣν προσυφαίνουσιν οἱ νέοι
5 θεοί[4], θνητὴν μὲν οὖσαν διότι τὸν μερισμὸν τοῦτον ἀποτίθεσθαί ποτε τὴν ψυχὴν ἀναγκαῖον, ὅταν ἀποκαταστῇ τυχοῦσα καθάρσεως, πολυχρονιωτέραν δὲ τῆς τοῦ σώματος τούτου ζωῆς· καὶ διὰ τοῦτο τὴν ψυχὴν καὶ ἐν Ἅιδου καὶ τοὺς βίους αἱρουμένην ἔχειν τὴν τοιαύτην ζωήν· κατὰ γὰρ αὐτὴν τὴν ῥοπὴν προσλαμβάνει τὴν θνητὴν ταύτην ζωὴν ἀπὸ νέων θεῶν.

---

[1] For the meaning of this term see *Gr. Ph.* II, nrs. **443b**, **559a**.
[2] Syrianus.
[3] Pr. holds that certain *apices* of unreasonable life are imperishable, together with the immaterial "vehicle", and caused by the Demiurge.
[4] The νέοι θεοί are the "created gods" addressed by the Demiurge in *Tim.* 41 (above, nr. **353**).

We found similar conceptions in Posidonius, Plutarchus, in the Hermetic writings and in Porphyrius. Cp. Dodds, *The Elements* p. 306 f. and *App*. II.

b. Pr. who holds the doctrine of an eternal alternation of ascent and descent of souls, excludes the possibility of either eternal bliss or eternal punishment. The man who is incurable (ἀνίατος) will perish as for his own doing, but he will be finally "saved" (i.e. brought back to the upperworld) by "that which comes to him from the Whole". This is illustrated by the famous case of Ardiaeus (*Resp*. 615c; above, nr. **307**).

Proclus, *In Rempubl*. II p. 178, l. 5 - 179, 2 Kroll:

Eternal Speaking of the ἀνίατοι ψυχαί in the myths of *Gorg*. 525c and *Phaed*. 113e the
punishment author says:
excluded

Καὶ ἡμεῖς ἐδείκνυμεν καὶ ἐν τοῖς εἰς ἐκείνους τοὺς μύθους εἰρημένοις, ὡς 5
ἄρα περίοδον ὅλην τινὰ κολάζων τὰς ἀνιάτους ψυχὰς τοιαῦτα φθέγγεται· τὸ
γὰρ παντελῶς ἀνίατον εἶναι ψυχὴν [ἄτοπον εἶναι ῥητέον]· τὸ γὰρ ἐν χρόνῳ
γεγονυῖ[αν ἀνίατον] μὴ καὶ ἐν χρόνῳ χωρίζεσθαι [τῶν νός]ων ἐκείνων ἀμήχανον. 10
καὶ εἰ μὲν [πᾶσα]ν ψυχὴν δυνατὸν τηλικαῦτα ἁμαρτεῖν καὶ [ἀνία]τον γενέσθαι,
πᾶν ἐπιλείψει τὸ πλῆθος τῶν ψυχῶν τὴν γένεσιν, ἐκεῖ γεγονυιῶν πασῶν ἐν
τῷ ἀπείρῳ χρόνῳ καὶ μὴ ἀνιουσῶν· εἰ δέ τι γένος ἐστὶν ἴδιον ψυχῶν τὸ ταῦτα
πάσχον, ἔσεσθαι χρόνον, ἐν ᾧ πᾶν τὸ τοιόνδε γένος ἐν τοῖς ὑπὸ γῆς τόποις 15
δεδεμένον ἐπιλείψει τὴν γένεσιν. τούτων δὲ ὄντων ἀτοπωτάτων ἐλέγομεν τὴν
ἀνίατον ζωὴν παρ᾽ ἑαυτῆς εἶναι τοιαύτην ὡς ἀμεταμέλητον· . . . τῆς δὲ οἰκείας
διορθώσεως ἀνῃρημένης αὐτὴ μέν ἐστιν παρ᾽ ἑαυτῆς ἀνίατος ἡ τοιαύτη πᾶσα 21
ζωή, τυγχάνει δὲ ἰάσεως ὑπὸ τῶν ὅλων κατά τινα περίοδον λύουσαν αὐτῆς τὴν
ἐκεῖ κατάταξιν. τὸ μὲν γὰρ ἀφ᾽ ἑαυτοῦ βοηθούμενον πολλῷ μειζόνως ἀπὸ τῶν
ὅλων βοηθεῖται κοσμικῶν περιόδων· τὸ δὲ ἀφ᾽ ἑαυτοῦ σωτηρίας οὐκ ἔχον 25
ἐλπίδα ἢ λαμβάνει σωτηρίας ἀφορμὴν ἀπὸ τῶν ὅλων, ἀΐδιον ὄν, ἢ ἀπόλλυται
παντελῶς, εἰ μὴ ἀΐδιον ὂν τυγχάνοι. Διὰ ταῦτα τοίνυν καὶ τοῦ Ἀρδιαίου πάντως
ἀπεγίγνωσκον ὡς ἀναβησομένου ποτέ, τὴν παροῦσαν ζωὴν γέμουσαν κακῶν 30
ὁρῶντες καὶ ἀνήκεστα πάσχουσαν, ὥσπερ καὶ ἔδρασεν· τὰ δὲ ὅλα τίνα p.
τρόπον σῴζει τὰς τοιαύτας ψυχάς, οὐχ ἑώρων.

See also p. 184, l. 25 f.:
Εἰ δὲ ὅπως οὖν ἰατρεύεται, παρ᾽ ἑαυτοῦ μὲν οὐκ ἂν πάσχοι τοῦτο ἀνίατος ὤν, παρὰ
δὲ τῶν ὅλων δυνάμεων.

Reincarna-   **c.** Pr. rejects the theory of reincarnation of human souls in animals.
tion in   He explains the passages of Plato relating to this in allegorical sense.
animals
rejected
Proclus, *In Rempubl*. II p. 312, l. 10-14; 313, 7-12:

Commenting on *Resp*. 620a-d, where it is said that the soul of Orpheus was re-incarnated in a swan, Pr. says:

"Ὅτι μὲν παντελῶς ταῦτα ἀτοπίας μεστὰ τοῖς ἀπερισκέπτως αὐτὰ μετιοῦσίν
ἐστιν, οὐδ' αὐτὸς ἄλλως ἂν εἴποιμι. τὸ γὰρ τὰς τῶν θείων ἀνδρῶν ψυχὰς εἰσοι-
κίζειν εἰς ἄλογα ζῷα καὶ τὰς ἡρωϊκὰς ὑπερβολὴν οὐ καταλιμπάνει τῆς περὶ
ἐκείνας πλημμελείας. —

313   Μήποτε οὖν, ἵνα καὶ τῷ μύθῳ χαρισώμεθα καὶ συγχωρήσωμεν ἃ βούλεται
πλάττειν καὶ τὸν Πλάτωνα τῆς εἰς τοὺς ἥρωας δυσφημίας ἐξέλωμεν, ἐκεῖνο
10 ῥητέον, ὡς ἄρα διὰ τῶν τοιούτων πλασμάτων οὐκ αὐτὰς θέλει τὰς ψυχὰς
ἐκείνας ὧν διαμνημονεύει νῦν ἡρώων εἰς τὰ ἄλογα κατασπᾶν, ἀλλὰ ζῴων
εἴδη αἰνίσσεσθαι διὰ τῶνδε τῶν ὀνομάτων.

1475—a. The Neoplatonism of Proclus came to Western Europe first of all
through the works of the Christian author of the early 6th century who called
himself Dionysius Areopagita and, from the 8th century onwards, was generally
accepted as such; next by the *Liber de causis*, which in the 12th was translated into
Latin. The original was an Arabic work of the 9th century, based on Proclus'
Elements. Finally in the 13th century, the *Elements* were translated into Latin by
William of Morbecca. Thus, Proclus' summary of Plotinus' doctrine was known
in Western Europe before the greater part of Plato's dialogues and before the
Enneads. Nicolaus Cusanus in the 15th century read William Morbecca's version
of the *Elements*, and to Ficino Proclus was as high an authority as Plato and Plotinus were. Still with the Cambridge Platonists, who in the 17th century opposed
a Neoplatonic spiritualism to the materialism of Hobbes, the influence of Proclus
and his *Elements* can be clearly traced. Dodds (*The Elements*, p. XXXII) finds
"a distant echo" of the *Elements* in the *Fairie Queen*, and a quotation of the *Theologia
Platonica* in Coleridge.

b.   Important parts of the Commentaries were translated into Syriac and
Arabic and diffused in the East during the early Middle Ages. The *Elements* were
also translated into Arabic, later into Georgian and Armenian (12th and 13th
centuries). Apparently they were still read and translated in the 18th and 19th
centuries.

c.   In Byzantium, Michael Psellus (11th cent.) was well up in Proclus.
He makes abundant use of the *Elements* in his *De omnifaria doctrina*. In the
12th cent. Nicolaus, bishop of Methone, wrote an Ἀνάπτυξις τῆς θεολογικῆς
στοιχειώσεως.

4—DAMASCIUS AND THE END OF THE SCHOOL OF ATHENS

1476—The last of Proclus' successors in the School of Athens was
Damascius. We cited his work Ἀπορίαι καὶ λύσεις περὶ τῶν πρώτων ἀρχῶν
εἰς τὸν Πλάτωνος Παρμενίδην in dealing with Iamblichus' doubling of
the First Principle. Dam. maintained with the greatest emphasis and
careful elaboration that the First Principle is beyond human knowledge.
He joins Iambl. in placing it above the One.

The First
Principle
beyond
human
language
and under-
standing
a. The First Principle cannot be named or conceived at all.

Damascius, *Dub. et sol.* 2, p. 4, l. 6-10 Ruelle:

Μαντεύεται ἄρα ἡμῶν ἡ ψυχὴ τῶν ὁπωσοῦν πάντων ἐπινοουμένων εἶναι ἀρχὴν
ἐπέκεινα πάντων ἀσύντακτον πρὸς πάντα. Οὐδὲ ἄρα ἀρχήν, οὐδὲ αἴτιον ἐκείνην
κλητέον, οὐδὲ πρῶτον, οὐδέ γε πρὸ πάντων, οὐδ' ἐπέκεινα πάντων· σχολῇ
γε ἄρα πάντα αὐτὴν ὑμνητέον· οὐδ' ὅλως * ὑμνητέον, οὐδ' ἐννοητέον, οὐδὲ
ὑπονοητέον.

b. Why a First Principle beyond the One?

Damascius, ib. p. 5, 2-9; c. 3, p. 5, 14-6, 7:

Ἀλλ' εἰ τὸ ἓν πάντων αἴτιον καὶ πάντων περιεκτικόν, τίς ἡ ἐπέκεινα καὶ
τούτου ἀνάβασις ἡμῶν; μήποτε γὰρ κενεμβατοῦμεν εἰς αὐτὸ τὸ οὐδὲν ἀνατει-
νόμενοι· ὁ γὰρ μηδὲ ἕν ἐστι, τοῦτο οὐδέν ἐστι κατὰ τὸ δικαιότατον· πόθεν γὰρ 5
ὅτι τὸ ἔστι τι τοῦ ἑνὸς ἐπέκεινα; ἄλλου γὰρ οὐδενὸς χρῄζει τὰ πολλὰ ἢ τοῦ
ἑνός· διὸ μόνον τὸ ἓν αἴτιον τῶν πολλῶν· διὸ καὶ τὸ ἓν πάντων αἴτιον, ὅτι τῶν
πολλῶν αἴτιον δεῖ μόνον εἶναι τὸ ἕν· οὔτε γὰρ τὸ οὐδὲν (τὸ γὰρ οὐδὲν αἴτιον
οὐδενός), οὔτε αὐτὰ τὰ πολλά. —

Εἰ δ' οὖν ταῦτά τις ἀπορούμενος λέγοι ἀρκεῖσθαι τῇ ἀρχῇ τοῦ ἑνὸς καὶ
προστιθείη τὸν κολοφῶνα ὡς οὐδὲ ἔννοιαν οὐδὲ ὑπόνοιαν ἔχομεν ἁπλουστέραν 15
τοῦ ἑνός, πῶς οὖν ὑπονοήσομεν ἐπέκεινά τι τῆς ἐσχάτης ὑπονοίας τε καὶ ἐννοίας; εἴ τις ταῦτα φάσκοι, συγγνωσόμεθα μὲν αὐτῷ τῆς ἀπορίας· ἄβατος
γὰρ ὡς ἔοικεν καὶ ἀμήχανος ἡ τοιάδε φροντίς. Ἀλλ' ὅμως ἐκ τῶν ἡμῖν γνωρι-
μωτέρων ἀνεθιστέον τὰς ἐν ἡμῖν ἀρρήτους ὠδῖνας εἰς τὴν ἄρρητον οὐκ οἶδα
ὅπως εἴπω συναίσθησιν τῆς ὑπερηφάνου ταύτης ἀληθείας· ἐπεὶ γὰρ ἐν τοῖς 20
τῇδε τὸ ἄσχετον πάντη τιμιώτερον τοῦ ἐν σχέσει καὶ τοῦ συντεταγμένου τὸ
ἀσύντακτον, ὡς ὁ θεωρητικὸς τοῦ πολιτικοῦ, καὶ ὁ Κρόνος φέρε εἰπεῖν τοῦ
δημιουργοῦ, καὶ τὸ ὂν τῶν εἰδῶν, καὶ τὸ ἓν τῶν πολλῶν, ὧν ἀρχὴ τὸ ἕν, οὕτω
καὶ ἁπλῶς αἰτίων καὶ αἰτιατῶν καὶ ἀρχῶν ἁπασῶν καὶ ἀρχομένων τὸ πάντα p. 6
τὰ τοιαῦτα ἐκβεβηκὸς καὶ ἐν οὐδεμιᾷ συντάξει καὶ σχέσει ὑποτιθέμενον, ὡς
τῷ λόγῳ φάναι· ἐπεὶ καὶ τὸ ἓν τῶν πολλῶν φύσει προέστηκεν καὶ τὸ ἁπλούστατον τῶν συνθετωτέρων ὁπωσοῦν, καὶ τὸ περιεκτικώτατον τῶν εἴσω περιεχο-
μένων· τόδ' εἰ θέλεις εἰπεῖν ἐπέκεινα πάσης ἐστὶν καὶ τῆς τοιαύτης ἀντιθέσεως, 5
ἐπέκεινα οὐ τῆς ἐν ὁμοταγέσι μόνον, ἀλλὰ καὶ τῆς ὡς πρώτου καὶ μετὰ τὸ
πρῶτον.

---

* ὅλως is the reading of a minority of Mss. I prefer it to ὅμως which is read in
most Mss. and in the edition of Ruelle.

1477—a. In what sense it is unknowable.

Damascius, c. 7, p. 12, l. 24-28 R.:

Πῶς οὖν ἀποδεικτὸν τό γε ὅσον ἐν ἡμῖν συνίσταται περὶ ἐκεῖνο ἀγνόημα;
πῶς γὰρ ἐκεῖνο ἄγνωστον λέγομεν; ἑνὶ μὲν λόγῳ τῷ ῥηθέντι, ὅτι ἀεὶ τὸ ὑπὲρ
τὴν γνῶσιν τιμιώτερον εὑρίσκομεν· ὥστε τὸ ὑπὲρ ἅπασαν γνῶσιν εἴπερ ἦν
εὑρετόν, εὑρέθη ἂν καὶ αὐτὸ τιμιώτατον.

b. Even the predicate *transcendent* (ἐξῃρημένον) is not adequate,
for it presupposes a relation to other things. Negation too is still a word
and as such insufficient. Only silence and the confession of complete
ignorance are fitting here.

Damascius, ib., p. 15, l. 11-25 R.:

Οὕτω δὴ καὶ πᾶν τὸ ὁπωσοῦν γνωστὸν καὶ ὑπονοητὸν λαβόντες ἐν τῷ νῷ,
μέχρι καὶ τοῦ ἑνὸς ἀξιοῦμεν, εἰ δεῖ φθέγγεσθαι τὰ ἄφθεγκτα καὶ ἐννοεῖν τὰ
ἀνεννόητα. Ἀξιοῦμεν ὅμως ὑποτίθεσθαι τὸ ἀσύμβατον πρὸς πάντα καὶ ἀσύντακτον καὶ οὕτως ἐξῃρημένον, ὥστε μηδὲ τὸ ἐξῃρημένον ἔχειν κατ' ἀλήθειαν·
15 ἐξῄρηται γὰρ ἀεί τινος τό γε ἐξῃρημένον καὶ οὐ πάντη ἐστὶν ἐξῃρημένον, ἅτε
σχέσιν ἔχον πρὸς τὸ οὗ ἐξῄρηται, καὶ ὅλως ἐν προηγήσει τινὶ σύνταξιν. Εἰ οὖν
μέλλοι τῷ ὄντι ἐξῃρημένον ὑποκεῖσθαι, μηδ' ἐξῃρημένον ὑποκείσθω· οὐ γὰρ
ἐπαληθεύει τῷ ἐξῃρημένῳ τὸ οἰκεῖον ὄνομα κατὰ ἀκρίβειαν· ἅμα γὰρ ἤδη
καὶ συντεταγμένον, ὥστε καὶ τοῦτο αὐτοῦ ἀποφῆσαι ἀνάγκη· ἀλλὰ καὶ ἡ
20 ἀπόφασις λόγος τις, καὶ τὸ ἀποφατὸν πρᾶγμα, τὸ δὲ οὐδὲν οὐδὲ ἄρα ἀποφατόν,
οὐδὲ λεκτὸν ὅλως, οὐδὲ γνωστὸν ὁπωσοῦν· ὥστε οὐδὲ ἀποφῆναι τὴν ἀπόφασιν
δυνατόν. Ἀλλὰ ἡ πάντη περιτροπὴ τῶν λόγων καὶ τῶν νοήσεων αὕτη ἐστὶν ἡ
ἐμφανταζομένη ἡμῖν ἀπόδειξις οὗ λέγομεν· καὶ τί πέρας ἔσται τοῦ λόγου,
πλὴν σιγῆς ἀμηχάνου καὶ ὁμολογίας τοῦ μηδὲν γιγνώσκειν, ὧν μηδὲ θέμις,
25 ἀδυνάτων ὄντων, εἰς γνῶσιν ἐλθεῖν;

1478—Damascius shows, if not an inclination towards irrationalism,
yet at any rate a strong feeling for the inadequacy of words.

a. Since the First Principle is beyond causation, another Ἀρχή
must be assumed which is described, however inadequately, as δύναμις
of the First and Cause of causes.

Damascius, c. 38, p. 78, l. 14-19, p. 79, 2-7 R.:

Ὡς οὖν πρὸς ἔνδειξιν ταύτης, διωρίσθω τινὰ τρόπον ἀσυμφανέστατον καὶ
ἥκιστά γε τρανῆ προσδιορισμόν. Καὶ τὸν πρώτιστον λέγω πάντων προσδιορισ-
μῶν καὶ σχεδὸν ὑπὸ τοῦ ἀδιορίστου καταπινόμενον, ὥστε δύναμιν τοῦ πρώτου
τὸ δεύτερον εἶναι δοκεῖν, δύναμιν τῇ ὑπάρξει συμπεπηγυῖαν, ὡς ἤδη τινὲς
ἱερολόγοι τοῦτο αἰνίττονται. —

Ἡ δὲ ἄλλη πρόοδος καὶ τάξις ἀπὸ τῶν ἄλλων αἰτίων ἐφήκει τοῖς πᾶσιν· ἀπὸ δὲ ἐκείνου καὶ ταῦτα μέν, ἀλλ' ὡς ἐν τοῖς πᾶσι καὶ ταῦτα. Διὸ μόνον ἐκεῖνο τῶν πάντων αἴτιον, ἄλλο δὲ ἄλλου τούτων πάντων. Ὅτι δὲ ὡς πάντων ὁμοῦ 5 ἐκεῖνο ἀρχή, δηλοῖ μὲν αὐτῆς καὶ τὸ παντελές, δηλοῖ δὲ τὸ ἀδιόριστον, οὐ μᾶλλον τοῦδε ὂν ἢ τοῦδε, δηλοῖ δὲ καὶ ἡ τῆς τοιαύτης αἰτίας ἐπιπόθησις τῆς πάντων, ὡς πάντων.

b. The procession of all things from this Principle is conceived by us, inadequately, as μονή - πρόοδος - ἐπιστροφή, though it is in fact beyond division and determination. The Principle of Being is also beyond the triad ὕπαρξις - δύναμις - ἐνέργεια. It is beyond production and is Cause in an unspeakable way.

The mode of procession

Damascius, c. 39, p. 79, l. 30-p. 80, 14 R.:

Μὴ τοίνυν ἀπορείτω τις εἰ τὰ ἄλλα ἀπ' αὐτοῦ πρόεισιν, ἐχωρίσθη αὐτοῦ· καὶ ἐκεῖνο ἄρα τούτων ἐχωρίσθη· εἰ δὲ ἥνωται, οὐ προῆλθεν· οὔτε γὰρ οὕτως p. ὡς ἡμεῖς νοοῦμεν, οὔτε προῆλθεν, οὔτε οὐ προῆλθεν. Ἄλλος γὰρ ὁ τρόπος ἐκεῖνος τῆς ἐνιαίας προόδου, ὃν ἡμεῖς οὔπω συννοοῦμεν, ἅτε μεμερισμένοι εἰς μονὴν καὶ πρόοδον καὶ ἐπιστροφήν, ὁ δέ ἐστιν ὑπὲρ τὸν διορισμὸν τῶν τοιούτων, οὔτε ἀναγκαῖον ἡνῶσθαι, εἰ μὴ διακρίνηται, οὔτε διακρίνεσθαι, εἰ μὴ ἥνωται· 5 ἐκεῖνο γὰρ τὴν πρὸ ἀμφοῖν ἀδιόριστον· τὰ δέ ἐστιν ἀντικείμενα. Μηδὲ αὖ ζητείτω τις εἰ παράγει, τὰ δὲ παράγεται· εἰ γὰρ ἐνεργεῖ, καὶ δύναται καὶ ὑπάρχει. Τρία οὖν τὰ πάντα, ἀλλ' οὐχ ἕν, ὕπαρξις, δύναμις, ἐνέργεια. Ἀλλ' εἴρηται ὅτι ἐκεῖνο πρὸ ἐνεργείας καὶ δυνάμεως καὶ ὑπάρξεως. ἓν γάρ, ἀλλ' οὐ τρία, πρὸ δὲ τῶν ἄλλων, ὡς ἓν καὶ τὰ τρία. Ἀπορίᾳ δὲ ἡμεῖς καὶ νοήσεως καὶ 10 ἐξηγήσεως παράγειν ὅμως αὐτὸ λέγομεν, διακαθαρτέον δὲ τὸν τρόπον τῆς παραγωγῆς, ὡς ὄντα ἀσύμφυλον ἡμῖν, καὶ οὔτε τῷ ἐνεργεῖν, οὔτε τῷ δύνασθαι, οὔτε τῷ ὑπάρχειν ἐπιτελούμενον, ἀλλὰ τῷ ἑνὶ πρὸ τῶν τριῶν ἀπορρήτῳ τρόπῳ.

c. Cp. also c. 54, cited above (nr. **1451a**), where it is said that the two ἀρχαί are neither ὁμοταγεῖς nor διωρισμέναι ἀπ' ἀλλήλων since they are beyond ταυτότης and ἑτερότης. The analogy is drawn with the triad πατήρ - δύναμις - νοῦς, but to this simile the author adds:

Πάντως δὲ φανερὸν ὅτι οὐδὲ ταῦτα ἀληθεύεται ἀληθῶς ἐπ' ἐκείνων.

The end of the School of Athens

1479—A.D. 529 the last School of philosophy at Athens was closed by the edict of the emperor Justinianus.

Joh. Malalas, *Chronogr.* XVIII p. 187:

Ἐπὶ δὲ τῆς ὑπατείας τοῦ αὐτοῦ Δεκίου ὁ αὐτὸς βασιλεὺς θεσπίσας πρόσταξιν ἔπεμψεν, ἐν Ἀθήναις κελεύσας μηδένα διδάσκειν φιλοσοφίαν μήτε νόμιμα ἐξηγεῖσθαι· —

1480—A.D. 531/2 seven Athenian philosophers, i.a. Damascius and Simplicius (the famous commentator on Aristoteles) emigrated to Persia, invited by the New Persian king Khosru Nuschirvan, an admirer of Greek culture and philosophy. The historian Agathias tells how, after a bitter disappointment and many difficulties, they came back to Athens (in the year 533). Khosru let them go after having made a treaty of peace with Justinian, to which a clause was added, stipulating that the philosophers should not be constrained to forsake their own opinions and the tradition handed down to them.

Agathias, *Hist.* II c. 30-31, p. 231 Dindorf:

Οὐ πολλῷ γὰρ ἔμπροσθεν Δαμάσκιος ὁ Σύρος καὶ Σιμπλίκιος ὁ Κίλιξ Εὐλά-
λιός τε ὁ Φρὺξ καὶ Πρισκιανὸς ὁ Λυδὸς Ἑρμείας τε καὶ Διογένης οἱ ἐκ Φοινίκης
καὶ Ἰσίδωρος ὁ Γαζαῖος, οὗτοι δὴ οὖν ἅπαντες τὸ ἄκρον ἄωτον, κατὰ τὴν
ποίησιν, τῶν ἐν τῷ καθ' ἡμᾶς χρόνῳ φιλοσοφησάντων, ἐπειδὴ αὐτοὺς ἡ
παρὰ Ῥωμαίοις κρατοῦσα ἐπὶ τῷ κρείττονι δόξα οὐκ ἤρεσκεν, ᾤοντό τε τὴν
Περσικὴν πολιτείαν πολλῷ εἶναι ἀμείνονα, τούτοις δὴ τοῖς ὑπὸ τῶν πολλῶν
περιᾳδομένοις ἀναπεπεισμένοι ὡς εἴη παρ' ἐκείνοις δικαιότατον μὲν τὸ ἄρχον
καὶ ὁποῖον εἶναι ὁ Πλάτωνος βούλεται λόγος, φιλοσοφίας τε καὶ βασιλείας ἐς
ταὐτὸ ξυνελθούσης, σῶφρον δὲ ἐς τὰ μάλιστα καὶ κόσμιον τὸ κατήκοον, καὶ
οὔτε φῶρες χρημάτων οὔτε ἅρπαγες ἀναφύονται, ἀτὰρ οὐδὲ τὴν ἄλλην μετιόντες
ἀδικίαν, ἀλλ' εἰ καί τι τῶν τιμίων κτημάτων ἐν ὅτῳ δὴ οὖν χώρῳ ἐρημοτάτῳ
καταλειφθείη, ἀφαιρεῖται ὅστις οὐδεὶς τῶν ἐντυγχανόντων, μένει δὲ οὕτως, εἰ
καὶ ἀφύλακτον ᾖ, σῳζόμενον τῷ λελοιπότι ἔστ' ἂν ἐπανήκοι· τούτοις δὴ οὖν
ὡς ἀληθέσιν ἀρθέντες, καὶ πρός γε ἀπειρημένον αὐτοῖς ἐκ τῶν νόμων ἀδεῶς
ἐνταῦθα ἐμπολιτεύεσθαι, ὡς τῷ καθεστῶτι[1] οὐχ ἑπομένοις, οἱ δὲ αὐτίκα
ἀπιόντες ᾤχοντο ἐς ἀλλοδαπὰ καὶ ἄμικτα ἤθη, ὡς ἐκεῖσε τὸ λοιπὸν βιωσόμενοι.
πρῶτον μὲν οὖν τοὺς ἐν τέλει ἀλαζόνας μάλα εὑρόντες καὶ πέρα τοῦ δέοντος
ἐξωγκωμένους, ἐβδελύττοντό γε αὐτοὺς καὶ ἐκάκιζον· ἔπειτα δὲ ἑώρων ὡς
τοιχωρύχοι τε πολλοὶ καὶ λωποδύται οἱ μὲν ἡλίσκοντο, οἱ δὲ καὶ διελάνθανον,
ἅπαν δὲ εἶδος ἀδικίας ἡμαρτάνετο. καὶ γὰρ οἱ δυνατοὶ τοὺς ἐλάττονας λυμαίνον-
ται, ὠμότητί τε πολλῇ χρῶνται κατ' ἀλλήλων καὶ ἀπανθρωπίᾳ, καὶ τὸ δὴ
πάντων παραλογώτερον· ἐξὸν γὰρ ἑκάστῳ μυρίας ὅσας ἄγεσθαι γαμετάς,
καὶ τοίνυν ἀγομένοις, ἀλλὰ μοιχεῖαί γε ὅμως τολμῶνται. τούτων δὴ οὖν ἁπάντων
ἕκατι οἱ φιλόσοφοι ἐδυσφόρουν καὶ σφᾶς αὐτοὺς ᾐτιῶντο τῆς μεταστάσεως.

(31) Ἐπεὶ δὲ καὶ τῷ βασιλεῖ διαλεχθέντες ἐψεύσθησαν τῆς ἐλπίδος, ἄνδρα
εὑρόντες φιλοσοφεῖν μὲν φρυαττόμενον, οὐδὲν δὲ ὅ τι καὶ ἐπαΐοντα τῶν αἰπυ-
τέρων, ὅτι τε αὐτοῖς οὐδὲ τῆς δόξης ἐκοινώνει, ἕτερα δὲ ἄττα ἐνόμιζεν ὁποῖα

---

[1] τῷ καθεστῶτι—"the established order", i.e. Christian religion.

Emigration of Athenian philosophers to Persia

ἤδη μοι εἴρηται [1], τήν τε τῶν μίξεων κακοδαιμονίαν οὐκ ἐνεγκόντες, ὡς τάχιστα ἐπανήεσαν. καίτοι ἔστεργέ τε αὐτοὺς ἐκεῖνος καὶ μένειν ἠξίου, οἱ δὲ ἄμεινον εἶναι σφίσιν ἡγοῦντο ἐπιβάντες μόνον τῶν Ῥωμαϊκῶν ὁρίων αὐτίκα οὕτω παρασχὸν καὶ τεθνάναι ἢ μένοντες παρὰ Πέρσαις τῶν μεγίστων γερῶν μεταλαγχάνειν. οὕτω τε ἅπαντες οἴκαδε ἀπενόστησαν, χαίρειν εἰπόντες τῇ τοῦ βαρβάρου φιλοξενίᾳ. ἀπώναντο δὲ ὅμως τῆς ἐκδημίας, οὐκ ἐν βραχεῖ τινι καὶ ἠμελημένῳ, ἀλλ᾽ ὅθεν αὐτοῖς ὁ ἐφεξῆς βίος εἰς τὸ θυμῆρές τε καὶ ἥδιστον ἀπετελεύτησεν. ἐπειδὴ γὰρ κατ᾽ ἐκεῖνο τοῦ χρόνου Ῥωμαῖοί τε καὶ Πέρσαι σπονδὰς ἔθεντο καὶ ξυνθήκας, μέρος ὑπῆρχε τῶν κατ᾽ αὐτὰς ἀναγεγραμμένων τὸ δεῖν ἐκείνους τοὺς ἄνδρας ἐς τὰ σφέτερα ἤθη κατιόντας βιοτεύειν ἀδεῶς τὸ λοιπὸν ἐφ᾽ ἑαυτοῖς, οὐδὲν ὁτιοῦν πέρα τῶν δοκούντων φρονεῖν ἢ μεταβάλλειν τὴν πατρῴαν δόξαν ἀναγκαζομένους. οὐ γὰρ ἀνῆκεν ὁ Χοσρόης μὴ οὐχὶ καὶ ἐπὶ τῷδε συστῆναι καὶ κρατεῖν τὴν ἐκεχειρίαν.

---

[1] In the preceding pages it was mentioned that Khosru had a Greek philosopher, named Uranius, in his house, a sceptic of apparently rather a bad reputation among the Athenian philosophers.

A SHORT BIBLIOGRAPHY [1]

I—THE HELLENISTIC-ROMAN AGE

A—GENERAL WORKS

P. Wendland, *Die hellenistisch-römische Kultur*, Tübingen 1912.
J. B. Bury, *The hellenistic age and the history of civilization* (The hellenistic age), Cambridge 1923.
K. J. Beloch, *Griechische Geschichte* IV, Leipzig-Berlin, [2]1925.
J. Kaerst, *Geschichte des Hellenismus* II, Leipzig-Berlin 1926.
J. Hatzfeld, *Histoire de la Grèce ancienne*, Paris 1932[2].
W. Tarn, *Hellenistic civilization*, London 1927. 3rd ed., revised by the Author and G. T. Griffith, London 1951.
U. Kahrstedt, *Kulturgeschichte der römischen Kaiserzeit*, München 1944.
W. Jaeger, *Paideia* II-III, Oxford 1944-45.
H. Meyer, *Geschichte der abendländischen Weltanschauung*, I-II, Würzburg 1947.
M. Rostovtzeff, *Social and economic history of the hellenistic world*, Oxford 1941.

R. Hirzel, *Der Dialog*, Leipzig 1895. Repr. in prep.
A. Oltramare, *Les origines de la diatribe romaine*, Genève 1926.

W. Nestle, *Die Nachsokratiker*, Jena 1923.

B—SPECIAL PROBLEMS

M. Heinze, *Die Lehre vom Logos in der griech. Phil.*, Oldenburg 1872. Repr. 1961.
A. Aall, *Geschichte der Logosidee in der griech. Phil.*, Leipzig 1896-1899 (2 vol.).
H. Meyer, *Die Lehre von den Keimkräften von der Stoa bis zum Ausgang der Patristik*, Bonn 1914.
H. Leisegang, *Der heilige Geist*, Leipzig 1919.
F. Rüsche, *Blut, Leben u. Seele*, Paderborn 1930 (Studien zur Geschichte u. Kultur d. Altertums, Ergänzungsband V).
—— *Das Seelenpneuma*. Seine Entwicklung von der Hauchseele zur Geistseele, Paderborn 1933 (ib. XVIII 3).
G. Verbeke, *L'évolution de la doctrine du pneuma du stoïcisme à S. Augustin*, Paris-Louvain 1945.

P. Rabbow, *Antike Schriften über Seelenheilung u. Seelenleitung* I, Leipzig 1914.
—— *Seelenführung*, Münster 1954.
J. Haussleiter, *Der Vegetarismus in der Antike*, Berlin 1935.
U. von Wilamowitz-Moellendorff, *Der Glaube der Hellenen*, Berlin 1931, 2 vol.
A. J. Festugière, *La religion de la Grèce*, Paris 1944 (Histoire générale de religion, Grèce-Rome).

---

[1] In this bibliography I follow as much as possible a systematical and chronological order.

C. Prantl, *Geschichte der Logik im Abendlande* I, Leipzig 1855.
H. Scholz, *Geschichte der Logik*, Berlin 1931.
I. M. Bochenski, *Ancient formal logic*, Amsterdam 1951.

H. Steinthal, *Geschichte der Sprachwissenschaft bei den Griechen u. Römern*, Berlin 1890 (2 vol.).
H. Dahlmann, *Varro u. die hellenistische Sprachtheorie*, Berlin 1932 (Problemata V).

2—EPICURUS AND HIS SCHOOL

Texts

H. Usener, *Epicurea*, Leipzig 1887 (Contains the preserved writings and the fragments, except the pap. fragm. of Π. φύσεως).
E. Bignone, *Epicuro* (Text with Italian transl., introd. and notes), Bari 1920.
P. von der Muehll, *Epicurus*, Lipsiae 1922 (Teubner).
C. Bailey, *Epicurus*, The extant remains, Oxford 1926. (Text with English transl.).
Diogenes Laërtius ed. R. D. Hicks, London 1925 (with Engl. transl., 2 vol.).

A survey of the fragments of the Π. φύσεως is found in Bailey, p. 391 f.
See further:
A. Vogliano, *Epicuri et Epicureorum scripta*, I, Berlin 1928.
W. Crönert, *Kolotes u. Menedemos*, Leipzig 1906.
C. Jensen, *Ein neuer Brief Epikurs* (Abh. Ges. Göttingen 1933).
F. Sbordone, *Philodemi adversus sophistas*. Napoli 1947.

Lucretius, *De rerum natura* ed. C. Bailey, Oxford 1898, 1921.
—— —— ed. A. Ernout, Paris 1920 (Budé) with French transl., 2 vol.
—— —— ed. J. Martin, Lipsiae 1934 (Teubner).
—— —— ed. C. Bailey, Oxford 1947, Vol. I: Prolegomena, Text, Transl.; II-III, Commentary.
Diogenes Oenoandensis ed. J. Williams, Lipsiae 1907.

Literature

C. Bailey, *The Greek Atomists and Epicurus*. Oxford 1928.
W. Schmid, *Epikurs Kritik der platonischen Elementenlehre*, Leipzig 1936.
E. Bignone, *L'Aristotele perduto e la formazione filosofica di Epicuro*, Firenze 1936, 2 vol.
    (Important, though often not sufficiently founded).
E. Bignone, *La dottrina epicurea del "clinamen"*, sua formazione e sua cronologia, in rapporto con la polemica con le scuole avversarie. Nuove luci sulla storia dell' atomismo Greco. Firenze 1940.
A. J. Festugière, *Epicure et ses Dieux*, Paris 1946. Engl. transl. Oxford 1955.
W. Schmid, *Götter u. Menschen in der Theologie Epikurs*, in: *Rhein. Mus.* 1951, pp. 97-156.
N. W. Dewitt, *Epicurus and his Philosophy*, Minneapolis 1954. See on this book the review of Ph. Merlan in *Phil. Review* 1955, p. 140-145.

3—THE STOA (THE ANCIENT STOA AND GENERAL WORKS)

Texts

A. C. Pearson, *The fragments of Zeno and Cleanthes*, London 1891.

J. von Arnim, *Stoicorum veterum fragmenta*, Leipzig 1903-1924 (4 vol.).
N. Festa, *I frammenti degli Stoici antichi*, Bari 1932-1935 (2 vol.) Italian transl. and notes.

LITERATURE

P. Barth, *Die Stoa*, Stuttgart, ^{1}1902, $^{3-4}$1921. Revised by A. Goedeckemeyer, 1941.
A. Dyroff, *Die Ethik der alten Stoa*, Berlin 1897.
E. Bréhier, *La théorie des incorporels dans l'ancien stoïcisme*, Paris 1908.
—— *Chrysippe*, Paris 1910. Revised ed. 1951.
E. Bevan, *Stoics and Sceptics*, Oxford 1913. Repr. Cambridge 1959.
R. M. Wenley, *Stoicism and its influence*, Boston 1924.
E. Grumach, *Physis u. Agathon in der älteren Stoa*, Berlin 1932 (Problemata, Heft 6).
O. Rieth, *Grundbegriffe der stoischen Ethik*, Berlin 1933.
E. Elorduy, *Die Sozialphilosophie der Stoa*, Philologus Suppl. XXVIII, 1936.
W. Wiersma, Περὶ τέλους, Diss. Groningen 1937.
M. Pohlenz, *Zenon u. Chrysipp*, Göttingen 1938. (Nachr. Gött. Ges., phil-hist. Kl., Fachgr. I, N.F. II 9).
—— *Die Begründung d. abendländischen Sprachlehre durch die Stoa*, Göttingen 1939 (ib. III 6).
—— *Grundfragen der stoischen Philosophie*, Göttingen 1940 (ib., 3. Folge 26).
K. H. E. de Jong, *De Stoa, Een wereld-philosophie*, Amsterdam (1937).
M. Pohlenz, *Die Stoa, Geschichte einer geistigen Bewegung*, Göttingen 1949 (2 vol.).
G. Verbeke, *Kleanthes van Assos*, Brussel 1949 (Verhandeling v. d. Kon. Vlaamse Ac.).
V. Goldschmidt, *Le système stoïcien et l'idée de temps*, Paris 1953. Interesting, but too speculative.
See also under 1B.

4—SCEPTICISM (INCLUDING THE MIDDLE AND NEW ACADEMY)

TEXTS AND TRANSLATIONS

U. v. Wilamowitz-Moellendorff, *Antigonos von Karystos* (Philol. Untersuch. IV) Berlin 1881. Repr. 1963.
Contains the texts, mainly of Diog. Laërt., concerning Pyrrho, Timon, Arcesilas a.o., with important critical studies.
H. Diels, *Poetarum philosophorum fragmenta*, Berlin 1901. Contains the fragments of Timon.
Sextus Empiricus ed. H. Mutschmann, vol. I, *Pyrrh. hyp.*, Leipzig 1912; vol. II, *Adv. dogmaticos* (= Adv. math. VII-IX), ib. 1914; vol. III, *Adv. math.* I-VI ed. J. Mau, ib. 1954; ^{2}1961. Vol. IV, indices on vol. I-III, coll. K. Janaček, ib. ^{2}1962.
Revised ed. of vol. I by Mau, 1958.
Sextus Empiricus, text (of Imm. Bekker, Berlin 1842) with Engl. transl. and notes by R. G. Bury, vol. I, *Outlines of Pyrrhonism*, London 1933, ^{2}1939; vol. II, *Against the logicians* (Adv. math. VII-VIII), ib. 1935; vol. III, *Against the physicists* (= Adv. math. IX-X), *Against the ethicists* (= Adv. math. XI), ib. 1936, ^{2}1953; vol. IV, *Against the professors* (= Adv. math. I-VI), ib. 1949.
Fragments in Cicero, Eusebius, *Praep. ev.*, Stobaeus and Photius.
For Carneades: Cicero, *De fato*, ed. A. Yon, Paris ^{2}1950 (Budé).
For the empirical school:
K. Deichgräber, *Die griechische Empirikerschule. Sammlung der Fragmente u. Darstellung der Lehre.* Berlin 1930.

BIBLIOGRAPHY

LITERATURE

Norman Maccoll, *The Greek sceptics from Pyrrho to Sextus*, London-Cambridge 1869.

Ch. Waddington, *Pyrrhon et le pyrrhonisme*, Paris 1877.

R. Hirzel, *Untersuchungen zu Ciceros phil. Schriften*, Leipzig 1883, vol. III, p. 1 ff., 39 ff. (The chapters concerning the origin and the development of the pyrrhonian skepsis).

P. Natorp, *Forschungen zur Geschichte des Erkenntnisproblems*, Berlin 1884, p. 63 ff.: Die Erfahrungslehre der Skeptiker u. ihr Ursprung.

E. Pappenheim, *Die Tropen der griechischen Skeptiker*, Gymn. Progr. Berlin, 1885.

—— *Der Sitz der Schule der pyrrhonischen Skeptiker*, in: *Archiv f. Gesch. d. Phil.* I, 1888, p. 37 ff.

—— *Der angebliche Heraklitismus des Skeptikers Aenesidemus*, Berlin 1889.

V. Brochard, *La méthode expérimentale chez les anciens*, in: *Revue philos.* I, 1887, p. 37-49.

—— *Les sceptiques grecs*, Paris 1887; reprinted 1923; [3]1959.
  Of great importance.

M. Patrick, *Sextus Empiricus and Greek scepticism*, Cambridge 1889.

L. Credaro, *Lo Scetticismo degli Academici*, Milano 1889-1893, 2 vol.

W. Vollgraff, *La vie de Sextus Empiricus*, in: *Rev. de Philologie* 1902, p. 195-210.

Ch. Waddington, *Le scepticisme après Pyrrhon. Les Nouveaux Académiciens; Enésidème et les nouveaux Pyrrhoniens* (Séances et travaux de l'Acad. des Sc. mor. et polit., 1902, p. 223 ff.).

A. Gödeckemeyer, *Die Geschichte der griechischen Skeptizismus*, Leipzig 1905.

R. Richter, *Der Skeptizismus in der Philosophie*, Leipzig 1904, vol. I. Repr. 1963.
  Superior to the work of Gödeckemeyer.

E. Bevan, *Stoics and Sceptics*, Oxford 1913; repr. Cambridge 1959.

E. Bréhier, *Les tropes d'Enésidème contre la logique inductive*, in: *Rev. des Etudes anciennes* XX, 1918, p. 69 ff.

P. Couissin, *La critique du réalisme des concepts chez Sextus Empiricus*, in: *Rev. d'histoire de la phil.*, 1927, p. 377-405.

—— *L'origine et l'évolution de l'ἐποχή* in: *Rev. des Etudes grecques* XLII, 1929, p. 373-397.

—— *Les sorites de Carnéade contre le polythéisme*, ib., LIV, 1941, p. 43-57.

J. Croissant, *La morale de Carnéade*, in: *Rev. internationale de phil.* 1939, p. 545-570.

L. Robin, *Pyrrhon et le scepticisme grec*, Paris 1944.
  Important.

K. Deichgräber, *Die griech. Empirikerschule*.
  Cited under Texts.

5—THE MIDDLE STOA AND FOURTH ACADEMY; CICERO

TEXTS

H. N. Fowler, *Panaetii et Hecatonis librorum fragmenta*, Bonn 1885.

M. van Straaten, *Panétius, sa vie, ses écrits et sa doctrine avec une édition des fragments*, Amsterdam 1946 (Diss. Nijmegen).
  A separate edition of the fragments:
  Panaetii Rhodii Fragmenta, coll. iterumque ed., Leiden 1952; [2]1962.

I. Bake, *Posidonii Rhodii reliquiae*, Lugd. Bat. 1820.

G. Luck, *Der Akademiker Antiochos*, Bern 1953.
  Contains an edition of the fragments.

Cicero, in *De officiis* I-II follows Panaetius, II. τοῦ καθήκοντος, with a certain liberty.

Teubner ed. by Atzert (1923, ²1932). Repr. 1958.

Ed. with a commentary by H. A. Holden, 1891.

Traces of Posidonius are found in many authors, i.a. (probably) in passages of the following works of Cicero:

Cicero, *Tusc. Disp.* I (Teubner-ed. by M. Pohlenz, 1918; by G. Fohlen and J. Humbert, Coll. Budé, Paris 1931;

ed. with a commentary by T. W. Dougan and R. H. Henry, 2 vol., Cambridge 1905, 1934).

—— *De natura deorum* II (Ed. O. Plasberg, Teubner 1908; W. Ax, 1961; commentary by J. B. Mayor, 1885, Comm. by A. S. Pease, Vol. II, Cambr. (Mass.) 1958).

—— *De divinatione* I (ed. O. Plasberg and W. Ax, Teubner 1938).

ed. with Commentary by A. S. Pease, Urbana, Univ. of Illinois, 1920-1923.

—— *De re publica* VI (ed. K. Ziegler, Teubner 1929, ⁵1960).

For Antiochus (more or less directly):

Cicero, *Academica*, ed. O. Plasberg, Teubner 1922; repr. 1961.

Ed. with commentary by J. S. Reid, London 1885.

—— *De finibus bonorum et malorum*, ed. J. Martha, Coll. Budé 1928-30; ²1955.

For Cicero's political philosophy:

—— *De legibus* (ed. K. Ziegler, Heidelberg 1950; ed. with Engl. translation by Clinton Walker Keyes, London (Loeb) 1928; G. de Plinval, Budé 1959).

—— *De re publica*. (ed. K. Ziegler, Teubner ⁵1960; with Engl. transl. by C. W. Keyes, London (Loeb) 1951).

—— *De officiis* III.

LITERATURE

A. Schmekel, *Die Philosophie der mittleren Stoa*, Berlin 1892.

B. N. Tatakis, *Panétius de Rhodes*, Paris 1931.

M. Pohlenz, *Antikes Führertum. Cicero de officiis u. das Lebensideal des Panaitios*, Leipzig 1934.

L. Labowsky, *Die Ethik des Panaitios*, Leipzig 1934.

M. van Straaten, *Panétius*, etc. (see texts).

W. Jaeger, *Nemesios von Emesa*, Quellenforschungen zum Neuplatonismus u.s. Anfängen bei Poseidonios, Berlin 1914.

K. Gronau, *Poseidonios u. die jüdisch-christliche Genesisexegese*, Leipzig 1914.

K. Reinhardt, *Poseidonios*, München 1921.

—— *Kosmos u Sympathie*, München 1926.

—— *Poseidonios über Ursprung u. Entartung*, Orient u. Antike VI, Heidelberg 1928.

I. Heinemann, *Poseidonios' metaphysische Schriften* I-II, Breslau 1921, 1928,

R. M. Jones, *Posidonius and Cicero's Tusc. disp.* I 17-81, in: *Class. Philol.* 1923, p. 202-228. See above, under **1192c**.

—— *Posidonius and the flight of the mind*, ib. 1926, p. 97-113.

—— *Posidonius and solar eschatology*, ib. 1936, p. 115 ff.

See above, under **1192b**.

W. Theiler, *Die Vorbereitung d. Neuplatonism.*, Berl. '30, p. 61-109. Repr. in prep.

R. E. Witt, *Plotinus and Posidonius*, in: *Class. Quart.* 1930, p. 198-207.

L. Edelstein, *The philosophical system of Posidonius*, in: *Amer. Journal of Philol.* 57 (1936), p. 286-325.

See above, nrs. **1192-1195**.

P. Boyancé, *Etudes sur le songe de Scipion*, Paris 1936.

M. van den Bruwaene, *La théologie de Cicéron*, Louvain 1937.

G. Nebel, *Zur Ethik des Poseidonios*, in: *Hermes* 1939, p. 34-57.

S. Blankert, *Seneca (Ep. 90) over natuur en cultuur en Posidonius als zijn bron.* Diss. Utrecht 1940.

On the Somnium Scipionis: see above, under nr. **959b**, VI.

An important chapter on Cicero and cosmic religion is found in:

A. J. Festugière, *La révélation d'Hermès Trismégiste* II, *Le Dieu cosmique*, Paris, 1949, p. 370-459.

On the sources of *Tusc.* I:

A. Barigazzi, *Sulle fonte del libro I delle Tusculane*, in: *Rivista di filologia* 1948, p. 161-163; 1950, p. 1-29.

A recent summary of Posidonius-studies is found in:

K. Reinhardt, Art. *Poseidonios* in Pauly-Wissowa RE vol. XXII 1, col. 558-826 (1953). Contains a detailed bibliography (col. 559-563).

Concerning Cicero:

P. Boyancé, *Le platonisme à Rome. Platon et Cicéron*, in the *Actes du Congrès Budé de Tours et Poitiers*, 3-9 Sept. 1953 (Paris 1954), p. 195-221.

On Antiochus:

R. Hoyer, *De Antiocho Ascalonita*, Diss. Bonn 1883.

E. Howald, *Das Compendium des Areios Didymos*, in: *Hermes* 55 (1920), p. 68 ff.

H. von Arnim, *Arius Didymus' Abriss der peripatetischen Ethik* (Sitz. ber. Wien 204.3, 1926).

W. Theiler, *Die Vorbereitung des Neuplatonismus*, Berlin 1930, p. 40 ff.

R. Philippson, *Das erste Naturgemässe*, in *Philologus* 87, 1932, p. 447 ff.

L. Edelstein, Review of P. Boyancé, *Etudes sur le Songe de Scipion*, in: *Amer. Journal of Philol.* 59, 1938, p. 360-364.

A. M. Lueder, *Die philosophische Persönlichkeit des Antiochos von Askalon*, Diss. Göttingen 1940.

G. Luck, *Der Akademiker Antiochos* (Noctes Romanae 7), Bern 1953.

6—THE STOA OF THE ROMAN EMPIRE

TEXTS AND TRANSLATIONS

Seneca, *Dialogi* ed. E. Hermes, Leipzig 1904.
—— *De beneficiis, De clementia* ed. C. Hosius, Leipzig ²1914.
—— *Epistulae* ed. O. Hense, Leipzig 1914.
—— *Naturales quaestiones* ed. A. Gercke, Leipzig 1907 (Teubner).
—— *Dialogues*, t. I-IV, text and French transl. by A. Bourgery and R. Waltz, Paris (Budé) 1922-1927; ²1942-45.
—— *Epistulae* ed. A. Beltrami, I, Brescia 1926, II, Bologna 1927; ²Rome, 1931.
Musonius Rufus ed. O. Hense, Leipzig 1905; Cora E. Lutz, New Haven 1947.
Epictetus ed. H. Schenkl, Leipzig 1894, ²1916 (Teubner).
With an English transl. by W. A. Oldfather, London 1925-1928 (2 vol.), Loeb Libr.
Marcus Aurelius (Antoninus) ed. H. Schenkl, Leipzig 1913 (Teubner).
New ed. with Engl. translation by A. S. L. Farquharson, *The meditations of the emperor Marcus Antoninus*, Oxford 1944, (2 vol.).

LITERATURE

C. Martha, *Les moralistes sous l'Empire romain*, Paris ⁷1900.
E. V. Arnold, *Roman Stoicism*, Cambridge 1911; repr. London 1958.
C. Marchesi, *Seneca*, Messina 1920, ²1934.
G. ten Veldhuys, *De misericordiae et clementiae apud Senecam philosophum usu atque ratione.* Diss. Utrecht 1935.

F. Smuts, *Die etiek van Seneca*. Diss. Utrecht 1948.
A. de Bovis, *La sagesse de Sénèque*, Paris 1948.
W. Klei, *Seneca De constantia sapientis*, with a commentary. Diss. Utrecht 1948.
A. C. van Geytenbeek, *Musonius Rufus en de Griekse Diatribe*, Diss. Utrecht 1948.
A. Bonhöffer, *Epiktet u. die Stoa*, Stuttgart 1890; repr. in prep.
—— *Die Ethik des Stoikers Epiktet*, Stuttgart 1894; repr. in prep.
    Still of great value.
Th. Colardeau, *Etude sur Epictète*, Paris 1903.
D. S. Sharp, *Epictetus and the New Testament*, London 1914.
H. D. Sedgwick, *Marcus Aurelius, A biography*, Oxford 1921.
U. von Wilamowitz-Moellendorf, *Kaiser Marcus*, Berlin 1931.
A. S. L. Farquharson, *Marcus Aurelius. His life and his world*, edited by D. A. Rees, Oxford 1951.

7—LATER CYNICS

Texts and Translations

Teletis reliquiae ed. O. Hense, Leipzig 1909 (Teubner).
The *Diogenes papyrus* of Vienna, ed. by C. Wessely in *Festschrift Th. Gomperz*, Wien 1902, p 68-72;
    by W. Crönert in *Kolotes u. Menedemos*, Leipzig 1906 (Stud. z. Palaeogr. u. Papyruskunde Bd. VI), p. 49-52.
Dio Chrysostomus ed. G. de Budé, Leipzig 1915-1919 (Teubner), 2 vol. With an English translation by J. W. Cohoon, London 1932-1951. 5 vol. (Loeb).
Lucianus ed. C. Jacobitz (Teubner), vol. II p. 195 ff. (*Demonax*);
    vol. III p. 271 ff. (*De morte Peregrini*);
    Vol. III p. 287 ff. (*Fugitivi*).
Eusebius, *Praep. ev.* V 18-36 (ed. Gifford vol. I).Contains fragments of Oenomaus of Gadara, Γοήτων φωρά (= κατὰ χρηστηρίων).
Favorinus Περὶ φυγῆς (Pap. Vat. 11).
Maximus Tyrius ed. H. Hobein, Leipzig 1910 (Teubner).
Asterius of Amesea in: Migne, Patrol. Gr. t. 40.
Damascius, *Vita Isidori*, in: Photius, *Bibl.* ed. Bekker (Berlin 1824) p. 342a, 27 ff.
    Speaks of Sallustius the Cynic. Budé edition by R. Henry, Paris 1960.
    The *Vita Isidori* of Damascius was also edited by Cobet and printed in the Didot edition of his *Diog. Laërt.* (1850).
    The passage on Sall. is found in § 89 ff.

Literature

H. von Arnim, *Leben u. Werke des Dio von Prusa*, Berlin 1898.
K. von Fritz, *Quellenuntersuchungen zu Leben u. Philosophie des Diogenes von Sinope*. Philologus, Suppl. Bd. 18, 2, Leipzig 1926.
D. R. Dudley, *A history of Cynicism*, London 1937.
R. Höistad, *Cynic Hero and Cynic King*, Uppsala 1948.
On Lucianus and Cynicism: see under nr. **1256b**; on Asterius sub **1260d**, on Favorinus sub **1260b**.

NEOPYTHAGOREANS

Texts

Alexander Polyhistor ap. Diog. Laërt. VIII 24.
    See under nr. **1279**.

Sextus Emp., *Adv. math.* X, 261 ff., 281 ff.
Pythagoreorum fragmenta ap. Mullach, *Fragm. phil. Gr.* II, Parisiis 1867.
Ocellus Lucanus, Text u. Kommentar von R. Harder, Berlin 1926 (Neue philol. Untersuch. 1).
Moderatus ap. Porphyr., *Vit. Pyth.*; Simplicius, *in Ar. Phys.*; Stob. *Ecl.*
Nicomachus, *Introd. arithmetica* ed. R. Hoche, Lipsiae 1866.
Iamblichi *in Nicomachi arithm. introd.* ed. H. Pistelli, Lipsiae 1894.
A commentary of Johannes Philoponus on the first book of Nicomachus' Intro-
ductio is edited by R. Hoche, Wesel 1864. On the second book, ib. 1867.
An epitome of Nicomachus' Ἀριθμητικὰ θεολογούμενα is found in Photius'
Bibliotheca, Vol. I ed. Bekker, Berolini 1824, p. 142b, 16-145b, 7.
Philostratus, *The life of Apollonius of Tyana, the Epistles of Apoll. and the Treatise
of Eusebius*, with an Engl. transl. of F. C. Conybeare, 2 vol., London 1912.
A complete list of the Pythagorean pseudepigrapha is found in Zeller, *Ph. d. Gr.*
III 2⁴, p. 115 n. 3 and 119 n. 1.

LITERATURE

Zeller, o.c., p. 114-175.
On Alexander Polyhistor's account of Pythagorean doctrine the studies of M.
Wellmann (in *Hermes* 1919, p. 225 ff.) A. Delatte (*La vie de Pyth. de Diog.
Laerce*, Bruxelles 1922, p. 198 ff.) and of W. Wiersma (in *Mnemosyne* 1941,
p. 97-112) are antiquated by A. J. Festugière in *Revue des Etudes grecques*
1945, pp. 1-65.
See also:
A. J. Festugière, *Le Dieu inconnu et la gnose*, Paris 1954, p. 1-53.
Of Nicomachus' *Introduction to Arithmetic* an English translation appeared by
M. L. d'Ooge (with studies in Greek mathematics by F. E. Robbins and L. C.
Karpinski), New York 1926.

PHILO

TEXTS

Opera Omnia ed. Thomas Mangey, 2 vol., Londini 1742.
A modern critical edition without the fragments:
    Philonis opera quae supersunt ed. L. Cohn, P. Wendland, S. Reiter, vol. I-VI,
    Berlin 1896-1915.
    Vol. VII, Indices by H. Leisegang, Berlin 1930. Repr. 1962.
(Editio minor without critical apparatus).
The fragments are found in the edition of Mangey. Further:
J. R. Harris, *Fragments of Philo Judaeus*, Cambridge 1896.
P. Wendland, *Neu entdeckte Fragmente Philos, nebst eine Unters. üb. d. urspr.
Gestalt d. Schr. De sacrificiis Abelis*, Berlin 1891.
K. Praechter, *Unbeachtete Philo-Fragmente*, in: *Archiv f. Gesch. d. Phil.* IX (1896),
p. 415-426.
H. Lewy, *Neue Philo-Texte*, Sitz. Ber. Akad., Berlin 1932, IV, p. 23-84.
The Armenian writings of Philo: ed. F. C. Conybeare, Venezia 1892.

TRANSLATIONS

Philos Werke hrsg. von L. Cohn u. J. Heinemann, 6 vol., Breslau, Münz 1909-1938.
Commentaire allégorique des saintes lois, texte et trad. par. E. Bréhier. Paris 1909.
Text and English transl. by F. H. Colson and G. H. Whitaker, vol. I-X, London
1929-1941.

Supplement I: *Questions and answers on Genesis* translated from the Armenian by R. Marcus, London 1943.
Supplement II: *Questions and answers on Exodus* transl. from the Armenian by R. Marcus, London 1943.

LITERATURE

E. Vacherot, *Histoire critique de l'Ecole d'Alexandrie*, 3 vol., Paris 1846.
P. Wendland, *Philo u. die Kynisch-Stoische Diatribe*, Berlin 1895.
A. Aall, *Der Logos*, Geschichte seiner Entwicklung in der griech. Phil. u. der christl. Literatur, Leipzig 1896-1899.
E. Bréhier, *Les idées philosophiques et religieuses de Philon d'Alexandrie*. Thèse, Paris 1907; ²1924. Repr. 1950.
W. Bousset, *Jüdisch-christlicher Schulbetrieb in Alexandria u. Rom*, Göttingen 1915.
H. Leisegang, *Der Heilige Geist*. Das Wesen u. Werden der mystisch-intuitiven Erkenntnis in der Phil. u. Religion der Griechen. Leipzig-Berlin 1919.
E. Turowski, *Die Wiederspiegelung des stoischen Systems bei Ph. v. A*. Diss. Königsb. 1927.
M. Adler, *Studien zu Ph. von Alex.*, Breslau 1929.
E. Stein, *Die alleg. Exegese des Ph. v. Alex.*, Beih. z. Zeitschr. f. alttest. Wiss. 51, Giessen 1929.
H. Lewy, *Sobria ebrietas*, Unters. z. Gesch. d. antiken Mystik, Beitr. z. Zeitschr. f. die neutest. Wiss. IX, Giessen 1929, p. 1-107.
J. Gross, *Philons v. Alex. Anschauungen über die Natur des Menschen*. Diss. Tübingen 1930.
M. J. Lagrange, *Le judaisme avant Jésus Christ*, Paris 1931.
E. R. Goodenough, *By Light Light*. The mystic gospel of hellenistic Judaism. New Haven, Yale Univ. Pr. 1935.
—— *The Politics of Philo Judaeus*. Practice and Theory. With a General Bibliogr. of Philo by H. L. Goodhart and E. R. Goodenough. 2 vol. New Haven, Yale Univ. Pr. 1938.
W. Völker, *Fortschritt u. Vollendung bei Ph. v. Alex.*, Leipzig 1938.
H. Leisegang, article *Philon* (Alex.) in Pauly-Wissowa XX 1, 1-50 (1941). See also Leisegang's article *Logos* in P.-W. XIII, 1047-1081 (on Philo: 1072-1078).
H. Wilms, *Eikoon*, Eine begriffsgeschichtliche Untersuchung zum Platonismus, 1. Teil: Philon von Alexandreia, mit einer Einleitung über Platon und die Zwischenzeit. Münster i. Westf. 1935.
H. A. Wolfson, *Philo*. Foundations of religious philosophy in Judaism, Christianity and Islam. 2 vol. Cambridge (Mass.) 1948.
To this work objections were made by:
I. Heinemann, *Philo als Vater der mittelalterlichen Philosophie?* in: Theologische Zeitschr. (Basel) 1950, p. 99-116.
See also Goodenough, *Wolfson's Philo* in: *Journal of Bibl. Litt.* 1948, p. 87;
    H. Chadwick in *Class. Review* 1949, p. 24 ff.;
    J. Daniélou in *Revue de l'histoire des religions*, 1950, p. 230.
R. Marcus gives an almost complete adhesion to Wolfson (*Wolfson's revaluation of Philo* in: *The Review of Religion*, 1949, p. 368-381).

PLUTARCHUS
TEXTEDITIONS
Vitae ed. Sintenis, Leipzig 1839 - 1846.
—— Lindskog-Ziegler, Leipzig 1914 - 1939.

Moralia ed. Deubner, Paris Didot 1839-1846.
—— Bernadakis, Leipzig Teubner 1888-1896.
—— Hubert, Nachstädt, Paton, Pohlenz etc. I-IV, Leipzig Teubner 1925-1938, V-VI, 1950-59.

SPECIAL EDITIONS WITH A COMMENTARY

Plutarque, *Sur l'E de Delphes* ed. R. Flacelière, Paris 1941 (Annales de l'université de Lyon, 3e série, Lettres, Fasc. 11).
—— *Sur la disparition des oracles* ed. R. Flacelière, Paris 1947 (Annales de l'université de Lyon, 3e série, Lettres, Fasc. 14).
Plutarch, *Ueber Isis u. Osiris.* Text, Uebersetzung u. Kommentar von Th. Hopfner, Prag 1940 (2 vol.) (Monographien des Archiv Orientālni, Prag).
Le Περὶ τοῦ προσώπου de Plutarque. Texte critique avec trad. et commentaire par P. Rainguard. Chartres 1934. (Thèse Paris 1934).

TRANSLATION AND COMMENTARY

G. Méautis, Plutarque, *Des délais de la justice divine.* Trad. nouvelle, introd. et notes explicatives. Lausanne 1935.

GENERAL WORKS

R. Hirzel, *Plutarch,* Leipzig 1912 (Das Erbe der Alten, Heft IV).
—— *Der Dialog,* Leipzig 1895, vol. 2, p. 124-239.
R. M. Jones, *The platonism of Plutarch,* diss. Chicago 1916.
G. Soury, *La démonologie de Plutarque,* Paris 1942.
K. Ziegler, *Ploutarchos von Chaironeia,* in Pauly-Wissowa, RE vol. XXI 1 (1951), col. 635-961). Also separatim.
Further literature is mentioned here.

MIDDLE PLATONISM

TEXTS

Atticus, fragm. ap. Euseb., *Praeparatio evangelica* XI 1-2; XV 4-9; 12 f.
Theo Smyrnaeus ed. E. Hiller, Leipzig 1878.
Albinus, *Prologus et Didascalicus* (= *Epitome*) ap. C. Fr. Hermann, *Platonis Dialogi* vol. VI, Leipzig 1853, pp. 152-189.
—— *Epitome* ed P. Louis, Rennes 1945 (Thèse compl., Paris).
Anonymer Kommentar zu Platons Theaetet ed. H. Diels, Berlin 1905.
Maximus Tyrius, *Philosophumena* ed. H. Hobein, Leipzig 1910.
Apuleius, *De philosophia libri* ed. P. Thomas, Leipzig 1908.

GENERAL WORKS

Zeller, *Ph. d. Gr.* III 2⁴, p. 219-234.
R. E. Witt, *Albinus and the history of Middle Platonism,* Cambridge 1937.
E. de Faye, *Origène, sa vie, son oeuvre, sa pensée.* Vol. II, *L'Ambiance philosophique.* Paris 1927, p. 154-164 (on Maximus of Tyrus).
A. J. Festugière, *Le Dieu inconnu et la Gnose,* Paris 1954, p. 92-140.

GNOSIS

General works are mentioned under **1332e**.
On the newly found manuscripts: **1332f**.

On Valentinus and Valentinians: **1332d**.
See further on Basilides:
P. Hendrix, *De Alexandrijnsche haeresiarch Basilides* Diss. Leiden 1926.
G. Quispel, *L'homme gnostique* (*La doctrine de Basilide*) in: *Eranos Jahrbuch* XVI,
    Zürich 1948, p. 89-140.
On Valentinus:
F. M. M. Sagnard, *La gnose valentinienne et le témoignage de Saint Irénée*, Paris
    1947. (Work of capital importance). With a bibliography.
G. Quispel, *The original doctrine of Valentine*, in: *Vigiliae Christianae* I 1947,
    p. 43-73.
—— *La conception de l'homme dans la gnose valentinienne* in: *Eranos Jahrb.* XV,
    Zürich 1947, p. 249-286.

HERMETICA

Corpus Hermeticum, tomes I-IV, ed. A. D. Nock, French transl. of A. J. Festugière.
    Paris 1945-54.
A. J. Festugière, *La révélation d'Hermes Trismegiste*
    I. *L'astrologie et les sciences occultes*. P². 1950.
    II. *Le Dieu cosmique*, P. 1949.
    III. *Les doctrines de l'âme*, P. 1953.
    IV. *Le Dieu inconnu et la gnose*, P. 1954.
Older literature is mentioned here and in the C.H. before each treatise.

NUMENIUS

E. A. Leemans, *Studie over den wijsgeer Numenius van Apamea* met *uitgave der
    fragmenten* (Kon. Belg. Akad., Afd. Letterk., Verhandelingen, Verzameling
    in 8°, Boek XXXVII, Afl. 2 en laatste). Brussel 1937.
H. Ch. Puech, *Numénius d'Apamée et les théologies orientales au second siècle* in:
    Annuaire de l'Institut de Philologie et d'histoire orientales (*Mélanges Bidez*),
    Tome II, Bruxelles 1934, p. 745-778.
    (Confounds Numenius' Noûs dèmiourgós with the gnostic demiurge.)
A. J. Festugière in the passage indicated under nr. 1345 (ad fin.).

PLOTINUS

TEXTS
Plotinus, *Enneades* ed. R. Volkmann, Lipsiae 1884, 2 vol. (with the vita by Por-
    phyrius).
Plotin, *Ennéades*. Texte établi et traduit par E. Bréhier, Paris 1924-1938, 6 vol.
    Contains a general introd., the Life of P. by Porph. and a short introd. to
    each treatise.
Plotini Opera ed. P. Henry et H.-R. Schwyzer, tom. I (Porph. Vita Plot., Enn.
    I-III), Paris-Bruxelles 1951.
    Critical edition. Vol. II 1959; Vol. III in preparation.

TRANSLATIONS
Engl. by S. MacKenna and B. S. Page. London 1917-1930. Revised edition 1956.
French by E. Bréhier, see above.
German by R. Harder, Lpz. 1930-37. Revised edition vol. I, Hamburg 1956.
    Continued by R. Beutler and W. Theiler.
A new Engl. transl. with notes by A. H. Armstrong is in preparation for the
    Loeb-collection.

LITERATURE

A—*General*
Th. Whittaker, *The Neoplatonists*. Cambridge [2]1918 (repr. 1928, 1961), pp. 40-106.
W. R. Inge, *The philosophy of Plotinus*, London, [2]1928, (reprinted 1948), 2 vol.
E. Bréhier, *La philosophie de Plotin*, Paris 1928.
F. Heinemann, *Plotin*, Leipzig 1921. (Attempts to trace a development in Plotinus' thought).

B. *Special subjects.*
R. Arnou, *Le Désir de Dieu dans la phil. de P.*, Paris 1921.
B. A. G. Fuller, *The problem of evil in P.*, Cambridge 1912.
E. Schröder, *P.'s Abhandlung Πόθεν τὰ κακά*; Diss. Rostock 1916.
G. Nebel, *P's Kategorien der intelligiblen Welt*, Tübingen 1929.
C. Schmidt, *P.'s Stellung zum Gnosticismus u. kirchlichen Christentum*. Leipzig 1901.
A. H. Armstrong, *The architecture of the intelligible universe in the phil. of P.* Cambridge 1940.
J. Trouillard, *La purification plotinienne*, Paris 1955.
—— *La procession plotinienne*, Paris 1955.
Eugénie de Keyser, *La signification de l'art dans les Ennéades de P.*, Louvain 1955.
On the problem of being in later Antiquity (Plotin - Marius Victorinus - Augustinus):
G. Huber, *Das Sein und das Absolute*. Studien zur Geschichte der ontologischen Problematik in der spätantiken Phil. (Studia philosophica, Jahrbuch der Schweizerischen phil. Gesellschaft, Supplementum 6), Basel 1955.

PORPHYRIUS

TEXTS

Eunapius, Βίοι φιλοσόφων καὶ σοφιστῶν, in: Philostratus and Eunapius, *The lives of the Sophists*, with an Engl. transl. by W. C. Wright, London 1922, pp. 352-362.
Porphyrius, Περὶ Πλωτίνου βίου, in the editions of Plotinus, *The Enneads*.
Porphyrius, Πυθαγόρου βίος (= *Vita Pythagorae*).
—— Περὶ τοῦ ἐν 'Οδυσσείᾳ τῶν νυμφῶν ἄντρου (= *De antro nympharum*).
—— Περὶ ἀποχῆς ἐμψύχων (*De abstinentia*) ll. IV.
—— Πρὸς Μάρκελλαν (*Ad Marcellam*).
These four writings are found in:
Porphyrii *Opuscula selecta* recogn. A. Nauck, Lipsiae 1886; repr. 1963.
Porphyrius, 'Αφορμαὶ πρὸς τὰ νοητά (= *Sententiae ad intelligibilia ducentes*) ed. B. Mommert, Lipsiae 1907.
Other works, see above, nr. *1445*.

LITERATURE

Zeller, *Phil. d. Gr.* III 2, pp. 693-735.
Th. Whittaker, *The Neoplatonists*, Cambridge [3]1928, p. 107-120.
J. Bidez, *Vie de Porphyre*, Gand-Leipzig 1913. Includes fragments of the Περὶ ἀγαλμάτων and *De regressu animae*.

IAMBLICHUS

TEXTS

Eunapius, *Vitae phil.*, p.362-378 Wright.
Iamblichus, Περὶ τοῦ Πυθαγορείου βίου (*De vita Pythagorica liber*) ed. L. Deubner, Lipsiae 1937.

Iamblichus, Προτρεπτικὸς ἐπὶ φιλοσοφίαν (Protrepticus) ed. H. Pistelli, Lipsiae 1888.
Three mathematical works, see above, nr. *1447c*.
De mysteriis ed. G. Parthey, Berlin 1857.
   On the authenticity see above, p. 557 n. 1.
   German translation and comm. by Th. Hopfner, 1922.

LITERATURE

Zeller, *Phil. d. Gr.* III 2, pp. 735-796.
Whittaker, *The Neoplatonists*, pp. 121-135.
E. R. Dodds, *Proclus' Elements of Theology*, Oxford 1933, p. XIX ff.

PROCLUS

TEXTS

Marinus, *Vita Procli* ed. J. F. Boissonade, Lipsiae 1814.
   Also in Cousin, *Procli opera inedita* (see below).
Proclus, Εἰς τὸν Τίμαιον Πλάτωνος (*In Platonis Timaeum commentaria*) ed. E. Diehl,
   Lipsiae 1903-1906, 3 vol.
—— Εἰς τὸν Πλάτωνος πρῶτον 'Αλκιβιάδην (*In Platonis primum Alcib.*).
—— Εἰς τὸν Πλάτωνος Παρμενίδην (*In Platonis Parmenidem*) ll. VII.
   These two commentaries were published by V. Cousin in *Procli philosophi
   Platonici opera inedita*, Paris 1864, together with the Vita of Marinus, Wil-
   liam Morbecca's translation of the treatises *De decem dubitationibus circa
   providentiam, De providentia et fato et eo quod in nobis, De malorum sub-
   sistentia*, and finally with the *Scholia in Parmenidem*. Repr. 1961.
   Cousin's edition of Proclus' *Commentary on the Parmenides* was not complete.
   It was completed by R. Klibansky and C. Labowski (*Corpus Platonicum
   medii aevi, Plato Latinus* vol. III), Warburg Institute, London 1953.
   This volume contains the Latin translation of the *Parm.*, probably of William
   of Morbecca (until p. 142A), the last part of the 7th book of Proclus' commentary, with an Engl. transl. of G. E. M. Anscombe and C. Labowsky,
   (the end of Proclus' commentary is preserved only in Latin; to the Greek
   part Morbecca's translation is added), and the marginal notes to Proclus'
   commentary by Nicolaus Cusanus.
   The *commentary on the Alcibiades Maior* was newly reedited by L. G. Westerink, Amsterdam 1954.

      (Dr. Westerink also edited the Scholia in Alcib. of Olympiodorus [1], Amster-
      dam 1956).

Proclus, Εἰς τὴν Πολιτείαν Πλάτωνος ὑπόμνημα (*In Platonis rem publicam com-
   mentarii*) ed. G. Kroll, Lipsiae 1899-1901, 2 vol.
   This is not a running commentary, as those on the *Tim., Alcib. Mai.*, and
   Parm., but a collection of essays on special subjects. The greater part of
   vol. I is taken by a defence of Homer against Plato.
'Εκ τῶν Πρόκλου σχολίων εἰς τὸν Κρατύλον τοῦ Πλάτωνος ἐκλογαὶ χρήσιμοι (*In
   Platonis Cratylum commentaria*) ed. G. Pasquali, Lipsiae 1808.

---

[1] This is not the Alexandrian O., who was the teacher of Proclus, but the
6th cent. Neoplatonician who was the author of the Comm. on the Phaedo, ed.
by Norvin.

Proclus, Εἰς τὴν Πλάτωνος θεολογίαν (*In Platonis theologiam*) ll. VI, with the
Latin transl. of Aemilius Portus and the Vita of Marinus, Hamburgi 1618.
Repr. Frankfurt 1960.
—— Στοιχείωσις θεολογική. The Elements of Theology. Text with an Engl.
transl., introd. and comm. by E. R. Dodds, Oxford 1933. Repr. 1963.
—— Στοιχείωσις φυσική (*Institutio physica*). Text with a German transl., a Latin
preface and a short comm. by Ritzenfeld, Lipsiae 1912.
Proclus also wrote a commentary on the first book of Euclides (Εἰς τὸ πρῶτον
τῶν Εὐκλείδου στοιχείων). This was recently translated into German by
L. Schoenberger, with an introd. and a commentary (Halle 1945). A French
transl. (with introd. and notes) by P. Vereecke appeared at Bruges, 1946.

LITERATURE

Zeller, *Phil. d. Gr.* III 2, pp. 834-890.
Whittaker, *The Neopl.*, pp. 157-180, 231-314.
E. R. Dodds, *The Elements*, introd.
L. J. Rosán, *The philosophy of Proclus*. The final phase of ancient thought. New
York 1949.

DAMASCIUS
TEXT

Damascius, Ἀπορίαι καὶ λύσεις περὶ τῶν πρώτων ἀρχῶν εἰς τὸν Πλάτωνος Παρμενίδην
(*Dubitationes et solutiones de primis principiis, in Platonis Parm.*) ed. C. A.
Ruelle, Paris 1889, 2 vol.

LITERATURE

C. A. Ruelle, *Le philosophe Damascius*; étude sur sa vie et ses ouvrages, suivie de
neuf morceaux inédits extraits du *Traité des premiers principes* et traduits
en Latin. *Revue archéologique*, 1860 et 1861.
Zeller, *Phil. der Gr.* III 2⁴, pp. 901-908.
Whittaker, *The Neopl.*, pp. 180 ff.

ADDITIONS TO THE BIBLIOGRAPHY

1. A—GENERAL WORK

Ph. de Lacy, *Some recent publications on hellenistic phil.* (1937-57). The class. World
1958-59.
Gnomologium Vaticanum ed. L. Sternbach, Berlin 1963.

1. B—SPECIAL PROBLEMS

S. Sambursky, *The physical world of late Antiquity*, London 1962.
W. & M. Kneale, *The development of logic*, Oxford 1962.
Galen, *Einführung in die Logik*, Kommentar mit deutscher Übersetzung von
J. Mau, Berlin 1960.
V. L. Schmidt, *Die Ethik der alten Griechen*, 2 vol. 1882; repr. in prep.

2. EPICURUS AND HIS SCHOOL

G. Arrighetti, *Epicurus, Opere*: introd., testo critico, trad. e note, Torino 1960.
Diogenes Oenoandensis ed. A. Grilli, Milano 1960.
P. Boyancé, *Lucrèce et l'Epicurisme*, Paris 1963.
Ph. Merlan, *Studies in Epicure and Aristotle*, Wiesbaden 1960.

R. D. Hicks, *Stoic and Epicurean*, N.Y. 1910; repr. 1963.

R. Westman, *Plutarch gegen Kolopes*. Die Schrift *Adv. Col.* als philosophiegeschicht-liche Quelle. (Acta philosophica Fennica), Helsinki 1955.

3. THE STOA

Les Stoïciens. Textes traduits par E. Bréhier, édités sous la direction de P.-M. Schuhl (Bibl. de la Pléiade), Paris 1962.

    Contains: A transl. of Cleanthes, *Hymn to Zeus*; Diog. Laert. b. VII; Plut., *De Stoic. repugn.* and *De comm. notionibus*.

    Cicero, *Acad. I, De fin.* III. *Tusc.* II 12-13, III from ch. 4, IV and V; *De nat. deorum* II, *De fato, De officiis*.

    Seneca, *De const. sapientis, De tranqu. animi, De brev. vitae, De vita beata, De prov.*; *Epist. ad Lucil.* 71-74;

    Epictetus and Marcus Aurelius (complete).

    All treatises are supplied with notes. Bibliogr. by P. M. Schuhl.

J. Christensen, *An essay on the Unity of Stoic philosophy*, Copenhagen 1962.

S. Sambursky, *Physics of the Stoics*, London 1959.

F. Solmsen, *Cleanthes or Posidonius?* The basis of Stoic physics. Amsterdam 1961 (Med. Kon. Acad.).

B. Mates, *Stoic logic*. Berkeley, Calif. 1953.

G. Pire, *Stoïcisme et pédagogie*. De Zénon à Marc Aurèle. De Sénèque à Montaigne et à J. J. Rousseau. Paris 1958.

4. SCEPTICISM

For Carneades:

    Cicero, *De fato* ed. A. Yon, Paris ²1950 (Budé).

    A. Weiche, *Cicero und die neue Akademie*. Untersuchungen zur Entstehung u. Geschichte des antiken Skepticismus. Münster i. W., 1961.

M. dal Pra, *Lo Scetticismo Greco*, Milano 1950.

W. Heinz, *Studien zu Sextus Empiricus*, Halle 1932.

5. THE MIDDLE STOA AND IVTH ACADEMY; CICERO

Cicero, *De natura deorum*, with a commentary by A. S. Pease, Cambr. (Mass.), 1956-58.

—— *De finibus* ed. Th. Schiche, Teubner 1915, repr. 1961.

—— *Hortensius* ed. A. Grilli, Milano 1962.

M. Ruch, *L'Hortensius de Cicéron*, Paris 1958.

A. Michel, *Rhétorique et philosophie chez Cicéron*, Paris 1960.

P. Milton Valente S.J., *L'éthique stoïcienne chez Cicéron*, Paris 1956.

A. Ronconi, *Cicero, Somnium Scip.*: introd. e commento (Bibl. Naz., Testi greci e latini con commento filologico) 1961.

A. J. Kleiwegt, *Ciceros Arbeitsweise im II. u. III. Buch der Schrift De nat. deorum* (Diss. Leiden) 1961.

G. Pfligersdorffer, *Studien zu Poseidonios*, Wien 1959.

M. Laffranque, *Posidonius*, in prep. (Paris).

6. THE STOA OF THE ROMAN EMPIRE

Sénèque, *Lettres*, t. I-IV, text and French transl. by F. Préchac and H. Noblot, Paris (Budé) 1956-62.

J. N. Sevenster, *Paul and Seneca*, Leiden 1961.

W. Trillitzsch, *Senecas Beweisführung*, Berlin 1962.

Cora M. Lutz, *Musonius Rufus* (Text, transl. and introd.), New Haven 1947.

A. C. van Geytenbeek, *Musonius Rufus and Greek diatribe*. Engl. ed. Assen 1963.
B. L. Hijmans, ΑΣΚΗΣΙΣ. Notes on Epictetus' educational system. Assen 1959.
W. Görlitz, *Marc-Aurèle, Empereur et philosophe*, Paris 1962.

7. LATER CYNICS

Favorin von Arelate, I. Teil der Fragmente ed. E. Mensching (with a commentary),
     Berlin 1963.

NEOPYTHAGOREANS

An important study on the dating of the Pythagorean pseudepigrapha was published
by H. Thesleff, *An introduction to the Pythagorean writings of the Hellenistic period*,
Åbo 1961.

PHILO

J. Daniélou, *Philon d'Alexandrie*, Paris 1958.
F. N. Klein, *Die Lichtterminologie bei Philo von Alexandrien u. in den hermetischen
     Schriften*, Leiden 1962.

GNOSIS

R. McL. Wilson, *The gnostic problem*, London 1958.
Frithjof Schuon, *Sentiers de gnose*, Paris 1957;
     Engl. transl.: *Gnosis, divine wisdom*, London 1959.
R. Ambelain, *La notion gnostique de démiurge*, Paris 1959.

HERMETICA

See F. N. Klein, under PHILO.

NUMENIUS, CHALCIDIUS

G. Martano, *Numenie d'Apamea*, un precursore del neoplatonismo, Napoli 1960.
A new edition of C(h)alcidius' translation of, and commentary on, the *Timaeus* was
     made by J. H. Waszink (Plato Latinus, vol. IV), London 1962.
J. C. M. van Winden, *Calcidius on Matter*, Leiden 1959.

PLOTINUS

K. H. Volkmann-Schluck, *Plotin als Interpret der Ontologie Platos*, Frankfurt, [2]1957.
Les sources de Plotin, Entretiens vol. V, Vandœuvres-Genève 1957.
J. Guitton, *Le temps et l'éternité chez Plotin et S. Augustin*, Paris 1933. Repr. 1961.
Ch. Rutten, *Les catégories du monde sensible dans les Ennéades de Plotin*, Paris 1961.
K. O. Weber, *Origenes der Neuplatoniker* (Zetemata 27), München 1962.

PORPHYRIUS

H. Dörrie, *Porphyrios' Symmikta Zetemata*, München 1959 (Zetemata, Heft 20).
Porphyrius, *De philosophia ex oraculis haurienda* ed. G. Wolff, Berlin 1856. Repr.
     1962.
J. J. O'Meara, *Porphyry's Philosophy from Oracles in Augustine*, Paris 1959.

IAMBLICHUS, SALLUSTIUS

Saloustios, *Des dieux et du monde*, text and transl. of G. Rochefort, Paris (Budé)
     1960.
Older literature on Sallustius:
     F. Cumont, *Salluste le philosophe*, in: *Rev. de philol.* 1892, pp. 49-56.

E. E. Passamonti, *La dottrina dei miti di Sallustio filosofo neoplatonico.*
Rendiconti accad. Lincei, ser. V 1, 1892, pp. 643-664.
—— *La dottrina morale e religiosa di Sall. fil. neopl.*, ib., pp. 712-727.
G. Murray, *Four stages of Greek Religion*, Oxford 1912, ch. 4. Ch. 5 contains
a translation of Sall., repr. in: *Five stages of Greek religion*, Oxford 1925.
Sallustius, *Concerning the gods and the universe* ed. A. D. Nock, Cambridge
1926. Edition of the text with a new Engl. transl., introd. and commentary.
French transl. by Mario Meunier, Paris 1931.

PROCLUS

Proclus, *Tria opuscula* (*De providentia*, *De libertate* and *De malo*), the Latin transl.
of G.van Moerbeke and the Greek fragments edited anew and collected
by H. Boese, Berlin 1960.
H. Boese, *Die mittelalterliche Übersetzung der* Στοιχείωσις φυσική *des Proklos*,
Berlin 1958 (Berl. Akad. d. Wiss.).
Procli *Hymni* ed. E. Vogt, Wiesbaden 1957.
Italian transl. of the *Theologia Plat.* by E. Tubolla, Bari 1959.

DAMASCIUS

Damascius, *Lectures on the Philebus* ed. L. G. Westerink, Amsterdam 1959.

INDICES

I—NAMES

Aratus 1175

Arcesilaus 805, 809, 896, 985, 1077, 1080, 1091, 1093, **1096-1107**, 1112, 1199

Archainetos 1281 b

Archedemus 898 c, 962 c, 1004, 1034 b, 1144, 1188 c

Archytas 1278, **1281**, 1288 a

Ardiaeus 1474 b

Ares 1314 c, 1356 b

Ariarathes of Cappadocia 1108

Aristarchus of Samos 943 n. 2

Aristarchus of Alexandria 972

Aristippus 880, 1087 a

Aristo of Chios 889, 896, 1021, 1028 c, 1030 a b, 1088 b c, 1096 b

Aristocles 861 c, 905 a, 1082 a, 1087 a, 1129 b

Ariston 1360 a

Aristotle 806, 807, 810 a, 811 a, 812, 822, 848 n. 1, 849 n. 2, 859, 879 c, 899 c, 903, 907, 941 a, 959, 960 d, 964 b, 967, 969, 971, 979 n. 3, 982, 989, 991, 997, 998, 1003, 1011 b, 1017 b, 1023, 1024, 1026, 1028 a, 1032 a b, 1034 d, 1035 b, 1049 b, 1050 b, 1051, 1058 b, 1059, 1066 c, 1074 b, 1076, 1077 a, 1111 a, 1114, 1123 c, 1125, 1133 b, 1134, 1135 a, 1150, 1160 a, 1182 b, 1184 b, 1192 b, 1199, 1200 b, 1214, 1221 a, 1236 c, 1278, 1279 a, 1280 b, 1281, 1285 b n. 2, 1290 a n. 1, 1305 a, 1314 c, 1322, 1325, 1327 d, 1352 b, 1353 e, 1385 b, 1394 c, 1400 n. 1, 1412 a n. 1, 1413 a, 1419 a, 1426 b, 1434 b, 1445 a, 1446 c, 1453 b, 1454 e, 1455 a b, 1457

Aristoxenus 1278

Arius Didymus 945 c, 957 b, 999 c, 1026 c, 1180 a, 1279 f, 1325, 1326 b

Armstrong, A. H., 1432 c

Arnim, H. von, 893, 943, 945 c, 999 c, 1181

Arnobius 1336 c, 1356 b

Arrianus 1231

Artemidorus 1226 b

Ascanius of Abdera 1082 a

Asklepiades 1132 b

Asklepios 925 b, 1338, 1340 a n. 2, 1440 a

Asmus 1261

Aspasius 1058 b, 1362 b

Asterius 1260 d

Athanasius 1300 c, 1302 a

Athena 1326 b

Athenaeus 863 a, 1012 a, 1042 b, 1172

Athenagoras 919 a, 924 b

Attagas 1095

Atticus Platonicus 856 b, **1325**, 1353 a n. 6, 1354 b, 1362 b

Augustinus 1003 n. 1, 1077, 1107 c, 1194 a, 1198 c, 1311 b, 1326 b, 1332 c, 1393 d, 1419 a, 1435 a b, 1442 b

Augustus 1284

Bacon, Francis, 845, 998

Bailey, C., frequently cited in ch. XX

Bardesanes 1340 a n. 3

Barth, P., 939 d, 994 b, 998

Barwick, K., 961

Basilides 1332 a c, 1336 b

Battos 1099 b

Bäumker, C., 1353 a n. 4

Bekker 1129 c

Benson, R. H., 935 n. 1

Berkeley 992 b, 1112 b, 1134

Bernays, J., 1256 b

Bidez 1457

Bier, Aug., 999 n. 1

Bion of Borysthenes 806, 1249, 1316 a

Blankert, S., 1192 b d, 1194 a, 1196 c d

Blossius, C., of Cumae, 936

Boëthius 975 b, 982, 1445 a

Boëthus of Sidon 990, 1143 b, 1151 b

Bonhöffer, A., 990 n. 2

Bousset, W., 1332 e, 1342 b n. 3, 1345 c

Boyancé, P., 959 b

Bréhier, E., 983, 1438

Bretz, A., 1260 d

Brieger 832 n. 1, 849 n. 4

Brochard, V., 983, 1078 b, 1080, 1086, 1089, 1106 a, 1107 d, 1116 b

Brutus 1197 b, 1198 c

Bryson 1082 a

Buecheler 1285 n. 1

Bury, R. G., 987 n. 1, 1094 n. 1

Bythos 1333 a c, 1336 a

Caesar, C. Julius, 1163

Calanos 1082 a n. 2

Caligula [Gaius] 1251, 1287, 1289 a

Callicles 875 c

Calvisius Taurus 1325

Harnack 1332 d
Häsle, B., 1260 b
Hecataeus of Abdera 1090 n. 3
Hecabe 1124, 1192 d, 1318 b, 1319 b, 1457
Hecaton 1018, 1145 b, 1162 b
Hector 1246 a
Heine, H., 932 a
Heinemann 1151 c, 1289, 1294 n. 1, 1311
Heinze 1318 d, 1320
Helen 987 n. 2, 1333 a, n. 4
Helios 925 b
Helvidius Priscus 1012 c
Hephaestus 924 c
Hera 924 c
Heracleon 1318 d, 1319 b, 1332 d
Heracles 905 b, 908 b, 924 a, 1044 n. 1, 1104, 1112 a, 1253, 1254 c, 1440 a
Heraclides Ponticus 810, 959 b, 1078 b, 1320, 1356 a
Heracleides of Tarentum 1137
Heraclitus 812, 904 a, 920 c, 941, 1066 c, 1080, 1195 b, 1267 b, 1311 b, 1314 c, 1353 c
Heraclitus Tyrius 1198 a
Herillus 889, 896, 1021
Hermarchos 813 c, 815 a, 1049 b, 1113 b
Hermeias 1480
Hermes (Mercurius) 924 a, 1356 b, 1437 c
Hermes Trismegistus **1338-1344**
Hermodorus 1352 a n. 8, 1410 b n. 4
Hermogenes 1249 a
Hero 1455
Herodotus (disciple and friend of Epicurus) 806, 820, 823 b, 824 n. 1, 827 a, 829, 832 a, 833, 836 a c, 837, 840 a b, 843
Herodotus (the historian) 1123 b
Herodotus of Tarsus 1078 b, 1079 b
Herophilus of Alexandria 948 c, 950, 1132 b, 1137 a, 1141 a.
Hesiod 810 a b, 938, 1288 c, 1311 a, 1318 a, 1330 e
Hicks, R. D., 827 b, 1095
Hierocles 945 c, 999 c
Hieronymus 880 a
Hilgenfeld 1332 d
Hipparchus 1172 c
Hippobotus 1078 b, 1129 a
Hippolytus 944 b, 1332 c, 1336 b, 1343
Hipponicus 1100 c
Hirzel, R., 1320, 1323 c

Hobbes 1475 a
Höistad, R., 1044 a, 1045 b, 1250 b, 1253 c, 1254 b c
Homer 918 a, 944 a, 949 d, 1254 c, 1269 n. 1, 1311 a, 1314 a n. 2, 1318 a, 1353 c, 1445 d
Hopfner, Th., 1314 b
Horace 879 a, 1149 c
Hornsby, H. M., 1256 b
Horus 1313 b, 1334 b d, 1337 c
Hultsch 1179 a
Hume 1134
Hypatia 1455

Iamblichus 1001 a, 1339 a n. 2, 1340 a n. 2, 1354 b, 1355 a b, 1360 a, 1436, 1440 f, 1445 c, **1446-1454**, 1457, 1462 f, 1476
Iccius 1149 c
Idomeneus 814 a, 819, 820, 880 a
Irenaeus 1332 c d, 1333 a b, 1334 a c d, 1335 a b, 1337 b, 1339 c n. 1
Isaak 1301 a
Isidorus 1261, 1480
Isis 1313
Iuno see Hera
Iuppiter see Zeus

Jacob 1301 a b
Jaeger, W., 1181 b
Jahweh 1301 b
Jesus see Christ
Jensen, Chr., 816 n. 2, 817, 858
Jeû 1332 c
John, St., 1304 b
Jonas, H., 1332 e
Jones, R. M., 959 b, 1192 b c d, 1193 a, 1319 c, 1320, 1321
Jong, Dr. K. H. E., 1358 a
Josephus 1289 a n. 2
Julianus 879 a, 1260 a, 1436, 1446 d, 1451 c, 1454 c f
Justinianus 1479, 1480

Kaibel 1231 d
Kant 1134
Kepler 960 d
Kern, O., 1340 a n. 2, 1437 c n. 2
Khosru Nuschirvan 1480
Krantor see Crantor
Kranz, W., 1279
Kroll, J., 1345 c

1015 b, 1018, 1021, 1022, 1028
a b c, 1035 a, 1041 a, 1042 a, 1044,
1049 a b, 1050 b, 1051, 1052, 1053,
1055, 1056 a, 1058 a, 1061 a, 1073,
1075
ridiculed by Timon 1092
criticized by Arcesilaus 1104
criticized by Carneades 1117 a, 1118a;
newly interpreted by Panaetius 1156;
basis of Posidonius' vitalism 1176;
other Zenonian tenets adopted by
Posidonius 1178 a, 1185 n. 1,
1185 c, 1196 a
cited by Antiochus of Ascalon
1197 d; cf. 1199

admired by Seneca 1207; cf. 1215;
1251 a
cited by Epictetus 1234 b
opposed by Plotinus 1415 c
Zeno of Elea 1121 n. 1
Zeus 908 n. 2, 918 a c d, 924 a b c, 925 a c,
927, 938, 942, 943, 944 c, 989 b,
1011 a, 1045 b, 1066 c, 1121 a, 1243a,
1245 a, 1246 b, 1254 b, 1256 a, 1271
d, 1284 c, 1314 c, 1340 a n. 2, 1356 b,
1451 b
Zeuxippus 1078 b
Zeuxis 1078 b
Ziegler, K., 1321
Zoè 1333 a

II—CONCEPTS

Abstinence
of animal food etc. (Neopyth.) **1279 f**
defended by Porph. against the Stoics
1444
practised bij Procl. **1416 a**
See also asceticism
Academy
the Middle A. **1096-1107**
the Third (New) A. **1108-1128**
the Fourth A. **1197-1205**
the A. of the second century **1325**
active principle
in nature acc. to the Stoa **899-902,
917**
aequalitas
men equal by nature **1069, 1071**
a. in the sense of ὁμολογία or constantia **1215 c**
aequitas **1065 b**
aether
called anima tenuis **1192 c**; cp.
1196 a
in Diog. Laërt. VIII 25 **1279 c**
in Basilides **1336 b**
aetheric body see ὄχημα
affection see oikeiosis
air
by Zeno identified with Hera **924 c**
crassus aer **1192 c**
in Neopyth. physics **1279 c**
full of souls and daemons **1279 e**
cp. Philo **1304**
Plut. **1318 b**

Apuleius **1331 a-c**
In the Valentinian psalm **1336 a**
in Basilides **1336 b**
allegoric interpretation
in the Stoa **924 c**
in Philo **1311 a**
in Porph. **1445 d**
ambition
warning against a. **1160 b**
amicitia see friendship
analogy
in Stoic grammar **972**
angels
with Neopyth. **1279 e**, with comments
in Philo Alex. **1306 a, c**
in Valentinus **1337 b, c**
See also demons
in Proclus **1472**
animals
distinguished from man by the Stoics
946
man has no duties towards a. **1001**
intermediate forms between plants
and a. **1182 b**
intelligent a. **1182 c**
instinct distinguished from reason
1183
treatment of a. (Plut.) **1323 b**
the Stoic theory opposed by Porphyry
1444
anomaly **972**
aoristus **970 a**
apprehension see κατάληψις

arrogance
  warning against a. **1160 b**; **1411 a**
ars
  per quam humana et divina noscantur
    1215 c; cp. **897 b**
  a. vivendi **1204 b**
asceticism
  of Epicurus **867**
  rejected by Panaet. **1165**
  practised by Sallustius **1261**
  See also abstinence and ἐπιθυμία
(askesis)
  in Musonius **1228**
  for Epictetus see **1247 a**
  for Plotinus **1411**; **1419** f.
  for Porphyrius **1440**
assensio **985 a**
assensus **985 b**
assent
  whether συγκατάθεσις is a ἑτεροίωσις
    ἐν ἡγεμονικῷ **956 a**
  the Stoic doctrine of a. (συγκατάθεσις)
    985 a b c; **987 a**
  the Stoic doctrine criticized by the
    Sceptics **1102**; **1103**
astrology
  accepted by the Stoics **937 b**
  criticized by the Sceptics **1139**
  by Panaetius **1153**
  Plotinus' attitude towards a. **1413 b**,
    the end, with n. 9; **1425 b**; **1431 d**
  For later Neoplatonists see **1356**
atomic theory
  of Epicurus **829-844**
atoms vid. ἄτομα
autarchy see αὐτάρκεια

Being
  four kinds of b. distinguished by
    Chrysippus **915**
  a hierarchy of b. admitted by Posi-
    donius **1196 d**
  generally found in the first centuries
    Ch. XXIV, introd.
  in Moderatus **1285 b**
  in Plutarch **1321**
  in Albinus **1327 b**
  in Gnosis **1332 b**, sub 3
  in Valentinus **1336**
  in Plotinus **1365-1370**
  in Proclus **1458-1470**
  A special kind of —s in each part of

  the cosmos **1280 c**; cp. **1304 a**
  See also ὄν, ὄντα, and οὐσία
beneficium **1217**
body
  —ies and space acc. to Epic. **829 a**
  motion in compound —ies **837**
  properties of compound —ies **838**
  the Stoa:
    everything which operates is a b.
      901
    virtues are —ies **914**
    four kinds of natural —ies **1181**
    b. and soul **1184 a** (Posid.), **1228**
      (Musonius), **1265 b c** (M. Aur.)
    Epict. **1232 a**, **1234 a**, **1235 a**
      (τὸ σαρκίδιον), **1236 b c** (τὸ σω-
      μάτιον), **1241 c** (τὸ σαρκίδιον)
    For a positive appreciation of the
      b., cp. **929 a**
    M. Aur.: τὰ τοῦ σώματος ποταμός
      1275 b
  Neopyth.:
    the origin of sensible —ies **1279 a**
  Philo:
    τὸ σῶμα οὐ θεοειδές **1296 a**; cp.
      1296 b c
    Plut. **1313 b** (Horus νενοθευμένος τῇ
      ὕλῃ διὰ τὸ σωματικόν)
    man consists of b., soul and spirit
      1319 a (cp. M. Aur. **1265 b**)
    the consequences of incarnation
      1320
  Herm.:
    how the spiritual man is joined to
      a b. **1341 b**
    the b. a burden **1344**
  Numenius:
    the ὄν cannot be a b. **1347 a b**
  Plotinus:
    soul and b. **1371 b c**; **1373 a** (the
      end), **1375 b** (the end); **1376 c**
      (l. 20), **1378 a** (τὸ ὄργανον τὸ
      σῶμα)
    μνήμη does not belong to the b.
      1378 b
    the b. of the universe **1373 c** (l. 6),
      1404 a c
    the b. always composite **1406 c**;
      1407 a
    ὕλη not a b. **1401 b c**; **1409 a**
    the b. not primarily bad **1410 c**
    man in a b. **1412-1424**

the b. should be accepted meekly
1424
See also ἀνάστασις
Porph.
personality defined as ὁ ἐπὶ πλεῖστον ἀφεστηκὼς τοῦ σώματος
1440 a (c. 8, sec. al.); cp. **1441**
the b. (σάρξ) not the cause of sin
1440 f; cp. Iambl. **1453 a**
Iambl.
his b. transfigured **1431 b**
Proclus
his comments on *Tim.* 43-44 (the
b. a cause of disturbance) **1453 a**;
(cp. Plot. **1412 e**)
the b. moved by soul **1459 d**
participates of being **1459 e**
θεῖον διὰ ψυχῆς **1465 a** (c. 129, 139);
cp. **1466 d** (c. 165)
periodical return of the soul into
a b. **1469 b**
ethereal or pneumatical b. see ὄχημα
celestial —ies see celestial
bona
in Stoic ethics **1012**; **1017 d**; **1022**;
1027 c
Pyrrho and Aristo **1288**
See also προηγμένον. For Plot. and
later Neoplat. see ἀγαθά
bonitas **876**
bonum
in the Stoa **1012**; **1015-1017**; **1021
c**; **1036**; **1062 c**
See also τέλος (summum bonum) and
honestum
bravery see ἀνδρεία

Caelum see οὐρανός
canon
the c. in Epicurus **821**; **823 a**
caritas
generis humani **1205**; cp. **1243**
(Epict.) and **1262 a**; **1272 a**; **1276
b** (Marc. Aur.); cp. also Iambl.
1448 c
casuistic
in the Stoa **1128**; **1145**
casus
conscientiae **1128**; **1145**
in grammar, vid. πτῶσις; c. rectus
969 b

categories
four c. admitted by the Stoics **915 a**
The Stoic theory of the c. criticized
by Plot. **915 a**, under the text.
For Plot. cp. **1433 b**, introd.
cause
in the Stoa, see active principle; also
919 b
Five or six c.s assumed in the later
Stoa **1305 a**, under the text
c. of evil, see evil
c. of the πάθη, see πάθη
the principle of causality denied by
the Sceptics **1131** f.
God the c. of the universe (Seneca)
1221
ps.-Archytas **1281**
one single c. admitted bij Plot. **1364 a**
a hierarchy of causes (Proclus) **1458 b**
See also αἰτία
celestial
the c. bodies
generally believed to be divine beings
848 b, introd., with n. 1
this belief rejected by Epic. **448 b**
accepted in the Stoa **902 a**
criticized by Carn. **1117 b**; **1121 c**
partly admitted by Boëthus of Sidon
1143 b
apparently rejected by Panaetius, cp.
1152; **1153**
the stars feeding on aether **1192 c**
(the end). See also sun and moon.
divine beings **1279 c**
ζῷα νοερά **1297 a** (l. 4)
God conducting the motion of the c.
bodies **1303 c** (see also sm. pr. under the text)
Plut. (Xenocr.): sun and stars εἰκόνες
of the Gods **1318 b**
the moon a μικτὸν σῶμα, see moon
Albinus: the stars are spiritual beings
and gods **1329 a**
Plotinus:
the star-souls **1376 b**
the stars divine beings **1381 a** (l. 40)
brother sun and brothers stars
1411 b
the stars a sign of future events, not
their cause **1413 b**, with n. 7;
cp. **1425 b**; **1431 d**; **1432 a** (the
end)

For the influence of the c. bodies on
earthly events, see astrology
the c. spheres: ascent of the soul
1342 b; decent **1356 b**
c. immortality **959**; **960**; **1192-
1194**; cp. **1319 b** and **1356**
See also sun, moon, and Milky Way
children
on having c., see marriage
circle
the simile of the c. in Plot. **1364 a b**;
1365 b, 1397 b (sm. pr.)
choice
deliberate c., see προαίρεσις
civitas
communis deorum atque hominum
1001; **1072**
climatic
c. influence on man **1184 a**
clinamen vid. παρέγκλισις
cognatio distantium rerum **935**
See further s.v. cosmic sympathy
coincidentia oppositorum **1398 c**, n. 1
collision
of the atoms acc. to Epic. **833**
colour
explained by Epic. **838**
kataleptic presentation of colour denied by the Sceptics **1112 b**
comitas **876**
commendatio **1000 a**
sibi commendari **945 b**
See also conciliatio and οἰκείωσις
common sense **1141 b**; **1142**
compassion
rejected in the Stoa **1064 b**
compound body, see body
comprehensio **985 a b**
See also κατάληψις
conciliatio **1003 b**
sibi conciliari **945 b**; **999 c**
See further οἰκείωσις
concilium, see compound body
conflagration, see ἐκπύρωσις
coniunctio
naturae **935**
See further cosmic sympathy
conscience
in Seneca **1218-1220**
consciousness, see self-consciousness
consensus
gentium **996 a b**

omnium **1122 b**
c. naturae **935**
consitus
the soul defined as c. spitirus **903 c**
consilium
ratio et c. the proprium of man **1001 c**
constantia
in Seneca **1006**
See also self-consistency
contemplation
of the intelligible World (θεάσασθαι)
1310 b (Philo)
In Plotinus: ἡ θέα, τὸ θέαμα (sc. of the
First Principle, called the Light),
θεάσασθαι **1389 a-c**; **1399 a, c-d**;
1400. Cp. Porph. **1441**, the beginning
See also ἐπιστροφή, ἐπιστρέφεσθαι
contingency
of all things acc. to Epic. **808**, sub (2)
contract
the social c. theory held by Epic. **875**
by Carneades **1126**
contradiction
the law of c. rejected by the Sceptics
1113
convenientia
= ὁμολογία **1003 b**
cosmic sympathy (συμπάθεια)
Chrysippus' view of c. s. **913**
artificial mantic based on c. s. **935**
(called cognatio distantium rerum,
coniunctio or consensus naturae)
this theory attacked by Carn. **1122**,
sub 3; also **935**
c. s. in Posid.' system **1177**; in M.
Aur. **1271-1272** (called ἐπισύνδη-
σις πάντων, σύμπνοια and ἕνωσις τῆς
οὐσίας); in Philo **1303 a**; in Plotinus
1431 a b; **1432 a**
cosmos
endowed with soul and reason acc. to
the Stoa **909**; divine **902 a**
three arguments **910**; **920 c**
unity of the c. **922**; **1271**
the Sceptic arguments against the
Stoic theory **1117** f.
the theory abandoned by Boëthus of
Sidon **1143 b**
eternity of the c. held by Panaetius
1151 b

desire, see ἐπιθυμία

dialectica **974**
See further διαλεκτική

diatribe
the genre defined **1249**

disease
man considered as suffering from a d. **883 b**
cp. **1160 b**: phil. medetur animis πάθη considered as a d. **1185**
sin regarded as a d. **1257 b**; **1316 a**, the beginning

divinatio **1122 a**
See further mantic

divisibility
infinite d. of atoms rejected by Epic. **832**

divisio
Carneadea **1111 b**

dogmatism
of Epic. and the Stoa, see theory of knowledge, s.v. knowledge
Stoic d. criticized by the Sceptics, ib.
Philo of Larisa did not return to d. **1197 c d**
Antiochus did **1198**

dolor
nihil agis, d. **1171 b**
See also πάθη, and pain

dreams **1123 c**; **1194 a**

dualism
of ps.-Archytas **1281**
of Plut. **1313**; **1314**
in gnosis **1332 a b**; **1334 ff.**
the *Poimandres*: **1339 a**, with n. 2
Numenius **1353 ff.**
For Plot. and Proclus see ὕλη. See also evil

duration
virtue not increased by d. **1036**

durativum **970 b**

dynamical
the One of Plot. a d. maximum **1398 b**
See further s.v. power

Earth
Posidonius' theories on form and circumference of the e. **1173-1176**
See further cosmos

effatum **974**

eidola, see εἴδωλα

elements, see στοιχεῖα

emanation, see ἐξερρύη

embryology
treatise of P.orph. on e. **1445 f.**

empiricism **809**; **1137-1139**. See also **1116**

end, see τέλος

enthusiasm
characteristic of the prophet **1310**

Epicureanism
in general **805-808**
See further Epicurus

equilibrium
in the universe acc. to Epic. **850**
in Diog. Laert. VIII 26 **1279 b**
in Philo **1306 b c**

eternity
defined by Plot. **1433**

ethereal, see aetheric

ethics
Epic.' e. connected with physics **834**
Epic.' e. **859-883**
its place in the system of phil. **898**
Stoic e. **999-1076**
Pyrrho's relation to e. **1088**
Carneades' position in e. **1125-1128**
Diog. and Antipater **1144-1147**
Panaetius **1156-1169**
Posidonius **1184-1191**
Antiochus of Ascalon **1201-1205**
Seneca **1206-1220**
Musonius **1227-1230**
Epictetus **1232-1248**
later Cynics **1249 b-1254**; **1257 f.**
Marc. Aur. **1262 ff.**
Philo **1309 f.**
Plutarch **1322 ff.**
Atticus **1325 b**
Hermetics **1341 f.**; **1344**
Numenius **1355 f.**
lack of e. in Gnosticism **1411**
Plotinus **1410-1424**
Porphyry **1439-1441**
Iambl. **1453**
Proclus **1456 b**; **1473 b**; **1474**

etymology **971 b**

evidence
practical e. **809**; cp. **1116**; **1137 ff.**

evil
the problem of e. in Epic. **853a**; cp. **865**; **883 a b**
in the Stoa **938-942**

Sceptic arguments against this **1119**
on moral evil, see sin
The Stoic tenet: There is no e. except
what is morally bad **1061 c**
Seneca's attitude towards e. **1207:
1210**
For Epictetus, cp. **1232** ff.; **1239**
The Cynics **1249 b**
Marc. Aur. **1270** f.
the problem of e. in Philo **1297**
the cause of e. acc. to Plut. **1314**
acc. to Plot. **1410 a-e**
e. defined as στέρησις **1410 e**
e. men have their function in the
whole **1429 c**
e. cannot be ascribed to the Gods
1431 c
Porphyry (man himself the cause of
e.) **1440 b**
Proclus **1479**
explorer
Posid. the greatest e. of Antiquity
1172 d
extasy
in Philo **1310**
for Plot., see ἔκστασις
externals, see outward things

Fasting **1456 a**
fatalism **808**
See further fate, εἱμαρμένη, and κοινὸς
νόμος s.v. law
fate, fatum
f. and liberty
in the Stoa **943** f.
Carneades **1124**
Plotinus **1413 b**, the end, with n.
10; **1418**; **1430**
Proclus **1473 b**
f. and providence
in Diog. Laërt. VIII 27 **1279 d**
in Philo **1302 b-d**
Plut. **1321**
Apuleius **1331 b**
Plot. **1421-1432**, esp. **1431**
Proclus **1471**
See further εἱμαρμένη, and κοινὸς
νόμος s.v. law
fear
in Epic.:
f. of death **844**; **865**
of the gods ib.

see also Cic. **1118 c**
f. of punishment **875**
in the Stoa:
one of the four πάθη **955**; **1057-
1060**; **1121 b**
Epict. mentions ἀφοβία as one of the
precious qualities of the "free"
man **1233 a**
See also the problem of evil s.v. evil
finalism
Zeno a finalist **808**
See further τέλος
finite
and infinite see πέρας and ἄπειρον
fire
in the Stoa **902** f.
See aslo πῦρ
fortitudo see ἀνδρεία
fortuita **1122**
freedom (ἐλευθερία)
in Epict. **1013 b**; **1234**; **1246**
free will
maintained by Epic. through the
clinamen theory **833-835**
in the early Stoa **943**; **944**
in Epict.: προαίρεσις the first characteristic of man **1236 d**; **1242** (init.)
Gnostics speak of τὸ αὐτεξούσιον **1335a**
Plotinus opposes the Stoic doctrine of
ἓν κ. πᾶν as abolishing f. w. **1425
a-d**. Cp. **1430**; **1432 c** (ἑκών,
οἰκεία φύσις, αὐτεξούσιος)
Iambl. **1453 a** (προαίρεσις)
Procl. **1473 b** (αἱρεῖσθαι, αἵρεσις)
See also fate (f. and liberty), and ἡμεῖς
friendship
in the School of Epic. **812 a b**; **813**;
815; **818**
Epic.' theory **877**
See also caritas, φιλανθρωπία, and φίλος

Generation
the g. of the universe acc. to the Stoa
904
See also regeneration and creation
gentleness **1160 b** (Panaetius); **1257 b**
(Demonax); **1424** (Plotinus)
gnosis
gnosticism } **1332-1337**
gnostics
Plotinus' arguments against g. **1411**;
1420 b; **1424**

indifferentism
  Pyrrho's i. **809**; **1082 b**; cp. **1089**
infinite, infinity, see ἄπειρον
injustice, see ἀδικία
instinct
  opposed to intellect **946**; **1183**
intellect, see comprehensio, κατάληψις,
  λόγος, διάνοια and νοῦς
intelligentia **1003 b**; see also ἔννοια
intelligible
  the i. world, see κόσμος νοητός (s.v.
  κόσμος) and ἰδέα. Also νοῦς.
intentio, spiritus, see τόνος
intention
  virtue essentially a question of i.
  1016, **1217**
intermundia, see μετακόσμια
international law **1070**
interpenetration of bodies **912**
  See also κρᾶσις δι' ὅλων s.v. κρᾶσις
irrational
  On the question whether there is an
  i. part in man acc. to the Stoa, see
  πάθος
  Numenius **1353 d**. See also ἄλογος
irrationalism
  detested by Plot. **1332 e**, the end
isonomy, see ἰσονομία
ius, see law

Justice, see δίκαιον and δικαιοσύνη

Kataleptic presentation, see κατάληψις
  and sense-impression
knowledge
  theory of k.: introd. remark **808**,
  sub (4); in Epic. **821**; in the Stoa
  984-997
  the Stoic theory criticized **1102-
  1104**; **1112** ff.
  For Plotinus, see **1414 c-1416**

Law
  of the universe **808**. By the Stoics
  called λόγος or κοινὸς νόμος **918 d**;
  943. See also logos
  the Stoic theory of natural l. **1065-
  1076**. Criticized by Carneades
  1125 ff.
  the immutable —s of nature (Philo)
  1302 c
  divinam legem esse fatum **1331 b**

the —s of the universe described by
  Plotinus **1431**
learning
  despised by Epic. **816**; **879 d**
  Epic. and Pyrrho **811 a**
  cultivated by Panaet. **1149**
  and Posid. **1170 c**; **1172**
  Nigidius praised for his l. **1278 b**
  See also παιδεία
lex, see law
liar
  the sophism of the l. **974**
libertas see ἐλευθερία
life
  a campaign (Epict.) **1247**
  full of deceit, wickedness and sorrow
  (Dio) **1253 c**
  human l. compared with eternity
  (M. Aur.) **1273 c**; is πόλεμος **1275 b**
  true l. is yonder (Plot.) **1400 a b**
  l. must bear witness to theory
  (Porph.) **1440 a**
  unparticipated l. (Procl.) **1463 c**
  See also ζωή
light
  in the vision of the *Poimandres* **1339**;
  frequently in Plotinus. See φῶς,
  ἐκλάμπειν, περίλαμψις, and creation
logic
  its place in the system of phil. **897** f.
  Stoic l. **973-983**
  the basis of logic attacked by Carn.
  1113
  arguments against proof **1114**
  against the Stoic criterium of truth
  1115
  later Sceptic arguments **1130-1136**;
  1141
  Stoic l. ridiculed by Lucianus **1050a**
  See further διαλεκτική
Logos (λόγος, ratio)
  Heraclitus' concept of universal Law
  adopted in the Stoa:
  the active principle in nature, God
  899 a; Zeus **904 a**; **925**; **943**
  pervading the universe and called
  εἱμαρμένη **900 a**; **904 a**
  material **901**; creative fire **902**
  l. spermatikos **904 a**; **919**
  contains the λ.οι σπερματικοί **902 a**;
  919 a-d

κοινός λ. **918 c**; **943** l. 12
also called noûs **920**; and πρόνοια
927 a; cp. **928-930**
identified with nature **921**
=speech **968**; defined **966**
λ. ἐνδιάθετος and προφορικός **965**;
cp. **991**
=argument **979-981**
λ. ἀπέραντος **980**; ἀναπόδεικτος **981**
λ. (ratio et consilium) the proprium
of man **1001 c**; **1002**
animals do not share in it **1001 b**
living acc. to nature=living acc. to
the l. **1003 a**
basis of morality and law **989 c**;
1065 a (ὀρθὸς λόγος)
cp. ratio summa **1066 a**; ratio recta
1066 b c
πάθος defined as a λ. πονηρός **1053 b**
ἀπειθὲς τῷ —ῳ **1056 a b**; cp. ἀποστρέφεσθαι τὸν —ν **1185 b**
the term λ. used by Orig. **1068 b**
divine L. the criterium of truth
1195 b (Posid.)
the L. governing the universe **1268**
(M. Aur.)
two —οι assumed by ps.-Archytas
1281
the term λ. used by Philo **1299**
l. described as rays of light **1300 c**
the elder son of God **1301 c**
the law immanent in nature **1302 c**
cyclic motion **1302 d**
l. spermatikos **1302 e**
transcendent l. an image of God
1303 b
the shepherd **1303 c**
instrumental cause of creation **1305**
the immanent l. **1306**
a double l., both in the cosmos and
in man **1307**
ὁ τῆς φύσεως ὀρθὸς λ., νόμος θεῖος ὤν
1308
By Plut. identified with Osiris **1313 b**
a twofold l. admitted by Albinus
1327 c
L. in Valentinus' pleroma **1333 a**
in the *Poimandres* **1339 b**; **1340 b**
in Plotinus: **1376 c**; **1381 b**; **1405 b**;
1427; **1428** f.
l. οἷον ἔκλαμψις ἐκ νοῦ κ. ψυχῆς **1427 b**

love
of ourselves and our fellow-men, see
oikeiosis and caritas
Also commendatio, conciliatio, φιλία
and φιλανθρωπία
sexual l., acc. to Epic. **866 b d**
Panaetius' attitude towards it **1167**
Musonius Rufus **1229**;
Plut. **1324 c**
l. of the spirit and the soul for its
Creator **1366**; **1367**; **1375 c**; **1389**
See also ἔρως and ἐρωτικὸν πάθημα
God's l. of man (τὸ φιλάνθρωπον) **995 b**
Lyceum **807**

Magic
in gnosis **1332 b**, sub 4
explained by Plotinus **1432 a**
magnanimus **1207**
magnitudo animi **1211** (Seneca)
animus magnus **1160 a** (Panaetius)
magnet
the m. a connecting link between
organic and anorganic nature **1182**
maius
(magnitudo) qua nihil m. cogitari
potest (of God) **1221 c**; cp **928**
malum
see evil and sin
man
the primary impulse of man acc. to
the Stoa **945**
m. opposed to animals **946**; **1001**
the soul of m. **947** ff.
natural bond of m. and m. **1000**;
1069 b; **1072**
reason the proprium of m. **1002** f.
the idea of humanity and humanitas
in Panaetius and Cicero **1161 b**;
1162
See further humanitas and caritas
The wise man, see wise
m. a psychophysical unity (Posid.)
1184
between God and the world **1181 b**
the Cynic ideal of m. **1253** f., **1257**
the moral task of m. according to
Seneca **1210**
acc. to Marc. Aur. **1275-1276**
Epict.' view of m. **1242**
m. a part of God **1244**

minimae partes
   (in the atomic theory of Epic.) **832**
miracles, see θεουργία
misericordia, see compassion
mixture
   Chrysippus' theory of m. **912-913**
modality
   (in Stoic logic) **973**; **975**
modestia
   defined by Panaetius **1161**
monism
   A tendency towards m. in the Stoa
      901 c, under the text
   in Diog. L. VIII 25 **1279 a**
   in Moderatus **1285 b**
   Nicomachus of Gerasa **1288 c**
   in the *Corp. Herm.* **1340 a**, with n. 2
   in Plotinus
      ὕλη αἰσθητή derived from the intel-
         ligible ἄπειρον **1408 c d**
      the indefinite Principle directly
         derived from the First **1408 e**
      one cause **1364 a-d**
   For Porph. cp. **1440 f**; Proclus **1470**
monotheism
   a monotheistic tendency in the Stoa
      922, but cp. **923**; **924 b**; **925**; **943**
   in Plut. **1312 c**
   in Max. Tyr. **1330**
   in the *Poimandres* **1343**
   in Valentinus and his followers
      1333 a, esp. n. 3
   opposed by Plot. **1411 a**
monstrosities **842**; **1121 a**
moon
   generally believed to be a divine being
      848 b, with n. 1
   this belief criticized by Carn. **1121 c**
   The moon produces new souls **1176 d**
   the phases of the m. connected with
      vegetation on earth and with tide
      1177 b
   Chrysippus' and Posid.' phys. theory
      1180
   soul springs from the m. and returns
      to it **1192 d**; **1319 a**
   the abode of souls, Philo **1304 b**;
      Plut. **1319 b**
   a μικτὸν σῶμα **1318 b**
   soul compared with the m. as a
      derived light (Plot.) **1370 b** (l. 17)

morality
   based on reason **1013 a**; **1015 a**
   basis of happiness **1013 c**; **1014**
   defends on the inner man **1035**
   absolute character of m. **1036**
   founded on nature **1065** sqq.
   moral character
      called χρηστότης καὶ καλοκάγαθία
         1227 c
   m. also called τὸ καλόν or καλὸν καὶ
      δίκαιον, cp. **873 c**; **874**
   See further ethics, bonum, honestum,
      and virtue
motion
   of Epic.' atoms **830 b**; **833 c**
   atomic speed **836 a**
   m. of atoms in compound bodies **837**
   In the Stoa πάθος defined as an irra-
      tional m. of the soul **1051 b**; cp.
      952
   the argument that m. is impossible
      and Herophilus' reply to this **1141 a**
   prolonged m. a therapy of passions
      1189 b
   the m. of the universe acc. to Plot.
      1431 a
multiplicity, see plurality
mysticism
   Epicurean m. **857**
   Posid. a mystic? **1195** (some com-
      ments under **b**)
   Philo **1310**
   Plotinus **1389**; **1395 b**; **1399 a-d**;
      1400
mythology
   in the Stoa allegorically explained **924**;
   by Philo **1311 a**
   the mythological element in Gnosis
      1332 a c
   in the *Corp. Herm.* **1338**
   for Plotinus' attitude towards m. see
      nr. **1411**, esp. sub 1-4 and sub 8;
      1350 a, under the text; **1352 a**

Names
   whether φύσει or θέσει **971**; **972**
nature (natura, φύσις)
   in the Stoa:
   two principles in n. (here called τὰ
      ὅλα; Lat.: natura rerum) **899 a**
   God and matter two aspects of the
      same n. **900 c**

n. defined as πῦρ τεχνικόν **902 b c**; **917**
identified with εἱμαρμένη **918 c**
= God or the Logos **921**; **924**
= Providence **927**; **928**
hierarchic order in n. (Marc. Aur.) **931**
teleology in n. **932**
the unity of n. viewed as cosmic sympathy **935**
the existence of evil in n., see evil
Zeus called φύσεως ἀρχηγός (Cleanthes) **943**, l. 2
living according to n. a moral principle **1003-1005**
the good defined as —al perfection **1017 b**
as that which is absolute by n. **1017c**
virtue a perfection of n. **1023**
man has by n. an aptitude to virtue **1025**; **1026**
sin a perversion of n. **1027**
πάθος defined as a motion against n. **1051**
n. the basis of morality and law **1065-1076**
this theory opposed by Carn. **1125-1128**
living acc. to n. interpreted in the Stoa after Carn. **1144**
phil. of n. basis of Panaetius' phil. **1151**
living acc. to n. explained by Panaetius **1156**; **1157**
Posid.' phil. of n. **1173-1182**
living acc. to n. explained by Posid. **1188 d**
φ. ranked second, after Zeus **1196 d**
vivere sec. n. explained by Antiochus **1201-1205**
satis nos instruxit n. (Seneca) **1214 b**
individual and universal n. connected (M. Aur.) **1262 c**
obedience to n. **1267**
the immanent law of n. (Philo) **1302**
not identified with God **1303 a**
God the conductor of the powers of n. **1303 b c**
the patriarchs an incarnation of the divine Law of n. **1309 a**
For Plut., Albinus, the gnostic and Hermetic view of n. see s.v. matter (ὕλη)
By Plotinus the term φ. is used and

denotes the lowest stage of soul **1405**
φ. called ἵνδαλμα φρονήσεως **1376 d**
n. should not be despised **1403 d**; **1411**; cp. **1424**; **1428 e-f**
negation
in Stoic logic **976**
Neo-pythagoreanism
Starts in the first century B.C., ch. XXIV I, introd.; **1278-1288**
Neo-platonism
preparation, ch. XXIV; the N. of Plotinus, ch. XXV; later N., ch. XXVI
notio
—es communes **995-997**; **1003 b**
See also ἔννοια
notitia, notities (= πρόληψις)
in Lucr. **825**; **854 b**
noûs
in the Stoa:
the Logos called n. **904 a**; **909**; **920 a-c**
= the cosmic pneuma **957**, introd.
διάνοια called n. **965 a**
ν. καὶ λόγος the dwelling-place of virtue and vice **1001 b**
Timon: spirit, understanding **1092 a**
Posidonius:
n. engendered by the sun **1176 d**
Cp. **1185** (a): the ἀρίστη φύσις is νοερά (with comments), and **1186 b**: νοεραὶ φύσεις
Cp. also **1192 b** (the end), and **1192 c**, with n. 4
n. ranked higher than soul **1192 d**, the beginning
cp. **1194 a** (comments), **1195 a b**
the universe governed by n. **1196 a**
M. Aur.:
1262 a; **1265 b** (of man); **1268 b** (ὁ τοῦ ὅλου ν.)
Cp. **1262 b**: νοερὰ κίνησις; **1262 c**: νοερὰ φύσις
Philo:
each of the angels is a n. ἀκραιφνέστατος **1304 a**
Plut.:
n. superior to soul **1192 d**; **1319 a**; called Daimon **1320**
Albinus:
the First Principle is N. ἀκίνητος

1327 b; δημιουργός 1327 d; 1328 ἄρρητος 1327 d e

cause of the n. of the whole ouranos 1327 b

cp. 1327 d: the First N. cause of the n. ἐν ψυχῇ (the world-soul)

Also a potential n. admitted 1327 b

n. in Valentinus' pleroma 1333 a b

a double n. assumed by Basilides 1336 b

in the *Poimandres* 1339 b; 1340

Numenius calls his First God N. 1350

Plotinus:

n. the first circle around the centre, φῶς ἐκ φωτός 1365 b

the second hypostasis 1370

plurality in n. 1374 b

light from Light 1382 a

a direct image of the Good 1382 b

multiplicity begins in n. 1382 c

the second God 1382 d

eternal 1383 a

= τὸ νοητόν or τὰ νοητά 1383 b-d

primary thinking 1383 d

= τὸ ὄν 1384 a

contains the νοητά as its eternal object 1384 b c; 1385 a

n. described 1385 b

the παντελὲς ζῷον 1386 a

contains number and all the Ideas 1386 b

double function 1389 a

why not the First Principle 1390

relation to the sensible world 1401 c

the archetypon of sensible things 1426 a

the power inherent in n. 1426 b; 1428 a b

Iambl. doubles the n. 1450

the first N. described as a triad 1451

Proclus:

unparticipated n. 1463 c

participated n. 1467 a

its knowledge 1467 b c

N. and the ideas 1467 d

divine and not-divine n. 1467 e

number

with Neopythagoreans 1279 a

Plato's metaphysical principles explained by n. 1285

n. a cosmic principle 1288 a

pre-existing in the mind of God 1288 b

in Plot.: ranked first in the intelligible world 1386 b

before being? 1387 a

being must be n. 1387 b

Obedience

to God and cosmic Law e.g. 943, 944 (Cleanthes); 1234 a, 1245 (Epict.); 1267, 1277 (M. Aur.)

occupations

vulgar and liberal, 1255 c

offerings

only accepted from good men 1254 b

should not be precious 1443

officium, see καθῆκον

oikeiosis (Gr. οἰκείωσις, Lat. commendatio, conciliatio; also caritas)

the o. theory in the Stoa; 945; 999-1003

whether the theory goes back to Theophr. 945 c, under the text

the term used by Plot. 1057

the theory of natural law based on the o. principle by Cic. 1065 b c; 1066-1067; 1070

opposed by Carn. 1125-1128

comments under 1128 c

renewed by Diog. and Antipater 1145

Panaetius 1159

Antiochus of Ascalon 1201 a; 1205

Musonius 1227 b

Philo 1290 b

See further love and caritas

omina 933

one

the o. as First Principle 1279 a (μονάς)

In Moderatus ἑνότης or ἕν 1285 a, and τὸ πρῶτον ἕν 1285 b

principle of number (Nicomachus) 1288 a; also called μονάς 1288 c

In Plotinus the first hypostasis 1370

contains everything within itself 1364 b c

contemplated by noûs 1389

the O. or the Good 1392-1400; beyond being 1392; 1398 a

infinite power 1398 b

By Iambl. the O. placed after the
ἄρρητος ἀρχή **1449 a**
Proclus: the O. and the many **1458 a**
the O. beyond the intelligible world
1459 d
a series of divine Henads ranked
under the O. **1464, a-k; 1466 b**
the scheme of the hierarchy **1466 d**,
under the text
Damascius: the First Principle beyond the O. **1476**
oracles
trustworthiness of o. **1123 b**
criticized by Oenomaus of Gadara
1260 a
o. explained by the interference of
demons **1319 c**
collected by Porph. **1445 g**
organism, organical unity
—s fortuitous combinations (Epic.) **808**
formation of —s **842**
The cosmos an organical unity, see
cosmos
outward things, outward conditions
(externals)
not needed for virtue **1022; 1035 b;
1036**
should not be cared for by the philosopher (Epict.) **1239; 1249** ff.
(later Cynics); **1264** (M. Aur.)
Epict. usually speaks of τὰ οὐκ ἐφ’
ἡμῖν **1232** ff.; but also of τὰ ἐκτός
× τὰ ἔσω, e.g. **1007 a; 1239 a b**
Plot.: τὰ ἄλλα or τὸ ἄλλο **1421**
See for Plot. also **1422-1423**
See also wise man s.v. wise

Pain
absence of p.=pleasure (Epic.) **860;
864**
In the Stoa, see πάθη
The attitude of the wise man towards
p., **1062 b** (Chrys.)
Seneca **1062 c**; also **1015 a** (tormentorum perpessio)
Panaetius **1166 c**
Posid.’ attitude towards p. **1171 b**
different reactions of individual men
1185
For Plotinus, see **1423** (the wise
man beyond outward things). Also
1414 (Does p. belong to the body
or to the soul?)

pantheism
For the Ancient Stoa, see **900-902**
Cleanthes? **943**; cp. **1196 a**
Posidonius? **1196**, esp. **b-d**
Seneca clearly not a pantheist **1221**
Neopythag. **1279 d**
For Plotinus see e.g. **1366** (clearly
no p.)
participation
natural law a p. of divine law **1076 c**
p. in the divine **1465** (Proclus)
grades of p. **1466 d**
For Plotinus see **1365 a; 1366-1369;
1370; 1401-1403**
The term μετέχειν occurs e.g. in **1401 b**
Plot. mostly speaks of εἰκών, μίμημα
and ἀρχέτυπον. See there
See also φῶς and φωτίζειν, πηγή and
ἐκρεῖ
passions, see πάθη
perception (αἴσθησις)
the basis of knowledge acc. to Epic.
822-828. See also πρόληψις
In the Stoa **984; 985-987; 990; 991**
See also κατάληψις, φαντασία, and
ἔννοια
The Stoic theory criticized by Arcesilaus **1102-1104**
by Carneades **1112**
p. analyzed by Plotinus **1378**, introd.;
1378 a
p. of the soul has nothing to do with
sense-impressions **1415**
sense-p. a kind of sleeping state of the
soul **1416 b**
perfectum (perfect tense) **970 a**
perpendiculum **835 a**. See also στάθμη
person, personality
By Panaetius called *propria natura*
(× natura communis) **1163**
In Plotinus: the higher soul of particular men **1373 a-c**
the inner man is the true self **1413**
Cp. **959 b**, l. 2 (mens cuiusque is est
quisque), with n. 3; **1265 c** (M.
Aur.)
Cp. ἡμεῖς, ἡμέτερον ἔργον **1425 a**;
οἰκεία φύσις **1430 c**, the end
Independence of the inner man from
outward things, see wise man s.v.
wise
For Plot. **1423, 1431 c** (the wise man
beyond the necessity of nature)

The individuality of the p. does not get lost ἐκεῖ: **1379 b**; **1380**

[Also *Enn.* IV 3, 5, l. 5-8: μένει ἕκαστον ἐν ἑτερότητι ἔχον τὸ αὐτὸ ὃ ἔστιν εἶναι.]

Porph.: ἐγὼ οὐχ ὁ ἁπτὸς οὗτος **1440 a** (c. 8, sec. al.)

See further the lemmata beginning by self-, such as self-knowledge, self-reflexion

See also man, virtue, ἦθος, προαίρεσις

For the social and religious side of human p. see κοινωνικός, πολιτικός, and religous

perversio

sin a p. naturae (διαστροφή) **1027**

perversion of reason **955 b**

phenomenism

the theoretical consequence of Pyrrho's view **1087 a**, under the text, sub (3)

Cp. Carneades' akatalepsia **1115**

Aenesidemus **1130-1132**

Menodotus and Sextus **1137-1142**

See also empiricism

philosophy

in the Hell.-Roman period **806**; **807**

ph. of life without scholarly pretentions (Epic.) **816**

φρόνησις φιλοσοφίας τιμιώτερον **872 b**

tripartition of ph. in the Stoa **897**; **898**

By Chrys. ph. called ἐπιτήδευσις λόγου ὀρθότητος **989 b**, small print; cp. **897 b**; **1215 c**

ph. the healing art of the soul **1060**

Scepticism a new ph.? **1081**

ph. of nature, see nature; also physics

a humanistic trend in ph., see humanitas and man

spiritualism in ph., see spiritualism

the aim of ph. according to Seneca **1207**

theoretical and practical ph. **1208**

ph. required for everybody (Musonius) **1227**

equally for men and women **1227 b**

defined as καλοκἀγαθίας ἐπιτήδευσις **1227 c**

first principles of ph. acc. to Epict. **1232**

character of M. Aur.' ph. **1262**, introd.

ph. of synthesis in the first centuries, ch. XXIV, introd. (p. 340)

number and mathematics in ph., see s.v. number and math.

a new element in ph. with Philo **1289**, introd.

Philo's appreciation of ph. **1289 b**

general character of Plut.' ph., p. 376, § 3, introd.

the part of ph. in gnosticism **1332 a**

in the Hermetica **1338**

in Numenius **1345 c**

Greek ph. versus mythology and popular religion **1411**; **1431-1432**

ph. (called dialectic) has to train man to virtue **1420 c**

ph. taken in the rational sense by Plot. and Porph., θεουργία preferred by Iambl. and later Neopl. **1446 c**

ph. promotes sympathy and mutual love (Iambl.) **1448 c**

ph. in Alexandria and Athens, 5th cent. **1455**, introd.

the end of Greek ph. **1479-1480**

physics

of Epicurus **829-844**

in the Stoa:

place of ph. in the system of phil. **897**; **898**

general principles **899-916**

God, providence, mantic **917-944**

soul and immortality **945-960**

Panaetius' interest in ph. **1151**

Posid. **1173-1182**; Seneca **1221**; M. Aur. **1267-1274**

Neopythag. phys. **1279**; **1280**; **1281**

See further nature

pleasure, see ἡδονή

pleroma

gnostic term for the spiritual world **1332 b**

described by Valentinus **1333 a**

plurality (πλῆθος)

how to explain p. (Plot.) **1364-1367**; **1370**; **1374**; **1382 c**

Whether p. is apostasy of the One **1398 b**, under the text

in the intelligible world always determined **1408 d**

Proclus: p. always participates of Unity **1458 a**; **1464 e**

See also s.v. quantity and ποσότης

pneuma

in the Ancient Stoa:

πνεῦμα διῆκον δι' ὅλου τοῦ κόσμου **902 a**

soul defined as π. ἔνθερμον **903 b**

the hegemonikon is p. **915 b**

soul is π. πως ἔχον **916 a**

the senses, voice and sperma are π. πως ἔχον **947 b**

the soul π. σύμφυτον **948 c**

πολυχρόνιον π. **957 a**

notion of God as π. νοερόν **995 a**

cp. Posid. **1196 b**; Cleom. **1177 a**

the definition of soul as π. ἔνθερμον found in Posid. **1192 a**

explained **1192 b-d**

Marc. Aur.: **1265 b** (πνευμάτιον for soul), **1271 a**

The Stoic p. theory with Neopythagoreans **1279 d**

Philo: **1295 a**, **1296 c**

In Valentinian gnosis p. is the instrument of spiritual knowledge; see **1336**. Also s.v. πνευματικοί

evil spirits called πνεύματα **1337 a b**

By Porph. p. is used frequently and can denote the ethereal or pneumatical body; see **1442 a**, with n. 1. Cp. **1356**, under the text. Also Procl. **1474 a**

See also s.v. body and ὄχημα

political

Epic.' attitude towards p. life compared with the Stoa **808**

the principle of avoiding p. life **879 d**

p. character of paideia in the Stoa **1045 a**

p. philosophy:

in the Stoa and of Cicero **1065-1075**

Plotinus' interest in politics **1361**

polytheism

in the Ancient Stoa **923**; in Seneca **924**

defended by Ocellus **1282** (some comments under the text)

Cp. e.g. Max. Tyr. **1330 a e**; Apuleius **1331 a**

Valentinus **1333 a**, with n. 3

Numenius **1345 c**; **1349-1352**

Plotinus defends p. explicitly **1411 a**

Cp. **1428 a**

Porph. **1442 a**; Iambl. **1451 b**; Procl. **1464**; **1472 a**

poor

the life of the p. **1255 a-c**

powers (δυνάμεις)

in Philo: ἀόρατοι δ. **1303 a**

conducted by the Logos **1303 b**

called angels **1304 a**

ψυχαὶ ἀσώματοι **1304 b**

in the *Poimandres*: innumerable p. in the Light **1339 c**

Plotinus: immense p. in the noûs **1426 b**

boundless p. **1428 a**

the —s in Noûs identified with the Ideas **1428 b**

the absolute p. of the First Principle **1398 b**; **1428 c**

this p. propagates itself throughout divine Nature **1365 a** (δύναμις ἄφατος) **1401 a**; **1428 d**

the —s of the sensible world **1428 e**

δ. ἄλογος **1428 f**; some comments under the text

praesens (present tense) **970 b**

prayer

of Cleanthes **943**; **944 c**

of Epict. see e.g. **929 a** (a hymn of praise), **1244**; **1245 a d**

For Seneca cp. **960 d**, under the text; **1215 c**; **1222**

Plut. **1312 c**; the *Poimandres* **1343** (a hymn); Numenius **1349 a**

Plotinus:

spiritual p., e.g. **1366** (εὔχεσθαι μόνους πρὸς μόνον)

formal p. (its influence explained by an automatical process) **1431 d**; **1432 a** l. 27

moral conditions of p. (Porph.) **1440 d** (the end); a p. of Proclus **1472 a**

preferential

(„le type préférentiel") in Stoic logic **977**

principle (ἀρχή),

principles (ἀρχαί)

In Epic.: τὰς —ᾰς ἀτόμους σωμάτων φύσεις **829 a** (the end)

ἡδονή is ἀ. καὶ τέλος **859**; **860**

In the Stoa: two —αἱ τῶν ὅλων **899 a**; ἀσώματοι **899 b**

the —αί of virtues **1026 c**

purification
ritualistic (διὰ καθαρμῶν) **1279 f**
moral (κάθαρσις) in Plot. and Porph.
condition to higher virtue **1419 a b**
the virtues themselves are —εις
1420 b; Porph. **1439**
Proclus **1474 a**
Pythagoreanism
the revival of P. **1279 ff.**

Quality (τὸ ποιόν, ποιότης)
Epic.: the atoms do not possess any
—ies except shape, weight and
size ·**831 a**
Zeno: —ies mix together as substances do **913 a**
the —ies of the soul are bodies **914 a**
προσηγορία defined as indicating a
common q. **967**
q. (τὸ ποιόν) admitted as a category
915 a
equilibrium of opposite —ies **1279 b**
(with comments); cp. **1306 b**
quantity (τὸ ποσόν, ποσότης)
Epic.: pleasure must be selected
according to q. **862 c**
In the Stoa: q. not admitted as a
category **915 a**
q. (ποσότης) term used by Moderatus
to indicate the principle of multiplicity **1285 b** = ἄπειρον and ὕλη
νοητή in Plotinus. See s.v. ἄπειρον
and ὕλη
absolute and relative q. **1288 a**
quantitative ("le type quantitatif")
propositions **977**

Radiation
of the divine Light (First Principle -
Noûs - Soul) see φῶς.
Also creation
ratio, the Lat. term for λόγος
the proprium of man **1001 c**; **1002**;
1013 a; **1157**
pars divini spiritus **1015**;
nullum bonum sine —ne, ib.
the unity of virtue founded on the
unity of r. **1028**
=lex recta, naturae congruens **1066 c**
does the cosmos possess r.? **1117 a**
appetitus oboediens —ni **1155 b**
ira non exaudit —nem **1214 a**

cum r. suadet finire se **1224 a**
ea pars philosophiae quae est in —ne
et in disserendo **1200 a**
reality
grades of r., see hierarchy of being
s.v. being
reason (λόγος, ratio)
see s.v. logos, λόγος and ratio; also
s.v. nature
obedience to r. condition for a happy
life, see s.v. happiness, virtue and
wise (man)
r. the basis of morality, see s.v.
bonum, morality, and virtue
r. and revelation in Philo **1289**, introd.
recordatio, see memory
redemption
by Christ through the gift of gnosis
1332 b, sub 4
regeneration
of the universe after the conflagration
905; **907**; **908**; **1273** (M. Aur.)
reincarnation
the doctrine of r. found in Tim. Locr.
1283; in Plut. **1318 a**; **1319 c**
explained by Proclus **1474 c**
religion
Epic.' attitude towards popular r.
845, introd.
of the Stoa, see allegorical interpretation s.v. allegorical
on the cosmic r. of the Stoa, see **805**
sub (2), and especially **943**; **944**;
also **1262 e**; **1269 c**
the part of r. in Gnosis **1332 a**
in the Hermetica **1338**
in Numenius **1345 c**
Plotinus' attitude towards popular
r. may be seen in his reaction
against the gnostics **1411**; **1420 d**;
1424
Porph. **1440 d e**; Procl. **1456**
See further God, gods, monotheism,
and polytheism
religious
For the r. character of the Stoa, see
esp. **943**; **944**; also **1045 b**
r. character of Posid.' philosophy
1192-1196
Was Seneca a r. man? **1222**; cp.
1215 c: incipis deorum socius esse,
non supplex

punishment of —s (Plut.) **1192 d**; **1315-1317**

acc. to Tim. Locr. **1283**

By Philo ascribed to subordinate powers **1297**

By Plot. s. ascribed to what is inferior to soul **1417 a**

only the soul with "additions" can sin **1417 b**

Porph.: the body not the cause of s. **1440 f** (but cp. Plot. **1377 a**: soul in a body does not sin by necessity)

Iambl.: the soul sins by free will and is therefore not without s. **1453 a**

Procl.: not matter, but the soul itself is the cause of s. **1470 c d**

size (μέγεθος)

Epic.' atoms differ by s. **831 a**

slave

defined by Chrys. **1071 b**

nobody a s. by nature **1071 c**

social

Epic.: man not naturally a social being (κοινωνικόν) **879 c**

the Stoa: see oikeiosis. Also s.v. political

the s. character of Stoic phil. is clearly seen in Cicero **1065-1075**

s. virtues ranked higher than theoretical **1075 b**; cp. **1159**

and in Marc. Aur.: **1262**; **1276 b**

the Spirit of the whole (the Logos) is "social" **1268 b**

Man an organical part of the whole **1272 a**

Social virtues, see πολιτικός

societas

humani generis **1000 b**; **1001 a c**. See also civitas

somnium

the S. Scipionis **959 b** (with some comments and bibliogr.)

soritai **1121**

sorrow, see λύπη and suffering

soul

Epic.: the s. a body consisting of fine atoms **843**

The Stoa: s. is fire or pneuma **903 a**

πνεῦμα ἔνθερμον **903 b**

consitus spiritus **903 c**; πνεῦμά πως ἔχον **916 a**

s. is "cooled pneuma" **916 a**, under

the text, with n. 1; **957** (introd.)

M. Aur.: s. originates from the Logos spermatikos and returns to it **919 d**

the parts or faculties of s. **947**; see also hegemonikon

Chrys.' theory of ἑτεροίωσις τῆς ψυχῆς **951**

no irrational part in man **952-956**

the s. not immortal acc. to Ancient Stoics **957**

not immortal acc. to Panaetius **958**

Posid. believes in celestial immortality **959**; cp. **1192**

Seneca **960**; **1223 b-c**

An irrational part in the s. admitted by Panaet. **1155**

by Posid. **1184 b**; **1185-1190**

Intellectual interpretation of passions by Epict. **1238**

S. defined as ἰδέα τοῦ πάντη διαστατοῦ **1193 a**

Intellectual interpretation of passions by Epict. **1238**

S. (the inner man) a part of God **1244** (frequently called νοῦς or ἡγεμονικόν)

the tripartition body, s., spirit **1265 b** (M. Aur.)

—s or daemons in the air **1279 e**; **1280 c**; **1283**; **1304**; **1318 b**; **1331 c**

s. a harmony (Moderatus) **1286**

The s. of man a copy of the Logos **1298** (Philo)

the world-soul **1303 a** (l. 23). Cp. **1327 d** (Albinus)

Two principles present in the soul of man (Plut.) **1314 d**

Noûs superior to s. **1319 a**; —s on the moon **1319 b**

the soul's immortality maintained by Atticus against Ar. **1325 e**

In Gnosis s. the lower level under the pleroma (Valentinus) **1334 d**

Cp. the term ψυχικοί

ψ. in the hymn of Valentinus **1336**

in Basilides **1336 b**

in the Chald. oracles **1336 c**

The s. of man drawn down by the body (Herm.) **1344** (some comments under the text)

Numenius: work Π. ἀφθαρσίας —ῆς **1345 c**

identified with virtue **1031 a**; with eudaimonia **1105**

explained by Chrys.' successors **1144**; by Panaetius **1156**; **1157**; by Posid. **1188 c d**; by Antiochus **1201-1205**; by Seneca **1215 c** pleasure cannot be the t. (Epict.) **1240 a**

temperantia
defined by Panaetius **1161**. See further virtues

tempora
the system of t. created by Stoics **970**

theodicy, see s.v. evil

theology, see s.v. God, gods

theurgy, see θεουργία

thinking
intuitive, not discursive **1383 a**
primary **1383 d**

tide
explained by Posid. **1177 b**

time
defined by Epic. **839**; infinite t. does not increase pleasure (Epic.) **870**
in the Stoa
virtue not increased by t. **1036**
passions soothed by t. **1189 b**; cp. **1185 c**
in Plut. **1312 b**
T. analyzed and defined by Plot. **1434 a** distention of the soul **1435 a** engendered together with the sensible universe **1435 b**
For Proclus see **1469 b**, **1474 b**

transcendentalism
extreme t. of ps.-Archytas **1281 b** (remark under the text)
cp. s.v. God: the notion of God from Philo onwards
also First Principle s.v. principle

truth
standard of t. see criterium

Universalism **805**, sub (2)
universe
the u.: κόσμος, τὰ ὅλα, τὸ ὅλον, τὸ πᾶν; universum, frequently in Stoic writers; in Plot. τὰ πάντα
E.g. M. Aur.: everyone has his function in the u. **1267**
imperfection in the u. **1270**
Neopyth.: the u. is imperishable **1280**

Philo: the Logos a bond of the u. **1306**; Plut.: the u. does not float reasonless and ungoverned **1314 a**
Plotinus: πάντα, not πᾶν **1425 a** (the Stoic conception criticized)
the laws of the u. **1431 a**
one living being **1431 b**
See also s.v. cosmos, universum, ὅλα, πᾶν

universum
in Seneca e.g. **918 d**; **928**; **1221 c**
See further cosmos and universe

Vibration (παλμός)
interior v. of a compound body (Epic.) **837**

vice, see κακία. Also s.v. sin

virtue (ἀρετή)
By Epic. subordinated to pleasure **808**, sub 1; **873**
nothing in itself **873 b**; **875** (based on social contract), **876**
the correlate of pleasure **874**
In the Stoa:
—s are bodies **914**; animals do not share in v. and vice **1001 b**
living acc. to nature (reason) **1003-1011**; **1013 a**
v. the only good **1012**; implies freedom **1013 b**, and happiness **1013 c**; autarkeia of v. **1014**; **1022**; no degrees **1015**; the intention is essential **1016**; defined as ὄφελος (ὠφέλεια) **1017 a**; a natural perfection **1017 b**; absolute character of v. **1017 c d**
perfectio naturae **1003** n. 1 (the precedents); **1023**
not a ἕξις but a διάθεσις **1024**
natural aptitude for v. **1025**; **1026**
the unity of v. **1028 a**; **1031**; the four main —s **1028 b**
Cleanthes' definition **1029 a**
Chrysippus' definition **1030**
v. cannot be lost **1032**
καθήκοντα and κατορθώματα **1033-1037**
v. not increased by duration **1036**
no medium between v. and vice **1038**
the wise man possesses all —s **1043 b**
the katorthoma a commandment of law **1068**

For Pyrrho v. = indifferentism **1088 c**, under the text

Carn. attacks the idea of v. as a perfection of nature **1125-1128**

By Panaetius —s are founded on natural strivings **1157**
the —s described **1158-1162**
the autarchy of v. abandoned **1165**

Antiochus: the germ of v. must be developed by personal energy **1204**
justice the leading v. **1205**

Seneca: the cult of v. is true religion **1209**
v. cannot be increased **1212 a b**
inner character of v. **1217**

Epict.: aidoos and pistis are cardinal —s **1240**

Philo: higher and lower —s **1297 b**

Plotinus: Is v. κάθαρσις? **1419 a b**;
a spiritualized state of the soul **1419 d**
higher and lower —s **1420 a b**
dialectic a training to v. **1420 c**
no cult of God without v. **1420 d**

Porph.' classification of —s **1439**
v. the only way to God **1440 c**

Procl. ranked θεουργικὴ ἀρετή higher than θεωρητική **1456 b**

vis
v. vitalis (Posid.) **1176**; **1192**

visum, Lat. term for φαντασία **985 a b**

vitalism
of Zeno **808**, sub (2); cp. **899-916** (the term ζωτικὴ δύναμις does not occur)
of Posid. **1176** (with notes); **1192**

vitium
defined as quod contra naturam est **1003** n. 1 (p. 132)
identified with inconstantia **1006**, introd.

void
τὸ κενόν (Epic.) **829 b**

voluntas, see will

voluptas, see ἡδονή

Weight
of Epic.' atoms **831 a b**

will
in the Stoa:
virtue essentially a question of the w. (intention) **1016**; **1217**

velle, θέλειν, βούλεσθαι **1006**; **1007**; **1008 a**; **1009**
nihil invitum (in the life of the wise man) **1010 a**; voluntas **1011 b**
voluntary surrender to the w. of God **943**; **944 b c** (Cleanthes); **1011 a** (Chrys.); **1245** (Epict.); **1267** (Marc. Aur.)
the part of the w. in wisdom **1215 a**
in moral progress **1216**
virtue a question of the will (inner man, *mens*) **1035**; **1037**; **1217**
See also προαίρεσις (deliberate choice)
w. of the First Noûs (Albinus) **1327 d**, **1329 b**

in Plotinus:
of the One **1393 b**
free w. of man **1418 a b**; **1425**; **1430-1432**

Iambl.:
man sins by free w. (προαίρεσις) **1453 a**

Procl.:
ad deterius impetus et appetitus **1470 d**
free w. maintained against ἀνάγκη **1473 b**

wise (sapiens, σοφός, σπουδαῖος)
the ideal of the w. man in the Stoa **1038-1050**; **1062**
only the w. man possesses ἐπιστήμη **985 b**; **1042**; **1043 a**
and virtue **1042**; **1043 b**
he is ἀπαθής **1062**
The Stoic conception of the w. man criticized **1050**; **1103**; **1112 a**
Pyrrho's ideal of the w. man **1084 b**
Plotinus **1423**
See also sapientia, σοφός and σπουδαῖος

women
in the School of Epic. **813 a b**
in the School of Musonius **1227**
in the School and house of Plot. **1360 a b**
Cp. Porph.' letter to his wife **1440**
Hypatia head of the School of Alexandria **1455**, introd.
For the appreciation of women, see e.g. **1147 b**: the wife a most important help to her husband (Antipater)

and **1324 d**: a man should share his spiritual life with his wife (Plut.)
See also marriage and love

world
see cosmos and universe

the inhabited w. (ἡ οἰκουμένη) **1174**

Zones
Posid.' theory of the five z. **1173**
zoöphyta, **1182 b**

III—GREEK WORDS

'Αγαθόν
Epic.: ἡδονή the πρῶτον —, **862 a**
The pleasure of the body the root of all —, **863**
πᾶν — ἐν αἰσθήσει, **865 b**
In the Stoa:
— defined, **1017**; the προηγμένον not an —, **1020 a**, cp. **1023 a**, **1028 a**, **1034 b**, **1234 a**
the field of morals indicated as περὶ —ῶν κ. κακῶν, **1066 d**, **1185 a**, **1191 b**, **1252 a**, **1262 a**
ἀνθρώπεια — ά, **1259 c**
the essence of the — is προαίρεσις ποιά, **1236 a**
οἱ —οί, **1254 b**
Philo distinguishes between πρεσβύτερα and νεώτερα —ά, **1297 b**
Numenius wrote a work Π. τἀγαθοῦ, **1348**, cp. **1350 a**
Plotinus:
the — not a predicate, **1394 a**; not a primary genus, **1394 b**; a hierarchy of —α, **1394 c**
the — is the Light, **1395**; beyond beauty **1396**
ἀγαθοποιόν **1281 a**
ἄγαλμα
Plot.: νοῦς an —, **1366** (l. 14), **1382 b**, sm. pr.
the sensible world an —, **1403 a** (l. 15)
ἄγγελοι, see angels
ἀγλαΐα
Plot.: the — in noûs, **1385 b** (l. 12), **1395 a** (l. 6)
ἡ ἐκεῖ —, **1399 a** (l. 18)
of the sensible world, **1401 c** (l. 7)
Cp. **1348** (Num.)
ἁγνεία
defined, **1063 b**
ἀγωγεύς
God called the — of sun and moon **1303 c** (small print, under the text)

ἀδελφός
the fellow-man called —, **1242**, **1243**
Sun and stars **1411 b**
ἄδηλα
τὰ —, **829 a**
proof is an ἄδηλον (ap. Sext. Emp.) **1114**
τὰ φύσει ἀ., **1142**
ἀδιάφορα
the Stoic doctrine of —, **1012 b c**, **1018-1022**, **1030 b**, **1034 b**, **1050 a**; (Pyrrho) **1087 a**, **1088 b**
ἀδιαφορία **1084 a**
ἀδικία
not an evil in itself (Epic.), **875 c**
mentioned among κακά in the Stoa, **1012 b**
Plot.: What about the — in the world? **1430**
ἀήρ
frequently mentioned as one of the elements
distinguished from αἰθήρ and full of mortal living beings, **1279 c e**, **1304 a**; by Philo identified with the Jacob's ladder **1304 b**; Basilides **1336 b**
ἀθανασία
τοῦ κόσμου, **1404 a**
ἄθροισμα (also written ἄθροισμα), see compound body, s.v. body
ἀίδιος **1461 e** (49)
αἰδώς
defined, **1063 b**
one of the cardinal virtues acc. to Epic., **1233 a**, **1240 a**; cp. **1241 c** (τὸν αἰδήμονα)
αἰθήρ
ἡγεμονικὸν τοῦ κόσμου acc. to Antipater, **1196 a**
noûs feeds on — (=anima tenuis) **1192 c**

feeds the heavenly bodies, **1279 c**, under the text
cp. the tripartition οὐρανός, γῆ, μετάρσιον mentioned under **1280 c**
Basilides, **1336 b**

αἵρεσις
in Epic.: **862 a, 872 b**
in the Stoa:
— κ. φυγή, e.g. **1030 b**
ap. Sext. Emp., **1105**
—έσεις κ. ἐκκλίσεις, e.g. **1029 a**
in the sense of School, e.g. **1073 b, 1137 a b**

αἱρετέος
virtues are αἱρετέα, e.g. **1028 a**
Also αἱρετά × φευκτά

αἴσθησις
in Epic.: **827 b, 828**
πᾶν ἀγαθὸν κ. κακὸν ἐν αἰσθήσει **865 b**
in the Stoa: **984, 985 a**, n. 1, **991, 1003 a, 1039 b, 1095, 1176 d, 1265 b**
Plot.: What is —?, **1415, 1416**
See also perception

αἰσθήσεις **823, 829**
See also sense-impressions and senses. The latter are also called τὰ αἰσθητήρια, e.g. **947 b**

αἰσθητά
in Epic.: **822**
in the Stoa: **990, 1057**
Aenesidemus: **1130, 1135 a**
with Neopythag.: τὰ — σώματα **1279 a**
in Numenius **1349 a**
in Plotinus: τὸ —όν the final term of creation, **1401 a**

αἰσθητικόν
when acquired by the soul in its descent? **1356 b**

αἰτία
the form is — (ps.-Archytas), **1281 a**
— πρὸ —ας, **1281 b**
Num. speaks of a first and a second αἴτιον, **1349 a**
See also cause

αἴτιος
ὁ — τοῦ εἶναι, **1408 e**

αἰτιῶδες
term in Stoic grammar and logic, **977**

αἰών
1273 c (M. Aur.), **1280 a** (Ocellus), **1312 c** (Plut.)
in Valentinus: **1333 a- c**
defined by Plot., **1433**
Cp. **1383 a**, l. 17 ff.

ἀκαταληψία **1077 a, 1082 a, 1115**
ἀκατάληπτος (-λημπτος), **1197 a**

ἀκοή
explained by Chrys., **947 b, 948 c**

ἀκολασία **1012 b, 122**

ἀκολουθία
in the universe, **1302 b, 1309 a, 1429 a, 1473 b**
In logic **1430 c** (l. 17)
See also ἐπακολούθησις

ἀκόλουθος
τὸ —ν (constantia), **1033 a**

ἀλαμπία
of ὕλη, **1288 c**

ἀλγεῖν **860, 872 b, 1062 b**
τὸ ἀλγοῦν, **864 a b, 869, 872 a**

ἀλγηδών, ἄλγος
in Epic.: **826 a, 862 b, 880 c**
Plotinus: **1422, 1423 a**
See also dolor and pain.

ἀλήθεια
one of the four principles of Porph., **1440 e**
ἡ περὶ τοῦ παντός (Iambl.), **1448 a**

ἀλλοτρίωσις
the opp. of οἰκείωσις, **999 c**, sm. pr.; **1057**

ἀλογία **1061 a, 1441, 1453 a**

ἄλογος
ἀ. κίνησις τῆς ψυχῆς, **1051 a b**, cp. **1058 c**
τὸ —ν τῆς ψυχῆς, **1053 a, 1055, 1056 b**
— ζωή, **1469 c** (209), **1474 a**
incarnation of souls into —α, **1474 c**
See also irrational, and animal

ἁμάρτημα, see sin
ἀμέθεκτος, see s.v. μεθεκτός

ἀμέριστος
τὸ —ν, **1374 c**
See also s.v. μεριστόν

ἄμεσα **1114**, under the text

ἀμετάβλητος
of Epic.' atoms, **829 a**
in Plut. (of God) the notion is circumscribed, e.g. **1312 b**
also **1313 b** (μεταβολῆς κρεῖττον)

ἀρετή, see virtue
ἄρθρον
  (grammatical term in the Stoa), **967**
ἀριθμός, see number
ἁρμονία **1279 f, 1281 a**
  — μαθηματική, **1286**
  = the celestial spheres, **1341 b, 1342 b**
  τὴν ὕλην —ᾳ συνδησάμενος, **1351**
  μία — καὶ τάξις in the universe, **1431 b**
ἄρνησις **1077**
ἀρνητικός **976**
ἀρρενόθηλυς (or ἀρσενόθηλυς)
  μονὰς —, **1288 c** (with some comments)
  Valentinus' aeons, **1333 a**
  Νοῦς —, **1340 a**
ἀρρεψία
  in Sceptical terminology, **1087 c**
ἄρρητον
  the First Principle as —, **1281 b**
  (comm. under the text)
  1327 a d e (Albinus), **1330 c** (Max. Tyr.), **1449 a** (Iambl.)
  Procl. **1464 i**
  cp. **1476-1477** (Damasc.)
  Cp. Plotinus **1392 b - d, 1394**
ἀρρώστημα **1185 a**. See also disease
ἀρχάγγελοι
  the highest of the good demons (Porph.), **1442 a**, under the text
  [By Philo the Logos is sometimes called —ος; not in this vol.]
ἀρχέτυπος
  Philo: — ἰδέα **1293 a**; σφραγίς **1293 d**; νοῦς **1296 a**; αὐγή **1300 c**
  τὸ —ν εἶδος (*Poim.*), **1339 c**
  the —α of all things in Νοῦς (Plot.), **1369 c**
  See also **1366 a** (l. 33), **1372 b** (l. 35), **1401 c** (l. 15 ff.), **1408 c** (l. 22), **1426 a** (l. 25)
ἀρχή, see principle
ἄσκησις **1187 b, 1228, 1253**, introd.
  See also asceticism, askesis
ἀστάθμητα **1087 a**
ἀσχημάτιστον
  (of ὕλη), **1285 b**
ἀσώματος
  Acc. to Epic. only the void is —ν, **843 c**
  in the Stoa: the ἀρχαί are —οι, **899 b**
  Moderatus: —α εἴδη, **1285 a**
  Numenius: τὸ —ν, **1347 b**

Plotinus: ὕλη is an —ν, **1409 a**
ἄτακτος
  τὰ —α κ. ἀόριστα, Ps.-Archytas, **1281 a**
  cp. Numenius, **1347 b**
ἀταραξία
  Epic.: **852, 860, 880**
  Seneca: (*animus impatiens*), **1062 c**
  Epict.: **1233 a**
  Pyrrho: **1084 b**, 10 7 a
  Arcesilaus: **1098**
ἄτομα
  Epic.: **829** ff.
  Aenesidemus' criticism of Epic.' theory, **1131**
  Marc. Aur., **1269, 1271**
αὐγή
  ἀρχέτυπος —, **1300 c, 1310 b**
αὐθάδεια **1411 a**, l. 55
αὐθυπόστατα
  Proclus' doctrine of self-constituted principles, **1461, 1468 c**
αὐτάρκεια, αὐτάρκης
  acc. to Epic., **814 c, 872 a**
  in the Stoa: the — of virtue, **1014**, cp. **1022**
  In Cynicism, **1253**, introd.
  Plotinus: the — of spiritual life, **1421**, the end, **1422, 1423**
αὐτεξούσιος
  944 b (Hippolytus)
  in Valentinian gnosis: only the ψυχικοί are —οι, **1332 b**, sub 3, **1335 a**
  Plot. **1377 a, 1430 c**; the end
αὐτοπάτωρ
  in Valentinus **1333 a**
  in Iambl. *De Myst.*, **1449 c**
ἀφασία **1087 a**
ἀφή
  defined by Chrysippus, **947 b, 948 c**
ἀφθαρσία
  τοῦ κόσμου, **1290 a**, n. 1
  See also ἀνώλεθρος
  περὶ —ς ψυχῆς (Num.), **1345 b**
ἄφθαρτος **1461 e** (46), **1468 b** (187)
ἀφοβία
  mentioned by Epict. among the prerogatives of the "free" man, **1233 a**
ἀφορμή
  1019 c (sm. pr.), **1025, 1137 a, 1156**

earth a prison and —οἱ ἀλιτρῶν σωμάτων, **1330 e**

Plotinus:
—οἱ τοῦ σώματος, **1375 c** (l. 22 ff.)
soul παντὸς —οῦ κρείττων, **1404 b**

Porph.:
— ψυχῆς, **1441** (init.)

δεύτερος, θεός,
Philo: the Logos a second God, **1300 c**, sm. pr., **1301 a**, with sm. pr., **1301 b**, **1305 a b**, **1306 b d**
Cp. Plut. **1320**; Albinus, **1326 b**; Herm. **1340**; Num. **1349**, **1352 a**; Plot. **1382 d**
δευτέρα φύσις, **1382 a**, **1426 b**, **1429 a**
τὰ δεύτερα, (secondary beings), **1464 h i**, **1472 b** (Proclus)

δημιουργός
God — τοῦ ὅλου, **899 a** (δημιουργεῖν)
Cp. **911 a**: *artifex universitatis*. See further Demiurge
Nemesius: **1181 b**
Philo: **1297 a**, **1303 a**, **1304 a**, **1305 a**
Albinus: **1327 d**, **1328**
Max. Tyr.: **1330 e**
Gnostics: **1332 b**, **1334 c e**, **1336 a**, **1337 b**
Herm.: **1340 a b**
Numenius: **1349 b c**, **1350 a b**, **1351**, **1352**
Plotinus:
νοῦς —, **1402 b** (l. 15)
cp. **1405 b** (ἡ δημιουργουμένη ὕλη, l. 24)
Iambl.: **1451 b c**

διάθεσις
virtue a — of the hegemonikon, **986 d**, **1005 a**, **1024**, **1033**, **1040 b**, **1053 b**, **1135 a**

διαιτητής
—αἱ λόγοι (Philo), **1306 c**

διαλεκτική
acc. to Zeno linked with rhetoric, **964 a**
cultivated by Arcesilaus, **1096 b**
later Sceptics dislike —, **1141**
in Plotinus: — a training to virtue, **1420 c**

διάλεκτος
defined in the Stoa, **966**

διάνοια
in Epic.: **869**

in the Stoa: **949 a b**, **951 c**, **953 a**, **963**, **966**, **986 d**, **990** (small print), **991**, **992 b**, **1053 b**, **1263 b** (small print), **1266 b**
Philo: **1296 c**, the end.
in Plotinus: as a purely intellectual function opposed to αἴσθησις, **1415 b**. [Elsewhere distinguished from noûs which is intuitive thinking]

διαστροφή
—αἱ τοῦ λόγου, **955 a**
(*perversio naturae*), **1027**
See also s.v. sin

διαφωνία
the first trope of Agrippa: ὁ ἀπὸ —ας, **1136 a**
πόλεμος καὶ — (in the cosmos), **1330 a**

διεζευγμένον
disjunctive, **977**

δικαιοσύνη (also: τὸ δίκαιον)
in Epic.: **875 a b**
in the Anc. Stoa: **914 c**, **1012 b**, **1028 b c**, **1029 a** (def. by Cleanthes), **1030** (def. by Chrys.), **1050**, **1065**, **1066**, **1073**
Carneades' disputation on —, **1111 a**, — not based on nature, **1125-1128**
Panaetius: **1159**
Antiochus of Ascalon: **1205 a**
Bion: **1249 b**
Plotinus: **1420 a**
Porph.: **1439**

δόγμα
our —τα about things (judgments) decisive in life (Epict.), **1237**

δόξα
the problem of ψευδὴς —, **828** (under the text)
λύπη defined as — πρόσφατος (Chrys.), **955**, **1061 a** (under the text), **1185 c**
λατρεία δοξῶν (Timon), **1085 a**
— defined by Arcesilaus, **1103 b**
the tenet that πάθη are δόξαι rejected by Posid., **1185**, esp. **c**
Chrysippus' theory criticized by Plotinus, **1414 b**

δοξάζω
"οὐ δοξάσει ὁ σοφός", **1043 a**
criticized, **1103 b**

δοξαστά

αἰσθητὰ κ. —, **1288 a**

δοῦλος

the non-philosophical man called — by Epict., **1013 b**

Cp. **1243 a** (ἀνδράποδον)

Opp. to ἐλεύθερος

See also slave

δυάς

ἀόριστος —, **1279 a**, **1285 a**, **1314 c**; **1349 a**, **1353 a**, with n. 2 and 3; **1408 e** (with comments)

δυνάμεις, see powers

Ἑβδομάς

a νοερὰ ἑβδομάς (Procl.), **1451 b**

ἐγκόσμιος **1466 d**, **1467 a**, **1469 a**

ἐγκράτεια, ἐγκρατής **1029 a**, **1190**, **1289 b**

ἐγκύκλια

declined by Epic., **879 d**

relation to phil. acc. to Philo, **1289 b**

See also learning and παιδεία

ἐγώ

εἶμι ὁ ὤν, **1292**

οὐχ ὁ ἁπτὸς οὗτος, **1440 a** (c. 8, sec. al.)

εἶδος, see ἰδέα

εἰδητικός

—ὰ μέτρα, **1285 b**, with n. 1

εἴδωλον

—α (*imagines*) explaining the human notion of gods (Epic.), **827 b**, sm. pr., **849**

in Plotinus:

αἴσθησις κ. φύσις an εἴδωλον of soul, **1370 a**

ὕλη an εἴδωλον of soul, **1402 c**, **1408 c**

— καὶ φάντασμα ὄγκου, **1409 a** (c. 7, l. 13)

—α ἐν εἰδώλῳ, ib., l. 24

τῶν ὄντων μιμήματα καὶ —α, l. 28 — οὐκ ἀληθές, **1409 a**

ὕλη an — ὡς πρὸς τὰ ὄντα, **1410 b**, l. 37

εἰκών

in Philo:

the sensible world a μίμημα θείας εἰκόνος, **1293 d**

the invisible light an — of the Logos, **1295 b**

man created κατ' —όνχ θεοῦ, **1296**

the εἶδος in sensible things an — τελείου λόγου, **1302 a**

Plut.:

— οὐσίας ἡ γένεσις, **1313 a**

Horus an — of the intelligible world, **1313 b**; cp. **1314 d**

αἰσθηταὶ —όνες, **1318 b**

Herm.:

the archetypal man an — τοῦ πατρός, **1341 a**

οὗ πᾶσα φύσις —, **1343**

Plotinus:

— οἷον ἀρχετύπων, **1366** (l. 33), **1369 a** (l. 15)

soul an — of noûs, **1381 b** (l. 7)

the sensible world an — of its Father, **1401 c** (l. 10)

an — ἀεὶ εἰκονιζόμενος, **1402 b**

time and —, **1434 c**

εἱμαρμένη (*fatum*)

in Epicurean texts: **834 a** (Diog. Oen.), **835 a** (Cic. on Epic.' doctrine)

in the Stoa:

ἡ πολυθρύλητος αὐτοῖς —, **912 c**

— = Zeus, **918**, **919 a**; θεός, νοῦς, **920 a**

κινητικὴ τῆς ὕλης, **927 a**

Posid.' conception of — differs from the Ancient Stoic one, **1196 d**

On πρόνοια and — in later Antiquity: **1279 d** (with some comments under the text), a.o. passages cited under "fate and providence" s.v. *Fate*

in Philo: **1302 b**, **1303 a**

Herm. **1340 a**

in Plot.: **1413 b**, **1425 a**

See also Fate

εἶναι (εἶ)

only to be said of God (Philo), **1292**

cp. **1303 b**: ὁ ἔστιν ἀψευδῶς

Plut. **1312 a**

a gift of grace (Plot.), **1401 b** (l. 23)

ἐκεῖ

τὰ — (= τὰ νοητά), **1403 b**

τὸ — ζῆν, **1400 a**

— ἅμα πάντα, **1406 a** (l. 13)

ὁ — κόσμος, **1406 e**

opposed to the soul and its virtues, **1420 b**

to the sensible world, **1427 a**
ἡ δύναμις ἡ —, **1428 a**, the end
ἡ ζωὴ ἡ —, **1434 c** (l. 48)
ἐκλάμπειν **1365 c**, **1449 c**
ἔκλαμψις **1427 b**
ἐκλογή
τῶν κατὰ φύσιν, **999**, **1004**, **1034 b**,
1144
ἐκμαγεῖον **1280 b**, **1294**, **1302 a**, **1326 a**
ἐκπύρωσις
the ancient Stoic doctrine of —, **905 a**,
907, **925 b**, **938**, **957 c**
the theory abandoned by Diog. Bab.,
1143 a
and by Panaetius, **1151 b**
restored by Posid., **1178**
ἐκρεῖ, see ἐξερρύη
ἔκστασις
in Philo: **1310 d**
By Plotinus the term — is used once
only in the sense of ἐνθουσιασμός:
Enn. VI 9, 11, l. 23 (not in this vol.)
ἐκτός
τὰ —, term frequently used by Epict.,
e.g. **1236 a**, **1239**
M. Aur., **1264 a**
See also outward things
ἔλεος **953 b**, **1044 b**
Cp. **1064 b** (*misericordia*)
ἐλευθερία
characteristic of the wise man in the
Stoa: **1044 a**, **1046 a**
frequently found in Epict., e.g.
1233 a (the end), **1245 a**
of Demonax, **1257 a**
ἐλεύθερος
—α κίνησις (of the atoms), **833 a**
in the Stoa: μόνον τὸν σοφὸν —ν,
e.g. **1044 a**
ἐλλάμπειν **1404 c d**, **1466 d**, **1467 a**
ἔλλαμψις **1464 b**
ἔλλειψις, evil defined as — (Plot.),
1410 c d
ἑλληνισμός **968**
ἐλπίς **1440 e f**
ἐμπειρία **991**, **1004**
ἐμπειρικός
ἡ —ἡ αἵρεσις, **1137 a**
defined, **1137 b**
ἕν, see One
ἑνάς (-άδες), **1464 b c**, **1465 a** (139),
1466 b d

ἐνδιάθεσις
ὁ κατὰ —ν λόγος, **991**
Also λόγος ἐνδιάθετος. See logos
In Philo: **1307**
ἐνέργεια
in Plotinus:
the One is —, **1393 a**, l. 22-25
— ἄνευ οὐσίας, **1398 a**
noûs is —, **1385 b**, l. 25
τὸ ὄν is —, **1385 ι**, l. 15
spiritual life is νοῦ —, **1400 a**, l. 17
διάνοια is —, **1415 b**, l. 21
αἰσθήσεις are —αι, **1415 c**
the essence of soul is —, **1416 a**, l. 42
πᾶσα ζωὴ —, **1427 b**, l. 17 sq.
ἡ τοῦ παντὸς —, **1431 b**, l. 15
time an — of soul, **1435 b**
ἐνέργημα **1033**, **1034**
ἐννόημα **991**, **992**. See also ἔννοια
ἔννοια
in the Stoa: the notion of God a
κοινὴ —, **846**, n. 3; **995**
the — described, **991**
κοιναὶ —αι = προλήψεις, **993**
their subject, **994-996**
Cp. **1003 b**, **1138 a**, **1200 a**, n. 3
τοῦ τριγώνου, **1285 a**
τοῦ ἑνός, **1476 b**
ἑνότης **1285 a**. See also One
ἐνσφραγίζεσθαι **1293 b**. Cp. σφραγίς
ἐνσωματῶσις **1355 a**
ἕνωσις
M. Aur.: τῆς οὐσίας, **1271 b**
Iambl.: τοῦ κόσμου, τοῦ παντός,
1448 a c
Procl.: **1464 i**
ἐξαγωγή
the εὔλογος —, **1047**, **1224**
Cp. Epict., **1007 b** (ἀποκαρτερεῖν)
ἐξάγειν ἑαυτόν, **1047 c d**
ἐξερρύη (for emanation), **1366**
The substantive does not occur in
Plot.
ἐξηρημένον
τὸ —, **1477 b**
ἕξις **1024**, **1032 b**, **1053 b**, **1181**, **1187 c**
ἐπακολούθησις **939 c**
See also παρακολούθησις
ἐπακτός
ἡ φαντασία σύνεσις —οῦ, **1405 a**
The universal soul creates οὐκ —ῷ
γνώμῃ, **1376 c**

ψυχή —ν νοῦν ἔχει, **1370 b**; cp. **1426 b** (l. 15)

ἐπέκεινα **1366** (l. 13), **1382 a, 1410 a** (c. 3, init.), **1433 a** (l. 8), **1449 b, 1450 b, 1459 d, 1464 a c, 1476 a b**

ἐπιβολαί
τῆς διανοίας, **823 a e, 824** n. 1, **827**

ἐπιθυμητικόν
The — impassible acc. to Plot., **1414 b** when acquired by the soul in its descent? **1356 b**

ἐπιθυμία
in Epic. :
  814 a, 866-867; cp. **869**
in the Stoa:
  one of the four main πάθη, **1058 a b** defined **1058 c**
  Cp. **1060 b** (*philosophia cupiditatibus liberat*)
In Plotinus: **1414 b**. See further πάθη

ἐπιστήμη
θείων κ. ἀνθρωπίνων, **897 b**; cp. **1215 c, 1289 b**
Zeno called virtue not — but φρόνησις, **1028 c**
Aristo of Chios called it —, **1028 c** (small print)
Chrysippus: **1030, 1031 a**
the wise man alone possesses —, **1043 a**
Posid.: not every virtue is —, **1190 b**
Plotinus: αἱ ἐπιστῆμαι, **1419 a**, the end
See further knowledge

ἐπιστροφή, ἐπιστρέφεσθαι
ἐπὶ τὸν ζωοποιήσαντα, **1334 d** (Valent. ap. Iren.)
Numenius:
  God ἐπέστραπται πρὸς ἕκαστον ἡμῶν (with comm.), **1350 b**
Plotinus:
  of the One to itself, **1366**
  of things becoming (τὸ γενόμενον) to Noûs (τὸ ὄν), **1370 b**
  of noûs to the One, often called θέα, e.g. **1370 a**
  of soul to noûs, e.g. **1375 c**; also called βλέπειν πρός, e.g. **1375 a**
  virtue defined as being turned to Noûs (ἐπέστραπται), **1419 a**
Porph. :
  ἀρετή arises μετὰ τὴν —ν, **1439**
  μόνη σωτηρία ἡ πρὸς θεὸν —, **1440 e**

in Procl. frequently, e.g.: **1460** (c. 32, 33), **1461** (c. 42, 43), **1466 a, 1472 b**
Also ἐπιστρέφεσθαι, ἐπιστρεπτικός:
  πρὸς ἑαυτό, **1459 b c, 1461 c d**
  to its source, **1460**
  νοῦς εἰς τὸ νοητόν, **1466 d**
  ψυχὴ πρὸς ἑαυτήν, **1468 c**
  —κὴ προμήθεια, **1472 b**
in Damasc. : **1478 b**. See also στροφή.

ἐπιστρέφω
the First Noûs ἐπέστρεψε τὴν ψυχὴν τοῦ κόσμου εἰς ἑαυτόν, **1327 d**

ἐπισύνδεσις πάντων **1271 b**

ἐπιτήδευσις
λόγου ὀρθότητος, definition of phil., **989 b**

ἐπιφορά **979**

ἐποχή **809, 1077, 1082 a, 1135 b**

ἐρημία **925 b**

ἑρμηνευτικόν
τὸ —, when acquired by the soul? **1356 b**

ἔρως
of matter for the First principle, **1313 a**
man's love of God's image (*Poimandres*), **1341 b**
Plotinus:
  of soul for noûs, **1395 a**, l. 11
  τοῦ καλοῦ, **1396 a**, l. 14 ff.; **b**, l. 26 ff.
Porph. :
  one of the four principles, **1440 e**; cp. **1441**

ἐρωτικὸν πάθημα (Plot.), of the soul seeing the object of its love, **1399 a**

ἐρώτημα, **973 b**

ἐστώ
ἁ — = οὐσία, acc. to ps.-Archytas = τὸ ὑποκείμενον, **1281 a**

ἑτεροίωσις
τῆς ψυχῆς (Chrysippus), **951, 986 a**
ἐν ἡγεμονικῷ, **986 b**

ἑτερότης
opp. of ταὐτότης, **1285 a** (Moderatus)
Cp. Plut. **1312 c** (the end)
in Plotinus:
  principle of plurality in Noûs, **1374 b c**; cp. **1385 b**
  principle of individual existence, **1380**
  ὕλη eternally produced by —, **1406 e**

one of the aspects of the intelligible
world, **1433 b**, **1434 c**
Iambl., **1451 a**
ἐτυμολογία **1200 a**
εὐδαιμονία (εὐδαίμων εἶναι, εὐδαιμονεῖν)
in Epic.: **814 b**
in the Stoa:
a concomitant state, **1011 b**
virtue the only condition, **1014 a**,
1046 c
— called the telos, **1105**
the consequence of voluntary obedience to divine Law, **1234 b**
(small print)
τὸ εὔρουν καὶ τὸ εὐδαιμονικόν, **1252 a**
in Plotinus:
εὐδαίμων εἶναι, εὐδαιμονεῖν, **1421**,
1422 a b, **1423 b c**
—ία, **1423 a**
εὐδοξία, **1146**
εὐθεῖα
—ν περαίνειν (to achieve a straight
course), **1008 a**
εὔλογον
τὸ —, a rule for practical life, **1105**,
1106 (Arcesilaus)
εὐλόγως **1190 b**
—ς ἐξαγωγή, **1224**
εὐπάθεια
The three —αι acc. to the Stoa, **1063**
in Plotinus: happiness, joy, **1400 b**,
the end
εὐπραγία **1037 a**
εὔροια
—βίου, term used for happiness both
by Zeno and Chrysippus, **989 b**,
1011 a, **1234 b**, **1252 a**
εὐρόως **1252 b**
εὐροεῖν **1271 c**
εὐστάθεια **881**
εὐχή, εὔχεσθαι
Plot.: **1366** (l. 10 f.), **1428 a**, **1431 d**,
1432 a (l. 27)
Porph.: **1440 b** , c (c. 15), **d** (c. 24)
Iambl.: **1446 b**
Cp. Procl., **1456 b**, sm. pr.; **1472 a**
ἐφεκτική
sc. ἀγωγή or αἵρεσις, synonym of
σκεπτική, **1077 b**
ἐφ' ἡμῖν, οὐκ ἐφ' ἡμῖν
primary distinction made by Epict.,
1007 a, **1232 a**

Ζητητική
sc. ἀγωγή or αἵρεσις, synonym of
σκεπτική, **1077 b**
ζωή
in the Stoa classed as adiaphoron,
1012 b
Plotinus: created by soul, **1381 a**
ἡ τελεία —, **1421**
πᾶσα — ἐνέργεια, **1427 b**
Proclus: **1468 c**
ζώνη
αἱ πέντε —αι, **1173** (Posid.)
Herm.: the soul has to cross seven
—αι before reaching God, **1342 b**
ζῷον
in the Stoa:
virtues considered as ζῷα, **914 b**
difference between λογικόν and
ἄλογον —, **946**, **1182 c**
man called a ἥμερον κ. φιλάλληλον —
by Epict., **1243**, introd.
νοερὸν κ. πολιτικὸν — (M. Aur.),
1263 b
the cosmos the τέλειον —, **1272 b**
the stars νοερὰ —α, **1297 a** (Philo),
1329 a (Albinus)
in Plotinus:
παντελὲς —, **1385 b**, **1386 a**
one —, **1431 b**
See also animal

Ἡγεμονικόν
Zeno's doctrine of the —, **947 a**
Chrysippus **947 b**
the — placed in the heart, **914 b**,
948-950
Chrysippus' doctrine of the — πως
ἔχον, **953**, **956**, **986 b-d**, **1030 a**
(introd.), **1053 b**, **1056 a**, **1213**
at birth the — a tabula rasa, **991**
Chrys. seems to have identified the —
with an inward δαίμων, **989 b**
Cp. Posid., **989 a**
Epict.: λοκιγὸν —, **1009**
the — as the inner man opposed to
τὰ ἐκτός, **1239 a**; cp. **1252 a**,
introd.
M. Aur.: **1263**
ἡδονή
Acc. to Epic. the telos: **808**, **812 b**,
859-862
the — of the body comes first, **863**

Philo:
  ἀσώματοι —αι, **1293 b**, **1307**
  ἀρχέτυπος —, **1302 b**
  τὰ παραδείγματα κ. τὰς —ας, **1310 b**
  the —αι identified with the Powers
    of God, **1294**, **1299**
  See also κόσμος νοητός, Logos, and
    power(s)
Albinus: **1326 b**
Numenius: **1350 a**, **1351**
Plotinus:
  ὁ νοῦς καὶ τὰ εἴδη, **1392 a**
  the εἴδη contained in noûs but not
    νοήσεις in the usual sense, **1384 b**
  the purified soul becomes an εἶδος,
    1419 b (l. 13 f.)
  ἰδέαι, e.g. **1406 e** (l. 25)
  Frequently called τὰ νοητά, τὸ
    νοητόν or τὰ ὄντα, and identified
    with noûs, **1383 a-d**
  called τὸ παντελὲς ζῷον, **1385 b**,
    1386 a
  τὸ αὐτοζῷον, **1386 b**
  the εἴδη are henads and numbers,
    basis and principle of being, **1387 b**
Frequently in Proclus' *Elementa*, e.g.
  1467 d, **1468 e**
ἱερός
  the stone on which Demonax used to
    sit down, **1259 c**
ἵλεως **1262 b**, **1275 b**, **1277**
ἴνδαλμα
  Plot.:
    — καὶ εἰκών, **1369 a**, l. 15
    of soul, **1372 b**, l. 33
    cp. **1402 b**, l. 12, **1410 c**, l. 30
    of Aphr. Our., **1373 a**, sm. pr.
    — φρονήσεως ἡ φύσις, **1376 d**, l. 3
  Porph.: τὰ τῆς ψυχῆς —άλματα, **1454 c**
ἰνδαλμοί **1094**
ἰσονομία
  in Epic.' physics, **850 a b**, **851**
ἰσοταχεῖς
  the atoms are —, **836 a**, **837**
ἴχνος
  —η of Noûs in the sensible world,
    1402 b

Κάθαρσις
  acc. to Plotinus essential condition
    of the ὁμοίωσις τῷ θεῷ, **1419 b**
  Porph.: **1439**; Proclus: **1474 a**

See also virtue
καθῆκον
  in the Stoa: **1003 b**, **1004** (small
    print), **1033-1034**, **1047 c d** (*of-
    ficium*), **1099 a**
  Arcesilaus: **1105** (with comments)
  Important place of —ήκοντα in the
    Stoa after Carn., **1144** (with com-
    ments), cp. **1145-1147**
  Panaetius' work Π.τ.κ., **1149 a b**
κάθοδος
  the descent of the soul
  By Numenius considered as essential-
    ly an evil, **1355**
  The — of the soul through the celestial
    spheres, **1356 b**
  Acc. to Plotinus the — not as such
    an evil, **1375 c**; cp. **1424**
  Cp. Porph., **1440 f**, Iambl. **1453**,
    Procl. **1470 d**
  Proclus' theory of periodical ascents
    and descents of the soul, **1469**
κακία
  the wickedness of man, **938** (small
    print). Also called κακουργία, **939 c**
  evil in general, **941 b**
  vice (of speech), **968**
  animals do not share in —, **1001 b**
  — a *perversio naturae*, **1027**
  no medium between ἀρετή and —,
    1038, **1042**
  ἀρετή and —, **1044 a**, **1047 b**, **1053 b**,
    1075 b, **1254 b**, **1268 a**, **1297 a**
  — has its roots within the soul, **1186**
  — ψυχῆς, **1410 c**
  πόλεως καὶ ἐκκλησίας, **1412 e** (l. 31)
  See also s.v. evil, and sin
κακόν
  Plutarchus' theory on the origin of
    evil, **1314**
  Plotinus: **1410**, **1431 c**
κακοποιόν **1281 a**
κακός, κακοί
  Frequently. E.g. **943**, l. 17, **944 c**
  Cp. **1186** (οἱ πονηροί)
  In Plot.: **1403 d**, **1432 b**
κάλλος
  of the Logos and in nature (Philo), **1298**
  of the Ideas, **1310 b**
  Max. Tyr.: πᾶν — ἐκεῖθεν ῥεῖ, **1330 d**
  Herm.: of God and intelligible being,
    1341 b

λήμματα
in Stoic logic = premisses, **979**
See also **1133 b**, **1134**

λογικός
τὸ —ν, **910 a**, **1412 c**

λογισμός
By Epic. and in the Stoa frequently
used for reasoning and the r.
faculty
Epic.: e.g. **870**, **872 b** (νήφων —)
By Cleanthes opposed to θυμός, **953 c**
this passage commented on by
Posid. **1054**
Cp. **1037 a**, **1189 b**, **1190 a**
Moderatus: — νόθος, **1285 b**
Also **1326 a** (Albinus)
Philo: **1293 c**, **1298**, **1310 c**
Cp. also διάνοια
In Plotinus frequently for delibera-
tion, e.g. **1426 b**, **1429 b**
Cp. **1385 b** (l. 32 ff.): discursive
reasoning

λογιστικόν
Platonic term used by Posid., e.g.
1190 b
When acquired by the soul in its
descent, **1356 b**

λόγος, see Logos

λογωθῆναι **1405 b** (l. 25)

λύπη
defined by Zeno, **955 a**
one of the four main πάθη, **1058**
how to treat it, **1061 a**
life full of — (Dio), **1253 c**
— explained by Plotinus, **1414 b**

Μαθηματικοί
professors of Arts and Sciences
Pyrrho and Epicurus hostile towards
the —, **811 a**
See also s.v. learning

μακάριος
τὸ —ν, of the gods, **852**
—α φύσις, **1296 c**
τὸ —ν, of noûs (Plot.), **1383 a** (l. 17)
— βίος, **1410 a** (init.)

μᾶλλον
"Οὐδὲν —", a sceptic rule, **1087 c**
— καὶ ἧττον (in the description of the
ἄπειρον), **1408 c**

μανία **1310 d**

μεγαλοψυχία **1160**, introd.

See also magnanimus
defined by Plotinus, **1419 b**

μέγεθος
of Epic.' atoms, **831 a**
in Plotinus: — not required as a
substrate for Form, **1407 c**

μεθεκτός
and ἀμέθεκτος, **1466**, **1467**, **1468 c d**

μέθεξις **1458 a**, **1459 e**, **1465**, **1466**,
1467 a, **1468 c**
See also μετέχειν, μεταλαμβάνειν, and
participation

μέλος
man a — of a whole (M. Aur.), **1272**

μερισμός **1474 a**

μεριστός
Plot.:
—ή and ἀμέριστος φύσις in soul, **1371 b**
—ν τὸ σῶμα, **1371 c**
the intelligible world is in a sense —,
1406 b (l. 12)
Iambl. **1453 b**
Procl. **1459 b**

μέρος
opposed to μέλος, **1272**

μεσίται
(διαιτηταὶ) λόγοι,̈ **1306 c**
—ης, Mithras called — by the Per-
sians, **1314 b**

μεταβολή
of the hegemonikon, διόλου τρεπόμενον
κ. μεταβάλλον, **986 d**, **1053 b**
of the transition from φαυλότης to
wisdom, **1039 c**
of the cosmos, **1181**
of the ever changing stream of things,
1273 b
of the succession of sovereignties,
1274 b
τῶν στοιχείων, **1280 b**
Plut.: τὸ ὂν —ῆς κρείττων, **1313 b**
Plot.:
not in the intelligible world, **1388**
— τῶν στοιχείων, **1407 a**

μετακόσμια
= *intermundia*, **808**, **840 c**

μεταλαμβάνειν, μετάληψις, see μετέχειν

μεταμέλεια
not considered as a virtue in the Stoa,
1010 a- d
This view criticized by Cic., **1050 b**
— defined, **1064 b**

μετάπτωσις
   ἀξιωμάτων ἐξ ἀληθῶν εἰς ψεύδη, **975 a**
μετάρσιον
   τὸ —, **1280 c**
   τὰ —α, **1351**
μετέχειν
   Philo: **1296 b, 1297 a**
   Plot.: **1401 b** (l. 19), **1410 c** (l. 1),
     1427 a (the end), **b** (l. 20)
   Procl.: **1458 a, 1462 c d f, 1463,
     1465, 1466, 1467, 1468 c**
   Cp. μεταλαμβάνειν, **1371 c** (l. 51),
     1372 a (l. 3), **1401 b** (l. 17), **1404 c**
     (l. 7), **1409 b** passim, **c** (l. 53),
     1410 d (l. 44)
μετάληψις **1371 c** (l. 50), **1409 b** (l. 39)
μετουσία **1462 f.**
μέτρον
   the Idea with regard to matter,
     1326 b
   πᾶς θεὸς — τῶν ὄντων, **1464 e**
μὴ ὄν
   τὸ —, (ὕλη), Moderatus, **1285 b**
   Plut.: **1312 b c**
   Plotinus: ὕλη ἀληθινῶς —, **1409 a**
     (l. 13), **1409 c, 1410 a**
   Cp. **1381 a** (l. 26 f.)
   an εἴδωλον ψυχῆς, **1402 c**
   See also ὄν
μίμημα
   ἤχου —, **943**, l. 4, with n. 1; cp. **971 a**
   Philo called the sensible world re-
     peatedly an ἀπεικόνισμα or — of
     the intelligible archetypon, e.g.
     1293 a b d
   cp. **1302**, introd., **1302 a, 1307**
   the soul of man an ἀπεικόνισμα and —
     of the Logos, **1298**
   Plut.:
   — τοῦ ὄντος τὸ γινόμενον, **1313 a**
   Horus a — of Osiris, **1313 b**, sm. pr.
   the moon a — δαιμόνιον, **1318 b**
   Numenius: the cosmos a — of in-
     telligible being, **1350 a**
   Plotinus:
   the sensible world, **1401 c** (l. 15 f.),
     1406 b (l. 8)
   τῶν ὄντων —ήματα, **1409 a** (l. 28)
μίμησις, μιμεῖσθαι
   (of time), **1434 c** (l. 28, 59)
   See also εἰκών and ἴνδαλμα
μίξις **912 b, 993 a**

μνήμη
   a θησαυρισμὸς φαντασιῶν (Zeno), **986**
     introd.
   For the Sceptic argument against this
     idea cp. **1134**
   Plotinus: by what faculty of the soul
     do we remember? **1378 b c**
μονάς
   ἀρχὴ ἀπάντων, **1279 a**. Cp. **1288 c**
   See also s.v. one
μοναδικός
   ἀριθμὸς —, **1387 b**, l. 35
μονογενής
   noῦs called — by Valent., **1333 a b**
μορφή (μορφώ)
   one of the ἀρχαί assumed by ps.-
     Archytas, **1281 a**

Νοερός
   in Proclus: **1459 c, 1463 d, 1466 d,
     1467 e** (183), **1468 c** (188), **1472
     a b**
νόησις
   Albinus: the Idea a — of God,
     1326 b (with sm. pr.)
   In Plotinus frequently for thinking,
     e.g. **1383 c d, 1384 b, 1385 a b,
     1397 a**
   φαντασίας κρείττων, **1405 a**
νοητός
   τὰ —ά, **1327 a, 1336 c**
   τὸ —ν identified with noῦs, **1383 c**
   τὰ —ά, **1384 c**
   —ἡ φύσις, **1402 b, 1403 a, 1433 a**
   —οἱ θεοί, **1403 a, 1411 a**
   —ἡ οὐσία, **1409 a**
   —αἱ ἑνάδες, **1466 d, 1472 a b**
   For κόσμος νοητός see cosmos (Philo-
     Plotinus) and noῦs (Plot.)
   Also the nrs. **1433 a** (l. 9) and **1453 b**
νόμος, see law
νοῦς, see noῦs
νοωθῆναι **1419 d**

Ξενία
   better practised by the poor than by
     wealthy people, **1255 a**

Ὀγδοατικὴ φύσις, **1342 b**
ὄγκος
   Term frequently found in Epic., see
     e.g. **832 a**

Rarely in Stoic authors
ὕλη distinguished by — (Moderatus),
1285 b (sm. pr., introd.)
the —οι of the body, **1344**
In Plotinus:
ὕλη has only the appearance of —,
1407 c
εἴδωλον κ. φάντασμα —ου, **1409 a**
ὁδὸς κάτω ἄνω, **904 b**; cp. **1274 a**
οἰκειοπραγία **1420 a b**, **1439**
οἰκεῖος
—εία φύσις (*propria natura*)
Panaetius, **1163**
Plotinus, **1430 c**, the end
See also person, personality
οἰκείωσις, see oikeiosis
ὅλος
τὰ ὅλα, frequently in the Stoa, e.g.
899 a, **1267 b**, **1268 a**, **1270**,
1273 a
Neopyth.: **1279 f**, **1280 a**
Philo: **1302 b**, **1303 b**, **1306 a**
Num.: ἡ τῶν —ων φύσις, **1347 b**
Plot.: ἡ τῶν —ων ψυχή, **1375 b**
Iambl.: **1453 b**
Procl.: **1474 b**
τὸ ὅλον
e.g. **1262 b**, **1277 b** (M. Aur.);
1302 c (Philo); **1375 c**, **1412 d**
(l. 21), **1413 b**, **1429 c** (Plot.)
See further universe, universum,
nature
ὁμοίωσις
τῷ θεῷ, **857** (Epic.)
Plotinus: higher virtue is ὁμοιωθῆναι
θεῷ, **1419 a b**
Porph.: **1440 c** (c. 15)
ὁμολογία (*convenientia*), **1003 b**; cp.
1215 (introd.)
ὁμολογουμένως (τῇ φύσει) ζῆν
the telos formula in the Stoa:
1003-1005; cp. **1012**, **1020 b**
See also telos
virtue defined as a διάθεσις — μένη,
1024 a
ὁμοούσιος **1340 b**
ὁμόφωνος
νόμος κ. λόγος, **1330 a**
ὄν, τὸ —, τὰ —τα
In the Stoa not a frequent term.
E.g. **1018**

[σώματα μόνον τὰ — εἶναι, SVF II 320,
525; not in this vol.]
Neopyth.:
δύο ἀρχὰς τῶν —των, **1281 a**
τὸ ὄντως —, **1285 b**
τὸ μὴ —, ib.
τὰ τοῦ —τος εἴδη, **1288 a**
Plut.:
God alone is the ὄντως —, **1312 a b**
cp. **1313 a b**
the — must be one, **1312 c**
Num.:
τί ἐστι τὸ —, **1347 c**
Plotinus:
the — identified with noûs, **1383 a**
(l. 25 ff.), **1384 a**
τὰ ὄντα **1382 d**
in noûs, **1384 c**, **1385 a**
is ἐνέργεια, **1385 a**
immutable and ἀπαθές, **1388**
τὸ μὴ — produced by the particular
soul, **1402 c**
the ὕλη is ἀληθινῶς μὴ —, **1409 a c**
εἰκὼν τοῦ —τος, **1410 a**
Procl.:
participated — depends on unparticipated —, **1463 c**
τὸ ὄντως ὄν
Iambl.: **1449 c**, **1453 b**
Procl.: **1462 c**, **1466 d** (164)
ὄνομα
(as a grammatical term) **967**
ὅρασις
defined by Chrys., **947 b**; cp. ὄψις
ὀργή **1057**, **1079 a**
ὄρεξις
a προσθήκη of soul, **1375 b**
ὀρθός
—λόγος, see logos
—νόμος, see law
ὀρίζω
the Sceptic rule "οὐδὲν ὁρίζομεν",
1087 c
ὁρμή
πάθη καὶ —αί, **914 b**, **951-953**
explained as ἑτεροιώσεις, **956 a**; cp.
986 b, **1053 b**
the πρώτη — of man, **999 a**; **1003 a**
— and ἀφορμή, **1019 c**, **1030 b**
Panaetius' theory, **1155-1157**
Posidonius: **1185**
Antiochus: **1201 a c**

ὄφελος
  virtue defined as —, 1017 a
ὄχημα
  σῶμα αἰθερικόν or πνευματικόν, 1356
    (comments), 1442 a, with n. 1
  ἄϋλον, 1469 c, 1474 a
ὄψις 948 c

Πάθη
  in Epic.: 823 a b, 826
  in the Stoa: 914 b, 951-956, 989 a,
    1051-1064, 1079 a
  Carneades: 1115, 1121 b
  Posid.: 1185, 1187-1190, 1191
  Seneca: 1213
  Epictetus: 1238 a
  Plut.: 1320
  Plotinus: 1413 b, 1414
  Porph.: the — not rejected as such,
    1440 a (c. 9), 1441
παίγνιον
  sensible things called —α, 1409 a
    (l. 23 f.)
παιδεία
  Epic.: 816
  the Stoa: 1044 a (sm. pr.), 1045 a
  Panaetius: 1159 b
  Posid: 1187
  Dio of Prusa: 1253 a - c
  Philo: 1289 a
  See also learning
παλιγγενεσία 1151 b
  See also regeneration, and renewal
  For — in the sense of metempsychosis,
    see reincarnation
παλμός, see vibration
πᾶν
  τὸ —, τὰ πάντα
  frequently in the Stoa, e.g. 918 b
  cp. 943: πᾶς ὅδε κόσμος (l. 7), πάντα
    κυβερνῶν (Zeus, l. 2), etc.
  M. Aur.: 1267 b, sm. pr.
  Neopyth.: 1280 a, 1282
  Philo: 1296 c, 1302 c, 1303 a b,
    1304 c, 1306 a (also τὰ ὅλα), 1307
  Plut.: 1314 a (τὸ π. does not float
    reasonless and ungoverned)
  ἡ ψυχὴ τοῦ —τός, 1314 d
  Orac. Chald.: τὰ —, 1336 c
  Plotinus:
    τὸ πᾶν 1357 b, 1368 b, 1369 a c

ψυχὴ τοῦ —τός, 1373 a b, 1376 d,
    1402 b, 1403 b, 1418 a
διοίκησις τοῦ —τός, 1403 a
ὕλη κ. σῶμα τοῦ —τός, 1404 a, cp.
    1373 c (l. 6), 1404 c
The Stoic conception of ἕν κ. πᾶν
    criticized, 1425 a
τόδε τὸ —, 1426 a, 1427 a
ποικιλώτατον γὰρ τὸ —, 1428 e
ἐν τῷ —τί, 1428 f, 1430 a c
ἡ ἐνέργεια τοῦ —τός, 1431 b (l. 15)
ἡ φύσις τοῦ —τός, 1432 b (l. 17),
    1402 a, 1403 c
Iambl.:
  ἕνωσις τοῦ —τός, 1448 c
  ἡ τοῦ —τὸς θεωρία, 1448 a
Procl.: 1472 c
τὰ πάντα, 1370 a
  ἐξ ἑνός, 1371 a (l. 5)
  cp. 1390 d: ἐξ ἀρχῆς τὰ —.
  ὁ νοῦς —, 1383 a, cp. 1385 b,
    1390 c (τὸ ὂν —)
  νοῦς ὁμοῦ —, 1428 b
  τὸ ἕν ≠ τὰ —, 1398 d
See also universe, universum, nature
πανδεχής
  of the material principle, 1280 b, 1285 b;
  Isis (Plut.), 1313 a
  See also ὑποδοχή
πανδοχεῖον
  ἡ καρδία, 1337 a
πανδοχεύς 1288 c
παντελής
  βίος (Epic.), 871
  —ἐς ζῷον, 1385 b (l. 57), 1386 a (l. 15)
παντοκράτωρ 1334 c
παράδειγμα
  Nicomachus: 1288 b
  Philo: 1293 a b d, 1298, 1305 a (sm.
    pr.)
  Plut.: 1315 b
  Albinus: 1326 b (the Idea = π. τῶν
    κατὰ φύσιν αἰώνιον)
  Plot.: 1419 e, 1420 b, 1426 a, 1433 a
  Porph.: 1439, the end
  Iambl.: 1449 c, 1450 b
  See also ἀρχέτυπον
παράθεσις
  of bodies, 912 b, 913 b
παρακολούθησις
  κατὰ —ιν (Chrys. ap. Gell.), 939 d
  Also κατ' ἐπακολούθησιν, 939 c

In Plot. — means self-consciousness, and παρακολουθεῖν = to be conscious, esp. self-conscious : **1422 a c, 1428 f**

See also s.v. self-consciousness

παρασυνημμένον
inferential **977**

παρέγκλισις (*clinamen*)
of the atoms acc. to Epic., **833, 835 a**

παρουσία
τοῦ Πατρός (*Poim.*), **1342 b**
the First Principle known by — (Plot.), **1399 a**
—τῶν θεῶν (Procl.), **1465 b**

παρρησία **1257 a**

πάσχον, τό,
Stoic term for the material principle, opp. of τὸ ποιοῦν, **899 a**
The Stoic conception criticized by Plotinus, **1425 a**, l. 17 ff.

πατήρ
God called —:
by Cleanthes, **943** (l. 34)
Epictetus, **1242** (πάντα τὰ αὑτοῦ ἡγεῖσθαι τοῦ πατρός)
Philo:
τὸν πατέρα κ. ποιητήν, **1290 b, 1296 c, 1297 a**
ὁ γεννήσας — (of the Logos), **1306 a**, cp. **1306 c**
Albinus: the first Noûs, **1327 d**
Max. Tyr.: **1330 a**
Valentinus: **1333 a - c, 1334 a b**
Herm.: ὁ νοῦς — θεός, **1339 b, 1341 a, 1342 a b, 1343**
Num.: the first God, **1352 a**
Plot.: **1375 c** n. 1, **1381 a b** (νοῦς —), **1403 d** (the end), **1393 d** (the First Principle), **1401 c** (Nous)
Iambl.: **1451 a**
See also προπάτωρ and οὐσιοπάτωρ
Iambl. **1449 c** speaks also of αὐτοπάτωρ and μονοπάτωρ

πενία
the life of the poor, **1255 a - c**

πέρας
καὶ ἄπειρον, **1281 b**
— τα, **1397 b, 1410 b** (l. 36)
ἀρχὴ καὶ —, **1396 b**
ἄπειρον and —, **1410 b** (l. 14)
Proclus: — and ἄπειρον basic prin-

ciples, **1462 c** (89), **d** (90), **f** (92), **1466 c, 1470 a**, sm. pr.

περιγραφή **913 b**

περίλαμψις **1366**

περίοδοι
in M. Aur., **1267 b**, sm. pr.
in Proclus, **1469 a b, 1474 b**

περιοδικῶς **1469 a**

πηγή
ἦθος — βίου (Zeno), **1035 a**
ἡ πάντων — (M. Aur.), **939 c**
the λόγος ἐνδιάθετος is οἷά τις — (Philo) **1307**
the ὀρθὸς λόγος — ἀρετῶν, **1309 b**
— ἀέναος καὶ ἀκήρατος (Max. Tyr.), **1330 d**
— ζωῆς, — νοῦ (Plot.), **1367**
— ἀρχὴν ἄλλην οὐκ ἔχουσα, **1398 d**
— τοῦ καλοῦ, **1419 b**
— τῶν πάντων (Iambl.), **1449 c**
— τῶν ὄντων (Procl.), **1472 b**

πιθανόν
τὸ —, probability (Carn.), **1116**, cp. **1106**

πίστις
cardinal virtue in Epict.' ethics, **1240, 1241**
one of the four principles of Proclus, **1440 e f**

πλάγια (πτῶσις), **969 a**

πλῆθος, see plurality. Also τὸ πολύ

πλήρωμα
1333 (Valentinus)
cp. **1467 d** (Proclus), **1453 b** (Iambl.)

πνεῦμα, see pneuma

πνευματικοί
the class of spiritual men acc. to Valentinian gnosis, **1332 b** (sub 4), **1335 a**
imperishable by nature, **1335 b**

πνευμάτιον
for soul, **1265 b**

ποικίλος
the intelligible world ἓν —ν, **1406 b** (l. 16)
—ώτατον τὸ πᾶν, **1428 e**

ποιμήν
God called —, **1303 c**

ποιοῦν, τό,
Stoic term for the active principle in the Universe, **899 a, 917**

ποιός, τὸ —ν, see quality

ποιότης, ib.

πόλεμος
ὁ βίος (M. Aur.), **1275 b**
everywhere on earth (Max. Tyr.),
1330 a

πόλις
defined by the Stoics, **1074 b**
See also political philosophy, s.v.
political

πολιτικά, ib.
πολιτικαὶ ἀρεταί, social virtues, Porph.
1439
Cp. Plotinus **1420**

πόνος
in the Stoa classed as adiaphoron,
1012 b
praised by Porph., **1440 a**

ποσός
τὸ —ν, see quantity

ποσότης
ἄμορφος, the indefinite principle (ὕλη),
1285 b. Cp. **1339 a**, n. 2

ποταμός
τὰ τοῦ σώματος, **1275 b**
ἡ ὕλη, **1347 a**

πρακτικόν
τὸ —, when acquired by the soul in its
descent, **1356 b**

πρέπον
τὸ —, in speech, **968**
the *decorum*, **1161**

προαίρεσις
the essense of morality acc. to Epict.:
1236, **1237**, **1239 b**
the first characteristic of man, **1242**
Plotinus: not every part of the universe has its own —, **1428 e**, l. 25 sq.,
1428 f, l. 13 sqq., **1431 b**, l. 5 sqq.,
1432 a, l. 24
Iambl.: By what do we sin? Not by
—?, **1453 a**

προηγμένα
τὰ —, a class of ἀδιάφορα, **1018-1020**,
1022, **1033 a**, **1034 b**, **1144**

προκοπή
moral progress (profectus), **1020 c**

προκόπτων
ὁ —, not of the level of the wise man,
1034 b, **1039**, **1189 a**, **1239 b**
See also *profectus*, *proficere*
Porph. οἱ πρὸς θεωρίαν —οντες, **1439**

πρόληψις
acc. to Epic.: **823 a**, **824**, **825**, **846**,
847, **848 a b**
Cp. **854 b** (νοτιτιες)
in the Stoa: **990-995**, cp. **996**;
1141 b, **1200 c**

πρόνοια, see Providence

πρόοδος, προϊέναι, see procession (emanation)

προόρασις **1426 a**
προπάθεια **1213**
προπάτωρ **1333 a**

προσγεγενημένα
τὰ —, see προσθῆκαι

προσηγορία **967**

προσθήκη
—αι of the soul (Plot.), **1375 b**, **1417 b**
Also called τὰ προσγεγενημένα, **1413 b**
Cp. **1356 b**: *incrementa corporis*

πρός τί πως ἔχον
one of the four categories in Stoic
logic, **915 a**

προφήτης **1310 a**

πρῶτα
in the Stoa: τὰ — κατὰ φύσιν, **1003 b**
(introd.), **1004** (sm. pr.), **1020 b**
(sm. pr.), **1021** (prima naturae),
1047 d, **1165**, **1188 c**
in Plotinus: τὰ — = intelligible Being
ὁ νοῦς ἐστιν αὐτὰ τὰ —, **1384 b**,
cp. **1369 c**

πρώτη ὕλη
900 a (is the οὐσία of everything);
πως ἔχουσα, **916**

πρωτόγονος
λόγος, **1306 d**, cp. **1303 c**

πτοία **952 d**, **1052**

πτῶσις
(grammatical term) **967**, **969**
πτώσεις τῆς ψυχῆς, **1053 a**

πῦρ
τεχνικόν, **902**, **907**, **917**
νοερόν, **916 a**, **957**

πυρίγονα **1304 a**

πύσμα **973 b**

πως ἔχον
one of the four categories in Stoic
logic, **915 c**
the hegemonikon —, see ἡγεμονικόν

Ῥεῖ
ἐν τῷ κόσμῳ, **1404 a**

ῥῆμα
in Stoic grammar, **967**
ῥητορική **964 a**

Σάρξ
Epic.: **866 d**, **867 b**
Epict.: (σαρκίδιον) **1235 a**, **1241 c**
Plut.: **1320**
Porph.: **1440 f**
σαφήνεια **968**
σελήνη, see moon
σημεῖα
given by the Gods to man, **933**
the doctrine of — as a basis of inference criticized, **1132**, **1133**,
1142
(in the math. sense) **1279 a**
σκοπός (propositum), intention
acc. to the Stoa the essential of an act,
1016 a, **1144** (sm. pr., n. 1), **1188 c**
σκότος
in the *Poimandres*, **1339 a**
in Plotinus frequently for ὕλη
(also τὸ σκοτεινόν): **1365 c**, **1381 a**
(l. 26), **1410 d** (l. 40), **1402 c**
(l. 13), **1406 d** (l. 13)
(ὕλη) σκοτεινὴ πᾶσα, **1406 c** (l. 7)
σκοτωδία
1288 c, with sm. pr.
Also ἀλαμπία
σκότωσις **1344**, **1356 b**
σολοικισμός **968**
σοφία
in the Stoa defined as θείων τε καὶ
ἀνθρωπίνων ἐπιστήμη, **897 a**
Cp. **1030 a**, **1289 b**
transcendent and created — distinguished (Philo), **1302 a**, sm. pr.
Plot.: **1419 e**, **1420 b**
Porph.: **1439**
σοφός
in the Stoa: **1042 b**, **1046**, **1050 a**,
1062, **1075 b**
Pyrrho: **1084 b**
Arcesilaus: **1103 b**
Philo: φαῦλος opp. to σοφός, **1310 d**
σπέρμα
explained by Chrysippus, **947 b**, cp.
948 c
cosmic —, **908 a**
ἀρχαὶ κ. σπέρματα (of virtues), **1026 c**

σπερματικός
(λόγος), **919** (introd.), **919 d**
Philo **1302 e**
Plot. **1365 d**
—οἱ (λόγοι), **902 a**, **919 a - d**
Plot. **1425 c**
σπουδαῖος
in the Stoa: **957 b**, **1032 a**, **1038 b**,
1042, **1043 a**, **1046 c**, **1048 a**,
1050 a
Carneades: **1112 a**
Philo: **1297 a**
Plotinus: **1423**
στάθμη
κατὰ —ν, **833 a b**, **835 a**
στάσις,
opp. of κίνησις, **1433 a b**, **1434 c**,
1435 b
σταλαγμός
οἴνου ἕνα —ν, **913 c**
στερέμνια
(solid bodies), **849**
στερητικόν
(γένος), **976**
στέρησις
in Stoic logic, **972 b**
in Moderatus (of the indefinite principle in metaphysics), **1285 b**, cp.
1288 c, sm. pr.
Plotinus, **1410 e**
στοιχεῖα
τὰ τέσσαρα —, **899 b**, **904 a** (Zeno);
916 b (Stoics); **1100 a** (Arcesilaus),
1181 b (Nemesius); Neopyth.
1279 a, **1285 a**
ὁ θάνατος οὐδὲν ἄλλο ἢ λύσις —είων,
1275 b
Philo: **1305 a**
Valentinus: **1334 d**
Herm.: **1339 c**, **1340 b**
Num.: **1347 a**
στροφή
ἡ πρὸς νοῦν, **1420 a**
συγγένεια
of man with God, **1297 a**. Cp. **1330 c**
συγκατάθεσις
914 b, **953 d**, **956 a**, **975 a**, **985 a**,
n. 2, **985 b**, **986 b**, **989 b**, **1103 b**,
1106 b, **1112 a**, **1185**
See also assent
σύγκρασις **1288 c**, sm. pr.
σύγχυσις **1288 c**, sm. pr.

συλλαβή **967**
σύμβαμα
and παρασύμβαμα, **1050 a**
συμβεβηκότα
(Epic.), **829 a**
συμμετρία
ὁ πρῶτος νοῦς, **1327 d**
συμπάθεια **912**, **935**, **1125**, **1177**, **1285 a**
See also cosmic sympathy, s.v. cosmic
σύμπνοια
(other term for cosmic sympathy), **1271 b**, **1285 a**, **1448 c**
συμπτώματα
(Epic.), **829 a**
συμφυής **1177**
σύμφωνος
διάθεσις —, **1005 b**
Also κατὰ συμφωνίαν, **1011 a**
συναγωγή, συνακτικός **979**
συναίσθησις
(αὑτῆς) of the soul, **1379 b**, **1405 d**, **1415 b**
συναμφότερον
τὸ — (the human compositum) frequently in Plot., e.g. **1378 a**, **1412 a**, **1414 b c**
Also τὸ κοινόν, **1413 d**
See further body, λεοντῶδες, θηρίον or τὸ σύνθετον: **1413 b**, **1417 b**
συνάμφω
τὸ —, **1412 d**
σύνδεσμος **967**
συνείδησις **999 a**. See also self-consciousness
συνεργία
M. Aur.: γενόναμεν πρὸς —ν, **1262 a**. See also κοινωνικός
συνεργός
—οί (in the work of creation), **1297 a b**
σύνεσις
Athena explained as ἡ τοῦ Διὸς —, **1326 b**, sm. pr.
συνημμένον **977**, **1133 b**
σύνθετος
Plut.:
man — of three parts, **1319 a**
Plot.:
the body always a —ν, **1406 c**, **1407 a**
man in a body, **1413 b**, **1417 b**
the sensible world, **1406 b**

συντομία **968**
σφραγίς
the Logos called ἀρχέτυπος — (Philo). **1293 d**
the powers of God compared with —ῖδες, **1294**
the archetypal man, **1296 b**
the Logos, **1302 a b**
σχῆμα
of Epic.' atoms, **830 a**, **831 a**
ἐπίπεδα κ. στερεὰ σχήματα (Neopyth.), **1279 a**
σῴζειν
ἀνθρώπους, **1276 b** (M. Aur.)
σῶμα, see body
σωτήρ
civilized men —ῆρες τῶν πολέων (Dio), **1253 a**
the good demons appear as —ῆρες for man, **1319 c**
ὁ —, **1335 a**
σωτηρία
God αἴτιον τῆς —ς for earthly beings, **1303 c**, sm. pr. (p. 369)
God procures — to those who are obedient, **1330 e**
no — for χοϊκοί, **1335 b**
τῆς ψυχῆς, **1440 a** (c. 9)
μόνη — ἡ πρὸς θεὸν ἐπιστροφή, **1440 e**
— coming from "the Whole", **1474 b**
σωτήριος
ἡ γνῶσις τοῦ θεοῦ —ν ἀνθρώπῳ (Herm.), **1344**
σωφροσύνη
one of the four cardinal virtues, mentioned **1012 b**, **1028 b-1030**, **1190**, **1249 b**
Defined by Cleanthes, **1029 a**
by Chrys., **1030 c**
by Plot., **1419 b**, **1420 a b**
by Porph., **1439**

Tαὐτότης
Moderatus: **1285 a**
Plotinus: **1385 b**, **1433 b**, **1434 c**
Iambl.: **1451 a**
τέλειος
in the Stoa: τὸ —ν κατὰ φύσιν (def. of virtue), **1017 b**
the cosmos a —ν ζῷον, **1272 b**
Philo: — λόγος, **1302 a**
Albinus: ὁ πρῶτος νοῦς —, **1327 d**

Plotinus:
  everything in noûs is —ν, **1383 a**
  noûs itself, **1385 b** (l. 30)
  πάντα ὅσα —α γεννᾷ, **1366** (l. 37 f.),
    cp. **1370 a**
  ἡ τελεία ψυχή, **1410 c**, l. 25
  τελεία ζωή, **1421**
  —αι ἀρεταί, **1420**
τελειότης **1023 b**
τελείωσις **1003** n. 1, **1023 a**
τέλος, see telos
τεταγμένα
  τὰ — καὶ ὁριστά, **1281 a**
τέχνη
  virtues as ἐπιστῆμαι κ. —αι, **1031 a**
τομή, see divisibility
τόνος **908 a**, **1029**
τρέπεσθαι δι' ὅλων
    1279 a (with comm.). Cp. **913**
  See also μεταβολή
τριάς
  ἡ νοητὴ —, **1449 a b**
  νοεραὶ —άδες (Iambl.), **1451 b**
  the triadic system applied to soul, **1452**
  noûs conceived as a — (Procl.), **1463 c**
τρόπος
  the ten —οι of Aenesidemus, **1135**
  the five —οι of Agrippa, **1136**
τύποι, τύπωσις
  ἐν ψυχῇ, **951**, **956 a**, **984 a**
  Plotinus: τύποι, **1415 a**
  τυπώσεις (ἐνέργειαι), **1415 c**

'Υγίεια
  classed among adiaphora, **1012 b**,
    1018, **1030 b**
  explained as ἁρμονία, **1279 f**
  Plotinus: **1423 a**
ὑγρός
  —ὰ φύσις, **1339 a**
ὕλη, see matter
ὑλικοί **1332 b**, **1335**
ὕπαρξις **1451 a**, **1464 g h**, **1467 a**,
    1470 a (sm. pr.), **1478 b**
ὑπεράγαθον **1394 a**
ὑπεραποφατικόν **976**
ὑπερβολή
  and ἔλλειψις, **1410 c**, with n. 3
ὑπέρζωος **1464 c**
ὑπερκόσμιος **1466 d**, **1467 a**
ὑπέρνους **1464 c**
ὑπερούσιος **1464 c f**

ὑπεροχή
  God is πάσης —ῆς μείζων, **1343**
ὑπερρεῖν
ὑπερερρύη **1370 a** (l. 8)
ὑποδοχή
  (the ὕλη), **1407 a**, **1409 c**
ὑποκείμενον
  first category in Stoic logic, **997**
  Cp. ὕλη and οὐσία, **900 a**, **916 b**
  Ps.-Archytas: ἀ ὠσία τὸ —, **1281 a**
  Albinus: (ὕλη), **1326 a**
  Plot.: **1406 b d**, **1407 a**, **1408 a**,
    1433 b
  Procl.: **1460 b**
ὑπόληψις
  in Epic.: —λήψεις ψευδεῖς, **848 b**
    (introd.)
  Epict.: **1232 a**
  M. Aur.: **1264 c**
  Porph.: **1440 d**
ὑπομνήματα
  Πυθαγορικά, **1279**
ὑπόνοια
  τοῦ ἑνός, **1476 b**
ὑπόστασις
  Valent. ap. Iren.: πνευματικὴ —.,
    1334 c, **1335 b**
  τῆς πονηρίας, **1337 d**
  Plot.: **1366**, **1375 a**, **1381 b**, **1387 a**,
    1398 a, **1409 a c**, **1410 b**
  Iambl.: **1450**, **1453 b**
  Procl.: **1459 d**, **1461 d**, **1464 b**
  See also αὐθυπόστατον.

Φαντασία
  in the Stoa: **914 b**, **951**, **953 d**,
    956 a, **965 b**
  φ. καταληπτική, **984-986**; cp. **988**,
    991
  the Sceptics: **1104**, **1112**, **1115**,
    1116, **1135 a**, **1138 a**
  Antiochus: **1197 d**
  Epict.: **1233 a b**
  M. Aur.: **1262 c**
  Plotinus: — μεταξὺ φύσεως τύπου καὶ
    νοήσεως, **1405 a**
φάντασμα
  in the Stoa: **991**, **992 a**, **1050 a**
  in Plot.: **1378 c**,
    — ὄγκου (ὕλη), **1407 c** (l. 27 ff.),
      1409 a (l. 13)
    —άσματα τῆς αἰσθήσεως, **1416 b** (l. 67)

φανταστικόν
τὸ —, when acquired by the soul in its descent, **1356 b**
Plot.: **1378** introd., **1378 c**

φαῦλος
by the Stoics opp. to σοφός. See there

φῆμαι **934**

φιλανθρωπία
812 a (of Epic.); **1159 b** (Panaetius); **1322, 1324** (Plut.)

φιλάνθρωπος **883 b, 1448 c**
τὸ —ν (for God's love of man), **995 b**

φιλία
in Epic., **877**
Cp. **812 a** (φιλανθρωπία) and **b** (φίλοι); also **813**
Epict.: **1241 a**
Neopyth.: defined as ἐναρμόνιος ἰσότης, **1279 f**

φίλος, φιλεῖν
Epic.: **812, 813**
M. Aur.: **1272 a, 1276 b** sm. pr.

φιλοσοφία
Epic.: φρόνησις τιμιώτερον —ας, **872 b**
defined in the Stoa, **897 b**, cp. Philo, **1289 b**
opposed to ἱερατική, **1446 c**
See further philosophy

φόβος, see fear

φορά, ἡ τῶν ἀτόμων, see motion

φρήν **965 a**

φρόνησις
acc. to Epic., **872 b**
in the Stoa: **1012 b, 1023 a, 1028 b c, 1030**
Arcesilaus: **1105**
Plot.:
φύσις ἴνδαλμα —ήσεως, **1376 d**
one of the ἀρεταὶ τῆς ψυχῆς, **1419 b e, 1420 b**
Porph.: **1439**

φυγή
Epic.: αἵρεσις καὶ —, **862 a, 872 b** (exilium) **1260 b**

φύσις
in the Stoa identified with the Logos, **921**
By Plotinus sometimes used in a general sense, almost identical with God, e.g. **1413 b**, l. 15 f.: ἔδωκεν ἡ —; cp. l. 17 f.: θεὸς ἔδωκεν

Cp. Marc. Aur. **1267 a**
δευτέρα —, **1382 a**
cp. δεύτερος θεός
What is —?, **1405**
ποιητὴς ἔσχατος, **1402 b**
See further Nature

φυτικόν
τὸ —, when acquired by the soul in its descent, **1356 b**
(Plot.) **1416 a**

φωνή
explained by Chrys., **947 b, 948 c**
defined, **962 a b**
corporeal, **962 c**
ὅθεν ἡ —, **963**
in other definitions, **966**

φῶς
καὶ σκότος, **1279 b, 1280 b**
Philo: τὸ ἀόρατον κ. νοητὸν —, **1295 b**
cp. also **1300 c** (ἀρχέτυπος αὐγή)
Plut.: — κ. σκότος, **1314 b**
Valentinus: **1334 d, 1335 a** (τὸ φῶς τοῦ κόσμου), **1337 c** (Jesus)
the *Poim.*:
— καὶ σκότος, **1339 a**
τὸ —= Νοῦς ὁ θεός, **1339 b**
ζωὴ κ. —, **1340 a, 1341 a**, cp. **1342 a**
Plotinus:
πολὺ — ἐκλάμψαν, **1365 c, 1366**
— in three stages, **1370 b**
the First Principle is — πρὸ —τός, **1382 a**, cp. **1389 b**
νοῦς is — ἐκ —τός, **1365 b**
— τὸ νοεῖν, **1391 b**
— coming from the ἀγαθόν to the soul, **1395 a b**
from soul to the sensible world, **1404 c**
to ὕλη, **1406 e**
to the body, **1414 c**
τὸ — itself is seen, **1395 b, 1400 c**
Proclus:
τὸ θεῖον —, **1465 b**
τῆς ἀληθείας, **1472 a**

φωτίζειν
—εται ἡ ψυχή, **1402 c, 1395 b**; cp. **1419 a**
πεφωτισμένος, **1370 b, 1389 b, 1406 d**
See also ἀφώτιστον, and ἐλλάμπειν

Χάος **1288 c**, sm. pr.

χαρά **953 b**, **1063 b**
χάρις **1299 b**, **1323 b**, **1395 a**, **1401 b**
χάσμα **1288 c** sm. pr., **1356 a**
χείμων
    ὁ τῆς ψυχῆς, **860**
χορεία
    ἔνθεος, of the Spirit around the One, **1400 a**
    the motion of the universe, **1431 a**
χρηστήρια
    κατὰ τῶν —ίων, **1260 d**
    See further oracles
χρηστότης
    καὶ καλοκἀγαθία, **1227 c**
    covers a larger field than δικαιοσύνη, **1323 b**
χρόνος, see time, and tense, s.v. tempora
χώρα **1409 c**
χωρίζειν
    ἑαυτοὺς ἀπὸ τῶν προσγεγενημένων, **1413 b**
χωρισμός
    ἀπὸ τοῦ σώματος, **1423 a**; cp. **1417 b**, l. 18
χωριστός
    —ἡ οὐσία, **1459 c**
    —ἡ σώματος, **1468 b**

τὸ —ὸν τοῦ κόσμου, **1467 a**

Ψευδής
    δόξα, **828**, sm. pr.
    συγκατάθεσις, **1043 a**
    δόξαι —εῖς, **1410 c**, l. 11
    See also δόξα, δοξάζειν and ψεῦδος
ψεῦδος
    the Stoa: no degrees of —, **1040 a**
    Herm.: Inhabits the seventh zone, **1342 b**
    Plot.:
        (of ὕλη and what enters into it), **1409 a** (l. 38-41)
        τὸ ἀνομοίως μεμιμῆσθαι —, **1403 a** (l. 18)
    Iambl.: πολυσχιδὲς τὸ —, **1448 b**
ψυχή, see soul
ψυχικοί
    a particular class of mankind acc. to the Gnostics, **1332 b** (sub 4), **1335**

Ὠφέλεια
    Epic.: friendship starts from —, **877 b**
    the Stoa: the ἀγαθόν defined as —, **1017 a**
    in the first trope of Aenesidemus, **1135 a**

ADDENDA

p. 562, nr. **1454 f,** the end, *supply*: New edition with prolegomena and Engl. translation by A. D. Nock, Cambridge 1926. French transl. by Mario Meunier, Paris 1931.

p. 647, col. 2, between l. 8 and 9: Fate and free w. (Carn. adv. Chrys.) **1124.**

p. 661, col. 1, l. 5 from bottom: οὐ — **1082a, 1087a.**

p. 670, col. 1, l. 3 from bottom: ὑπερνόησις **1368a.**